IJCAI-99

Proceedings of the Sixteenth International
Joint Conference on Artificial Intelligence

Stockholm, Sweden
July 31–August 6, 1999

VOLUME 1

Sponsored by the
International Joint Conferences on Artificial Intelligence, Inc. (IJCAII)
The Scandinavian AI Societies

Edited by Thomas Dean

Distributed by
Morgan Kaufmann Publishers, Inc.
340 Pine Street, 6th Floor
San Francisco, CA 94104
http://www.mkp.com

Printed in the United States

Design, composition, production, and manufacturing management by
Professional Book Center, Denver, Colorado

BRIEF CONTENTS

VOLUME 1

VOLUME 2

ORDERING INFORMATION

The following is a list of proceedings of IJCAI conferences available from Morgan Kaufmann. To place an order or inquire about these and other Morgan Kaufmann publications, please use the following information:

Telephone: 800-745-7323 (from within the U.S. and Canada) and 407-345-3800 (international);
FAX: 800-874-6418 or 407-345-4060; Web: http://www.mkp.com; Email: orders@mkp.com;
Post: Morgan Kaufmann, Attention: Order Fulfillment Department, 6277 Sea Harbor Drive, Orlando, FL 32887 USA

Shipping is free from Morgan Kaufmann within the U.S. on prepaid orders. International shipping is $7 per volume via DHL/local post combination, or $20 per volume via overnight courier. Morgan Kaufmann accepts credit card payments: The buyer should provide card number, expiration date, and name as it appears on the card for Visa, MasterCard, or American Express. Morgan Kaufmann also accepts checks or money orders in U.S. dollars drawn on a U.S. bank.

Lower price listed below available to IJCAI conference registrants and members of national/regional AI societies only.

IJCAI-99
Stockholm, Sweden
2 volumes; ISBN 1-55860-613-0
$85/$63.75

IJCAI-97
Nagoya, Japan
2 volumes; ISBN 1-55860-480-4
$85/$63.75

IJCAI-95
Montréal, Québec
2 volumes; ISBN 1-55860-363-8
$75/$56.25

IJCAI-93
Chambéry, France
2 volumes, ISBN 1-55860-300-X
$75/$56.25

IJCAI-91
Sydney, Australia
2 volumes, ISBN 1-55860-160-0
$75/$56.25

IJCAI-89
Detroit, Michigan
2 volumes, ISBN 1-55860-094-9
$75/$56.25

IJCAI-87
Milan, Italy
2 volumes; ISBN 0-934613-43-5
$69/$51.75

IJCAI-85
Los Angeles, California
2 volumes; ISBN 0-934613-02-8
$69/$51.75

IJCAI-83
Karlsruhe, West Germany
2 volumes; ISBN 1-55860-043-4
$65/$48.75

IJCAI-81
Vancouver, British Columbia
2 volumes; ISBN 1-55860-044-2
$65/$48.75

IJCAI-79
Tokyo, Japan
2 volumes; ISBN 0-934613-47-8
$65/$48.75

IJCAI-77
Cambridge, Massachusetts
2 volumes; ISBN 0-934613-48-6
$65/$48.75

IJCAI-75
Tbilisi, Georgia USSR
ISBN 0-934613-20-6
$65/$48.75

IJCAI-73
Stanford, California
ISBN 0-934613-58-3
$65/$48.75

IJCAI-71
London, England
ISBN 0-934613-34-6
$65/$48.75

IJCAI 5-Year Set
1991–1999
10 volumes, ISBN 1-55860-620-3
$355/$266.25

IJCAI 10-Year Set
1981–1999
20 volumes; ISBN 1-55860-629-7
$657/$493.75

IJCAI 15-Year Set
1971–1999
27 volumes; ISBN 1-55860-628-9
$950/$712

FOREWORD

This proceedings contains the papers accepted for presentation at the Sixteenth International Joint Conference on Artificial Intelligence (IJCAI) held in Stockholm, July 31–August 6, 1999. IJCAI is the premier international forum for AI research and the papers in these proceedings attest to its high standards.

Seven hundred fifty papers were submitted for review and each paper was reviewed by three experts. This year the 37 members of the Program Committee essentially served as associate editors, recruiting their own reviewers and taking responsibility for their assigned papers. Collectively they recruited over 400 reviewers, whose considerable efforts are much appreciated. This year, 195 papers were accepted, for an overall acceptance rate of 26 percent. These proceedings also include papers that accompany selected invited and award talks.

This year we highlight responses to the challenges issued in the 1997 conference and proceedings. Papers responding to the IJCAI-97 challenges were reviewed on the same high standards for regular submissions, except that a certain narrowness in addressing the specifics of a challenge was tolerated. Not all the 1997 challenges generated papers accepted at IJCAI-99, but several of them attracted high-quality submissions that appear in the proceedings. If this challenge–response process appears to have produced significant progress that would probably not have occurred otherwise, we may well try it again.

We continue IJCAI's tradition of identifying papers for special attention. Reviewers are asked to recommend papers for distinction and then a subcommittee of the Program Committee decides which of them should be highlighted at the conference. This year Dan Geiger, Robert Milne, Maria-Teresa Pazienza, and Toby Walsh helped in choosing the distinguished papers. Highlighting individual papers is always difficult, because such papers tend to receive increased scrutiny, but we see this exercise as yet another way to promote quality and encourage the community to sharpen its criteria for identifying significant contributions to the field.

Putting together a program for a large conference such as IJCAI is a massive undertaking, and this year's program owes its high quality to many people. The members of the Program Committee deserve great credit, for it is their dedication that makes IJCAI the high-quality conference it is. Carol Hamilton, Rick Skalsky, and all the staff at AAAI merit special thanks for their professionalism and extraordinary effort throughout the reviewing process. The staff at Professional Book Center, for the first time offering an option for all-electronic submission of final papers, provided the skill and time required to turn the individual contributions into a book. Vibhu Mittal did a wonderful job of enhancing and adapting the software originally developed by Ramesh Patil for assisting in the assignment of papers.

Gigina Aiello, Anita Kollerbaur, the IJCAI, Inc. trustees, and the members of the IJCAI-99 Advisory Committee provided timely advice at critical junctures. The final selection of papers and the organization of the paper sessions owe a great deal to the efforts of Randy Goebel, Daphne Koller, Maria-Teresa Pazienza, Daniela Rus, Marco Schaerf, and Noel Sharkey, who traveled to Providence last February to help finalize the program. Boi Faltings and Sebastian Thrun were extremely effective in putting together, respectively, the tutorial programs and workshop programs. At Brown University, Katrina Avery, Kee-Eung Kim, Jennet Kirschenbaum, Sonia Leach, and Soren Spies helped in ways too numerous to count.

Thomas Dean
Providence, Rhode Island, USA

Conference Committee

Conference Chair
Luigia Carlucci Aiello
Università di Roma "La Sapienza" (Italy)

Program Chair
Thomas Dean
Brown University (USA)

Secretary-Treasurer
Ronald J. Brachman
AT&T Labs—Research (USA)

Conference Arrangements Chair
Anita Kollerbaur
Stockholm University and
Royal Institute of Technology (Sweden)

Local Arrangements Chair
Carl Gustaf Jansson
Stockholm University and
Royal Institute of Technology (Sweden)

**Nordic IJCAI Scientific Advisory
Committee Chair**
Erik Sandewall
Linköping University (Sweden)

Advisory Committee

Chair: Luigia Carlucci Aiello, Università di Roma "La Sapienza" (Italy)
Maria Gini, University of Minnesota (USA)
Hiroaki Kitano, Sony Computer Science Laboratory (Japan)
Teuvo Kohonen, Helsinki University of Technology (Finland)
Jean Claude Latombe, Stanford University (USA)
Nada Lavrac, J. Stefan Institute (Slovenia)
Juzar Motiwalla, Kent Ridge Digital Labs (Singapore)
Bernd Neumann, Universität Hamburg (Germany)
Karen Sparck Jones, FBA, University of Cambridge (England)
Pietro Torasso, University of Turin (Italy)
J. R. Quinlan, RuleQuest Research Pty Ltd and University of New South Wales (Australia)
Tibor Vámos, Hungarian Academy of Sciences (Hungary)
David Waltz, NEC Research Institute (USA)

LOCAL ARRANGEMENTS COMMITTEE

Chair: Carl Gustaf Jansson, Stockholm University and Royal Institute of Technology (Sweden)

Vice Chair and Conference Arrangements Chair: Anita Kollerbaur, Stockholm University
and Royal Institute of Technology (Sweden)

Subcommittee Chairs: Tord Dahl, Financial Chair, Stockholm University and Royal Institute of Technology (Sweden);
Lars Mollberg, Fund-Raising Chair, Ericsson Telecom (Sweden); Kersti Hedman, Exhibition Chair, SITI (Sweden);
Henrik Eriksson, Affiliate Events Chair, Linköping University (Sweden)

Liasion Officers & Representatives for AI Societies: Erik Sandewall, NISAC Liaison, Linköping University (Sweden);
Silvia Coradeschi, RoboCup Liaison, Linköping University (Sweden); Agnar Aamodt, NAIS, Norwegian University of Science
and Technology (Norway); Patrick Doherty, SAIS, Linköping University (Sweden); Timo Honkela, FAIS, Helsinki University
of Technology (Finland); Brian Mayoh, DAIS, Aarhus University (Denmark)

Other Members: Sture Hägglund, Linköping University (Sweden); Rune Gustavsson, University College of
Carlskrona/Ronneby (Sweden); Åsa Rudström, Stockholm University and Royal Institute of Technology (Sweden);
Diana Molero, Royal Institute of Technology (Sweden); Enn Tyugu, Royal Institute of Technology (Sweden);
Peter Wahlgren, Stockholm University (Sweden)

PROGRAM COMMITTEE

Program Chair: Thomas Dean, Brown University (USA)
Agnar Aamodt, Norwegian University of Science and Technology (NTNU, Norway)
Susanne Biundo, University of Ulm (Germany)
Joost Breuker, University of Amsterdam (Netherlands)
Joachim M. Buhmann, University of Bonn (Germany)
Eugene Charniak, Brown University (USA)
Henrik Christensen, Royal Institute of Technology (Sweden)
Rina Dechter, University of California/Irvine (USA)
Pedro Domingos, Instituto Superior Tecnico (Portugal)
Boi Faltings, Ecole Polytechnique Federale de Lausanne (EPFL, Switzerland)
Ian Frank, Electrotechnical Laboratory (Japan)
Dan Geiger, Technion (Israel) and Microsoft Research (USA)
Malik Ghallab, LAAS-CNRS (Centre National de la Recherche Scientifique, France)
Randy Goebel, University of Alberta (Canada)
Radu Horaud, CNRS and INRIA Rhone-Alpes (France)
Liliana Ironi, Consiglio Nazionale delle Ricerche (CNR, Italy)
Finn V. Jensen, Aalborg University (Denmark)
Peter Jonsson, Linköping University (Sweden)
Hiroaki Kitano, Sony Computer Science Laboratory (Japan)
Daphne Koller, Stanford University (USA)
Sarit Kraus, Bar-Ilan University (Israel) and University of Maryland (USA)
David Leake, Indiana University (USA)
David McAllester, AT&T Labs—Research (USA)
Robert Milne, Intelligent Applications (UK)
Andrew Moore, Carnegie Mellon University (USA)
Leora Morgenstern, IBM (USA)
Maria Teresa Pazienza, University of Rome "Tor Vergata" (Italy)
Henri Prade, Institute Recherche en Informatique de Toulouse (IRIT, France)
Daniela Rus, Dartmouth College (USA)
Claude Sammut, University of New South Wales (Australia)
Marco Schaerf, University of Rome "La Sapienza" (Italy)
Noel Sharkey, University of Sheffield (UK)
Sam Steel, University of Essex (UK)
Kilian Stoffel, University of Neuchatel (Switzerland)
Peter Struss, Technical University of Munich and OCC'M Software (Germany)
Moshe Tennenholtz, Technion (Israel)
Volker Tresp, Siemens AG (Germany)
Toby Walsh, University of Strathclyde (UK)

Tutorial Chair: Boi Faltings, Ecole Polytechnique Federale de Lausanne (EPFL, Switzerland)

Workshop Chair: Sebastian Thrun, Carnegie Mellon University (USA)

Additional Volunteer Help to Program Committee: Kee-Eung Kim, Brown University (USA) and
Vibhu O. Mittal, Just Research and Carnegie Mellon University (USA)

IJCAII ORGANIZATION

NISAC (NORDIC IJCAI SCIENTIFIC ADVISORY COMMITTEE)

Chair: Erik Sandewall, Linköping University (Sweden)
Agnar Aamodt, NTNU, Trondheim (Norway)
Niels Ole Bernsen, Odense University (Denmark)
Henrik Christensen, Royal Institute of Technology, Stockholm (Sweden)
Patrick Doherty, Linköping University (Sweden)
Patrik Eklund, University of Umeå (Sweden)
Joergen Fischer Nilsson, Technical University of Denmark (Denmark)
Peter Gärdenfors, University of Lund (Sweden)
Lars Kai Hansen, Denmark's Technical University (Denmark)
Timo Honkela, Helsinki University of Technology (Finland)
Sture Hägglund, Linköping University (Sweden)
Peter Johansen, University of Copenhagen (Denmark)
Christen Krogh, University of Oslo (Norway)
Jan Komorowski, The Norwegian Institute of Technology (Norway)
Bente Maegaard, University of Copenhagen (Denmark)
Brian Mayoh, Aarhus University (Denmark)
Ilkka Niemelä, Helsinki University of Technology (Finland)
John Perram, University of Odense (Denmark)
Anna Sågvall-Hein, Uppsala University (Sweden)
Annika Waern, Swedish Institute of Computer Science (SICS)/ SITI (Sweden)
Karl Johan Åström, Lund Institute of Technology (Sweden)

IJCAI-99 AWARDS

The IJCAI-99 Award for Research Excellence
Reasoning with Cause and Effect
Judea Pearl

The IJCAI-99 Computers and Thought Award
Agent-Based Computing: Promise and Perils
Nicholas R. Jennings

IJCAI-99 Distinguished Papers
Learning in Natural Language
Dan Roth, University of Illinois at Urbana-Champaign

A Distributed Case-Based Reasoning Application for Engineering Sales Support
Ian Watson, AI-CBR University of Salford
Dan Gardingen, Western Air Ltd.

IJCAI Awards Selection Committee
Chair: Wolfgang Wahlster (Saarbruecken, Germany)
Daniel Bobrow (Palo Alto, USA)
C. Raymond Perrault (Palo Alto, USA)
Ross Quinlan (Sydney, Australia)
Erik Sandewall (Linköping, Sweden)

INVITED SPEAKERS*

Minoru Asada (Osaka University) and
Henrik I. Christensen (The Royal Institute of Technology, Stockholm,
and Centre for Autonomous Systems)
Robotics in the Home, Office, and Playing Field

Luca Console (Università di Torino)
and Oskar Dressler (Technical University of Munich)
Model-based Diagnosis in the Real World: Lessons Learned and Challenges Remaining

Neil Gershenfeld (Physics and Media Group at the MIT Media Lab)
Natural Intelligence

Stig B. Hagström (Stanford University)
From Teaching to Learning: The Role of AI in an Education Paradigm Shift

David Heckerman (Microsoft Research)
Learning Bayesian Networks

John Hooker (Carnegie Mellon University)
Unifying Optimization and Constraint Satisfaction

Radu Horaud (CNRS and INRIA Rhone-Alpes)
Non-Metric Dynamic Vision: A Paragdigm for Representing Motion in Perception Space

Lydia Kavraki (Rice University)
Computational Approaches to Drug Design

Robert E. Schapire (AT&T Labs—Research)
Theory and Practice of Boosting

Donia R. Scott (University of Brighton)
The Multilingual Generation Game: Authoring Fluent Texts in Unfamiliar Languages

Oliviero Stock (IRST, Istituto per la Ricerca Scientifica e Technologica)
Was the Title of This Talk Generated Automatically? Prospects for Intelligent Interfaces and Language

Moshe Tennenholtz (Technion Israel Institute of Technology)
Realizing Electronic Commerce: From Economic and Game-Theoretic Models to Working Protocols

* Not all invited speakers elected to submit a paper for publication in the conference proceedings.

Anne Abeille
John Mark Agosta
Robert Aiken
Akiko Aizawa
Rachid Alami
Kamal Ali
Peter Allen
Jose Luis Ambite
Eyal Amir
Alessandro Armando
Kevin Ashley
Chris Atkeson
Ruth Aylett
Franz Baader
Fahiem Bacchus
Marko Balabanovic
Christian Barillot
Claude Barrouil
Roberto Basili
Mathias Bauer
Jon Baxter
Roberto Bayardo
Don Beal
Michael Beetz
Rachel Ben-Eliyahu-Zohary
Massimo Benerecetti
Salem Benferhat
Yoshua Bengio
Belaid Benhamou
Carlos Bento
Ralph Bergmann
Christian Bessiere
Gautam Biswas
Marcus Bjäreland
Yngvi Bjornsson
Alan Blair
Jim Blythe
Mark Boddy
Karl F. Bohringer
Gregory W. Bond
Daniel Borrajo
Craig Boutilier
Liz Bradley
Ronen Brafman
Bertrand Braunschweig
Pavel Brazdil
Bert Bredeweg
Paolo Bresciani
John Bresina
Gerhard Brewka
Amy Briggs

Chris Brown
Gordon Brown
Joachim Buhmann
Wray Buntine
Wolfram Burgard
Robin Burke
Jay Burmeister
Michael Buro
Hilary Buxton
Marco Cadoli
Diego Calvanese
Francisco Cantu
Sharon Caraballo
Jaime Carbonell
Janette Cardoso
John Carroll
Nuria Castell
Amedeo Cesta
Nick Chater
Francois Chaumette
Ken Chen
Yves Chiaramella
Howie Choset
Berthe Y. Choueiry
Ron Chrisley
Daniel J. Clancy
Keith Clark
Peter Clark
Axel Cleeremans
David Cohn
Tony Cohn
Luca Console
Roger Cooke
Silvia Coradeschi
Marie-Odile Cordier
Ulises Cortes
Fabio G. Cozman
Mark Craven
Susan Craw
Bruce Croft
James L. Crowley
Joseph Culberson
Fred Cummins
Bruce D'Ambrosio
Ido Dagan
Kostas Daniilidis
Adnan Darwiche
Ernest Davis
Gert de Cooman
Giuseppe De Giacomo
Johan de Kleer

Hans de Nivelle
Joris De Schutter
Keith Decker
Anatoli Degtyarev
James Delgrande
Thierry Denoeux
Michel Devy
Thomas Dietterich
Yannis Dimopoulos
Clare Dixon
Stephane Donikian
Francesco Donini
Brian Drabble
Mark Drummond
Werner Dubitzky
Phan Minh Dung
Ed Durfee
Pete Edwards
Uwe Egly
Thomas Eiter
Jan-Olof Eklundh
Clark Elliott
Susan L. Epstein
Francesc Esteva
Oren Etzioni
Helene Fargier
Adam Farquhar
Ariel Felner
George Ferguson
Nicola Ferrier
Eugene Fink
Michael Fisher
Peter A. Flach
David Fogel
Norman Foo
Ken Forbus
Maria Fox
Aviezri S. Fraenkel
Enrico Franconi
Jeremy Frank
Eugene C. Freuder
Nir Friedman
Gerhard Friedrich
Daniel Frost
Norbert Fuhr
Cesare Furlanello
Daniel Gaines
Robert Gaizauskas
Joao Gama
Catherine Garbay
Erann Gat

Michael Gelfond
James Geller
Ian P. Gent
Alfonso Gerevini
Felix Gers
Fredric Gey
Aditya K. Ghose
Angelo Gilio
Paolo Giorgini
Enrico Giunchiglia
Robert Givan
Oren Glickman
Ashok Goel
Claudia Goldman
Robert P. Goldman
Moises Goldszmidt
Martin Charles Golumbic
Paulo Gomes
Joshua Goodman
Richard Goodwin
Scott Goodwin
Monique Grandbastien
Jim Greer
Niall Griffith
Reijer Grimbergen
Ralph Grishman
Atanas Gueorguiev
Joakim Gustafsson
Merav Hadad
Peter Haddawy
Othar Hansson
Patrik Haslum
David Hawking
Marti Hearst
Marcus Held
Laurent Henocque
Joachim Hertzberg
Andreas Herzig
Katsutoshi Hirayama
Haym Hirsh
Steffen Hoelldobler
Achim Hoffmann
Reimar Hofmann
Thomas Hofmann
Robert Holte
Ian Horrocks
Ian Horswill
Jeff Horty
Eric Horvitz
Adele Howe
David Hull

Luke Hunsberger
Anthony Hunter
Robert Hyatt
Hiroyuki Iida
Felix Ingrand
Nathan Intrator
Toru Ishida
Hiroshi Ishiguro
Yumi Iwasaki
Jean-Yves Jaffray
Peter Jarvis
Peter Jeavons
Philippe Jegou
David Jensen
Finn V. Jensen
Frank Jensen
Yan-Bin Jia
Radim Jirousek
W. Lewis Johnson
Alipio Jorge
Leo Joskowicz
Andreas Junghanns
Frederic Jurie
Leslie Pack Kaelbling
A.C. Kakas
Subbarao Kambhampati
Gal A. Kaminka
Lars Karlsson
G. Neelakantan Kartha
Simon Kasif
Henry Kautz
Lydia Kavraki
Deepak Khemani
Dennis Kibler
Lefteris Kirousis
Yasuhiko Kitamura
Uffe Kjaerulff
Mark Klein
Kevin Knight
Craig Knoblock
Sven Koenig
Richard E. Korf
Jana Kosecka
Manolis Koubarakis
John Koza
Kazuhiro Kuwabara
James Tin-Yau Kwok
Rex Kwok
Simon Lacroix
Gerhard Lakemeyer
Jerome Lang
Javier Larrosa
Christian Laugier
Jean-Paul Laumond
Steven M. LaValle

Nada Lavrac
Claude Le Pape
John Lee
Daniel Lehmann
Roy Leitch
Maurizio Lenzerini
Ales Leonardis
Frederic Lerasle
Leonardo Lesmo
Yves Lesperance
Paolo Liberatore
Vladimir Lifschitz
Marc Light
Gerard Ligozat
Dekang Lin
Fangzhen Lin
Michael Lindenbaum
Michael Littman
Vincenzo Lombardo
Derek Long
Alneu Lopes
Ramon Lopez de Mantaras
Guy Lorette
Witold Lukaszewicz
Sean Luke
Kevin Lynch
Ann Macintosh
David Madigan
Anders Madsen
Sridhar Mahadevan
Stephen Majercik
Andreas Malik
Shaul Markovitch
Fabio Massacci
Hitoshi Matsubara
Shigeo Matsubara
Robert Matzinger
Jakob Mauss
Norman McCain
Andrew McCallum
Thomas Leo McCluskey
Drew McDermott
Deborah McGuinness
Sheila McIlraith
Christopher Meek
Erica Melis
Robert E. Mercer
Pedro Meseguer
Stefano Messelodi
Silvia Miksch
Alain Mille
Ruslan Mitkov
Riichiro Mizoguchi
Paul-Andre Monney
Serafin Moral

Paul Morris
Steve Moyle
Martin Muehlenbrock
Klaus Robert Mueller
Jean-Pierre Müller
Martin Müller
Philippe Muller
Remi Munos
Hector Munoz-Avila
Tom Murray
Nicola Muscettola
Karen Myers
Daniele Nardi
Abhaya Nayak
Pandurang Nayak
Bernhard Nebel
Ralph Neuneier
Bertrand Neveu
Ann Nicholson
Thomas Nielsen
Ilkka Niemela
Lars Niklasson
Sergei Nirenburg
Toyoaki Nishida
Toshikazu Nishimura
Itsuki Noda
Tim Oates
Klaus Obermayer
Angelo Oddi
Hans Juergen Ohlbach
Hiroshi G. Okuno
Kristian G. Olesen
Charles Ortiz
David Page
Maurice Pagnucco
Luigi Palopoli
Massimo Paolucci
Lynne E. Parker
Ronald Parr
Rupert Parsons
Peter F. Patel-Schneider
Xavier Pennec
David Pennock
Mark Peot
Fernando Pereira
Patrick Perez
Bernhard Pfahringer
Emanuele Pianta
Javier Pinto
Aske Plaat
Enric Plaza
Andreas Podelski
Paolo Pogliano
Lech Polkowski

David Poole
Luigi Portinale
Henri Prade
Patrick Prosser
Foster Provost
Arun K. Pujari
James Pustejovsky
Yang Qiang
Long Quan
Ronan Reilly
Thomas Richardson
Michael Richter
Martin Riedmiller
Jussi Rintanen
Stephen Robertson
Erich Rome
Riccardo Rosati
Jeff Rosenschein
Francesca Rossi
Martin Sachenbacher
Elisha Sacks
Alessandro Saffiotti
Gerhard Sagerer
Lorenza Saitta
Anthony Sanford
Ken Satoh
Abdul Sattar
Tony Savage
Jacques Savoy
Stefan Schaal
Jonathan Schaeffer
Torsten Schaub
Thomas Schiex
Juergen Schmidhuber
Sascha Schmitt
Dale Schuurmans
Eddie Schwalb
Daniel Schwartz
David Schwartz
Rina Schwartz
Michele Sebag
Bart Selman
Sandip Sen
Luciano Serafini
Amanda Sharkey
Onn Shehory
Solomon Eyal Shimony
Candy Sidner
Carles Sierra
Munindar Singh
John Slaney
Philippe Smets
Barbara M. Smith
Stephen F. Smith
Barry Smyth

Wayne Snyder
Liz Sonenberg
Jon Edward Spragg
Ashwin Srinivasan
Mark E. Stickel
Oliviero Stock
Peter Stone
Tomek Strzalkowski
Milan Studeny
Jaap Suermondt
Kurt Sundermeyer
Katia P. Sycara
Patrick Taillibert
Hozumi Tanaka
Katsumi Tanaka
Gerald Tesauro
Sergio Tessaris
Bjørnar Tessem
Sylvie Thiebaux
Michael Thielscher

Bo Thiesson
John Thornton
Sebastian Thrun
Gil Tidhar
Massimo Tistarelli
Hans Tompits
Luis Torgo
Geoffrey Towell
Louise Trave-Massuyes
Paolo Traverso
Gilles Trombettoni
Andre Trudel
Edward Tsang
Peter Turney
Howard Turtle
Paul Utgoff
Marco Valtorta
Johan van Benthem
Michel Van Caneghem
Linda C. van der Gaag

Manuela Veloso
Gerard Verfaillie
Thierry Vidal
Lluis Vila
Michele Vindigni
Ivo Vollrath
Andrei Voronkov
Gerd Wagner
Mark Wallace
Rich Washington
Ian Watson
Geoff Webb
Frank Weberskirch
Gerhard Weiss
Michael Werman
Stefan Wermter
Dietrich Wettschereck
Richard Wheeler
Gerhard Widmer
David E. Wilkins

Mary-Anne Williams
Steven Willmott
Radboud Winkels
Sharon Wood
Franz Wotawa
Yang Xiang
Osher Yadgar
Masayuki Yamamura
Qiang Yang
Mark Yim
Makoto Yokoo
Jia-Huai You
Massimo Zancanaro
Richard Zemel
Nevin L. Zhang
Yan Zhang
Tom Ziemke
Shlomo Zilberstein

CONTENTS

COMPUTER GAME PLAYING

KNOWLEDGE-BASED APPLICATIONS

VOLUME 2

MACHINE LEARNING

AUTOMATED REASONING

AUTOMATED REASONING

Theorem Proving

Lemma Generation for Model Elimination by Combining Top-Down and Bottom-Up Inference

Marc Fuchs

Fakultät für Informatik

TU München

80290 München, Germany

fuchsm@informatik.tu-muenchen.de

Abstract

A very promising approach for integrating top-down and bottom-up proof search is the use of bottom-up generated lemmas in top-down provers. When generating lemmas, however, the currently used lemma generation procedures suffer from the well-known problems of forward reasoning methods, e.g., the proof goal is ignored. In order to overcome these problems we propose two relevancy-based lemma generation methods for top-down provers. The first approach employs a bottom-up level saturation procedure controlled by top-down generated patterns which represent promising subgoals. The second approach uses evolutionary search and provides a self-adaptive control of lemma generation and goal decomposition.

1 Introduction

Top-down and bottom-up approaches for automated theorem proving in first-order logic each have specific advantages and disadvantages. Top-down approaches (like model elimination (ME) [9] or the connection tableau calculus (CTC) [8]) are goal oriented but suffer from long proof lengths and the lack of an effective redundancy control. Bottom-up approaches (like superposition [2]) provide more simplification power but lack in their purest form any kind of goal orientation. Thus, an integration of these two paradigms is desirable.

Two approaches have been in the focus of interest in the last years. The methods from [14; 10] are bottom-up theorem proving approaches. There, the bottom-up inferences are restricted to the use of *relevant clauses* which are detected by additional top-down computations. Thus, goal orientation is combined with redundancy control. In other approaches top-down provers are assisted by *lemmas* ([12; 1; 5]). Also these methods combine goal orientation with redundancy control provided by the lemmas. The use of additional clauses can also reduce the proof length which may lead to large search reductions. But this has to be paid for by an increase of the branching rate of the search space. Thus, mechanisms for selecting relevant clauses are needed.

Our integration approach is based on [12; 5] where lemmas have been used in the CTC. There, in order to refute a set of *input clauses* with the CTC, in a preprocessing phase the input clauses are augmented by bottom-up generated clauses (lemmas). Then, the prover tries to refute this augmented clause set. Lemmas are obtained by creating a pool of possible lemmas which are able to shorten the proof length (*generation step*). Then, in the *selection step* some possibly relevant lemmas are selected which are then used for refuting the given proof task. In [5] it is concentrated on the selection of lemmas and rather simple lemmas have successfully been used. In order to speed-up the proof search in a more effective manner harder lemmas are needed. The generation approaches as used in [12; 5], however, have severe difficulties in generating harder lemmas in a controlled way. They suffer from the earlier mentioned problems of saturation based proving.

Thus, we focus now on the aspect of the generation of possible lemmas and propose two new approaches for a *controlled generation of lemmas for top-down provers* based on the combination of top-down and bottom-up search. The first technique generates lemmas in a systematic way based on some kind of level saturation (as in [12; 5]). The lemma generation, however, is combined with a decomposition of generalized proof goals which represent possibly solvable subgoals in a compact way. These generalized goals are used for detecting possibly irrelevant lemmas. The other approach uses *genetic programming* [7]. In the evolution process simultaneously top-down and bottom-up inferences are performed which are controlled by a fitness function which measures the similarity between open subgoals and derived lemmas. Thus, lemma generation and goal decomposition are focused on promising clauses in a self-adaptive way. We evaluate the usefulness of the new methods at hand of experiments performed with the prover SETHEO [11].

2 Connection Tableau Calculus

In order to refute a set C of clauses the CTC works on *connected (clause) tableaux* for C (see [8]). The inference rules are *start*, *extension*, and *reduction*. The start rule allows a so-called tableau expansion that can only be applied to a trivial tableau, i.e., one consisting of only one node. An expansion step means selecting a variant of a clause from $\mathcal{C}$ and attaching for each of its literals a node (labeled with the respective literal) to a leaf node of an *open* branch, i.e., a branch that does not contain two complementary literals. The start rule can be restricted to some *start clauses*, e.g., the set of negative clauses may be used (see [11]). Tableau reduction closes a branch by unifying a *subgoal s* (the literal at the leaf of the open branch) with the complement of a literal r (denoted by $\sim r$) on the same branch, and applying the substitution to the whole tableau. For defining extension we need the notion of a contrapositive. If $C = l_1 \vee \ldots \vee l_n$ is a clause then each sequence $l_i \leftarrow \sim l_1, \ldots, \sim l_{i-1}, \sim l_{i+1}, \ldots, \sim l_n$, $1 \le i \le n$, is a *contrapositive* of C with *head* l_i and *tail* $\sim l_1, \ldots, \sim l_{i-1}, \sim l_{i+1}, \ldots, \sim l_n$. Extension with a contrapositive $h \leftarrow t_1, \ldots, t_n$ of a clause from $\mathcal{C}$ is performed by selecting a subgoal s, unifying s and $\sim h$ with σ, instantiating the tableau with σ, attaching $h\sigma, \sim t_1\sigma, \ldots, \sim t_n\sigma$ below $s\sigma$, and closing the branch which ends with $h\sigma$.

We say $T \vdash_\mathcal{C} T'$ if and only if tableau T' can be derived from T by applying a start rule (if T is the trivial tableau) or an extension/reduction rule to a subgoal in T. In order to refute an inconsistent clause set $\mathcal{C}$, a search tree has to be examined in a *fair* way (each tree node must finally be visited) until a closed tableau occurs. A *search tree* $\mathcal{T}^\mathcal{C}$ defined by a set of clauses $\mathcal{C}$ is a tree, whose root is labeled with the trivial tableau. Each node in $\mathcal{T}^\mathcal{C}$ labeled with tableau T has as immediate successors the maximal set of nodes $\{v_1, \ldots, v_n\}$, where v_i is labeled with T_i and $T \vdash_\mathcal{C} T_i$, $1 \le i \le n$.

In order to enumerate a search tree implicit enumeration procedures are normally in use that apply *iterative deepening search* with backtracking. Iteratively increasing finite initial parts of the search tree are explored in depth-first search (cp. [13]). For instance, for clause sets $\mathcal{D}$ and $\mathcal{S}$, $\mathcal{T}^{\mathcal{D},\mathcal{S},n}$ denotes the finite initial part of $\mathcal{T}^{\mathcal{D} \cup \mathcal{S}}$ where all tableaux are obtained by using only clauses from $\mathcal{S}$ for the start expansion, only the clauses from $\mathcal{D}$ for extensions, and where the tree depth of each tableau does not exceed a value of $n \in I\!N$. (The root node has depth 0, its successor nodes depth 1, and so on).

3 Goal Decomposition and Saturation

We provide some basic notions regarding the decomposing and saturating capabilities of the CTC which will be used in the following. We start by demonstrating how to extract *query* and *lemma* clauses from a given connection tableau. At first we introduce a method for extracting valid clauses from a connection tableau.

Definition 3.1 (subgoal clause) Let $\mathcal{C}$ be a set of clauses. Let T be a connection tableau for $\mathcal{C}$. Let $s_1, \ldots, s_n$, $n \ge 1$, be the subgoals of T. Then we call $s_1 \vee \ldots \vee s_n$ the *subgoal clause* of T.

The subgoal clause of a connection tableau T for a clause set $\mathcal{C}$ is a logical consequence of $\mathcal{C}$ (see e.g., [8]). Subgoal clauses may be considered to be top-down generated queries or bottom-up generated lemmas depending

on the form of the tableaux they are derived from. First, we consider the analytic character of subgoal clauses and define query clauses as follows (see also [3]).

Definition 3.2 (query tableau, query clause) Let $\mathcal{C}$ be a set of clauses. Let T be a connection tableau for $\mathcal{C}$. Let $\mathcal{S} \subseteq \mathcal{C}$ be a set of start clauses. Let S be the clause below the unlabeled root of T. If S is an instance of a clause from $\mathcal{S}$ we call T a *query tableau* (w.r.t. $\mathcal{S}$) and the subgoal clause of T a *query clause* (w.r.t. $\mathcal{S}$).

Essentially CTC based proof procedures implicitly enumerate query clauses w.r.t. the chosen start clauses $\mathcal{S} \subseteq \mathcal{C}$ until the empty query clause is derived. Lemmas introduce a bottom-up element into the top-down oriented CTC. We employ the following definition of a lemma which extends and generalizes the notions of lemmas used in [12; 1; 5].

Definition 3.3 (lemma tableau, lemma clause) Let $\mathcal{C}$ be a clause set. Let T be a connection tableau for $\mathcal{C}$. Let $C = s_1 \vee \ldots \vee s_n$ be the subgoal clause of T. Let $\mathcal{H}$ be the set of subgoals which are immediate successors of the root. If $\mathcal{H} \ne \emptyset$ we call T a *lemma tableau*. Then, let s_i, $1 \le i \le n$, be the element of $\mathcal{H}$ which is left-most in T. We call the contrapositive $s_i \leftarrow \sim s_1, \ldots, \sim s_{i-1}, \sim s_{i+1}, \ldots, \sim s_n$ of C the *lemma clause* of T.

Example 3.1 Let $\mathcal{C} = \{\neg p(X), p(X) \vee \neg q(X) \vee \neg r(X), r(X) \vee \neg h(X), q(a)\}$. Let $\mathcal{S} = \{\neg p(X)\}$ be the set of start clauses. The left tableau is a query tableau representing the query $\neg q(X) \vee \neg r(X)$ (w.r.t. $\mathcal{S}$), the right tableau is no query tableau but a lemma tableau which represents the lemma $p(a) \leftarrow h(a)$.

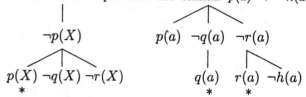

A lemma application transforms a subgoal into a (possibly empty) set of new subgoals. An application of a lemma L to a subgoal s can be viewed as attaching the instantiated lemma tableau of L below s. Thus, it works as a macro operator in the search space. The use of a bottom-up created lemma can close a subgoal by an extension with the lemma and performing reduction steps into the introduced subgoals (tail literals) and thus reduces the proof length. In the following we will always employ such a purely bottom-up oriented view on lemmas, i.e., they replace deductions at the "tableau front". Extension steps to instantiated tail literals of lemmas are forbidden. This provides a controlled use of lemmas and prevents a nesting of lemma applications when dealing with non-unit lemmas.

4 Pattern Controlled Level Saturation

Our first method for generating lemmas is based on a combined *systematic* goal decomposition and lemma saturation. The basic idea is to employ iterative top-down and bottom-up generation procedures which produce in iteration step (level) $i > 1$ all query and lemma tableaux of depth i by the decomposition or saturation of the queries and lemmas of the previous level, respectively. Initial queries and lemmas (created in step 1) are the start clauses and the contrapositives of the input clauses, respectively. Then, after each iteration step subsumed tableaux are deleted (a notion of tableau subsumption can be found, e.g., in [8]). Thus, a proof of depth d can be obtained in $\lceil \frac{d}{2} \rceil$ top-down and bottom-up iteration steps. It is obtained by closing a query tableau generated in step $\lceil \frac{d}{2} \rceil$ using bottom-up lemmas (by extension of the query literals with lemmas and closing the introduced subgoals with reductions) which have been created in the steps $1, \ldots, \lceil \frac{d}{2} \rceil$.

This combined bottom-up and top-down proof search has several theoretical advantages compared to a pure bottom-up or top-down search. The top-down search is improved by bottom-up processing which avoids the recomputation of solutions for multiple occurring subgoals in query clauses. Moreover, the method improves on a pure bottom-up computation because it is more goal oriented and thus the production of a large number of irrelevant clauses may be avoided.

In practice, however, such an approach does not appear to be reasonable (for "harder problems"). An explicit storage of all generated tableaux is not sensible when dealing with ME based provers because of the huge increase of the number and size of the generated tableaux. Thus, we have to focus only on some few relevant query tableaux (or query clauses when dealing with Horn problems) and lemmas which are maintained after each level for further decomposition or saturation in the next iteration, respectively. Heuristic selection criteria for query tableaux and lemma clauses are needed. When using such normally fuzzy criteria, however, it is not guaranteed any longer that a query tableau which can be closed with lemmas can be produced after $\lceil \frac{d}{2} \rceil$ iterations. It is probable that useful queries or lemmas are discarded such that more than $\lceil \frac{d}{2} \rceil$ iterations are needed. Then, the process may be more costly than conventional top-down or bottom-up deduction. Because of the deletion of query tableaux and lemmas it is even possible that no proof can be found by clc ing a maintained query tableau with derived lemma clauses.

Thus, we employ a slightly different (lemma oriented) method which we will explain only for *Horn clauses and unit lemmas* for simplicity reasons. Instead of employing a complete top-down enumeration of all query clauses we work in an abstracted top-down search space. Literals of specific query clauses are generalized to so-called *patterns*. Patterns are literals which cover the form of several subgoals. Specifically, we try to guarantee that subgoals occurring in a proof are subsumed by some patterns. Patterns are created in $d-1$ steps. As initial patterns, in step 1, the literals occurring in start clauses are created. Then, in each step $i > 1$ we successively decompose patterns of the previous step $i-1$ into new subgoals

and generalize then the subgoals to new patterns. Thus, patterns created in step i generalize subgoals of depth i which occur in query clauses. These top-down generated patterns cannot be used for finishing a proof task (with the help of lemmas). However, they provide relevancy criteria for lemmas. If a lemma is not unifiable with the complement of a specific pattern it can be discarded. Thus, we can work with a conventional iterated lemma generation procedure whose maintenance criteria for lemmas are assisted by top-down inferences. Finally, the lemmas are used in a top-down proof run for refuting the input clauses.

We make our method more concrete. We start with the top-down goal decomposition. First, we show how to generalize literals occurring in a set $\mathcal{Q}$ of subgoal clauses to patterns. We use as patterns $N \in \mathbb{N}$ literals from the set $Lit_{<L}$ for $L \in \mathbb{N}$. $Lit_{<L}$ is the set of all literals where each literal has a length (no. of symbols) $l \leq L$ and cannot be specialized to a literal with length $l' > l$ and $l' \leq L$. Patterns should generalize the subgoals of clauses from $\mathcal{Q}$ which are the most likely to occur in a proof. In order to determine the literals to be used as patterns we employ a function $qual_{\mathcal{Q}}$ on literals. This function is based on a notion of quality $qual_{sg}$ on subgoals. $qual_{sg}$ is used to estimate whether a subgoal may occur in a proof. Then, $qual_{\mathcal{Q}}$ expresses how many subgoals from $\mathcal{Q}$ of a high quality are generalized by a pattern.

$qual_{sg}(s)$ of a subgoal s is a value which represents the "generality" of s since we assume that more general subgoals can more easily be solved. For instance, small subgoals with many variables may get large values by $qual_{sg}$ (cp. [5]). $qual_{\mathcal{Q}}$ is defined using $qual_{sg}$ as follows.

Definition 4.1 (pattern quality) For a literal l let $Inst(l)$ be the multi-set $\{s : C_1 \vee s \vee C_2 \in \mathcal{Q}, \exists \mu : l\mu = s\}$. We define the pattern quality $qual_{\mathcal{Q}}(l)$ of a literal l w.r.t. $\mathcal{Q}$ by $qual_{\mathcal{Q}}(l) = \sum_{s \in Inst(l)} qual_{sg}(s)$.

The best N literals from $Lit_{<L}$ w.r.t. $qual_{\mathcal{Q}}$ form the set $pat_{L,N}(\mathcal{Q})$ of patterns for $\mathcal{Q}$. Patterns which generalize subgoals which are part of a proof provide an exact criterion for discarding irrelevant lemmas. A pattern must be unifiable with the complement of a lemma. L and N are responsible for providing a compromise between a large pruning effect of the patterns on the number of generated lemmas (L large, N small) or a high probability that no useful lemmas are discarded (L small, N large). We employ a query generation algorithm which gets as input a clause set $\mathcal{C}$, start clauses $\mathcal{S}$, and an iteration number $I \geq 1$. As output the sets of patterns $\mathcal{P}_1, \ldots, \mathcal{P}_I$ are delivered.

Procedure 4.1 (query generation)

1. $\mathcal{P}_1 := \{l : C_1 \vee l \vee C_2 \in \mathcal{S}\}$.

2. *for $i := 2$ to I do:*

   (a) *let $\mathcal{Q}$ be the set of the most general query clauses of query tableaux from $\mathcal{T}^{\mathcal{C}, \mathcal{P}_{i-1}, 2}$ which are not part of $\mathcal{T}^{\mathcal{C}, \mathcal{P}_{i-1}, 1}$.*

   (b) $\mathcal{P}_i := pat_{L,N}(\mathcal{Q})$.

The lemma generation algorithm enumerates lemma tableaux in a similar way as in [12; 5] but additionally uses the generated patterns. It can be applied after the generation of the query pattern sets $\mathcal{P}_1, \ldots, \mathcal{P}_I$. A further input of the algorithm is again an iteration number $J \leq I$ and the set of input clauses $\mathcal{C}$. As output a lemma set $\mathcal{L}$ is delivered.

Procedure 4.2 (lemma generation)

1. $\mathcal{L} := \{l \in \mathcal{C} : |l| = 1, \exists \mu : l\mu = {\sim}s\mu, s \in \bigcup_{j=1}^{I} \mathcal{P}_j\}.$

2. $\mathcal{M}_1 := \{l \in \mathcal{C} : |l| = 1\}.$

3. *for* $i := 2$ *to* J *do:*

   (a) *let* $\mathcal{M}_i$ *be the set of the most general lemma clauses of lemma tableaux from* $\mathcal{T}^{\mathcal{C} \cup \mathcal{L}, \mathcal{C}, 2}$ *which are not in* $\bigcup_{j=1}^{i-1} \mathcal{M}_j$.

   (b) $\mathcal{L} := \{l \in \mathcal{M}_i : |l| = 1, \exists \mu : l\mu = {\sim}s\mu,$
   $s \in \bigcup_{j=1}^{I-i+1} \mathcal{P}_j\} \cup \mathcal{L}.$

The chance for easy lemmas to be maintained is higher than for hard lemmas since more patterns are used. This is because easy lemmas may be applicable in more depth levels of a proof. The pattern-based criterion discards lemmas immediately after their generation and thus saves space. The set $\mathcal{L}$ forms the set of possible lemmas which may finally be used in the proof run in addition to the input clauses. We consider a closed tableau for a Horn clause set of a depth of d. If $I \geq d - 1$ and the patterns from $\mathcal{P}_i$ cover the form of the subgoals with depth i which are needed to find the closed tableau, the lemma generation method is complete. This means that it can be guaranteed that $\mathcal{L}$ contains all lemmas needed to reduce the proof depth by an amount of $J - 1$. Specifically, it is also possible to reduce the proof length. In practice after the execution of the generation procedure lemmas are selected from $\mathcal{L}$ with a selection function Φ (see [5]). These lemmas are used in a final proof run.

5   Evolutionary Lemma Generation

The pattern-based method has the pleasant property that it provides a systematic generation of lemmas which can guarantee the generation of useful lemmas under certain conditions. A practical advantage is that highly efficient model-elimination provers can be employed for top-down as well as bottom-up inferences.

But if the choice of the patterns is not optimal the method works as a *local optimization method* because lemmas are discarded. Lemma tableaux whose derivations require the use of (small quality) lemmas which are discarded at a certain moment cannot be generated later. Thus, it is rather probable that the generation of useful and also well judged lemmas is prevented because the generation of such lemmas may require the use of other discarded clauses.

Our solution to this problem is the use of evolutionary techniques for lemma generation which are based on the genetic programming (GP) paradigm. For a detailed introduction to genetic algorithms or genetic programming

we refer to [6] or [7], respectively. Our application of GP combines the evolution of query and lemma tableaux. The abstract principles of our method are as follows. An individual corresponds to a connection tableau which represents a lemma or a query clause. Thus, we work with (possibly) partial solutions (lemmas) of our initial problem and with goal decompositions which represent problems which are still open. The fitness of one lemma is given by its ability to solve or "almost" solve an open subproblem. A tableau which represents a query is the fitter the more subgoals are solvable (almost solvable) by lemmas. The genetic operators are based on the exchange of subtableaux. Thus, good subdeductions which may be part of a proof are used in order to create new (and possibly fitter) individuals. Building blocks (subtableaux) of the fittest individuals persist with a high probability and can contribute to a generation of lemmas or query clauses which appear in a proof.

Thus, the lemma and query tableaux used for GP are used in a deductive sense by producing new lemma and query clauses in order to solve the original problem or at least to generate useful lemmas. Further, they play a role as control elements. The lemma production influences the query decomposition and vice versa. This is similar to our first pattern-based approach. But now also the top-down decomposition is influenced by some kind of distance to given valid lemmas. Hence the search is concentrated on "interesting" regions of the search space in a self-adaptive way. Furthermore, the probabilistic character of GP offers the chance to avoid a naive hill climbing based search and can produce needed lemmas although ancestors are judged by low fitness values.

The technical realization of these ideas is as follows. As already mentioned we use a fixed sized population of tableaux. Each tableau represents a query or a lemma. The population is initialized using the given input clauses to be refuted. Each query tableau obtainable by applying the start rule with a clause allowed as a start clause is added to the population. Analogously for each contrapositive of an input clause a lemma tableau is built. Additionally, it is possible to use some further selected lemma or query clauses in the initial population (see Section 6).

We employ three genetic operators, namely *reproduction*, and variants of *crossover* and *mutation*. Reproduction copies one element from the old population to the next. Our crossover operator differs from standard GP where two randomly chosen subtrees of two ancestor individuals are exchanged. Since such an operation would normally not result in a connection tableau crossover has to be constrained. One approach is to allow crossover at nodes v_1 and v_2 (labeled with l_1 and l_2) of two individuals T_1 and T_2, respectively, only if $\mu = mgu(l_1, l_2)$ exists. Then, an exchange of the subtrees could take place and the resulting tableaux are instantiated with μ. As appealing as this sounds it neglects the fact that a re-use of a subdeduction below v_1 in tableau T_1 may be possible below v_2 in T_2 although the above criterion is not applicable. This is because the subdeduction may be more general when viewed in an isolated way and is "over-instantiated" in T_1. Consider following example.

Example 5.1 Let $\mathcal{C} \supseteq \{q(a) \vee \neg p(f(a)), p(f(X)), p(a), \neg p(X) \vee \neg r(X)\}$. The following figure shows two connection tableaux for $\mathcal{C}$. The arrow (which is also called *link*) shows that the subdeduction below $\neg p(f(a))$ which represents a proof for $p(f(X))$ can be used below the goal $\neg p(a)$ which would take the form $\neg p(Y)$ when deleting the subproof below the subgoal.

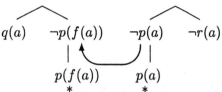

Thus, *asymmetric link relations* between tableaux can be built which show which subdeductions can replace others (see also [4]). Our crossover variant produces *one* new individual. Consistently with the link relation in a *destination* tableau a (possibly empty) subdeduction is replaced by a subdeduction in a *source tableau*. Then, the modified destination tableau is instantiated in an appropriate manner (more details can be found in [4]). In the above example the left and the right tableau serve as source and destination tableau, respectively. The tableau resulting from crossover represents the query $\neg r(f(X))$. The crossover operator can be viewed as a *generalized extension step* which allows us to attach subdeductions and not only clauses to (inner) nodes. We use a mutation operator which serves as a *generalized reduction step* (see [4]). It is needed in the non-Horn case to preserve the completeness of the genetic operators in order to create each useful lemma.

The genetic operators are applied to individuals chosen probabilistically proportionate to their fitness. We use a similarity measure between query and lemma tableaux for computing fitness. In the Horn case only the query and lemma clauses are considered. In the non-Horn case we may also consider open branches for judging the similarity. We use a similarity measure which considers certain syntactic properties of literals (cp. [4]).

The evolutionary search stops if a query tableau can be extended to a closed tableau using the lemma tableaux or a given maximal number of generations is reached. In the latter case a selection function Φ (see [5]) chooses lemma clauses of the current population which are used in the final proof run. In summation the GP approach cannot guarantee that useful lemmas are generated during the search. But at least one can show that when fulfilling weak conditions each needed lemma can be created with a probability greater than 0 [4]. The self-adaptation capabilities and randomized effects can allow the solution of problems which are out of reach of conventional search techniques (see Section 6).

6 Experimental Results

We want to analyze the performance of the newly developed lemma generation procedures. We have chosen the

Table 1: Experimental Results in the TPTP library

domain		SETHEO	SETHEO/PAT	SETHEO/GP
BOO	≤ 5	6	12	12
	≤ 10	10	14	14
	≤ 15	11	14	14
CAT	≤ 5	3	5	5
	≤ 10	3	5	5
	≤ 15	3	5	5
COL	≤ 5	10	29	27
	≤ 10	27	32	32
	≤ 15	28	33	33
GRP	≤ 5	9	11	15
	≤ 10	9	11	15
	≤ 15	9	11	15
SET	≤ 5	36	48	50
	≤ 10	39	50	52
	≤ 15	41	50	54

high performance model elimination prover SETHEO for the final top-down proof run as well as for the pattern based lemma generation procedure.

As test set domains of the problem library TPTP v2.0.0 [15] are used. The domains BOO, CAT, COL, GRP, and SET have been chosen. BOO, COL, and GRP mostly contain Horn problems whereas in the other domains often non-Horn problems occur. We tackled only "hard problems". These problems cannot be solved with the conventional SETHEO system within 10 seconds. We have used a SUN Ultra 2 and a run time limit of 15 minutes for each problem. This includes the time for the lemma generation and the final refutation run.

In Table 1 one can find the performance of the newly developed systems in comparison with SETHEO. SETHEO is configured as described in [11]. Specifically, this includes the use of *folding-up* (see [8]) in the proof run. SETHEO/PAT generates lemmas based on our first method. The lemmas are then added to SETHEO. The final proof run is done with the same version of SETHEO which is used without lemmas. We restrict the lemma generation to unit lemmas which are sufficient to obtain good results in the considered domains. The lemma generation Procedure 4.2 is employed with iteration number $J = 3$. The iteration number for the pattern generation was set to $I = 6$. We used for the pattern length L and the pattern number N the combinations $(L, N) = (3, 3)$ and $(L, N) = (7, 10)$. We depict for each example the best result which could be obtained with a configuration. The selection function Φ is defined using the *lemma delaying method* as introduced in [5]. SETHEO/GP is based on genetic programming. We have initialized the evolutionary lemma generation in such a manner that the lemmas which are produced by the pattern based method with two bottom-up iteration steps are used in the initial population. Furthermore, we use some selected queries (see [4]). Thus, the procedure can start at an interesting point in the search space. Unit lemmas are selected from the final population using the lemma delaying method. We show the best results obtained in 5 runs for each problem. The exact configuration of our genetic algorithm can be found in [4].

In the table we have depicted the number of problems which can be solved by the considered approaches after 5, 10, and 15 minutes. We can see that all lemma methods improve on the conventional SETHEO system in a stable way. Often lemma tableaux of a proof depth of 2, sometimes of a depth of 3 and 4, can be used in a proof. The use of these lemmas leads to a proof length reduction and significantly smaller search spaces which have to be traversed by the iterative deepening search procedure. In comparison with the already successful conventional lemma generation approaches (without top-down assistance) as described in [12; 5] all of our methods improve on results obtained with these methods. The level saturation procedure can be improved by the top-down generated patterns. E.g., in the SET domain where a lot of predicate and function symbols occur the pattern use is indispensable. In domains like BOO, however, the patterns cannot incorporate additional potential for deleting lemmas. The GP approach significantly improves on the level saturation method. A not fitness controlled randomized method achieves worse results (see [4]).

Considering the pattern based method and GP one can recognize that with GP generated lemmas the proof length can often be reduced in a more effective manner. The pattern based method has some difficulties in producing sufficiently specific patterns well-suited for the first iteration steps since the probability that such patterns match needed query literals decreases from iteration to iteration. GP can overcome the problem that in its initial population some useful lemmas may be missing. It can re-compute these lemmas. Furthermore, we could observe that GP sometimes generates well-suited rather hard lemmas (with depth 4).

7 Conclusion and Future Work

We presented two methods for combining top-down and bottom-up proof search aiming at generating a set of well-suited lemmas. The lemmas are then used in a final top-down proof run in addition to the given input clauses. We have seen that an evaluation of an abstracted top-down search space (with patterns) and a partial evaluation of interesting regions of the complete top-down search space (by genetic programming) is indeed able to provide sufficient information in order to control bottom-up inferences. As the experiments show the criteria are strong enough to generate interesting hard lemmas which provide large search reductions.

The study reveals that the use of our techniques in a parallel proof environment is desirable. The pattern based approach can work with different parameters for L, N, I, and J in parallel. Also the GP algorithm can profit when different incarnations run in parallel. Specifically, the evolutionary approach offers the possibility to develop high performance parallel systems which may scale up to a large number of processors.

References

[1] O. Astrachan and D. Loveland. The Use of Lemmas in the Model Elimination Procedure. *Journal of Automated Reasoning*, 19(1):117–141, 1997.

[2] L. Bachmair and H. Ganzinger. Rewrite-based equational theorem proving with selection and simplification. *Journal of Logic and Computation*, 4(3):217–247, 1994.

[3] D. Fuchs. Cooperation of Top-Down and Bottom-Up Theorem Provers by Subgoal Clause Transfer. In *Proceedings of AISC-98*, pages 157–169. Springer, LNAI 1476, 1998.

[4] M. Fuchs. An Evolutionary Approach for Combining Top-down and Bottom-up Proof Search. AR-Report AR-98-04, 1998, Technische Universität München, Institut für Informatik, 1998.

[5] M. Fuchs. Relevancy-Based Lemma Selection for Model Elimination using Lazy Tableaux Enumeration. In *Proceedings of ECAI-98*, pages 346–350. John Wiley & Sons, Ltd., 1998.

[6] J. Holland. *Adaptation in natural and artificial systems*. Ann Arbor: Univ. of Michigan Press, second edition, 1992.

[7] J. Koza. *Genetic Programming: On the Programming of Computers by Means of Natural Selection*. MIT Press, Cambridge, MA, 1992.

[8] R. Letz, K. Mayr, and C. Goller. Controlled Integration of the Cut Rule into Connection Tableau Calculi. *Journal of Automated Reasoning*, 13:297–337, 1994.

[9] D. Loveland. *Automated Theorem Proving: a Logical Basis*. North-Holland, 1978.

[10] D. Loveland, D. Reed, and D. Wilson. SATCHMORE: SATCHMO with RElevancy. *Journal of Automated Reasoning*, 14:325–351, 1995.

[11] M. Moser, O. Ibens, R. Letz, J. Steinbach, C. Goller, J. Schumann, and K. Mayr. The Model Elimination Provers SETHEO and E-SETHEO. *Journal of Automated Reasoning*, 18(2), 1997.

[12] J. Schumann. Delta - a bottom-up preprocessor for top-down theorem provers. system abstract. In *Proceedings of CADE-12*, pages 774–777. Springer, LNAI 814, 1994.

[13] M. Stickel. A prolog technology theorem prover: Implementation by an extended prolog compiler. *Journal of Automated Reasoning*, 4:353–380, 1988.

[14] M. Stickel. Upside-Down Meta-Interpretation of the Model Elimination Theorem-Proving Procedure for Deduction and Abduction. *Journal of Automated Reasoning*, 13:189–210, 1994.

[15] G. Sutcliffe, C. Suttner, and T. Yemenis. The TPTP Problem Library. In *Proceedings of CADE-12*, pages 252–266. LNAI 814, 1994.

Cooperation of Heterogeneous Provers

Jörg Denzinger and **Dirk Fuchs**
Fachbereich Informatik
Universität Kaiserslautern
67663 Kaiserslautern, Germany
{denzinge, dfuchs}@informatik.uni-kl.de

Abstract

We present a methodology for achieving co-operation between already existing theorem provers employing different proof paradigms and/or different search controls, and using different but related logics. Cooperation between the provers is achieved by periodically interchanging clauses which are selected by so-called referees. By employing referees both on the side of a sending prover and a receiving prover the communication is both success- and demand-driven, which results in a rather small communication overhead and synergetical effects.

We report on experiments regarding the cooperation of the provers SPASS, SETHEO and DISCOUNT in domains of the TPTP library and with problems stemming from an application in software component retrieval. The experiments show significant improvements in the number of problems solved as well as in the solution times.

1 Introduction

Search is a central problem solving method employed in AI systems. For most problem areas there exist many systems based on different search paradigms like branch-and-bound, evolutionary algorithms, or problem decomposition. All these paradigms have different strengths and weaknesses and much effort has been invested in implementing systems suitable for dealing with hard and interesting problem instances.

An example for such a problem area is automated deduction. The paradigms used are problem decomposition in analytical provers and (intelligent) enumeration of logical consequences in saturation-based provers. For each paradigm there are several calculi and for each calculus different implementations, typically with many parameters allowing for different incarnations of a prover.

Many experimental studies and prover competitions have shown that it is very difficult to find a priori the best prover for a given problem instance. Therefore competition approaches where several incarnations of one prover or several provers run on different machines until one prover is successful have been proposed (see [Ertel, 1992]) and are used in applications. However, from an economical point of view such approaches are not very efficient, since only one machine contributes to solving the instance. A *cooperation* of the provers would be more interesting and should also lead to finding solutions faster by achieving synergetical effects.

There are approaches for cooperation of homogeneous search systems that have been used for coupling different incarnations of the same prover. Further, Sutcliffe [1992] proposed a concept for heterogeneous provers but failed to deliver convincing results. The problems to solve in order to achieve a successful cooperation of different provers are (1) finding appropriate types of results to interchange, (2) selecting useful results out of the large number of produced results, and (3) having efficient implementations of the provers.

In this paper, we present a general approach for achieving cooperation between search systems using different paradigms that tackles the problems mentioned above for automated deduction. Our TECHS approach (**TE**ams for **C**ooperative **H**eterogeneous **S**earch) allows us to use existing provers with only small modifications, limits the amount of communication by filtering the results of a sending prover, does not unnecessarily disturb the work of receiving provers since received data is filtered with respect to current and future needs, and has the ability to integrate specialized provers.

Our experiments with three state-of-the-art provers, namely SPASS, SETHEO and DISCOUNT, show that their cooperation indeed outperforms the simple competition approach for all tested domains and all time limits. In the tested domains of the TPTP ([Sutcliffe *et al.*, 1994]) TECHS solves up to twice as many hard problems as can be solved by the individual provers taken together.

2 The TECHS Approach

The general idea of the TECHS approach is to interchange selected results between the search agents of a search team in regular time intervals. The search agents are incarnations of the search systems that have been integrated into the distributed system by enhancing them with communication facilities. If there is more than one incarnation of a search system in the team then the incarnations have to differ in their search control. We call the phases where the search agents independently work on their problem *working phases*, the phases where information is exchanged *cooperation phases*.

To start the team, each agent is given either the whole problem instance to solve or the parts of the instance it can work with. The selection process of results takes place both on the side of a sending agent, by a so-called *send-referee*, and on the side of the receiving agent, by a so-called *receive-referee*. Each search agent may have between 1 and $n - 1$ send-referees, if there are n agents in the team, and 1 or no receive-referee.

The task of a send-referee is to select results from the current search state of its agent that should be communicated to the other agents the send-referee is responsible for. The criteria used by a send-referee are either totally based on the success the results have had for its agent or include some general knowledge about the demands of the receiving agents. If a send-referee is responsible for the selection of results for more than one receiving agent, in most cases only success-based criteria can be used. Typically send-referees evaluate results with respect to their syntactic structure and the search steps the results were involved in.

The task of a receive-referee is to select those results sent to its agent that are considered useful for its agent in its current state or in future states. Therefore the criteria used by receive-referees either reflect the current demands and needs of its agent or try to anticipate future demands and needs. Because an agent receives only a small number of results, the criteria used by receive-agents can involve more expensive computations, like the impact of a result on the current search state, than in the case of send-referees.

3 TECHS in Theorem Proving

In theorem proving, the TECHS approach requires different provers running in parallel on different computing nodes. Proof problems are specified in first-order clausal logic. The provers employ either calculi which are complete for first-order logic (*universal provers*) or calculi which are complete for a sub-logic of first-order logic (*specialized provers*). We allow the use of saturation-based and analytic calculi.

In the following, we first introduce the saturation-based calculi *superposition* and *unfailing completion*, and the analytical *connection tableau calculus*. This is because we employ provers based on these calculi in our experiments. After that, we explain in detail how the TECHS concept can be instantiated for provers based on the introduced calculi. Since clauses are to be exchanged between the provers we must at first cope with the topic of how to *extract clauses from the proof search*. After that, we proceed by introducing several methods for *selecting clauses*, i.e. we describe possible send- and receive-referees. Finally, we explain how a prover can *integrate received clauses* into its search state.

3.1 Basics of Theorem Proving

The superposition calculus ([Bachmair and Ganzinger, 1994]) contains several inference rules which can be applied to a set of clauses that constitute a search state. Generally, its inference rules are *expansion* inference rules (superposition left and right, equality resolution, and equality factoring). These rules allow the generation of new clauses that are added to the search state. All inference rules are well-suited for handling equality, i.e. no equality axioms are needed. In addition to expansion rules contraction rules like rewriting or subsumption can be employed. These rules delete redundant clauses or replace clauses by simpler ones.

In order to show the inconsistency of a clause set $\mathcal{C}$, starting with $\mathcal{C}$ derivations of clause sets have to be performed until a set $\mathcal{D}$ is derived which contains the empty clause. A theorem prover based on superposition usually maintains a set $\mathcal{F}^P$ of so-called *passive clauses* from which it selects and removes one clause C at a time. This clause is put into the set $\mathcal{F}^A$ of *activated clauses*. Activated clauses are, unlike passive clauses, allowed to produce new clauses via the application of some inference rules. The inferred new clauses are put into $\mathcal{F}^P$. Initially, $\mathcal{F}^A = \emptyset$ and $\mathcal{F}^P = \mathcal{C}$. The search stops if the empty clause is derived. The indeterministic selection or *activation step* is realized by heuristic means. A heuristic $\mathcal{H}$ associates a number $\omega_C \in \mathbb{N}$ with each $C \in \mathcal{F}^P$, and the $C \in \mathcal{F}^P$ with the smallest *weight* ω_C is selected.

The unfailing completion procedure ([Bachmair *et al.*, 1989]) essentially is a restriction of superposition to unit equations and allows for the development of efficient provers for pure equational logic.

The connection tableau calculus (*CTC* for short) works on *connection tableaux* for a clause set $\mathcal{C}$ (see [Letz *et al.*, 1994]). It employs three inference rules in order to transform one tableau (tree of literals) into another. The *start rule* attaches the literals of an input clause beneath the unmarked root node. Tableau *reduction* unifies a literal s at the leaf of an open branch with the complement of a literal r on the same branch, and applies the substitution to the whole tableau. Hence, by reduction branches can be closed. If a literal of an input clause is unifiable with the complement of the leaf literal of an open branch, *extension* can attach the literals of the input clause beneath the leaf literal. Since the tableau must remain connected after the extension step (each non-leaf literal must be identical to the complement of one of its immediate successors in the tree) the tableau must be instantiated with this unifier (see [Letz *et al.*, 1994]). Because the *CTC* has no specific rules for handling equality, equality axioms must possibly be added to the axiomatization.

In order to show the inconsistency of a set $\mathcal{C}$, all tableaux derivable from the trivial tableau have to be enumerated until a closed tableau appears. This search space can be represented by a search tree. Normally, tableaux enumeration procedures apply *consecutively bounded iterative deepening search with backtracking* ([Korf, 1985]). In this approach iteratively larger finite initial parts of the search tree are explored with depth-first search.

3.2 Extraction of clauses

The first step of an exchange of information is the extraction of clauses from the search states a prover has produced in a working phase. We distinguish between saturation-based and CTC-based provers.

The extraction of valid clauses from search states of saturation-based provers is very easy because search states are sets of clauses. Even more, a theorem prover can take all interesting clauses to be selected from the *actual search state* at the beginning of a cooperation phase. This is because the provers only derive new clauses, delete unnecessary clauses, or simplify clauses. Hence, the sequence of produced search states (clause sets) is not needed. It is sufficient to consider the most recently derived clause set. We restricted ourselves to the extraction of active clauses since these clauses are maximally contracted w.r.t. the current clause set.

CTC-based provers conduct a search with iterative deepening and backtracking in the search tree of all connection tableaux. A single search state is only one of these tableaux. Hence, it is only possible to extract information on *one* proof attempt from a search state. If the proof attempt represented by the search state does not lead to a proof it might be that all clauses which can be extracted from it are unnecessary. Then, send-referees might have to chose from a pool consisting of unnecessary clauses only. This shows that clauses must be extracted from *all* search states enumerated during a working phase, i.e. they must essentially be extracted from the search tree of all tableaux.

Because of the fact that the search tree of all tableaux is in general not given explicitly, clauses must be extracted from the enumerated tableaux during the search process. A possible method to do this is to utilize *bottom-up lemma mechanisms* (see, e.g., [Letz *et al.*, 1994]) of connection tableau-based theorem provers. We used a second variant and extracted *top-down lemmas*, so-called subgoal clauses (see [Fuchs, 1998a]), from a tableau. A subgoal clause is the clause of the open leaf literals of a tableau. Before a send-referee is applied to the set of extracted clauses it is reasonable to compute a *minimal* clause set by eliminating subsumed clauses.

3.3 Realization of send-referees

A send-referee in a system based on the TECHS approach consists of a pair (S, φ) of a *filter predicate S* and a *selection function φ*. The prover that receives the results of the send-referee obtains those clauses in the cooperation phases that pass through the filter and that are selected by φ. The filter predicate S limits the set of clauses that are eligible for transmission. Typically, clauses are filtered out that are redundant w.r.t. the receivers. Redundant means that a receiver cannot use the clauses in its inference mechanism due to its specific logic. The selection function φ can employ several

judgment functions $\psi_1, \ldots, \psi_n$. These functions ψ_i associate a natural number with each clause C, and C is considered the better the higher the value $\psi_i(C)$ is. φ eventually selects the clauses with the best judgments.

Firstly, we have developed a judgment function ψ_{gen} which considers *syntactic features of clauses*. It computes a weighted sum of the number of variables and two times the number of function symbols of a clause and hence prefers general short clauses which contain many variables and only few function symbols. These clauses are useful for saturation-based provers because they might often take part in contracting inferences (subsumption, rewriting). They are often also useful for CTC-based provers because open tableau branches might be closed by extending the branches with them and closing the introduced literals with reduction steps.

Secondly, function ψ_{hist} judges the *role of clauses in the search process* conducted so far. It is defined by $\psi_{hist}(C) = \alpha_1 \cdot \mathsf{sub}(C) + \alpha_2 \cdot \mathsf{exp}(C)$, $\alpha_1 > 0 > \alpha_2$. For a saturation-based prover, $\mathsf{sub}(C)$ denotes the number of clauses subsumed by C, $\mathsf{exp}(C)$ is the number of expansion inferences C was involved in. For a CTC-based prover, $\mathsf{sub}(C)$ is the number of clauses subsumed by C after the extraction and $\mathsf{exp}(C)$ is the number of extension or reduction inferences applied to (instances) of literals of C. If the receiver of clauses is a saturation-based prover the idea is to select clauses which may reduce the search space by subsuming other clauses without simultaneously introducing many new clauses by expanding inferences. The criterion is also sensible for receiving CTC-based provers because an uncontrolled increase of the search space caused by the additional clauses might be prevented.

Finally, we employ the function ψ_{deriv} that *judges the derivation tree of a clause* w.r.t. its possible usefulness for the receiver. The derivation tree of a clause taken from a clause set of a saturation-based prover can partially be constructed by tracing back the inferences needed to infer the clause as far as possible (recall that clauses may be deleted during the derivation). The derivation tree of a subgoal clause of a CTC-based prover is represented by the tableau the clause was extracted from. If a clause is selected for a saturation-based prover utilizing heuristic $\mathcal{H}$ the function ψ_{deriv} considers whether clauses with a high heuristic weight regarding $\mathcal{H}$ are part of the derivation tree. If this is the case, it might be difficult for the receiver to infer the clause on its own and hence the proof search can drastically be reduced if the clause is needed in a proof. If the receiver of a clause is a CTC-based prover and the sender a saturation-based prover, we consider whether the clause is the result of an equality inference like superposition. Such clauses are especially useful for CTC-based provers since they have difficulties handling equality. If sender and receiver are CTC-based provers, such subgoal clauses are useful whose respective tableaux can only be inferred by the receiver if a high resource value is employed. Then, high speed-ups can occur if such clauses can be used in a proof.

Due to lack of space we cannot describe the referees in detail. Exact descriptions of send-referees for superposition and unfailing completion provers can be found in [Fuchs and Denzinger, 1997], descriptions of send-referees for CTC-based provers in [Fuchs, 1998a] and [Fuchs, 1999].

3.4 Realization of receive-referees

A receive-referee is a selection function φ which also uses judgment functions for measuring the quality of clauses.

Our first function ψ_{pop} judges whether a received clause may be *part of a proof* that can quickly be found. For a saturation-based prover ψ_{pop} is defined by $\psi_{pop}(C) = \sum_{C' \in \mathcal{F}\mathcal{A}} \nu(C, C')$. ν judges whether both C and C' contribute to a proof. E.g., for superposition-based provers ν judges whether many short clauses can be derived from C and C'. Exact definitions of the function ν for superposition and unfailing completion provers can be found in [Fuchs and Denzinger, 1997]. In our approach, CTC-based provers employ receive-referees only if they receive clauses from saturation-based provers. Then, we define ψ_{pop} as follows. If $\mathcal{S}$ is the set of extracted subgoal clauses of the receiving prover, $\psi_{pop}(C) = \sum_{C' \in \mathcal{S}} \nu(C, C')$. There, ν judges whether C might contribute to close the tableau represented by the subgoal clause C'. The function simply computes the difference of the number of tableau branches which can be closed by C and the number of branches that remain open.

The second judgment function ψ_{dse} prefers clauses which need not be part of a proof but are nevertheless *able to decrease the search effort* in future. We use this function for saturation-based provers only. The function ψ_{dse} produces higher values if many contracting inferences are possible with a clause. Again, exact definitions can be found in [Fuchs and Denzinger, 1997].

3.5 Integration of clauses

The integration of clauses into the search state of a superposition-based prover is very simple since it works on sets of clauses. Thus, a clause can be integrated by adding it to the set of active clauses and performing all inferences possible with it (see [Fuchs, 1998b]).

For the integration of clauses into the search state of a CTC-based prover there exist two possibilities. The first is to add the new clauses to the old axioms and to perform a re-start of the proof run. The second is to avoid a re-start, to add the new clauses to the old axioms, and to continue the search at the current choice point. The first variant has the disadvantage that the whole search of a CTC-based prover is lost and must possibly be repeated. However, the variant has the advantage that it can be implemented very easily. Moreover, in contrast to the second variant it guarantees that during the iterative deepening process a proof can be found in *a minimal segment of the search space*. Since the segments usually grow exponentially, despite the repetition of parts of the work done so far proofs may then be found faster. Therefore, we decided to employ the simple first variant.

4 Experiments

In order to reveal the power of our cooperation approach we conducted experimental studies with the well-known theorem provers SPASS, SETHEO, and DISCOUNT running on different workstations of a prover network. We have chosen two different test areas: on the one hand several domains from the TPTP problem library v.1.2.1., on the other hand problems stemming from an application in software component retrieval. In the following, all time limits or intervals are measured as wall clock time, which means that for the cooperative runs also the time needed for communication is included. Communication was implemented in the simplest way possible, via reading from and writing in files.

4.1 Experiments with TPTP domains

We have chosen the domains BOO, CAT, COL, and GRP as our test domains. These domains cover a large number of problems with different difficulty. Most problems contain unit equations so that the equational prover DISCOUNT can at least obtain parts of the proof problems.

We coupled the provers SPASS, SETHEO, and DISCOUNT in the following way. SPASS and SETHEO run in their standard settings (that were used for the CADE competition CASC-13). Since the DISCOUNT standard heuristic AddWeight is very similar to that of SPASS, we used a goal-oriented heuristic for DISCOUNT as described in [Denzinger and Fuchs, 1994]. This heuristic is not as powerful as the AddWeight heuristic when working alone but is well-suited for cooperation purposes. We allowed for a bidirectional information exchange between SPASS and SETHEO and between SPASS and DISCOUNT every 5 seconds. SETHEO and DISCOUNT did not exchange information. This is because subgoal clauses of SETHEO are mainly non-unit clauses which are useless for DISCOUNT. Further, it is not sensible to add too many equations to the input set of SETHEO because this increases the branching rate of the search tree too much. The referees were parameterized as follows. SPASS and DISCOUNT selected 10 clauses for each other via send-referees, 5 of these clauses were finally selected by their receive-referees. For achieving cooperation between SPASS and SETHEO, their send-referees selected 40 clauses. Then, their receive-referees selected from these clauses 10 clauses in the domains COL and GRP, 30 clauses in the domains CAT and BOO.

Table 1 presents the results obtained in form of the number of hard problems solved within a certain time limit. A problem is 'hard' if none of the provers alone can solve it within 10 seconds. Table 1 displays the results of the single provers, of a competitive parallel system consisting of the three provers (comp), and the results of cooperative systems consisting of SPASS and SETHEO (SP-SE), SPASS and DISCOUNT (SP-DI), and of all provers (all).

In all tested domains, the cooperation of all provers outperforms the competitive approach for all time limits, for domain CAT it even solves twice the number of problems. Even with only one cooperation phase (i.e.

BOO	SP	SE	DI	comp	SP-SE	SP-DI	all
$\leq 10s$	0	0	0	0	2	0	2
$\leq 100s$	0	3	2	5	4	5	9
$\leq 500s$	4	3	2	7	6	8	10
COL	SP	SE	DI	comp	SP-SE	SP-DI	all
$\leq 10s$	0	0	0	0	1	0	1
$\leq 100s$	2	6	0	8	14	2	14
$\leq 500s$	2	10	0	12	17	2	17

CAT	SP	SE	DI	comp	SP-SE	SP-DI	all
$\leq 10s$	0	0	0	0	6	0	6
$\leq 100s$	5	3	0	7	14	5	14
$\leq 500s$	6	4	0	7	14	5	14
GRP	SP	SE	DI	comp	SP-SE	SP-DI	all
$\leq 10s$	0	0	0	0	5	0	7
$\leq 100s$	28	0	2	28	32	33	37
$\leq 500s$	31	1	4	31	39	44	49

Table 1: Experiments with the TPTP library: numbers of hard problems solved

with a $\leq 10s$ time limit) the results are already better than the results of the single provers and the competitive approach. The BOO and GRP domains show that all systems contribute to the improvement in performance.

It should be noted that the performance of DISCOUNT alone (and in comp) is very bad due to the fact that the results of the goal-oriented heuristic are reported. But even if we "cheat" and report the results of AddWeight, the results of comp still are worse than the TECHS cooperation (while the results in CAT and COL would remain unchanged, for BOO 9 and for GRP 43 problems would be solved within the 500 seconds).

4.2 Experiments with software component retrieval

Besides the use of TPTP domains, we have evaluated TECHS with problems stemming from a concrete application, namely software component retrieval. These problems are generated by the NORA/HAMMR tool that tries to retrieve software components with deductive techniques (see [Schumann and Fischer, 1997]). There, we have the following situation. Software components are available in a software library and specified by their pre- and postconditions. Queries are also formulated by pre- and postconditions. In order to find a suitable library component for a given query proof tasks are constructed that check for each library component whether or not it matches the query (via *plug-in compatibility*). We have chosen a library and queries of list processing functions and constructed several proof problems from it. All in all, we tackled 81 provable problems.

In order to solve these problems, we coupled SPASS, DISCOUNT, and SETHEO in the following way. We used all provers in their standard settings. Whereas SPASS and DISCOUNT were coupled in a bidirectional manner as before, we only allowed SPASS to send selected clauses to SETHEO. The integration of subgoal clauses of SETHEO into the search states of SPASS and DISCOUNT decreased the performance. Again, we let the provers cooperate every 5 seconds. The referees were parameterized as for domains CAT and BOO.

Table 2 presents the results obtained in form of the number of problems solved within certain time limits. Again, we observe a significantly better performance by the cooperation of all systems than by the competitive approach. While the competitive approach can merely

slightly increase the number of problems solvable in the time limit, all cooperative combinations significantly increase the success rate. Note again that the best performance is achieved if all systems are working together.

5 Related Work

Distribution and cooperation concepts for search systems have mainly been developed as homogeneous concepts. This is also true for automated theorem proving, as several overview paper indicate (see, for example, [Bonacina and Hsiang, 1994]). A concept, that is by many considered heterogeneous, is A-Teams (see [Talukdar *et al.*, 1993]). A-Teams is a shared-memory, data flow architecture like approach in which agents working on the same type of results use the appropriate part of the shared memory as a common search state. So far, no effort has been undertaken to include tree- or graph-based search paradigms in A-Teams. Also, the cooperation of A-Team agents is much closer than the cooperation of TECHS agents, since an A-Teams agent communicates the results of each search step it has performed. This does not allow to use existing search systems as agents easily. In A-Teams there is also no referee concept for limiting communication.

Another concept, that has a certain heterogeneous flavor, is Teamwork [Denzinger, 1995]. Teamwork has been developed to distribute automated deduction [Denzinger *et al.*, 1997] and has some similarities to TECHS. In Teamwork, periodically the work of the search agents is evaluated by referees that use success-based criteria to judge the whole agent and to select good results. In contrast to TECHS, for all agents a new common start state is generated by using the state of the best agent and the selected results of the other agents. So, most of the agents are different incarnations of one search systems. Other agents, called specialists, can only contribute certain results that are used to direct the search of all agents. Due to the common new start state, there is no use of demand-based criteria for selecting results.

A truly heterogeneous search system was presented in [Hogg and Williams, 1993] for solving graph coloring problems. The system consisted of a tree-based search agent that heuristically constructed the possible colorings and a repair agent, that worked on inconsistent colorings in order to generate a consistent one. The agents communicate via a blackboard on which partial color-

T_{max} (secs.)	SPASS	SETHEO	DISCOUNT	competitive	SP-SE	SP-DI	all
10	37	39	0	48	49	37	49
30	47	39	0	54	57	47	57
60	48	45	0	55	57	50	58
120	50	48	0	56	60	54	63

Table 2: Experiments with software component retrieval: numbers of problems solved

ings (called hints) are written in random intervals. The tree-based agent also randomly reads hints and chooses its node that fits to the hint to work on instead of the node its heuristic would choose. Whenever the repair agent is stuck, it uses with a certain probability a hint to generate a new coloring instead of generating a random one. Obviously, a knowledge-based selection using referees is not included in this approach.

In [Sutcliffe, 1992] a heterogeneous cooperation concept for automated deduction was proposed. The central concept was a distributed implementation of a shared memory (a so-called tuple-space), in which each agent wrote all formulas generated by it. No selection process was involved and no existing provers could be used. Therefore the experiments were not convincing.

6 Future Work

We have presented a cooperation methodology for existing search systems and we have demonstrated that this methodology yields significant improvements in the area of automated deduction. Besides testing the methodology for other areas of search (cooperation of genetic algorithms with branch and bound, for example), future work will also be directed to using other types of information than clauses. These other types include selected *negative results* and various *control information*.

Negative results of an agent may be used by other agents to either avoid producing such results or to remove them from their search states. Control information can mostly be used by agents of the same type so as to improve their search focus or to avoid searching in the same parts of the search space. But also agents of different types may gain from certain control information.

References

[Bachmair et al., 1989] L. Bachmair, N. Dershowitz, and D.A. Plaisted. Completion without Failure. In *Coll. on the Resolution of Equations in Algebraic Structures*. Academic Press, Austin, 1989.

[Bachmair and Ganzinger, 1994] L. Bachmair and H. Ganzinger. Rewrite-based equational theorem proving with selection and simplification. *Journal of Logic and Computation*, 4(3):217–247, 1994.

[Bonacina and Hsiang, 1994] M.P. Bonacina and J. Hsiang. Parallelization of deduction strategies: an analytical study. *Journal of Automated Reasoning* 13:1-33, 1994.

[Denzinger, 1995] J. Denzinger. Knowledge-Based Distributed Search Using Teamwork. In *Proc. ICMAS-95*, San Francisco, AAAI-Press, 1995, pp. 81–88.

[Denzinger and Fuchs, 1994] J. Denzinger and M. Fuchs. Goal-oriented equational theorem proving using teamwork. In *Proc. 18th KI-94*, Saarbrücken, LNAI 861, 1994, pp. 343–354.

[Denzinger et al., 1997] J. Denzinger, Marc Fuchs, and Matthias Fuchs. High Performance ATP Systems by Combining Several AI Methods. In *Proc. IJCAI-97*, Nagoya, Morgan Kaufmann, 1997, pp. 102–107.

[Ertel, 1992] W. Ertel. OR-parallel theorem proving with random competition. In *Proc. LPAR'92*, St. Petersburg, LNAI 624, 1992, pp. 226–237.

[Fuchs and Denzinger, 1997] D. Fuchs and J. Denzinger. Knowledge-based cooperation between theorem provers by TECHS. *Technical Report SR-97-11*, U. Kaiserslautern, 1997.

[Fuchs, 1998a] D. Fuchs. Cooperation between Top-Down and Bottom-Up Theorem Provers by Subgoal Clause Transfer. In *Proc. AISC-98*, Plattsburgh, NY, USA, LNAI 1476, 1998, pp. 157-169.

[Fuchs, 1998b] D. Fuchs. Coupling Saturation-Based Provers by Exchanging Positive/Negative Information. In *Proc. RTA-98*, Tsukuba, LNCS 1379, 1998, pp. 317-331.

[Fuchs, 1999] D. Fuchs. On the Use of Subgoal Clauses in Bottom-up and Top-down Calculi. *Fundamenta Informaticae*, to appear, 1999.

[Hogg and Williams, 1993] T. Hogg and C.P. Williams. Solving the Really Hard Problems with Cooperative Search. In *Proc. AAAI-93*, Washington, AAAI-Press, 1993, pp. 231–236.

[Korf, 1985] Richard E. Korf. Depth-First Iterative-Deepening: An Optimal Admissible Tree Search. *AI*, 27:97 – 109, 1985. Elsevier Publishers B.V. (North-Holland).

[Letz et al., 1994] R. Letz, K. Mayr, and C. Goller. Controlled Integration of the Cut Rule into Connection Tableau Calculi. *Journal of Automated Reasoning*, 13:297-337, 1994.

[Schumann and Fischer, 1997] Schumann, J.; Fischer, B.: Making Deduction-Based Software Component Retrieval Practical. Proc. 12th Intl. Conf. Automated Software Engineering, Lake Tahoe, 1997, pp. 246-254.

[Sutcliffe, 1992] G. Sutcliffe. A Heterogeneous Parallel Deduction System. In Proc. Workshop on Automated Deduction: Logic Programming and Parallel Computing Approaches, *FGCS'92*, Tokyo, 1992.

[Sutcliffe et al., 1994] G. Sutcliffe, C.B. Suttner, and T. Yemenis. The TPTP Problem Library. In *Proc. 12th CADE*, Nancy, LNAI 814, 1994, pp. 252–266.

[Talukdar et al., 1993] S.N. Talukdar, P.S. de Souza, and S. Murthy. Organizations for Computer-based Agents. *Journal of Engineering Intelligent Systems*, 1993.

UPML: A framework for knowledge system reuse

Dieter Fensel
Institute AIFB
Univ. of Karlsruhe
76128 Karlsruhe
Germany

V. Richard Benjamins
Dep. SWI
Univ. of Amsterdam
1018 WB Amsterdam
The Netherlands

Enrico Motta
Knowledge Media Institute
The Open University
MK7 6AA, Milton Keynes
United Kingdom

Bob Wielinga
Dep. SWI
Univ. of Amsterdam
1018 WB Amsterdam
The Netherlands

Abstract

Problem-solving methods provide reusable architectures and components for implementing the reasoning part of knowledge-based systems. The *Unified Problem-solving Method Development Language, UPML*, has been developed to describe and implement such architectures and components and to facilitate their semiautomatic reuse and adaptation. In a nutshell, UPML is a framework for developing knowledge-intensive reasoning systems based on libraries of generic problem-solving components. The paper describes the components, architectural constraints, development guidelines, and tools provided by UPML. Our focus is hereby on the meta ontology that has been developed to formalize the architectural structure and elements of UPML.

1 Introduction

Problem-solving methods (*PSMs*) for knowledge-based systems (KBSs) (cf. [Schreiber et al., 1994]; [Benjamins & Fensel, 1998]) decompose the reasoning task of a KBS in a number of *subtasks* and *inference actions* that are connected by knowledge roles. Several problem solving method libraries are now available [Breuker & van de Velde, 1994], [Motta & Zdrahal, 1998]. The IBROW project [Benjamins et al., 1998] has been set up with the aim of enabling semiautomatic reuse of PSMs. This reuse is provided by integrating PSM libraries in an internet-based environment. A *software broker* selects and combines PSMs from different libraries and provides a knowledge engineer with semi-automated support for configuring a reasoning system. Hence, a description language for these reasoning components (i.e., PSMs) must provide human-understandable, high-level descriptions, which should also be grounded on a formal representation, to allow automated support by the broker. To this purpose we have developed the *Unified Problem-Solving Method Development Language, UPML* [Fensel et al., 1999b]. UPML is a software architecture for knowledge-based systems providing *components*, *adapters* and a configuration (called *architectural constraints*) of how the components should be connected using the adapters. Finally *design guidelines* specify how to develop a system constructed from the components and connectors that satisfies the architectural constraints.

In knowledge engineering terms UPML provides a *meta-ontology* for describing knowledge-based systems. The different elements of a specification correspond to concepts of this ontology and the architectural constraints are axioms in this ontology.

In this paper we outline the main features of the approach we have taken to define a framework for knowledge sharing and reuse. In particular we illustrate the basic meta-ontology of UPML, its underlying architecture, support tools and development guidelines. Because of space constraints we can only provide a limited number of technical details. Hence, the paper is better seen as an overview report on the main issues we are facing and the solutions we are developing.

The paper is organized as follows. In Section 2, we will briefly sketch the overall structure of UPML. Then we will discuss the (meta-)ontology that can be used to formalize UPML. Section 4 introduces the architectural constraints of UPML and Section 5 shows various ways in which tools for developing, selecting, and combining PSMs can make use of the (meta-)ontology. Section 6 briefly mentions the development guidelines of UPML. Conclusions, related work and outlook are discussed in Section 7.

2 The Overall Structure of UPML

[Fensel et al., 1999a] introduce the four components types of a UPML specification:

- *Tasks* define the problems that should be solved by the KBS.
- *PSMs* define the reasoning process of a KBS in domain-independent terms.
- *Domain models* describe the domain knowledge of the KBS.
- *Ontologies* provide the terminology used in tasks, PSMs and domain definitions.

Each of these elements is described independently to enable the reuse of task descriptions in different domains, the reuse of PSMs across different tasks and domain, and the reuse of domain knowledge for different tasks and PSMs. Therefore,

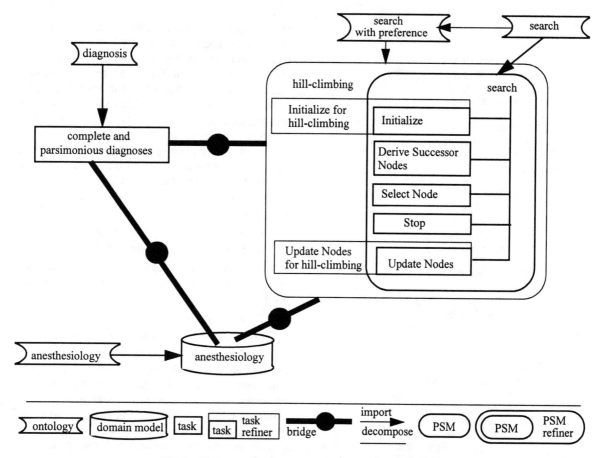

Fig 1. The overall structure of a UPML specification.

adapters are required to adjust the (reusable) parts to each other and to the specific application problem. UPML provides two types of adapters: *bridges* and *refiners*.

- *Bridges* explicitly model the relationships between two distinct parts of an architecture, e.g. between domain and task or task and PSM.

- *Refiners* can be used to express the stepwise specialization of a class of elements of a specification, e.g. a task is refined or a PSM is refined.

Very generic PSMs and tasks can be refined to more specific ones by applying a sequence of refiners (cf. [Fensel, 1997]). Again, separating generic and specific parts of a reasoning process maximizes reusability.

Together, the six UPML building blocks define a *software architecture*. The overall structure of a UPML specification is presented in Figure 1 (a more detailed discussion of the example can be found in [Fensel et al., 1999b]). A task called "complete and parsimonious diagnoses" is defined by importing an ontology called "diagnosis". The PSM applied to solve the task is "hill climbing". A bridge is required to connect the generic terminology of hill climbing with the diagnostic task: states and states transitions of the method have to be rephrased in terms of the task ontology.

Hill climbing is only one possible refinement of a generic search method that decomposes an entire search task into five more elementary subtasks: Initialize, Derive Successor Nodes, Select Node, Stop and Update Nodes. Hill climbing can be derived from this generic search method by (i) refining one of its subtasks (i.e., update node forgets all earlier nodes and only processes the currently derived successors further) and (ii) introducing a preference ordering.

*PSM-mediated task decomposition and PSM specialization through a refiner are analogous to the **part-of** and **is-a** constructs of knowledge representation formalisms.* Subtasking corresponds to the part-of construct because it decomposes a task into subtasks. The refinement of problem-solving methods, as introduced in [Fensel, 1997], corresponds to the is-a relationship of knowledge representation formalisms - e.g., Hill-climbing is a specialization of a general search method by refining some of its attributes (i.e., subtasks).

3 The Meta Ontology of UPML

We used PROTÉGÉ-II [Puerta et al., 1992] to develop a *meta* ontology of UPML. PROTÉGÉ-II is a knowledge acquisition tool-generator. After defining an ontology it semiautomatically generates a graphical interface for collecting the knowledge that is described by the ontology. The ontology can be described in terms of classes and

```
Root
    Competence
        Competence CPSM
        Competence Task
            Competence PPSM
    Cost expression
    Formula
    MCL-Program
    Operational Description
    Pragmatics
    Renaming
    Role
        Input/Output Role
            Input Role
            Output Role
        Intermediate Role
        Knowledge Role
    Signature
    Specification Units
        Bridge
            PSM-Domain Bridge
            PSM-Task Bridge
            Task-Domain Bridge
        Domain Model
            Domain Refiner
        Ontology
            Ontology Refiner
        PSM
            Complex PSM
            Primitive PSM
            PSM Refiner
                Complex PSM Ref.
                Primitive PSM Ref.
        Task
            Task Refiner
        UPML Specification
```

Fig 2. The class hierarchy of the UPML meta ontology.

attributes and organized with an is-a hierarchy and attribute inheritance. Viewing UPML as an ontology and structuring this ontology with the help of PROTÉGÉ-II, helped us to realize some missing elements in sub-specifications and we obtained a much clearer view of the overall structure of UPML. It turned out that the two adapter types, refiners and bridges are rather different entities in the ontology. Refiners are a subconcept of the specification element they refine, while bridges are a class by themselves. Figure 2 provides the class hierarchy of the UPML meta ontology. The organizational principle of the class hierarchy was to minimize the definitions of attributes, i.e. to maximize attribute inheritance. The definitions of the attributes of the class *task* and *task competence* are provided in Figure 3. This ontology has been used to formulate architectural constraints, and to develop tools like editors, browsing, querying and reasoning services for UPML.

4. Architectural Constraints

Architectural constraints ensure well-defined components and composed systems. The conceptual model of UPML decomposes the overall specification and verification tasks

into subtasks of smaller grainsize and clearer focus. The architectural constraints of UPML consist of requirements that are imposed on the intra- and interrelationships of the different parts of the architecture. They either ensure a valid part (for example, a task or a problem-solving method) by restricting possible relationships between its subspecifications or they ensure a valid composition of different elements of the architecture (for example, constraints on connecting a problem-solving method with a task). These architectural constraints can be formulated as axioms of the UPML meta ontology.

For example, we require the consistency of a task specification, i.e.

T_1 *ontology axioms* $\cup$ *preconditions*
$\cup$ *assumptions* must have a model.

Otherwise we would define an inconsistent task specification which would never be solved. In addition, it must hold:

T_2 $\forall x_1,..,x_n$ (*ontology axioms* $\cup$ *preconditions* $\cup$
assumptions $\rightarrow$ $\exists y_1,..,y_m$ *goal*)

That is, if the ontology axioms, preconditions, and assumptions are fulfilled by a domain and the provided case data then the goal of a task must be achievable. This constraint ensures that the task model makes the underlying assumption of a task explicit. For example, when defining a global optimum as a goal of a task it must be ensured that a preference relation exists and that this relation has certain properties. For example that x < y and y < x (i.e., reflexivity) is prohibited because otherwise the existence of a global optimum cannot be guaranteed.

These are the two architectural constraints UPML imposes to guarantee well-defined task specifications. A third optional constraint ensures minimality of assumptions and preconditions (called *weakest preconditions* in software engineering) and therefore maximizes the reusability of the task specification. It prevents overspecialization of assumptions and preconditions (i.e., it ensures that a task is not applied to an unsuitable domain).

T_3 $\forall x_1,..,x_n$ $\exists y_1,..,y_m$ (*goal* $\rightarrow$
ontology axioms $\cup$ *preconditions* $\cup$ *assumptions*)

Similar constraints have been developed for the other components. Correct relationships between components are formalized as axioms concerning the relevant bridges. For

```
Task[
    pragmatics → Pragmatics
    ontologies → Ontology
    import → Task
    competence → Competence Task]

Competence Task[
    goal → Formula
    precondition → Formula
    roles → Input/Output Role
    assumptions → Formula]
```

Fig 3. The attributes of the UPML meta ontology.

example

TPB₂

renaming(*PSM preconditions* ∪ *PSM assumptions* ∪
PSM postconditions) ∪
task ontology ∪ *task preconditions* ∪ *task assumptions* ∪
bridge ontology ∪ *mapping axioms* ∪ *bridge assumptions*
→ *task goal*

ensures that the goal of the task is fulfilled by the postcondition of the selected method. Further axioms can be found in [Fensel et al., 1999b].

5. Tool Support

We used PROTÉGÉ-II to implement an editor for UPML specifications. First PROTÉGÉ-II helps to define an ontology (in our case the meta ontology of UPML). In a second step it automatically derives an editor from it that requires some human interaction to derive a suitable tool from it.

The output of the UPML editor delivers files of the ontology and UPML specifications in a lisp-like syntax. We implemented a tool that translates these files into *Frame Logic* [Kifer et al., 1995]. The reason for this is to be able to use *On2broker*[1] as a browsing and query interface for UPML specifications. On2broker (cf. [Fensel et al., 1998]) is an advanced tool for browsing and querying WWW information sources. It provides a hyperbolic browsing and querying interface for formulating queries, an inference engine used to derive answers, and a webcrawler used to collect the required knowledge from the web. Figure 4 provides the hyperbolic presentation of the UPML meta ontology: classes in the center are depicted with a large circle, whereas classes at the border of the surrounding circle are only marked with a small circle. The visualization technique allows a quick navigation to classes far away from the center as well as a closer examination of classes and their vicinity. The structure of the frame-based representation language is used to define a tabular querying interface that frees users from typing logical formulas (see Figure 4). When a user selects a class from the hyperbolic ontology view, the class name appears in the class field of the tabular query interface and the user can select one of the attributes from the attribute choice menu because the pre-selected class determines the possible attributes. The discussed tool set is implemented in Java and available via the WWW.

However, typical UPML queries may be more complex. For example, Figure 5 shows parts of an On2broker's answer to a complex query which asks for all attribute values of a task specification. Such queries are closer to short logical programs than to typical database queries. To ameliorate this problem we have used the UPML meta-ontology to define generic query patterns such as the one shown in

Figure 5 which are instantiated for specific queries. Moreover, because the query interface is implemented as a Java Remote Method Invocation (RMI) Server.

6. Development Guidelines

Design guidelines define a process model for building complex KBSs out of elementary components. In general, the guidelines of UPML fall into three categories (cf. [Fensel et al., 1999b]):

- How to develop an application system out of reusable components. Guidelines describe the sequence and interrelationships of component selection and adaptation in developing an application system.

- How to develop a library of reusable task definitions and problem-solving methods. A three dimensional design space with predefined transition types provides structured support in developing and refining PSMs according to algorithmic paradigms, task terminologies and assumptions on domain knowledge.

- Which components of UPML correspond to an implementation and how can such components be implemented in an object-oriented framework. We developed and refined some *Design Patterns* that guide this translation process and defined certain interface guidelines.

7. Conclusions

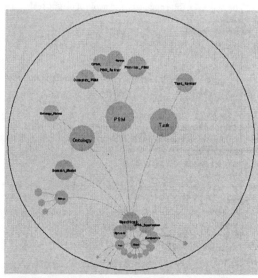

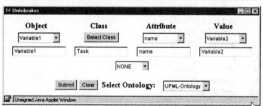

Fig 4. Hyperbolic Query Interface of On2broker.

---

[1]. http://www.aifb.uni-karlsruhe.de/www-broker.

```
FORALL V₁,V₂,V₃,...,V₃₉,V₄₀    <-
V₃₉:UPML_Specification[V1->>V2] &
V₂:Task[name->>"Complete and parsimonious diagnosis"] &
V₂:Task[name->>V₄] & V₂:Task[pragmatics->>V₃₂] &
V₂:Task[V₅->>V₃₂] & V₃₂:Pragmatics[explanation->>V₉] &
V₃₂:Pragmatics[V₈->>V₉] & V₃₂:Pragmatics[V₁₀->>V₁₁] &
V₃₂:Pragmatics[author->>V₁₁] &
V₃₂:Pragmatics[last_date_of_modification->>V₁₃] &
V₃₂:Pragmatics[V₁₂->>V₁₃] & V₃₂:Pragmatics[V₁₄->>V₁₅] &
V₃₂:Pragmatics[reference->>V₁₅] &
V₃₂:Pragmatics[URL->>V₁₇] & V₃₂:Pragmatics[V₁₆->>V₁₇] &
V₂:Task[imported_ontologies->>V₂₈] &
V₂:Task[competence->>V34] &
V₃₄:Competence[postconditions_goal->>V₃₅] &
V₃₄:Competence[V₁₈->>V₃₅] & V₃₅:Formula[formula->>V₁₉] &
V₃₄:Competence[preconditions->>V₃₆] &
V₃₄:Competence[V₂₀->>V₃₆] & V₃₆:Formula[formula->>V₂₁] &
V₃₄:Competence[assumptions->>V₃₇] &
V₃₄:Competence[V22->>V₃₇] & V₃₇:Formula[formula->>V23] &
V₃₄:Competence[roles->>V₃₈] & V₃₄:Competence[V24->>V₃₈] &
V₃₈:Input_Role[name->>V₂₅] & V₃₄:Competence[roles->>V₄₀] &
V₄₀:Output_Role[name->>V₂₆] & V₂:Task[V₂₇->>V₂₈] &
V₂₈:Ontology[name->>V₃₀] & V₂₈:Ontology[V₂₉->>V₃₀].
```

Ontobroker found the following:

```
V1 = task
V2 = "instance_00003"
V4 = "Complete and parsimonious diagnosis"
V5 = pragmatics
V8 = explanation
V9 = "The task asks for a complete and minimal diagnoses"
V10 = author
V11 = "Dieter Fensel"
V12 = last_date_of_modification
V13 = "May 2, 1998"
V14 = reference
V15 = "D. Fensel: Understanding, Developing and Reusing Problem-Sol
Universitaet Karlsruhe, 1998."
V16 = URL
V17 = " http://www.psm-library.com "
V18 = postconditions_goal
V19 = "complete(diagnosis, observations) & parsimonious(diagnosis)"
V20 = preconditions
V21 = "observations <> empty"
V22 = assumptions
V23 = "If we receive input there must be   complete hypothesis. observe
V24 = roles
V25 = "observations"
V26 = "diagnosis"
V27 = imported_ontologies
V28 = "instance_00004"
V29 = name
V30 = "diagnoses"
V32 = "instance_00046"
V34 = "instance_00150"
V35 = "instance_00153"
V36 = "instance_00154"
V37 = "instance_00155"
V38 = "instance_00151"
V39 = "instance_00001"
V40 = "instance_00152"
```

Fig 5. Querying the specification of a task.

Ontologies were introduced as means to support knowledge sharing and reuse (cf. [Gruber, 1993]). UPML provides an ontology for sharing and reusing knowledge-based systems. That is, it provides a (meta-)ontology for describing tasks, PSMs, domain models, ontologies, their mappings via bridges and refiners that express adaptation of the components. A number of tools have been developed and configured for supporting the definition and use of UPML components. A PROTÉGÉ-II based editor enables the development of UPML descriptions, while On2broker can be used to browse and query such descriptions. In addition, the IBROW broker matches user requirements with knowledge components specified in UPML and supports their distributed execution.

Related Work

UPML is close in spirit to CML which has been developed in the CommonKADS project (cf. [Schreiber et al., 1994]). CML provides a layered conceptual model of KBS by distinguishing between domain, inference, and task layers according to the CommonKADS model of expertise. UPML took this model as a starting point, but refined it according to the component-oriented style of software architectures. UPML decomposes a knowledge-based system - via an architecture - into a set of related elements: tasks, problem-solving methods, domain models and bridges that define their relationships. CML does not provide task-independent specification of problem-solving methods nor the encapsulation mechanism of UPML for problem-solving method. In UPML, the operational specification of a method is an internal aspect that is externally described by the competence of the method. In addition, CML does not provide means to refine tasks and problem-solving methods. In general, UPML is much more oriented to problem-solving method reuse (i.e., component reuse) than CML. Finally, CML is a semiformal language whereas UPML can be used as a semiformal language (using its structuring primitives) and as a formal language (UPML provides logical formalisms to formally define the elementary slots).

UPML has also many similarities with other standardization efforts in the area of knowledge-based systems. OKBC [Chaudhri et al., 1998] jointly developed at SRI International and Stanford University, provides a set of functions that support a generic interface to underlying frame representation systems. The *Knowledge Interchange Format* [KIF] is a computer-oriented first-order language for the interchange of knowledge among disparate programs. [KQML] or the *Knowledge Query and Manipulation Language* is a language and protocol for exchanging information and knowledge. KQML can be used as a language for an application program to interact with an intelligent system or for two or more intelligent systems to share knowledge in support of cooperative problem solving. The distinctive feature of UPML is that it is about sharing and exchange of problem-solving methods, i.e. software components that realize complex reasoning tasks of knowledge-based systems. Moreover, UPML is less a standardization *formalism* than a standard *architecture*, which is defined by its meta-ontology. A similar approach is taken in Ontolingua [Gruber, 1993], which defines a meta-ontology for describing frame-based ontologies. Although UPML aims for a much broader scope, Ontolingua could be used at the object level of UPML for describing the elementary attribute values of specifications.

Finally, [Fensel et al., 1999b] put UPML in the general context of software architectures and also sketch how it can be translated into UML.

Outlook

An important issue concerns the integration of components subscribing to different ontologies. This integration can be specified by means of bridges. Bridges can either be defined by hand (i.e. by library providers or application developers) or can be generated automatically by an intelligent broker (cf. [Benjamins et al., 1999]). However, the automatic generation of bridges requires that the library providers do not only agree on a shared language (i.e., UPML) but also on a shared vocabulary, i.e., they do not only have to use the same UPML meta-ontology but also partially the same ontology at the object level.

Acknowledgment. We thank Igor Becker, Stefan Decker, Mauro Gaspari, John Gennari, Rix Groenboom, William Grosso, Frank van Harmelen, Mark Musen, John Park, Rainer Perkun, Enric Plaza, Guus Schreiber, Rudi Studer, Annette ten Teije, and Andre Valente for valuable comments on early drafts of the paper.

References

[Benjamins & Fensel, 1998] V. R. Benjamins and D. Fensel: Special issue on problem-solving methods of the *International Journal of Human-Computer Studies (IJHCS)*, 49(4), 1998.

[Benjamins et al., 1998] V. R. Benjamins, E. Plaza, E. Motta, D. Fensel, R. Studer, B. Wielinga, G. Schreiber, Z. Zdrahal, and S. Decker: An Intelligent Brokering Service for Knowledge-Component Reuse on the World-WideWeb. In *Proceedings of the 11th Banff Knowledge Acquisition for Knowledge-Based System Workshop (KAW'98)*, Banff, Canada, April 18-23, 1998.

[Benjamins et al., 1999] V. R. Benjamins, B. Wielinga, J. Wielemaker, and D. Fensel: Brokering Problem-Solving Knowledge at the Internet. In *Proceedings of the European Knowledge Acquisition Workshop (EKAW-99)*, D. Fensel et al. (eds.), Lecture Notes in Artificial Intelligence, Springer-Verlag, May 1999.

[Breuker & van de Velde, 1994] J. A. Breuker and W. van de Velde: *CommonKADS Library for Expertise Modelling*. IOS Press, Amsterdam, The Netherlands.

[Chaudhri et al., 1998] V. K. Chaudhri, A. Farquhar, R. Fikes, P. D. Karp, and J. P. Rice: *Open Knowledge Base Connectivity 2.0*, Knowledge Systems Laboratory, KSL-98-06, January 1998. http://www-ksl-svc.stanford.edu:5915/doc/project-papers.html

[Fensel, 1997] D. Fensel: The Tower-of-Adapter Method for Developing and Reusing Problem-Solving Methods. In E. Plaza et al. (eds.), *Knowledge Acquisition, Modeling and Management*, Lecture Notes in Artificial Intelligence (LNAI) 1319, Springer-Verlag, 1997.

[Fensel et al., 1998] D. Fensel, S. Decker, M. Erdmann, and R. Studer: Ontobroker: The Very High Idea. In *Proceedings of the 11th International Flairs Conference (FLAIRS-98)*, Sanibal Island, Florida, USA, 131-135, May 1998.

[Fensel et al., 1999a] D. Fensel, V. R. Benjamins, S. Decker, M. Gaspari, R. Groenboom, W. Grosso, M. Musen, E. Motta, E. Plaza, G. Schreiber, R. Studer, and B. Wielinga: The Component Model of UPML in a Nutshell. In *WWW Proceedings of the 1st Working IFIP Conference on Software Architectures (WICSA1)*, San Antonio, Texas, USA, February 1999.

[Fensel et al., 1999b] D. Fensel, E. Motta, V. R. Benjamins, S. Decker, M. Gaspari, R. Groenboom, W. Grosso, M. Musen, E. Plaza, G. Schreiber, R. Studer, and B. Wielinga: *The Unified Problem-solving Method development Language UPML*. ESPRIT project number 27169, IBROW3, Deliverable 1.1, Chapter 1. http://www.aifb.uni-karlsruhe.de/WBS/dfe/publications99.html.

[Gruber, 1993] T. R. Gruber: A Translation Approach to Portable Ontology Specifications, *Knowledge Acquisition*, 5:199—220, 1993.

[KIF] KIF: http://logic.stanford.edu/kif/kif.html.

[Kifer et al., 1995] M. Kifer, G. Lausen, and J. Wu: Logical Foundations of Object-Oriented and Frame-Based Languages, *Journal of the ACM*, vol 42, 1995.

[KQML] KQML: http://www.cs.umbc.edu/kqml/.

[Motta & Zdrahal, 1998] E. Motta and Z. Zdrahal: An approach to the organization of a library of problem solving methods which integrates the search paradigm with task and method ontologies. In [Benjamins & Fensel, 1998].

[Puerta et al., 1992] A. R. Puerta, J. W. Egar, S. W. Tu, and M.A. Musen: A Multiple-method Knowledge-Acquisition Shell for the Automatic Generation of Knowledge-acquisition Tools, *Knowledge Acquisition*, 4(2):171—196, 1992.

[Schreiber et al., 1994] A. TH. Schreiber, B. Wielinga, J. M. Akkermans, W. Van De Velde, and R. de Hoog: CommonKADS. A Comprehensive Methodology for KBS Development, *IEEE Expert*, 9(6):28—37, 1994.

AUTOMATED REASONING

Nonmonotonic Reasoning 1

Complexity results for propositional closed world reasoning and circumscription from tractable knowledge bases

Sylvie Coste-Marquis
CRIL/Université d'Artois et IUT de Lens
rue de l'Université, S.P. 16
62307 Lens cedex - France

Pierre Marquis
CRIL/Université d'Artois
rue de l'Université, S.P. 16
62307 Lens cedex - France

Abstract

This paper presents new complexity results for propositional closed world reasoning (CWR) from tractable knowledge bases (KBs). Both (basic) CWR, generalized CWR, extended generalized CWR, careful CWR and extended CWR (equivalent to circumscription) are considered. The focus is laid on tractable KBs belonging to target classes for exact compilation functions: Blake formulas, DNFs, disjunctions of Horn formulas, and disjunctions of renamable Horn formulas. The complexity of inference is identified for all the forms of CWR listed above. For each of them, new tractable fragments are exhibited. Our results suggest knowledge compilation as a valuable approach to deal with the complexity of CWR in some situations.

1 Introduction

Closed world reasoning (CWR) is a widely used inference technique in Artificial Intelligence, Database Theory and Logic Programming. It relies on the idea that negative information is often not represented in an explicit way; in this situation, every piece of positive information which cannot be deduced from a knowledge base (KB) is assumed false.

In order to define CWR in a formal way, an approach consists in characterizing the formulas which must be assumed false in the KB: CWR is then viewed as deduction from the closure of the KB, i.e., the KB completed with these assumptions. Several policies for characterizing such assumptions have been developed so far, giving rise to several forms of CWR. Let us mention the (basic) closed world assumption (CWA) [Reiter, 1978], the generalized closed world assumption (GCWA) [Minker, 1982], the extended generalized closed world assumption (EGCWA) [Yahya and Henschen, 1985], the careful closed world assumption (CCWA) [Gelfond and Przymusinska, 1986], and the extended closed world assumption (ECWA) [Gelfond *et al.*, 1989]. The most sophisticated closed world assumption is ECWA; in the propositional case, Gelfond, Przymusinska and Przymusinski

[1989] show it is equivalent to circumscription, as defined in [McCarthy, 1986].

The complexity of propositional CWR has already been investigated by several researchers. Eiter and Gottlob [1993] show that CWR is hard in the general case: typically at the second level of the polynomial hierarchy. Cadoli and Lenzerini [1994] focus on the complexity of CWR from various fragments of propositional logic for which clause deduction is tractable, especially the Horn CNF class, the reverse Horn CNF class and the Krom one. For such classes of formulas, the complexity of CWR falls one level down in the polynomial hierarchy.

The aim of this paper is to complete the complexity results pointed out in [Cadoli and Lenzerini, 1994] by focusing on some other tractable fragments of propositional logic. Especially, four classes are considered:

- The *Blake* class is the set of formulas given in prime implicates normal form,

- the *DNF* class is the set of formulas given in disjunctive normal form (DNF),

- the *Horn cover* class is the set of disjunctions of Horn CNF formulas,

- the *renamable Horn cover* class is the set of disjunctions of renamable Horn CNF formulas.

As a main contribution, the complexity of clause inference is identified for each form of CWR and each tractable class listed above. Several new tractable subcases are exhibited for each form of CWR; some new intractable subcases are presented as well.

Interestingly, our tractability results for CWR apply to classes of formulas strictly more expressive than some of the most expressive tractable fragments for CWR pointed out up to now. In particular, some of the classes we focus on include classes considered in [Cadoli and Lenzerini, 1994] as strict subcases. Additionally, the fragments we consider are target classes for exact knowledge compilation functions. Thus, every propositional formula can be turned ("compiled") into a formula from the Blake class (the target class for the compilation function given in [Reiter and de Kleer, 1987]), the DNF class (the target class for the function given in [Schrag, 1996]), the Horn cover class and the renamable Horn cover class (which are specific instances of the class of tractable covers considered in [Boufkhad *et al.*, 1997]). Since CWR from such tractable formulas is shown computationally easier than CWR from unconstrained formulas, our study suggests a two step approach to compute CWR: the KB is first compiled off-line, giving rise to a formula from one of the target classes, then queries are addressed on-line w.r.t. the compiled KB. While such a pre-processing is known as not computationally helpful in the general case, our results indicate that it can prove valuable when CWR from the compiled KB can be achieved in polynomial time, as long as the KB does not often change and the size of its compiled form remains "small enough".

The rest of this paper is organized as follows. Some formal preliminaries are given in Section 2. Basic definitions and complexity results about CWR are recalled in Section 3. Section 4 presents the complexity of CWR for each of the fragments we focus on. Section 5 concludes the paper. Proofs are given in [Coste-Marquis and Marquis, 1999] available from the authors.

2 Formal Preliminaries

$PROP_{PS}$ denotes the propositional language built up from a denumerable set PS of symbols and the connectives in the standard way. The size of a formula Σ from $PROP_{PS}$, noted $|\Sigma|$, is the number of signs (symbols and connectives) used to write it. Every propositional symbol of PS is also called a positive literal and a negated one a negative literal. For every subset V of PS, L_V (resp. L_V^+, L_V^-) is the set of literals (resp. positive literals, negative literals) built up from the propositional symbols of V. $Var(\Sigma)$ denotes the set of propositional symbols occurring in Σ.

Formulas are interpreted in the classical way. Every set of formulas is interpreted conjunctively. A formula is Horn CNF (resp. reverse Horn CNF) iff it is a CNF formula s.t. every clause in it contains at most one positive (resp. negative) literal. A Krom formula is a CNF formula in which every clause contains at most two literals. A renamable Horn CNF formula Σ is a CNF formula which can be turned into a Horn CNF formula by substituting in a uniform way in Σ some literals of $L_{Var(\Sigma)}$ by their negation.

We assume that the reader is familiar with some basic notions of computational complexity, especially the complexity classes P, NP, and coNP, and the classes Δ_k^p, Σ_k^p and Π_k^p of the polynomial hierarchy PH (see [Papadimitriou, 1994] for details). The class $P^{X[O(log n)]}$ contains the decision problems which can be solved in polynomial time with no more than $O(log\,n)$ calls to an oracle for deciding a problem $Q \in X$ for "free" (i.e., within a constant time), n representing the size of the problem instance. Let us recall that a decision problem is said at the kth level of PH iff it belongs to Δ_{k+1}^p, and is either Σ_k^p-hard or Π_k^p-hard. It is strongly believed that PH does not collapse (at any level), i.e., is a truly infinite hierarchy (for every integer k, PH $\neq \Sigma_k^p$).

3 Closed World Reasoning

All the forms of CWR pointed out so far can be characterized through the notions of *closure* and *free for negation formula*. A clause γ is then considered as a (non monotonic) consequence of a KB Σ interpreted under some closed world assumption policy $*CWA$ (where the generic character $*$ can be replaced by G, EG, CC, E or the empty string) iff it is a logical consequence of the closure of Σ w.r.t. the policy. Both the CCWA and ECWA policies require $Var(\Sigma)$ to be partitioned into three sets, P, Q, and Z. P contains the symbols preferred false, Z contains the symbols the truth value of which can vary when trying to falsify the symbols from P, and Q contains the symbols the truth value of which cannot vary.

Definition 3.1 (closure of a KB)
Let $*CWA$ be any closed world assumption policy among (basic) CWA, $GCWA$, $EGCWA$, $CCWA$ and $ECWA$. Let Σ be a formula from $PROP_{PS}$ and $\langle P, Q, Z\rangle$ a partition of $Var(\Sigma)$. The closure $*CWA(\Sigma, \langle P, Q, Z\rangle)^1$ of Σ given $\langle P, Q, Z\rangle$ w.r.t. $*CWA$ is the formula $\Sigma \cup \{\neg\alpha \; ; \; \alpha \text{ is a } *CWA\text{-free for negation formula w.r.t. } \Sigma \text{ and } \langle P, Q, Z\rangle\}$.

The $*CWA$-free for negation formulas w.r.t. Σ are the negations of the formulas which are assumed false when they are not deducible from Σ. They vary according to the closed world assumption policy under consideration:

Definition 3.2 (*CWA-free for negation formula)
Let Σ and α be two formulas from $PROP_{PS}$ and let $\langle P, Q, Z\rangle$ be a partition of $Var(\Sigma)$.

- *α is CWA-free for negation iff α is a positive literal s.t. $\Sigma \not\models \alpha$ holds.*
- *α is $GCWA$-free for negation iff α is a positive literal and for each positive clause γ s.t. $\Sigma \not\models \gamma$ holds, $\Sigma \not\models \alpha \vee \gamma$ holds.*
- *α is $EGCWA$-free for negation iff α is a conjunction of positive literals and for each positive clause γ s.t. $\Sigma \not\models \gamma$ holds, $\Sigma \not\models \alpha \vee \gamma$ holds.*
- *α is $CCWA$-free for negation iff α is a literal from L_P^+ and for each clause γ containing only literals from $L_P^+ \cup L_Q$ and s.t. $\Sigma \not\models \gamma$ holds, $\Sigma \not\models \alpha \vee \gamma$ holds.*
- *α is $ECWA$-free for negation iff $Var(\alpha) \cap Z = \emptyset$ and for each clause γ containing only literals from $L_P^+ \cup L_Q$ and s.t. $\Sigma \not\models \gamma$ holds, $\Sigma \not\models \alpha \vee \gamma$ holds.*

Let us note that every symbol not belonging to $Var(\Sigma)$ is CWA, $GCWA$ and $EGCWA$-free for negation. As to $CCWA$ and $ECWA$, every symbol from $PS \setminus Var(\Sigma)$ is assumed to belong to P.

In the rest of this paper, the following decision problems are considered:

Definition 3.3 (*CWA clause inference)
Let $*CWA$ be any closed world assumption policy among

---

[1] The partition of $Var(\Sigma)$ is not significant for the CWA, $GCWA$ and $EGCWA$ policies.

(basic) *CWA, GCWA, EGCWA, CCWA and ECWA.
∗*CWA* CLAUSE INFERENCE *is the following decision problem:*

- **Input:** *A formula* Σ *and a clause* γ *from* $PROP_{PS}$, *a partition* $\langle P, Q, Z \rangle$ *of* $Var(\Sigma)$ *and a CWA policy* ∗*CWA*.
- **Query:** *Does* ∗$CWA(\Sigma, \langle P, Q, Z \rangle) \models \gamma$ *hold?*

∗*CWA* LITERAL INFERENCE is the restriction of the corresponding ∗*CWA* CLAUSE INFERENCE problem where γ is restricted to be a literal.

The complexity of propositional CWR has been investigated by several researchers, especially Eiter and Gottlob [1993] and Cadoli and Lenzerini [1994]. CWR has been shown hard: all the forms of CWR except basic CWA are at the second level of the polynomial hierarchy. Thus, CWR is computationally harder than deduction in the general case (CLAUSE DEDUCTION is "only" coNP-complete), unless PH collapses.

In order to circumvent this complexity, several approaches can be considered. One of them is centered around the idea of exact *knowledge compilation*. Knowledge compilation can be viewed as a form of preprocessing (see [Cadoli and Donini, 1998] for a survey): the original KB is turned into a compiled one during an off-line compilation phase and this compiled KB is used to answer the queries on-line. Assuming that the KB does not often change and that answering queries from the compiled KB is computationally easier than answering them from the original KB, the compilation time can be balanced over a sufficient number of queries.

Existing researches about knowledge compilation can be split into two categories. The first category gathers theoretical works about *compilability*, which indicates whether or not the objective can be expected to be reached in the general case by focusing on the size of the compiled form (see e.g., [Cadoli *et al.*, 1997a; Liberatore, 1998]). Indeed, if the size of the compiled form is exponentially larger than the size of the original KB, significant computational improvements are hard to be expected. Some decision problems are compilable, while others are (probably) not compilable. Thus, CLAUSE DEDUCTION (from a fixed KB) is (probably) not compilable: the existence of an equivalence-preserving compilation function $COMP$ s.t. it is guaranteed that for every propositional CNF formula Σ, CLAUSE DEDUCTION from $COMP(\Sigma)$ is in P and $|COMP(\Sigma)|$ is polynomially bounded in $|\Sigma|$ would make PH to collapse at the second level (see [Kautz and Selman, 1992; Cadoli *et al.*, 1997a] for more details). The second category contains works that are much more oriented towards the design of compilation algorithms, and their empirical evaluations (see e.g. [Reiter and de Kleer, 1987; Schrag, 1996; Boufkhad *et al.*, 1997; Boufkhad, 1998]).

The compilability of CWR has been analyzed in depth in [Cadoli *et al.*, 1996; 1997b]. The results are typically negative. In a nutshell, inference under ECWA from a fixed KB is shown (probably) not compilable. Contrastingly, it is shown that CWA CLAUSE INFERENCE and CCWA CLAUSE INFERENCE from Horn CNF, reverse Horn CNF or Krom formulas are compilable (the fixed part of the problem is the KB plus the partition in the CCWA case).

From the practical side, Nerode, Ng and Subrahmanian [1995] present an algorithm for compiling a KB interpreted under circumscription into the set of its minimal models. The algorithm is based on a mixed integer linear programming. The circumscription policy (i.e., the partition of the symbols) is fixed. Several other approaches show how CWR can be reduced to deduction through the computation of the closure of the KB (or the computation of any equivalent formula), see e.g. [Raiman and de Kleer, 1992; Castell *et al.*, 1996]. All these approaches confirm the (probable) non compilability of the most sophisticated forms of CWR in the sense that in the worst case, the compilation phase outputs a formula that is not polynomially bounded in the size of the original KB.

4 Complexity Results

In the following, the complexity of CWR is investigated for some KBs for which CLAUSE DEDUCTION is tractable (tractable KBs for short):

Definition 4.1 (some tractable classes)
Let Σ *be a formula from* $PROP_{PS}$.

- Σ *is a Blake formula iff* Σ *is a CNF formula and for every implicate* γ *of* Σ, *there exists a clause* π *in* Σ *s.t.* $\pi \models \gamma$ *holds.*
- Σ *is a DNF formula iff* Σ *is a (finite) disjunction of terms.*
- Σ *is a Horn cover formula iff* Σ *is a (finite) disjunction of Horn CNF formulas.*
- Σ *is a renamable Horn cover formula iff* Σ *is a (finite) disjunction of renamable Horn CNF formulas.*

Blake formulas [Blake, 1937] are CNF formulas given by their prime implicates. Clearly enough, they are tractable since for every clause γ, $\Sigma \models \gamma$ holds iff there exists π in Σ s.t. $\pi \models \gamma$ holds and this test can be easily achieved in time polynomial in $|\pi| + |\gamma|$. Indeed, many algorithms for computing prime implicates have been proposed so far (see [Marquis, 1999] for a survey).

DNF formulas are tractable since for every clause γ, $\Sigma \models \gamma$ holds iff for every term δ in Σ, $\delta \models \gamma$ holds and this test can be easily achieved in time polynomial in $|\delta| + |\gamma|$. Several algorithms for turning a formula into DNF can be found in the literature, e.g. [Schrag, 1996].

Horn (resp. renamable Horn) cover formulas are tractable since for every clause γ, $\Sigma \models \gamma$ holds iff for every Φ in Σ, $\Phi \models \gamma$ holds and this test can be easily achieved in time polynomial in $|\Phi| + |\gamma|$ when Φ is a Horn CNF formula [Dowling and Gallier, 1984] (resp. a renamable Horn CNF formula [Lewis, 1978]). Note that Horn CNF formulas and renamable Horn CNF formulas can be recognized (and checked for satisfiability) in polynomial time. Note also that every term is a Horn CNF formula, every Horn CNF formula and every satisfiable Krom formula is a renamable Horn CNF formula, and every term (resp. Horn CNF formula, renamable Horn CNF formula) is a DNF formula (resp. a Horn cover formula, a renamable Horn cover formula). Hence every DNF formula is a Horn cover formula and every Horn cover formula is a renamable Horn cover formula. Algorithms for computing Horn cover formulas and renamable Horn cover formulas can be found in [Boufkhad et al., 1997; Boufkhad, 1998].

The next proposition is the central result of this paper:

Proposition 4.1 (complexity of CWR)

The complexity of ∗CWA CLAUSE INFERENCE *and* ∗CWA LITERAL INFERENCE *from a Blake formula, a DNF formula, a Horn cover formula and a renamable Horn cover formula is reported in Tables 1 and 2*[2].

Intuitively, the fact that CWR typically is at the second level of PH can be explained by the presence of two independent sources of complexity. One of them lies in deduction and the other one in model minimization. As Proposition 4.1 illustrates it, focusing on tractable KBs enables ruling out one source of difficulty in the general case, and both sources in some specific cases.

This work can be related to several studies in which the complexity of non monotonic inference from tractable fragments of propositional logic is analyzed, for instance [Kautz and Selman, 1991; Cadoli and Lenzerini, 1994; Ben-Eliyahu and Dechter, 1996]. Cadoli and Lenzerini [1994] investigate the complexity of CWR from Horn CNF, reverse Horn CNF and Krom formulas. Interestingly, the tractable classes for CWR we consider are strictly more expressive than some of the most expressive tractable classes pointed out up to now. Especially, they include some of the tractable classes given in [Cadoli and Lenzerini, 1994] as subcases. Thus, every Krom formula can be turned into its prime implicates normal form in polynomial time (just because a set of binary clauses has a polynomially bounded number of resolvents). Additionally, every Horn CNF formula belongs to the Horn cover class. However, the converse does not hold: the fragments studied here are strictly more expressive that those given in [Cadoli and Lenzerini, 1994]. For instance, every monotonic CNF formula (i.e., a CNF formula in which every symbol occurs only positively or negatively) can be put into prime implicates normal form in polynomial time but is not equivalent to a Horn CNF or a Krom formula in the general case.

Another significant difference w.r.t. [Cadoli and Lenzerini, 1994] is that our study is directly related to exact knowledge compilation in the sense that the fragments

of propositional logic we consider are target classes for exact compilation functions. Thus, every propositional formula can be turned into a Blake formula, a DNF formula, a Horn cover formula and a renamable Horn cover formula without modifying the set of its models. This contrasts with the fragments considered in [Cadoli and Lenzerini, 1994] since some formulas cannot be represented either as a Horn CNF, a reverse Horn CNF or a Krom formula while preserving logical equivalence.

Accordingly, the tractability results given in Proposition 4.1 can be exploited to draw some new conclusions about the usefulness of knowledge compilation for CWR. From the theoretical side, the compilability results for CWR given in [Cadoli et al., 1996] can be completed at the light of our results. Indeed, every polynomially solvable problem is compilable, even if its fixed part is empty since the compilation phase can be achieved in polynomial time. More interestingly, from the practical side, the connection with knowledge compilation suggests a two step process for computing CWR: the KB is first made tractable through knowledge compilation, then CWR is achieved from the compiled KB. The first step is performed off-line and done once at all (unless the KB is modified). Using such an approach, the closed world assumption policy adopted can vary with the queries that are considered; for instance, the set of symbols to be minimized can change with time, without requiring the KB to be re-compiled each time such a modification occurs. This flexibility is particularly interesting when the KB, representing "hard" constraints, is shared by several agents, and different agents may have different preferences, encoded as a CWA policy. Each time an agent asks the KB, the corresponding preferences can be taken into account without requiring any re-compilation of the KB.

At the light of the complexity results given in Proposition 4.1, our claim is that *some* approaches to knowledge compilation can prove helpful in practice for *some* forms of CWR, *provided that the compiled KB remains "small enough"*. For instance, compiling a KB into a Horn cover formula so as to interpret it under EGCWA reduces the complexity of inference from Π_2^p-complete to P. Thus, if the compilation phase does not result in an exponential blow up in the size of the KB, the time needed for inference from the compiled KB can be much lower than the corresponding time from the original KB; subsequently, the compilation time can be balanced. Let us stress that our claim concerns some specific cases only, not the general one: since CWR is (probably) not compilable [Cadoli et al., 1996; 1997b], knowledge compilation cannot be expected as valuable for improving CWR in the general case. Nevertheless, it is worth noting that, while compilability results for CWR are mainly negative, they do not prevent from exhibiting some instances for which knowledge compilation proves helpful. Accordingly, many experiments with various compilation functions show the practical utility of such an approach for improving CLAUSE DEDUCTION (see e.g., [Schrag, 1996; Boufkhad et al., 1997]), though the problem is known as

---

[2]Some tractability results reported in the two tables can be generalized to any tractable KB. To be more precise, CWA CLAUSE INFERENCE and both CCWA CLAUSE INFERENCE and ECWA CLAUSE INFERENCE under the restriction $P = \emptyset$ are in P whenever Σ belongs to a class for which CLAUSE DEDUCTION is tractable.

Tractable KB	*CWA	CLAUSE INFERENCE	LITERAL INFERENCE
Blake	CWA	in P	in P
Blake	GCWA	in P	in P
Blake	EGCWA	coNP-complete	in P
Blake	CCWA	in P	in P
Blake	ECWA	coNP-complete	coNP-complete
DNF	CWA	in P	in P
DNF	GCWA	in P	in P
DNF	EGCWA	in P	in P
DNF	CCWA	coNP-hard and in $P^{NP[O(\log n)]}$	coNP-hard and in $P^{NP[O(\log n)]}$
DNF	ECWA	coNP-complete	coNP-complete
Horn cover	CWA	in P	in P
Horn cover	GCWA	in P	in P
Horn cover	EGCWA	in P	in P
Horn cover	CCWA	coNP-hard and in $P^{NP[O(\log n)]}$	coNP-hard and in $P^{NP[O(\log n)]}$
Horn cover	ECWA	coNP-complete	coNP-complete
renamable Horn cover	CWA	in P	in P
renamable Horn cover	GCWA	coNP-hard and in $P^{NP[O(\log n)]}$	coNP-hard and in $P^{NP[O(\log n)]}$
renamable Horn cover	EGCWA	coNP-complete	coNP-complete
renamable Horn cover	CCWA	coNP-hard and in $P^{NP[O(\log n)]}$	coNP-hard and in $P^{NP[O(\log n)]}$
renamable Horn cover	ECWA	coNP-complete	coNP-complete

Table 1: The complexity of CWR from some tractable KBs.

(probably) not compilable. Our results show that, in the many situations in which some compilation techniques are computationally profitable for CLAUSE DEDUCTION, they can be profitable as well for some forms of CWR, with only a polynomial extra cost.

5 Conclusion

In this paper, the complexity of CWR has been investigated for some tractable fragments of propositional logic. Several new tractable cases have been identified, and some new intractability results have been provided as well. Interestingly, the tractable fragments we have focused on are target classes for some compilation functions; such a connection with exact knowledge compilation can prove valuable from a computational point of view in the situations in which the size of the compiled KB remains "small enough".

Due to close connections between CWR and abduction and between CWR and some simple forms of default reasoning, complexity results for these additional forms of non monotonic inference from tractable KBs can be derived from the results presented in this paper. This is an issue for further research.

Acknowledgements

This work has been supported by the Ganymède II project of the "Contrat de plan État/Région Nord Pas-de-Calais".

References

[Ben-Eliyahu and Dechter, 1996] R. Ben-Eliyahu and R. Dechter. Default reasoning using classical logic. *Artificial Intelligence*, 84:113–150, 1996.

[Blake, 1937] A. Blake. *Canonical expressions in boolean algebra*. PhD thesis, University of Chicago, Chicago (IL), 1937.

[Boufkhad et al., 1997] Y. Boufkhad, E. Grégoire, P. Marquis, B. Mazure, and L. Saïs. Tractable cover compilations. In *Proc. of IJCAI'97*, pages 122–127, Nagoya, 1997.

[Boufkhad, 1998] Y. Boufkhad. Algorithms for propositional KB approximation. In *Proc. of AAAI'98*, pages 280–285, Madison (WI), 1998.

[Cadoli and Donini, 1998] M. Cadoli and F.M. Donini. A survey on knowledge compilation. *AI Communications*, 1998. (in press).

[Cadoli and Lenzerini, 1994] M. Cadoli and M. Lenzerini. The complexity of propositional closed world reasoning and circumscription. *Journal of Computer and System Sciences*, 48:255–310, 1994.

[Cadoli et al., 1996] M. Cadoli, F.M. Donini, and M. Schaerf. Is intractability of non-monotonic reasoning a real drawback? *Artificial Intelligence*, 88:215–251, 1996.

[Cadoli et al., 1997a] M. Cadoli, F.M. Donini, P. Liberatore, and M. Schaerf. Preprocessing of intractable problems. Technical Report DIS 24-97, Dipartimento di Informatica e Sistemistica, Università di Roma "La Sapienza", 1997.

[Cadoli et al., 1997b] M. Cadoli, F.M. Donini, M. Schaerf, and R. Silvestri. On compact representations of propositional circumscription. *Theoretical Computer Science*, 182:183–202, 1997.

Tractable KB	*CWA	CLAUSE INFERENCE	LITERAL INFERENCE
Blake	ECWA	in P when $P = \emptyset$	in P when $P = \emptyset$ or $Z = \emptyset$
Blake	ECWA	coNP-hard when $Q = Z = \emptyset$	coNP-hard when $Q = \emptyset$
DNF	CCWA	in P when $P = \emptyset$ or $Q = \emptyset$	in P when $P = \emptyset$ or $Q = \emptyset$
DNF	CCWA	coNP-hard when $Z = \emptyset$	coNP-hard when $Z = \emptyset$
DNF	ECWA	in P when $P = \emptyset$ or $Q = \emptyset$	in P when $P = \emptyset$ or $Q = \emptyset$
DNF	ECWA	coNP-hard when $Z = \emptyset$	coNP-hard when $Z = \emptyset$
Horn cover	CCWA	in P when $P = \emptyset$ or $Q = \emptyset$	in P when $P = \emptyset$ or $Q = \emptyset$
Horn cover	CCWA	coNP-hard when $Z = \emptyset$	coNP-hard when $Z = \emptyset$
Horn cover	ECWA	in P when $P = \emptyset$ or $Q = \emptyset$	in P when $P = \emptyset$ or $Q = \emptyset$
Horn cover	ECWA	coNP-hard when $Z = \emptyset$	coNP-hard when $Z = \emptyset$
renamable Horn cover	CCWA	in P when $P = \emptyset$	in P when $P = \emptyset$
renamable Horn cover	CCWA	coNP-hard when $Q = Z = \emptyset$	coNP-hard when $Q = Z = \emptyset$
renamable Horn cover	ECWA	in P when $P = \emptyset$	in P when $P = \emptyset$
renamable Horn cover	ECWA	coNP-hard when $Q = Z = \emptyset$	coNP-hard when $Q = Z = \emptyset$

Table 2: Complexity bounds for CCWA and ECWA inference from tractable KBs in some restricted cases.

[Castell et al., 1996] Th. Castell, C. Cayrol, M. Cayrol, and D. Le Berre. Using the Davis and Putnam procedure for an efficient computation of preferred models. In *Proc. of ECAI'96*, pages 350–354, Budapest, 1996.

[Coste-Marquis and Marquis, 1999] S. Coste-Marquis and P. Marquis. Complexity results for propositional closed world reasoning and circumscription from tractable knowledge bases. Technical Report 99-SC/PM-01, CRIL, Université d'Artois, 1999.

[Dowling and Gallier, 1984] W. Dowling and J.H. Gallier. Linear time algorithms for testing the satisfiability of propositional Horn formulae. *Journal of Logic Programming*, 1(3):267–284, 1984.

[Eiter and Gottlob, 1993] Th. Eiter and G. Gottlob. Propositional circumscription and extended closed-world reasoning are Π_2^p-complete. *Theoretical Computer Science*, 114:231–245, 1993.

[Gelfond and Przymusinska, 1986] M. Gelfond and H. Przymusinska. Negation as failure: careful closure procedure. *Artificial Intelligence*, 30:273–287, 1986.

[Gelfond et al., 1989] M. Gelfond, H. Przymusinska, and T. Przymusinski. On the relationship between circumscription and negation as failure. *Artificial Intelligence*, 38:49–73, 1989.

[Kautz and Selman, 1991] H.A. Kautz and B. Selman. Hard problems for simple default logic. *Artificial Intelligence*, 49:243–279, 1991.

[Kautz and Selman, 1992] H.A. Kautz and B. Selman. Forming concepts for fast inference. In *Proc. of AAAI'92*, pages 786–793, San Jose (CA), 1992.

[Lewis, 1978] H.R. Lewis. Renaming a set of clauses as a horn set. *Journal of the Association for Computing Machinery*, 25:134–135, 1978.

[Liberatore, 1998] P. Liberatore. On the compilability of diagnosis, planning, reasoning about actions, belief revision, etc. In *Proc. of KR'98*, pages 144–155, Trento, 1998.

[Marquis, 1999] P. Marquis. *Consequence finding algorithms*, volume 5 of *The Handbook for Uncertain and Defeasible Reasoning*, chapter Algorithms for Uncertain and Defeasible Reasoning. Kluwer Academic Publishers, 1999. (to appear).

[McCarthy, 1986] J. McCarthy. Applications of circumscription to formalizing common-sense knowledge. *Artificial Intelligence*, 28:89–116, 1986.

[Minker, 1982] J. Minker. On indefinite databases and the closed world assumption. In *Proc. of CADE'82*, pages 292–308, 1982.

[Nerode et al., 1995] A. Nerode, R.T. Ng, and V.S. Subrahmanian. Computing circumscriptive databases. i: Theory and algorithms. *Information and Computation*, 116:58–80, 1995.

[Papadimitriou, 1994] Ch. H. Papadimitriou. *Computational complexity*. Addison–Wesley, 1994.

[Raiman and de Kleer, 1992] O. Raiman and J. de Kleer. A minimality maintenance system. In *Proc. of KR'92*, pages 532–538, Cambridge (MA), 1992.

[Reiter and de Kleer, 1987] R. Reiter and J. de Kleer. Foundations of assumption-based truth maintenance systems: preliminary report. In *Proc. of AAAI'87*, pages 183–188, Seattle (WA), 1987.

[Reiter, 1978] R. Reiter. *Logic and Data Bases*, chapter On closed world data bases, pages 119–140. Plenum Press, 1978.

[Schrag, 1996] R. Schrag. Compilation for critically constrained knowledge bases. In *Proc. of AAAI'96*, pages 510–515, Portland (OR), 1996.

[Yahya and Henschen, 1985] A. Yahya and L.J. Henschen. Deduction in non-Horn databases. *Journal of Automated Reasoning*, 1:141–160, 1985.

Credulous Nonmonotonic Inference

Alexander Bochman

Department of Computerized Systems
Center for Technological Education Holon
52 Golomb St., P.O.B. 305, Holon 58102, Israel
bochman@macs.biu.ac.il

Abstract

We present a formal characterization and semantic representation for a number of credulous inference relations based on the notion of an epistemic state. It is shown, in particular, that credulous inference can be naturally represented in terms of expectations (see [Gärdenfors and Makinson, 1994]). We describe also the relationships between credulous and usual skeptical nonmonotonic inference and show how they can facilitate each other.

1 Introduction

The approach to nonmonotonic and commonsense reasoning based on describing associated inference relations forms one of the most influential and effective tools in studying such a reasoning in AI. A number of fundamental works in this area have reached its first 'saturation' in the so-called KLM theory [Kraus *et al.*, 1990]. In these works a semantic representation of nonmonotonic inference relations was developed based on sets of states ordered by a preference relation: a nonmonotonic inference rule $A \hspace{0.3em}\mid\hspace{-0.5em}\sim\hspace{0.3em} B$ was assigned a meaning that B should be true in all preferred states satisfying A.

The above notion of nonmonotonic inference was designed to capture a *skeptical approach* to nonmonotonic reasoning, according to which if there is a number of equally preferred alternatives, we infer only what is common to all of them. However, works in nonmonotonic reasoning have suggested also an alternative approach, usually called *credulous* or *brave* reasoning, according to which each of the preferred alternatives is considered as an admissible solution to the nonmonotonic reasoning task. Actually, there are many important reasoning problems in AI and beyond, such as diagnosis, abduction and explanation, that are best seen as involving search for particular preferred solutions. This idea is implicit also in the notion of an extension in default logic [Reiter, 1980] as well as in similar constructs in autoepistemic and modal nonmonotonic logics.

There have been a few attempts in the literature to investigate the properties of credulous inference, mainly with negative conclusions that such an inference does not satisfy practically all 'respectable' rules (see, e.g., [Brass, 1993; Cayrol and Lagasquie-Shiex, 1995]). For example, a distinctive feature of credulous reasoning is that it does not allow to conjoin different conclusions derivable from the same premises (because they might be grounded on different preferred solutions). In other words, it renders invalid the following well-known rule:

(And) If $A \hspace{0.3em}\mid\hspace{-0.5em}\sim\hspace{0.3em} B$ and $A \hspace{0.3em}\mid\hspace{-0.5em}\sim\hspace{0.3em} C$, then $A \hspace{0.3em}\mid\hspace{-0.5em}\sim\hspace{0.3em} B \wedge C$.

In fact, we will establish below that And can be seen as a culprit distinguishing credulous and skeptical nonmonotonic inference. Accordingly, inference relations satisfying this rule will be called *skeptical* in what follows.

We suggest below both a formal characterization and semantic interpretation for a number of systems of credulous nonmonotonic inference based on the notion of an epistemic state. The latter are quite similar to cumulative models of skeptical nonmonotonic inference, described in [Kraus *et al.*, 1990], though they will be used in a somewhat different way. Despite this, we will see that skeptical inference is also definable in the framework of epistemic states, and this will give us a good opportunity to compare these two kinds of inference and study their relationship.

We will establish also a close connection between credulous inference relations and ordinary Tarski consequence relations. In fact, we will see that practically all kinds of nonmonotonic inference relations, both skeptical and credulous, can be described in these terms. Among other things, this will allow us to give a representation of credulous inference in the expectation-based framework suggested in [Gärdenfors and Makinson, 1994].

Below we will follow David Makinson in distinguishing monotonic Tarski *consequence* relations from nonmonotonic *inference* relations. This terminological distinction will be especially suitable in the present context.

2 Preliminaries: supraclassical consequence relations

In what follows we will use ordinary Tarski consequence relations defined in a language containing the classical connectives $\{\vee, \wedge, \neg, \rightarrow\}$. $\vDash$ will denote the classical entailment with respect to these connectives. Also, $A, B, C, \ldots$ will denote propositions, while $a, b, c, \ldots$ finite sets of propositions.

A Tarski consequence relation $\vdash$ will be called *supraclassical* if it satisfies

(Supraclassicality) If $a \vDash A$, then $a \vdash A$

Thus, a consequence relation is supraclassical if it subsumes classical entailment. Supraclassicality requires all theories of a consequence relation to be deductively closed. It allows for replacement of classically equivalent formulas in premises and conclusions of the rules. In addition, it allows to replace sets of premises by their classical conjunctions: $a \vdash A$ will be equivalent to $\bigwedge a \vdash A$. This implies, in particular, that any supraclassical consequence relation can be seen also as a certain binary relation among propositions. In fact, such binary relations are partial orders that will be used below as a 'partial' generalization of *expectation orders* from [Gärdenfors and Makinson, 1994], since they have all the properties of the latter except connectivity.

3 Epistemic states

The notion of an epistemic state, defined below, will provide a uniform semantic framework for representing nonmonotonic inference relations. It is based on a quite common understanding that nonmonotonic reasoning uses not only known facts, but also *defaults* or *expectations* we have about the world. Such defaults are used as auxiliary assumptions that allow us to 'jump' to useful conclusions and beliefs that are not logical consequences of the facts alone. Such conclusions are defeasible and can be retracted when further facts become known. This indicates that our epistemic states can be seen as structured entities determined, or generated, by admissible sets of defaults. Furthermore, our defaults and expectations are often conflict with each other, and this may create situations in which we have a number of different plausible 'views of the world'. Such situations are actually quite common in nonmonotonic reasoning. In addition, not all defaults or expectations are equally plausible or acceptable, and this creates, in turn, priorities and preferences among otherwise admissible combinations of defaults. If we identify each such admissible set of defaults with the (deductively closed) set of its consequences, we will arrive at the following picture:

Definition 3.1. An *epistemic state* $\mathcal{E}$ is a triple $\langle S, \prec, l \rangle$, where S is a set of objects called *admissible belief states*, $\prec$ is a *preference relation* on S, while l is a labeling function assigning each admissible state a deductively closed theory.

Epistemic states turn out to be quite similar to *preferential models* of Makinson [Makinson, 1994] and *cumulative models* from [Kraus et al., 1990]. Indeed, labeling with a deductively closed theory can be equivalently described using labeling with a set of worlds, as in [Kraus et al., 1990] (see [Dix and Makinson, 1992] for the relation between these two kinds of representation). Epistemic states in which l is an injective function will be

called *standard*. Clearly, for standard epistemic states, admissible belief states can be safely identified with their associated theories. So, a standard epistemic state can be described as a pair $\langle \mathcal{T}, \prec \rangle$, where $\mathcal{T}$ is a set of deductively closed theories and $\prec$ is a preference relation on $\mathcal{T}$.

A state $s \in S$ will be said to *support* a proposition A if $A \in l(s)$. A state s will be said to be *consistent with* A if $\neg A \notin l(s)$. The set of states consistent with A will be denoted by $\langle A \rangle$.

According to [Kraus et al., 1990], a subset P of states is called *smooth* with respect to $\prec$ if, for any $s \in P$, either s is $\prec$-minimal in P or there exists $t \prec s$ such that t is $\prec$-minimal in P. An epistemic state will be said *(negatively) smooth* if any set of states $\langle A \rangle$ is smooth.

Skeptical and credulous validity. The informal understanding of epistemic states, sketched earlier, gives raise to the notions of skeptical and credulous validity, given below. To begin with, A sceptically entails B if all preferred sets of defaults that are consistent with A, taken together with A itself, logically imply B. This leads to the following definition of skeptical validity that is somewhat different from the standard one, given in [Kraus et al., 1990].

Definition 3.2. A conditional $A \mathrel{|\!\sim} B$ will be said to be *sceptically valid* in an epistemic state $\mathcal{E}$ if all preferred states in $\langle A \rangle$ support $A \rightarrow B$.

Similarly, A credulously entails B if A allows to *explain* B in the sense that there exists a preferred set of defaults that is consistent with A and, taken together with A, will logically imply B. An inessential modification of this description will give us

Definition 3.3. A conditional $A \mathrel{|\!\sim} B$ will be said to be *credulously valid* in an epistemic state $\mathcal{E}$ if either $\langle A \rangle$ is empty or at least one preferred state in $\langle A \rangle$ supports $A \rightarrow B$.

We will provide below a syntactic characterization for the above two kinds of validity.

4 Basic inference relation

As we mentioned, credulous nonmonotonic inference invalidates the basic postulates of skeptical nonmonotonic inference, such as Cut, Cautious Monotony or And. This means that in order to obtain a broader picture of nonmonotonic inference that would encompass both credulous and skeptical kinds, we need to find an alternative ground for classifying inference relations. Below we take as a basis a system suggested in [Benthem, 1984]. The latter will give us a rather rich and neat picture that avoids complications and fancy elaborations created by alternative approaches.

The main idea behind van Benthem's approach is that a conditional can be seen as a special kind of a *generalized quantifier* representing a relation between the respective sets of instances or situations supporting its premise and conclusion. In this setting, the nature of a conditional can be described in terms of possible changes made to these sets of situations that still preserve its validity. Such changes can involve adding new confirming instances, deleting refuting ones, etc. As is shown in [Benthem, 1984], this naturally leads to the set of postulates, given below.

By a *basic inference relation* $\mathcal{B}$ we will mean a relation on propositions satisfying the following postulates:

(Reflexivity) $A \mathrel{\vdash\mkern-10mu\sim} A$;

(Left Logical Equivalence) If $\models A \leftrightarrow B$ and $A \mathrel{\vdash\mkern-10mu\sim} C$, then $B \mathrel{\vdash\mkern-10mu\sim} C$;

(Right Weakening) If $A \mathrel{\vdash\mkern-10mu\sim} B$ and $B \models C$, then $A \mathrel{\vdash\mkern-10mu\sim} C$;

(Antecedence) If $A \mathrel{\vdash\mkern-10mu\sim} B$, then $A \mathrel{\vdash\mkern-10mu\sim} A \wedge B$;

(Deduction) If $A \wedge B \mathrel{\vdash\mkern-10mu\sim} C$, then $A \mathrel{\vdash\mkern-10mu\sim} B \to C$;

(Conjunctive Cautious Monotony) If $A \mathrel{\vdash\mkern-10mu\sim} B \wedge C$, then $A \wedge B \mathrel{\vdash\mkern-10mu\sim} C$.

The most salient feature of the above list is that all the above postulates involve no more than one conditional premise. Consequently, the system says nothing about how to combine different conditionals. As a result, a conditional is derivable in $\mathcal{B}$ from a set of conditionals only if it is derivable from one of them. The following result gives a direct characterization of this derivability relation.[1]

Theorem 4.1. *$C \mathrel{\vdash\mkern-10mu\sim} D$ is derivable from $A \mathrel{\vdash\mkern-10mu\sim} B$ in $\mathcal{B}$ iff either $C \models D$, or $A \wedge B \models C \wedge D$ and $C \wedge \neg D \models A \wedge \neg B$.*

Using the terminology of [Benthem, 1984], the above theorem says that a conditional implies another one if all confirming instances of the former are confirming instances of the latter and all refuting instances of the latter are refuting instances of the former.

As we will see, the system $\mathcal{B}$ is sufficiently powerful to capture exactly the one-premise fragment of both credulous and skeptical inference relations, and hence can be seen as their common core.

Regularity. An inference relation will be called *regular* if it satisfies the rules of $\mathcal{B}$ and the following rule (where **f** denotes an arbitrary contradiction):

(Preservation) If $A \mathrel{\vdash\mkern-10mu\sim} \mathbf{f}$ and $B \mathrel{\vdash\mkern-10mu\sim} C$, then $B \mathrel{\vdash\mkern-10mu\sim} \neg A \wedge C$.

The conditional $A \mathrel{\vdash\mkern-10mu\sim} \mathbf{f}$ says, in effect, that A is seen as impossible with respect to the inference relation, that is, no imaginable situation assumed by $\mathrel{\vdash\mkern-10mu\sim}$ is compatible with A. It is reasonable to conclude then that $\neg A$ should hold in all situations, and consequently it can be conjoined to consequences of any proposition.

Duality. It turns out that, for any regular inference relation $\mathrel{\vdash\mkern-10mu\sim}$ we can define a *dual* inference relation as follows:

(Dual) $\qquad A \mathrel{\vdash\mkern-10mu\sim}^{\diamond} B \quad \equiv \quad A \mathrel{\not\vdash\mkern-10mu\sim} \neg B$ or $A \mathrel{\vdash\mkern-10mu\sim} \mathbf{f}$

---
[1] Due to space limitations, we omit all proofs.

The above notion of duality can be seen as an abstract form of the relation between ordinary conditionals and their corresponding *might*-conditionals, well-known in the literature on conditional logic at least since the time of David Lewis.

The following result can be proved by a straightforward check of the relevant rules. It shows that the set of regular inference relations is closed with respect to taking duals.

Theorem 4.2. *If $\mathrel{\vdash\mkern-10mu\sim}$ is a regular inference relation, then $\mathrel{\vdash\mkern-10mu\sim}^{\diamond}$ is also a regular inference relation. Moreover, $\mathrel{\vdash\mkern-10mu\sim}^{\diamond\diamond}$ coincides with $\mathrel{\vdash\mkern-10mu\sim}$.*

5 Credulous nonmonotonic inference

In this section we will give a characterization of a basic credulous inference relation.

Definition 5.1. A nonmonotonic inference relation will be called *credulous* if it is regular and satisfies Rational Monotony:

(RM) If $A \mathrel{\vdash\mkern-10mu\sim} B$ and $A \mathrel{\not\vdash\mkern-10mu\sim} \neg C$, then $A \wedge C \mathrel{\vdash\mkern-10mu\sim} B$.

So, credulous inference is a subsystem of rational inference from [Kraus *et al.*, 1990]. As we will see, the latter can be obtained simply by adding the rule And.

The following theorem shows that the semantic definition of credulous validity, given earlier, determines a credulous inference relation.

Theorem 5.1. *If $\mathcal{E}$ is a smooth epistemic state, then the set of conditionals that are credulously valid in $\mathcal{E}$ forms a credulous inference relation.*

In the next section we will show that our postulates provide a complete description of credulous validity.

6 Credulous inference generated by consequence relations

In this section we introduce an alternative representation of credulous inference relations as generated by supraclassical Tarski consequence relations.

For any supraclassical consequence relation define the following inference relation:

(IC) $\qquad A \mathrel{\vdash\mkern-10mu\sim}^{c}_{\vdash} B \quad$ iff $\quad A \to B \not\vdash \neg A$ or $\vdash \neg A$

As can be easily seen, $A \mathrel{\vdash\mkern-10mu\sim}^{c}_{\vdash} B$ holds if either no theory of $\vdash$ is consistent with A or $A \to B$ belongs to at least one maximal theory of $\vdash$ that is consistent with A. Now we may consider the set of theories of $\vdash$ as a standard epistemic state ordered by set inclusion. Then the above description will immediately give us that the above definition provides a description of a credulous inference with respect to this epistemic state. As a result, we obtain the following

Corollary 6.1. *If $\vdash$ is a supraclassical consequence relation, then $\mathrel{\vdash\mkern-10mu\sim}^{c}_{\vdash}$ is a credulous inference relation.*

It turns out that a credulous inference relation determines, in turn, its generating Tarski consequence relation via the following equivalence:

(CI) $A \vdash_{\vdash} B \quad \equiv \quad \neg(A \wedge B) \vdash A$ or $\neg(A \wedge B) \vdash \mathbf{f}$

The following result shows that Tarski consequence relations are strongly equivalent to credulous inference relations.

Theorem 6.2. *1. If $\vdash$ is a supraclassical consequence relation, then $\vdash_{\vdash}$ is a credulous inference relation. Moreover, the corresponding consequence relation determined by (CI) coincides with $\vdash$.*

2. If $\vdash$ is a credulous inference relation, then $\vdash_{\vdash}$ is a supraclassical consequence relation. Moreover, the credulous inference relation generated by $\vdash_{\vdash}$ via (IC) coincides with $\vdash$.

An important consequence of the above result is that any credulous inference relation is generated by an epistemic state (corresponding to theories of the associated consequence relation). Therefore, we have the following

Representation Theorem 1. *An inference relation $\vdash$ is credulous if and only if there exists a smooth epistemic state $\mathcal{E}$ that credulously validates conditionals from $\vdash$.*

7 Credulous inference based on expectations

There exists a strong connection between the above representation of credulous inference in terms of consequence relations and representation of nonmonotonic inference relations based on *expectation orders* described in [Gärdenfors and Makinson, 1994].

At the beginning of their paper, Gärdenfors and Makinson suggested two general ways of understanding nonmonotonic inference. The first formulation was as follows:

> *A nonmonotonically entails B iff B follows logically from A together with "as many as possible" of the set of our expectations as are compatible with A.*

On the other hand, expectations can be reflected in the form of an ordering between propositions, and then this relation can be used in the nonmonotonic inference as follows:

> *A nonmonotonically entails B iff B follows logically from A together with all those propositions that are "sufficiently well expected" in the light of A.*

As was rightly noted by the authors, though the two ideas are closely related, the former tends to suggest a multiplicity of possible sets of auxiliary premises, while the second formulation points towards a unique set of such premises. In other words, the first formulation admits a credulous reading, while the second formulation is primary a skeptical one. Nevertheless, the authors have shown that the two formulations can be 'reconciled' in

a single framework. As we will see, however, this possibility depends on a particular structure of expectations chosen that gives rise to rational inference relations; for the latter, credulous validity will actually coincide with the skeptical one.

As we mentioned, a supraclassical consequence relation (viewed as a binary relation among propositions) is actually a 'partial' generalization of an *expectation order* from [Gärdenfors and Makinson, 1994]. Moreover, the above definition (IC) of credulous inference relation generated by a consequence relation can be equivalently expressed as follows:

$A \vdash B$ iff either $\vdash A \rightarrow B$ or $A \rightarrow B \nvdash \neg A$.

As was shown in [Gärdenfors and Makinson, 1994], Theorem 3.5, the above description is equivalent to the 'standard' definition of expectation inference relations. Thus, our notion can be considered as a generalization of the corresponding interpretation for expectation inference given in [Gärdenfors and Makinson, 1994]. Informally, it corresponds to the following modification of the second formulation above:

> *A nonmonotonically entails B if B follows logically from A together with some consistent set of propositions that are "sufficiently well expected" in the light of A.*

8 Permissive inference

In this section we will describe another interesting kind of brave nonmonotonic inference.

Definition 8.1. An inference relation will be called *permissive* if it satisfies the basic postulates and the Cut rule:

(Cut) If $A \vdash B$ and $A \wedge B \vdash C$, then $A \vdash C$.

It can be shown that, in the context of $\mathcal{B}$, Cut implies the rule Or:

(Or) If $A \vdash C$ and $B \vdash C$, then $A \vee B \vdash C$.

The following theorem gives a more 'traditional' characterization of permissive inference relations:

Theorem 8.1. *Permissive inference relations are completely characterized by the postulates Reflexivity, Left Logical Equivalence, Right Weakening, Conjunctive Cautious Monotony, Cut and Or.*

If we compare the above list of postulates with the characterization of preferential inference, given in [Kraus *et al.*, 1990], we can notice that the distinction of permissive inference from preferential one amounts simply to replacement of standard Cautious Monotony by Conjunctive Cautious Monotony. Still, permissive inference is not skeptical, since it does not satisfy And.

The following result shows that permissive and credulous inference relations are duals.

Theorem 8.2. *$\vdash$ is a permissive inference relation iff $\vdash^{\diamond}$ is a credulous inference relation.*

Using the above duality, we can immediately obtain the following semantic characterization of permissive inference in epistemic states:

Definition 8.2. A conditional $A \mathrel{|\!\sim} B$ will be said to be *permissively valid* in an epistemic state $\mathcal{E}$ if any preferred state in $\langle A \rangle$ is consistent with $A \wedge B$.

So, permissive conditional says informally "*A is normally consistent with B*".

Again, the duality of credulous and permissive inference immediately implies that any supraclassical consequence relation generates a permissive inference relation via

(PC) $A \mathrel{|\!\sim} B \quad \equiv \quad \neg(A \wedge B) \vdash \neg A$

and that any permissive inference relation can be produced in this way from some consequence relation.

X-logics. [Siegel and Forget, 1996] suggested a new description of nonmonotonic inference relations that they called *X-logics*. For any set of propositions X, they defined an inference relation $\vdash_X$ as follows:

$$A \vdash_X B \text{ iff } \mathrm{Th}(A, B) \cap X \subseteq \mathrm{Th}(A) \cap X$$

A detailed study of such inference relations and their use for describing circumscriptions is given in [Moinard and Rolland, 1998]. The latter authors have established, in effect, that any X-logic is a permissive inference relation in our sense. Actually, the following result shows that, for finite languages, the two notions turn out to coincide.

Theorem 8.3. *Any X-logic is a permissive inference relation. Moreover, for any permissive inference relation* $\mathrel{|\!\sim}$ *in a finite language there exists a set of propositions* X *such that* $\mathrel{|\!\sim}$ *coincides with* $\vdash_X$.

Since any preferential inference relation is permissive, the above result immediately implies that in the finite case any preferential inference relation will also coincide with some X-logic.

9 Preferential and rational inference relations

Preferential inference relation $\mathcal{P}$ from [Kraus *et al.*, 1990] can be obtained by adding the rule And to the postulates of $\mathcal{B}$.

It has been shown already in [Adams, 1975] that the condition described in Theorem 4.1 is actually necessary and sufficient for 'one-premise' derivability in preferential inference relations. Consequently, we immediately obtain that preferential inference is a 'conservative extension' of the derivability in $\mathcal{B}$:

Theorem 9.1. *A conditional* $C \mathrel{|\!\sim} D$ *is derivable from* $A \mathrel{|\!\sim} B$ *in* $\mathcal{P}$ *if and only if it is derivable already in* $\mathcal{B}$.

The next result shows that our modified definition of skeptical validity is nevertheless adequate for characterizing preferential inference.

Representation Theorem 2. *An inference relation* $\mathrel{|\!\sim}$ *is preferential iff there exists a smooth epistemic state* $\mathcal{E}$ *that sceptically validates conditionals from* $\mathrel{|\!\sim}$.

As a result, both skeptical and credulous inference acquire a semantic representation in the same framework of epistemic states. We will use this fact in the next section.

Rational inference. Rational inference relations (see [Kraus *et al.*, 1990]) are preferential inference relations that satisfy also Rational Monotony. So, they are both credulous and skeptical, and hence obliterate, in effect, the distinction between skeptical and credulous inference. A semantic representation of such inference relations can be obtained by restricting epistemic states to standard states in which the set of admissible theories is linearly ordered by set inclusion. As can be easily checked, a conditional $A \mathrel{|\!\sim} B$ will be sceptically valid in such a state iff it is credulously valid in it.

10 Interplay

In this section we will invariably use $\mathrel{|\!\sim}$ to denote a skeptical (preferential) inference relation, while $\mathrel{|\!\approx}$ will denote a credulous inference relation.

Any epistemic state determines both a credulous and skeptical inference relation. Clearly, the two will be related. Below we will give a number of conditions that relate the two kinds of inference.

To begin with, skeptical consequences of some proposition can always be added to its credulous consequences:

Lemma 10.1. *If* $\mathrel{|\!\approx}$ *and* $\mathrel{|\!\sim}$ *are, respectively, a credulous and skeptical inference relations determined by the same epistemic state, then*

If $A \mathrel{|\!\sim} B$ *and* $A \mathrel{|\!\approx} C$, *then* $A \mathrel{|\!\approx} B \wedge C$.

Strengthening the Antecedent. There are some useful conditions allowing strengthening the antecedent for skeptical conditionals - a well-known problem for defeasible inference. To begin with, we have the following

Lemma 10.2. *If* $\mathrel{|\!\sim}$ *and* $\mathrel{|\!\approx}^{\circ}$ *are, respectively, skeptical and permissive inference relation determined by some epistemic state, then*

If $A \mathrel{|\!\sim} B$ *and* $A \mathrel{|\!\approx}^{\circ} C$, *then* $A \wedge C \mathrel{|\!\sim} B$.

The above condition is a kind of a 'mixed' Cautious Monotony rule that is valid for any skeptical inference relation. In this rule the 'permissibility claim' $A \mathrel{|\!\approx}^{\circ} C$ serves precisely the same role as *irrelevance conditions* in [Geffner, 1992].

Unlike credulous inference, skeptical inference relations do not satisfy, in general, Rational Monotony. Still, the following lemma establish two weaker variants of 'rational monotony' that hold for skeptical inference relations and their credulous counterparts:

Lemma 10.3. *If* $\mathrel{|\!\sim}$ *and* $\mathrel{|\!\approx}$ *are, respectively, skeptical and credulous inference relation determined by some epistemic state, then*

1. If $A \vdash B$ and $A \not\approx \neg C$, then $A \wedge C \vdash B$.

2. If $A \vdash B$ and $A \not\sim \neg C$, then $A \wedge C \not\approx B$.

The last condition above is especially interesting, since it describes a transition from skeptical to credulous inference. The following example of *Nixon Diamond* illustrates the use of these rules.

Example 10.1. Let P, Q and R denote, respectively, "Nixon is a pacifist", "Nixon is a quaker" and "Nixon is a republican". Assume that $Q \vdash P$ and $R \vdash \neg P$ are sceptically acceptable conditionals. Then if Q and R are compatible, that is $Q \not\sim \neg R$ and $R \not\sim \neg Q$, we can use the above rule to conclude both $Q \wedge R \not\approx P$ and $Q \wedge R \not\approx \neg P$. Thus, in this situation we can credulously infer incompatible conclusions.

Credulous rules as defeaters. Credulous inference rules $A \not\approx B$ can be considered as *might*-conditionals saying that if A holds then it might be the case that B. Such conditionals play an important role in Nute's *defeasible logic* [Nute, 1990] where they function primarily as *defeaters* that block applications of skeptical defeasible rules. This function can be justified via the following condition relating skeptical inference and its counterpart credulous inference:

If $A \not\approx \neg B$ and $A \not\approx \mathbf{f}$, then $A \vdash B$.

The above condition says that if, given A, it might be the case that $\neg B$, then A should not sceptically entail B. Actually, instead of credulous inference in the above condition, we could as well use permissive inference. So, brave inference rules can indeed function as defeaters of ordinary skeptical rules.

11 Conclusion and perspectives

The main conclusion of this study is that credulous nonmonotonic inference admits a rigorous semantic and syntactic characterization. Moreover, both credulous and ordinary skeptical inference are representable in the same semantic framework of epistemic states.

As is well-known, common systems of skeptical inference, namely preferential and rational entailment, are too weak (too skeptical) to account for some natural forms of *defeasible inference*. In this respect, the most promising perspective suggested by the present study (briefly sketched in the last section) consists in a joint use of skeptical and brave inference rules in order to achieve a more fine-grained representation framework for nonmonotonic inference. As has been shown in the last section, brave inference rules can be used both for deriving new plausible skeptical inferences and for defeating implausible ones. Accordingly, brave conditionals can be used as additional assumptions that allow, e.g., strengthening antecedents of skeptical rules with irrelevant propositions or sanction certain instances of transitive chaining for such rules, etc. In short, brave inference can facilitate skeptical one in order to achieve an adequate representation of defeasible inference. Further

work is needed, however, in order to clarify the perspectives of this approach.

References

[Adams, 1975] E. W. Adams. *The Logic of Conditionals.* Reidel, Dordrecht, 1975.

[Benthem, 1984] J. Van Benthem. Foundations of conditional logic. *J. of Philosophical Logic,* 13:303–349, 1984.

[Brass, 1993] S. Brass. On the semantics of supernormal defaults. In *Proceedings IJCAI-93,* pages 578–583, 1993.

[Cayrol and Lagasquie-Shiex, 1995] C. Cayrol and M.-C. Lagasquie-Shiex. Non-monotonic syntax-based entailment: A classification of consequence relations. In C. Froidevaux and J. Kohlas, editors, *Symbolic and Qualitative Approaches to Reasoning and Uncertainty, ECSQARU'95,* pages 107–114, Fribourg, Switzerland, July 1995. Springer Verlag. Lecture Notes in AI, 946.

[Dix and Makinson, 1992] J. Dix and D. Makinson. The relationship between KLM and MAK models for nonmonotonic inference operations. *J. of Logic and Computation,* 1:131–140, 1992.

[Gärdenfors and Makinson, 1994] P. Gärdenfors and D. Makinson. Nonmonotonic inference based on expectations. *Artificial Intelligence,* 65:197–245, 1994.

[Geffner, 1992] H. Geffner. *Default Reasoning. Causal and Conditional Theories.* MIT Press, 1992.

[Kraus *et al.*, 1990] S. Kraus, D. Lehmann, and M. Magidor. Nonmonotonic reasoning, preferential models and cumulative logics. *Artificial Intelligence,* 44:167–207, 1990.

[Makinson, 1994] D. Makinson. General patterns in nonmonotonic reasoning. In D. M. Gabbay and Others, editors, *Handbook of Logic in Artificial Intelligence and Logic Programming, Vol. 3, Nonmonotonic and Uncertain Reasoning,* volume 2, pages 35–110. Oxford University Press, Oxford, 1994.

[Moinard and Rolland, 1998] Y. Moinard and R. Rolland. Circumscriptions from what they cannot do (Preliminary report). In *Working papers of Common Sense'98,* pages 20–41, University of London, 1998.

[Nute, 1990] D. Nute. Defeasible logic and the frame problem. In R. Loui H. Kyburg and G. Carlson, editors, *Knowledge Representation and Defeasible Reasoning,* pages 3–24. Kluwer Academic Publishers, Boston MA, 1990.

[Reiter, 1980] R. Reiter. A logic for default reasoning. *Artificial Intelligence,* 13:81–132, 1980.

[Siegel and Forget, 1996] P. Siegel and L. Forget. A representation theorem for preferential logics. In L. C. Aiello, J. Doyle, and S. C. Shapiro, editors, *Principles of Knowledge Representation and Reasoning. Proc. Fifth Int. Conference, KR'96,* pages 453–460. Morgan Kaufmann, 1996.

Preferred Arguments are Harder to Compute than Stable Extensions

Yannis Dimopoulos
University of Cyprus
Dept. of Computer Science
75 Kallipoleos Street
Nicosia P.O. Box 537
Cyprus
yannis@cs.ucy.ac.cy

Bernhard Nebel
Universität Freiburg
Institut für Informatik
Am Flughafen 17
D-79110 Freiburg
Germany
nebel@informatik.uni-freiburg.de

Francesca Toni
Imperial College
Dept. of Computing
180 Queen's Gate
London SW7 2BZ
United Kingdom
ft@doc.ic.ac.uk

Abstract

Based on an abstract framework for nonmonotonic reasoning, Bondarenko *et al.* have extended the logic programming semantics of *admissible* and *preferred arguments* to other nonmonotonic formalisms such as circumscription, auto-epistemic logic and default logic. Although the new semantics have been tacitly assumed to mitigate the computational problems of nonmonotonic reasoning under the standard semantics of *stable extensions*, it seems questionable whether they improve the worst-case behaviour. As a matter of fact, we show that credulous reasoning under the new semantics in propositional logic programming and propositional default logic has the same computational complexity as under the standard semantics. Furthermore, sceptical reasoning under the admissibility semantics is easier – since it is trivialised to monotonic reasoning. Finally, sceptical reasoning under the preferability semantics is harder than under the standard semantics.

1 Introduction

Bondarenko *et al.* [1997] show that many logics for nonmonotonic reasoning, in particular default logic (DL) [Reiter, 1980] and logic programming (LP), can be understood as special cases of a single abstract framework. The standard semantics of these logics can be understood in terms of *stable extensions* of a given theory, where a stable extension is a set of assumptions that does not *attack* itself and it attacks every assumption not in the set. In abstract terms, an assumption is attacked if its *contrary* can be proven, in some appropriate underlying monotonic logic, possibly with the aid of other conflicting assumptions.

Bondarenko *et al.* [1997] also propose two new semantics generalising, respectively, the *admissibility semantics* [Dung, 1991] and the *semantics of preferred extensions* [Dung, 1991] and *partial stable models* [Saccà and Zaniolo, 1990] for LP. In abstract terms, a set of assumptions is an *admissible argument* of a given theory, iff it does not attack itself and it attacks all sets of

assumptions which attack it. A set of assumptions is a *preferred argument* iff it is a maximal (wrt. set inclusion) admissible argument.

The new semantics are more general than the stability semantics since every stable extension is a preferred (and admissible) argument, but not every preferred argument is a stable extension. Moreover, the new semantics are more liberal because for most concrete logics for nonmonotonic reasoning, admissible and preferred arguments are always guaranteed to exist, whereas stable extensions are not. Finally, reasoning under the new semantics appears to be computationally easier than reasoning under the stability semantics. Intuitively, to show that a given sentence is justified by a stable extension, it is necessary to perform a global search amongst all the assumptions, to determine for each such assumption whether it or its contrary can be derived, independently of the sentence to be justified. For the semantics of admissible and preferred arguments, however, a "local" search suffices. First, one has to construct a set of assumptions which, together with the given theory, (monotonically) derives the sentence to be justified, and then one has to augment the constructed set with further assumptions to defend it against all attacks.

However, from a complexity-theoretic point of view, it seems unlikely that the new semantics lead to better lower bounds than the standard semantics since all the "sources of complexity" one has in nonmonotonic reasoning are present. There are potentially exponentially many assumption sets sanctioned by the semantics. Further, in order to test whether a sentence is entailed by a particular argument one has to reason in the underlying monotonic logic. For this reason, one would expect that reasoning under the new semantics has the same complexity as under the stability semantics, i.e., it is on the first level of the polynomial hierarchy for LP and on the second level for logics with full propositional logic as the underlying logic [Cadoli and Schaerf, 1993]. However, previous results on the expressive power of DATALOG⁻ queries by Saccà [1997] suggest that this is not the case for LP. Indeed, these results imply that reasoning under the preferability semantics for LP is at the second level of the polynomial hierarchy.

In this paper, we extend these results and show that

for LP and DL

- *credulous* reasoning under the *admissibility* and *preferability semantics* has the same complexity as under the stability semantics,

- *sceptical* reasoning under the *admissibility semantics* is easier than under the stability semantics – since it reduces to monotonic reasoning with the given theory, and, finally,

- *sceptical* reasoning under the *preferability semantics* is harder than under the stability semantics. In other words, here intuition seems to clash severely with the complexity-theoretic results.

The paper is organised as follows. Section 2 summarises the abstract framework introduced by Bondarenko *et al.* [1997], its semantics and concrete instances capturing LP and DL. Section 3 gives complexity theory background and introduces the reasoning problems. Section 4 gives abstract upper bounds for credulous and sceptical reasoning, parametric wrt. the complexity of the underlying monotonic logic. Section 5 gives the completeness results. Section 6 discusses the results and concludes.

2 Default Reasoning via Argumentation

Assume a **deductive system** $(\mathcal{L}, \mathcal{R})$ where $\mathcal{L}$ is some formal language with countably many sentences and $\mathcal{R}$ is a set of inference rules inducing a monotonic derivability notion $\vdash$. Given a theory $T \subseteq \mathcal{L}$ and a formula $\alpha \in \mathcal{L}$, $Th(T) = \{\alpha \in \mathcal{L} \mid T \vdash \alpha\}$ is the deductive closure of T. Then, an **abstract (assumption-based) framework** is a triple $\langle T, A, {}^{-} \rangle$, where $T, A \subseteq \mathcal{L}$ and ${}^{-}$ is a mapping from A into $\mathcal{L}$. T, the **theory**, is a (possibly incomplete) set of beliefs, formulated in the underlying language, and can be extended by subsets of A, the set of **assumptions**. An **extension** of an abstract framework $\langle T, A, {}^{-} \rangle$ is a theory $Th(T \cup \Delta)$, with $\Delta \subseteq A$ (sometimes an extension is referred to simply as $T \cup \Delta$ or Δ). Finally, given an assumption $\alpha \in A$, $\overline{\alpha}$ denotes its **contrary**.

LP is the instance of the abstract framework $\langle T, A, {}^{-} \rangle$ where T is a logic program, the assumptions in A are all negations *not p* of atomic sentences *p*, and the contrary $\overline{not\,p}$ of an assumption *not p* is *p*. $\vdash$ is Horn logic provability, with assumptions, *not p*, understood as new atoms, p^*.

DL is the instance of the abstract framework $\langle T, A, {}^{-} \rangle$ where the monotonic logic is classical logic augmented with domain-specific inference rules of the form

$$\frac{\alpha_1, \ldots, \alpha_m, M\beta_1, \ldots, M\beta_n}{\gamma}$$

where $\alpha_i, \beta_j, \gamma$ are sentences in classical logic. T is a classical theory and A consists of all expressions of the form $M\beta$ where β is a sentence of classical logic. The contrary $\overline{M\beta}$ of an assumption $M\beta$ is $\neg\beta$.

In the remainder of the paper, without loss of generality, we will assume that the set of assumptions A in the abstract framework for DL consists of all assumptions $M\beta$ occurring in the domain-specific inference rules.

Given an abstract framework $\langle T, A, {}^{-} \rangle$ and an assumption set $\Delta \subseteq A$, Δ **attacks an assumption** $\alpha \in A$ iff $\overline{\alpha} \in Th(T \cup \Delta)$ and Δ **attacks an assumption set** $\Delta' \subseteq A$ iff Δ attacks some assumption $\alpha \in \Delta'$.

The standard semantics of extensions of DL [Reiter, 1980] and stable models of LP [Gelfond and Lifschitz, 1988] correspond to the "stability" semantics of abstract frameworks, where an assumption set $\Delta \subseteq A$ is **stable** iff

1. Δ does not attack itself, and
2. Δ attacks each assumption $\alpha \notin \Delta$.

A **stable extension** is an extension $Th(T \cup \Delta)$ for some stable assumption set Δ.

Bondarenko *et al.* define new semantics for the abstract framework, e.g., by generalising the admissibility semantics originally proposed for LP by Dung [1991]. An assumption set $\Delta \subseteq A$ is **admissible** iff

1. Δ does not attack itself, and
2. for all $\Delta' \subseteq A$, if Δ' attacks Δ then Δ attacks Δ'.

Maximal (wrt. set inclusion) admissible assumption sets are called **preferred**. In this paper we use the following terminology: an **admissible (preferred) argument** is an extension $Th(T \cup \Delta)$ for some admissible (preferred) assumption set Δ. Bondarenko *et al.* show that preferred arguments correspond to preferred extensions [Dung, 1991] and partial stable models [Saccà and Zaniolo, 1990] for LP.

In order to illustrate the effects of the different semantics, let us consider the following logic program:

$p \leftarrow not\,p$;	$r \leftarrow not\,q$;
$s \leftarrow not\,r$;	$q \leftarrow not\,r$.

This logic program has no stable extension, two preferred arguments ($\{not\,r\}$ and $\{not\,q, not\,s\}$) and four admissible arguments (additionally $\emptyset$ and $\{not\,q\}$). If we drop the clause "$p \leftarrow not\,p$," we get the same admissible and preferred arguments. In addition, the preferred arguments are also stable.

In [Bondarenko *et al.*, 1997], the definition of stable and admissible sets includes a third condition, namely, that the set Δ must be **closed**, i.e., $\Delta = A \cap Th(T \cup \Delta)$, and in part 2 of the definition of admissible sets all Δ' are required to be closed. Here we omit these conditions because in the LP and DL instances of the framework every set is guaranteed to be closed. Frameworks with this property are called **flat**.

In the sequel we will use the following properties:

Prop₁: Every preferred assumption set is (trivially) admissible and every admissible assumption set is a subset of some preferred assumption set [Bondarenko *et al.*, 1997, Theorem 4.8];

Prop₂: The empty assumption set is always admissible, trivially, for all concrete LP and DL frameworks.

3 Reasoning Problems and Complexity

We will analyse the *computational complexity* of the following reasoning problems for the propositional variants of the frameworks for LP and DL under admissibility and preferability semantics:

- the **credulous reasoning problem**, i.e., the problem of deciding for any given sentence φ in the set of possible queries whether $\varphi \in Th(T \cup \Delta)$ for *some* assumption set Δ sanctioned by the semantics;

- the **sceptical reasoning problem**, i.e., the problem of deciding for any given sentence φ in the set of possible queries whether $\varphi \in Th(T \cup \Delta)$ for *all* assumption sets Δ sanctioned by the semantics.

The set of possible queries consists of (variable-free conjunctions of) literals in the LP case and formulas in propositional logic in the DL case.

Instead of the sceptical reasoning problem, we will often consider its complementary problem, i.e.

- the **co-sceptical reasoning problem**, i.e, the problem of deciding for any given sentence φ (in a set of possible queries) whether $\varphi \notin Th(T \cup \Delta)$ for *some* assumption set Δ sanctioned by the semantics.

The computational complexity[1] of the above problems for all frameworks and semantics we consider is located at the lower end of the *polynomial hierarchy*. This is an infinite hierarchy of complexity classes above NP defined by using *oracle machines*, i.e. Turing machines that are allowed to call a subroutine—the *oracle*—deciding some fixed problem in constant time. Let $\mathcal{C}$ be a class of decision problems. Then, for any class $\mathcal{X}$ defined by resource bounds, $\mathcal{X}^{\mathcal{C}}$ denotes the class of problems decidable on a Turing machine with an oracle for a problem in $\mathcal{C}$ and a resource bound given by $\mathcal{X}$. Based on these notions, the sets Δ_k^p, Σ_k^p, and Π_k^p are defined as follows:

$$\Delta_0^p = \Sigma_0^p = \Pi_0^p = \mathsf{P}$$
$$\Delta_{k+1}^p = \mathsf{P}^{\Sigma_k^p}, \quad \Sigma_{k+1}^p = \mathsf{NP}^{\Sigma_k^p}, \quad \Pi_{k+1}^p = \mathsf{co\text{-}NP}^{\Sigma_k^p}.$$

The "canonical" complete problems are SAT for $\Sigma_1^p = \mathsf{NP}$ and k-QBF for Σ_k^p ($k > 1$), where k-QBF is the problem of deciding whether the quantified boolean formula

$$\underbrace{\exists \vec{p} \forall \vec{q} \ldots}_{k \text{ alternating quantifiers starting with } \exists} \Phi(\vec{p}, \vec{q}, \ldots).$$

is true. The complementary problem, denoted by co-k-QBF, is complete for Π_k^p.

All problems in the polynomial hierarchy can be solved in polynomial time iff $\mathsf{P} = \mathsf{NP}$. Further, all these problems can be solved by worst-case exponential time algorithms. Thus, the polynomial hierarchy might not seem too meaningful. However, different levels of the hierarchy differ considerably in practice, e.g. methods working for moderately sized instances of NP-complete problems do not work for Σ_2^p-complete problems.

The complexity of the problems we are interested in has been extensively studied for existing logics for nonmonotonic reasoning under the standard, stability

---

[1]For the following, we assume that the reader is familiar with the basic concepts of complexity theory [Papadimitriou, 1994], i.e., the complexity classes P, NP, and co-NP and the notion of completeness with respect to log-space reductions.

semantics [Cadoli and Schaerf, 1993; Gottlob, 1992; Niemelä, 1990; Marek and Truszczynski, 1993; Stillman, 1992]. In particular, the credulous reasoning problem is NP-complete for LP and Σ_2^p-complete for DL, and the sceptical reasoning problem is co-NP-complete for LP and Π_2^p-complete for DL.

4 Generic Upper Bounds

We identify upper bounds for the credulous and sceptical reasoning problems by exploiting the following *guess-and-verify algorithm* that, in order to decide these problems, guesses an assumption set, verifies that it is sanctioned by the semantics, and verifies that the formula under consideration is derivable or not derivable, respectively, from the set of assumptions and the given theory in the underlying monotonic logic. The upper bounds are parametric on the complexity of the **derivability problem** in the underlying monotonic logic. Moreover, the upper bounds are determined by exploiting upper bounds for their sub-problem that an assumption set is sanctioned by the semantics, called the **assumption set verification problem**.

In LP, the underlying logic is (propositional) Horn logic, hence the derivability problem is P-complete (under log-space reductions) [Papadimitriou, 1994, p.176]. In DL, the underlying logic is classical (propositional) logic extended with domain-specific inference rules. However, these extra inference rules do not increase the complexity of reasoning. It is known (e.g. see [Gottlob, 1995, p.90]) that for any DL like propositional monotonic rule system S, checking whether $S \not\models \varphi$ is NP-complete. Therefore, the following proposition follows immediately.

Proposition 1 *Given a DL framework* $\langle T, A, \overline{} \rangle$, *deciding for a sentence* $\varphi \in \mathcal{L}$ *and an assumption set* $\Delta \subseteq A$ *whether* $\varphi \in Th(T \cup \Delta)$ *is* co-NP-*complete*.

We now prove the basic membership result for flat frameworks in general and LP and DL in particular. In fact, flatness seems to be a computationally important property. For non-flat frameworks, the assumption set verification problem under the admissibility and preferability semantics seems to become harder in general.

Theorem 2 *Given a flat framework with derivability problem in* $\mathcal{C}$, *the assumption set verification problem is*

1. *in* $\mathsf{P}^{\mathcal{C}}$ *under the stability semantics,*

2. *in* $\mathsf{P}^{\mathcal{C}}$ *under the admissibility semantics, and*

3. *in* $\mathsf{co\text{-}NP}^{\mathcal{C}}$ *under the preferability semantics.*

Proof: 1. Only polynomially many $\mathcal{C}$-oracle calls are needed to verify that a given assumption set Δ does not attack itself and it attacks all assumptions $\alpha \notin \Delta$.

2. The following deterministic, polynomial-time algorithm using a $\mathcal{C}$-oracle decides whether a given assumption set Δ is admissible:

(a) Verify that Δ does not attack itself ($|\Delta|$ calls to a $\mathcal{C}$-oracle).

is often easier than constructing stable extensions. For example, given the propositional logic program $P \cup \{p\}$, with P any set of clauses not defining the atom p, the empty set is an admissible argument for the query p that can be constructed "locally", without accessing P. Moreover, if $P \cup \{p\}$ is stratified or order-consistent [Bondarenko et al., 1997], p is guaranteed to be a credulous consequence of the program under the stability semantics. Indeed, in all cases where the stability semantics coincides with the preferability semantics (e.g. for stratified and order-consistent abstract frameworks) any sound (and complete) computational mechanism for the admissibility semantics is sound (and complete) for the stability semantics.

The "locality" feature of the admissibility semantics renders it a feasible alternative to the stability semantics in the first-order case, when the propositional version of the given abstract framework is infinite. For example, given the (negation-free) logic program: $\{q(f(X)); \ p(0)\}$, the empty set of assumptions is an admissible argument for the query $p(0)$ that can be constructed "locally", even though the propositional version of the corresponding abstract framework is infinite.

The complexity results in this paper discredit sceptical reasoning under admissibility and preferability semantics as trivial and "unnecessarily" complex, respectively. However, this does not seem to matter for the envisioned applications of this semantics, because credulous reasoning only is required for these applications [Kowalski and Toni, 1996]. For example, in argumentation in practical reasoning in general and legal reasoning in particular, unilateral arguments are put forwards and defended against all counterarguments, in a credulous manner. Indeed, these domains appear to be particularly well suited for credulous reasoning under the admissibility semantics.

Acknowledgements

The first author has been partially supported by the DFG as part of the graduate school on *Human and Machine Intelligence* at the University of Freiburg and the third author has been partially supported by the UK EPSRC project "Logic-based multi-agent systems." We would also like to thank the anonymous reviewers for their comments on an earlier version of this paper.

References

[Bondarenko et al., 1997] Andrei Bondarenko, Phan Minh Dung, Robert A. Kowalski, and Francesca Toni. An abstract, argumentation-theoretic framework for default reasoning. *Artificial Intelligence*, 93(1–2):63–101, 1997.

[Cadoli and Schaerf, 1993] Marco Cadoli and Marco Schaerf. A survey of complexity results for nonmonotonic logics. *The Journal of Logic Programming*, 17:127–160, 1993.

[Dung, 1991] Phan Minh Dung. Negation as hypothesis: an abductive foundation for logic programming. In K. Furukawa, editor, *Proceedings of the 8th International Conference on Logic programming*, pages 3–17, Paris, France, 1991. MIT Press.

[Eiter et al., 1998] Thomas Eiter, Nicola Leone, and Domenico Saccà. Expressive power and complexity of partial models for disjunctive deductive databases. *Theoretical Computer Science*, 206:181–218, 1998.

[Gelfond and Lifschitz, 1988] Michael Gelfond and Vladimir Lifschitz. The stable model semantics for logic programming. In K. Bowen and R. A. Kowalski, editors, *Proceedings of the 5th International Conference on Logic programming*, pages 1070–1080, Seattle, WA, 1988. MIT Press.

[Gottlob, 1992] Georg Gottlob. Complexity results for nonmonotonic logics. *Journal for Logic and Computation*, 2(3):397–425, 1992.

[Gottlob, 1995] Georg Gottlob. The complexity of default reasoning under the stationary fixed point semantics. *Information and Computation*, 121:81–92, 1995.

[Kowalski and Toni, 1996] Robert A. Kowalski and Francesca Toni. Abstract argumentation. *Journal of Artificial Intelligence and Law*, 4(3–4):275–296, 1996.

[Marek and Truszczynski, 1993] Victor W. Marek and Miroslaw Truszczynski. *Nonmonotonic logic: context-dependent reasoning*. Springer-Verlag, Berlin, Heidelberg, New York, 1993.

[Niemelä, 1990] Ilkka Niemelä. Towards automatic autoepistemic reasoning. In *Logics in AI*, volume 478 of *Lecture Notes in Artificial Intelligence*. Springer-Verlag, Berlin, Heidelberg, New York, 1990.

[Papadimitriou, 1994] Christos H. Papadimitriou. *Computational Complexity*. Addison-Wesley, Reading, MA, 1994.

[Reiter, 1980] Raymond Reiter. A logic for default reasoning. *Artificial Intelligence*, 13(1):81–132, April 1980.

[Saccà and Zaniolo, 1990] Domenico Saccà and Carlo Zaniolo. Stable models and non-determinism in logic programs with negation. In *Proceedings of the 9th ACM SIGACT-SIGMOD-SIGART Symposium on Principles of Database-Systems (PODS-90)*, pages 205–217, 1990.

[Saccà, 1997] Domenico Saccà. The expressive power of stable models for bound and unbound DATALOG queries. *Journal of Computer and System Sciences*, 54:441–464, 1997.

[Stillman, 1992] J. Stillman. The complexity of propositional default logics. In *Proceedings of the 10th National Conference of the American Association for Artificial Intelligence (AAAI-92)*, pages 794–799, San Jose, CA, July 1992. MIT Press.

AUTOMATED REASONING

Nonmonotonic Reasoning 2

Abducing Priorities to Derive Intended Conclusions

Katsumi Inoue
Dept. Electrical and Electronics Engineering
Kobe University
Rokkodai, Nada, Kobe 657-8501, Japan
inoue@eedept.kobe-u.ac.jp

Chiaki Sakama
Dept. Computer and Communication Sciences
Wakayama University
Sakaedani, Wakayama 640-8510, Japan
sakama@sys.wakayama-u.ac.jp

Abstract

We introduce a framework for finding preference information to derive desired conclusions in nonmonotonic reasoning. A new abductive framework called *preference abduction* enables us to infer an appropriate set of priorities to explain the given observation skeptically, thereby resolving the multiple extension problem in the answer set semantics for extended logic programs. Preference abduction is also combined with a usual form of abduction in abductive logic programming, and has applications such as specification of rule preference in legal reasoning and preference view update. The issue of learning abducibles and priorities is also discussed, in which abduction to a particular cause is equivalent to abduction to preference.

1 Introduction

In commonsense reasoning, it is important to represent and reason about preference in order to reduce nondeterminism due to incomplete knowledge. To represent such knowledge about preference, it is required that priorities among commonsense knowledge are to be found out. For example, to get the desired result of the *Yale shooting problem* [Hanks and McDermott, 1987], an adequate priority should be expressed according to our commonsense. The essence of this problem can be represented by the following *extended logic program*, P, where $ab1$ and $ab2$ are abnormality predicates, $loaded_i$ and $alive_j$ denote that the gun is loaded at the time T_i and the turkey is alive at the time T_j, respectively. We also assume that some unknown action *wait* is done at T_0, and that the *shoot* action, which causes the turkey dead whenever the gun is loaded, is done at T_1.

$$P: \quad loaded_1 \leftarrow loaded_0, not\, ab1, \quad (1)$$
$$alive_2 \leftarrow alive_1, not\, ab2, \quad (2)$$
$$\neg alive_2 \leftarrow loaded_1,$$
$$\neg loaded_1 \leftarrow alive_2,$$
$$ab1 \leftarrow loaded_0, \neg loaded_1,$$
$$ab2 \leftarrow loaded_1,$$

$$loaded_0 \leftarrow ,$$
$$alive_1 \leftarrow .$$

Here, *not* denotes negation as failure, and (1) and (2) represent the inertia of actions. Without any priority information, we do not know which default of (1) or (2) should take precedence. Then, to the contrary of our intention that $\neg alive_2$ should be inferred, neither $alive_2$ nor $\neg alive_2$ is decided from the above program. In fact, there are two answer sets of P, one including $loaded_1, ab2, \neg alive_2$ (intended), and the other containing $alive_2, \neg loaded_1, ab1$.

Historically, the Yale shooting problem revealed the so called *multiple extension problem*. In this case, we should decide which $ab1$ or $ab2$ must have a higher priority for minimization. Using *prioritized circumscription* [Lifschitz, 1985], for example, the criterion can be manually given for the Yale shooting problem that $ab1$ should be minimized with a higher priority than $ab2$ in order to derive $\neg alive_2$. Other than circumscription, recent development in the field of logic programming and nonmonotonic reasoning has provided a number of mechanisms for freely specifying preference on multiple extensions in default reasoning. Such prioritized reasoning systems include *prioritized default logics* and *prioritized logic programs* [Brewka, 1994; Baader and Hollunder, 1995; Dimopoulos and Kakas, 1995; Sakama and Inoue, 1996; Brewka and Eiter, 1998]. For the Yale shooting problem, we would like to prefer the default (1) to (2), and then a higher priority is given to (1) in these frameworks.

Although the Yale shooting problem is so simple that we can find the proper priority manually, it becomes more complicated and difficult to find priorities among many complex default knowledge in the real world's commonsense reasoning. Hence, a framework and a method for automatic finding of such priority information are highly required.

In this paper, we provide a framework for finding priorities as a part of a *prioritized logic program* [Sakama and Inoue, 1996] in order to derive an intended conclusion as a theorem of the logic program. To this end, we introduce the notion of *preference abduction*, which infers a sufficient priority relation to make the intended conclusion hold. This inference is in fact a form of abduction, i.e., abduction of meta-knowledge which is preference in this case. We further provide an integrated framework of abduction, in which both literals and priorities can be abduced. Using such an abductive framework, we can infer *skeptical explanations* of an observation even when only credulous explanations are obtained due to non-determinism of a given abductive program.

There are many applications of nonmonotonic reasoning that require to find out priorities among conflicting rules. For example, in the legal domain, priorities among the conflicting laws are often required for disputants to derive their desired conclusion, which give them the advantage in the argumentation of a court. The proposal in this paper enables us to derive a desired conclusion by abducing appropriate priorities in such cases. An interesting application is *preference view*, which transfers a given priority relation among observations into a priority relation among base abducible literals.

This paper is organized as follows. Section 2 introduces the theoretical background in this paper. Section 3 provides the framework for preference abduction. Section 4 goes on elaborating on preference abduction. Section 5 discusses related work, and Section 6 is the conclusion. Due to the lack of space, we will omit proofs of propositions and theorems in this paper.

2 Background

2.1 Extended Logic Programs

An *extended logic program* (ELP) [Gelfond and Lifschitz, 1990] is a set of rules of the form

$$L_0 \leftarrow L_1, \ldots, L_m, \text{not } L_{m+1}, \ldots, \text{not } L_n \qquad (3)$$

where L_i's $(0 \leq i \leq n; n \geq m)$ are literals. Here, the left-hand side L_0 is called the *head* of the rule (3), and the right-hand side is called the *body* of the rule. The head is possibly empty. A rule with an empty body is called a *fact*, and each fact $L \leftarrow$ is identified with the literal L. Two kinds of negation appear in a program: *not* is the *negation as failure* (NAF) operator, and $\neg$ is *classical negation*. Intuitively, the rule (3) can be read as: if $L_1, \ldots, L_m$ are believed and $L_{m+1}, \ldots, L_n$ are not believed then L_0 is believed.

The semantics of an ELP P is given by the *answer set semantics* [Gelfond and Lifschitz, 1990], which is defined by the following two steps. Let $\mathcal{L}_P$ be the set of all ground literals in the language of P, and let $S \subseteq \mathcal{L}_P$. First, let P be a *not*-free ELP (i.e., for each rule $m = n$). Then, S is an *answer set* of P if S is a minimal set satisfying the conditions:

1. For each ground rule $L_0 \leftarrow L_1, \ldots, L_m$ from P, $\{L_1, \ldots, L_m\} \subseteq S$ implies $L_0 \in S$.

2. If S contains a pair of complementary literals L and $\neg L$, then $S = \mathcal{L}_P$.

Second, let P be any ELP and $S \subseteq \mathcal{L}_P$. Then, define a *not*-free ELP P^S as follows: a rule

$$L_0 \leftarrow L_1, \ldots, L_m$$

is in P^S iff there is a ground rule of the form (3) from P such that $\{L_{m+1}, \ldots, L_n\} \cap S = \emptyset$. For P^S, its answer sets have already been defined. Then, S is an *answer set* of P if S is an answer set of P^S.

The class of ELPs is a subset of Reiter's *default logic* [Gelfond and Lifschitz, 1990]. An answer set of an ELP P is *consistent* if it is not $\mathcal{L}_P$. P is *consistent* if it has a consistent answer set. An ELP P *(skeptically) entails* a literal L, written as $P \models L$, if L is included in every answer set of P. On the other hand, P *credulously infers* L if L is included in an answer set of P.

2.2 Abductive Logic Programs

An *abductive (extended) logic program* (ALP) is a pair $\langle P, \Gamma \rangle$, where P is an ELP and Γ is a set of literals from the language of P. The set Γ is identified with the set of ground instances from Γ, and each literal in Γ is called an *abducible*. The model-theoretic semantics for ALPs is given in [Inoue and Sakama, 1996]. A set $S \subseteq \mathcal{L}_P$ is called a *belief set* of $\langle P, \Gamma \rangle$ if S is a consistent answer set of $P \cup A$ for some $A \subseteq \Gamma$. Note that belief sets reduce to consistent answer sets when $\Gamma = \emptyset$.

Let O be a ground literal called an *observation*. $A \subseteq \Gamma$ is an *skeptical explanation* of O (wrt $\langle P, \Gamma \rangle$) if $P \cup A \models O$ and $P \cup A$ is consistent. On the other hand, $A \subseteq \Gamma$ is a *credulous explanation* of O (wrt $\langle P, \Gamma \rangle$) if there is a belief set S of $\langle P, \Gamma \rangle$ such that $O \in S$ and S is a consistent answer set of $P \cup A$. A skeptical/credulous explanation A of O is *minimal* if no $A' \subset A$ is a skeptical/credulous explanation of O.

In an ALP $\langle P, \Gamma \rangle$, each abducible in Γ is a literal. Often however, we would like to introduce rules of the form (3) with $n \geq m \geq 1$ in Γ. Such a rule, called an *abducible rule*, intuitively means that if the rule is abduced then it is used for inference together with background knowledge P. This extended abductive framework is introduced in [Inoue, 1994] as a *knowledge system*. Any knowledge system $\langle P, \Gamma \rangle$, where both P and Γ are ELPs, can be translated into an ALP $\langle P', \Gamma' \rangle$ where Γ' is a set of literals [Inoue, 1994]: For each abducible rule R in Γ, a new *naming* atom δ_R is associated with R, and let

$$P' = P \cup \{(H \leftarrow B, \delta_R) \mid R = (H \leftarrow B) \in \Gamma\},$$
$$\Gamma' = \{\delta_R \mid R \in \Gamma\}.$$

2.3 Prioritized Logic Programs

A reflexive and transitive relation $\preceq$ is defined on $\mathcal{L}_P$. Each $e_1 \preceq e_2$ is called a *priority*, and we say e_2 *has a priority over* e_1. We write $e_1 \prec e_2$ if $e_1 \preceq e_2$ and $e_2 \npreceq e_1$. When $\mathbf{x}$ and $\mathbf{y}$ are tuples of variables, $e_1(\mathbf{x}) \preceq e_2(\mathbf{y})$ stands for any priority $e_1(\mathbf{s}) \preceq e_2(\mathbf{t})$ for any instances $\mathbf{s}$ of $\mathbf{x}$ and $\mathbf{t}$ of $\mathbf{y}$.

A *prioritized (extended) logic program* (PLP) by [Sakama and Inoue, 1996] is given as a pair (P, Φ), where P is an ELP and Φ is a set of priorities on $\mathcal{L}_P$.[1] The

---

[1]In [Sakama and Inoue, 1996], a PLP (P, Φ) is defined with a *general extended disjunctive program* P, which allows NAF and disjunctions in heads of rules, and Φ may contain NAF formulas. Here, we consider a subset of their PLPs.

declarative semantics of PLP is defined using the answer sets. Given a PLP (P, Φ), suppose that S_1 and S_2 are two distinct answer sets of P. Then, S_2 is *preferable to* S_1, written as $S_1 \preceq S_2$, if for some element $e_2 \in S_2 \setminus S_1$, (i) there is an element $e_1 \in S_1 \setminus S_2$ such that $e_1 \preceq e_2$, and (ii) there is no element $e_3 \in S_1 \setminus S_2$ such that $e_2 \prec e_3$. Here, the relation $\preceq$ on answer sets is also defined as reflexive and transitive. Note that the condition (ii) is automatically satisfied if there is no priority chained on more than two different elements (i.e., $e_1 \preceq e_2 \preceq e_3$ implies either $e_1 = e_2$ or $e_2 = e_3$). An answer set S of P is called a *preferred answer set* (or *p-answer set*, for short) of P (wrt Φ) if $S \preceq S'$ implies $S' \preceq S$ for any answer set S' of P.

By definition, (P, Φ) has a p-answer set if P has a finite number of answer sets. In particular, the p-answer sets of (P, Φ) coincide with the answer sets of P when $\Phi = \emptyset$. It is also clear that if a program P has the unique answer set, it also becomes the unique p-answer set of (P, Φ) for any Φ. We say (P, Φ) *entails* a literal L, written as $P \models_\Phi L$, if L is included in every preferred answer set of P.

Using PLPs, we can represent preference knowledge naturally, and it is helpful to reduce non-determinism in logic programming. Moreover, various forms of commonsense reasoning such as (prioritized) minimal abduction, (prioritized) default reasoning, and prioritized circumscription can be realized in terms of PLP. In particular, the mapping from prioritized circumscription of any clause set to a PLP is given in [Sakama and Inoue, 1996], which much extends the previous translation into a stratified logic program by Gelfond and Lifschitz [1988].

3 Preference Abduction

In this section, we introduce *preference abduction*, which is the process of abducing priorities to explain given observations.

3.1 Basic Framework

Given an ELP P and a literal O, we first consider the case that O is credulously inferred by P but is not skeptically entailed by P. In this case, there exists a multiple extension problem, that is, both answer sets containing O and answer sets not containing O coexist. Let AS^+ be the set of answer sets containing O, and AS^- the set of answer sets not containing O. A direct way to prefer answer sets containing O is to construct priorities between answer sets in AS^+ and AS^-, so that some subset of AS^+ are made the set of preferred answer sets of P. However, there are many ways to associate priorities between AS^+ and AS^-. Hence, we assume the existence of some set Ψ of pre-specified candidate hypotheses for priorities in the following abductive framework.

Definition 3.1 Let P be a consistent ELP, and O a literal. Suppose that Ψ is a set of candidate priorities on $\mathcal{L}_P$. A set ψ of priorities is a *(skeptical) explanation* of O (wrt $\langle P, \Psi \rangle$) if

1. $\psi \subseteq \Psi$, and

2. $P \models_\psi O$.

Also, ψ is a *minimal explanation* of O if no $\psi' \subset \psi$ is an explanation of O.

Given a pair $\langle P, \Psi \rangle$ for preference abduction, let S_1 and S_2 be two distinct answer sets of P. Then, in order to find priorities ψ from Ψ such that $S_1 \preceq S_2$ holds, one should select a literal $e_1 \in S_1 \setminus S_2$ and another literal $e_2 \in S_2 \setminus S_1$ such that (i) $e_1 \preceq e_2$ and (ii) for any literal $e_3 \in S_1 \setminus S_2$, $e_2 \not\prec e_3$, i.e., $e_2 \preceq e_3$ implies $e_3 \preceq e_2$.

Example 3.1 Suppose that the ELP P is given as

$$p \leftarrow not\, q, \quad q \leftarrow not\, p, \quad o \leftarrow p, \quad \neg o \leftarrow q,$$

and $\Psi = \{p \preceq q, q \preceq p\}$. There are two answer sets of P: $S1 = \{p, o\}$ and $S2 = \{q, \neg o\}$. Suppose we want to find an explanation of o. Abducing the priority $q \preceq p$, we get the relation $S2 \preceq S1$, hence $P \models_{\{q \preceq p\}} o$.

Example 3.2 (Yale shooting) Consider the ELP P introduced in Section 1. The candidate hypotheses for this problem can be supplied as $\Psi = \{ab1 \preceq ab2, ab2 \preceq ab1\}$. Then, $\{ab1 \preceq ab2\}$ is the explanation of $\neg alive_2$. This abduced priority corresponds to our commonsense that the abnormality wrt the *shoot* action should be stronger than that wrt the *wait* action.

3.2 Combining with Credulous Abduction

When an observation O cannot be credulously inferred by P, the basic framework in Section 3.1 cannot give a sufficient explanation of O. In such a case, we can combine preference abduction with ordinary abduction in Section 2.1 so that O gets a skeptical explanation. An extended abductive framework is given as follows.

Definition 3.2 A *preference abduction framework* is a triple $\langle P, \Gamma, \Psi \rangle$, where P is an ELP, $\Gamma \subseteq \mathcal{L}_P$ is a set of abducibles, and Ψ is a set of candidate priorities on $\mathcal{L}_P$. A pair (A, ψ) is a *(skeptical) explanation* of a literal O (wrt $\langle P, \Gamma, \Psi \rangle$) if

1. $A \subseteq \Gamma$,

2. $\psi \subseteq \Psi$,

3. $P \cup A$ is consistent, and

4. $P \cup A \models_\psi O$.

Also, (A, ψ) is a *minimal explanation* of O if for any explanation (A', ψ') of O, $A' \subseteq A$ and $\psi' \subseteq \psi$ imply $A' = A$ and $\psi' = \psi$.

Note that the basic framework of preference abduction in Section 3.1 is a special case of Definition 3.2, where $\Gamma = \emptyset$. Moreover, the traditional ALP framework in Section 2.2 is also a special case, where $\Psi = \emptyset$. We can also consider an abductive framework $\langle P, \Gamma, \Psi \rangle$ in which Γ is a set of abducible rules and Ψ includes priorities on such abducible rules. In that case, a naming technique similar to the one in Section 2.2 can be applied to abducible rules, and then priorities among rules are translated into priorities among rule names, thereby reducing such an abductive framework to that in Definition 3.2.

Example 3.3 Let us consider the abductive framework $\langle P, \Gamma, \Psi \rangle$, where

$$
\begin{aligned}
P : \quad & p \leftarrow a, \, not \, q, \\
& q \leftarrow not \, p, \\
& \neg q \leftarrow b, \\
\Gamma : \quad & a, \, b, \\
\Psi : \quad & p \preceq q, \, q \preceq p.
\end{aligned}
$$

There are four belief sets of $\langle P, \Gamma \rangle$: $S1 = \{q\}$, $S2 = \{a, p\}$, $S3 = \{a, q\}$, $S4 = \{a, b, p, \neg q\}$. Then, both $E1 = (\{a\}, \{q \preceq p\})$ and $E2 = (\{a, b\}, \emptyset)$ are the minimal explanations of p. In fact, $P \cup \{a\} \models_{\{q \preceq p\}} p$ and $P \cup \{a, b\} \models p$. For $E1$ the p-answer set of $P \cup \{a\}$ is $S2$, while $S4$ is the unique answer set of $P \cup \{a, b\}$ for $E2$.

Note in the above example that explanations are obtained either from credulous explanations with abduced priorities or from skeptical explanations wrt the given ELP. Hence, a naive procedure to compute preference abduction is as follows.

Procedure 3.1 $PrefAbd(P, \Gamma, \Psi, O, E)$

Input: a preference abduction framework $\langle P, \Gamma, \Psi \rangle$, a literal O (observation).

Output: a skeptical explanation E of O wrt $\langle P, \Gamma, \Psi \rangle$.

1. Compute a credulous explanation A of O wrt $\langle P, \Gamma \rangle$;

2. If A is a skeptical explanation of O wrt $\langle P, \Gamma \rangle$, then return $E = (A, \emptyset)$;

3. Otherwise, compute the answer sets of $P \cup A$; $AS^+ :=$ the set of answer sets containing O; $AS^- :=$ the set of answer sets not containing O;

4. Find priorities $\psi \subseteq \Psi$ and $P\text{-}AS \subseteq AS^+$ such that $T \preceq S$ for any $S \in P\text{-}AS$ and any $T \in AS^-$; Then, ψ is an explanation of O wrt $\langle P \cup A, \Psi \rangle$; Return $E = (A, \psi)$.

In Procedure 3.1, computing credulous explanations of O at Step 1 can be realized by existing abductive procedures such as [Kakas and Mancarella, 1990; Inoue and Sakama, 1996]. At Step 2, each credulous explanation A is checked to see whether it is skeptical or not. This test can easily be realized by checking the consistency of $P \cup A \cup \{\leftarrow O\}$. At Step 3, the answer sets of $P \cup A$ or belief sets of $\langle P, \Gamma \rangle$ can be computed by some bottom-up procedures, e.g., [Inoue and Sakama, 1996]. At Step 4, it can be shown that: if ψ is an explanation of O wrt $\langle P \cup A, \Psi \rangle$, then (A, ψ) is an explanation of O wrt $\langle P, \Gamma, \Psi \rangle$. Hence, the next theorem holds.

Theorem 3.1 *Procedure $PrefAbd(P, \Gamma, \Psi, O, E)$ is sound. That is, if it terminates, its output E is a skeptical explanation of O wrt $\langle P, \Gamma, \Psi \rangle$.*

The completeness of Procedure 3.1 holds for a ground ELP P and finite Γ and Ψ if we assume (i) the existence of an abductive procedure that is complete for computing credulous explanations at Step 1, and (ii) the exhaustive search for finding ψ at Step 4. However, since many

existing abductive procedures are designed to compute credulous explanations, it is more difficult to compute skeptical explanations directly. In fact, the skeptical explanation $\{a, b\}$ of p wrt $\langle P, \Gamma \rangle$ in Example 3.3 cannot be obtained by top-down abductive procedures in general. In this sense, to compute skeptical explanations of an observation, it is easier to compute credulous explanations first, then priorities are added to make explanations skeptical as in Procedure 3.1.

4 Finding Further Preference

In Section 3.2, we considered an abductive framework $\langle P, \Gamma, \Psi \rangle$ in which Γ and Ψ are pre-specified. However, such candidate hypotheses are often insufficiently given so that we cannot explain an observation skeptically.

Example 4.1 (legal reasoning [Kowalski and Toni, 1996]) Suppose that the ELP P is given as:

$$inherits(x, y) \leftarrow beneficiary(x, y), \, not \, \neg inherits(x, y), \quad (4)$$
$$\neg inherits(x, y) \leftarrow murder(x, y), \, not \, inherits(x, y). \quad (5)$$
$$beneficiary(a, b) \leftarrow, \quad murder(c, d) \leftarrow,$$
$$beneficiary(j, h) \leftarrow, \quad murder(j, h) \leftarrow,$$

Rule (4) indicates that a person inherits an estate if he/she is the beneficiary of a valid will and it cannot be shown that the person does not inherit it. Rule (5) says that a person usually does not inherit an estate if he/she murders the owner of the estate. The program P has two answer sets, one containing $inherits(j, h)$ and the other $\neg inherits(j, h)$. Given the observation $\neg inherits(j, h)$, we cannot get any explanation wrt $\langle P, \emptyset, \emptyset \rangle$.

In this section, we consider a method to generate new abducibles for obtaining further preference.

4.1 Generating New Abducibles

A method to discover new abducibles is considered in [Inoue and Haneda, 1999], where abducibles are newly invented in learning ALPs. Here, we modify their method by associating priorities with new abducibles.

Firstly, notice that rules (4) and (5) in Example 4.1 are the source of non-determinism in the program. Then, these *non-deterministic rules* are converted into abducible rules. Without loss of generality, we assume that such rules in an ELP P are of the form:[2]

$$
\begin{aligned}
\alpha &\leftarrow B_1, \, not \, \beta, \\
\beta &\leftarrow B_2, \, not \, \alpha,
\end{aligned}
\quad (6)
$$

where α and β are literals and both B_1 and B_2 are conjunctions of literals and NAF formulas. Here, we assume that neither α nor β appears in the head or the body of any rule other than (6) in P. Now, let N_1 be a pair of rules of the form (6), and $P_1 = P \setminus N_1$. Also, let E_1 be the set of ground instances of α and β that are entailed by P. Then, Γ_1 is obtained by converting N_1 into abducible rules:

$$
\begin{aligned}
\alpha &\leftarrow B_1, \\
\beta &\leftarrow B_2.
\end{aligned}
\quad (7)
$$

---

[2]Using the unfolding operation, we can get pairs of rules of the form (6) which cause non-determinism in P.

Next, using the translation in Section 2.2, each abducible rule R of the form (7) in Γ_1 can be named with a new atom δ_R, and put $P_2 = P_1 \cup \{ (H \leftarrow B, \delta_R) \mid R = (H \leftarrow B) \in \Gamma_1 \}$ and $\Gamma_2 = \{ \delta_R \mid R \in \Gamma_1 \}$. Then, compute the set E_2 of instances of new abducibles in Γ_2 such that $P_2 \cup E_2 \models e$ for every $e \in E_1$. This identification of E_2 from E_1 is easy, and it is used to assure that the literals in E_1 can also be entailed by the new program. We now obtain the ALP $\langle P', \Gamma' \rangle = \langle P_2 \cup E_2, \Gamma_2 \rangle$.

Proposition 4.1 *Let P be an ELP, and $\langle P', \Gamma' \rangle$ the ALP constructed as above. Then, for every consistent answer set S of P, there is a belief set S' of $\langle P', \Gamma' \rangle$ such that $S = S' \setminus \Gamma'$.*[3]

Example 4.2 (cont. from Example 4.1)
Let N_1 be the last two rules (4,5) in P, $P_1 = P \setminus N_1$, and $E_1 = \{ inherits(a, b), \neg inherits(c, d) \}$. Then, non-deterministic rules N_1 are converted into abducible rules:

$$\Gamma_1: \quad inherits(x, y) \leftarrow beneficiary(x, y),$$
$$\neg inherits(x, y) \leftarrow murder(x, y).$$

By naming these abducible rules with $\delta_{inherit}(x, y)$ and $\delta_{\neg inherit}(x, y)$, the ALP $\langle P', \Gamma' \rangle$ is obtained as:

$$P' = \{ \quad inherits(x, y) \leftarrow beneficiary(x, y), \delta_{inherit}(x, y),$$
$$\neg inherits(x, y) \leftarrow murder(x, y), \delta_{\neg inherit}(x, y),$$
$$\delta_{inherit}(a, b) \leftarrow , \quad \delta_{\neg inherit}(c, d) \leftarrow \quad \} \cup P_1,$$
$$\Gamma' = \{ \quad \delta_{inherit}(x, y), \quad \delta_{\neg inherit}(x, y) \quad \}.$$

In the ALP, $inherits(j, h)$ is concluded by abducing $\delta_{inherit}(j, h)$, while $\neg inherits(j, h)$ is skeptically explained by $\delta_{\neg inherit}(j, h)$.

4.2 From Abducibles to Priorities

So far, we have not yet introduced new priorities into the process of finding new abducibles. That is, appropriate literals are just abduced to explain the observation. *Such a right selection of hypotheses in abduction can be considered as our preference of some particular causes over others*. With this regard, we can acquire new preference information from abductive programs as follows.

Suppose that δ_α and δ_β are the naming atoms for a pair of abducible rules of the form (7). Then, the ALP $\langle P', \Gamma' \rangle$ in Section 4.1 can be further translated into the semantically equivalent ELP P^* by replacing each pair of abducibles δ_α and δ_β in Γ' with the pair of rules:

$$\delta_\alpha \leftarrow not\, \delta_\beta, \tag{8}$$
$$\delta_\beta \leftarrow not\, \delta_\alpha.$$

This time, we have the following relationship between the answer sets of the original ELP P and those of P^*.

Proposition 4.2 *Let P be a consistent ELP, and P^* the ELP constructed as above. Then, for every answer*

set S of P, there is an answer set S^* of P^* such that $S = S^* \setminus \Gamma'$, where Γ' is the same as in Proposition 4.1. Conversely, for every answer set S^* of P^*, there is an answer set S of P such that $S = S^* \setminus \Gamma'$.

Using the above new P^*, it is easy to associate priorities on the newly introduced abducibles. Once the ALP $\langle P', \Gamma' \rangle$ is constructed, we can just consider the abductive framework $\langle P^*, \Psi^* \rangle$, where Ψ^* is the candidate priorities on Γ'. In this way, abduction to particular causes and preference abduction are made transferable into each other.

Theorem 4.3 *Let $\langle P', \Gamma' \rangle$ and $\langle P^*, \Psi^* \rangle$ be the same as in the above discussion, and O be an observation. Then, there is a skeptical explanation of O wrt $\langle P', \Gamma' \rangle$ iff there is a skeptical explanation of O wrt $\langle P^*, \Psi^* \rangle$.*

Example 4.3 (cont. from Example 4.2)
The ALP $\langle P', \Gamma' \rangle$ constructed in Example 4.2 can be now translated into the ELP $P^* = P' \cup P_{\Gamma'}$ where $P_{\Gamma'}$ is given as:

$$\delta_{inherit}(x, y) \leftarrow not\, \delta_{\neg inherit}(x, y),$$
$$\delta_{\neg inherit}(x, y) \leftarrow not\, \delta_{inherit}(x, y).$$

Then, P^* has two answer sets, one containing $\delta_{inherit}(j, h)$ and $inherits(j, h)$, and the other containing $\delta_{\neg inherit}(j, h)$ and $\neg inherits(j, h)$.

Now, let us consider the preference abduction $\langle P^*, \Psi^* \rangle$, where Ψ^* contains the candidate priorities:

$$\delta_{inherit}(x, y) \preceq \delta_{\neg inherit}(x, y),$$
$$\delta_{\neg inherit}(x, y) \preceq \delta_{inherit}(x, y).$$

Given the observation $\neg inherits(j, h)$, we have the explanation $\{ \delta_{inherit}(j, h) \preceq \delta_{\neg inherit}(j, h) \}$.

4.3 Preference View Updates

The advantage of the above translation into preference abduction is that priorities do not have to be given on the target observations but are given on the source hypotheses. In this sense, we call such inference to preference *preference view updates*, which are analogous to the notion of *view updates* in deductive databases. In preference view updates, the priority request on given observations $O_1 \preceq O_2$ is translated into priorities on their causes $\psi \subseteq \Psi^*$. A typical application of this kind is abduction to *rule preference* in the legal domain.

Example 4.4 (cont. from Example 4.3)
Suppose that one rather prefers the conclusion $inherits(j, h)$ to the opposite $\neg inherits(j, h)$. This preference view:

$$\neg inherits(j, h) \preceq inherits(j, h)$$

can be translated into the priority between the hypotheses:

$$\delta_{\neg inherit}(j, h) \preceq \delta_{inherit}(j, h).$$

This last relation indicates that she/he should prefer the rule (4) to the other rule (5) in her/his argument.

It should be noted that, as view updates in databases can be characterized through abduction [Kakas and Mancarella, 1990], our formulation of preference view updates are also based on preference abduction.

---

[3]The converse of Proposition 4.1 does not hold. In Example 4.2, the ALP $\langle P', \Gamma' \rangle$ has a belief set containing neither $inherits(j, h)$ nor $\neg inherits(j, h)$, which is not an answer set of P.

5 Related Work

As far as the authors know, there are very few work on abducing priorities to derive desired conclusion. Zhang and Foo [1998] associate priorities to resolve conflicts between rules in updating ELPs. Their framework can be regarded as a kind of preference abduction to be applied to theory updates. In general, preference information is helpful to resolve contradiction in a program. Priorities on defaults specify the guideline that some defaults are to be kept but some are discarded in restoring the consistency. Wakaki *et al.* [1998] present a method of finding priorities as a part of the circumscription policy to be used in prioritized circumscription. In their method, priorities are selected from the set of all possible orderings on minimized predicates. On the other hand, our method can discover new priorities on literals for PLPs as shown in Section 4.

There are a lot of recent work on introducing priorities into abductive and nonmonotonic reasoning. Eiter and Gottlob [1995] discuss the computational complexity of a form of *prioritized abduction*, whose prioritization is similar to that of prioritized circumscription. Sakama and Inoue [1996] propose a different kind of prioritied abduction in the context PLPs, in which priorities are used to select desired abducibles from multiple explanations. Priorities have also been used to represent preference between conflicting default rules in PLPs and prioritied default logics [Brewka, 1994; Baader and Hollunder, 1995; Dimopoulos and Kakas, 1995; Sakama and Inoue, 1996; Brewka and Eiter, 1998]. None of these work, however, discusses how to find an appropriate set of priorities to derive desired conclusions.

Brewka [1994] argues the importance of the ability of using defaults that reason about preference between other defaults. Our preference abduction would also be extended by introducing such dynamic preference into not only deduction but abduction on PLPs, but the issue is not addressed in this paper.

6 Conclusion

This paper introduced a novel framework for finding preference to derive intended conclusions in nonmonotonic reasoning. Preference abduction is not only an extension of traditional ALPs, but much extends the reasoning ability of PLPs. Applications of preference abduction include the resolution of the multiple extension problem, skeptical abduction, preference view updates, and abduction to rule preference in legal reasoning.

In this paper, we also presented an interesting fact that abduction to a particular cause and abduction to preference are sometimes transferable to each other. This line of research would extend the applicability of existing frameworks for ALPs as computational tools for prioritied default reasoning. The design of a more sophisticated algorithm to compute preference abduction also remains to be explored.

References

[Baader and Hollunder, 1995] F. Baader and B. Hollunder. Priorities on defaults with prerequisites, and their application in treating specificity in terminological default logic. *J. Automated Reasoning*, 15(1):41–68, 1995.

[Brewka, 1994] G. Brewka. Reasoning about priorities in default logic. In: *Proc. AAAI-94*, pages 940–945.

[Brewka and Eiter, 1998] G. Brewka and T. Eiter. Preferred answer sets for extended logic programs. In: *Proc. KR '98*, pages 86–97, 1998.

[Dimopoulos and Kakas, 1995] Y. Dimopoulos and A. C. Kakas. Logic programming without negation as failure. In: *Proc. Int'l Logic Programming Symp. '95*, pages 369–383, 1995.

[Eiter and Gottlob, 1995] T. Eiter and G. Gottlob. The complexity of logic-based abduction. *J. ACM*, 42(1):3–42, 1995.

[Gelfond and Lifschitz, 1988] M. Gelfond and V. Lifschitz. Compiling circumscriptive theories into logic programs. In: *Proc. AAAI-88*, pages 455–459, 1988.

[Gelfond and Lifschitz, 1990] M. Gelfond and V. Lifschitz. Logic programs with classical negation. In: *Proc. 7th Int'l Conf. on Logic Programming*, pages 579–597, 1990.

[Hanks and McDermott, 1987] S. Hanks and D. McDermott. Nonmonotonic logic and temporal projection. *Artificial Intelligence*, 33:379–412, 1987.

[Inoue, 1994] K. Inoue. Hypothetical reasoning in logic programs. *J. Logic Programming*, 18(3):191-227, 1994.

[Inoue and Haneda, 1999] K. Inoue and H. Haneda. Learning abductive and nonmonotonic logic programs. In: P. Flach and A. Kakas, editors. *Abductive and Inductive Reasoning—Essays on their Relation and Integration*, pages 241–262, Kluwer Academic, 1999.

[Inoue and Sakama, 1996] K. Inoue and C. Sakama. A fixpoint characterization of abductive logic programs. *J. Logic Programming*, 27(2):107–136, 1996.

[Kakas and Mancarella, 1990] A. C. Kakas and P. Mancarella. Database updates through abduction. In: *Proc. 16th Int'l Conf. Very Large Databases*, pages 650–661, 1990.

[Kowalski and Toni, 1996] R. A. Kowalski and F. Toni. Abstract argumentation. *Artificial Intelligence and Law*, 4:275–296, 1996.

[Lifschitz, 1985] V. Lifschitz. Computing circumscription. In: *Proc. IJCAI-85*, pages 121–127, 1985.

[Sakama and Inoue, 1996] C. Sakama and K. Inoue. Representing priorities in logic programs. In: *Proc. 1996 Joint Int'l Conf. and Symp. on Logic Programming*, pages 82–96, 1996.

[Wakaki et al., 1998] T. Wakaki, K. Satoh, K. Nitta and S. Sakurai. Finding priorities of circumscription policy as a skeptical explanation in abduction. *J. IEICE Trans. Information and Systems*, E-81D(10), 1998.

[Zhang and Foo, 1998] Y. Zhang and N. Y. Foo. Updating logic programs. In: *Proc. 13th European Conf. on Artificial Intelligence*, pages 403-407, 1998.

Maximum Entropy and Variable Strength Defaults

Rachel A. Bourne and **Simon Parsons**
Department of Electronic Engineering
Queen Mary & Westfield College
University of London
London E1 4NS, UK
r.a.bourne,s.d.parsons@elec.qmw.ac.uk

Abstract

A new algorithm for computing the maximum entropy ranking over models is presented. The algorithm handles arbitrary sets of propositional defaults with associated strength assignments and succeeds whenever the set satisfies a robustness condition. Failure of this condition implies the problem may not be sufficiently specified for a unique solution to exist. This work extends the applicability of the maximum entropy approach detailed in [Goldszmidt et al., 1993], and clarifies the assumptions on which the method is based.

1 Introduction

There have been several suggestions of what might constitute the best consequence relation to be associated with a set of propositional defaults. The weakest, and most widely accepted, is System P [Adams, 1975], [Kraus et al., 1990]. Of those which handle the more complex default interactions, such as exceptional inheritance, correctly, the maximum entropy approach (me) has, arguably, the clearest objective justification being derived from a well understood principle of indifference. In this paper, the me-approach of [Goldszmidt et al., 1993] is extended so that the me-ranking for an arbitrary set of variable strength defaults can be found. A new algorithm is presented along with a sufficient condition for its successful computation. As well as handling the usual examples from the literature in a satisfactory way, this extended framework provides a flexible method for handling default knowledge through its use of variable strength defaults which sheds some light on previously ambiguous examples. Indeed, the results suggest that some examples are inherently ambiguous. However, the clear underlying principle of the me-approach clarifies why this ambiguity arises, and suggests how it might be resolved.

2 Deriving the me-ranking

Consider a set of defaults, $\Delta = \{r_i : a_i \Rightarrow b_i\}$ where a, b, c, are formulæ of a finite propositional language,

$\mathcal{L}$, with the usual connectives $\wedge$, $\vee$, $\neg$, $\rightarrow$. The symbol, $\Rightarrow$, denotes a default connective. The models of $\mathcal{L}$ are contained in the set $\mathcal{M}$. A model, $m \in \mathcal{M}$, is said to *verify* a default, $a \Rightarrow b$, if $m \models a \wedge b$. Conversely, a model, m, is said to *falsify* a default, $a \Rightarrow b$, if $m \models a \wedge \neg b$.

The semantics of defaults is given in terms of conditional probabilities. Each default $a \Rightarrow b$ is supposed to constrain a set of probability distributions. For example, if it were assumed that $P(\neg b|a) = 0.05$, then the set $\{a \Rightarrow b\}$ would define all those probability distributions which satisfied the constraint imposed by the default. However, in this context no actual conditional probabilities are specified only the (fixed) relationships between the defaults in a given set.

The entropy of a probability distribution over a set of models $\mathcal{M}$ is given by

$$H[P] = -\sum_{m \in \mathcal{M}} P(m) \log P(m) \qquad (1)$$

The problem is to select that probability distribution which maximises (1) subject to constraints imposed by the defaults. The main supposition underlying this formalism is that specifying relative orders of magnitude for the conditional probabilities corresponding to each default implies a similar order of magnitude description of the probabilities of each model. This is achieved by parameterising the conditional probabilities and examining the behaviour as the parameter tends to zero. Intuitively, this can be thought of as taking a set of assumptions to the extreme in order to ascertain what other information is implied. The intuitive interpretation of the relative orders of magnitude between defaults is that one is required to specify their relative *strengths*; that is, numerically higher strength defaults can be thought of as holding more strongly than, or as having priority over, those of lower strength. Note that the symbol $\sim$ will be used to denote asymptotic equality since, for the purposes of this analysis, it is only the asymptotic behaviour of the probabilities that is important not their actual values, nor indeed the actual value of entropy.

Goldszmidt *et al.* [1993] originally chose to use inequalities for the default constraints but were unable to obtain results except for a small class of default sets, termed minimal core sets, which were guaranteed to sat-

Note that given two distinct rankings, κ and κ', it may still be the case that $\kappa(m) = \kappa'(m)$ for all m, i.e., the ranking over models may be unique despite there being multiple solutions for the $\kappa(r_i)$ to the constraint equations (5) and (6). For example, the set $\{r_1 : a \Rightarrow b, r_2 : \neg b \Rightarrow \neg a\}$, produces the two equations

$$\kappa(r_1) + \kappa(r_2) = s_1$$
$$\kappa(r_1) + \kappa(r_2) = s_2$$

which have no solution unless $s_1 = s_2$ in which case there are an infinite number of solutions. However, all solutions lead to the same unique ranking over models. Refining the robustness condition and understanding its significance in such cases is the subject of ongoing research.

4 Computing the me-ranking

Using the robustness condition and equation (4), it is possible to determine the me-ranking over defaults one by one. Robustness guarantees that for at least one default the currently computed minimal ranks of models are indeed their genuine ranks in the me-ranking.

Let the function $\mathrm{MINV}(r)$ (respectively, $\mathrm{MINF}(r)$) be defined so that it returns the rank of the current minimal verifying model of r (respectively, the rank of the current minimal falsifying model of r *excluding its own contribution*) using equation (5). Then equation (6) can be re-written as

$$\kappa(r) = s_r + \kappa(v_r) - (\kappa(f_r) - \kappa(r)) \qquad (9)$$

which in the algorithm is used to assign the rank of a default using

$$\kappa(r) := s_r + \mathrm{MINV}(r) - \mathrm{MINF}(r) \qquad (10)$$

```
Algorithm to compute me-ranking
```

```
Input: a set of defaults, {r_i}, and associated
strength assignments, {s_i}.
Output: the me-ranking, κ, or an exception if the
set is p-inconsistent, or if the robustness
condition is violated.
```

[1] Initialise all $\kappa(r_i) = \infty$.

[2] From all r_i with $\kappa(r_i) = \infty$, find the minimal value of $s_i + \mathrm{MINV}(r_i)$ and select any r_i for which this holds, say r.

[3] If $\mathrm{MINV}(r) = \infty$ then the input set is p-inconsistent. Output an exception.

[4] Find $\mathrm{MINF}(r)$.

[5] If $\mathrm{MINF}(r) = \infty$ the robustness condition is violated. Output an exception.

[6] Let $\kappa(r) := s_r + \mathrm{MINV}(r) - \mathrm{MINF}(r)$.

[7] If any $\kappa(r_i) = \infty$ goto step 2.

[8] Assign ranks to models using equation (5).

[9] Validate the ranking by ensuring both that the constraints (4) and that the robustness condition are satisfied. Output either the me-ranking or an exception.

This algorithm clearly terminates at step 3, if the input set is probabilistically inconsistent, or at step 5, or at step 9. Termination does not guarantee that a valid ranking has been found but this is checked for and reported at step 9. The following theorem proves that, provided the robustness condition is satisfied, the algorithm will compute the unique me-ranking. That the algorithm works given certain pre-conditions can be verified if the two ranks in the assignment (10) can be shown to be valid. This requires that the ranks selected for $\mathrm{MINV}(r)$ and $\mathrm{MINF}(r)$ when the assignment is made are indeed the minimal ranks for r.

Theorem 4.1 *Given a finite set of defaults, $\{r_i\}$, with associated strengths, $\{s_i\}$, the algorithm computes the unique me-ranking, κ, if it is robust.*

Proof. The theorem is proved by induction. On the first pass of the loop no rules have been ranked and so the ranks of each rule ranked (i.e. none) are correct. The inductive hypothesis assumes that at the nth pass of the loop all rules ranked in the previous $(n-1)$ passes have been assigned their correct me-ranks. Consider that on the nth pass of the loop, rule r, with minimal $s_i + \mathrm{MINV}(r_i)$, is selected to be ranked.

Let v_c be a verifying model of r such that $\kappa(v_c) = \mathrm{MINV}(r)$. Suppose that v_c is not a minimal verifying model of r, so there exists v_r, such that $\kappa(v_r) < \kappa(v_c)$. Now, $\kappa(v_r) < \mathrm{MINV}(r)$, the computed minimal verifying rank for r, so it must be the case that v_r falsifies some rule, $r' \neq r$, which has not yet been ranked, and since r' was not selected to be ranked in this pass of the loop it follows that

$$s_r + \mathrm{MINV}(r) \leq s_{r'} + \mathrm{MINV}(r')$$

Then, since v_r falsifies r', $\kappa(f_{r'}) \leq \kappa(v_r)$, in particular, using (6)

$$s_{r'} + \kappa(v_{r'}) = \kappa(f_{r'}) < s_r + \kappa(v_r) <$$
$$s_r + \mathrm{MINV}(r) \leq s_{r'} + \mathrm{MINV}(r')$$

so that $\kappa(v_{r'}) < \mathrm{MINV}(r')$. It follows that $v_{r'}$, too, must falsify some rule, $r'' \neq r' \neq r$, which has not yet been ranked. Then, since $v_{r'}$ falsifies r'', $\kappa(f_{r''}) \leq \kappa(v_{r'})$. Continuing in this way, an infinite descending chain of distinct unranked rules is constructed. This contradicts the finite size of the original default set, and therefore v_c must be a minimal verifying model of r.

Let f_c be a falsifying model of r such that $\kappa(f_c) = \kappa(r) + \mathrm{MINF}(r)$. Suppose that f_c is not a minimal falsifying model of r, so there exists f_r, such that $\kappa(f_r) < \kappa(f_c)$. Now, since $\kappa(f_r) - \kappa(r) < \mathrm{MINF}(r)$, the computed minimal falsifying rank for r, it must be the case that f_r falsifies some rule, $r' \neq r$, which has not yet been ranked, and since r' was not selected to be ranked in this pass of the loop it follows that

$$s_r + \mathrm{MINV}(r) \leq s_{r'} + \mathrm{MINV}(r')$$

Now, f_r falsifies r', and under the assumption that the robustness condition holds, no two defaults share a common minimal falsifying model in the me-ranking. Therefore, $\kappa(f_{r'}) < \kappa(f_r)$, and the following inequality holds

$$s_{r'} + \kappa(v_{r'}) = \kappa(f_{r'}) < \kappa(f_r) =$$
$$s_r + \text{MINV}(r) \leq s_{r'} + \text{MINV}(r')$$

so that $\kappa(v_{r'}) < \text{MINV}(r')$, the computed minimal verifying rank for r'. It follows that $v_{r'}$, too, must falsify some rule, $r'' \neq r' \neq r$, which has not yet been ranked. Then, since $v_{r'}$ falsifies r'', $\kappa(f_{r''}) \leq \kappa(v_{r'})$. Continuing in this way, an infinite descending chain of distinct unranked rules is constructed. This contradicts the finite size of the original default set and therefore f_c must be a minimal falsifying model of r.

Given that for the selected rule, r, the values $\text{MINV}(r)$ and $\text{MINF}(r)$ calculated at this pass of the loop represent the me-ranks of its minimal verifying and falsifying models (excluding its own contribution), respectively, it follows that the assignment

$$\kappa(r) := s_r + \text{MINV}(r) - \text{MINF}(r) \qquad (11)$$

is valid and r is assigned its correct me-rank. The theorem follows by induction.   •

5 Examples

In the first example, the solution is tabulated explictly to illustrate the method of finding the me-ranking but later this is omitted to save space.

Example 5.1 (Exceptional inheritance)

$$\Delta = \{r_1 : b \Rightarrow f, r_2 : p \Rightarrow b, r_3 : p \Rightarrow \neg f, r_4 : b \Rightarrow w\}$$

The intended interpretation of this knowledge base is that birds fly, penguins are birds, penguins do not fly and birds have wings; each r_i has strength s_i. The table shows whether a model falsifies or verifies each default. The column headed $\kappa(m)$ gives the me-rank of each model in terms of the $\kappa(r_i)$ using equation (5).

m	b	f	p	w	r_1	r_2	r_3	r_4	$\kappa(m)$
m_1	0	0	0	0	-	-	-	-	0
m_2	0	0	0	1	-	-	-	-	0
m_3	0	0	1	0	-	f	v	-	$\kappa(r_2)$
m_4	0	0	1	1	-	f	v	-	$\kappa(r_2)$
m_5	0	1	0	0	-	-	-	-	0
m_6	0	1	0	1	-	-	-	-	0
m_7	0	1	1	0	-	f	f	-	$\kappa(r_2) + \kappa(r_3)$
m_8	0	1	1	1	-	f	f	-	$\kappa(r_2) + \kappa(r_3)$
m_9	1	0	0	0	f	-	-	f	$\kappa(r_1) + \kappa(r_4)$
m_{10}	1	0	0	1	f	-	-	v	$\kappa(r_1)$
m_{11}	1	0	1	0	f	v	v	f	$\kappa(r_1) + \kappa(r_4)$
m_{12}	1	0	1	1	f	v	v	v	$\kappa(r_1)$
m_{13}	1	1	0	0	v	-	-	f	$\kappa(r_4)$
m_{14}	1	1	0	1	v	-	-	v	0
m_{15}	1	1	1	0	v	v	f	f	$\kappa(r_3) + \kappa(r_4)$
m_{16}	1	1	1	1	v	v	f	v	$\kappa(r_3)$

Substituting the $\kappa(m)$ into the reduced constraint equations (4) gives rise to:

$$\kappa(r_1) = s_1$$

$$\kappa(r_2) = s_2 + \min(\kappa(r_1), \kappa(r_3))$$
$$\kappa(r_3) = s_3 + \min(\kappa(r_1), \kappa(r_2))$$
$$\kappa(r_4) = s_4$$

Clearly, the only solution to these equations is $\kappa(r_1) = s_1$, $\kappa(r_2) = s_1 + s_2$, $\kappa(r_3) = s_1 + s_3$, and $\kappa(r_4) = s_4$.

To determine default consequences it is necessary to compare the ranks of a default's minimum verifying and falsifying models. Since the solution holds for any strength assignment (s_1, s_2, s_3, s_4), it follows that some default conclusions may hold in general. In particular, it can be seen that the default $p \wedge b \Rightarrow \neg f$ is me-entailed since

$$\kappa(p \wedge b \wedge \neg f) < \kappa(p \wedge b \wedge f)$$
$$s_1 < s_1 + s_3$$

This result is unsurprising since $p \wedge b \Rightarrow \neg f$ is a preferential consequence of Δ. A more interesting general conclusion is $p \Rightarrow w$, which follows since

$$\kappa(p \wedge w) = s_1 < \kappa(p \wedge \neg w) = s_1 + \min(s_2, s_4) \qquad (12)$$

Again this result holds regardless of the strength assignments and illustrates that, for this example, the inheritance of w to p via b is uncontroversial.   •

Example 5.2 (Nixon diamond)

$$\Delta = \{r_1 : q \Rightarrow p, r_2 : r \Rightarrow \neg p\}$$

The intended interpretation is that quakers are pacificists whereas republicans are not pacifists. Given a strength assignment of (s_1, s_2) is easily shown that $\kappa(r_1) = s_1$ and $\kappa(r_2) = s_2$. The classical problem associated with this knowledge base is to ask whether Nixon, being a quaker and a republican, is pacifist or not. This is represented by the default $r \wedge q \Rightarrow p$. The two relevant models to compare are $r \wedge q \wedge p$ and $r \wedge q \wedge \neg p$ whose me-ranks in the general me-solution are

$$\kappa(r \wedge q \wedge p) = s_2 \quad \text{and} \quad \kappa(r \wedge q \wedge \neg p) = s_1 \qquad (13)$$

Clearly either $r \wedge q \Rightarrow p$ or $r \wedge q \Rightarrow \neg p$, or neither, may be me-entailed depending on the comparative strengths s_1 and s_2. This result is in accordance with the "intuitive" solution that no conclusion should be drawn regarding Nixon's pacifist status unless there is reason to suppose that one default holds more strongly than the other. In the case of one default being stronger, the conclusion favoured by the stronger would prevail.   •

Example 5.3 (Royal elephants/marine chaplains)

$$\Delta = \{r_1 : a \Rightarrow b, r_2 : c \Rightarrow b, r_3 : b \Rightarrow d, r_4 : a \Rightarrow \neg d\}$$

There are two interpretations of this knowledge base. In the first, the propositions a, b, c, and d, stand for royal, elephant, african and grey, respectively; in the second, the propositions stand for chaplain, man, marine and beer drinker, respectively. The constraint equations (4) give rise to:

$$\kappa(r_1) = s_1 + \min(\kappa(r_3), \kappa(r_4))$$
$$\kappa(r_2) = s_2$$
$$\kappa(r_3) = s_3$$
$$\kappa(r_4) = s_4 + \min(\kappa(r_1), \kappa(r_3))$$

which have the unique solution $\kappa(r_1) = s_1 + s_3$, $\kappa(r_2) = s_2$, $\kappa(r_3) = s_3$, and $\kappa(r_4) = s_3 + s_4$.

The key question relating to this knowledge base is "Are elephants which are both royal and african, not grey?", or alternatively, "Don't marine chaplains drink beer?" This translates into the default $a \wedge c \Rightarrow \neg d$ which is me-entailed in general as can be seen from:

$$\begin{aligned} \kappa(a \wedge c \wedge \neg d) &< \kappa(a \wedge c \wedge d) \\ s_3 &< s_3 + \min(s_4, s_1 + s_2 + s_3) \end{aligned}$$

The result in this example is unambiguous, that is, it holds for all strength assignments[2]. However, [Touretzky et al., 1987] were not entirely happy about the conclusion that marine-chaplains do not drink beer. They argued that if the rate of beer drinking amongst marines was significantly higher than normal, then this might alter the behaviour associated with marine-chaplains.

Now, the default $r_5 : c \Rightarrow d$ (marines drink beer) is in fact me-entailed by Δ, but adding it to the database with all defaults having equal strength violates the robustness condition. If, however, r_5 were added with a higher strength, so that it represented a new constraint for the purposes of maximising entropy, a robust solution would result and the status of the default $a \wedge c \Rightarrow \neg d$ would depend on the relative strengths s_4 and s_5.

So, Touretzky et al. were correct to suppose that if marines were heavier drinkers than men in general then it may not be clear whether marine chaplains are beer drinkers or not. However, it seems they were expecting too much of a default reasoning mechanism (a path-based inheritance reasoner in their case) in assuming it could draw such conclusions since this would involve using information *which it had never been told*. •

It is interesting to note that many of the more complex examples from the literature (for example, see [Makinson and Schlechta, 1991]), which have been devised deliberately to overcome any intuitive biases, fail to satisfy the robustness condition when all defaults are assigned equal strengths. If a set is probabilistically consistent it is usually possible to restore robustness by altering the strengths. This suggests that some sets may be too complex for the human intuition to disentangle because they are ambiguous or underspecified. By requiring more information from the knowledge engineer, in terms of a strength assignment over defaults, some of these ambiguities can be cleared up and the hitherto implicit biases made explicit.

6 Conclusions

This paper has refined and extended the work of Goldszmidt et al. [1993] on applying the principle of maximum entropy to probabilistic semantics for default rules to enable it to be applied to a much wider class of default sets. A new algorithm was presented which finds the

maximum entropy ranking for a set of variable strength defaults that satisfy a sufficient condition for a unique solution to exist. The output is a consequence relation based on a total ordering of models—a *rational consequence relation* in the sense of Lehmann and Magidor [Lehmann and Magidor, 1992]. Some extreme technical cases remain to be investigated.

Using the me-approach for default reasoning provides the same benefits as its use in statistical problems. As Jaynes [1979] suggests, by encoding all known relevant information and finding the maximum entropy distribution, any observations which differ significantly from the result imply that other constraints, in this case defaults, exist. A closer approximation is obtained by adding more defaults or by adjusting the strengths. Instead of questioning the conclusions of a default reasoning system, one should ensure that all relevant information has been encoded — the maximum entropy formalism enables the precise and explicit representation of this as default knowledge. The main disadvantage of the me-approach is its intractability, however, this extension to arbitrary sets has shed some light onto the causes of controversy among classical examples from the literature and pointed to ways of resolving them.

References

[Adams, 1975] E. Adams. *The Logic of Conditionals*. Reidel, Dordrecht, Netherlands, 1975.

[Bacchus et al., 1996] F. Bacchus, A. J. Grove, J. Y. Halpern, and D. Koller. From statistical knowledge bases to degrees of belief. *Artificial Intelligence*, 87:75–143, 1996.

[Goldszmidt et al., 1993] M. Goldszmidt, P. Morris, and J. Pearl. A maximum entropy approach to nonmonotonic reasoning. *IEEE Transactions on Pattern Analysis and Machine Intelligence*, 15:220–232, 1993.

[Kraus et al., 1990] S. Kraus, D. Lehmann, and M. Magidor. Nonmonotonic reasoning, preferential models and cumulative logics. *Artificial Intelligence*, 44:167–207, 1990.

[Lehmann and Magidor, 1992] D. Lehmann and M. Magidor. What does a conditional knowledge base entail? *Artificial Intelligence*, 55:1–60, 1992.

[Makinson and Schlechta, 1991] D. Makinson and K. Schlechta. Floating conclusions and zombie paths: two deep difficulties in the "directly skeptical" approach to defeasible inheritance nets. *Artificial Intelligence*, 48:199–209, 1991.

[Touretzky et al., 1987] D. S. Touretzky, J. F. Horty, and R. H. Thomason. A clash of intuitions: the current state of nonmonotonic multiple inheritance systems. In *Proceedings of the International Joint Conference on Artificial Intelligence*, pages 476–482, 1987.

---

[2]In fact all these examples have general solutions since they are minimal core sets as defined by Goldszmidt et al. [1993].

On the Relationship between Probabilistic Logic and π-CMS

P. HANSEN

GERAD and Dept. Méthodes Quantitatives de Gestion

Ecole des Hautes Etudes Commerciales

pierreh@crt.umontreal.ca

B. JAUMARD

GERAD and Dept. Math. and Ind. Eng.

Ecole Polytechnique de Montréal

brigitt@crt.umontreal.ca

A. D. PARREIRA

Dept. Math. and Ind. Eng.

Ecole Polytechnique de Montréal

anderson@crt.umontreal.ca

Abstract

We discuss the relationship between probabilistic logic and π-CMS. Given a set of logical sentences and their probabilities of being true, the outcome of a probabilistic logic system consists of lower and upper bounds on the probability of an additional sentence to be true. These bounds are computed using a linear programming formulation. In π-CMS systems, the outcome is defined by the probabilities of the support and the plausibility (with the assumptions being independent) after a first phase which consists of computing the prime implicants depending only on the variables of the assumptions. We propose to reformulate a π-CMS system without independence conditions on the assumptions, using the linear programming framework of probabilistic logic, and show how to exploit its particular structure to solve it efficiently. When an independence condition is imposed on the assumptions the two systems give different results. Comparisons are made on small problems using the assumption-based evidential language program (ABEL) of [Anrig *et al.*, 1998] and the PSAT program of [Jaumard *et al.*, 1991].

1 Introduction

Many different models have been proposed for reasoning under uncertainty in expert systems. Among those based on the use of logic and probability theory which require a moderate amount of input data, two important families are the probabilistic Clause Maintenance Systems (π-CMS) [Reiter and de Kleer, 1987; de Kleer and Williams, 1987], and the probabilistic logic models [Nilsson, 1986; Jaumard *et al.*, 1991; Hansen *et al.*, 1995]. While these families have been developed separately, they have much in common, with however the difference that models of the former family usually suppose independence of their assumptions, while those of the latter do not. In this paper, we explore π-CMS systems, with and without independence of the assumptions, from the probabilistic logic viewpoint. The main results are the following: (i) when relaxing the independence condition, two formulations can be proposed for π-CMS systems; (ii) the second formulation suggests an algorithm which exploits the particular structure of π-CMS and is, on large instances, 7000 times faster than the column generation algorithm for probabilistic logic of [Jaumard *et al.*, 1991] applied to the first formulation; (iii) with the independence condition, probability intervals of an additional proposition obtained by π-CMS may overlap with those of the corresponding probabilistic logic model, which suggests that π-CMS systems do not exploit the available information to its fullest degree.

The paper is organized as follows: probabilistic logic models and π-CMS systems are briefly reviewed in the next two sections. The two probabilistic logic models for π-CMS systems are presented in Section 4. Algorithms are discussed in Section 5 and computational results in Section 6. Brief conclusions are drawn in the last section.

2 Probabilistic Logic

Nilsson [Nilsson, 1986] has presented a semantical generalization of propositional logic in which the truth values of sentences are probability values (*probabilistic logic*, also called *probabilistic satisfiability* or PSAT for short).

Let $X = \{x_1, x_2, \ldots, x_n\}$ denote a set of propositional variables and $S = \{S_1, S_2, \ldots, S_m\}$ a set of propositional sentences over X defined with the usual operators $\vee$ (disjunction), $\wedge$ (conjunction), and $\neg$ (negation). A literal y_k is a propositional variable ($y_k = x_k$) or its negation ($y_k = \neg x_k$). Propositional sentences are assumed to be written using a DNF (Disjunctive Normal Form) expression in this paragraph.

Let $w = (w_1, \ldots, w_m)$ be a valuation for S, where w_i is equal to 1 if S_i has value true, and to 0 otherwise. w is a *possible world* if there exists a truth assignment over X which leads to w over S and it is an *impossible world* otherwise. Observe that two different truth assignments on X may lead to the same possible world. Let W denote the set of possible worlds and set k to $|W|$ (note that $k \leq$

2^n). To illustrate, if $X = \{x_1, x_2\}$ and $S = \{x_1, x_1 \vee x_2\}$, we have $W = \{w^1 = (0,0); w^2 = (0,1); w^3 = (1,1)\}$, $k = 3 < 2^2$, and $w^4 = (1,0)$ is an impossible world.

Let $p = (p_1, p_2, \ldots, p_k)$ be a probability distribution on W, with $0 \leq p_j \leq 1$ $(j = 1, \ldots, k)$ and $\sum_j p_j = 1$. Let $\pi = (\pi_1, \ldots, \pi_m)$ be a probability vector such that π_i denotes the probability of sentence S_i in S, $i = 1, \ldots, m$.

The probability distribution p is *consistent* if it satisfies the set of logical sentences together with their probabilities, i.e., if for each sentence S_i, the sum of p_j's over all truth assignment w^j that satisfy S_i (i.e., $w_i^j = 1$) equals π_i.

For a given set S of sentences, let A^S be an $m \times k$ matrix such that a_{ij}^S is equal to 1 if S_i is true for w^j, and equal to 0 otherwise. This leads to the following linear programming formulation of the PSAT problem (in decision form):

$$
\begin{aligned}
\mathbb{1}\, p &= 1 \\
A^S p &= \pi \\
p &\geq 0
\end{aligned}
\qquad (1)
$$

where $\mathbb{1}$ is a unit row k-vector. The problem PSAT thus reduces to determining whether there exists or not a vector p satisfying (1). Observe that (PSAT) is completely determined by the pair (S, π).

Let us assume that the PSAT problem defined by (1) is consistent. Let S_{m+1} denote an additional logical sentence, with an unknown probability π_{m+1}. The optimization form of PSAT (also known as *probabilistic entailment*, see [Nilsson, 1986]), is to determine the range $[\underline{\pi}_{m+1}, \overline{\pi}_{m+1}]$ of values of the probability π_{m+1} such that $(S \cup \{S_{m+1}\}, (\pi, \pi_{m+1}))$ is consistent. Consider the objective function $A_{m+1} p$ (with $A_{m+1} = (a_{m+1,j})$, where $a_{m+1,j}$ is equal to 1 if S_{m+1} is true for the possible word w^j and equal to 0 otherwise). PSAT corresponds to determining $\underline{\pi}_{m+1} = \min \{A_{m+1} p : \text{constraints (1)}\}$ and $\overline{\pi}_{m+1} = \max \{A_{m+1} p : \text{constraints (1)}\}$.

2.1 Numerical solution of PSAT

The linear program which expresses the PSAT problem in its decision or optimization form has an exponential number of variables in the size of the input; for this reason, in the sequel we will speak of Generalized Linear Programming (GLP for short) formulation. So writing explicitly PSAT already requires exponential time. This led Nilsson [Nilsson, 1986] to suggest looking for heuristic solution methods only.

Such a view is overly pessimistic since, although writing large PSAT problems explicitly is impossible, they can be solved quite efficiently by keeping them implicit. This can be done using the so-called column generation technique [Lasdon, 1970]. It extends the revised simplex method, in which only a small number of columns are kept explicitly. This technique makes use of a master problem which implies an objective and constraints related to the probabilities of the possible worlds, and a subproblem which determines the entering column for the master problem. This last subproblem depends on the structure of the original problem and has quite often a combinatorial nature. For more details see [Jaumard et al., 1991].

3 CMS and π-CMS models

The Assumption-based Truth Maintenance Systems (or ATMS for short) [de Kleer, 1986] and later the CMS (Clause Maintenance Systems) [Reiter and de Kleer, 1987] can be viewed as symbolic algebra systems for producing a set of statements (Boolean expressions) in which one can believe. A brief description of the CMS is given below; details can be found in [Reiter and de Kleer, 1987].

Given a set of propositional variables X, a CMS consists of a set of *assumptions* $A = \{a_1, a_2, \ldots, a_m\}$ supposed to be such that $A \subset X$ and a set of propositional sentences $H = \{h_1, h_2, \ldots, h_r\}$ (also called *justifications*, see [de Kleer, 1986]) such that the h_i are clauses. Propositional sentences are assumed to be written using a CNF (Conjunctive Normal Form) expression in this paragraph. Therefore, a clause is a finite disjunction of literals with no literal repeated, also represented as a set of literals.

A clause $\mathcal{L}(h)$ is a support for a clause h with respect to H iff $H \not\models \mathcal{L}(h)$ (i.e., $H \cup \{\neg\mathcal{L}(h)\}$ is satisfiable) and $H \models \mathcal{L}(h) \cup h$ (i.e., $H \models \neg\mathcal{L}(h) \supset h$). $\mathcal{L}(h)$ is a minimal support for h with respect to H iff no proper subset of $\mathcal{L}(h)$ is a support for h with respect to H. The CMS is a database management system which, given a set H of propositional sentences computes a minimal support clause, $\mathcal{L}(h)$, for a clause h. $\mathcal{L}(h)$ summarizes a list of sets of nonredundant assumptions (in terms of a Boolean formula), each of which is sufficient to support a proof of h. The $\mathcal{L}(h)$ for a clause h is related with a prime implicant for H. This relationship is given as follows [Reiter and de Kleer, 1987]: $\mathcal{L}(h)$ is a minimal support clause for h with respect to H iff there is a prime implicant σ for H such that $h \cap \sigma \neq \varnothing$ and $\mathcal{L}(h) = \sigma \setminus h$. Conversely, if σ is a prime implicant for H such that $h \subseteq \sigma$ then $\sigma \setminus h$ is a minimal support clause for h with respect to H.

3.1 CMS Algorithms

The prime implicants can be used to implement CMSs [Reiter and de Kleer, 1987]. The prime implicants of a set of clauses can be computed by repeatedly resolving pairs of clauses, adding the resulting resolvents to the set and removing subsumed clauses. This method is known to be a brute-force approach and performs far more resolution steps than necessary. The running time of this algorithm depends on the number and expense of the subsumption checks required. De Kleer [de Kleer, 1992] describes an improved algorithm for generating the prime implicants of a set of clauses.

3.2 Adding Numerical Uncertainties

From a logical viewpoint, the $\mathcal{L}(h)$ that the ATMS/CMS attaches to a clause yield only three possible truth values for h: believed, disbelieved, and unknown. This three-value logic cannot rate the degree of uncertainty associated with unknown clauses, and thus may lead to a stalemate whenever a decision is to be made whose outcome depends critically on the truth of these propositions. For this and others reasons, several attempts have been made to augment ATMS/CMS with a numerical measure of uncertainty. Several authors use probability theory to deal with uncertainty associated with assumptions for ATMS (De Kleer and Williams [de Kleer and Williams, 1987] and Liu *et al.* [Liu *et al.*, 1993]) or CMS (Kohlas *et al.* [Kohlas and Haenni, 1996]). In all extensions the probabilities assigned to assumptions must be independent (see [Hansen *et al.*, 1999] for details) in order to calculate the degree of belief.

The quantitative judgment of belief can be measured by the degree of support and plausibility. The degree of support of h (*dsp* for short) is the probability of arguments ($\mathcal{L}(h)$) in favor of it. Similarly, the degree of plausibility (*dpl* for short) of h is 1 minus the probability of arguments ($\mathcal{L}(\neg h)$) against it.

As next shown, π-CMS without independence condition can be reformulated using the linear programming expression of the PSAT problem.

4 Using PSAT Linear Programming expression to reformulate a π-CMS model

Consider the PSAT problem (S, π') defined as follows: $S = A \cup H$ where $S_i = a_i$ ($i = 1, 2, \ldots, m$) and $S_{i+m} = h_i$ ($i = 1, 2, \ldots, r$); $\pi' = (\pi, \mathbb{1})$, where π is a probability m-vector associated with the set A of assumptions and $\mathbb{1}$ is a unit r-vector (all the probabilities are equal to 1 for the set H of clauses). Note that $|S| = m'$ with $m' = m + r$. The clause h with unknown probability is associated with $S_{m'+1}$. Denote by $Y_i \subseteq Y$ the set of literals of clause h_i, i.e., $h_i = \bigvee_{y_j \in Y_i} y_j$.

First Formulation (F_1)

The π-CMS problem can be expressed using the GLP formulation of the PSAT problem:
Master problem:

$$\text{min/max} \quad A_{m'+1}p \quad (2)$$

subject to:

$$\mathbb{1} p = 1 \quad (3)$$
$$A^A p = \pi \quad (4)$$
$$A^H p = \mathbb{1} \quad (5)$$
$$p \geq 0 \quad (6)$$

Subproblem:

$$\text{min/max}_j \; \bar{c}_j = c_j - \left(1, (A^A)^j, (A^H)^j\right)(u_0, u_A, u_H) \quad (7)$$

where u_0, u^A and u^H are the dual variables associated with the constraints (3)-(5), respectively.

This reformulation results in a PSAT problem with a subproblem corresponding to an unconstrained nonlinear program in 0-1 variables.

Note that the set of propositional sentences of H has a specific structure, in that its probabilities are all equal to 1, i.e., these propositional sentences are always true. Exploring this structure leads to a second formulation.

Second Formulation (F_2)

There is a natural partitioning of the constraints of the GLP defined by formulation F_1. Observe that satisfying the constraint (5) is equivalent to satisfying the equation:

$$\bigwedge_{i=1,\ldots,r} h_i = 1,$$

i.e., to solving a satisfiability problem (SAT).

Hence, constraints (5) can be transferred to the subproblem, which then leads to consider in the master problem only the solutions of (5) which satisfy (3), (4), (6) and minimize or maximize (2).

We thus obtain the following GLP reformulation. Master problem:

$$\text{min/max} \quad A_{m'+1}p \quad (8)$$

subject to:

$$\mathbb{1} p = 1 \quad (9)$$
$$A^A p = \pi \quad (10)$$
$$p \geq 0 \quad (11)$$

Subproblem:

$$\text{min/max}_j \; \bar{c}_j = c_j - (1, (A^A)^j)(u_0, u^A)$$
$$\text{subject to:}$$
$$\sum_{y_j \in Y_i} y_j \geq 1 \quad i = 1, 2, \ldots, r \quad (12)$$
$$x_i + \bar{x}_i = 1 \quad x_i \in X$$

The subproblem is now a linear program in the $2n$ 0-1 variables x_i, $\bar{x}_i$ (as the y_j are either variables x_l or $\bar{x}_l$) with linear constraints.

Each column of (10) corresponds to a possible world w^j, or equivalently a subset of assumptions with true/false values, which may imply $S_{m'+1}$, imply $\neg S_{m'+1}$ or neither. In the first two cases there is one corresponding column in (8)-(11), and in the latter two. When minimizing $A_{m'+1}p$, columns which have $a_{m'+1,j} = 1$ will have probability 0 if there are twin columns with $a_{m'+1,j'} = 0$. So $\underline{\pi}_{m+1}$ will correspond to the sum of probabilities of those clauses which imply $S_{m'+1}$, i.e., to the degree of support of $S_{m'+1}$. When maximizing $A_{m'+1}p$, columns which have $a_{m'+1,j} = 0$ will have probabilities 0 if there are twin columns with $a_{m'+1,j'} = 1$. So $\overline{\pi}_{m+1}$ will correspond to 1 minus the sum of probabilities of those clauses which imply $\neg S_{m'+1}$, i.e., to the degree of plausibility of $S_{m'+1}$.

5 Solution Method

The method is an iterative one (in fact, the revised simplex algorithm [Chvátal, 1983]) where at each iteration, we determine the column with the minimum (maximum) reduced cost by solving (7) in the case of F_1, i.e.,

$$\min/\max_j \bar{c}_j = a_{m'+1,j} - u_0 - \sum_{i=1}^{m'} u_i a_{ij} \qquad (13)$$

where the u_0 and u_i are the current dual variables associated with the tautology S_0 and with the propositional sentences S_i, $i = 1, \ldots, m'$, respectively. By associating the logical values true with 1 and false with 0 in each logical proposition, one can rewrite (13) as:

$$\min/\max_j \bar{c}_j = S_{m'+1} - u_0 - \sum_{i=1}^{m'} u_i S_i.$$

This optimization problem can be reformulated using arithmetic expressions of the propositional variables of X. This can easily be done with the convention $1 \equiv$ true and $0 \equiv$ false and the relations $x_i \vee x_j \equiv x_i + x_j - x_i \times x_j$, $x_i \wedge x_j \equiv x_i \times x_j$ and $\neg x_i \equiv 1 - x_i$, where the left-hand side variables are logical ones, and the right-hand side variables are integer ones. The choice of the entering column is thus reduced to a problem of minimizing (maximizing) an unconstrained nonlinear function in 0-1 variables (PNL-0/1). In formulation F_2 the subproblem is a constrained linear program in 0-1 variables (CPL-0/1).

5.1 Basic Algorithm

We assume that the optimization problem is a minimization one. Algorithm 1 provides a description of the column generation method for Formulation F_1 or F_2.

Phase-1 is not detailed as it proceeds in a similar way than Phase-2, i.e., through STEP 3 to STEP 7.

5.2 Solution of the Subproblems

Again assume that the optimization problem is a minimization one. At each iteration a column with a negative reduced cost must be found by a heuristic or an exact algorithm. Exact solution of the subproblem is not necessary at each iteration to guarantee convergence. As long as a negative reduced cost is found by the heuristic an iteration of the revised simplex algorithm may be done. If a feasible solution is obtained in that way, the decision version of the satisfiability problem is solved, but finding none when choosing the entering column in a heuristic way cannot guarantee that none exists. So, when no more negative reduced cost is obtained by the heuristic it is necessary to turn to an exact algorithm to prove that there is no feasible solution for the decision version of PSAT, nor feasible solution giving a better bound than the incumbent one for the optimization version. We use a Steepest Ascent Mildest Descent (SAMD) or Tabu Search (TS) heuristic ([Hansen and Jaumard, 1990; Glover and Laguna, 1997]) for PNL-0/1, and a variant of Tabu Search for CPL-0/1 with constraints to find an approximately optimal solution. We also use a method based on linearization for PNL-0/1, and branch-and-bound for CPL-0/1, to find an exact optimal solution.

Algorithm 1 Column Generation Method

STEP 1. Using phase-1 of the simplex algorithm (see, e.g. [Chvátal, 1983] for details), build an initial matrix B_0 associated with a feasible solution.

STEP 2. If there is no such matrix B_0 then the problem is inconsistent: Stop.

STEP 3. Solve the master problem to compute the dual variables (phase-2 of the simplex algorithm).

STEP 4. Solve the subproblem to compute a column with negative reduced cost $\bar{c}_t$ using a heuristic;

STEP 5. If $\bar{c}_t < 0$ then add the corresponding column to the master problem, reoptimize it, and go to STEP 3.

STEP 6. Solve the subproblem to compute the column with the most negative reduced cost using an exact algorithm.

STEP 7. If $\bar{c}_t < 0$ then add the corresponding column to the master problem, reoptimize it, and go to STEP 3.

STEP 8. Stop: the optimal solution has been reached.

PNL-0/1 without constraints

The Tabu Search (TS) heuristic proceeds to a local optimum by moving at each iteration from one feasible solution to another in its neighborhood (here the vectors at Hamming distance 1 from the current one). We then pick the solution in the neighborhood that produces the best improvement in the objective function. If there is no improving solution (a local optimum was reached assuming we use aspiration, see page 50 in [Glover and Laguna, 1997]) then we choose that one which degrades the objective function least. In order to avoid returning to the local optimum just visited, or cycling, the reverse move is forbidden for a given number of iterations ($SizeMaxTabu$).

The steps of TS are presented in Algorithm 2. The parameters T_j denote the remaining number of iterations during which a local change in direction j is forbidden. When a change in an ascent direction j is done T_j is set at the value $tabu$. That value is chosen by random selection among integers in the range $[1, SizeMaxTabu]$. The stopping condition may be, e.g., maximum computing time allowed, maximum number of iterations, or maximum number of iterations between two improvements.

The linearization method works by replacing in a standard way each product of variables by a new 0-1 variable and adding constraints to ensure that the values agree in 0-1 variables.

The size of the resulting linear 0-1 variables increases rapidly with m, n and the number of nonzero dual variables u_i.

Algorithm 2 Tabu Search

STEP 1. Select a feasible solution x and let $z(x)$ be the value associated with x. Set $x_{opt} := x$, $z_{opt} := z(x)$, and T empty, the directions where changes are forbidden. Choose a stopping condition.

STEP 2. Transform x into the solution x_j modified in the jth direction and evaluate $\delta_j := z(x_j) - z(x)$ with $T_j = 0$. Let $\delta_k := min\{\delta_j : T_j = 0\}$. If $\delta_k \leq 0$, $T_k := tabu$. Set $x := x_k$.

STEP 3. If $z(x_k) < z_{opt}$ then update $x_{opt} := x_k$ and $z_{opt} := z(x_k)$.

STEP 4. If the stopping condition is met then STOP.
Otherwise, update T and return to STEP 2.

Algorithm 3 Tabu Search-Constrained

STEP 1. Select a solution x (not necessarily feasible) and let $z(x)$ denote the value associated with x. Set $x_{opt} := x$, $z_{opt} := z(x)$, $iter := 1$ and T empty. Choose the values of $UnsatMax$, REP and a stopping condition.

STEP 2. Transform x into the solution x^j modified in the jth direction and evaluate $\delta_j := z(x^j) - z(x)$ with $T_j = 0$. Let $\delta_k := min\{\delta_j : T_j = 0 \text{ and } unsat < UnsatMax\}$. If $\delta_k \leq 0$, $T_k := tabu$. Set $x := x^k$.

STEP 3. If $z(x^k) < z_{opt}$ and x^k feasible then update $x_{opt} := x^k$ and $z_{opt} := z(x^k)$.

STEP 4. If the stopping condition is met then Stop. Otherwise, update T and return to STEP 2.

STEP 5. If x^k is feasible then $UnsatMax := UnsatMax - \beta * UnsatMax$.
Otherwise $UnsatMax = \alpha * UnsatMax$.

STEP 6. $iter := iter + 1$.

STEP 7. If $iter < REP$ then return to STEP 2. Otherwise Stop.

CPL-0/1 with constraints

Heuristic solution of CPL-0/1 is again done by a SAMD or TS algorithm. The idea behind this algorithm is to allow infeasibility. However it must be limited, therefore for each sequence of iterations a move is allowed only if the resulting number of unsatisfied clauses (or violated constraints) is smaller than a given threshold $UnsatMax$. After a number of iterations we verify if the current solution is feasible. In the affirmative we reduce the value of $UnsatMax$ by β and another sequence of iterations is performed. In the negative the value of $UnsatMax$ is increased by α, we apply a transformation to get a feasible solution and another sequence of iterations is performed. The overall algorithm has a maximum number of REP iterations. Steps of the TS-Constrained heuristic are presented on Algorithm 3.

The constrained linear 0-1 program (12) has the form of a combined set covering and set partitioning problem. Exact solution is based on the algorithm of [Fisher and Kedia, 1990]. The main feature of this algorithm is the use of dual variables in the linear programming relaxation to provide lower bounds for a branch-and-bound algorithm.

6 Computational Experiments

The algorithms for π-CMS/PSAT described in the previous sections have been coded in C and tested on a Ultra-2 SUN SPARC computer. The resulting program uses the CPLEX 6.0 package for linear programming. The problems for π-CMS/PSAT were randomly generated in the following way: (i) the numbers m of assumptions, r of justifications, which here are clauses, n of variables (assumptions and propositional symbols) are parameters; (ii) the clauses contain at most 4 literals. There is an uniform distribution of clauses with 1, 2, 3 and 4 literals as well as of uncomplemented and complemented variables. Probabilities $\pi_i(A)$ corresponding to feasible problems were obtained by generating randomly

$max(2^{10}; 2^n)$ Boolean vectors x, constructing the corresponding possible worlds, associating with them positive numbers summing up to 1 (i.e., probabilities for these worlds to occur), and then summing for each clause the probabilities of the worlds in which it is true.

Results of the comparison between the two π-CMS/PSAT models are given in Table 1 and 2, which detail problem sizes, total cpu time, number of columns generated, cpu time for the tabu search and the exact algorithms for the subproblems. Each line corresponds to averages over five problems. Note than the number of propositions m' in the first formulation is equal to the number of assumptions (propositions in the master problem) plus the number of justifications (considered only in the subproblems) in the second formulation. Clearly the second formulation is by far superior to the first one: computation times for the larger instances are 7000 times smaller.

If an independence condition is imposed on the assumptions, only much smaller instances of π-CMS are solvable in reasonable time. If columns corresponding to feasible worlds are considered explicitly, each has a positive probability and their number increases exponentially. This contrast with the linear programming model of PSAT, where the number of columns with positive probability in a basic, and hence in an optimal, solution is at most equal to the number of lines. Using Boolean simplifications we may reduce somewhat the computational burden but it often remains too high to solve large instances.

Intervals $[\underline{\pi}_{m+1}, \overline{\pi}_{m+1}]$ for π-CMS/PSAT and

Problems		tcpu		Column		TS Heuristic			Exact Algorithm		
n	m'	tcpu μ (s)	σ	μ	σ	tcpu μ (s)	σ	Iter	tcpu μ (s)	σ	Iter
				Maximization+Minimization							
100	100	17.278	6.376	712.80	140.599	1.96	0.41	714.80	0.01	0.01	3.60
100	150	3307.274	743.309	3863.00	255.948	12.66	0.95	3865.00	0.01	0.03	3.20
150	200	10890.038	3779.051	4464.00	208.784	22.51	1.70	4466.00	0.01	0.02	3.40

Table 1: Formulation-1

Problems			tcpu		Column		TS Heuristic			Exact Algorithm		
n	m	r	tcpu μ (s)	σ	μ	σ	tcpu μ (s)	σ	Iter	tcpu μ (s)	σ	Iter
					Maximization+Minimization							
100	50	50	0.532	0.043	20.20	1.939	0.41	0.03	22.20	0.05	0.15	2.20
100	50	100	0.984	0.183	26.80	4.308	0.82	0.12	28.80	0.08	0.21	2.80
150	100	100	1.532	0.136	32.80	3.370	1.24	0.11	34.80	0.09	0.22	2.20

Table 2: Formulation-2

$[dsp, dpl]$ for π-CMS with independence condition (obtained with the ABEL program [Anrig *et al.*, 1998]) are given in Table 3. It appears that in some cases the intervals of π-CMS with the independence conditions overlap in part with those of π-CMS/PSAT instead of being included in them, as one would have expected. This indicates π-CMS does not exploit the available information to its fullest degree. Reasons why this is so will be explored in future work.

Problems			PSAT	ABEL
n	m	r	$\underline{\pi}_{m+1}$-$\overline{\pi}_{m+1}$	dsp-dpl
15	10	20	0.0000-0.5513	0.000-0.313
15	10	20	0.1046-1.0000	0.037-1.000
15	10	20	0.3666-1.0000	0.473-1.000
15	10	20	0.4301-1.0000	0.601-1.000

Table 3: Comparison of bounds

7 Conclusions

π-CMS systems can be expressed in two ways as a PSAT problem, when the independence condition on the assumptions is removed. Then the lower and upper bounds on the probability of the additional propositional sentence coincide with its support and plausibility. The second formulation, which keeps the justifications implicit (or transfer them to the subproblem when using column generation as solution method), is much more efficient than the first, direct one. If the independence condition is kept in π-CMS, solution becomes more cumbersome and probability intervals for the objective function clause provided by both methods may overlap.

Acknowledgments

Research of the authors was supported by DREV-Valcartier contract. Work of the first and second authors was supported by FCAR grants 92-EQ-1048 and 95-ER-1048. Work of the first has also been supported by NSERC grant to HEC and NSERC grant GP0105574. Work of the second author was also supported by NSERC grants GP0036426 and EQP0157431. Work of the third author has also been supported by CNPq (Conselho Nacional de Desenvolvimento Científico e Tecnológico), Brazil, grant 200722/95-6.

References

[Anrig *et al.*, 1998] Bernhard Anrig, Roman Bissig, Rolf Haenni, Jürg Kohlas, and Nobert Lehmann. Probabilistic Argumentation Systems: Introduction to Assumption-Based Modeling using ABEL. Technical report, Institute of Informatics, University of Fribourg, September 1998.

[Chvátal, 1983] Vasek Chvátal. *Linear Programming.* Freeman, New York, NY, 1983.

[de Kleer and Williams, 1987] Johan de Kleer and Brian C. Williams. Diagnosing Multiple Faults. *Artificial Intelligence*, 32(1):97–130, 1987.

[de Kleer, 1986] Johan de Kleer. An Assumption-based TMS. *Artificial Intelligence*, 28:127–162, 1986.

[de Kleer, 1992] Johan de Kleer. An Improved Incremental Algorithm for Generating Prime Implicates. In *Proc. of the 10th Nat. Conf. on Artificial Intelligence*, pages 780–785, San Jose, California, July 1992. AAAI.

[Fisher and Kedia, 1990] Marchall L. Fisher and Pradeep Kedia. Optimal Solution of Set Covering/Partitioning Problems Using Dual Heuristics. *Management Science*, 36(6):674–688, June 1990.

[Glover and Laguna, 1997] Fred Glover and Manuel Laguna. *Tabu Search.* Kluwer, 1997.

[Hansen and Jaumard, 1990] Pierre Hansen and Brigitte Jaumard. Algorithms for the Maximum Satisfiability Problem. *Computing*, 44:279–303, 1990.

[Hansen *et al.*, 1995] Pierre Hansen, Brigitte Jaumard, and Marcus V. Poggi de Aragão. Boole's Conditions of Possible Experience and Reasoning Under Uncertainty. *Discrete Applied Mathematics*, 60:181–193, 1995.

[Hansen *et al.*, 1999] Pierre Hansen, Brigitte Jaumard, Anderson D. Parreira, and Marcus V. Poggi de Aragão. Difficulties of Conditioning and Conditional Independence in Probabilistic Satisfiability. Technical Report G-99-16, Cahiers du GERAD, February 1999.

[Jaumard *et al.*, 1991] Brigitte Jaumard, Pierre Hansen, and Marcus V. Poggi de Aragão. Column Generation Methods for Probabilistic Logic. *ORSA Journal on Computing*, 3:135–148, 1991.

[Kohlas and Haenni, 1996] Jürg Kohlas and Rolf Haenni. Assumption-based Reasoning and Probabilistic Argumentation Systems. In J. Kohlas and S. Moral, editors, *Defeasible Reasoning and Uncertainty Management Systems: Algorithms*. Oxford University Press, 1996.

[Lasdon, 1970] Leon S. Lasdon. *Optimization Theory for Large Systems*. MacMillan, New York, 1970.

[Liu *et al.*, 1993] Weiru Liu, Alan Bundy, and Dave Robertson. On the Relations between Incidence Calculus and ATMS. In *Symbolic and Quantitative Approaches to Reasoning and Uncertainty (Granada, 1993)*, pages 249–256. Springer-Verlag, Berlin, 1993.

[Nilsson, 1986] Nils J. Nilsson. Probabilistic Logic. *Artificial Intelligence*, 28:71–87, 1986.

[Reiter and de Kleer, 1987] Raymond Reiter and Johan de Kleer. Foundations of Assumption-Based Truth Maintenance Systems: Preliminary Report. In *Proc. of the 6th Nat. Conf. on Artificial Intelligence*, volume 1, pages 183–188, Seattle, Washington, July 1987.

AUTOMATED REASONING

Nonmonotonic Reasoning 3:
Model Checking Methods

On the Complexity of Model Checking for Propositional Default Logics: New Results and Tractable Cases

Robert Baumgartner*
Institut für Informationssysteme
Technische Universität Wien
A-1040 Vienna, Austria
baumgart@dbai.tuwien.ac.at

Georg Gottlob*
Institut für Informationssysteme
Technische Universität Wien
A-1040 Vienna, Austria
gottlob@dbai.tuwien.ac.at

Abstract

We analyse the complexity of standard and weak model checking for propositional default logic; in particular, we solve the open problem of complexity in case of normal default theories and introduce a new ample class of default theories with a tractable model checking problem.

1 Introduction and Overview of Results

The complexity of default reasoning is already well understood, however, in search of model-based representations, the complexity of the model checking problem instead of the inference problem needs to be analysed.

As Halpern and Vardi [1991] argue, model checking is a beneficial alternative simplifying reasoning tasks (for instance, in classical propositional logic, model checking can be done using an easy polynomial algorithm, however reasoning is **coNP**-complete) and allowing for representing the agent's knowledge as a semantic structure instead of a collection of formulae and additionally, this approach introduces a kind of closed-world assumption. Furthermore, the complexity of model checking is closely related to the notion of *representational succinctness* [Gogic *et al.*, 1995] of non-monotonic formalisms.

1.1 Complexity of Inference

Gottlob [1992] and Stillman [1992] showed that the complexity of *brave (cautious) reasoning*, i.e. to decide, given a formula f and a default theory $\langle D, W \rangle$, if f is in at least one (all) extension(s) of $\langle D, W \rangle$ is Σ_2^P-complete (Π_2^P-complete), even in case of normal and prerequisite-free default theories, and even if f is a single literal. For related results, see [Papadimitriou and Sideri, 1992].

The complexity decreases one level if *disjunction-free* default theories are considered, i.e. only conjunctions of literals and negated literals are allowed. Kautz and Selman [1991] dealt with the inference problem for such theories: Brave reasoning (for disjunction-free formulae) is **NP**-complete, even in the case of normal default theories (although finding an extension is polynomial in that

case) and even if the formula to be inferred of at least one extension is a single literal. If W is a Horn theory, **NP**-completeness holds even in the case of prerequisite-free normal default theories [Stillman, 1990].

1.2 Complexity of Model Checking

An interpretation is a model of a default theory iff it satisfies at least one extension of the theory. Liberatore and Schaerf [1998] show that model checking is Σ_2^P-complete, even for semi-normal prerequisite-free default theories. In the case of normal default theories, model checking is easier than the corresponding reasoning task - they show that the problem is in Δ_2^P and $\Delta_2^P[O(\log n)]$-hard, and **coNP**-complete if defaults are also prerequisite-free.

In general, model checking suffers from two sources of hardness: On the one hand there are $2^{|G|}$ (with $G = \{d \mid \mathcal{M} \models c(d)\}$) possible sets of generating defaults, and the other source of intractability is the hardness of propositional inference. In case of normal default theories, given a particular model, only one subset of G needs to be considered and therefore the initial guessing stage is eliminated. In Theorem 4.1 we show with a non-trivial membership proof that this problem is in $\Delta_2^P[O(\log n)]$ and hence due to earlier results $\Delta_2^P[O(\log n)]$-complete. To obtain this theorem we improve techniques of Gottlob [1995] for guessing data-structures.

If the defaults are restricted in such a way that propositional satisfiability and inference are polynomial, the other source of intractability is affected and the problem is due to the necessary guessing of generating defaults **NP**-complete. If such a default theory is restricted to normal defaults, complexity of model checking is even polynomial. Therefore, in Chapter 5, we introduce the class of *default theories in extended Horn normal form* (abbreviated as "EHNF default theories"), a class containing disjunction-free default theories, for which model checking is still one level easier than for arbitrary default theories. A default theory $\langle D, W \rangle$ is in EHNF iff W and all elements of each justification are disjunctions of Horn theories, each prerequisite is a conjunction of dual Horn theories, and each consequent is a Horn theory. This is an ample class of default theories with a tractable model checking problem and hence very useful in practical applications.

---
*This work was supported by the Austrian Science Fund Project N Z29-INF.

	General/Semi-N.	Normal
General	Σ_2^P-complete*	$\Delta_2^P[O(\log n)]$-cpl.
Prerequisite-free	Σ_2^P-complete*	coNP-complete*
EHNF	NP-complete	P-complete
EHNF/Prer.-free	NP-complete	P-complete

Table 1: Complexity of Model Checking

	General/Semi-N.	Normal
General	Σ_2^P-complete	Σ_2^P-complete
Prerequisite-free	Σ_2^P-complete	coNP-complete
EHNF	NP-complete	NP-complete
EHNF/Prer.-free	NP-complete	P-complete

Table 2: Complexity of Weak Model Checking

1.3 Weak Model Checking and AEL

In Chapter 6 we recall the notion of *weak extensions* and show that *weak model checking*, i.e. deciding if an interpretation satisfies at least one weak extension of a default theory, is, due to the non-constructive nature of the problem, even Σ_2^P-complete for normal default theories and hence strictly harder than model checking. This issue is also connected to the fact that no modular translation from default logic into autoepistemic logic (AEL) exists [Gottlob, 1995b], since prerequisites are treated in a very different way. The objective parts of stable expansions (N-expansions) of the translated default theory correspond to weak extensions (extensions) of the default theory, therefore we obtain the complexity of model checking for AEL (nonmonotonic logic N) in Chapter 7.

1.4 Summary

In Table 1 and Table 2 a summary of our results for model checking and weak model checking with Reiter's default logic is presented (the results already present in [Liberatore and Schaerf, 1998] are marked with ⋆). Additionally, the main contributions of this paper are:

- We solve the open problem of the exact complexity of model checking for normal default theories.
- We introduce a new ample class of default theories with a tractable model checking problem.
- We show that weak model checking is Σ_2^P-complete, even if restricted to normal default theories.
- We generalize these results to Σ_2^P-completeness of model checking with AEL and N.
- Finally, in Chapter 8 the complexity results of model checking are used to draw some interesting conclusions in translatability issues.

2 Basic Concepts

A **propositional default theory** [Reiter, 1980] is a pair $\langle D, W \rangle$ where W is a finite set of propositional sentences and D is a finite set of defaults. Whenever we use the term *default theory* in the rest of the paper, we mean propositional default theory.

A *default* d is a configuration of the form $\frac{p(d):\beta_1,\ldots,\beta_n}{c(d)}$ where $p(d), \beta_i, c(d)$ are propositional sentences. $p(d)$ is called the prerequisite of d, the (non-empty) set $\{\beta_1, \ldots, \beta_n\}$ is referred to as the justification of d and denoted by $j(d)$; $c(d)$ is called the consequent of the default d. For convenience we define $c(H) = \{c(d) \mid d \in H\}$ and if $j(d)$ is a singleton we identify it with its only element.

Since Reiter's original definition of extensions [1980] a great number of equivalent characterizations has been introduced. In this paper we normally use a finite quasi-inductive characterization, based on the operator B^D due to Marek and Truszczyński [1993].

We define $cons(A)$ as usual as $\{\Phi \mid A \models \Phi\}$. Let H be a subset of D: $H_0 = \emptyset, H_{k+1} =$

$$\{d \in D \mid W \cup c(H_k) \models p(d), \forall \beta_i \in j(d)\ W \cup c(H) \not\models \neg\beta_i\}.$$

As we limit ourselves to finite default theories, it can easily be seen that at latest after $|D|$ steps a fixed point has been reached. $E = cons(W \wedge c(H_{|D|}))$ is an extension of $\langle D, W \rangle$ iff $H = H_{|D|}$. Every extension is of the form $E = cons(W \cup c(GD(D, E)))$ with GD being called the generating defaults of the extension.

In a *normal default theory* $j(d) = c(d)$ for each default. A *semi-normal default theory* is a theory in which each $j(d)$ is of the form $f(d) \wedge c(d)$ where $f(d)$ are arbitrary propositional formulae.

Definition 2.1 *An interpretation (valuation) $\mathcal{M}$ is a model of $\langle D, W \rangle$ iff $\mathcal{M}$ is model of at least one (consistent) extension of $\langle D, W \rangle$.*

Whenever we use the term *model* we refer to *propositional Herbrand model*. The *Model Checking* problem for default logic is to decide, given an interpretation $\mathcal{M}$ and a default theory $\langle D, W \rangle$, if $\mathcal{M} \models \langle D, W \rangle$.

Short Review of Relevant Complexity Concepts: The notion of completeness we employ is based on many-one polynomial transformability. Recall that the classes Δ_k^P, Σ_k^P and Π_k^P of the polynomial time hierarchy (PH)[1] are defined as $\Delta_0^P = \Sigma_0^P = \Pi_0^P = \mathbf{P}$ and for all $k \geq 0$, $\Delta_{k+1}^P = \mathbf{P}^{\Sigma_k^P}, \Sigma_{k+1}^P = \mathbf{NP}^{\Sigma_k^P}, \Pi_{k+1}^P = \mathrm{co}-\Sigma_{k+1}^P$. In particular, $\mathbf{NP} = \Sigma_1^P, \mathbf{coNP} = \Pi_1^P$ and $\Delta_2^P = \mathbf{P}^{\mathbf{NP}}$ (see [Papadimitriou, 1993] for details). Δ_2^P is the class of decision problems that are solvable in polynomial time on a deterministic oracle Turing machine calling an **NP**-oracle polynomially often.

The classes Δ_k^P have been refined, depending of how many oracle calls are needed: Of special interest in this paper is the class $\Delta_2^P[O(\log n)]$, also known as $\mathbf{P}^{\mathbf{NP}[O(\log n)]}$ - this is the class of decision problems solvable with a logarithmic number of calls to an **NP**-oracle.

A survey on already known complexity results for several non-monotonic logics can be found in [Cadoli and Schaerf, 1992].

---

[1] We always implicitly assume that $\mathbf{P} \neq \mathbf{NP}$ and that the PH does not collapse.

3 Some Useful Tools

Due to lack of space, some proofs in the following chapters are sketched or omitted.

Lemma 3.1 *Let $\langle D, W \rangle$ be a normal default theory. If $W \wedge c(D)$ is consistent, then there are no mutually incompatible defaults and thus only one generating set.*

Lemma 3.2 *Let $\langle R, W \rangle$ be a monotonic rule-system (or a normal or justification-free default theory) where W and the consequents b_i of $R = \{\frac{a_1}{b_1}, \ldots \frac{a_n}{b_n}\}$ are jointly consistent. Then the statement: "At least k rules do not fire" is equivalent to "It is possible to choose a set $B \subseteq R$ with $|B| = k$ and k interpretations $\mathcal{I}_1, \ldots \mathcal{I}_k$ in such a way that $\forall j (1 \leq j \leq k) : \mathcal{I}_j \models W, \forall j \, \forall b \in R \backslash B : \mathcal{I}_j \models b, \forall a \in B \, \exists j : \mathcal{I}_j \not\models a."*

The following proposition formalizes a technique (binary search) that is well known in the literature [Wagner, 1990; Papadimitriou, 1993].

Proposition 3.3 *Let $a(I_1, \ldots, I_n)$ be a function of n instances of a problem and $a(I_1, \ldots, I_n)$ be polynomially bounded in n, i.e. $a(I_1, \ldots, I_n) \leq p(n)$. If the problem of deciding $a(I_1, \ldots, I_n) \leq r$ (or $a \geq r$) is in **NP**, then the computation of $a(I_1, \ldots, I_n)$ is in $\Delta_2^P[O(\log n)]$.*

Proposition 3.4 *$\mathcal{M}$ is a model of a default theory $\langle D, W \rangle$ iff there exists an extension of $\langle D, W \rangle$ generated by a subset $G_1 \subseteq G$ where $G = \{d \mid \mathcal{M} \models c(d)\}$. In a normal default theory at most one extension E such that $\mathcal{M} \models E$ exists.*

Proposition 3.5 *Let E be an extension of the default theory $\langle G, W \rangle$ and $G \subseteq D$. Then, E is an extension of $\langle D, W \rangle$ iff for each default in $D \backslash G$ it holds that $W \wedge c(GD(G, E)) \not\models p(d)$ or $W \wedge c(GD(G, E)) \models \neg \beta_i$ for at least one i with $\beta_i \in j(d)$.*

4 Model Checking for Normal Default Theories is $\Delta_2^P[O(\log n)]$-complete

Theorem 4.1 *Let $\mathcal{M}$ be an interpretation and $\langle D, W \rangle$ be a normal default theory. Deciding whether $\mathcal{M} \models \langle D, W \rangle$ is in $\Delta_2^P[O(\log n)]$.*

Proof. We describe a Turing machine M which decides this problem in polynomial time using an **NP**-oracle for only $O(\log n)$ times where n is the number of defaults. M works in four steps.

Step 1: M rejects if $\mathcal{M} \not\models W$. Let $G \subseteq D$ be the set of all defaults d with $\mathcal{M} \models c(d)$. This step determines G by sorting out all unwanted ("bad") defaults $B = D \backslash G$. None of the defaults of B shall fire or $\mathcal{M}$ is not a model of this extension (Proposition 3.4). Checking if $\mathcal{M} \models W$ and constructing G can be achieved in polynomial time. In the following, let m be the cardinality of G.

Step 2: M computes the cardinality of the set G_1 of generating defaults of the extension, i.e. those defaults in G which are applicable because their prerequisites can be inferred; due to Lemma 3.1, G_1 is unique. M assumes that $E = cons(W \cup c(G_1))$ is an extension, and in step 3 and 4 M will verify if no "bad" defaults have to be

used. To compute the cardinality of G_1, M determines the number $|G_2| = |G \backslash G_1|$ of defaults that do not fire. We can identify $\langle D, W \rangle$ with a monotonic rule-system $\langle R, W \rangle$ in which all consequents are jointly consistent.

Claim The problem to decide if at least r rules of a monotonic rule-system (in n rules) do not fire is in **NP**.

Proof of Claim: Machine M guesses a data-structure $\langle G_2', \{\mathcal{I}_1, \ldots, \mathcal{I}_r\} \rangle$ with $|G_2'| = r$. G_2' is a set of defaults (rules), the $\mathcal{I}_j (1 \leq j \leq r)$ are interpretations, and proves in polynomial time (using the monotonic rule system syntax of Lemma 3.2): $\forall j : \mathcal{I}_j \models W$, $\forall j \, \forall b \in R \backslash G_2' : \mathcal{I}_j \models b, \forall a \in G_2' \, \exists j : \mathcal{I}_j \not\models a$. Due to Lemma 3.2, this is equivalent to the question if at least r rules do not fire, i.e. if $|G_2| \geq r$. $\diamond$

From Proposition 3.3 the number t of defaults which do not fire can be computed in polynomial time using $O(\log m)$ calls to an **NP**-oracle. After concluding this step M knows $|G_2| = t$, hence $|G_1| = m - t$.

Step 3: If it can be shown that $W \cup c(G_1) \models p(d)$ and $W \wedge c(G_1) \wedge j(d)$ is consistent for at least one $d \in B$, then G_1 is not a set of generating defaults and the given interpretation $\mathcal{M}$ is not a model for $\langle D, W \rangle$ (Proposition 3.5). Two types of "bad" defaults need to be distinguished: B_1 is consisting of defaults in which the prerequisites are not applicable, formally $B_1 = \{d \in B \mid W \cup c(G_1) \not\models p(d)\}$; and $B_2 = B \backslash B_1$. M determines the exact number u of defaults in B_1 and in the fourth step will check for each default in B_2, if the justifications are consistent with $W \wedge c(G_1)$ (after guessing the right G_1 and B_1).

Claim The problem to decide, given $|G_1|$, if the number of defaults in B_1 is at least s, is in **NP**.

Proof of Claim: For a given s, M guesses a data-structure $\langle G_1 \subseteq G, \{\mathcal{N}_1, \ldots, \mathcal{N}_t\}, B_1' \subseteq B, \{\mathcal{O}_1, \ldots, \mathcal{O}_s\} \rangle$ with $|G_1| = m - t$, $|B_1'| = s$ and $\mathcal{N}_e$ and $\mathcal{O}_y$ are interpretations. Now M proves:

- $\forall d \in G_2 \, \exists \mathcal{N}_e (1 \leq e \leq t) : \mathcal{N}_e \not\models p(d), \forall e : \mathcal{N}_e \models W \wedge c(G_1)$ (In step 2 M was provided with the information of the cardinality of G_1, therefore M now just has to guess a G_1 of suitable cardinality and check if it is the right one.).

- $\forall d \in B_1' \, \exists \mathcal{O}_y (1 \leq y \leq s) : \mathcal{O}_y \not\models p(d), \forall y : \mathcal{O}_y \models W \wedge c(G_1)$. If it is possible to choose the $\mathcal{O}_y$ this way, then there are at least s not applicable prerequisites of defaults, hence $|B_1| \geq s$ (This statement is equivalent to $\forall d \in B_1' : W \cup c(G_1) \not\models p(d)$.).

Both steps can be concluded in polynomial time and are due to the initial guess in **NP**. $\diamond$

Hence, $u = |B_1|$ can be computed with $\lceil \log(n - m) \rceil$ oracle calls (Proposition 3.3).

Step 4: In the previous steps M has determined the cardinality of B_1 and G_1. Now M finally has to check that $W \wedge c(G_1) \wedge j(d)$ is inconsistent for all defaults $d \in B_2$ (if *yes*, then G_1 is a generating set). To this aim, let us show that the converse problem is in **NP** and introduce a machine N solving it.

Claim The problem to decide if $W \wedge c(G) \wedge j(d)$ is consistent for at least one $d \in B_2$, given the cardinality of G_1 and B_1, is in **NP**.

Proof. Hardness: Weak extensions (extensions) of a default theory correspond to objective parts of stable expansions (N-expansions) of the translated theory [Marek and Truszczyński, 1989; 1993].

Membership: In [Gottlob, 1992] it is shown that deciding if a formula is not occuring in all extensions is in Σ_2^P (using the finitary characterization of Niemelä [1991] with modal subformulae). Consider the propositional language $\{a_1, \ldots, a_n\}$ and any model $\mathcal{M}$ containing some of these atoms. Then $\mathcal{M} \models E$ iff $E \not\models l_1 \vee \ldots \vee l_n$ with $l_i = \neg a_i$ if $a_i \in \mathcal{M}$ and $l_i = a_i$ if $a_i \notin \mathcal{M}$. $\square$

8 Translatability Issues

A pfm-function $f : A \mapsto B$ is a function embedding formalism A into formalism B fulfilling the additional criteria of **p**olynomiality, **f**aithfulness (extensions/expansions coincide in some way) and **m**odularity (a propositional subtheory can independently be translated) [Janhunen, 1998; Gottlob, 1995b].

We refer to [Eiter and Gottlob, 1995] for details of disjunctive logic programming (DLP) (reasoning is as hard as in default logic) and to [Inoue and Sakama, 1993] for results that DLP can be pfm-embedded into default logic.

Theorem 8.1 *Unless the PH collapses, there exists no pfm-function embedding default logic, normal default logic or disjunction-free default logic into DLP.*

Proof. Assume the existence of a pfm-function embedding default logic into disjunctive logic programming; then a given default theory would admit the same models as a pfm-translation into a corresponding disjunctive program. However, as model checking with disjunctive logic programming is only **coNP**-complete, this implies that $\Sigma_2^P = \mathbf{coNP}$. Contradiction. $\square$

9 Future Research

We plan to investigate the complexity of model checking for further interesting variants of default logic and other nonmonotonic logics. We hope that this will allow us to clarify a number of translatability issues, akin the result of Chapter 8.

Acknowledgments

The authors are grateful to C. D. Koutras and R. Rosati for reading an earlier version of this paper and suggesting improvements, and to the referees for several comments.

References

[Cadoli and Schaerf, 1992] M. Cadoli and M. Schaerf. A Survey on Complexity Results for Non-monotonic Logics. *J. Logic Program.* 17 (1993) 127-160.

[Dantsin *et al.*, 1997] E. Dantsin, T. Eiter, G. Gottlob and A. Voronkov. Complexity and Expressive Power of Logic Programming. *Proc. of the IEEE Conf. on Computational Complexity '97* (1997).

[Eiter and Gottlob, 1995] T. Eiter and G. Gottlob. On the computational cost of disjunctive logic programming: Propositional case. *Annals of Math. and AI* 15(3/4) (1995) 289-323.

[Gelfond *et al.*, 1991] M. Gelfond, H. Przymusińska, V. Lifschitz and M. Truszczyński. Disjunctive defaults. *Proc. of KR-2* (1991).

[Gogic *et al.*, 1995] G. Gogic, H. Kautz, C. Papadimitriou, B. Selman. The Comparative Linguistics of Knowledge Representation. *Proc. of IJCAI'95* (1995).

[Gottlob, 1992] G. Gottlob. Complexity Results for Nonmonotonic Logics. *J. Logic and Comput.* 2(3) (1992) 397-425.

[Gottlob, 1995] G. Gottlob. The Complexity of Default Reasoning under the Stationary Fixed Point Semantics. *Inform. and Comput.* 121 (1995) 81-92.

[Gottlob, 1995b] G. Gottlob. Translating Default Logic into Standard Autoepistemic Logic. *J. of the ACM* 42/4 (1995) 712-740.

[Halpern and Vardi, 1991] J. Y. Halpern and M. Y. Vardi. Model Checking vs. Theorem Proving: A Manifesto. *Proc. of KR-2* (1991) 325-333.

[Inoue and Sakama, 1993] K. Inoue and C. Sakama. Relating Disjunctive Logic Programs to Default Theories. *Logic Programming and Non-monotonic Reasoning* (1993) 266-282.

[Janhunen, 1998] T. Janhunen. On the Intertranslatability of Autepistemic, Default and Priority Logics, and Parallel Circumscription. *Proc. of JELIA'98* (1998).

[Kautz and Selman, 1991] H. A. Kautz and B. Selman. Hard Problems for Simple Default Logics. *Artificial Intelligence* 49 (1991) 243-279.

[Liberatore and Schaerf, 1998] P. Liberatore and M. Schaerf. The Complexity of Model Checking for Propositional Default Logics. *Proc. of ECAI'98* (1998).

[Marek and Truszczyński, 1989] W. Marek and M. Truszczyński. Relating Autoepistemic and Default Logic. *Proc. of KR-1* (1990).

[Marek and Truszczyński, 1993] W. Marek and M. Truszczyński. *Nonmonotonic Logics - Context Dependent Reasoning* (1993). Springer Verlag.

[Niemelä, 1991] I. Niemelä. Towards Automatic Autoepistemic Reasoning. In *Logics in AI* (1991) 428-443. Springer Verlag.

[Papadimitriou and Sideri, 1992] C. H. Papadimitriou and M. Sideri. On Finding Extensions of Default Theories. *ICDT '92* (1992) 276-281. Springer LNCS 646.

[Papadimitriou, 1993] C. H. Papadimitriou. *Computational Complexity* (1993). Addison Wesley.

[Reiter, 1980] R. Reiter. A logic for Default Reasoning, *Artificial Intelligence* 13 (1980) 81-132.

[Stillman, 1990] J. Stillman. It's not my Default: The Complexity of Membership Problems in Restricted Propositional Default Logic. *Proc. of AAAI-90* (1990) 571-578.

[Stillman, 1992] J. Stillman. The Complexity of Propositional Default Logics. *Proc. of AAAI-92* (1992) 794-799.

[Wagner, 1990] K. Wagner. Bounded query classes. *SIAM J. Comput.* 19(5) (1990) 833-846.

Stable Model Checking Made Easy*

Christoph Koch and Nicola Leone
Information Systems Dept.
Technical University of Vienna
A-1040 Vienna, Austria
{koch, leone}@dbai.tuwien.ac.at

Abstract

Disjunctive logic programming (DLP) with stable model semantics is a powerful nonmonotonic formalism for knowledge representation and reasoning. Reasoning with DLP is harder than with normal (∨-free) logic programs; because *stable model checking* – deciding whether a given model is a stable model of a propositional DLP program – is co-NP-complete, while it is polynomial for normal logic programs.

This paper proposes a new transformation $\Gamma_M(\mathcal{P})$, which reduces stable model checking to UNSAT – i.e., to deciding whether a given CNF formula is unsatisfiable. Thus, the stability of a model M for a program $\mathcal{P}$ can be verified by calling a Satisfiability Checker on the CNF formula $\Gamma_M(\mathcal{P})$. The transformation is parsimonious and efficiently computable, as it runs in logarithmic space. Moreover, the size of the generated CNF formula never exceeds the size of the input.

The proposed approach to stable model checking has been implemented in a DLP system, and a number of experiments and benchmarks have been run.

1 Introduction

Disjunctive logic programming (DLP) with stable model semantics is a powerful nonmonotonic formalism for knowledge representation and commonsense reasoning [Baral and Gelfond, 1994; Lobo *et. al.*, 1992]. DLP has a very high expressive power [Eiter *et. al.*, 1997a], and it allows to represent complex problems in a simple and easy-to-understand fashion [Eiter *et. al.*, 1998]. As for the other main nonmonotonic formalisms, reasoning with DLP (under stable model semantics) is very hard. The high complexity of DLP reasoning depends also on the hardness of *stable model checking* – deciding whether a given model is a stable model of a propositional DLP program – which is co-NP-complete. The hardness of

---

*Research supported by FWF (Austrian Science Fund) under the projects P11580-MAT and Z29-INF.

this problem has discouraged the implementation of DLP engines. Indeed, at the time being only one system, namely the `dlv` system [Eiter *et. al.*, 1998], is available which fully supports (function-free) DLP with stable model semantics.

This paper proposes a new transformation, which reduces stable model checking to UNSAT – i.e., to deciding whether a given CNF formula is unsatisfiable – the complement of Satisfiability, a problem for which very efficient systems have been developed in AI.

Besides providing an elegant characterization of stable models, which sheds new light on their intrinsic nature, the proposed transformation has also a strong practical impact. Indeed, by using this transformation, the huge amount of work done in AI on the design and implementation of efficient algorithms for checking Satisfiability can be profitably used for the implementation of DLP engines supporting stable model semantics. Thus, this transformation opens "new frontiers" in the implementation of Disjunctive Logic Programming which can benefit now from efficient AI techniques and implementations.

We have implemented the proposed technique in the DLP system `dlv`, and we have run a number of experiments and benchmarks.

In sum, the main contributions of this paper are the following:

• We define a new transformation from stable model checking for general DLP with negation to UNSAT of propositional CNF formulas. The transformation is parsimonious (i.e., it does not add any new symbol) and efficiently computable, since it runs in logspace (and, therefore, in polynomial time). Moreover, the size of the generated CNF formula never exceeds the size of the input (it is usually much smaller).

• We realize our approach in the DLP system `dlv`, by using an implementation of the Davis-Putnam procedure as the Satisfiability checker.

Our implementation exploits also novel modular evaluation techniques, which follow from our main results.

• We carry out an experimental activity which witnesses the efficiency of our approach to stable model checking.

It is worth noting that, since stable model checking of DLP programs generalizes minimal model checking for Horn CNF formulas, our results can be employed also for reasoning with minimal models and with circumscription.

The dlv system, which implements the results described in this paper, can be downloaded from www.dbai.tuwien.ac.at/proj/dlv. From the same Web page, one can also retrieve the benchmark problems that we used in our experiments.

The remainder of the paper is organized as follows: Setions 2 and 3 contain preliminary notions on DLP, stable model semantics, and its characterization in terms of unfounded sets. Section 4 describes our new reduction from stable model checking to UNSAT. Section 5 reports on our experiments.

2 Disjunctive Logic Programming with Stable Model Semantics

In this section, we provide an overview of disjunctive logic programming with stable model semantics. (For further details, see [Lobo *et. al.*, 1992].)

The terms of the language are inductively defined. A variable or constant is a *term*; a function symbol with terms as arguments is a term. An *atom* is $a(t_1, ..., t_n)$, where a is a *predicate* of arity n and $t_1, ..., t_n$ are terms. A *literal* is either a *positive literal* p or a *negative literal* $\neg p$, where p is an atom.

A *(disjunctive) rule* r is a clause of the form

$$a_1 \vee \cdots \vee a_n \leftarrow b_1 \wedge \cdots \wedge b_k \wedge \neg b_{k+1} \wedge \cdots \wedge \neg b_m \quad n \geq 1, \, m \geq 0$$

where $a_1, \cdots, a_n, b_1, \cdots, b_m$ are atoms. The disjunction $a_1 \vee \cdots \vee a_n$ is the *head* of r, while the conjunction $b_1 \wedge ... \wedge b_k \wedge \neg b_{k+1} \wedge ... \wedge \neg b_m$ is the *body* of r. We denote by $H(r)$ the set $\{a_1, ..., a_n\}$ of the head atoms, and by $B(r)$ the set $\{b_1, ..., b_k, \neg b_{k+1}, ..., \neg b_m\}$ of the body literals. $B^+(r)$ (resp., $B^-(r)$) denotes the set of atoms occurring positively (resp., negatively) in $B(r)$. A *(disjunctive) program* (also called DLP program) is a set of rules. A $\neg$-free (resp., $\vee$-free) program is called *positive* (resp., *normal*). A term, an atom, a literal, a rule, or a program is *ground* if no variables appear in it. A finite ground program is also called a *propositional* program. A *function-free* program is a finite program where no function symbol occurs.

Let $\mathcal{P}$ be a program. The *Herbrand universe* and the *Herbrand base* of $\mathcal{P}$ are defined in the standard way and denoted by $U_{\mathcal{P}}$ and $B_{\mathcal{P}}$, respectively. Given a rule r occurring in a $\mathcal{P}$, a *ground instance* of r is a rule obtained from r by replacing every variable X in r by $\sigma(X)$, where σ is a mapping from the variables occurring in r to the terms in $U_{\mathcal{P}}$. We denote by *ground*($\mathcal{P}$) the set of all the ground instances of the rules occurring in $\mathcal{P}$.

An *interpretation* for $\mathcal{P}$ is a set of ground atoms, that is, an interpretation is a subset I of $B_{\mathcal{P}}$. A ground positive literal A is *true* (resp., *false*) w.r.t. I if $A \in I$ (resp., $A \notin I$). A ground negative literal $\neg A$ is *true* w.r.t. I if A is false w.r.t. I; otherwise $\neg A$ is false w.r.t. I.

Let r be a ground rule in *ground*($\mathcal{P}$). The head of r is *true* w.r.t. I if $H(r) \cap I \neq \emptyset$. The body of r is *true* w.r.t. I if all body literals of r are true w.r.t. I (i.e.,

$B^+(r) \subseteq I$ and $B^-(r) \cap I \neq \emptyset$) and is *false* w.r.t. I otherwise. The rule r is *satisfied* (or *true*) w.r.t. I if its head is true w.r.t. I or its body is false w.r.t. I.

A *model* for $\mathcal{P}$ is an interpretation M for $\mathcal{P}$ such that every rule $r \in$ *ground*($\mathcal{P}$) is true w.r.t. M. A model M for $\mathcal{P}$ is *minimal* if no model N for $\mathcal{P}$ exists such that N is a proper subset of M. The set of all minimal models for $\mathcal{P}$ is denoted by MM($\mathcal{P}$).

A generally acknowledged semantics for DLP programs is the extension of the stable model semantics to take into account disjunction [Gelfond and Lifschitz, 1991; Przymusinski, 1991]. Given a program $\mathcal{P}$ and an interpretation I, the *Gelfond-Lifschitz (GL) transformation* of $\mathcal{P}$ w.r.t. I, denoted $\mathcal{P}^I$, is the set of positive rules defined as follows:

$$\mathcal{P}^I = \{ \; a_1 \vee \cdots \vee a_n \leftarrow b_1 \wedge \cdots \wedge b_k \; | \;$$
$$a_1 \vee \cdots \vee a_n \leftarrow b_1 \wedge \cdots \wedge b_k \wedge \neg b_{k+1} \wedge \cdots \wedge \neg b_m$$
$$\text{is in ground}(\mathcal{P}) \text{ and } b_i \notin I, \text{ for all } k < i \leq m \}$$

Definition 2.1 [Przymusinski, 1991; Gelfond and Lifschitz, 1991] Let I be an interpretation for a program $\mathcal{P}$. I is a *stable model* for $\mathcal{P}$ if $I \in$ MM($\mathcal{P}^I$) (i.e., I is a minimal model of the positive program $\mathcal{P}^I$). □

Example 2.2 Let $P = \{a \vee b \leftarrow c; \quad b \leftarrow \neg a \wedge \neg c; \quad a \vee c \leftarrow \neg b\}$ and $I = \{b\}$. Then, $P^I = \{a \vee b \leftarrow c; \quad b \leftarrow\}$.

It is easy to verify that I is a minimal model for P^I; thus, I is a stable model for P. □

Clearly, if $\mathcal{P}$ is positive, then $\mathcal{P}^I$ coincides with *ground*($\mathcal{P}$). It turns out that for a positive program, minimal and stable models coincide.

3 Stable Models and Unfounded Sets

Next, we present a characterization of the stable models of disjunctive logic programs in terms of unfounded sets. This characterization will be used to prove the correctness of our reduction from stable model checking to UNSAT in the next section.

The characterization presented here is obtained by slight modifications of the results presented in [Leone *et. al.*, 1997]. In particular, providing the notion of unfounded sets directly for total (2-valued) interpretations, we obtain a simpler characterization than in [Leone *et. al.*, 1997], where unfounded sets were defined w.r.t. partial (3-valued) interpretations.

Definition 3.1 (Definition 3.1 in [Leone *et. al.*, 1997]) Let I be an interpretation for a program $\mathcal{P}$. A set $X \subseteq B_{\mathcal{P}}$ of ground atoms is an *unfounded set* for $\mathcal{P}$ w.r.t. I if, for each rule $r \in$ *ground*($\mathcal{P}$) such that $X \cap H(r) \neq \emptyset$, at least one of the following conditions holds:
1. $(B^+(r) \nsubseteq I) \vee (B^-(r) \cap I \neq \emptyset)$, that is the body of r is false w.r.t. I.
2. $B^+(r) \cap X \neq \emptyset$, that is, some positive body literal belongs to X.
3. $(H(r) - X) \cap I \neq \emptyset$, that is, an atom in the head of r, distinct from the elements in X, is true w.r.t. I. □

Input: A ground DLP program $\mathcal{P}$ and a model M for $\mathcal{P}$.
Output: A propositional CNF formula $\Gamma_M(\mathcal{P})$ over M.
var $\mathcal{P}'$: DLP Program; S: Set of Clauses;
begin
1. Delete from $\mathcal{P}$ each rule whose body is false
   w.r.t. M;
2. Remove all negative literals from the (bodies of the)
   remaining rules;
3. Remove all false atoms (w.r.t. M) from the heads
   of the resulting rules;
4. $S := \emptyset$;
5. Let $\mathcal{P}'$ be the program resulting from steps 1–3;
6. **for** each rule $a_1 \vee \cdots \vee a_n \leftarrow b_1 \wedge \cdots \wedge b_m$ in $\mathcal{P}'$ **do**
7. $\qquad S := S \cup \{ \; b_1 \vee \cdots \vee b_m \leftarrow a_1 \wedge \cdots \wedge a_n \; \}$;
8. **end for**;
9. $\Gamma_M(\mathcal{P}) := \bigwedge_{c \in S} c \; \wedge \; (\bigvee_{x \in M} x)$;
10. **output** $\Gamma_M(\mathcal{P})$
end.

Figure 1: *The transformation $\Gamma_M(\mathcal{P})$*

Definition 3.2 An interpretation I for a program $\mathcal{P}$ is
unfounded-free iff no nonempty subset of I is an unfounded set for $\mathcal{P}$ w.r.t. I. □

The unfounded-free condition singles out precisely the
stable models.

Theorem 3.3 *(Theorem 4.6 in [Leone et. al., 1997])*
Let M be a model for a program $\mathcal{P}$. M is a stable model
for $\mathcal{P}$ iff M is unfounded-free.

Example 3.4 Let $\mathcal{P} = \{a \vee b \leftarrow\}$. $M_1 = \{a\}$ is a
stable model of $\mathcal{P}$, since there is no nonempty subset of
M_1 which is an unfounded set. On the other hand, for
$M_2 = \{a, b\}$, due to Condition 3, both $\{a\}$ and $\{b\}$ are
unfounded sets. M_2 is not unfounded-free, and therefore,
it is not a stable model. □

4   From Stable Model Checking to UNSAT

In this section we present a reduction from stable model
checking to UNSAT, the complement of Satisfiability, a
problem which is better explored in AI and for which
efficient algorithms and systems are available.

Recall that a CNF formula over a set A of atomic
propositions is a conjunction of the form $\phi = c_1 \wedge \cdots \wedge$
c_n, where $c_1, \cdots, c_n$ are clauses over A. Without loss of
generality, in this paper a clause $c = a_1 \vee \cdots \vee a_m \vee \neg b_1 \vee$
$\cdots \vee \neg b_r$ will be written as $a_1 \vee \cdots \vee a_m \leftarrow b_1 \wedge \cdots \wedge b_r$;
thus, a CNF ϕ will be a conjunction of these implications.

A formula ϕ is *satisfiable* if there exists a truth assignment to the propositions of A which makes ϕ true;
otherwise, ϕ is *unsatisfiable* (or *inconsistent*).
UNSAT is the following decision problem.

> Given a CNF formula ϕ, is it true that ϕ is
> unsatisfiable?

Our reduction from stable model checking to UNSAT
is implemented by the algorithm shown in Figure 1.

Example 4.1 Let $\mathcal{P} = \{a \vee b \vee c \leftarrow; \quad a \leftarrow b; \quad a \leftarrow$
$c; \quad b \leftarrow a \wedge \neg c\}$. Consider model $M_1 = \{a, b\}$ of $\mathcal{P}$.

In the first step of the algorithm shown in Figure 1, the
rule $a \leftarrow c$ is deleted. In the second step, $\neg c$ is removed
from the body of the last rule of $\mathcal{P}$; while the third step
removes c from the head of the first rule. Thus, after Step
3, the program becomes $\{a \vee b \leftarrow; \quad a \leftarrow b; \quad b \leftarrow a\}$.
Steps 4 to 8 switch the bodies and the heads of the rules,
yielding the set of clauses $S = \{\leftarrow a \wedge b; \quad b \leftarrow a; \quad a \leftarrow$
$b\}$. Finally, Step 9 constructs the conjunction of the
clauses in S plus the clause $a \vee b \leftarrow$. Therefore, the
output of the algorithm is $(\leftarrow a \wedge b) \bigwedge (b \leftarrow a) \bigwedge (a \leftarrow$
$b) \bigwedge (a \vee b \leftarrow)$.
Now consider model $M_2 = \{a, c\}$. Here, the first three
steps simplify $\mathcal{P}$ to $\{a \vee c \leftarrow; \quad a \leftarrow c\}$. Steps 4 to 8
swap the heads and bodies of the rules to get $\{\leftarrow a \wedge$
$c; \quad c \leftarrow a\}$, and Step 9 adds $a \vee c \leftarrow$. So the outcome
for M_2 is $(\leftarrow a \wedge c) \bigwedge (c \leftarrow a) \bigwedge (a \vee c \leftarrow)$. □

Theorem 4.2 *Given a model M for a ground DLP pro-*
gram $\mathcal{P}$, let $\Gamma_M(\mathcal{P})$ be the CNF formula computed by the
algorithm of Figure 1 on input $\mathcal{P}$ and M.
Then, M is a stable model for $\mathcal{P}$ if and only if $\Gamma_M(\mathcal{P})$ is
unsatisfiable.

In the remainder of this section we demonstrate The-
orem 4.2 (i.e., we show the correctness of our $\Gamma_M(\mathcal{P})$
reduction). For space limitation, we do not include the
proofs of the two lemmas here; but we illustrate their
validity on a running example.

To better illustrate the $\Gamma_M(\mathcal{P})$ transformation, we proceed in an incremental way, dividing the transformation
into three steps, and showing the correctness of each of
them.

Definition 4.3 Let $\mathcal{P}$ be a ground DLP program and
M be a model for $\mathcal{P}$. Define the *simplified version* $\alpha_M(\mathcal{P})$
of $\mathcal{P}$ w.r.t M as:

$$\alpha_M(\mathcal{P}) = \{ \; \bigvee_{x \in (H(r) \cap M)} x \leftarrow \bigwedge_{x \in B^+(r)} x \mid \; r \in \mathcal{P},$$
$$\text{the body of } r \text{ is true w.r.t. M} \} \quad □$$

Thus, $\alpha_M(\mathcal{P})$ coincides with the program $\mathcal{P}'$ obtained
by steps 1–3 of Figure 1. Observe that every rule in
$\alpha_M(\mathcal{P})$ has a non-empty head. Indeed, if $\alpha_M(\mathcal{P})$ would
contain a rule r with an empty head, then M would not
be a model for $\mathcal{P}$, as the rule of $\mathcal{P}$ corresponding to r
would have a true body and a false head. Moreover, the
simplified program $\alpha_M(\mathcal{P})$ is positive ($\neg$-free) and it only
contains atoms that are true w.r.t. M.

Next, we observe that $\alpha_M(\mathcal{P})$ is equivalent to $\mathcal{P}$ as far
as the stability of M is concerned.

Lemma 4.4 *Let $\mathcal{P}$ be a DLP program and M be a model*
for $\mathcal{P}$. Then, M is a stable model for $\mathcal{P}$ if and only if it
is a stable model for $\alpha_M(\mathcal{P})$.

Example 4.5 Take $\mathcal{P}$ and the two models M_1 and M_2
from Example 4.1. M_1 is a stable model for $\mathcal{P}$, while
M_2 is not. Indeed, M_1 is a stable model for $\alpha_{M_1}(\mathcal{P}) =$
$\{a \vee b \leftarrow; \quad a \leftarrow b; \quad b \leftarrow a\}$ and M_2 is not a stable
model for $\alpha_{M_2}(\mathcal{P}) = \{a \vee c \leftarrow; \quad a \leftarrow c\}$. □

Next, we show that by simply swapping the heads and
bodies of the rules of the simplified program $\alpha_M(\mathcal{P})$, we

get a set of clauses whose models correspond to the unfounded sets of $\mathcal{P}$ w.r.t. M.

Definition 4.6 Let $\mathcal{P}$ be a DLP program and M be a model for $\mathcal{P}$. Define $\beta_M(\mathcal{P})$ as the following set of clauses over M:

$$\beta_M(\mathcal{P}) = \{ \bigvee_{x \in B(r)} x \leftarrow \bigwedge_{x \in H(r)} x \mid r \in \alpha_M(\mathcal{P}) \} \qquad \square$$

Observe that $\beta_M(\mathcal{P})$ coincides with the set of clauses S constructed after steps 1–8 of Figure 1.

Lemma 4.7 *Let $\mathcal{P}$ be a ground DLP program, M be a model for $\mathcal{P}$, and $X \subseteq M$. Then X is a model for $\beta_M(\mathcal{P})$ iff it is an unfounded set for $\mathcal{P}$ w.r.t. M.*

Example 4.8 $\beta_{M_1}(\mathcal{P})$ is $\{\leftarrow a \wedge b; \quad b \leftarrow a; \quad a \leftarrow b\}$, The only subset of M_1 which is a model for $\beta_{M_1}(\mathcal{P})$ is $\emptyset$. Indeed, $\emptyset$ is the only unfounded set for $\mathcal{P}$ w.r.t. M_1 (contained in M_1).

$\beta_{M_2}(\mathcal{P})$ is equal to $\{\leftarrow a \wedge c; \quad c \leftarrow a\}$. $\emptyset$ and $\{c\}$ are the subsets of M_2 which are models of $\beta_{M_2}(\mathcal{P})$. Indeed, they are precisely the unfounded sets for $\mathcal{P}$ w.r.t. M_2 (contained in M_2). $\qquad \square$

We are now in a position to demonstrate our main theorem.

Proof of Theorem 4.2 *(Sketch)* In the following, we show that $\Gamma_M(\mathcal{P})$ is unsatisfiable iff $\mathcal{P}$ is unfounded-free; the statement will then follow from Theorem 3.3.

It is easy to see that the output $\Gamma_M(\mathcal{P})$ of the algorithm of Figure 1 coincides with the conjunction of all clauses in $\beta_M(\mathcal{P})$ and the clause $\bigvee_{x \in M} x$. From Lemma 4.7, the models of $\beta_M(\mathcal{P})$ are precisely the unfounded sets of $\mathcal{P}$ w.r.t. M. Therefore, the models of $\Gamma_M(\mathcal{P})$ are exactly the non-empty unfounded sets of $\mathcal{P}$ w.r.t. M, since every model of $\Gamma_M(\mathcal{P})$ must satisfy also the clause $\bigvee_{x \in M} x$. Thus, M contains no *nonempty* unfounded set for $\mathcal{P}$ (i.e., it is unfounded-free) iff $\Gamma_M(\mathcal{P})$ has no model (i.e., it is unsatisfiable). $\qquad \square$

Example 4.9 $M_1 = \{a, b\}$ is a stable model for $\mathcal{P}$. Indeed, $\Gamma_{M_1}(\mathcal{P}) = (\leftarrow a \wedge b) \bigwedge (b \leftarrow a) \bigwedge (a \leftarrow b) \bigwedge (a \vee b \leftarrow)$ is unsatisfiable.

Differently, $M_2 = \{a, c\}$ is not stable for $\mathcal{P}$. Indeed, $\Gamma_{M_2}(\mathcal{P}) = (\leftarrow a \wedge c) \bigwedge (c \leftarrow a) \bigwedge (a \vee c \leftarrow)$ is satisfied by model $\{c\}$. $\qquad \square$

The next theorem shows that $\Gamma_M(\mathcal{P})$ is also an efficient transformation.

Theorem 4.10 *Given a model M for a ground DLP program $\mathcal{P}$, let $\Gamma_M(\mathcal{P})$ be the CNF formula computed by the algorithm of Figure 1 on input $\mathcal{P}$ and M. Then, the following holds.*

1. *$\Gamma_M(\mathcal{P})$ is logspace computable from $\mathcal{P}$ and M.*

2. *$\Gamma_M(\mathcal{P})$ is a parsimonious transformation.*

3. *$|\Gamma_M(\mathcal{P})| \leq |\mathcal{P}| + |M|$.*

Proof *(Sketch)* $\Gamma_M(\mathcal{P})$ is the conjunction of the clauses in $\beta_M(\mathcal{P})$ plus the disjunction of the propositions in M. The size of $\beta_M(\mathcal{P})$ is equal to the size of $\alpha_M(\mathcal{P})$, which is smaller than the size of $\mathcal{P}$. Thus, $|\Gamma_M(\mathcal{P})| \leq |\mathcal{P}| + |M|$.

$\Gamma_M(\mathcal{P})$ is clearly parsimonious, as it is a formula over the propositions of M only.

Finally, it is easy to see that $\Gamma_M(\mathcal{P})$ can be computed by a logspace Turing Machine. Indeed, $\Gamma_M(\mathcal{P})$ can be generated by dealing with one rule of $\mathcal{P}$ at a time, without storing any intermediate data apart from a (fixed) number of indices. $\qquad \square$

5 Implementation and Benchmarks

In order to check the concrete usability of our results, we have implemented our approach to stable model checking in the disjunctive logic programming system `dlv` [Eiter *et. al.*, 1997b; 1998].

`dlv` is a knowledge representation system which has been developed at Technische Universität Wien. Recent comparisons [Eiter *et. al.*, 1998] have shown that `dlv` is nowadays a state-of-the-art implementation of disjunctive logic programming. To our knowledge, `dlv` is the only publicly available system which supports full (function-free) disjunctive logic programming under stable model semantics.

The computational engine of `dlv` implements the theoretical results achieved in [Leone *et. al.*, 1997]. Roughly, the system consists of two main modules: the Model Generator (MG) and the Model Checker (MC). MG produces stable model candidates, whose stability is then checked by the MC.

We have replaced the Model Checker of `dlv` by new modules implementing the results of the previous section, running some benchmark problems and comparing the execution times.

Overview of the Compared Methods

We have compared the following methods for stable model checking (the labels below are used in Figures 2, 3, and 4).

• (Old Checker.) The old model checker of the `dlv` system [Leone *et. al.*, 1997; Eiter *et. al.*, 1997b]. Its strong points are the efficient evaluation of head cycle free (HCF) programs [Ben-Eliyahu and Dechter, 1994] and the use of modular evaluation techniques. Indeed, HCF programs are evaluated in polynomial time and, if the program is not HCF, the inefficient part of the computation is limited only to the subprograms[1] which are not HCF (while the polynomial time algorithm is applied to the HCF subprograms). Polynomial space and single exponential time bounds are always guaranteed.

• (Γ_M+DP.) Given a program $\mathcal{P}$ and a model M to be checked for stability, an implementation of the algorithm of Figure 1 generates the CNF formula $\Gamma_M(\mathcal{P})$, which is then submitted to a Satisfiability checker. If the Satisfiability checker returns true ($\Gamma_M(\mathcal{P})$ is satisfiable), then M is not a stable model of $\mathcal{P}$; otherwise ($\Gamma_M(\mathcal{P})$ is unsatisfiable), M is a stable model of $\mathcal{P}$. For checking

---

[1] A subprogram of $\mathcal{P}$ is the set of rules defining the atoms of the same strongly connected component of the dependency graph of $\mathcal{P}$ [Leone *et. al.*, 1997].

Satisfiability of $\Gamma_M(\mathcal{P})$, we have used an efficient implementation of the Davis-Putnam procedure called SATO [Zhang, 1997].

- (Γ_M+DP+Mod.) This is an improved version of the method above, enhanced by modular evaluation techniques derived from the combination of Lemma 4.4 with the modularity results of [Leone *et. al.*, 1997]. Roughly, given $\mathcal{P}$ and M, $\mathcal{P}$ is first simplified (steps 1–3 of Figure 1) computing the program $\alpha_M(\mathcal{P})$. The subprograms of $\alpha_M(\mathcal{P})$ are then evaluated one-at-a-time. A polynomial time method is applied to HCF subprograms (as in *Old Checker*); while the Γ_M+DP method is applied to non-HCF subprograms.

Benchmark Problem

In order to generate some co-NP-hard model checking instances, which could better highlight the differences between the model checking techniques, we needed to run Σ_2^P-hard problems on the DLP system at hand. Thus, we have compared the performance of the different model checking methods by running various instances of the Σ_2^P-complete problem *Strategic Companies* on the `dlv` system.

The strategic companies problem is from [Cadoli *et. al.*, 1997]; it is, to the best of our knowledge, the only Σ_2^P-complete KR problem from the business domain. No experimental results for any Σ_2^P-complete KR problems are known.

Briefly, a holding owns companies, each of which produces some goods. Moreover, several companies may have joint control over another company. Now, some companies should be sold, under the constraint that all goods can be still produced, and that no company is sold which would still be controlled by the holding after the transaction. A company is *strategic*, if it belongs to a *strategic set*, which is a minimal set of companies satisfying these constraints. Those sets are expressed by the following natural program:

```
strategic(C1) ∨ strategic(C2) ←
     produced_by(P,C1,C2).
strategic(C) ← controlled_by(C,C1,C2,C3) ∧
     strategic(C1) ∧ strategic(C2) ∧
     strategic(C3).
```

Here $\mathtt{strategic}(C)$ means that C is strategic, $\mathtt{produced\_by}(P,C1,C2)$ that product P is produced by companies $C1$ and $C2$, and $\mathtt{controlled\_by}(C,C1,C2,C3)$ that C is jointly controlled by $C1,C2$ and $C3$; we have adopted here from [Cadoli *et. al.*, 1997] that each product is produced by at most two companies and each company is under joint control of at most three other companies.

The problem is to find out the set of all strategic companies (i.e., under brave reasoning, for which C the fact $\mathtt{strategic}(C)$ is true).

Note that this problem cannot be expressed by a fixed normal (∨-free) logic program uniformly on all collections of facts $\mathtt{produced\_by}(p,c1,c2)$ and $\mathtt{controlled\_by}(c,c1,c2,c3)$ (unless NP $= \Sigma_2^P$, an unlikely event). Thus, Strategic Companies is an example of a relevant problem where the expressive power of disjunctive logic programming is really needed.

Benchmark Data

We have generated tests with instances for n companies and $3n$ products.

We have uniform randomly chosen the `produced_by` and the `controlled_by` relations, where each company is controlled by one to five companies (Obeying the obvious constraints that no company can control itself, and that two consortia have to have at least one member in common). On average there are 1.5 `controlled_by` relationships per company.

Discussion of Results

Our experiments were run on a 133 MHz i486-compatible PC under Linux, using egcs-2.91.14 C++ compiler.

The results are displayed in the graphs of Figures 2– 4. Execution times are reported on the vertical axis, while the horizontal axis displays the size of the problem instance (number of companies of the instance of Strategic Companies to be solved). We have run instances of a size increasing a step of 5 companies, up to 100 companies.

The graph of Figure 2 shows the total time employed by the (stable) Model Checkers for the computation of all stable models of the program (i.e., for the generation of all sets of strategic companies). Note that a program having n stable models requires $m \geq n$ calls to the Model Checker ($m - n$ is the number of calls on models which are not stable); the sum of the times employed for checking the stability of all m models is displayed in the graph. For each problem size (number of companies) x, we have run 25 instances of size x and reported the average time. Thus, this graph shows the practical impact of the various model checking strategies on the computation.

Γ_M+DP clearly outperforms `Old Checker`: the time employed by Γ_M+DP to solve an instance of 100 companies is not sufficient for `Old Checker` even to solve instances of 25 companies. Interestingly, modular evaluation techniques appear very useful: Γ_M+DP+Mod takes less than 5% of Γ_M+DP to solve problems of size 100.

The graph in Figure 3 refers to the same runs of the previous graph; but it shows the longest times required

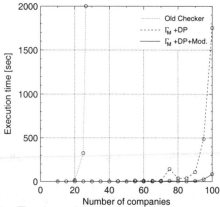

Figure 2: Total model checking time required for the computation of all stable models

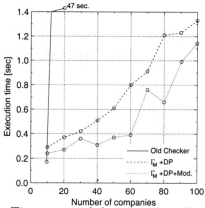

Figure 3: Time required for a single call to the MC (worst case)

by each method for checking the stability of a single model. This time, the curves are not very regular, because they visualize times of single calls (rather than average times as in Figure 2) of randomly generated instances. Also in this graph the new strategies show better performances than the old `dlv` checker. Surprisingly, the difference between the times of Γ_M+DP and Γ_M+DP+Mod is much smaller than in the previous graph. We have the following explanation for this phenomenon. Modular evaluation techniques speed up the computation of most instances. (Thus, modularity significantly affects total model checking time.) However, very hard instances cannot be "decomposed" by modular evaluation techniques. (Thus, the worst case times for single calls to the model checker are similar.)

Finally, the graph in Figure 4 refers to the computation of *one* stable model (i.e., to the computation of one set of strategic companies – sufficient to solve the corresponding Σ_2^P decision problem). It compares the overall execution time (model generation + model checking time) taken by the `dlv` system when the (old) model checker is replaced by our new model checkers. The advantage of using Γ_M+DP+Mod is very evident: by using Γ_M+DP+Mod an instance of size 100 is solved more quickly than an instance of size 20 with the old system. This graph also shows the time taken by `dlv` for model generation alone. Most of the execution time needed for

computing one stable model is consumed for the generation of the models; only a very low percentage of the time is consumed by the Model Checker Γ_M+DP+Mod itself.

In conclusion, observe that we have also compared the model checking strategies on a number of problems "easier" than Stategic Companies (at most NP-complete); as expected, the methods behaved very similarly.

References

[Apt and Bol, 1994] K.R. Apt, R.N. Bol (1994), Logic Programming and Negation: A Survey, *Journal of Logic Programming*, **19/20**, 9–71.

[Baral and Gelfond, 1994] C. Baral, M. Gelfond (1994), Logic Programming and Knowledge Representation *Journal of Logic Programming*, **19/20**, 73–148.

[Ben-Eliyahu and Dechter, 1994] R. Ben-Eliyahu, R. Dechter (1994), Propositional Semantics for Disjunctive Logic Programs, *Annals of Mathematics and Artificial Intelligence*, Baltzer, **12**, pp. 53–87.

[Cadoli *et. al.*, 1997] M. Cadoli, T. Eiter, G. Gottlob. (1997), Default Logic as a Query Language. *IEEE-TKDE*, 9(3):448-463.

[Eiter *et. al.*, 1997a] T. Eiter, G. Gottlob, H. Mannila. (1997) Disjunctive Datalog. *ACM-TODS*, 22(3):315–363.

[Eiter *et. al.*, 1997b] T. Eiter, N. Leone, C. Mateis, G. Pfeifer, F. Scarcello. (1997) A Deductive System for Nonmonotonic Reasoning. *Proc. LPNMR'97*, pp. 363-374.

[Eiter *et. al.*, 1998] T. Eiter, N. Leone, C. Mateis, G. Pfeifer, F. Scarcello. The KR System `dlv`: Progress Report, Comparisons and Benchmarks. *Proc. KR'98*, pp. 406-417.

[Gelfond and Lifschitz, 1991] M. Gelfond, V. Lifschitz (1991), Classical Negation in Logic Programs and Disjunctive Databases, *New Generation Computing*, **9**, 365–385.

[Gottlob, 1992] G. Gottlob. (1992) Complexity Results for Nonmonotonic Logics. *Journal of Logic and Computation*, 2(3):397–425.

[Leone *et. al.*, 1997] N. Leone, P. Rullo, F. Scarcello. (1997) Disjunctive stable models: Unfounded sets, fixpoint semantics and computation. *Information and Computation*, 135(2):69–112.

[Lobo *et. al.*, 1992] J. Lobo, J. Minker, A. Rajasekar (1992), "Foundations of disjunctive logic programming," The MIT Press.

[Przymusinski, 1991] T. Przymusinski. (1991), Stable Semantics for Disjunctive Programs, *New Generation Computing*, **9**, 401–424.

[Zhang, 1997] H. Zhang. (1997), SATO: An Efficient Propositional Prover. *Proc. CADE-97*.

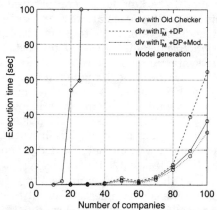

Figure 4: Overall time to compute one stable model

Model checking for nonmonotonic logics: algorithms and complexity

Riccardo Rosati

Dipartimento di Informatica e Sistemistica

Università di Roma "La Sapienza"

Via Salaria 113, 00198 Roma, Italy

rosati@dis.uniroma1.it

Abstract

We study the complexity of model checking in propositional nonmonotonic logics. Specifically, we first define the problem of model checking in such formalisms, based on the fact that several nonmonotonic logics make use of interpretation structures (i.e. default extensions, stable expansions, universal Kripke models) which are more complex than standard interpretations of propositional logic. Then, we analyze the complexity of checking whether a given interpretation structure satisfies a nonmonotonic theory. In particular, we characterize the complexity of model checking for Reiter's default logic and its restrictions, Moore's autoepistemic logic, and several nonmonotonic modal logics. The results obtained show that, in all such formalisms, model checking is computationally easier than logical inference.

1 Introduction

In recent years the problem of model checking has been widely studied in knowledge representation and AI [Levesque, 1986; Halpern and Vardi, 1991]. Informally, model checking for a logical formalism L corresponds to the following problem: given an interpretation structure I and a logical formula Σ, does I satisfy Σ according to the semantics of L?

Model checking has been convincingly advocated as an alternative to classical reasoning, i.e. logical inference. The main advantage of model checking lies in the fact that in general it is computationally easier than logical inference: For instance, it is well-known that, in first-order logic, model checking is polynomial in the size of the interpretation structure. Besides "classical" application domains (like hardware verification), model checking techniques have been recently employed in the field of planning and cognitive robotics [Cimatti *et al.*, 1997].

Lately, model checking has been studied in some propositional nonmonotonic settings [Cadoli, 1992; Liberatore and Schaerf, 1998]. In particular, [Liberatore and Schaerf, 1998] analyze the problem of checking whether a classical (propositional) interpretation "satisfies" a given default theory, in the sense that such interpretation satisfies at least one extension of the default theory.

The results obtained show that for propositional default logic this kind of model checking is in general as hard as logical inference, hence the computational advantages of model checking over theorem proving do not seem to hold in the case of default logic.

The work presented in this paper originates from a different definition of model checking for default logic and several other nonmonotonic logics. Such a notion is an immediate consequence of the fact that many nonmonotonic formalisms make use of interpretation structures (i.e. default extensions, autoepistemic expansions, universal Kripke models) which are more complex than standard interpretations of classical logic, and which can be represented in a compact way by means of logical formulas. Hence, we argue that model checking in such frameworks corresponds to verify whether a given interpretation structure of this form satisfies a nonmonotonic theory, according to the semantics of the formalism. E.g., according to this notion, a *model* of a default theory is a default extension, and model checking for propositional default logic corresponds to verify whether a given propositional *formula* represents an extension of a given default theory. Hence, the notion of model checking in such nonmonotonic formalisms is peculiar in the sense that the interpretation structure is represented by means of a logical formula.

We thus provide a computational analysis of the above notion of model checking for several propositional nonmonotonic logics. In particular, we characterize the complexity of model checking in Reiter's default logic [Reiter, 1980], *disjunctive* default logic [Gelfond *et al.*, 1991], and for several syntactic restrictions of such formalisms; we also study model checking in Moore's autoepistemic logic AEL [Moore, 1985], and in several other nonmonotonic modal logics, including McDermott and Doyle's (MDD) modal logics [Marek and Truszczyński, 1993], the modal logic of minimal knowledge $S5_G$ [Halpern and Moses, 1985], and the logic of minimal knowledge and negation as failure MKNF [Lifschitz, 1991].

Our analysis shows that the problem of model checking is easier than logical inference in all the cases examined: typically, model checking for propositional nonmonotonic formalisms is complete with respect to the class Θ_2^p [Eiter and Gottlob, 1997], while logical inference is typically Π_2^p-complete in such logics. We also provide model checking algorithms for both default logic and several nonmonotonic modal logics.

In the following, we first briefly recall Reiter's default logic and Moore's autoepistemic logic. Then, in Section 3 we analyze model checking in default logic, and in Section 4 we study model checking in nonmonotonic modal logics. Finally, in Section 5 we compare our approach with recent related work, and conclude in Section 6.

2 Preliminaries

We start by briefly recalling Reiter's default logic [Reiter, 1980]. Let $\mathcal{L}$ be the usual propositional language. A *default rule* is a rule of the form

$$\frac{\alpha : \beta_1, \dots, \beta_n}{\gamma} \tag{1}$$

where $n \geq 0$ and α (called the *prerequisite*), $\beta_1, \dots, \beta_n$ (called *justifications*), and γ (called the *conclusion*) are all formulas from $\mathcal{L}$. A *default theory* is a pair $\langle D, W \rangle$ where $W \in \mathcal{L}$ and D is a set of default rules.

Default theories in which each rule is of the form $\frac{\alpha : \beta}{\beta}$ are called *normal* (i.e. the justification is equal to the consequence of the default). Moreover, if each default is of the form $\frac{: \beta}{\beta}$, then the default theory is called *super-normal*.

The characterization of default theories is given through the notion of *extension*, i.e. a deductively closed set of propositional formulas. In the following, given a set of propositional formulas G, we denote with $Cn(G)$ the deductive closure of G, i.e. the set of propositional formulas logically implied by G.

Let $E \subseteq \mathcal{L}$, and let D be a set of default rules. We denote with $D(E)$ (and say that $D(E)$ is the *reduct* of D with respect to E) the set

$$\left\{ \frac{\alpha :}{\gamma} : \frac{\alpha : \beta_1, \dots, \beta_n}{\gamma} \in D \text{ and } \neg\beta_i \notin E \text{ for each i} \right\}$$

We say that a set $E \subseteq \mathcal{L}$ is closed under a set of justification-free default rules D if, for each $\frac{\alpha:}{\gamma} \in D$, if $\alpha \in E$ then $\gamma \in E$.

Definition 1 *[Gelfond et al., 1991, Theorem 2.3] Let $\langle D, W \rangle$ be a default theory, and let $E \subseteq \mathcal{L}$. E is an extension for $\langle D, W \rangle$ iff $W \in E$ and E is the minimal set closed under deduction and closed under the set $D(E)$.*

We recall that each extension is fully characterized by the set of conclusions of the default rules applied during this construction: in fact, it is easy to see that, for each extension of $\langle D, W \rangle$, there exists a subset G of the set of conclusions $\{\gamma_1, \dots, \gamma_k\}$ of the default rules in D (which is denoted as $Con(D)$) such that $E = Cn(W \wedge \bigwedge_{\gamma_i \in G} \gamma_i)$. Hence, each extension of a given default theory can be represented in terms of a propositional formula f (or

any propositional formula equivalent to f). Moreover, the propositional formula $f = W \wedge \bigwedge_{\gamma_i \in G} \gamma_i$ provides a *finite* representation of an infinite structure (i.e. the extension).

In [Gelfond et al., 1991] default logic has been extended to the case of disjunctive conclusions, in the following way. A *disjunctive default rule* is a rule of the form

$$\frac{\alpha : \beta_1, \dots, \beta_n}{\gamma_1 | \dots | \gamma_m}$$

where $n, m \geq 0$ and $\alpha, \beta_1, \dots, \beta_n, \gamma_1, \dots, \gamma_m \in \mathcal{L}$. A disjunctive default theory is a pair $\langle D, W \rangle$ where $W \in \mathcal{L}$ and D is a set of disjunctive default rules. The characterization of disjunctive default theories is given by changing (in a conservative way) the above notion of extension as follows.

The reduct $D(E)$ wrt $E \subseteq \mathcal{L}$ of a set of disjunctive defaults D is the set

$$\left\{ \frac{\alpha :}{\gamma_1 | \dots | \gamma_m} : \frac{\alpha : \beta_1, \dots, \beta_n}{\gamma_1 | \dots | \gamma_m} \in D \text{ and } \neg\beta_i \notin E \text{ for each i} \right\}$$

We say that a set $E \subseteq \mathcal{L}$ is closed under a set of justification-free disjunctive default rules D if, for each $\frac{\alpha:}{\gamma_1|\dots|\gamma_m} \in D$, if $\alpha \in E$ then $\gamma_i \in E$ for some i such that $1 \leq i \leq m$. $E \subseteq \mathcal{L}$ is an extension for a disjunctive default theory $\langle D, W \rangle$ iff $W \in E$ and E is a minimal set closed under deduction and under the set $D(E)$.

We finally briefly recall Moore's autoepistemic logic (AEL). We denote with $\mathcal{L}_K$ the modal extension of $\mathcal{L}$ with the modality K. Moreover, we denote with $\mathcal{L}_K^F$ the set of *flat* modal formulas, that is the set of formulas from $\mathcal{L}_K$ in which each propositional symbol appears in the scope of exactly one modality.

Definition 2 *A consistent set of formulas T from $\mathcal{L}_K$ is a* stable expansion *for a formula $\Sigma \in \mathcal{L}_K$ if T satisfies the following equation:*

$$T = Cn_{\mathsf{KD45}}(\{\Sigma\} \cup \{\neg K\varphi \mid \varphi \notin T\})$$

where Cn_{KD45} is the logical consequence operator of modal logic KD45.

Given $\Sigma, \varphi \in \mathcal{L}_K$, $\Sigma \models_{\mathsf{AEL}} \varphi$ iff φ belongs to all the stable expansions of Σ. Notably, each stable expansion T is a *stable set*, i.e. (i) T is closed under propositional consequence; (ii) if $\varphi \in T$ then $K\varphi \in T$; (iii) if $\varphi \notin T$ then $\neg K\varphi \in T$. We recall that each stable set S corresponds to a *maximal* universal S5 model $\mathcal{M}_S$ such that S is the set of formulas satisfied by $\mathcal{M}_S$ (see e.g. [Marek and Truszczyński, 1993]).

With the term AEL *model* for Σ we will refer to an S5 model whose set of theorems corresponds to a stable expansion for Σ in AEL: without loss of generality, we will identify such a model with the set of interpretations it contains. Moreover, each S5 model corresponding to a stable expansion S of a formula Σ can be characterized by a propositional formula f such that $\mathcal{M}_S = \{I : I \models f\}$; f is called the *objective kernel* of the stable expansion S. As in the case of default logic, f provides a finite representation of an infinite structure.

Finally, notice that, as in e.g. [Marek and Truszczyński, 1993], we have adopted the notion of *consistent* autoepistemic logic, i.e. we do not allow the inconsistent theory consisting of all modal formulas to be a (possible) stable expansion. The results we present can be easily extended to this case (corresponding to Moore's original proposal).

We finally briefly introduce the complexity classes mentioned throughout the paper (we refer to [Johnson, 1990] for further details). All the classes we use reside in the *polynomial hierarchy*. In particular, the complexity class Σ_2^p is the class of problems that are solved in polynomial time by a nondeterministic Turing machine that uses an NP-oracle (i.e., that solves in constant time any problem in NP), and Π_2^p is the class of problems that are complement of a problem in Σ_2^p. The class Θ_2^p [Eiter and Gottlob, 1997] (also known as $\Delta_2^p[O(\log n)]$) is the class of problems that are solved in polynomial time by a *deterministic* Turing machine that makes a number of calls to an NP-oracle which is logarithmic in the size of the input. Hence, the class Θ_2^p is "mildly" harder than the class NP, since a problem in Θ_2^p can be solved by solving "few" (i.e. a logarithmic number of) instances of problems in NP. It is generally assumed that the polynomial hierarchy does not collapse, and that a problem in the class Θ_2^p is computationally easier than a Σ_2^p-hard or Π_2^p-hard problem.

3 Model checking in default logic

In this section we analyze the complexity of model checking for propositional default logic. We start by proving that such a problem belongs to the complexity class Θ_2^p. To this aim, we define the algorithm DL-Check (reported in Figure 1) for checking whether a propositional formula f represents an extension of a default theory $\langle D, W \rangle$. The algorithm first computes D', the reduct of D with respect to f, then computes a formula representing the extension of $\langle D', W \rangle$, and finally checks whether such a formula is equivalent to f.

In the algorithm, we make use of the well-known fact that a justification-free default theory $\langle D', W \rangle$ has exactly one extension. We denote as $Ext(\langle D', W \rangle)$ the propositional formula representing such an extension, which can be naively computed through a quadratic (in the cardinality of D') number of NP-calls, starting from $Ext(\langle D', W \rangle) = W$ and conjoining to $Ext(\langle D', W \rangle)$ the conclusions γ_i of each default rule $d_i = \frac{\alpha_i}{\gamma_i}$ in D' such that α_i is logically implied by $Ext(\langle D', W \rangle)$.

Correctness of the algorithm follows immediately from Definition 1.

Lemma 3 *Let $\langle D, W \rangle$ be a default theory, and let $f \in \mathcal{L}$. Then, $Cn(f)$ is an extension of $\langle D, W \rangle$ iff DL-Check($\langle D, W \rangle, f$) returns* true.

The computational analysis of the algorithm DL-Check provides an upper bound for the model checking problem in default logic.

```
Algorithm DL-Check(⟨D, W⟩, f)
Input: default theory ⟨D, W⟩, formula f ∈ L;
Output: true if Cn(f) is an extension of ⟨D, W⟩,
           false otherwise
begin
    D' = ∅;
    for each d = α:β₁,...,βₙ / γ ∈ D do
        if f ⊭ ¬βᵢ for each i = 1, ..., n
        then add α: / γ to D';
    compute Ext(⟨D', W⟩);
    if ⊨ f ≡ Ext(⟨D', W⟩)
    then return true
    else return false
end
```

Figure 1: Algorithm DL-Check.

Theorem 4 *Let $\langle D, W \rangle$ be a default theory, and let $f \in \mathcal{L}$. Then, the problem of establishing whether $Cn(f)$ is an extension of $\langle D, W \rangle$ is in Θ_2^p.*

Proof sketch. First, we prove that it is possible to compute the formula $Ext(\langle D', W \rangle)$ through a *linear* number (in the cardinality of D') of calls to an NP-oracle, by using the following procedure:

$Ext(\langle D', W \rangle) := W$;
for each $\gamma_i \in Con(D')$ **do**
    if for each partition (P, N) of $Con(D')$
        $(\gamma_i \in P)$ **or**
        (there exists $\gamma_j \in N$ s. t. $(W \wedge \bigwedge_{\gamma \in P} \gamma) \models \alpha_j$)
    then $Ext(\langle D', W \rangle) := Ext(\langle D', W \rangle) \wedge \gamma_i$

Then, based on the use of the above procedure for computing $Ext(\langle D', W \rangle)$, we show that the algorithm DL-Check can be reduced to an *NP-tree* [Eiter and Gottlob, 1997], which immediately implies an upper bound of Θ_2^p for the problem of model checking in propositional default logic. □

We now turn our attention to establishing lower bounds for model checking in default logic. We first prove that such a problem is Θ_2^p-hard even if default rules are normal.

Theorem 5 *Let $\langle D, W \rangle$ be a normal default theory, and let $f \in \mathcal{L}$. Then, the problem of establishing whether $Cn(f)$ is an extension of $\langle D, W \rangle$ is Θ_2^p-hard.*

Proof sketch. We reduce the Θ_2^p-complete problem PARITY(SAT) [Eiter and Gottlob, 1997] to model checking for a normal default theory. Informally, an instance of PARITY(SAT) is a set of propositional formulas $\varphi_1, \ldots, \varphi_n$, such that if φ_i is not satisfiable then, for each $j \geq i$, φ_j is not satisfiable. The problem is to establish if the number of satisfiable formulas is odd.

Given an instance of such a problem, in which we assume n odd without loss of generality, we construct the normal default theory $\langle D, W \rangle$, in which $W = \mathsf{true}$ and

$$D = \left\{ \frac{\neg\varphi_1 : p'}{p'}, \frac{\neg\varphi_3 : \varphi_2 \wedge p'}{\varphi_2 \wedge p'}, \ldots, \frac{\neg\varphi_n : \varphi_{n-1} \wedge p'}{\varphi_{n-1} \wedge p'} \right\}$$

where p' is a propositional symbol not appearing in $\varphi_1, \ldots, \varphi_n$.

We prove that there is an odd number of satisfiable formulas in $\varphi_1, \ldots, \varphi_n$ iff true is an extension of $\langle D, W \rangle$. Informally, this is due to the fact that the number of satisfiable formulas is even if and only if either all formulas are not satisfiable (i.e. φ_1 is not satsfiable) or, for some even i, it holds that φ_i is satisfiable and φ_{i+1} is not satisfiable. Now, the rules in D are built in such a way that, if this situation occurs, then there is a default rule which is applied, thus forcing knowledge of p' in the extension. Therefore, in this case true is not an extension for $\langle D, W \rangle$. $\square$

The above property, together with Theorem 4, immediately implies that model checking is Θ_2^p-complete both for general propositional default theories and for normal default theories.

Then, with a proof similar to the previous one, it is possible to show that model checking is Θ_2^p-hard also in the case of prerequisite-free default theories.

Theorem 6 *Let* $\langle D, W \rangle$ *be a prerequisite-free default theory, and let* $f \in \mathcal{L}$. *Then, the problem of establishing whether* $Cn(f)$ *is an extension of* $\langle D, W \rangle$ *is* Θ_2^p-hard.

Again, the above theorem and Theorem 4 prove that model checking is Θ_2^p-complete for prerequisite-free default theories.

We now turn our attention to supernormal (i.e. both normal and prerequisite-free) default theories, and prove that in this case model checking is computationally easier than for unrestricted default theories.

Theorem 7 *Let* $\langle D, W \rangle$ *be a supernormal default theory, and let* $f \in \mathcal{L}$. *The problem of establishing whether* $Cn(f)$ *is an extension of* $\langle D, W \rangle$ *is coNP-complete.*

Proof sketch. As for membership in coNP, we reduce the problem to a propositional validity problem. The key property is the fact that, given

$$D = \left\{ \frac{: \beta_1}{\beta_1}, \ldots, \frac{: \beta_n}{\beta_n} \right\},$$

$Cn(f)$ is an extension of $\langle D, W \rangle$ iff the following two conditions hold:

1. for each i, either $f \models \beta_i$ or $f \models \neg\beta_i$;

2. $W \wedge \bigwedge_{f \models \beta_i} \beta_i$ is equivalent to f.

We prove that it is possible to encode each of the two above conditions in terms of a propositional validity problem, through two polynomial transformation of the input. We thus obtain two propositional formulas $\tau_1(\langle D, W \rangle, f)$ and $\tau_2(\langle D, W \rangle, f)$ such that condition 1. holds iff $\tau_1(\langle D, W \rangle, f)$ is valid and condition 2. holds iff $\tau_1(\langle D, W \rangle, f)$ is valid. Then, by simply using two distinct alphabets for the two formulas, it is possible to reduce the two problems to a single validity problem.

Hardness with respect to coNP follows from the fact that propositional validity of a formula f can be reduced to the problem of establishing whether f is an extension of $\langle \emptyset, \text{true} \rangle$. $\square$

```
Algorithm AEL-Check(Σ, f)
Input: formula Σ ∈ 𝓛_K, formula f ∈ 𝓛;
Output: true if M = {I : I ⊨ f} is AEL model for Σ,
         false otherwise
begin
   while Σ ∉ 𝓛 do begin
      choose a subformula Kφ from Σ
            such that φ ∈ 𝓛;
      if f ⊨ φ
      then Σ := Σ(Kφ → true)
      else Σ := Σ(Kφ → false)
   end;
   if ⊨ f ≡ Σ
   then return true
   else return false
end
```

Figure 2: Algorithm AEL-Check.

As for disjunctive default logic, the easiest way to characterize model checking is to exploit known correspondences between such a formalism and nonmonotonic modal logic MKNF [Lifschitz, 1991]. In particular, the existence of a polynomial embedding of disjunctive default theories in the flat fragment of the logic MKNF makes it possible to show that model checking is in Θ_2^p. Moreover, Θ_2^p-hardness follows from Theorem 5 and from the fact that disjunctive default logic is a conservative generalization of default logic. Hence, the following property holds.

Theorem 8 *Let* $\langle D, W \rangle$ *be a disjunctive default theory, and let* $f \in \mathcal{L}$. *Then, the problem of establishing whether* $Cn(f)$ *is an extension of* $\langle D, W \rangle$ *is* Θ_2^p-complete.

The above property and Theorem 6 also imply Θ_2^p-completeness of model checking for prerequisite-free disjunctive default theories.

In Table 1 we summarize the complexity results described in this section. Each column of the table corresponds to a different condition on the conclusion part of default rules.

The results reported in the table, together with known complexity characterizations of the inference problem in default logic (for a survey see [Cadoli and Schaerf, 1993]), show that model checking is easier than logical inference in all the cases considered. In fact, logical inference is already Π_2^p-hard (skeptical reasoning) or Σ_2^p-hard (credulous reasoning) for supernormal default theories, while model checking is always in Θ_2^p.

4 Model checking in nonmonotonic modal logics

In this section we analyze model checking for nonmonotonic modal logics. Due to lack of space, in the following we only sketch our complexity analysis, and refer to [Marek and Truszczyński, 1993; Lifschitz, 1991] for a formal definition of MDD logics and MKNF: all the results obtained are summarized in Table 2.

	General	Normal	Disjunctive
General	Θ_2^p-complete	Θ_2^p-complete	Θ_2^p-complete
Prerequisite-free	Θ_2^p-complete	coNP-complete	Θ_2^p-complete

Table 1: Complexity of model checking for default logic

	AEL	S4F$_{\mathrm{MDD}}$	SW5$_{\mathrm{MDD}}$	S5$_G$	MKNF
General	Θ_2^p-complete	Θ_2^p-complete	Θ_2^p-complete	Σ_2^p-complete	Σ_2^p-complete
Flat	Θ_2^p-complete	Θ_2^p-complete	Θ_2^p-complete	Θ_2^p-complete	Θ_2^p-complete

Table 2: Complexity of model checking for nonmonotonic modal logics

We start by examining the case of autoepistemic logic. In Figure 2 we report the algorithm AEL-Check for checking whether a propositional formula represents an autoepistemic model of a modal formula. In the algorithm, $\Sigma(K\varphi \rightarrow \mathsf{true})$ represents the formula obtained from Σ by replacing each occurrence of the subformula $K\varphi$ with true, while $\Sigma(K\varphi \rightarrow \mathsf{false})$ represents the formula obtained from Σ by replacing each occurrence of the subformula $K\varphi$ with false.

Informally, the algorithm iteratively computes the value of all modal subformulas (without nested occurrences of the modality) in Σ according to f, until all modal subformulas have been replaced by a truth value. The resulting propositional formula is compared with f, and the algorithm returns true if and only if the two formulas are equivalent.

Correctness of the algorithm can be established by means of previous results on reasoning in autoepistemic logic [Marek and Truszczyński, 1993].

Lemma 9 *Let* $\Sigma \in \mathcal{L}_K$, $f \in \mathcal{L}$. *Then,* $M = \{I : I \models f\}$ *is an* AEL *model of* Σ *iff* AEL-Check(Σ, f) *returns* true.

The above property allows us to prove Θ_2^p-completeness of model checking in AEL.

Theorem 10 *Let* $\Sigma \in \mathcal{L}_K$, $f \in \mathcal{L}$. *Then, the problem of establishing whether* $M = \{I : I \models f\}$ *is an* AEL *model of* Σ *is* Θ_2^p-complete.

Proof sketch. Membership in Θ_2^p follows from Lemma 9 and from the fact that the algorithm AEL-Check can be polynomially reduced to an NP-tree. Hardness follows from the fact that it is possible to reduce an instance of the problem of model checking for prerequisite-free default theories to model checking in AEL: the reduction is based on the correspondence between the prerequisite-free default $\frac{:\beta}{\gamma}$ and the modal formula $\neg K \neg \beta \supset \gamma$ in autoepistemic logic. $\square$

It can actually be shown that model checking for AEL is Θ_2^p-hard (and thus, from the above theorem, Θ_2^p-complete) even under the restriction that the formula Σ is *flat*, i.e. each propositional symbol in Σ lies within the scope of exactly one modality. The proof of this property can be obtained through a reduction from PARITY(SAT).

A similar analysis allows for establishing the same complexity characterization for the problem of model checking in two well-known nonmonotonic modal formalisms of the McDermott and Doyle's (MDD) family, i.e. the nonmonotonic logics based on the modal systems SW5 and S4F [Marek and Truszczyński, 1993].

Theorem 11 *Let* $\Sigma \in \mathcal{L}_K$, $f \in \mathcal{L}$. *Then, the problem of establishing whether* $M = \{I : I \models f\}$ *is an* S4F$_{\mathrm{MDD}}$ *model (or an* SW5$_{\mathrm{MDD}}$ *model) of* Σ *is* Θ_2^p-complete.

As in the case of autoepistemic logic, the above property also holds if we restrict to flat formulas.

For modal logics based on the *minimal knowledge* paradigm, we prove that model checking is harder than for the above presented nonmonotonic logics. In particular, it is a Σ_2^p-complete problem. However, logical inference in such logics of minimal knowledge is harder than in default logic and autoepistemic logic, since it is a Π_3^p-complete problem both in MKNF and in S5$_G$ [Donini *et al.*, 1997; Rosati, 1997]. Hence, also in such formalisms model checking is easier than logical inference. We first analyze modal logic S5$_G$, i.e. the logic of minimal knowledge introduced in [Halpern and Moses, 1985].

Theorem 12 *Let* $\Sigma \in \mathcal{L}_K$, $f \in \mathcal{L}$. *Then, the problem of establishing whether* $M = \{I : I \models f\}$ *is an* S5$_G$ *model of* Σ *is* Σ_2^p-complete.

Interestingly, if we impose that the modal formula Σ is flat, then model checking in S5$_G$ becomes easier.

Theorem 13 *Let* $\Sigma \in \mathcal{L}_K^F$, $f \in \mathcal{L}$. *Then, the problem of establishing whether* $M = \{I : I \models f\}$ *is an* S5$_G$ *model of* Σ *is* Θ_2^p-complete.

The same computational characterization of model checking can be shown for the logic MKNF, i.e. the logic of minimal knowledge and negation as failure introduced in [Lifschitz, 1991], which extends S5$_G$ with a second modal operator interpreted in terms of negation as failure.

Comparing the above results with known computational characterizations of the inference problem in nonmonotonic modal logics, it turns out that model checking is easier than logical inference in all the cases considered. Moreover, we remark that logical inference in the flat fragment of S5$_G$ and MKNF is Π_2^p-complete. This implies that, for each of the cases reported in the table, if logical inference is Π_2^p-complete, then model checking is Θ_2^p-complete, and if logical inference is Π_3^p-complete, then model checking is Σ_2^p-complete.

5 Related work

Model checking has been recently studied in some non-monotonic settings (see e.g. [Cadoli, 1992; Liberatore and Schaerf, 1998]). In particular, the work reported in [Liberatore and Schaerf, 1998] is the closest to the approach presented in this paper, since it deals with the model checking problem for propositional default logic.

The notion of model checking introduced in [Liberatore and Schaerf, 1998] for default logic corresponds to check whether a propositional interpretation I "satisfies" a given default theory $\langle D, W \rangle$, in the sense that I satisfies at least one extension of $\langle D, W \rangle$. Such a notion of model checking relies on the usage of standard propositional interpretations, thus avoiding the need to resort to the representation of an interpretation structure in terms of a logical formula. On the other hand, a propositional interpretation cannot be considered as a "model" of a default theory: in fact, model-theoretic characterizations of default logic are based on possible-world structures analogous to universal S5 models introduced for autoepistemic logic. Hence, a propositional interpretation is a *component* of an interpretation structure of a default theory. Instead, our formulation of the model checking problem is based on the idea of checking a whole interpretation structure of this form against a nonmonotonic theory: in this sense, our notion is a more natural extension to nonmonotonic logics of the "classical" notion of model checking.

From the computational viewpoint, it turns out that Liberatore and Schaerf's notion of model checking is harder than the one presented in this paper. In fact, comparing Table 1 with the results reported in [Liberatore and Schaerf, 1998], it can be seen that our formulation of model checking is computationally easier in almost all the cases examined, with the exception of normal and supernormal default theories, for which the complexity of the two versions of model checking is the same.

6 Conclusions

In this paper we have studied the complexity of model checking in several nonmonotonic logics. Our results show that, as in classical logic, model checking is computationally easier than logical inference in many nonmonotonic formalisms. We have also provided algorithms for model checking in default logic and nonmonotonic modal logics.

Our results provide a positive answer to the question whether it is convenient to use "model-based" representations of knowledge in the case of nonmonotonic logics. It therefore appears possible to use the analysis presented in this paper as the basis for the development of model checking techniques in knowledge representation systems with nonmonotonic abilities.

Acknowledgments

The author wishes to thank Paolo Liberatore for useful discussions about the subject of this paper.

References

[Cadoli and Schaerf, 1993] M. Cadoli and M. Schaerf. A survey of complexity results for non-monotonic logics. *J. of Logic Programming*, 17:127–160, 1993.

[Cadoli, 1992] M. Cadoli. The complexity of model checking for circumscriptive formulae. *Information Processing Letters*, 44:113–118, 1992.

[Cimatti *et al.*, 1997] A. Cimatti, E Giunchiglia, F. Giunchiglia, and P. Traverso. Planning via model checking. In *Proc. of ECP-97*, 1997.

[Donini *et al.*, 1997] F. M. Donini, D. Nardi, and R. Rosati. Ground nonmonotonic modal logics. *J. of Logic and Computation*, 7(4):523–548, 1997.

[Eiter and Gottlob, 1997] T. Eiter and G. Gottlob. The complexity class Θ_2^p: Recent results and applications in AI and modal logic. In *Proc. of FCT-97*, LNAI 1279, pages 1–18, 1997.

[Gelfond *et al.*, 1991] M. Gelfond, V. Lifschitz, H.Przymusinska, and M. Truszczynski. Disjunctive defaults. In *Proc. of KR-91*, pages 230–237, 1991.

[Halpern and Moses, 1985] J. Y. Halpern and Y. Moses. Towards a theory of knowledge and ignorance: Preliminary report. In K. Apt, editor, *Logic and models of concurrent systems*. Springer-Verlag, 1985.

[Halpern and Vardi, 1991] J. Y. Halpern and M. Y. Vardi. Model checking vs. theorem proving: A manifesto. In *Proc. of KR-91*, 1991.

[Johnson, 1990] D. S. Johnson. A catalog of complexity classes. In J. van Leuven, editor, *Handbook of Theoretical Computer Science*. Elsevier, 1990.

[Levesque, 1986] H. J. Levesque. Making believers out of computers. *Artif. Intell.*, 30:81–108, 1986.

[Liberatore and Schaerf, 1998] P. Liberatore and M. Schaerf. The complexity of model checking for propositional default logics. In *Proc. of ECAI-98*, pages 18–22, 1998.

[Lifschitz, 1991] V. Lifschitz. Nonmonotonic databases and epistemic queries. In *Proc. of IJCAI-91*, pages 381–386, 1991.

[Marek and Truszczyński, 1993] W. Marek and M. Truszczyński. *Nonmonotonic Logics–Context-Dependent Reasoning*. Springer-Verlag, 1993.

[Moore, 1985] R. C. Moore. Semantical considerations on nonmonotonic logic. *Artif. Intell.*, 25:75–94, 1985.

[Reiter, 1980] R. Reiter. A logic for default reasoning. *Artif. Intell.*, 13:81–132, 1980.

[Rosati, 1997] R. Rosati. Reasoning with minimal belief and negation as failure: Algorithms and complexity. In *Proc. of AAAI-97*, pages 430–435, 1997.

AUTOMATED REASONING

Description Logics 1

Reasoning in Expressive Description Logics with Fixpoints based on Automata on Infinite Trees

Diego Calvanese, Giuseppe De Giacomo, Maurizio Lenzerini
Dipartimento di Informatica e Sistemistica
Università di Roma "La Sapienza"
Via Salaria 113, 00198 Roma, Italy
`lastname@dis.uniroma1.it`
`http://www.dis.uniroma1.it/~lastname`

Abstract

In the last years, the investigation on Description Logics (DLs) has been driven by the goal of applying them in several areas, such as, software engineering, information systems, databases, information integration, and intelligent access to the web. The modeling requirements arising in the above areas have stimulated the need for very rich languages, including fixpoint constructs to represent recursive structures. We study a DL comprising the most general form of fixpoint constructs on concepts, all classical concept forming constructs, plus inverse roles, n-ary relations, qualified number restrictions, and inclusion assertions. We establish the EXPTIME decidability of such logic by presenting a decision procedure based on a reduction to nonemptiness of alternating automata on infinite trees. We observe that this is the first decidability result for a logic combining inverse roles, number restrictions, and general fixpoints.

1 Introduction

Description Logics (DLs) allow one to represent a domain of interest in terms of *concepts* and *roles*, where concepts model classes of individuals, and roles model relationships between classes [Woods and Schmolze, 1992; Donini *et al.*, 1996; Borgida and Patel-Schneider, 1994]. A knowledge base expressed in a DL is constituted by inclusion assertions that state the properties of concepts and roles. Various reasoning tasks can be carried out on a knowledge base. The most fundamental one consists in checking whether a certain assertion is logically implied by a knowledge base. A DL is characterized by three aspects: the language used to form complex concepts and roles, the kind of assertions that are used to express properties of concepts and roles, and the inference mechanisms provided for reasoning on the knowledge bases expressible in the system.

In the last years, the investigation on DLs has been driven by the goal of applying them in several areas, such as planning [Weida and Litman, 1992], action representation [Artale and Franconi, 1994], software engineering [Devanbu and Jones, 1997], information systems [Catarci and Lenzerini, 1993], databases [Borgida, 1995; Bergamaschi and Sartori, 1992; Sheth *et al.*, 1993], information integration [Calvanese

et al., 1998c], and intelligent access to the web [Levy *et al.*, 1996; Blanco *et al.*, 1994]. The modeling requirements arising in the above areas have stimulated the need for incorporating increasingly expressive representation mechanisms:

- The goal of capturing the semantics of database models and reasoning about data schemas has stressed the importance of number restrictions, n-ary relations, and cyclic assertions in the knowledge base [Calvanese *et al.*, 1994].

- Information integration systems require inclusion assertions not only on concepts, but also on relations [Ullman, 1997].

- Semi-structured data, used in applications such as digital libraries, internet information systems, etc., require the ability to represent data whose structure is not rigid and strictly typed as in conventional database systems. Models for semi-structured data represent data as graphs with labeled edges, and adopt flexible typing schemes in order to classify data [Buneman, 1997]. A special case of such models is XML [Bray *et al.*, 1998], which is becoming the standard for exchanging data on the web. In general, correctly modeling such typing schemes calls for the use of fixpoints in the representation formalism [Calvanese *et al.*, 1998b].

- UML [Booch *et al.*, 1998] is nowadays the standard language for the analysis phase of software and information system development. CASE tools that perform automated reasoning on UML schemas (for example, to test consistency or redundancy) would be of great interest. Fully capturing UML schemas in DLs requires inverse roles, n-ary relations, number restrictions, and general fixpoints on concepts for modeling recursive structures (both inductive and coinductive), such as lists, trees, streams, etc..

DLs that capture all requirements above except fixpoints are known (see e.g. [Calvanese *et al.*, 1998c]). However, fully capturing fixpoints in DLs has been an open problem for a long time. Fixpoints incorporated directly in the semantics have been first studied in [Nebel, 1991; Baader, 1996] for simple DLs. DLs with regular expressions, which can be seen as a form of fixpoints, have been studied in [Baader, 1991], and exploiting the correspondence with Propositional Dynamic Logics in [Schild, 1991; De Giacomo and Lenzerini, 1994]. In [Calvanese *et al.*, 1995] another form of fixpoints, capturing well-foundedness, has been considered. While such logics got increasingly expressive, they all include fixpoint of a limited form only. Fixpoints on concepts in their full generality have been investigated in [Schild, 1994; De Giacomo and Lenzerini, 1997] developing a correspondence with modal μ-calculus [Kozen, 1983]. However these logics lack inverse roles (and number restrictions on them) which are essential to deal with n-ary relations.

The work presented in this paper closes the gap between the two lines of research, presenting a logic with general fixpoints on concepts that includes all the constructs mentioned above. Specifically, we consider a DL, called $\mathcal{DLR}_\mu$, that includes:

- a very rich language, comprising all classical concept forming constructs, plus inverse roles, n-ary relations, and the most general form of number restrictions;

- the most general form of inclusion assertions, without any limitations on the presence of cycles;

- the most general form of fixpoint on concepts.

We characterize reasoning in such a DL as EXPTIME-complete[1], by presenting a decision procedure based on reducing inference to nonemptiness of two-way alternating automata on infinite trees [Vardi, 1998]. We observe that this is the first decidability result for a logic combining inverse roles, number restrictions, and general fixpoints.

2 The Description Logic $\mathcal{DLR}_\mu$

Traditionally, description logics (DLs) allow one to represent a domain of interest in terms of concepts and roles, which model classes of individuals and binary relationships between classes, respectively. More recently DLs comprising relations of arbitrary arity have been introduced, e.g., $\mathcal{DLR}$ [Calvanese et al., 1998c]. We present the DL $\mathcal{DLR}_\mu$ which extends $\mathcal{DLR}$ by least and greatest fixpoint constructs.

We make use of the standard first-order notions of scope, bound and free occurrences of variables, closed formulae, etc., treating μ and ν as quantifiers.

Concepts and relations (of arity between 2 and n_{max}) are built according to the following syntax:

$$R ::= \top_n \mid P \mid (\$i/n{:}C) \mid \neg R \mid R_1 \sqcap R_2$$
$$C ::= \top_1 \mid A \mid X \mid \neg C \mid C_1 \sqcap C_2 \mid$$
$$\exists[\$i]R \mid (\leq k\,[\$i]R) \mid \mu X.C$$

where P and A denote *atomic relations* and *atomic concepts* respectively, R and C denote arbitrary *relations* and *concepts*, i denotes components of relations, i.e., an integer between 1 and n_{max}, n denotes the arity of a relation, i.e., an integer between 2 and n_{max}, k denotes a nonnegative integer, $\top_1$ denotes the top concept, $\top_n$, for $n = 2, \ldots, n_{max}$, denotes the top relation of arity n, X denotes a concept variable, and the restriction is made that every free occurrence of X in $\mu X.C$ is in the scope of an even number of negations ($(\leq k\,[\$i]R)$ counts as one negation).

Concepts and relations must be *well-typed*, which means that (i) only relations of the same arity n can be combined to

[1]The same computational complexity of reasoning with inclusion assertions in the basic DL $\mathcal{ALC}$.

$$(\top_n)^{\mathcal{I}}_\rho = \top_n^{\mathcal{I}} \subseteq (\Delta^{\mathcal{I}})^n \qquad (\neg R)^{\mathcal{I}}_\rho = \top_n^{\mathcal{I}} \setminus R_\rho^{\mathcal{I}}$$
$$P_\rho^{\mathcal{I}} = P^{\mathcal{I}} \subseteq \top_n^{\mathcal{I}} \qquad (R_1 \sqcap R_2)_\rho^{\mathcal{I}} = (R_1)_\rho^{\mathcal{I}} \cap (R_2)_\rho^{\mathcal{I}}$$
$$(\$i/n{:}C)_\rho^{\mathcal{I}} = \{(d_1, \ldots, d_n) \in \top_n^{\mathcal{I}} \mid d_i \in C_\rho^{\mathcal{I}}\}$$

$$(\top_1)_\rho^{\mathcal{I}} = \Delta^{\mathcal{I}} \qquad\qquad X_\rho^{\mathcal{I}} = \rho(X) \subseteq \Delta^{\mathcal{I}}$$
$$A_\rho^{\mathcal{I}} = A^{\mathcal{I}} \subseteq \Delta^{\mathcal{I}} \qquad (\neg C)_\rho^{\mathcal{I}} = \Delta^{\mathcal{I}} \setminus C_\rho^{\mathcal{I}}$$
$$(C_1 \sqcap C_2)_\rho^{\mathcal{I}} = (C_1)_\rho^{\mathcal{I}} \cap (C_2)_\rho^{\mathcal{I}}$$
$$(\exists[\$i]R)_\rho^{\mathcal{I}} = \{d \mid \exists(d_1, \ldots, d_n) \in R_\rho^{\mathcal{I}}.d_i = d\}$$
$$(\leq k\,[\$i]R)_\rho^{\mathcal{I}} = \{d \mid \#\{(d_1, \ldots, d_n) \in R_\rho^{\mathcal{I}} \mid d_i = d\} \leq k\}$$
$$(\mu X.C)_\rho^{\mathcal{I}} = \bigcap\{\mathcal{E} \subseteq \Delta^{\mathcal{I}} \mid C_{\rho[X/\mathcal{E}]}^{\mathcal{I}} \subseteq \mathcal{E}\}$$

$P, R, R_1,$ and R_2 have arity n

Figure 1: Semantic rules for $\mathcal{DLR}_\mu$

form expressions of type $R_1 \sqcap R_2$ (which inherit the arity n), and (ii) $i \leq n$ whenever i denotes a component of a relation of arity n.

We make use of the standard abbreviations, including $\nu X.C$ for $\neg \mu X.\neg C[X/\neg X]$, where $C[X/C']$ denotes the concept obtained from C by substituting all free occurrences of X with C'. We use λ to denote either μ or ν.

An *interpretation* $\mathcal{I} = (\Delta^{\mathcal{I}}, \cdot^{\mathcal{I}})$ consists of an *interpretation domain* $\Delta^{\mathcal{I}}$, and an *interpretation function* $\cdot^{\mathcal{I}}$, which maps every atomic concept to a subset of $\Delta^{\mathcal{I}}$, and every atomic relation of arity n to a subset of $(\Delta^{\mathcal{I}})^n$. The presence of free variables does not allow us to extend $\cdot^{\mathcal{I}}$ directly to every concept and relation. For this reason we introduce valuations. A *valuation* ρ on $\mathcal{I}$ is a mapping from concept variables to subsets of $\Delta^{\mathcal{I}}$. Given a valuation ρ, we denote by $\rho[X/\mathcal{E}]$ the valuation identical to ρ except for $\rho[X/\mathcal{E}](X) = \mathcal{E}$.

Let $\mathcal{I}$ be an interpretation and ρ a valuation on $\mathcal{I}$. We assign meaning to concepts and relations of the logic by associating to $\mathcal{I}$ and ρ an *extension function* $\cdot_\rho^{\mathcal{I}}$, mapping concepts to subsets of $\Delta^{\mathcal{I}}$ and relations of arity n to subsets of $(\Delta^{\mathcal{I}})^n$, as shown in Figure 1. Observe that the semantics assigned to $\nu X.C$ is

$$(\nu X.C)_\rho^{\mathcal{I}} = \bigcup\{\mathcal{E} \subseteq \Delta^{\mathcal{I}} \mid \mathcal{E} \subseteq C_{\rho[X/\mathcal{E}]}^{\mathcal{I}}\}$$

The expression $C_{\rho[X/\mathcal{E}]}^{\mathcal{I}}$ can be seen as an operator from subsets $\mathcal{E}$ of $\Delta^{\mathcal{I}}$ to subsets of $\Delta^{\mathcal{I}}$, and, by the syntactic restriction enforced on variables, such an operator is guaranteed to be monotonic wrt $\subseteq$. The constructs $\mu X.C$ and $\nu X.C$ denote respectively the *least fixpoint* and the *greatest fixpoint* of the operator (see [De Giacomo and Lenzerini, 1997] for a discussion on the use of fixpoints in DLs). The extension of closed concepts and relations is independent of the valuation, and therefore for closed concepts and relations we do not consider the valuation explicitly. A closed concept or relation L is *satisfiable* if there exists an interpretation $\mathcal{I}$ such that $L^{\mathcal{I}} \neq \emptyset$.

A $\mathcal{DLR}_\mu$ *knowledge base* is a finite set of *assertions* of the form $L_1 \sqsubseteq L_2$ where L_1 and L_2 are either two closed concepts of $\mathcal{DLR}_\mu$ or two closed relations of the same arity. We use $L_1 \equiv L_2$ as an abbreviation for the assertions $L_1 \sqsubseteq L_2$ and $L_2 \sqsubseteq L_1$. An interpretation $\mathcal{I}$ *satisfies an assertion* $L_1 \sqsubseteq L_2$, if $L_1^{\mathcal{I}} \subseteq L_2^{\mathcal{I}}$. $\mathcal{I}$ is a *model* of a knowledge base

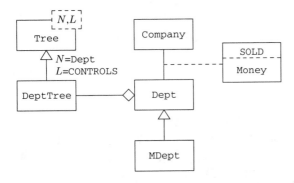

Figure 2: An UML diagram

$$\begin{aligned}
\alpha(\top_n) &= A_{\top_n} & \alpha(\top_1) &= A_{\top_1} \\
\alpha(P) &= A_P & \alpha(A) &= A \\
\alpha((i/n\colon C)) &= A_{\top_n} \sqcap \forall F_i.\alpha(C) & \alpha(X) &= X \\
\alpha(\neg R) &= A_{\top_n} \sqcap \neg\alpha(R) & \alpha(\neg C) &= A_{\top_1} \sqcap \neg\alpha(C) \\
\alpha(R_1 \sqcap R_2) &= \alpha(R_1) \sqcap \alpha(R_2) & \alpha(C_1 \sqcap C_2) &= \alpha(C_1) \sqcap \alpha(C_2)
\end{aligned}$$

$$\alpha(\exists[\$i]R) = \exists F_i^-.\alpha(R)$$
$$\alpha((\leq k\,[\$i]R)) = (\leq k\,F_i^-.\alpha(R))$$
$$\alpha(\mu X.C) = \mu X.\alpha(C)$$
$$\alpha(L_1 \sqsubseteq L_2) = \alpha(L_1) \sqsubseteq \alpha(L_2)$$

Figure 3: Mapping $\alpha(\cdot)$ from $\mathcal{DLR}_\mu$ to $\mu\mathcal{ALCQI}$

$\mathcal{K}$, if it satisfies all assertions in $\mathcal{K}$. An assertion $L_1 \sqsubseteq L_2$ is *logically implied* by a knowledge base $\mathcal{K}$ if $L_1^{\mathcal{I}} \subseteq L_2^{\mathcal{I}}$ for every model $\mathcal{I}$ of $\mathcal{K}$.

Example 2.1 Figure 2 shows an UML diagram which is part of a Telecom Italia application monitoring departments. Departments other than Main Departments are controlled by other departments, in a purely hierarchical fashion (see the use of the concept Tree). Moreover, Departments can be sold to companies for a certain amount of money. There are further constraints in the application (not shown in the diagram): First, if a Main Department is sold, then all Departments directly or indirectly controlled by it are also sold. Second, if a Department is sold, then its controlling Main Department is also sold.

We provide the formalization in $\mathcal{DLR}_\mu$ of the UML diagram in Figure 2. Tree$[N, L]$ represents a concept parameterized on N and L, to be used as a template, according to the following inductive definition of tree: (i) an empty tree is a tree; (ii) a node with at most one predecessor, at least one successor, and such that all successors are trees, is a tree; (iii) nothing else is a tree. Tree$[\text{Dept}, \text{CONTROLS}]$ represents the concept obtained by syntactically substituting Dept and CONTROLS for the parameters N and L in Tree$[N, L]$.

$$\begin{aligned}
\text{Tree}[N, L] &\stackrel{def}{=} \mu X.(\text{EmptyTree} \sqcup \\
&(N \sqcap (\leq 1\,[\$2]L) \sqcap \exists[\$1]L \sqcap \\
&\neg\exists[\$1](L \sqcap (\$2/2\colon \neg X)))) \\
\text{DeptTree} &\equiv \text{Tree}[\text{Dept}, \text{CONTROLS}] \\
\text{SOLD} &\sqsubseteq (\$1\colon \text{Dept}) \sqcap (\$2\colon \text{Company}) \sqcap (\$3\colon \text{Money}) \\
\text{CONTROLS} &\sqsubseteq (\$1\colon \text{Dept}) \sqcap (\$2\colon \text{Dept}) \\
\text{MDept} &\sqsubseteq \text{Dept} \sqcap \neg\exists[\$2]\text{CONTROLS}
\end{aligned}$$

The additional constraints mentioned above are formalized as follows:

$$\begin{aligned}
\text{MDept} \sqcap \exists[\$1]\text{SOLD} &\sqsubseteq \nu X.(\exists[\$1]\text{SOLD} \sqcap \\
&\neg\exists[\$1](\text{CONTROLS} \sqcap (\$2\colon \neg X))) \\
\text{Dept} \sqcap \exists[\$1]\text{SOLD} &\sqsubseteq \mu X.((\text{MDept} \sqcap \exists[\$1]\text{SOLD}) \sqcup \\
&\exists[\$2](\text{CONTROLS} \sqcap (\$1\colon X)))
\end{aligned}$$

3 The DLs $\mu\mathcal{ALCQI}$ and $\mu\mathcal{ALCI}_f$

Below we also consider the DL $\mu\mathcal{ALCQI}$, which extends $\mu\mathcal{ALCQ}$, studied in [De Giacomo and Lenzerini, 1997], by the inverse operator on roles. Concepts in $\mu\mathcal{ALCQI}$ are built as follows (R is an atomic or inverse atomic role):

$$C ::= A \mid X \mid \neg C \mid C_1 \sqcap C_2 \mid \exists R.C \mid (\leq k\,R.C) \mid \mu X.C$$

$\mu\mathcal{ALCQI}$ can be viewed as a syntactic variant of *modal μ-calculus* [Kozen, 1983] extended both with *graded modalities* (see e.g., [Van der Hoek and De Rijke, 1995]) and with *backward modalities* [Vardi, 1985].

We observe that $\mu\mathcal{ALCQI}$ can also be considered as a sublanguage of $\mathcal{DLR}_\mu$ by restricting relations to be binary and allowing their use only according to the following abbreviations:

$$\begin{aligned}
\exists P.C &\quad\text{for}\quad \exists[\$1](P \sqcap (\$2/2\colon C)) \\
\exists P^-.C &\quad\text{for}\quad \exists[\$2](P \sqcap (\$1/2\colon C)) \\
(\leq k\,P.C) &\quad\text{for}\quad (\leq k\,[\$1](P \sqcap (\$2/2\colon C))) \\
(\leq k\,P^-.C) &\quad\text{for}\quad (\leq k\,[\$2](P \sqcap (\$1/2\colon C)))
\end{aligned}$$

Finally, we call $\mu\mathcal{ALCI}_f$ the restriction of $\mu\mathcal{ALCQI}$ obtained by forcing all atomic and *inverse* roles to be functional.

4 Encoding $\mathcal{DLR}_\mu$ into $\mu\mathcal{ALCI}_f$

Next we turn to reasoning in $\mathcal{DLR}_\mu$. In particular, we present a technique to decide logical implication in $\mathcal{DLR}_\mu$. In this section we show how to encode $\mathcal{DLR}_\mu$ into $\mu\mathcal{ALCQI}$ and then into $\mu\mathcal{ALCI}_f$. In Section 5 we study reasoning in $\mu\mathcal{ALCI}_f$ by adopting automata theoretic techniques.

Since we can define an atomic relation to be equivalent to any complex relation, we assume wlog that all qualified number restrictions are of the form $(\leq k\,[\$i]P)$, where P is an atomic relation. We also use the standard abbreviations.

To reduce logical implication in $\mathcal{DLR}_\mu$ to logical implication in $\mu\mathcal{ALCQI}$ we extend the technique in [Calvanese *et al.*, 1998a]. We make use of the mapping $\alpha(\cdot)$ defined in Figure 3, and define the $\mu\mathcal{ALCQI}$ knowledge base $\alpha(\mathcal{K})$ by applying α to all assertions in $\mathcal{K}$ and adding:

$$\begin{aligned}
\top &\sqsubseteq A_{\top_1} \sqcup \cdots \sqcup A_{\top_{n_{max}}} \\
\top &\sqsubseteq (\leq 1\,F_i.\top) \quad\text{for each } i \in \{1, \ldots, n_{max}\} \\
\forall F_i.\bot &\sqsubseteq \forall F_{i+1}.\bot \quad\text{for each } i \in \{1, \ldots, n_{max}\} \\
A_{\top_n} &\equiv \exists F_1.A_{\top_1} \sqcap \cdots \sqcap \exists F_n.A_{\top_1} \sqcap \forall F_{n+1}.\bot \\
&\qquad\text{for each } n \in \{2, \ldots, n_{max}\} \\
A_P &\sqsubseteq A_{\top_n} \quad\text{for each atomic relation } P \text{ of arity } n \\
A &\sqsubseteq A_{\top_1} \quad\text{for each atomic concept } A
\end{aligned}$$

Intuitively, $\alpha(\mathcal{K})$ makes use of *reification* of n-ary relations, i.e. a tuple in a model of $\mathcal{K}$ is represented in a model of $\alpha(\mathcal{K})$ by an individual having one functional role F_i for each tuple component $\$i$.

Although atomic roles in $\alpha(\mathcal{K})$ are functional their inverses are not. Next we further transform $\alpha(\mathcal{K})$ to get a $\mu\mathcal{ALCI}_f$

$$\beta(\top) = \top \qquad\qquad \beta(\neg C) = \neg\beta(C)$$
$$\beta(A) = A \qquad\qquad \beta(C_1 \sqcap C_2) = \beta(C_1) \sqcap \beta(C_2)$$
$$\beta(X) = X \qquad\qquad \beta(\mu X.C) = \mu X.\beta(C)$$
$$\beta(\exists F_i^-.C) = \exists f_i.\exists g_i^*.\beta(C)$$
$$\beta(\exists F_i.C) = \exists f_i^-.\exists (g_i^-)^*.\beta(C)$$
$$\beta((\leq 1\, F_i.\top)) = \top$$
$$\beta((\leq k\, F_i^-.A)) = \forall f_i.\forall g_i^*.(\neg\beta(A) \sqcup \forall g_i^+.\neg\beta(A) \sqcup$$
$$\forall g_i^+.(\cdots(\neg\beta(A) \sqcup \forall g_i^+.\neg\beta(A))\cdots))$$
$$\beta(C_1 \sqsubseteq C_2) = \beta(C_1) \sqsubseteq \beta(C_2)$$

where in the second last equation the number of nested concepts of the form $\neg\beta(A) \sqcup \forall g_i^+.C$ is k, and the following abbreviations are used: $\forall g_i^*.C$ for $\nu X.(C \sqcap \forall g_i.X)$, $\forall g_i^+.C$ for $\forall g_i.\forall g_i^*.C$, $\exists g_i^*.C$ for $\mu X.(C \sqcup \exists g_i.X)$, and $\exists (g_i^-)^*.C$ for $\mu X.(C \sqcup \exists g_i^-.X)$.

Figure 4: Mapping $\beta(\cdot)$ from $\mu\mathcal{ALCQI}$ to $\mu\mathcal{ALCI}_f$

knowledge base $\beta(\alpha(\mathcal{K}))$ (in which also all inverse roles are functional). Intuitively, following [De Giacomo and Lenzerini, 1995], we represent the role F_i^-, $i = 1, \ldots, n_{max}$, by the role $f_i \circ g_i^*$, where f_i, g_i are new functional roles and g_i^* is the reflexive-transitive closure of g_i. Now qualified number restrictions can be encoded as constraints on the chain $f_i \circ g_i^*$. Formally, we make use of the mapping $\beta(\cdot)$ defined in Figure 4.

We define $\beta(\alpha(\mathcal{K}))$ as the $\mu\mathcal{ALCI}_f$ knowledge base obtained by applying β to all assertions in $\alpha(\mathcal{K})$ and adding the assertion $\top \sqsubseteq \neg(\exists f_i^-.\top \sqcap \exists g_i^-.\top)$.

Theorem 4.1 *Given a $\mathcal{DLR}_\mu$ knowledge base $\mathcal{K}$ and a $\mathcal{DLR}_\mu$ assertion $L_1 \sqsubseteq L_2$,*

$$\mathcal{K} \models L_1 \sqsubseteq L_2 \quad \text{iff} \quad \beta(\alpha(\mathcal{K})) \models \beta(\alpha(L_1 \sqsubseteq L_2)).$$

Since the mappings α and β are polynomial we get the following result.

Theorem 4.2 *Logical implication in $\mathcal{DLR}_\mu$ can be polynomially reduced to logical implication in $\mu\mathcal{ALCI}_f$.*[2]

Finally we observe, that since $\mu\mathcal{ALCI}_f$ has the *connected-model property*, we can internalize assertions and polynomially reduce logical implication to concept satisfiability. Namely, $\mathcal{K} \models C_1 \sqsubseteq C_2$ iff

$$C_1 \sqcap \neg C_2 \sqcap \nu X.(C_\mathcal{K} \sqcap (\sqcap_{i=1}^q (\forall P_i.X \sqcap \forall P_i^-.X)))$$

is unsatisfiable, where $C_\mathcal{K} = \sqcap_{[C \sqsubseteq C' \in \mathcal{K}]}(\neg C \sqcup C')$ and $P_1, \ldots, P_q$ are the atomic roles in $\mathcal{K}, C_1$ and C_2. Therefore, in the following we concentrate on concept satisfiability in $\mu\mathcal{ALCI}_f$.

5 Automata Techniques for $\mu\mathcal{ALCI}_f$

We now study concept satisfiability in $\mu\mathcal{ALCI}_f$ following the techniques based on *two-way alternating automata on infinite trees* (TWAA) introduced in [Vardi, 1998]. Indeed, Vardi used TWAAs to derive a decision procedure for modal μ-calculus with backward modalities. Here we exploit them

---

[2]Under the usual assumption that numbers in number restrictions are coded in unary.

to derive a reasoning procedure for $\mu\mathcal{ALCI}_f$, which corresponds to a modal μ-calculus with backward modalities in which both forward and backward modalities are functional.

5.1 Automata on Infinite Trees

Infinite trees are represented as prefix closed (infinite) sets of words over $\mathbb{N}$ (the set of positive natural numbers). Formally, an *infinite tree* is a set of words $T \subseteq \mathbb{N}^*$, such that if $x \cdot c \in T$, where $x \in \mathbb{N}^*$ and $c \in \mathbb{N}$, then also $x \in T$. The tree is *full* if also $x \cdot c' \in T$ for all $0 < c' < c$. The elements of T are called *nodes*, the empty word ε is the *root* of T, and for every $x \in T$, the nodes $x \cdot c$, with $c \in \mathbb{N}$, are the *successors* of x. By convention we take $x \cdot 0 = x$, and $x \cdot i \cdot -1 = x$. The *branching degree* $d(x)$ denotes the number of successors of x. If $d(x) = k$ for all nodes x, then we say that the tree is k-*ary*. An *infinite path* P of T is a prefix-closed set $P \subseteq T$ such that for every $i \geq 0$ there exists a unique node $x \in P$ with $|x| = i$. A *labeled tree* over an alphabet Σ is a pair $\langle T, V \rangle$ where T is a tree and $V : T \to \Sigma$.

Alternating automata on infinite trees are a generalization of nondeterministic automata on infinite trees, introduced in [Muller and Schupp, 1987]. They allow for an elegant reduction of decision problems for temporal and program logics [Emerson and Jutla, 1991; Bernholtz *et al.*, 1994]. Let $\mathcal{B}^+(I)$ be the set of positive boolean formulas over I, including also **true** and **false**. For a set $J \subseteq I$ and a formula $\varphi \in \mathcal{B}^+(I)$, we say that J *satisfies* φ iff assigning **true** to the elements in J and **false** to those in $I \setminus J$ makes φ true. Let $[k] = \{-1, 0, 1, \ldots, k\}$. A *two-way alternating automaton* over infinite k-ary trees is a tuple $\mathbf{A} = \langle \Sigma, Q, \delta, q_0, F \rangle$, where Σ is the input alphabet, Q is a finite set of states, $\delta : Q \times \Sigma \to \mathcal{B}^+([k] \times Q)$ is the transition function, $q_0 \in Q$ is the initial state, and F specifies the acceptance condition.

The transition function maps a state $q \in Q$ and an input letter $\sigma \in \Sigma$ to a positive boolean formula over $[k] \times Q$. Intuitively, if $\delta(q, \sigma) = \varphi$, then each pair (c, q') appearing in φ corresponds to a new copy of the automaton going to the direction suggested by c and starting in state q'. For example, if $k = 2$ and $\delta(q_1, \sigma) = (1, q_2) \wedge (1, q_3) \vee (-1, q_1) \wedge (0, q_3)$, when the automaton is in the state q_1 and is reading the node x labeled by the letter σ, it proceeds either by sending off two copies, in the states q_2 and q_3 respectively, to the first successor of x (i.e., $x \cdot 1$), or by sending off one copy in the state q_1 to the predecessor of x (i.e., $x \cdot -1$) and one copy in the state q_3 to x itself (i.e., $x \cdot 0$).

A run of a TWAA $\mathbf{A}$ over a labeled tree $\langle T, V \rangle$ is a labeled tree $\langle T_r, r \rangle$ in which every node is labeled by an element of $T \times Q$. A node in T_r labeled by $\langle x, q \rangle$ describes a copy of $\mathbf{A}$ that is in the state q and reads the node x of T. The labels of adjacent nodes have to satisfy the transition function of $\mathbf{A}$. Formally, a run $\langle T_r, r \rangle$ is a $T \times Q$-labeled tree satisfying:

1. $\varepsilon \in T_r$ and $r(\varepsilon) = \langle \varepsilon, q_0 \rangle$.

2. Let $y \in T_r$, with $r(y) = \langle x, q \rangle$ and $\delta(q, V(x)) = \varphi$. Then there is a (possibly empty) set $S = \{\langle c_1, q_1 \rangle, \ldots, \langle c_n, q_n \rangle\} \subseteq [k] \times Q$ such that:

   - S satisfies φ and
   - for all $1 \leq i \leq n$, we have that $y \cdot i \in T_r$, $x \cdot c_i$ is defined, and $r(y \cdot i) = \langle x \cdot c_i, q_i \rangle$.

A run $\langle T_r, r \rangle$ is *accepting* if all its infinite paths satisfy the acceptance condition. Given an infinite path $P \subseteq T_r$, let $inf(P) \subseteq Q$ be the set of states that appear infinitely often in P (as second components of node labels). We consider here *parity* acceptance conditions. A parity condition over a state set Q is a finite sequence $F = (G_1, \ldots, G_m)$ with $G_1 \subseteq G_2 \subseteq \cdots \subseteq G_m = Q$, and a path P satisfies F if there is an even i for which $inf(P) \cap G_i \neq \emptyset$ and $inf(P) \cap G_{i-1} = \emptyset$.

5.2 Reasoning in $\mu\mathcal{ALCI}_f$

First we observe that $\mu\mathcal{ALCI}_f$ has the *tree model property*, which states that if a $\mu\mathcal{ALCI}_f$ concept C is satisfiable then it is satisfied in an interpretation which has the structure of an infinite tree of bounded degree. In particular, the degree is bounded by $2 \cdot n$, where n is the number of atomic roles appearing in C. The tree model property can be shown following the lines of the proof in [Vardi, 1998] for the modal μ-calculus with backward modalities. Next we define a TWAA that accepts exactly the trees that are models of a concept.

The closure $cl(C)$ of a $\mu\mathcal{ALCI}_f$ concept C (which extends the one in [Kozen, 1983] for the modal μ-calculus) is defined as the smallest set $cl(C)$ of closed concepts that satisfies:

$C \in cl(C)$
$C' \in cl(C)$ implies $\neg C' \in cl(C)$ (we identify $\neg\neg C$ and C)
$C_1 \sqcap C_2, C_1 \sqcup C_2 \in cl(C)$ implies $C_1 \in cl(C)$ and $C_2 \in cl(C)$
$\exists R.C', \forall R.C' \in cl(C)$ implies $C' \in cl(C)$
$\lambda X.C' \in cl(C)$ implies $C'[X/\lambda X.C'] \in cl(C)$

Note that the cardinality of $cl(C)$ is linear in the length of C.

Let C be the $\mu\mathcal{ALCI}_f$ concept we want to check for satisfiability, which wlog we assume to be in negation normal form. Let $\mathcal{A}$ be the set of atomic concepts, and $\mathcal{P} = \{P_1, \ldots, P_n\}$ the set of atomic roles appearing in C. We construct from C a TWAA $\mathbf{A}_C$ which checks that C is satisfied at the root of the input tree. For technical reasons it is useful to consider trees where all nodes have the same branching degree $2n$. To this end we introduce dummy nodes in the tree. We use the symbols A_g and $\neg A_g$ to distinguish nodes that correspond to elements of the model from those that do not. We also represent in the nodes of the tree the information about the labeling of the edges by introducing for each role P_i four symbols $A_i, \neg A_i, A_i^-$, and $\neg A_i^-$. Intuitively, A_i labels $x \cdot i$ if $(x, x \cdot i) \in P_i^{\mathcal{I}}$ and $\neg A_i$ labels $x \cdot i$ if not. Similarly A_i^- labels $x \cdot i$ if $(x \cdot i, x) \in P_i^{\mathcal{I}}$ and $\neg A_i^-$ labels $x \cdot i$ if not.

Since all roles (both direct and inverse) are deterministic, we can assume that for each node x, each P_i and each P_i^- successor appears in a fixed position. In particular, $x \cdot i$ is labeled with A_i and $x \cdot (i+n)$ is labeled with A_i^-. Let det and ini be two new symbols, and $\mathcal{A}_{aux} = \{A_g, \neg A_g\} \cup \bigcup_{i=1}^n \{A_i, \neg A_i, A_i^-, \neg A_i^-\} \cup \{det\}$.

The automaton $\mathbf{A}_C = \langle \Sigma, S, \delta, ini, F \rangle$, where $\Sigma = 2^{\mathcal{A} \cup \mathcal{A}_{aux}}$, $S = cl(C) \cup \mathcal{A}_{aux} \cup \{ini, det\}$, the acceptance condition F is as in [Vardi, 1998] and the transition function δ is defined as follows. For all $\sigma \in \Sigma$: for all $A \in \mathcal{A} \cup \mathcal{A}_{aux}$ we have $\delta(A, \sigma) = \mathbf{true}$ if $A \in \sigma$, $\delta(A, \sigma) = \mathbf{false}$ if $A \notin \sigma$,

$\delta(\neg A, \sigma) = \mathbf{true}$ if $A \notin \sigma$, $\delta(\neg A, \sigma) = \mathbf{false}$ if $A \in \sigma$, and

$\delta(C_1 \sqcap C_2, \sigma) = (0, C_1) \wedge (0, C_2)$
$\delta(C_1 \sqcup C_2, \sigma) = (0, C_1) \vee (0, C_2)$
$\delta(\lambda X.C_1, \sigma) = (0, C[X/\lambda X.C_1])$
$\delta(\exists P_i.C_1, \sigma) = ((-1, C_1) \wedge (0, A_i^-)) \vee ((i, A_g) \wedge (i, C_1))$
$\delta(\exists P_i^-.C_1, \sigma) = ((-1, C_1) \wedge (0, A_i)) \vee ((i+n, A_g) \wedge (i+n, C_1))$
$\delta(\forall P_i.C_1, \sigma) = ((-1, C_1) \vee (0, \neg A_i^-)) \wedge ((i, \neg A_g) \vee (i, C_1))$
$\delta(\forall P_i^-.C_1, \sigma) = ((-1, C_1) \vee (0, \neg A_i)) \wedge ((i+n, \neg A_g) \vee (i+n, C_1))$
$\delta(det, \sigma) = \bigwedge_{i=1}^{2n}(i, det) \wedge$
$\qquad \bigwedge_{i=1}^{n}((i, \neg A_g) \vee (i, A_i) \wedge (i+n, \neg A_g) \vee (i+n, A_i^-)) \wedge$
$\qquad \bigwedge_{i=1}^{n}((0, \neg A_i) \vee (n+i, \neg A_g) \wedge (0, \neg A_i^-) \vee (i, \neg A_g))$
$\delta(ini, \sigma) = (0, det) \wedge (0, C)$

Intuitively, the automaton starts in the initial state ini and spawns two copies of itself: one verifies that the tree has the right structure wrt functionality, and one checks C on such structure.

Theorem 5.1 *A $\mu\mathcal{ALCI}_f$ concept C is satisfiable iff the set of trees accepted by $\mathbf{A}_C$ in not empty.*

Since nonemptiness of TWAA can be decided in EXPTIME [Vardi, 1998] we get the following upper bound.

Corollary 5.2 *Concept satisfiability in $\mu\mathcal{ALCI}_f$ can be decided in EXPTIME.*

Since the reduction in the previous section is polynomial, we get a worst case deterministic exponential time decision procedure for logical implication in $\mathcal{DLR}_\mu$. Moreover, since logical implication in $\mathcal{DLR}_\mu$ is EXPTIME-hard (it is so already for $\mathcal{ALC}$) we get the following tight complexity bound.

Theorem 5.3 *Logical implication in $\mathcal{DLR}_\mu$ is EXPTIME-complete.*

6 Conclusions

By addressing general fixpoints on concepts, in addition to more standard constructs, DLs finally meet the modeling requirements of advanced applications. The EXPTIME reasoning procedure for $\mathcal{DLR}_\mu$ is the first decidability result for a logic combining inverse roles, number restrictions, and general fixpoints. In particular, since modal μ-calculus extended both with graded and backward modalities corresponds to $\mu\mathcal{ALCQI}$, the result here applies to such logic as well.

We observe that reasoning in the presence of extensional information (ABox) remains an open problem for $\mathcal{DLR}_\mu$.

References

[Artale and Franconi, 1994] A. Artale and E. Franconi. A computational account for a description logic of time and action. In *KR-94*, pages 3–14, 1994.

[Baader, 1991] F. Baader. Augmenting concept languages by transitive closure of roles: An alternative to terminological cycles. In *IJCAI-91*, 1991.

[Baader, 1996] F. Baader. Using automata theory for characterizing the semantics of terminological cycles. *Ann. of Math. and AI*, 18:175–219, 1996.

[Bergamaschi and Sartori, 1992] S. Bergamaschi and C. Sartori. On taxonomic reasoning in conceptual design. *ACM TODS*, 17(3):385–422, 1992.

[Bernholtz et al., 1994] O. Bernholtz, M. Y. Vardi, and P. Wolper. An automata-theoretic approach to branching-time model checking. In *CAV-94*, LNCS 818, pages 142–155, 1994.

[Blanco et al., 1994] J. L. Blanco, A. Illarramendi, and A. Goñi. Building a federated relational database system: An approach using a knowledge-based system. *J. of Intelligent and Cooperative Information Systems*, 3(4):415–455, 1994.

[Booch et al., 1998] G. Booch, J. Rumbaugh, and I. Jacobson. *Unified Modeling Language User Guide*. Addison Wesley, 1998.

[Borgida and Patel-Schneider, 1994] A. Borgida and P. F. Patel-Schneider. A semantics and complete algorithm for subsumption in the CLASSIC description logic. *JAIR*, 1:277–308, 1994.

[Borgida, 1995] A. Borgida. Description logics in data management. *IEEE Trans. on Knowledge and Data Engineering*, 7(5):671–682, 1995.

[Bray et al., 1998] T. Bray, J. Paoli, and C. M. Sperberg-McQueen. *Extensible Markup Language (XML) 1.0 – W3C Recommendation*, 1998.

[Buneman, 1997] P. Buneman. Semistructured data. In *PODS-97*, pages 117–121, 1997.

[Calvanese et al., 1994] D. Calvanese, M. Lenzerini, and D. Nardi. A unified framework for class based representation formalisms. In *KR-94*, pages 109–120, 1994.

[Calvanese et al., 1995] D. Calvanese, G. De Giacomo, and M. Lenzerini. Structured objects: Modeling and reasoning. In *DOOD-95*, LNCS 1013, pages 229–246, 1995.

[Calvanese et al., 1998a] D. Calvanese, G. De Giacomo, and M. Lenzerini. On the decidability of query containment under constraints. In *PODS-98*, pages 149–158, 1998.

[Calvanese et al., 1998b] D. Calvanese, G. De Giacomo, and M. Lenzerini. What can knowledge representation do for semi-structured data? In *AAAI-98*, pages 205–210, 1998.

[Calvanese et al., 1998c] D. Calvanese, G. De Giacomo, M. Lenzerini, D. Nardi, and R. Rosati. Description logic framework for information integration. In *KR-98*, pages 2–13, 1998.

[Catarci and Lenzerini, 1993] T. Catarci and M. Lenzerini. Representing and using interschema knowledge in cooperative information systems. *J. of Intelligent and Cooperative Information Systems*, 2(4):375–398, 1993.

[De Giacomo and Lenzerini, 1994] G. De Giacomo and M. Lenzerini. Boosting the correspondence between description logics and propositional dynamic logics. In *AAAI-94*, pages 205–212, 1994.

[De Giacomo and Lenzerini, 1995] G. De Giacomo and M. Lenzerini. What's in an aggregate: Foundations for description logics with tuples and sets. In *IJCAI-95*, pages 801–807, 1995.

[De Giacomo and Lenzerini, 1997] G. De Giacomo and M. Lenzerini. A uniform framework for concept definitions in description logics. *JAIR*, 6:87–110, 1997.

[Devanbu and Jones, 1997] P. Devanbu and M. A. Jones. The use of description logics in KBSE systems. *ACM Trans. on Software Engineering and Methodology*, 6(2):141–172, 1997.

[Donini et al., 1996] F. M. Donini, M. Lenzerini, D. Nardi, and A. Schaerf. Reasoning in description logics. In *Principles of Knowledge Representation*, pages 193–238. 1996.

[Emerson and Jutla, 1991] E. A. Emerson and C. S. Jutla. Tree automata, mu-calculus and determinacy. In *FOCS-91*, pages 368–377, 1991.

[Kozen, 1983] D. Kozen. Results on the propositional μ-calculus. *Theor. Comp. Sci.*, 27:333–354, 1983.

[Levy et al., 1996] A. Y. Levy, A. Rajaraman, and J. J. Ordille. Query answering algorithms for information agents. In *AAAI-96*, pages 40–47, 1996.

[Muller and Schupp, 1987] D. E. Muller and P. E. Schupp. Alternating automata on infinite trees. *Theor. Comp. Sci.*, 54:267–276, 1987.

[Nebel, 1991] B. Nebel. Terminological cycles: Semantics and computational properties. In *Principles of Semantic Networks*, pages 331–361. Morgan Kaufmann, 1991.

[Schild, 1991] K. Schild. A correspondence theory for terminological logics: Preliminary report. In *IJCAI-91*, pages 466–471, 1991.

[Schild, 1994] K. Schild. Terminological cycles and the propositional μ-calculus. In *KR-94*, pages 509–520, 1994.

[Sheth et al., 1993] A. P. Sheth, S. K. Gala, and S. B. Navathe. On automatic reasoning for schema integration. *J. of Intelligent and Cooperative Information Systems*, 2(1):23–50, 1993.

[Ullman, 1997] J. D. Ullman. Information integration using logical views. In *ICDT-97*, LNCS 1186, pages 19–40, 1997.

[Van der Hoek and De Rijke, 1995] W. Van der Hoek and M. De Rijke. Counting objects. *J. of Log. and Comp.*, 5(3):325–345, 1995.

[Vardi, 1985] M. Y. Vardi. The taming of converse: Reasoning about two-way computations. In LNCS 193, pages 413–424, 1985.

[Vardi, 1998] M. Y. Vardi. Reasoning about the past with two-way automata. In *ICALP'98*, LNCS 1443, pages 628–641, 1998.

[Weida and Litman, 1992] R. Weida and D. Litman. Terminological reasoning with constraint networks and an application to plan recognition. In *KR-92*, pages 282–293, 1992.

[Woods and Schmolze, 1992] W. A. Woods and J. G. Schmolze. The KL-ONE family. In *Semantic Networks in Artificial Intelligence*, pages 133–178. Pergamon Press, 1992.

Reasoning with Concrete Domains

Carsten Lutz

RWTH Aachen, LuFg Theoretical Computer Science

Ahornstr. 55, 52074 Aachen, Germany

`clu@cantor.informatik.rwth-aachen.de`

Abstract

Description logics are formalisms for the representation of and reasoning about conceptual knowledge on an abstract level. Concrete domains allow the integration of description logic reasoning with reasoning about concrete objects such as numbers, time intervals, or spatial regions. The importance of this combined approach, especially for building real-world applications, is widely accepted. However, the complexity of reasoning with concrete domains has never been formally analyzed and efficient algorithms have not been developed. This paper closes the gap by providing a tight bound for the complexity of reasoning with concrete domains and presenting optimal algorithms.

1 Introduction

Description logics are knowledge representation and reasoning formalisms dealing with conceptual knowledge on an abstract logical level. However, for a variety of applications, it is essential to integrate the abstract knowledge with knowledge of a more concrete nature. Examples of such "concrete knowledge" include all kinds of numerical data as well as temporal and spatial information. Important application areas which have been found to depend on integrated reasoning with concrete knowledge are, e.g., mechanical engineering [Baader and Hanschke, 1993], reasoning about aggregation in databases [Baader and Sattler, 1998], as well as temporal and spatial reasoning (see [Haarslev *et al.*, 1998] and [Lutz, 1998]). Many description logic systems such as e.g. CLASSIC and $\mathcal{KRIS}$ (see [Borgida *et al.*, 1989], [Baader and Hollunder, 1991], resp.), provide interfaces that allow the attachment of external reasoning facilities which deal with concrete information. Surprisingly, the complexity of combined reasoning with abstract and concrete knowledge has, to the best of our knowledge, never been formally analyzed and provably optimal algorithms have not been developed. Recent efficient implementations of expressive description logics like FACT (see [Horrocks, 1998]) concentrate on logics for which reasoning is in PSPACE. An important reason why these systems fail to integrate concrete knowledge is that no complexity results and no efficient algorithms are available.

Baader and Hanschke [1991] extend description logics by concrete domains, a theoretically well-founded approach to integrated reasoning with abstract and concrete knowledge. On basis of the well-known description logic $\mathcal{ALC}$, they define the description logic $\mathcal{ALC}(\mathcal{D})$, which can be parameterized by a concrete domain $\mathcal{D}$. In this paper, we extend $\mathcal{ALC}(\mathcal{D})$ by the operators feature agreement and feature disagreement. This leads to the new logic $\mathcal{ALCF}(\mathcal{D})$, which combines $\mathcal{ALC}(\mathcal{D})$ with the logic $\mathcal{ALCF}$ [Hollunder and Nutt, 1990]. Algorithms for deciding the concept satisfiability and ABox consistency problems for the logic $\mathcal{ALCF}(\mathcal{D})$ are given. Furthermore, the complexity of reasoning with $\mathcal{ALCF}(\mathcal{D})$ is formally analyzed. Since reasoning with $\mathcal{ALCF}(\mathcal{D})$ involves a satisfiability check for the concrete domain, the complexity of the combined formalism depends on the complexity of reasoning in the concrete domain. The proposed algorithms are proved to need polynomial space which implies that, first, reasoning with $\mathcal{ALCF}(\mathcal{D})$ is PSPACE-complete provided that reasoning with the concrete domain is in PSPACE, and, second, the devised algorithms are optimal. The obtained complexity results carry over to the description logic $\mathcal{ALC}(\mathcal{D})$. The algorithmic techniques introduced in this paper are vital for efficient implementations of both $\mathcal{ALCF}(\mathcal{D})$ and $\mathcal{ALC}(\mathcal{D})$.

As a simple example illustrating the expressivity of $\mathcal{ALCF}(\mathcal{D})$, consider the concept *Man* $\sqcap$ *wife*$\downarrow$*boss* $\sqcap$ $\exists$*wage*, *(wife wage)*. $>$. In this example, *Man* is a primitive concept, *wife* and *wage* are features (i.e., single valued roles), and $>$ is a concrete predicate. The given concept describes the set of men whose boss coincides with their wife and who, furthermore, have a higher wage than their wife. In this example, the wage of a person is knowledge of a concrete type while being a man is knowledge of a more abstract nature. The coincidence of wife and boss is described using the feature agreement operator $\downarrow$ and cannot be expressed in $\mathcal{ALC}(\mathcal{D})$. The syntax used is defined in the next section.

2 The Description Logic $\mathcal{ALCF}(\mathcal{D})$

In this section, the description logic $\mathcal{ALCF}(\mathcal{D})$ is introduced. We start the formal specification by recalling the definition of a concrete domain given in [Baader and Hanschke, 1991].

Definition 1. A *concrete domain* $\mathcal{D}$ is a pair $(\Delta_{\mathcal{D}}, \Phi_{\mathcal{D}})$, where $\Delta_{\mathcal{D}}$ is a set called the domain, and $\Phi_{\mathcal{D}}$ is a set of predicate names. Each predicate name P in $\Phi_{\mathcal{D}}$ is associated with an arity n and an n-ary predicate $P^{\mathcal{D}} \subseteq \Delta_{\mathcal{D}}^n$. A concrete domain $\mathcal{D}$ is called *admissible* iff (1) the set of its predicate names is closed under negation and contains a name $\top_{\mathcal{D}}$ for $\Delta_{\mathcal{D}}$ and (2) the satisfiability problem for finite conjunctions of predicates is decidable.

On the basis of concrete domains, the syntax of $\mathcal{ALCF}(\mathcal{D})$ concepts can be defined.

Definition 2. Let C, R, and F be disjoint sets of concept, role, and feature names[1]. A composition $f_1 f_2 \cdots f_n$ of features is called a *feature chain*. Any element of C is a *concept*. If C and D are concepts, R is a role or feature, $P \in \Phi_{\mathcal{D}}$ is a predicate name with arity n, and $u_1, \ldots, u_n$ are feature chains, then the following expressions are also concepts:

- $\neg C$ (negation), $C \sqcap D$ (conjunction), $C \sqcup D$ (disjunction), $\forall R.C$ (value restriction), $\exists R.C$ (exists restriction),
- $\exists u_1, \ldots, u_n.P$ (predicate operator)
- $u_1 \downarrow u_2$ (feature agreement), $u_1 \uparrow u_2$ (feature disagreement).

A simple feature is a feature chain of length one. For a feature chain $u = f_1 \cdots f_n$, $\exists u.C$ and $\forall u.C$ will be used as abbreviations for $\exists f_1 \ldots \exists f_n.C$ and $\forall f_1 \ldots \forall f_n.C$, respectively. As usual, a set theoretic semantics is given.

Definition 3. An *interpretation* $\mathcal{I} = (\Delta_{\mathcal{I}}, \cdot^{\mathcal{I}})$ consists of a set $\Delta_{\mathcal{I}}$ (the abstract domain) and an interpretation function $\cdot^{\mathcal{I}}$. The sets $\Delta_{\mathcal{D}}$ and $\Delta_{\mathcal{I}}$ must be disjoint. The interpretation function maps each concept name C to a subset $C^{\mathcal{I}}$ of $\Delta_{\mathcal{I}}$, each role name R to a subset $R^{\mathcal{I}}$ of $\Delta_{\mathcal{I}} \times \Delta_{\mathcal{I}}$, and each feature name f to a partial function $f^{\mathcal{I}}$ from $\Delta_{\mathcal{I}}$ to $\Delta_{\mathcal{D}} \cup \Delta_{\mathcal{I}}$, where $f^{\mathcal{I}}(a) = x$ will be written as $(a, x) \in f^{\mathcal{I}}$. If $u = f_1 \cdots f_k$ is a feature chain, then $u^{\mathcal{I}}$ is defined as the composition $f_1^{\mathcal{I}} \circ \cdots \circ f_k^{\mathcal{I}}$ of the partial functions $f_1^{\mathcal{I}}, \ldots, f_k^{\mathcal{I}}$. Let the symbols C, D, R, P, and $u_1, \ldots, u_n$ be defined as in Definition 2. Then the interpretation function can be extended to complex concepts as follows:

$$(C \sqcap D)^{\mathcal{I}} := C^{\mathcal{I}} \cap D^{\mathcal{I}}$$
$$(C \sqcup D)^{\mathcal{I}} := C^{\mathcal{I}} \cup D^{\mathcal{I}}$$
$$(\neg C)^{\mathcal{I}} := \Delta_{\mathcal{I}} \setminus C^{\mathcal{I}}$$
$$(\exists R.C)^{\mathcal{I}} := \{a \in \Delta_{\mathcal{I}} \mid \exists b \in \Delta_{\mathcal{I}}:$$
$$(a, b) \in R^{\mathcal{I}} \wedge b \in C^{\mathcal{I}}\}$$
$$(\forall R.C)^{\mathcal{I}} := \{a \in \Delta_{\mathcal{I}} \mid \forall b: (a, b) \in R^{\mathcal{I}} \rightarrow b \in C^{\mathcal{I}}\}$$
$$(\exists u_1, \ldots, u_n.P)^{\mathcal{I}} := \{a \in \Delta_{\mathcal{I}} \mid \exists x_1, \ldots, x_n \in \Delta_{\mathcal{D}}:$$
$$(a, x_1) \in u_1^{\mathcal{I}} \wedge \cdots \wedge (a, x_n) \in u_n^{\mathcal{I}} \wedge$$
$$(x_1, \ldots, x_n) \in P^{\mathcal{D}}\}$$
$$(u_1 \uparrow u_2)^{\mathcal{I}} := \{a \in \Delta_{\mathcal{I}} \mid \exists b_1, b_2 \in \Delta_{\mathcal{I}}: b_1 \neq b_2 \wedge$$
$$(a, b_1) \in u_1^{\mathcal{I}} \wedge (a, b_2) \in u_2^{\mathcal{I}}\}$$
$$(u_1 \downarrow u_2)^{\mathcal{I}} := \{a \in \Delta_{\mathcal{I}} \mid \exists b \in \Delta_{\mathcal{I}}: (a, b) \in u_1^{\mathcal{I}} \wedge$$
$$(a, b) \in u_2^{\mathcal{I}}\}$$

---

[1]In the following, the notion *role* (*feature*) is used synonymously for role name (feature name).

An interpretation $\mathcal{I}$ is a *model* of a concept C iff $C^{\mathcal{I}} \neq \emptyset$. A concept C is *satisfiable* iff there exists a model $\mathcal{I}$ of C. A concept C *subsumes* a concept D (written $D \preceq C$) iff $D^{\mathcal{I}} \subseteq C^{\mathcal{I}}$ for all interpretations $\mathcal{I}$.

Subsumption can be reduced to satisfiability since $D \preceq C$ iff the concept $D \sqcap \neg C$ is unsatisfiable. Please note that the feature agreement and feature disagreement operators consider only objects from $\Delta_{\mathcal{I}}$ and no objects from $\Delta_{\mathcal{D}}$. Agreement and disagreement over concrete objects can be expressed by using a concrete domain which includes an equality predicate. Using disjunction, "global" agreement and disagreement over both the concrete and the abstract domain can then also be expressed (see [Lutz, 1998]). This approach was chosen since global agreement and disagreement are not considered to be very "natural" operators. We will now introduce the assertional formalism of $\mathcal{ALCF}(\mathcal{D})$.

Definition 4. Let O_D and O_A be disjoint sets of object names. Elements of O_D are called *concrete objects* and elements of O_A are called *abstract objects*. If C, R, f, and P are defined as in Definition 2, a and b are elements of O_A and x, $x_1, \ldots, x_n$ are elements of O_D, then the following expressions are *assertional axioms*:

$$a{:}C, \quad (a,b){:}R, \quad (a,x){:}f, \quad a \neq b, \quad (x_1, \ldots, x_n){:}P$$

A finite set of assertional axioms is called an $\mathcal{ALCF}(\mathcal{D})$ *ABox*. An interpretation for the concept language can be extended to the assertional language by mapping every object name from O_A to an element of $\Delta_{\mathcal{I}}$ and every object name from O_D to an element of $\Delta_{\mathcal{D}}$. The unique name assumption is not imposed, i.e. $a^{\mathcal{I}} = b^{\mathcal{I}}$ may hold even if a and b are distinct object names. An interpretation satisfies an assertional axiom

$$a{:}C \quad \text{iff} \quad a^{\mathcal{I}} \in C^{\mathcal{I}},$$
$$(a,b){:}R \quad \text{iff} \quad (a^{\mathcal{I}}, b^{\mathcal{I}}) \in R^{\mathcal{I}},$$
$$(a,x){:}f \quad \text{iff} \quad (a^{\mathcal{I}}, x^{\mathcal{I}}) \in f^{\mathcal{I}},$$
$$a \neq b \quad \text{iff} \quad a^{\mathcal{I}} \neq b^{\mathcal{I}},$$
$$(x_1, \ldots, x_n){:}P \quad \text{iff} \quad (x_1^{\mathcal{I}}, \ldots, x_n^{\mathcal{I}}) \in P^{\mathcal{D}}.$$

An interpretation is a *model* of an ABox $\mathcal{A}$ iff it satisfies all assertional axioms in $\mathcal{A}$. An ABox is *consistent* iff it has a model.

Satisfiability of concepts, as introduced in Definition 3, can be reduced to ABox consistency since a concept C is satisfiable iff the ABox $\{a{:}C\}$ is consistent. In the next section, an algorithm for deciding the consistency of $\mathcal{ALCF}(\mathcal{D})$ ABoxes is presented.

3 Algorithms

Completion algorithms, also known as tableau algorithms, are frequently used to decide concept satisfiability and ABox consistency for various description logics. Completion algorithms work on (possibly generalized) ABoxes and are characterized by a set of completion rules and a strategy to apply these rules to the assertional axioms of an ABox. The algorithm starts with an initial ABox $\mathcal{A}_0$ whose consistency is to be decided. If the satisfiability of a concept C is to be decided, the ABox $\{a\!:\!C\}$ is considered. The algorithm repeatedly applies completion rules adding new axioms, and, by doing so, makes all knowledge implicitly contained in the ABox explicit. If the algorithm succeeds to construct an ABox which is complete (i.e., to which no more completion rules are applicable) and which does not contain an obvious contradiction, then $\mathcal{A}_0$ has a model. Otherwise, $\mathcal{A}_0$ does not have a model.

In [Hollunder and Nutt, 1990], a completion algorithm for deciding the satisfiability of $\mathcal{ALCF}$ concepts is given which can be executed in polynomial space. In [Baader and Hanschke, 1991], an algorithm for deciding the consistency of $\mathcal{ALC}(\mathcal{D})$ (i.e., $\mathcal{ALCF}(\mathcal{D})$ without feature agreement and disagreement) ABoxes is given. However, this algorithm needs exponential space in the worst case. This is due to the fact that the algorithm collects *all* axioms of the form $(x_1, \ldots, x_n)\!:\!P$ (*concrete domain axioms*) obtained during rule application, conjoins them into one big conjunction c, and finally tests c for satisfiability w.r.t. the concrete domain. Unfortunately, the size of this conjunction may be exponential in the size of $\mathcal{A}_0$ (see [Lutz, 1998] for an example). To obtain a polynomial space algorithm for deciding the consistency of $\mathcal{ALCF}(\mathcal{D})$ ABoxes, the concrete domain satisfiability test has to be broken up into independent "chunks" of polynomial size.

The completion algorithm for deciding the consistency of $\mathcal{ALCF}(\mathcal{D})$ ABoxes is developed in two steps: First, an algorithm for deciding the satisfiability of $\mathcal{ALCF}(\mathcal{D})$ concepts is devised. Second, an algorithm is given which reduces ABox consistency to concept satisfiability by constructing a number of "reduction concepts" for a given ABox $\mathcal{A}_0$. A similar reduction can be found in [Hollunder, 1994].

Before giving a formal description of the completion algorithms themselves, the completion rules are defined. To define the rules in a succinct way, the functions $succ_\mathcal{A}$ and $chain_\mathcal{A}$ are introduced. Let $\mathcal{A}$ be an ABox. For an object $a \in \mathsf{O}_A$ and a feature chain u, $succ_\mathcal{A}(a, u)$ denotes the object b that can be found by following u starting from a in $\mathcal{A}$. If no such object exists, $succ_\mathcal{A}(a, u)$ denotes the special object ϵ that cannot be part of any ABox. An object name $a \in \mathsf{O}_A$ is called *fresh* in $\mathcal{A}$ if a is not used in $\mathcal{A}$. Let a be an object from O_A, x be an object from O_D, and $u = f_1 \cdots f_k$ be a feature chain. The function *chain* is defined as follows:

$chain_\mathcal{A}(a, x, u) := \{(a, c_1)\!:\!f_1, \ldots, (c_{k-1}, x)\!:\!f_k\}$
where the $c_1, \ldots, c_{k-1} \in \mathsf{O}_A$ are distinct and fresh in $\mathcal{A}$.

Now, the set of completion rules can be formulated. Please note that the completion rule R⊔ is nondeterministic, i.e., there is more than one possible outcome of a rule application.

Definition 5. The following *completion rules* replace a given ABox $\mathcal{A}$ nondeterministically by an ABox $\mathcal{A}'$. An ABox $\mathcal{A}$ is said to contain a *fork* (for a feature f) iff it contains the two axioms $(a, b)\!:\!f$ and $(a, c)\!:\!f$ or the two axioms $(a, x)\!:\!f$ and $(a, y)\!:\!f$, where $b, c \in \mathsf{O}_A$ and $x, y \in \mathsf{O}_D$. A fork can be eliminated by replacing all occurrences of c in $\mathcal{A}$ with b, or of x with y, resp. It is assumed that forks are eliminated as soon as they appear (as part of the rule application) with the proviso that newly generated objects are replaced by older ones and not vice versa. In the following, C and D denote concepts, $\hat{R}$ a role, f a feature, P a predicate name from $\Phi_\mathcal{D}$

with arity n, $u_1, \ldots, u_n$ feature chains, a and b objects from O_A, and $x_1, \ldots, x_n$ objects from O_D.

R⊓ The conjunction rule.
If $a\!:\!C \sqcap D \in \mathcal{A}$, $\{a\!:\!C,\ a\!:\!D\} \not\subseteq \mathcal{A}$
then $\mathcal{A}' = \mathcal{A} \cup \{a\!:\!C,\ a\!:\!D\}$

R⊔ The (nondeterministic) disjunction rule.
If $a\!:\!C \sqcup D \in \mathcal{A}$, $\{a\!:\!C,\ a\!:\!D\} \cap \mathcal{A} = \emptyset$
then $\mathcal{A}' = \mathcal{A} \cup \{a\!:\!C\} \ \vee \ \mathcal{A}' = \mathcal{A} \cup \{a\!:\!D\}$

Rr∃C, Rf∃C The role/feature exists restriction rule.
If $a\!:\!\exists \hat{R}.C \in \mathcal{A}$, $\nexists b \in \mathsf{O}_A : \{(a,b)\!:\!\hat{R},\ b\!:\!C\} \subseteq \mathcal{A}$
then $\mathcal{A}' = \mathcal{A} \cup \{(a,b)\!:\!\hat{R},\ b\!:\!C\}$ where $b \in \mathsf{O}_A$ is fresh in $\mathcal{A}$.
This is the Rr∃C rule. To obtain Rf∃C, replace $\hat{R}$ by f.

Rr∀C, Rf∀C The role/feature value restriction rule.
If $a\!:\!\forall \hat{R}.C \in \mathcal{A}$, $\exists b \in \mathsf{O}_A : (a,b)\!:\!\hat{R} \in \mathcal{A} \wedge b\!:\!C \notin \mathcal{A}$
then $\mathcal{A}' = \mathcal{A} \cup \{b\!:\!C\}$
This is the Rr∀C rule. To obtain Rf∀C, replace $\hat{R}$ by f.

R∃P The predicate exists restriction rule (may create forks).
If $a\!:\!\exists u_1, \ldots, u_n.P \in \mathcal{A}$, $\nexists x_1, \ldots, x_n \in \mathsf{O}_D :$
$\quad (succ_\mathcal{A}(a, u_1) = x_1 \wedge \ldots \wedge succ_\mathcal{A}(a, u_n) = x_n \wedge$
$\quad (x_1, \ldots, x_n)\!:\!P \in \mathcal{A})$
then $\mathcal{C}_0 := \mathcal{A} \cup \{(x_1, \ldots, x_n)\!:\!P\}$
$\quad$ where the $x_i \in \mathsf{O}_D$ are distinct and fresh in $\mathcal{A}$.
$\quad \mathcal{C}_1 := chain_{\mathcal{C}_0}(a, x_1, u_1), \ldots, \mathcal{C}_n := chain_{\mathcal{C}_{n-1}}(a, x_n, u_n)$
$\quad \mathcal{A}' = \bigcup_{i=0 \ldots n} \mathcal{C}_i$

R↓ The agreement rule (may create forks).
If $a\!:\!u_1 \downarrow u_2 \in \mathcal{A}$, $\nexists b \in \mathsf{O}_A : succ_\mathcal{A}(a, u_1) = succ_\mathcal{A}(a, u_2) = b$
then $\mathcal{C} = \mathcal{A} \cup chain_\mathcal{A}(a, b, u_1)$ where $b \in \mathsf{O}_A$ is fresh in $\mathcal{A}$.
$\quad \mathcal{A}' = \mathcal{C} \cup chain_\mathcal{C}(a, b, u_2)$

R↑ The disagreement rule (may create forks).
If $a\!:\!u_1 \uparrow u_2 \in \mathcal{A}$, $\nexists b_1, b_2 \in \mathsf{O}_A :$
$\quad (succ_\mathcal{A}(a, u_1) = b_1 \wedge succ_\mathcal{A}(a, u_2) = b_2 \wedge b_1 \neq b_2 \in \mathcal{A})$
then $\mathcal{C} = \mathcal{A} \cup chain_\mathcal{A}(a, b_1, u_1)$
$\quad \mathcal{A}' = \mathcal{C} \cup chain_\mathcal{C}(a, b_2, u_2) \ \cup \ \{b_1 \neq b_2\}$
$\quad$ where $b_1, b_2 \in \mathsf{O}_A$ are distinct and fresh in $\mathcal{A}$.

Rule applications that generate new objects are called *generating*. All other rule applications are called *non-generating*. All applications of the Rr∃C rule are generating. Application of the rules Rf∃C, R∃P, R↓, R↑ are usually generating but may be non-generating if fork elimination takes place.

A formalized notion of contradictory and of complete ABoxes is introduced in the following.

Definition 6. Let the same naming conventions be given as in Definition 5. An ABox $\mathcal{A}$ is called *contradictory* if one of the following *clash triggers* is applicable. If none of the clash triggers is applicable to an ABox $\mathcal{A}$, then $\mathcal{A}$ is called *clash-free*.

- *Primitive clash*: $\{a\!:\!C,\ a\!:\!\neg C\} \subseteq \mathcal{A}$
- *Feature domain clash*: $\{(a,x)\!:\!f,\ (a,b)\!:\!f\} \subseteq \mathcal{A}$
- *All domain clash*: $\{(a,x)\!:\!f,\ a\!:\!\forall f.C\} \subseteq \mathcal{A}$
- *Agreement clash*: $a \neq a \in \mathcal{A}$

An ABox to which no completion rule is applicable is called *complete*. An ABox $\mathcal{A}$ is called *concrete domain satisfiable* iff there exists a mapping δ from O_D to $\mathcal{D}$, such that $\bigwedge_{(x_1, \ldots, x_n)P \in \mathcal{A}} (\delta(x_1), \ldots, \delta(x_n)) \in P^\mathcal{D}$ is true in $\mathcal{D}$.

define procedure sat($\mathcal{A}$)
$\quad$ $\mathcal{A}' :=$ feature-complete($\mathcal{A}$)
$\quad$ **if** $\mathcal{A}'$ contains a clash **then**
$\quad\quad$ **return** *inconsistent*
$\quad$ $\mathcal{C} := \{\alpha \in \mathcal{A}' \mid \alpha$ is of the form $(x_1, \ldots, x_n) : P\}$
$\quad$ **if** satisfiable?($\mathcal{D},\mathcal{C}$) = *no* **then**
$\quad\quad$ **return** *inconsistent*
$\quad$ **forall** $a : \exists \hat{R}.D \in \mathcal{A}'$, where $\hat{R}$ is a role, **do**
$\quad\quad$ Let b be an object name from O_A.
$\quad\quad$ **if** sat($\{b : D\} \cup \{b : E \mid a : \forall \hat{R}.E \in \mathcal{A}'\}$)
$\quad\quad\quad$ returns *inconsistent* **then**
$\quad\quad\quad\quad$ **return** *inconsistent*
$\quad$ **return** *consistent*

define procedure feature-complete($\mathcal{A}$)
$\quad$ **while** a rule r from the set $\{$R$\sqcap$, R$\sqcup$, Rf$\exists$C, Rf$\forall$C,
$\quad\quad$ R$\exists$P, R$\downarrow$, R$\uparrow\}$ is applicable to $\mathcal{A}$, **do**
$\quad\quad$ $\mathcal{A} := \mathcal{A} \cup apply(\mathcal{A}, r)$
$\quad$ **return** $\mathcal{A}$

Figure 1: The sat algorithm.

We are now ready to define the completion algorithm sat for deciding the satisfiability of $\mathcal{ALCF(D)}$ concepts. Sat takes an ABox $\{a : C\}$ as input, where C has to be in *negation normal form*, i.e., negation is allowed only in front of concept names. Conversion to NNF can be done by exhaustively applying appropriate rewrite rules to push negation inwards. We only give the conversion rules needed for the new constructors feature agreement and feature disagreement, and refer to [Baader and Hanschke, 1991] for the $\mathcal{ALC(D)}$ rule set.

$$\neg(u_1 {\downarrow} u_2) = \exists u_1.\top_{\mathcal{D}} \sqcup \exists u_2.\top_{\mathcal{D}}$$
$$\sqcup \; \forall u_1.\bot \sqcup \forall u_2.\bot \sqcup u_1 {\uparrow} u_2$$
$$\neg(u_1 {\uparrow} u_2) = \exists u_1.\top_{\mathcal{D}} \sqcup \exists u_2.\top_{\mathcal{D}}$$
$$\sqcup \; \forall u_1.\bot \sqcup \forall u_2.\bot \sqcup u_1 {\downarrow} u_2$$

Any $\mathcal{ALCF(D)}$ concept can be converted into an equivalent concept in NNF in linear time. Some comments about the application of nondeterministic completion rules are in order. The application of the nondeterministic rule R$\sqcup$ yields more than one possible outcome. It is not specified which possibility is chosen in a given run of a completion algorithm. This means that the algorithms to be specified are nondeterministic algorithms. Such algorithms returns a positive result if there is *any* way to make the nondeterministic decisions such that a positive result is obtained.

The satisfiability algorithm makes use of two auxiliary functions which will be described only informally. The function *apply* takes two arguments, an ABox $\mathcal{A}$ and a completion rule r. It applies r once to arbitrary axioms from $\mathcal{A}$ matching r's premise and (nondeterministically) returns a descendant of $\mathcal{A}$ that is obtained by rule application. The function satisfiable? takes as arguments a concrete domain $\mathcal{D}$ and a set $\mathcal{C}$ of concrete domain axioms. It returns *yes* if the conjunction of all axioms in $\mathcal{C}$ is satisfiable w.r.t. $\mathcal{D}$ and *no* otherwise. The sat algorithm is given in figure 1. Based on sat, we define the ABox-cons algorithm for deciding ABox consistency. This algorithm can be found in figure 2.

A formal correctness proof for the algorithms is omitted for the sake of brevity and can be found in [Lutz, 1998]. A

define procedure ABox-cons($\mathcal{A}$)
$\quad$ eliminate forks in $\mathcal{A}$ (see Definition 5)
$\quad$ $\mathcal{A} :=$ preprocess($\mathcal{A}$)
$\quad$ $\mathcal{C} := \{\alpha \in \mathcal{A} \mid \alpha$ is of the form $(x_1, \ldots, x_n) : P\}$
$\quad$ **if** $\mathcal{A}$ contains a clash **then**
$\quad\quad$ **return** *inconsistent*
$\quad$ **if** satisfiable?($\mathcal{D},\mathcal{C}$) = *no* **then**
$\quad\quad$ **return** *inconsistent*
$\quad$ **forall** $a : \exists \hat{R}.D \in \mathcal{A}$, where $\hat{R}$ is a role, **do**
$\quad\quad$ Let b be an object name from O_A.
$\quad\quad$ **if** sat($\{b : (D \sqcap \bigsqcap\limits_{a : \forall R.E \in \mathcal{A}} E)\}$)
$\quad\quad\quad$ returns *inconsistent* **then**
$\quad\quad\quad\quad$ **return** *inconsistent*
$\quad$ **return** *consistent*

define procedure preprocess($\mathcal{A}$)
$\quad$ **while** a rule r from the set $\{$R$\sqcap$, R$\sqcup$, Rr$\forall$C, Rf$\exists$C,
$\quad\quad$ Rf$\forall$C, R$\exists$P, R$\downarrow$, R$\uparrow\}$ is applicable to $\mathcal{A}$, **do**
$\quad\quad$ $\mathcal{A} := \mathcal{A} \cup apply(\mathcal{A}, r)$
$\quad$ **return** $\mathcal{A}$

Figure 2: The ABox-cons algorithm.

short, informal discussion of the employed strategies is given instead. The sat algorithm performs depth-first search over role successors. This technique, first introduced by Schmidt-Schauß and Smolka [1991] for the logic $\mathcal{ALC}$, allows to keep only a polynomial fragment (called "trace") of the model in memory, although the total size of the model may be exponential. Tracing algorithms usually expand the axioms belonging to a single object, only, and make a recursive call for each role successor of this object. This is not feasible in the case of $\mathcal{ALCF(D)}$ since more than a single object may have to be considered when checking concrete domain satisfiability. The central idea to overcome this problem is to expand axioms not for single objects but for "clusters" of objects which are connected by features. This is done by the feature-complete function. During cluster expansion, chunks of concrete domain axioms are collected. Any such chunk can separately be checked for satisfiability. To see this, it is important to note that roles are not allowed inside the predicate operator, and thus concrete domain axioms cannot involve objects from different clusters (which are connected by roles). A similar strategy is employed for $\mathcal{ALCF}$ in [Hollunder and Nutt, 1990]. The ABox-cons reduces ABox consistency to satisfiability by performing preprocessing on the initial ABox and then constructing a reduction concept for each role successor of any object in the resulting ABox. In the next section, the complexity of both algorithms is analyzed.

4 Complexity of Reasoning

To characterize space requirements, a formal notion for the size of an ABox is introduced.

Definition 7. The *size* $\|C\|$ of a concept C is defined inductively. Let C and D be concepts, A a concept name, R a role or feature, $u = f_1 \cdots f_k$ a feature chain, and let $u_1, \ldots, u_n$ also be feature chains.

$$||A|| = ||\neg A|| = 1 \qquad ||f_1 \cdots f_k|| = k$$
$$||C \sqcap D|| = ||C \sqcup D|| = ||C|| + ||D|| + 2$$
$$||\forall R.C|| = ||\exists R.C|| = ||C|| + 1$$
$$||\exists u_1, \ldots, u_n.P|| = ||u_1|| + \cdots + ||u_n|| + 1$$
$$||u_1 \downarrow u_2|| = ||u_1 \uparrow u_2|| = ||u_1|| + ||u_2|| + 1$$

The size of an axiom α is $||C||$ if α is of the form $x : C$ and 1 otherwise. The size of an ABox $\mathcal{A}$ is the sum of the sizes of all axioms in $\mathcal{A}$.

For the analysis of the space needed by sat, two lemmata are needed.

Lemma 8. *For any input $\mathcal{A}$, the function* feature-complete *constructs an ABox $\mathcal{A}'$ with $||\mathcal{A}'|| \leq ||\mathcal{A}||^2 + ||\mathcal{A}||$.*

Proof: The upper bound for the size of $\mathcal{A}'$ is a consequence of the following two points:

1. feature-complete generates no more than $||\mathcal{A}||$ new axioms.

2. For each axiom α, we have $||\alpha|| \leq ||\mathcal{A}||$.

The second point is obvious, but the first one needs to be proven. The rules Rr$\exists$C and Rr$\forall$C will not be considered since they are not applied by feature-complete. For all other completion rules, the most important observation is that they can be applied at most once per axiom $a : C$. This is also true for axioms $a : \forall f.C$ and the Rf$\forall$C rule since there is at most one axiom $(a, b) : f$ per feature f and object a. We make the simplifying assumption that the premise of the Rf$\forall$C rule does *only* contain the axiom $a : \forall f.C$, i.e., that it is applied to *every* axiom of this form regardless if there is an axiom $(a, b) : f$ or not. This may result in too high an estimation of the number of generated axioms but not in one that is too low. We now prove the first point from above by showing that, for each axiom α in $\mathcal{A}$, no more than $||\alpha||$ axioms are generated by feature-complete.

No new axioms are generated for axioms of the form $(a, b) : R$, $(a, x) : f$, $a \neq b$, and $(x_1, \ldots, x_n) : P$ since they do not appear in the premise of any completion rule (please recall the simplification we made about Rf$\forall$C). The remaining axioms are of the form $a : C$. For these axioms, the property in question can be proved by induction on the structure of C.

For the induction start, let C be $\exists u_1, \ldots, u_n.P$, $u_1 \downarrow u_2$, $u_1 \uparrow u_2$, $\exists \hat{R}.C$, $\forall \hat{R}.C$, or a concept name. In any of these cases, it is trivial to verify that at most $||C||$ new axioms may be generated. For the induction step, we need to make a case distinction according to the form of C. Let C be of the form $D \sqcap E$. The application of the R$\sqcap$ rule generates two axioms $a : D$ and $a : E$. By induction hypothesis, from these two axioms, at most $||D||$ and $||E||$ axioms may be generated, respectively. Hence, from $a : D \sqcap E$, at most $||D|| + ||E|| + 2 = ||D \sqcap E||$ new axioms may be generated. The cases for the remaining operators $D \sqcup E$, $\exists f.C$, and $\forall f.C$ are analogous. Because of the simplifying assumptions made, the $\forall f.C$ case does not need a special treatment. ∎

Lemma 9. *For any input $\mathcal{A}_0$, the recursion depth of* sat *is bounded by $||\mathcal{A}_0||$.*

Proof: The *role depth* of a concept C is the maximum nesting depth of exists and value restrictions in C. The role depth of an ABox $\mathcal{A}$ is the maximum role depth of all concepts occurring in $\mathcal{A}$. As an immediate consequence of the way in which the input ABoxes of recursive calls are constructed, we have that the role depth of the arguments ABoxes strictly decreases with recursion depth. ∎

The space requirements of sat can now be settled.

Proposition 10. *For any input $\mathcal{A}_0$,* sat *can be executed in space polynomial in $||\mathcal{A}_0||$, provided that this also holds for the function* satisfiable?.

Proof: We will first analyze the maximum size of the arguments passed to sat in recursive calls. The argument to sat is an ABox which contains axioms $a : C$ for a single object a. It is obvious that there can be at most as many such axioms per object as there are distinct (sub)concepts appearing in $\mathcal{A}_0$. This number is bounded by $||\mathcal{A}_0||$. Furthermore, the size of any axiom is at most $||\mathcal{A}_0||$. It follows that the maximum size of arguments given in a recursive call is $||\mathcal{A}_0||^2$. Using feature-complete, the argument ABox is extended by new axioms. Combining the argument size with the result from Lemma 8, we find that the maximum size of ABoxes constructed during recursive calls is $||\mathcal{A}_0||^4 + ||\mathcal{A}_0||^2$. Together with Lemma 9, it follows that sat can be executed in $||\mathcal{A}_0||^5 + ||\mathcal{A}_0||^3$ space. ∎

This result completes the analysis of the sat algorithm. The ABox-cons algorithm performs some preprocessing on the input ABox and then repeatedly calls sat. Its space requirements are investigated in the next Proposition.

Proposition 11. *Started on input $\mathcal{A}$,* ABox-cons *can be executed in space polynomial in $||\mathcal{A}||$, provided that this also holds for the function* satisfiable?.

Proof: It was already proven that sat can be executed in polynomial space if this also holds for satisfiable?. Thus, it remains to be shown that, for an ABox $\mathcal{A}$, the size of $\mathcal{A}' := \text{preprocess}(\mathcal{A})$ is polynomial in $||\mathcal{A}||$. We will only give a sketch of the proof, for the full version see [Lutz, 1998]. Objects are called *old* if they are used in $\mathcal{A}$ and *new* if they are used in $\mathcal{A}'$ but not in $\mathcal{A}$. The proof relies on the fact that the preprocess function is identical to the feature-complete function except that preprocess does also apply the Rr$\forall$C rule. An upper bound for the number of Rr$\forall$C applications performed by preprocess can be given as follows: If Rr$\forall$C is applied to axioms $a : \forall \hat{R}.C$ and $(a, b) : \hat{R}$, then both a and b are old objects. This is the case since preprocess does not apply Rr$\exists$C, and, hence, no new axioms of the form $(a, b) : \hat{R}$, where $\hat{R}$ is a role, are generated. Furthermore, there are at most $||\mathcal{A}||$ old objects which means that the number of Rr$\forall$C applications is bounded by $||\mathcal{A}||^2$. Together with Lemma 8, it can be shown that $||\mathcal{A}'||$ is of order $\mathcal{O}(||\mathcal{A}||^k)$. ∎

The results just obtained allows us to determine the formal complexity of reasoning with concrete domains.

Theorem 12. *Provided that the satisfiability test of the concrete domain $\mathcal{D}$ is in* PSPACE, *the following problems are* PSPACE-*complete:*

1. *Consistency of $\mathcal{ALCF(D)}$ ABoxes.*
2. *Satisfiability and subsumption of $\mathcal{ALCF(D)}$ concepts.*
3. *Satisfiability and subsumption of $\mathcal{ALC(D)}$ concepts.*
4. *Consistency of $\mathcal{ALC(D)}$ and $\mathcal{ALCF}$ ABoxes.*

If the satisfiability test of $\mathcal{D}$ is in a complexity class X *with* PSPACE $\subseteq$ X, *then all of the above problems are* PSPACE-*hard.*

Proof: (1) Since $\mathcal{ALC}$ is a proper subset of $\mathcal{ALCF(D)}$ and the satisfiability problem for $\mathcal{ALC}$ is PSPACE-complete [Schmidt-Schauß and Smolka, 1991], deciding the consistency of $\mathcal{ALCF(D)}$ ABoxes is PSPACE-hard. It remains to be shown that it is in PSPACE if this is also the case for the concrete domain satisfiability test. This follows from Proposition 11 together with the well-known fact that PSPACE = NPSPACE [Savitch, 1970]. (2) is true since satisfiability as well as subsumption can be reduced to ABox consistency, cf. Section 2. (3) and (4) hold since $\mathcal{ALC}$ is a proper subset of both logics $\mathcal{ALC(D)}$ and $\mathcal{ALCF}$ which are in turn proper subsets of $\mathcal{ALCF(D)}$. ∎

Examples of useful concrete domains for which the satisfiability test is in PSPACE are given in [Lutz, 1998].

5 Conclusions and Future Work

We have presented optimal algorithms for deciding the concept satisfiability and the ABox consistency problems for the logic $\mathcal{ALCF(D)}$. In contrast to existing decision procedures, the devised algorithms can be executed in polynomial space provided that this does also hold for the concrete domain satisfiability test. Based on this result, it was proven that reasoning with $\mathcal{ALCF(D)}$ is a PSPACE-complete problem. The rule application strategy used by the proposed algorithm is vital for efficient implementations of description logics with concrete domains. An interesting new result in this context is that in the case of $\mathcal{ALC(D)}$ and $\mathcal{ALCF}$, satisfiability w.r.t. TBoxes is a NEXPTIME-hard problem [Lutz, 1998]. As future work, we will consider the combination of concrete domains with more expressive logics for which reasoning is in PSPACE, see e.g. [Sattler, 1996]. Furthermore, the logic $\mathcal{ALCF(D)}$ seems to be a promising candidate for the reduction of some temporal description logics in order to obtain complexity results for them.

Acknowledgments I would like to thank Ulrike Sattler and Franz Baader for enlightening discussions and helpful comments. The work in this paper was supported by the "Foundations of Data Warehouse Quality" (DWQ) European ESPRIT IV Long Term Research (LTR) Project 22469.

References

[Baader and Hanschke, 1991] F. Baader and P. Hanschke. A scheme for integrating concrete domains into concept languages. In John Mylopoulos and Ray Reiter, editors, *Proc. of IJCAI-91*, pages 452–457, Sydney, Australia, August 24–30, 1991.

[Baader and Hanschke, 1993] F. Baader and P. Hanschke. Extensions of concept languages for a mechanical engineering application. In *Proc. of GWAI-92*, volume 671 of *LNCS*, pages 132–143, Bonn, Germany, 1993. Springer–Verlag.

[Baader and Hollunder, 1991] F. Baader and B. Hollunder. KRIS: Knowledge representation and inference system. *SIGART Bulletin*, 2(3):8–14, 1991. Special Issue on Implemented Knowledge Representation and Reasoning Systems.

[Baader and Sattler, 1998] F. Baader and U. Sattler. Description logics with concrete domains and aggregation. In Henri Prade, editor, *Proc. of ECAI-98*, Brighton, August 23–28, 1998. John Wiley & Sons, New York, 1998.

[Borgida *et al.*, 1989] A. Borgida, R.J. Brachman, D.L. McGuiness, and L. Alpern Resnick. CLASSIC: A structural data model for objects. In *Proc. of 1989 ACM SIGMOD*, pages 59–67, Portland, OR, 1989.

[Haarslev *et al.*, 1998] V. Haarslev, C. Lutz, and R. Möller. A description logic with concrete domains and role-forming predicates. *Journal of Logic and Computation*, 1998. To appear.

[Hollunder and Nutt, 1990] B. Hollunder and W. Nutt. Subsumption algorithms for concept languages. DFKI Research Report RR-90-04, German Research Center for Artificial Intelligence, Kaiserslautern, 1990.

[Hollunder, 1994] B. Hollunder. *Algorithmic Foundations of Terminological Knowledge Representation Systems*. PhD thesis, Universität des Saarlandes, 1994.

[Horrocks, 1998] I. Horrocks. Using an expressive description logic: Fact or fiction? In A.G. Cohn, L.K. Schubert, and S.C. Shapiro, editors, *Proc. of KR'98*, pages 636–647, Trento, Italy, 1998. Morgan Kaufmann Publ. Inc., San Francicso, CA, 1998.

[Lutz, 1998] C. Lutz. The complexity of reasoning with concrete domains. LTCS-Report 99-01, LuFG Theoretical Computer Science, RWTH Aachen, Germany, 1999.

[Lutz, 1998] C. Lutz. On the Complexity of Terminological Reasoning. LTCS-Report 99-04, LuFG Theoretical Computer Science, RWTH Aachen, Germany, 1999. To appear.

[Sattler, 1996] U. Sattler. A concept language extended with different kinds of transitive roles. In G. Görz and S. Hölldobler, editors, *20. Deutsche Jahrestagung für KI*, volume 1137 of *Lecture Notes in Artificial Intelligence*, 1996.

[Savitch, 1970] W. J. Savitch. Relationsship between nondeterministic and deterministic tape complexities. *Journal of Computer and System Sciences*, 4:177–192, 1970.

[Schmidt-Schauß and Smolka, 1991] M. Schmidt-Schauß and G. Smolka. Attributive concept descriptions with complements. *Artificial Intelligence*, 48(1):1–26, 1991.

Computing Least Common Subsumers in Description Logics with Existential Restrictions*

Franz Baader, Ralf Küsters, and Ralf Molitor

LuFg Theoretische Informatik, RWTH Aachen
email: {baader,kuesters,molitor}@informatik.rwth-aachen.de

Computing the least common subsumer (lcs) is an inference task that can be used to support the "bottom-up" construction of knowledge bases for KR systems based on description logics. Previous work on how to compute the lcs has concentrated on description logics that allow for universal value restrictions, but not for existential restrictions. The main new contribution of this paper is the treatment of description logics with existential restrictions. Our approach for computing the lcs is based on an appropriate representation of concept descriptions by certain trees, and a characterization of subsumption by homomorphisms between these trees. The lcs operation then corresponds to the product operation on trees.

1 Introduction

Knowledge representation systems based on description logics (DL) can be used to describe the knowledge of an application domain in a structured and formally well-understood way. Traditionally, the knowledge base of a DL system is built in a "top-down" fashion by first formalizing the relevant concepts of the domain (its terminology) by *concept descriptions*, i.e., expressions that are built from atomic concepts (unary predicates) and atomic roles (binary predicates) using the concept constructors provided by the DL language. In a second step, the concept descriptions are used to specify properties of objects and individuals occurring in the domain. DL systems provide their users with inference services that support both steps: classification of concepts and of individuals. Classification of concepts determines subconcept/superconcept relationships (called subsumption relationships) between the concepts of a given terminology, and thus allows one to structure the terminology in the form of a subsumption hierarchy. Classification of

individuals (or objects) determines whether a given individual is always an instance of a certain concept (i.e., whether this instance relationship is implied by the descriptions of the individual and the concept).

This traditional "top-down" approach for constructing a DL knowledge base is not always adequate, however. On the one hand, it need not be clear from the outset which are the relevant concepts in a particular application. On the other hand, even if it is clear which (intuitive) concepts should be introduced, it is sometimes difficult to come up with formal definitions of these concepts within the available description language. For example, in one of our applications in chemical process engineering [Sattler, 1998; Baader and Sattler, 1996], the process engineers prefer to construct the knowledge base (which consists of descriptions of standard building blocks of process models, such as reactors) in the following "bottom-up" fashion: first, they introduce several "typical" examples of the standard building block as individuals, and then they generalize (the descriptions of) these individuals into a concept description that (i) has all the individuals as instances, and (ii) is the most specific description satisfying property (i). The task of computing a description satisfying (i) and (ii) can be split into two subtasks: computing the most specific concept of a single individual, and computing the least common subsumer of a given finite number of concepts. The *most specific concept* (msc) of an individual b is the most specific concept description C (expressible in the given DL) that has b as an instance, and the *least common subsumer* (lcs) of n concept descriptions $C_1, \ldots, C_n$ is the most specific concept description in the given DL that subsumes $C_1, \ldots, C_n$.

The present paper investigates the second subtask for the sub-language $\mathcal{ALE}$ of the DL employed in our process engineering application. This language allows both for value restrictions and existential restrictions, but not for full negation and disjunction (since the lcs operation is trivial in the presence of disjunction, and thus does not provide useful information). It can, e.g., be used to introduce the concept of a reactor with cooling jacket by the description Reactor $\sqcap$ $\exists$connected-to.Cooling-Jacket $\sqcap$ $\forall$functionality.$\neg$Vaporize, where Vaporize is a primitive concept (i.e., not further defined). Previous work on

*This work was partially supported by the EC Working Group CCL II, the *Studienstiftung des deutschen Volkes*, and the *Deutsche Forschungsgemeinschaft* Grant No. GRK 185/3-98.

how to compute the lcs [Cohen and Hirsh, 1994; Frazier and Pitt, 1996] has concentrated on sub-languages of the DL used by the system CLASSIC [Brachman *et al.*, 1991], which allows (among other constructors) for value restrictions, but not for existential restrictions. Thus, the main new contribution of the present paper is the treatment of existential restrictions.

For didactic reasons, we will start by showing how to compute the lcs in the small language $\mathcal{EL}$, which allows for conjunction and existential restrictions only and extend our treatment in two steps to $\mathcal{FLE}$ by adding value restrictions, and then to $\mathcal{ALE}$ by further adding primitive negation. For all three languages, we proceed in the following manner. First, we introduce an appropriate data structure for representing concept descriptions (so-called description trees), and show that subsumption can be characterized by the existence of homomorphisms between description trees. From this characterization we then deduce that the lcs operation on concept descriptions corresponds to the product operation on description trees, which can easily be computed. We will also comment on the complexity of subsumption and the lcs for the languages under consideration. Because of the space limitation, we cannot give all the technical details. These details as well as complete proofs can be found in [Baader *et al.*, 1998].

2 Preliminaries

Concept descriptions are inductively defined with the help of a set of *constructors*, starting with a set N_C of *primitive concepts* and a set N_R of *primitive roles*. The constructors determine the expressive power of the DL. In this paper, we consider concept descriptions built from the constructors shown in Table 1. In the description logic $\mathcal{EL}$, concept descriptions are formed using the constructors top-concept ($\top$), conjunction ($C \sqcap D$) and existential restriction ($\exists r.C$). The description logic $\mathcal{FLE}$ additionally provides us with value restrictions ($\forall r.C$), and $\mathcal{ALE}$ allows for all the constructors shown in Table 1.

The semantics of a concept description is defined in terms of an *interpretation* $\mathcal{I} = (\Delta, \cdot^I)$. The domain Δ of $\mathcal{I}$ is a non-empty set of individuals and the interpretation function $\cdot^I$ maps each primitive concept $P \in N_C$ to a set $P^I \subseteq \Delta$ and each primitive role $r \in N_R$ to a binary relation $r^I \subseteq \Delta \times \Delta$. The extension of $\cdot^I$ to arbitrary concept descriptions is inductively defined, as shown in the third column of Table 1.

One of the most important traditional inference services provided by DL systems is computing the subsumption hierarchy. The concept description C is *subsumed* by the description D ($C \sqsubseteq D$) iff $C^I \subseteq D^I$ holds for all interpretations $\mathcal{I}$. The concept descriptions C and D are *equivalent* ($C \equiv D$) iff they subsume each other.

In this paper, we are interested in the non-standard inference task of computing the *least common subsumer* (lcs) of concept descriptions. Given $n \geq 2$ concept descriptions $C_1, \ldots, C_n$ in a description logic $\mathcal{L}$, a concept description C of $\mathcal{L}$ is an lcs of $C_1, \ldots, C_n$ (for short,

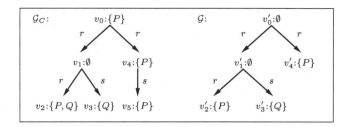

Figure 1: $\mathcal{EL}$-description trees.

$C = \mathsf{lcs}(C_1, \ldots, C_n)$) iff (i) $C_i \sqsubseteq C$ for all $1 \leq i \leq n$, and (ii) C is the least concept description with this property, i.e., if C' satisfies $C_i \sqsubseteq C'$ for all $1 \leq i \leq n$, then $C \sqsubseteq C'$.

Depending on the DL under consideration, the lcs of two or more descriptions need not always exist, but if it exists, then it is unique up to equivalence. In the following, we will show that, for the DLs $\mathcal{EL}$, $\mathcal{FLE}$, and $\mathcal{ALE}$, the lcs always exists and can effectively be computed. We will mostly restrict the attention to the problem of computing the lcs of two concept descriptions, since the lcs of $n > 2$ descriptions can be obtained by iterated application of the binary lcs operation.

3 Getting started – the lcs in $\mathcal{EL}$

As mentioned in the introduction, our method for computing the lcs is based on an appropriate representation of concept descriptions by trees. In the case of the small DL $\mathcal{EL}$, these trees, called $\mathcal{EL}$-*description trees*, are of the form $\mathcal{G} = (V, E, v_0, \ell)$, where $\mathcal{G}$ is a tree with root v_0 whose edges $vrw \in E$ are labeled with primitive roles $r \in N_R$, and whose nodes $v \in V$ are labeled with sets $\ell(v)$ of primitive concepts from N_C. The empty label corresponds to the top-concept.

Intuitively, such a tree is merely a graphical representation of the syntax of the concept description. More formally, every $\mathcal{EL}$-concept description C can be written (modulo equivalence) as $C \equiv P_1 \sqcap \ldots \sqcap P_n \sqcap \exists r_1.C_1 \sqcap \ldots \sqcap \exists r_m.C_m$ with $P_i \in N_C \cup \{\top\}$. This description can now be translated into an $\mathcal{EL}$-description tree $\mathcal{G}_C = (V, E, v_0, \ell)$ as follows. The set of all primitive concepts occurring in the top-level conjunction of C yields the label $\ell(v_0)$ of the root v_0, and each existential restriction $\exists r_i.C_i$ in this conjunction yields an r_i-successor that is the root of the tree corresponding to C_i. For example, the $\mathcal{EL}$-concept description

$$C := P \sqcap \exists r.(\exists r.(P \sqcap Q) \sqcap \exists s.Q) \sqcap \exists r.(P \sqcap \exists s.P)$$

yields the tree $\mathcal{G}_C$ depicted on the left-hand side of Fig. 1.

Conversely, every $\mathcal{EL}$-description tree $\mathcal{G} = (V, E, v_0, \ell)$ can be translated into an $\mathcal{EL}$-concept description $C_\mathcal{G}$. Intuitively, the primitive concepts in the label of v_0 yield the primitive concepts in the top-level conjunction of $C_\mathcal{G}$, and each r-successor v of v_0 yields an existential restriction $\exists r.C$ where C is the $\mathcal{EL}$-concept description obtained by translating the subtree of $\mathcal{G}$ with root v. For a leaf $v \in V$, the empty label is translated into the top-concept. For example, the $\mathcal{EL}$-description tree $\mathcal{G}$ in

name of constructor	Syntax	Semantics	$\mathcal{EL}$	$\mathcal{FLE}$	$\mathcal{ALE}$
primitive concept $P \in N_C$	P	$P^I \subseteq \Delta$	x	x	x
top-concept	$\top$	Δ	x	x	x
conjunction	$C \sqcap D$	$C^I \cap D^I$	x	x	x
existential restriction for $r \in N_R$	$\exists r.C$	$\{x \in \Delta \mid \exists y : (x,y) \in r^I \wedge y \in C^I\}$	x	x	x
value restriction for $r \in N_R$	$\forall r.C$	$\{x \in \Delta \mid \forall y : (x,y) \in r^I \rightarrow y \in C^I\}$		x	x
primitive negation for $P \in N_C$	$\neg P$	$\Delta \setminus P^I$			x
bottom-concept	$\bot$	$\emptyset$			x

Table 1: Syntax and semantics of concept descriptions.

Fig. 1 yields the $\mathcal{EL}$-concept description

$$C_{\mathcal{G}} = \exists r.(\exists r.P \sqcap \exists s.Q) \sqcap \exists r.P.$$

These translations preserve the semantics of concept descriptions in the sense that $C \equiv C_{\mathcal{G}_C}$.

Subsumption in $\mathcal{EL}$ can be characterized using the following notion: a *homomorphism* from an $\mathcal{EL}$-description tree $\mathcal{H} = (V_H, E_H, w_0, \ell_H)$ to an $\mathcal{EL}$-description tree $\mathcal{G} = (V_G, E_G, v_0, \ell_G)$ is a mapping $\varphi : V_H \longrightarrow V_G$ such that (1) $\varphi(w_0) = v_0$, (2) $\ell_H(v) \subseteq \ell_G(\varphi(v))$ for all $v \in V_H$, and (3) $\varphi(v)r\varphi(w) \in E_G$ for all $vrw \in E_H$.

Theorem 1 *Let C, D be $\mathcal{EL}$-concept descriptions and $\mathcal{G}_C, \mathcal{G}_D$ the corresponding $\mathcal{EL}$-description trees. Then $C \sqsubseteq D$ iff there exists a homomorphism from $\mathcal{G}_D$ to $\mathcal{G}_C$.*

In our example, the $\mathcal{EL}$-concept description $C_{\mathcal{G}}$ subsumes C, because mapping v'_i onto v_i for all $0 \le i \le 4$ yields a homomorphism from $\mathcal{G} = \mathcal{G}_{C_{\mathcal{G}}}$ to $\mathcal{G}_C$ (see Fig. 1).

Theorem 1 is a special case of the characterization of subsumption between simple conceptual graphs in [Chein and Mugnier, 1992], and of the characterization of containment of conjunctive queries in [Abiteboul *et al.*, 1995]. In the more general setting of simple conceptual graphs and conjunctive queries, testing for the existence of a homomorphism is an NP-complete problem. In the restricted case of $\mathcal{EL}$-description trees, however, testing for the existence of a homomorphism can be realized in polynomial time [Reyner, 1977; Baader *et al.*, 1998], which shows that subsumption between $\mathcal{EL}$-concept descriptions is a tractable problem.

Least common subsumer in $\mathcal{EL}$

The characterization of subsumption by homomorphisms allows us to characterize the lcs by the product of $\mathcal{EL}$-description trees. The *product* $\mathcal{G} \times \mathcal{H}$ of two $\mathcal{EL}$-description trees $\mathcal{G} = (V_G, E_G, v_0, \ell_G)$ and $\mathcal{H} = (V_H, E_H, w_0, \ell_H)$ is defined by induction on the depth of the trees. Let $\mathcal{G}(v)$ denote the subtree of $\mathcal{G}$ with root v. We define (v_0, w_0) to be the root of $\mathcal{G} \times \mathcal{H}$, labeled with $\ell_G(v_0) \cap \ell_H(w_0)$. For each r-successor v of v_0 in $\mathcal{G}$ and w of w_0 in $\mathcal{H}$, we obtain an r-successor (v, w) of (v_0, w_0) in $\mathcal{G} \times \mathcal{H}$ that is the root of the product of $\mathcal{G}(v)$ and $\mathcal{H}(w)$.

For example, consider the $\mathcal{EL}$-description tree $\mathcal{G}_C$ (Fig. 1) and the $\mathcal{EL}$-description tree $\mathcal{G}_D$ (Fig. 2), where $\mathcal{G}_D$ corresponds to the $\mathcal{EL}$-concept description $D :=$

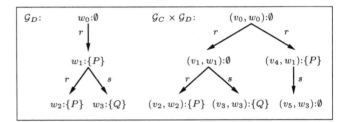

Figure 2: The product of $\mathcal{EL}$-description trees.

$\exists r.(P \sqcap \exists r.P \sqcap \exists s.Q)$. The product $\mathcal{G}_C \times \mathcal{G}_D$ is depicted on the right-hand side of Fig. 2.

Theorem 2 *Let C, D be two $\mathcal{EL}$-concept descriptions and $\mathcal{G}_C$, $\mathcal{G}_D$ the corresponding $\mathcal{EL}$-description trees. Then $C_{\mathcal{G}_C \times \mathcal{G}_D}$ is the lcs of C and D.*

In our example, we thus obtain

$$\mathsf{lcs}(C, D) = \exists r.(\exists r.P \sqcap \exists s.Q) \sqcap \exists r.(P \sqcap \exists s.\top).$$

The size of the lcs of two $\mathcal{EL}$-concept descriptions C, D can be bounded by the size of $\mathcal{G}_C \times \mathcal{G}_D$, which is polynomial in the size of $\mathcal{G}_C$ and $\mathcal{G}_D$. Since the size of the description tree corresponding to a given description is linear in the size of the description, we obtain:

Proposition 3 *The size of the lcs of two $\mathcal{EL}$-concept descriptions C, D is polynomial in the size of C and D, and the lcs can be computed in polynomial time.*

In our process engineering application, however, we are interested in the lcs of $n > 2$ concept descriptions $C_1, \ldots, C_n$. This lcs can be obtained from the product $\mathcal{G}_{C_1} \times \cdots \times \mathcal{G}_{C_n}$ of their corresponding $\mathcal{EL}$-description trees. Therefore, the size of the lcs can be bounded by the size of this product. It has turned out [Baader *et al.*, 1998] that, even for the small DL $\mathcal{EL}$, this size cannot be polynomially bounded.

Proposition 4 *The size of the lcs of n $\mathcal{EL}$-concept descriptions $C_1, \ldots, C_n$ of size linear in n may grow exponential in n.*

4 Extending the results to $\mathcal{FLE}$

Our goal is to obtain a characterization of the lcs in $\mathcal{FLE}$ analogous to the one given in Theorem 2 for $\mathcal{EL}$. To achieve this goal, we first extend the notion of a description tree from $\mathcal{EL}$ to $\mathcal{FLE}$. In order to cope with value

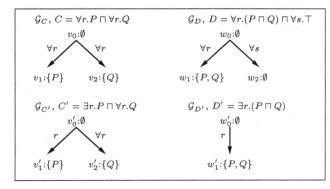

$$\mathcal{G}_C, C = \forall r.P \sqcap \forall r.Q$$
$$\mathcal{G}_D, D = \forall r.(P \sqcap Q) \sqcap \forall s.\top$$

$$\mathcal{G}_{C'}, C' = \exists r.P \sqcap \forall r.Q$$
$$\mathcal{G}_{D'}, D' = \exists r.(P \sqcap Q)$$

Figure 3: $\mathcal{FLE}$-description trees.

restrictions occurring in $\mathcal{FLE}$-concept descriptions, we allow for two types of edges, namely those labeled with a primitive role $r \in N_R$ (corresponding to existential restrictions of the form $\exists r.C$) and those labeled with $\forall r$ for $r \in N_R$ (corresponding to value restrictions of the form $\forall r.D$). Just as for $\mathcal{EL}$, there is a 1–1 correspondence between $\mathcal{FLE}$-concept descriptions and $\mathcal{FLE}$-description trees.

The notion of a homomorphism also extends to $\mathcal{FLE}$-description trees in a natural way. A homomorphism from an $\mathcal{FLE}$-description tree $\mathcal{H} = (V_H, E_H, w_0, \ell_H)$ into an $\mathcal{FLE}$-description tree $\mathcal{G} = (V_G, E_G, v_0, \ell_G)$ is a mapping $\varphi : V_H \longrightarrow V_G$ that satisfies the conditions (1)–(3) on homomorphisms between $\mathcal{EL}$-description trees, and additionally (4) $\varphi(v) \forall r \varphi(w) \in E_G$ for all $v \forall r w \in E_H$.

However, these straightforward extensions are not sufficient to obtain a sound and complete characterization of subsumption in $\mathcal{FLE}$ based on homomorphisms between $\mathcal{FLE}$-description trees. For example, consider the $\mathcal{FLE}$-concept descriptions and their translations into $\mathcal{FLE}$-description trees depicted in Fig. 3. It is easy to see that $C \sqsubseteq D$ and $C' \sqsubseteq D'$, but there exists neither a homomorphism from $\mathcal{G}_D$ to $\mathcal{G}_C$ nor one from $\mathcal{G}_{D'}$ to $\mathcal{G}_{C'}$.

To avoid these problems, we must normalize the $\mathcal{FLE}$-concept descriptions before translating them into $\mathcal{FLE}$-description trees. The *normal form* of an $\mathcal{FLE}$-concept description C is obtained from C by exhaustively applying the following *normalization rules*:

$$
\begin{aligned}
\forall r.E \sqcap \forall r.F &\longrightarrow \forall r.(E \sqcap F) \\
\forall r.E \sqcap \exists r.F &\longrightarrow \forall r.E \sqcap \exists r.(E \sqcap F) \\
\forall r.\top &\longrightarrow \top \\
E \sqcap \top &\longrightarrow E
\end{aligned}
$$

Since each normalization rule preserves equivalence, the resulting normalized $\mathcal{FLE}$-concept description is equivalent to the original one. The rules should be read modulo commutativity of conjunction; e.g., $\exists r.E \sqcap \forall r.F$ is also normalized to $\exists r.(E \sqcap F) \sqcap \forall r.F$.

Now, the *$\mathcal{FLE}$-description tree $\mathcal{G}_C$ corresponding to C* is obtained from C by first normalizing C, and then translating the resulting normalized $\mathcal{FLE}$-concept description into a tree. Each $\mathcal{FLE}$-description tree $\mathcal{G} = (V, E, v_0, \ell)$ obtained this way satisfies the following properties [Baader *et al.*, 1998]:

- For each node $v \in V$ and each primitive role $r \in N_R$, v has at most one outgoing edge labeled $\forall r$.
- Let $\{vrw, v\forall rw'\} \subseteq E$, and let C denote the $\mathcal{FLE}$-concept description corresponding to the subtree of $\mathcal{G}$ with root w, and C' the one corresponding to the subtree of $\mathcal{G}$ with root w'. Then $C \sqsubseteq C'$.
- Leaves in $\mathcal{G}$ labeled with the empty set cannot be reached via an edge labeled $\forall r$ for some $r \in N_R$, i.e., $C_{\mathcal{G}}$ does not contain a subconcept of the form $\forall r.\top$.

The proof of soundness and completeness of the characterization of subsumption in $\mathcal{FLE}$ stated in the next theorem makes heavy use of these properties [Baader *et al.*, 1998].

Theorem 5 *Let C, D be two $\mathcal{FLE}$-concept descriptions and $\mathcal{G}_C$, $\mathcal{G}_D$ their corresponding $\mathcal{FLE}$-description trees. Then $C \sqsubseteq D$ iff there exists a homomorphism from $\mathcal{G}_D$ to $\mathcal{G}_C$.*

It should be noted that there is a close relationship between the normalization rules introduced above and some of the so-called *propagation rules* employed by tableaux-based subsumption algorithms, as e.g. introduced in [Donini *et al.*, 1992]. The main idea underlying our second normalization rule and the propagation rule treating value restrictions is to make the knowledge implicitly given by a conjunction of the form $\forall r.E \sqcap \exists r.F$ explicit by propagating E onto the existential restriction according to the equivalence $\forall r.E \sqcap \exists r.F \equiv \forall r.E \sqcap \exists r.(E \sqcap F)$. As shown in [Donini *et al.*, 1992], this propagation rule may lead to an exponential blow-up of the tableau, and the same is true for our normalization rule. More precisely, applying the normalization rules introduced above to an $\mathcal{FLE}$-concept description C may lead to a normalized concept description, and hence a corresponding $\mathcal{FLE}$-description tree $\mathcal{G}_C$, of size exponential in the size of C. This exponential blow-up cannot be avoided since (i) as for $\mathcal{EL}$, existence of a homomorphism between $\mathcal{FLE}$-description trees can be tested in polynomial time; and (ii) subsumption in $\mathcal{FLE}$ is an NP-complete problem [Donini *et al.*, 1992].

Least common subsumer in $\mathcal{FLE}$

Just as for $\mathcal{EL}$, we can now use the characterization of subsumption in $\mathcal{FLE}$ by homomorphisms to characterize the lcs of two $\mathcal{FLE}$-concept descriptions by the product of $\mathcal{FLE}$-description trees. The *product $\mathcal{G} \times \mathcal{H}$* of two $\mathcal{FLE}$-description trees $\mathcal{G} = (V_G, E_G, v_0, \ell_G)$ and $\mathcal{H} = (V_H, E_H, w_0, \ell_H)$ is again defined by induction on the depth of the trees. As before, (v_0, w_0) is the root of $\mathcal{G} \times \mathcal{H}$, and r-successors of (v_0, w_0) are obtained in the same way as for $\mathcal{EL}$. Additionally, we now obtain a $\forall r$-successor (v, w) of (v_0, w_0) in $\mathcal{G} \times \mathcal{H}$ if v is the $\forall r$-successor of v_0 in $\mathcal{G}$ and w the one of w_0 in $\mathcal{H}$, and (v, w) is the root of the product of $\mathcal{G}(v)$ and $\mathcal{H}(w)$.

Theorem 6 *Let C, D be two $\mathcal{FLE}$-concept descriptions and $\mathcal{G}_C$, $\mathcal{G}_D$ their corresponding $\mathcal{FLE}$-description trees. Then $C_{\mathcal{G}_C \times \mathcal{G}_D}$ is the lcs of C and D.*

As mentioned above, $\mathcal{FLE}$ differs from $\mathcal{EL}$ in that the $\mathcal{FLE}$-description tree $\mathcal{G}_C$ corresponding to an $\mathcal{FLE}$-concept description C may be of size exponential in the size of C. Therefore, even for *two* $\mathcal{FLE}$-concept descriptions C, D, the size of their lcs cannot be polynomially bounded by the size of C and D [Baader *et al.*, 1998].

Proposition 7 *The size of the lcs of two $\mathcal{FLE}$-concept descriptions C, D may be exponential in the size of C and D.*

5 Extending the results to $\mathcal{ALE}$

In order to characterize the lcs of two $\mathcal{ALE}$-concept descriptions by the product of description trees, we must adapt the notions description tree, homomorphism, and product appropriately, taking into account the additional constructors primitive negation and bottom-concept.

First, we extend the notion of $\mathcal{FLE}$-description trees to $\mathcal{ALE}$-*description trees* by additionally allowing for negated primitive concepts $\neg P$ and the bottom-concept $\bot$ in the labels of nodes. Again, as for $\mathcal{EL}$ and $\mathcal{FLE}$, there is a 1–1 correspondence between $\mathcal{ALE}$-concept descriptions and $\mathcal{ALE}$-description trees.

Since $\mathcal{ALE}$ is an extension of $\mathcal{FLE}$, and since we are again interested in a characterization of subsumption by homomorphisms, we must normalize $\mathcal{ALE}$-concept descriptions before translating them into their corresponding $\mathcal{ALE}$-description trees. In addition to the normalization rules for $\mathcal{FLE}$, we need three more rules, which deal with the fact that $\mathcal{ALE}$-concept descriptions may contain inconsistent sub-descriptions (i.e., $\bot$ and $P \sqcap \neg P$ for $P \in N_C$):

$$
\begin{aligned}
P \sqcap \neg P &\longrightarrow \bot, \text{ for each } P \in N_C \\
\exists r.\bot &\longrightarrow \bot \\
E \sqcap \bot &\longrightarrow \bot
\end{aligned}
$$

Starting with an $\mathcal{ALE}$-concept description C, the exhaustive application of these rules, together with the rules for $\mathcal{FLE}$, yields an equivalent $\mathcal{ALE}$-concept description in normal form, which is used to construct the $\mathcal{ALE}$-description tree $\mathcal{G}_C$ corresponding to C.

In addition to the conditions for $\mathcal{FLE}$-description trees, the $\mathcal{ALE}$-description trees obtained this way satisfy the following condition: if the label of a node contains $\bot$, then its label is $\{\bot\}$ and it is a leaf that cannot be reached by an edge with label $r \in N_R$.

Unfortunately, the straightforward adaptation of the notion of a homomorphism from $\mathcal{FLE}$-description trees to $\mathcal{ALE}$-description trees does not yield a sound and complete characterization of subsumption in $\mathcal{ALE}$. As an example, consider the following $\mathcal{ALE}$-concept descriptions:

$$
\begin{aligned}
C &:= (\forall r.\exists r.(P \sqcap \neg P)) \sqcap (\exists s.(P \sqcap \exists r.Q)), \\
D &:= (\forall r.(\exists r.P \sqcap \exists r.\neg P)) \sqcap (\exists s.\exists r.Q).
\end{aligned}
$$

The description D is already in normal form, and the normal form of C is $C' := \forall r.\bot \sqcap \exists s.(P \sqcap \exists r.Q)$. The corresponding $\mathcal{ALE}$-description trees $\mathcal{G}_C$ and $\mathcal{G}_D$ are depicted in Figure 4.

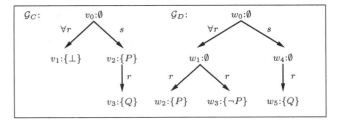

Figure 4: $\mathcal{ALE}$-description trees.

It is easy to see that there does not exist a homomorphism (in the sense of Section 4) from $\mathcal{G}_D$ into $\mathcal{G}_C$, although we have $C \sqsubseteq D$. In particular, the $\mathcal{ALE}$-concept description $\exists r.P \sqcap \exists r.\neg P$ corresponding to the subtree with root w_1 of $\mathcal{G}_D$ subsumes $\bot$, which is the concept description corresponding to the subtree with root v_1 in $\mathcal{G}_C$. Therefore, a homomorphism from $\mathcal{G}_D$ into $\mathcal{G}_C$ should be allowed to map the whole tree corresponding to $\exists r.P \sqcap \exists r.\neg P$, i.e., the nodes w_1, w_2, w_3, onto the tree corresponding to $\bot$, i.e., onto v_1.

A *homomorphism* from an $\mathcal{ALE}$-description tree $\mathcal{H} = (V_H, E_H, w_0, \ell_H)$ into an $\mathcal{ALE}$-description tree $\mathcal{G} = (V_G, E_G, v_0, \ell_G)$ is a mapping $\varphi : V_H \longrightarrow V_G$ such that (1) $\varphi(w_0) = v_0$, (2) $\ell_H(v) \subseteq \ell_G(\varphi(v))$ or $\ell_G(\varphi(v)) = \{\bot\}$ for all $v \in V_H$, (3) for all $vrw \in E_H$, either $\varphi(v)r\varphi(w) \in E_G$, or $\varphi(v) = \varphi(w)$ and $\ell_G(\varphi(v)) = \{\bot\}$, and (4) for all $v \forall rw \in E_H$, either $\varphi(v)\forall r\varphi(w) \in E_G$, or $\varphi(v) = \varphi(w)$ and $\ell_G(\varphi(v)) = \{\bot\}$.

In our example, if we map w_0 onto v_0; w_1, w_2, and w_3 onto v_1; w_4 onto v_2; and w_5 onto v_3, then the above conditions are satisfied, i.e., this mapping yields a homomorphism from $\mathcal{G}_D$ into $\mathcal{G}_C$.

With this new notion of a homomorphism between $\mathcal{ALE}$-description trees, we can again characterize subsumption in $\mathcal{ALE}$ in a sound and complete way [Baader *et al.*, 1998].[1]

Theorem 8 *Let C, D be two $\mathcal{ALE}$-concept descriptions and $\mathcal{G}_C$, $\mathcal{G}_D$ the corresponding $\mathcal{ALE}$-description trees. Then $C \sqsubseteq D$ iff there exists a homomorphism from $\mathcal{G}_D$ into $\mathcal{G}_C$.*

Least common subsumer in $\mathcal{ALE}$

The definition of the product of $\mathcal{ALE}$-description trees must be adapted to the modified notion of a homomorphism. In particular, this definition must treat leaves with label $\{\bot\}$ in a special manner. In fact, such a leaf corresponds to the bottom-concept, and since $\bot \sqsubseteq C$ for all $\mathcal{ALE}$-concept descriptions C, we have $\mathsf{lcs}(\bot, C) \equiv C$. Thus, our product operation should be defined such that $C_{\mathcal{G}_\bot \times \mathcal{G}_C} \equiv C$.

More precisely, the *product* $\mathcal{G} \times \mathcal{H}$ of two $\mathcal{ALE}$-description trees $\mathcal{G} = (V_G, E_G, v_0, \ell_G)$ and $\mathcal{H} = (V_H, E_H, w_0, \ell_H)$ is defined as follows. If $\ell_G(v_0) = \{\bot\}$ ($\ell_H(w_0) = \{\bot\}$), then we define $\mathcal{G} \times \mathcal{H}$ by replacing each node w in $\mathcal{H}$ (v in $\mathcal{G}$) by (v_0, w) ((v, w_0)). Otherwise, we

---

[1]Note that subsumption in $\mathcal{ALE}$ is also an NP-complete problem [Donini *et al.*, 1992].

define $\mathcal{G} \times \mathcal{H}$ by induction on the depth of the trees analogous to the definition of the product of $\mathcal{FLE}$-description trees.

In the example, $\mathcal{G}_C \times \mathcal{G}_D$ can be obtained from $\mathcal{G}_D$ by replacing w_0 by (v_0, w_0), w_i by (v_1, w_i) for $i = 1, 2, 3$, w_4 by (v_2, w_4), and w_5 by (v_3, w_5) (see Fig. 4).

Theorem 9 *Let C, D be two $\mathcal{ALE}$-concept descriptions and $\mathcal{G}_C$, $\mathcal{G}_D$ their corresponding $\mathcal{ALE}$-description trees. Then $C_{\mathcal{G}_C \times \mathcal{G}_D}$ is the lcs of C and D.*

The proof of Proposition 7 also works if we view the $\mathcal{FLE}$-concept descriptions used in this proof as special $\mathcal{ALE}$-concept descriptions. Thus, we have:

Proposition 10 *The size of the lcs of two $\mathcal{ALE}$-concept descriptions C, D may be exponential in the size of C, D.*

6 Conclusion and future work

We have described a method for computing the least common subsumer in the description logic $\mathcal{ALE}$. In the worst case, the result of this computation may be exponential in the size of the input descriptions. However, the examples that show this exponential behavior [Baader *et al.*, 1998] are rather artificial, and thus we believe that this complexity will not pose a problem in practice.

Our method depends on the characterization of subsumption by homomorphisms on description trees, because this allows us to construct the lcs as the product of the description trees. For sub-languages of CLASSIC, a similar method has been used to construct the lcs [Cohen and Hirsh, 1994; Frazier and Pitt, 1996], even though the characterization of subsumption (via a structural subsumption algorithm [Borgida and Patel-Schneider, 1994]) is not explicitly given in terms of homomorphisms. The main difference is that these languages do not allow for existential restrictions. The results for simple conceptual graphs (conjunctive queries) mentioned below Theorem 1 characterize subsumption (resp. containment) with the help of homomorphisms, but they do not consider the lcs, and they cannot handle value restrictions.

The language $\mathcal{ALE}$ is expressive enough to be quite useful in our process engineering application. In fact, the descriptions of standard building blocks of process models that we currently represent in our DL system can all be expressed within this language. However, in order to support the "bottom-up" approach for constructing knowledge bases outlined in the introduction, we must also be able to compute the most specific concept for individuals. Unfortunately, the msc need not always exist in $\mathcal{ALE}$. For the DL $\mathcal{ALN}$, it was shown in [Baader and Küsters, 1998] that this problem can be overcome by allowing for cyclic concept descriptions, but $\mathcal{ALN}$ does not allow for existential restrictions. Thus, we must either extend the approach of [Baader and Küsters, 1998] to $\mathcal{ALE}$, or resort to an approximation of the msc, as proposed in [Cohen and Hirsh, 1994]. In the process engineering application, we can also use the lcs operation directly to structure the existing knowledge base.

In fact, it has turned out that the subsumption hierarchy obtained from the knowledge base of standard building blocks is rather flat. To obtain a deeper hierarchy (which better supports search and hence reuse of building blocks), we will try to construct intermediate levels of concepts by applying the lcs operation. Of course, this only makes sense if the lcs yields concepts that have an intuitive meaning in the application domain.

References

[Abiteboul *et al.*, 1995] S. Abiteboul, R. Hull, and V. Vianu. *Foundations of Databases*. Addison-Wesley, 1995.

[Baader and Küsters, 1998] F. Baader and R. Küsters. Computing the least common subsumer and the most specific concept in the presence of cyclic $\mathcal{ALN}$-concept descriptions. In *Proc. of KI'98*, LNCS 1504, 1998.

[Baader and Sattler, 1996] F. Baader and U. Sattler. Knowledge representation in process engineering. In *Proc. of DL'96*, 1996.

[Baader *et al.*, 1998] F. Baader, R. Küsters, and R. Molitor. Computing least common subsumers in description logics with existential restrictions. LTCS-Report 98-09. See http://www-lti.informatik.rwth-aachen.de/Forschung/Papers.html.

[Borgida and Patel-Schneider, 1994] A. Borgida and P. Patel-Schneider. A semantics and complete algorithm for subsumption in the CLASSIC description logic. *J. of AI Research*, 1, 1994.

[Brachman *et al.*, 1991] R. J. Brachman, D. McGuinness, P. Patel-Schneider, L. Resnick, and A. Borgida. Living with CLASSIC: When and how to use a KL-ONE-like language. In *Principles of Semantic Networks*. Morgan Kaufmann, 1991.

[Chein and Mugnier, 1992] M. Chein and M. Mugnier. Conceptual graphs: Fundamental notions. *Revue d'Intelligence Artificielle*, 6(4), 1992.

[Cohen and Hirsh, 1994] W. W. Cohen and H. Hirsh. Learning the CLASSIC description logic: Theoretical and experimental results. In *Proc. of KR'94*. Morgan Kaufmann, 1994.

[Donini *et al.*, 1992] F.M. Donini, M. Lenzerini, D. Nardi, B. Hollunder, W. Nutt, and A.M. Spaccamela. The complexity of existential quantification in concept languages. *Journal of Artificial Intelligence*, 52, 1992.

[Frazier and Pitt, 1996] M. Frazier and L. Pitt. CLASSIC learning. *Machine Learning*, 25, 1996.

[Reyner, 1977] S. Reyner. An analysis of a good algorithm for the subtree problem. *SIAM Journal of Computing*, 6(4), 1977.

[Sattler, 1998] U. Sattler. *Terminological Knowledge Representation Systems in a Process Engineering Application*. PhD thesis, RWTH Aachen, 1998.

AUTOMATED REASONING

Description Logics 2

Multi-dimensional description logics

Frank Wolter
Institut für Informatik
Universität Leipzig
Augustus-Platz 10-11
04109 Leipzig, Germany
e-mail: wolter@informatik.uni-leipzig.de

Michael Zakharyaschev
Institute of Applied Mathematics
Russian Academy of Sciences
Miusskaya Square 4
125047 Moscow, Russia
e-mail: mz@spp.keldysh.ru

Abstract

In this paper, we construct a new concept description language intended for representing dynamic and intensional knowledge. The most important feature distinguishing this language from its predecessors in the literature is that it allows applications of modal operators to *all* kinds of syntactic terms: concepts, roles and formulas. Moreover, the language may contain both local (i.e., state-dependent) and global (i.e., state-independent) concepts, roles and objects. All this provides us with the most complete and natural means for reflecting the dynamic and intensional behaviour of application domains. We construct a satisfiability checking (mosaic-type) algorithm for this language (based on $\mathcal{ALC}$) in (i) arbitrary multimodal frames, (ii) frames with universal accessibility relations (for knowledge) and (iii) frames with transitive, symmetrical and euclidean relations (for beliefs). On the other hand, it is shown that the satisfaction problem becomes undecidable if the underlying frames are arbitrary linear orders or the language contains the common knowledge operator for $n \geq 2$ agents.

1 Introduction

Description logics are often characterized as logic-based formalisms intended for representing knowledge about concept hierarchies and supplied with effective reasoning procedures and a Tarski-style declarative semantics. A standard example is the description logic $\mathcal{ALC}$ (see [Schmidt-Schauß and Smolka, 1991]) in the syntax of which the "definition" above can be represented as follows:

Description_logic = Knowledge_representation_language ∧ Logic ∧ ∃is_decided_by.Algorithm ∧ ∃has.Tarski_semantics,

$$\mathcal{ALC} : \text{Description\_logic}$$

(here Description_logic, Knowledge_representation_language, Logic, Algorithm, Tarski_semantics are concept names (unary predicates), is_decided_by and has are role names (binary predicates) and $\mathcal{ALC}$ is an object name (individual constant)).

Created in the 1980s as a direct successor of semantic networks and Minsky frames, description logic has found numerous applications and given rise to a rich family of languages (see e.g. [Brachman and Schmolze, 1985; Donini *et al.*, 1996]). But as the application areas are becoming more and more sophisticated, new, more expressive description logics are being called for. Sometimes it is possible to comply with the application demands by enriching a "standard" description language with new constructs and retaining basically the same semantical paradigm. E.g., De Giacomo and Lenzerini [1996] extend $\mathcal{ALC}$ by providing means to form the union, composition, inversion, transitive reflexive closure of roles and to use the number restrictions for quantification over roles; Baader and Hanschke [1991] add concrete domains to $\mathcal{ALC}$. However, some constructs require more drastic changes in the standard semantics. This happens, for instance, when one has to take into account various dynamic aspects of knowledge representation, say time- or agent-dependence of knowledge like

Received = Mail ∧ ⟨*sometime in the past*⟩∃is_in.Mailbox,

John : ∃[*always*]loves.Woman,

[*John believes*]⟨*eventually*⟩(∃loves.⊤ = ⊤),

i.e., a received mail has been put into the mailbox some time ago, John will always love the same woman, and John believes that sometime in the future everybody will love somebody.

Several approaches to the design of "dynamic" description logics were developed in the 1990s (see e.g. [Schmiedel, 1990; Schild, 1993; Baader and Ohlbach, 1995; Baader and Laux, 1995; Donini *et al.*, 1992; Wolter and Zakharyaschev, 1998a; 1998b; 1998c]), and all of them share one important feature: their models become multi-dimensional in the sense that besides the usual "object dimension" they may contain a time axis, possible worlds or states for beliefs or actions, etc.

Perhaps the most general multi-dimensional perspective was proposed by Baader and Ohlbach [1993; 1995]. Roughly, each dimension (object, time, belief, etc.) is represented by a set D_i (of objects, moments of time, possible worlds, etc.), concepts are interpreted as subsets of the Cartesian product $\prod_{i=1}^{n} D_i$ and roles of dimension i as binary relations between n-tuples that may differ only in the ith coordinate. And one can quantify over roles not only concepts, but also roles themselves and concept equations. However, the constructed language turned out to be too expressive. At least no sound and complete reasoning procedure for it has appeared (Baader and Ohlbach provide only a sound satisfiability algorithm for a restricted fragment of their language). Moreover, under the natural assumption that some dimensions may be "independent" the language becomes undecidable.[1]

Trying to simplify this semantics, Baader and Laux [1995] noticed that different dimensions may have a different status. For instance, time should probably be the same for all objects inhabiting the object dimension of our knowledge base. This observation led to a somewhat more transparent semantics: models now consist of worlds (or states) which represent—in terms of some standard description logic—the "current state of affairs"; these worlds may change with time passing by or under certain actions, or they may have a number of alternative worlds reflecting the beliefs of agents, and the connection between concepts and roles from different worlds is described by means of the corresponding temporal, dynamic, epistemic, or some other "modal" operators.

There are several "degrees of freedom" within this semantical paradigm.

1. The worlds in models may have arbitrary, or expanding (with respect to the accessibility relation between worlds), or constant domains. Of course, the choice depends on the application we deal with. However, from the technical point of view the most important is the *constant domain assumption*: as was shown in [Wolter and Zakharyaschev, 1998b], if the satisfaction problem is decidable in models with constant domains then it is decidable in models with varying or expanding domains as well. This is the reason why in this paper we adopt the constant domain assumption.

2. The concept, role and object names of the underlying description language may be *local* or *global*. Global names have the same extensions in all worlds, while local ones may have different extensions. (For example, an agent A may regard the role loves to be local, while the role believes to be global.) In principle, we may need both kinds of names. However technically, local object names present no difficulty as compared with global ones, and global concepts are expressible via local concepts and the modal operators.

3. As we saw above, in general one may need modal operators applicable to concepts, roles and formulas.

And finally, depending on the application domain we may choose between various kinds of modal operators (e.g. temporal, epistemic, action, etc.), the corresponding accessibility relations (say, linear for time, universal

_____

[1] Franz Baader has kindly informed us that the language is undecidable without this assumption as well.

for knowledge, arbitrary for actions), and between the underlying pure description logics.

The main objective of this paper is to analyze a number of basic multi-dimensional modal description logics based on $\mathcal{ALC}$ and having the most expressive combination of the listed parameters. In particular, we show that the satisfaction problem (and so many other reasoning problems as well) for the logics with modal operators applicable to arbitrary concepts, (local and global) roles and formulas is *decidable* in the class of all (multi-modal) frames, in the class of universal frames (corresponding to the modality "agent A knows") and in the class of transitive, symmetrical and euclidean frames (corresponding to the modality "agent A believes").

Multi-dimensional modal description logics of such a great expressive power have never been considered in the literature. Languages with modal operators applicable only to axioms were studied by Finger and Gabbay [1992] and Laux [1994]; Schild [1993] allows applications of temporal operators only to concepts. Baader and Laux [1995] prove the decidability of the satisfaction problem for $\mathcal{ALC}$ extended with modal operators applicable to concepts and axioms, but only in the class of arbitrary frames and under the expanding domain assumption. Wolter and Zakharyaschev [1998a; 1998b; 1998c] have obtained a series of decidability results for the most important epistemic, temporal and dynamic description logics (based on the description logic $\mathcal{CIQ}$ of [De Giacomo and Lenzerini, 1996]) under the constant domain assumption and with modal operators applicable to both concept and formulas.

However, the computational behaviour of the modalized roles (i.e., binary predicates) has remained unclear. It should be emphasized that this problem is not of only technical interest. Modalized roles are really required for expressing the dynamic features of roles while passing from one state to another (which is usually much more difficult than to reflect the dynamic behaviour of concepts). For instance, to describe the class of people always voting for the same party we can use the axiom

Faithful_voter = Voter $\land \exists[always]$votes.Party.

(By swapping $\exists$ and $[always]$ we get the class of people always voting for *some* party.)

The price we have to pay for this extra expressive power is that only a limited number of logics in this language enjoy decidability. We show, for instance, that the satisfaction problem in linear frames or in universal frames with the common knowledge operator for $n \geq 2$ agents is undecidable (but it becomes decidable if the language contains neither global nor modalized roles).

To simplify presentation, we will be considering first description logics with only one modal operator and then generalize the obtained results to systems of multi-modal description logic. A full version of the paper is at http://www.informatik.uni-leipzig.de/~wolter.

2 The language and its models

The primitive symbols of the *modal description language* $\mathcal{ALC_M}$ we deal with in this paper are: *concept names* $C_0, C_1, \ldots$, *role names* $R_0, R_1, \ldots$, and *object names* $a_0, a_1, \ldots$. Starting from these we construct compound *concepts* and *roles* in the following way. Let R be a role, C, D concepts, and let $\square$ and $\diamond$ be the (dual) modal "necessity" and "possibility" operators, respectively. Then $\diamond R$, $\square R$ are roles, and $\top$, $C \wedge D$, $\neg C$, $\diamond C$, $\exists R.C$ are concepts. *Atomic formulas* are expressions of the form $\top$, $C = D$, aRb, $a : C$, where a, b are object names. If φ and ψ are *formulas* then so are $\diamond\varphi$, $\neg\varphi$, and $\varphi \wedge \psi$.

The intended semantics of $\mathcal{ALC_M}$ is a natural combination of the standard Tarski-type semantics for the description part of $\mathcal{ALC_M}$ and the Kripke-type (possible world) semantics for the modal part.

Definition 1 (model). An $\mathcal{ALC_M}$-*model* based on a frame $\mathfrak{G} = \langle W, \lhd \rangle$[2] is a pair $\mathfrak{M} = \langle \mathfrak{G}, I \rangle$ in which I is a function associating with each $w \in W$ an $\mathcal{ALC}$-model

$$I(w) = \left\langle \Delta, R_0^{I,w}, \ldots, C_0^{I,w}, \ldots, a_0^{I,w}, \ldots \right\rangle,$$

where Δ is a non-empty set, the *domain* of $\mathfrak{M}$, $R_i^{I,w}$ are binary relations on Δ, $C_i^{I,w} \subseteq \Delta$, and $a_i^{I,w}$ are objects in Δ such that $a_i^{I,u} = a_i^{I,v}$, for any $u, v \in W$. The *values* $C^{I,w}$, $R^{I,w}$ of a concept C and a role R in a world $w \in W$, and the *truth-relation* $(\mathfrak{M}, w) \models \varphi$ (or simply $w \models \varphi$) are defined inductively as follows:

1. $x(\diamond R)^{I,w} y$ iff $\exists v \rhd w \; x R^{I,v} y$;
2. $x(\square R)^{I,w} y$ iff $\forall v \rhd w \; x R^{I,v} y$;
3. $(C \wedge D)^{I,w} = C^{I,w} \cap D^{I,w}$;
4. $(\neg C)^{I,w} = \Delta - C^{I,w}$;
5. $x \in (\diamond C)^{I,w}$ iff $\exists v \rhd w \; x \in C^{I,v}$;
6. $x \in (\exists R.C)^{I,w}$ iff $\exists y \in C^{I,w} \; x R^{I,w} y$;
7. $w \models C = D$ iff $C^{I,w} = D^{I,w}$;
8. $w \models a : C$ iff $a^{I,w} \in C^{I,w}$;
9. $w \models aRb$ iff $a^{I,w} R^{I,w} b^{I,w}$;
10. $w \models \diamond\varphi$ iff $\exists v \rhd w \; v \models \varphi$;
11. $w \models \varphi \wedge \psi$ iff $w \models \varphi$ and $w \models \psi$;
12. $w \models \neg\varphi$ iff $w \not\models \varphi$.

A formula φ is *satisfiable* if there is a model $\mathfrak{M}$ and a world w in $\mathfrak{M}$ such that $w \models \varphi$.

Since many reasoning tasks are reducible to the satisfaction problem for formulas (see e.g. [Donini *et al.*, 1996] and [Wolter and Zakharyaschev, 1998b]), in this paper we focus attention only on the latter. Our first aim is to show that the satisfaction problem is decidable in the class of all $\mathcal{ALC_M}$-models.

By the *modal depth* $md(\varphi)$ of a formula φ we mean the length of the longest chain of nested modal operators in

---

[2]W is a non-empty set of *worlds* and $\lhd$ a binary *accessibility* relation on W.

φ (including those in the concepts and roles occurring in φ). It is well known from modal logic (see e.g. [Chagrov and Zakharyaschev, 1997]) that every satisfiable purely modal formula φ can be satisfied in a finite intransitive tree of depth $\leq md(\varphi)$. We remind the reader that a frame $\mathfrak{G} = \langle W, \lhd \rangle$ is called a *tree* if (i) $\mathfrak{G}$ is *rooted*, i.e., there is $w_0 \in W$ (a *root* of $\mathfrak{G}$) such that $w_0 \lhd^* w$ for every $w \in W$, where $\lhd^*$ is the transitive and reflexive closure of $\lhd$, and (ii) for every $w \in W$, the set $\{v \in W : v \lhd^* w\}$ is finite and linearly ordered by $\lhd^*$. The *depth* of a tree is the length of its longest branch. And by the *co-depth* of w we mean the number of worlds in the chain $\{v \in W : v \lhd^* w\}$. A tree $\mathfrak{G}$ is *intransitive* if every world v in $\mathfrak{G}$, save its root, has precisely one predecessor, i.e., $|\{u \in W : u \lhd v\}| = 1$, and the root w_0 is *irreflexive*, i.e., $\neg w_0 \lhd w_0$. Using the standard technique of modal logic one can prove the following lemma.

Lemma 2. *Every satisfiable formula is satisfied in a model based on an intransitive tree of depth $\leq md(\varphi)$ (but possibly with infinitely many branches).*

3 Quasimodels

Fix an $\mathcal{ALC_M}$-formula φ. Let $ob\varphi$ be the set of all object names in φ, and by $con\varphi$, $rol\varphi$ and $sub\varphi$ we denote the sets of all concepts, roles, and subformulas occurring in φ, respectively.

In general, $\mathcal{ALC_M}$-models are rather complex structures with rich interactions between worlds, concepts and roles. That is why standard methods of establishing decidability (say, filtration) do not go through for them. Our idea is to factorize the models modulo φ in such a way that the resulting structures—we will call them *quasimodels*—can be constructed from a finite number of relatively small finite pieces called *blocks*.

Definition 3 (types). A *concept type* for φ is a subset t of $con\varphi$ such that

- $C \wedge D \in t$ iff $C, D \in t$, for every $C \wedge D \in con\varphi$;
- $\neg C \in t$ iff $C \notin t$, for every $\neg C \in con\varphi$.

A *named concept type* is the pair $t_a = \langle t, a \rangle$, where t is a concept type and $a \in ob\varphi$. A *formula type* and a *named formula type* for φ are defined analogously as saturated subsets of $sub\varphi$. Finally, by a *type* for φ we mean the pair $\tau = (t, \Xi)$, where t is a concept type and Ξ a formula type for φ; $\tau_a = (t_a, \Xi_a)$ is a *named type* for φ.

To simplify notation we write $C \in \tau$ and $\psi \in \tau$ whenever $\tau = (t, \Xi)$, $C \in t$ and $\psi \in \Xi$. Two types $\tau_1 = (t_1, \Xi_1)$ and $\tau_2 = (t_2, \Xi_2)$ are *formula-equivalent* if $\Xi_1 = \Xi_2$.

Let $\mathfrak{M} = \langle \mathfrak{G}, I \rangle$ be a model over Δ and $\mathfrak{G} = \langle W, \lhd \rangle$ an intransitive tree of depth $\leq md(\varphi)$. Without loss of generality we may assume also that $ob\varphi \subseteq \Delta$ (and $a_i^{I,w} = a_i$). For every pair $x \in \Delta$, $w \in W$, let $\tau(x, w) = (t(x, w), \Xi(w))$, where

$$t(x, w) = \{C \in con\varphi : x \in C^{I,w}\},$$
$$\Xi(w) = \{\psi \in sub\varphi : w \models \psi\}.$$

Clearly, $\tau(x, w)$ is a type for φ. The set of (labelled) types $\tau(x, w)$, $w \in W$, with the relation $<_x$ defined by $\tau(x, u) <_x \tau(x, v)$ iff $u \lhd v$ is a tree isomorphic to $\mathfrak{G}$. But modulo φ only a finite part of this tree is enough to represent all the essential information it contains.

Definition 4 (type tree). By a *type tree* for φ we mean a structure of the form $\mathfrak{T} = \langle T, < \rangle$, where T is a finite set of labelled types for φ (so that one type may have many occurrences in T) and $<$ an intransitive tree order on T such that

(a) for all $\tau \in T$ and $\diamond C \in con\varphi$, we have $\diamond C \in \tau$ iff $\exists \tau' > \tau \ C \in \tau'$;

(b) for all $\tau \in T$ and $\diamond \psi \in sub\varphi$, we have $\diamond \psi \in \tau$ iff $\exists \tau' > \tau \ \psi \in \tau'$;

(c) $\mathfrak{T}$ is of depth $\leq md(\varphi)$;

(d) if $\tau < \tau'$, $\tau < \tau''$ and $\tau' \neq \tau''$ then the subtrees of $\mathfrak{T}$ generated by τ' and τ'' are not isomorphic.

It should be clear that there exist at most $N_d(\varphi)$ pairwise non-isomorphic type trees of depth d, where

$$N_1(\varphi) = 2^{|con\varphi|} \cdot 2^{|sub\varphi|},$$

$$N_{n+1}(\varphi) = 2^{|con\varphi|} \cdot 2^{|sub\varphi|} \cdot 2^{N_n(\varphi)}.$$

So the number of types in each type tree for φ does not exceed $\sharp(\varphi) = (N_{md(\varphi)}(\varphi))^{md(\varphi)}$.

Definition 5 (type forest). A *type forest of depth d* over Δ is a set $\mathfrak{F} = \{\mathfrak{T}_x : x \in \Delta\}$, where all $\mathfrak{T}_x = \langle T_x, <_x \rangle$ are type trees for φ of the same depth d and $\mathfrak{T}_a$, for every $a \in \Delta \cap ob\varphi$, consists of only named types of the form τ_a.

To represent worlds in models with their inner complex structure we require the following definition.

Definition 6 (run). A *run of co-depth d* through a type forest $\mathfrak{F}$ over Δ is a pair of the form

$$r = \langle \Delta_r, \{R_r : R \in rol\varphi\} \rangle$$

in which Δ_r contains precisely one type $r(x) \in T_x$ of co-depth d for every $x \in \Delta$ (so that $\Delta_r = \{r(x) : x \in \Delta\}$) and $R_r \subseteq \Delta_r \times \Delta_r$ such that:

(e) all types in Δ_r are formula-equivalent to each other;

(f) $\exists R.C \in r(x)$ iff $\exists y \in \Delta \ (r(x)R_r r(y) \ \& \ C \in r(y))$, for every $\exists R.C \in con\varphi$;

(g) $C = D \in r(x)$ iff $\forall y \in \Delta \ (C \in r(y) \Leftrightarrow D \in r(y))$, for every $C = D \in sub\varphi$;

(h) $a : C \in r(x)$ iff $C \in r(a)$, for every $a : C \in sub\varphi$ provided that $a \in \Delta$;

(i) $aRb \in r(x)$ iff $r(a)R_r r(b)$, for every $aRb \in sub\varphi$ provided that $a, b \in \Delta$.

If only the ($\Leftarrow$)-part of (f) holds, we call r a *weak run* of co-depth d. And if a weak run r satisfies (f) for some particular x in Δ, then r is called a *weak x-saturated run* of co-depth d. Instead of $\psi \in r(x)$ we will write $r \models \psi$.

Models as a whole are represented in the form of quasimodels.

Definition 7 (quasimodel). A triple $\mathfrak{m} = \langle \mathfrak{F}, \mathfrak{R}, \lhd \rangle$ is called a *quasimodel* for φ if $\mathfrak{F}$ is a type forest of depth $m \leq md(\varphi)$ for φ over some $\Delta \supseteq ob\varphi$, $\mathfrak{R}$ a set of runs through $\mathfrak{F}$ and $\lhd$ is an intransitive tree order on $\mathfrak{R}$ such that the following conditions hold:

(j) for every $d \leq m$, the set $\mathfrak{R}^d$ of runs of co-depth d in $\mathfrak{R}$ is non-empty;

(k) for any $r, r' \in \mathfrak{R}$, if $r \lhd r'$ then $r(x) <_x r'(x)$ for all $x \in \Delta$;

(l) for all $r \in \mathfrak{R}^d$, $x \in \Delta$, and $\tau \in T_x$, if $r(x) <_x \tau$ then there is $r' \in \mathfrak{R}^{d+1}$ such that $r'(x) = \tau$ and $r \lhd r'$;

(m) for all $x, y \in \Delta$, $d \leq m$, $\diamond R \in rol\varphi$, and $r \in \mathfrak{R}^d$, we have $r(x)(\diamond R)_r r(y)$ iff $\exists r' \rhd r \ r'(x)R_{r'} r'(y)$;

(n) for all $x, y \in \Delta$, $d \leq m$, $\Box R \in rol\varphi$, and $r \in \mathfrak{R}^d$, we have $r(x)(\Box R)_r r(y)$ iff $\forall r' \rhd r \ r'(x)R_{r'} r'(y)$.

We say $\mathfrak{m}$ *satisfies* φ if $r \models \varphi$ for some $r \in \mathfrak{R}$.

To reconstruct the model $\mathfrak{M} = \langle \mathfrak{G}, I \rangle$ factorized in a quasimodel $\mathfrak{m} = \langle \mathfrak{F}, \mathfrak{R}, \lhd \rangle$ over domain Δ, one can take $\mathfrak{G} = \langle W, \lhd \rangle$, $W = \bigcup \mathfrak{R}$, and put $x R_i^{I,r} y$ iff $r(x)(R_i)_r r(y)$, $x \in C_i^{I,r}$ iff $C_i \in r(x)$, $a_i^{I,r} = a_i$,

$$I(r) = \langle \Delta, R_0^{I,r}, \ldots, C_0^{I,r}, \ldots, a_0^{I,r}, \ldots \rangle,$$

Thus we obtain:

Theorem 8. *A formula φ is satisfiable iff φ is satisfied in some quasimodel for φ.*

Let $\mathfrak{m} = \langle \mathfrak{F}, \mathfrak{R}, \lhd \rangle$ be a quasimodel over Δ, $x \in \Delta$, $R \in rol\varphi$ and let $R = MR_i$ for some (possibly empty) string M of $\diamond$ and $\Box$, R_i a role name. Consider $\mathfrak{T}_x = \langle T_x, <_x \rangle$ as a usual Kripke frame. If $(\mathfrak{T}_x, r(x)) \models M\bot$, $r \in \mathfrak{R}$, then we say that R is *r-universal*. This name is explained by the fact that if R is r-universal then we have $R_r = \Delta_r \times \Delta_r$, which can be easily established by induction on the length of M. Using the standard unravelling technique of modal logic (see e.g. [Chagrov and Zakharyaschev, 1997]) one can prove

Lemma 9. *Every satisfiable φ is satisfied in a quasimodel $\langle \mathfrak{F}, \mathfrak{R}, \lhd \rangle$ for φ in which the set of pairs $\langle x, y \rangle$ such that $x, y \notin ob\varphi$ and $r(x)R_r r(y)$ for some R that is not r-universal, $r \in \mathfrak{R}$, is an intransitive forest order on the set of objects involved in this relation.*

4 Satisfiability checking

We are in a position now to show that a formula φ is satisfiable iff one can construct a (possibly infinite) quasimodel satisfying φ out of a finite set of finite pattern blocks.

Definition 10 (block). Let $\mathfrak{F}$ be a type forest for φ of depth $m \leq md(\varphi)$ over a finite Δ which is disjoint from $ob\varphi$, x an object in Δ, $\mathfrak{R}$ a set of weak x-saturated runs through $\mathfrak{F}$ such that the set of pairs $\langle x, y \rangle$ with $r(x)R_r r(y)$ for some R that is not r-universal, $r \in \mathfrak{R}$, is an intransitive tree order on Δ with root x, and let $\lhd$ be an intransitive tree order on $\mathfrak{R}$. We say $\langle \mathfrak{F}, \mathfrak{R}, \lhd \rangle$ is a $\mathfrak{T}_x$-*block* for φ if it satisfies conditions (j)–(n).

Definition 11 (kernel block). A *kernel block* over $ob\varphi \neq \emptyset$ is a structure of the form $\langle \mathfrak{F}, \mathfrak{R}, \lhd \rangle$ in which $\mathfrak{F}$ is a type forest over $ob\varphi$ of depth $m \leq md(\varphi)$ (it contains only type trees named by the elements of $ob\varphi$), $\mathfrak{R}$ a set of weak runs through $\mathfrak{F}$ and $\lhd$ an intransitive tree order on $\mathfrak{R}$ satisfying (j)–(n).

Definition 12 (satisfying set). A set of blocks $\mathcal{S}$ for φ is called a *satisfying set* for φ if

(o) $\mathcal{S}$ contains one kernel block for φ whenever $ob\varphi \neq \emptyset$;

(p) in every block $\langle \mathfrak{F}, \mathfrak{R}, \lhd \rangle \in \mathcal{S}$ there is $r \in \mathfrak{R}$ such that $r \models \varphi$;

(q) for every $\langle \mathfrak{F}, \mathfrak{R}, \lhd \rangle$ in $\mathcal{S}$ and every $\mathfrak{T}_x \in \mathfrak{F}$, there is precisely one $\mathfrak{T}_x$-block in $\mathcal{S}$.

Theorem 13. *A formula φ is satisfiable iff there is a satisfying set for φ the domain of each (non-kernel) block in which contains at most $\sharp(\varphi) \cdot |con\varphi| \cdot (md(\varphi) + 1) + 1$ objects.*

As an immediate consequence we obtain:

Theorem 14. *The satisfaction problem for $\mathcal{ALC}_\mathcal{M}$-formulas is decidable.*

So far we were considering satisfiability in *arbitrary* $\mathcal{ALC}_\mathcal{M}$-models. However, various specializations of the modal operators may impose different restrictions on the structure of underlying frames in our models. For instance, if we understand $\square$ as "it is known", we may need frames that are transitive, reflexive and symmetrical, i.e., **S5**-frames in the modal logic terminology, and if $\square$ is intended to stand for "it is believed", then we may need **KD45**-frames which have the form of an **S5**-frame possibly with one irreflexive predecessor.

It is not hard to adopt the developed technique to prove the following:

Theorem 15. *There is an algorithm which is capable of deciding, given an arbitrary $\mathcal{ALC}_\mathcal{M}$-formula φ, whether φ is satisfiable in an $\mathcal{ALC}_\mathcal{M}$-model based upon (i) an **S5**-frame or (ii) a **KD45**-frame.*

In some applications we may need $\mathcal{ALC}_\mathcal{M}$-models with *global roles*, i.e., roles R which are interpreted by the same binary relation in every world of a model. In quasi-models, we can reflect this by requiring that $r(x)R_r r(y)$ implies $r'(x)R_{r'}r'(y)$ for all $x, y \in \Delta$, $r, r' \in \mathfrak{R}$; in other words, global roles correspond to binary relations between type trees. By a straightforward modification of the proof of Theorem 14 one can show the following:

Theorem 16. *There is an algorithm which is capable of deciding, given an arbitrary $\mathcal{ALC}_\mathcal{M}$-formula φ with global roles, whether φ is satisfiable in an $\mathcal{ALC}_\mathcal{M}$-model based upon (i) an arbitrary frame, (ii) an **S5**-frame or (iii) a **KD45**-frame.*

When dealing with intensional knowledge, one usually needs one modal operator $\square_i$ for each agent i (meaning that "agent i knows" or "agent i believes"); see e.g. [Fagin *et al.*, 1995] for a discussion of propositional multimodal epistemic logics. Let $\mathcal{ALC}_{\mathcal{M}_n}$ denote the modal description language with n modal operators, so that

$\mathcal{ALC}_{\mathcal{M}_n}$-models are based on Kripke frames with n accessibility relations $\lhd_1, \ldots, \lhd_n$. These frames are called *n-frames*. **S5**$_n$-frames and **KD45**$_n$-frames are those n-frames all monomodal fragments of which are **S5**-frames and **KD45**-frames, respectively. The developed technique provides a satisfiability checking algorithm for this multimodal case as well.

Theorem 17. *For every $n \geq 1$, there is an algorithm which is capable of deciding, for an arbitrary $\mathcal{ALC}_{\mathcal{M}_n}$-formula φ with global roles, whether φ is satisfiable in an $\mathcal{ALC}_{\mathcal{M}_n}$-model based upon (i) an arbitrary n-frame, (ii) an **S5**$_n$-frame or (iii) a **KD45**$_n$-frame.*

It would also be of interest to extend the constructed epistemic description language $\mathcal{ALC}_{\mathcal{M}_n}$ with the *common knowledge operator* **C** which is interpreted by the transitive and reflexive closure of the union $\lhd_1 \cup \ldots \cup \lhd_n$. (For various applications of **C** in the analysis of multi-agent systems see [Fagin *et al.*, 1995].) Another important kind of modality often used in applications is the temporal operator "always in the future" (or the operators "Since" and "Until") interpreted in linearly ordered sets of worlds (see e.g. [Gabbay *et al.*, 1994]). The satisfaction problem for these languages without global and modalized roles is known to be decidable (see [Wolter and Zakharyaschev, 1998a; 1998b; 1998c]). However, this is not the case for the language constructed in this paper:

Theorem 18. (i) *The satisfaction problem for $\mathcal{ALC}_\mathcal{M}$-formulas in linearly ordered transitive frames is undecidable; it is undecidable in $\langle \mathbb{N}, < \rangle$ as well.*

(ii) *The satisfaction problem for the epistemic description formulas with $n \geq 2$ agents and the common knowledge operator is undecidable in the class of **S5**$_n$-frames.*

5 Discussion and open problems

This paper makes one more step in the study of concept description languages of high expressive power that are located near the border between decidable and undecidable. We have designed a "full" multidimensional modal description language which imposes no restrictions whatsoever on the use of modal operators (they can be applied to all types of syntactic terms: concepts, roles and formulas) and contains both local and global object, concept and role names. Using the mosaic technique we have proved that the satisfaction problem for the formulas of this language (and so many other reasoning tasks as well) is decidable in some important classes of models. On the other hand, it was shown that the language becomes undecidable when interpreted on temporal structures or augmented with the common knowledge operator.

The obtained results demonstrate a principle possibility of using this highly expressive language in knowledge representation systems. Further investigations are required to make it really applicable. In particular, it would be of interest to answer the following questions:

(1) Do the logics considered above have the finite model property?

Our conjecture is that they do have this property, and so the finite model reasoning in those logics is effective.

(2) What is the complexity of satisfiability checking in these logics?

We only know that the satisfaction problem in all of them is NEXPTIME-hard.

To increase the language's capacity of expressing the dynamics of relations between individual objects in application domains it would be desirable also

(3) to extend $\mathcal{ALC_{M_n}}$ with (some of) the booleans operating on roles,

(4) to extend the underlying description logic with new constructs

and, of course, retain decidability.

Acknowledgements

The work of the second author was supported by U.K. EPSRC grant no. GR/M36748.

References

[Baader and Hanschke, 1991] F. Baader and P. Hanschke. A scheme for integrating concrete domains into concept languages. In *Proceedings of the 12th International Joint Conference on Artificial Intelligence*, pages 452–457, Sydney, 1991.

[Baader and Laux, 1995] F. Baader and A. Laux. Terminological logics with modal operators. In *Proceedings of the 14th International Joint Conference on Artificial Intelligence*, pages 808–814, Montreal, Canada, 1995. Morgan Kaufman.

[Baader and Ohlbach, 1993] F. Baader and H. Ohlbach. A multi-dimensional terminological knowledge representation language. In *Proceedings of the 13th International Joint Conference on Artificial Intelligence*, pages 690–695, Chambery, 1993.

[Baader and Ohlbach, 1995] F. Baader and H.J. Ohlbach. A multi-dimensional terminological knowledge representation language. *Journal of Applied Non-Classical Logic*, 5:153–197, 1995.

[Brachman and Schmolze, 1985] R.J. Brachman and J.G. Schmolze. An overview of the KL-ONE knowledge representation system. *Cognitive Science*, 9:171–216, 1985.

[Chagrov and Zakharyaschev, 1997] A.V. Chagrov and M.V. Zakharyaschev. *Modal Logic*. Clarendon Press, Oxford, 1997.

[De Giacomo and Lenzerini, 1996] G. De Giacomo and M. Lenzerini. TBox and ABox reasoning in expressive description logics. In *Proceedings of the fifth Conference on Principles of Knowledge Representation and Reasoning*, Montreal, Canada, 1996. Morgan Kaufman.

[Donini et al., 1992] F. Donini, M. Lenzerini, D. Nardi, A. Schaerf, and W. Nutt. Adding epistemic operators to concept languages. In *Principles of Knowledge Representation and Reasoning*, pages 342–353, Cambridge, 1992.

[Donini et al., 1996] F. Donini, M. Lenzerini, D. Nardi, and A. Schaerf. Reasoning in description logics. In G. Brewka, editor, *Principles of Knowledge Representation*, pages 191–236. CSLI Publications, 1996.

[Finger and Gabbay, 1992] M. Finger and D. Gabbay. Adding a temporal dimension to a logic system. *Journal of Logic, Language and Information*, 2:203–233, 1992.

[Fagin et al., 1995] R. Fagin, J. Halpern, Y. Moses, and M. Vardi. *Reasoning about Knowledge*. MIT Press, 1995.

[Gabbay et al., 1994] D. Gabbay, I. Hodkinson, and M. Reynolds. *Temporal Logic*. Oxford University Press, 1994.

[Laux, 1994] A. Laux. Beliefs in multi-agent worlds: a terminological approach. In *Proceedings of the 11th European Conference on Artificial Intelligence*, pages 299–303, Amsterdam, 1994.

[Schild, 1993] K. Schild. Combining terminological logics with tense logic. In *Proceedings of the 6th Portuguese Conference on Artificial Intelligence*, pages 105–120, Porto, 1993.

[Schmidt-Schauß and Smolka, 1991] M. Schmidt-Schauß and G. Smolka. Attributive concept descriptions with complements. *Artificial Intelligence*, 48:1–26, 1991.

[Schmiedel, 1990] A. Schmiedel. A temporal terminological logic. In *Proceedings of the 9th National Conference of the American Association for Artificial Intelligence*, pages 640–645, Boston, 1990.

[Wolter and Zakharyaschev, 1998a] F. Wolter and M. Zakharyaschev. Dynamic description logic. In *Proceedings of AiML'98*, pages 290–300, Uppsala, 1998. To appear in *Advances in Modal Logic II*, CSLI Publishers, Stanford, 1999.

[Wolter and Zakharyaschev, 1998b] F. Wolter and M. Zakharyaschev. Satisfiability problem in description logics with modal operators. In *Proceedings of the sixth Conference on Principles of Knowledge Representation and Reasoning* (KR'98), pages 512–523, Montreal, Canada, 1998. Morgan Kaufman.

[Wolter and Zakharyaschev, 1998c] F. Wolter and M. Zakharyaschev. Temporalizing description logics. In *Proceedings of FroCoS'98*, pages 312–332, Amsterdam, 1998. To appear in *Frontiers of Combining Systems*, Kluwer Academic Publishers, 1999.

On the Relation of Resolution and Tableaux Proof Systems for Description Logics

Ullrich Hustadt and **Renate A. Schmidt**

Department of Computing and Mathematics, Manchester Metropolitan University,
Chester Street, Manchester M1 5GD, UK

U.Hustadt@doc.mmu.ac.uk, R.A.Schmidt@doc.mmu.ac.uk

Abstract

This paper investigates the relationship between resolution and tableaux proof system for the satisfiability of general knowledge bases in the description logic $\mathcal{ALC}$. We show that resolution proof systems can polynomially simulate their tableaux counterpart. Our resolution proof system is based on a selection refinement and utilises standard redundancy elimination criteria to ensure termination.

1 Introduction

Recently a number of results concerning resolution decision procedures for subclasses of first-order logic have been obtained. The considered subclasses are expressive enough to encompass a variety of non-classical logics, in particular, description logics and extended modal logics. De Nivelle [1998] describes a resolution decision procedure for the guarded fragment using a non-liftable ordering refinement. The guarded fragment is a generalisation of the restricted quantifier fragment corresponding to basic modal logic and allows for the embedding of a variety of extended modal logics and description logics [Grädel, 1998]. Expressions and knowledge bases of the description logic $\mathcal{ALC}$ can also be embedded into Maslov's class K and its subclasses One-Free [Fermüller et al., 1993] and the class of DL-clauses [Hustadt and Schmidt, 1999]. Again, ordering refinements of resolution provide decision procedures for these classes. A nonstandard translation into the Bernays-Schönfinkel class combined with resolution and arbitrary refinements provide decision procedures for the satisfiability of $\mathcal{ALC}$ expressions [Schmidt, 1999]. This approach was adopted in the experiments of Hustadt, Schmidt, and Weidenbach [1997; 1998]. Experiments using the standard translation and a combination of a first-order theorem prover augmented with a finite-model finder are described in [Paramasivam and Plaisted, 1998].

The problem of empirical investigations based on competitive testing is the difficulty in identifying the major factors having a positive or negative influence on the performance of a theorem prover. As long as the theorem provers which are being compared follow different proof strategies this difference is likely to have a dominating effect on the overall performance. This has two consequences. One, we can say little about the other factors influencing the performance, for example, fundamental differences between the underlying proof systems or sophisticated redundancy elimination techniques used by the theorem prover. Two, while it is easy to find benchmark problems illustrating the superiority of one theorem prover it is just as easy to find benchmark problems showing the opposite. Therefore, it is always advisable to complement empirical investigations with a theoretical analysis of the relative proof and search complexity of the underlying proof systems. In the first case, the task is to determine whether a proof system $\mathcal{A}$ is able to polynomially simulate a proof system $\mathcal{B}$. This is to say, for any given theorem ϕ there is a function g, computable in polynomial time, mapping proofs of ϕ in $\mathcal{B}$ to proofs of ϕ in $\mathcal{A}$. In the second case, the task is to determine the relative size of the search space, that is the potential number of inference steps performed until a proof is found [Plaisted and Zhu, 1997].

In this paper we focus on the aspect of relative proof complexity of tableaux proof systems and resolution proof systems for the description logic $\mathcal{ALC}$ with general terminological sentences and ABox elements. This logic is of particular interest, since all tableaux proof systems presented in the literature require some form of blocking or loop-checking to force termination [Buchheit et al., 1993; Donini et al., 1996; Horrocks, 1997]. We describe a resolution proof system based on a selection refinement of resolution, instead of an ordering refinement, which provides a new resolution decision procedure for this logic. We show that this proof system is able to polynomially simulate tableaux proof systems for this logic. The technique for simulating blocking described in this paper can also be applied for obtaining other simulation results, for example, analytic modal KE tableaux proof systems or sequent proof systems for modal logics.

The structure of the paper is as follows. Section 2 defines the syntax and semantics of $\mathcal{ALC}$ and describes a standard tableaux proof system. We adopt the resolution framework of Bachmair and Ganzinger [1998] which is described briefly in Section 3. Section 4 presents the simulation result for the tableaux proof system and Section 5 shows how termination of the resolution proof system can be enforced in analogy to blocking in tableaux systems. In Section 6 we discuss some optimisations which are naturally available in the resolution framework and can be transferred to the corresponding tableaux proof systems.

2 Inference for $\mathcal{ALC}$

We work with a *signature* given by a tuple $\Sigma = (\mathsf{O}, \mathsf{C}, \mathsf{R})$ of three disjoint alphabets, the set C of *concept symbols*, the set R of *role symbols*, and the set O of *objects*. *Concept terms* (or just *concepts*) are defined as follows. Every concept symbol is a concept. If C and D are concepts, and R is a role symbol, then $\top, \bot, C \sqcap D, C \sqcup D, \neg C, \forall R.C$, and $\exists R.C$ are concept terms. A concept symbol is also called a *primitive concept*.

A *knowledge base* has two parts: A *TBox* comprising of terminological sentences of the form $C \sqsubseteq D$ and an *ABox* comprising of assertional sentences of the form $a \in C$ and $(a,b) \in R$, where C and D are concepts, R is a role, and a and b are objects.

Although the language does contain any role forming operators, it is still possible to express properties of the domain and range of a role R [Buchheit *et al.*, 1993].

The semantics is specified by the embedding into first-order logic as follows. For sentences:

$$\Pi(C \sqsubseteq D) = \forall x\colon \pi(C,x) \to \pi(D,x)$$
$$\Pi(a \in C) = \pi(C,\underline{a})$$
$$\Pi((a,b) \in R) = \pi(R,\underline{a},\underline{b})$$

where $\underline{a}$ and $\underline{b}$ are constants uniquely associated with a and b. For terms:

$$\pi(A,X) = p_A(X)$$
$$\pi(R,X,Y) = p_R(X,Y)$$
$$\pi(\neg C,X) = \neg\pi(C,X)$$
$$\pi(\top,X) = \top$$
$$\pi(\bot,X) = \bot$$
$$\pi(C \sqcap D,X) = \pi(C,X) \wedge \pi(D,X)$$
$$\pi(C \sqcup D,X) = \pi(C,X) \vee \pi(D,X)$$
$$\pi(\forall R.C,X) = \forall y\colon \pi(R,X,y) \to \pi(C,y)$$
$$\pi(\exists R.C,X) = \exists y\colon \pi(R,X,y) \wedge \pi(C,y)$$

where X and Y are meta-variables for variables and constants, and p_A (respectively p_R) denotes a unary (binary) predicate symbol uniquely associated with the concept symbol A (role symbol R). The variable y is distinct from X.

All common inferential services for knowledge bases, like subsumption tests for concepts, TBox classification, realization, retrieval, can be reduced to tests of the satisfiability of a knowledge base. Our definition of a tableaux proof system, also called a constraint system, largely follows Buchheit *et al.* [1993]. All terminological sentences $C \sqsubseteq D$ are assumed to have been replaced by $\top \sqsubseteq \neg C \sqcup D$ and all concepts in the resulting knowledge based are assumed to have been transformed into negation normal form.

Let I be a subset of O such that no element of I occurs in Γ. Let $\prec_{\mathsf{I}}$ be a well-founded total ordering on I. The elements of I are called *introduced objects*. We assume that the elements of I are introduced during inference according to $\prec_{\mathsf{I}}$, that is, if a is introduced into Γ, then for all $b \in \mathsf{I}$ with $b \prec_{\mathsf{I}} a$, b already occurs in Γ.

Following Buchheit *et al.* [1993] we define the following set of transformation rules for the purpose of testing the satisfiability of a knowledge base:

1. $\Gamma \Rightarrow_{\sqcap} \Gamma \cup \{a \in C, a \in D\}$, if $a \in (C \sqcap D)$ is in Γ, and $a \in C$ and $a \in D$ are not both in Γ.

2. $\Gamma \Rightarrow_{\sqcup} \Gamma \cup \{a \in E\}$, if $a \in (C \sqcup D)$ is in Γ, neither $a \in C$ nor $a \in D$ is in Γ, and $E = C$ or $E = D$.

3. $\Gamma \Rightarrow_{\exists} \Gamma \cup \{(a,b) \in R, b \in C\}$, if $a \in \exists R.C$ is in Γ, there is no d such that both $(a,d) \in R$ and $d \in C$ are in Γ, $b \in \mathsf{I}$ is a newly introduced object.

4. $\Gamma \Rightarrow_{\forall} \Gamma \cup \{b \in C\}$, if $a \in \forall R.C$ and $(a,b) \in R$ are in Γ, and $b \in C$ is not in Γ.

5. $\Gamma \Rightarrow_{\bot} \Gamma \cup \{a \in \bot\}$, if $a \in A$ and $a \in \neg A$ are in Γ, where A is a concept symbol.

6. $\Gamma \Rightarrow_{\sqsubseteq} \Gamma \cup \{a \in C\}$, if a occurs in Γ and a sentence $\top \sqsubseteq C$ is in Γ, and $a \in C$ is not in Γ.

Let $\Rightarrow_{\mathit{TAB}}$ be the transitive closure of the union of the transformation rules given above. A knowledge base Γ contains a *clash* if $a \in \bot$ is in Γ. A knowledge base Γ is satisfiable if there exists a knowledge base Γ' such that (i) $\Gamma \Rightarrow_{\mathit{TAB}} \Gamma'$, (ii) no further applications of $\Rightarrow_{\mathit{TAB}}$ to Γ' are possible, and (iii) Γ' is clash-free. Note that the rule $\Rightarrow_{\sqcup}$ is don't know nondeterministic.

3 The Resolution Framework

As usual clauses are assumed to be multisets of literals. The components in the variable partition of a clause are called split components, that is, split components do not share variables. A clause which is identical to its split component is indecomposable. The condensation $\mathrm{Cond}(C)$ of a clause C is a minimal subclause of C which is a factor of C.

The calculus is parameterised by an ordering $\succ$ and a selection function S. The ordering has to satisfy certain restrictions as detailed in [Bachmair and Ganzinger, 1998], in particular, it is required to be a reduction ordering. A *selection* function assigns to each clause a possibly empty set of occurrences of negative literals. If C is a clause, then the literal occurrences in $S(C)$ are *selected*. No restrictions are imposed on the selection function.

The calculus consists of general *expansion rules* (over clause sets)

$$\frac{N}{N_1 \mid \cdots \mid N_n},$$

each representing a finite derivation of the leaves $N_1, \ldots, N_k$ from the root N. The following rules describe how derivations can be expanded at leaves.

Deduce:
$$\frac{N}{N \cup \{\mathrm{Cond}(C)\}}$$

if C is either a resolvent or a factor of clauses in N.

Delete:
$$\frac{N \cup \{C\}}{N}$$

if C is a tautology or N contains a clause which is a variant of C.

Split:
$$\frac{N \cup \{C \cup D\}}{N \cup \{C\} \mid N \cup \{D\}}$$

if C and D are variable-disjoint.

Resolvents and factors are derived by the following rules.

Ordered Resolution:
$$\frac{C \cup \{A_1\} \quad D \cup \{\neg A_2\}}{(C \cup D)\sigma}$$

where (i) σ is the most general unifier of A_1 and A_2, (ii) no literal is selected in C and $A_1\sigma$ is strictly $\succ$-maximal with respect to $C\sigma$, and (iii) $\neg A_2$ is either selected, or $\neg A_2\sigma$ is maximal in $D\sigma$ and no literal is selected in D. $C \vee A_1$ is called the *positive premise* and $D \vee \neg A_2$ the *negative premise*.[1]

Ordered Factoring:
$$\frac{C \cup \{A_1, A_2\}}{(C \cup \{A_1\})\sigma}$$

where (i) σ is the most general unifier of A_1 and A_2; and (ii) no literal is selected in C and $A_1\sigma$ is $\succ$-maximal with respect to $C\sigma$.

Let N be a set of ground clauses. A ground clause C is *redundant* in N if there are clauses $C_1, \ldots, C_n$ in N such that $C_1, \ldots, C_n$ are smaller than C with respect to $\succ$ and logically imply C. The notion of redundancy is lifted to the non-ground case in the expected way. An inference is redundant if one of the parent clauses or its conclusion is redundant.

Theorem 1 (Bachmair and Ganzinger [1998]).
Let N be a set of clauses. Then N is unsatisfiable iff the saturation of N up to redundancy contains the empty clause.

4 Simulation by Resolution

Our intention is to restrict resolution inferences in such a way that admissible resolution steps correspond to inference steps in tableaux proof systems. Furthermore, the resolution proof system will be a decision procedure whenever the tableaux system terminates without the help of loop-checking or blocking techniques.

It is necessary to modify the translation mapping Π slightly. Without loss of generality, all expressions occurring in Γ are assumed to be in negation normal form. Let $\blacktriangledown$ be a concept symbol not occurring in Γ. Intuitively, $\blacktriangledown$ has the same semantics as the concept symbol $\top$. But while $\top$ is translated to the true formula and will vanish during the conversion to clausal form, the translation treats $\blacktriangledown$ as an ordinary concept symbol. By adding certain formulae to the translation of the knowledge base we provide sufficient information about $\blacktriangledown$ to

---

[1] As usual we implicitly assume that the premises have no common variables.

ensure that the introduction of $\blacktriangledown$ preserves satisfiability equivalence. This allows us to obtain the desired computational behaviour in our resolution proof system.

The modified translation $\overline{\Pi}$ is defined as follows.

$$\overline{\Pi}(C \sqsubseteq D) = \forall x \colon \pi(\blacktriangledown, x) \to \pi(\mathrm{nnf}(\neg C) \sqcup D, x)$$

$$\overline{\Pi}(a \in C) = \pi(C, \underline{a}) \wedge \pi(\blacktriangledown, \underline{a})$$

$$\overline{\Pi}((a,b) \in R) = \pi(R, \underline{a}, \underline{b}) \wedge \pi(\blacktriangledown, \underline{a}) \wedge \pi(\blacktriangledown, \underline{b})$$

The occurrence of $\pi(\blacktriangledown, x)$ on the left-hand side of the implication ensures that all clauses in the clausal form contain the negative literal $\neg p_\blacktriangledown(x)$. Since

$$\overline{\Pi}(C \sqsubseteq D) = \overline{\Pi}(\top \sqsubseteq \mathrm{nnf}(\neg C) \sqcup D)$$

it is immaterial whether the terminological sentences in Γ take the first or second form.

The conversion to clausal form of first-order formulae resulting from the translation of $\mathcal{ALC}$ knowledge bases, makes use of a particular form of structural transformation Ξ [Baaz *et al.*, 1994], which is based on two mappings Ξ_1 and Ξ_2.

Let $\mathrm{Pos}(\phi)$ be the set of positions of a formula ϕ. If λ is a position in ϕ, then $\phi|_\lambda$ denotes the subformula of ϕ at position λ and $\phi[\lambda \leftarrow \psi]$ is the result of replacing ϕ at position λ by ψ. We associate with each element λ of $\Lambda \subseteq \mathrm{Pos}(\phi)$ a predicate symbol Q_λ and a literal $Q_\lambda(x_1, \ldots, x_n)$, where the x_i are the free variables of $\phi|_\lambda$, Q_λ does not occur in ϕ and two symbols Q_λ and $Q_{\lambda'}$ are equal iff ϕ_λ and $\phi_{\lambda'}$ are variant formulae. Ξ_1 uses *definitions* of the form

$$\mathrm{Def}_\lambda(\phi) = \forall x_1, \ldots, x_n \colon Q_\lambda(x_1, \ldots, x_n) \to \phi|_\lambda.$$

Now, define $\mathrm{Def}_\Lambda(\phi)$ inductively by: $\mathrm{Def}_\emptyset(\phi) = \phi$ and

$$\mathrm{Def}_{\Lambda \cup \{\lambda\}}(\phi) = \mathrm{Def}_\Lambda(\phi[\lambda \leftarrow Q_\lambda(x_1, \ldots, x_n)]) \wedge \mathrm{Def}_\lambda(\phi),$$

where λ is maximal in $\Lambda \cup \{\lambda\}$ with respect to the prefix ordering on positions. Let $\mathrm{Pos}_d(\phi)$ be the set of positions of subformulae of ϕ corresponding to positions of non-primitive concepts in the knowledge base Γ. By Ξ_1 we denote the transformation taking $\overline{\Pi}(\Gamma)$ to its *definitional form*

$$\mathrm{Def}_{\mathrm{Pos}_d(\overline{\Pi}(\Gamma))}(\overline{\Pi}(\Gamma)).$$

Note that in this case, every predicate symbol Q_λ is a unary predicate associated with a concept C (although not necessarily uniquely associated). Thus, we will henceforth denote Q_λ by p_C. By Ξ_2 we denote the function which produces for every unary predicate symbol p occurring in $\Xi_1\overline{\Pi}(\Gamma)$ the conjunction of all formulae

$$\forall x \colon p(x) \to p_\blacktriangledown(x).$$

Finally, let $\Xi\overline{\Pi}(\Gamma) = \Xi_1\overline{\Pi}(\Gamma) \wedge \Xi_2\Xi_1\overline{\Pi}(\Gamma)$.

Theorem 2. *Let Γ be any knowledge base. $\Xi\overline{\Pi}(\Gamma)$ can be computed in polynomial time, and Γ is satisfiable iff $\Xi\overline{\Pi}(\Gamma)$ is satisfiable.*

The clausal form of $\Xi\overline{\Pi}(\Gamma)$ consists of three types of clauses: (i) clauses stemming from terminological axioms which all contain an occurrence of the negative literal $\neg p_{\blacktriangledown}(x)$, (ii) clauses stemming from formulae introduced by Ξ_1 and Ξ_2 which all contain an occurrence of some negative literal $\neg p_C(x)$, and (iii) clauses originating from the translation of assertional sentences which are ground unit clauses.

Our selection function $S_{\mathcal{TAB}}$ selects the literal $\neg p_{\blacktriangledown}(x)$ in clauses of type (i) and $\neg p_C(x)$ in clauses of types (ii). In addition, a binary literal of the form $\neg p_R(s, t)$ is selected whenever s is a ground term and t is a variable. All clauses stemming from a terminological sentence or from an additional formula introduced by $\overline{\Xi}$ contain negative literals, one of which is selected. We will mark selected literals by $\cdot_+$. For Theorem 3 an arbitrary reduction ordering $\succ$ may be used.

For every concept C and every role R, which may possibly occur in a knowledge base during a satisfiability test, there exist corresponding predicate symbols p_C and p_R in the clausal form of $\overline{\Xi}\Pi(\overline{\Gamma})$. Likewise every object a is associated with a term t_a.

We show that every application of one of the transformation rules is simulated by at most two resolution inference steps.

1. The $\Rightarrow_\sqcap$ rule, by two resolution inference steps between the ground clause $\{p_{C \sqcap D}(t_a)\}$ and clauses $\{\neg p_{C \sqcap D}(x)_+, p_C(x)\}$ and $\{\neg p_{C \sqcap D}(x)_+, p_D(x)\}$, generating the resolvents $\{p_C(t_a)\}$ and $\{p_D(t_a)\}$.

2. The $\Rightarrow_\sqcup$ rule, by an inference step between the ground unit clause $\{p_{C \sqcup D}(t_a)\}$ and $\{\neg p_{C \sqcup D}(x)_+, p_C(x), p_D(x)\}$, followed by an application of the splitting rule to the conclusion $\{p_C(t_a), p_D(t_a)\}$ which will generate two branches, one on which the set of clauses contains $\{p_C(t_a)\}$ and one on which it contains $\{p_D(t_a)\}$.

3. The $\Rightarrow_\exists$ rule, by resolution inference steps between the clauses $\{p_{\exists R.C}(t_a)\}$, $\{\neg p_{\exists R.C}(x)_+, p_R(x, f(x))\}$, and $\{\neg p_{\exists R.C}(x)_+, p_C(f(x))\}$. This will add $\{p_R(t_a, f(t_a))\}$ and $\{p_C(f(t_a))\}$ to the clause set. The term $f(t_a)$ corresponds to the object $b \in \mathsf{I}$ introduced by the $\Rightarrow_\exists$ rule, that is, $t_b = f(t_a)$.

4. The $\Rightarrow_\forall$ rule, by two consecutive resolution inference steps. Here, the set of clauses contains $\{p_{\forall R.C}(t_a)\}$ and $\{p_R(t_a, t_b)\}$. First, the clause $\{p_{\forall R.C}(t_a)\}$ is resolved with $\{\neg p_{\forall R.C}(x)_+, \neg p_R(x, y), p_C(y)\}$ to obtain the clause $\{\neg p_R(t_a, y)_+, p_C(y)\}$. Then the conclusion is resolved with $\{p_R(t_a, t_b)\}$ to obtain $\{p_C(t_b)\}$.

5. The $\Rightarrow_\perp$ rule, by two consecutive inference steps using $\{p_A(t_a)\}$, $\{p_{\neg A}(t_a)\}$, and $\{\neg p_{\neg A}(x)_+, \neg p_A(x)\}$ (which is the clausal form of the definition of $\neg A$) to derive the empty clause.

6. The $\Rightarrow_\sqsubseteq$ rule is simulated as follows. Since the object a occurs in Γ, the corresponding term t_a occurs in our set of clauses. In particular, there is a ground unit clause $\{p_D(t_a)\}$, a clause $\{\neg p_D(x)_+, p_{\blacktriangledown}(x)\}$ introduced by Ξ_2, and a clause $\{\neg p_{\blacktriangledown}(x)_+, p_C(x)\}$ stemming from the translation of the terminological sentence $\top \sqsubseteq C$. By two resolution inference steps we obtain $\{p_C(t_a)\}$ which corresponds to the sentence $a \in C$ added by $\Rightarrow_\sqsubseteq$ to Γ.

Note that all the inference steps strictly obey the restrictions enforced by the selection function $S_{\mathcal{TAB}}$ and are in accordance with the resolution calculus. This proves:

Theorem 3. *The resolution proof system with selection function $S_{\mathcal{TAB}}$ p-simulates the tableaux proof system for $\mathcal{ALC}$.*

Interestingly, factoring plays no role for the clause sets under consideration, that is, the only possible factoring steps are condensations of ground conclusions. Moreover, no resolution inference steps other than those of the simulation are possible. Thus, the following stronger result holds.

Theorem 4. *Let Γ be a knowledge base and N the clausal form of $\overline{\Xi}\Pi(\overline{\Gamma})$. Then the search space of the resolution procedure for N can be polynomially reduced to the search space of the tableaux procedure for Γ.*

5 Termination

By $\mathsf{C}(\Gamma, a)$ we denote the set of all concep? ? such that $a \in C$ is an element of the knowledge . .e Γ. Two objects $a, b \in \mathsf{I}$ are Γ-*equivalent*, denoted by $a \equiv_\Gamma b$, if $\mathsf{C}(\Gamma, a) = \mathsf{C}(\Gamma, b)$. If $b \prec_\mathsf{I} a$ and $a \equiv_\Gamma b$, then b is a *witness* for a. Similarly, let $\mathsf{P}(N, t)$ denote the set of predicate symbols $\{p \mid \{p(t)\} \in N\}$ in a clause set N. (Remember whenever $a \in \neg A$ is an element of Γ, then the positive clause $\{p_{\neg A}(t_a)\}$ is an element of N.)

The strategy (S) employed by Buchheit et al. [1993] restricts the application of rules as follows: (i) apply a transformation to an introduced object only if no rule is applicable to an object $a \in \mathsf{O} \setminus \mathsf{I}$, (ii) apply a rule to an introduced object a only if no rule is applicable to an introduced object b such that $b \prec_\mathsf{I} a$, (iii) apply $\Rightarrow_\exists$ only if no other rule is applicable, and (iv) apply $\Rightarrow_\exists$ to an introduced object a in Γ only if there is no witness for a. Restrictions (i)–(iii) ensure that whenever $\Rightarrow_\exists$ becomes applicable to an introduced object a in a knowledge base Γ, then for every Γ' with $\Gamma \Rightarrow^*_{\mathcal{TAB}} \Gamma'$ we have $\mathsf{C}(\Gamma, a) = \mathsf{C}(\Gamma', a)$. The strategy guarantees the termination of the tableaux proof system.

Restriction (iv) may be viewed as an instance of the Leibniz principle, identifying two objects which are indistinguishable with respect to their properties. Since we confine ourselves to applications of this principle to introduced objects, it is sufficient to consider properties expressible by concepts. In this case, the principle can be expressed as a set of first-order formulae of the form

$$\forall x, y \colon p_{C_1}(x) \wedge \ldots \wedge p_{C_n}(x) \wedge \\ p_{C_1}(y) \wedge \ldots \wedge p_{C_n}(y) \to x = y,$$

with the antecedents representing all possible truth assignments to concepts and subconcepts occurring in Γ. (That is, each p_{C_i} corresponds to a concept C_i in Γ and for every subconcept C in Γ, either p_C or $p_{\neg C}$ occurs in each formula.) The notion of $\equiv_\Gamma$-equivalence also has a non-monotonic aspect: During a tableaux derivation it can happen that $a \equiv_\Gamma b$ at one state and $a \not\equiv_\Gamma b$ at a later state. But restrictions (i)–(iii) ensure that eventually either $a \equiv_\Gamma b$ or $a \not\equiv_\Gamma b$ holds for all future states in the derivation. Furthermore, it is assumed that for concepts

C not occurring in $\mathsf{C}(\Gamma, a)$ or $\mathsf{C}(\Gamma, b)$ we can assume that neither a nor b are in the semantical interpretation of C.

To account for these aspects and to reduce the computational overhead introduced by these formulae we choose to add a special expansion rule instead.

Blocking: $$\frac{N}{N \cup \{t_a \approx t_b\}}$$

where (i) t_a and t_b are distinct ground, functional terms, and (ii) $\mathsf{P}(N, t_a) = \mathsf{P}(N, t_b)$. ('$\approx$' is the equality symbol.)

This rule is sound. Using the correspondence between the application of one of the propagation rules and particular resolution inference steps, we can restrict ourselves to a corresponding strategy in the resolution proof system. It follows that whenever resolution inference steps corresponding to $\Rightarrow_\exists$ become applicable to a term t_a in the clause set N, then for every clause set N' derivable from N we have $\mathsf{P}(N, t_a) = \mathsf{P}(N', t_a)$.

On the basis of the ordering $\prec_\mathsf{I}$ on introduced objects we will now define a reduction ordering $\succ_{\mathcal{TAB}}$. Suppose a and b are introduced objects and t_a and t_b are the corresponding terms according to the simulation result above. Let $\succ_{\mathcal{TAB}}$ be a reduction ordering with the following properties: (i) if $b \prec_\mathsf{I} a$ then $t_a \succ_{\mathcal{TAB}} t_b$, and (ii) for arbitrary non-equality atoms A, if $t_a \succ_{\mathcal{TAB}} t_b$, then $A[t_a] \succ_{\mathcal{TAB}} A[t_b]$ and $A[t_a] \succ_{\mathcal{TAB}} (t_a \approx t_b)$. It is not difficult to show that such a reduction ordering exists. Note that it is sufficient that only ground expressions are ordered by $\succ_{\mathcal{TAB}}$.

Assume now that by restriction (iv) of strategy (S) the rule $\Rightarrow_\exists$ is not applicable to an introduced object a in Γ, because there is a witness b for a. Then there are terms t_a and t_b such that $\mathsf{P}(N, t_a) = \mathsf{P}(N, t_b)$. In this situation an application of the blocking expansion rule will add an equation $\{t_a \approx t_b\}$ to N. Since $b \prec_\mathsf{I} a$, it follows $t_a \succ_{\mathcal{TAB}} t_b$, and the ground clauses $\{p_C(t_b)\}$ and $\{t_b \approx t_a\}$ are smaller than $\{p_C(t_a)\}$ with respect to $\succ_{\mathcal{TAB}}$. Also, $\{p_C(t_b)\}$ and $\{t_b \approx t_a\}$ logically imply $\{p_C(t_a)\}$. Consequently, the clause $\{p_C(t_a)\}$ is redundant and does not participate in any further inferences. This mimics restriction (iv) of strategy (S). To establish logical implications of this form, the redundancy elimination algorithm will require some form of equality reasoning, for example, superposition. In our special case, all that is required are one-step rewrite transformations.

Theorem 5. *The strategy (S) for tableaux proof systems can be polynomially simulated by blocking and redundancy elimination as outlined above.*

It is now straightforward to show that any inference in our resolution proof system terminates.

Theorem 6. *Let Γ be a knowledge base and let N be the clausal form of $\Xi\overline{\Pi}(\overline{\Gamma})$. Then any derivation from N by (ordered) resolution with selection as determined by $S_{\mathcal{TAB}}$ and blocking following the strategy outlined above terminates.*

Corollary 7. *The resolution proof system and the tableaux proof system have the same time complexity, namely NEXPTIME [Buchheit et al., 1993].*

6 Optimisations

In practice a principal cause for intractability is the presence of a large number of terminological sentences. Every application of the $\Rightarrow_\sqsubseteq$ rule to an object a and terminological sentence $\top \sqsubseteq \neg C \sqcup D$ will be followed by an application of $\Rightarrow_\sqcup$ to $a \in \neg C \sqcup D$. The number of branches in the search space generated in this way is too large to be manageable for implementations relying on chronological backtracking to systematically investigate all the branches.

As indicated by Horrocks and Patel-Schneider [1998] and Hustadt and Schmidt [1998] one possible optimisation is the use of more sophisticated backtracking techniques like backjumping or branch condensing. However, it is even more desirable to avoid unnecessary branching in the first place. A closer look at the intention behind the introduction of $\blacktriangledown$ in the modified translation $\overline{\Pi}$ reveals one possible optimisation in this direction. Suppose the knowledge base contains a terminological sentence of the form $\neg A \sqsubseteq C$. Using the standard embedding Π we obtain a clause $\{p_A(x), p_C(x)\}$ which contains no negative literal we could select. Using $\overline{\Pi}$ we obtain $\{\neg p_\blacktriangledown(x), p_A(x), p_C(x)\}$ which contains a selectable literal. However, whenever for a terminological sentence $C \sqsubseteq D$, the concept $\mathrm{nnf}(\neg C) \sqcup D$ contains a negative occurrence of a primitive concept A, the corresponding clauses under the standard embedding Π will contain a selectable negative literal $\neg p_A(x)$. The transformation Ξ_1 is modified such that these occurrences are preserved. Now the selection function can select an arbitrary negative literal. For example, if we have a terminological sentence of the form $A_1 \sqcap \ldots \sqcap A_n \sqsubseteq C$, the selection function can choose an arbitrary $\neg p_{A_i}(x)$ among the negative literals in $C_1 = \{\neg p_{A_1}(x), \ldots, \neg p_{A_n}(x), p_C(x)\}$. This prevents any inference with C_1 until a unit clause $\{A_i(t_a)\}$ has been derived. Independent of these consideration, this optimisation has been incorporated in the FaCT system [Horrocks, 1997].

From correspondences with propositional dynamic logic it is known that the satisfiability problem for general $\mathcal{ALC}$ knowledge bases is in EXPTIME. The algorithms presented in Sections 2 and 4 require double exponential time in the worst case. Buchheit et al. [1993] note that this can be improved by caching contradictory sets $\mathsf{C}(\Gamma, a)$ of previously investigated branches introduced by applications of the $\Rightarrow_\sqcup$ rule. This has been formalised in [Donini et al., 1996]. Evidently, this form of caching will have the same effects for the resolution procedure described in this paper.

7 Conclusion

The prime motivation for this work has been our interest in possible links between different proof systems for description logics and modal logics. This paper focuses on a particular tableaux proof system for description logics with general inclusion sentences and shows how this system and certain optimisations can be simulated with polynomial overhead in the context of resolution. Our results provide new insight into the relative proof complexity of these systems similar to corresponding results for propositional logic. Although we have considered only the logic $\mathcal{ALC}$, our results may be extended to description logics with role conjunction and role hierarchies. We expect similar results can also be obtained for other forms of tableaux proof systems or sequent calculi. Resolution procedures following tableaux proof strategies have the advantage that proofs may be easily translated back into tableaux or sequent-style proofs of the original source logic. Related work on backward translation is by Caferra and Demri [1993; 1995].

The resolution decision procedure described in this paper offers just one of many possible search strategies. Other resolution strategies utilised in the literature, mentioned in the Introduction, are implemented by ordering strategies which do not rely on blocking or loop-checking techniques. Such techniques are also not needed in the ordered chaining calculus for modal logics with transitive modalities, or $\mathcal{ALC}$ with transitive roles [Ganzinger et al., 1999].

Although experimental results with SPASS using ordered resolution are encouraging [Hustadt and Schmidt, 1997; Hustadt et al., 1998], there are classes of problems on which tableaux proof systems have better performance. The results of this paper now provide a basis for the scientific testing of the comparative performance of the two orthogonal strategies for resolution proof systems, and for establishing guidelines indicating which strategy is most appropriate for particular classes of problems.

References

[Baaz et al., 1994] M. Baaz, C. Fermüller, and A. Leitsch. A non-elementary speed-up in proof length by structural clause form transformation. In Proc. LICS'94, pages 213–219. IEEE Computer Society Press, 1994.

[Bachmair and Ganzinger, 1998] L. Bachmair and H. Ganzinger. Equational reasoning in saturation-based theorem proving. In W. Bibel and P. Schmitt, eds., Automated Deduction: A Basis for Applications, Vol. I, pages 353–397. Kluwer, 1998.

[Buchheit et al., 1993] M. Buchheit, F. M. Donini, and A. Schaerf. Decidable reasoning in terminological knowledge representation systems. J. Aritificial Intelligence Research, 1:109–138, 1993.

[Caferra and Demri, 1993] R. Caferra and S. Demri. Cooperation between direct method and translation method in non classical logics: Some results in propositional S5. In R. Bajcsy, ed., Proc. IJCAI-93, pages 74–79. Morgan Kaufmann, 1993.

[de Nivelle, 1998] H. de Nivelle. A resolution decision procedure for the guarded fragment. In C. Kirchner and H. Kirchner, eds., Proc. CADE-15, volume 1421 of LNAI, pages 191–204. Springer, 1998.

[Demri, 1995] S. Demri. A hierarchy of backward translations: Applications to modal logics. In M. de Glas and Z. Pawlak, eds., Proc. WOCFAI 95, pages 121–132. Angkor, 1995.

[Donini et al., 1996] F. M. Donini, G. De Giacomo, and F. Massacci. EXPTIME tableaux for $\mathcal{ALC}$. In L. Padgham, et al., ed., Proc. DL'96, AAAI Technical Reports Series WS-96-05, pages 107–110, 1996.

[Fermüller et al., 1993] C. Fermüller, A. Leitsch, T. Tammet, and N. Zamov. Resolution Method for the Decicion Problem, volume 679 of LNCS. Springer, 1993.

[Ganzinger et al., 1999] H. Ganzinger, U. Hustadt, C. Meyer, and R. A. Schmidt. A resolution-based decision procedure for extensions of K4. To appear in volume 2 of Advances in Modal Logic. CSLI Publications, 1999.

[Grädel, 1998] E. Grädel. Guarded fragments of first-order logic: A perspective for new description logics? In Proc. DL'98, volume 11 of CEUR Electronic Workshop Proceedings, 1998.

[Horrocks and Patel-Schneider, 1998] I. Horrocks and P. F. Patel-Schneider. Optimising propositional modal satisfiability for description logic subsumption. In Proc. AISC'98, 1998.

[Horrocks, 1997] I. Horrocks. Optimising Tableaux Decision Procedures for Description Logics. PhD thesis, University of Manchester, Manchester, UK, 1997.

[Hustadt and Schmidt, 1997] U. Hustadt and R. A. Schmidt. On evaluating decision procedures for modal logic. In M. E. Pollack, ed., Proc. IJCAI-97, pages 202–207. Morgan Kaufmann, 1997.

[Hustadt and Schmidt, 1998] U. Hustadt and R. A. Schmidt. Simplification and backjumping in modal tableau. In H. de Swart, ed., Proc. TABLEAUX'98, volume 1397 of LNAI, pages 187–201. Springer, 1998.

[Hustadt and Schmidt, 1999] U. Hustadt and R. A. Schmidt. Issues of decidability for description logics in the framework of resolution. To appear in R. Caferra and G. Salzer, eds., Proc. FTP'98, LNAI. Springer, 1999.

[Hustadt et al., 1998] U. Hustadt, R. A. Schmidt, and C. Weidenbach. Optimised functional translation and resolution. In H. de Swart, ed., Proc. TABLEAUX'98, volume 1397 of LNAI, pages 36–37. Springer, 1998.

[Paramasivam and Plaisted, 1998] M. Paramasivam and D. A. Plaisted. Automated deduction techniques for classification in description logic systems. J. Automated Reasoning, 20(3):337–364, 1998.

[Plaisted and Zhu, 1997] D. A. Plaisted and Y. Zhu. The Efficiency of Theorem Proving Strategies. Vieweg, 1997.

[Schmidt, 1999] R. A. Schmidt. Decidability by resolution for propositional modal logics. To appear in J. Automated Reasoning, 1999.

AUTOMATED REASONING

Semantics and Models

Preferential Semantics for Causal Systems

Pavlos Peppas and **Maurice Pagnucco**
Computational Reasoning Group
Department of Computing
Division of ICS
Macquarie University
NSW, 2109, Australia
{pavlos, morri}@ics.mq.edu.au

Mikhail Prokopenko
CSIRO Mathematical and Information Sciences
Locked Bag 17
North Ryde
NSW, 2113, Australia
mikhail.prokopenko@cmis.csiro.au

Norman Y. Foo
Knowledge Systems Group
Department of AI
School of CSE
The University of New South Wales
2052, NSW, Australia
norman@cse.unsw.edu.au

Abhaya Nayak
Computational Reasoning Group
Department of Computing
Division of ICS
Macquarie University
NSW, 2109, Australia
abhaya@ics.mq.edu.au

Abstract

In the present work we examine the causal theory of actions put forward by McCain and Turner [McCain and Turner, 1995] for determining *ramifications*. Our principal aim is to provide a characterisation of this causal theory of actions in terms of a Shoham-like *preferential semantics* [Shoham, 1988]. This would have a twofold advantage: it would place McCain and Turner's theory in perspective, allowing a comparison with other logics of action; and, it would allow us to glean further insights into the nature of causality underlying their work. We begin by showing that our aim is not attainable by a preferential mechanism alone. At this point we do not abandon preferential semantics altogether but augment it in order to arrive at the desired result. We draw the following moral which is at the heart of our paper: *two components — minimal change under a preferential structure and causality — are required to provide a concise solution to the frame and ramification problems.*

1 Introduction

One of the cornerstone developments in the field of reasoning about action (and nonmonotonic reasoning) was Shoham's *preferential semantics* [Shoham, 1988]. While work in this area has since progressed, preferential semantics remain an important and intuitively appealing concept. It furnishes a semantics for a class of nonmonotonic logics. Under this idea an ordering is placed over the class of interpretations. The models corresponding to a particular inference are then identified as the minimal models under this ordering that satisfy the premises. In an intuitive sense, the ordering represents a preference or plausibility ordering over interpretations with only the most preferred (most plausible) being countenanced as serious possibilities. At the heart of this approach lies the *principle of minimal change*: consider only the minimal (i.e., most preferred) models.

In more recent times the notion of causality has attracted much attention [McCain and Turner, 1995; Thielscher, 1997; Sandewall, 1996] in an attempt to provide a concise solution to the *frame problem* (and, more specifically, the *ramification problem*). This is mainly in response to the recognition that traditional *domain constraints* alone are not sufficient for providing compact solutions to these problems.

In this work we focus on a proposal by McCain and Turner [McCain and Turner, 1995] which includes a causal component. McCain and Turner introduce causal laws of the form $\phi \Rightarrow \psi$ where ϕ and ψ are fluent formulae (i.e., they do not contain further instances of $\Rightarrow$ but only classical truth functional connectives). From an intuitive standpoint these formulae can be read as 'ϕ *causes* ψ'. In this way they express 'a relation of determination between states of affairs that make ϕ and ψ true' [McCain and Turner, 1995, p. 1979]. In fact, it is possible to do away with traditional domain constraints altogether in deference to these causal laws [McCain and Turner, 1995, Proposition 3]. An important point to note is that causal laws function as 'uni-directional' implications — the contrapositive ($\neg\psi \Rightarrow \neg\phi$) does not hold in general.

The principal aim of this paper is to determine whether it is possible to supply McCain and Turner's causal theory of actions with a preferential-style semantics. More specifically, the contributions of this paper are as follows. We show that it is not possible to characterise McCain and Turner's causal theory via a traditional preferential semantics applied to interpretations of the original (unaugmented) language. We rectify this, not by abandoning preferential semantics but by augmenting it with a further relational structure. A similar result was sought by Peppas et al. [Peppas *et al.*, 1997] but the counterexample they present assumes a transitive and total ordering where we only assume transitivity, and the semantics they develop only characterises a subset of the possible McCain and Turner causal systems whereas the semantics we present captures all.

In arriving at this result we introduce two state-selection mechanisms: *state elimination systems* and *state transition systems*. State transition systems enhance a preference structure, based on symmetric difference, with a binary relation on states. State elimination systems function as a way of tying together McCain and Turner causal systems and state transition systems. Both state elimination systems and state transition systems give a clearer insight into the nature of causality at play in McCain and Turner's causal theory of actions.

The results contained herein are significant on a number of fronts. They allow us to gain a deeper understanding of the nature of causality underpinning McCain and Turner's framework. They also permit us to place McCain and Turner's causal theory in the context of other nonmonotonic logics whose semantics make use of preferential structures. It has previously been suggested that minimal change and causality are interreducible (for instance [Gustafsson and Doherty, 1996]). However, such works make use of an expanded language. In doing so they move away from the ideal of a *concise* solution to the frame and ramification problems. We, on the contrary, claim that minimal change and causality can coexist in separate roles and, moreover, can complement each other.

This paper is structured as follows. In the next two sections we shall outline some basic terminology and notation followed by a brief overview of McCain and Turner's [McCain and Turner, 1995] causal theory of action. In section 4 we shall show that it is not possible to supply a straightforward preferential semantics to capture McCain and Turner's approach. The solution we suggest here is not to abandon preferential semantics entirely but rather to augment it. In sections 5—7 we investigate the different state selection mechanisms, giving the desired result. We end with a discussion of the significance of these results and our conclusions.

2   Technical Preliminaries

Throughout this paper we shall be working with a fixed finitary propositional language $\mathcal{L}$ whose propositional letters we shall call *fluents*. The set of all fluents is denoted by $\mathcal{F}$. A *literal* is a fluent or the negation of a fluent. A *state* (or *world*) is defined as a maximal consistent set of literals. The set of all literals will be denoted $\mathcal{N}$. The set of all states will be denoted $\mathcal{W}$. By $[\phi]$ we denote all states consistent with the

sentence $\phi \in \mathcal{L}$ (i.e., $[\phi] = \{w \in \mathcal{W} : w \vdash \phi\}$). Occasionally we will refer to $[\phi]$ as the *ϕ-states* (or *ϕ-worlds*).

3   Causal Systems

In this section we briefly review McCain and Turner's [McCain and Turner, 1995] causal theory of actions. In so doing we shall introduce some further notation that will be useful for the remainder of the paper.

As outlined above, McCain and Turner introduce a new connective $\Rightarrow$ to stand for the existence of a causal relationship between sentences ϕ and ψ of the underlying language $\mathcal{L}$. This allows for expressions of the form $\phi \Rightarrow \psi$ (where $\phi, \psi \in \mathcal{L}$)[1] which are termed *causal laws* (or *casual rules*).[2] A set of causal laws $\mathcal{D}$ is referred to as a *causal system*. Given any set of sentences $\Gamma \subseteq \mathcal{L}$ and a causal system $\mathcal{D}$, the (causal) *closure* of Γ in $\mathcal{D}$ is denoted $C_\mathcal{D}(\Gamma)$ and defined to be the smallest superset of Γ closed under classical logical consequence and such that for any $\phi \Rightarrow \psi \in \mathcal{D}$, if $\phi \in C_\mathcal{D}(\Gamma)$, then $\psi \in C_\mathcal{D}(\Gamma)$. We also say that Γ *causally implies* ϕ with respect to $\mathcal{D}$ if and only if $\phi \in C_\mathcal{D}(\Gamma)$ and denote this $\Gamma \vdash_\mathcal{D} \phi$.

Another notion that will be of importance is that of a *legitimate state* with respect to a causal system $\mathcal{D}$. Any state r is legitimate with respect to $\mathcal{D}$ if and only if $r = C_\mathcal{D}(r) \cap \mathcal{N}$. That is, a state is legitimate if and only if it does not contravene any causal laws of $\mathcal{D}$. The set of legitimate states with respect to $\mathcal{D}$ is denoted by $Legit_\mathcal{D}$.

McCain and Turner's aim is to determine the set of possible next (or resultant) states $\text{Res}_\mathcal{D}(E, w)$ given an initial state w and the direct effects (or post-conditions) of an action represented by the sentence E.[3] Formally speaking, we have for any causal system $\mathcal{D}$ a function $\text{Res}_\mathcal{D}$ mapping a legitimate (initial) state w and sentence E (direct effects) to the set of states $\text{Res}_\mathcal{D}(E, w)$ according to the definition [McCain and Turner, 1995]:

$$r \in \text{Res}_\mathcal{D}(E, w) \text{ iff } r = \{\mathtt{f} \in \mathcal{N} : (w \cap r) \cup \{E\} \vdash_\mathcal{D} \mathtt{f}\}$$

We often refer to the elements of $\text{Res}_\mathcal{D}(E, w)$ as *causal fixed-points*. Note that it follows from this definition that if $r \in \text{Res}_\mathcal{D}(E, w)$, then $r \in [E]$ (i.e., r must satisfy the direct effects of the action). Intuitively speaking, the elements of $\text{Res}_\mathcal{D}(E, w)$ are simply those E-states where all changes with respect to w can be justified by the underlying causal system.

We are now in a position to state our aims more clearly. The desire is to mimic McCain and Turner's fixed-point definition using a preference ordering over states and in such a way as not to introduce auxiliary sentences into our language. More specifically, we wish to investigate whether this is at all possible; whether we can provide a preferential-style semantics characterising $\text{Res}_\mathcal{D}(E, w)$ for any legitimate state w and sentence E.

---

[1]Note that nesting of $\Rightarrow$ is not permitted.

[2]For the sake of simplicity we shall assume here that the antecedent of any causal law is consistent.

[3]We shall refer to actions only through their direct effects as they play no direct role in McCain and Turner's framework.

4 Impossibility Results

In this section we clearly specify what we mean by a preferential semantics. We then present an impossibility result showing that a traditional preferential semantics is not capable of characterising McCain and Turner's fixed-point definition.

We are given an initial state $w \in \mathcal{W}$ and a (strict) preference ordering $<_w \subseteq \mathcal{W} \times \mathcal{W}$ on states. The only restriction we place on $<_w$ is that it satisfy transitivity. Adhering to the essence of preferential semantics [Shoham, 1988] we seek to define those states resulting from the occurrence of an action with direct effects E at initial state w as the minimal E-states under $<_w$. The following condition expresses these desiderata:

$$(\text{P}) \quad \text{Res}_\mathcal{D}(E, w) = min([E], <_w)$$

Now, according to McCain and Turner, there is no need to consider illegitimate states as possible resultant states since they contradict the causal laws. Hence, we begin by focusing on a variant of condition (P):

$$(\text{P}') \quad \text{Res}_\mathcal{D}(E, w) = min([E], <_w) \cap Legit_\mathcal{D}$$

We are now in a position to state a fundamental result of this section; that, in general, it is not possible to satisfy the condition (P') (with transitive $<_w$). Note firstly that a *non-trivial language* is one with at least three fluents.

Theorem 4.1 *(First Impossibility Theorem)*
Given a non-trivial language $\mathcal{L}$, there exists a causal system $\mathcal{D}$ and (initial) state $w \in \mathcal{W}$ such that no ordering $<_w$ on states (generated by $\mathcal{L}$) satisfies (P').

Proof: Assume that $\mathcal{L}$ has three propositional letters a, b, c. Let the initial state be $w = \{a, b, c\}$ and define s_1, s_2, s_3 and s_4 to be the following states: $s_1 = \{\neg a, b, c\}$, $s_2 = \{a, \neg b, c\}$, $s_3 = \{\neg a, \neg b, c\}$ and $s_4 = \{\neg a, b, \neg c\}$. Finally let $\mathcal{D}$ be the following causal system: $\mathcal{D} = \{\neg a \wedge c \Rightarrow \neg b, \neg b \wedge c \Rightarrow \neg a, \neg a \wedge b \Rightarrow \neg c\}$.

Consider now the following direct effects (post-conditions) of actions. $\Delta_1 = \neg a \wedge c$, $\Delta_2 = \neg b \wedge c$, $\Delta_3 = (b \leftrightarrow \neg c)$ and $\Delta_4 = (\bigwedge s_1) \vee (\bigwedge s_2) \vee (\bigwedge s_3) \vee (\bigwedge s_4)$. Clearly, states s_1 and s_3 satisfy Δ_1; s_2 and s_3 satisfy Δ_2; s_3 and s_4 satisfy Δ_3; and all four states s_1, s_2, s_3, s_4 satisfy Δ_4.

Suppose a (transitive) ordering on states $<_w$ satisfying condition (P') exists. Now, the following is easily (albeit tediously) verified. $\text{Res}_\mathcal{D}(\Delta_1, w) = \{s_3\}$ from which we conclude $s_1 \not<_w s_3$. $\text{Res}_\mathcal{D}(\Delta_2, w) = \{s_3\}$, therefore $s_2 \not<_w s_3$. $\text{Res}_\mathcal{D}(\Delta_3, w) = \{s_3, \{a, b, \neg c\}\}$, therefore $s_4 \not<_w s_3$. Finally, $\text{Res}_\mathcal{D}(\Delta_4, w) = \{s_4\}$ from which it follows that $(s_1 <_w s_3) \vee (s_2 <_w s_3) \vee (s_4 <_w s_3)$. This leads us to a contradiction. ∎

The following impossibility result now follows quite straightforwardly and is more appropriate for our purposes given that condition (P) is a more faithful rendering of the spirit of preferential semantics than condition (P'). It allows us to conclude that a traditional preferential semantics (captured by condition (P)) cannot, in general, be given to McCain and Turner's causal theory of actions.

Theorem 4.2 *(Second Impossibility Theorem)*
Given a non-trivial language $\mathcal{L}$, there exists a causal system $\mathcal{D}$ and (initial) state $w \in \mathcal{W}$ such that no ordering $<_w$ on states (generated by $\mathcal{L}$) satisfies (P).

We shall not give away preferential semantics entirely however. Our aim now becomes to retain as much of preferential semantics as possible and include a further mechanism to capture the influence of causality. To this end we investigate separate (though related) mechanisms for selecting possible resultant states.

5 State-Selection Mechanisms

Taking a step backwards for a moment, we can simply view McCain and Turner's approach as a *state-selection mechanism*. More specifically, McCain and Turner's causal theory of actions, given some domain knowledge in terms of a causal theory $\mathcal{D}$, specifies a way of selecting a subset $\text{Res}_\mathcal{D}(E, w)$ of $[E]$ given an initial state w and direct effects E. $\text{Res}_\mathcal{D}(E, w)$ returns exactly those states that are possible upon the occurrence of an action with direct effects E at state w.

Viewing this as a *selection function* however, we consider $\text{Res}_\mathcal{D}(E, w)$ to be a function selecting the 'best' states from among $[E]$ (with respect to w). This is the view we shall adopt here in presenting two further state-selection mechanisms: *state elimination systems* and *state transition systems*. State transition systems will provide the augmented preferential semantics we seek in terms of our aims.

This desired result is achieved in two steps. We begin by showing how to intertranslate McCain and Turner causal systems and state elimination systems in a way that preserves the selection process. We then show how to intertranslate state elimination systems and state transition systems (again preserving the selection process). In truth, we could do away with state elimination systems and simply translate directly between causal systems and state transition systems. However, we choose not to do so because it simplifies the proofs and provides further insight into the nature of causality captured by McCain and Turner's approach.

6 Mechanism 1: State Elimination Systems

In this section we describe our first state-selection mechanism: state elimination systems. The underlying idea is to use *state elimination rules* to discard E-states from further consideration for we have noted above that in McCain and Turner's [McCain and Turner, 1995] causal theory $\text{Res}_\mathcal{D}(E, w) \subseteq [E]$. A state rejected or eliminated by a state elimination rule is one which contravenes a causal relationship deemed to hold in the resultant state (in fact, in the causal system as a whole).

Definition 6.1 *(State elimination rule)*
A state elimination rule (or simply, elimination rule) is an expression of the form $\{r_1, r_2, \cdots, r_k, r_{k+1}, \cdots, r_n\} \triangleright \{r_1, r_2, \cdots, r_k\}$ where each r_i is a state.

A state elimination system $\mathcal{S}$ is a set of state elimination rules. An elimination rule functions by rejecting certain states from among those currently considered possible. Suppose that according to an agent's current beliefs it considers the states that are possible to be among $\{r_1, \cdots, r_n\}$. An elimination rule like that in Definition 6.1 allows the agent to reject states $r_{k+1}, \cdots, r_n$.

Let us briefly consider the mechanics of a state elimination system. At any point we are working with the set of states currently being entertained (a subset of $[E]$). We repeatedly apply elimination rules to this set of states to reject the illegitimate ones (those not possible) focusing on the possible resultant states. All elimination rules need to be applied until no further states can be rejected to ensure that all illegitimate states have been purged and only definite possibilities remain. To put it another way, a state elimination system acts as a *filtering* mechanism; illegitimate states are successively filtered out through use of elimination rules.

Definition 6.2 ($\leadsto$ *and* $\stackrel{*}{\leadsto}$)
In a state elimination system S, we shall say that a set of states Q yields a set of states R in one step, denoted by $Q \leadsto R$, iff there exists an elimination rule $X \triangleright Y$ such that $Q \subseteq X$ and $R = Q \cap Y$. We define $\stackrel{*}{\leadsto}$ to be the reflexive transitive closure of $\leadsto$.

After the application of certain elimination rules we find that any further application does not result in the rejection of additional states. At this point we reach a *compact set of states*; a point of equilibrium.

Definition 6.3 *(Compact state)*
A set of states Q is compact (in S) iff for any R such that $Q \stackrel{*}{\leadsto} R$, it follows that $Q = R$. If Q is a singleton and compact, we will call the state in Q compact.

One last notion that we require is that of an *E-predecessor* of a given state; those E-states preceding the given state with respect to an ordering based on symmetric difference. More formally:

Definition 6.4 *(E-predecessor)*
Given any two states w, r and any sentence E, the E-predecessors of r with respect to w is defined to be the set $\langle r, E \rangle_w = \{r' : r' \in [E] \text{ and } Diff(w, r') \subseteq Diff(w, r)\}$ where $Diff(x, y)$ denotes the symmetric difference of states x and y (i.e., $(x \setminus y) \cup (y \setminus x)$) as in the PMA [Winslett, 1988].

It is clear that any $r \in [E]$ is an E-predecessor of itself with respect to w (i.e., $r \in \langle r, E \rangle_w$). The E-predecessors of r with respect to w are just the E-states which agree with w on at least those fluents where w and r agree and possibly others. If one considers a PMA ordering [Winslett, 1988] of states $\leq_w$ (i.e., $r \leq_w s$ iff $Diff(w, r) \subseteq Diff(w, s)$), then the E-predecessors are those E-states at least as close to w as r.

We are now in a position to define a state-selection mechanism based on state elimination systems.

Definition 6.5 ($\text{Next}_S(E, w)$)
With any state elimination system S we associate a result function Next_S (mapping a compact (in S) state w and a sentence E to the set of states $\text{Next}_S(E, w)$) defined as follows: $\text{Next}_S(E, w) = \{r \in [E] : r \text{ is compact (in } S) \text{ and } \langle r, E \rangle_w \stackrel{*}{\leadsto} \{r\} \}$.

In the following section we characterise $\text{Res}_D(E, w)$ in terms of $\text{Next}_S(E, w)$. First, however, let us briefly consider the definition of $\text{Next}_S(E, w)$. According to the definition above, a state r is a possible resultant state if and only if all its E-predecessors (with respect to w) are rejected by

elimination rules in S but r and only r is retained. If r is retained along with some other state, then there is some closer state (one with 'less' change) consistent with the state elimination system S (and, therefore, causal system D) under consideration. Moreover, it means that there is something in the state(s) for which causality cannot account. If r is rejected on the other hand, it must violate a causal relationship. For these reasons we only consider the E-predecessors of r to determine whether it belongs to $\text{Next}_S(E, w)$; we need to determine whether r is illegitimate or whether a 'closer' state satisfies the causal relationships. If either is the case, we can safely reject the state. Otherwise, we can retain the state.

6.1 Causal Systems and State Elimination Systems

We now establish the interrelationship between causal systems and state elimination systems. This will give us a way of moving back and forth between the two systems facilitating the final intertranslation between causal systems and state transition systems. The following definition will prove useful.

Definition 6.6 *(Selection-equivalent)*
A causal system D is selection-equivalent to a state elimination system S iff $\text{Res}_D(E, w) = \text{Next}_S(E, w)$, for every sentence E and state w.

The notion of selection-equivalence will be useful in relating causal systems and state elimination systems. Moreover, it will be useful in relating any two state-selection mechanisms (in an obvious way).

We now turn to the main result of this section. A state elimination system can exactly capture a causal system (and vice versa).

Theorem 6.7 *For every causal system there exists a selection-equivalent state elimination system. Conversely, for every state elimination system there exists a selection-equivalent causal system.*

Proof (Sketch)
($\Rightarrow$) Let D be an arbitrary causal system. For every causal law $\varphi \Rightarrow \psi$ in D, produce the elimination rule $[\varphi] \triangleright [\varphi \wedge \psi]$. Call S the set of elimination rules so produced. It is not difficult to verify that for any legitimate state w and sentence E, $\text{Res}_D(E, w) = \text{Next}_S(E, w)$ (simply notice that for any state r, $[(w \cap r) \cup \{E\}] = \langle r, E \rangle_w$).

($\Leftarrow$) Let S be an arbitrary state elimination system. For every elimination rule $X \triangleright Y$ produce the causal law $\dot{\varphi} \Rightarrow \psi$, where φ, ψ are such that $[\varphi] = X$ and $[\psi] = Y$ (since our language is a finitary propositional one, such φ and ψ always exist). The set of causal laws so produced, call it D, is selection-equivalent to S. ∎

Of particular note in this proof is the relationship between causal laws and elimination rules: $\phi \Rightarrow \psi$ if and only if $[\phi] \triangleright [\phi \wedge \psi]$ (or, equivalently, $[\phi] \triangleright [\phi] \cap [\psi]$).

We can also identify an important class of state elimination systems that will be useful later (in the proof of Theorem 7.3).

Definition 6.8 *(S Unary)*
A state elimination system S is unary iff every elimination rule eliminates precisely one state, i.e. for all $(X \triangleright Y) \in S$, $X \setminus Y$ is a singleton.

The following result reveals an interesting and important aspect of unary state elimination systems.

Theorem 6.9 *Every state elimination system is selection-equivalent to a unary state elimination system.*

7 Mechanism 2: State Transition Systems

In this section we consider our second (and last) state-selection mechanism: state transition systems. Again, we shall obtain a direct characterisation of causal systems (and state elimination systems). In this case we have a preferential mechanism augmented by further structure to achieve the result we desire in this paper.

A state transition system consists of a binary relation on states intended to represent possible transitions between states due to the presence of causality. It is this relation that, together with a preferential ordering based on symmetric difference, will be used to determine possible resultant states.

We begin with some requisite definitions.

Definition 7.1 *A state transition system $\mathcal{M}$ is a binary relation on the set $\mathcal{W}$ of states (i.e., $\mathcal{M} \subseteq \mathcal{W} \times \mathcal{W}$). Whenever $\langle r, r' \rangle \in \mathcal{M}$ we will write $r \rightharpoonup r'$. We shall say that a state r is final (in $\mathcal{M}$) iff for any r' such that $r \rightharpoonup r'$, $r = r'$.*

The binary relation $\mathcal{M}$ can be considered to represent state transitions due to the influence of causality.

We are now in a position to define the mechanism for selecting possible resultant states (or *successor states*) $\mathrm{Succ}_{\mathcal{M}}(E, w)$ for a state transition system $\mathcal{M}$ given initial state w and action with direct effects E.

Definition 7.2 ($\mathrm{Succ}_{\mathcal{M}}(E, w)$)
To any state transition system $\mathcal{M}$ we associate a function $\mathrm{Succ}_{\mathcal{M}}$ (mapping a final (in $\mathcal{M}$) state w and a sentence E to the set of states $\mathrm{Succ}_{\mathcal{M}}(E, w)$) defined as follows: $\mathrm{Succ}_{\mathcal{M}}(E, w) = \{r' \in [E] : r'$ is final (in $\mathcal{M}$) and there is a Hamiltonian path through states in $\langle\!\langle r', E \rangle\!\rangle_w \}$.

A Hamiltonian path is one which traverses every vertex (here states) of a graph [Wilson, 1985]. In this case, the graph's vertices are the E-predecessors of r' and the edges are given by the binary relation $\mathcal{M}$ (i.e., there is an edge between states r' and s iff $\langle r', s \rangle \in \mathcal{M}$). The significance of a Hamiltonian path will be considered further in the next section.

It is important to notice that $\mathrm{Succ}_{\mathcal{M}}(E, w)$ is determined by two components: a preference ordering on states, based on symmetric difference, used to derive the E-predecessors of r' with respect to w (i.e., $\langle\!\langle r', E \rangle\!\rangle_w$) and the binary relation on states $\mathcal{M}$. We maintain that the preference ordering captures the principle of minimal change while the binary relation captures the effect of causality. Notice firstly that a state must be reachable via a Hamiltonian path through all E-predecessors ending in r'. If this is not possible, either a 'closer' E-state is consistent with the causal relationships that hold (absence of Hamiltonian path) or r' violates a causal relationship (path does not end at r'; i.e., r' is not final). Another important point is that, like state elimination systems, we only need consider E-predecessors of r' (with respect to w) to determine whether it is a possible resultant state.

7.1 State Elimination Systems and State Transition Systems

In this section we establish an intertranslation between state elimination systems and state transition systems. We can then use the results of Section 6.1 to establish a correspondence between causal systems and state transition systems. This gives us the result we seek: an augmented preferential semantics for McCain and Turner's causal theory of actions.

Theorem 7.3 *For every state elimination system $\mathcal{S}$ there is a selection-equivalent state transition system $\mathcal{M}$. Conversely, for every state transition system $\mathcal{M}$ there is a selection-equivalent state elimination system $\mathcal{S}$.*

Proof. (Sketch)

($\Rightarrow$) Let $\mathcal{S}$ be a state elimination system. Let $\mathcal{S}'$ be a unary state elimination system that is selection-equivalent to $\mathcal{S}$. From $\mathcal{S}'$ we construct a selection-equivalent state transition system $\mathcal{M}$. First we require some definitions.

Consider an arbitrary set of states Q with cardinality $n + 1$. We shall say that the string of elimination rules $\sigma_1; \sigma_2; \cdots; \sigma_n$ *dissolves* Q iff after applying these rules successively (in the order given), all but one of the states of Q are eliminated and, furthermore, the one remaining state is compact.

Assume that $\sigma_1; \sigma_2; \cdots; \sigma_n$ dissolves Q and for all $1 \leq i \leq n$, let r_i be the state of Q that is eliminated by the rule σ_i; let us also call w the one state of Q that is not eliminated. We shall call the sequence of states $r_1; r_2; \cdots; r_n; w$ a *trace* for Q (in $\mathcal{S}'$).

We now construct from $\mathcal{S}'$ a state transition system $\mathcal{M}$ in the following manner. For any two states r, r', $\langle r, r' \rangle \in \mathcal{M}$ if and only if there is a dissolvable set of states Q containing r and r', such that for some trace of Q in $\mathcal{S}'$, r' appears immediately after r. It can be shown that $\mathcal{M}$ is selection-equivalent to $\mathcal{S}'$.

($\Leftarrow$) Essentially proved by reversing the construction presented above. ∎

The central result of this paper, as expressed by the following corollary, is now obtained by combining theorems 6.7 and 7.3.

Corollary 7.4 *For every causal system $\mathcal{D}$ there exists a selection-equivalent state transition system $\mathcal{M}$. Conversely, for every state transition system $\mathcal{M}$ there exists a selection-equivalent causal system $\mathcal{D}$.*

This result states that it is possible to exactly characterise McCain and Turner's causal theory of actions via a preferential-style semantics (defined in terms of symmetric difference) augmented with a binary relation on states and through the notion of a Hamiltonian path.

8 Discussion

One of the morals that we have attempted to stress in this work is that it is possible to retain preferential semantics and augment it in capturing the causal theory of McCain and Turner. We maintain that the preferential component of state transition systems relates to the principle of minimal change while the binary relation on states relates to the causal system. It is our contention that both of these components — minimal change and causality — are required if one is to supply a *concise* solution to the frame problem; the two can co-exist and, in fact, complement each other.

It has been suggested that other preferential-style approaches to reasoning about action are capable of capturing McCain and Turner's causal theory of actions (for instance, [Gustafsson and Doherty, 1996]); an apparent contradiction of what is suggested by our impossibility theorems in Section 4. However, this and similar approaches are able to do so only by augmenting the original language $\mathcal{L}$ (with, for instance, predicates like *occludes* or so-called frame fluents). At the outset we made clear that we did not wish to adopt this tactic. To do so would be to call into question our adherence to the quest for conciseness in seeking a solution to the frame problem and, more specifically, the ramification problem. Moreover, the ontological status of added predicates is not always clear and places a huge burden on the designer who must determine whether and when to occlude predicates.

The notion of a Hamiltonian path through E-predecessors in a state transition system to determine possible resultant states is an interesting one. Essentially, a Hamiltonian path serves as a contextual mechanism much in the same way that augmenting the underlying language through the addition of extra predicates does. The additional information allows the effects of causality to contribute in certain situations and not in others.

9 Conclusion and Future Work

In this paper we set out to determine whether it is possible to furnish McCain and Turner's [McCain and Turner, 1995] causal theory of actions with a preferential semantics in the spirit of Shoham [Shoham, 1988]. We demonstrated, through use of an impossibility theorem (Theorem 4.2), that this is not possible in general when we do not embellish the original language $\mathcal{L}$ and assume the preferential ordering satisfies transitivity. Choosing not to abandon preferential semantics entirely, we then adopted an abstract view in terms of state-selection mechanisms introducing two such systems: state elimination systems and state transition systems. The latter of these provides the sought after semantics augmenting a preferential structure based on symmetric difference with a binary relation on states and making use of the notion of a Hamiltonian path. The former provides a stepping stone and, of equal importance, gives further insight into the nature of causality at play in McCain and Turner's approach. Significantly, we show that causal systems, state elimination systems and state transition systems, as defined here, are (selection) equivalent. That state transition systems augment a preferential structure with a binary relation on states demonstrates, we claim, that minimal change and causality — the former captured by preferential semantics and the latter by a binary relation — together are essential in furnishing a concise solution to the frame and ramification problems.

Providing McCain and Turner's causal theory of action with an augmented preferential semantics allows comparison with other logics of action and provides an interesting direction for future work. Another avenue for future work would be a contrast of Sandewall's *causal propagation semantics* [Sandewall, 1996] and our state transition systems. This would indirectly link Sandewall's semantics with McCain and Turner's causal theory of actions giving further insight into causal approaches to reasoning about action. It may also be possible to modify the approach here in terms of state transition systems and Hamiltonian paths to capture other causal approaches such as that of Thielscher [Thielscher, 1997]. Note, however, that Thielscher's system does not satisfy the property that the possible resultant states lie among the E-states. This suggests that such a result is not likely to be a straightforward extension of the current work.

Acknowledgements

The authors would like to thank members of the School of Computing Science at Simon Fraser University for their comments on this work.

References

[Gustafsson and Doherty, 1996] Joakim Gustafsson and Patrick Doherty. Embracing occlusion in specifying the indirect effects of actions. In L. Aiello, J. Doyle, and S. Shapiro, editors, *Proceedings of the Fifth International Conference on Knowledge Representation and Reasoning*. Morgan-Kaufmann, 1996.

[McCain and Turner, 1995] Norman McCain and Hudson Turner. A causal theory of ramifications and qualifications. In *Proceedings of the Fourteenth International Joint Conference on Artificial Intelligence*, pages 1978–1984. Montreal, 1995.

[Peppas *et al.*, 1997] Pavlos Peppas, Maurice Pagnucco, Mikhail Prokopenko, and Norman Foo. Preferential semantics for causal fixpoints. In Abdul Sattar, editor, *Proceedings of the Tenth Australian Joint Conference on Artificial Intelligence*, pages 197–206, Perth, Australia, 1997.

[Sandewall, 1996] Erik Sandewall. Assessments of ramification methods that use static domain constraints. In L. Aiello, J. Doyle, and S. Shapiro, editors, *Proceedings of the Fifth International Conference on Knowledge Representation and Reasoning*. Morgan-Kaufmann, 1996.

[Shoham, 1988] Yoav Shoham. *Reasoning About Change*. MIT Press, Cambridge, Massachusetts, 1988.

[Thielscher, 1997] Michael Thielscher. Ramification and causality. *Artificial Intelligence*, 89:317–364, 1997.

[Wilson, 1985] Robin J. Wilson. *Introduction to Graph Theory*. Longman Scientific and Technical, 3rd edition, 1985.

[Winslett, 1988] Marianne Winslett. Reasoning about actions using a possible models approach. In *Proceedings of the Seventh National Artificial Intelligence Conference*, San Mateo, CA., 1988. Morgan Kaufmann Publishers.

Query Evaluation and Progression in $\mathcal{AOL}$ Knowledge Bases

Gerhard Lakemeyer
Department of Computer Science
Aachen University of Technology
D-52056 Aachen
Germany
gerhard@cs.rwth-aachen.de

Hector J. Levesque
Department of Computer Science
University of Toronto
Toronto, Ontario
Canada M5S 3A6
hector@cs.toronto.edu

Abstract

Recently Lakemeyer and Levesque proposed the logic $\mathcal{AOL}$, which amalgamates both the situation calculus and Levesque's logic of only knowing. While very expressive the practical relevance of the formalism is unclear because it heavily relies on second-order logic. In this paper we demonstrate that the picture is not as bleak as it may seem. In particular, we show that for large classes of $\mathcal{AOL}$ knowledge bases and queries, including epistemic ones, query evaluation requires first-order reasoning only. We also provide a simple semantic definition of progressing a knowledge base. For a particular class of knowledge bases, adapted from earlier results by Lin and Reiter, we show that progression is first-order representable and easy to compute.

1 Introduction

A knowledge-based agent in a dynamic environment needs powerful facilities to query its knowledge base. In particular, it does not suffice to only ask what the world is like after any number of actions have occurred. As has been argued both in the case of static knowledge bases [6; 9] and in the context of reasoning about action [15; 17; 4], the query language should be able to explicitly refer to the agent's *knowledge*[1] in order to make distinctions such as knowing that versus knowing who [2] which otherwise cannot be made. This is best illustrated by an example.

Suppose we have a simple, stationary mail sorting robot whose task it is to pick up only the red letters in front of it. Initially the robot has no letters and it is told that there are two letters C and D and that at least one of them is red. (Let us also assume that, unbeknownst to the robot, both letters are red.) Then the robot should be able to answer the following queries:

1. Is there a red letter? Answer: *yes.*

2. Do you *know* which one is red? Answer: *no.*

3. Assume the robot now senses the colour of C.
   Do you now know of a particular letter that it is red?

Answer: *yes.* (Note that even if C were not red, the answer would still be *yes.*)

4. The robot now picks up C.
   Are you holding all the red letters? Answer: *unknown.* (For all the robot knows, D could be red or not.)

5. Are you holding all the known red letters? Answer: *yes.* (C is the only letter known to be red.)

Recently, Lakemeyer and Levesque [4] have proposed the logic $\mathcal{AOL}$, which amalgamates the situation calculus [14] and Levesque's logic of only-knowing [7] and which has the expressiveness to handle queries such as the above. However, $\mathcal{AOL}$ employs heavy second-order machinery to achieve this and it is not clear how to use the logic in practice other than for specification purposes. In this paper we show that the picture is not as bleak as it may seem. In particular, we show that in $\mathcal{AOL}$ the evaluation of queries like those in the example requires first-order reasoning only.

Another important issue is knowledge base progression. In principle, the only information necessary to answer queries after a number of actions have occurred is the initial knowledge base together with the action sequence and the outcome of sensing actions. However, for long sequences of actions this seems hopelessly unrealistic from a computational point of view. It seems much more sensible to update the knowledge base appropriately after each action has occurred. Lin and Reiter [13] studied progression in the context of the situation calculus without sensing and epistemic notions. They show that progression can only be represented using second-order logic in general, but they identify interesting classes of theories where it remains first-order. Here we show how their approach can be applied to the more expressive language of $\mathcal{AOL}$ both at the semantic and the representational level. In particular, we adapt Lin and Reiter's definition of context-free action theories and show that progression remains first-order and efficiently computable in corresponding $\mathcal{AOL}$ knowledge bases.

The rest of the paper is organized as follows. In Section 2, we introduce the logic $\mathcal{AOL}$. In Section 3, we define how to query and progress an agent's knowledge at an abstract level. In Section 4, we consider concrete knowledge bases and discuss the issue of first-order query evaluation and progression there. The paper ends with some concluding remarks.[2]

---

[1] While we freely use the term knowledge, we really mean belief, but the difference is not important for the purposes of this paper.

[2] Some preliminary ideas about first-order query processing in

2 The Logic $\mathcal{AOL}$

Here we only give a brief introduction to the semantics of $\mathcal{AOL}$. The reader is referred to [4] for a more detailed account including a characterization using foundational axioms, which we omit here. (We also assume a basic familiarity with the situation calculus.)

The language of $\mathcal{AOL}$ is a dialect of the second-order predicate calculus with equality and has all the primitives of the situation calculus, and some more. There are three sorts of individuals: ordinary objects, actions, and situations. For each sort there is an infinite supply of variables. The situation variable *now* is reserved for special use. As in the situation calculus, we have the following primitives: the constant S_0 denotes the situation which corresponds to the real world before any actions have taken place; if a is an action and s a situation, then $do(a, s)$ denotes the situation resulting from doing a in s; the special predicate $Poss(a, s)$ has the intended meaning that a is executable in s; fluents like $Red(x, s)$ are relations, which have ordinary objects as arguments plus a situation argument in their final position, and are used to express how the world evolves from situation to situation; there are only finitely many fluents and action function symbols.

We also require two new special predicates, $SF(a, s)$ and $K_0(s)$, normally not present in the situation calculus, which are used to model sensing and knowledge and will be discussed in more detail in Section 2.2.

For simplicity, we also make the following restrictions: there are no constants or functions of the situation sort other than S_0 and do; action functions do not take situations as arguments; there are no function symbols of type object; and all predicates other than those mentioned above are fluents.

The language also includes a set of so-called standard names $\mathcal{N} = \{^\#1, ^\#2, \ldots\}$. The intended use of a standard name is to uniquely identify an object across all possible interpretations, which is useful when dealing with concepts like knowing that versus knowing who. Indeed, the semantics assumes a fixed domain of objects and these are isomorphic with the standard names. (See [6; 9] for more details.)

Atomic formulas are obtained in the usual way from the above primitives and formulas are built using the connectives $\neg$, $\wedge$, and $\forall$. Other connectives like $\supset$ and $\exists$ will be used as abbreviations in the usual way. We will use the following conventions: let $\vec{a} = a_1 \cdot a_2 \cdot \ldots \cdot a_n$ be a sequence of actions and s a situation. Then $do(\vec{a}, s)$ stands for $do(a_n, do(a_{n-1} \ldots, do(a_1, s) \ldots))$. ϵ denotes the empty sequence and we sometimes write $do(\epsilon, s)$ for s. Finally, we use TRUE as an abbreviation for $\forall x.(x = x)$ and FALSE for $\neg$TRUE.

2.1 Semantics

Rather than appealing to the standard semantics of FOL, $\mathcal{AOL}$ comes equipped with a nonstandard semantics derived from possible-world semantics [3], in particular, the semantics of the logic $\mathcal{OL}$ [7], which was developed to specify static

knowledge bases.[3] As in possible-world semantics, the basic semantic building-block is a world. However, unlike the static case, a world in $\mathcal{AOL}$ determines what is true initially and after any number of actions have occurred. A situation is then interpreted simply as a world w indexed by a sequence of actions $\vec{a}$. In particular, every world "starts" with an initial situation where no actions have occurred yet. Besides the *real* world, whose initial situation serves as the denotation of S_0, a model in $\mathcal{AOL}$ also features a set of worlds e. As in modal logics of knowledge like $\mathcal{OL}$, e should be understood as the set of worlds which the agent considers epistemically possible. In Section 2.2, we will see how, using the special predicate K_0, the worlds in e can be accessed and how this gives us a way to define knowledge in dynamic domains.

To simplify the semantics, we assume that besides the standard names for objects there are also standard names for actions. These are terms of the form $A(n_1, \ldots, n_k)$ where A is an action function and each n_i is a standard name of an object. A primitive formula is an atom of the form $F(n_1, \ldots, n_k)$ where each n_i is a standard name, and $F(x_1, \ldots, x_k, s)$ is a relational fluent, or of the form $Poss(A)$ or $SF(A)$, where A is a standard name for an action. The set of all primitive formulas is $\mathcal{P}$.

Let Act^* be the set of all sequences of standard names for actions including the empty sequence ϵ.

Definition 2.1: A *world* w is a function:

$$w : \mathcal{P} \times Act^* \longrightarrow \{0, 1\}$$

Let $\mathcal{W}$ denote the set of all worlds.

Definition 2.2: A *situation* is a pair $(w, \vec{a})$, where $w \in \mathcal{W}$ and $\vec{a} \in Act^*$. An *initial* situation is one where $\vec{a} = \epsilon$.

Definition 2.3: An *action model* M is a pair $\langle e, w \rangle$, where $w \in \mathcal{W}$ and $e \subseteq \mathcal{W}$.

w is taken to specify the actual world, and e specifies the *epistemic state* as those worlds an agent has not yet ruled out as being the actual one. As we will see below, a situation term s will be interpreted semantically as a situation $(w, \vec{a})$, consisting of a world and a sequence of actions that have happened so far. A fluent $p(s)$ will be considered true if $w[p, \vec{a}] = 1$.

A variable map ν is a function that maps object, action, and situation variables into standard names for objects and actions, and into situations, respectively. In addition, ν assigns relations of the appropriate type[4] to relational variables. For a given ν, ν^x_o denotes the variable map which is like ν except that x is mapped into o.

The meaning of terms

We write $|\cdot|_{M,\nu}$ for the denotation of terms with respect to an action model $M = \langle e, w \rangle$ and a variable map ν. Then

$|n|_{M,\nu} = n$, where n is a standard name;

$|A(\vec{t})|_{M,\nu} = A(|\vec{t}|_{M,\nu})$, where $A(\vec{t})$ is an action term;

---

[3]The reader who prefers classical logic is referred to [4], where we provide a second-order axiomatization which is sound and complete with respect to the nonstandard semantics.

[4]Since the type will always be obvious from the context, we leave this information implicit.

$\mathcal{AOL}$ first appeared in [5]. Progression was not handled at all in that paper.

$|S_0|_{M,\nu} = (w, \epsilon)$;

$|do(t_a, t_s)|_{M,\nu} = (w', \vec{a} \cdot a)$, where $|t_s|_{M,\nu} = (w', \vec{a})$, and $|t_a|_{M,\nu} = a$;

$|x|_{M,\nu} = \nu(x)$, where x is any variable, including predicate variables.

Observe that in a model $M = \langle e, w \rangle$, the only way to refer to a situation that does not use the given world w is to use a situation variable.

The meaning of formulas

We write $M, \nu \models \alpha$ to mean formula α comes out true in action model M and variable map ν:

$M, \nu \models F(\vec{t}, t_s)$ iff $w'[F(|\vec{t}|_{M,\nu}), \vec{a}] = 1$, where $F(\vec{t}, t_s)$ is a relational fluent, and $|t_s|_{M,\nu} = (w', \vec{a})$;

$M, \nu \models X(\vec{t})$ iff $|\vec{t}|_{M,\nu} \in \nu(X)$ with X a relational var.;

$M, \nu \models Poss(t_a, t_s)$ iff $w'[Poss(|t_a|_{M,\nu}), \vec{a}] = 1$, where $|t_s|_{M,\nu} = (w', \vec{a})$;

$M, \nu \models SF(t_a, t_s)$ iff $w'[SF(|t_a|_{M,\nu}), \vec{a}] = 1$, where $|t_s|_{M,\nu} = (w', \vec{a})$;

$M, \nu \models K_0(t_s)$ iff $|t_s|_{M,\nu} = (w', \epsilon)$ and $w' \in e$;

$M, \nu \models t_1 = t_2$ iff $|t_1|_{M,\nu} = |t_2|_{M,\nu}$;

$M, \nu \models \neg \alpha$ iff $M, \nu \not\models \alpha$;

$M, \nu \models \alpha \wedge \beta$ iff $M, \nu \models \alpha$ and $M, \nu \models \beta$;

$M, \nu \models \forall x. \alpha$ iff $M, \nu_o^x \models \alpha$ for all o of the appropriate sort (object, action, situation, relation).

If α does not mention K_0, that is, the truth of α does not depend on e, we also write $w, \nu \models \alpha$ instead of $M, \nu \models \alpha$. Similarly, if α does not mention S_0 and, hence, does not depend on the real world, we write $e, \nu \models \alpha$. If α mentions neither S_0 nor K_0, we simply write $\nu \models \alpha$. Also, if α is a sentence, we omit the variable map and write, for example, $M \models \alpha$.

Finally, a formula α is valid in $\mathcal{AOL}$ if for all action models $M = \langle e, w \rangle$ and variable maps ν, $M, \nu \models \alpha$.

2.2 Knowledge and Action

To determine what is known initially (that is, in situation S_0), we only need to consider K_0. More precisely, a sentence is known initially just in case it holds in all situations s for which $K_0(s)$ holds. To find out what holds in successor situations, we use the predicates SF and $Poss$. First note that the logic itself imposes no constraints on either SF or $Poss$; it is up to the user in an application to write appropriate axioms. For $Poss$, these are the precondition axioms, which specify necessary and sufficient conditions under which an action is executable. So we might have, for example,

$$Poss(\mathsf{pickup}(x), s) \equiv Letter(x, s)$$

as a way of saying that the robot is able to pick up only letters. For SF, the user must write *sensed fluent axioms*, one for each action type, as discussed in [8]. The idea is that $SF(A, s)$ gives the condition sensed by action A in situation s. So we might have, for example,

$$SF(\mathsf{senseRed}(x), s) \equiv Red(x, s)$$

as a way of saying that the senseRed action in situation s tells the robot whether or not x is red. In case the action A has no sensing component (as in simple physical actions, like dropping an object), we require as a convention that the axiom states that $SF(A, s)$ is identically TRUE. Actions without a sensing component are referred to as *ordinary* actions.

With these terms, we can now define $K(s', s)$ as an abbreviation for a formula that characterizes when a situation s' is accessible from an arbitrary situation s:[5]

$$K(s', s) \doteq \forall R[\ldots \supset R(s', s)]$$

where the ellipsis stands for the conjunction of

$$\forall s_1, s_2. \, Init(s_1) \wedge Init(s_2) \wedge K_0(s_2) \supset R(s_2, s_1)$$
$$\forall a, s_1, s_2. \, R(s_2, s_1) \wedge (SF(a, s_2) \equiv SF(a, s_1)) \wedge$$
$$(Poss(a, s_2) \equiv Poss(a, s_1)) \supset$$
$$R(do(a, s_2), do(a, s_1)).$$

Here $Init(s)$ stands for $\neg \exists a, s'. s = do(a, s')$.

If s is an initial situation, then the situations which are K-related to s are precisely those initial situations s' for which $K_0(s')$ holds. The general picture, after some actions have occurred, is best reflected by the following theorem, which shows that our definition yields the successor state axiom for a predicate K proposed in [17] as a solution to the frame problem for knowledge.[6]

Theorem 2.4: *[4]. The following sentence is valid:*
$$\forall a, s, s'. \, Poss(a, s) \supset K(s', do(a, s)) \equiv$$
$$\exists s''. \, s' = do(a, s'') \wedge K(s'', s) \wedge Poss(a, s'')$$
$$\wedge \, [SF(a, s) \equiv SF(a, s'')].$$

In other words, s' is K-related to $do(a, s)$ just in case there is some other s'' which is K-related to s and from which s' can be reached by doing a. Furthermore s and s'' must agree on the values of SF and $Poss$ for action a.

Given K, knowledge can then be defined in a way similar to possible-world semantics [3; 1; 15] as truth in all accessible situations. Knowing is then denoted using the following macro, where α may contain the special situation variable *now*. Let α_s^{now} refer to α with all occurrences of *now* replaced by s. Then

$$\mathsf{Knows}(\alpha, \mathsf{s}) \doteq \forall \mathsf{s}' K(\mathsf{s}', \mathsf{s}) \supset \alpha_{\mathsf{s}'}^{now}$$

where s' is a new variable occurring nowhere else in α.

Note that α itself may contain Knows with the understanding that macro expansion works from the innermost occurrence of Knows to the outside. For example, $\mathsf{Knows}(\neg\mathsf{Knows}(Red(\mathrm{x}, now), now), \mathsf{S_0})$ stands for

$$\forall s K(s, S_0) \supset (\neg \forall s' K(s', s) \supset Red(x, s'))$$

and should be read as "the agent knows in S_0 that it does not know that x is red."

---

[5] We could have defined K as a predicate in the language as is usually done, but we have chosen not to in order to keep the formal apparatus as small as possible.

[6] Here we follow the notation from [8].

3 Queries and Progression

In this section, we will consider two related ways of answering queries in $\mathcal{AOL}$. For our purposes, a query is any formula with a single free situation variable, *now*. An example is $\exists x Red(x, now) \land \neg \text{Knows}(Red(x, now), now)$, which asks whether it is *now* the case that there is a red object which is not known yet. The *now* in this query is intended to refer to a particular situation, either an initial situation or one that is the result of a sequence of actions. With this view, it is not possible to answer queries wrt an action model $M = \langle e, w \rangle$ alone, since we also need to specify what sequence of actions to use.

In our first specification of query answering, we are given an initial M, and a sequence of actions $\vec{a}$, and we answer according to what would be known in the situation resulting from doing $\vec{a}$. In other words, we answer a query α with *yes* if according to M, α is known in $do(\vec{a}, S_0)$:

$$\text{ASK}_0[\alpha, M, \vec{a}] = \begin{cases} yes \text{ if } M \models \text{Knows}(\alpha, do(\vec{a}, S_0)) \\ no \text{ if } M \models \text{Knows}(\neg\alpha, do(\vec{a}, S_0)) \\ unknown \text{ otherwise.} \end{cases}$$

Note the difference between $\text{Knows}(\alpha[now], do(\vec{a}, S_0))$ as above, and $\text{Knows}(\alpha[do(\vec{a}, now)], S_0)$. In the former, we are asking if α would be known after doing $\vec{a}$; in the latter, we are asking if it is known initially that α would be true after doing $\vec{a}$. It is not hard to show that the former is implied by the latter, but not vice-versa.

While this is a simple form of query answering, note that it needs to use the world w in M to decide what is known. If $\vec{a}$ consists of a single sensing action like $\text{senseRed}(C)$, then after doing the sensing, the agent should know whether C is red or not. But which one is known is determined by w, which specifies (via SF) how sensing will turn out.

There is, however, a different view where we only need the epistemic state e to answer a query. The idea is that while an agent performs her actions, her epistemic state gets updated to reflect the changes caused by those actions. In particular, a sensing action leads to the removal of worlds which contradict the sensed value. We can define $\text{SUCC}[e, w, \vec{a}]$ to be the epistemic state that results from executing $\vec{a}$ starting with initial state e with sensing as specified by w, by the following:

1. $\text{SUCC}[e, w, \epsilon] = e$.
2. If $\text{SUCC}[e, w, \vec{a}] = e'$, then $\text{SUCC}[e, w, \vec{a} \cdot A] = \{w' \mid w' \in e' \text{ and}$
$\nu^s_{(w,\vec{a})}{}^{s'}_{(w',\vec{a})} \models [SF(A, s) \equiv SF(A, s')] \land$
$[Poss(A, s) \equiv Poss(A, s')]\}$

Now given an e that is equal to $\text{SUCC}[e_0, w_0, \vec{a}]$, we can define a new query operation for any query α which does not mention S_0:

$$\text{ASK}[\alpha, e, \vec{a}] = \begin{cases} yes \text{ if for all } w \in e, \ e, \nu^{now}_{(w,\vec{a})} \models \alpha. \\ no \text{ if for all } w \in e, \ e, \nu^{now}_{(w,\vec{a})} \models \neg\alpha. \\ unknown \text{ otherwise.} \end{cases}$$

Restricting ourselves to queries that do not mention S_0 is necessary since ASK does not carry with it the real world, which is needed as the denotation of S_0. In fact, mentioning S_0 within a query does not make much sense in the first place.

Consider, for example, $\alpha = P(S_0)$. Asking whether α is true is completely independent of any epistemic state e and depends only on the initial state of the real world.

In order to compare our two notions of ASK, it is necessary to restrict the class of queries even further. In fact, we restrict ourselves to queries whose only situation term is *now*. In particular, this has the effect that we cannot ask about other past or future situations.

Definition 3.1: The interaction language $\mathcal{IL}$.
Atomic formulas whose only situation term is *now* are $\mathcal{IL}$-formulas. If α and β are $\mathcal{IL}$-formulas, then $\neg\alpha$, $\alpha \land \beta$, $\forall x \alpha$, where x is an object variable, and $\text{Knows}(\alpha, now)$ are $\mathcal{IL}$-formulas. Nothing else is an $\mathcal{IL}$-formula. From now on, unless stated otherwise, a *query* is an $\mathcal{IL}$-formula where *now* is the only free variable.

An example query in $\mathcal{IL}$ is

$$\exists x Red(x, now) \land \neg \text{Knows}(Red(x, now), now).$$

The formula

$$\exists x Red(x, now) \land$$
$$\neg \text{Knows}(Red(x, now), do(\text{senseRed}, now)),$$

on the other hand, is not in $\mathcal{IL}$.

The formulas of $\mathcal{IL}$ are interpreted by first converting them into $\mathcal{AOL}$-formulas using the definition of Knows introduced in the previous section.

We then have the following relationship between ASK_0 and ASK:

Theorem 3.2: *For any* $\alpha \in \mathcal{IL}$, e, w *and* $\vec{a}$,

$$\text{ASK}_0[\alpha, \langle e, w \rangle, \vec{a}] = \text{ASK}[\alpha, \text{SUCC}[e, w, \vec{a}], \vec{a}].$$

The theorem can be strengthened considerably as it holds for many queries outside of $\mathcal{IL}$ as well. In a nutshell, the only restriction needed is that a query does not refer to what is known *before* the actions $\vec{a}$ have occurred. Roughly, this is because $\text{SUCC}[e, w, \vec{a}]$ knows more about the past than e because it has fewer worlds than e. However, the formulation of a broader class of queries for which the theorem holds turns out to be somewhat awkward. $\mathcal{IL}$, on the other hand, is simple and intuitive. Moreover, it is $\mathcal{IL}$ for which we develop a first-order query evaluation method in Section 4.2.

3.1 Progression

For ASK to make sense, we needed to assume that e reflected the epistemic changes that occurred during the execution of $\vec{a}$, as reflected in SUCC. In a different context, Lin and Reiter (LR) [13] have called the process of updating a knowledge base of an acting agent *progression* and they studied it in detail in the framework of the standard situation calculus.

One major difference between progression and the SUCC operation above is that in the former we attempt to forget the history of actions, and treat the resulting knowledge base as if it were an initial one.[7] Indeed, for many applications, it is sufficient to maintain information about a single "current" situation. Our definition of progression below adapts the ideas of LR to the more expressive language of $\mathcal{AOL}$. In fact, our

---

[7] See [12] for a formalization of forgetting.

formulation is somewhat simpler, which is possible because the semantics assumes a fixed set of worlds. It is also more general because LR do not deal with sensing.

We can define a progression operator $\text{PROG}[e, w, \vec{a}]$ analogous to SUCC that produces a new epistemic state, but which loses information about the past. Given worlds w and w', we say that w' *agrees with* w *after* $\vec{a}$ if for all $\vec{c}$ and p, $w'[p, \vec{a} \cdot \vec{c}] = w[p, \vec{a} \cdot \vec{c}]$. Note that w and w' may differ arbitrarily in all situations before the last action of $\vec{a}$ has been performed. Then we define PROG by the following:

1. $\text{PROG}[e, w, \epsilon] = e$.
2. If $\text{PROG}[e, w, \vec{a}] = e'$, then $\text{PROG}[e, w, \vec{a} \cdot A] = \{w'' \mid \exists w' \in e', w' \text{ agrees with } w'' \text{ after } \vec{a} \cdot A \text{ and }$
$$\nu^s_{(w,\vec{a})} {}^{s'}_{(w',\vec{a})} \models [SF(A, s) \equiv SF(A, s')] \land$$
$$[Poss(A, s) \equiv Poss(A, s')]\}$$

When $e = \text{PROG}[e_0, w_0, \vec{a}]$, we say that e is a *progression* at $\vec{a}$ wrt $\langle e_0, w_0 \rangle$.

The following theorem states that progression is faithful in that it agrees with the original epistemic state for queries in $\mathcal{IL}$ about what is true after a sequence of actions has occurred.

Theorem 3.3: *Let $M = \langle e, w \rangle$ and $M_{\vec{a}} = \langle e_{\vec{a}}, w \rangle$, where $e_{\vec{a}}$ is a progression at $\vec{a}$ wrt M. Then for all queries $\alpha \in \mathcal{IL}$,*

1. $\text{ASK}_0[\alpha, M, \vec{a} \cdot \vec{c}] = \text{ASK}_0[\alpha, M_{\vec{a}}, \vec{a} \cdot \vec{c}]$.
2. $\text{ASK}_0[\alpha, M, \vec{a}] = \text{ASK}[\alpha, e_{\vec{a}}, \vec{a}]$.

Note that in the case of the empty sequence of actions, $\text{ASK}_0[\alpha, M, \epsilon] = \text{ASK}[\alpha, e, \epsilon]$ follows immediately.

4 $\mathcal{AOL}$ Knowledge Bases

So far, we have only talked about the agent's knowledge in the abstract, namely as a set of worlds, which include all possible ways they could evolve in the future. Let us now turn to representing the agent's knowledge symbolically and see how this connects with the semantic view taken so far.

In the situation calculus an application domain is typically characterized by the following types of axioms: action precondition axioms, successor state axioms, and axioms describing the current (often initial) situation. Successor state axioms were proposed by Reiter as a solution to the frame problem [16]. When there are sensing actions, there is also a fourth type called *sensed fluent axioms* specifying what the outcome of sensing is.

$\mathcal{AOL}$-knowledge bases, as we envisage them, consist of formulas of these types and they have a special syntactic form. We call a formula *objective* if it does not mention the predicate K_0.

A formula ϕ is called *simple* in t_s if ϕ is first-order and objective, t_s is the only situation argument occurring in any of the predicates, and any variable in t_s occurs only free in α. ($\exists x.Red(x, do(A, s))$ is simple in $do(A, s)$, whereas $\exists s, x.Red(x, do(A, s))$ is not.)

In the following, let A be an action and F a fluent. Let $\phi(\vec{u})$ denote a formula whose free variables are among the variables in $\vec{u}$.

Let $s \preceq s'$ denote that situation s' is a successor of s, which is defined as:

$$s \preceq s' \doteq \forall R[\ldots \supset R(s, s')]$$

with the ellipsis standing for the conjunction of

$\forall s_1.\ R(s_1, s_1)$
$\forall a, s_1.\ R(s_1, do(a, s_1))$
$\forall s_1, s_2, s_3.\ R(s_1, s_2) \land R(s_2, s_3) \supset R(s_1, s_3)$

Action Precondition Axioms:
$\forall s \forall \vec{x}. now \preceq s \supset [Poss(A(\vec{x}), s) \equiv \phi(\vec{x}, s)]$,[8]
where $\phi(\vec{x}, s)$ is simple in s.

Sensed Fluent Axioms:
$\forall s \forall \vec{x}. now \preceq s \supset [SF(A(\vec{x}), s) \equiv \phi(\vec{x}, s)]$
where $\phi(\vec{x}, s)$ is simple in s.

Successor State Axioms:
$\forall s \forall a \forall \vec{x}. now \preceq s \supset [Poss(a, s) \supset [F(\vec{x}, do(a, s)) \equiv \phi(\vec{x}, a, s)]]$, where $\phi(\vec{x}, a, s)$ is simple in s.

Current State Axioms:
ϕ, where ϕ is simple in $do(\vec{a}, now)$.

A knowledge base (at $\vec{a}$) is then a collection of formulas

$$\text{KB} = \text{KB}_{cur} \cup \text{KB}_{Poss} \cup \text{KB}_{SF} \cup \text{KB}_{ss},$$

where KB_{Poss}, KB_{SF}, and KB_{ss} contain the action preconditions, sensed fluent axioms, and successor state axioms, respectively, and KB_{cur} is the set of current state axioms for a fixed $\vec{a}$. A knowledge base at ϵ is called an *initial knowledge base*.

We define the epistemic state corresponding to a KB as the set of all worlds satisfying the formulas in KB, where *now* is interpreted by initial situations. Formally,

$$\Re[\![\text{KB}]\!] = \{w \mid w, \nu^{now}_{(w, \epsilon)} \models \text{KB}\}.$$

Defining the epistemic state this way reflects the intuition that the KB is *all* the agent knows, hence she cannot rule out any world compatible with the sentences in KB. (See [4] for how to formalize "all I know" in $\mathcal{AOL}$.)

4.1 An Example KB

Here we consider the mail-sorting robot example in more detail. There are letters of different colours laid out in front of the robot and its task is to pick up only the red letters. To keep matters simple, there are only two actions, pickup(x), which is possible if x is a letter, and senseRed(x), which tells the robot whether the sensed object is red and which is always possible. There are three fluents, *Letter*, *Red*, and *HoldRLs*. *Letter* and *Red* never change and *HoldRLs*(x, s) is true if the robot is holding the red letter x in situation s.

We can formalize this by defining appropriate precondition axioms, sensed fluent axioms and successor state axioms, all parameterized by *now*.

Let *ALL*(*now*) stand for the set of these formulas:

---

[8]In the situation calculus without epistemic concepts, s ranges over all situations, namely those reachable from S_0. Here we need to relativize quantification wrt *now* because there are initial situations other than S_0.

$$\forall s, x. now \preceq s \supset Poss(\mathsf{pickup}(x), s) \equiv Letter(x, s)$$
$$\forall s, x. now \preceq s \supset Poss(\mathsf{senseRed}(x), s) \equiv \mathsf{TRUE}$$
$$\forall s, x. now \preceq s \supset SF(\mathsf{pickup}(x), s) \equiv \mathsf{TRUE}$$
$$\forall s, x. now \preceq s \supset SF(\mathsf{senseRed}(x), s) \equiv Red(x, s)$$
$$\forall s, a, x. now \preceq s \supset Letter(x, do(a, s)) \equiv Letter(x, s)$$
$$\forall s, a, x. now \preceq s \supset Red(x, do(a, s)) \equiv Red(x, s)$$
$$\forall s, a, x. now \preceq s \supset HoldRLs(x, do(a, s)) \equiv$$
$$[(a = \mathsf{pickup}(x) \wedge Red(x, s)) \vee HoldRLs(x, s)]$$

Initially, the robot knows that there are at least two letters C and D and that one of them is red. Hence let

$$\mathrm{KB}_{cur} = \left\{ \begin{array}{l} Letter(C, now), Letter(D, now), \\ (Red(C, now) \vee Red(D, now)), \\ \forall x. \neg HoldRLs(x, now). \end{array} \right\}$$

Let $\mathrm{KB} = ALL(now) \cup \mathrm{KB}_{cur}$.

Let the real world w be any world such that $w \models ALL(now)^{now}_{S_0} \wedge Letter(C, S_0) \wedge Red(C, S_0) \wedge Letter(D, S_0) \wedge Red(D, S_0)$, that is, the actions indeed behave as the robot expects them to and there are at least two red letters C and D. Finally, let $M = \langle \Re[\mathrm{KB}], w \rangle$ be our action model.

4.2 First-Order Query Evaluation

By lifting results from Levesque [6; 9], we show that answering epistemic queries for KB's like the above requires only first-order reasoning.

For any formula α simple in $do(\vec{a}, now)$ let $\alpha\!\downarrow$ be α with all occurrences of $do(\vec{a}, now)$ removed. For example, $Red(C, now)\!\downarrow = Red(C)$. Let S_U denote the set of sentences expressing the unique names assumption for standard names and actions, and let $\models_{\mathrm{FOL}}$ denote classical first-order logical implication.

The following definition of $\mathrm{RES}[\phi, \mathrm{KB}]$ shows how to compute in FOL the known instances of ϕ and representing it as a first-order equality expression.

Definition 4.1: Let $\mathrm{KB} = \mathrm{KB}_{cur} \cup \mathrm{KB}_{Poss} \cup \mathrm{KB}_{SF} \cup \mathrm{KB}_{ss}$ and ϕ an objective query and let $n_1, \ldots, n_k$ be all the standard names occurring in KB and ϕ and let n' be a name not occurring in KB or ϕ. Then $\mathrm{RES}[\phi, \mathrm{KB}]$ is defined as:

1. If $\phi\!\downarrow$ has no free variables, then $\mathrm{RES}[\phi, \mathrm{KB}]$ is
   TRUE, if $\mathrm{KB}_{cur}\!\downarrow \cup S_\mathrm{U} \models_{\mathrm{FOL}} \phi\!\downarrow$, and
   FALSE, otherwise.

2. If x is a free variable in $\phi\!\downarrow$, then $\mathrm{RES}[\phi, \mathrm{KB}]$ is
   $((x = n_1) \wedge \mathrm{RES}[\phi^x_{n_1}, \mathrm{KB}]) \vee \ldots$
   $((x = n_k) \wedge \mathrm{RES}[\phi^x_{n_k}, \mathrm{KB}]) \vee$
   $((x \neq n_1) \wedge \ldots \wedge (x \neq n_k) \wedge \mathrm{RES}[\phi_{n'}, \mathrm{KB}]^{n'}_x).$

If we consider our example KB, then $\mathrm{RES}[Letter(x, now)]$ reduces (after simplification) to $(x = C) \vee (x = D)$ whereas $\mathrm{RES}[Red(x, now)]$ reduces to FALSE because there are no known red things. The next definition applies RES to all occurrences of Knows within a query using a recursive descent denoted by $\| \cdot \|_{\mathrm{KB}}$. The idea is that any occurrence of $\mathrm{Knows}(\alpha, now)$ in a query is replaced by an equality expression describing the known instances of α.

Definition 4.2:
Given a KB as defined above and an arbitrary query α, $\|\alpha\|_{\mathrm{KB}}$ is the objective formula simple in *now* defined by

$\|\alpha\|_{\mathrm{KB}} = \alpha$, when α is objective;
$\|\neg\alpha\|_{\mathrm{KB}} = \neg\|\alpha\|_{\mathrm{KB}}$;
$\|(\alpha \wedge \beta)\|_{\mathrm{KB}} = (\|\alpha\|_{\mathrm{KB}} \wedge \|\beta\|_{\mathrm{KB}})$;
$\|\forall x \alpha\|_{\mathrm{KB}} = \forall x \|\alpha\|_{\mathrm{KB}}$;
$\|\mathrm{Knows}(\alpha, now)\|_{\mathrm{KB}} = \mathrm{RES}[\|\alpha\|_{\mathrm{KB}}, \mathrm{KB}]$.

Theorem 4.3: *Let* KB *be a knowledge base at* $\vec{a}$ *with current state axioms* KB_{cur}. *Then* $\mathrm{ASK}[\alpha, \Re[\mathrm{KB}], \vec{a}] = yes$ *iff*

$$\mathrm{KB}_{cur}\!\downarrow \cup S_\mathrm{U} \models_{\mathrm{FOL}} \|\alpha\|_{\mathrm{KB}}\!\downarrow .$$

In essence, the theorem says that answering an epistemic query can be achieved by computing a finite number of first-order implications. Restricting ourselves to queries in $\mathcal{IL}$ is essential in this case.

To illustrate what this theorem says consider the example KB and the query $\alpha = \exists x Red(x, now) \wedge \neg\mathrm{Knows}(Red(\mathrm{x}, now))$. Then $\mathrm{ASK}[\alpha, \Re[\mathrm{KB}], now] = yes$ because of the following: $\mathrm{RES}[Red(x, now), \mathrm{KB}]$ simplifies to FALSE because there are no known instances of red objects. Hence $\|\alpha\|_{\mathrm{KB}}\!\downarrow$ is equivalent to $\exists x Red(x) \wedge \neg\mathsf{FALSE}$ and, furthermore, $\mathrm{KB}_{cur}\!\downarrow \cup S_\mathrm{U} \models_{\mathrm{FOL}} \exists x Red(x)$.

Being able to reduce query evaluation in $\mathcal{AOL}$ to first-order reasoning under certain restrictions is somewhat analogous to a result by Lin and Reiter [13] for the standard (non-epistemic) situation calculus. They show that, even though their foundational axioms for the situation calculus include a second-order axiom to characterize the set of all situations, this axiom is not needed when doing temporal projection, that is, when inferring whether a formula ϕ simple in $do(\vec{a}, S_0)$ follows from the domain theory together with the foundational axioms. There are also other examples such as [11] which show that theories which are inherently second-order nevertheless have interesting special cases where first-order reasoning alone suffices.

4.3 Context-Free Knowledge Bases

Lin and Reiter showed that in their framework, progression is not always first-order definable. We conjecture that the same is true in $\mathcal{AOL}$, but just as in LR's case there are interesting classes of knowledge bases which are not only first-order representable but where progression is also easily computable. LR discuss in particular the classes they call *relatively-complete* and *context-free* action theories. Here we adapt and extend context-free action theories for $\mathcal{AOL}$ and obtain very similar results. (The same is true for relatively complete theories, but we omit them for space reasons.)

A fluent F is called *situation independent* if its successor state axiom has the form $\forall s \forall a \forall \vec{x}. now \preceq s \supset [Poss(a, s) \supset [F(\vec{x}, do(a, s)) \equiv F(\vec{x}, s)]]$, that is, F never changes. Otherwise F is called situation dependent. A formula is called situation independent if it contains only situation independent fluents.

Definition 4.4: [Lin and Reiter] A KB is *context-free* if

- KB_{ss} consists of successor state axioms of the form $\forall s \forall a \forall \vec{x}. now \preceq s \supset [Poss(a, s) \supset [F(\vec{x}, do(a, s)) \equiv \gamma_F^+(\vec{x}, a, s) \vee (F(\vec{x}, s) \wedge \neg\gamma_F^-(\vec{x}, a, s))]]$, where $\gamma_F^+(\vec{x}, a, s)$ and $\gamma_F^-(\vec{x}, a, s)$ are situation independent.[9]

---

[9]The idea is that γ_F^+ describes the conditions which cause F to be true and γ_F^- those which cause it to be false.

- KB_{cur} consists of situation independent formulas and formulas of the form $\forall \vec{x}.\psi \; \supset \; F(\vec{x}, do(\vec{a}, now))$ or $\forall \vec{x}.\psi \supset \neg F(\vec{x}, do(\vec{a}, now))$, where ψ is a situation independent formula with free variables in $\vec{x}$ and now.

- For every action precondition axiom
$\forall s \forall \vec{x}.now \preceq s \supset [Poss(A(\vec{x}), s) \equiv \phi(\vec{x}, s)]$,
$\phi(\vec{x}, s)$ is situation independent.

- For every sensed fluent axiom
$\forall s \forall \vec{x}.now \preceq s \supset [SF(A(\vec{x}), s) \equiv \psi(\vec{x}, s)]$,
$\psi(\vec{x}, s)$ is situation independent.

The conditions on the sensed fluent and action precondition axioms are missing in LR's definition because they do not deal with sensing and they do not consider the case where an agent successfully performs an action even though she does not know that it is possible. In a sense, finding out that an action is possible by doing it can be thought of as a special form of sensing. Note also that SF and $Poss$ are treated completely symmetricly in our semantic definition of progression.

Definition 4.5: Let $\mathrm{KB} = \mathrm{KB}_{cur} \cup \mathrm{KB}_{Poss} \cup \mathrm{KB}_{SF} \cup \mathrm{KB}_{ss}$ be a context-free knowledge base at $\vec{a}$, w_0 a world, $A = Act(\vec{n})$ an action, and let $s_1 = do(\vec{a}, now)$ and $s_2 = do(\vec{a} \cdot A, now)$. Let the action precondition and sensed fluent axioms for A be

$\quad \forall s \forall \vec{x}.now \preceq s \supset [Poss(Act(\vec{x}), s) \equiv \phi_A(\vec{x}, s)]$ and
$\quad \forall s \forall \vec{x}.now \preceq s \supset [SF(Act(\vec{x}), s) \equiv \psi_A(\vec{x}, s)]$.

Then let $\mathrm{KB}^A = \mathrm{KB}^A_{cur} \cup \mathrm{KB}_{Poss} \cup \mathrm{KB}_{SF} \cup \mathrm{KB}_{ss}$, where KB^A_{cur} is constructed as follows:

1. Let A be a sensing action. Then:
   - If $\phi \in \mathrm{KB}_{cur}$ then $\phi^{s_1}_{s_2} \in \mathrm{KB}^A_{cur}$;
   - if $w_0 \models Poss(A, do(\vec{a}, S_0))$ then $\phi_A(\vec{n}, s_2) \in \mathrm{KB}^A_{cur}$ else $\neg \phi_A(\vec{n}, s_2) \in \mathrm{KB}^A_{cur}$;
   - if $w_0 \models SF(A, do(\vec{a}, S_0))$ then $\psi_A(\vec{n}, s_2) \in \mathrm{KB}^A_{cur}$ else $\neg \psi_A(\vec{n}, s_2) \in \mathrm{KB}^A_{cur}$.

2. Let A be an ordinary action. Then:
   - If $\phi \in \mathrm{KB}_{cur}$ is sit. independent, then $\phi^{s_1}_{s_2} \in \mathrm{KB}^A_{cur}$;
   - for any situation dependent fluent F add to KB^A_{cur}
     $\forall \vec{x}.\gamma^+_F(\vec{x}, A, s_2) \supset F(\vec{x}, s_2)$ and
     $\forall \vec{x}.\gamma^-_F(\vec{x}, A, s_2) \supset \neg F(\vec{x}, s_2)$;
   - If $\forall \vec{x}.\psi \supset F(\vec{x}, s_1)$ is in KB_{cur}, then add
     $\forall \vec{x}.\psi^{s_1}_{s_2} \wedge \neg \gamma^-_F(\vec{x}, A, s_2) \supset F(\vec{x}, s_2)$;
   - If $\forall \vec{x}.\psi \supset \neg F(\vec{x}, s_1)$ is in KB_{cur}, then add
     $\forall \vec{x}.\psi^{s_1}_{s_2} \wedge \neg \gamma^+_F(\vec{x}, A, s_2) \supset \neg F(\vec{x}, s_2))$;
   - if $w_0 \models Poss(A, do(\vec{a}, S_0))$ then $\phi_A(\vec{n}, s_2) \in \mathrm{KB}^A_{cur}$ else $\neg \phi_A(\vec{n}, s_2) \in \mathrm{KB}^A_{cur}$.

Note the different treatment depending on whether A is a sensing action or not. In the former case, the old contents of KB_{cur} is simply copied to the new knowledge base with the new situation s_2 replacing the old s_1. If A is an ordinary action, we need to treat the situation dependent fluents in KB_{cur} in a special way in order to reflect the changes that result from doing A. In the case of a sensing action we also need to record the values of ϕ_A and ψ_A depending on the

truth value of $Poss(A)$ and $SF(A)$ at $(w_0, \vec{a})$. If A is an ordinary action, this needs to be done only for ϕ_A because we assume that ψ_A is equivalent to TRUE for ordinary actions.

It is not hard to see that the property of being context-free is preserved by our syntactic form of progression.

Lemma 4.6: *Let* KB, KB^A, *and* A *be as in Definition 4.5. Then* KB^A *is context-free.*

In their paper [13], LR describe some very simple (and reasonable) consistency requirements for context-free knowledge bases.[10] We will not repeat those conditions here and simply refer to them as LR-consistency. We are now ready to show that syntactic progression of context-free KB's conforms with our semantic definition.

Theorem 4.7: *Let* KB_0 *be an initial knowledge base,* w_0 *a world and* $e_0 = \Re[\![\mathrm{KB}_0]\!]$. *Let* KB, KB^A *and* A *be as in Definition 4.5 such that* $\Re[\![\mathrm{KB}]\!]$ *is a progression at* $\vec{a}$ *wrt* $\langle e_0, w_0 \rangle$.

If KB *is LR-consistent, then* $\Re[\![\mathrm{KB}^A]\!]$ *is a progression of* $\Re[\![\mathrm{KB}]\!]$ *at* $\vec{a}$ *wrt* $\langle e_0, w_0 \rangle$.

Note that, by definition, KB_0 is itself a progression at ϵ wrt $\langle e_0, w_0 \rangle$. Hence, the theorem tells us that, starting in an initial context-free knowledge base, doing an action A will lead to a progression which itself is represented by a context-free knowledge base, and this process iterates.

To illustrate how progression works, let us consider the initial KB and the corresponding action model $M = \langle \Re[\![\mathrm{KB}]\!], w \rangle$ from Section 4.1. First, it is easy to verify that it conforms to the definition of a context-free KB.

1. Let us consider progressing KB by $A = \mathsf{senseRed}(C)$ resulting in KB^A with corresponding KB^A. Let s_1 stand for $do(\mathsf{senseRed}(C), now)$.
Since A is a sensing action (case (1) of Def. 4.5), we obtain KB^A_{cur} simply by replacing every occurrence of now in KB_{cur} by s_1 and adding $Red(C, s_1)$ to it, because we assume that $M \models SF(\mathsf{senseRed}(C), S_0)$. Then $\Re[\![\mathrm{KB}^A]\!]$ is a progression at A.
Let $\alpha = \exists x Red(x, now) \wedge Knows(Red(x, now), now)$. Then $\mathrm{ASK}[\alpha, \Re[\![\mathrm{KB}^A]\!], A] = yes$ because now there is a known red letter, namely C.

2. Let us now progress KB^A by $A' = \mathsf{pickup}(C)$ resulting in $\mathrm{KB}^{AA'}$ with corresponding $\mathrm{KB}^{AA'}_{cur}$. Let s_2 stand for $do(\mathsf{pickup}(C), s_1)$.

Starting with the empty set we construct $\mathrm{KB}^{AA'}_{cur}$ by adding the following sentences:[11]

- $Letter(C, s_2), Letter(D, s_2), Red(C, s_2)$

(The disjunction $(Red(C, s_2) \vee Red(D, s_2))$ is omitted because it is clearly subsumed by $Red(C, s_2)$.)

Given the successor state axiom for $F = HoldRLs$, we obtain

$\gamma^-_F = \mathrm{FALSE}$ and
$\gamma^+_F(x, A, s_2) = [pickup(C) = pickup(x) \wedge Red(x, s_2)]$.

---

[10]One such requirement is that γ^+_F and γ^-_F may never be true simultaneously. The example KB is LR-consistent.

[11]For simplicity, we omit adding sentences that turn out to be valid or subsumed by others.

Hence we add

- $\forall x. \gamma_F^+(x, A, s_2) \supset HoldRLs(x, s_2)$

Finally, the last case of Definition 4.5 applies and we add

- $\forall x. \neg \gamma_F^+(x, A, s_2) \supset \neg HoldRLs(x, s_2)$

Given the unique names assumption for standard names of objects and actions, $\gamma_F^+(x, A, s_2)$ is true just in case $x = C$, that is, the agent is holding precisely C in s_2.

Given this progressed knowledge base it is then not hard to show that the robot does not know in s_2 whether it is holding all the red letters. Formally, let

$$\alpha = \forall x. Red(x, now) \wedge Letter(x, now) \supset$$
$$\mathtt{Knows}(Red(\mathtt{x}, now) \wedge Letter(\mathtt{x}, now), now).$$

Then $\mathrm{ASK}[\alpha, \Re[\![\mathrm{KB}^{AA'}]\!], A \cdot A'] = unknown$. This is because there are worlds in $\Re[\![\mathrm{KB}^{AA'}]\!]$ where C is the only red letter and others where there are red letters other than C after doing $A \cdot A'$.

5 Conclusions

Using the second-order logic $\mathcal{AOL}$, we specified a query facility for knowledge bases in dynamic worlds. Despite the expressiveness of the logic, we showed that query evaluation often requires only first-order reasoning. Moreover, by adapting and extending results by Lin and Reiter, we gave a semantic definition of progression and showed that it is first-order representable in the case of context-free knowledge bases.

Future work includes finding more powerful classes of knowledge bases with first-order progressions and applying the results to the action programming language GOLOG [10]. We defined progression in a way that is very close to the original definition by Lin and Reiter. The exact relationship between the two still needs to be determined. Also, our earlier definition of SUCC can be thought of as a progression operator in its own right. It is more powerful in that nothing about the past is forgotten. It is an interesting open problem to determine syntactic variants of this notion of progression.

References

[1] Hintikka, J., *Knowledge and Belief: An Introduction to the Logic of the Two Notions*. Cornell University Press, 1962.

[2] Kaplan, D., Quantifying In, in L. Linsky (ed.), *Reference and Modality*, Oxford University Press, Oxford, 1971.

[3] Kripke, S. A., Semantical considerations on modal logic. *Acta Philosophica Fennica* **16**, 1963, pp. 83–94.

[4] Lakemeyer, G. and Levesque, H. J. $\mathcal{AOL}$: a logic of acting, sensing, knowing, and only knowing. *Proc. of the Sixth International Conference on Principles of Knowledge Representation and Reasoning*, Morgan Kaufmann, San Francisco, 1998.

[5] Lakemeyer, G. and Levesque, H. J. Querying $\mathcal{AOL}$ Knowledge Bases. Preliminary Report. Festschrift in Honour of W. Bibel, Kluwer Academic Press, to appear.

[6] Levesque, H. J., Foundations of a Functional Approach to Knowledge Representation, *Artificial Intelligence*, **23**, 1984, pp. 155-212.

[7] Levesque, H. J., All I Know: A Study in Autoepistemic Logic. *Artificial Intelligence*, North Holland, **42**, 1990, pp. 263–309.

[8] Levesque, H. J., What is Planning in the Presence of Sensing. AAAI-96, AAAI Press, 1996.

[9] Levesque, H. J. and Lakemeyer, G., *The Logic of Knowledge Bases*, Monograph, forthcoming.

[10] Levesque, H. J., Reiter, R., Lespérance, Y., Lin,F. and Scherl., R. B., GOLOG: A logic programming language for dynamic domains. *Journal of Logic Programming*, **31**, 59-84, 1997.

[11] Lifschitz, V., Computing Circumscription, *Proceedings of the 9th International Joint Conference on Artificial Intelligence*, Morgan Kaufmann, San Francisco, 1985, pp. 121–127.

[12] Lin, F. and Reiter, R., Forget It!, in *Proc. of the AAAI Fall Symposium on Relevance*, New Orleans, 1994, pp. 154–159.

[13] Lin, F. and Reiter, R., How to Progress a Database. *Artificial Intelligence*, **92**, 1997, pp.131-167.

[14] McCarthy, J., *Situations, Actions and Causal Laws*. Technical Report, Stanford University, 1963. Also in M. Minsky (ed.), *Semantic Information Processing*, MIT Press, Cambridge, MA, 1968, pp. 410–417.

[15] Moore, R. C., A Formal Theory of Knowledge and Action. In J. R. Hobbs and R. C. Moore (eds.), *Formal Theories of the Commonsense World*, Ablex, Norwood, NJ, 1985, pp. 319–358.

[16] Reiter, R., The Frame Problem in the Situation Calculus: A simple Solution (sometimes) and a Completeness Result for Goal Regression. In V. Lifschitz (ed.), *Artificial Intelligence and Mathematical Theory of Computation*, Academic Press, 1991, pp. 359–380.

[17] Scherl, R. and Levesque, H. J., The Frame Problem and Knowledge Producing Actions. in *Proc. of the National Conference on Artificial Intelligence (AAAI-93)*, AAAI Press, 1993, 689–695.

Axiomatic Foundations for Qualitative/Ordinal Decisions with Partial Preferences

Adriana Zapico*
Institut d'Investigacio en Intel.ligència Artificial (IIIA)-CSIC
Campus UAB s/n.
08193 Bellaterra, Barcelona.
Spain.
zapico@iiia.csic.es

Abstract

The representational issues of preferences in the framework of a possibilistic (qualitative/ordinal) decision model under uncertainty, were originally introduced few years ago by Dubois and Prade, and more recently linked to case-based decision problem by Dubois et al.. In this approach, the uncertainty is assumed to be of possibilistic nature. Uncertainty (or similarity) and preferences on consequences are both measured on commensurate ordinal scales. However, in case-based decision problems, similarity or preferences on consequences may sometimes take values that are incomparable. In order to cope with some of these situations, we propose an extension of the model where both preferences and uncertainty are graded on distributive lattices, providing axiomatic settings for characterising a pessimistic and an optimistic qualitative utilities. Finally, we extend our proposal to also include belief states that may be partially inconsistent, supplying elements for a qualitative case-based decision methodology.

1 Introduction

Assuming that uncertainty about the actual state may be represented by possibility distributions, Dubois and Prade [1995] proposed a qualitative counterpart to Von Neumann and Morgenstern's Expected Utility Theory [Von Neumann and Morgenstern, 1944]. Both uncertainty and preferences are valued on linear ordinal scales of plausibility and preferences on decision consequences.

Gilboa and Schmeidler [1995] have proposed a Case-Based Decision Theory (CBDT) based on the choice of decisions according to their performance in previously experienced decision problems. This theory assumes a set **M** of decision problem instances storing the performance of decisions taken in different past situations as triples (*situation, decision, consequence*), and some measure **Sim** of similarity between situations. The Decision Maker (DM), in face of a new situation s_0, is proposed to choose a decision d which maximises a counterpart of the expected utility, namely the expression

$$U_{s_0,M}(d) = \Sigma_{(s,d,x) \in M} \ Sim(s_0,s) \cdot u(x)$$

where *Sim* is a non-negative function which estimates the similarity of situations and u provides a numerical utility for each consequence x. Gilboa and Schmeidler axiomatically characterise the preference relation induced by this U-maximisation.

In a recent paper [Dubois *et al*, 1998], an adaptation of the mentioned possibilistic decision model to the framework of case-based decision problems was suggested. But it was pointed out that some problems may appear in doing that. In order to cope with such problems, it has been proposed [Zapico and Godo, 1998] an extension of the possibilistic decision model to deal with non-normalised possibility distributions, i.e. distributions accounting for partial information that can be inconsistent to some extent.

In these proposals it is assumed that both uncertainty (similarity) and preferences are measured on linearly ordered scales, however, these hypotheses may not hold in many problems. There are real problems where we are not able to measure similarity and preferences in such linearly ordered sets but only in partially ordered ones. This situation may occur in case-based decision when the degrees of similarity on problems are only partially ordered. For example, consider that each situation is described as s = $(s^1,...,s^b)$. Suppose we are provided with a similarity function on situations $Sim: S \times S \rightarrow V$, defined in function of the b-features similarity functions. That is, let $S=S^1 x...x S^b$, given $\mathcal{S}^k: S^k \times S^k \rightarrow E$, that measures the degree of similarity between two k-features, where E is a finite linear scale, the similarity on situations is defined by $Sim(s,s') = (\mathcal{S}^1(s^1,s'^1),..., \mathcal{S}^b(s^b,s'^b))$, being V= E x...x E, with $\leq_V$ the product ordering on V. In this case, the set of values for similarity, $(V, \leq_V)$, is a lattice. If we are not provided with an aggregation criterion for similarity vectors that summarises the criteria on an ordinal linear scale, we are not able to apply the previously mentioned models. In a similar way, we may have that DM's preferences on consequences are only partially ordered, maybe as a consequence of a previous aggregation of various criteria. Indeed, a preference relation among consequences is usually modelled by a utility function u: $X \rightarrow U$, where U is a preference scale, frequently a (numerical or a qualitative) linear scale.

---

*On leave from Universidad Nacional de Río Cuarto (Argentina)

However, in many cases, this preference function may be a vectorial one on a lattice. Hence, we are now interested in a qualitative decision model that let us make decisions in cases where the DM's preferences on consequences are only partially ordered or when the uncertainty on the consequences is valued on a lattice.

In this work, we propose axiomatic settings for qualitative decision making under uncertainty, requiring only finite distributive lattices for valuing uncertainty and preferences. Two qualitative criteria are axiomatized: a pessimistic and an optimistic one, respectively obeying an uncertainty aversion axiom and an uncertainty-attraction axiom. In order to be able to apply the model to case-based decision, we extend our initial proposal to include belief states that may be partially inconsistent.

In the following section we provide a background on lattices. In section 3 we propose two axiomatic settings for characterising both pessimistic and optimistic qualitative utilities, requiring only finite distributive and commensurate lattices for assessing uncertainty and preferences. An extension that lets us make decisions in contexts in which possibly partially inconsistent belief states are involved, is summarised in section 4. In section 5, it is shown how this extended model may be applied to case-based decision problems.

2 Background on Lattices

Lets us recall many definitions related with lattices (for more details [Davey and Priestley, 1990]), that we will use in the following.

2.1 Some Previous Definitions and Results

$(L, \wedge, \vee)$ is a *lattice* if $\wedge$, $\vee$ are associative, commutative, satisfy idempotency and the absorption laws. The induced order in a lattice is: $x \leq y$ iff $x \wedge y = x$.

$(L, \wedge, \vee, n_L, 0, 1)$ will denote a *bounded lattice with involution*, i.e. L satisfies that $0, 1 \in L$ and $0 \leq x \leq 1$ $\forall x \in L$, being $n_L: L \to L$ a decreasing function s.t. $n_L(n_L(x)) = x$.

Observations. Given $(L, \wedge, \vee)$ a lattice, then

- $\vee$ and $\wedge$ are non-decreasing.
- If $(L, \wedge, \vee, n_L, 0, 1)$ is a lattice with involution, n_L satisfies that $n_L(0) = 1$ and $n_L(1) = 0$, $n_L(x \wedge y) = n_L(x) \vee n_L(y)$ and $n_L(x \vee y) = n_L(x) \wedge n_L(y)$.

Definition. Given a partially pre-ordered set $(L, \leq)$, i.e. $\leq$ is reflexive and transitive, the associated *indifference relation* $\sim$ is defined by $a \sim b$ iff $a \leq b$ and $b \leq a$.

Now we introduce some results that will be used in our proposal.

Proposition 1. Let $(L, \leq)$ be a partially pre-ordered set, then $\sim$ is an equivalence relation.

Definition. Given $(L, \leq)$ a partially pre-ordered set, we denote by $L/\sim$ the quotient set w.r.t. $\sim$. $(L, \leq)$ is a *pre-lattice* iff $(L/\sim, \sqsubseteq)$ is a lattice, defining $\sqsubseteq$ as: $[a] \sqsubseteq [b]$ iff $a \leq b$.

Theorem 1. $(A, \leq)$ is a pre-lattice iff $(A, \leq)$ is a partially pre-ordered set, such that satisfies

I) For all $a, b \in A$ there exists an unique not empty subset $SUP(a,b) \subseteq A$ s.t.
- the $SUP(a,b)$ elements are indifferent one to each other, i.e. $c \sim d$, $\forall c, d \in SUP(a,b)$.
- if $c \in SUP(a,b)$, $c \sim d$, then $d \in SUP(a,b)$.
- $\forall c \in SUP(a,b)$, $a \leq c$ and $b \leq c$.
- if $a \leq e$ and $b \leq e$, then $(e \sim c \ \forall c \in SUP(a,b))$ or $(e >^1 c \ \forall c \in SUP(a,b))$.

II) For all $a, b \in A$ there exists an unique not empty subset $INF(a,b) \subseteq A$ s.t.
- the $INF(a,b)$ elements are indifferent one to each other, i.e. $c \sim d$ for all $c, d \in INF(a,b)$.
- if $c \in INF(a,b)$, $c \sim d$ then $d \in INF(a,b)$.
- if $e \leq a$ and $e \leq b$ then, $(e \sim c \ \forall c \in INF(a,b))$ or $(c > e$ for all $c \in INF(a,b))$.
- $\forall c \in INF(a,b)$, $c \leq a$ and $c \leq b$.

2.2 Possibility Distributions and Lattices

Now, let us introduce the context of our work. Let $X = \{x_1, \dots, x_p\}$ be a finite *set of consequences*. We will denote by $(V, \vee, \wedge, 0, 1, n_V)$ a *finite distributive lattice of uncertainty values* with minimum 0, maximum 1 and an involution n_V, and $\leq_V$ the order induced by $\wedge$ in V. $(U, \leq_U, 0, 1, n_U)$ will be a *finite distributive lattice of preference values* with involution n_U. The *indifference* and *incomparability relations* are:

- $\lambda \sim \lambda'$ iff $\lambda \leq_V \lambda'$ and $\lambda' \leq_V \lambda$.
- $\lambda <> \lambda'$ iff $\lambda \not\leq_V \lambda'$ and $\lambda' \not\leq_V \lambda$.

Now, we consider the set of *consistent possibility distributions* on X over V, i.e.

$$Pi(X) = \{\pi: X \to V \mid \bigvee_{x \in X} \pi(x) = 1\}.$$

As usual, $\pi \leq \pi'$ iff $\forall x \in X$ $\pi(x) \leq_V \pi'(x)$, with $\leq_V$ the order induced by $\wedge$ in V.

At first, we will be interested in a subset of Pi(X), the set of *normalised possibility distributions*, i.e.

$$Pi^*(X) = \{\pi \in Pi(X) / \exists x \text{ s.t. } \pi(x) = 1\}.$$

For the sake of simplicity, we shall use x for denoting both an element belonging to X and the normalised possibility distribution on X such that $\pi(x) = 1$ and $\pi(z) = 0$ for $z \neq x$. In general, we shall also denote by A both a subset $A \subseteq X$ and the normalised possibility distribution on X such that $\pi(x) = 1$ if $x \in A$ and $\pi(x) = 0$ otherwise. Hence, we can consider X as included in $Pi^*(X)$.

Given $x, y \in X$, $x \neq y$, $\lambda, \mu \in V$ s.t. $\lambda \vee \mu = 1$, the *qualitative lottery* $(\lambda/x, \mu/y)$ is the consistent possibility distribution on X, defined as $(\lambda/x, \mu/y)(z) = \lambda$ if $z = x$, equal to μ if $z = y$ and 0 otherwise.

The so-called *Possibilistic Mixture* is an operation defined on Pi(X) that combines two consistent possibility distributions π_1 and π_2 into a new one, denoted $(\lambda/\pi_1, \mu/\pi_2)$, with $\lambda, \mu \in V$ and $\lambda \vee \mu = 1$, and defined as

$$(\lambda/\pi_1, \mu/\pi_2)(x) = (\lambda \wedge \pi_1(x)) \vee (\mu \wedge \pi_2(x)).$$

---

[1] $e > c$ iff $c \leq e$ and $e \not\leq c$.

In order to have a closed operation on Pi*(X), the mixture operation is restricted to Pi*(X) requiring the scalars to satisfy an additional condition, i.e., if π, $\pi' \in$ Pi*(X), we consider $(\lambda/\pi, \mu/\pi')$ with $\lambda, \mu \in V$ and $\lambda = 1$ or $\mu = 1$.

It is not difficult to verify that *reduction of lotteries* always holds, i.e. $\forall \lambda_1, \lambda_2 \in V$ s.t. $\lambda_1 \vee \lambda_2 = 1$, $\forall \pi \in$ Pi(X)

$$(\lambda_1/(1/\pi, \mu_1/X), \lambda_2/(1/\pi, \mu_2/X)) =$$
$$= (1/\pi, \ (\lambda_1 \wedge \mu_1) \vee (\lambda_2 \wedge \mu_2)/X).$$

Note. In order to simplify notation, we use $\wedge$, $\vee$ for denoting both operations on V and U, although they may be different, hoping they may be understood by the context.

3 Our Proposal

Consider **u**: $X \to U$ a preference function that assigns to each consequence of X a preference level of U, requiring V and U to be commensurate, i.e. there exists **h**:$V \to U$ a {0,1}-homomorphism relating both lattices V and U. Let **n** be the reversing homomorphism **n**: $V \to U$ defined as $n(\lambda) = n_U(h(\lambda))$. It also verifies $n(0) = 1$, $n(1) = 0$. For any $\pi \in$ Pi*(X), consider the qualitative utility functions

$$QU^-(\pi) = \bigwedge_{x \in X} (n(\pi(x)) \vee u(x)),$$
$$QU^+(\pi) = \bigvee_{x \in X} (h(\pi(x)) \wedge u(x)).$$

Now, we will introduce the axioms that characterise the preferences relations induced by these functions and some results that we need for the representation theorems proofs.

Note. As U is a distributive lattice with involution, QU^- and QU^+ preserve the possibilistic mixture in the sense that the following expressions hold,

$QU^-(\lambda/\pi_1, \mu/\pi_2) = (n(\lambda) \vee QU^-(\pi_1)) \wedge (n(\mu) \vee QU^-(\pi_2))$,
$QU^+(\lambda/\pi_1, \mu/\pi_2) = (h(\lambda) \wedge QU^+(\pi_1)) \vee (h(\mu) \wedge QU^+(\pi_2))$.

Proposition 2. Let (Pi*(X), $\sqsubseteq$), satisfying

- **A1**: (Pi*(X), $\sqsubseteq$) is a pre-lattice.

- **A2** (uncertainty aversion): if $\pi \leq \pi' \Rightarrow \pi' \sqsubseteq \pi$.

Then
a) The maximal[2] elements of (Pi*(X), $\sqsubseteq$) are equivalent.
b) The maximal elements of (X, $\sqsubseteq$) are equivalent, and they are equivalent to the maximal ones of (Pi*(X), $\sqsubseteq$).

Axiomatic setting. Let **AXP** be the following set of axioms on (Pi*(X), $\sqsubseteq$):

- **A1**: (Pi*(X), $\sqsubseteq$) is a pre-lattice.

- **A2** (uncertainty aversion): if $\pi \leq \pi' \Rightarrow \pi' \sqsubseteq \pi$.

- **A3** (independence):

  $\pi_1 \sim \pi_2 \Rightarrow (\lambda/\pi_1, \mu/\pi) \sim (\lambda/\pi_2, \mu/\pi)$.

- **A4**: if $\pi_\lambda \sqsubseteq \pi_{\lambda'} \Rightarrow \pi_{n_V(\lambda)} \sqsupseteq \pi_{n_V(\lambda')}$,

  with $\pi_\lambda = (1/\overline{\pi}, \lambda/X)$ and $\overline{\pi}$ a maximal element of (Pi*(X), $\sqsubseteq$).

- **A5**: if $\lambda <> \lambda' \Rightarrow \pi_\lambda \sqsubset \sqsupset \pi_{\lambda'}$.

- **A6**: $\forall \pi \in$ Pi*(X), $\exists \lambda \in V$, such that $\pi \sim (1/\overline{\pi}, \lambda/X)$.

Observation. If A4 holds then, $\pi_\lambda \sim \pi_{\lambda'} \Rightarrow \pi_{n_V(\lambda)} \sim \pi_{n_V(\lambda')}$.

---

[2] π is a maximal element iff $\forall \pi' \in$ Pi*(X), $\pi \sqsubseteq \pi' \Rightarrow \pi \sim \pi'$.

Lemma 1. Let $(U, \leq_U, 0, 1, n_U)$ and $(V, \leq_V, 0, 1, n_V)$ be two distributive lattices with involution, n: $V \to U$ a reversing epimorphism, and **u**: $X \to U$. Consider $QU^-(\pi) = \bigwedge_{x \in X} (n(\pi(x)) \vee u(x))$, if $(QU^-)^{-1}(1) \neq \emptyset$ and $(QU^-)^{-1}(0) \neq \emptyset$, then

a) there exists $x \in X$ s.t. $u(x) = 1$ and $\bigwedge_{x \in X} u(x) = 0$.
b) QU^- is onto.

Lemma 2. Let n: $V \to U$ be an onto decreasing function also satisfying that if $\lambda <> \lambda'$ then $n(\lambda) <>_U n(\lambda')$. Then, n is a reversing epimorphism.

Finally, let $\leq_{QU^-}$ be the preference ordering on Pi*(X) induced by QU^-, i.e. $\pi \leq_{QU^-} \pi'$ iff $QU^-(\pi) \leq_U QU^-(\pi')$. In the following, we state that the set of axioms AXP characterise these preference orderings

Representation Theorem 2. *(Pessimistic Utility)* A preference relation (Pi*(X), $\sqsubseteq$) satisfies axioms AXP iff there exist
(i) a finite distributive utility lattice $(U, \wedge, \vee, n_U, 0, 1)$.
(ii) a preference function u: $X \to U$, s.t. $u^{-1}(1) \neq \emptyset$ and $\bigwedge_{x \in X} u(x) = 0$,
(iii) an onto order reversing function n: $V \to U$ s.t. $n(0) = 1$ and $n(1) = 0$, also satisfying

  if $\lambda <> \lambda'$ then $\quad n(\lambda) <>_U n(\lambda')$, (1)
  and $n_U \circ n \circ n_V = n$, (2)
in such a way that it holds:
$$\pi' \sqsubseteq \pi \quad \text{iff} \quad \pi' \leq_{QU^-} \pi.$$

<u>Proof</u>: $\leftarrow$) Now, we verify that the preference ordering on Pi*(X) induced by QU^- satisfies the above set of axioms.

As $\leq_U$ is a partial order, $\leq_{QU^-}$ is reflexive and transitive. QU^- is onto, so we may define $SUP(\pi, \pi') = (QU^-)^{-1}(QU^-(\pi) \vee QU^-(\pi'))$, and $INF(\pi, \pi') = (QU^-)^{-1}(QU^-(\pi) \wedge QU^-(\pi'))$. Then, by theorem 1, (Pi*(X), $\leq_{QU^-}$) is a pre-lattice.

A2 results from the fact that $\vee$ and $\wedge$ are non-decreasing in U and n is a reversing function. While, A3 is a consequence of the fact that QU^- preserves mixtures.

A4: if $\pi_\lambda \leq_{QU^-} \pi_{\lambda'} \Rightarrow \pi_{n_V(\lambda)} \geq_{QU^-} \pi_{n_V(\lambda')}$.

Let $\overline{\pi}$ be a maximal element of Pi*(X), so $QU^-(\overline{\pi}) = 1$. As QU^- preserves mixtures and $QU^-(X) = 0$, we have that $QU^-(\pi_\lambda) = n(\lambda)$. As $n_U \circ n \circ n_V = n$, and n_V and n_U are involutive, if $n(\lambda) \leq n(\lambda')$, then $n(n_V(\lambda)) = n_U(n(\lambda)) \geq n_U(n(\lambda')) = n(n_V(\lambda'))$.

A5 is a consequence of $<>_{QU^-}$ definition and that n satisfies (1). Now, we check A6. Let $\overline{\pi}$ be maximal element of Pi*(X) w.r.t. $\leq_{QU^-}$. As $QU^-(1/\overline{\pi}, \lambda/X) = n(\lambda)$, then $QU^-(\pi) = n(\lambda) = QU^-(1/\overline{\pi}, \lambda/X) \ \forall \lambda \in n^{-1}(QU^-(\pi))$.

$\rightarrow$) The proof is analogous with the one given in [Dubois *et al*, 1998] for the linear case. We structure the proof in the following three steps.
I) We define the distributive utility lattice U, with involution n_U, and a reversing mapping n from V to U, satisfying if $\lambda <> \lambda'$ then $n(\lambda) <>_U n(\lambda')$, and $n_U \circ n \circ n_V = n$. By lemma 2, n results a reversing epimorphism.
II) A function QU^-: Pi*(X) $\to U$ representing $\sqsubseteq$, i.e. such that $QU^-(\pi) \leq QU^-(\pi')$ iff $\pi \sqsubseteq \pi'$, is defined.

III) Finally, we prove that $QU^-(\pi) = \bigwedge_{x \in X}(n(\pi(x)) \vee u(x))$, where u: $X \to U$ is the restriction of QU^- on X. u also satisfies that $u^{-1}(1) \neq \varnothing$ and $\bigwedge_{x \in X} u(x) = 0$.

Now, we develop these steps.

I) We consider on Pi*(X) the equivalence relation ~, defined as $\pi \sim \pi'$ iff $\pi \sqsubseteq \pi'$ and $\pi' \sqsubseteq \pi$, by A1 Pi*(X)/~ is a lattice. As in the linear case, we take as utility lattice U = Pi*(X)/~. As Theorem 1 guarantees the existence of SUP and INF, we consider in U the operations $\wedge$ and $\vee$ induced by SUP and INF, i.e.

$$[\pi] \vee [\pi'] = SUP(\pi, \pi') \text{ and } [\pi] \wedge [\pi'] = INF(\pi, \pi').$$

The $\leq_U$ induced from $\vee$ coincides with $\sqsubseteq$. It is not difficult to verify that [X] is minimum of U, and if $\bar{\pi}$ is a maximal element of Pi*(X), as all maximal elements are equivalent, $[\bar{\pi}]$ is maximum on U.

Let $\pi_\lambda = (1/\bar{\pi}, \lambda/X)$, and let n: $V \to U$ be defined as $n(\lambda) = [\pi_\lambda]$. It is not difficult to see that n is onto, n(1) = 0, n(0) = 1, and that n actually reverses the order. Now, we define n_U from n and n_V. Given $w \in U$, there exists $\lambda \in V$ s.t. $n(\lambda) = w$. We define $n_U(w) = n(n_V(\lambda))$.

By A5, n satisfies if $\lambda \Leftrightarrow \lambda'$ then $n(\lambda) \Leftrightarrow_U n(\lambda')$, and by definition of n_U, $n_U \circ n \circ n_V = n$. Hence, as n is a reversing epimorphism, and V is distributive, so is U.

II) As usual, QU^- may be defined on Pi*(X) in two steps. First, we define it on lotteries of type π_λ, as $QU^-(1/\bar{\pi}, \lambda/X) = n(\lambda)$. A6 lets us to extend this definition. Since $\forall \pi \exists \lambda$ s.t. $\pi \sim (1/\bar{\pi}, \lambda/X)$, we define $QU^-(\pi) = n(\lambda)$.

It is not difficult to verify that QU^- represents $\sqsubseteq$.

III) Consider u: $X \to U$ defined as $u(x) = QU^-(x)$.

It remains to prove that $QU^-(\pi) = \bigwedge_{x \in X}(n(\pi(x)) \vee u(x))$. To verify this, we will prove the following equality:

• $QU^-(\lambda_1/\pi_1, \lambda_2/\pi_2) = (n(\lambda_1) \vee QU^-(\pi_1)) \wedge (n(\lambda_2) \vee QU^-(\pi_2))$ with $\lambda_1 = 1$ or $\lambda_2 = 1$.

By A6, $\exists \mu, \gamma$ s.t. $\pi_1 \sim (1/\bar{\pi}, \mu/X)$ and $\pi_2 \sim (1/\bar{\pi}, \gamma/X)$ by A3, $(\lambda_1/\pi_1, \lambda_2/\pi_2) \sim (\lambda_1/(1/\bar{\pi}, \mu/X), \lambda_2/(1/\bar{\pi}, \gamma/X))$, and reducing lotteries we obtain

$$(\lambda_1/\pi_1, \lambda_2/\pi_2) \sim (1/\bar{\pi}, ((\lambda_1 \wedge \mu) \vee (\lambda_2 \wedge \gamma))/X).$$

Therefore, as n is distributive,
$QU^-(\lambda_1/\pi_1, \lambda_2/\pi_2) = n((\lambda_1 \wedge \mu) \vee (\lambda_2 \wedge \gamma)) =$
$= (n(\lambda_1) \vee n(\mu)) \wedge (n(\lambda_2) \vee n(\gamma)) =$
$= (n(\lambda_1) \vee QU^-(\pi_1)) \wedge (n(\lambda_2) \vee QU^-(\pi_2))$
Hence, $QU^-(\pi_1 \vee \pi_2)) = QU^-(\pi_1) \wedge QU^-(\pi_2))$

More generally, $QU^-(\bigvee_{i=1,p} \pi_i) = \bigwedge_{i=1,p} QU^-(\pi_i)$.

• $QU^-(\pi) = \bigwedge_{i=1,p} (n(\pi(x_i)) \vee u(x_i))$.

As $\pi \in$ Pi*(X), then $\exists x_j \in X$ s.t. $\pi(x_j) = 1$, without loss of generality assume j = 1. Let $\pi_i = (1/x_1, \pi(x_i)/x_i)$. As $\pi = \bigvee_{i=1,p} \pi_i$, we have that
$QU^-(\pi) = QU^-(\bigvee_{i=1,p} \pi_i) =$
$= \bigwedge_{i=1,p} \{(u(x_1) \wedge (n(\pi(x_i)) \vee u(x_i))\} =^3$
$= \bigwedge_{i=1,p} (n(\pi(x_i)) \vee u(x_i))$.

Finally, as $\bar{\pi}$ is normalised, exists $x_0 \in X$ s.t. $\bar{\pi}(x_0) = 1$, so $x_0 \leq \bar{\pi}$. Then by A2, $x_0 \sqsupseteq \bar{\pi}$. As QU^- represents $\sqsubseteq$, $QU^-(x_0) \geq QU^-(\bar{\pi}) = n(0) = 1$, hence $u(x_0) = 1$, so $u^{-1}(1) \neq \varnothing$. As $QU^-(X) = n(1) = 0$, and $QU^-(X) = \bigwedge_{x \in X} u(x)$, then $\bigwedge_{x \in X} u(x) = 0$. This ends the proof. $\square$

---

[3] Note that $\pi(x_1) = 1$, so $u(x_1) = u(x_1) \vee n(\pi(x_1))$.

In order to represent an optimistic preference criterion, we consider now the distribution π_λ defined as $\pi_\lambda = (\lambda/X, 1/\underline{\pi})$, where $\underline{\pi}$ is minimal of (Pi*(X), $\sqsubseteq$), and we have to change the uncertainty aversion axiom A2 by an uncertainty-prone postulate

• **A2⁺**: if $\pi \leq \pi'$ then $\pi \sqsubseteq \pi'$,

and to modify the continuity axiom A6 into

• **A6⁺**: $\forall \pi \in$ Pi*(X) $\exists \lambda \in V$ such that $\pi \sim (\lambda/X, 1/\underline{\pi})$, where $\underline{\pi}$ is minimal of (Pi*(X), $\sqsubseteq$).

For an optimistic behaviour, we consider $\lesssim_{QU^+}$ the preference ordering on Pi*(X) induced by QU^+, i.e.

$$\pi \lesssim_{QU^+} \pi' \text{ iff } QU^+(\pi) \leq_U QU^+(\pi').$$

Representation Theorem 3. (*Optimistic Utility*) A preference relation $\sqsubseteq$ on Pi*(X) satisfies axioms set AXP⁺ = {A1, A2⁺, A3, A4, A5, A6⁺} iff there exist
(i) a finite distributive utility lattice (U, $\vee$, $\wedge$, 0, 1, n_U),
(ii) a preference function u: $X \to U$, s.t. $u^{-1}(0) \neq \varnothing$ and $\bigvee_{x \in X} u(x) = 1$,
(iii) an onto order preserving function h: $V \to U$, s.t. h(0)=0, h(1) = 1, $n_U \circ h \circ n_V = h$, and also satisfying $\lambda \Leftrightarrow \lambda'$ then $h(\lambda) \Leftrightarrow_U h(\lambda')$,

in such a way that it holds:

$$\pi' \sqsubseteq \pi \quad \text{iff} \quad \pi' \lesssim_{QU^+} \pi.$$

The proof is very analogous to the one for pessimistic utility, hence it is omitted.

Observation. As n is onto and decreasing, if V is linear, so is U (i.e. U non linear, then V is non linear). Moreover, as a consequence of the condition "if $\lambda \Leftrightarrow \lambda'$ then $n(\lambda) \Leftrightarrow_U n(\lambda')$", if V is non linear so is U. Hence, V and U are both linear lattices or both non linear lattices.

4 Extension for Partially Inconsistent Belief States

Sometimes, the Decision Maker may only have partial information about the possible consequences of decisions, for example, by having the performance of decisions taken in different past situations stored as a set M of triples (*situation, decision, consequence*). As previously mentioned, in such a framework, Gilboa and Schmeidler [1995] proposed a case-based decision model where the Decision Maker, faced with a new situation s_0, is supposed to choose a decision d which maximises a counterpart of classical expected utility. Another approach to Case-Based Decision, which proposes looking for decisions that always gave good results in similar experienced situations, was suggested by Dubois and Prade [1997].

In [Dubois *et al*, 1998] a link is established between Case-based Decision Theory and Qualitative Decision Theory by estimating how much plausible x is a consequence of a decision d in the current situation s_0 in terms of what extent s_0 is similar to situations in which x was experienced after taking the decision d. Being U and V finite linearly ordered scales that are commensurate, they consider a similarity function on situations *Sim*: $S \times S \to V$, and a preference function ü: $X \to U$ which represents DM's preferences on consequences. So, a decision or action d can be identified with a possibility distribution on consequences. They define the *distribution associated to d and s_0* (and obviously depending on *Sim* and M) $\pi_{d,s_0}: X \to V$ on the set of consequences, as

$$\pi_{d,s_0}(x) = \max\{Sim(s_0, s) \mid (s, d, x) \in M\},$$

where, by convention, max $\emptyset = 0$. $\pi_{d,s_0}(x)$ represents the plausibility of x of being the consequence of s_0 by d. Hence, the proposal was to evaluate d, in terms of π_{d,s_0}.

If π_{d,s_0} is normalised, then it is always the case that optimistic criterion scores a decision higher than the pessimistic one, but if the distribution is not normalised it may not. This problem is solved in [Zapico and Godo, 1998] extending the model to include non-normalised distributions that represent belief states that may be partially inconsistent. A similar analysis is valid for our work, hence, in order to apply the model to case-based decision that may involve non-normalised distributions, we provide now the corresponding extension of our proposal. First, let us introduce the concepts of normalisation and height of a distribution. Define h, the *height of a distribution*, as $h(\underline{\pi}) = \bigvee_{x \in X} \underline{\pi}(x)$, and for each distribution consider the subset of consequences with maximal plausibility

$$X_{h(\underline{\pi})} = \{ x \in X / \forall\ y \in X\ \underline{\pi}(y) \not> \underline{\pi}(x)\}.$$

We define $N(\underline{\pi})$, *the normalisation of* $\underline{\pi}$, as the normalised distribution

$$N(\underline{\pi})(x) = \begin{cases} 1 & \text{if} \quad x \in X_{h(\underline{\pi})} \\ \underline{\pi}(x) & \text{otherwise.} \end{cases}$$

We extend the set of possibilistic lotteries to the set $Pi^{ex}(X)$ of non necessarily normalised distributions on V. Hence, we need to extend the concept of possibilistic mixture PME on $Pi^{ex}(X)$ to combine $\underline{\pi}_1$ and $\underline{\pi}_2$ with $(\lambda, \mu) \in \Phi_V$, with $\Phi_V = \{(\alpha, \beta) \in V \times V \mid \alpha \vee \beta = 1\}$, i.e.
PME: $Pi^{ex}(X) \times Pi^{ex}(X) \times \Phi_V \to Pi^{ex}(X)$,

$$PME(\underline{\pi}_1,\underline{\pi}_2,\lambda,\mu) = (\lambda/\underline{\pi}_1,\mu/\underline{\pi}_2) = (\lambda\wedge\underline{\pi}_1(x)) \vee (\mu\wedge\underline{\pi}_2(x))$$

Given a function F: $V \to V$, such that F(1) = 0, now we may consider the qualitative (or ordinal) utility functions on $Pi^{ex}(X)$, corresponding to those considered previously

$$QU_F^-(\underline{\pi}) = QU^-(N(\underline{\pi})) \wedge n(F(h(\underline{\pi})))$$
$$QU_F^+(\underline{\pi}) = QU^+(N(\underline{\pi})) \vee h(F(h(\underline{\pi}))).$$

Let $\sqsubseteq_F$ be a preference relation in $Pi^{ex}(X)$. We will denote by $\sqsubseteq$ its restriction to $Pi^*(X)$, $\sim_F$ and $\sim$ the corresponding indifference relations. In order to characterise the preference orderings induced by the utilities QU_F^- and QU_F^+, we extend the axiom sets AXP and AXP^+, defined on $(Pi^*(X), \sqsubseteq)$ in Section 3, with

• **A7PF**: for all $\underline{\pi} \in Pi^{ex}(X)$ $\underline{\pi} \sim_F (1/N(\underline{\pi}), F(h(\underline{\pi}))/X)$.

The intuitive idea behind this axiom is that, according to the above utility functions, a non-normalised possibilistic lottery $\underline{\pi}$ is indifferent to the corresponding normalised lottery $N(\underline{\pi})$ provided that this is modified in terms of an uncertainty level related with the normality degree of the lottery expressed by its height $h(\underline{\pi})$. For, example if we consider F= n_V, $N(\underline{\pi})$ is weighted by the "negation" of the height of the original distribution.

We say that a preference relation $\sqsubseteq_F$ on $Pi^{ex}(X)$ satisfies axiom set $\underline{AXP}=$ AXP$\cup\{\underline{A7PF}\}$ ($\underline{AXP^+}=$ AXP$^+\cup\{\underline{A7PF}\}$

resp.) iff its restriction to $Pi^*(X)$, denoted by $\sqsubseteq$, satisfies AXP (AXP$^+$ resp.) and $\sqsubseteq_F$ also satisfies $\underline{A7PF}$.

Representation Theorem 4 . A preference relation $\sqsubseteq_F$ on $Pi^{ex}(X)$ satisfies axiom set $\underline{AXP}$ ($\underline{AXP^+}$ resp.) iff there exist
(i) a finite distributive utility lattice (U, $\vee$, $\wedge$, 0, 1) with involution n_U,
(ii) a preference function u: $X \to U$, s.t. $u^{-1}(1) \neq \emptyset$ and $\bigwedge_{x \in X} u(x) = 0$,
(iii) an onto order preserving function h: $V \to U$ s.t. h(0)=0, h(1) =1, and $n_U \circ h \circ n_V$=h, also satisfying
$$\text{if } \lambda \ll \lambda' \text{ then} \quad h(\lambda) \ll_U h(\lambda'),$$
in such a way that it holds:
$$\underline{\pi}' \sqsubseteq_F \underline{\pi} \text{ iff } \underline{QU_F^-}(\underline{\pi}') \leq_U \underline{QU_F^-}(\underline{\pi})$$
($\underline{\pi}' \sqsubseteq_F \underline{\pi}$ iff $\underline{QU_F^+}(\underline{\pi}') \leq_U \underline{QU_F^+}(\underline{\pi})$ resp.), with n = $n_U \circ h$.

5 Case-based Decision: an Application of the Model

Now, we may apply this model to case-based decision, for example, in the context[4] of the *COMRIS Project* [Plaza, *et al.,* 1998]. Suppose we have different agents, called Personal Representative Agents (PRA for short), each of one pursuing a different interest for a same user, and a PA (Personal Assistant) agent coordinating the proposals presented by PRAs. Each PRA presents its most relevant proposal among one of the following :

• an appointment with a person (app)
• an alert about the proximity of a person or event of interest for the user (pro)
• a proposal of receiving propaganda related with events like demonstrations, future conferences, etc. (rp)
• a reminder of an event that will happen soon (rem),

together with a degree of the estimated proposal relevance: great importance (gi), moderate importance (mi), doubtful importance (di), null. (For more details see [Plaza, *et al.,* 1998]).

The PA has to choose one of the PRAs' proposals to send it to the user, with its own evaluation of relevance: gi, mi, di, null.

Suppose we have a memory of cases storing the performance of proposals made in the past by the PA with the respective user opinions about PA's behaviour. A case is represented as a triple **c = (vs, winner, x)**, with:

• **vs** = $((d^1, rel_1),\dots, (d^n, rel_n))$, where (d^i,rel_i) describes the proposal made by the PRA$_i$ and the importance that it assigned to its proposal,
• **winner** = (PA's proposal, PA's evaluation of the importance of its proposal).
• Finally, **x** is a pair reflecting the user opinion. Its first component is user's evaluation on PA's proposal, while the second one is his evaluation of the relevance PA has assigned to it. User opinion is measured on U = E x E, being E= $\{0, \lambda, \mu, 1\}$, with $0 < \lambda < \mu < 1$, and n_E its reversing involution.

---

[4] Actually, we will consider a simplified perspective of the problems involved in this project.

The similarity function on proposals, S_prop, defined over E, is described in Table 1,

Table 1: similarity on proposals

S_prop	app	pro	rem	rp
app	1	μ	λ	0
pro	μ	1	λ	0
rem	λ	λ	1	0
rp	0	0	0	1

while the similarity on labels of relevance, S_rel, is defined in Table 2.

Table 2: similarity on relevance labels.

S_rel	gi	mi	di	null
gi	1	μ	λ	0
mi	μ	1	λ	0
di	λ	λ	1	0
null	0	0	0	1

Now, we define the similarity on states as:

$\mathrm{SIM}(vs,vs') = \bigwedge_{i=1,n}(S\_prop(d^i, d'^i), S\_rel(rel_i, rel'_i))$.

Suppose there are 3 PRAs, being available the memory of cases M described in Table 3.

Table 3: Memory of cases

cases	vs	winner	user_ opinion
c1	((app1,gi),(app2,gi), (app3,gi))	(app2,gi)	(1, 1)
c2	((app1,gi),(rem2,gi), (app3,gi))	(rem2,mi)	(1, μ)
c3	((rp1,di),(rem2,di), (pro3,di))	(pro3,mi)	(μ, λ)
c4	((app1,gi),(rem2,di), (rp3,di)	(rem2,mi)	(λ, λ)
c5	((pro1,mi), (pro2, di), (app3,mi))	(pro1,di)	(1, λ)
c6	((pro1,di),(rem2,di), (app3, mi))	(pro1,di)	(λ, μ)
c7	((app1,mi),(rem2,null), (app3,mi))	(rem2,di)	(0, 0)
c8	((app1,gi)(rem2,di) (rem3, null))	(app1,gi)	(1, μ)

Let $vs_0 = ((app1, mi),(rem2, mi), (rem3, di))$. Now, we evaluate some of PA's available options. As we may see, many of these distributions are non-normalised, so we apply $\underline{QU_F}^+$ and $\underline{QU_F}^-$. Consider $F = n_\vee$, with $n_\vee = (n_E, n_E)$. So, $U_{F s_0}^-(d) = \underline{Q U_F}^-(\pi_{d,vs_0}) = h(\pi_{d,s_0})) \wedge QU^-(N(\pi_{d,s_0}))$ and $U_{F s_0}^+(d) = QU^+(N(\pi)) \vee n_\vee(h(\pi))$.

The distributions associated to PA's proposals not made before, like (rp3, mi), (app2, di), are null. Hence, their utilities are 0 and 1 w.r.t. pessimistic and optimistic criteria respectively. While for (app1,gi), $\pi_{d,vs_0}(1, \mu) = (1, 0)$ and $(0, 0)$ otherwise, so $\underline{QU_F}^-(\pi_{d,vs_0}) = (1, 0) \wedge (1, \mu) = (1, 0)$, while $\underline{QU_F}^+(\pi_{d,vs_0}) = (1, 0) \vee n_\vee(1, \mu) = (1, \lambda)$.

6   Conclusions

In this paper, we propose a framework that allows us to make decisions in contexts in which we only have partially ordered information, in the sense that DM's preferences are valued on a distributive lattice, and that the valuation set of uncertainty (or similarity) is partially ordered too.

We axiomatically characterise these criteria.

As the problem of partially ordered information may have been originated in a case-based decision problem with similarity degrees valued on a lattice involving belief states partially inconsistent, we extended our initial proposal to non-normalised distributions, obtaining two criteria for case-based decisions.

Up to now, we have considered $\wedge$ and $\vee$ as the available operations, now we are considering other operations defined in the lattices, letting us defining other utility functions which we are characterising.

Acknowledgements

The author wishes to thank the valuable support of her advisor Lluís Godo. She is also grateful to J. Arcos for his comments on COMRIS project, and to the three anonymous referees for their comments that have helped to improve the paper. This research is partially supported by the Universidad Nacional de Río Cuarto (Argentina) and by the CICYT project SMASH (TIC96-1138-C04-01).

References

[Davey and Priestley, 1990] B. Davey and H. Priestley. *Introduction to Lattices and Order.* Cambridge Univ. Press.

[Dubois *et al*, 1998] Didier Dubois, Lluís Godo, Henri Prade and Adriana Zapico. Making decision in a qualitative setting: from decision under uncertainty to case-based decision. In *Proce. of the Sixth International Conference on Principles of Knowledge Representation and Reasoning*, pages 594 - 605. Trento.

[Dubois and Prade, 1997] Didier Dubois and Henri Prade. A fuzzy set approach to case-based decision. In *Proc. of the Second European Workshop on Fuzzy Decision Analysis and Neural networks for Management, Planning and Optimization* , pages 1-9. Dortmund, 1997.

[Dubois and Prade, 1995] Didier Dubois and Henri Prade. Possibility theory as a basis for qualitative decision theory, *Proc. of the 14th Int. Joint Conf. on Artificial Intelligence*, pages 1924-1930, Montreal. 1995.

[Gilboa and Schmeidler, 1995] Itzhak Gilboa and David Schmeidler .Case-based Theory, *The Quarterly Journal of Economics, 110* : 607-639. 1995.

[Plaza *et al.*, 1998] Enric Plaza, Josep Ll. Arcos. Pablo Noriega and Carles Sierra. Competing Agents in Agent-Mediated Institutions. Personal Technologies, 2: 1-9.

[von Neumann and Morgenstern, 1944] John von Neumann and Oscar Morgenstern.*Theory of Games and Economic Behaviour* . Princeton Univ. Press, Princeton.

[Zapico and Godo, 1998] Adriana Zapico and Lluís Godo. On the possibilistic-based decision model: preferences under partially inconsistent belief states. *Proc of the Workshop on Decision theory meets artificial intelligence: qualitative and quantitative approaches. ECAI'98* . pages 99-109.

AUTOMATED REASONING

Reasoning about Action 1

The Ramification Problem in the Event Calculus

Murray Shanahan

Department of Electrical and Electronic Engineering,
Imperial College,
Exhibition Road,
London SW7 2BT,
England.
m.shanahan@ic.ac.uk

Abstract

Finding a solution to the frame problem that is robust in the presence of actions with indirect effects has proven to be a difficult task. Examples that feature the instantaneous propagation of interacting indirect effects are particularly taxing. This article shows that an already widely known predicate calculus formalism, namely the event calculus, can handle such examples with only minor enhancements.

Introduction

The *ramification problem*, that is to say the frame problem in the context of actions with indirect effects, has attracted considerable attention recently [McCain & Turner, 1995], [Lin, 1995], [Gustafsson & Doherty, 1996], [Sandewall, 1996], [Shanahan, 1997], [Thielscher, 1997], [Kakas & Miller, 1997], [Denecker, et al., 1998]. The purpose of this paper is to demonstrate that the standard benchmark scenarios for the ramification problem can be handled by the event calculus, as presented in Chapter 16 of [Shanahan, 1997], without introducing any significant new logical machinery.

Following [Shanahan, 1997], this article presents the event calculus in the first-order predicate calculus, augmented with circumscription. In this form, it can be used to represent a variety of phenomena, including concurrent action, actions with non-deterministic effects, and continuous change [Shanahan, 1997].

The event calculus can also be used to represent actions with indirect effects, as shown in [Shanahan, 1997]. However, certain types of domains are problematic. These involve the instantaneous propagation of interacting indirect effects, as exemplified by Thielscher's circuit benchmark [1997]. Staying within the framework of the event calculus, and introducing just two new predicates and two new axioms, this article presents a general technique for representing actions with indirect effects that encompasses such domains.

1 Event Calculus Basics

The event calculus used in this paper is drawn directly from Chapter 16 of [Shanahan, 1997]. Its ontology includes actions (or events), fluents and time points. The formalism's basic predicates are as follows. Initiates(α,β,τ) means fluent β starts to hold after action α at time τ, Terminates(α,β,τ) means fluent β ceases to hold after action α at time τ, Releases(α,β,τ) means fluent β is not subject to inertia after action α at time τ, Initially$_P$(β) means fluent β holds from time 0, Initially$_N$(β) means fluent β does not hold from time 0, Happens(α,τ) means action α occurs at time τ, and HoldsAt(β,τ) means fluent β holds at time τ.

Given a collection of *effect axioms*, expressed as Initiates, Terminates and Releases formulae, and a *narrative* of events, expressed as Happens, Initially$_N$, Initially$_P$ and temporal ordering formulae, the axioms of the event calculus yields HoldsAt formulae that tell us which fluents hold at what time points. Here are the axioms, whose conjunction will be denoted EC.

$$\text{HoldsAt}(f,t) \leftarrow \text{Initially}_P(f) \wedge \neg \, \text{Clipped}(0,f,t) \qquad \text{(EC1)}$$

$$\text{HoldsAt}(f,t2) \leftarrow \qquad \text{(EC2)}$$
$$\text{Happens}(a,t1) \wedge \text{Initiates}(a,f,t1) \wedge$$
$$t1 < t2 \wedge \neg \, \text{Clipped}(t1,f,t2)$$

$$\text{Clipped}(t1,f,t3) \leftrightarrow \qquad \text{(EC3)}$$
$$\exists \, a,t2 \, [\text{Happens}(a,t2) \wedge t1 < t2 \wedge t2 < t3 \wedge$$
$$[\text{Terminates}(a,f,t2) \vee \text{Releases}(a,f,t2)]]$$

$$\neg \, \text{HoldsAt}(f,t) \leftarrow \qquad \text{(EC4)}$$
$$\text{Initially}_N(f) \wedge \neg \, \text{Declipped}(0,f,t)$$

$$\neg \, \text{HoldsAt}(f,t2) \leftarrow \qquad \text{(EC5)}$$
$$\text{Happens}(a,t1) \wedge \text{Terminates}(a,f,t1) \wedge$$
$$t1 < t2 \wedge \neg \, \text{Declipped}(t1,f,t2)$$

$$\text{Declipped}(t1,f,t3) \leftrightarrow \qquad \text{(EC6)}$$
$$\exists \, a,t2 \, [\text{Happens}(a,t2) \wedge t1 < t2 \wedge t2 < t3 \wedge$$
$$[\text{Initiates}(a,f,t2) \vee \text{Releases}(a,f,t2)]]$$

The frame problem is overcome using circumscription.

Given a conjunction Σ of Initiates, Terminates and Releases formulae, a conjunction Δ of Initially$_P$, Initially$_N$, Happens and temporal ordering formulae, and a conjunction Ω of uniqueness-of-names axioms for actions and fluents, we're interested in,

$$\text{CIRC}[\Sigma \, ; \text{Initiates, Terminates, Releases}] \wedge$$
$$\text{CIRC}[\Delta \, ; \text{Happens}] \wedge \text{EC} \wedge \Omega.$$

In all the cases we're interested in, Σ and Δ are in a form which, according to a theorem of Lifschitz, guarantees that these circumscriptions are equivalent to the predicate completions of Initiates, Terminates, Releases and Happens.

2 State Constraints

The *ramification problem* is the frame problem for actions with indirect effects, that is to say actions with effects beyond those described explicitly by their associated effect axioms. Although it's always possible to encode these indirect effects as direct effects instead, the use of constraints describing indirect effects ensures a modular representation and can dramatically shorten an axiomatisation. One way to represent actions with indirect effects is through *state constraints*, the focus of this section. These express logical relationships that have to hold between fluents at all times.

In the event calculus, state constraints are HoldsAt formulae with a universally quantified time argument. Here's an example, whose intended meaning should be obvious.

$$\text{HoldsAt(Happy}(x),t) \leftrightarrow \qquad\qquad \text{(H1.1)}$$
$$\neg \text{ HoldsAt(Hungry}(x),t) \wedge \neg \text{ HoldsAt(Cold}(x),t)$$

Note that this formula incorporates fluents with arguments. Actions may also be parameterised, as in the following effect axioms.

$$\text{Terminates(Feed}(x),\text{Hungry}(x),t) \qquad\qquad \text{(H2.1)}$$

$$\text{Terminates(Clothe}(x),\text{Cold}(x),t) \qquad\qquad \text{(H2.2)}$$

Here's a narrative for this example.

$$\text{Initially}_P(\text{Hungry(Fred)}) \qquad\qquad \text{(H3.1)}$$

$$\text{Initially}_N(\text{Cold(Fred)}) \qquad\qquad \text{(H3.2)}$$

$$\text{Happens(Feed(Fred)},10) \qquad\qquad \text{(H3.3)}$$

Finally we need some uniqueness-of-names axioms.

$$\text{UNA[Feed, Clothe]} \qquad\qquad \text{(H4.1)}$$

$$\text{UNA[Hungry, Cold]} \qquad\qquad \text{(H4.2)}$$

The incorporation of state constraints has negligible impact on the solution to the frame problem already presented. However, state constraints must be conjoined to the theory outside the scope of any of the circumscriptions. Given a conjunction Σ of Initiates, Terminates and Releases formulae, a conjunction Δ of Initially$_P$, Initially$_N$, Happens and temporal ordering formulae, a conjunction Ψ of state constraints, and a conjunction Ω of uniqueness-of-names axioms for actions and fluents, we're interested in,

$$\text{CIRC}[\Sigma \text{ ; Initiates, Terminates, Releases}] \wedge$$
$$\text{CIRC}[\Delta \text{ ; Happens}] \wedge \text{EC} \wedge \Psi \wedge \Omega.$$

For the current example, if we let Σ be the conjunction of (H2.1) and (H2.2), Δ be the conjunction of (H3.1) to (H3.3), Ψ be (H1.1), and Ω be the conjunction of (H4.1) and (H4.2), we have,

$$\text{CIRC}[\Sigma \text{ ; Initiates, Terminates, Releases}] \wedge$$
$$\text{CIRC}[\Delta \text{ ; Happens}] \wedge \text{EC} \wedge \Psi \wedge \Omega \models$$
$$\text{HoldsAt(Happy(Fred)},11).$$

State constraints must be used with caution. As can be seen by inspection, Axioms (EC1) to (EC6) enforce the following principle: *a fluent that has been initiated/terminated directly through an effect axiom cannot then be terminated/initiated indirectly through a state constraint, unless it is released beforehand.* Similarly, a fluent that holds at time 0 because of an Initially$_P$ formula cannot then be terminated indirectly through a state constraint, unless it's released beforehand, and a fluent that does not hold at time 0 because of an Initially$_N$ formula cannot then be initiated indirectly through a state constraint, unless it's released beforehand.

Suppose, in the present example, we introduced an Upset(x) event whose effect is to terminate Happy(x). Then the addition of Happens(Upset(Fred),12) would lead to contradiction. Similarly, the addition of Initially$_N$(Happy(Fred)) would lead to contradiction.

State constraints are most useful when there is a clear division of fluents into *primitive* and *derived*. Effect axioms are used to describe the dynamics of the primitive fluents and state constraints are used to describe the derived fluents in terms of the primitive ones.

3 Effect Constraints

State constraints aren't the only way to represent actions with indirect effects, and often they aren't the right way, as emphasised by Lin [1995] and McCain and Turner [1995]. To see this, we'll take a look at the so-called "walking turkey shoot", a variation of the Yale shooting problem in which the Shoot action, as well as directly terminating the Alive fluent, indirectly terminates a fluent Walking.

The effect axioms are inherited from the Yale shooting problem.

$$\text{Initiates(Load,Loaded},t) \qquad\qquad \text{(W1.1)}$$

$$\text{Terminates(Shoot,Alive},t) \leftarrow \text{HoldsAt(Loaded},t) \quad \text{(W1.2)}$$

The narrative of events is as follows.

$$\text{Initially}_P(\text{Alive}) \qquad\qquad \text{(W2.1)}$$

$$\text{Initially}_P(\text{Loaded}) \qquad\qquad \text{(W2.2)}$$

$$\text{Initially}_P(\text{Walking}) \qquad\qquad \text{(W2.3)}$$

$$\text{Happens(Shoot,T1)} \qquad\qquad \text{(W2.4)}$$

$$\text{T1} < \text{T2} \qquad\qquad \text{(W2.5)}$$

We have two uniqueness-of-names axioms.

$$\text{UNA[Load, Shoot]} \qquad\qquad \text{(W3.1)}$$

$$\text{UNA[Loaded, Alive, Walking]} \qquad\qquad \text{(W3.2)}$$

Now, how do we represent the dependency between the Walking and Alive fluents so as to get the required indirect effect of a Shoot action? The obvious, but incorrect, way is to use a state constraint.

$$\text{HoldsAt(Alive},t) \leftarrow \text{HoldsAt(Walking},t)$$

The addition of this state constraint to the above formalisation would yield inconsistency, because it violates the rule that a fluent, in this case Walking, that holds directly through an Initially$_P$ formula cannot be terminated indirectly through a state constraint. (The same problem would arise if the Walking fluent had been initiated directly by an action.)

A better way to represent the relationship between the Walking fluent and the Alive fluent in the walking turkey shoot is through an *effect constraint*. Effect constraints are Initiates and Terminates formulae with a single universally quantified action variable. The constraint we require for this example is the following.

Terminates(a,Walking,t) ← Terminates(a,Alive,t) (W4.1)

Notice that effect constraints are weaker than state constraints: the possibility of resurrecting a corpse by making it walk, inherent in the faulty state constraint, is not inherent in this formula.

Let Σ be the conjunction of (W1.1), (W1.2) and (W4.1). Let Δ be the conjunction of (W2.1) to (W2.5), and Ω be the conjunction of (W3.1) and (W3.2). We have,

CIRC[Σ ; Initiates, Terminates, Releases] ∧
    CIRC[Δ ; Happens] ∧ EC ∧ Ω ⊨
       ¬ HoldsAt(Walking,T2).

Effect constraints are adequate for the representation of many actions with indirect effects. But there is still a class of examples for which they don't work. Consider the following benchmark problem due to Thielscher [1997]. A circuit comprising a battery, three switches, a relay, and a light bulb is wired up as in Figure 1.

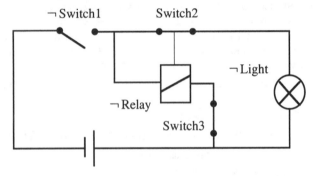

Figure 1: Thielscher's Circuit

Five fluents represent the state of each component in the circuit: Switch1, Switch2, Switch3, Relay, and Light. Their initial configuration is as in Figure 1. There are various dependencies among the fluents. The light is on if switches one and two are closed. Switch two is open if the relay is on. Finally, the relay is on if switches 1 and 3 are closed. When switch 1 is closed, the relay becomes activated, switch 2 will open, and the light stays off. The awkward nature of this example derives from the fact that closing switch 1 has one indirect effect (closing the relay, which opens switch 2) that disables another indirect effect (the light coming on).

A first, naive attempt to formalise this example might include an effect constraint like the following.

Initiates(a,Light,t) ←
    Initiates(a,Switch1,t) ∧ HoldsAt(Switch2,t)

But this formula is obviously a false start, because in this scenario, initiating Switch1 also indirectly terminates Switch2, and the event calculus axioms entail that Switch2

still holds at the instant of termination. A better attempt would be the following effect constraint.

Initiates(a,Light,t) ←
    Initiates(a,Switch1,t) ∧ HoldsAt(Switch2,t) ∧
       ¬ Terminates(a,Switch2,t)

This formula is adequate for this particular scenario, but doesn't fully capture the dependency between the fluents. Suppose, for example, that switch 1 is initially closed, while switch 2 and switch 3 are initially open. Then closing switch 2 causes the light to go on, something not captured by this constraint. We need a counterpart to the above formula for this case.

Initiates(a,Light,t) ←
    Initiates(a,Switch2,t) ∧ HoldsAt(Switch1,t) ∧
       ¬ Terminates(a,Switch1,t)

Once again, while this is adequate for the present example, it's not a general solution. In particular, neither of these formulae accounts for the possibility of independent but concurrent switch events.

In the following section, a method for representing the indirect effects of actions is presented whose generality is comparable to that of other recently published solutions to the ramification problem, but which doesn't require the development of significantly more logical machinery than is already present in the event calculus defined above.

4 Causal Constraints

Following a common practise in recent literature on the ramification problem, let's introduce some shorthand notation for expressing dependencies between fluents.

Definition 4.1. A *fluent symbol* is any string of characters starting with an upper-case letter. □

Definition 4.2. Any fluent symbol is also a *fluent formula*. If φ and ψ are fluent formulae, then so are ¬ φ, φ ∧ ψ, φ ∨ ψ, φ ← ψ, φ → ψ and φ ↔ ψ. □

Definition 4.3. Following the notation of [Denecker, *et al.*, 1998], a *causal constraint* is a formula of the form,

    <u>initiating</u> Π <u>causes</u> β

or,

    <u>initiating</u> Π <u>causes</u> ¬ β

where Π is a fluent formula and β is a fluent symbol. □

Here's a subset of the fluent dependencies in Thielscher's circuit expressed using this notation.

    <u>initiating</u> Switch1 ∧ Switch2 <u>causes</u> Light

    <u>initiating</u> Relay <u>causes</u> ¬ Switch2

    <u>initiating</u> Switch1 ∧ Switch3 <u>causes</u> Relay

There are other dependencies in the circuit. For example, this set of dependencies neglects to specify the conditions under which the light goes off. But these can be ignored for the example narrative we're interested in here.

Formulae like these are intended to have an intuitive meaning. The translation into the event calculus detailed below could be thought of as one attempt to give them a precise semantics. Alternatively, these formulae can be thought of simply as syntactic sugar for more long-winded event calculus formulae of the particular form defined below.

4.1 Causal Constraints in the Event Calculus

The key to correctly representing causal constraints in the event calculus is first to introduce new events that update each fluent whose value is dependent on other fluents, and second to write formulae ensuring that these events are triggered whenever those influencing fluents attain the appropriate values. (A related proposal is made by Pinto [1998] in the context of the situation calculus.)

To guarantee the instantaneous propagation of the effects of such events, they must be triggered not just when the influencing fluents already have their appropriate values, but also when they are *about to get* those values thanks to other events occurring at the same time. This motivates the introduction of four new predicates, Started, Stopped, Initiated and Terminated. The formula $\text{Started}(\beta,\tau)$ means that either β already holds at τ or an event occurs at τ that initiates β. Conversely, the formula $\text{Stopped}(\beta,\tau)$ means that either β already does not hold at τ or an event occurs at τ that terminates β. The predicates Started and Stopped are defined by the following axioms.

$$\text{Started}(f,t) \leftrightarrow \qquad \text{(CC1)}$$
$$\text{HoldsAt}(f,t) \lor$$
$$\exists a\, [\text{Happens}(a,t) \land \text{Initiates}(a,f,t)]$$

$$\text{Stopped}(f,t) \leftrightarrow \qquad \text{(CC2)}$$
$$\neg\, \text{HoldsAt}(f,t) \lor$$
$$\exists a\, [\text{Happens}(a,t) \land \text{Terminates}(a,f,t)]$$

Note that at the instant of a fluent's transition from one value to another, we have both Stopped and Started at the same time.

The formula $\text{Initiated}(\beta,\tau)$ means that β has been "started" at τ in the above sense, and furthermore no event occurs at τ that terminates β. Likewise, the formula $\text{Terminated}(\beta,\tau)$ means that β has been "stopped" at τ in the above sense, and no event occurs at τ that initiates β. The predicates Initiated and Terminated are defined by the following axioms.

$$\text{Initiated}(f,t) \leftrightarrow \qquad \text{(CC3)}$$
$$\text{Started}(f,t) \land$$
$$\neg\, \exists a\, [\text{Happens}(a,t) \land \text{Terminates}(a,f,t)]$$

$$\text{Terminated}(f,t) \leftrightarrow \qquad \text{(CC4)}$$
$$\text{Stopped}(f,t) \land$$
$$\neg\, \exists a\, [\text{Happens}(a,t) \land \text{Initiates}(a,f,t)]$$

To represent the causal constraints in Thielscher's circuit example, we introduce three events, LightOn, Open2 and CloseRelay, which are triggered under conditions described by the following formulae.

$$\text{Happens}(\text{LightOn},t) \leftarrow \qquad \text{(L1.1)}$$
$$\text{Stopped}(\text{Light},t) \land \text{Initiated}(\text{Switch1},t) \land$$
$$\text{Initiated}(\text{Switch2},t)$$

$$\text{Happens}(\text{Open2},t) \leftarrow \qquad \text{(L1.2)}$$
$$\text{Started}(\text{Switch2},t) \land \text{Initiated}(\text{Relay},t)$$

$$\text{Happens}(\text{CloseRelay},t) \leftarrow \qquad \text{(L1.3)}$$
$$\text{Stopped}(\text{Relay},t) \land \text{Initiated}(\text{Switch1},t) \land$$
$$\text{Initiated}(\text{Switch3},t)$$

These triggered events govern the *transition* of fluents from one value to another when certain conditions come about, as prescribed by the corresponding causal constraints. Hence the need for the Stopped and Started conditions in the above formulae. These ensure that an event occurs *only* at the time of the transition in question. The effects of these events are as follows. A Close1 event is also introduced.

$$\text{Initiates}(\text{LightOn},\text{Light},t) \qquad \text{(L2.1)}$$

$$\text{Terminates}(\text{Open2},\text{Switch2},t) \qquad \text{(L2.2)}$$

$$\text{Initiates}(\text{CloseRelay},\text{Relay},t) \qquad \text{(L2.3)}$$

$$\text{Initiates}(\text{Close1},\text{Switch1},t) \qquad \text{(L2.4)}$$

The circuit's initial configuration, as shown in Figure 1, is as follows.

$$\text{Initially}_N(\text{Switch1}) \qquad \text{(L3.1)}$$

$$\text{Initially}_P(\text{Switch2}) \qquad \text{(L3.2)}$$

$$\text{Initially}_P(\text{Switch3}) \qquad \text{(L3.3)}$$

$$\text{Initially}_N(\text{Relay}) \qquad \text{(L3.4)}$$

$$\text{Initially}_N(\text{Light}) \qquad \text{(L3.5)}$$

The only event that occurs is a Close1 event, at time 10.

$$\text{Happens}(\text{Close1},10) \qquad \text{(L3.6)}$$

Two uniqueness-of-names axioms are required.

$$\text{UNA}[\text{LightOn, Close1, Open2, CloseRelay}] \qquad \text{(L4.1)}$$

$$\text{UNA}[\text{Switch1, Switch2, Switch3, Relay, Light}] \qquad \text{(L4.2)}$$

As the following proposition shows, this formalisation of Thielscher's circuit yields the required logical consequences. In particular, the relay is activated when switch 1 is closed, causing switch 2 to open, and the light does not come on.

Proposition 4.4. Let Σ be the conjunction of (L2.1) to (L2.4), Δ be the conjunction of (L1.1) to (L1.3) with (L3.1) to (L3.6), Ψ be the conjunction of (CC1) to (CC4), and Ω be the conjunction of (L4.1) and (L4.2). We have,

$$\text{CIRC}[\Sigma\,;\,\text{Initiates, Terminates, Releases}] \land$$
$$\text{CIRC}[\Delta\,;\,\text{Happens}] \land \text{EC} \land \Psi \land \Omega \models$$
$$\text{HoldsAt}(\text{Relay},20) \land \neg\, \text{HoldsAt}(\text{Switch2},20) \land$$
$$\neg\, \text{HoldsAt}(\text{Light},20).$$

Proof. From $\text{CIRC}[\Sigma\,;\,\text{Initiates, Terminates, Releases}]$ we get the completions of Initiates, Terminates and Releases. From $\text{CIRC}[\Delta\,;\,\text{Happens}]$ we get the completion of Happens, namely,

$$\text{Happens}(a,t) \leftrightarrow \qquad [4.5]$$
$$[a = \text{Close1} \land t = 10] \lor$$
$$[a = \text{LightOn} \land \text{Stopped}(\text{Light},t) \land$$
$$\text{Initiated}(\text{Switch1},t) \land \text{Initiated}(\text{Switch2},t)] \lor$$
$$[a = \text{Open2} \land \text{Started}(\text{Switch2},t) \land \text{Initiated}(\text{Relay},t)] \lor$$
$$[a = \text{CloseRelay} \land \text{Stopped}(\text{Relay},t) \land$$
$$\text{Initiated}(\text{Switch1},t) \land \text{Initiated}(\text{Switch3},t)].$$

At the time of the first event, the fluents Switch2 and Switch3 hold and the fluents Switch1, Relay and Light don't hold.

First we prove that the Close1 event at time 10 is the first event. Consider any t < 10. There can't be a Close1 event at t, since, from [4.5], the only Close1 event is at 10. Since we have ¬ HoldsAt(Switch1,t) and only a Close1 event can initiate Switch1, we have ¬ Initiated(Switch1,t), so, from [4.5], there can't be a LightOn or CloseRelay event at t. Since we have ¬ HoldsAt(Relay,t) and there can't be a CloseRelay event at t, we have ¬ Initiated(Relay,t), and therefore, from [4.5], there can't be an Open2 event at t. From [4.5], this exhausts all the possible types of event, so there can't be any event occurrence at time t. So the Close1 event at time 10 is the first event.

Now we prove that a Close1 event, a CloseRelay event and an Open2 event all occur at time 10, but that no LightOn event occurs at time 10. We know directly from [4.5] that a Close1 event occurs at 10. Therefore, since there is no type of event that can terminate Switch1, we have Initiated(Switch1,10), given (L2.4). We know that Stopped(Relay,10) since we have ¬ HoldsAt(Relay,10), and since we have HoldsAt(Switch3,10), we also have Initiated(Switch3,10). So, from [4.5], we know that a CloseRelay event occurs at 10. Since a CloseRelay event occurs at 10 and there is no type of event that can initiate Relay, we have Initiated(Relay,10), given (L2.3). We also know that HoldsAt(Switch2,10) and therefore Started(Switch2,10). So, from [4.5], we know that an Open2 event occurs at time 10. Since there is an Open2 event at 10, which, from (L2.2), terminates Switch2, we have ¬ Initiated(Switch2,10), and therefore, from [4.5] there cannot be a LightOn event at 10.

Using a similar argument to the paragraph before last, we can show that no events occur after time 10. Given the events that occur at time 10, it's then straightforward to prove, from Axioms (EC2) and (EC5), that the fluent Relay holds at time 20, but the fluents Switch2 and Light do not.□

Let's briefly consider a couple of minor variations on this example. First, suppose we augment the formalisation with a Close2 action which initiates Switch2. Then the addition of the formula Happens(Close2,15) will give rise to a contradiction, since we would have both a Close2 event at time 15 and, from (L1.2), an Open2 event, enabling us to prove, for any time t after 15, both HoldsAt(Switch2,t) and ¬ HoldsAt(Switch2,15). In other words, switch 2 cannot be manually closed while switches 1 and 3 are closed, thanks to the relay.

Now consider the original narrative of events, but with a different initial situation, one in which switch 3 is open, then, as desired, we get a different result: the relay isn't activated, switch 2 doesn't open, so the light does come on.

Initially$_N$(Switch1)	(L5.1)
Initially$_P$(Switch2)	(L5.2)
Initially$_N$(Switch3)	(L5.3)
Initially$_N$(Relay)	(L5.4)
Initially$_N$(Light)	(L5.5)

Proposition 4.6. Retaining Σ, Δ, Ψ and Ω as above, let Δ be the conjunction of (L5.1) to (L5.5) with (L3.5). Then we have,

CIRC[Σ ; Initiates, Terminates, Releases] $\wedge$
   CIRC[Δ ; Happens] $\wedge$ EC $\wedge$ Ψ $\wedge$ Ω $\vDash$
HoldsAt(Light,20).

Proof. The proof is similar to that of Proposition 4.4.   □

5 From Causal Constraints to Event Calculus

This section presents a general translation from the shorthand notation for causal constraints presented above into the event calculus, along the lines suggested by the preceding example.

Definition 5.1. A *negated fluent symbol* is a fluent formula of the form ¬ β where β is a fluent symbol.   □

First we define the function T_c, which translates a single causal constraint into a pair of event calculus formulae.

Definition 5.2. Let ψ be a causal constraint of the form,

   initiating Π causes γ

where Π is a fluent formula and γ is either a fluent symbol or a negated fluent symbol. The *translation* $T_c(\psi)$ *of* ψ *with new action name* α is the pair $\langle\sigma,\delta\rangle$, where δ and σ are defined as follows. Let Π' be Π with every negated fluent symbol ¬ β replaced by Terminated(β,t) and every other fluent symbol β replaced by Initiated(β,t). If γ is a negated fluent symbol ¬ β, then σ is,

   Terminates(α,β,t)

and δ is,

   Happens(α,t) ← Started(β,t) $\wedge$ Π'.

Otherwise σ is,

   Initiates(α,γ,t)

and δ is,

   Happens(α,t) ← Stopped(γ,t) $\wedge$ Π'.   □

Next we define the function Tc*, which translates a set of causal constraints into a pair of conjunctions of event calculus formulae.

Definition 5.3. Let Φ be a finite set of causal constraints {ψ_1, ..., ψ_n}. The *translation* $T_c^*(\Phi)$ *of* Φ *with new action names* α_1 to α_n is the pair $\langle\Sigma,\Delta\rangle$, where Σ is $\sigma_1 \wedge ... \wedge \sigma_n$ and Δ is $\delta_1 \wedge ... \wedge \delta_n$, given that for any $1 \leq i \leq n$, $T_c(\psi_i)$ with new action name α_i is $\langle\sigma_i,\delta_i\rangle$.   □

5.1 Limitations: The Gear Wheels Example

Although the technique described here can represent the indirect effects of many different types of actions, it does *not* work well in scenarios involving mutually dependent fluents, such as the following example, which is taken from [Denecker, *et al.*, 1998]. There are two interlocking gear wheels. If one is turning, the other must be turning, and if one is stationary, the other must be stationary. The example is formalised using two fluents, Turning1 and Turning2.

   initiating Turning1 causes Turning2

   initiating Turning2 causes Turning1

   initiating ¬ Turning1 causes ¬ Turning2

initiating ¬ Turning2 causes ¬ Turning1

The proposed event calculus translation of these causal constraints does not yield the desired conclusions, as it cannot rule out phantom self-starting events that cause the wheel to turn. (Note, however, that this example can be correctly formalised using the state constraints of Section 2.) As illustrated in the next section, other examples with cycles of dependencies are handled more satisfactorily.

6 Vicious Cycles

Consider the modification of Thielscher's circuit depicted in Figure 2. This circuit incorporates a potentially vicious cycle of fluent dependencies. If switch 1 is closed, the relay is activated, opening switch 2, which prevents the relay from being activated. Given Axioms (CC1) to (CC4) in their present form, the formalisation of this scenario using causal constraints will yield inconsistency.

Here are the causal constraints Φ.

initiating Relay causes ¬ Switch2

initiating Switch1 ∧ Switch2 ∧ Switch3 causes Relay

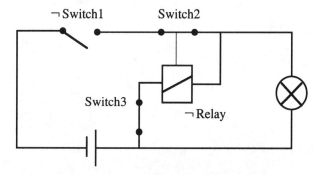

Figure 2: A Modification of Thielscher's Circuit

Let $\langle \Sigma, \Delta \rangle$ be $T_c^*(\Phi)$ with new action names Open2 and CloseRelay. Then Δ is the conjunction of the following Happens formulae, and Σ is the conjunction of the following Initiates and Terminates formulae.

Happens(Open2,t) ←   (V1.1)
   Started(Switch2,t) ∧ Initiated(Relay,t)

Happens(CloseRelay,t) ←   (V1.2)
   Stopped(Relay,t) ∧ Initiated(Switch1,t) ∧
   Initiated(Switch2,t) ∧ Initiated(Switch3,t)

Terminates(Open2,Switch2,t)   (V2.1)

Initiates(CloseRelay,Relay,t)   (V2.2)

Initiates(Close1,Switch1,t)   (V2.3)

The circuit's initial configuration is as follows.

$\text{Initially}_N(\text{Switch1})$ (V3.1)

$\text{Initially}_P(\text{Switch2})$ (V3.2)

$\text{Initially}_P(\text{Switch3})$ (V3.3)

$\text{Initially}_N(\text{Relay})$ (V3.4)

The only event that occurs is a Close1 event, at time 10.

Happens(Close1,10)   (V3.5)

Here are the customary uniqueness-of-names axioms.

UNA[Close1, Open2, CloseRelay]   (V4.1)

UNA[Switch1, Switch2, Switch3, Relay]   (V4.2)

Proposition 6.1. Let Σ be the conjunction of (V1.1) and (V1.2), Δ be the conjunction of (V1.1) and (V1.2) with (V3.1) to (V3.5), Ψ be the conjunction of (CC1) to (CC4), and Ω be the conjunction of (V4.1) and (V4.2). The following formula is inconsistent.

CIRC[Σ ; Initiates, Terminates, Releases] ∧
   CIRC[Δ ; Happens] ∧ EC ∧ Ψ ∧ Ω.

Proof. From CIRC[Δ ; Happens] we get,

Happens(a,t) ↔   [6.2]
   [a = Close1 ∧ t = 10] ∨
   [a = Open2 ∧ Started(Switch2,t) ∧ Initiated(Relay,t)] ∨
   [a = CloseRelay ∧ Stopped(Relay,t) ∧
     Initiated(Switch1,t) ∧ Initiated(Switch2,t) ∧
     Initiated(Switch3,t)].

Using the techniques of the proof of Proposition 4.4, we can show that the formula entails that the first event occurs at time 10. At time 10, Switch2 and Switch3 hold, but Switch1 and Relay do not hold. We know that a Close1 event occurs at 10. Now suppose no Open2 event occurs at 10. Then, since Open2 is the only event type that can terminate Switch2, we have Initiated(Switch2,10), which, since we have Stopped(Relay,10), Initiated(Switch1,10) and Initiated(Switch3,10), entails that a CloseRelay event occurs at 10 from [6.2]. But if a CloseRelay event occurs at 10, then we have Initiated(Relay,10) and, from [6.2], an Open2 event also occurs at 10, which contradicts out initial assumption.

So an Open2 event must occur at 10. But then, from [6.2], we must have Initiated(Relay,10). From (CC3) and [6.2], this entails that a CloseRelay event must occur at 10. From [6.2], this gives us Initiated(Switch2,10). But since an Open2 event occurs at 10, which terminates Switch2, this contradicts (CC3). Therefore the formula has no models. □

Note that the cycle in this example is only "dangerous" if switch 3 is initially closed. If switch 3 is initially open, the correspondingly modified theory is consistent, and yields the expected conclusion that the relay remains inactive after the Close1 event.

Arguably, inconsistency is not the most desirable response to an example with a vicious cycle. A formalisation that yielded non-determinism instead would at least permit other useful conclusions to be drawn. Moreover, suppose the initial state of switch 3 is unknown, and (V3.3) is omitted. Then, the threat of inconsistency ensures that $\text{Initially}_N(\text{Switch3})$ follows from the theory, even though no Initially_N formula to that effect is included. This seems a little counter-intuitive.

On the other hand, the aim of formalisation should be to avoid inconsistency. The fact that inconsistency can result here simply from selecting an inappropriate initial state for switch 3 indicates that the wrong level of abstraction has been chosen for representing this particular domain. If we want to represent it in earnest (not just for illustrative purposes), a level of abstraction should be chosen in which every possible narrative that is itself consistent results in a consistent theory. (In the present case, this would demand the inclusion of explicit delays in the model.)

Concluding Remarks

The works of Lin [1995], of Gustafsson and Doherty [1996], and of Thielscher [1997] all share an important feature with the present paper. In each case, an existing predicate calculus-based action formalism, respectively the situation calculus, the fluent calculus, and PMON, is extended to handle actions with indirect effects. Moreover, in [Lin, 1995] and [Gustaffson & Doherty, 1996], as in the present article, circumscription policies are deployed which minimise parts of the theory separately.

The solution to the ramification problem offered in the present article is also based on an existing predicate calculus action formalism, namely the event calculus. As such, it doesn't demand the introduction of any new semantic machinery. Moreover, the proposal is conservative in the sense that it only adds to the existing calculus, the extension comprising four new axioms and four new predicates. With these axioms in place, the proposed solution is little more than a novel style of writing certain event calculus formulae.

No formal assessment has yet been undertaken of the range of applicability of the proposed solution to the ramification problem, as recommended by [Sandewall, 1996]. This, along with a more formal comparison with other approaches, would be a good topic for future research.

Acknowledgments

Thanks to Patrick Doherty, Rob Miller, Michael Thielscher, Kristof Van Belleghem and Mark Witkowski for discussions related to the topic of this paper. Thanks also to the anonymous referees who spotted flaws in an earlier version of the paper.

References

[Denecker, *et al.*, 1998] M.Denecker, D.Theseider Dupré and K.Van Belleghem, An Inductive Definition Approach to Ramifications, *Electronic Transactions on Artificial Intelligence*, to appear.

[Gustafsson & Doherty, 1996] J.Gustafsson and P.Doherty, Embracing Occlusion in Specifying the Indirect Effects of Actions, *Proceedings 1996 Knowledge Representation Conference (KR 96)*, pp. 87–98.

[Kakas & Miller, 1997] A.Kakas and R.S.Miller, Reasoning about Actions, Narrative and Ramification, *Electronic Transactions on Artificial Intelligence*, vol. 1 (1997), pp. 39–72.

[Lin, 1995] F.Lin, Embracing Causality in Specifying the Indirect Effects of Actions, *Proceedings IJCAI 95*, pp. 1985–1991.

[McCain & Turner, 1995] N.McCain and H.Turner, A Causal Theory of Ramifications and Qualifications, *Proceedings IJCAI 95*, pp. 1978–1984.

[Pinto, 1998] J.Pinto, Concurrent Actions and Interacting Effects, *Proceedings 1998 Knowledge Representation Conference (KR 98)*, pp. 292–303.

[Sandewall, 1996] E.Sandewall, Assessments of Ramification Methods that Use Static Domain Constraints, *Proceedings 1996 Knowledge Representation Conference (KR 96)*, pp. 99–110.

[Shanahan, 1997] M.P.Shanahan, *Solving the Frame Problem: A Mathematical Investigation of the Common Sense Law of Inertia*, MIT Press, 1997.

[Thielscher, 1997] M.Thielscher, Ramification and Causality, *Artificial Intelligence*, vol. 89 (1997), pp. 317–364.

Logic-Based Subsumption Architecture

Eyal Amir and Pedrito Maynard-Reid II
Computer Science Department
Stanford University
Stanford, CA 94305
{eyala,pedmayn}@cs.stanford.edu

Abstract

We describe a logic-based AI architecture based on Brooks' subsumption architecture. In this architecture, we axiomatize different layers of control in First-Order Logic (FOL) and use independent theorem provers to derive each layer's outputs given its inputs. We implement the subsumption of lower layers by higher layers using circumscription to make assumptions in lower layers, and nonmonotonically retract them when higher layers draw new conclusions. We also give formal semantics to our approach. Finally, we describe four layers designed for the task of robot control and an experiment that empirically shows the feasibility of using fully expressive FOL theorem provers for robot control with our architecture.

1 Introduction

In [Brooks, 1986], Rodney Brooks provided a decomposition of the problem of robot control into layers corresponding to levels of behavior, rather than a sequential, functional form. Within this setting, he introduced the idea of subsumption, that is, that more complex layers not only depend on lower, more reactive layers, but could also influence their behavior. The resulting architecture was one that could simultaneously service multiple, potentially conflicting goals in a reactive fashion, giving precedence to high-priority goals.

Because of its realization in hardware, the architecture lacks declarativeness, making it difficult to implement higher-level reasoning and making its semantics unclear. The increasing hardware complexity with new layers introduces scaling problems. And, relying on hardware specifications, the architecture is specifically oriented towards robot control and is not applicable to software-based intelligent agents. The problem of extending similar architectures to more complex tasks and goals and to agents that are not necessarily physical has already been raised and discussed in general terms by [Minsky, 1985] and [Stein, 1997], but to our knowledge, no practical AI architecture has been developed along these lines.

In this paper we describe an architecture that is modeled in the spirit of Brooks' subsumption architecture but relies on a logical framework and has wider applicability and extendibility in the manner described above. Our *Logic-Based Subsumption Architecture* (LSA) includes a set of First-Order Logic (FOL) theories, each corresponding to a layer in the sense of Brooks' architecture. Each layer is supplied with a separate theorem prover, allowing the system of layers to operate concurrently. We use nonmonotonic reasoning to model the connections between the theories. In addition, by allowing the layers to make nonmonotonic assumptions, we have made each layer's performance independent of the performance of other layers, thus supporting reactivity.

We demonstrate our architecture by modeling four layers for the task of robot control, the bottom two of which are Brooks' first two layers. We show empirically that the layer in greatest need of reactivity is sufficiently fast (0.1–0.3 seconds per control-loop cycle). This result shows that general-purpose theorem provers can be used in intelligent agents without sacrificing reactivity.

The remainder of the paper is organized as follows: After giving a brief introduction to Brooks' system and behavioral decomposition, we describe the LSA and give formal semantics to the approach using circumscription. We then describe the robot control system we have implemented using the architecture. We conclude with a discussion of implementation issues, comparisons to related work and a description of future directions.

2 Subsumption and Decomposition

2.1 Brooks' Subsumption Architecture

Brooks showed that it is often advantageous to decompose a system into parallel tasks or behaviors of increasing levels of competence rather than the standard functional decomposition. Whereas a typical functional decomposition might resemble the sequence

sensors → perception → modeling → planning → task recognition → motor control,

Brooks would decompose the same domain as

avoid objects < wander < explore < build maps < monitor changes < identify objects < plan actions < reason about object behavior where < denotes increasing levels of competence. Potential benefits from this approach include increased robustness, concurrency support, incremental construction and ease of testing.

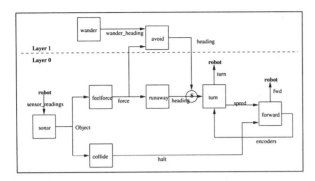

Figure 1: Layers 0 and 1 of Brooks' subsumption architecture robot control system.

In general, the different layers are not completely independent. In the decomposition above, wandering and exploring depend on the robot's ability to avoid objects. But the system may be able to service multiple goals in parallel, despite the dependence. The goals of one layer will occasionally conflict with those of another layer, in which case higher-priority goals should override lower-priority ones. Consequently, the subsumption architecture provides mechanisms by which higher, more competent layers may observe the state of lower layers, inhibit their outputs and override their inputs, thus adjusting their behavior. High-priority tasks in lower layers (such as reflexively halting when an object is dead ahead) will still have a default precedence if the designer disallows any tampering with these particular tasks.

Brooks implemented a control system of layers corresponding to the first three levels of competence described above (avoidance, wandering and exploration). The first two layers are shown in Figure 1. Briefly, the `avoid` layer endows the robot with obstacle avoidance capabilities by moving it in directions that avoid obstacles as much as possible and forcing it to stop if a head-on collision is imminent. The `wander` layer causes the robot to move around aimlessly when it is not otherwise occupied. The `explore` layer gives the robot some primitive goal-directed behavior by periodically choosing a location in the distance and heading the robot towards it if idle. While in explore mode, this layer inhibits the `wander` layer so that the robot remains on track towards its destination. When either the `wander` or the `explore` layer is active, it overrides the default heading computed by the `avoid` layer, but the `avoid` layer still ensures that the robot does not have a collision. We refer the reader to [Brooks, 1986] for further details.

2.2 Behavioral Decomposition

The first important idea we borrow from Brooks' architecture is that of decomposing the domain along behavioral lines rather than along the standard, sequen-

tial functional lines. A *Logic-Based Subsumption Architecture* (LSA) is composed of a sequence of FOL theories. Each represents a layer with an axiomatization of the layer's behavior, that is, the layer's inputs, outputs (goal), state and any dependencies between them. The inputs are axioms coming from either the sensors or higher layers. The outputs are proved theorems determined by running a separate theorem prover for that layer only. These outputs may be sent to lower layers or to the robot effectors.

Because the axiomatization of a layer is usually much smaller than that of the whole system, each cycle is less computationally expensive than running one theorem prover over the whole compound axiomatization, leading to an overall higher performance. Another advantage of the layer-decoupling is the possibility of achieving more reactive behavior. As in Brooks' system, lower layers controlling basic behaviors are trusted to be autonomous and do not need to wait on results from higher layers (they assume some of them by default) before being able to respond to situations. Because these layers typically have simpler axiomatizations, and given the default assumptions, the cycle time to compute their outputs can be shorter than that of the more complex layers.

2.3 Subsumption Principles

Of course, the layers are *not* fully independent. We adopt the view that, together with the task-based decomposition idea, the coupling approach represented by subsumption in the subsumption architecture is an important and natural paradigm for intelligent agents in general, and robot control in particular (see [Stein, 1997]). We want each layer in an LSA to be able to communicate with those underneath it in the hierarchy.

In general, however, when one layer overrides another, the two disagree on what some particular input should be. In a classical logic setting, the two corresponding theories will be inconsistent. We need to formalize the higher-layer theory's precedence over the lower layer's in such a way that (a) if there is no conflict, both layers keep their facts and the higher layer asserts its relevant conclusions in the lower layer, and (b) if there is conflict, the lower layer tries to give up some assumptions to accommodate the higher layer's conclusions. A number of techniques developed in the logic community are applicable, e.g., nonmonotonic techniques and belief revision. We have chosen to use circumscription, although other approaches may be equally interesting and appropriate.

3 Logical Subsumption

This section describes in detail how we implement the principles discussed above.

3.1 Basic Machinery

We distinguish three parts of the logical theory associated with each layer: (1) the *Body* of the layer, (2) the *Sensory and Input Latches*, and (3) the *Output*. The *Body* of the layer is the invariant theory for that layer.

The *Latches* are used to accept the input and replace it at the beginning of every cycle (rather than accumulate it). The *Output* is the set of *goal* sentences proved from the layer's theory (including the latches).

The processing loop of each layer proceeds as follows: First, collect any pertinent sensor data and assert it in the form of logical axioms. Simultaneously, assert any inputs from higher-level theories. The theorem prover of that layer then attempts to prove the layer's goal. Upon reaching the conclusions, transmit the relevant ones either to the layer below or (in the case of layer 0) to the robot manipulators. Figure 2 illustrates this process.

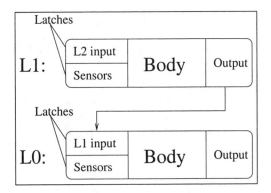

Figure 2: A detailed look at two layers.

3.2 Circumscription-Based Subsumption

In the logical paradigm, McCarthy's circumscription [McCarthy, 1986] is one of the first major nonmonotonic reasoning tools. McCarthy's circumscription formula

$$Circ[A(P, Z); P; Z] = \\ A(P, Z) \wedge \forall p, z \ (A(p, z) \Rightarrow \neg(p < P))$$

says that in the theory A, with parameter relations and function sequences P, Z, P is a minimal element such that $A(P, Z)$ still holds while Z is allowed to vary in order to allow P to become smaller.

Take, for example, the theory $T \equiv block(B_1) \wedge block(B_2)$. The circumscription of $block$ in T, varying nothing, is $Circ[T; block;] = T \wedge \forall p \ [T_{[block/p]} \Rightarrow \neg(p < block)]$ and is equivalent to $\forall x \ (block(x) \Leftrightarrow (x = B_1 \vee x = B_2))$. By minimizing $block$, we have concluded that there are no other blocks in the world besides those mentioned in the original theory T.

In the LSA, we use circumscription for two distinct tasks: assuming defaults in the layers and giving semantics to the system of layers as one big logical system.

To implement the idea of subsumption, we let each layer make default "assumptions" about the inputs that later may be adjusted by other (higher-level) layers. These assumptions take the form of the Closed-World Assumption (CWA) by minimizing a predicate in the layer's input language (Extended CWA, a generalization of CWA, was shown to be equivalent to circumscription [Gelfond *et al.*, 1989]).

More formally, let $Layer_i$ be the theory of layer i, and C_i, a set of predicates in $\mathcal{L}(Layer_i)$, for which we wish to assert CWA. Then, subsumption is achieved for layer i by using the parallel circumscription policy

$$Circ[Layer_i; C_i; \mathcal{L}(Layer_i)]$$

When implemented, this formula often can be substituted with a simple (external to the logic) mechanical interference determining the value of the minimized predicates; we discuss this issue in section 5.

3.3 Semantics for LSA

If we ignore the time differences between the theorem provers in different layers and consider the entire system of layers as one logical theory, we can give the system a simple semantics. Let $Layer_i$ be the theory of layer i (including any CWA as a FOL schemata), $G_i(x)$ be the goal formula of layer i (i.e., the formula that we try to prove in that layer) and $G'_i(f_i(x))$ be its translation to $Layer_{i-1}$'s input. We call such a system of layers T a *layered theory*. For $\varphi \in \mathcal{L}(Layer_i)$, we write $T \vdash \varphi$ if the mechanical entailment we described above derives φ.

Let $\varphi_i^{ab} = \forall x. \neg ab_i(x) \Rightarrow (G_i(x) \Rightarrow G'_i(f_i(x)))$, where every ab_i is a relation symbol that does not show in T.

Definition 3.1 (Semantics for Layered Theories) $\mathcal{M}$ *is a model of the layered theory T (written $\mathcal{M} \models_c T$) iff it is a first-order model of the circumscriptions*

$$\bigwedge_{i \leq n} Circ[Layer_i \cup Layer_{i-1} \cup \{\varphi_i\}; ab_i; \mathcal{L}(Layer_{i-1})]$$

This semantics assumes (1) we are interested in the set of results $\varphi \in \mathcal{L}(Layer_i)$ for some i (as opposed to $\varphi \in \mathcal{L}(Layer_i \cup Layer_j)$, for example) and (2) all the symbols in the various theories are different (e.g., the symbol 1 actually has the name $L_0.1$ in layer 0 and $L_2.1$ in layer 2).

Let $\mathcal{L}_i^I$ be the FOL language including only G_i, $=$, and the constant and function symbols of $\mathcal{L}(Layer_i)$. For a sentence $\phi \in \mathcal{L}_i^I$, let ϕ' be the translation of ϕ by replacing G with G' and every term t by $t' = f_i(t)$. The following theorem validates the semantics for our proof-theoretic system of transferring goals from one layer to another.

Theorem 3.2 (Completeness) *Assume that $T = \{Layer_i\}_{i \leq m}$ is a layered theory and φ is a formula in the language $\mathcal{L}(Layer_0)$. If $T \vdash \varphi$, then there is $k \geq 0$ and a sequence of sentences $\varphi_k, \ldots, \varphi_0$ s.t. $\varphi = \varphi_0$, $Layer_k \models \varphi_k$, and $1 \leq \forall i \leq k \ \varphi_i \in \mathcal{L}_i^I$ and $Layer_{i-1} \models \varphi'_i \Rightarrow \varphi_{i-1}$.*

Our LSA obeys this semantics, assuming that transferring a single instantiation of the goal between any pair of layers is sufficient. In case one layer proves only a disjunction of goal instantiations, we need to refine our LSA to support such a transfer, but this refinement can be done for any size of disjunctions. Additionally, there is no need to consider quantification in our LSA since we assume skolemization of the clauses (see Section 5).

We omit the proof for lack of space, but mention that it relies on Craig's Interpolation Theorem for FOL and on the following lemma.

Lemma 3.3 *If* $Circ[Layer_1 \cup Layer_0 \cup \{\varphi_1^{ab}\}; ab_1;$ $\mathcal{L}(Layer_0)] \not\models \forall x \neg ab_1(x)$, *then there is a formula* $\phi \in \mathcal{L}_1^I$, *negative in* G_1, *s.t.* $Layer_1 \not\models \phi$ *and* $Layer_0 \models \phi'$.

Furthermore, if $Layer_1'$ *is the result of adding all such* ϕ's *to* $Layer_1$, *then* $Circ[Layer_1' \cup Layer_0 \cup \{\varphi_1^{ab}\}; ab_1; \mathcal{L}(Layer_0)] \models \forall x \neg ab(x)$.

For soundness, we need to assume that the set of layers of T is consistent with $\{\varphi_i, \forall x \neg ab_i(x)\}_{i \leq n}$ and that all the circumscriptions in $\models_c$ for T have *smooth* preference relations (i.e., every model is either minimal or has a minimal model that is preferred to it).

Theorem 3.4 (Soundness) *Assume that there are* $\varphi_k, ..., \varphi_l$ *s.t.* $k \geq l$ *and* $Layer_k \models \varphi_k$ *and* $k \geq \forall i > l$, $\varphi_i \in L_i^I$, *positive in* G_i, *and* $Layer_i \models \varphi_{i+1}' \Rightarrow \varphi_i$, *where* φ_i' *is the translation of* φ_i *from layer* i *to layer* $i - 1$. *Then,* $T \models_c \varphi_l$.

4 A Model of Brooks' System

We briefly describe the logical theories for a control system we have implemented for a robot operating in a multi-story office building. The first two layers correspond roughly to the first three layers in Brooks' system. For simplicity, we list only selected axioms from the theories and refer the reader to the full version of the paper for the complete system.

We assume the architecture is used to control a cylindrical robot with sonar sensors on its perimeter and wheels that control its motion. We also assume that it is able to determine its current location and orientation.

4.1 LAYER 0: Obstacle-avoidance

Layer 0 takes its input, asserted in the form of the axiom schema $SonarReading(sonar\_number) = dist$, from the physical sonars and translates it into a map of objects, recording their distance and direction (relative to the robot)[1]. It may also discover "virtual" objects by way of layer 1's subsumption latch.

$$\forall dist, dir. \ (\exists sonar\_number.$$
$$SonarReading(sonar\_number) = dist \wedge$$
$$SonarDirection(sonar\_number) = dir \wedge$$
$$dist \geq 0 \wedge dir > -\pi \wedge dir \leq \pi) \Rightarrow$$
$$(\exists obj. \ Object(obj) \wedge Distance(obj) = dist \wedge$$
$$Direction(obj) = dir).$$

Layer 0 checks to see if it has detected objects lying directly in front of it, and halts the robot if it has.

$$ObjectAhead \iff$$
$$(\exists obj. \ (Object(obj) \wedge Distance(obj) < MIN\_DIST \wedge$$
$$Direction(obj) = dir \wedge dir > -\frac{\pi}{4} \wedge dir < \frac{\pi}{4}).$$

$$ObjectAhead \Rightarrow HaltRobot.$$

[1] The robot's 0-radians reference point is straight ahead, the front sonar is numbered 0, and the sonars are numbered consecutively, counter-clockwise from 0 to $NSONARS - 1$.

Using the map, layer 0 executes the function *GetForce*, computing the combined "repulsive force" exerted on the robot by the detected objects as *Force_direction* and *Force_strength*. It uses the former to specify a heading angle for the robot away from this force. Once headed in the right direction, the robot is commanded to move away at a speed proportional to the strength of the force, slowing down as it moves farther away from the objects.

$$Heading\_angle = (Force\_direction \mod 2\pi) - \pi.$$
$$Heading\_speed = Force\_strength.$$

$$NeedTurn(Heading\_angle) \Rightarrow Turn(Heading\_angle).$$

$$\neg HaltRobot \wedge \neg NeedTurn(Heading\_angle) \wedge$$
$$NeedFwd(Heading\_speed) \Rightarrow Fwd(Heading\_speed).$$
$$HaltRobot \vee NeedTurn(Heading\_angle) \Rightarrow Fwd(0).$$

During each cycle of layer 0, it applies the CWA to the symbols *HaltRobot*, *Object*, *Distance*, *Direction* in the input language. It then uses its theorem prover to try to prove $Fwd(speed)$ and $Turn(angle)$, where *speed* and *angle* are instantiated by the proof. The results are translated into the appropriate actuator commands.

4.2 LAYER 1: Destination-seeking

Layer 1 supports simple movements towards a goal location, more closely resembling the exploration layer of Brooks' system than the wandering layer. Given a particular pair of coordinates specified by the input *MoveCmd* from layer 2 and given the robot's current location,[2] it makes a simple calculation to find in which of the eight quadrants surrounding the robot this goal position is, and asserts the existence of a "virtual pushing object" in the opposing quadrant.

$$Object(PUSH\_OBJECT).$$

$$\forall x_0, y_0, x, y. \ CurrLoc = \{x_0, y_0\} \wedge MoveCmd(x, y) \Rightarrow$$
$$HasPushObject(Quadrant(x_0 - x, y_0 - y)).$$

$$\forall quad. \ HasPushObject(quad) \Rightarrow$$
$$Direction(PUSH\_OBJECT) = quad * \frac{2\pi}{NQUADS} \wedge$$
$$Distance(PUSH\_OBJECT) = PUSH\_OBJ\_DIST.$$

During each cycle, layer 1's theorem prover attempts to prove $Object(obj)$, $Direction(obj) = dir$, and $Distance(obj) = dist$, and introduces them into layer 0's input latch if successful. The avoidance capabilities of layer 0 effectively push the robot away from the object in the direction of the goal, although it may deviate from a direct path if there are physical objects in the vicinity.

4.3 LAYER 2: Mid-Level Planning

Layer 2 performs two tasks: (1) translate logical locations into Cartesian coordinates and (2) reason in the situation calculus [McCarthy and Hayes, 1969] about using the elevators.

[2] These coordinates are with respect to the fixed coordinate system of the domain.

The inputs for this layer are the current location data from the robot ($CurrLandmark$) and the output from layer 3 ($TargetLandmark$). During each cycle, it tries to plan for the next landmark and prove $MoveCmd(next\_landmark)$.

$Cartesian(RM218, [0, 0]).$

$\forall x, y, lm.\ \neg NeedElevPlan \wedge TargetLandmark(lm) \wedge$
$Cartesian(lm, [x, y]) \Rightarrow MoveCmd(x, y).$

$\forall x, y, lm, s_{l1}, inter, s_1.\ NeedElevPlan \wedge$
$TargetLandmark(lm) \wedge At(ROBOT, lm, s_{l1}) \wedge$
$FirstSit(s_{l1}, s_1) \wedge At(ROBOT, inter, s_1) \wedge$
$Cartesian(inter, [x, y]) \Rightarrow MoveCmd(x, y).$

The situation calculus theory includes three fluents: the two elevators' locations and the robot's location (we explicitly state frame axioms). Since the domain and depth are small, planning here is simple.

4.4   LAYER 3: High-level planning

Layer 3 performs high-level robot motion planning using situation calculus. Here there is only one fluent (the robot's location); thus, deeper reasoning can be performed in a reasonable time.

The input for this layer is the current location of the robot. The goal is $TargetLandmark(landmark)$.

$Room(RM218) \wedge Room(ELEV1) \ldots$
$Corridor(C2A1) \wedge Corridor(C2AELEV) \ldots$
$InCorridor(Front(RM218), C2A1) \ldots$

$\forall l, l', s.At(ROBOT, l, s) \wedge VConnected(l, l') \Rightarrow$
$At(ROBOT, l', Result(MoveTo(l'), s)).$

$\forall l.Room(l) \Rightarrow VLinked(l, Front(l)).$

5   Implementation Issues

We have implemented the above theory using the PTTP theorem prover ([Stickel, 1988], [Stickel, 1992]) on a Sun Sparc station, running Quintus Prolog as the underlying interpreter for PTTP. PTTP (Prolog Technology Theorem Prover) is a model-elimination theorem prover. Given a theory made of clauses (not necessarily disjunctive) without quantifiers, PTTP produces a set of Prolog-like Horn clauses, makes sure only sound unification is produced, and avoids the negation-as-failure proofs that are produced by the Prolog inference algorithm. It is sound and complete.

We subjected our system to a battery of experiments in a simulated office building environment. Figure 3 summarizes the results for three scenarios of varying difficulty: (1) planning a path towards a location on the same floor as the robot, (2) creating a plan that requires a low-level plan for using the elevator, and (3) planning a path towards a location on a different floor. In each scenario, we experimented with various robot orientations and obstacle positions in the robot's vicinity. For

each layer, we measured the number of inference steps and time taken to prove its goal.[3]

Layer 0, the critical layer, achieved its results in an average of 0.1 seconds when a turn action was required, and 0.3 seconds when a forward action was required. (Because of space concerns, we have included in Figure 3 only the data for cases of the former kind.) Layers 1, 2, and 3 worked fairly fast, although the long planning involved in Scenario 1 took more than 10 seconds (for a depth of 30 in the proof space). However, because we rely on the speed of only layer 0, safety is not compromised; the avoidance capabilities ensure that the robot does not fall off a cliff while planning a way to avoid the cliff edge.

We attribute the speed achieved to three optimizations. First, we used a few semantic attachments in Layer 0. In particular, the predicate $GetForce$ was embodied in a C function that returns the force vector $[Strength, Direction]$. It calls Prolog's bagof operator to collect all the objects for which existence proofs can be found, then computes the sum of the forces contributed by each object. This CWA is achieved by limiting proofs to be no longer than a specified constant (after some experimentation, we settled on a constant of 20.)

Second, we applied caching to the proof of $GetForce$. Since every proof "re-proved" $GetForce$ many times, this improved the performance of Layer 0 significantly (from approximately 10 seconds to 0.1 seconds per proof).

Third, we divided the planning so that layer 2 executes "local planning" for the elevator domain. This allowed layer 3 to avoid an explosion of the proof space, which otherwise would have occurred since there are four principal actions as well as a number of frame axioms associated with the robot and the elevator. The separation also helped prevent complex unifications.

6   Related Work

Compared to other approaches to agent architecture and robot control using logic, LSA is the only one using full FOL theorem provers for the low-level control loop and the first one to propose an architecture built on theorem provers that is suitable for realizing complex tasks.

[Shanahan, 1996] describes a map-building process using abduction, but then implements his theory in an algorithm that is proved to have his abductive semantics. [Baral and Tran, 1998] define control modules to be of a form of Stimulus-Response (S-R) agents (see [Nilsson, 1998]), relating them to the family of action languages $\mathcal{A}$ (e.g., [Gelfond and Lifschitz, 1993], [Giunchiglia et al., 1997]). They provide a way to check that an S-R module is correct with respect to an action theory in $\mathcal{A}$ or $\mathcal{AR}$ and provide an algorithm to create an S-R agent from an action theory. [Levesque et al., 1997], [Giacomo et al., 1998], and other work in the GOLOG project have a planner that computes/plans the GOLOG program offline, only later letting the robot execute the GOLOG

---

[3]We do not list averages or standard deviations for layers 2 and 3 because their performances are independent of both the robot's orientation and sonar readings.

| | Layer 0 | | | | Layer 1 | | | | Layer 2 | | Layer 3 | |
| | Time | | Infer. | | Time | | Infer. | | Time | Infer. | Time | Infer. |
	Mean	SD	Mean	SD	Mean	SD	Mean	SD				
Scen. 1	0.09	0.02	3598	629	0.02	0.01	394	2	0.01	4	0.00	20
Scen. 2	0.10	0.01	3703	613	0.02	0.01	384	4	0.52	27184	0.47	34056
Scen. 3	0.09	0.02	3575	640	0.02	0.01	389	1	0.00	4	11.24	694966

Figure 3: Proof time and inference steps measurements for the LSA during experiments in three different scenarios: (1) single-floor planning, (2) lower-level elevator planning, and (3) multi-floor planning. (*SD* is *standard deviation*.)

program on-line. Here again, logic is used only to give semantics for GOLOG programs by way of situation calculus ([McCarthy and Hayes, 1969]).

None of this work uses FOL theorem provers for controlling robots at run-time. To our knowledge, there has been no such system since Shakey [Nilsson, 1984].

7 Conclusion

We have shown that theorem provers can be used for robot control by employing them in a layered architecture. We demonstrated that the architecture and the versatility of theorem provers allow us to realize complex tasks, while keeping individual theories simple enough for efficient theorem proving. Furthermore, we have grounded our proposal by giving it formal semantics based on circumscription.

At this time, the system is implemented in four layers on a simulating computer. Besides installing the system on a mobile robot, our future work plan includes adding layers that create maps and layers that reason about and update explicit beliefs about the world. We are currently working on incorporating vision sensory capabilities and implementing concurrency.

This work is a first step towards our long-term goal of creating a general logic-based AI architecture that is efficient and scalable, and that supports reactivity.

8 Acknowledgments

We wish to thank Mark Stickel for allowing us to use his PTTP sources (both for PROLOG and LISP) and providing helpful answers to our inquiries regarding its use. This research was supported by an ARPA (ONR) grant N00014-94-1-0775 and by a National Physical Science Consortium (NPSC) fellowship.

References

[Baral and Tran, 1998] C. Baral and S.C. Tran. Relating theories of actions and reactive control. *Electronic Trans. on Artificial Intelligence*, 1998. Under review.

[Brooks, 1986] Rodney A. Brooks. A robust layered control system for a mobile robot. *IEEE J. Robotics and Automation*, RA-2(1):14–23, March 1986.

[Gelfond and Lifschitz, 1993] M. Gelfond and V. Lifschitz. Representing actions and change by logic programs. *J. Logic Programming*, 17:301–322, 1993.

[Gelfond et al., 1989] M. Gelfond, H. Przymusinska, and T. C. Przymusinski. On the relationship between circumscription and negation as failure. *Artificial Intelligence*, 38(1):75–94, February 1989.

[Giacomo et al., 1998] G. De Giacomo, R. Reiter, and M. Soutchanski. Execution monitoring of high-level robot programs. In *Proc. KR-98*, pages 453–464, 1998.

[Giunchiglia et al., 1997] E. Giunchiglia, G.N. Kartha, and V. Lifschitz. Representing action: Indeterminacy and ramifications. *Artificial Intelligence*, 95(2):409–438, 1997.

[Levesque et al., 1997] H.J. Levesque, R. Reiter, Y. Lesperance, F. Lin, and R. Scherl. Golog: A logic programming language for dynamic domains. *J. Logic Programming*, 31:59–84, 1997.

[McCarthy and Hayes, 1969] J. McCarthy and P.J. Hayes. Some philosophical problems from the standpoint of artificial intelligence. In *Machine Intelligence*, volume 4, pages 463–502. 1969.

[McCarthy, 1986] John McCarthy. Applications of Circumscription to Formalizing Common Sense Knowledge. *Artificial Intelligence*, 28:89–116, 1986.

[Minsky, 1985] M. Minsky. *The Society of Mind*. Simon and Schuster, 1985.

[Nilsson, 1984] N. J. Nilsson. Shakey the robot. Technical Report 323, SRI International, CA, 1984.

[Nilsson, 1998] N.J. Nilsson. *Artificial Intelligence: A New Synthesis*. Morgan-Kaufmann, 1998.

[Shanahan, 1996] M. P. Shanahan. Robotics and the common sense informatic situation. In *Proc. ECAI-96*, pages 684–688, 1996.

[Stein, 1997] L.A. Stein. Postmodular systems: Architectural principles for cognitive robotics. *Cybernetics and Systems*, 28(6):471–487, September 1997.

[Stickel, 1988] M.E. Stickel. A Prolog Technology Theorem Prover: implementation by an extended Prolog compiler. *J. Automated Reasoning*, 4:353–380, 1988.

[Stickel, 1992] M.E. Stickel. A Prolog Technology Theorem Prover: a new exposition and implementation in Prolog. *Theoretical Computer Science*, 104:109–128, 1992.

Automata Theory for Reasoning about Actions

Eugenia Ternovskaia
Department of Computer Science,
University of Toronto
Toronto, ON, Canada, M5S 3G4
eugenia@cs.toronto.edu

Abstract

In this paper, we show decidability of a rather expressive fragment of the situation calculus. We allow second order quantification over finite and infinite sets of situations. We do not impose a domain closure assumption on actions; therefore, infinite and even uncountable domains are allowed. The decision procedure is based on automata accepting infinite trees.

1 Introduction

During the last decade, several action formalisms have been developed: [Reiter, 1991, Gelfond and Lifschitz, 1993, Sandewall, 1994, Miller and Shanahan, 1994], to mention a few. The ultimate goal of developing these formalisms is to perform reasoning about actions, which generally amounts to computing answers to queries. More precisely, given action description theory T and query ϕ, we are interested whether ϕ is a logical consequence of T. Obviously, for some theories (in expressive languages) logical consequence — and thus query answering — will not be decidable. It is important to establish under what restrictions on the language one can obtain an answer for an arbitrary query. We solve this question positively for a rather expressive fragment of the situation calculus[1]. This language is second order, with quantification over finite and infinite sets of situations. The domain closure axiom for actions is not assumed, therefore infinite and even uncountable action domains are allowed.

Similar work has been done for the action language $\mathcal{A}$ proposed in [Gelfond and Lifschitz, 1993]. Liberatore [Liberatore, 1997] studied the complexity of deciding whether a set of statements in this language is consistent, and specified which restrictions of $\mathcal{A}$ lead to tractability and which do not. The author describes a reduction from propositional satisfiability to consistency in $\mathcal{A}$ thus showing NP-completeness of the problem. It follows that the entailment problem for the language $\mathcal{A}$ is co-NP-complete. Since the language of the situation

---

[1] We use the dialect of the situation calculus developed by the members of the Cognitive Robotics group in Toronto.

calculus is more expressive (we allow second order quantification), the reduction from propositional satisfiability cannot be applied.

Here, we reduce the problem of decidability of the basic action theory $\mathcal{D}$ (cf. [Pirri and Reiter, 1999]) to the emptiness problem for a tree automaton. The emptiness problem is to determine whether the language accepted by a tree automaton is empty. From our construction it follows that if the accepted language is empty, then $\mathcal{D} \cup \{\neg\phi\}$ is unsatisfiable which is equivalent to the fact that ϕ is logically implied by $\mathcal{D}$. Since the emptiness problem for tree automata is decidable, the problem $\mathcal{D} \models \phi$ is decidable as well.

In the following section, we specify the language $\mathcal{L}^{sc}$ of the situation calculus. Section 3 describes the basic action theory $\mathcal{D}$. Section 4 surveys basic definitions of automata theory on infinite trees. Then, in Section 5, we construct a tree automaton corresponding to the basic action theory $\mathcal{D}$. Section 6 is devoted to the main step in the proof of decidability — translating an arbitrary formula in the language of the situation calculus to a tree automaton. Finally, in Section 7, we discuss the implications of this work and outline directions for future research.

2 The Language

We consider a two-sorted version $\mathcal{L}^{sc}$ of the language of the situation calculus with equality and with sorts for actions and situations. The primitive non-logical symbols of sort *actions* consist of variables $a, a_1, a_2, \ldots$, and constants $A_0, A_1, A_2, \ldots$ The primitive non-logical symbols of sort *situations* consist of variables $s, s', s'', \tilde{s}, \ldots$, constant S_0, binary function $do(a, s)$, where a is an action, s is a situation. This function defines a successor situation in terms of a current situation and a performed action. Finitely many unary predicate symbols $F_1, \ldots, F_n$ called *fluents* represent properties of the world and have situations as their arguments. We allow quantification over finite and infinite sets of situations, i.e., over unary predicate variables. Sometimes it is convenient to view a situation as a string of performed actions. We shall use binary relation $s \sqsubset s'$ to represent the prefix relation on the corresponding strings of actions. Below, in Section 3, it will be seen that $\sqsubset$ is second order definable in terms of function $do(a, s)$ and hence is inessential. The logical symbols of the language are $\neg, \supset, \exists, =$. Other logical connectives and the universal quantifier $\forall$ are the usual abbreviations. Note that we do not include the predicate $Poss$ (cf. [Pirri and Reiter, 1999]). Including it is unproblematic, but would complicate the exposition.

It is convenient to introduce the following shorthands.

$$\mu_{X,s'}\Phi(X, s')(s) \stackrel{\text{def}}{=} \forall X[\forall s'[\Phi(X, s') \supset X(s')] \supset X(s),$$

$$\nu_{X,s'}\Phi(X, s')(s) \stackrel{\text{def}}{=} \exists X[\forall s'[X(s') \supset \Phi(X, s')] \wedge X(s)].$$

These sentences introduce notations for least and greatest fixed points respectively. In these sentences, $\Phi(X, s)$ is any formula in the language $\mathcal{L}^{sc}$ with no free variables other than X and s. The following examples demonstrate the expressive power of this language. Property "there is a path in the tree of situations where fluent F holds in infinitely many situations" is expressible by $\nu_{X,s'}\ \mu_{Y,s'}\ [\exists s'\ \exists a\ s' = do(a, s) \wedge [F(s') \wedge X(s') \vee Y(s')]](s)$. Formula $F_1(s) \supset \mu_{X,s'}\ [\exists a\ s' = do(a, s) \wedge F_2(s') \vee \forall a\ X(do(a, s'))](s)$ says that "every occurrence of a situation where fluent F_1 holds, is eventually followed by a situation where F_2 holds". Property "there is a path in the tree of situations where fluent F holds in every situation" is represented by $\nu_{X,s'}\ F(s') \wedge [\exists a\ s'' = do(a, s') \wedge X(s'')](s)$.

3 Basic Action Theories

A basic action theory is a set of axioms

$$\mathcal{D} = \mathcal{D}_f \cup \mathcal{D}_{ss} \cup \mathcal{D}_{una} \cup \mathcal{D}_{S_0},$$

where $\mathcal{D}_f$ is the set of foundational axioms for situations, $\mathcal{D}_{ss}$ is the set of successor state axioms, one for each fluent, $\mathcal{D}_{una}$ is the set of unique name axioms for actions, and $\mathcal{D}_{S_0}$ is the description of the initial situation.

First we consider the foundational axioms for the situation calculus, $\mathcal{D}_f$. The unique name axioms for situations are

$$S_0 \neq do(a, s),$$
$$do(a_1, s_1) = do(a_2, s_2) \supset a_1 = a_2 \wedge s_1 = s_2. \quad (1)$$

The induction principle for situations is

$$\forall P\ [P(S_0) \wedge \forall s'\ \forall a\ P(s') \supset P(do(a, s'))] \supset \forall s\ P(s)]. \quad (2)$$

These axioms guarantee that situations compose an infinitely branching tree. Indeed, it can be shown that the class of tree-like structures is completely characterized by the induction principle on situations and unique name assumptions for situations [Ternovskaia, 1998]. The properties of the prefix relation $\sqsubset$ are as follows.

$$s \not\sqsubset S_0,$$
$$s \sqsubset do(a, s') \equiv s \sqsubseteq s'. \quad (3)$$

Formula $s \sqsubseteq s'$ is an abbreviation for $s \sqsubset s' \vee s = s'$. Relation $s \sqsubset s'$ can be defined by

$$\forall X\{\exists a X(do(a, s)) \wedge \forall \tilde{s} \exists \tilde{a}[X(\tilde{s}) \supset X(do(\tilde{a}, \tilde{s}))] \supset X(s')\}.$$

We use it for easier formalizations. The foundational axioms for situations, $\mathcal{D}_f$, are (1), (2) and (3).

Successor state axioms, $\mathcal{D}_{ss}$, have the form

$$\forall a\ \forall s\ F(do(a, s)) \equiv [\gamma_F^+(a, s) \vee F(s) \wedge \neg \gamma_F^-(a, s)]. \quad (4)$$

Formula $\gamma_F^+(a, s)$ (respectively, $\gamma_F^-(a, s)$) denotes a first order formula specifying the conditions under which fluent F is true (respectively, false) in the successor situation [Reiter, 1991]. The only free variables of these formulae are those among a, s. Function symbol do does not occur in these formulae.

The unique name axioms, $\mathcal{D}_{una}$, specify that any two actions with different names are not equal. The description of the initial situation, $\mathcal{D}_{S_0}$, is a set of first order sentences that are uniform in S_0, i.e., contain no situation term other than S_0. We shall call $\mathcal{D}_{S_0}$ the initial database. For simplicity, we assume that the initial database is first order and does not contain sentences mentioning no situation term at all. We do not require completeness of $\mathcal{D}_{S_0}$.

4 Tree Automata

Let $\sigma = \{A_0, \dots, A_{k-1}\}$ be a finite set. Later, in sections 5 and 6, we shall associate the elements of this set with actions. An *unlabeled k-ary tree* is specified by its set of nodes; each node is a string in σ^*. The empty string ε corresponds to the root of the tree. If w is a node, then wA_i is the i-th son of w. Notice that this set of strings is prefix-closed, and each string uniquely determines a node in the tree. Suppose a finite alphabet Σ of *labels* is given. A *k-ary Σ-labeled tree* t is specified by its set of nodes (the "domain" $dom(t) \subseteq \sigma^*$) and a valuation of the nodes (the "labeling function" $t : dom(t) \to \Sigma$). By T_Σ^ω we denote the set of infinite Σ-labeled trees with domain σ^*. A subset T of T_Σ^ω will be called a *tree language*. An example of a tree language is the language

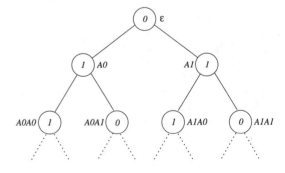

Figure 1: An infinite labeled tree $t : \{A_0, A_1\}^* \to \{0, 1\}$ with the set of nodes $dom(t) = \{A_0, A_1\}^*$ and labels from $\{0, 1\}$.

$T_\mathcal{D}$ defined in Section 5. This language is determined by the basic action theory $\mathcal{D}$. Another example of a tree language is the language T_ϕ associated with an arbitrary formula ϕ in the language $\mathcal{L}^{sc}$. We define T_ϕ in Section 6.

Both languages, $T_\mathcal{D}$ and T_ϕ, are sets of trees of situations labeled with tuples of fluent values.

Let us review definitions from the general theory of automata on infinite k-ary trees. A Büchi tree automaton $\mathbf{A}$ over alphabet Σ is a quadruple $\mathbf{A} = (Q, Q_0, \Delta, F)$ where

- Q is a finite set of states,
- $Q_0 \subseteq Q$ is the set of initial states,
- $F \subseteq Q$ is the set of final (or accepting) states,
- $\Delta \subseteq Q \times \Sigma \times Q^k$ is the transition relation.

The transition relation specifies which tuples $\langle q_1, \ldots, q_k \rangle$ of states of $\mathbf{A}$ can be assumed at the k sons of a node, given the node's label in Σ and the state of the automaton assumed there. A *run* of $\mathbf{A}$ on a tree $t \in T_\Sigma^\omega$ is a map $r : \sigma^* \to Q$ with $r(\varepsilon) \in Q_0$, and $\langle r(w), t(w), r(wA_0), \ldots, r(wA_{k-1}) \rangle \in \Delta$, for $w \in \sigma^*$. In other words, a run is a labeling of the nodes of the tree t with the states of the automaton $\mathbf{A}$ that obeys the transition function. Let $\sqsubset$ be the proper prefix relation over σ^*. A path through t is a maximal subset of $dom(t)$ linearly ordered by $\sqsubset$. If π is a *path* through t, then $t|\pi$ denotes the restriction of the function t to the set π. Let Q^ω be the set of infinite strings over the set of states Q. For an ω-sequence $\delta = \delta(0), \delta(1), \ldots$ from Q^ω, the "infinity set" of δ is $In(\delta) = \{q \in Q \mid$ there exist infinitely many n such that $\delta(n) = q\}$. The run r is *successful* if on each path some final state occurs infinitely often, i.e., for all paths π, $In(r|\pi) \cap F \neq \emptyset$.

A *Rabin tree automaton over* Σ has the form $\mathbf{A} = (Q, q_0, \Delta, \Omega)$, where Q, q_0, Δ are as before, and $\Omega = \{(L_1, U_1), \ldots, (L_n, U_n)\}$ is a collection of "accepting pairs" of state sets $L_i, U_i \subseteq Q$. A run r of the Rabin automaton $\mathbf{A}$ is *successful* if for all paths π there exists an $i \in \{1, \ldots, n\}$ with $In(r|\pi) \cap L_i = \emptyset$ and $In(r|\pi) \cap U_i \neq \emptyset$.

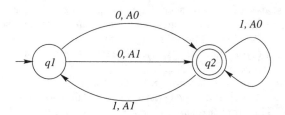

Figure 2: A graphical representation of a Büchi automaton accepting the tree from Figure 1.

A tree $t \in T_\Sigma^\omega$ is *accepted* by a Büchi, respectively Rabin tree automaton $\mathbf{A}$, if some run of $\mathbf{A}$ is successful in the corresponding sense. A set $T \subseteq T_\Sigma^\omega$ is *Büchi recognizable*, respectively *Rabin recognizable*, if it consists of the trees accepted by a Büchi, respectively Rabin tree automaton. Since any Büchi tree automaton may be regarded as a Rabin tree automaton (set $\Omega = \{(\emptyset, F)\}$), any Büchi recognizable set of infinite trees is Rabin recognizable. Both Büchi and Rabin tree automata are closed under union, intersection and projection. The famous Rabin complementation theorem holds for Rabin

tree automata, but fails for Büchi tree automata. More information about tree automata can be found in the excellent survey [Thomas, 1990].

Example 1 Consider the infinite labeled tree represented in Figure 1. This tree has the following property. The label of the root is 0. The son wA_0 of every node w is always labeled with 1. If the label of a current node w is 1 (0, respectively), then the label of the node wA_1 is 0 (1, respectively). A deterministic tree automaton accepting this tree is represented in Figure 2. The initial state is q_1, and the accepting state is q_2. Notice that we could rename state q_1 of the automaton as 0 and state q_2 as 1. The input label then would always coincide with the current state of the automaton. An automaton having this property is called *input-free*. The automata from Section 5 are input-free. This is not the case, however, for automata considered in Section 6.

5 Translating $\mathcal{D}$ to a Tree Automaton

In the remaining part of the paper, we shall consider the trees of situations. The set of nodes, the domain, of such a tree is the set of strings of actions. The empty string ε corresponds to the initial situation S_0. If w is a string representing situation s, then string wA_i, where A_i is an action, represents $do(A_i, s)$. Let the language include n fluents, then the alphabet of labels Σ^n is the set of all tuples of length n over alphabet $\{0, 1\}$. Position i of the tuple corresponds to the i-th fluent, $1 \leq i \leq n$. The labeling function maps each node of the tree, a situation, to an element of Σ^n.

In this section, we demonstrate a connection between the structures of the basic action theory $\mathcal{D}$ and the trees accepted by a Büchi tree automaton. The main difficulty in proving such a connection is that the universe of actions may be infinite, or even uncountable. To approach this problem, we first introduce a structure $\mathfrak{U}$ of $\mathcal{D}$ such that if $\mathcal{D}$ is satisfiable then this structure is a model of $\mathcal{D}$. Let $\sigma_\mathcal{A} = \{A_0, \ldots, A_{k-1}\}$ be the set of all constants of sort action in the language $\mathcal{L}^{sc}$. Let $\mathfrak{U}$ be a structure with the universe of actions $U_\mathcal{A} = \{A_0, A_0', \ldots, A_{k-1}, A_{k-1}'\}$. The universe of situations, $U_\mathcal{S}$, is constructed by applying function do starting from the initial situation. The basic action theory $\mathcal{D}$ is satisfiable if and only if $\models_\mathfrak{U} \mathcal{D}$.

Given $\sigma_\mathcal{A} = \{A_0, \ldots, A_{k-1}\}$, we consider infinite $2|\sigma_\mathcal{A}|$-ary trees where the domain (i.e., the set of nodes) is the set of strings over $\sigma = \{A_0, A_0', \ldots, A_{k-1}, A_{k-1}'\}$. Let Σ be $\{0, 1\}$, Σ^n be the n-fold Cartesian product of Σ. Every tuple $\langle V_1, \ldots, V_n \rangle$ of sets of situations yields a tree $t(V_1, \ldots, V_n)$ that labels each node $w \in \sigma^*$ with tuple $\langle c_{V_1}(w), \ldots, c_{V_n}(w) \rangle \in \Sigma^n$, where $c_V(w)$ is the characteristic function of V. Notice that each fluent F can be seen as the set of situations where it is true. Thus, every tuple $\langle F_1, \ldots, F_n \rangle$ of fluents yields a $2|\sigma_\mathcal{A}|$-ary tree $t_\mathcal{D}(F_1, \ldots, F_n)$ labeled with the elements of Σ^n. Notice further that the characteristic function $c_F(w)$ of F specifies whether fluent F holds in the situation represented by string w. The characteristic function for each fluent is determined by successor state axioms, $\mathcal{D}_{ss}$, and by the initial database, $\mathcal{D}_{S_0}$. With every set of axioms $\mathcal{D}$, we shall associate a Büchi tree automaton $\mathtt{A}_{\mathcal{D}}$ that accepts a tree language $T_{\mathcal{D}}(F_1, \ldots, F_n)$. This automaton depends on the description of the initial situation $\mathcal{D}_{S_0}$ and the choice of successor state axioms $\mathcal{D}_{ss}$.

Theorem 1 *Let $\mathfrak{U}$ be the model of $\mathcal{D}$ defined above. With every set of axioms $\mathcal{D}$ one can effectively associate a tree Büchi automaton $\mathtt{A}_{\mathcal{D}}$ labeled with the elements of Σ^n such that*

$$\models_{\mathfrak{U}} \mathcal{D} \text{ iff } \mathtt{A}_{\mathcal{D}} \text{ accepts } T_{\mathcal{D}}(F_1, \ldots, F_n).$$

Proof We shall construct a Büchi tree automaton $\mathtt{A}_{\mathcal{D}}$ that accepts trees labeled with tuples $\langle c_{F_1}(w), \ldots, c_{F_n}(w) \rangle$, for each node w. The set of states Q of $\mathtt{A}_{\mathcal{D}}$ is the set of all possible n-tuples over $\{0, 1\}$.

First, we define the set of initial states Q_0. Note that we have restricted $\mathcal{D}_{S_0}$ to be a collection of ground formulae. Find the set of satisfying truth assignments for $\mathcal{D}_{S_0}$, or determine that no such assignment exists. In the latter case $\mathcal{D}$ is unsatisfiable, and $\mathtt{A}_{\mathcal{D}}$ is an automaton without final states. This means that the set of trees it accepts is empty. The set of truth assignments corresponds to the set of tuples $\langle c_{F_1}(\varepsilon), \ldots, c_{F_n}(\varepsilon) \rangle$ of characteristic functions specifying which fluents hold in the initial situation. Each such tuple is an element of Q_0.

Second, we define the transition relation $\Delta \subseteq Q \times \Sigma^n \times Q^{2|\sigma_{\mathcal{A}}|}$. This relation specifies what tuples of automaton states may be assumed at the $2|\sigma_{\mathcal{A}}|$ sons of the node, i.e., what states (tuples of fluent values) are reached by performing each action A_i. A transition exists if and only if the state of the automaton is the same as the label of the current node. It is easy to see that the set of all truth assignments satisfying successor state axioms determines the transition relation. The computability of this set of truth assignments is guaranteed by the definition of $\mathcal{L}^{sc}$ and the form of γ^+, γ^-. If this set does not exist we, again, construct $\mathtt{A}_{\mathcal{D}}$ so that it accepts the empty language.

Example 2 Suppose $\mathcal{D}$ includes two successor state axioms:

$$\forall a \forall s F_1(do(a, s)) \equiv [F_2(s) \wedge a = A_0 \vee F_1(s) \wedge a \neq A_1],$$

$$\forall a \, \forall s \, F_2(do(a, s)) \equiv [F_2(s) \wedge a \neq A_0],$$

The transition function is determined by the truth assignments that satisfy the successor state axioms. For example, suppose F_1 is false and F_2 is true in a situation. This corresponds to the label $\langle 0, 1 \rangle$ of the tree of situations and to a state of the automaton with the same name. (Recall that all automata considered in this section are input-free.) Now we have to specify which tuples of states may be assumed at the four sons of this node. Suppose A_0 is performed. According to the successor state axioms, F_1 will be true and F_2 will be false in the successor situation. This corresponds to state $\langle 1, 0 \rangle$ of the automaton. We map all actions different from A_0 to the action A_0'. Thus, whenever $a \neq A_0$, we consider the transition from node w to node wA_0'. This transition leads to state $\langle 0, 1 \rangle$ if A_0' equals A_1 and to state

$\langle 1, 1 \rangle$ otherwise. For actions A_1 and A_1' the construction is similar. A tree automaton corresponding to these successor state axioms is represented in Figure 3.

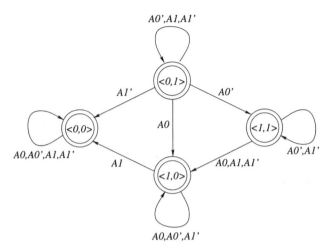

Figure 3: A Büchi tree automaton where the transition function is determined by the successor state axioms from Example 2.

Now we continue defining $\mathtt{A}_{\mathcal{D}}$. The set F of final states of this automaton coincides with the set of all states, Q. We impose Büchi acceptance condition: a tree over Σ^n is accepted by $\mathtt{A}_{\mathcal{D}}$ if there is a run such that in all possible paths some final state occurs infinitely often. We claim that $\models_{\mathfrak{U}} \mathcal{D}$ if and only if $\mathtt{A}_{\mathcal{D}}$ accepts $T_{\mathcal{D}}(F_1, \ldots, F_n)$.

Suppose $\models_{\mathfrak{U}} \mathcal{D}$. Then $\mathcal{D}_f$ is satisfied by $2|\sigma_{\mathcal{A}}|$-ary trees of situations; $\mathcal{D}_{S_0}$ specifies the set of initial states of $\mathtt{A}_{\mathcal{D}}$; and $\mathcal{D}_{ss}$ is satisfied by the truth assignment which determines the transition relation Δ of the automaton. The number of states of $\mathtt{A}_{\mathcal{D}}$ is finite. Therefore the only way to obtain infinite computations is by looping. Since all states of $\mathtt{A}_{\mathcal{D}}$ are accepting, all paths starting at one of the initial states contain at least one accepting state infinitely often. Therefore $\mathtt{A}_{\mathcal{D}}$ accepts trees labeled with tuples $\langle c_{F_1}(w), \ldots, c_{F_n}(w) \rangle$, for each node w. The set of these trees is $T_{\mathcal{D}}(F_1, \ldots, F_n)$.

Suppose $\mathtt{A}_{\mathcal{D}}$ accepts all trees from $T_{\mathcal{D}}(F_1, \ldots, F_n)$. These $2|\sigma_{\mathcal{A}}|$-ary trees satisfy the foundational axioms $\mathcal{D}_f$. The label $\langle c_{F_1}(w), \ldots, c_{F_n}(w) \rangle$ of each node w determines fluent values in the corresponding situation. The transition relation for $\mathtt{A}_{\mathcal{D}}$ is represented by a set of tuples which determines the set of satisfying truth assignments for $\mathcal{D}_{ss}$. The set of initial states of $\mathtt{A}_{\mathcal{D}}$ specifies the initial database $\mathcal{D}_{S_0}$. Therefore, $\mathcal{D}$ is satisfiable, and it follows that $\models_{\mathfrak{U}} \mathcal{D}$. □

6 Translating ϕ to a Tree Automaton and Decidability of $\mathcal{D}$

With every formula ϕ in the language $\mathcal{L}^{sc}$, we shall associate a Rabin tree automaton $\mathtt{A}_{\phi}$. This automaton accepts labeled $2|\sigma_{\mathcal{A}}|$-ary trees determined by the formula ϕ if and only if $\models_{\mathfrak{U}} \phi$, where $\mathfrak{U}$ is a structure constructed as in the previous section. Notice that it is sufficient to consider structures of this form — we are interested in satisfying $\mathcal{D}$ and ϕ simultaneously. For easier exposition, we restrict to the case where $\sigma_{\mathcal{A}} = \{A_0, A_1\}$ are the only actions occurring in $\mathcal{D}$. The proof generalizes easily for the case with any number of actions.

Let $\phi[F_1, \ldots, F_m]$ be a formula in the language of the situation calculus $\mathcal{L}^{sc}$ with fluents $F_1, \ldots, F_m$, where $m \leq n$ and n is the total number of fluents.

Theorem 2 *Let $\sigma_{\mathcal{A}} = \{A_0, A_1\}$. Let $\mathfrak{U}$ be the model of $\mathcal{D}$ defined in section 5. With every formula $\phi[F_1, \ldots, F_m]$ in the language $\mathcal{L}^{sc}$ one can effectively associate a Σ^m-tree Rabin automaton $\mathtt{A}_\phi$ such that for all $F_1, \ldots, F_m \subseteq \{A_0, A_0', A_1, A_1'\}^*$,*

$$\models_{\mathfrak{U}} \phi[F_1, \ldots, F_m] \text{ iff } \mathtt{A}_\phi \text{ accepts } T_\phi(F_1, \ldots, F_m).$$

Proof In the proof of this theorem we use techniques similar to those used in the proof of Rabin's result about the decidability of S2S, the second order monadic logic of two successors.

For every formula ϕ we construct an equivalent formula ϕ' in a (formally first order) language with binary predicates $\subseteq$, $Succ_0$, $Succ_0'$, $Succ_1$, $Succ_1'$, with variables ranging over subsets of $\{A_0, A_0', A_1, A_1'\}^*$, with the obvious interpretation of $\subseteq$, and with

$$Succ_i(U, V), \text{ iff } U = \{w\} \text{ and } V = \{wA_i\};$$
$$\text{and, similarly,}$$
$$Succ_i'(U, V), \text{ iff } U = \{w\} \text{ and } V = \{wA_i'\},$$
$$\text{for some } w \in \{A_0, A_0', A_1, A_1'\}^*.$$

Carry out the following steps, starting with a given formula ϕ in the language $\mathcal{L}^{sc}$.

(i) Eliminate superpositions of "do" by introducing additional variables of sort situations. For example,

$$F(do(A_1, do(A_0, s))) \text{ becomes}$$
$$\exists s' \, \exists s'' \, do(A_0, s) = s' \wedge do(A_1, s') = s'' \wedge F(s'').$$

(ii) Eliminate universal and existential quantification over actions by using conjunctions and disjunctions, respectively. For example, $\forall s \, \forall a \, F(do(a, s))$ becomes

$$\forall s \, F(do(A_0, s)) \wedge F(do(A_0', s))$$
$$\wedge F(do(A_1, s)) \wedge F(do(A_1', s)).$$

$\exists a \, a = A_1 \wedge \phi(a)$ will be rewritten as
$$A_0 = A_1 \wedge \phi(A_0) \vee A_0' = A_1 \wedge \phi(A_0')$$
$$\vee A_1 = A_1 \wedge \phi(A_1) \vee A_1' = A_1 \wedge \phi(A_1').$$

(iii) Eliminate occurrences of action symbols other than as arguments of function do. For example,

$$A_0 = A_1 \text{ becomes } \forall s \, do(A_0, s) = do(A_1, s).$$

(iv) Eliminate the symbol S_0 by using the property that no situation is a proper prefix of S_0. For example,

$$F(S_0) \text{ will be rewritten as } \exists s' \, F(s') \wedge \neg \exists s \, s \sqsubset s'.$$

We arrive at a formula with atomic formulae of the form $s = s'$, $do(A_i, s) = s'$, and $F(s)$ only.

For the remaining step we use the shorthands

$$F = F' \text{ for } F \subseteq F' \wedge F' \subseteq F,$$

$$F \neq F' \text{ for } \neg F = F',$$

$$Sing(F) \ (F \text{ is a singleton}) \text{ for}$$
$$\exists F' \, \{F' \subseteq F \wedge F' \neq F$$
$$\wedge \neg \exists \tilde{F} \, [\tilde{F} \subseteq F \wedge \tilde{F} \neq F \wedge \tilde{F} \neq F']\}$$

(there is exactly one proper subset of F).

(v) Eliminate variables ranging over situations and function $do(a, s)$ by using relations $Sing$ and $Succ$. For example,

$$\forall s \, do(A_0, s) = do(A_1, s) \text{ becomes}$$
$$\forall F \, \forall F_1 \, \forall F_2 \, [Sing(F) \wedge Sing(F_1) \wedge Sing(F_2)$$
$$\wedge Succ_0(F, F_1) \wedge Succ_1(F, F_2) \supset F_1 = F_2].$$

$$\forall s \, \exists s' \, do(A_0, s) = s' \wedge \tilde{F}(s') \text{ becomes}$$
$$\forall F \, \{Sing(F) \supset$$
$$\exists F' \, [Sing(F') \wedge Succ_0(F, F') \wedge F' \subseteq \tilde{F}]\}.$$

We obtain a formula ϕ' equivalent over tree-like structures to the given formula ϕ in the following sense: if $\mathfrak{U}$ is the structure with the domain of actions $\{A_0, A_0', A_1, A_1'\}$, as defined in the previous section, and if $\mathfrak{U}' = (\{A_0, A_0', A_1, A_1'\}^*, \subseteq, \mathsf{succ}_0, \mathsf{succ}_0', \mathsf{succ}_1, \mathsf{succ}_1')$, then $\models_{\mathfrak{U}} \phi$ if and only if $\models_{\mathfrak{U}'} \phi'$.

For each formula ϕ' in the language with binary predicates $\subseteq$, $Succ_0$, $Succ_0'$, $Succ_1$, $Succ_1'$, one can effectively construct a tree automaton $\mathtt{A}_{\phi'}$ satisfying the conditions of the claim. We show this by induction over ϕ'.

For atomic formulae the construction is easy. Let $\Sigma^2 = \{0, 1\} \times \{0, 1\}$. In this case, each node w is labeled with tuple $\langle c_F(w), c_{F'}(w) \rangle$. For $F \subseteq F'$ we need a tree automaton $\mathtt{A}$ that accepts a Σ^2-tree t if and only if t avoids the label $\langle 0, 1 \rangle$, i.e., $t(w) \neq \langle 0, 1 \rangle$ for all nodes w. This is achieved by an automaton with a single state q (which is initial and final) and transition (q, α, q) for all $\alpha \neq \langle 0, 1 \rangle$.

For $Succ_i(F, F')$ the automaton $\mathtt{A}_i$ has three states, q_0, q_1, q_2, where q_0 is the initial state and q_2 is the final state; the transitions are $(q_0, \langle 0, 0 \rangle, q_0), (q_0, \langle 1, 0 \rangle, q_1), (q_1, \langle 0, 1 \rangle, q_2), (q_2, \langle 0, 0 \rangle, q_2)$. Automaton $\mathtt{A}_i$ accepts t if and only if there exist a node $w \in \{A_0, A_0', A_1, A_1'\}^*$ such that $t(w) = \langle 1, 0 \rangle$, $t(wA_i) = \langle 0, 1 \rangle$ and $t(w') = \langle 0, 0 \rangle$ for any other node w'. In other words, $\mathtt{A}_i$ accepts if and only if there is a situation s such that F holds in s, F' holds in $do(A_i, s)$, and these fluents do not hold anywhere else. In the case if there are more than two fluents, the construction is essentially the same except for each additional fluent, say F_i, we replace each transition with two transitions, one with 1 on the i-s position, one with 0. The induction step for $\phi' = \psi \vee \nu$, $\phi' = \exists X \, \psi$ and $\phi' = \neg \psi$ follows from the fact that (nondeterministic) tree automata are closed under union, projection and complementation. $\square$

Recall that theory T in language $\mathcal{L}$ is *decidable* if and only if there is an algorithm to determine whether any given sentence ϕ of $\mathcal{L}$ is a logical consequence of T.

Theorem 3 *The basic action theory $\mathcal{D}$ in language $\mathcal{L}^{sc}$ is decidable.*

Proof We shall use the fact that $\mathcal{D} \models \phi$ if and only if $\mathcal{D} \cup \neg\phi$ is unsatisfiable. From the construction of $\mathtt{A}_{\mathcal{D}}$ and $\mathtt{A}_{\neg\phi}$, it follows that

$$\mathcal{D} \models \phi \quad \text{iff} \quad L(\mathtt{A}_{\mathcal{D}}) \cap L(\mathtt{A}_{\neg\phi}) = \emptyset.$$

Every Büchi tree automaton is also a Rabin tree automaton. Rabin tree automata are closed under complementation and intersection. The emptiness problem for Rabin tree automata is decidable. It follows that there is an algorithm to determine $\mathcal{D} \models \phi$ for an arbitrary ϕ in $\mathcal{L}^{sc}$, i.e., theory $\mathcal{D}$ in language $\mathcal{L}^{sc}$ is decidable. $\square$

7   Conclusions

We have proven the decidability of the basic action theory $\mathcal{D}$ in the second order language of the situation calculus. This language allows one to reason about quite sophisticated properties of the trees of situations, such as, for example, "there is a path in the tree of situations where fluent F holds in infinitely many situations" or "every occurrence of a situation where fluent F_1 holds, is eventually followed by a situation where fluent F_2 holds". Reasoning about such properties is especially important when one has to address the verification of high-level programs for robotics.

Of course, expressiveness never comes for free. The decision procedure described in this paper is non-elementary. Each level of negation in the given formula $\neg\phi$ requires a corresponding complementation of a Rabin automaton and hence an at least exponential blow-up in the size of the query. A nice improvement of our result would be a decision procedure of elementary time complexity (i.e., of time complexity bounded by the composition of a fixed number of exponential functions), or a proof that no such procedure exists. This direction of research is interesting because in practice queries tend to be relatively small.

Our decision procedure can be easily generalized for the case of concurrent actions. Each transition to a son of a node would be performed if a corresponding group of concurrent actions is executed. It is also straightforward to incorporate actions with non-deterministic effects. This would amount to redefining the automaton $\mathtt{A}_{\mathcal{D}}$ from Section 5 as non-deterministic. Introducing indirect effects is a more complicated problem. Extending our decision procedure to handle ramifications would be an interesting exercise.

For many practical problems we need to study the entailment of restricted classes of queries. Such queries might be, for example, those expressible using fixed point operators μ and ν, or those where set quantifiers refer to chains in trees of situations (i.e., sets of situations linearly ordered by the prefix relation $\sqsubseteq$), or to paths of situations (i.e., maximal chains). Developing decision procedures for these subproblems would be useful. The impact of incorporating more information about the theory $\mathcal{D}$ on the complexity of the decision procedure is also

of interest. Another intriguing direction of research is to further investigate the boundary between decidable and undecidable fragments of the situation calculus.

In our proofs, we have used automata on infinite trees. To our knowledge, this is the first time that automata theory has been applied to the problems of reasoning about actions. We consider automata-theoretic techniques useful for the following reasons. First, automata bear an obvious relation to action theories. Transition diagrams for tree automata are closely connected to successor states axioms specifying the effects of actions. Second, automata-theoretic techniques provide the only known methods of obtaining elementary time decision procedures for some very expressive logics. Therefore, they bear great potential for automating reasoning.

Acknowledgments

Thanks to Ray Reiter and to the anonymous referees for helpful comments.

References

[Gelfond and Lifschitz, 1993] M. Gelfond and V. Lifschitz. Representing action and change by logic programs. *J. of Logic Programming*, 17:301–322, 1993.

[Liberatore, 1997] P. Liberatore. The complexity of the language $\mathcal{A}$. *Linköping Electronic Articles in Computer and Information Science*, 2, 1997.

[Miller and Shanahan, 1994] R. Miller and M. Shanahan. Narratives in the situation calculus. *J. of Logic and Computation (Special Issue on Actions and Processes)*, 4(5):513–530, 1994.

[Pirri and Reiter, 1999] F. Pirri and R. Reiter. Some contributions to the metatheory of the situation calculus. *J. of ACM, to appear*, 1999.

[Reiter, 1991] R. Reiter. The frame problem in the situation calculus: a simple solution (sometimes) and a completeness result for goal regression. In Vladimir Lifschitz, editor, *Artificial Intelligence and Mathematical Theory of Computation: Papers in Honor of John McCarthy*, pages 359–380. Academic Press, San Diego, CA, 1991.

[Sandewall, 1994] E. Sandewall. *Features and Fluents: The Representation of Knowledge about Dynamic Systems*. Oxford University Press, 1994.

[Ternovskaia, 1998] E. Ternovskaia. Inductive definability and the situation calculus. In *Transaction and Change in Logic Databases*, volume 1472 of *Lecture Notes in Computer Science*. Springer-Verlag, 1998.

[Thomas, 1990] W. Thomas. Automata on infinite objects. In J. van Leeuwen, editor, *Handbook of Theoretical Computer Science*, pages 134–191. 1990.

AUTOMATED REASONING

Reasoning about Action 2

Projection using Regression and Sensors

Giuseppe De Giacomo
Dipartimento di Informatica e Sistemistica
Università di Roma "La Sapienza"
Via Salaria 113, 00198 Roma, Italy
degiacomo@dis.uniroma1.it

Hector J. Levesque
Department of Computer Science
University of Toronto
Toronto, ON, Canada M5S 3H5
hector@cs.toronto.edu

Abstract

In this paper, we consider the projection task (determining what does or does not hold after performing a sequence of actions) in a general setting where a solution to the frame problem may or may not be available, and where online information from sensors may or may not be applicable. We formally characterize the projection task for actions theories of this sort, and show how a generalized form of regression produces correct answers whenever it can be used. We characterize conditions on action theories, sequences of actions, and sensing information that are sufficient to guarantee that regression can be used, and present a provably correct regression-based procedure in Prolog for performing the task under these conditions.

1 Introduction

One of the most fundamental tasks concerned with reasoning about action and change is the *projection task*: determining whether a fluent[1] does or does not hold after performing a sequence of actions. In the usual formulation, we are given a characterization of the initial state of the world and a specification of some sort of what each action does. The projection task requires us to determine the cumulative effects (and non-effects) of sequences of actions.

Projection is clearly a prerequisite to *planning*: we cannot figure out if a given goal is achieved by a sequence of actions if we cannot determine what holds after doing the sequence. Similarly, the *high-level program execution task* [6], which is that of finding a sequence of actions constituting a legal execution of a high-level program, also requires projection: to execute a program like "while there is a block on the table, pick up a block and put it away," one needs to be able to determine after various sequences of actions if there is still a block on the table.

A perennial stumbling block in the specification of the projection task is the frame problem [4]: for each action, we need to specify somehow not only what changes as the result of performing the action, but the much larger number of fluents unaffected by the action. One solution to this difficulty is

[1]By a fluent, we mean a property of the world that changes as the result of performing actions.

make a STRIPS assumption [2]: what will be known about a state of the world will be representable as a database of simple atomic facts, and we specify actions as operators on such a database, adding or removing just what changes.

A much more expressive and declarative solution to the frame problem is presented in [10]. There, the situation calculus is used to specify the effects of actions, and then a simple syntactic procedure is provided for combining the effects for each fluent into a so-called *successor state axiom* that logically entails not only the effect axioms, but all the frame axioms for that fluent as well.

However, this solution to the frame problem makes a strong completeness assumption: after specifying the (perhaps conditional) effects of the given actions on fluents, and then allowing for possible ramifications of these actions (*e.g.*, [7]), it is then assumed that a fluent changes *only if* it has been affected in one of these ways. Thus, it is assumed that each fluent can be *regressed* in the sense that whether or not it holds after performing an action can be determined by considering the action in question and what was true just before.

What is not allowed, in other words, are cases where the value of a fluent does not depend in this way on the previous state. This can arise in at least two ways. First, a fluent might change as the result of an action that is exogenous to the system, *i.e.*, not represented in the action theory. If a robot opens a door in a building, then when nobody else is around, it is justified in concluding that the door remains open until the robot closes it. But in a building with other occupants, doors will be opened and closed unpredictably. Similarly, the robot may be able to determine that a warning light is on simply because it was on in the previous state and the robot is the only one who can turn it off; but it may not be able to predict when the warning light goes on. Secondly, the robot might have incomplete knowledge of the fluent in question. For example, a robot normally would not be able to infer the current temperature outdoors, since this is the result of a large number of unknown events and properties. Even when a fluent is expected to stay relatively constant, like the depth of water in a swimming pool, the robot may not know what that value is.

In cases such as these, the only way we can expect a robot to be able to perform the projection task is if it has some other way of determining the current value of certain fluents in the world. To this effect, we assume that not only can the robot use regression, it can use a collection of onboard *sensors*. In [5], sensing is modeled as an action performed by a robot that returns a binary measurement. The robot then uses so-called *sensed fluent axioms* to correlate the value returned with the state of various fluents. However, in this account, no attempt is made to be precise about the exact relation between sensing and regression. Moreover, there is no possibility of saying that only under certain conditions can regression be used, and in others, sensing. On the other hand, the knowledge or belief of an agent is modeled explicitly in [5] as a fluent that can be changed by sensing actions, while for our purposes, knowledge will be left implicit.

What we propose in this paper is this: a formal specification of a changing world that generalizes Reiter's solution to the frame problem (and hence STRIPS also) to allow conditional successor state axioms, and generalizes Levesque and others' treatment of sensors (*e.g.*, [1; 3; 9; 12]) to allow conditional sensing axioms. Our specification will be sufficiently general that in some cases, there will simply not be enough information to perform the projection task even with sensing. However, in many cases, we will be able to do projection using a combination of sensing and regression. In addition to this specification, we propose a reasoning method for performing projection under these general circumstances which is guaranteed to be sound, and in many cases of interest, complete. We provide a Prolog evaluation procedure for the projection task and prove its soundness and under suitable circumstances its completeness.

2 Basic action theories

Our account of action, sensing, and change is formulated in the language of the situation calculus [4; 11]. We will not go over the language here except to note the following components: there is a special constant S_0 used to denote the *initial situation*, namely the one in which no actions have yet occurred; there is a distinguished binary function symbol *do* where $do(a, s)$ denotes the successor situation to s resulting from performing action a; relations whose truth values vary from situation to situation, are called (relational) *fluents*, and are denoted by predicate symbols taking a situation term as their last argument; and there is a special predicate $Poss(a, s)$ used to state that action a is executable in situation s.

Within this language, we can formulate action theories that describe how the world changes as the result of the available actions. One such is a theory of the following form [10; 11]:

- Axioms describing the initial situation S_0, and axioms not mentioning situations at all, which form together the initial database.

- Action precondition axioms, one for each primitive action a, characterizing $Poss(a, s)$.

- Successor state axioms, one for each fluent F, stating under what conditions $F(\vec{x}, do(a, s))$ holds as function of what holds in situation s. These take the place of the so-called effect axioms, but also provide a solution to the frame problem [10].

- Unique names axioms for the primitive actions.

- Some foundational, domain independent axioms.

For example, the successor state axiom[2]

$$Broken(x, do(a, s)) \equiv$$
$$a = drop(x) \land Fragile(x)$$
$$\lor \ \exists b \left[a = explode(b) \land Bomb(b) \land Near(x, b, s) \right]$$
$$\lor \ a \neq repair(x) \land Broken(x, s)$$

states that an object x is broken after doing action a if a is dropping it and x is fragile, a is exploding a bomb near it, or it was already broken, and a is not the action of repairing it.

In [5], to characterize the result of sensing, it is assumed that each primitive action can return a binary sensing result, and that there is a special predicate $SF(a, s)$ used to state that action a returns value 1 in situation s. To relate this sensing result to fluents, the following are added to basic action theories:

- Sensed fluent axioms, one for each primitive action a, characterizing SF.

For example, the sensed fluent axiom

$$SF(readHeatGauge, s) \equiv \exists n. \ RobotTemp(n, s) \land n > 25$$

states that reading the heat gauge returns 1 iff the temperature around the robot exceeds 25 degrees.

3 Guarded action theories

In what follows we will be replacing successor state and sensed fluent axioms by more general versions. To this effect, instead of assuming that actions return a binary sensing value, we assume that a robot has a number of onboard sensors that provide sensing readings at any time. Thus, we drop SF from the language of the situation calculus, and introduce instead a finite number of *sensing functions*: unary functions whose only argument is a situation. For example, thermometer(s), sonar(s), depthGauge(s), might all be real-valued sensing functions.[3]

We then define a *sensor-fluent formula* to be a formula of the language (without *Poss*, for simplicity) that uses at most a single situation term, which is a variable, and that this term only appears as the final argument of a fluent or sensor function. We write $\phi(\vec{x}, s)$ when ϕ is a sensor-fluent formula with free variables among the $\vec{x}$ and s, and $\phi(\vec{t}, t_s)$ for the formula that results after the substitution of $\vec{x}$ by the vector of terms $\vec{t}$ and s by the situation term t_s. A *sensor formula* is a sensor-fluent formula that mentions no fluents, and a *fluent formula* is one that mentions no sensor functions.

We then define our generalized version of successor state and sensed fluent axioms as follows:

A *guarded successor state axiom* (GSSA) is a formula of the form

$$\alpha(\vec{x}, a, s) \supset [F(\vec{x}, do(a, s)) \equiv \gamma(\vec{x}, a, s)]$$

and a *guarded sensed fluent axiom* (GSFA) is a formula of the form

$$\alpha(\vec{x}, s) \supset [F(\vec{x}, s) \equiv \rho(\vec{x}, s)]$$

---

[2]Here and below, formulas should be read as universally quantified from the outside.

[3]Syntactically, these look like functional fluents, so to avoid confusion, we only deal with relational fluents in this paper.

where α is a sensor-fluent formula called the *guard* of the axiom, F is a relational fluent, γ is a fluent formula, and ρ is a sensor formula.

An action theory can contain any number of GSSAs and GS-FAs for each fluent. We can handle a universally applicable successor state axiom like the one for *Broken* above by using the guard **True**. We no longer have sensing actions, but we can achieve much the same effect using a GSFA with guard **True**. For example,

$$\textbf{True} \supset [RobotTemp(n,s) \equiv \mathsf{thermometer}(s) = n]$$

says that the on board thermometer always measures the temperature around the robot.

3.1 Some examples

We now proceed to consider examples that cannot be represented in the basic action theories from Section 2.

1. The outdoor temperature is unpredictable from state to state. However, when the robot is outdoors, its onboard thermometer measures that temperature.

$$Outdoors(s) \supset$$
$$OutdoorTemp(n,s) \equiv \mathsf{thermometer}(s) = n$$

   Note that when the guard is false, *i.e.*, when the robot is indoors, nothing can be concluded regarding the outdoor temperature.

2. The indoor temperature is constant when the climate control is active, and otherwise unpredictable. However, when the robot is indoors, its onboard thermometer measures that temperature:

$$ClimateControl(s) \supset$$
$$IndoorTemp(n, do(a,s)) \equiv IndoorTemp(n,s)$$

$$Indoors(s) \supset$$
$$IndoorTemp(n,s) \equiv \mathsf{thermometer}(s) = n$$

   Note that in this case, if the climate control remains active, then a robot that goes first indoors and then outdoors will still be able to infer the current indoor temperature using both sensing and regressing. To our knowledge, no other representation for reasoning about action and change can accommodate this combination.

3. The distance between a (1-dimensional) robot and the wall is affected only by the moving actions. Also, the onboard sonar correctly measures the distance to the wall, but only when the reading is within a certain interval.

$$\textbf{True} \supset$$
$$WDist(n, do(a,s)) \equiv$$
$$a = forward \wedge WDist(n+1,s)$$
$$\vee \ a = backward \wedge WDist(n-1,s)$$
$$\vee \ a \neq forward \wedge a \neq backward \wedge WDist(n,s)$$

$$\theta_1 \leq \mathsf{sonar}(s) \leq \theta_2 \supset$$
$$WDist(n,s) \equiv \mathsf{sonar}(s) = n$$

   In this case, the successor state axiom is universally applicable, meaning we can always regress all the way to S_0 to determine the distance to the wall. However, if the distance to the wall in S_0 is unknown, we would still not know the current value, and so it much more useful to be able to regress to a situation where the sonar reading was within its operating range.

4. If the robot is alone in the building, the state of the door is completely determined by the robot's *open* and *close* actions. Either way, any time the robot is in front of the door, its onboard door sensor correctly determines the state of the door.

$$Alone(s) \supset$$
$$DoorOpen(x, do(a,s)) \equiv$$
$$a = open(x)$$
$$\vee \ a \neq close(x) \wedge DoorOpen(x,s)$$

$$InFrontOf(x,s) \supset$$
$$DoorOpen(x,s) \equiv \mathsf{doorSensor}(s) = 1$$

   One intriguing possibility offered by this example is that on closing a door, and later coming back in front of the door to find it open, a security guard robot would be able to infer that $\neg Alone$.

5. A warning light for an alarm can go on unpredictably. Once it is on, however, it will stay on until the robot turns it off. Also, the robot can determine the state of the warning using its onboard light sensor, provided it is looking at the light.

$$LightOn(x,s) \vee a = turnoff(x) \supset$$
$$LightOn(x, do(a,s)) \equiv$$
$$a \neq turnoff(x) \wedge LightOn(x,s)$$

$$LookingAt(x,s) \supset$$
$$LightOn(x,s) \equiv \mathsf{lightSensor}(s) = 1$$

   In this case, we need a complex guard for the successor state axiom, since we can only regress when the light was on previously or when the action is to turn it off.

3.2 Histories and the projection task

We are now ready to define the projection task formally. Obviously, to be able to determine if a fluent holds at some point, it is no longer sufficient to know just the actions that have occurred; we also need to know the readings of the sensors along the way. Consequently, we define a *history* as a sequence of the form $(\vec{\mu_0}) \cdot (A_1, \vec{\mu_1}) \cdots (A_n, \vec{\mu_n})$ where A_i $(1 \leq i \leq n)$ is a ground action term and $\vec{\mu_i} = \langle \mu_{i1}, \ldots, \mu_{im} \rangle$ $(0 \leq i \leq n)$ is a vector of values, with μ_{ij} understood as the reading of the j-th sensor after the i-th action. If λ is such a history, we then recursively define a ground situation term $end[\lambda]$ by $end[(\vec{\mu_0})] = S_0$ and $end[\lambda \cdot (A, \vec{\mu})] = do(A,t)$ where $t = end[\lambda]$. We also define a ground sensor formula $Sensed[\lambda]$ as $\bigwedge_{i=0}^{n} \bigwedge_{j=1}^{m} h_j(end[\lambda_i]) = \mu_{ij}$ where λ_i is the subhistory up to action i, $(\vec{\mu_0}) \cdots (A_i, \vec{\mu_i})$, and h_j is the j-th sensor function. So $end[\lambda]$ is the situation that results from doing the actions in λ and $Sensed[\lambda]$ is the formula that states that the sensors had the values specified by λ[4]. The projection task, then, is this:

Given an action theory Σ as above, a history λ, and a formula $\phi(s)$ with a single free variable s, determine whether or not $\Sigma \cup Sensed[\lambda] \models \phi(end[\lambda])$.

---

[4]Obviously interesting histories λ have to satisfy certain legality criteria such as consistency of $\Sigma \cup Sensed[\lambda]$ and conformance to *Poss*.

4 Generalized regression

In principle, the projection task as formulated can be solved using a general first-order theorem prover. But the ineffectiveness of this approach in an even simpler setting is arguably what led many to abandon the situation calculus and take up STRIPS. Our goal here is to keep the logical framework, but show that in common cases, projection can be reduced using a form of regression to reasoning about the initial situation, as done in [11]. The reduction is tricky, however, because of the interaction between the various GSFAs and GSSAs, requiring us to solve (auxiliary) projection tasks at each step.

What we propose is a generalized form of regression that is a sensible compromise between syntactic transformations and logical reasoning. Specifically we require the latter only in evaluating the *guards* to decide which GSFAs and GSSAs to apply (see Section 4.1 where regression is again used).

In the following we assume that Σ is an action theory as above, λ is a history, and $\phi(\vec{x}, s)$ and $\psi(\vec{x}, s)$ are sensor-fluent formulas, $\rho(\vec{x}, s)$ is a sensor formula, and $\gamma(\vec{x}, s)$ is a fluent formula. We use the notation $\phi \backslash \lambda$ to mean the formula that results from replacing every sensor function $h_j(s)$ in ϕ by the j-th component of the final sensor reading in λ. We denote by Σ_0 the part of Σ formed by the initial database and the unique name axioms for actions as above.

Lemma 1 *Let $\rho(\vec{x}, s)$ be a sensor formula. Then for every history λ the following statement is valid:*[5]

$$Sensed[\lambda] \supset \forall\vec{x}.\rho(\vec{x}, end[\lambda]) \equiv \rho(\vec{x}, s)\backslash\lambda$$

Proof: By induction on the structure of $\rho(\vec{x}, s)$. ∎

To begin, we consider simplifications to formulas resulting from sensing, using the guarded sensed fluent axioms.

Definition 4.1 $\phi(\vec{x}, s)$ *simplifies to* $\psi(\vec{x}, s)$ *at* λ *iff there are fluents* $F_1(\vec{t_1}, s), \ldots F_k(\vec{t_k}, s)$ *in* $\phi(\vec{x}, s)$ *with* $k \geq 0$, *and for every* $1 \leq i \leq k$, *there is a GSFA in* Σ

$$\alpha_i(\vec{z}, s) \supset [F_i(\vec{z}, s) \equiv \rho_i(\vec{z}, s)]$$

where $\Sigma \cup Sensed[\lambda] \models \forall\alpha_i(\vec{t_i}, end[\lambda])$, *and* $\psi(\vec{x}, s)$ *is the result of replacing each* $F_i(\vec{t_i}, s)$ *in* $\phi(\vec{x}, s)$ *by* $\rho_i(\vec{t_i}, s)\backslash\lambda$.

Definition 4.2 $\phi(\vec{x}, s)$ *fully simplifies to* $\psi(\vec{x}, s)$ *at* λ *iff* $\phi(\vec{x}, s)$ *simplifies to* $\psi'(\vec{x}, s)$ *at* λ, $\psi'(\vec{x}, s)$ *simplifies only to itself at* λ, *and* $\psi(\vec{x}, s) = \psi'(\vec{x}, s)\backslash\lambda$.

Lemma 2 *If* $\phi(\vec{x}, s)$ *simplifies to* $\psi(\vec{x}, s)$ *at* λ, *then*

$$\Sigma \cup Sensed[\lambda] \models \forall\vec{x}.\phi(\vec{x}, end[\lambda]) \equiv \psi(\vec{x}, end[\lambda])$$

Proof: By logical manipulation and Lemma 1. ∎

Next, we consider simplifications involving reasoning backwards using the guarded successor state axioms.

Definition 4.3 $\phi(\vec{x}, s)$ *rolls back to* $\psi(\vec{x}, s)$ *from a nonempty history* $\lambda = \lambda' \cdot (A, \vec{\mu})$ *iff* $\phi(\vec{x}, s)$ *fully simplifies to* $\phi'(\vec{x}, s)$ *at* λ, *and for every fluent* $F_1(\vec{t_1}, s), \ldots F_k(\vec{t_k}, s)$ *in* $\phi'(\vec{x}, s)$ *with* $k \geq 0$, *there is a GSSA in* Σ

$$\alpha_i(\vec{z}, a, s) \supset [F_i(\vec{z}, do(a, s)) \equiv \gamma_i(\vec{z}, a, s)]$$

where $\Sigma \cup Sensed[\lambda'] \models \forall\alpha_i(\vec{t_i}, A, end[\lambda'])$, *and* $\psi(\vec{x}, s)$ *is the result of replacing each* $F_i(\vec{t_i}, s)$ *in* $\phi'(\vec{x}, s)$ *by* $\gamma_i(\vec{t_i}, A, s)$.

Lemma 3 *If* $\phi(\vec{x}, s)$ *rolls back to* $\psi(\vec{x}, s)$ *from a nonempty history* $\lambda = \lambda' \cdot (A, \vec{\mu})$, *then*

$$\Sigma \cup Sensed[\lambda] \models \forall\vec{x}.\phi(\vec{x}, end[\lambda]) \equiv \psi(\vec{x}, end[\lambda'])$$

Proof: By logical manipulation and Lemma 2. ∎

Putting both forms of simplification together we get:

Definition 4.4 $\phi(\vec{x}, s)$ *regresses to* $\psi(\vec{x}, s)$ *from* λ *iff either:*

- $\lambda = (\vec{\mu_0})$ *and* $\phi(\vec{x}, s)$ *fully simplifies to* $\psi(\vec{x}, s)$ *at* λ.
- $\lambda = \lambda' \cdot (A, \vec{\mu})$ *and* $\phi(\vec{x}, s)$ *rolls back to* $\psi'(\vec{x}, s)$ *from* λ, *and* $\psi'(\vec{x}, s)$ *regresses to* $\psi(\vec{x}, s)$ *from* λ'.

Theorem 4 *If* $\phi(\vec{x}, s)$ *regresses to* $\psi(\vec{x}, s)$ *from* λ *then*

$$\Sigma \cup Sensed[\lambda] \models \forall\vec{x}.\phi(\vec{x}, end[\lambda]) \equiv \psi(\vec{x}, S_0)$$

Proof: By induction on the number of actions in λ using Lemma 2 and Lemma 3. ∎

Observe that a formula $\phi(\vec{x}, s)$ can regress to zero, one, or more formulas $\psi(\vec{x}, s)$ from λ, depending on how many entailed guards we can find for the fluents at each stage.

When a formula with a single free variable does regress, then, as a consequence of Theorem 4, we get the following:

Corollary 5 *Under plausible consistency conditions for* $\Sigma \cup Sensed[\lambda]$,[6] *if* $\phi(s)$ *regresses to* $\psi(s)$ *from* λ *then*

$$\Sigma \cup Sensed[\lambda] \models \phi(end[\lambda]) \quad iff \quad \Sigma_0 \models \psi(S_0)$$

This provides a *soundness* result for regression: to perform the projection task, it is sufficient to regress the formula, and check the result against the initial database.

Unfortunately, regression in general cannot be *complete*. To see why, suppose nothing is known about fluent F; then a formula like $(F(s) \vee \neg F(s))$ will not regress even though it will be entailed at any history. In Section 5, we show that for certain histories (namely those where enough useful sensing information is available), regression will be complete.

The other drawback of regression as defined is that we need to evaluate guards. However, evaluating a guard is just a sub-projection task, and so for certain "well structured" action theories, we can again apply regression, as we now show.

4.1 Acyclic action theories and g-regression

We now restrict our interest to action theories Σ that are acyclic, in the following sense. Let $\prec$, called the *dependency relation*, be a binary relations over fluents s.t. $F' \prec F$ iff there is a GSFA $\{\alpha(\vec{z}, s) \supset [F(\vec{z}, s) \equiv \rho(\vec{z}, s)]\}$ in Σ where F' occurs in $\alpha(\vec{z}, s)$. An action theory Σ *is acyclic* iff the dependency relation $\prec$ is well-founded. When it is, we call the *level* of a fluent F the maximal distance in terms of $\prec$-chains from a bottom element of $\prec$.

Definition 4.5 *Let* Σ *be acyclic. The sensor-fluent formula* $\phi(\vec{x}, s)$ *g-regresses to* $\psi(\vec{x}, s)$ *from* λ *iff* $\phi(\vec{x}, s)$ *regresses to* $\psi(\vec{x}, s)$ *and*

---

[5]We assume a logic with equality.

[6]We will elaborate on this in a longer version of the paper.

- *for every simplification step, where a GSFA in Σ*

$$\alpha(\vec{z}, s) \supset [F(\vec{z}, s) \equiv \rho(\vec{z}, s)]$$

is used to replace $F(\vec{t}, s)$ by $\rho(\vec{t}, s) \backslash \lambda'$ for some subhistory λ', we have that the guard $\alpha(\vec{t}, s)$ g-regresses to some $\alpha'(\vec{t}, s)$ from λ' s.t. $\Sigma_0 \models \forall \alpha'(\vec{t}, S_0)$;

- *for every roll back step, where a GSSA in Σ*

$$\alpha(\vec{z}, a, s) \supset [F(\vec{z}, do(a, s)) \equiv \gamma(\vec{z}, a, s)]$$

is used to replace $F(\vec{t}, s)$ by $\gamma(\vec{t}, A, s)$ for a subhistory $\lambda' \cdot (A, \vec{\mu})$, we have that the guard $\alpha(\vec{t}, A, s)$ g-regresses to some $\alpha'(\vec{t}, A, s)$ from λ' s.t. $\Sigma_0 \models \forall \alpha'(\vec{t}, A, S_0)$.

The trickiest aspect of this definition is to show that the recursion is indeed well-founded. This is done by simultaneous induction on the length of λ and the level of the fluents. Clearly, if a formula g-regresses to another, then it regresses also (although not vice-versa). The main point however is that we only ever need to evaluate formulas at S_0:

Theorem 6 *For an acyclic Σ, under plausible consistency conditions for $\Sigma \cup Sensed[\lambda]$, if $\phi(s)$ g-regresses to some formula from λ, then the only theorem-proving needed to perform projection is to evaluate formulas in Σ_0.*

Proof: By induction on the total number of simplification and roll back steps used to g-regress ϕ, using Corollary 5. ∎

5   JIT-histories

As noted above, we cannot expect to use regression to evaluate sensor-fluent formulas in general: a tautology might be entailed even though nothing is entailed about the component fluents. However, in a practical setting, we can imagine never asking the robot to evaluate a formula unless the history is such that it knows enough about the component fluents, using the given GSSAs and GSFAs, and their component fluents.

For example, assume we have the indoor temperature axioms from Section 3.1. We might only ask the robot to evaluate a formula that mentions the indoor temperature for those histories where the climate control is known to have remained on from some earlier point in the history where the robot was known to be indoors. We do not require the robot to know whether the climate control was on before then (since this may have required going to a control panel), or even whether it is indoors now. In general, we call a history *just-in-time* for a formula, if the actions and sensing readings it contains are enough to guarantee that suitable formulas (including guards) can be evaluated at appropriate points to determine the truth value of all the fluents in the formula. More precisely:

Definition 5.1 *An history λ is a* just-in-time-history *(JIT-history) for a sensor-fluent formula $\phi(\vec{x}, s)$ iff:*

- $\phi(\vec{x}, s) = \neg\phi_1(\vec{x}, s) \mid \phi_1(\vec{x}, s) \wedge \phi_2(\vec{x}, s)$ *and λ is a JIT-history for $\phi_1(\vec{x}, s)$ and $\phi_2(\vec{x}, s)$;*

- $\phi(\vec{x}, s) = \exists y.\phi_1(y, \vec{x}, s)$ *and λ is a JIT-history for the (open) formula $\phi_1(y, \vec{x}, s)$;*

- $\phi(\vec{x}, s)$ *is a sensor formula;*

- $\phi(\vec{x}, s) = F(\vec{t}, s)$, *where F is a fluent, and for some GSFA $\{\alpha(\vec{z}, s) \supset [F(\vec{z}, s) \equiv \rho(\vec{z}, s)]\}$, λ is a JIT-history for $\alpha(\vec{t}, s)$, and $\Sigma \cup Sensed[\lambda] \models \forall \alpha(\vec{t}, end[\lambda])$;*

- $\phi(\vec{x}, s) = F(\vec{t}, s)$, *a fluent, λ is an empty history ($\vec{\mu}_0$), and either $\Sigma_0 \models \forall F(\vec{t}, S_0)$ or $\Sigma_0 \models \forall\neg F(\vec{t}, S_0)$;*

- $\phi(\vec{x}, s) = F(\vec{t}, s)$, *a fluent, $\lambda = \lambda' \cdot (A, \vec{\mu})$, and for some GSSA $\{\alpha(\vec{z}, a, s) \supset [F(\vec{z}, do(a, s)) \equiv \gamma(\vec{z}, a, s)]\}$, λ' is a JIT-history both for $\alpha(\vec{t}, A, s)$ and for $\gamma(\vec{t}, A, s)$, and $\Sigma \cup Sensed[\lambda'] \models \forall \alpha(\vec{t}, A, end[\lambda'])$.*

For JIT-histories we have the following theorem:

Theorem 7 *Let Σ be an action theory as above, and $\phi(\vec{x}, s)$ a sensor-fluent formula. If λ is a JIT-history for $\phi(\vec{x}, s)$, then there exists a formula $\psi(\vec{x}, s)$ such that:*

1. *$\phi(\vec{x}, s)$ regresses to $\psi(\vec{x}, s)$ from λ, and*

2. *if Σ is acyclic, then $\phi(\vec{x}, s)$ g-regresses to $\psi(\vec{x}, s)$ from λ, and either $\Sigma_0 \models \forall \vec{x}.\psi(\vec{x}, S_0)$ or $\Sigma_0 \models \forall \vec{x}.\neg\psi(\vec{x}, S_0)$.*

Proof: (1) is proven by induction on the length of λ and induction on the structure of $\phi(\vec{x}, s)$; (2) is proven by simultaneous induction on the length of λ and the (max) level of the fluents in the $\phi(\vec{x}, s)$, and induction on the structure of $\phi(\vec{x}, s)$. ∎

This theorem shows that for JIT-histories, regression is both a sound and complete way of performing projection.

6   An evaluation procedure for projection

Although our action theories are assumed to be *open-world*, a JIT-history provides a sort of *dynamic* closed world assumption in that it ensures that the truth value of any fluent will be known whenever it is part of a formula whose truth value we need to determine. This allows us to evaluate complex formulas as we would if we had a normal closed world assumption. We now consider a Prolog procedure that does this.

We assume the user provides the following clauses:[7]

- `fluent`(F), for each fluent F,
- `sensor`(h), for each sensor function h,
- `ini`(F), for each fluent F such that $\Sigma_0 \models F(S_0)$,
- `closed`(F), for each fluent F such that $\Sigma_0 \models F(S_0)$ or $\Sigma_0 \models \neg F(S_0)$,
- `gsfa`(α, F, ρ), for each GSFA,
- `gssa`(a, α, F, γ), for each GSSA, where a is the distinguished action term quantified in α and γ

Formulas are expressed using `and`(ϕ, ψ), `neg`(ϕ), `equ`(t, t'), and `some`(v, ϕ) where v is a Prolog constant. We drop the situation arguments from fluents and sensor functions in formulas (and keep track of the situation in the history).

Histories are represented as lists. For brevity, we assume a predicate `last`(λ, h, r) which extracts the last value r for sensor function h in history λ. We assume also a predicate `sub`(v, x, ϕ, ϕ') with the meaning that ϕ' is the formula obtained by substituting x for v in the formula ϕ (see [6]). Now we define `eval`(λ, ϕ, b), with the intended meaning that the formula ϕ evaluates to the truth-value b (`tt`/`ff`) for the history λ, as follows:

---

[7]For simplicity in what follows, we do not distinguish between situation calculus formulas and their representations as Prolog terms.

```
eval(H,and(P1,P2),tt) :-
    eval(H,P1,tt), eval(H,P2,tt).
eval(H,and(P1,P2),ff) :-
    eval(H,P1,ff); eval(H,P2,ff).
eval(H,neg(P),tt) :- eval(H,P,ff).
eval(H,neg(P),ff) :- eval(H,P,tt).
eval(H,some(V,Pv),tt) :-
    sub(V,_,Pv,Px), eval(H,Px,tt).
eval(H,some(V,Pv),ff) :-
    not(sub(V,_,Pv,Px), not eval(H,Px,ff)).
    /* double negation for ``for all'' */
    /* so not eval(H,Px,ff) flounders!  */
eval(H,equ(E,V),tt) :-
    sensor(E), last(H,E,R), R=V.
eval(H,equ(E,V),ff) :- /* Neg as failure */
    sensor(E), last(H,E,R), not R=V.
eval([[(Mu)]],F,tt) :- fluent(F), ini(F).
eval([[(Mu)]],F,ff) :- /* Neg as failure */
    fluent(F), closed(F), not ini(F).
eval(H,F,B) :-
    fluent(F), gsfa(Alpha,F,Rho),
    eval(H,Alpha,tt), eval(H,Rho,B).
eval([[(A,Mu)|H],F,B) :-
    fluent(F), gssa(A,Alpha,F,Gamma),
    eval(H,Alpha,tt), eval(H,Gamma,B).
```

Observe that a formula $\texttt{eval}(\lambda, \phi, b)$ can either succeed returning $\texttt{tt}$, succeed returning $\texttt{ff}$, fail, or not terminate. Under the assumption that all the auxiliary predicates are correct and terminating, we get the following soundness and a weak form of completeness for $\texttt{eval}$:

Theorem 8 *Assume that* $\texttt{eval}(\lambda, \phi(\vec{x}, s), \texttt{B})$ *succeeds with computed answer* $\vec{x} = \vec{t}$, $\texttt{B} = b$. *If* $b = \texttt{tt}$, *then* $\Sigma \cup Sensed[\lambda] \models \forall\phi(\vec{t}, end[\lambda])$; *if* $b = \texttt{ff}$ *then* $\Sigma \cup Sensed[\lambda] \models \forall\neg\phi(\vec{t}, end[\lambda])$.

Proof: By induction on the structure of $\phi(\vec{x}, s)$. ∎

Theorem 9 *Let* λ *be a JIT-history for* $\phi(\vec{x}, s)$. *Then,* $\texttt{eval}(\lambda, \phi(\vec{x}, s), \texttt{B})$ *does not finitely fail.*

Proof: By induction on the structure of $\phi(\vec{x}, s)$. ∎

Note that we cannot guarantee termination since we can get into a loop evaluating guards of GSFAs or GSSAs, or by floundering in trying to evaluate to $\texttt{ff}$ an existential. We can eliminate the first problem by using acyclic action theories. For the second, we can close the domain. Let $\texttt{domain}(o)$ be a user-defined predicate over a finite domain. We can then change the definition of $\texttt{eval}$ for existentials as follows:

```
eval(H,some(V,Pv),tt) :-
    domain(O), sub(V,O,Pv,Po), eval(H,Po,tt).
eval(H,some(V,Pv),ff) :-
    not(domain(O), sub(V,O,Pv,Po),
        not eval(H,Po,ff)).
```

For this new version of $\texttt{eval}$ we get a completeness result:

Theorem 10 *Let* Σ *be acyclic, let* $\phi(s)$ *be a sensor-fluent formula with no free variables except the situation argument* s, *and let* λ *be a JIT-history for* $\phi(s)$. *Then,* $\texttt{eval}(\lambda, \phi(s), \texttt{B})$ *always succeeds, returning either* $\texttt{tt}$ *or* $\texttt{ff}$.

So under these circumstances, $\texttt{eval}$ is a sound and complete implementation of projection.

7 Conclusions

We have given a formal definition of projection for a generalized action theory where successor state axioms and sensing information are only conditionally applicable. We also showed that in certain circumstances, a regression-based evaluation procedure could correctly perform the task.

Many open problems remain, however. How can we decide in an automated but practical way when regression can be used? It may be expecting too much of a conditional planner to determine what actions it should perform now to permit it to later use sensing information in this way. An interesting alternative is offered by the high-level program execution model. Given a program like "if ϕ then do δ_1 else do δ_2," the *user* can take the responsibility of inserting a prior program ensuring that the resulting history is just in time for ϕ.

Another related problem is the projection of initial databases. Once a robot actually performs a sequence of actions in the world, we would prefer to no longer regress all the way back to the initial situation, but instead to project the database forward to the current state [8]. How this can be done for the action theories we are proposing remains to be seen.

References

[1] C. Baral and T.C. Son. Approximate reasoning about actions in presence of sensing and incomplete information. In *Proc. of ILPS'97*, 387–401.

[2] R. Fikes and N. Nilsson. STRIPS: a new approach to the application of theorem proving to problem solving. In *Artificial Intelligence*, 2, 189–208, 1971.

[3] K. Golden and D.S. Weld. Representing sensing actions: the middle ground revisited. In *Proc. of KR'96*, 174–185.

[4] J. McCarthy and P. Hayes. Some philosophical problems from the standpoint of artificial intelligence. In *Machine Intelligence*, vol. 4, Edinburgh University Press, 1969.

[5] H. Levesque. What is planning in the presence of sensing? In *Proc. of AAAI'96*, 1139–1146.

[6] H. Levesque, R. Reiter, Y. Lespérance, F. Lin, and R. B. Scherl. GOLOG: A logic programming language for dynamic domains. In *Journal of Logic Programming*, 31, 59–84, 1997.

[7] F. Lin and R. Reiter. State constraints revisited. *Journal of Logic and Computation*, 4(5), 655–678, 1994.

[8] F. Lin and R. Reiter. How to progress a database. *Artificial Intelligence*, 92, 131–167, 1997.

[9] D. Poole. Logic programming for robot control. In *Proc. IJCAI'95*, 150–157.

[10] R. Reiter. The frame problem in the situation calculus: A simple solution (sometimes) and a completeness result for goal regression. In *Artificial Intelligence and Mathematical Theory of Computation*, 359–380. Academic Press, 1991.

[11] R. Reiter. *Knowledge in Action: Logical Foundation for Describing and Implementing Dynamical Systems*. In preparation.

[12] D.S. Weld, C.R. Anderson, D.E. Smith. Extending graphplan to handle uncertainty and sensing actions. In *Proc. of AAAI'98*, 897–904.

Expressive Reasoning about Action in Nondeterministic Polynomial Time

Thomas Drakengren
Laxgatan 4, 2tr
S-133 43 Saltsjöbaden, Sweden
thodr@fjuk.org

Marcus Bjäreland[*]
Dept of Comp and Info Science
Linköping University
S-581 83 Linköping, Sweden
marbj@ida.liu.se

Abstract

The rapid development of efficient heuristics for deciding satisfiability for propositional logic motivates thorough investigations of the usability of NP-complete problems in general. In this paper we introduce a logic of action and change which is expressive in the sense that it can represent most propositional benchmark examples in the literature, and some new examples involving parallel composition of actions, and actions that may or may not be executed. We prove that satisfiability of a scenario in this logic is NP-complete, and that it subsumes an NP-complete logic (which in turn includes a nontrivial polynomial-time fragment) previously introduced by Drakengren and Bjäreland.

1 Introduction

The rapid development of efficient heuristics for deciding satisfiability for propositional logic (GSAT and similar heuristics [Selman *et al.*, 1992]) motivates thorough investigations of the usability of NP-complete problems in general. In this paper we introduce a logic of action and change which is expressive in the sense that it can represent most propositional[1] benchmark examples in the literature, and some new examples involving parallel composition of actions, and actions that may or may not be executed. We prove that this logic extends a previous formalism, where satisfiability for scenarios is NP-complete, and for which reasoning could be done in polynomial time in a fragment of the logic [Drakengren and Bjäreland, 1997]. Although the polynomial class they characterize is nontrivial, its expressiveness is very limited. This also holds for the tractable fragments of the action description language $\mathcal{A}$ [Gelfond and Lifschitz, 1993], found by Liberatore [1997]. In that work, Liberatore showed that satisfiability of $\mathcal{A}$ is NP-complete, and

---

[*]This research has been supported in parts by the Swedish Research Council for Engineering Sciences (TFR), the Knut and Alice Wallenberg Foundation, and ASEA Brown Bovery (dept ISY/AMC).

[1]This means that fluents are propositional.

he provided an encoding of $\mathcal{A}$ into propositional logic in order to able to use e.g. GSAT. There seems to be no other analyses of computational complexity for similar formalisms, for instance for the Situation Calculus [McCarthy and Hayes, 1969].

2 Overview

We will develop a logic for action and change in similar spirit as in Drakengren and Bjäreland [1997] (henceforth, for convenience we shall denote this paper *DB97*), i.e. we will define the syntax and semantics of a temporal propositional logic (syntactically, but not semantically related to TPTL [Alur and Henzinger, 1989]) with the possibility of expressing time points as linear polynomials with rational coefficients. Then we introduce the notion of a *scenario description*, which is basically a set of formulae in the temporal logic, and formulae that describe the change of fluent values over time. An *interpretation* of a scenario description is a function, which given a set of formulae yields the possibilities as to what *combinations of changes* are allowed by the set of formulae. For instance, a scenario description may allow either the combination of changes that the feature *loaded* and *alive* both are set to false at time 3, or the combination that *gunnerSleeps* is set to true at time 3. A *model* of a scenario description is defined as an interpretation such that for some possible combination of changes, fluents change values iff they are explicitly stated to change by this combination of changes. This way of defining interpretations enables us to (semantically) model composition of actions as operations on sets of combinations of changes, and to (syntactically) model them on the object-level. In fact, we will view every Boolean combination of changes as an object-level composition of separate actions, in an arbitrary number of levels. The basis case is then the *change features*, which are syntactical constructs that state that the value of one feature changes to true or false.

For the results regarding computation, the NP-hardness of satisfiability in our logic is obvious, since we can encode propositional logic in it. NP-membership, on the other hand, is more tricky to prove: the obvious way of guessing an interpretation and a combination of changes and verifying that the interpretation is a model using this combination of changes in polynomial time fails, since the set of combinations of changes can be exponentially large. Instead, we guess also *how* a combination of changes is obtained from the interpretation, and this solves the problem. However, this proof technique fails if we introduce quantification over time points, which is used in approaches to ramification (see e.g. Gustafsson and Doherty [1996]).

3 Scenario Descriptions

This section defines syntax and semantics of the logic together with some illustrating examples.

3.1 Syntax

We begin by defining a slight (syntactical) extension of the temporal logic in DB97. What differs is that the binary operator $\vee_x$ for *exclusive or* is included, but it is straightforward to check that all relevant results of DB97 hold with this extension.

Definition 1 A *signature* is a tuple $\sigma = \langle \mathcal{T}, \mathcal{F} \rangle$, where $\mathcal{T}$ is a finite set of time point variables and $\mathcal{F}$ is a finite set of propositional features. A *time point expression* is a linear polynomial over $\mathcal{T}$ with rational coefficients. We denote the set of time point expressions over $\mathcal{T}$ by $\mathcal{T}^*$. □

Definition 2 Let $\sigma = \langle \mathcal{T}, \mathcal{F} \rangle$ be a signature, let $\alpha, \beta \in \mathcal{T}^*$, $f \in \mathcal{F}$, $R \in \{=, \leq, <, \geq, >\}$, $\oplus \in \{\wedge, \vee, \vee_x, \rightarrow, \leftrightarrow\}$, and define the *scenario description language* Σ over σ by

$$\Sigma ::= \text{T} \mid \text{F} \mid f \mid \alpha R \beta \mid \neg \Sigma \mid \Sigma_1 \oplus \Sigma_2 \mid [\alpha]\Sigma.$$

A formula $[\alpha]\gamma$ expresses that at time α, γ is true. The remaining connectives are standard (the notation for exclusive or, $\vee_x$, is however nonstandard). Whenever we say "formula", we mean a formula in Σ, for a given σ.

Let γ be a formula. A feature $f \in \mathcal{F}$ occurs *free* in γ iff it does not occur within the scope of a $[\alpha]$ expression in γ. If no feature occurs free in γ, γ is *closed*.

The *size* of a set of formulae is the sum of the lengths of the formulae in the set. □

We shall be informal with respect to specifying over what signature the language Σ is defined, when it is clear what signature is intended.

In DB97 a special language for expressing action scenarios, extending the basic temporal logic, is defined. In this paper, we shall not need that; we just modify the semantics of the temporal logic, and identify a distinguished set of features which designate *change* of another feature. This is the natural generalisation of Sandewall's concept of *occlusion*, which in turn is equivalent to what is accomplished by a *release* statement in the language $\mathcal{AR}$ [Giunchiglia *et al.*, 1997].

Definition 3 (Scenario description) Let $\sigma = \langle \mathcal{T}, \mathcal{F} \rangle$ be a signature, $\mathcal{I} \subseteq \mathcal{F}$, $\Delta = \{\delta(f, \text{T}), \delta(f, \text{F}) \mid f \in \mathcal{F}\}$, $\sigma' = \langle \mathcal{T}, \mathcal{F} \cup \Delta \rangle$ (that is, we consider $\delta(f, \text{T})$ and $\delta(f, \text{F})$ to be features themselves), and Γ a finite set of closed formulae over σ'. Then $\Upsilon = \langle \sigma, \Gamma, \mathcal{I} \rangle$ is said to be

a *scenario description*. We will call features of the form $\delta(f, \text{T})$ and $\delta(f, \text{F})$ *change features*. Given Υ, the set Δ is denoted $\Delta(\Upsilon)$. □

The set $\mathcal{I}$ consists of all fluents that are supposed to be inert, i.e. features that will not change value over time, unless explicitly stated. The fluents not in $\mathcal{I}$ are non-inert. Intuitively, the set Δ of features is intended to model that the corresponding features in $\mathcal{I}$ can be subject to change, and remain unchanged otherwise.

We now present some examples in order to present some properties of our formalism, and to try to convince the reader that most propositional benchmark examples in the literature (see e.g. Sandewall [1994] for a list) can be represented.

Example 4 We take an example, the Russian Turkey Shoot (RTS), by Sandewall [1994], where we initially (at time point 0) assume that a turkey is alive, and that a gun is unloaded. Then we load the gun (at time point 1), spin the chamber (at 3), and fire the gun (between 4 and 5). The intended conclusion of this scenario is that we cannot prove that the turkey is alive, or dead, after the firing action has been executed. Semantically we want one model where the turkey is dead, and one where it is alive, after the execution of the firing action. We now formalise the scenario:

$$\Upsilon_{RTS} = \langle \langle \emptyset, \{alive, loaded\}\rangle, \ \Gamma_{RTS}, \{alive, loaded\}\rangle,$$

where

$$
\begin{aligned}
\Gamma_{RTS} \ = \ \{ & [0]alive \wedge \neg loaded, \\
& [1]\delta(loaded, \text{T}), \\
& [3]\delta(loaded, \text{T}) \vee \delta(loaded, \text{F}), \\
& [4]loaded \rightarrow \\
& \qquad [5]\delta(alive, \text{F}) \wedge \delta(loaded, \text{F})\}.
\end{aligned}
$$

□

Example 5 As an example of parallel composition we use the Balls and Boxes Scenario (BBS): We have two non-empty boxes on the ground, standing side by side. Our first action, a_1 is to drop a ball between the boxes, so that it is unknown in which box the ball will end up. The second action, a_2, is to throw a ball into the left box. Initially both boxes are empty. We are interested in the case when both a_1 and a_2 happen. We use the features *leftEmpty*, and *rightEmpty*, which are true if the left, or the right box is empty, respectively.

$$
\begin{aligned}
\Gamma_{Boxes} \ = \ \{ & [0]leftEmpty \wedge rightEmpty, \\
& [\text{t}]\delta(leftEmpty, \text{F}) \vee_x \\
& \qquad \delta(rightEmpty, \text{F}), \\
& [\text{t}]\delta(leftEmpty, \text{F})\}.
\end{aligned}
$$

The effect of both a_1 and a_2 happening, as described by the second and third formulae in the set above, as we will see below, will be

$$[\text{t}](\delta(leftEmpty, \text{F}) \vee_x \delta(rightEmpty, \text{F})) \wedge \delta(leftEmpty, \text{F}).$$

The intended conclusion is that either only the right box is empty, or both boxes are nonempty. We cannot get the second case by formulating the composite action in a straightforward manner in e.g. PMON[2] [Doherty, 1994], since

$$((\neg H(\mathbf{t}, \textit{leftEmpty}) \vee_x \neg H(\mathbf{t}, \textit{rightEmpty})) \wedge$$
$$\neg H(\mathbf{t}, \textit{leftEmpty})) \wedge$$
$$Occlude(\mathbf{t}, \textit{leftEmpty}) \wedge Occlude(\mathbf{t}, \textit{rightEmpty})$$

is equivalent to

$$(\neg H(\mathbf{t}, \textit{leftEmpty}) \wedge H(\mathbf{t}, \textit{rightEmpty})) \wedge$$
$$Occlude(\mathbf{t}, \textit{leftEmpty}) \wedge Occlude(\mathbf{t}, \textit{rightEmpty}),$$

i.e. the box to the right will be empty. □

Example 6 Finally, we model actions that may or may not be executed as $[\mathbf{t}](A \vee \mathtt{T})$, where A is describes an action, and $\mathtt{T}$ the truth value *true*. When we define the semantics of scenario descriptions, the intuition behind this syntax will be clear. Logics like PMON will have similar problems with this construct, but for reasons of space, an example of that is omitted. □

For an example with interactions between concurrently executed actions, see DB97 (which is the *soup bowl lifting* example of [Baral and Gelfond, 1997]).

3.2 Semantics

We now define the semantics of the temporal logic. The semantics will be directly defined in terms of scenario descriptions; note however that the semantics will be identical to the standard semantics of the basic temporal logic of DB97 if we set $\mathcal{I} = \emptyset$.

Definition 7 Let $\sigma = \langle \mathcal{T}, \mathcal{F} \rangle$ be a signature. A *state* over σ is a function from $\mathcal{F}$ to the set $\{\mathtt{T}, \mathtt{F}\}$ of truth values. A *history* over σ is a function h from $\mathbb{R}$ to the set of states. A *valuation* ϕ is a function from $\mathcal{T}$ to $\mathbb{R}$. It is extended in a natural way, giving e.g. $\phi(3t+4.3) = 3\phi(t)+4.3$. An *interpretation* over σ is a tuple $I = \langle h, \phi \rangle$ where h is a history and ϕ is a valuation.

Similarly for a scenario description Υ with signature σ, I is an interpretation for Υ iff I is an interpretation over σ. □

In ordinary logic, we use the notion of *truth value* for a formula in a model. Here we shall genereralise this, so that we instead obtain a set of *possible combinations of changes*, where an empty such set corresponds to F, and a nonempty set corresponds to T, but with possibly several alternatives for changes of actions (this is nondeterminism on the semantical level).

Definition 8 (Combination of changes, possible combinations of changes) Let $\Upsilon = \langle \sigma, \Gamma, \mathcal{I} \rangle$ be a scenario description, $\gamma = \bigwedge \Gamma$, and let $I = \langle h, \phi \rangle$ be an interpretation over σ. A set e of tuples $\langle t, f, \tau \rangle$, where $t \in \mathbb{R}$, $f \in \mathcal{I}$ and $\tau \in \{\mathtt{T}, \mathtt{F}\}$ is said to be a *combination of changes* (one tuple therein is said to be a *change*), and a set E of such combinations is said to be *a set of possible combinations of changes*.

---

[2]It seems that most other logics of action and change would have similar problems.

Given Γ, I and t, the set of *possible combinations of changes* of Γ in I for a time point $t \in \mathbb{R}$, denoted $I(\Gamma, t)$, is a set E (note that this is a set of *sets*) of possible combinations of changes is defined below. For this we first need an auxiliary function $condeff(B, E)$, taking a truth value B and a set E of possible combinations of changes, returning E if B is true, and $\emptyset$ otherwise.

Let $f \in \mathcal{F}$, $R \in \{=, \leq, <, \geq, >\}$, $\alpha, \beta \in \mathcal{T}^*$, $\gamma, \epsilon \in \Sigma$, $\oplus \in \{\wedge, \vee, \vee_x, \rightarrow, \leftrightarrow\}$, and $\tau \in \{\mathtt{T}, \mathtt{F}\}$. Now define

$$
\begin{aligned}
I(\Gamma, t) &= I(\bigwedge \Gamma), t) \\
I(\tau, t) &= condeff(\tau, \{\emptyset\}) \\
I(f, t) &= condeff(h(t)(f), \{\emptyset\}) \\
I(\delta(f, \mathtt{T}), t) &= \{\{\langle t, f, \mathtt{T} \rangle\}\} \\
I(\delta(f, \mathtt{F}), t) &= \{\{\langle t, f, \mathtt{F} \rangle\}\} \\
I(\alpha R \beta, t) &= condeff(\phi(\alpha) R \phi(\beta), \{\emptyset\}) \\
I(\neg \gamma, t) &= \neg I(\gamma, t) \\
I(\gamma \oplus \epsilon, t) &= I(\gamma, t) \oplus I(\epsilon, t) \\
I([\alpha]\gamma, t) &= I(\gamma, \phi(\alpha)),
\end{aligned}
$$

where the operators $\neg$, $\wedge$, $\vee$, $\vee_x$, $\rightarrow$ and $\leftrightarrow$ on sets E_1, E_2 of possible combinations of changes as follows.

$$
\begin{aligned}
\neg E_1 &= \begin{cases} \emptyset & \text{if } E_1 \neq \emptyset \\ \{\emptyset\} & \text{otherwise} \end{cases} \\
E_1 \wedge E_2 &= \{e_1 \cup e_2 \mid e_1 \in E_1, e_2 \in E_2\} \\
E_1 \vee E_2 &= \{e_1, e_2, e_1 \cup e_2 \mid e_1 \in E_1, e_2 \in E_2\} \\
E_1 \vee_x E_2 &= \{e_1 \in E_1 \mid \neg \exists e_2 \in E_2.e_2 \subseteq e_1\} \cup \\
&\quad \{e_2 \in E_2 \mid \neg \exists e_1 \in E_1.e_1 \subseteq e_2\} \\
E_1 \rightarrow E_2 &= \begin{cases} E_2 & \text{if } E_1 \neq \emptyset \\ \{\emptyset\} & \text{otherwise} \end{cases} \\
E_1 \leftrightarrow E_2 &= (E_1 \rightarrow E_2) \wedge (E_2 \rightarrow E_1)
\end{aligned}
$$

□

Since the result of I does not depend on t when γ is closed, we can write $I(\gamma)$ in these cases. If $I(\gamma) \neq \emptyset$, we say that γ is *true* in I.

With this definition of interpretations, it is clear that we model *any* Boolean combination of combinations of changes as composition. For example, disjunction is non-deterministic composition, and conjunction is parallel composition (with "parallel" here, we denote that the changes could *possibly* be simultaneous). However, note that negated change features (e.g. as antecedents in implication) do *not* affect the resulting set of combinations of changes. For example, the formula $[\mathbf{t}]\delta(f_1, \mathtt{T}) \rightarrow \delta(f_2, \mathtt{T})$ is equivalent to $\mathtt{T} \rightarrow \delta(f_2, \mathtt{T})$, since a negated change is interpreted to $\emptyset$ or $\{\emptyset\}$: that is, we do not model that something should *not* change. This of course means that implication is *causal* and not material (see e.g. McCain and Turner [1995]).

Intuitively, we should interpret the empty set of possible combinations of changes so that there is no possible combination of effects that could have taken place, and the set *containing* only the empty set as its possible combination of changes that the only possibility with respect to changes is that *nothing* changes. This is coherent with how the *truth value* is defined above.

We will briefly discuss how our three examples are interpreted:

- For RTS, the interesting part to interpret is the spinning action, which yields:

$$I([3]\delta(loaded, \text{T}) \vee [3]\delta(loaded, \text{F})) =$$
$$I([3]\delta(loaded, \text{T})) \vee I([3]\delta(loaded, \text{F})) =$$
$$I(\delta(loaded, \text{T}), 3) \vee I(\delta(loaded, \text{F}), 3) =$$
$$\{\{\langle 3, loaded, \text{T}\rangle\}\} \vee \{\{\langle 3, loaded, \text{F}\rangle\}\} =$$
$$\{\{\langle 3, loaded, \text{T}\rangle\}, \{\langle 3, loaded, \text{F}\rangle\},$$
$$\{\langle 3, loaded, \text{T}\rangle, \langle 3, loaded, \text{F}\rangle\}\}$$

Thus, we have three possibilities of change due to the spinning action, that *loaded* becomes true, that it becomes false, or that it becomes both true and false (this is, of course, impossible, and it is taken care of by the histories, as we will see below).

- For BBS, we focus on the composite action $a_1 \wedge a_2$, i.e.

$$[\mathbf{t}](\delta(leftEmpty, \text{F}) \vee_x \delta(rightEmpty, \text{F})) \wedge$$
$$\delta(leftEmpty, \text{F}),$$

for which we get the following possible combinations of changes:

$$(\{\{\langle \mathbf{t}, leftEmpty, \text{F}\rangle\}\} \vee_x \{\{\langle \mathbf{t}, rightEmpty, \text{F}\rangle\}\}) \wedge$$
$$\{\{\langle \mathbf{t}, leftEmpty, \text{F}\rangle\}\}.$$

By definition of the operator $\vee_x$ on sets of possible combinations of changes, we get the following:

$$\{\{\langle \mathbf{t}, leftEmpty, \text{F}\rangle\}, \{\langle \mathbf{t}, rightEmpty, \text{F}\rangle\}\} \wedge$$
$$\{\{\langle \mathbf{t}, leftEmpty, \text{F}\rangle\}\} =$$
$$\{\{\langle \mathbf{t}, leftEmpty, \text{F}\rangle\},$$
$$\{\langle \mathbf{t}, rightEmpty, \text{F}\rangle, \langle \mathbf{t}, leftEmpty, \text{F}\rangle\}\}$$

There are two possibilities: in the first combination of changes, only the right box will be empty, whereas in the second, both boxes are nonempty.

- For the "maybe" action, we note that

$$I([\mathbf{t}]A \vee [\mathbf{t}]\text{T}) = I(A, \mathbf{t}) \vee I(\text{T}, \mathbf{t}) = I(A, \mathbf{t}) \vee \{\emptyset\}.$$

The resulting set will include $\{\emptyset\}$, which means that it is possible that the resulting action has no effects at all, which is what we intended.

Proposition 9 Let Γ be a set of formulae over a signature σ containing no formulae of the type $\delta(f, \text{T})$ or $\delta(f, \text{F})$. Then I is a model of Γ in the sense of DB97 iff $I(\Upsilon) \neq \emptyset$ for the scenario description $\Upsilon = \langle \sigma, \Gamma, \emptyset\rangle$.
Proof: An easy induction shows first that $I(\gamma) \in \{\emptyset, \{\emptyset\}\}$, and then that $\emptyset$ corresponds to F and $\{\emptyset\}$ to T according to the definitions of DB97. □

Finally, we need to code the fact that actions succeed, and *inertia* (the frame problem) into the formalism. This is done by identifying all time points where a feature f can possibly change its value, exactly as in DB97. During every interval where no such change time point exists, f has to have the same value throughout the interval.

When looking at the following definition, it is instructive to look at the corresponding definition in DB97.

Definition 10 Let $\Upsilon = \langle \sigma, \Gamma, \mathcal{I}\rangle$ be a scenario description. A *model*[3] of Υ is an interpretation $I = \langle h, \phi\rangle$ for which there exists an $e \in I(\Gamma)$ such that

- for each $f \in \mathcal{I}$ and $s, t \in \mathbb{R}$ with $s < t$ such that for no $t' \in (s, t]$ (half-open interval) $\langle t', f, \tau\rangle \in e$ holds (for some $\tau \in \{\text{T}, \text{F}\}$), we have $h(t)(f) = h(s)(f)$

- for each $\langle t, f, \tau\rangle \in e$, it holds that $h(t)(f) = \tau$.

Intuitively, this definition ensures that no change in the value of a feature occurs in an interval if nothing changes it explicitly, and all specified changes have effect. Note that e is always a finite set, so this definition makes sense[4].

Denote by $Mod(\Upsilon)$ the set of all models for a scenario description Υ.

A formula $\gamma \in \Sigma$ is *entailed* by a scenario description Υ, denoted $\Upsilon \models \gamma$, iff γ is true in all models of Υ. Υ is *satisfiable* iff $Mod(\Upsilon) \neq \emptyset$. □

Fact 11 If $\Upsilon = \langle \sigma, \Gamma, \mathcal{I}\rangle$ is a scenario description and $\gamma \in \Sigma$ a formula, then $\Upsilon \models \gamma$ iff $\langle \sigma, \Gamma \cup \{\neg\gamma\}, \mathcal{I}\rangle$ is unsatisfiable. □

Next we establish that this formalism indeed subsumes that of DB97. An auxiliary result is needed[5].

Definition 12 (Corresponding action formula)
Let a be the action expression $\phi \Rightarrow [\alpha]\psi\texttt{Infl}$ (in the sense of DB97). Then the formula

$$\phi \to [\alpha](\psi \wedge \bigwedge_{f \in \texttt{Infl}} (\delta(f, \text{T}) \vee_x \delta(f, \text{F})))$$

is said to be the *action formula* corresponding to a. □

The subsumption result follows.

Proposition 13 Let $\Upsilon' = \langle \sigma, \text{SCD}, \text{OBS}\rangle$ be a scenario description in the sense of DB97, let $\mathcal{A}$ be the set of action formlae corresponding to action expressions in SCD, and define the scenario description $\Upsilon = \langle \sigma, \text{OBS} \cup \mathcal{A}, \mathcal{F}\rangle$, where $\sigma = \langle \mathcal{T}, \mathcal{F}\rangle$. Then the set of models of Υ' is identical to the set of models of Υ.
Proof: Just compare the definitions. □

4 Complexity Results

The following result is easy.

Theorem 14 Deciding satisfiability of a scenario description is NP-hard.
Proof: NP-hardness follows, since we can express satisfiability of propositional logic formulae. □

---

[3]Often, the term *intended model* is used for models of scenario descriptions. However, it seems more philosophically correct to name it just *model*. We shall also name the intended models in DB97 just *models*.

[4]Infinite sets of changes could express open intervals of changes, which would require some more machinery to obtain a suitable definition.

[5]Due to space limitations, we refer the reader to the original paper instead of repeating the definitions here.

NP-membership, on the other hand, is more involved to prove. For instance, the obvious method of guessing a combination of changes and verifying that this set is a member of the set of possible combinations of changes, fails, since the set of sets can be exponentially large. We need some auxiliary notions.

Definition 15 Let Γ be a set of formulae. Then define $time(\Gamma)$ to be the set of time point expressions used in Γ. Also, for a scenario description $\Upsilon = \langle \sigma, \Gamma, \mathcal{I} \rangle$, define $time(\Upsilon) = time(\Gamma)$, and $changes(\Upsilon)$ to be the set $time(\Upsilon) \times \mathcal{I} \times \{\mathtt{T}, \mathtt{F}\}$.

Let I be an interpretation over σ and suppose that $e \in I(\Upsilon)$. For each $\langle t, f, \tau \rangle \in e$, find an $\alpha \in time(\Upsilon)$ such that $I(\alpha) = t$ (such an α always exists); collect these tuples $\langle \alpha, f, \tau \rangle$ in the set U. Now let $synteff$ be a function taking Υ, I and e, returning such an U, that is, $synteff(\Upsilon, I, e) = U$ (such a function clearly exists).

The function thus makes a syntactic representation of a set of changes, relative to a scenario description and an interpretation. Such a set is said to be a *syntactic combination of changes*. □

Next, we shall show how to represent an interpretation I in terms of a set of formulae.

Definition 16 ($A(T)$, *intrep*) Let $\sigma = \langle \mathcal{T}, \mathcal{F} \rangle$ be a signature, $T \subseteq \mathcal{T}^*$, and set $A(T) = \{[\alpha]f, \alpha R\beta \mid \alpha, \beta \in T, f \in \mathcal{F}, R \in \{<, \leq, =, \geq, >\}\}$.

Let $I = \langle h, \phi \rangle$ be an interpretation over σ. Then define $intrep(I, T) = \{\gamma \in A(T) \mid I(\gamma) \neq \emptyset\}$. Note that the sizes of A and thus $intrep(I, T)$ are polynomial in the sizes of T and $\mathcal{F}$. □

Thus $intrep(I, T)$ represents the interpretation I, given that only the time point expressions in T are important.

Proposition 17 Verifying for an arbitrary subset $B \subseteq A(T)$ whether $B = intrep(I, T)$ for some I and T can be done in time polynomial in the size of $A(T)$.
Proof: We use a result of DB97, saying that satisfiability of a set of *Horn formulae* can be solved in polynomial time. For this proof, it is enough to know that formulae in $A(T)$ and negations of such formulae are Horn formulae.

Construct the set $B' = B \cup \{\neg\gamma \mid \gamma \in A(T), \gamma \notin B\}$. Now it is clear that B' has a model I iff $B = intrep(I, T)$, and the result follows. □

Corollary 18 Let I be an interpretation over $\sigma = \langle \mathcal{T}, \mathcal{F} \rangle$, $T \subseteq \mathcal{T}^*$, and let $W = intrep(I, T)$. Then querying whether $I(\gamma) \neq \emptyset$ for $\gamma \in A(T)$ can be done in time polynomial in the size of $A(T)$.
Proof: Just check whether $\gamma \in W$. □

Definition 19 (Annotated formula) Let $\Upsilon = \langle \sigma, \Gamma, \mathcal{I} \rangle$ be a scenario description, $\gamma = \bigwedge \Gamma$, and let the formula γ' (which is never a member of Σ) be obtained from γ by replacing every subformula β of γ (γ is counted as a subformula of itself) by the expression $\langle \beta, E, \alpha \rangle$, for $E \subseteq \{e\}$, with some arbitrarily chosen $e \subseteq changes(\Upsilon)$, and $\alpha \in time(\Upsilon)$. Then γ' is said to be an *annotated formula* for Υ. Note that the size of γ' is polynomial in

the size of Υ, and that γ can always easily be recovered from γ'. Then we write $\gamma = unannotate(\gamma')$. □

Definition 20 (Syntactic scenario interpretation, syntactic scenario model) Let $\Upsilon = \langle \sigma, \Gamma, \mathcal{I} \rangle$ be a scenario description, $T = time(\Upsilon)$, S a pair $\langle W, \gamma' \rangle$, with $W \subseteq A(T)$ and $\gamma' = \langle \gamma, E, \alpha \rangle$ an annotated formula for Υ. Then S is said to be a *syntactic scenario interpretation* for Υ.

For the definition of a syntactic scenario model, we need an auxiliary definition: define the function $condeff_s(B, E)$ (a syntactic variant of the function $condeff$), taking a truth value B and a set E of possible syntactic combinations of changes, returning E if B is true, and $\emptyset$ otherwise.

Furthermore, for a syntactic scenario interpretation $S = \langle W, \gamma' \rangle$, we define a predicate S on γ' as follows, letting $\oplus \in \{\wedge, \vee, \vee_x, \rightarrow, \leftrightarrow\}$, $R \in \{=, \leq, <, \geq, >\}$, $\alpha, \beta \in \mathcal{T}^*$, $\alpha, \alpha', \alpha_i, \beta \in \mathcal{T}^*$, and $\tau \in \{\mathtt{T}, \mathtt{F}\}$. F should be a previously unused variable.

$$
\begin{aligned}
&S(\langle \tau, E, \alpha \rangle) \Leftrightarrow \\
&\qquad E = condeff_s(\tau, \{\emptyset\}) \\
&S(\langle f, E, \alpha \rangle) \Leftrightarrow \\
&\qquad E = condeff_s([\alpha]f \in W, \{\emptyset\}) \\
&S(\langle \delta(f, \mathtt{T}), E, \alpha \rangle) \Leftrightarrow \\
&\qquad E = \{\{\langle \alpha, f, \mathtt{T} \rangle\}\} \\
&S(\langle \delta(f, \mathtt{F}), E, \alpha \rangle) \Leftrightarrow \\
&\qquad E = \{\{\langle \alpha, f, \mathtt{F} \rangle\}\} \\
&S(\langle \alpha' R\beta, E, \alpha \rangle) \Leftrightarrow \\
&\qquad E = condeff_s(\alpha' R\beta \in W, \{\emptyset\}) \\
&S(\langle \neg \langle \gamma, E_\gamma, \alpha_\gamma \rangle, E, \alpha \rangle) \Leftrightarrow \\
&\qquad E = \neg E_\gamma \wedge \alpha = \alpha_\gamma \\
&S(\langle \langle \gamma, E_\gamma, \alpha_\gamma \rangle \oplus \langle \epsilon, E_\epsilon, \alpha_\epsilon \rangle, E, \alpha \rangle) \Leftrightarrow \\
&\qquad F = E_\gamma \oplus E_\epsilon \wedge E \subseteq F \wedge \\
&\qquad (E = \emptyset \Rightarrow F = \emptyset) \wedge \alpha = \alpha_\gamma = \alpha_\epsilon \\
&S(\langle [\alpha]\langle \gamma, E_\gamma, \alpha_\gamma \rangle, E, \alpha \rangle) \Leftrightarrow \\
&\qquad E = E_\gamma \wedge \alpha = \alpha_\gamma,
\end{aligned}
$$

where the operators $\neg, \wedge, \vee, \vee_x, \rightarrow$ and $\leftrightarrow$ on sets E_1, E_2 of possible syntactic combinations of changes are defined by

$$
\begin{aligned}
\neg E_1 &= \begin{cases} \emptyset & \text{if } E_1 \neq \emptyset \\ \{\emptyset\} & \text{otherwise} \end{cases} \\
E_1 \wedge E_2 &= \{e_1 \cup e_2 \mid e_1 \in E_1, e_2 \in E_2\} \\
E_1 \vee E_2 &= \{e_1, e_2, e_1 \cup e_2 \mid e_1 \in E_1, e_2 \in E_2\} \\
E_1 \vee_x E_2 &= \{e_1 \in E_1 \mid \neg\exists e_2 \in E_2 . e_2 \subseteq_s e_1\} \cup \\
&\qquad \{e_2 \in E_2 \mid \neg\exists e_1 \in E_1 . e_1 \subseteq_s e_2\} \\
E_1 \rightarrow E_2 &= \begin{cases} E_2 & \text{if } E_1 \neq \emptyset \\ \{\emptyset\} & \text{otherwise} \end{cases} \\
E_1 \leftrightarrow E_2 &= (E_1 \rightarrow E_2) \wedge (E_2 \rightarrow E_1),
\end{aligned}
$$

where the relation $\subseteq_s$ is defined such that $e_1 \subseteq_s e_2$ iff for each $\langle \alpha, f, \tau \rangle \in e_1$, there exists a $\langle \alpha', f, \tau \rangle \in e_2$, with $\alpha = \alpha' \in W$. The relation models inclusion of syntactic combinations of changes, taking into account which syntactically differing time points are semantically equal. Note that this relation can be computed in polynomial time, due to our assumptions.

Now, if the following conditions hold, then S is said to be a *syntactic scenario model* of Υ:

- $W = intrep(I, T)$ for some interpretation I
- $S(\beta)$ is true for every subformula β of γ'
- there exists an $e \in E$ such that
  - for each $\langle \alpha, f, \tau \rangle \in e$, $[\alpha]f \in W \Leftrightarrow \tau$
  - for each $f \in \mathcal{I}$ and $\alpha, \beta \in time(\Upsilon)$ with $\alpha < \beta \in W$ such that for no α' for which $\alpha < \alpha', \alpha' < \beta \in W$, $\langle \alpha', f, \tau \rangle \in e$ holds (for some $\tau \in \{\mathbf{T}, \mathbf{F}\}$), we have that $[\beta]f \in W \Leftrightarrow [\alpha]f \in W$.

It is clear that S can be computed in polynomial time, and similarly for the remaining checks, so checking wheter a syntactic scenario interpretation is a syntactic scenario model can be checked in polynomial time. $\square$

Theorem 21 Deciding satisfiability of a scenario description is NP-complete.

Proof (sketch): It remains to prove NP-membership, by Theorem 14. Now, we can use a syntactic scenario interpretation as a guess, and then verify whether it is a scenario model or not in polynomial time, by the previous results. The existence of a syntactical scenario model and the existence of a model of the scenario description can easily proved to be equivalent. $\square$

5 Discussion

We have expanded the expressivity boundaries for reasoning about action in NP time. This is a proof that a polynomial-time reduction exists to propositional logic, making stochastic search procedures like GSAT applicable to the problem. The formalism presented here is clearly more expressive than e.g. $\mathcal{A}$ in all aspects except that we do not have branching time (we can handle explicit, continuous time, nondeterministic actions, "maybe" actions and so on), so the result that computational complexity of satisfiability in the two formalisms is equivalent is somewhat surprising. Then a question is: how much further can one go? Since there is no precise measure for expressivity, this is a difficult question. Moreover, some extensions of the logic presented in this paper will not prove to be NP-complete with the proof technique we have employed. A basic tool in the NP-membership proof is to find a polynomially-sized representation of an interpretation. Now, if would extend the logic to allow quantification over time points (which could represent causal rules), we could have a scenario description $\Upsilon = \langle \sigma, \Gamma, \{f\} \rangle$ where

$$\Gamma = \{\forall t.t \neq 0 \rightarrow \\ (([t]f \rightarrow [2t]\delta(f, \mathbf{F})) \wedge \\ ([t]\neg f \rightarrow [2t]\delta(f, \mathbf{T})))\}.$$

This scenario description has uncountably many models, so the method of representing interpretations and changes in polynomial space will fail (there are only countably many representations of whatever needs to be represented). Thus, some new proof technique would have to be employed.

6 Conclusions

We have introduced a logic of action and change which is expressive in the sense that it can represent most propositional benchmark examples in the literature, and some new examples involving parallel composition of actions, and actions that may or may not be executed. We have proved that satisfiability of a scenario in this logic is NP-complete, and that it subsumes an NP-complete logic introduced by Drakengren and Bjäreland [1997]

References

[Alur and Henzinger, 1989] R. Alur and T.A. Henzinger. A really temporal logic. In *Proceedings of the 30th Annual IEEE Symposium on the Foundations of Computer Science*, pages 164–169. IEEE Computer Society, 1989.

[Baral and Gelfond, 1997] Chitta Baral and Michael Gelfond. Reasoning about effects of concurrent actions. *Journal of Logic Programming*, 31:85–118, 1997.

[Doherty, 1994] Patrick Doherty. Reasoning about action and change using occlusion. In *ECAI '94*.

[Drakengren and Bjäreland, 1997] Thomas Drakengren and Marcus Bjäreland. Reasoning about action in polynomial time. In *IJCAI '97*.

[Gelfond and Lifschitz, 1993] Michael Gelfond and Vladimir Lifschitz. Representing action and change by logic programs. *Journal of Logic Programming*, 17:301–321, 1993.

[Giunchiglia et al., 1997] Enrico Giunchiglia, G. Neelakantan Kartha, and Vladimir Lifschitz. Representing action: indeterminacy and ramifications. *Artificial Intelligence*, 95:409–438, 1997.

[Gustafsson and Doherty, 1996] J. Gustafsson and P. Doherty. Embracing occlusion in specifying the indirect effects of actions. In *KR '96*.

[Liberatore, 1997] P. Liberatore. The complexity of the language $\mathcal{A}$. *Linköping Electronic Articles in Computer and Information Science*, 2(2), July 1997. URL: http://www.ep.liu.se/ea/cis/1997/006.

[McCain and Turner, 1995] Norman McCain and Hudson Turner. A causal theory of ramifications and qualifications. In *IJCAI '95*.

[McCarthy and Hayes, 1969] J. McCarthy and P.J. Hayes. Some philosophical problems from the standpoint of Artificial Intelligence. *Machine Intelligence*, 4:463–502, 1969.

[Sandewall, 1994] Erik Sandewall. *Features and Fluents*. Oxford University Press, 1994.

[Selman et al., 1992] Bart Selman, Hector Levesque, and David Mitchell. A new method for solving hard satisfiability problems. In *AAAI '92*.

A Logic of Intention

Xiaoping Chen   **Guiquan Liu**
Dept. of Computer Science & Technology
Univ. of Science & Technology of China
He Fei, An Hui Province, 230027
P. R. China

Abstract

There is a lot of research on formalization of intention. The common idea of these theories is to interpret intention as an unary modal operator in Kripkean semantics. These theories suffer from the side-effect problem seriously. We introduce an alternative approach by establishing a non-classical logic of intention. This logic is based on a novel non-Kripkean semantics which embodies some cognitive features. We show that this logic does provide a formal specification and a decidable inference mechanism of intention consequences. All and only the instances of side-effects, except ones in absorbent forms, are forbidden in the logic.

1 Introduction

Formalization of intention has drawn the attention of researchers [Cohen and Levesque 1990; Rao and Georgeff 1991; Konolige and Pollack 1993; Wainer 1994; Linder *et al.*, 1995; Huang *et al.*, 1996; Singh, 1997; Schild, 1999]. The common idea is to formalize intention into a modal operator on the framework of Kripkean possible world semantics. Many varieties of the semantics have been put forward, and a lot of models of intention have been established. But all the formalizations suffer from the side-effect problem [Bratman, 1987]. The problem has two most difficult cases, the one concerning closeness of intention consequences under tautological implications and the other concerning closeness under logical equivalencies. The former is about the relation between tautological implications and intention consequences. It asks the question

(Q) Given ψ, a tautological implication of φ, whether intending that ψ is a consequence of intending that φ?

The latter is a special case of the former where "equivalence" is substituted for "implication" and "conse-quence".

To the question (Q), some of the previous theories answer "yes", most of the others answer "no", and the remainders give indefinite answers. We argue that both of the "yes" and the "no" answers are wrong. Moreover, the first answer causes confusion between an agent's goal and its side-effects, and the second answer results in forsaking the specification of intention consequences.

We provide an alternative approach to formalizing intention. The basic idea is to develop a novel semantics which introduce "cognitive abstraction" into interpretation rules. It turns out that the semantics produces an appropriate specification of intention consequences to the extent that all and only the instances of side-effects, except those in absorbent forms, are avoided. Besides that, the semantics supports a decision procedure for the intention consequences defined in the semantics.

In the next section, we examine the side-effect problem and previous work on it. Section 3 states our motivation and basic ideas. The semantics is developed in section 4 and discussed in depth in section 5. Finally, in section 6, we draw some conclusions and point the way toward further development of our logic of intention.

2 The Side-effect problem

The language we use in this section is a modal extension of a propositional language with operators **I** and **B**, where **I** and **B** represent intention and belief, respectively. φ and ψ are arbitrary formulas, $\supset$ and $\equiv$ represent material implication and equivalence, respectively. The so-called side-effect problem is captured by the following cases

(SEB) $\models \mathbf{B}(\varphi \supset \psi) \Rightarrow \models \mathbf{I}(\varphi) \supset \mathbf{I}(\psi)$

(SET) $\models \varphi \supset \psi \Rightarrow \models \mathbf{I}(\varphi) \supset \mathbf{I}(\psi)$

(SEL) $\models \varphi \equiv \psi \Rightarrow \models \mathbf{I}(\varphi) \equiv \mathbf{I}(\psi)$

(SEB) is the case of side-effect under belief implications. In this case, an agent's intentions are closed under his/her belief implications. (SET) is the case of side-effect under tautological implications (logical consequences), that is, an agent's intentions are closed under tautological implications. It can be regarded as a special case of the well-known problem of *logical omniscience* [Hintikka, 1962]. As pointed out in [Konolige and Pollack, 1993], this problem is more serious and harmful to intention than belief: logically consequential closure cannot be assumed for intention, even as an idealization; not all the consequences of an agent's intention are intentions of the agent, even the consequences he/she has anticipated. (SEL) is another case of the side-effect problem.

There are good solutions to (SEB), e.g. [Cohen and Levesque, 1990; Rao and Georgeff, 1991; Wainer, 1994], so we will not consider it in this paper. But, on the other hand, neither (SET) nor (SEL) has been solved satisfactorily. A major difficulty in dealing with (SET) comes from the fact that either of the following rules has exceptions,

(C1) $\forall \varphi, \psi: \models \varphi \supset \psi \Rightarrow \models \mathbf{I}(\varphi) \supset \mathbf{I}(\psi)$

(C2) $\forall \varphi, \psi: \models \varphi \supset \psi \Rightarrow \not\models \mathbf{I}(\varphi) \supset \mathbf{I}(\psi)$

That is, tautological implications cannot be transferred to intention consequences in a globally uniform manner.

Previous work concerning (SET) can be classified into three categories. The models of intention in the first category take (C1) and reject (C2) [Cohen and Levesque, 1990; Wainer, 1994]. These models employ normal modal logics to characterize cognitive states including intention. This makes them tolerate and hence suffer from (SET)(Strictly speaking, [Cohen and Levesque, 1990] takes some more constraints on (C1), which avoids (SET) in some way. But Cohen and Levesque did not consider the way satisfactory). The models in the second category take (C2) with constraint $\not\models \psi \supset \varphi$. For example, the representationalist theory of intention [Konolige and Pollack, 1993] employs the minimal model semantics [Chellas, 1980] to interpret the operator $\mathbf{I}$. The only way to infer formulas containing $\mathbf{I}$ is by using the rule $\varphi \equiv \psi / \mathbf{I}(\varphi) \equiv \mathbf{I}(\psi)$. Hence, if any intention is derivable from another in the theory, then their content must be logical equivalence. This means that both (SET) and the intention consequence are eliminated from the model. The models in the third category restrict both (C1) and (C2) such that neither of them are valid for all φ and ψ [Linder *et al.*, 1995; Huang *et al.*, 1996]. Obviously, these models are more appropriate than the ones in the other two categories. But these models are not self-contained: one could not employ these models by themselves to decide whether $\models \mathbf{I}(\varphi) \supset \mathbf{I}(\psi)$ holds for any φ and ψ. For instance, the model proposed in [Linder *et al.*, 1995] uses *awareness* [Fagin and Halpern, 1988] to define preferences, and then goals (intentions). Because the *explicit preferences* cannot be characterized by a formalized system, the intention consequences in the model are not specified. Moreover, no remedial measures to overcome this short-

age have been put forward in literature.

As for (SEL), it is usually considered harmless [Linder *et al.*, 1995]. But from the point of view of bounded rationality and resource-boundness, (SEL) is inappropriate and harmful: logical equivalencies are not "cognitive equivalencies". For example, from

$$\mathbf{I}(\varphi) \equiv \mathbf{I}((\varphi \wedge \psi) \vee (\varphi \wedge \neg \psi))$$

the side-effect ψ is introduced. Perhaps one may think the situation could be remedied by demanding that agents always take the "simplest" content of an intention. This requires the specification of "simplest content", the criterion of which has not been established definitely. It follows from the discussion above that all the models mentioned are inadequate. We believe the inadequacy results from the formal tools. We are to deal with these issues in depth.

3 Motivation

For simplicity, in this paper we only consider the formal specification of the intention consequence relation between the *content* of two intentions. Hence we assume in the rest of this paper that any formula in our formal language L_I represents the content of an intention. For any $\varphi, \psi \in L_I$, that ψ is an intention consequence of φ means that $\mathbf{I}(\psi)$ is an agent's intention whenever $\mathbf{I}(\varphi)$ is the agent's intention. Thus, L_I need not contain the modal operator $\mathbf{I}$. A binary operator '$\rightarrow$' is added into L_I and $\varphi \rightarrow \psi$ means that ψ is an intention consequence of φ.

In all existing theories, the semantic interpretation of an intention $\mathbf{I}(\varphi)$ is based on some set of the intended worlds, where each intended world is a classical possible world [Chellas 1980] satisfying φ, the content of the intention. However, classical possible worlds have following properties that are harmful to the appropriate specification of intention and intention consequences. Suppose φ is the formula representing the content of the intention being considered (and hence being satisfied by all the intended worlds).

(H1) All tautologies are satisfied by each classical possible world. Thus all tautologies are always intentions of any agent. This is a special case of (SET).

(H2) Any ψ logically equivalent to φ is satisfied by each of the intended worlds. So ψ is also an intention whenever φ is. This is (SEL).

(H3) Suppose formula ψ is stronger than φ. Then ψ may not be satisfied by an intended world, or even specified by a set of the intended worlds. This causes the failure to the specification of "strong consequences" (see below).

To overcome all the drawbacks, we introduce a new sort of possible worlds based on "cognitive abstraction". In our semantics, an intended world about φ is a "minimal model" of φ in the sense that only a possibly smallest number of propositional symbols occurring in φ are assigned classical truth values while others are assigned the same abstract value (0 or l). Any proposition assigned the abstract values are considered to be "abstracted cognitively" (neglected cognitively). A world of this sort is a cognitively finite object, just matching the ability or nature of resource-bounded agents. Based on the set of minimal models, the intention consequence defined in the next section will draw or extract ψ from φ such that ψ is a piece of "partial content" of φ. As a result, the semantics avoids all the harmful properties listed above and fits our purpose well. Most importantly, it supports a well-defined and decidable inference scheme that can derive both "strong consequences" and "weak consequences" of an intention. If an agent intend that φ∧ψ, then both φ and ψ are "partial content" (or "subgoals" as usually called) of the agent's intention. Generally, ψ is called a *weak consequence* of φ, if φ is stonger than ψ in the classical logic. Sometimes an agent need derive from his/her intention φ some ψ as a "means" to the "end" φ, where ψ is stronger than φ. We call such ψ a *strong consequence* of φ. The compositions of strong and weak consequences are called hybrid consequences. For example, given intention $(x_1 \lor x_2) \land x_3$, its weak consequences are $x_1 \lor x_2$ and x_3, strong consequences are $x_1 \land x_2$ and $x_2 \land x_3$, and hybrid consequences are x_1 and x_2.

We will establish a logic of intention, L_{mp4c}, and employ the set of the L_{mp4c}'s valid formulas of the form φ→ψ to provide a formal specification for the intention consequence. Therefore, for any $φ, ψ \in L_l$, the problem "if ψ is an intention consequence of φ" is reduced to the problem "if $\models φ→ψ$ holds in L_{mp4c}". The three kinds of intention consequence described above will be defined uniformly in L_{mp4c}, this makes it an uniform mechanism of inferring intention consequences. Moreover, we can also provide an algorithm to decide whether an intention consequence is a strong, weak, or hybrid one. If φ and ψ satisfy the single-level description assumption (SDA), i.e., all items of the primitive intention content (represented by proposition symbols in L_l) occurring in ψ also occur in φ, then that $\models φ→ψ$ holds in L_{mp4c} will guarantee that ψ will *realize or elaborate φ without side-effect*.

It follows from the discussion above that the validity characterized by our logic should conform to the following principles

(P1-1) $\models x_1 \land x_2 → x_1$

(P1-2) $\not\models (\neg x_1 \land x_1) → x_1$

(P1-3) $\models x_1 \land (x_1 \lor x_2) → x_1$

(P1-4) $\not\models x_1 \land (x_1 \lor x_2) → (x_1 \lor x_2)$

(P2-l) $\models (x_1 \lor x_2) → x_1$

(P2-2) $\not\models x_1 → (\neg x_1 \lor x_1)$

(P2-3) $\models x_1 \lor (x_1 \land x_2) → x_1$

(P2-4) $\not\models x_1 \lor (x_1 \land x_2) → (x_1 \land x_2)$

(P3) $\not\models x_1 → (x_1 \lor x_2)$

(P4) $\not\models (x_1 \land x_2) ↔ (x_1 \lor x_2)$

(P5-l) $\models x_1 \land (x_2 \land x_3) ↔ (x_1 \land x_2) \land x_3$

(P5-2) $\models x_1 \lor (x_2 \lor x_3) ↔ (x_1 \lor x_2) \lor x_3$

(P6-1) $\models x_1 \land x_2 ↔ x_2 \land x_1$

(P6-2) $\models x_1 \lor x_2 ↔ x_2 \lor x_1$

(P7-l) $\models x_1 \land (x_2 \lor x_3) ↔ (x_1 \land x_2) \lor (x_1 \land x_3)$

(P7-2) $\models x_1 \lor (x_2 \land x_3) ↔ (x_1 \lor x_2) \land (x_1 \lor x_3)$

(P8-l) $\models \neg(x_1 \land x_2) ↔ (\neg x_1 \lor \neg x_2)$

(P8-2) $\models \neg(x_1 \lor x_2) ↔ (\neg x_1 \land \neg x_2)$

(P9) $\models \neg\neg x_1 ↔ x_1$

(P10-1) $\models x_1 ↔ x_1 \land x_1$

(P10-2) $\models x_1 ↔ x_1 \lor x_1$

4 Formalization

Let L_l be the propositional language with a set of propositional symbols Atom=$\{x_1, x_2, \ldots\}$ and logical connectives $\neg$, $\land$, and $\lor$. The formulas of L_l are defined as usual. Let L, the language of L_{mp4c}, be an extension of L_l with only one additional operator →. Any formula of L has the form φ→ψ where $φ, ψ \in L_l$. The semantic interpretation of L_l is defined over the set **T**=$\{t, f, 0, 1\}$, where t and f mean truth and falsehood, respectively, and 0 and 1 represent two states of "cognitive abstraction".

Definition 1 (Assignment) A **0-assignment** is a mapping
　　g0: Atom→$\{t, f, 0\}$.
A **l-assignment** is a mapping
　　g1: Atom→$\{t, f, 1\}$.
An **assignment** is either a 0-assignment or a 1-assignment. □

We will use M_0 and M_1 to denote the set of 0-assignments and the set of l-assignments, respectively, and M to denote $M_0 \cup M_1$.

The connectives $\neg$, $\land$ and $\lor$ are interpreted by operators -, *, and + on **T**, respectively. These operators are defined in Figure 1.

x	-x		*	t	f	0	1		+	t	f	0	1
t	f		t	t	f	0	t		t	t	t	t	1
f	t		f	f	f	0	f		f	t	f	f	1
0	1		0	0	0	0	0		0	t	f	0	1
1	0		1	t	f	0	1		1	1	1	1	1

Figure 1. The definitions of -, * and +

terms of sets of belief sets. The final result essentially expresses a notion of transitivity in our representation theorem; this in turn is based on the fact that if $K \diamond \alpha \subseteq K \diamond \alpha \wedge \beta$ then any minimal belief set in which $\neg \alpha$ is consistent is also a minimal belief set in which $\neg (\alpha \wedge \beta)$ is consistent, justifying an assertion that $K \diamond \alpha \preceq_K K \diamond \beta$.

We obtain the following results relating the KB contraction postulates to similarity order models.

Theorem 3.2 *Let M be any similarity order model on belief sets centred on K. If $K \diamond \alpha$ is defined according to Definition 3.4 then the KB contraction postulates are satisfied in M.*

Theorem 3.3 *Let $\diamond$ be a function from $\mathcal{T} \times L$ to $2^{\mathcal{T}}$ satisfying the KB contraction postulates. Then for any fixed theory $K \in \mathcal{T}$ there is a similarity order model on belief sets centred on K satisfying Definition 3.4 for all $\alpha \in L$.*

We can determine what conditions are required to recover the other AGM postulates. This can be accomplished in two ways. First, we can consider criteria which satisfy individual postulates. Second, we can consider a criterion that would *en masse* as it were, yield the AGM postulates. (A third, and most interesting, possibility is given in Theorem 3.8 in the final subsection of this section.)

In the first case, for example, one can obtain a postulate equivalent to $(K \dot{-} 2)$ by restricting the similarity relation to belief sets strictly weaker than K. To obtain a postulate equivalent to $(K \dot{-} 1)$ there are various strategies that can be employed. To obtain a single belief set from a contraction, one could define some *selection function* that returns a single belief set given a set of equally-similar belief sets. For example, this function could select an arbitrary belief set, or it might select a belief set on the basis of some other criterion, for example, the overall *simplicity* of the belief set. Or it might determine some representative belief set, for example, the intersection of the set.

Alternately, one might decide that the semantics be refined so that the contraction function returns a single belief set. Again, there are various alternatives. For example, one could require that the similarity order be antisymmetric, so that if $K_i \preceq_K K_j$ then $K_j \not\preceq_K K_i$ unless $K_i = K_j$. Alternately, one could require that equally-similar belief sets be closed under intersection, so that if K_i and K_j were equally-similar to K then so would be $K_i \cap K_j$; the contraction then would return the minimal (in terms of containment) belief set. For either strategy, the imposition of additional constraints would not be ad hoc, but rather should reflect reasonable assumptions in the semantics. So if $\preceq_K$ were a total order on belief sets, then one would be compelled to accept the assumption that there are no "ties" in similarity of belief sets. If one decided that contraction is closed under intersections, then presumably one should be able to justify this choice. The point here is that the approach allows such distinctions to be made.

On the other hand, one obtains the full set of AGM contraction postulates by asserting that successive weakenings of K are less similar to K. This reflects a criterion of *informational economy*, that we retain as much as possible of our old beliefs. The use of a selection function, below, is one of a number of ways to guarantee that a single belief set results from a contraction. We obtain:

Theorem 3.4 *Let $M = \langle K, \mathcal{KB}, \preceq_K \rangle$ be a similarity order model on belief sets centred on K such that: $\mathcal{KB} = \{K' \in \mathcal{T} \mid K' \subseteq K\}$ and if $K' \subseteq K''$ then $K'' \preceq_K K'$. Let S be any selection function on $K \diamond \alpha$ such that $S(K \diamond \alpha) = \cap S'$ for some $S' \subseteq K \diamond \alpha$. Then the AGM contraction postulates are satisfied in M by the function $S(K \diamond \alpha)$.*

Note that in the above theorem, if we allowed an arbitrary similarity order model, and we defined a new contraction operator to be $\bigcap_{K' \in (K \diamond \alpha)} K'$ (as suggested for example in [Neb92]) that the only new AGM postulate satisfied is $(K \dot{-} 1)$.

3.3 Belief Change: Revision

We turn now to belief revision. The main result is that, surprisingly, this function is not interdefinable with contraction, and in fact is weaker.

Given a similarity order model M, we define $min(\alpha)$ as the least set of belief sets in which α is true, following which we define belief revision.

Definition 3.6 $min(\alpha) = \{K_1 \in KB(\alpha) \mid K_1 \preceq_K K_2 \text{ for every } K_2 \in KB(\alpha)\}$.

Definition 3.7 *The revision of theory K by α in M is given by: $K \dot{\circ} \alpha = min(\alpha)$.*

Revision postulates are given in the next definition, with numbering in reference to the corresponding (or most similar) AGM revision postulates.

Definition 3.8 *The following constitute the set of* KB *revision postulates.*

$(K \dot{\circ} 1)$ $K \dot{\circ} \alpha$ *is a non-empty set of belief sets.*

$(K \dot{\circ} 2)$ $K \dot{\circ} \alpha \subseteq KB(\alpha)$.

$(K \dot{\circ} 3)$ *If $K \vdash \alpha$ then $K \dot{\circ} \alpha = \{K\}$.*

$(K \dot{\circ} 6)$ *If $\vdash \alpha \equiv \beta$ then $K \dot{\circ} \alpha = K \dot{\circ} \beta$.*

$(K \dot{\circ} 7)$ *If $K \dot{\circ} \alpha \cap KB(\beta) \neq \emptyset$ then $K \dot{\circ} (\alpha \wedge \beta) = K \dot{\circ} \alpha \cap KB(\beta)$.*

$(K \dot{\circ} 8)$ *If $K \dot{\circ} \alpha_i \cap KB(\alpha_{i+1}) \neq \emptyset$ for $0 \leq i < n$, and $K \dot{\circ} \alpha_n \cap KB(\alpha_0) \neq \emptyset$ then $K \dot{\circ} (\alpha_0 \wedge \alpha_n) \subseteq K \dot{\circ} \alpha_0$.*

$(K \dot{\circ} 2)$ and $(K \dot{\circ} 6)$ are the only postulates the same as their AGM counterparts. For $(K \dot{\circ} 1)$, revision, like contraction, isn't guaranteed to result in a unique belief set. $(K \dot{\circ} 2)$ reflects the requirement that the revision be successful. $(K \dot{\circ} 3)$ is an obvious weakening of $(K \dot{+} 3)$; it is difficult to think of a situation where it shouldn't hold. In contrast, it seems feasible that a revision function may not satisfy the AGM postulates $(K \dot{+} 3)$ and $(K \dot{+} 4)$, since if α is consistent with K, it may be that $K + \alpha$ isn't the most similar belief set to K in which α is believed; for this to hold we could again bring in an assumption of informational economy. $(K \dot{+} 5)$ is missing: if $\not\vdash \neg\alpha$ there is nothing forbidding $K \dot{\Box} \alpha = K_\perp$. $(K \dot{\Box} 7)$ and $(K \dot{\Box} 8)$ again are dissimilar from their AGM counterparts.

Again, various reasonable and interesting results following from these postulates. Several examples are given in the following theorem.

Theorem 3.5

1. $K \dot{\Box} \alpha = K \dot{\Box} \beta$ iff $K \dot{\Box} \alpha \subseteq KB(\beta)$ and $K \dot{\Box} \beta \subseteq KB(\alpha)$.

2. If $K \dot{\Box} \alpha \subseteq KB(\beta)$ then $K \dot{\Box} (\alpha \wedge \beta) = K \dot{\Box} \alpha$.

3. If $K \dot{\Box} \alpha_i \subseteq KB(\alpha_{i+1})$ for $0 \leq i < n$ and $K \dot{\Box} \alpha_n \subseteq KB(\alpha_0)$ then $K \dot{\Box} \alpha_i = K \dot{\Box} \alpha_{i+1}$ for $0 \leq i < n$.

4. $K \dot{\Box} \alpha \cap K \dot{\Box} \beta = \emptyset$ or $K \dot{\Box} (\alpha \wedge \beta) \subseteq K \dot{\Box} \alpha$ or $K \dot{\Box} (\alpha \wedge \beta) \subseteq K \dot{\Box} \beta$.

For the third result, if $K \dot{\Box} \alpha_i \subseteq KB(\alpha_{i+1})$ then semantically (see below) the least α_i belief sets are no more similar to K than the least α_{i+1} belief sets. If a chain of such containments forms a "loop", then the revisions are equally similar and, in fact, equal. The final result provides a weaker version of the AGM "factoring" result (see [Gär88, p. 57 (3.16)]). It is also weaker than the corresponding result for contraction (Theorem 3.1.2). As well, the AGM postulates $(K \dot{+} 7)$ and $(K \dot{+} 8)$ are not logical consequences of the KB revision postulates, in contradistinction to the AGM contraction postulates $(K \dot{-} 7)$ and $(K \dot{-} 8)$ whose analogues are logical consequences of the KB contraction postulates.

In addition, we do not obtain the representation result for revision that we do for contraction. Define a *weak similarity order model on belief sets centred on K* to be a similarity order model on belief sets *except* rather than being connected, it is reflexive only. We obtain the following results relating the KB revision postulates to weak similarity order models.

Theorem 3.6 *Let M be a weak similarity order model on belief sets centred on K. If we define $K \dot{\Box} \alpha = min(\alpha)$ then the KB revision postulates are satisfied in M.*

Theorem 3.7 *Let $\dot{\Box}$ be a function from $\mathcal{T} \times L$ to $2^{\mathcal{T}}$ satisfying the KB revision postulates. Then for any fixed theory $K \in \mathcal{T}$ there is a weak similarity order model on belief sets centred on K satisfying $K \dot{\Box} \alpha = min(\alpha)$ for all $\alpha \in L$.*

As with contraction we can ask what conditions are required to recover the other AGM postulates. We can specify that revision has a unique belief set as its value via strategies sketched previously. To obtain an equivalent of $(K \dot{+} 5)$ we would require (and not unreasonably) that the inconsistent belief set be the most dissimilar of belief sets to any consistent belief set. Other postulates are dealt with by imposing similar conditions.

3.4   Discussion

As in the AGM approach, the present approach leaves open how a specific contraction or revision function may

be defined. Rather, the approach provides constraints that contraction and revision functions must obey. If one accepts that a notion of similarity as developed here underlies belief change then one presumably would accept the respective postulate sets that would limit properties of an acceptable change function. One can further restrict the class of acceptable functions by placing additional restrictions on the notion of similarity. Thus if the range of a contraction function for belief set K is restricted to be a subsumed belief set of K, this together with a selection function restricts the satisfying contraction functions to those satisfying the AGM postulates.

On the other hand, one could propose a specific metric of similarity for a (say) revision operator. For example, if we equated a belief set with a set of possible worlds rather than a set of sentences, then Dalal's approach [Dal88] is easily expressed using similarity: for belief set K the most similar belief sets to K not the same as K would be those composed of possible worlds differing in one literal from a world in K. The next closest set of belief sets would be those composed of worlds differing in two literals from a world in K, and so on. The result of revising K by α would be the maximal, nearest belief set in which α is true.

As mentioned, revision proves to be weaker than contraction. In detail, in the proof of Theorem 3.3 a similarity order model is defined such that for belief sets K_1 and K_2 there are α and β such that $K_1 \in K \dot{\diamond} \alpha$ and $K_2 \in K \dot{\diamond} \beta$. Theorem 3.1.2 yields that for every α and β: $K \dot{\diamond} \alpha \subseteq K \dot{\diamond} (\alpha \wedge \beta)$ or $K \dot{\diamond} \beta \subseteq K \dot{\diamond} (\alpha \wedge \beta)$. $K \dot{\diamond} \alpha \subseteq K \dot{\diamond} (\alpha \wedge \beta)$ for example asserts that every belief set in $K \dot{\diamond} \alpha$ is in $K \dot{\diamond} (\alpha \wedge \beta)$, or informally the belief sets in $K \dot{\diamond} \alpha$ and $K \dot{\diamond} (\alpha \wedge \beta)$ are equivalently similar, so the belief sets in $K \dot{\diamond} \beta$ are no more similar to K than the belief sets in $K \dot{\diamond} (\alpha \wedge \beta)$, whence $K_1 \preceq_K K_2$. For revision, there is no such relation among belief sets, and the belief sets in $K \dot{\Box} \alpha$, $K \dot{\Box} \beta$, $K \dot{\Box} (\alpha \wedge \beta)$, and $K \dot{\Box} (\alpha \vee \beta)$ may be distinct. We thus lose the capability to define connectivity in Theorem 3.7. This difference in turn relies on the fact that contraction yields belief sets *consistent* with a sentence, whereas revision yields belief sets in which a sentence is *provable*.

Interestingly, a revision operator satisfying the AGM postulates is obtained in terms of KB contraction and the Levi identity, but AGM contraction is not recoverable from KB revision using the Harper identity.

Theorem 3.8 *Let M be any similarity order model centred on K with $K \dot{\diamond} \alpha$ defined as in Definition 3.4 where*

1. $\dot{\diamond} : \mathcal{KB} \times L \mapsto \mathcal{KB}$

2. $K_1 \preceq_K K_\perp$ for every $K_1 \in \mathcal{KB}$.

Define $K \dot{\Box} \alpha = (K \dot{\diamond} \neg\alpha) + \alpha$. Then $K \dot{\Box} \alpha$ satisfies the AGM revision postulates.

See the discussion at the end of Section 3.2 for meeting the first proviso in the theorem; the second proviso states that the incoherent belief set is maximally dissimilar to K. The theorem is interesting, in that it arguably demonstrates that AGM revision is founded on assumptions of similarity (as given in KB contraction) *plus* informational economy (as implicit in the expansion in the Levi identity) *plus* uniqueness (proviso one) *plus* the avoidance of incoherent belief states (proviso two).

We don't obtain a similar result for revision and the Harper identity.

Theorem 3.9 *Let M be any similarity order model centred on K with $K \dot{\varpi} \alpha$ defined as in Definition 3.7 where*

1. $\dot{\varpi} : \mathcal{KB} \times L \mapsto \mathcal{KB}$

2. $K_1 \preceq_K K_\perp$ *for every $K_1 \in \mathcal{KB}$.*

Define $K \dot{\diamond} \alpha = K \cap (\dot{K} \dot{\varpi} \neg \alpha)$. Then $K \dot{\diamond} \alpha$ satisfies $(K \dot{-} 1)$, $(K \dot{-} 2)$, $(K \dot{-} 4)$ provided $K \neq K_\perp$, and $(K \dot{-} 6)$.

Not surprisingly, the KB contraction/revision functions are weaker than the corresponding AGM functions.

Theorem 3.10 *Let f be a function satisfying the AGM contraction (revision) postulates. Then f satisfies the KB contraction (revision) postulates.*

More surprising is the fact that the contraction postulates are not strictly weaker than the KM erasure postulates [KM92], in that $(K \dot{\diamond} 3)$ is not a consequence of the erasure postulates. However the KB revision postulates subsume the update postulates.

Theorem 3.11 *Let f be a function satisfying the KM update postulates. Then f satisfies the KB revision postulates.*

It is an interesting, but unexplored, question to determine whether there is anything about contraction and revision as defined here that lends them most naturally to the AGM and KM approaches respectively.

4 Conclusion

A foundational approach has been presented in which to investigate belief change. The central intuition is that change to a belief set K by a sentence α is with reference to the belief set(s) most similar to K. The approach is quite basic, in that various of the AGM postulates don't hold, or only hold in a weaker form. Arguably the approach is not too basic, in that interesting properties still obtain, as given in the set of KB contraction and revision postulates. Moreover, the approach allows fine-grained control over the properties of contraction and revision functions. This is illustrated by the fact that of the basic AGM postulates that don't hold in the approach, each may be independently satisfied in some augmentation of the approach. An advantage of the approach then, as a foundational approach to revision, is that while the semantic basis is intuitive, such additional assumptions must be explicitly recognised and made. As a corollary, the approach arguably demonstrates that AGM revision can be viewed as being founded on a number of distinct assumptions including similarity, informational economy, and the avoidance of incoherent belief states.

A further result of this inquiry is that it appears that, at their core, revision and contraction constitute distinct functions, with revision being the weaker. A question for future work to ask what it is about the AGM approach that leaves revision and contraction there interdefinable but not here. A second question concerns the relation of the approach to update and erasure.

There has been substantial recent interest in iterated belief revision. Iterated revision has not been addressed here, mainly because our foremost interest is in developing an approach that in some sense is more basic than the AGM approach. Clearly iteration could be addressed by investigating relations among similarity orders; in fact it may be that iterated change is more easily addressed here than in the AGM approach, primarily because here we have stepped back from some of the commitments of the AGM approach. A straightforward approach for incorporating iterated revision is, in a model, to define a mapping from pairs of belief sets to ordinals, giving the relative similarity of every pair of belief sets. From this it is an easy step to define an *epistemic state* for a belief set, K, corresponding to the total preorder expressing the relative similarity of each belief set to K.

Acknowledgements

I thank Maurice Pagnucco for his extensive and very helpful comments on an earlier version of this paper. As well I thank two reviewers for their comments.

References

[AGM85] C.E. Alchourron, P. Gärdenfors, and D. Makinson. On the logic of theory change: Partial meet contraction and revision functions. *Journal of Symbolic Logic*, 50(2):510–530, 1985.

[Dal88] M. Dalal. Investigations into theory of knowledge base revision. In *Proceedings of the AAAI National Conference on Artificial Intelligence*, pages 449–479, St. Paul, Minnesota, 1988.

[Gär88] P. Gärdenfors. *Knowledge in Flux: Modelling the Dynamics of Epistemic States*. The MIT Press, Cambridge, MA, 1988.

[Gro88] A. Grove. Two modellings for theory change. *Journal of Philosophical Logic*, 17:157–170, 1988.

[KM92] H. Katsuno and A. Mendelzon. On the difference between updating a knowledge base and revising it. In P. Gärdenfors, editor, *Belief Revision*, pages 183–203. Cambridge University Press, 1992.

[Lew73] D. Lewis. *Counterfactuals*. Harvard University Press, 1973.

[Neb92] B. Nebel. Syntax based approaches to belief revision. In P. Gärdenfors, editor, *Belief Revision*, pages 52–88. Cambridge University Press, 1992.

Postulates for conditional belief revision

Gabriele Kern-Isberner
FernUniversität Hagen
Dept. of Computer Science, LG Prakt. Informatik VIII
P.O. Box 940, D-58084 Hagen, Germany
e-mail: gabriele.kern-isberner@fernuni-hagen.de

Abstract

In this paper, we present a scheme of postulates for revising epistemic states by conditional beliefs. These postulates are supported mainly by following the specific, non-classical nature of conditionals, and the aim of preserving conditional beliefs is achieved by studying specific interactions between conditionals, represented properly by two relations. Because one of the postulates claims propositional belief revision to be a special case of conditional belief revision, our framework also covers the work of Darwiche and Pearl [Darwiche and Pearl, 1997], and we show that all postulates presented there may be derived from our postulates. We state representation theorems for the principal postulates, and finally, we present a conditional belief operator obeying all of the postulates by using ordinal conditional functions as representations of epistemic states.

1 Introduction

Belief revision deals with the *dynamics of belief* – how should currently held beliefs be modified in the light of new information? Results in this area are mainly influenced by the so-called *AGM theory*, named after Alchourron, Gärdenfors and Makinson who set up a framework of postulates for a reasonable change of beliefs (cf. [Alchourrón *et al.*, 1985], [Gärdenfors, 1988]). Usually, the *belief sets* in AGM theory are assumed to be deductively closed sets of propositional formulas, or to be represented by one single propositional formula, respectively, and the revising beliefs are taken to be propositional formulas. So the AGM postulates constrain revisions of the form $\psi \star A$, the revision operator $\star$ connecting two propositional formulas ψ and A, where ψ represents the initial state of belief and A stands for the new information. A representation theorem (cf. [Katsuno and Mendelzon, 1991]) establishes a relationship between AGM revision operators and total pre-orders $\leq_\psi$ on the set of possible worlds, proving the revised belief set $\psi \star A$ to be satisfied precisely by all minimal A-worlds.

Though belief sets representing what is known for certain are of specific interest they are only poor reflections of the complex attitudes an individual may hold. The limitation to propositional beliefs severely restricts the frame of AGM theory, in particular, when iterated revision has to be performed. So belief revision should not only be concerned with the revision of propositional beliefs but also with the modification of *revision strategies* when new information arrives (cf. [Darwiche and Pearl, 1997], [Boutilier, 1993], [Boutilier and Goldszmidt, 1993]). These revision strategies may be taken as conditional beliefs, therefore revision should be concerned with changes in conditional beliefs and, the other way around, with the preservation of conditional beliefs.

Darwiche and Pearl [Darwiche and Pearl, 1997] explicitly took conditional beliefs into account by considering epistemic states instead of belief sets, and they advanced four postulates in addition to the AGM axioms to model what may be called *conditional preservation* under revision by propositional beliefs.

In the present paper, we broaden the framework for revising epistemic states presented in [Darwiche and Pearl, 1997] so as to include also the *revision by conditional beliefs*. Thus belief revision is considered here in quite a general framework, exceeding the AGM-theory in two respects:

- We revise epistemic states; this makes it necessary to allow for the changes in conditional beliefs caused by new information.

- The new belief A may be of a conditional nature, thus reflecting a changed or newly acquired revision policy that has to be incorporated adequately.

We present a scheme of eight postulates appropriate to guide the revision of epistemic states by conditional beliefs. These postulates are supported mainly by following the specific, non-classical nature of conditionals, and the aim of preserving conditional beliefs is achieved by studying specific interactions between conditionals, represented properly by two relations. Because one of the postulates claims propositional belief revision to be a special case of conditional belief revision, our framework also covers the topic of Darwiche and Pearl's work [Darwiche and Pearl, 1997], and we show that all four postulates presented there may be derived from our postulates. We state representation theorems for the principal postulates, and finally, we present a conditional belief operator obeying all of the postulates by using ordinal conditional functions as representations of epistemic states.

The organization of this paper is as follows: In section 2, we briefly summarize the results of Darwiche and Pearl concerning the revision of epistemic states and lay down some foundations for this paper. In section 3, we describe conditionals as objects of a three-valued nature and introduce the relations $\perp$ and $\sqsubseteq$ between conditionals which play an important part for studying interactions between conditionals. Section 4 presents and explains the eight postulates for conditional revision and shows correspondences to the axioms of [Darwiche and Pearl, 1997]. Section 5 contains representation theorems and some consequences of the postulates. In section 6, we introduce a conditional revision operator for ordinal conditional functions that realizes the ideas of this paper, and section 7 concludes this paper with a short summary and an outlook.

2   Revising epistemic states

An epistemic state Ψ represents the cognitive state of some individual at a given time. In particular, beside the set of beliefs $Bel(\Psi)$ the individual accepts for certain, Ψ contains the revision policies the individual entertains at that time. These revision policies reflect the beliefs (B) the individual is inclined to hold if new information (A) becomes obvious, and are adequately represented by conditionals $(B \mid A)$, i.e. expressions of the form "*If A then B*", conjoining two propositional formulas A and B. So the conditional $(B \mid A)$ is accepted in the epistemic state Ψ iff revising Ψ by A yields belief in B. This defines a fundamental relationship between conditionals and the process of revision, known as the *Ramsey test* (cf. e.g. [Boutilier and Goldszmidt, 1993], [Gärdenfors, 1988]):

(RT) $\Psi \models (B \mid A)$ iff $Bel(\Psi \star A) \models B$

where $\star$ is a revision operator, taking an epistemic state Ψ and some new belief A as inputs and yielding a revised epistemic state $\Psi \star A$ as output.

Each epistemic state Ψ is associated with its belief set $Bel(\Psi)$ which is supposed to be a deductively closed set of formulas of a propositional language $\mathcal{L}$. The revision of Ψ by $A \in \mathcal{L}$ also yields a revised belief set $Bel(\Psi \star A) \subseteq \mathcal{L}$, and of course, this revision should obey the standards of the AGM theory. But the revision of epistemic states cannot be reduced to propositional revision because two *different* epistemic states Ψ_1, Ψ_2 may have *equivalent* belief sets $Bel(\Psi_1) \equiv Bel(\Psi_2)$. Thus an epistemic state is not described uniquely by its belief set, and revising Ψ_1 and Ψ_2 by new information A may result in different revised belief sets $Bel(\Psi_1 \star A) \not\equiv Bel(\Psi_2 \star A)$.

Example.   Two physicians have to make a diagnosis when confronted with a patient showing certain symptoms. They both agree that disease A is by far the most adequate diagnosis, so they both hold belief in A. Moreover, as the physicians know, diseases B and C might also cause the symptoms, but here the experts disagree: One physician regards B to be a possible diagnosis, too, but excludes C, whereas the other physician is inclined to take C into consideration, but not B.

Suppose now that a specific blood test definitely proves that the patient is not suffering from disease A. So both experts have to change their beliefs, the first physician now takes B to be the correct diagnosis, the second one takes C for granted. Though initially the physicians' opinions may be described by the same belief set, they end up with different belief sets after revision.

It is important to note that Gärdenfors' famous triviality result [Gärdenfors, 1988] complaining the incompatibility of the Ramsey test with some of the AGM-postulates does not hold if conditional beliefs are considered essentially different from propositional beliefs, as is emphasized here and elsewhere (cf. e.g. [Darwiche and Pearl, 1997]). Therefore obeying the difference between $Bel(\Psi_1) \equiv Bel(\Psi_2)$ and $\Psi_1 = \Psi_2$ makes the Ramsey test compatible with the AGM-theory for propositional belief revision: Whereas $Bel(\Psi_1) \equiv Bel(\Psi_2)$ only means that both epistemic states have equivalent belief sets, $\Psi_1 = \Psi_2$ requires the two epistemic states to be identical, i.e. to incorporate in particular the same propositional beliefs as well as the same conditional beliefs.

Darwiche and Pearl [Darwiche and Pearl, 1997] consider the revision of epistemic states with propositional beliefs, mainly concerned with handling iterated revisions. They generalize the AGM-postulates for belief revision to the framework of revising epistemic states (cf. [Darwiche and Pearl, 1997]):

Suppose Ψ, Ψ_1, Ψ_2 to be epistemic states and $A, A_1, A_2, B \in \mathcal{L}$;

(R*1) A is believed in $\Psi \star A$: $Bel(\Psi \star A) \models A$.

(R*2)   If $Bel(\Psi) \wedge A$ is satisfiable, then $Bel(\Psi \star A) \equiv Bel(\Psi) \wedge A$.

(R*3)   If A is satisfiable, then $Bel(\Psi \star A)$ is also satisfiable.

(R*4)   If $\Psi_1 = \Psi_2$ and $A_1 \equiv A_2$, then $Bel(\Psi_1 \star A_1) \equiv Bel(\Psi_2 \star A_2)$.

(R*5) $Bel(\Psi \star A) \wedge B$ implies $Bel(\Psi \star (A \wedge B))$.

(R*6)   If $Bel(\Psi \star A) \wedge B$ is satisfiable then $Bel(\Psi \star (A \wedge B))$ implies $Bel(\Psi \star A) \wedge B$.

Considered superficially, these postulates are exact reformulations of the AGM postulates, as stated in [Katsuno and Mendelzon, 1991], with belief sets replaced throughout by belief sets of epistemic states. So the postulates above ensure that the revision of epistemic states is in line with the AGM theory as long as the revision of the corresponding belief sets is considered. The most important new aspect by contrast with propositional belief revision is given by postulate (R*4): Only identical epistemic states are supposed to yield equivalent revised belief sets. This is a clear but adequate weakening of the corresponding AGM-postulate

(R4) If $Bel(\Psi_1) \equiv Bel(\Psi_2)$ and $A_1 \equiv A_2$, then
$$Bel(\Psi_1 \star A_1) \equiv Bel(\Psi_2 \star A_2)$$

which amounts to reducing the revision of epistemic states to propositional belief revision. As we explained above, such a reduction is inappropriate.

Darwiche and Pearl [Darwiche and Pearl, 1997] proved a representation theorem for their postulates which parallels the corresponding theorem in AGM theory (cf. [Katsuno and Mendelzon, 1991]), using the notion of *faithful assignments*:

Definition 1 ([Darwiche and Pearl, 1997]) Let W be the set of all worlds (interpretations) of the propositional language $\mathcal{L}$ and consider epistemic states Ψ the belief sets of which belong to $\mathcal{L}$.

A *faithful assignment* is a function that maps each such epistemic state Ψ to a total pre-order $\leq_\Psi$ on the worlds W satisfying the following conditions:

(1) $\omega_1, \omega_2 \models \Psi$ only if $\omega_1 =_\Psi \omega_2$;

(2) $\omega_1 \models \Psi$ and $\omega_2 \not\models \Psi$ only if $\omega_1 <_\Psi \omega_2$.

for worlds $\omega_1, \omega_2 \in W$ and epistemic states Ψ, Φ.

As usual, $\omega_1 <_\Psi \omega_2$ means $\omega_1 \leq_\Psi \omega_2$ and $\omega_2 \not\leq_\Psi \omega_1$; $\omega_1 =_\Psi \omega_2$ iff $\omega_1 \leq_\Psi \omega_2$ and $\omega_2 \leq_\Psi \omega_1$.

Given the set W of all worlds of the language $\mathcal{L}$ and a propositional formula $A \in \mathcal{L}$, we denote by $Mod(A)$ the set of all A-worlds, $Mod(A) = \{\omega \in W \mid \omega \models A\}$. If Ψ is an epistemic state, we set $Mod(\Psi) = Mod(Bel(\Psi))$.

Theorem 2 ([Darwiche and Pearl, 1997]) *A revision operator $\star$ satisfies postulates (R*1)-(R*6) precisely when there exists a faithful assignment that maps each epistemic state Ψ to a total pre-order $\leq_\Psi$ such that*

$$Mod(\Psi \star A) = \min(A; \Psi) := \min(Mod(A); \leq_\Psi)$$

i.e. the worlds satisfying $Bel(\Psi \star A)$ are precisely those worlds satisfying A that are minimal with respect to $\leq_\Psi$.

This theorem shows an important connection between the ordering $\leq_\Psi$ associated with an epistemic state Ψ and the process of revising Ψ by propositional beliefs. Therefore, at least in the context of revision, epistemic states are properly represented as pairs $(\Psi, \leq_\Psi)$ with a total pre-order $\leq_\Psi$ satisfying conditions (1)-(2) of definition 1 and the so-called *smoothness condition* $\min(A; \Psi) \neq \emptyset$ for any satisfiable $A \in \mathcal{L}$ (cf. e.g. [Boutilier and Goldszmidt, 1993]), and such that $Mod(\Psi) = \min(W; \leq_\Psi)$. Using the relationship (RT) between revision and conditionals, theorem 2 immediately yields

Lemma 3 *A conditional $(B \mid A)$ is accepted in an epistemic state $(\Psi, \leq_\Psi)$ iff all minimal A-worlds satisfy B, i.e. $\Psi \models (B \mid A)$ iff $\min(A; \Psi) \subseteq Mod(B)$.*

Thus the pre-order $\leq_\Psi$ encodes the conditional beliefs held in Ψ.

For two propositional formulas A, B, we define $A \leq_\Psi B$ iff for all $\omega \in \min(A; \Psi)$, $\omega' \in \min(B; \Psi)$, we have

$\omega \leq_\Psi \omega'$, i.e. iff the minimal A-worlds are at least as plausible as the minimal B-worlds. To simplify notations, we will replace a conjunction by juxtaposition and indicate the negation of a proposition by barring, i.e. $AB = A \wedge B$ and $\overline{B} = \neg B$. Using this, the lemma above may be reformulated as

Lemma 4 *A conditional $(B \mid A)$ is accepted in an epistemic state $(\Psi, \leq_\Psi)$ iff $AB <_\Psi A\overline{B}$.*

Boutilier (cf. e.g. [Boutilier, 1994]) also took conditional beliefs into account. He presented in [Boutilier, 1993] his *natural revision* that preserves as many conditional beliefs as possible, in accordance with the AGM postulates, and he generalized this approach to deal with the revision by conditional beliefs [Boutilier and Goldszmidt, 1993]. As Darwiche and Pearl emphasized, however, Boutilier's natural revision seems to be too restrictive in that it preserves conditional beliefs at the cost of compromising propositional beliefs (cf. [Darwiche and Pearl, 1997]). Thus the question which conditional beliefs should be kept under revision turns out to be a crucial problem when revising epistemic states. In the framework of iterated revision, Darwiche and Pearl [Darwiche and Pearl, 1997] proposed four postulates concerning the preservation of conditional beliefs under propositional revision:

(C1) If $C \models B$ then $\Psi \models (D \mid C)$ iff $\Psi \star B \models (D \mid C)$.

(C2) If $C \models \overline{B}$ then $\Psi \models (D \mid C)$ iff $\Psi \star B \models (D \mid C)$.

(C3) If $\Psi \models (B \mid A)$ then $\Psi \star B \models (B \mid A)$.

(C4) If $\Psi \star B \models (\overline{B} \mid A)$ then $\Psi \models (\overline{B} \mid A)$.

For discussion of these postulates, cf. the original paper [Darwiche and Pearl, 1997].

In this paper, we present postulates for the revision of epistemic states by *conditional beliefs* which generalize the postulates of Darwiche and Pearl and support them with new conditional arguments. The rationale behind these postulates is not to minimize conditional change, as in Boutilier's work, but to preserve the *conditional structure* of the knowledge, as far as possible, which is made obvious by studying interactions between conditionals.

3 Conditionals

Conditionals may be given a lot of different interpretations, e.g. as counterfactuals, as indicative, subjunctive or normative conditionals etc. (cf. e.g. [Nute, 1980], [Boutilier, 1994]). In the context of revision, a subjunctive meaning fits particularly well, in accordance with the Ramsey test (RT): *If A were true, B would hold*, implicitly referring to a revision of the actual epistemic state by A.

Independently of its given meaning, a conditional $(B \mid A)$ is an object of a three-valued nature, partitioning the set of worlds W in three parts: those worlds satisfying $A \wedge B$ and thus confirming the conditional, those worlds satisfying $A \wedge \neg B$, thus contradicting the conditional, and those worlds not fulfilling the premise A and so which the conditional may not be applied to at all. Therefore Calabrese represents a conditional as a *generalized indicator function* (cf. [Calabrese, 1991])

$$(B \mid A)(\omega) = \begin{cases} 1 & \text{if} \quad \omega \models AB \\ 0 & \text{if} \quad \omega \models A\overline{B} \\ u & \text{if} \quad \omega \models \overline{A} \end{cases}$$

where u means *undefined*. Two conditionals are considered to be equivalent iff they are identical as indicator functions, i.e. $(B \mid A) \equiv (D \mid C)$ iff $A \equiv C$ and $AB \equiv CD$ (cf. [Calabrese, 1991]). Usually, a propositional fact $A \in \mathcal{L}$ is identified with the conditional $(A \mid \top)$, where $\top$ is tautological.

For a conditional $(B \mid A)$, we define the *affirmative set* $(B \mid A)^+$ and the *contradictory set* $(B \mid A)^-$ of worlds as

$$(B \mid A)^+ = \{\omega \in W \mid \omega \models AB\} = Mod(AB)$$
$$(B \mid A)^- = \{\omega \in W \mid \omega \models A\overline{B}\} = Mod(A\overline{B})$$

Lemma 5 *Two conditionals $(B \mid A), (D \mid C)$ are equivalent iff their corresponding affirmative and contradictory sets are equal, i.e. $(B \mid A) \equiv (D \mid C)$ iff $(B \mid A)^+ = (D \mid C)^+$ and $(B \mid A)^- = (D \mid C)^-$.*

It is difficult to capture interactions between conditionals. In [Calabrese, 1991], logical connectives and implications between conditionals are defined and investigated. Here we will pursue a different idea of interaction. Having the effects of conditionals on worlds in mind, we define two relations $\sqsubseteq$ and $\bot$ between conditionals by

$$(D \mid C) \sqsubseteq (B \mid A) \quad \text{iff} \quad (D \mid C)^+ \subseteq (B \mid A)^+$$
$$\text{and} \quad (D \mid C)^- \subseteq (B \mid A)^-$$

and

$$(D \mid C) \bot (B \mid A) \quad \text{iff} \quad Mod(C) \subseteq (B \mid A)^+$$
$$\text{or} \quad Mod(C) \subseteq (B \mid A)^- \quad \text{or} \quad Mod(C) \subseteq Mod(\overline{A}).$$

Thus $(D \mid C) \sqsubseteq (B \mid A)$ if the effect of the former conditional on worlds is in line with the latter one, but $(D \mid C)$ applies to fewer worlds. Thus $(D \mid C)$ may be called a *subconditional* of $(B \mid A)$ in this case. In contrast to this, the second relation $\bot$ symbolizes a kind of *independency between conditionals*. We have $(D \mid C) \bot (B \mid A)$ if $Mod(C)$, i.e. the range of application of the conditional $(D \mid C)$, is completely contained in one of the sets $(B \mid A)^+, (B \mid A)^-$ or $Mod(\overline{A})$. So for all worlds which $(D \mid C)$ may be applied to, $(B \mid A)$ has the same effect and yields no further partitioning. Note, however, that $\bot$ is not a symmetric independence relation; $(D \mid C) \bot (B \mid A)$ rather expresses that $(D \mid C)$ is *not affected* by $(B \mid A)$.

Both relations may be expressed using the standard ordering $\leq$ between propositional formulas: $A \leq B$ iff $A \models B$, i.e. iff $Mod(A) \subseteq Mod(B)$.

Lemma 6 *(i) $(D \mid C) \sqsubseteq (B \mid A)$ iff $CD \leq AB$ and $C\overline{D} \leq A\overline{B}$; in particular, if $(D \mid C) \sqsubseteq (B \mid A)$ then $C \leq A$.*

(ii) $(D \mid C) \sqsubseteq (B \mid A)$ and $(B \mid A) \sqsubseteq (D \mid C)$ iff $(D \mid C) \equiv (B \mid A)$.

(iii) $(D \mid C) \bot (B \mid A)$ iff $C \leq AB$ or $C \leq A\overline{B}$ or $C \leq \overline{A}$.

4 Revision by conditionals

Revising an epistemic state Ψ by a conditional $(B \mid A)$ becomes necessary if a new conditional belief resp. a new revision policy should be included in Ψ, yielding a changed epistemic state $\Psi' = \Psi \star (B \mid A)$ such that $\Psi' \models (B \mid A)$, i.e. $\Psi' \star A \models B$. We will use the same operator $\star$ for propositional as well as for conditional revision, thus expressing that conditional revision should extend propositional revision in accordance with the Ramsey test (RT).

Boutilier and Goldszmidt [Boutilier and Goldszmidt, 1993] presented a generalized version of the natural revision operator of Boutilier to perform such an adaptation to conditional beliefs; their method minimizes changes in conditional beliefs in accordance with the AGM theory.

Below, we propose several postulates a revision of an epistemic state by a conditional should satisfy. The key idea is to follow the conditionals in Ψ as long as there is no conflict between them and the new conditional belief, and we will use $\sqsubseteq$ and $\bot$ to relate conditionals appropriately.

Postulates for conditional revision:

Suppose $(\Psi, \leq_\Psi)$ is an epistemic state and $(B \mid A)$, $(D \mid C)$ are conditionals. Let $\Psi \star (B \mid A)$ denote the result of revising Ψ by $(B \mid A)$.

(CR0) $\Psi \star (B \mid A)$ is an epistemic state.

(CR1) $\Psi \star (B \mid A) \models (B \mid A)$.

(CR2) $\Psi \star (B \mid A) = \Psi$ iff $\Psi \models (B \mid A)$.

(CR3) $\Psi \star B = \Psi \star (B \mid \top)$ induces a propositional AGM-revision operator.

(CR4) $\Psi \star (B \mid A) = \Psi \star (D \mid C)$ whenever $(B \mid A) \equiv (D \mid C)$.

(CR5) If $(D \mid C) \bot (B \mid A)$ then $\Psi \models (D \mid C)$ iff $\Psi \star (B \mid A) \models (D \mid C)$.

(CR6) If $(D \mid C) \sqsubseteq (B \mid A)$ and $\Psi \models (D \mid C)$ then $\Psi \star (B \mid A) \models (D \mid C)$.

(CR7) If $(D \mid C) \sqsubseteq (\overline{B} \mid A)$ and $\Psi \star (B \mid A) \models (D \mid C)$ then $\Psi \models (D \mid C)$.

Postulates (CR0) and (CR1) are self-evident. (CR2) postulates that Ψ should be left unchanged precisely if it already entails the conditional. (CR3) says that the induced propositional revision operator should be in accordance with the AGM postulates. (CR4) requires the result of the revision process to be independent of the syntactical representation of conditionals.

The next three postulates aim at preserving the conditional structure of knowledge:

(CR5) claims that revising by a conditional should preserve all conditionals that are independent of that conditional, in the sense given by the relation $\perp$. The rationale behind this postulate is the following: The validity of a conditional $(B \mid A)$ in an epistemic state Ψ depends on the relation between (some) worlds in $Mod(AB)$ and (some) worlds in $Mod(A\overline{B})$ (cf. lemmata 3, 4). So incorporating $(B \mid A)$ to Ψ may require a shift between $Mod(AB)$ on one side and $Mod(A\overline{B})$ on the other side, but should leave intact any relations between worlds within $Mod(AB)$, $Mod(A\overline{B})$, or $Mod(\overline{A})$. These relations may be captured by conditionals not affected by $(B \mid A)$, i.e. by conditionals $(D \mid C) \perp (B \mid A)$.

(CR6) states that conditional revision should bring about no change for conditionals that are already in line with the revising conditional, and (CR7) guarantees that no conditional change contrary to the revising conditional is caused by conditional revision.

An idea of *conditional preservation* is also inherent to the postulates (C1)-(C4) of Darwiche and Pearl [Darwiche and Pearl, 1997] which we will show to be generalized by our postulates.

Theorem 7 *Suppose $\star$ is a conditional revision operator obeying the postulates* (CR0)-(CR7). *Then for the induced propositional revision operator, postulates* (C1)-(C4) *are satisfied, too.*

Proof: Let $A, B, C, D \in \mathcal{L}$.

Suppose $C \leq B$ or $C \leq \overline{B}$. Then, according to lemma 6, $(D \mid C) \perp (\overline{B} \mid \top)$. (CR3) and (CR5) now imply (C1) and (C2).

(C3) and (C4) are direct consequences of (CR6) and (CR7) by using that $(B \mid A) \sqsubseteq (B \mid \top)$ and $(\overline{B} \mid A) \sqsubseteq (\overline{B} \mid \top)$, respectively, due to lemma 6. $\square$

This theorem provides further justifications for the postulates of Darwiche and Pearl from within the framework of conditionals.

5 Representation theorems

Postulates (CR5)-(CR7) claim specific connections to hold between Ψ and the revised $\Psi \star (B \mid A)$, thus relating $\leq_\Psi$ and $\leq_{\Psi \star (B \mid A)}$. We will elaborate this relationship in order to characterize those postulates by properties of the pre-orders associated with Ψ and $\Psi \star (B \mid A)$.

Postulate (CR5) proves to be of particular importance because it guarantees the ordering within $Mod(AB)$, $Mod(A\overline{B})$, $Mod(\overline{A})$, respectively, to be preserved:

Theorem 8 *The conditional revision operator $\star$ satisfies* (CR5) *iff for each epistemic state* $(\Psi, \leq_\Psi)$ *and for each conditional* $(B \mid A)$ *it holds that:*

$$\omega \leq_\Psi \omega' \quad iff \quad \omega \leq_{\Psi \star (B \mid A)} \omega' \qquad (1)$$

for all worlds $\omega, \omega' \in Mod(AB)$ $(Mod(A\overline{B}), Mod(\overline{A})$, *respectively).*

As an immediate consequence, (1) yields

Lemma 9 *Suppose* (1) *holds for all worlds* $\omega, \omega' \in Mod(AB)$ $(Mod(A\overline{B}), Mod(\overline{A})$, *respectively). Let proposition* $E \leq AB$ $(A\overline{B}, \overline{A}$, *respectively). Then*

$$min(E; \Psi) = min(E; \Psi \star (B \mid A))$$

Together with the Ramsey test (RT), (CR5) yields equalities of belief sets as stated in the following proposition:

Proposition 10 *If the conditional revision operator $\star$ satisfies postulate* (CR5), *then*

$$
\begin{aligned}
Bel((\Psi \star (B \mid A)) \star AB) &= Bel(\Psi \star AB) \\
Bel((\Psi \star (B \mid A)) \star A\overline{B}) &= Bel(\Psi \star A\overline{B}) \\
Bel((\Psi \star (B \mid A)) \star \overline{A}) &= Bel(\Psi \star \overline{A})
\end{aligned}
$$

For the representation theorems of postulates (C6) and (C7), we need postulate (CR5), respectively equation (1) and its consequence, lemma 9, to ensure that the property of being a minimal world in the affirmative or in the contradictory set associated with some conditionals is not touched under revision.

Theorem 11 *Suppose $\star$ is a conditional revision operator satisfying* (CR5). *Let Ψ be an epistemic state, and let $(B \mid A)$ be a conditional.*

1. *$\star$ satisfies* (CR6) *iff for all $\omega \in Mod(AB)$, $\omega' \in Mod(A\overline{B})$, $\omega <_\Psi \omega'$ implies $\omega <_{\Psi \star (B \mid A)} \omega'$.*

2. *$\star$ satisfies* (CR7) *iff for all $\omega \in Mod(AB)$, $\omega' \in Mod(A\overline{B})$, $\omega' <_{\Psi \star (B \mid A)} \omega$ implies $\omega' <_\Psi \omega$.*

6 Ordinal conditional functions

Ordinal conditional functions (rankings), as introduced by Spohn [Spohn, 1988], are functions κ from worlds to ordinals, i.e. to non-negative integers, such that some worlds are mapped to the minimal element 0. They are considered adequate representations of epistemic states (cf. e.g. [Spohn, 1988], [Darwiche and Pearl, 1997]), inducing a total pre-order on the set W of worlds by setting $\omega_1 \leq_\kappa \omega_2$ iff $\kappa(\omega_1) \leq \kappa(\omega_2)$. So the smaller $\kappa(\omega)$ is, the more plausible appears the world ω, and what is believed (for certain) in the epistemic state represented by κ is described precisely by the set $\{\omega \in W \mid \kappa(\omega) = 0\} =: Mod(Bel(\kappa))$. For a propositional formula $A \in \mathcal{L}$, we set $\kappa(A) = \min\{\kappa(\omega) \mid \omega \models A\}$, so that $\kappa(A \vee B) = \min\{\kappa(A), \kappa(B)\}$. In particular, $0 = \min\{\kappa(A), \kappa(\overline{A})\}$, so that at least one of A or $\overline{A}$ is considered mostly plausible. A proposition A is believed iff $\kappa(\overline{A}) > 0$ (which implies $\kappa(A) = 0$), so that A is believed iff $Bel(\kappa) \models A$. We abbreviate this again by $\kappa \models A$.

Let $\kappa \star A$ denote the revision of the ranking κ (of the corresponding epistemic state, respectively) by the proposition $A \in \mathcal{L}$ (for examples of such revision operators, cf. [Spohn, 1988], [Darwiche and Pearl, 1997]). For a conditional $(B \mid A)$, we set $\kappa \models (B \mid A)$ iff $\kappa \star A \models B$, that is iff $\kappa(AB) < \kappa(A\overline{B})$ (cf. lemma 4). Similar as in probability theory, we define $\kappa(B \mid A) = \kappa(AB) - \kappa(A)$

AUTOMATED REASONING

Resource-Bounded Reasoning

Programming Resource-Bounded Deliberative Agents

Michael Fisher and Chiara Ghidini*

Department of Computing and Mathematics
Manchester Metropolitan University
Manchester M1 5GD, United Kingdom

EMAIL: {M.Fisher,C.Ghidini}@doc.mmu.ac.uk

Abstract

This paper is concerned with providing a common framework for both the logical specification and execution of agents. While numerous high-level agent theories have been proposed in order to model agents, such as theories of intention, these often have little formal connection to practical agent-based systems. On the other hand, many of the agent-based programming languages used for implementing 'real' agents lack firm logical semantics. Our approach is to define a logical framework in which agents can be specified, and then show how such specifications can be directly executed in order to implement the agent's behaviour.

We here extend this approach to capture an important aspect of practical agents, namely their resource-bounded nature. We present a logic in which resource-boundedness can be specified, and then consider how specifications within this logic can be directly executed. The mechanism we use to capture finite resources is to replace the standard modal logic previously used to represent an agent's beliefs, with a *multi-context* representation of belief, thus providing tight control over the agent's reasoning capabilities where necessary.

This logical framework provides the basis for the specification and execution of agents comprising dynamic (temporal) activity, deliberation concerning goals, and resource-bounded reasoning.

1 Introduction

The METATEM [Barringer *et al.*, 1995] and Concurrent METATEM [Fisher, 1995] languages have been used as high-level mechanisms for specifying and executing individual agents and multi-agent systems, respectively. Both are based upon the principle of specifying an agent using temporal logic, and then *directly executing* this specification in order to provide the agent's behaviour. This approach provides a high-level programming notation, while maintaining a close link between the program and its specification.

---

*Visiting Research Fellow from University of Trento, Italy, supported by the Italian National Research Council (CNR)

While this approach has provided a useful basis for experimentation with both the logical representation and animation of agents, it has become clear that a more refined version of the specification language is required if this framework is to be used for 'real world' agents. In particular, the METATEM family of programming languages originally contained no sophisticated mechanisms for representing deliberation within an agent, i.e. the process that an agent carries out in order to decide which goal/action/plan to attempt.

Thus, inspired by the success of the BDI framework [Rao and Georgeff, 1991] in representing deliberation, the basic METATEM system was extended, in [Fisher, 1997b], with explicit mechanisms for ordering goals. Goals, corresponding to both desires and intentions in the BDI model were, in turn, represented by temporal eventualities. This then allowed deliberation to be represented using user defined functions providing an ordering on the satisfaction of eventualities.

While this provides a simple and concise mechanism for representing and implementing deliberative agents, it does not deal with a further important aspect of 'real' agents, namely their resource-bounded nature [Bratman *et al.*, 1988]. In particular, the representation of belief was given by extending the temporal basis with a standard modal logic having Kripke semantics [Halpern and Moses, 1992]. As is well known, this does not match the resource-bounded nature of 'real' reasoners [Giunchiglia *et al.*, 1993]. Indeed modal logics generally model logically omniscient agents which are forced to believe (and compute) all the logical consequences of their own beliefs.

Thus, in this paper we modify the logic used in [Fisher, 1997b] by replacing the standard KD45 modal logic with a *multi-context* representation of belief [Giunchiglia and Serafini, 1994; Benerecetti *et al.*, 1997]. This logic is a modification of KD45 which permits a simple execution mechanism to be employed over belief contexts. Consequently, it allows us to tightly control the use of belief contexts within deliberative agents and so to represent resource-bounded reasoning. In addition, we also investigate the resource-bounded aspects of *temporal* reasoning. Thus, rather than allowing the agent to reason about the full underlying temporal logic, we examine how the agent can be restricted so that it reasons with an *abstraction* of the underlying temporal model.

The paper is structured as follows. In §2, we define the syntax and semantics of the particular logic used to represent agents. This will combine a simple temporal logic [Emerson, 1990] with a multi-context logic of belief [Benerecetti *et al.*, 1997]. In order to provide the basis for the direct execution of this logic, we introduce, in §3, a particular normal form, that extends the Separated Normal Form used in the METATEM [Fisher, 1997a]. An algorithm which can be used to directly execute formulae in this normal form is defined in §4, while an example of such execution is given in §5. The correctness of the execution algorithm is considered in §6. In §7, we consider the effects of restricting both the hypothetical doxastic and temporal reasoning that can be carried out by an agent. Finally, in §8, we provide conclusions from this research and consider future work.

2 Temporal Logic of Bounded Belief

In this section, we give the syntax and semantics of our base logic (called a *Temporal Logic of Bounded Belief*, or TLBB for short) which combines propositional linear temporal logic, with a multi-context belief logic. While temporal reasoning is essentially infinite, reasoning about beliefs can be bounded. In this sense, the logic allows the representation of bounded reasoning.

Syntax We are considering a situation with an agent, a, observing and representing beliefs about a set $I = \{1, \ldots, n\}$ of agents. Formulae of TLBB are constructed using the following connectives and proposition symbols.

- A set, $\mathcal{P}$, of propositional symbols.
- Propositional connectives, **true**, **false**, $\neg$, $\vee$, $\wedge$, and $\Rightarrow$.
- Temporal connectives, $\bigcirc$, $\Diamond$, $\square$, $\mathcal{U}$, and $\mathcal{W}$.
- A set, $\{B_1, B_2, \ldots, B_n\}$, of belief operators.

Let I^k be the set the set of (possibly empty) strings of the form $i_1 \ldots i_h$ with $|i_1 \ldots i_h| \leq k$. We call any $\alpha \in I^k$ a *view*. Intuitively, each view in I^k represents a possible nesting of the belief operators. The empty string represents the view of the external agent a. The views[1] that a can build can be organized in a structure such as that presented in Figure 1.

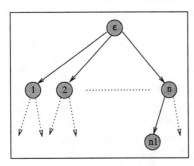

Figure 1: The structure of views

We associate a logical language L_α with each view. The set of well-formed formulae of L_α, denoted by WFF$_\alpha$, is inductively defined as the smallest set satisfying:

---

[1]A more detailed description of the structure of views we are using can be found in [Benerecetti *et al.*, 1997].

- Any element of $\mathcal{P}$ is in WFF$_\alpha$
- If ψ and φ are in WFF$_\alpha$ then so are

$$\neg\psi \quad \psi \vee \varphi \quad \psi \wedge \varphi \quad \psi \Rightarrow \varphi \quad \textbf{false} \quad \textbf{true}$$
$$\Diamond\psi \quad \square\psi \quad \psi \mathcal{U} \varphi \quad \psi \mathcal{W} \varphi \quad \bigcirc\psi$$

- $B_i\psi$ [for all $1 \leq i \leq n$] is an atomic formula in WFF$_\alpha$ if, and only if, ϕ is in WFF$_{\alpha i}$

The set of well-formed formulae of TLBB comprises the sets of well-formed formulae contained in each L_α.

Semantics The semantics of the TLBB language is based on the semantics for contextual reasoning proposed in [Giunchiglia and Ghidini, 1998; Benerecetti *et al.*, 1997]. Following this approach, the semantics of every formula is *local* to the view where we consider it. Therefore, we associate to each view α a discrete linear temporal model of time m_α with finite past and infinite future, e.g. $(\mathbb{N}, <)$, in order to interpret the temporal component of each language L_α. Each of these *moments* in time, represented by a temporal index $u \in \mathbb{N}$, provides also a valuation π_α for the propositional part of the language and for (atomic) formulae of the form $B_i\psi$. As usual, we define the semantics of each L_α via the satisfiability relation:

$\langle m_\alpha, u \rangle \models \textbf{true}$ $\langle m_\alpha, u_0 \rangle \models \textbf{start}$

$\langle m_\alpha, u \rangle \models p$ iff $\pi_\alpha(u, p) = T$ (where $p \in \mathcal{P}$ or p is of the form $B_i\psi$ with $B_i\psi \in L_\alpha$)

$\langle m_\alpha, u \rangle \models \neg A$ iff $\langle m_\alpha, u \rangle \not\models A$

$\langle m_\alpha, u \rangle \models A \vee B$ iff $\langle m_\alpha, u \rangle \models A$ or $\langle m_\alpha, u \rangle \models B$

$\langle m_\alpha, u \rangle \models \bigcirc A$ iff $\langle m_\alpha, u + 1 \rangle \models A$

$\langle m_\alpha, u \rangle \models \square A$ iff $\forall u' \in \mathbb{N}$. if $(u \leq u')$ then $\langle m_\alpha, u' \rangle \models A$

$\langle m_\alpha, u \rangle \models \Diamond A$ iff $\exists u' \in \mathbb{N}$. if $(u < u')$ then $\langle m_\alpha, u' \rangle \models A$

$\langle m_\alpha, u \rangle \models A \mathcal{U} B$ iff $\exists u' \in \mathbb{N}$. such that $(u' \geq u)$ and $\langle m_\alpha, u' \rangle \models B$, and $\forall u'' \in \mathbb{N}$, if $(u \leq u'' < u')$ then $\langle m_\alpha, u'' \rangle \models A$

$\langle m_\alpha, u \rangle \models A \mathcal{W} B$ iff $\langle m_\alpha, u \rangle \models A \mathcal{U} B$ or $\langle m_\alpha, u \rangle \models \square A$

Satisfiability and validity are defined in the usual way.

The second step in defining the semantics for TLBB is to formalize the relation existing among different views. Indeed only a certain combinations of temporal models are *compatible* and provide a model for TLBB. A *model* M for TLBB is a set $M = \{m_\alpha\}_{\alpha \in I^k}$ such that for all $\alpha \in I^k$:

1. if $m_\alpha \models B_i\phi$ then $m_{\alpha i} \models \phi$;
2. if $m_{\alpha i} \models \phi$ then $m_\alpha \models B_i\phi$;
3. if $m_\alpha \models B_i\phi$ and $B_i\phi \in L_{\alpha i}$ then $m_{\alpha i} \models B_i\phi$;
4. if $m_\alpha \models \neg B_i\phi$ and $B_i\phi \in L_{\alpha i}$ then $m_{\alpha i} \models \neg B_i\phi$;

M satisfies a formula $\phi \in L_\alpha$ if m_α satisfies it.

Let us write $\alpha : \phi$ to mean that ϕ is a formula in L_α. Each model M for TLBB satisfies the formulae $\alpha : B_i(\phi \Rightarrow \psi) \Rightarrow (B_i\phi \Rightarrow B_i\psi)$, $\alpha : B_i\phi \Rightarrow B_iB_i\phi$ and $\alpha : \neg B_i\phi \Rightarrow B_i\neg B_i\phi$. They are the TLBB versions of modal axioms K, 4, and 5, respectively, and are obtained from conditions 1–4 in the definition of M. Moreover M satisfies the formulae $\alpha : \neg B_i\neg\phi \Rightarrow B_i\phi$ and $\alpha : B_i\phi \Rightarrow \neg B_i\neg\phi$. These are a consequence of the fact that M associates a unique temporal model m_α to each view and ensures that '$\neg B_i \neg$' and 'B_i' are equivalent. While the fact that each view has exactly one B_i-accessible view enforces that each agent must either believe, or disbelieve, every atom, it does simplify the model structure, and hence the execution, required. As we will see in §5, typical examples of agent reasoning are not affected by this addition.

3 Normal Form for TLBB

Formulae in TLBB can be transformed into a normal form SNF_{BB} (Separated Normal Form for temporal logics of bounded belief). Separated Normal Form (SNF) is used as the basic normal form for linear-time temporal logics [Fisher, 1997a] and has been extended, for example to temporal logics of knowledge in [Dixon *et al.*, 1998]. The translation to SNF_{BB} uses the renaming technique [Plaisted and Greenbaum, 1986] where complex subformulae are replaced by new propositions and then the truth value of these propositions are linked, in all states, to the formulae they replaced. In linear time temporal logic this is achieved by ensuring that such formulae are in the scope of a '$\square$' operator, i.e. they hold at all reachable states. For TLBB we introduce the $\square^*$ operator, which allows arbitrary nesting of B_i and $\square$ operators to achieve the same effect. As in the case of temporal logics of knowledge, the $\square^*$ operator can be defined using fixpoints [Dixon *et al.*, 1998].

Formulae in SNF_{BB} are of the general form

$$\square^* \bigwedge_i T_i$$

where each T_i, known as a *rule*, must be in one of the varieties described in Figure 2. Note that k_a, l_b, and l are all literals,

$$\textbf{start} \Rightarrow \bigvee_{b=1}^{r} l_b \qquad \text{(an \textit{initial} rule)}$$

$$\bigwedge_{a=1}^{g} k_a \Rightarrow \bigcirc \left[\bigvee_{b=1}^{r} l_b \right] \qquad \text{(a \textit{step} rule)}$$

$$\bigwedge_{a=1}^{g} k_a \Rightarrow \lozenge l \qquad \text{(a \textit{sometime} rule)}$$

$$\bigwedge_{a=1}^{g} k_a \Rightarrow B_i \left[\bigvee_{b=1}^{r} l_b \right] \qquad \text{(a \textit{belief} rule)}$$

Figure 2: Rules in SNF_{BB}

and the outer '$\square^*$' operator that surrounds the conjunction of rules is usually omitted.

Example 3.1 Consider the TLBB formula

$$(\bigcirc B_2 \psi) \Rightarrow ((B_1(B_2 \varphi)) \wedge \lozenge(B_1(\psi \vee B_2 \chi))) . \quad (1)$$

We can go through the following stages to transform this into SNF_{BB}:

a) rename $(\bigcirc B_2 \psi)$ by p and add $\neg p \Rightarrow \bigcirc \neg B_2 \psi$;

b) rename $\neg B_2 \psi$ above by q and add $q \Rightarrow B_2 \neg \psi$;

c) rename $B_2 \varphi$ in (1) by r and add $r \Rightarrow B_2 \varphi$;

d) rename $B_1(\psi \vee B_2 \xi)$ in (1) by s and add $s \Rightarrow B_1(\psi \vee B_2 \xi)$;

e) rename $(\psi \vee B_2 \xi)$ in the above formula by t and add $(t \wedge \neg \psi) \Rightarrow B_2 \xi$.

The original formula is now $p \Rightarrow B_1 r \wedge \lozenge s$, which can be split giving the final set of rules in SNF_{BB} as:

1.	p	$\Rightarrow$	$B_1 r$
2.	p	$\Rightarrow$	$\lozenge s$
3.	$\neg p$	$\Rightarrow$	$\bigcirc q$
4.	q	$\Rightarrow$	$B_2 \neg \psi$
5.	r	$\Rightarrow$	$B_2 \varphi$
6.	s	$\Rightarrow$	$B_1 t$
7.	$(t \wedge \neg \psi)$	$\Rightarrow$	$B_2 \chi$.

The key properties of the translation to SNF_{BB}, characterised by the function 'τ' are as in the temporal case [Fisher, 1997a].

Theorem 1 *If TLBB formula φ is satisfiable, then $\tau(\varphi)$ is satisfiable.*

Theorem 2 *If M is a model for $\tau(\varphi)$ then M is also a model for φ.*

Consequently, as execution is essentially model building in our framework, then we can execute $\tau(\varphi)$ in place of φ.

4 Execution of SNF_{BB}

In this section we give an algorithm for executing a set of SNF_{BB} rules. Since lack of space precludes us from providing the algorithm in full detail, we will first present an outline of the execution mechanism for temporal logic, based on [Barringer *et al.*, 1995] and [Fisher, 1997b], and will follow this with a more detailed account of the execution of the belief element of the logic.

4.1 Executing Temporal Logic

The basic idea underlying METATEM [Barringer *et al.*, 1995] is to directly execute a temporal formula, by attempting to build a model for the formula in a simple forward-chaining fashion. This is extended, in [Fisher, 1997b], whereby the choice of which formulae to satisfy is provided by user defined deliberation functions, rather than by a fixed ordering heuristic. An outline of the basic approach, assuming that we are executing the set of rules, R, is given below.

1. By examining the *initial* rules, constraints on the possible start states for the temporal model can be generated.

   We choose one of these possible start states, deriving its valuation from the initial rules.

   If all the possible start states have been explored, then we terminate stating that the set of rules, R, is unsatisfiable.

2. Generate constraints on *next* states, C_n, and constraints on *future* states, C_f, by checking applicability in current state of step and sometime rules, respectively.

   C_n represents all the possible choices of valuations for the next state, while C_f provides the set of eventualities that must be satisfied at some time in the future.

$v(A)$ – which is defined as follows: Let $\Gamma_A = \bigcup T_i : L_i \cap L(A) \neq \emptyset$, where $L(A)$ is the *smallest language* in which A can be expressed (cf. Lemma LS2).
If Γ_A is consistent, then

   if $\Gamma_A \vdash A$, then $v(A) = true$
   if $\Gamma_A \vdash \neg A$, then $v(A) = false$, and
   $v(A) = \bot$ otherwise.

If Γ_A is inconsistent, then $v(A) = \top$.

Intuitively we see *which* of the theories T_i *could be* relevant to A and put them together to get Γ_A. Γ_A is used to answer questions about A and the rest of the theories T_j are *not* brought into play.

Controlling Inconsistency: Our approach, while seeking to handle this problem, is distinct from the usual paraconsistent approach in that we do allow full use of classical logic, albeit locally.

Limited consistency: Suppose that A has at most l distinct symbols, the L_i are a k-partition, and $m \geq k \times l$. Then Γ_A will be a union of at most m of the theories T_i. If the collection $\{T_i : i \leq n\}$ is m-consistent, then Γ_A will be consistent and *exactly one* of the first three values will be given. In other words, an agent whose B-structure is *fairly consistent*, and who is responding to a *short* query, will *always* give a consistent response.

We say that the person with belief base B *implicitly believes* A if $v(A) = true$. If so, it is true that A follows from her explicit beliefs but the converse does not hold in general. If the explicit beliefs are jointly inconsistent, then their consequences will include all formulae, but the agent may still have implicit beliefs which are a reasonable set. The implicit beliefs will always include the explicit ones and will be *locally* closed under logical rules.

What about adjunction? If an agent implicitly believes A and B, i.e. if the answers to A and B are both *true* and $L(A \wedge B)$ has no more than l symbols, then the answer to $A \wedge B$ will also be *true*. However, cases can arise where the longer formula $A \wedge B$ forces the agent to simultaneously consider several of his beliefs and the underlying inconsistency is detected. Let $L_1 = \{P, R\}$, $L_2 = \{Q, R\}$, $T_1 = Cn(P, R)$ and $T_2 = Cn(Q, \neg R)$. Then the answers to the queries 'P?' and 'Q?' will both be *yes*, but to '$P \wedge Q$?' it will be $\top$.

5   Base Refinement

A person who has explicit beliefs Γ in language L may organize these beliefs in smaller or larger chunks. Clearly if Γ is inconsistent, then it is un-workable to organize them in a single chunk. Moreover, organizing in larger chunks can make the computational problems harder. On the other hand it does have the advantage that more implicit beliefs can be derived in the sense described below.

Definition 4: A B-structure B *refines* another, B' if (i) every language L_i is a subset of another L_j', (ii) every $L_j' = \bigcup L_i | L_i \subseteq L_j'$, and (iii) every $T_j' = Cn(\bigcup T_i | L_i \subseteq L_j')$.

Example: Suppose that the B-structure B has the three languages $\{P, Q\}, \{Q, R\}, \{R, S\}$ and theories $T_i : i \leq 3$ generated by the formulae $P \rightarrow Q$, $\neg Q \wedge R$ and $R \wedge S$ respectively. the B-structure B' has the two languages $\{P, Q, R\}, \{R, S\}$. and theories $T_j' : j \leq 2$ generated by the formulae $\neg P \wedge \neg Q \wedge R$ and $R \wedge S$ respectively. Clearly B refines B'. Now to the query 'P?', B will give the answer $\bot$ and B' will give the answer 'yes' or *true*.

Theorem 1: Let B refine B' and A be a formula. Then $v(A) \leq_k v'(A)$ where $v(A), v'(A)$ respectively stand for $v_B(A)$ and $v_{B'}(A)$.
Proof: Given a formula A and B-structure B the query "A?" is answered by giving the value $v_B(A) = v(A)$ which is defined using $\Gamma_A = \bigcup T_i : L_i \cap L(A) \neq \emptyset$, where $L(A)$ is the language of A. Similarly for B'.

Now we note that if $L_i \subseteq L_j'$ and $L(A)$ intersects L_i then it also intersects L_j'. Hence $\Gamma_A \subseteq \Gamma_A'$. This immediately yields $v(A) \leq_k v'(A)$. $\square$

In other words, B' always yields more information than B. The downside is that B' may give the inconsistent answer $\top$ to a query A whereas B may have given a *true* or *false* answer to it. The partitioning of information into separate languages may on occasion miss some answers which might have been obtained without such partitioning, but it is more likely to be consistent in particular queries.

6 B-Structure Revision

What will happen to a B-structure when an agent receives some information which overlaps two sub-languages? One possibility is that the agent accepts the consequences *within* each sub-language while still keeping them separate. If I learn that both Beijing and London had cold winters, I am not likely to merge all my other beliefs about the two cities. However, if I repeatedly receive information which overlaps two sub-languages, I may decide that the division is artificial and should be abandoned. Options A and B below correspond to these two different attitudes.

option A - the non-merging option: Assume that each of the languages L_i has its own AGM style revision operator. Given a belief structure B and a new input A, define, for each i, the *i-shadow* of A to be the set $\{B | B \in L_i \wedge A \vdash B\}$. This will be a theory T_i' in L_i. T_i' is what A has to say about the language L_i. Let $A_i \in L_i$ be such that $T_i' = Cn(A_i)$. Now define the theories T_i'' by:

$T_i'' = T_i \dotplus A_i$ if A_i is consistent with T_i, and
$T_i'' = T_i *_i A_i$ otherwise where $*_i$ is a local revision operator for L_i.
Then the revised B-structure $B * A$ will equal $\{(L_1, T_1''), ..., (L_n, T_n'')\}$.

In practice, if $L(A) \cap L_i$ is empty, we can just leave T_i unchanged, saving computational time. We define $B \dotplus A$ analogously, except that we use the operator $\dotplus$ on the various T_i.

option B - the merging option: Given a formula

A as input and a belief base $\mathcal{B}$, assume without loss of generality that A has been written in the *smallest language* in which it can be expressed [Parikh, 1996]. Let as before $\Gamma_A = \bigcup T_i : L_i \cap L(A) \neq \emptyset$, where $L(A)$ is the language of A. Let T_A be $Cn(\Gamma_A)$ and $L_A = \bigcup L_i | L_i \cap L(A) \neq \emptyset$. Now replace all those languages L_i such that $L_i \cap L(A) \neq \emptyset$ by the single language $\bigcup L_i : L_i \cap L(A) \neq \emptyset$, which is their union. At the same time, replace all the corresponding T_i by the theory $T_A * A$. This new way will specialize to the procedure in [Parikh, 1996] where the languages were all assumed to be disjoint but the receipt of information resulted in joining those theories whose languages overlapped the language of the new information.

6.1 Properties of B-structure revision

Both options A and B are *computationally efficient*. Generally we assume that each L_i has relatively small size, say under some fixed p, while the cardinality n of the whole language $L = \bigcup L_i$ might be quite large. Then given a k-partition and a formula A with at most l distinct symbols, the query answering procedures run in time which is exponential in $l \times k \times p$, but *linear in n*. (For option A, the procedure is linear in n, k and exponential only in $l + p$). Thus if $k \times l \times p$ – the number of atomic propositions *relevant* to A – is small compared to n, as is usually the case, the computational cost will be much smaller than that of usual update procedures which are exponential in n.

The update procedures need not preserve refinements. If $\mathcal{B}$ refines $\mathcal{B}'$ and there is new information A, it may reveal an inconsistency in $\mathcal{B}'$, even though $\mathcal{B}$ is unfazed. It may seem foolish not to notice one's own inconsistencies, but these are often unavoidable, as with the well known Preface and Lottery paradoxes [Kyburg, 1961], [Kyburg, 1997]. The ability to retain a measure of consistency and act on the basis of one's implicit beliefs may have much to say in its favour.

Option B results in two formally distinct subject areas merging as the result of some new information which straddles them. In real life this is likely to happen only occasionally. Suppose I have a B-structure which keeps my beliefs about Turkey, Iraq and Iran separate. If I now receive a great many pieces of information about the Kurds who are scattered over these three countries then I may simply create the new subject *Asia Minor* and give up my attempt to deal with the three countries separately.

6.2 Analogues of the AGM axioms

Let $\mathcal{B} * A$ denote the revision of B-structure $\mathcal{B}$ by the formula A according to option B. The axioms B1-B5 below hold. The set theoretic notions $\in, \subseteq$ used in stating the AGM axioms are now replaced by more sophisticated generalizations which enter in with Belnap's four truth values. For option A, axiom **B2** needs the caveat that $A \in L_i$ for some i or, at least that $A \Leftrightarrow B_1 \wedge ... \wedge B_p$ where each B_k is in some L_i and p is small. However *dis-*

junctive information which straddles two of the L_i may be lost if we insist, as we do in option A, on keeping the L_i separate.

Let $\mathcal{B}$ be a belief structure, A a new piece of information, $*$ the revision operator. We then have the following axioms: (read $A \in \mathcal{B}$ as 'A is an implicit belief according to $\mathcal{B}$'.)

B1. $\mathcal{B} * A$, the revision of $\mathcal{B}$ by A, is a belief structure.

B2. $A \in \mathcal{B} * A$

B3. If $A \Leftrightarrow B$, then $\mathcal{B} * A = \mathcal{B} * B$

B4. $\mathcal{B} * A \subseteq \mathcal{B} \dotplus A$. i.e. if $\mathcal{B} * A$ and $\mathcal{B} \dotplus A$ give values v, v' to A, then $v <_k v'$.

B5. If A is consistent with $\mathcal{B}$, i.e it is not the case that $v_B(A) \in \{false, \top\}$, then $\mathcal{B} * A = \mathcal{B} \dotplus A$

Other Issues: Issues commonly raised in belief revision literature include, for instance, the axiom of recovery, revision by conjunctions, by sets of propositions etc. Most of these properties *will* hold at the local level provided that the original local operations have them. At the non-local level when several of the T_i interact in a particular case of a belief revision, more complex patterns of behaviour will emerge. These require further investigation.

6.3 Review of Previous Work

We briefly discuss how other authors have addressed the issues mentioned at the outset.

Work on the minimal change model has concentrated on minimizing the number of beliefs given up during the *contraction* operation. To this end, operations such as partial meet contraction using selection functions were defined in [Alchourron *et. al*, 1985]. A motivation for the choice of beliefs to be dropped is given by the notion of *epistemic entrenchment* introduced by [Gärdenfors and Makinson, 1988] and refined for iterated belief change by [Nayak, 1994], [Darwiche and Pearl, 1994], [Lehmann, 1995]. [Williams, 1996] uses the concept of *maxi-adjustment* to achieve maximal inertia of information under iterated belief revision. [Georgatos, 1999] presents a generalization of entrenchment that serves as a representation of the AGM axioms. The notion of *epistemic relevance* is used for minimal contraction in [Hansson, 1992] and [Nebel, 1992].

The distinction between implicit and explicit beliefs, has been explored by the proponents of the *belief base* method such as [Fuhrmann, 1991], [Nebel, 1992], [Hansson 1991;1992]. [Rott, 1992] combines some intuitions in showing how epistemic entrenchment orderings can be carried out for *safe contractions* for belief bases.

Belief revision for inconsistent belief bases has been studied in an alternative approach by [Brewka, 1991]. The possibility of paraconsistent belief revision is explored by [Tanaka, 1997] while [Restall and Slaney, 1995] have developed a paraconsistent semantical representation based on the revision of models approach suggested in [Grove, 1988]. The work of [Schotch and Jennings,

1980] predates the AGM approach to belief revision. They consider an approach based on giving up the adjunction rule: from $\Gamma \vdash A$ and $\Gamma \vdash B$ conclude $\Gamma \vdash A \wedge B$. As we saw, our treatment retains this rule at the local level.

The investigation of complexity procedures in [Nebel, 1992], via a fine-grained set of complexity classes, has shown that the complexity of base revision procedures satisfying AGM postulates is that of ordinary propositional derivability. Nebel's comparison of different revision methods shows that model-based revision methods such as those of [Dalal, 1988] have a complexity which exceeds both **NP** and **co-NP**.

Conclusion: We started this paper by indicating four desiderata which a framework for answering queries and for belief revision should try to meet. The B-structures framework meets all four. In future work we intend to carry out a thorough study of this interesting new model for belief representation and revision and to implement the query answering and revision procedures.

Acknowledgements: This research was supported in part by a grant from the Research Foundation of CUNY. We thank Ron Fagin, Melvin Fitting, Konstantinos Georgatos, Henry Kyburg, Graham Priest and the referees for helpful comments.

References:

[Alchourron et. al, 1985] Alchourron, C., Gärdenfors, P. and Makinson, D. (1985) On the logic of theory Change: partial meet functions for contraction and revision. *Journal of Symbolic Logic*, Vol 580, pp 510-530.

[Belnap, 1977] Belnap, N.D. A useful four-valued logic. *Modern Uses of Multiple-Valued Logic*, J.M Dunn and G. Epstein eds., D. Reidel.

[Brewka, 1991] Brewka, G., Belief revision in a framework for default reasoning. *The Logic of Theory Change*, A. Fuhrmann and M Morreau, editors, LNAI 465, Springer.

[Dalal, 1988] Dalal, M. Investigations into a theory of knowledge base revision. *Proceedings of the Seventh National Conference of the American Association for Artificial Intelligence*, Saint-Paul, MN, pp 475-479.

[Darwiche and Pearl, 1994] Darwiche, A, Pearl J. On the logic of iterated belief revision. *Proceedings of Theoretical Aspects of Rationality and Knowledge*, 1994, pages 5-23.

[Fitting, 1989] Fitting, Melvin. Bilattices and the theory of truth. *Journal of Philosophical Logic*, Vol 18, 225-256, 1989.

[Fuhrmann, 1991] Fuhrmann, Andre. Theory contraction through base revision. *Journal of Philosophical Logic*, Vol 20, pp175-203, 1991.

[Gärdenfors and Makinson, 1988] Gärdenfors P., Makinson, D. Revisions of knowledge systems using epistemic entrenchment. *Proceedings of Theoretical Aspects of Reasoning about Knowledge*, Moshe Vardi ed., Morgan-Kaufmann, pp 83-96, 1988.

[Gärdenfors, 1988] Gärdenfors, Peter. *Knowledge in Flux: Modeling the Dynamics of Belief States*, Bradford Books, MIT Press, Cambridge, MA, 1988.

[Georgatos, 1999] Georgatos, Konstantinos. To preference via entrenchment. *Annals of Pure and Applied Logic*, to appear.

[Grove, 1988] Grove, A. Two modellings for theory change. *Journal of Philosophical Logic*, 17:157-170, 1988.

[Hansson, 1992] Hansson, S.O. A dyadic representation of belief. *Belief Revision*, Gärdenfors, P. ed., Cambridge, 1992.

[Hansson, 1991] Hansson, S.O. In defense of base contraction. *Synthese*, 91:239-245, 1992.

[Kyburg, 1961] Kyburg, Henry, *Probability and the Logic of Rational Belief*, Middletown, CT: Wesleyan, 1961

[Kyburg, 1997] Kyburg, Henry. The rule of adjunction and reasonable inference. *Journal of Philosophy*, **XCIV**, 3, 1997, pages 109-125.

[Lehmann, 1995] Lehmann, D. Belief revision, revised. *Proceedings of the Fourteenth International Joint Conference on Artificial Intelligence 1995*, pages 1534-1540.

[Minsky, 1986] Minsky, M., *The Society of Mind*, Simon and Schuster.

[Nayak, 1994] Nayak, Abhaya. Foundational belief change. *Journal of Philsophical Logic*, Vol. 23, pp 495-533, 1994

[Nebel, 1992] Nebel, B. Syntax based approaches to belief revision. *Belief Revision*, Gärdenfors, P. ed., Cambridge, 1992.

[Parikh, 1996] Parikh, Rohit. Beliefs, belief revision and splitting languages. *Preliminary Proceedings of Information Theoretic Approaches to Logic, Language and Computation*, 1996, editors L. Moss, M. de Rijke and J. Ginzburg. Final version to appear, CSLI, 1999.

[Restall and Slaney, 1995] Restall, G and Slaney, J. Realistic belief revision. *Technical Report: TR- ARP-2-95*, Automated Reasoning Project, Australian National University, 1995.

[Rott, 1992] Rott, Hans. Preferential belief change using generalized epistemic entrenchment, *Journal of Logic, Language and Information*, 1:45-78, 1992.

[Schotch and Jennings, 1980] Schotch P.K, Jennings R. Inference and necessity. *Journal of Philosophical Logic*, 9 (1980), 327-340.

[Tanaka, 1997] Tanaka, Koji. What does paraconsistency do? The case of belief revision. *The Logica Yearbook*, Timothy Childers ed., Praha, 1997, pp 188-197.

[Williams, 1996] Williams, Mary-Anne. A practical approach to belief revision: Reason-based change, in L. Aiello and S. Shapiro eds. *Principles of Knowledge Representation and Reasoning: Proceedings of the Fifth International Conference*, Morgan-Kaufmann, San Mateo, CA, 412-421, 1996.

3. Make a choice from C_n and check that the chosen valuation is consistent. If there are no unexplored choices, return to a choice point in a previous state.

   The choice mechanism takes into account a combination of C_f, the outstanding eventualities, and the deliberation ordering functions [Fisher, 1997b].

4. Generate a new state, s, from the choice made in (3). Note that, by default, if propositions are not constrained we choose to leave them unsatisfied.

   Define s as being a successor to the current state and record the eventualities that are still outstanding (i.e. previously generated eventualities that were not satisfied in s); call this set of eventualities Evs.

   If any member of Evs has been continuously outstanding for more than $2^{5|R|}$ states, then return to a previous choice point and select a different alternative.

5. With current state, s, and the set of outstanding eventualities, Evs, go to (2).

The key result here is that, under certain constraints on the choice mechanism within (3), this execution algorithm represents a decision procedure (previously presented in [Barringer *et al.*, 1995]).

Theorem 3 *If a set of SNF rules, R, is executed using the above algorithm, with the proviso that the choice in (3) ensures that the oldest outstanding eventualities are attempted first at each step, then a model for R will be generated if, and only if, R is satisfiable.*

The above proviso ensures that, if an eventuality is outstanding for an infinite number of steps, then it will be attempted an infinite number of times. Once the choice mechanism is extended to include arbitrary ordering functions, as in [Fisher, 1997b], then a more general version of the above theorem can be given wherein we only require a form of *fairness* on the choice mechanism. While the above proviso effectively means that we *can* potentially explore every possibility, the incorporation in the algorithm of a bound on the number of states that eventualities can remain outstanding, together with the finite model property of the logic, ensures that all of the possible states in the model will be explored if necessary.

4.2 Extending Execution

We now extend the above algorithm to handle the execution of SNF_{BB}. The two main elements of the algorithm affected by this are that the execution process now builds a labelled tree, rather than a sequence, and that once a new belief state is built it must be checked for equivalence with previously generated states. Thus, rather than just generating a set of choices based upon temporal rules, we must now consider both temporal and belief rules. This will (often) lead to the construction of a number of belief contexts and (simulated) temporal sequences in order to derive these choices. For example, in Figure 3 the basic temporal sequence (labelled by 'TL') is being constructed. However, at certain points, belief contexts (e.g. B1 and B2) must be explored in order to decide how to proceed. In addition, within these belief contexts, temporal execution itself can be simulated, e.g. B2(TL). Note

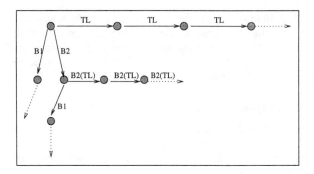

Figure 3: Typical Model Exploration

that exploration of everything within a belief context will be carried out within a finite amount of time.

In order to incorporate the execution of belief operators into the algorithm described in §4.1, we add the following to the end of step (4).

> For all belief operators, B_i, if $expand(B_i, R, s, 0)$ returns **false**, then return to a previous choice point and select a different alternative.

The function '$expand$' explores belief contexts and attempts to build a model for the multi-context beliefs as follows.

$expand(B_i, R, s, D) : Boolean$

1. Let $C_{B_i} = \bigwedge F$, where $(P \Rightarrow B_i F) \in R$ and $s \models P$; if there are no such rules $P \Rightarrow B_i F$, return **true**.
   Let C'_{B_i} be DNF version of C_{B_i}, and remove all inconsistent disjuncts from C'_{B_i}.

2. Choose a disjunct, d, from C'_{B_i}; if no unexplored disjuncts are available then immediately return **false**.

3. If $D \neq \emptyset$, then conjoin the formulae in D with d to give d'; otherwise, let $d' = d$. Note that D contains the belief constraints from the last state and this operation corresponds to the persistence of beliefs given by axioms 4 and 5, e.g. $\vdash B_i\varphi \Rightarrow B_i B_i\varphi$.

4. Generate a new state, t, with valuation based on d'. If a state equivalent to t has occurred previously within this exploration from a basic temporal state, then make a B_i edge from s to this previous state and return **true**.
   If no such equivalent state exists, then make a B_i edge from s to t

5. For all belief operators, B_i, if any of $expand(B_i, R, t, \{d'\})$ returns **false**, then return to (2) and select a different alternative.

6. If $tl\_expand(R, t, \emptyset)$ returns **false**, then return to choice point (2) and select a different alternative.

7. Return **true**.

The function $tl\_expand(Rules, State, Eventualities)$ effectively carries out temporal reasoning in a belief context. However, rather than continuing indefinitely, as the base-level algorithm does, it uses a tableau-like produce to ensure that a finite structure is constructed if the formula is satisfiable.

Rather than giving the detail of *tl_expand*, we note that it is very similar to the base-level temporal execution algorithm, although it does try to recognise repeated temporal states and so construct a finite graph rather than an infinite sequence. We will consider this temporal reasoning aspect further in §7.2.

5 Example

Consider the following example of an agent acting as a travel information provider (note that, for reasons of space, the example is represented in predicate logic where variables range over finite domains).

A) $ask(you, x) \Rightarrow B_{me} \Diamond go(you, x)$

   i.e., "if you ask for information about destination x, then I believe that you will holiday in x in the future"

B) $B_{me}[\Diamond go(you, x) \Rightarrow \Diamond buy(you, holiday, x)]$

   i.e., "I believe that, if you will holiday in x in the future, then you will buy a holiday for x in the future"

C) $B_{me} \Diamond buy(you, holiday, x) \Rightarrow \bigcirc send\_info(you, x)$

   i.e., "if I believe that you will buy a holiday for x in the future, I will send you information about holidays at x":

D) $ask(you, x)$

   i.e., "you ask for information on destination x":

These translate to the following SNF_{BB} rules.

A1.	$ask(you, x)$	$\Rightarrow$	$B_{me} a$
A2.	a	$\Rightarrow$	$\Diamond go(you, x)$
B3.	b	$\Rightarrow$	$B_{me} c$
B4.	c	$\Rightarrow$	$\Diamond buy(you, holx)$
B5.	$\neg b$	$\Rightarrow$	$B_{me} d$
B6.	$\neg b$	$\Rightarrow$	$B_{me} \neg go(you, x)$
B7.	d	$\Rightarrow$	$\bigcirc \neg go(you, x)$
B8.	d	$\Rightarrow$	$\bigcirc d$
C9.	e	$\Rightarrow$	$\bigcirc send\_info(you, x)$
C10.	$\neg e$	$\Rightarrow$	$B_{me} f$
C11.	$\neg e$	$\Rightarrow$	$B_{me} \neg buy(you, holx)$
C12.	f	$\Rightarrow$	$\bigcirc \neg buy(you, holx)$
C13.	f	$\Rightarrow$	$\bigcirc f$
D14.	**start**	$\Rightarrow$	$ask(you, x)$

Execution begins by ensuring that $ask(you, x)$ is true in the initial temporal state and then exploring other choices. Thus, if we choose b to be false here, then we get a contradiction in the $B_{me}(TL)$ simulation with (effectively) $\Box \neg go(you, x)$ (from rules B5–B8) and $\Diamond go(you, x)$ (from rule A2).

Similarly, if we choose e to be false, we get a contradiction in the $B_{me}(TL)$ simulation with (effectively) $\Box \neg buy(you, holx)$ (from rules C10–C13) and $\Diamond buy(you, holx)$ (from rule B4).

Thus, we eventually choose to satisfy $ask(you, x)$, b and e together in the initial state, which in turn leads to the execution of $send\_info(you, x)$ in the next state.

The model eventually produced is given in Figure 4.

6 Correctness

As in the case with the basic METATEM system, we can show that the extended system can be used as a decision procedure for TLBB if necessary.

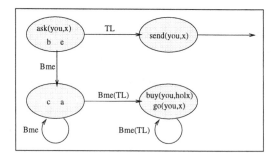

Figure 4: Example Execution

Theorem 4 *If a set of SNF_{BB} rules, R, is executed using the above algorithm, and the choices made by the temporal component ensure that the oldest outstanding eventualities are attempted first at each step, then a model for R will be generated if, and only if, R is satisfiable.*

The proof follows by showing that the above execution mechanism will (eventually) explore all the tableau structure for TLBB [Ghidini, 1998; Wooldridge *et al.*, 1998]. In particular, the execution within belief contexts explores potential linear sequences of such contexts until either a model is found, or until no unexplored possibilities remain and so the belief formula is unsatisfiable.

In general, the mechanisation of such a logic is relatively easy since there are no axioms defining interactions between the different belief/temporal operators. Thus, the sub-logics within TLBB can effectively be treated separately, and decidability of TLBB is retained [Blackburn and de Rijke, 1997].

7 Resource-Bounded Reasoning

In §4.2, we considered the execution of the temporal logic of bounded belief with (effectively) infinite bounds on belief reasoning capabilities. Now we will examine how the effect that introducing resource bounds of various kinds will have on this execution mechanism.

7.1 Bounded Reasoning

The most obvious thing to do (and indeed this was the main motivation for this work) is to set an explicit bound on the depth of belief reasoning allowed. In order to modify the execution mechanism, we just need to add an extra argument to the *expand* and *tl_expand* functions. This argument will represent the depth of nesting of belief contexts. Thus, in the first call to *expand* (from the basic temporal execution), the depth is 0. In the definition of the *expand* function itself, the depth is incremented when the function is invoked recursively. Finally, we require an additional condition in *expand* stating that backtracking will occur if the depth bound reaches its limit (i.e. the maximum depth of nested beliefs allowed).

Given that we can bound the agent's ability to reason about belief, then can we do the same with temporal reasoning? In principle, yes. However, a bounded multi-context semantics for the type of temporal logic we use is quite complex, and we have not yet considered restricting the logic in this way.

7.2 Abstract Temporal Reasoning

From a practical point of view, carrying out hypothetical reasoning within propositional linear-time temporal logic is quite expensive. While the logic is decidable, the decision problem is PSPACE-complete [Emerson, 1990]. Also, although the execution mechanism for METATEM is complete, and thus could be used as a (naive) theorem-prover for the logic, the execution mechanism is not at all efficient in this respect. We propose a modified logical framework which consists of three elements: (full) propositional linear temporal logic for the agent's basic execution; bounded (multi-context) belief; and 'simulated' temporal logic, comprising only '$\Diamond$', but no '$\bigcirc$' operator (this logic is only used within belief contexts and is equivalent to KDT4 modal logic). The *tl_expand* function described in §4.2 now executes the KDT4 logic, rather than temporal logic.

While the restriction of the capability of an agent to reason only about 'abstract' elements of time in a belief context may seem too extreme, it does significantly reduce the complexity of the execution mechanism. In addition, it is debatable whether an agent *should* be able to reason about the exact detail of the time structure in which it is situated. Further, if an agent wishes to reason about the temporal behaviour of another agent, then the asynchronous nature of agent execution means that a step in one agent will not necessarily match a step in the other. Thus, perhaps an agent should only be able to reason about another agent reaching a certain state at *some* point in the future. Hence the use, within hypothetical temporal reasoning, of just the '$\Diamond$' operator.

8 Conclusions and Future Work

We have considered the extension of basic executable temporal logic (of the METATEM style) with bounded reasoning about belief and time. In particular, we have proposed the version of the logic in §7.2 as a practical basis for the high-level logic-based programming of resource-bounded agents.

It is important to note that we are not interested in generating alternative mechanisms for undertaking temporal/modal proof. The main element we are concerned with is the execution of temporal formulae in order to generate an infinite sequence. However, at certain points hypothetical reasoning needs to be carried out and belief contexts must be explored. We could have used standard proof mechanisms for non-interacting temporal and doxastic logics [Wooldridge *et al.*, 1998] at this point (and, indeed, our intention is to provide this possibility within the full implementation). However, (a) we would like to retain the common execution mechanism throughout, (b) by representing belief exploration in terms of execution the whole process should be more amenable to meta-level control, and (c) while belief exploration is neither very common nor very complex, it makes sense to keep the execution mechanism simple.

Finally, the execution mechanism described in this paper provides a way to execute multi-context logics of this form [Giunchiglia and Serafini, 1994] using the Imperative Future [Barringer *et al.*, 1996] style of executable logics.

Future work includes testing a full implementation on larger examples, incorporating belief revision and persistence, and investigating the addition of real-time aspects.

References

[Barringer *et al.*, 1995] H. Barringer, M. Fisher, D. Gabbay, G. Gough, and R. Owens. METATEM: An Introduction. *Formal Aspects of Computing*, 7(5):533–549, 1995.

[Barringer *et al.*, 1996] H. Barringer, M. Fisher, D. Gabbay, R. Owens, and M. Reynolds, editors. *The Imperative Future: Principles of Executable Temporal Logics*. Research Studies Press, 1996.

[Benerecetti *et al.*, 1997] M. Benerecetti, F. Giunchiglia, and L. Serafini. Model Checking Multiagent Systems. To appear in Journal of Logic and Computation, 1997.

[Blackburn and de Rijke, 1997] P. Blackburn and M. de Rijke. Why Combine Logics? *Studia Logica*, 59:5–27, 1997.

[Bratman *et al.*, 1988] M. E. Bratman, D. J. Israel, and M. E. Pollack. Plans and resource-bounded practical reasoning. *Computational Intelligence*, 4:349–355, 1988.

[Dixon *et al.*, 1998] C. Dixon, M. Fisher, and M. Wooldridge. Resolution for Temporal Logics of Knowledge. *Journal of Logic and Computation*, 8(3):345–372, 1998.

[Emerson, 1990] E. A. Emerson. Temporal and Modal Logic. In J. van Leeuwen, editor, *Handbook of Theoretical Computer Science*, pages 996–1072. Elsevier, 1990.

[Fagin *et al.*, 1996] R. Fagin, J. Halpern, Y. Moses, and M. Vardi. *Reasoning About Knowledge*. MIT Press, 1996.

[Fisher, 1995] M. Fisher. Representing and Executing Agent-Based Systems. In M. Wooldridge and N. R. Jennings, editors, *Intelligent Agents*. Springer-Verlag, 1995.

[Fisher, 1997a] M. Fisher. A Normal Form for Temporal Logic and its Application in Theorem-Proving and Execution. *Journal of Logic and Computation*, 7(4), 1997.

[Fisher, 1997b] M. Fisher. Implementing BDI-like Systems by Direct Execution. In *Proc. IJCAI-97*. Morgan-Kaufmann, 1997.

[Ghidini, 1998] C. Ghidini. Tableaux for Multi-Context Logics. (Unpublished manuscript.), 1998.

[Giunchiglia and Ghidini, 1998] F. Giunchiglia and C. Ghidini. Local Models Semantics, or Contextual Reasoning = Locality + Compatibility. In *Proc. KR-98*. Morgan Kaufmann, 1998.

[Giunchiglia and Serafini, 1994] F. Giunchiglia and L. Serafini. Multilanguage hierarchical logics (or: how we can do without modal logics). *Artificial Intelligence*, 65:29–70, 1994.

[Giunchiglia *et al.*, 1993] F. Giunchiglia, L. Serafini, E. Giunchiglia, and M. Frixione. Non-Omniscient Belief as Context-Based Reasoning. In *Proc. IJCAI-93*. Morgan-Kaufmann, 1993.

[Halpern and Moses, 1992] J. Y. Halpern and Y. Moses. A guide to completeness and complexity for modal logics of knowledge and belief. *Artificial Intelligence*, 54:319–379, 1992.

[Plaisted and Greenbaum, 1986] D. A. Plaisted and S. A. Greenbaum. A Structure-Preserving Clause Form Translation. *Journal of Symbolic Computation*, 2(3):293–304, 1986.

[Rao and Georgeff, 1991] A. S. Rao and M. P. Georgeff. Modeling Agents within a BDI-Architecture. In *Proc. KR-91*. Morgan Kaufmann, 1991.

[Wooldridge *et al.*, 1998] M. Wooldridge, C. Dixon, and M. Fisher. A Tableau-Based Proof Method for Temporal Logics of Knowledge and Belief. *Journal of Applied Non-Classical Logics*, 8(3):225–258, 1998.

Exploiting a Common Property Resource under a Fairness Constraint: a Case Study

Michel Lemaître and Gérard Verfaillie
ONERA CERT
2, avenue Édouard Belin (BP 4025)
31055 – Toulouse Cedex – France

Nicolas Bataille
Centre National d'Études Spatiales
18, avenue Édouard Belin
31055 – Toulouse Cedex – France

Abstract

Resources co-funded by several agents must be exploited in such a way that three kinds of constraints are met: (1) physical problem (hard) constraints; (2) efficiency constraints, aiming at maximizing the satisfaction of each agent; (3) a fairness constraint, which is ideally satisfied when each agent receives an amount of the resource exactly proportional to its financial contribution. This paper investigates a decision problem for which the common property resource is an earth observation satellite. The problem is to decide on the daily selection of a subset of pictures, among a set of candidate pictures which could be taken the next day considering the satellite trajectory. This subset must satisfy the three kinds of constraints stated above. Although fair division problems have received considerable attention for a long time, especially from microeconomists, this specific problem does not fall entirely within a classical approach. This is because the candidate pictures may be incompatible, and because a picture is only of value to the agent requesting it. As in the general case, efficiency and fairness constraints are antagonistic. We propose three ways for solving this share problem. The first one gives priority to fairness, the second one to efficiency, and the third one computes a set of compromises.

1 Introduction

Due to their cost, large research or industrial projects are often co-funded by several agents (countries, companies, entities ...). Space projects such as earth observation satellites, space stations or space probes are good examples. Once constructed and made operational, the common property resource must be exploited and shared in a way which satisfies three kinds of constraints :

- *physical* constraints: the exploitation of the resource must obey hard constraints;

- *efficiency* constraints: each agent wants to get the highest possible satisfaction in return;

- a *fairness* constraint: each agent must get a return on investments proportional to its financial contribution to the project; the better the proportionality of returns is achieved, the more the share quality improves.

The first kind of constraints must absolutely be met (hard constraints) whereas the two others are preference constraints (soft constraints). As it can be easily guessed, the efficiency and fairness constraints are antagonistic: the search for a perfect share may lead to poorly efficient decisions, and conversely, decisions which maximize the global satisfaction of agents are often unfair. So, a compromise between the best satisfaction of both constraints must be found.

The usual case involving only one agent (in which case there is no share problem) is a difficult combinatorial discrete optimization problem (NP-hard). Nevertheless, it is a perfectly well stated problem. The multiagent case is also a discrete combinatorial problem, but is actually a multi-objective optimization problem [Keeney and Raiffa, 1976]; the first difficulty arises when searching for a meaningful and principled definition of a good compromise between efficiency and fairness.

This article sums up a study, the aim of which was to propose methods to solve a specific share problem, namely the fair and efficient exploitation of an earth observation satellite owned in common by several agents. It is organized as follows. The next section sets the problem more formally. Then we present three quite different methods devoted to the resolution of this share problem. These methods have been simulated on the basis of the expected data for the future Spot5 satellite. The section after reports these simulations. Lastly, we state our conclusions.

2 An Earth Observation Satellite Scheduling and Sharing Problem

The studied problem is the following: an earth observation satellite, co-funded by several agents, is exploited in common. These agents make daily requests for pictures they would like to be taken by the satellite. Roughly speaking, the problem consists in selecting each day, among the set of candidate pictures which could be taken

values for λ would allow to get other compromises : this is also of interest in this method.

7 Summary and conclusions

We have described a specific share decision problem involving multiple agents, in which the satisfaction of two kinds of constraints poses a dilemma: efficiency constraints aim at satisfying the agents the most, whereas a fairness constraint watches over equity among agents.

We proposed three different methods to solve this problem. The first method searches for fairness first, and then for efficiency. It is a simple *a priori* sharing method, allocating observation windows to each agent in turn.

The second method is based on the opposite view : first efficiency, fairness if possible. A global satisfaction criterion is defined and maximized. A "minimal fair share" for each agent is defined *a priori* but only checked *a posteriori*.

The third approach does not favor one constraint or the other, but computes a set of good compromise decisions. This is a multi-criteria approach, based on the computation of the set of Pareto-optimal decisions in the two-dimensional space (global-satisfaction, quality-of-share). This set is computed exactly by a branch-and-bound search, or approached by an adapted local search method when the search space is too large.

These three methods have been simulated on the basis of the expected data for the future Spot5 satellite. In short:

- the first method results in very good shares, but inefficient decisions,

- the second one delivers quite good decisions (minimal fair shares are always achieved and the global satisfaction is high), and uses a tolerable amount of computational resources,

- the last one is very costly in computational resources, but allows a human decision-maker to preview a set of interesting non-dominated compromise decisions.

The overall conclusions of this work are:

- no method can be indisputably put forward; the problem is not to choose a method against another one, it is to present to the agents a set of methods and their properties and to let them decide according to the properties they consider the most important[3];

- whereas general methods of sharing can be stated, each share problem is specific and must be studied carefully;

- discrete share problems like this one are computationally very consuming; more specialized combinatorial optimization algorithms are needed to solve them.

---

[3]See [Rosenschein and Zlotkin, 1994] for a discussion about this point. What we call a method is called by them a

Acknowledgments

The authors would like to thank the anonymous reviewers for their useful comments, as well as Lionel Lobjois and Loïc Trégan for their help in the simulation work.

References

[Bistarelli *et al.*, 1995] S. Bistarelli, U. Montanari, and F. Rossi. Constraint solving over semirings. In *Proceedings of the Fourteenth International Joint Conference on Artificial Intelligence*, pages 624–630, Montréal, Québec, Canada, August 1995. International Joint Commitee on Artificial Intelligence.

[Brams and Taylor, 1996] S. J. Brams and A. D. Taylor. *Fair Division — From cake-cutting to dispute resolution.* Cambridge University Press, 1996.

[Freuder and Wallace, 1992] E. Freuder and R. Wallace. Partial Constraint Satisfaction. *Artificial Intelligence*, 58(1-3):21–70, December 1992.

[Keeney and Raiffa, 1976] R. L. Keeney and H. Raiffa. *Decisions with Multiple Objectives: Preferences and Value Tradeoffs.* John Wiley and Sons, 1976.

[Larrosa *et al.*, 1998] J. Larrosa, P. Messeguer, T Schiex, and G. Verfaillie. Reversible DAC and Other Improvements for Solving Max-CSP. In *Proceedings of the Fifteenth National Conference on Artificial Intelligence*, pages 347–352, Madison, Wisconsin, July 1998. American Association for Artificial Intelligence.

[Moulin, 1988] H. Moulin. *Axioms of Cooperative Decision Making.* Cambridge University Press, 1988.

[Moulin, 1995] H. Moulin. *Cooperative Microeconomics, A Game-Theoretic Introduction.* Prentice Hall, 1995.

[Rosenschein and Zlotkin, 1994] J. S. Rosenschein and G. Zlotkin. *Rules of Encouter.* MIT Press, Cambridge, Massachusetts, 1994.

[Schiex *et al.*, 1995] T. Schiex, H. Fargier, and G. Verfaillie. Valued Constraint Satisfaction Problems: Hard and Easy Problems. In *Proceedings of the Fourteenth International Joint Conference on Artificial Intelligence*, pages 631–637, Montréal, Québec, Canada, August 1995. International Joint Commitee on Artificial Intelligence.

[Verfaillie *et al.*, 1996] G. Verfaillie, M. Lemaître, and T. Schiex. Russian Doll Search for Solving Constraint Optimization Problems. In *Proceedings of the Thirteen National Conference on Artificial Intelligence*, pages 181–187, Portland, Oregon, August 1996. American Association for Artificial Intelligence.

[Wallace, 1994] R. Wallace. Directed Arc Consistency Preprocessing. In *Constraint Processing*, pages 121–137. Lecture Notes in Computer Science 923, Springer, 1994.

[Young, 1994] H. P. Young. *Equity in Theory and Practice.* Princeton University Press, 1994.

Maximization of the Average Quality of Anytime Contract Algorithms over a Time Interval

Arnaud Delhay*
LIFL - ISEN
F-59046 Lille
adel@isen.fr

Max Dauchet
LIFL
F-59655 Villeneuve
d'Ascq
Max.Dauchet@lifl.fr

Patrick Taillibert
Thomson-CSF Detexis
F-78190 Trappes
*Patrick.Taillibert@
detexis.thomson-csf.com*

Philippe Vanheeghe
ISEN
F-59046 Lille
pva@isen.fr

Abstract

Previous studies considered quality optimization of anytime algorithms by taking into account the quality of the final result. The problem we are interested in is the maximization of the average quality of a contract algorithm over a time interval. We first informally illustrate and motivate this problem with few concrete situations. Then we prove that the problem is NP-hard, but quadratic if the time interval is large enough. Eventually we give empirical results.

1 Introduction

Hard problems like planning or decision making cannot be reasonably treated by complete methods. That is the reason why [Dean and Boddy, 1988] first considered anytime algorithms, also called flexible algorithms in [Horvitz, 1988]. These algorithms offer a trade-off between time and performance. They are characterized by a *Performance Profile* [Grass, 1996] that enables a prediction about the quality of the results given by the algorithm depending on the execution time duration. This method has been used to solve several problems in various domains like robot control [Zilberstein and Russel, 1993], knowledge-based computation [Mouaddib and Zilberstein, 1995] and reactive agents [Adelantado and de Givry, 1995].

Quality is not the essential characteristic of a computation result: what really matters is its utility. The intuitive idea is that, in many situations, the utilit· of a result decreases over time, and a result of medium quality rapidly obtained is more useful than a result of high quality obtained after a long time [Zilberstein and Russel, 1996]. But, when the algorithm operates on an uncertain environment, utility can be of another nature. This is the case in the following examples, which are all associated to a "crisis situation":

- a person (P) has to give his boss (B) a report in the morning. P only knows that B will ask for the report at some time between 8 a.m. and 11 a.m. The problem for P is that trying to achieve the best quality would be a good

strategy only if the report were claimed at 11. If it is not the case, no report at all is available! Hence it seems better to ensure a medium quality draft for 8 a.m. and, once the draft is ready, to start to write a better quality report, expecting that the claim will occur late in the morning.

- Every time the enemy is going to launch a satellite, only the temporal window on which the event will occur is known in advance. To perturb the launching, some electromagnetic jamming action must be set up (planes have to take-off, lures must be activated...). All these actions take time and the best jamming is useless if achieved after the launch. What could be considered is to set up the jamming in order to ensure the best *average* quality on the time interval, then to maximize the utility (in the long term).

- When a tornado is announced, very little time is available to prepare oneself (and one's house) for any possible destruction. Hence it is important to achieve the best "utility" of the protections set in place, e.g. to ensure that minimal actions have been taken first (securing the kids), before improving the quality of the protections (nailing down the shutters).

In the previously described situations, an interruptible algorithm would be the best solution: at the time of the event, the best possible quality would be achieved. Unfortunately, interruptible algorithms are not always available since:
- none of the available algorithms might be interruptible,
- anytime algorithms might result from the composition of elementary interruptible algorithms. In that case, the result is of the contract kind [Zilberstein and Russel, 1996],
- contract algorithms can be transformed into interruptible ones [Zilberstein and Russel, 1996] but, notwithstanding the fact that the execution time is 4 times longer, this method only applies if the contract durations can be chosen freely (exponential series) which is generally not the case.

Finally, even with a genuine interruptible algorithm, situations exist in which the contract case re-occurs: if applying the results of the algorithm causes a change in the environment, it is no longer possible to let the algorithm continue in order to improve the solution from the previously

---

* This author is supported by the *Délégation Générale pour l'Armement (DGA)*, French Ministry of Defense

obtained one; it must be restarted from scratch. For instance, this might occur in counter-measure applications, if the result of the interruptible algorithm is a jamming action which itself provokes a counter-jamming decision from the enemy.

In [Delhay *et al*, 1998], we proposed partial solutions to solve these kinds of problems consisting of maximizing the average quality over a time interval. But the results achieved are limited to convex quality functions (whose second derivative is positive) which are the less probable ones in real applications.

In this paper, after restating the problem of maximizing the average quality of an anytime contract algorithm over a time interval (section 2), we present general results about any kind of quality function approximated by a stepwise function. We prove that the problem is NP-hard, but becomes quadratic if the time interval is large enough (section 3). We then present empirical results which augurs well for the practical applicability of the approach (section 4).

2   Maximizing the average quality over a time interval

We use the notion of contract algorithms which was first coined by Zilberstein [Zilberstein, 1993], even though they appeared before, like RTA* [Korf, 1985]. Contract algorithms can also result from the composition of anytime modules. In this paper, we assume that the performance profiles are deterministic functions of time. It is sometimes difficult to construct them with such a confidence, but they are good approximations of the performance profiles used in real situations.

2.1   Informal presentation

A typical example is the following: an attack might happen with a uniform probability over a given time interval, and a contract algorithm, whose performance profile is increasing over time (figure 1) is available to counter-attack. The problem then consists in determining how to best prepare the counter-attack in order to get the best chance of survival over the time interval.

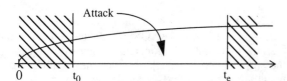

figure 1: The attack might happen at any time over $[t_0, t_e]$

An answer to the attack must be given between t_0 and t_e and it is possible to begin the computation at time $t = 0$. To answer to this problem, several solutions can be considered.

First (figure 2) we activate the algorithm for a short contract (t_1); in that case, the result has a relatively poor quality but this quality is available on a relatively long time interval ($t_e - t_1$).

figure 2: short but bad preparation

To get a better quality, we have to start the algorithm with a longer contract (t_2): the quality of the result is better, but most of the time, on $[t_0, t_2]$, no "quality" (that is, no protection from the attack) is available (figure 3).

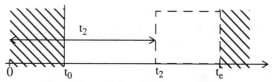

figure 3: good but slow preparation

These two cases lead to a simple observation: if the algorithm starts with a (sufficiently) short contract (t_1), then the remaining time can be used to restart the algorithm with a contract t'_2, to get a better result.

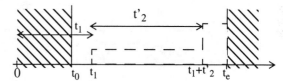

figure 4: mixed preparation

Hence an effective method is to start the contract algorithm several times to get a good cover of the time interval and a minimal quality early. We only have to respect two conditions:

- The sum of all contracts must be strictly lower than the length of the interval where it is possible to compute
- Every new contract must be longer than the previous one to improve the quality of the result

Remark:

Note that to maximize the average quality, we never execute more than one contract before t_0. Should we do that, all contracts before t_0, except the last, would be useless.

2.2   Formalization

Now let us give the definition of the average quality over an interval where $<\Theta_n> = \{\theta_1, \theta_2, ..., \theta_n\}$ denotes the duration of successive runs of the algorithm (contracts).

definition 1 : *integral quality*

Let f be the performance profile of a contract algorithm A. The integral quality *of A over a time interval $[t_0, t_e]$, relative to a choice $<\Theta_n>$ of n contracts with performance profile f, is defined as follows:*

$$Q(f, \langle \Theta_n \rangle) = min(0, \theta_1 - t_0) \cdot f(\theta_1) + \sum_{i=1}^{n-1} f(\theta_i) \cdot \theta_{i+1}$$

$$+ f(\theta_n) \cdot \left(t_e - \sum_{i=1}^{n} \theta_i \right)$$

The above definition is only usable if the contracts respect the sum constraint, that is: $\sum_{i=1}^{n} \theta_i < t_e$

The average quality $\overline{Q}(f, \langle \Theta_n \rangle)$ *is equal to the integral quality divided by the length of the interval* $[t_0, t_e]$.
$Q(f)$ *is the supremum of the integral quality, and* $\overline{Q}(f)$ *the supremum of the average quality.*

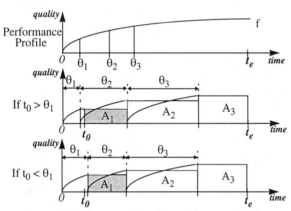

figure 5: Performance Profile and Average Quality

2.3 The analytic case

In [Delhay *et al.*, 1998], we studied the maximization of the average quality for continuous and derivable performance profiles, leading to preliminary analytic results that partially cover functions with constant curvature, that is the convex case and the concave case for one contract. These results are shown below.

A first theorem gives the value of a single contract. The linear performance profile is a limit and the single contract equals $t_e/2$. For convex performance profiles, the single contract is greater than $t_e/2$. In the concave case, it is lower than $t_e/2$. A second theorem states that, for convex performance profiles, there is no need to start several contracts over $[0, t_e]$, as a single contract always gives the best average quality. The value of this contract θ_1 is analytically defined by a simple equation.

$$\theta_1 = t_e - \frac{f(\theta_1)}{f'(\theta_1)}$$

The point we can add is that there is at least two contracts in the concave case because of the first theorem. As a matter of fact, as the single contract is lower than $t_e/2$, it is possible to add a contract greater than the first one, but respecting the sum constraint, that improves the average quality.

3 Average quality for stepwise constant performance profiles

Because of the difficulties involved in solving this problem in the continuous and derivable case, we chose to solve the problem by approximating the performance profile in order to get a discrete problem. We first tried using a stepwise linear function. Even with this approximation, we did not manage to exhibit interesting properties. Then we approximated the performance profiles with stepwise constant functions. This approach not only enables us to avoid difficulties due to the continuous and derivable performance profiles, but also makes sense in the common representation of performance profiles, that is the discrete tabular representation. Moreover, lemma 1 states that the average quality is approximated with the same error as the error on performance profile itself. In particular, this is true when approximating the continuous performance profile f with a stepwise function.

lemma 1 : *approximation lemma*
   If $|f - g| < \varepsilon$ *then* $|\overline{Q}(f) - \overline{Q}(g)| < \varepsilon$
Proof: This is a property of integrals applied to definition 1.

So, hereafter the performance profiles are stepwise constant functions, either originally, or by approximation. A stepwise constant function is a function such as, for a finite set of thresholds $\{\theta_1, ..., \theta_n\}$, f is constant on every interval $[\theta_i, \theta_{i+1})$. The following lemma allows us to treat the maximization problem as a discrete problem, by only examining the steps of the performance profile instead of all values in the interval $[0, t_e]$.

lemma 2 : *(stepwise function lemma)*
   To maximize average quality, it is sufficient to choose all contracts θ_i *in the set of thresholds of the stepwise function.*
Proof:
   If a contract θ is in the interval (θ_i, θ_{i+1}), replacing θ by θ_i increases the average quality. It can be checked by calculating the difference between the two average qualities (with and without θ).

Thanks to lemma 2, we call this (discrete) problem MAXQSF (MAXimization of the average Quality for a Stepwise Function). MAXQSF(f,t_e) denotes the maximum of the integral quality of an increasing stepwise function f over the time interval $[0, t_e]$. In the next subsections, the tractability of MAXQSF is considered.

3.1 MAXQSF is NP-hard

The following theorem states that the MAXQSF problem is intractable in general.

theorem 1 : *MAXQSF(f, t_e) is NP-hard*

The proof consists in reducing polynomially the Knapsack problem to MAXQSF. The Knapsack (<A>,b) problem is to find a part of <A>={$a_1, a_2, ..., a_n$}, a set of naturals, whose sum of its elements is maximal and lower than a natural b. We assume that the a_i are sorted and distinct. This restriction is still NP-complete. The reduction consists in building a stepwise constant function $f_{<A>}$ of $2n+1$ steps that gives an instance of $MAXQSF(f, t_e)$ for any instance of $Knapsack(<A>, b)$.

To do so, we use the fact that the increase of average quality obtained by adding a contract θ' between two consecutive contracts θ and θ'' only depends on θ and θ'' and θ_φ (the last contract).

The variation of the average quality induced by the choice of introducing a threshold as a contract depends on the other choices and is not easy to evaluate. That is why $f_{<A>}$ is constructed by alternating the thresholds (odd numbers) that corresponds to the elements of $<A>$, and thresholds (even numbers) **that are chosen to necessary belong to the optimal choice of the best average quality**. The even thresholds "isolate" the effects of a choice in the set of odd thresholds; hence, the improvement of the average quality obtained by adding an odd threshold (element of $<A>$) only depends on the two even thresholds surrounding it[1]. That is the reason why we chose them so that if the corresponding element α of $<A>$ is in the solution, the improvement of the average quality is α. As a consequence, maximizing the average quality will maximize the load of the knapsack.

The reduction also requires that optimizing the average quality satisfies the sum constraint of the Knapsack problem. This is obtained by choosing t_e, the end of the time interval, such that:

$$t_e = b + \sum_{i \text{ even}} s_i + 0.5$$

Since the sum of all contracts in MAXQSF must be less than t_e and that all the even thresholds belong to the solution by construction, we therefore have:

$$\sum_{i \text{ odd}} s_i \le b$$

which is the sum constraint of the Knapsack problem.

We do not have enough space to include all the steps necessary to perform the reduction we have presented. Let's just say that the choice of the f function is done such that $f_i - f_{i-1} = K^{4n-i}$ with K great enough (but polynomially linked to the size of $<A>$) and that the s_{2i} are chosen such that $s_{2i} < a_i + 1/(3nK^{2n})$. This construction is polynomial in the size of $<A>$ which proves that MAXQSF is NP-hard. For a detailed proof, see [Delhay and Dauchet, 1999].

Theorem 1 looks like an instance of theorem 4.2 presented by [Zilberstein and Russel, 1996] in the framework of composition of anytime algorithms. However, it is not the case: we look for the best average quality, whereas they look for the best final quality after a fixed contract, the most important difference being that we do not know the number of contracts necessary to get the best average quality.

1.*also on the last contract* (θ_φ), *but, since it's an even one, it belongs to the optimal choice.*

3.2 MAXQSF with no sum constraint is quadratic

Our problem is intractable in general. The main difficulty comes from the search over the set of thresholds assuming that the sum constraint does not allow to take any subset of thresholds. As in Knapsack, it is necessary to judiciously choose the candidate contracts. So we could suppose that:

$$\sum_{i=1}^{p} s_i < t_e \text{ where } s_i \text{ is a threshold of the performance profile f.}$$

Hence it is possible to add any contract because the time interval is large enough to contain all contracts. That restricts MAXQSF and leads to a lower complexity algorithm.

The idea of this dynamic programming algorithm is founded on lemma 3 which allows the division of the set of combinations of thresholds into distinct subsets composed of the combinations finishing by a fixed threshold s_i. The lemma allows to iteratively compute $Q(f, <\Theta|\{s_i\}>)$, noted $MAXQ(s_i)$ for subset of combinations finishing by s_i, with s_i from s_1 to s_p, to finally give $MAXQ(s_p) = Q(f, <\Theta|\{s_i\}>)$ is the ordered set Θ finishing by s_i.

lemma 3 :

Let s_i and s_j be two thresholds of $<s>$, the set of thresholds of f, with $j<i$.
For any s_i, let $MAXQ(s_i)$ be the maximum of integral quality with s_i as the last contract and $TR(s_i) = (t_e - \theta_1 - ... - s_i)$ the remaining time for the optimal choice of contracts with s_i as the last contract.
Then $MAXQ(s_i) = max_{s_j}(MAXQ(s_j)$
$+ (TR(s_j) - s_i) \cdot (f(s_i) - f(s_j)))$

and especially: $MAXQ(s_p) = Q(f)$, where s_p is the last threshold of $<s>$.

Proof:

- It can be immediately proved that $Q(f, <\Theta|\{s_j, s_i\}>) = Q(f, <\Theta|\{s_j\}>) + (TR(s_j) - s_i).(f(s_i) - f(s_j))$. By using the maximum for both members, the result of the lemma comes as $TR(s_j)$ only depends on s_j. Indeed, $TR(s_j)$ is the remaining time for the optimal choice of contracts with s_j as the last contract.

- For the second part of the lemma, note that s_p is necessary in the optimal choice of contracts. It could always be added to the choice of contracts (as there is no sum constraint) and improves the quality. By definition, $MAXQ(s_p)$ gives the maximal integral quality at the last step of iteration.

The complexity of the algorithm is $O(n^2)$, with n the number of thresholds.

Algorithm:

Only one threshold $\theta_1 \leftarrow s_1$ and $TR(s_1) \leftarrow t_e - max(t_0, s_1)$
$MAXQ(s_1) \leftarrow TR(s_1) \cdot f(s_1)$
$CHOICE(s_i)$ denotes the optimal choice of contracts with s_i as the last contract.

For i *from* 2 *to* p *Do*

   $Q_{temp} \leftarrow 0$

   $TR_{temp} \leftarrow 0$

   $CHOICE_{temp} \leftarrow \emptyset$

   For j *from* 1 *to* i-1 *Do*

      If $MAXQ(sj) + (TR(s_j) - s_i) \cdot (f(s_i) - f(s_j)) > Q_{temp}$

      Then

        $Q_{temp} \leftarrow MAXQ(s_j) + (TR(s_j) - s_i) \cdot (f(s_i) - f(s_j))$

        $TR_{temp} \leftarrow TR(s_j) - s_i$

        $CHOICE_{temp} \leftarrow CHOICE(s_j) \cup \{s_i\}$

      Endif

   Endfor

   $MAXQ(s_i) \leftarrow Q_{temp}$

   $TR(s_i) \leftarrow TR_{temp}$

   $CHOICE(s_i) \leftarrow CHOICE_{temp}$

Endfor

$Q(f) \leftarrow MAXQ(s_i)$

$CHOICEMAX \leftarrow CHOICE(s_i)$

4 Empirical results

The results obtained so far do not take into account the duration of the deliberation itself. It might be a serious impediment to the practical application of our approach since we proved that the general problem is NP-hard! Fortunately, achieving the optimal solution is not a necessary condition for applying our method: a set of contracts approaching the optimal value of the average quality on the time interval is sufficient. That is the reason why we conducted a set of experiments designed to estimate the practical complexity of our problem. And the result was far better than expected: for all the cases we studied, the average quality achieved by the best choice of a set of 2 contracts was always at a distance lower than 2.75% from the quality of the optimal choice.

These results concern a family of monotonic functions which approximate the quality functions most often encountered in practical cases. That is the reason why we think that these results can be of some general interest.

The experiment was twofold. First, we studied the contribution of the shape of the quality function to the value of the average quality. For that, we considered the family of functions defined by the following equation where the parameter "a" permits the control of the curvature of the function as shown in the associated graphics.

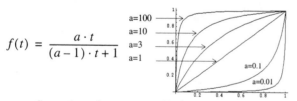

$$f(t) = \frac{a \cdot t}{(a-1) \cdot t + 1}$$

figure 6: performance profile for experiments

Every function ("a" varying from 1 to 205 incremented by 5) was approximated by a stepwise function of 50 steps for

which we computed the optimal average quality; we also computed the error w.r.t. this optimal value when considering smaller sets of contracts. We relied upon integer programming in order to avoid the classic problems of floating point numbers and took advantage of the sum constraint to limit the computation time. The results are summarized in the following table where a is the curvature, n is the number of contracts and ✹ is the optimal solution:

a \ n	1	2	3	4	5	6
0.1	✹					
1	✹					
5	10.83%	0.23%	✹			
25	12.33%	2.47%	0.25%	✹		
45	11.59%	2.71%	0.59%	✹		
65	10.75%	2.63%	0.6%	0.01%	✹	
85	9.97%	2.44%	0.53%	✹		
105	9.52%	2.36%	0.46%	0.01%	✹	
125	8.98%	2.29%	0.45%	0.02%	✹	
145	8.55%	2.22%	0.39%	0.02%	✹	
165	8.29%	2.02%	0.35%	0.01%	✹	
185	7.96%	1.83%	0.28%	✹		
205	7.54%	1.68%	0.31%	✹		

table 1: Error for limited number of contracts

For $a \leq 1$ the optimal quality is obtained with only one contract which was the expected result because of theorem 2. In the other cases, it is clear that the optimal quality obtained with 2 contracts is very close to the best result obtained notwithstanding the number of contracts.

We also investigated the influence of the temporal location of the time interval (t_0), which was set to 0 in the first experiment, while $t_e - t_0$ remained equal to 1. This might be of importance for many applications when time is available before the "attack" might occur. Here again, as shown on the following figure, restricting the deliberation to the computation of only 2 contracts gives very accurate results (even if only one contract rapidly gives very good results):

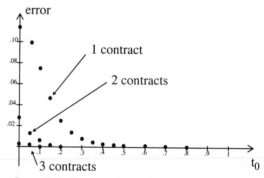

figure 7: Influence of t_0 on the number of contracts

In that experiment, the curvature was set to 51 and, since t_e was increased, the "sum constraint heuristic" became less efficient; hence we operated with a stepwise function of only 30 steps to keep the computation of optima tractable.

5 Conclusion

The aim of this paper was to present an **off-line** optimization of the time allocation for a contract algorithm so as to get the best chance of survival over a time interval. So far, no analytical method for solving the problem of maximizing the average quality over a time interval is known in the general case. That is the reason why we proposed solutions for discrete performance profiles. This restriction is not a real impediment since:

- a discrete tabular representation for the performance profiles is not a rare occurrence,
- the average quality resulting from a discrete performance profile can be as close as necessary to a given continuous performance profile (lemma 1).

We showed that the so-called MAXQSF problem is NP-hard in general, and quadratic if the time interval is large enough. This, unfortunately, is not frequently encountered in practical applications. Nonetheless, the experiments we carried out lead us to think that the "practical" complexity of that problem is quite low, which makes it possible to use the approach in real-time applications. Further studies to find a theoretical explanation of this behavior could prove very interesting.

The average quality of a contract algorithm A can be defined by:

$$\frac{1}{t_e - t_0} \cdot \int_{t_0}^{t_e} f^*(t)dt$$

where f^* is the quality of an interruptible algorithm A^* associated to A by the relation: $A^*(t) = A(\theta_i)$ where θ_i is the last contract executed at t.

[Zilberstein and Russel, 1996] gives a simple construction to transform a contract algorithm A of quality f into an interruptible algorithm A^* of quality f^* such as $f^*(4t) > f(t)$. The first difference with our study is that we consider the case of a given time interval to optimize the average quality. In our case, this leads to a construction of A^* which optimizes the average quality. The second difference is that our problem permits cases where the length of each contract is imposed by a method, when Zilberstein and Russel assume that the length of each contract can be arbitrarily chosen.

Note that a uniform probability of appearance of the attack over the interval has been considered. There are situations where this probability is not constant, such as with a gaussian. A future study could concentrate on this point.

Another extension could concentrate on our evaluation criteria, that is the average quality. Even if this criteria gives the best statistical results, there could exist others, for example that could take the number of contracts into account (a good solution therefore is a choice of few contracts).

Acknowledgments

I am especially appreciative of the discussions I had with Dominique Lohez at different stages of this work. His remarks and suggestions were very valuable.

References

[Adelantado and De Givry, 1995] M. Adelantado, S. De Givry, *Reactive/anytime Agents, Towards Intelligent Agents with Real-Time Performance*, IJCAI'95, Workshop on Anytime Algorithms and Deliberation Scheduling, August 21-25, 1995, Montreal, Canada.

[Dean and Boddy, 1988] Thomas Dean and Mark Boddy, *An Analysis of Time-Dependent Planning*, AAAI 88, August 1988, Saint Paul Minnesota.

[Delhay *et al.*, 1998] Arnaud Delhay, Max Dauchet, Patrick Taillibert, Philippe Vanheeghe, *Optimization of the Average Quality of Anytime Algorithms*, Workshop on Monitoring and control of real-time intelligent systems, ECAI'98, August 1998, Brighton, pp. 1-4.

[Delhay and Dauchet, 1999] Arnaud Delhay and Max Dauchet, *Complexity of the maximization of the average quality of anytime contract algorithms*, Internal Report LIFL-99-09, Laboratoire d'Informatique Fondamentale de Lille, 1999, ftp://ftp.lifl.fr/pub/reports/internal/1999-09.ps.gz

[Grass, 1996] Joshua Grass, *Reasoning about computational resource allocation, An introduction to anytime algorithms*, Crossroads, ACM student magazine, University of Massachusetts, September 1996, http://anytime.cs.umass.edu/~jgrass/school/papers/racra.html.

[Horvitz, 1988] Eric J. Horvitz, *Reasoning under varying and uncertain resource constraints*, Proceedings of the Seventh National Conference on Artificial Intelligence, Minneapolis, MN. August 1988, Morgan Kaufmann, San Mateo, CA. pp. 111-116.

[Korf, 1985] Richard E. Korf, *Real-Time Heuristic Search*, Artificial Intelligence vol. 42, 1985, pp. 189-211.

[Mouaddib and Zilberstein, 1995] Abdel-Illah Mouaddib, Shlomo Zilberstein, *Knowledge-Based Anytime Computation*, in Proceedings of the 14th IJCAI, Montreal, Canada, 1995, pp 775-781.

[Zilberstein and Russel, 1993] Shlomo Zilberstein, Stuart J. Russel, *Anytime Sensing, Planning and Action: A Practical Model for Robot Control*, in Proceedings of the 13th IJCAI, Chambery, France, 1993.

[Zilberstein and Russel, 1996] Shlomo Zilberstein, Stuart J. Russel, *Optimal composition of real-time systems*, Artificial Intelligence vol. 82, 1996, pp. 181-213.

CASE-BASED REASONING

CASE-BASED REASONING

Case-Based Reasoning 1

Demand-Driven Discovery of Adaptation Knowledge

David McSherry

School of Information and Software Engineering
University of Ulster
Coleraine BT52 1SA
Northern Ireland

Abstract

A case-based approach to adaptation for estimation tasks is presented in which there is no requirement for explicit adaptation knowledge. Instead, a target case is estimated from the values of three existing cases, one retrieved for its similarity to the target case and the others to provide the knowledge required to adapt the similar case. With recursive application of the adaptation process, any problem space can be fully covered by fewer than nk selected cases, where n is the number of case attributes and k is the number of values of each attribute. Moreover, a $k \times k$ problem space is fully covered by any set of $2k - 1$ known cases provided there is no redundancy in the case library. Circumstances in which the approach is appropriate are identified by theoretical analysis and confirmed by experimental results.

1 Introduction

Addressing the problems of automatic adaptation has been identified as a central problem for the future of CBR [Leake, 1996]. Recent advances promise to reduce the overhead associated with the acquisition of adaptation knowledge by automating its discovery from case data [Hanney and Keane, 1996; Smyth and Keane, 1998], or by a case-based approach to adaptation in which *adaptation cases* are acquired from user adaptations or learned from adaptation experience [Leake *et al.*, 1996; Leake *et al.*, 1997].

This paper presents a case-based approach to adaptation for estimation tasks that differs from other approaches to adaptation in that there is no requirement for explicit adaptation knowledge. Instead, a target case is estimated from the values of three existing cases, one retrieved for its similarity to the target case and the others to provide the knowledge required to adapt the similar case. The transformation applied to the similar case is based on a simple adaptation heuristic called the *difference heuristic* [McSherry, 1998] or an alternative called the *ratio heuristic*.

The demand-driven discovery of adaptation knowledge that characterizes the approach is consistent with the demand-driven approach to problem solving that characterizes CBR itself [Aha, 1998]. The techniques presented have been implemented in a case-based reasoner for estimation tasks called CREST (Case-based Reasoning for ESTimation). Estimation tasks to which CBR has been applied include cost estimation of software projects [Bisio and Malabocchia, 1995], property valuation [Gonzalez and Laureano-Ortiz, 1992], and estimation of sentence duration in JUDGE [Riesbeck and Schank, 1989].

The retrieval criteria and adaptation heuristics used in CREST are presented in the following section. In Section 3, coverage of the problem space is shown to be significantly increased by recursive application of the adaptation process. In Section 4, experimental results are presented which show that certain departures from the assumptions on which the difference heuristic is based can be tolerated at the expense of some loss of coverage.

2 Case Retrieval and Adaptation

The value of a case is assumed to be determined by an unknown function f of its attributes $x_1, x_2, ..., x_n$, all of which are assumed to be discrete. The task of the case-based reasoner is to estimate the value of the case function for a target case from the values of existing cases in a case library. A problem space P of dimensions $k_1 \times k_2 \times ... \times k_n$ is defined by the cartesian product of the attribute domains $D_1, D_2, ..., D_n$. A case is represented in CREST as a tuple $C = (a_1, a_2, ..., a_n)$, where for $1 \leq i \leq n$, a_i is the value of the attribute x_i for C. The known (or estimated) value of each case is also stored in the case library.

Table 1. Example library of 7 cases in the cylinder volume domain.

r	h	Volume
1	1	3.14
1	2	6.28
2	4	50.24
3	2	56.52
3	3	84.78
4	1	50.24
4	4	200.96

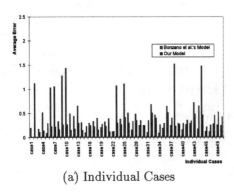 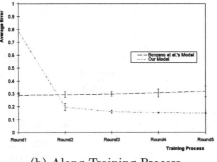

(a) Individual Cases   (b) Along Training Process

Figure 5: Comparisons between Bonzano et al.'s Model and Our Model (In (a), each case has two bars. The left bar corresponds to Bonzano et al.'s model while the right bar corresponds to ours)

different features. The effects of such interaction could be possibly reduced by introducing stronger bias factors into the system. We are also seeking other efficient and effective techniques to deal with the problem. In addition, one of the assumptions of our learning model is that the user of our system should be consistently one person in a certain period. If a different user comes to use the system, s/he might not satisfy and thus destroy the previous optimal case retrieval result, requiring the whole case base be retrained.

We will further explore, for our model, the more accurate relationship between the average running time and the size of a case base (including the number of feature-value pairs and cases). In the future, we hope to address these problems by introducing more effective learning and feedback control mechanisms and architectures into CBR.

References

[Bonzano et al., 1997] A. Bonzano, P. Cunningham, and B. Smyth. Using introspective learning to improve retrieval in CAR: A case study in air traffic control. In *Proceedings of the Second International Conference on Case-Based Reasoning, ICCBR-97*, pages 291–302, Providence RI, USA, 1997.

[Fox and Leake, 1995] S. Fox and D.B. Leake. Learning to refine indexing by introspective reasoning. In *Proceedings of the 14th International Joint Conference on Artificial Intelligence*, Montreal, Canada, August 1995.

[Gupta and Ding, 1994] M.M. Gupta and H. Ding. Foundations of fuzzy neural computation. In Fred Aminzadeh and Mohaamad Jamshidi, editors, *Soft Computing, Fuzzy Logic, Neural Networks, and Distributed Artificial Intelligence*, pages 165–200. PTR Prentice Hall, Englewood Cliffs, New Jersey, USA, 1994.

[Kolodner, 1993] J.L. Kolodner. *Case-Based Reasoning*. Morgan Kaufmann Publishers, Inc., 1993.

[Leake and Ram, 1993] D.B. Leake and A. Ram. Goal-driven learning: Fundamental issues (a symposium report). *AI Magazine*, 14(4):67–72, 1993.

[Leake et al., 1995] D.B. Leake, A. Kinley, and D. Wilson. Learning to improve case adaptation by introspective reasoning and CBR. In *Proceedings of the First International Conference on Case-Based Reasoning*, pages 229–240, Sesimbra, Portugal, 1995. Springer-Verlag.

[Munoz-Avilz and Huellen, 1996] H. Munoz-Avilz and J. Huellen. Feature weighting by explaining case-based reasoning planning episodes. In *Proceedings of Third European Workshop on Case-Based Reasoning (EWCBR-96)*, 1996.

[Ram and Cox, 1993] A. Ram and M. Cox. Introspective reasoning using meta-explanations for multistrategy learning. In R. Michalski and G. Tecuci, editors, *Machine Learning: A Multistategy Approach*. Morgan Kaufmann, San Mateo, USA, 1993.

[Smyth and Keane, 1995] B. Smyth and M.T. Keane. Remembering to forget. In *Proceedings of the 14th International Joint Conference on Artificial Intelligence*, pages 377–382, Montreal, Canada, August 1995.

[Wettschereck et al., 1997] D. Wettschereck, D.W. Aha, and T. Mohri. A review and comparative evaluation of feature weighting methods for lazy learning algorithms. *Artificial Intelligence Review*, 11:273–314, 1997.

[Zhang and Yang, 1998] Z. Zhang and Q. Yang. Towards lifetime maintenance of case based indexes for continual case-based reasoning. In *Proceedings of the Eighth International Conference on Artificial Intelligence: Methodology, Systems, Applications*, Sozopol, Bulgaria, 1998.

[Zurada, 1992] J.M. Zurada. *Introduction to Artificial Neural Systems*. West Publishing Company, 1992.

Remembering to Add: Competence-preserving Case-Addition Policies for Case-Base Maintenance

Jun Zhu and **Qiang Yang**

School of Computing Science

Simon Fraser University

Burnaby, British Columbia

Canada, V5A 1S6

Abstract

Case-base maintenance is gaining increasing recognition in research and the practical applications of case-based reasoning (CBR). This intense interest is highlighted by Smyth and Keane's research on case deletion policies. In their work, Smyth and Keane advocated a case deletion policy, whereby the cases in a case base are classified and deleted based on their coverage potential and adaptation power. The algorithm was empirically shown to improve the competence of a CBR system and outperform a number of previous deletion-based strategies.

In this paper, we present a different case-base maintenance policy that is based on case addition rather than deletion. The advantage of our algorithm is that we can place a lower bound on the competence of the resulting case base; we demonstrate that the coverage of the computed case base cannot be worse than the optimal case base in coverage by a fixed lower bound, and the coverage is often much closer to optimum. We also show that the Smyth and Keane's deletion based policy cannot guarantee any such lower bound. Our result highlights the importance of finding the right case-base maintenance algorithm in order to guarantee the best case-base coverage. We demonstrate the effectiveness of our algorithm through an experiment in case-based planning.

1 Introduction

Case-base maintenance refers to the task of adding, deleting and updating cases, indexes and other knowledge in a case base in order to guarantee the ongoing performance of a CBR system. Case-base maintenance is particularly important when a case based reasoning system becomes a critical problem solving system for an organization. This is because for any such organization, the knowledge may change over time and the need for different knowledge structures for problem solving may vary. The case-base size will increase with time, creating significant barrier to reasoning efficiency and the user's ability to understand the results.

In response to these problems, there has been a significant increase in case-base maintenance research. One branch of research has focused on the ongoing maintenance of case-base indexes through training and case base usage [Cunningham et al., 1997; Fox and Leake, 1995; Aha and Breslow, 1997; Zhang and Yang, 1998]. Another branch of research have focused on increasing the overall competence of the case base through case deletion [Smyth and Keane, 1995; Markovich and Scott, 1988; Domingos, 1995; Aha et al., 1991; Smyth and Keane, 1995; Racine and Yang, 1997] in a way similar to utility-based control-rule deletion policies [Minton, 1990]. Excellent surveys of this field can be found in [Leake and Wilson, 1998] and [Watson, 1997].

This recent surge of interest in case-base maintenance is highlighted by Smyth and Keane seminal work on competence-preserving case-deletion policy [Smyth and Keane, 1995]. In this work, the cases in a case base are classified into a type hierarchy based on their coverage potential and adaptation power. The deletion policy then selectively deletes cases from a case base guided by the classification of the cases until a limit on the case base size is reached. The algorithm was empirically shown to preserve the competency of a CBR system and to outperform a number of previous deletion based strategies.

In this paper, we present a detailed analysis of Smyth and Keane's deletion based policy and show that this policy does not always guarantee the competence preserving property. In particular, we show that using this policy can potentially result in a case base with significantly decreased performance. In response, we develop a different case-base maintenance policy that is based on case addition rather than deletion. By this policy, cases in an original case base are repeatedly selected and *added* to an empty case base until a certain size limit is reached, producing an updated case base which high coverage guarantee. The addition based policy will allow a more global view of the case base as a result of the maintenance operations. We show that both the Smyth and Keane's deletion-based policies and our addition-based policies have the same time complexity. The advantage

the role and use of abstract cases, e.g., [Bergmann and Wilke, 1996]. Abstract cases represent cases at a higher level of abstraction. Through abstract cases, the CBR process can be supported in several ways [Bergmann and Wilke, 1996]; those ways pertinent to the discussion in this paper are outlined below:

- Abstract cases can reduce the complexity of a casebase by substituting sets of concrete cases and thereby significantly reducing the size of the casebase. A drastically reduced casebase can improve retrieval efficiency, reduce maintenance costs, and eliminate or alleviate the notorious swamping problem [Smyth and Keane, 1995].

- Cases at higher levels of abstraction can serve as prototypes for indexing larger sets of more detailed cases. This can have profound effects on reducing retrieval times, maintenance costs, and it can promote a better user understanding of the casebase content, and facilitate explanations for the system's reasoning process.

In most situations, abstract cases are not readily available, they must be generated – manually or automatically – from concrete cases. To manually construct abstract cases will require a very high knowledge engineering effort for most applications. Whereas an automatic generation procedure requires general domain knowledge about ways of mapping concrete cases onto higher levels of abstraction.

The abstract case construct proposed in this paper is based on the concept of hypertuples. Hypertuples, i.e., abstract cases, are automatically generated through a so-called domain lattice, which is implied in a problem domain. The extraction and retrieval of abstract cases are achieved in domain lattice using the Lattice Machine.

3 Definitions and notation

To present our findings concisely and within the given page limit, we briefly introduce some notational conventions and definitions that are used throughout the paper.

3.1 Decision systems

An *information system* is a tuple $\mathcal{I} = \langle U, \Omega, V_x \rangle_{x \in \Omega}$, where $U = \{a_0, \ldots, a_N\}$ is a nonempty finite set and $\Omega = \{x_0, \ldots, x_T\}$ is a nonempty finite set of mappings $x_i : U \to V_{x_i}$ [1].

We interpret U as a set of objects and Ω as a set of attributes or features, each of which assigns to an object a its value under the respective attribute. Let $\mathbf{V} \stackrel{\text{def}}{=} \prod_{x \in \Omega} V_x$. For $a \in U$, we let $\Omega(a) \stackrel{\text{def}}{=} \langle x(a) \rangle_{x \in \Omega} \in \mathbf{V}$. Each $\Omega(a)$ is called a *tuple*, and the collection of all tuples is denoted by $\mathbf{D}$. Thus, for each $t \in \mathbf{D}$, there is at least one $a \in U$ such that $\Omega(a) = t$.

---

[1] Note V_{x_i} can be finite or infinite. For the latter case the domain lattice is infinite. However we are only interested in the *finite* sublattice generated from a finite casebase.

A *decision system* $\mathcal{D}$ is a pair $\langle \mathcal{I}, d \rangle$, where $\mathcal{I}$ is an information system as above, and $d : \mathbf{D} \twoheadrightarrow V_d = \{d_0, \ldots, d_\mathbf{K}\}$ is an onto mapping, called a *labeling* of $\mathbf{D}$; the value $d(t)$ is called the *label of* t.

The mapping d induces a partition $\mathcal{P}_d$ of $\mathbf{D}$ with the classes $\{\mathbf{D}_0, \ldots, \mathbf{D}_\mathbf{K}\}$, where $t \in \mathbf{D}_i \iff d(t) = d_i$.

In this paper we consider a dataset represented as a decision system $\mathcal{D}$, which can be regarded as an *initial casebase* consisting of concrete cases. Then $\mathbf{D}$ is the set of (descriptions of) concrete cases, d is the case solution, and $\mathbf{V}$ is the set of all possible concrete cases in a problem domain. Therefore each $t \in \mathbf{D}$ is associated with a solution in the form of a class label $d(t)$.

3.2 Order and lattices

Let $\mathcal{P} = \langle P, \leq \rangle$ be a partially ordered set and $T \subseteq P$. We let $\downarrow T \stackrel{\text{def}}{=} \{y \in P : (\exists x \in T)\, y \leq x\}$. If no confusion can arise, we shall identify singleton sets with the element they contain.

Let $\mathcal{L}$ be a lattice, partially ordered by $\leq$. For $x, y \in \mathcal{L}$, the least upper bound (or sum) is written by $x + y$ and the greatest lower bound (or product) by $x \times y$. For $A \subseteq \mathcal{L}$, its least upper bound and greatest lower bound are denoted by $\text{lub}(A)$ and $\text{glb}(A)$ respectively. An element $a \in A$ is called *maximal* in A, if for all $x \in A$, $a \leq x$ implies $x = a$.

For $A, B \subseteq \mathcal{L}$, we say that B *covers* A or A *is covered by* B, written as $A \preccurlyeq B$ if for each $s \in A$ there is some $t \in B$ such that $s \leq t$.

The *sublattice* of $\mathcal{L}$ generated from $M \subseteq \mathcal{L}$, written by $[M]$, is $[M] = \{t \in \mathcal{L} : \exists X \subseteq M \text{ such that } t = \text{lub}(X)\}$. The greatest element in $[M]$ is $\text{lub}(M)$. If M is finite, $[M]$ is also finite.

A comprehensive discussion on lattice theory can be found in [Grätzer, 1978].

4 The Lattice Machine

This section introduces the Lattice Machine, a construct which facilitates the discovery of abstract cases from a given dataset. The discussion should also make apparent how the Lattice Machine is linked to machine learning concepts.

4.1 Domain lattice

We have found that, given a dataset expressed as a decision system, an elegant mathematical structure (lattice) is implied. This structure makes it possible to investigate CBR, machine learning, as well the relationship between the two from an algebraic perspective. In the sequel, we shall use $\mathcal{D}$ as described above as a generic decision system representing a dataset.

Let $\mathcal{L} \stackrel{\text{def}}{=} \prod_{x \in \Omega} 2^{V_x}$. Then $t \in \mathcal{L}$ is a vector $\langle t(x) \rangle_{x \in \Omega}$, where $t(x) \subseteq V_x$ are sets of values [2]. The elements of $\mathcal{L}$ are called *hypertuples*; the elements t of $\mathcal{L}$ with $|t(x)| = 1$ for all $x \in \Omega$ are called *simple tuples*. Any set of

---

[2] Note that if $t \in \mathcal{L}$ and $x \in \Omega$, then $t(x)$ is the projection of t to its x–th component.

hypertuples is called a *hyperrelation* [3]. Note that $\mathbf{V}$ is a set of *all* simple tuples for a given problem domain, and $\mathbf{D}$ is the set of simple tuples described in the dataset $\mathcal{D}$.

$\mathcal{L}$ is a lattice under the ordering

$$(1) \qquad t \leq s \Longleftrightarrow t(x) \subseteq s(x)$$

with the sum and product operations, and the maximal element (i.e., 1) given by

$$(2) \qquad t + s = \langle t(x) \cup s(x) \rangle_{x \in \Omega}.$$
$$(3) \qquad t \times s = \langle t(x) \cap s(x) \rangle_{x \in \Omega},$$
$$(4) \qquad 1 = \langle V_x \rangle_{x \in \Omega}.$$

$\mathcal{L}$ is called *domain lattice* for $\mathcal{D}$.

There is a natural embedding of $\mathbf{D}$ into $\mathcal{L}$ by assigning

$$\Omega(a) \mapsto \langle \{x_0(a)\}, \{x_1(a)\}, \dots, \{x_T(a)\} \rangle.$$

and we shall identify $\mathbf{D}$ with the image of this embedding. Then $\mathbf{D} \subseteq \mathbf{V} \subseteq \mathcal{L}$.

In the context of CBR, simple tuples are concrete cases whereas hypertuples are abstract cases since hypertuples cover multiple simple tuples hence they are "abstractions" of simple tuples.

Table 1(a) is a dataset (decision system) consisting of three simple tuples, where $V_{X_1} = \{a, b\}$ and $V_{X_2} = \{0, 1\}$, and d is the labeling. Table 1(b) and (c) are sets of hypertuples, which are the least and greatest E-sets respectively for the dataset, to be defined later.

$$\mathbf{D} = \{\langle a, 0 \rangle, \langle a, 1 \rangle, \langle b, 0 \rangle\};$$
$$\mathbf{V} = \{\langle a, 0 \rangle, \langle a, 1 \rangle, \langle b, 0 \rangle, \langle b, 1 \rangle\};$$
$$\mathcal{L} = \{\langle \emptyset, \emptyset \rangle, \langle \emptyset, \{0\} \rangle, \langle \emptyset, \{1\} \rangle, \langle \emptyset, \{0, 1\} \rangle,$$
$$\langle \{a\}, \emptyset \rangle, \langle \{a\}, \{0\} \rangle, \langle \{a\}, \{1\} \rangle, \langle \{a\}, \{0, 1\} \rangle,$$
$$\langle \{b\}, \emptyset \rangle, \langle \{b\}, \{0\} \rangle, \langle \{b\}, \{1\} \rangle, \langle \{b\}, \{0, 1\} \rangle,$$
$$\langle \{a, b\}, \emptyset \rangle, \langle \{a, b\}, \{0\} \rangle, \langle \{a, b\}, \{1\} \rangle, \langle \{a, b\}, \{0, 1\} \rangle\}.$$

U	X_1	X_2	d
u_0	a	0	α
u_1	a	1	α
u_2	b	0	β

(a)

U	2^{X_1}	2^{X_2}	d
u_0'	$\{a\}$	$\{0, 1\}$	α
u_1'	$\{b\}$	$\{0\}$	β

(b)

U	2^{X_1}	2^{X_2}	d
u_0'	$\{a\}$	V_{X_2}	α
u_1'	$\{b\}$	V_{X_2}	β

(c)

Table 1: *(a) A set of simple tuples in a decision system. (b) A set of hypertuples as the least E-set. (c) A set of hypertuples as the greatest E-set.*

---

[3]The concept of hyperrelation has been used before in e.g. [Orlowska, 1985; Wang *et al.*, 1998].

4.2 Equilabelledness and generalization

A dataset imposes a labeling d of $\mathbf{D}$ on the domain lattice $\mathcal{L}$. Thus all elements in $\mathbf{D}$ are *labeled*, and those in $\mathbf{V} \setminus \mathbf{D}$ are *unlabeled*. This labeling can be generalized to elements in the lattice which cover $\mathbf{D}$. This generalization must be consistent with d in the sense that the generalized labeling must be the same as d for $t \in \mathbf{D}$. This renders only those generalizations acceptable which generalize d to *equilabeled* elements. Intuitively, an equilabeled element is $t \in \mathcal{L}$ which covers at least one labeled element and all labeled elements covered by t have the same label.

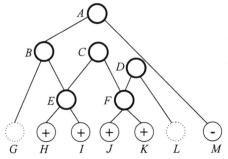

Legend:
○ *hyper tuple*   ○ *simple tuple*   ⋯ *unseen simple tuple*
+ - *class labels*

Figure 1: A running example.

For an illustrative example, consider the diagram in Figure 1, which depicts a small part of a domain lattice. The bottom elements (thin-lined circles) in the diagram represent simple tuples. All other elements (bold-lined circles) represent hypertuples. The original labeling d is defined only for the elements $\{H, I, J, K, M\}$. Here, B is equilabeled as H and I are all labeled positive by d while G is unlabelled. In fact, all elements in Figure 1 are equilabeled except A, G and L: A covers elements with different labels whereas G and L cover no labeled element.

Formally, we call an element $r \in \mathcal{L}$ *equilabeled* with respect to $\mathbf{D}_q$, if $\emptyset \neq \downarrow r \cap \mathbf{D}$, $\downarrow r \cap \mathbf{D} \subseteq \mathbf{D}_q$. In other words, r is equilabeled if $\downarrow r$ intersects $\mathbf{D}$, and every element in this intersection is labeled d_q for some $q \leq \mathbf{K}$. Recall that $\mathbf{K}$ is the number of classes. In this case, we say that r *G-belongs to* $\mathbf{D}_q$. We denote the set of all equilabeled elements G-belonging to $\mathbf{D}_q$ by $\mathcal{E}_q$, and let $\mathcal{E}$ be the set of all equilabeled elements. Note that $\mathbf{D} \subseteq \mathcal{E}$, and that $q, r \leq \mathbf{K}, q \neq r$ implies $\mathcal{E}_q \cap \mathcal{E}_r = \emptyset$.

We will now extend d over all of $\mathcal{L}$ by setting

$$d(r) = \begin{cases} d_q, & \text{if } r \in \mathcal{E}_q, \\ unknown, & \text{otherwise.} \end{cases}$$

Now $\mathcal{E}$, along with the extended labeling, can be regarded as a casebase of abstract cases (hypertuples). This is clearly too large. Since the elements in $\mathcal{E}$ are partially ordered – some are covered by some others –

we need only look at those which are not covered by any; they are *maximal*. Our wish to find maximal elements in some context leads to the following notions.

Def. 4.1. A *(generalization) context* (for learning) is a set P such that $\mathbf{D} \subseteq P \subseteq \mathbf{V}$. We let

$$\mathbf{M}(P) \stackrel{\text{def}}{=} \{h \in \mathcal{E} : \exists X \subseteq P, h = \text{lub}(X)\}$$

$$\mathbf{E}(P) \stackrel{\text{def}}{=} \{t : t \text{ is maximal in } \mathbf{M}(P)\}.$$

$\mathbf{E}(P)$ is called the *E–set for* P, and $t \in \mathcal{L}$ is said to be *in context* P if $t \in \mathbf{M}(P)$.

We observe the following lemma [4]:

Lemma 4.2. $A \subseteq B \subseteq \mathcal{L}$ *implies* $\mathbf{M}(A) \preccurlyeq \mathbf{M}(B)$ *and* $\mathbf{E}(A) \preccurlyeq \mathbf{E}(B)$.

This lemma implies $\mathbf{E}(\mathbf{D}) \preccurlyeq \mathbf{E}(P) \preccurlyeq \mathbf{E}(\mathbf{V})$ for $\mathbf{D} \subseteq P \subseteq \mathbf{V}$. We then call $\mathbf{E}(\mathbf{D})$ *least E-set* and $\mathbf{E}(\mathbf{V})$ *greatest E-set*, which are denoted by $\mathbf{E}$ and $\mathbb{E}$ respectively. It is not hard to see that $\mathbb{E}$ is the set of all maximal elements in $\mathcal{E}$.

Consider Figure 1 again. $\mathbf{E}(\{H, \cdots, K, M\}) = \{C, M\}$, and $\mathbf{E}(\{G, \cdots, M\}) = \{B, C, D, M\}$.

4.3 Interpretation of a domain lattice

Given a hypertuple t in a context P (i.e., $t \in \mathbf{M}(P)$), we need a calculus to get the remaining hypertuples in the same context (see Theorem 4.1 below). We therefore need to interpret the domain lattice in a suitable way.

Formally, let $t = \langle e_0, \ldots, e_T \rangle$ be a hypertuple, with $e_i = \{e_{i_0}, \ldots, e_{i_{t(i)}}\}$. We think of t as an (undeterministic) description of some object a in the following way:

$$(x_0(a) = e_{0_0} \vee \ldots \vee x_0(a) = e_{0_{t(0)}}) \wedge \cdots$$

$$\ldots \wedge (x_T(a) = e_{T_0} \vee \ldots \vee x_T(a) = e_{T_{t(T)}}).$$

In short we have $t = e_0 \wedge \cdots \wedge e_T$.

Each e_i stands as a hypertuple on its own, which is interpreted as $\langle V_0, \cdots, V_{i-1}, e_i, V_{i+1}, \cdots, V_T \rangle$; and $e_j \wedge e_k$ is interpreted as $\text{glb}(e_j, e_k)$.

Consider a hypertuple $t = \langle e_0, \cdots, e_T \rangle$. The *relative complement* or, simply, *R-complement* of t with respect to the greatest element in $\mathcal{L}$ (i.e., 1) is $\bar{t} = \overline{e_0} \vee \cdots \vee \overline{e_T}$, and $\overline{e_j}$ is interpreted as $V_j \setminus e_j$.

Given a hyperrelation $R = \{t_0, \cdots, t_n\}$, where $t_i = \langle e_{i0}, \cdots, e_{iT} \rangle$, we wish to calculate its R-complement $\overline{R}$ in such a way that $R \cup \overline{R} \succcurlyeq \mathbf{V}$ and $\downarrow R \cap \downarrow \overline{R} = \emptyset$. For this purpose we interpret R as $t_0 \vee \cdots \vee t_n$. Using the propositional calculus we can calculate the R-complement of R as follows. Let $X = \{\bigwedge_{i=0}^{n} \overline{e_{ij_i}} : \text{ for } j_i \in \{0, \cdots, T\}\}$. $\overline{R} = \bigwedge_{i=0}^{n} \overline{t_i} = \bigvee_{x \in X} x$. If follows $|X| = (T+1)^{(n+1)}$. Clearly the calculation of R-complement is exponential, which makes this not practical for large R.

The above R-complement calculus can be generalized as follows. Let $t = \langle e_{t0}, \cdots, e_{tT} \rangle$ and $h = \langle e_{h0}, \cdots, e_{hT} \rangle$. If $t \leq h$ then the R-complement of t with respect to h, denoted by $\overline{t|h}$, is calculated similarly except that $\overline{e_{tj}} = e_{hj} \setminus e_{tj}$.

[4]Due to lack of space, we omit all proofs throughout the paper.

Lemma 4.3. *For* $R \subseteq \mathcal{L}$,

1. $R \cup \overline{R} \succcurlyeq \mathbf{V}$.
2. $\downarrow R \cap \downarrow \overline{R} = \emptyset$.
3. *Let* $W \stackrel{\text{def}}{=} \{w \in \mathcal{L} : \downarrow w \cap \downarrow R = \emptyset\}$. *Then* $\overline{R}$ *is the set of all maximal elements in* W.

The first two properties guarantee that $\overline{R}$ is exclusively complementary to R with respect to the maximal element of the domain lattice. For an example, consider Table 1(a). The table is interpreted as $u_0 \vee u_1 \vee u_2$. u_0 is interpreted as $(X_1 = a) \wedge (X_2 = 0)$. $\overline{u_0} = \langle a, 0 \rangle = \bar{a} \vee \bar{0} = \langle \bar{a}, V_2 \rangle \vee \langle V_1, \bar{0} \rangle$. Let $V_1 = \{a, b\}$ and $V_2 = \{0, 1\}$. Then $\overline{u_0} = \langle b, \{0, 1\} \rangle \vee \langle \{a, b\}, 1 \rangle$, which clearly covers u_1 and u_2, as well as an unseen tuple $\langle b, 1 \rangle$.

The third property says that $\overline{R}$ is the set of maximal elements not covered by R. Consider Figure 1. Let $R = \{E\}$. Then $\overline{R} = \{G, D, M\}$.

4.4 Hypothesis space and casebase

Given a dataset we wish to have a *hypothesis* to replace the entire dataset. The hypothesis should not only cover the dataset but also generalize it. As discussed earlier, a dataset $\mathcal{D}$ imposes a labeling on the underlying domain lattice. The labeling can then be generalized to elements in $\mathbf{M}(P)$ for a given context P. However we do not need to use the whole $\mathbf{M}(P)$ as the hypothesis; a proper subset of it will suffice. Then a hypothesis is just a set of hypertuples, each of which is more informative than the simple tuples in the original dataset. Therefore, it is possible to consider a *casebase* as a hypothesis for a dataset. In this section we will introduce and justify some concepts through which we can precisely describe what kind of hypothesis we are aiming for.

Note that, by Lemma 4.2, $\mathbf{M}(\mathbf{D}) \preccurlyeq \mathbf{M}(P) \preccurlyeq \mathbf{M}(\mathbf{V})$ for $\mathbf{D} \subseteq P \subseteq \mathbf{V}$. Therefore $H \subseteq \mathbf{M}(P) \Rightarrow H \subseteq \mathbf{M}(\mathbf{V})$. Then we have

Def. 4.4. A *hypothesis for* $\mathbf{D}$ is a $H \subseteq \mathbf{M}(\mathbf{V})$ such that $\mathbf{D} \preccurlyeq H$. We use $\text{GEN}(\mathbf{D})$ to denote the set of all hypotheses for $\mathcal{D}$.

Similarly, we define a *hypothesis for* $\mathbf{D}_q$. Note that for a hypothesis H for $\mathbf{D}$, $H \cap \mathcal{E}_q$ is a hypothesis for $\mathbf{D}_q$. Conversely, if H_q is a hypothesis for $\mathbf{D}_q$ for each $q \leq \mathbf{K}$, then $H \stackrel{\text{def}}{=} \bigcup_{q \leq \mathbf{K}} H_q$ is a hypothesis for $\mathbf{D}$.

Since $\mathbf{M}(P)$ contains only equilabeled elements, H is *consistent* with the dataset. Since $\mathbf{D} \preccurlyeq H$, H covers all simple tuples in the dataset.

Def. 4.5. Let H_j and H_k be two hypotheses for $\mathbf{D}$. Then H_j is **more general than** H_k if and only if $H_k \preccurlyeq H_j$. H_j is **(strictly) more general than** H_k, written $(H_k \prec H_j)$, if and only if $(H_k \preccurlyeq H_j) \wedge (H_j \not\preccurlyeq H_k)$.

A hypothesis H for $\mathbf{D}$ is *maximally general* if and only if $H \in \text{GEN}(\mathbf{D})$ and there is no $H' \in \text{GEN}(\mathbf{D})$ such that $H \prec H'$. We denote by $\mathbf{G}$ the set of all maximally general hypotheses for $\mathbf{D}$. In [Mitchell, 1997] $\mathbf{G}$ is called the *general boundary* for $\mathbf{D}$.

The following lemma establishes the equivalence between $\mathbf{G}$ and the greatest E-set ($\mathbb{E}$).

Lemma 4.6. $G = \{\mathbb{E}\}$.

This lemma says that, although there are many possible hypotheses for a given dataset, there is only one maximally general hypothesis – the greatest E-set. This hypothesis is consistent with the dataset but has the maximal coverage of unseen simple tuples (because it has the maximal context $\mathbf{V}$). General boundary is a well established concept in the field of concept learning, and it has been used as an inductive bias in some concept learning algorithms [Mitchell, 1997]. The equivalence of the greatest E-set and the general boundary enables us to use the same inductive bias in automatic casebase design. Therefore our objective is to find the greatest E-set for a dataset. Our casebase design and retrieval are both associated with the greatest E-set.

However, as shown in [Haussler, 1988], the size of the general boundary can grow exponentially in the number of training examples. In the context of domain lattice, calculating the greatest E-set needs $\mathbf{V}$, which is not explicitly available; instead it has to be calculated from $\mathbf{D}$ using the R-complement calculus discussed above. This involves calculating $\overline{\mathbf{D}}$, which has been shown exponential in $|\mathbf{D}|$. It is then not practical to directly use the greatest E-set as the casebase. The following theorem guarantees that we can use a much smaller hypothesis as the casebase, but we can still use the general boundary as inductive bias. In effect it establishes the relationship between the casebase and the greatest E-set.

Theorem 4.1. *Let H be hypothesis for $\mathcal{D}$, as defined in Def. 4.4. Let $\mathbf{V}_{\mathbb{E}} = \downarrow \mathbb{E} \cap \mathbf{V}$, and $\mathbf{V}_H = \{t \in \mathbf{V} : \exists h \in H, \exists g \in \overline{(h|h+t)} \cup h, \text{ such that } t \leq g, \text{ and } g \text{ is equilabeled or unknown}\}$. Then $\mathbf{V}_{\mathbb{E}} \subseteq \mathbf{V}_H$.*

This theorem says that if a case (simple tuple) t is covered by $\mathbb{E}$, then there must be h such that $t \leq h$ or $t \leq g$ for $g \in \overline{h|h+t}$ with g being either equilabeled or unknown. Note that $\overline{h|h+t}$ is the R-complement of h with respect to $h+t$, which is the set of all elements covered by $h+t$ but not covered by h. The CaseRetrieve algorithm in Section 6 exploits this theorem to retrieve cases to classify new cases.

Theorem 4.1 says that any hypothesis can be used as a casebase that serves as an intermediary between a new case and the greatest E-set. Classification of a new case can then be made based on its relationship to the greatest E-set, which employs the general boundary inductive bias.

5 Case extraction

As indicated in Theorem 4.1, an expected casebase can be any hypothesis as defined in Def. 4.4. The simplest one is the dataset itself. However, checking whether the conditions are satisfied requires computing R-complements of the tuples. It is usually the case that datasets are large hence the computation cost is high. Therefore we need an algorithm to efficiently find a hypothesis, other than the dataset itself, satisfying the con-

ditions. The least E-set seems ideal since it is the E-set in the minimal context ($\mathbf{D}$). However calculating the least E-set is computationally expensive. The following algorithm, CaseExtract, finds, given the minimal context $\mathbf{D}$, the set of elements in $\mathbf{M}(\mathbf{D})$ which have disjoint coverage of $\mathbf{D}$.

Given $\mathbf{D}_q$ and $\mathcal{E}_q$ as defined above.

- Initialization: let $X = \mathbf{D}_q, H = \emptyset$.
- Repeat until X is empty:
  1. Let $h \in X$ and $X = X \setminus \{h\}$.
  2. For $g \in X$, let $X = X \setminus g$. If $h+g$ is equilabeled then $h = h + g$.
  3. Let $H = H \cup \{h\}$.

This algorithm bi-partitions X into a set of elements the sum of which is an equilabeled element, and a new X consisting of the rest of the elements. The new X is similarly bi-partitioned until X becomes empty. This process leads to a binary tree, the depth of which is a measure of the time complexity of the algorithm. In the worst case the time complexity for building the casebase for class $\mathbf{D}_q$ is in the order of $O(|\mathbf{D}_q|)$. Therefore the worst case complexity for building the whole casebase is $O(\mathbf{K} \times |\mathbf{D}_q|)$, where $\mathbf{K}$ is the number of classes.

Consider Figure 1. CaseExtract gives the hypothesis $\{E, F, M\}$ which has disjoint coverage of the labeled elements.

6 Case retrieval

The retrieval of relevant cases from the casebase is arguably the most important process in CBR. In this section we discuss how to retrieve cases from a casebase to classify new instances. Having a casebase H as discovered by the CaseExtract algorithm, we can associate a new instance $t \in \mathbf{V}$ with a case $h \in H$ by checking whether t is covered by $\mathbb{E}$ through h. Then t is regarded as being in the same class as h. The CaseRetrieve algorithm is as follows.

- Sort the elements in H in decreasing order of $|X|$ for $h \in H$ and $h = \text{lub}(X)$, which results in $H = \{h_0, \cdots, h_n\}$ with h_0 having the largest coverage of $\mathbf{D}$ elements.
- t is classified by the first h_i in the sorted H such that the conditions in Theorem 4.1 are satisfied.
- If there is no such h_i, label t by $d(h_0)$.

The time complexity of this algorithm is dominated by calculating the R-complement of $h \in H$, as needed in Theorem 4.1. This is in the order of $O(T)$, where T is the number of attributes. In the worst case we need to do so for all h_i in H, $i = 0, \cdots, n$. Therefore the overall time complexity of the algorithm is $O(nT)$ in the worst case.

To illustrate the CaseRetrieve algorithm, consider Figure 1. The casebase is now $\{E, F, M\}$, as discovered by CaseExtract. Consider a new case G. The sum of G and E is B, which is equilabeled. Then E is retrieved and G is labeled as positive. Clearly $G \leq B$, hence $G \preceq \mathbb{E}$.

7 Experiment

CASEEXTRACT and CASERETRIEVE are implemented in our CBR system, called LM. We compared LM with C4.5 using public datasets. The datasets are described in Table 2. Datasets in the upper half are from UC Irvine Machine Learning Repository; and those in the lower half are collections of documents which are used as benchmark for text mining study [Cohen and Hirsh, 1998]. The results are shown in Table 3.

Datasets	#Features #Terms	#Train	#Test	#Class
Annealing	38	798	5cv	6
Auto	25	205	5cv	6
Diabetes	8	768	5cv	2
Glass	9	214	5cv	6
Iris	4	150	5cv	3
Sonar	60	208	5cv	2
Vote	18	232	5cv	2
Memos	1014	334	10cv	11
CDroms	1133	798	10cv	6
Birdcom	674	914	10cv	22
Birdsci	1738	914	10cv	22

Table 2: Description of the datasets.

Dataset	Prediction accuracy	
	C4.5	LM
Annealing	91.8	93.6
Auto	72.2	76.1
Diabetes	72.9	71.7
Glass	81.3	82.7
Iris	94.0	96.0
Sonar	69.4	69.7
Vote	95.1	97.0
memos	57.5	59.8
cdroms	39.2	40.0
birdcom	79.6	90.4
birdsci	83.3	92.3
Average	76.0	79.0

Table 3: Prediction accuracy of C4.5 and LM.

8 Summary and conclusion

The paper proposed a promising model for automating the design of CBR systems. Revolving around the notion of hypertuples (abstract cases), the proposed model presents a successful attempt at combining powerful eager techniques from machine learning with the flexible "defer-processing" philosophy characteristic for lazy methods [Aha, 1997]. On the basis of concise formal argument and empirical evaluation, it has been demonstrated that the Lattice Machine approach constitutes an effective and efficient mechanism to discover abstract cases in a given dataset. Abstract cases have been shown to be an effective alternative to representing the knowledge held in CBR systems [Bergmann and Wilke, 1996].

They can provide answers to issues such as casebase complexity, maintenance costs, retrieval efficiency, and user acceptance. In addition to the discovery of abstract cases, an algorithm was presented, which employs the general boundary inductive bias and ensures that the retrieval of relevant abstract cases is within the limits of reasonable time constraints. The main contribution of this work lies in the Lattice Machine's ability to discover abstract cases within a given dataset *without* requiring difficult-to-obtain domain knowledge.

References

[Aha, 1997] D. Aha, editor. *Lazy Learning*. Kluver Academic Pub., 1997.

[Bergmann and Wilke, 1996] R. Bergmann and W. Wilke. On the role of abstraction in case-based reasoning. In *Proc. Advances in Case-Based Reasoning, 3rd EWCBR-96*, pages 28–41, 1996.

[Cohen and Hirsh, 1998] William W. Cohen and Haym Hirsh. Joins that generalize: Text classification using whirl. In *Proc. KDD-98, New York*, 1998.

[Grätzer, 1978] George Grätzer. *General Lattice Theory*. Birkhäuser, Basel, 1978.

[Haussler, 1988] D. Haussler. Quantifying inductive bias: Ai learning algorithms and valiant's learning framework. *Artificial Intelligence*, 36:177–221, 1988.

[Leake and Wilson, 1998] D.B. Leake and D.C. Wilson. Categorizing case base maintenance: Dimensions and directions. In *Proc. Advances in Case-Based Reasoning,4th EWCBR-98*, pages 196–207, 1998.

[Leake, 1996] D.B. Leake, editor. *Case-Based Reasoning: Experiences, Lessons & Future Directions*. MIT Press, MA, 1996.

[Lenz et al., 1998] M. Lenz, B. Bartsch-Spörl, H-D. Burkhard, and S. Wess, editors. *Case-Based Reasoning Technology: From Foundations to Applications*. Springer-Verlag, 1998.

[Mitchell, 1997] T. M. Mitchell. *Machine Learning*. The McGraw-Hill Companies, Inc, 1997.

[Orlowska, 1985] Ewa Orlowska. Logic of nondeterministic information. *Studia Logica*, 44:93–102, 1985.

[Patterson et al., 1998] D. Patterson, W. Dubitzky, S.S. Anand, and J.G. Hughes. On the automation of case base development from large databases. In *Proc. AAAI Workshop: Case-Based Reasoning Integrations*, pages 126–130, 1998.

[Smyth and Keane, 1995] B. Smyth and M.T. Keane. Remembering to forget: A competence-preserving case deletion policy for case-based reasoning systems. In *Proc. 14th IJCAI-95*, pages 337–382, 1995.

[Wang et al., 1998] Hui Wang, Ivo Düntsch, and David Bell. Data reduction based on hyper relations. In *Proceedings of KDD98, New York*, pages 349–353, 1998.

CHALLENGE PAPERS

new insights and subject to review much in the manner described by Medawar.

This paper reports on the machine learning (ML) submissions made to this IJCAI challenge from its inception in August, 1997 to December, 1998. The paper is organised as follows. Section 2 summarises the course of the challenge from 1997, and presents the models selected for further evaluation. Section 3 contains an assessment of the accuracies of the ML models in comparison to those developed under the guidance of expert toxicologists (this includes toxicology expert systems). Section 4 contains an appraisal of the explanatory value of the ML models[2]. Section 5 concludes this paper.

2 The IJCAI PTE Challenge: details and submissions

As part of the NTP, the National Institute of Environmental Health Sciences (NIEHS) organises the Predictive Toxicology Evaluation (or PTE) project. The project [Bristol et al., 1996] is concerned with predicting the outcome of rodent bioassays measuring the cancerous activity of a pre-specified set of compounds. In its simplest setting, predictions are restricted to either "POS" to denote carcinogenic, or "NEG" if otherwise. There is no restriction on the type of method used to construct the toxicity model. The PTE project accepted predictions until late 1996 for 30 compounds (collectively known as PTE2) undergoing bioassays within the NTP – the last of these assays being completed by June, 1998.

The relevance of the PTE project to programs concerned with "knowledge discovery" directly led to the PTE Challenge in IJCAI-97. Here, it was proposed to collect submissions from AI techniques. Submissions were to be made at a prescribed Internet site (www.comlab.ox.ac.uk/oucl/groups/machlearn/PTE) and consisted of two parts: (1) prediction: POS and NEG classification for the PTE2 compounds; and (2) description: details of the materials and methods used, and results obtained with the technique. The former was needed to assess model accuracy, and the latter for replicability of results and evaluations of model comprehensibilty.

The site accepted submissions from August 29, 1997 (one week after the challenge was announced at IJCAI-97). Submissions received up to November 15, 1998 were eligible for assessments of chemical comprehensibility. The challenge was regularly advertised at major AI conferences and in electronic newsgroups, and our records indicate that the data provided by the challenge site were retrieved over 100 times[3]. By November 15

1998, 9 legal submissions were received (by legal here we mean that both "prediction" and "description" parts of the submission were in order). These are summarised in Figure 1. Space restrictions prevent us from providing a description here of each entry – the reader is directed to the Internet site under the "Description" column for complete details[4].

At this point, it is worth noting an important point of difference between the submissions made to the NTP's PTE project, and those in Figure 1. All predictions by the former were made before true classifications on any chemical in PTE2 were known. The timing and duration of the IJCAI challenge has precluded the possibility of such a truly blind trial. We rely on submissions to abide by challenge regulations that prevent the use of PTE2 classifications in any way to direct model formation or selection.

3 Assessment of predictive accuracy

At the time of writing this paper, the classification of 23 of the 30 compounds had become available. Figure 2 tabulates the predictive accuracies achieved by the models described in the submissions in Figure 1 (henceforth called "ML-derived models").

Benigni [Benigni, 1998] provides a tabulation of the predictions made by several toxicity prediction methods on a subset of the PTE2 compounds. We concentrate here on those techniques that involve substantial input from experts. These include models devised directly by toxicologists or those that rely on the application of compilations of such specialist knowledge (that is, expert systems). In [Benigni, 1998], there are 9 such "expert-derived" models due to: Huff et al. (HUF, [Huff et al., 1996]), OncoLogic (ONC, [Woo et al., 1997]), Bootman (BOT, [Bootman, 1996]), Tennant et al. (TEN, [R.W. Tennant, 1996]), Ashby (ASH, [Ashby, 1996]), Benigni et al. (BEN, [R.Benigni et al., 1996]), Purdy (PUR, [Purdy, 1996]), DEREK (DER, [Marchant, 1996]), and COMPACT/HAZARDEXPERT (COM, [Lewis et al., 1996]). Excluding missing entries, predictions are available from these methods for 18 PTE2 compounds. A comparative tabulation on this subset against the ML-derived models is in Figure 3.

Comparisons based on predictive accuracy overlook an important practical concern, namely that the costs of different types of errors may be unequal. In toxicology modelling, the cost of false negatives is usually higher than those of false positives. Borrowing from terminology in signal-detection, "sensitivity" refers to the fraction of POS chemicals classified as POS by a model; and "specificity" refers to the fraction of NEG chemicals

---

[2]Performed by one of the authors (D.W.B.), who is a toxicologist.

[3]Clearly, only very limited conclusions can be drawn from this figure. Our records suggest that the data were extracted by groups with a wide range of research interests. However, the reader will note that the final submissions appear to be largely from those interested in Inductive Logic Programming (ILP). While it is possible that the emphasis on a descriptive

component discouraged the use of methods like neural networks, we have no way of knowing why some ML researchers failed to respond to the challenge.

[4]The reader should note that the submission OU2 was from two of the authors here (A.S. and R.D.K.). As far as we are aware, none of the submissions appear to have involved a toxicologist during model-development.

Submission	Method	Description
LE1	ILP	*www.cs.kuleuven.ac.be/~hendrik/PTE/PTE1.html*
LE2	ILP	*www.cs.kuleuven.ac.be/~ldh/PTE/PTE2.html*
LE3	ILP	*www.cs.kuleuven.ac.be/~wimv/PTE/PTE2.html*
LRD	Stochastic voting technique	*www.lri.fr/~fabien/PTE/Distill/*
LRG	Stochastic rule construction	*www.lri.fr/~fabien/PTE/GloBo/*
OAI	Decision tree and Naive Bayes	*www.ai.univie.ac.at/~bernhard/pte2/pte2.html*
OU1	Decision tree and ILP	*www.comlab.ox.ac.uk/oucl/groups/machlearn/PTE/oucl1.html*
OU2	Decision tree and ILP	*www.comlab.ox.ac.uk/oucl/groups/machlearn/PTE/oucl2.html*
TA1	Genetic search	*ailab2.cs.nthu.edu.tw/pte*

Figure 1: Legal submissions to the PTE Challenge. Here "ILP" stands for Inductive Logic Programming.

Submission	Accuracy
LRD	0.87 (0.07)
LRG	0.78 (0.09)
OU2	0.78 (0.09)
OAI	0.74 (0.09)
LE3	0.70 (0.10)
LE2	0.65 (0.10)
OU1	0.57 (0.10)
TA1	0.52 (0.10)
LE1	0.48 (0.10)
DEF	0.74 (0.10)

Figure 2: Estimated accuracies of submissions made to the PTE Challenge. Here, accuracy refers to the fraction of PTE2 compounds correctly classified by the ML-derived model. The quantity in parentheses next to the accuracy figure is the estimated standard error. The classifications are based on the outcome of 23 of the 30 PTE2 bioassays. The classification of remaining 7 is yet to be decided. "DEF" refers to the simple rule that states that all compounds will be "POS". This was not an official submission to the challenge and is only included here for completeness.

classified as NEG by a model. Figure 4 is a scatter-diagram that shows the position of each model in this two-dimensional probability space.

Complementary to sensitivity and specificity are: the fraction of POS predictions that are actually POS, and the fraction of NEG predictions that are actually NEG. Termed here as "positive predictivity" and "negative predictivity", these measure the accuracy of each type of prediction. Good models should exhibit high predictivity values. Figure 5 shows the scatter-diagram of the models along these dimensions.

Keeping in mind the mandatory caution that must be exercised when interpreting figures derived from such small test-sets, Figures 2, 3, 4 and 5 appear to suggest that ML-derived models are able to at least match the performance attained by their expert counterparts. As is evident, 7 of the 9 ML-derived models achieve the predictive accuracy threshold set by the DEF model. This is in contrast to 3 of the 9 expert-derived models. 6 ML-derived models (LE2, LE3, LRD, LRG, OAI, OU2) achieve false-negative error rates of at most 0.25 with false-positive rates of no more than 0.50. This is matched by only 1 expert-derived model (ONC). 7 ML-derived models (the previous 6 and OU1) also achieve positive and negative predictive rates of at least 0.50

(Figure 5). This is in contrast to 4 expert-derived models. Elsewhere, we present a more detailed assessment of these trends based on a cost-sensitive technique termed ROC-analysis [Srinivasan *et al.*, 1999]. Due to space restrictions, a summary has to suffice here. The analysis shows the ML-derived models to be extremely competitive, with LRG being the pick of the best across a range of reasonable error-costs and prior distributions over class values. LRG was obtained with a stochastic technique which resulted in rules that use, amongst others, attributes encoding the results from ILP methods.

4 Assessment of explanatory value

At the outset of this section, it is worth emphasising that as submitted, none of the ML-derived models would be considered toxicology acceptable. This comment extends even to the most transparent submission like OU2, which presents a relatively simple (by ML standards) decision-tree obtained from a well-known algorithm (C4.5). Much of this probably stems from a lack of toxicology expertise amongst the program users, and the lack of any "client specifications" in the statement of the challenge. We intend to rectify the latter in future experiments (PTE-3, see [Srinivasan *et al.*, 1999]). However, some attempt by all developers at improving clarity by including tables of

Model	Type	Accuracy
LRD	ML	0.89 (0.07)
LRG	ML	0.84 (0.09)
HUF	Expert	0.78 (0.10)
LE3	ML	0.78 (0.10)
OAI	ML	0.78 (0.10)
ONC	Expert	0.78 (0.10)
OU2	ML	0.78 (0.10)
LE2	ML	0.72 (0.11)
BEN	Expert	0.67 (0.11)
OU1	ML	0.67 (0.11)
TA1	ML	0.62 (0.11)
ASH	Expert	0.56 (0.12)
LE1	ML	0.56 (0.12)
TEN	Expert	0.56 (0.12)
BOT	Expert	0.50 (0.12)
COM	Expert	0.50 (0.12)
DER	Expert	0.50 (0.12)
PUR	Expert	0.28 (0.11)
DEF	–	0.67 (0.11)

Figure 3: Comparison of estimated accuracies of expert and ML-derived models. The figures are based on the classification of 18 of the 30 PTE2 compounds for which predictions are available from all models. As before, estimates of standard errors are in parentheses. Some expert-derived models include a third category of classification called "borderline carcinogen." These are simply taken as a POS classification here. As before DEF predicts all chemicals as POS.

names and structures identified by the rules, clear statements of their reliability etc., would have greatly assisted the evaluation exercise. The application of ML techniques to modelling toxicity endpoints is a relatively new research development in toxicology, and it is essential that descriptions of representations used and results obtained are as thorough as possible (see for example, [Bristol, 1995] for an appraisal of the requirements of models from both developer and prospective-client points of view). Nevertheless, the performance of the models have been sufficiently intriguing to foster further examination.

In performing an evaluation of the explanatory value provided by the ML-derived models, we have found it instructive to examine their contributions in the following categories:

A. Those that suggest any new lines of investigation for toxicology modelling;

B. Those that confirm, clarify or contribute to current ideas in toxicology; and

C. Those that are uninteresting or unlikely.

Our examination is restricted to the models that showed the most promise in the previous section, namely: LE2, LE3, LRG, OAI, OU2. Unfortunately, the most accurate model (LRD) could not be considered, as no explicit model was provided. Further, it is not our intention to single out any one model as being the "best" – rather, it is to provide an overall assessment of the value of using ML methods in toxicology.

Of most interest is the frequent use of combinations, in models like LRG, of chemical structure and biological tests. For some time, there has been vigourous debate on how classical structure-activity modelling can be applied to toxicity problems. This form of modelling relates chemical features to activity, and works well *in-vitro*. The extent to which these ideas transfer to toxicity modelling – which deals with the interaction of chemical factors with biological systems – is not evident. By using a combination of chemical features and biological test outcomes, the ML-derived models provide one possible method for dealing with the chemical effects in such "open" systems. If the accuracies obtained with such rules are borne out on larger datasets, then this would constitute a significant advance in structure-activity modelling for toxicology. This is certainly worth further investigation and falls in Category A.

A number of aspects of some of the models can be categorised in Category B. As an example, OU2 selects a combination of mouse lymphoma and Drosophilla tests as a strong indicator of carcinogenicity. Many toxicologists believe that relationships exist between genotoxicity and carcinogenicity. While the only accepted correlation involves the Salmonella assay, this rule suggests a different combination of short-term tests could be equally, or more effective. Similar comments could be made on a number of other fronts: the presence of methoxy groups, sulphur compounds, and biphenyl groups are all identified in various ways as being related to toxicity. These are in line with what is currently

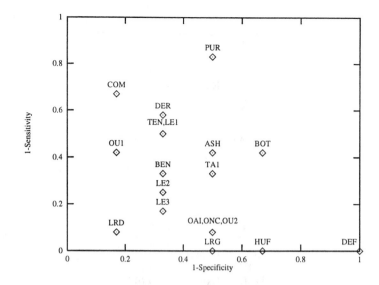

Figure 4: Scatter-diagram showing the performance of expert and ML-derived models based on their false positive (*x*-) and false negative (*y*-) error rates. For two models with the same *x*-value, the one with the smaller *y*-value is preferable.

known in toxicology.

Given the relative opaqueness of the output, it is hard to judge the extent to which the models have identified aspects in Category C. The general approach in toxicology is to be wary of "explanations" that only pertain to a few or uninteresting chemical structures. These do occur in the models submitted, and appear to have been ignored (except in the case of OU2, where some editing attempt is undertaken). We do not enumerate examples of this here.

5   Conclusions

Toxicology is a young science that is primarily driven by intense health and industrial interests focused on specific chemical substances. A practicing toxicologist is regularly confronted with urgent requests to provide reliable information about the next substance of interest – whatever it might be. This situation demands that the toxicologist be able to call on, or develop, predictive models that are not only accurate, but also cover an extremely wide range of noncongeneric dissimilar chemicals. These range from pure organic and inorganic compounds to polymers and complex mixtures. Predictions also need to be generated for a variety of toxicity endpoints [Bristol, 1995]. Aspiring assistants – human or otherwise – seeking to aid an expert toxicologist in this model-building endeavour, must be capable of suggesting robust solutions that are accurate and understandable. This forms the crux of the PTE Challenge – do AI programs meet these requirements when constrained to the task of predicting chemical carcinogenesis? The short answer, for the submissions participating in the challenge, is: "not yet." The qualifier is important though, as they do show considerable potential to achieve this goal. This opinion is based on the evidence that (a) mod-els developed by these programs are clearly competitive on accuracy terms with those derived with significant expert assistance; and (b) even with almost no effort made to render the output chemically understandable the models have still suggested unusual ways to proceed with toxicology modelling. Whether such programs can make the transition from promising apprentices to valuable assistants will depend on whether their developers recognise the paramount importance of ensuring that the models are phrased in terms familiar to a toxicologist, and on continued good results with larger datasets.

Acknowledgements

The authors would like to acknowledge the significant effort made by the Machine Learning community in responding to the PTE Challenge. In particular, sincere thanks are due to the groups whose models we have used in the analysis here, namely those at Leuven (Belgium), LRI (France), OFAI (Austria), and the AI Lab, Taiwan. At Oxford, the model OU1 was largely developed by Ngozi Dozie, a MSc student in Computation. A.S currently holds a Nuffield Trust Research Fellowship at Green College, Oxford. During the first six months of the PTE Challenge, he was supported by Smith-Kline Beecham. A.S. and R.D.K would also like to thank Donald Michie, Stephen Muggleton, and Michael Sternberg for interesting and useful discussions concerning the use of machine learning for predicting biological activity. We thank the support staff of the Computing Laboratory, Oxford – in particular, Ian Collier – for his help with the Web pages related to the PTE Challenge.

References

[Ashby, 1996] J. Ashby. Predictions of rodent carcinogenicity for 30 compounds. *Environmental Health Perspectives*, pages 1101–1104, 1996.

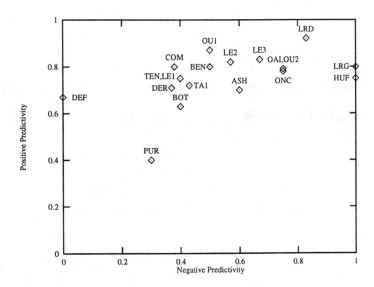

Figure 5: Scatter-diagram showing the performance of expert and ML-derived models based on their negative (x-) and positive (y-) predictivity. Models in the upper right are preferable to those in the lower left. The x-value for DEF has been taken as 0, as no chemicals are classified NEG by this rule.

[Benigni, 1998] R. Benigni. (Q)sar prediction of chemical carcinogenicity and the biological side of the structure activity relationship. In *Proceedings of The Eighth International Workshop on QSARs in the Environmental Sciences*, 1998. Held in Baltimore, May 16–20, 1998.

[Bootman, 1996] J. Bootman. Speculations on the carcinogenicity of 30 chemicals currently under review in rat and mouse bioassays organised by the us national toxicology program. *Mutagenesis*, 27:237–243, 1996.

[Bristol et al., 1996] D.W. Bristol, J.T. Wachsman, and A. Greenwell. The NIEHS Predictive-Toxicology Evaluation Project. *Environmental Health Perspectives*, pages 1001–1010, 1996. Supplement 3.

[Bristol, 1995] D.W. Bristol. Summary and Recommendations: Activity Classification and Structure-Activity Relationship Modeling for Human Health Risk Assessment of Toxic Substances. *Toxicology Letters*, pages 265–280, 1995.

[Huff et al., 1996] J. Huff, E. Weisburger, and V.A. Fung. Multicomponent criteria for predicting carcinogenicity: dataset of 30 ntp chemicals. *Environmental Health Perspectives*, 104:1105–1112, 1996.

[Lewis et al., 1996] D.F.V. Lewis, C. Ioannides, and D.V. Parke. COMPACT and molecular structure in toxicity assessment: a prospective evaluation of 30 chemicals currently being tested for rodent carcinogenicity by the NCI/NTP. *Environmental Health Perspectives*, pages 1011–1016, 1996.

[Marchant, 1996] C.A. Marchant. Prediction of rodent carcinogencity using the DEREK system for 30 chemicals currently being tested by the National Toxicology Program. *Environmental Health Perspectives*, pages 1065–1074, 1996.

[Medawar, 1984] P.B. Medawar. *Pluto's Republic*. Oxford University Press, Oxford, 1984.

[Purdy, 1996] R. Purdy. A mechanism-mediated model for carcinogenicity: model content a prediction of the outcome of rodent carcinogencity bioassays currently being conducted on 25 organic chemicals. *Environmental Health Perspectives*, pages 1085–1094, 1996.

[R.Benigni et al., 1996] R.Benigni, C. Andreoli, and R.Zito. Prediction of the carcinogenicity of further 30 chemicals bioassayed by the US National Toxicology Program. *Environmental Health Perspectives*, pages 1041–1044, 1996.

[R.W. Tennant, 1996] J. Spalding R.W. Tennant. Predictions for the outcome of rodent carcinogenicity bioassays: identification of trans-species carcinogens and non-carcinogens. *Environmental Health Perspectives*, pages 1095–1100, 1996.

[Srinivasan et al., 1997] A. Srinivasan, R.D. King, S.H. Muggleton, and M.J.E. Sternberg. The Predictive Toxicology Evaluation Challenge. In *Proceedings of the Fifteenth International Conference on Artificial Intelligence (IJCAI-97)*. Morgan Kaufmann, Los Angeles, CA, 1997.

[Srinivasan et al., 1999] A. Srinivasan, R.D. King, and D.W. Bristol. An assessment of ILP-assisted models for toxicity and the PTE-3 experiment. In *Proceedings of the Ninth International Workshop on Inductive Logic Programming*, LNAI, Berlin, 1999. Springer-Verlag. (to appear).

[Woo et al., 1997] Y.T. Woo, D.Y. Lai, J.C. Arcos, M.F. Argus, M.C. Cimino, S. DeVito, and L. Keifer. Mechanism-based structure-activity relationship (SAR) analysis of 30 NTP test chemicals. *Environ. Carcino. Ecotox. Revs. C*, 15:139–160, 1997.

Two Fielded Teams and Two Experts:
A RoboCup Challenge Response from the Trenches

Milind Tambe, Gal A. Kaminka, Stacy Marsella, Ion Muslea, Taylor Raines

Information Sciences Institute and Computer Science Department

University of Southern California

4676 Admiralty Way

Marina del Rey, CA 90292, USA

{tambe,galk,marsella,muslea,raines}@isi.edu

Abstract

The RoboCup (robot world-cup soccer) effort, initiated to stimulate research in multi-agents and robotics, has blossomed into a significant effort of international proportions. RoboCup is simultaneously a fundamental research effort and a set of competitions for testing research ideas. At IJ-CAI'97, a broad research challenge was issued for the RoboCup synthetic agents, covering areas of multi-agent learning, teamwork and agent modeling. This paper outlines our attack on the entire breadth of the RoboCup research challenge, on all of its categories, in the form of two fielded, contrasting RoboCup teams, and two off-line soccer analysis agents. We compare the teams and the agents to generalize the lessons learned in learning, teamwork and agent modeling.

1 Introduction

Increasingly, multi-agent systems are being designed for a variety of complex, dynamic domains. To stimulate and pursue research towards such multi-agent systems, the *RoboCup* initiative has proposed simulation and robotic soccer as a common, unified domain for multi-agent research[Kitano *et al.*, 1997]. RoboCup has now blossomed into a significant effort of international proportions.

At IJCAI'97, a broad research challenge was issued for the RoboCup synthetic agents[Kitano *et al.*, 1997]. This paper responds to this challenge, in the form of research lessons drawn from several systems we have constructed for RoboCup. In particular, we fielded the ISIS97 and ISIS98 teams, which won third place and fourth place at RoboCup97 and RoboCup98 respectively (out of 30 to 35 participating teams). We have also constructed two experts, ISAAC and TEAMORE, for off-line review of RoboCup. Our response draws from these multiple systems for two reasons. First, the RoboCup challenge covers a broad spectrum of multi-agent research, and requires teams and off-line experts to be built. Indeed, it proposes three separate challenge areas, *learning, teamwork* and *agent modeling*. Second, these challenge areas often do not have just one right answer, rather, they point to tradeoffs, which we explore via multiple systems.

Our challenge response also attempts to extract general lessons from RoboCup. Indeed, despite the RoboCup aim to stimulate general multi-agent research, few RoboCup researchers have extracted domain-independent research lessons (there are a few notable exceptions[Stone and Veloso, 1998b]). This paper attempts to remedy this situation.

2 Background: Domain and Agents

The RoboCup simulation league uses a complex, dynamic, noisy soccer simulation, called the *soccerserver*, which simulates the players' (22) bodies, the ball and the soccer field with goals and flags. Software agents (11 agents per team) provide the "brains" for the simulated bodies. Visual and audio information as "sensed" by the player's body are sent to the player agent ("brain"), which can then send action commands to control the simulated body (e.g., kick, dash, turn, say, etc.). The server constrains an agent's actions (one action per 100ms) and sensory updates (one perceptual update every 150-300ms). The players also have limited stamina.

The software agents we constructed to control the player bodies are based on a two-tier architecture. The lower-level, developed in C, processes input received from the simulator, and together with recommendations of an intercept micro-plan and possible kicking directions, sends the information up to the higher-level. The higher-level is implemented in the Soar integrated architecture[Newell, 1990]. Soar uses the information it receives to reach a decision about the next action and communicates its decision to the lower-level, which then forwards the relevant action to the simulator. Soar's operation involves dynamically executing an operator (reactive plan) hierarchy. The operator hierarchy shown in Figure 1 illustrates a portion of the operator hierarchy for ISIS player-agents. Only one path through this hierarchy is typically active at a time in a player agent. The hierarchy has two types of operators. Team operators constitute activities that the agent takes on as part of a team or subteam, shown in [] (e.g., [Play]). In contrast, the "normal" individual operators are ones that players execute as individuals (e.g., Intercept). The implication of this distinction will be clarified later.

3 Response to the Learning Challenge

ISIS teams have addressed the problems of off-line skill learning and on-line adversarial learning, with results used in actual

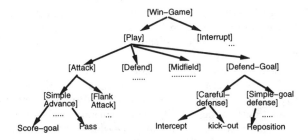

Figure 1: Operator hierarchy for player-agents.

competitions. Different learning algorithms are integrated in ISIS via a *divide-and-conquer* approach, i.e., different modules (skills) within individual agents are learned separately.

3.1 Offline Skill Learning

Shooting a ball to score a goal is clearly one of the critical skills in soccer. Yet, our initial, heuristic, hand-coded approaches (e.g., shoot to a corner of the goal) failed, because (i) small variations in shooter-position sometimes had dramatic effects on the best shooting direction and (ii) large number of heuristic rules were needed.

We addressed these problems via automated, *off-line* learning of the shooting rules. A human specialist created a set of 3000 shooting situations (each of them labeled with an optimal shooting direction: UP, DOWN, and CENTER) that were used as training examples for C4.5[Quinlan, 1993]. Each such shooting scenario was used as a training case described by 40 attributes: the recommended kicking direction, the shooter's facing direction, and the shooter's angles to the visible players, flags, lines, ball, and goal. The system was trained on 1600 randomly chosen examples, and the other 1400 examples were used for testing. We repeated this procedure 50 times, and the average accuracy of the rules on the testing sets was 70.8%. Even though the predictive power appears low, the kicking rules were quite efficient in practice. This is because learned-rules covered far more difficult shots than were actually used in practice.

While the C4.5 learned rules dramatically improved shooting skills, in the competitions, the rules sometimes appeared to take unnecessarily risky shots on the goal. This occurred because offline learning assumed the worst about the opponents' level of play, while in practice, weaker teams provided easier opportunities that did not justify such risks. Thus, while one key lesson learned here is that a divide-and-conquer learning technique may be promising for agent design, another key lesson is that off-line learning in dynamic multi-agent contexts must be sensitive to the varying capabilities of other agents.

3.2 Online Adversarial Learning

A key skill in RoboCup where adaptation to the opponent is critical is that of intercepting the ball. In particular, an opponent may kick/pass/run harder than normal, thereby requiring a player to adapt by running harder, modifying their path or forgoing interception. To enable players to adapt their intercept online to adversaries, ISIS exploits reinforcement learning.

One key difficulty in applying reinforcement learning however is rapid adaptation — in the course of a game, there are not many opportunities to intercept the ball. To address this concern, our approach employs intermediate reinforcement, rather than waiting for the end of the intercept. A player intercepts the ball by stringing together a collection of micro-plans of a turn followed by one or two dashes. For every step in a micro-plan, ISIS98 has an expectation as to what any new information from the server should inform it as to the ball's location. Failure to meet that expectation results in a learning opportunity. To allow transfer to similar states, the input conditions are clustered. Repeated failures lead to changes in the plan assigned to an input condition. In particular, the turn increment specific to that input condition is adjusted either up or down upon repeated failure. Typically, the actual turn is calculated from the turn increment in the following fashion:

$$Turn = BallDir + (TurnIncrement * ChangeBallDir)$$

Experiments: In accordance with the IJCAI challenge, experiments were performed against publicly available teams, specifically CMUnited97 (team of Stone and Veloso of Carnegie Mellon, 4th at RoboCup'97) Andhill97 (team of T. Andou of NTT labs, 2nd at RoboCup'97). In each experiment, each player started with a default value of 2.0 for their turn increment across all input conditions. The online learning in these games results in turn increment values that range from +5 down to -1, across input conditions. While these may appear small numbers, because of the multiplicative factors, and since the intercept plan is invoked repeatedly, even a small change is overall very significant.

The results show some surprising differences in what is learned. For instance, the same player may learn very different turn increments against different teams. Figure 2 compares the mean results for Player 1, a forward, in games against CMUnited97 with games against Andhill97. The mean for all players is also shown. The x-axis plots the clock ticks (continued until 15000) and the y-axis plots the turn increment. This data is for the input condition of balls moving across the player's field of vision, a middling-to-close distance away. Against Andhill97, the player is learning a turn increment similar to the mean across all players for this input condition. However, against CMUnited97, the player is learning a considerably larger increment (difference in means is significant using a Welch two-sided t-test, p-value=.0447). Figure 3 shows that different players against the same team do learn different increments. It plots mean turn-increments for Player 1 and Player 10 for the the same input condition as above, against CMUnited97. The difference in the means is significant (using a Welch two-sided t-test, p-value = 6.36e-06)

Lessons learned: Player 1 distinctly tailors its intercept to its role and particular opponents. This occurs because CMUnited97's defenders often clear the ball with a strong sideways kick, which player 1 continuously faces. Player 1's adaptation not only illustrates the benefits of on-line learning, but also a general point: it shows a high specialization of (intercept) skills according to the role and situations faced. Thus, sharing experiences of individuals in different roles or training individual across roles would appear to be detrimental, i.e., *there are key limits to social learning*. Of course, it does not rule

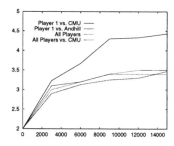

Figure 2: Player 1 against CMUnited97 & Andhill97.

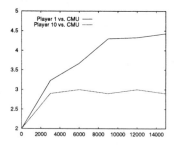

Figure 3: Players 1 & 10 against CMUnited97.

out social learning. Indeed, in the results above, the trends of the changes were shared across players, so that some social learning can be carried out. Thus, our goalee agents, which tend not to get as many intercept opportunities during the game, rely on mean intercept values from the other players.

4 Teamwork Challenge Response

The teamwork challenge covers team planning, plan decomposition, execution, etc. There is not necessarily one best answer to this challenge, and our two RoboCup teams present at least some of the tradeoffs.

4.1 Team Plan Execution

Our response to the team plan execution challenge is a key distinction of our ISIS teams — the use of a general-purpose teamwork model called STEAM[Tambe, 1997]. Based on the notion of joint commitments[Cohen and Levesque, 1991], STEAM enables team members to autonomously reason about coherence during team plan execution. It also enables team reorganization upon disablemen of a team member and selective communication. STEAM's reasoning is instigated by a (sub)team's execution of a team operator. For an example of STEAM in operation, consider the SIMPLE-DEFENSE team operator executed by the goalee subteam to position themselves on the field and watch out for the ball (Fig 1). Each player sees only within its limited cone of vision, and can be unaware at times of the approaching ball. If any one of these players sees the ball as being close, it declares the SIMPLE-DEFENSE team operator to be irrelevant. Its teammates now focus on defending the goal in a coordinated manner via the CAREFUL-DEFENSE team operator. Specifically this includes intercepting the ball and then clearing it. Should any one player in the goalee subteam see the ball move sufficiently far away, it again alerts its team mates (that

CAREFUL-DEFENSE is achieved). The subteam players once again revert to SIMPLE-DEFENSE. All the communication decisions for the subteam coordination here are handled automatically by STEAM.

For teamwork, one evaluation criteria in [Kitano *et al.*, 1997] is generality, i.e., reuse of the teamwork capability across applications. STEAM was originally used in battlefield simulations[Tambe, 1997], and its generality is illustrated in its reuse in RoboCup. We may measure this reuse in terms of the number of STEAM rules reused. STEAM originally had 283 rules, of which 35%-45% are used in ISIS. Without STEAM reuse, communication in ISIS would have required dozens of domain-specific coordination plans.

A second evaluation criteria is general performance. To this end, we measure impact of STEAM on ISIS97, by experimenting with different settings of communication cost in STEAM. In particular, at "low" communication cost, ISIS97 agents communicate a significant number of messages, while at "high" communication cost, ISIS agents communicate no messages. Since the portion of STEAM in use in ISIS is effective only with communication, a "high" communication cost essentially nullifies the effect of STEAM. Table 1 below shows the results of games for the two settings of communication cost, illustrating the usefulness of STEAM. It compares the performance of the two settings against Andhill97 and CMUnited97 in approximately 60 games. It shows that the mean goal difference between ISIS97 and Andhill97 was -3.38 per game for "low" cost, and was -4.36 per game for "high" cost. This difference in the means is significant using a t-test (null hypothesis p=0.032). It also shows a similar comparison for 30 games between ISIS97 and CMUnited97. It shows that the mean goal difference between ISIS97 and CMUnited97 for "low" was 3.27, and was 1.73 for "high" (again, using a t-test, p=0.022). Thus in both cases, STEAM's communication (low cost) helped to significantly improve ISIS's performance.

Comm cost	Mean goal difference against Andhill97	Mean goal difference against CMUnited97
Low	-3.38	3.27
High	-4.36	1.73
p(null hypo)	0.032	0.022

Table 1: ISIS97: Mean goal difference with/without STEAM.

4.2 Team Monitoring Challenge

In response to the team monitoring challenge (part of the team plan execution challenge), we contrast ISIS98 with ISIS97. Our individual ISIS98 players very precisely monitored their own and the ball's x,y positions on the RoboCup field. In contrast, ISIS97 players only approximately (and often inaccurately) estimated their own or the ball position (without x,y). Thus, ISIS98 players were individually more situationally aware, and were expected to outperform ISIS97 players.

The surprise: In actual games (e.g., against CMUnited97) however, ISIS97 players appeared to be as effective as ISIS98 players. Our analysis revealed that ISIS97 players were compensating for their lack of individual monitoring by relying on their teammates. Consider for instance the CAREFUL-DEFENSE team operator discussed earlier. This operator is terminated if the ball is sufficiently far away. In ISIS97, without x,y locations, individually recognizing such termination was difficult. However, one of the players in the subteam would just happen to stay at a fixed known location (e.g., the goal), acting as a reference. When it recognized that the ball was far away, it would inform the teammates, as per its joint commitments in the team operator. Thus, other players, who were not situationally well-aware, would now know the ball is far away. In contrast, ISIS98 players, with x,y computations, would individually quickly recognize the termination of this operator.

Table 2 shows the means of goal differences for ISIS98 with differing communication costs and different opponents (over 170 games against CMUnited97, 60 against Andhill97). STEAM's communication ("low" communication cost) does not provide a statistically significant improvement over no-communication (using a two-tailed t-test). This indicates decreased reliance on communication among teammates, and contrasts with results for ISIS97 from Table 1.

Comm cost	Mean goal difference against Andhill97	Mean goal difference against CMUnited97
Low	-1.53	4.04
High	-2.13	3.91
p(null hypo)	0.58	0.13

Table 2: Impact of STEAM in ISIS98.

Thus, the response to the team monitoring challenge is the discovery of a general tradeoff: one monitoring approach provides individual agents with complex monitoring capabilities, making them situationally well-aware and hence independent of others (for monitoring). Another approach provides simpler monitoring capabilities to agents, but they must now rely on teammates to compensate for the lack of own capabilities.

4.3 Plan Decomposition Challenge

The RoboCup challenge of team plan decomposition focuses on designing *roles* for individual agents in a team. Ideally, roles should divide the team responsibilities fairly, avoid conflicts, and conserve resources by avoiding redunducies. Indeed, in ISIS98, these factors led to players' roles being defined in terms of non-overlapping regions of the soccer field, in which they were responsible for intercepting and kicking the ball. These regions were flexibly changed, if the team went from attack to defense mode. In contrast, in ISIS97, players' roles (also defined in terms of regions), had a significant overlap, possibly wasting stamina. Thus, the role non-overlap plan decomposition of ISIS98 was expected to be significantly superior to the *role overlap* style of ISIS97.

The surprise: When we played ISIS97 and ISIS98 against CMUnited97, however, ISIS97 was not outperformed as expected. In particular, ISIS97 managed to attain a reasonable division of responsibilities, via *competition within collabora-*

tion. Essentially, multiple players in ISIS97 would chase the ball, competing for opportunities to intercept the ball. Players that were out of stamina, or those that lost sight of the ball etc., would all fall behind, and the player best able to compete (i.e., get close to the ball first) would get to kick the ball.

Thus, a key lesson is tradeoff in role design: a flexible, role no-overlap design reduces conflicts, conserves resources, but requires careful off-line role planning. It can also fail in dynamic load balancing, e.g., an ISIS98 player, even if very tired, is still solely responsible for its region. In contrast, ISIS97's role overlap can exploit *competition within collaboration* to more autonomously plan its role division, and attain more dynamic load balancing, e.g., if a player is tired, a teammate with more stamina will get to the ball quicker. However, role overlap may waste resources, due to redundant actions.

5 Agent Modeling Response

The agent modeling area provides a key difficult RoboCup challenge: *off-line review* by an expert to analyze teams. We have constructed two contrasting agents in response to this challenge. Both agents use a domain-independent approach that avoids the encoding of extensive domain knowledge and rely instead on extensive data-mining. These agents are thus collaborative *assistants*, relying on the "knowledge-rich" human observer to complete the analysis. Since both agents rely on data-mining, they excel at uncovering unexpected phenomena. Within the complexity of the RoboCup environment, these off-line review agents appear capable of capturing novel regularities that escape unaided human observers.

5.1 Off-line Expert Agent

ISAAC is a web-based off-line soccer expert (Fig. 4, http://coach.isi.edu). It is focused on automated analysis to aid in improving a team's behavior. ISAAC approaches the problem by investigating actions that did not produce the desired result and then classifying the contexts in which failures occured. Based on that classification, ISAAC recommends changes in behavior to avoid the failures: either the team should perform a different action in that context or should perform the action in a modified context. More specifically, ISAAC's analysis starts with logs of a particular team's games. From the logs, ISAAC extracts interesting behaviors and the outcomes of those behaviors. For instance, shots on own or opponent goals are interesting behaviors, so ISAAC gathers data on such shots, and whether they succeed. ISAAC then classifies these successes and failures into subclasses with similar contexts. For instance, a subclass might be all goal shots with a near-by opponent, that fail. Currently, C4.5 is used to induce these subclasses by generating rules that classify the successes and failures of the shooting team.

ISAAC's next step is to formulate suggestions that may improve the team's performance, once again, using a knowledge-lean approach. To that end, ISAAC formulates and analyzes perturbations of the rules. Each rule consists of a number of conditions that must be satisfied for the rule to be valid. We define a perturbation to be the rule that results from reversing one condition. Thus a rule with N conditions will have N perturbations. The successes and failures governed by the

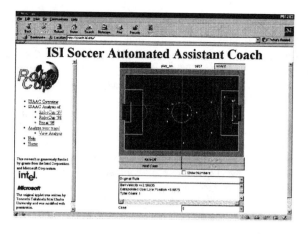

Figure 4: ISAAC exists on the web.

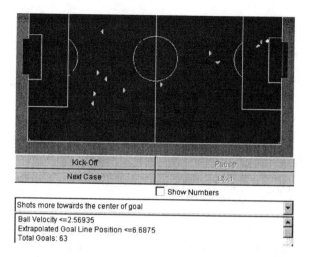

Figure 5: ISAAC's rule perturbations for Andhill'97.

perturbations of a rule are examined to determine which conditions have the most effect in changing the outcome of the original rule, turning a failure into a success.

Let us consider a simple example of ISAAC's analysis of Andhill97 against other teams in the RoboCup '97 tournament. One of ISAAC's learned rules states that when taking shots on goal, the Andhill97 team often fails to score when (i) ball velocity is less than 2.57 meters per time tick and (ii) the shot is aimed at greater than 6.7 meters from the center of goal (which is just inside the goalpost). ISAAC reveals that shots governed by this rule score once, and fail to score 70 times. That Andhill97, the 2nd place winner of 97 had so many goal-shot failures, and that poor aim was at least a factor was a surprising revelation to the human observers. The user can review the "video" of these shots on goal in ISAAC's log monitor to better appreciate what is occurring in these cases. Perturbations of this rule can also be considered. In cases where the rule is perturbed so that ball velocity is greater than 2.57m/t and the shot aim is still greater than 6.7m, Andhill scores once and fails to score 3 times. In another perturbation, where ball velocity is again less than 2.57m/t, but now shot aim is equal to or less than 6.7m (see Figure 5), Andhill is now scoring 63 times and failing to score 106 times. These perturbations suggest that improving Andhill97's shot aiming capabilities can significantly improve performance.

More recently, ISAAC has been extended to analyze sequences of behaviors (again using C4.5), such as sequences of actions (e.g., assists) that lead up to successes or failures. This analysis has revealed that out of the top four teams of RoboCup'97, ISIS is at one extreme with little or no emergent pattern of assists, while CMUnited shows deeper patterns of assists and secondary assists.

5.2 Teamwork Review Agent

TEAMORE (or TEAmwork MOnitoring REview) is an agent that performs off-line review via a contrast of the behaviors of the agents in a team. TEAMORE is based in *socially-attentive monitoring*, originally applied in battlefield simulations[Kaminka and Tambe, 1998], underscoring its generality. In RoboCup, TEAMORE complements the use of goals scored as a measure of teamwork.

TEAMORE currently assumes that it has access to plans or behaviors executed by agents during a game (via agents' execution traces). TEAMORE then compares the plans being executed by different team members, identifying *discrepant* situations, where team-members failed to agree on the joint team-plan that they should have been executing together. For instance, suppose the forwards are to execute a team tactic together, but one forward fails to execute it — this is a team discrepancy. TEAMORE uses this discrepancy information over time as the basis for a quantitative measure of teamwork.

TEAMORE uses several measures of discrepancy, but one particularly useful is the average time that it takes for a sub-team (e.g., forwards) to switch from one team plan to another. In perfect teamwork situations, all team-members switch team plans (tactics) together, moving in unison from one agreed upon team plan to another. Thus, the perfect team-plan switch time is exactly one time unit. The worst possible switch is if one team member never makes the switch and the sub-team never establishes agreement.

Earlier in this paper, ISIS97 was shown (Table 1) to have significantly different score-differences with and without communications, while even a large number of games (over 230) of ISIS98 resulted in no statistically significant difference (Table 2). Table 3 presents the results of TEAMORE's analysis for the ISIS98-Andhill97 and ISIS97-Anghill97 games. The average time per switch for two sub-teams (defenders and goalees) is shown for the two settings of the communication cost (approximately half of the games were played in each setting). These results show that communications (when cost is low) do reduce the average time per switch for each of the sub-teams. This reduction is statistically significant (two tailed t-test values are shown in the table), hinting at an improvement in the quality of teamwork with communication.

The first two columns of table 3 show that while ISIS98 had no statistically significant difference in the goal-difference for these games, TEAMORE is able to confirm that in fact STEAM is still making a statisically significant impact on the quality of teamwork, allowing validation of design objectives. Moreover, as the last two columns (presenting TEAMORE's analysis of the ISIS97-Andhill97 games) show, the difference in quality of teamwork that STEAM makes for ISIS97 is much greater than it is for ISIS98, supporting our hypothesis that ISIS98's superior monitoring capabilities reduced its dependency on teamwork. In fact, the average-time-per-switch values for ISIS97 using communications lie in between the values for ISIS98 with and without communications. However, the values for ISIS97 without communications are much greater then those for ISIS98, explaining the much bigger impact communication had on ISIS97.

Comm cost	ISIS98 Goalees	ISIS98 Defenders	ISIS97 Goalees	ISIS97 defenders
High	13.28	12.99	32.80	57.5
Low	3.65	3.98	5.79	6.81
p(null-hypo)	9.26E-16	7.13E-5	7.13E-13	1.45E-10

Table 3: Ave time per switch in games against Andhill97.

6 Lessons Learned

Our research in RoboCup has been fueled by the IJCAI'97 challenge. We have responded to the challenge in all three categories of learning, teamwork and agent modeling. Few other RoboCup teams have attacked the IJCAI'97 challenge in this much breadth. One possible exception is [Stone and Veloso, 1998b], who have focused on layered learning for agent design, and an approach to teamwork based on *locker-room arrangements*[Stone and Veloso, 1998a]. In their teamwork approach, agents synchronize their individual beliefs periodically in a fixed manner, in contrast with ISIS's STEAM in which communications are issued dynamically. Indeed, in comparison with [Stone and Veloso, 1998a] and other teams, ISIS stands alone in its use of a domain-independent teamwork model, with its demonstrated reuse. Other RoboCup researchers have investigated individual research areas. For instance, [Luke *et al.*, 1998] have investigated an innovative approach to learning in RoboCup, but they have yet to address the agent modeling and teamwork challenge of RoboCup. Others have investigated teamwork via explicit team plans and roles[Ch'ng and Padgham, 1998], but not learning or agent modeling, and they fail the *basic performance* requirement of the RoboCup challenge, i.e., the team must be able to play reasonably well. ISIS passes this test, given its third- and fourth-place in RoboCup'97 and RoboCup'98.

In conclusion, in responding to the IJCAI challenge, we have been able to extract the following general lessons in multi-agent learning, teamwork, and agent modeling:

- Some multi-agent environments require a significant role specialization of individuals. Thus, sharing experiences of individuals in different roles can sometimes be significantly *detrimental* to team performance, placing key limits on social learning.

- Divide-and-conquer learning can be used to enable different learning techniques to co-exist, reducing the complexity of the learning problem.

- Reuse of general teamwork models can improve performance and reduce development time.

- Tradeoffs exist in individual and team monitoring, e.g., responsible team behavior enables the design of simpler monitoring capabilities for individuals.

- *Competition within collaboration* can provide a simple but powerful technique for designing role responsibilities for individuals.

- In analyzing agent behavior in complex multi-agent environments, data-driven analysis combined with human oversight appears promising.

- Comparison of the behavior of team members can provide a useful teamwork monitoring tool.

Acknowledgements

This research is supported in part by NSF grant IRI-9711665, and in part by a generous gift from the Intel Corporation.

References

[Ch'ng and Padgham, 1998] S. Ch'ng and L. Padgham. Team description: Royal merlbourne knights. In *RoboCup-97: The first robot world cup soccer games and conferences*. Springer-Verlag, Heidelberg, Germany, 1998.

[Cohen and Levesque, 1991] P. R. Cohen and H. J. Levesque. Teamwork. *Nous*, 35, 1991.

[Kaminka and Tambe, 1998] G. Kaminka and M. Tambe. What is wrong with us? improving robustness through social diagnosis. In *Proceedings of the National Conference on Artificial Intelligence (AAAI)*, August 1998.

[Kitano *et al.*, 1997] H. Kitano, M. Tambe, P. Stone, S. Coradesci, H. Matsubara, M. Veloso, I. Noda, E. Osawa, and M. Asada. The robocup synthetic agents' challenge. In *Proceedings of the International Joint Conference on Artificial Intelligence (IJCAI)*, August 1997.

[Luke *et al.*, 1998] S. Luke, Hohn C., J. Farris, G. Jackson, and J. Hendler. Co-evolving soccer softbot team coordination with genetic programming. In *RoboCup-97: The first robot world cup soccer games and conferences*. Springer-Verlag, Heidelberg, Germany, 1998.

[Newell, 1990] A. Newell. *Unified Theories of Cognition*. Harvard Univ. Press, Cambridge, Mass., 1990.

[Quinlan, 1993] J. R. Quinlan. *C4.5: Programs for machine learning*. Morgan Kaufmann, San Mateo, CA, 1993.

[Stone and Veloso, 1998a] P. Stone and M. Veloso. Task decomposition and dynamic role assignment for real-time strategic teamwork. In *Proceedings of the international workshop on Agent theories, Architectures and Languages*, 1998.

[Stone and Veloso, 1998b] P. Stone and M. Veloso. Using decision tree confidence factors for multiagent control. In *RoboCup-97: The first robot world cup soccer games and conferences*. Springer-Verlag, Heidelberg, Germany, 1998.

[Tambe, 1997] M. Tambe. Towards flexible teamwork. *Journal of Artificial Intelligence Research (JAIR)*, 7:83–124, 1997.

CHALLENGE PAPERS

Challenge Papers 2:
Propositional Reasoning and Search

Compiling Knowledge into Decomposable Negation Normal Form

Adnan Darwiche
Cognitive Systems Laboratory
Department of Computer Science
University of California
Los Angeles, CA 90024
darwiche@cs.ucla.edu

Abstract

We propose a method for compiling propositional theories into a new tractable form that we refer to as decomposable negation normal form (DNNF). We show a number of results about our compilation approach. First, we show that every propositional theory can be compiled into DNNF and present an algorithm to this effect. Second, we show that if a clausal form has a bounded treewidth, then its DNNF compilation has a linear size and can be computed in linear time — treewidth is a graph-theoretic parameter which measures the connectivity of the clausal form. Third, we show that once a propositional theory is compiled into DNNF, a number of reasoning tasks, such as satisfiability and forgetting, can be performed in linear time. Finally, we propose two techniques for approximating the DNNF compilation of a theory when the size of such compilation is too large to be practical. One of the techniques generates a sound but incomplete compilation, while the other generates a complete but unsound compilation. Together, these approximations bound the exact compilation from below and above in terms for their ability to answer queries.

1 Introduction

Compiling propositional theories has emerged as a new technique for enhancing the computational efficiency of automated reasoning systems. The basic idea here is to split the computational effort of such systems into two phases, off-line and on-line. In the off-line phase, a propositional theory is compiled into a tractable form which is then used in an on-line phase to answer multiple queries. The main value of such compilation is that most of the computational overhead is shifted into the off-line phase, which is amortized over all on-line queries.

One of the key approaches for compiling propositional theories has been proposed in [7]. Here, a propositional theory is compiled in an off-line phase into a Horn theory, which is used in an on-line phase to answer multiple queries. As it is not always possible to compile a propositional theory into a Horn theory, the propositional theory is generally compiled into two Horn theories, which approximate the original theory from below and above in terms of logical strength.

In this paper, we propose to compile propositional theories into a new form, which we call *decomposable negation normal form (DNNF)*. This form is a generalization of disjunctive normal form (DNF) and a specialization of *negation normal form (NNF)* [1]. DNNF is tractable as the satisfiability of theories expressed in DNNF can be decided in linear time. In fact, a number of other interesting reasoning tasks, such as *forgetting* [6], can also be performed in linear time on theories expressed in DNNF.

We show a number of results about our compilation approach. First, contrary to compilations into Horn theories, we show that every propositional theory can be compiled into DNNF and present an algorithm to this effect. Second, we show that if a clausal form has a bounded treewidth, then it has a linear DNNF compilation which can be computed in linear time. Here, treewidth is a graph-theoretic parameter which measures the connectivity of a given clausal form. Even when the clausal form does not have a bounded treewidth, we show that its DNNF compilation is exponential only in its treewidth and linear in all other aspects. Finally, we present two techniques for approximating the DNNF compilation of a propositional theory in case such compilation is too large to be practical. One of the techniques generates a sound but incomplete compilation, while the other generates a complete but unsound compilation. Together, these approximations bound the exact compilation from below and above in terms of their ability to answer queries.

This paper is structured as follows. Section 2 introduces DNNF and its various properties. Section 3 discusses the compilation of propositional theories into DNNF. Section 4 discusses the two techniques for approximating a DNNF compilation and Section 5 focuses on the operation of forgetting. Finally, Section 6 closes with some concluding remarks. Proofs of theorems can be found in the long version of the paper [4].

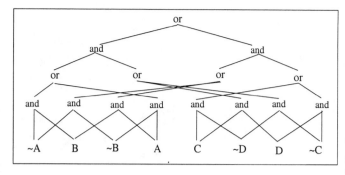

Figure 1: A propositional sentence in DNNF.

2 Decomposable NNF

A propositional sentence is in negation normal form (NNF) if it is constructed from literals using only the conjoin and disjoin operators [1]. Figure 1 shows a sentence in NNF depicted as a rooted, directed acyclic graph where the children of each node are shown below it in the graph. Each leaf node represents a literal and each non-leaf node represents a conjunction or a disjunction. We will also allow *true* and *¬false* to appear as leaves in a DNNF to denote a conjunction with no conjuncts. Similarly, we will allow *false* and *¬true* as leaves to represent a disjunction with no disjuncts. The size of an NNF is measured by the number of edges in its graphical representation. Note that every disjunctive normal form (DNF) is an NNF, and that every conjunctive normal form (CNF) is an NNF. There are NNFs, however, that are neither DNFs nor CNFs.

Our concern here is mainly with a subclass of NNFs:

Definition 1 *A* decomposable negation normal form *(DNNF) is a negation normal form satisfying the decomposability property: for any conjunction $\bigwedge_i \alpha_i$ appearing in the form, no atoms are shared by the conjuncts α_i.*

The NNF in Figure 1 is decomposable. It has ten conjunctions and the conjuncts of each share no atoms. Decomposability is the property which makes DNNF tractable. We will explore this property at length later, but we first note that every DNF is also a DNNF.[1] Therefore, all properties that we shall prove of DNNFs also hold for DNFs. A question that may arise then is why not compile propositional theories into DNFs? As it turns out, there are propositional theories that have linear DNNF representations, yet exponential DNF representations. For example, consider a propositional theory Δ over n atoms, which is satisfied exactly by models in which an odd number of atoms is set to true (Δ represents the odd-parity function). The DNF representation of this theory is known to be exponential in n. However, the theory has a DNNF representation which is linear in n. Figure 1 depicts such representation for $n = 4$.

Propositional theories in DNNF are tractable:

---

[1]We assume that in the DNF $\alpha_1 \vee \ldots \vee \alpha_n$, no atoms are shared by the literals in α_i.

1. Deciding the satisfiability of a DNNF can be done in linear time.

2. Forgetting about some atoms in a DNNF can be done in linear time [6].

3. Computing the minimum cardinality of models that satisfy a DNNF can be done in linear time, where cardinality is the number of atoms that are set to true (or false) by the model [3].

The last task has applications to model-based diagnosis and is outside the scope of this paper. Our focus here will be on the first two tasks, which we consider next.

By a <u>clause</u> (over distinct atoms $p_1, \ldots, p_n$), we will mean a disjunction $l_1 \vee \ldots \vee l_n$, where l_i is either p_i or $\neg p_i$. By an <u>instantiation</u> (of distinct atoms $p_1, \ldots, p_n$), we will mean a conjunction $l_1 \wedge \ldots \wedge l_n$. We start with a linear test for deciding the satisfiability of NNFs.

Definition 2 *Let* SAT? *be a predicate over NNFs defined as follows.* SAT?(l) *is true where l is a literal.* SAT?$(\bigwedge_i \alpha_i)$ *is true iff each* SAT?(α_i) *is true.* SAT?$(\bigvee_i \alpha_i)$ *is true iff some* SAT?(α_i) *is true.*

It should be clear that the predicate SAT?(α) can be evaluated in time which is linear in the size of NNF α. The previous test is sound and complete for DNNFs:

Theorem 1 *DNNF α is satisfiable iff* SAT?(α) *is true.*

Now that we have a satisfiability test, we can also define an entailment test. Specifically, to test whether α entails clause β, we only need to test whether $\alpha \wedge \neg\beta$ is satisfiable. Note, however, that even though both α and $\neg\beta$ may be in DNNF, their conjunction $\alpha \wedge \neg\beta$ is not guaranteed to be in DNNF as α and $\neg\beta$ may share atoms. This can be easily dealt with, however, using the notion of conditioning:

Definition 3 *Let α be a propositional sentence and let γ be an instantiation. The* <u>conditioning</u> *of α on γ, written $\alpha \mid \gamma$, is the sentence which results from replacing each atom p in α with true if the positive literal p appears in γ and with false if the negative literal $\neg p$ appears in γ.*

For example, conditioning the DNNF $(\neg A \wedge \neg B) \vee (B \wedge C)$ on instantiation $B \wedge D$ gives $(\neg A \wedge \neg true) \vee (true \wedge C)$ and conditioning it on $\neg B \wedge D$ gives $(\neg A \wedge \neg false) \vee (false \wedge C)$. Conditioning allows us to eliminate reference to atoms while preserving satisfiability:

Theorem 2 *For DNNF α and instantiation γ, $\alpha \mid \gamma$ is in DNNF, and $\alpha \mid \gamma$ is satisfiable iff $\alpha \wedge \gamma$ is satisfiable.*

Therefore, to test whether DNNF α entails clause β, we only need to test whether $\alpha \mid \neg\beta$ is satisfiable, which is guaranteed to be in DNNF. We can now define a linear entailment test for DNNFs. Actually, we will (more generally) define it for NNFs:

Definition 4 *For NNF α and clause β, define $\alpha \vdash \beta$ to be true when* SAT?$(\alpha \mid \neg\beta)$ *is false, where $\neg\beta$ is the instantiation negating clause β.*

This linear test is both sound and complete for DNNFs:

Theorem 3 *For DNNF α and clause β, $\alpha \vdash \beta$ iff $\alpha \models \beta$.*

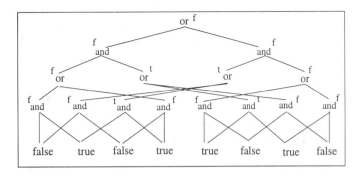

Figure 2: A propositional sentence in DNNF.

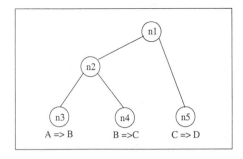

Figure 3: A decomposition tree.

Consider the DNNF α in Figure 1, the clause $\beta = \neg A \lor \neg B \lor \neg C \lor \neg D$, and suppose we want to test whether $\alpha \models \beta$. Theorem 3 suggests that we condition α on $\neg \beta$, to yield $\alpha \mid \neg \beta$, and then test whether $\text{SAT}?(\alpha \mid \neg \beta)$ is false. Figure 2 depicts the conditioning of α on $\neg \beta$ and the result of applying the SAT? test. Since $\text{SAT}?(\alpha \mid \neg \beta)$ is false, we conclude $\alpha \vdash \beta$ and also $\alpha \models \beta$.

Before we close this section, we present three important results on DNNF entailment. First, that the entailment test $\vdash$ is sound with respect to sentences in NNF:

Theorem 4 *For NNF α, $\alpha \vdash \beta$ only if $\alpha \models \beta$.*

That is, even though α may not be decomposable, the entailment test $\vdash$ is still sound, but not necessarily complete. Even completeness of this test, however, can be guaranteed under the following condition.

Definition 5 *NNF α is decomposable except on atoms X iff for any conjunction $\bigwedge_i \beta_i$ that appears in α, only atoms in X are shared by the conjuncts β_i.*

For example, the NNF $(\neg A \lor B) \land (\neg B \lor C)$ is decomposable except on B.

Theorem 5 *Let α be an NNF which is decomposable except on X. Let β be a clause which mentions all atoms in X. Then $\alpha \vdash \beta$ iff $\alpha \models \beta$.*

Consider the NNF $\alpha = (\neg A \lor B) \land (\neg B \lor C)$ and the queries $A \supset B$, $B \supset A$ and $A \supset C$. Since α is decomposable except on B, the test $\vdash$ is sound and complete with respect to the first two queries but is only sound with respect to the third query. Partial decomposability is extremely important in practice since the less decomposable a sentence is, the smaller its size will be. Finally:

Theorem 6 *For NNF α, which is decomposable except on X, and for clause β, $\alpha \models \beta$ iff $\alpha \vdash \gamma_i \lor \beta$ for each clause γ_i over atoms appearing in X but not in β.*

Therefore, if the size of X is bounded by a constant, then $\alpha \models \beta$ can be decided in linear time for any query β, even though α itself is not decomposable.

3 Compiling Knowledge into DNNF

We established two main results in the previous section. First, we identified the class of DNNF theories. Second,

we showed that satisfiability and entailment can be decided in linear time with respect to DNNF theories. Our goal in this section is two fold. First, to prove that every propositional theory can be expressed in DNNF. Second, to provide an algorithm for this purpose.

The following theorem is the key to proving that every propositional theory can be converted into DNNF.

Theorem 7 *Let Δ_1 and Δ_2 be two propositional sentences in DNNF. Let Δ be the sentence $\bigvee_\beta (\Delta_1 \mid \beta) \land (\Delta_2 \mid \beta) \land \beta$, where β is an instantiation of all atoms shared by Δ_1 and Δ_2. Then Δ is in DNNF and Δ is equivalent to $\Delta_1 \land \Delta_2$.*

Here is a recursive algorithm $\text{DNNF1}(\Delta)$, based on the above theorem, which converts any clausal form Δ into an equivalent theory in DNNF:

1. If Δ contains a single clause α, $\text{DNNF1}(\Delta) \leftarrow \alpha$.

2. Otherwise, $\text{DNNF1}(\Delta) \leftarrow \bigvee_\beta \text{DNNF1}(\Delta_1 \mid \beta) \land \text{DNNF1}(\Delta_2 \mid \beta) \land \beta$, where Δ_1 and Δ_2 is a partition of the clauses in Δ, and β is an instantiation of the atoms shared by Δ_1 and Δ_2.

This algorithm converts any theory in clausal form into an equivalent theory in DNNF, but at the expense of increasing the theory size. The increase in size comes mainly from the case analysis performed on the atoms shared by the sub-theories Δ_1 and Δ_2. Consider the theory $\Delta = (A \supset B) \land (B \supset C)$ and let $\Delta_1 = A \supset B$ and $\Delta_2 = B \supset C$. Then $\text{DNNF1}(\Delta) = (\text{DNNF1}(\Delta_1 \mid B) \land \text{DNNF1}(\Delta_2 \mid B) \land B) \lor (\text{DNNF1}(\Delta_1 \mid \neg B) \land \text{DNNF1}(\Delta_2 \mid \neg B) \land \neg B)$, which simplifies to $(C \land B) \lor (\neg A \land \neg B)$.

We have two key observations about the above procedure. First, the size of resulting DNNF is very sensitive to the way we split the theory Δ into two sub-theories Δ_1 and Δ_2. Second, the above procedure is not deterministic since it does not specify how to split the theory Δ into two sub-theories. To make the procedure deterministic, we will utilize a decomposition tree, which represents a recursive partitioning of the clauses in Δ.

Definition 6 *A decomposition tree T for clausal form Δ is a full binary tree whose leaves correspond to the clauses in Δ. If N is the leaf node corresponding to clause α in Δ, then $\Delta(N) \overset{def}{=} \{\alpha\}$.*

```
┌─────────────────────────────────────────┐
│           Algorithm DNNF1                 │
├─────────────────────────────────────────┤
│ /* N is a tree node ; α is an instantiation */
│ DNNF1(N, α)
│   if N is a leaf node & Δ(N) = {φ}, then γ←φ | α
│   else γ← ⋁_β DNNF1(N_l, α ∧ β) ∧ DNNF1(N_r, α ∧ β) ∧ β
│     where β ranges over all instantiations
│     of atoms(N_l) ∩ atoms(N_r) − atoms(α)
│   return γ
└─────────────────────────────────────────┘
```

Figure 4: Compiling a theory into DNNF.

```
┌─────────────────────────────────────────┐
│           Algorithm DNNF2                 │
├─────────────────────────────────────────┤
│ DNNF2(N, α)
│   ψ←project(α, atoms(N))
│   if CACHE_N(ψ) ≠ NIL, return CACHE_N(ψ)
│   if N is a leaf node & Δ(N) = {φ}, then γ←φ | α
│   else γ← ⋁_β DNNF2(N_l, α ∧ β) ∧ DNNF2(N_r, α ∧ β) ∧ β
│     where β ranges over all instantiations
│     of atoms(N_l) ∩ atoms(N_r) − atoms(α)
│   CACHE_N(ψ)←γ
│   return γ
└─────────────────────────────────────────┘
```

Figure 5: Compiling a theory into DNNF.

Figure 3 depicts a decomposition tree for the theory Δ which contains the clauses $A \supset B$, $B \supset C$ and $C \supset D$.

For a decomposition tree to be useful computationally, we need to associate some information with each of its nodes. First, for every internal node N: N_l and N_r denote the left and right children of N, respectively, and $\Delta(N) \stackrel{def}{=} \Delta(N_l) \cup \Delta(N_r)$. Second, $atoms(N)$ is defined as the set of atoms appearing in clauses $\Delta(N)$. For example, in Figure 3, $\Delta(n_2)$ contains the clauses $A \supset B$ and $B \supset C$ and $atoms(n_2)$ contains the atoms A, B and C.

Given a decomposition tree for theory Δ, Figure 4 depicts an algorithm which compiles Δ into DNNF.

Theorem 8 DNNF1(N, α) returns $\Delta(N) \mid \alpha$ in DNNF.

Therefore, to convert a theory Δ into DNNF, we first construct a decomposition tree T for Δ and call DNNF1$(N, true)$ with N being the root of tree T. The following is an important observation about DNNF1:

Theorem 9 If α and α' agree on $atoms(N)$, then DNNF1(N, α) is equivalent to DNNF1(N, α').

Therefore, we can improve on DNNF1 by associating a cache with each node N to store the result of DNNF1(N, α) indexed by the projection of instantiation α on $atoms(N)$, denoted $project(\alpha, atoms(N))$. When another recursive call DNNF1(N, α') is made, we first check the cache of node N to see whether we have an entry for $project(\alpha', atoms(N))$. If we do, we return it. Otherwise, we continue with the recursion. This improvement leads to the refined algorithm in Figure 5. We now address the complexity of DNNF2.

Definition 7 Let N be a node in a decomposition tree T. The <u>cluster</u> of node N is defined as follows:

- If N is a leaf node, then its cluster is $atoms(N)$.
- If N is an internal node, then its cluster is the set of atoms that appear either
  - above and below node N in the tree; or
  - in the left and right subtrees of node N.

The <u>width</u> of a decomposition tree is the size of its maximal cluster minus one.

In Figure 3, we have $cluster(n_1) = \{C\}$, $cluster(n_2) = \{B, C\}$, $cluster(n_3) = \{A, B\}$, $cluster(n_4) = \{B, C\}$ and $cluster(n_5) = \{C, D\}$. Therefore, the decomposition tree has width 1.

Theorem 10 Let T be the decomposition tree used in Figure 5. The time and space complexity of the algorithm in Figure 5 is $O(nw2^w)$, where n is the number of leaf nodes in tree T and w is its width.[2]

Therefore, the complexity of compiling a propositional theory into DNNF depends crucially on the quality (width) of decomposition tree used. The question now is how to construct good decomposition trees (ones with small width)? As it turns out, there is a device in the literature on graph-based reasoning, known as a jointree, which can be easily converted into a decomposition tree. A jointree also has a width and good jointrees are those with small width. We can easily convert a jointree into a decomposition tree while maintaining its width. Therefore, any good method for constructing jointrees is also a good method for constructing decomposition trees. A jointree, however, is constructed for an undirected graph while a decomposition tree is constructed for a propositional theory. The following definition makes the connection.

Definition 8 [5] Let Δ be a propositional theory in clausal form. The <u>interaction graph</u> for Δ is the undirected graph G constructed as follows. The nodes of G are the atoms of Δ. There is an edge between two atoms in G iff the atoms appear in the same clause of Δ.

Theorem 11 Let Δ be a propositional theory in clausal form and let G be its interaction graph. Let J be a jointree for G with width w. There is a decomposition tree for Δ which has width $\leq w$ and which can be constructed from J in time linear in the size of J.

The width of the best jointree for a graph G is known as the *treewidth* of G. If the treewidth of a graph is bounded by a constant w, then one can construct an optimal jointree in linear time [2]. A major implication of this result is that if a clausal form Δ has an interaction graph with a bounded treewidth, then (a) computing an optimal decomposition tree (jointree) for that theory, (b) compiling the theory based on the computed decomposition tree, and (c) answering queries based on

---

[2]Note that if T is a decomposition tree for a clausal form Δ, then n is also the number of clauses in Δ.

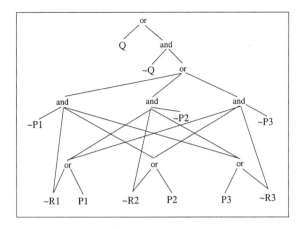

Figure 6: A propositional sentence in DNNF.

the resulting compilation, can all be done in linear time. This is our central result on the complexity of compiling theories into DNNF.[3]

We stress, however, that the interaction graph of a theory may not have a bounded treewidth, yet the theory may have a polynomial compilation into DNNF. Consider the theory $\Delta = \{P_1 \wedge \ldots \wedge P_n \supset Q, R_1 \wedge \neg P_1 \supset Q, \ldots, R_n \wedge \neg P_n \supset Q\}$. The interaction graph of this theory has treewidth n, yet it has a DNNF compilation of size $O(n^2)$ (shown in Figure 6 for $n = 3$).

The theory we just considered is not equivalent to any Horn theory. In fact, even its Horn approximation is known to be exponential in n [7]. This shows that there are theories with exponential Horn approximations, yet polynomial DNNF representations.

4 Approximate Compilation

What if we have a theory Δ for which the best decomposition tree has an unacceptable width? We have two key choices to address this problem. First, we can try to improve on algorithm DNNF2. Second, we can try to generate an approximate compilation, which is the direction we shall peruse in this section.

Consider the algorithm DNNF2 in Figure 5. It should be clear that the reason for possible intractability in this algorithm is the size of $\mathcal{S}(N, \alpha) \stackrel{def}{=} atoms(N_l) \cap atoms(N_r) - atoms(\alpha)$, which contains some of the atoms shared by sub-theories $\Delta(N_l)$ and $\Delta(N_r)$. Specifically, the algorithm will consider a number of instantiations β which is exponential in the size of $\mathcal{S}(N, \alpha)$. Therefore, we can control the size of resulting compilation by reducing the number of instantiations considered. We can do this in two ways:

1. *Ignoring atoms:* We can ignore some of the atoms in $\mathcal{S}(N, \alpha)$ by performing a case analysis on only a subset of $\mathcal{S}(N, \alpha)$. That is, we consider all instan-

---

[3]The satisfiability of this class of theories can also be decided in linear time using directional resolution [5].

tiations β of a <u>subset</u> of $\mathcal{S}(N, \alpha)$. This leads to a variation on algorithm DNNF2 which we call DNNF$_u$.

2. *Ignoring instantiations:* We can ignore some of the instantiations β. That is, we only consider <u>some</u> instantiations β of $\mathcal{S}(N, \alpha)$. This leads to a variation on algorithm DNNF2 which we call DNNF$_l$.

In either case, we can control the size of resulting compilation and to the degree we wish. In fact, using either technique we can ensure a linear compilation if we decide to ignore enough atoms or instantiations. This leaves two questions. First, what atoms or instantiations should we ignore? Second, what can we guarantee about the resulting compilations?

The choice of atoms or instantiations to ignore is typically heuristic and will not be addressed in this paper. We only address the second question here.

Theorem 12 DNNF$_u(N, \alpha)$ *is in NNF and is equivalent to* DNNF2(N, α).

That is, ignoring atoms preserves equivalence to the exact compilation, but compromises the decomposability property. The more atoms we ignore, the less decomposable the approximation is. But in all cases, the compilation generated by DNNF$_u$ is sound, although not necessarily complete, with respect to entailment.

Corollary 1 DNNF$_u(N, \alpha) \vdash \beta$ *only if* DNNF2$(N, \alpha) \vdash \beta$.

Here is the guarantee about the second approximation:

Theorem 13 DNNF$_l(N, \alpha)$ *is in DNNF and* DNNF$_l(N, \alpha) \models$ DNNF2(N, α).

That is, ignoring instantiations preserves the decomposability property but could lead to strengthening the compilation. The more instantiations we ignore, the stronger the approximate compilation is. But in all cases, the compilation generated by DNNF$_l$ is complete, although not necessarily sound, with respect to entailment.

Corollary 2 DNNF$_l(N, \alpha) \nvdash \beta$ *only if* DNNF2$(N, \alpha) \nvdash \beta$.

Therefore, if the size of a DNNF compilation Γ is too large, we can replace it with two approximations Γ_l and Γ_u. Given a query β, we first test whether $\Gamma_l \vdash \beta$ and $\Gamma_u \vdash \beta$. We have three possibilities: If $\Gamma_l \nvdash \beta$, then $\Delta \not\models \beta$. If $\Gamma_u \vdash \beta$, then $\Delta \models \beta$. If $\Gamma_l \vdash \beta$ and $\Gamma_u \nvdash \beta$, then the approximations are not good enough to answer this query. Note that the case $\Gamma_l \nvdash \beta$ and $\Gamma_u \vdash \beta$ is impossible.

The bounds Γ_l and Γ_u are inspired by the lower and upper Horn approximations proposed in [7]. In their approach, however, these bounds are crucial since not every theory has a Horn representation. In our case, however, the approximations are only meant to address intractability; our compilation approach would continue to be meaningful without them.

5 Compiling Out Atoms

Given a theory Δ, we may only be interested in queries β which do not mention atoms X. In this case, it makes sense to compile Δ into a theory which does not mention atoms X either, yet is equivalent to Δ with respect to

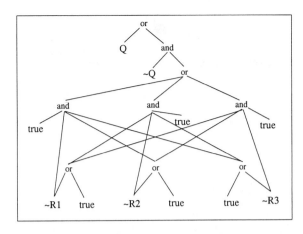

Figure 7: Forgetting atoms in a DNNF.

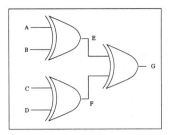

Figure 8: An odd-parity circuit.

queries β. Such theory is the result of forgetting about atoms X in Δ [6]. As it turns out, once a theory is converted into DNNF, forgetting takes linear time:

Definition 9 *For DNNF α and atoms X, define* FORGET(α, X) *as the result of replacing each literal in α with true iff that literal refers to an atom in X.*

The following theorem shows that the above linear operation does correspond to forgetting as defined in [6]:

Theorem 14 *Let α be a sentence in DNNF and let β be a clause that does not mention atoms X. Then $\alpha \models \beta$ iff* FORGET$(\alpha, X) \models \beta$.

Consider the DNNF in Figure 6, which is equivalent to the theory $\Delta = \{P_1 \wedge P_2 \wedge P_3 \supset Q, R_1 \wedge \neg P_1 \supset Q, R_2 \wedge \neg P_2 \supset Q, R_3 \wedge \neg P_3 \supset Q\}$. Forgetting about atoms P_1, P_2, P_3 in this theory gives the DNNF in Figure 7, which can be easily simplified to $R_1 \wedge R_2 \wedge R_3 \supset Q$.

Forgetting has three major applications. First, reducing the size of a DNNF compilation by forgetting about atoms that would never appear in queries. Second, computing DNNF representations of Boolean functions. Consider the circuit in Figure 8 which implements the odd-parity function, and let Δ be a theory representing this circuit. If we compile $\Delta \cup \{G\}$ into DNNF, and then forget atoms E, F and G, we obtain a DNNF representation of this Boolean function. This technique can be used to compile any circuit representation of a Boolean function into its DNNF representation.[4] A final application of forgetting is in computing the implications of a given theory on a particular set of atoms X (by forgetting about all atoms other than X). This has proven to be very useful in model–based diagnosis [3].

6   Conclusion

We have proposed an approach for compiling propositional theories into a tractable form, which we refer to as decomposable negation normal form (DNNF). We have

---

[4]In [4], we compare DNNFs with Binary Decision Diagrams (BDDs) as a representation of Boolean functions.

shown that once a theory is compiled into that form, a number of reasoning tasks including entailment, satisfiability and forgetting can be accomplished in linear time. We have shown that every propositional theory can be compiled into DNNF and presented an algorithm to this effect. We then presented a key result according to which the time and space complexity of our compilation technique is linear given that the propositional theory has a clausal form with bounded treewidth. Finally, we presented two techniques for approximating DNNF compilations. One of the techniques generates sound compilations, the other generates complete compilations. Together, the two approximations bound the original theory from below and above in terms of their ability to answer queries. There are at least three key distinctions between our compilation approach and the one proposed in [7]. First, every theory has a DNNF representation, while not every theory has a Horn representation. Second, there are theories with exponential Horn approximations, yet polynomial DNNF representations. Third, we have characterized a class of theories which is guaranteed to have linear DNNF compilations. We are not aware of a similar guarantee on the Horn approximations of this class of theories.

References

[1] Jon Barwise, editor. *Handbook of Mathematical Logic*. North-Holland, Amsterdam, 1977.

[2] Hans. L. Bodlaender. A linear time algorithm for finding tree-decompositions of small treewidth. *SIAM Journal of Computing*, 25(6):1305–1317, 1996.

[3] Adnan Darwiche. Compiling devices: A structure-based approach. In *KR98*, pages 156–166, 1998.

[4] Adnan Darwiche. Compiling knowledge into decomposable negation normal form. Technical Report R–262, Cognitive Systems Laboratory, UCLA, 1999.

[5] Rina Dechter and Irina Rish. Directional resolution: The davis-putnam procedure, revisited. In *KR94*, pages 134–145, 1994.

[6] Fangzhen Lin and Ray Reiter. Forget it! In *Working notes: AAAI Fall Symposium on Relevance*, 1994.

[7] Bart Selman and Henry Kautz. Knowledge compilation and theory approximation. *Journal of the ACM*, 43(2):193–224, March, 1996.

Using Walk-SAT and Rel-SAT for Cryptographic Key Search

Fabio Massacci*

Dip. di Informatica e Sistemistica
Univ. di Roma I "La Sapienza"
via Salaria 113, I-00198 Roma, Italy
email: massacci@dis.uniroma1.it
url: http://www.dis.uniroma1.it/~massacci

Abstract

Computer security depends heavily on the strength of cryptographic algorithms. Thus, cryptographic key search is often THE search problem for many governments and corporations.

In the recent years, AI search techniques have achieved notable successes in solving "real world" problems. Following a recent result which showed that the properties of the U.S. Data Encryption Standard can be encoded in propositional logic, this paper advocates the use of cryptographic key search as a benchmark for propositional reasoning and search. Benchmarks based on the encoding of cryptographic algorithms optimally share the features of "real world" and random problems.

In this paper, two state-of-the-art AI search algorithms, Walk-SAT by Kautz & Selman and Rel-SAT by Bayardo & Schrag, have been tested on the encoding of the Data Encryption Standard, to see whether they are up the task, and we discuss what lesson can be learned from the analysis on this benchmark to improve SAT solvers.

New challenges in this field conclude the paper.

1 Introduction

Securing one's data and communication from unauthorized access in large open networks such as the Internet is of the main issues for computer science today [Anderson & Needham, 1996; G10, 1996; OECD, 1998].

Yet security depends heavily on the strength of cryptographic algorithms: security protocols which have been formally proved correct may be broken by the choice of a bad cipher [Ryan & Schneider, 1998]. Thus, cryptographic key search is often the search problem for many government and large corporations; and the ability of law enforcement officers to perform key search becomes the main concern behind the licensing of encryption technology [OECD, 1998].

Search, although in different settings, has also been a problem at the heart of AI research for many years. Recently propositional search has received attention for a number of factors [Selman *et al.*, 1997]:

> First new algorithms were discovered ... based on stochastic local search as well as systematic search [...]. Second, improvements in machine speed, memory size and implementations extended the range of the algorithms. Third, researchers began to develop and solve propositional encodings of interesting, real-world problems [...] Between 1991 and 1996 the size of hard satisfiability problems grew from ones involving less than 100 variables to ones involving over 10,000 variables.

Following a seminal proposal from [Cook and Mitchel, 1997], an application comes to one's mind: *can we encode cryptographic key search as a SAT-problem so that AI search techniques can solve it?*

A recent result in automated reasoning makes this possible. In [Marraro & Massacci, 1999] it has been show that, by combining clever reverse engineering, advanced CAD minimization, and propositional simplification, it is possible to encode in propositional logic the properties of the U.S. Data Encryption Standard, DES for short, [NIST, 1997; Schneier, 1994]. An encoding whose size is within reach of current AI search techniques: the encoding of a cryptographic search problem (finding a model is equivalent to finding a key) for the commercial version of DES requires slightly more than 10,000 variables and 6 times many clauses.

Although DES is currently under review, it is still the most widely used cryptographic algorithm within banks, financial institutions, and governments. It is the algorithm on which cryptanalysts tested the final success of their techniques (see [Schneier, 1994] or Sect. 2 for further references). Even partial successes with AI techniques can be relevant.

In this paper we claim that this problem should be one of the reference SAT-benchmarks. In particular, it gives the possibility of generating as many random instances as one wants and still each instance is as "real-world" as any instance that can be met in commercial cryptographic applications. It provides a neat answer to the last challenge for propositional reasoning and search proposed by Selman, Kautz and McAllester [1997] at IJCAI-97.

---
*Supported by CNR fellowship 201-15-9. This work has been partly supported by ASI, CNR and MURST grants. I would like to thank L. Carlucci Aiello, P. Liberatore, and L. Marraro for useful comments and discussions.

To check the potential effectiveness of AI techniques on this problem, two state-of-the-art SAT solvers have been tested for cryptographic key search using the propositional encoding. The choices are Walk-SAT, a local search algorithm proposed in [Selman *et al.*, 1994] as an improvement of GSAT, and Rel-SAT, a combination of the traditional Davis-Putnam Algorithm with back-jumping and learning proposed in [Bayardo & Schrag, 1997] to solve real-world problems.

In the experiments on the Data Encryption Standard, one shouldn't expect to be immediately competitive with twenty years of advanced cryptanalysis techniques, especially because AI Labs are not equally well funded to afford a specialized hardware machine of 250.000 USD or the exclusive use of a network of workstations for 50 days which have been used to break DES in the last years. Still, general purpose search algorithm using off-the-shelf hardware (Sparcs and Pentium II) can crack limited versions of DES without being told any problem-dependent information. Ad-hoc cryptographic techniques are still better since the first success with the limited version of DES we can solve was obtained in 1982 [Andleman & Reeds, 1982] and modern cryptographic approaches [Biham & Shamir, 1991; Matsui, 1994a] obtain the same results with better scaling properties. Still, the result is promising and points out at weaknesses of AI search algorithms that we need tackle to solve hard problems.

In the next section (§2) we introduce some basic preliminaries on cryptography and the Data Encryption Standard. Then we discuss the features of the encoding (§3). This is followed by the experimental analysis with Walk-SAT (§4) and Rel-SAT (§5). Few lessons for SAT solvers we can learn (§6) and new challenges (§7) conclude the paper.

2 Cryptography and DES

To make the paper self-contained for the non-security expert we sketch some preliminaries about cryptography and DES (for an introduction see [Schneier, 1994]).

Following [Schneier, 1994], we denote vector of bits by P (the plaintext), C (the ciphertext), and K (the secret key). At an abstract level, a cryptographic algorithm is simply a function $C = E_K(P)$ that transforms a sequence of bits (the plaintext) into another sequence of bits (the ciphertext) with certain (desirable) properties by using some additional (possibly secret) bits K. To decrypt we use another function that maps back C into P using K (or its inverse).

The important property of the encryption algorithm is that *security of the algorithm must reside in the (secret) key*. If one does not know K, it must be difficult to recover P from C, even if the algorithm has been public for years. In the ideal case, the only way to recover the plaintext must be by brute force "generate-and-test": try out all possible keys and see which yields an acceptable plaintext. The need to hinder brute force attacks has therefore generated hot debates on the minimum size of a key [Schneier, 1994].

Exhaustive search is not so impossible as it seems if one can use (and pay for) specialized hardware: last year a machine costing 250.000 USD broke the Data Encryption Standard finding a 56 bits key in 56 hours [DES Search, 1998a].

Search can be cut down if the cryptanalyst knows a suf-

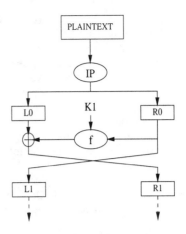

Figure 1: DES Algorithm

ficient number of blocks of plaintext with the corresponding ciphertext (known plaintext attack). This is a reasonable hypothesis: almost all messages and files have fixed parts. Using a network of 12 workstation and 2^{47} (randomly generated) plaintexts, Matsui [1994a] broke DES in 50 days.

As the reader might now want to know how DES works, we start by saying that DES is a block cipher, which encipher *blocks* (sequences) of 64 bits into blocks of 64 bits using a key of 56 bits[1]. DES and almost all symmetric ciphers are built following an architecture which is due to Feistel and his group [Feistel *et al.*, 1975]. After some initial preprocessing, the following operations are executed:

1. break the plaintext in two halves,

2. combine one half with the key using a clever function,

3. XOR the combination with the other half

4. swap the two parts.

These 4 operations constitutes a *round* and are repeated a suitable number of times. Figure 1 exemplifies the idea.

DES has 16 rounds which are almost identical except for the way in which the key is fed into the f function (Fig. 1): for each round a different subset of the 56 keybits is selected and combined with the input of the previous round. The strength of the cipher depends on the number of rounds and on f. Its design is, to quote Ron Rivest, "part art, part science".

As we have mentioned already, the basic way to break DES is by exhaustive search but there are other techniques.

Differential cryptanalysis was introduced by Biham and Shamir [1991]. It assumes that the cryptanalyst can choose ciphertext and plaintext pairs presenting particular fixed differences. Then, it analyzes the evolution of these differences through the rounds of DES. Using the differences resulting from ciphertexts, different probabilities are assigned to different keys. By analyzing a large number of ciphertext and plaintext pairs (2^{47} for the commercial version), a key will emerge as the most probable. This attack is only practical for less than 12 rounds. After that, it requires too many resources.

---

[1]The key is usually expressed as a 64 bits number, in which every eighth bit is a parity bit ignored by the algorithm.

Matsui's *linear cryptanalysis* [Matsui, 1994a; 1994b] works better. This method uses linear approximations (xor) to describe the behavior of the round function f (Fig. 1). By xoring together some plaintext bits with some ciphertext bits, one can get a bit that is the xor of some key bits. This is a linear approximation of a round that is true with a certain probability. Again, by analyzing a large number of plain/ciphertext pairs (2^{43} are needed for DES at 16 rounds), it is possible to guess the value of some key bits with 80% success rate. A refinement of this method approximates the internal 14-round and then guesses the results of the first and last round. It can find 26 keybits and uses exhaustive search for the rest.

A key aspect of cryptanalytic attacks (beside brute force) is that they are probabilistic. No deterministic method is known.

3 DES as a SAT Problem

Recently, an encoding of the U.S. Data Encryption Standard in propositional logic has been proposed in [Marraro & Massacci, 1999]. Before discussing how the encoding can be used to generate random problems, we sketch its functioning:

- each bit of the ciphertext, the plaintext, and the key is encoded as a propositional variable;

- the operations corresponding to the round function f (Fig. 1) are transformed into boolean formulae and minimized off-line with CAD tools;

- then the encoding algorithm "runs" DES at the meta-level, and generates formulae corresponding to each DES operation on the way;

- since the straightforward application of this method would generate a huge formula, clever optimizations are used so that some operations are encoded as formulae and some operations are computed.

For instance, operations corresponding to permutations of bits are not encoded as formulae; rather the propositional variables describing the inputs are permuted. Further details can be found in [Marraro & Massacci, 1999].

The outcome[2] of the algorithm is a formula $\mathcal{E}(P, K, C)$ which represent the logical relations between the key bits K, the plaintext bits P and the ciphertext bits C.

In a traditional plaintext attack we know the value of some plaintext and ciphertext bits so, if we replace the variables by the corresponding truth value, we have a formula whose structure is shown in Fig. 2. The K_i are the key bits while the other variables M_i^r, S_i^r, X_i^r are introduced to denote intermediate results and make the formula simpler. We use the superscripts r to denote the results produced at the r-th round and the subscript i to the denote the i-th bit produced at corresponding intermediate stage (i ranges from 1 to 64). Loosely speaking, and looking at Fig. 1, we may say that each X_i^r represents an output of the r-th round and thus an input of the $r + 1$-th round of the algorithm. The value $lastr$ is the number of rounds of DES for which the encoding has been done. The actual formulae have more definitions to ease the subsequent (polynomial) translation into CNF.

---

[2]The algorithm in [Marraro & Massacci, 1999] takes less than 1 sec (3 rounds) up to 25 seconds (16 rounds) to generate the encoding. Memory requires a peak of 135M for the full 16 rounds.

Figure 2: The Encoding for a known-plaintext attack

Definitions
$$
\begin{aligned}
M_i^r &- \bigwedge_j \pm X_j^r & 2 \le r \le lastr - 1 \\
S_i^r &- \bigvee_j M_j^r & 2 \le r \le lastr \\
X_i^{r+1} &- S_j^r \oplus K_h & 1 \le r \le lastr - 1
\end{aligned}
$$

Constraints
$$
\begin{aligned}
M_i^1 &- \bigwedge_j \pm K_j \\
M_i^{lastr} &- \bigwedge_j \pm K_j \\
\pm S_i^{lastr-1} &- \bigoplus_r S_j^r & r \text{ even} \\
\pm S_i^{lastr} &- \bigoplus_r S^r & r \text{ odd}
\end{aligned}
$$

Table 1: Formula size per single plain/ciphertext pair

R	−	⊕	∧	∨	Clauses	Vars	C/V
1	520	0	504	16	1645	243	6.77
2	1042	0	1010	32	3304	489	6.75
3	1738	48	1609	80	9064	1430	6.34
4	2432	96	2208	128	14811	2368	6.25
5	3096	176	2760	160	18738	3032	6.18
6	3760	256	3312	192	22665	3696	6.13
7	4424	336	3864	224	26592	4360	6.10
8	5088	416	4416	256	30519	5024	6.07
9	5752	496	4968	288	34446	5688	6.06
10	6416	576	5520	320	38373	6352	6.04
11	7080	656	6072	352	42300	7016	6.03
12	7744	736	6624	384	46227	7680	6.02
13	8408	816	7176	416	50154	8344	6.01
14	9072	896	7728	448	54081	9008	6.00
15	9736	976	8280	480	58008	9672	6.00
16	10400	1056	8832	512	61935	10336	5.99

Table 1, taken from [Marraro & Massacci, 1999], shows some quantitative data for the encoding of a single pair constituted by a known block of plaintext and a block of cipher text, for an increasing number of rounds (R).

For random formulae, the ratio of c/v is an indicator of the hardness of the formula. In this case, it is not so. For instance, using the data of Table 1 for 3 rounds or more, we can see that if we use one block or an "infinite" number of blocks, the value of c/v changes by less than 4%. This would seem to imply that adding more blocks should not make the problem neither much easier nor much harder. As we shall see, the experimental results contradict this hypothesis.

In the introduction, it has been claimed that this encoding can be used to combine the contrasting needs of using "real-world" problems (possibly with lot of structure) and of generating a huge number of instances which can only be (pseudo)randomly generated. It might solve the dilemma pointed out in [Bayardo & Schrag, 1997]:

Care must be taken when experimenting with real world instances because the number of instances available for experimentation is often limited

whereas [Crawford & Auton, 1996] noted that

[...] random problems are readily available in any given size and virtually inexhaustible numbers. For example, ... [their experiments] required several million problems and it is hard to imagine collecting that many problems any other way.

How do we generate a random SAT problem based on cryptography? At first we generate a random key v_K and a plaintext block v_P (just vectors of 0/1). Then we use the cryptographic algorithm itself to get $v_C = E_{v_K}(v_P)$. Finally we substitute in $\mathcal{E}(P, K, C)$ the corresponding boolean values v_P and v_C that we have so far generated. Then the pair $\langle v_K, \mathcal{E}(v_P, K, v_C) \rangle$ is a *solved instance* of the SAT problem. Notice that $\mathcal{E}(v_P, K, v_C)$ might contain other variables than K but the latter are the only independent variables. If we have n blocks of plaintext (and the corresponding ciphertext) we can constrain the search further by conjoining the corresponding formulae $\bigwedge_{i=1}^{n} \mathcal{E}(v_P^i, K, v_C^i)$.

So we have encoded cryptographic key search, a known plaintext attack to DES, as a SAT problem. Since ciphers are designed to be hard to break, this will provide us with the hard solved instances asked for in [Cook and Mitchel, 1997]. We can generate generic instances by randomly generating both the plaintext and the ciphertext.

The main point here is that by changing the plaintext and the key we can generate an endless stream[3] of different solved instances either with the same solution or with different solutions. At 16 rounds, it would be exactly identical to an actual plaintext and ciphertext used by a bank, financial institution or government department.

4 Walk-SAT on DES

The first tested algorithm is a local search one: Walk-SAT [Selman *et al.*, 1994]. It is only briefly recalled:

- the algorithm starts from a random assignment;

- then it flips the value of some propositional variables (usually one) trying to increase the value of an objective function (here the number of satisfied clauses);

- when a local minimum is reached, the algorithm restart the search with another random assignment.

Variants of this basic approach include the possibility of making random moves from time to time and of continuing the search after a local minimum by using a tabu-list[4]. For more details see [Selman *et al.*, 1994; 1997].

Experiments were run on a Pentium II running Linux (with 64MB) and a Sun Sparc running Solaris (with 64M) with qualitatively and quantitatively similar results. To generate an instance we simply follow the recipe above: generate randomly a key (discarding weak keys [Schneier, 1994]) and then some hundred blocks of plaintext. For each plaintext block we generate the corresponding ciphertext and then substitute the value of the pair in the formula. An instance is finally created by conjoining the formulae corresponding to the desired number of plain/ciphertext pairs (or blocks).

The initial settings of Walk-SAT were the recommend standard: hill-climbing with some random perturbations. The performance improved by using a random flip every 16 moves

---

[3]For DES we have $2^{56} \times 2^{64}$ instances if we consider the encryption of binary data. If we restrict ourselves to ASCII plaintexts, the number of different plaintexts only shifts from 2^{64} to 2^{56}.

[4]A tabu-list is a list of variables which have just been flipped and which cannot be immediately re-flipped

Table 2: Performance of Walk-SAT

R	B	% Succ	Kbits	Sec	# Bad
1	1	100%	31.4	0.03	-
1	2	100%	46.8	0.53	-
1	4	100%	52	1.67	-
1	8	100%	52.4	7.24	-
2	1	100%	53.8	21.8	-
2	2	100%	55.8	2.63	-
2	4	100%	56	3.16	-
2	8	100%	56	4.29	-
3	1	0%	-	1227.20	15.4
3	2	0%	-	3695.23	35.7

and the final result is reported in Table 2. R denotes the number of rounds on which DES has been limited and B the number of blocks which have been conjoined to produce the instance (to get the size of an instance, multiply the values of Table 1 for the number of blocks). Sec. is the average running time and Kbits tells on average how many bits of the solution found by Walk-SAT coincided with the known solution. For unsuccessful attempts we also report the lowest number of unsatisfied clauses found.

Walk-SAT can crack DES up to 2 rounds, and compares favorably with the results of SATO and TABLEAU reported in [Marraro & Massacci, 1999]. At three rounds Walk-SAT cannot crack any instance, even with a number of flips hundreds times the number of clauses and a few hundreds tries. Moreover, adding more constraints (blocks) makes the search harder and not easier.

Why doesn't Walk-SAT solve the problem well?

The first problem has been already pointed out in [Selman *et al.*, 1997]: the difficulty of local search algorithms to run around *dependent* variables. Recall that here almost all variables are dependent. The dagsat approach proposed in [Kautz *et al.*, 1997] might prove to be more successful.

The second problem is the presence of wide "rugged" plateaus at the bottom of the search space: the number of unsatisfied clauses goes quickly down from thousands to few tens per block and stays there, with Walk-SAT flipping (in vain) a lot of dependent variables and moving from a local minima to the next. The lowest number of bad clauses was decreased by re-engineering Walk-SAT as follows:

- the first time a local minimum is reached, its value is stored as a reference value and the search continues;

- after the search visited n local minima with value higher than the reference value, all keybits were randomly flipped (with a probability $\frac{1}{n}$ all variables were flipped);

- each time a lower minimum was reached, n was reset and that minimum considered the new reference value;

The idea was to escape the plateaus by exploiting the domain knowledge that the keybits were the only independent variables. In this way, the search converges to a much lower value of bad clauses (usually from 40-100 bad clauses per block to less than 10), but we are still stuck there.

Table 3: Performance of Rel-SAT

		General			No Learning		
R	B	Kbit	Branch	Sec	Kbit	Branch	Sec
1	1	31	28	0.02	-	-	-
1	2	49	104	0.11	-	-	-
1	4	51	104	0.22	53	112	4.44
1	8	52	83	0.45	53	184	6.18
2	1	54	20841	32.43	-	-	-
2	2	56	40122	111.15	-	-	-
2	4	56	4050	18.39	56	157	4.98
2	8	56	57	0.81	56	103	8.00
3	1	-	-	$\geq$ 1h	-		
3	2	56	173075	976.28	-		
3	4	56	19311	159.13	56	75538	$\geq$ 1h
3	8	56	3594	75.02	56	8153	822

5 Rel-SAT on DES

The second algorithm is a systematic one: Rel-SAT from [Bayardo & Schrag, 1997]. It is a variant of the Davis-Putnam algorithm, enhanced with conflict directed back-jumping and learning. It works as follows:

- unit propagation is applied to the clause set;

- if no contradiction is found a new literal is selected and added either positively or negatively to the clause set;

- if a contradiction is found then the algorithm backtracks to the literal that caused the contradiction;

- the clause responsible for the contradiction is resolved with a clause representing the temporary assignment; the resolvent is thus learned as a reason to avoid the corresponding assignment;

- the procedure is iterated until all literals have been assigned (SAT) or no backtrack is possible (UNSAT).

For more details see [Bayardo & Schrag, 1997].

The instance generation method, the architecture, and operating systems were the same used for Walk-SAT. Also in this case, the experiment started with the recommend standard: a small learning factor (4), using relevance-based learning.

Up to 2 rounds, Rel-SAT cracks DES only slightly faster than SATO and TABLEAU (see [Marraro & Massacci, 1999]) or Walk-SAT. However, it is the only algorithm which cracks three round of DES in less than ten minutes. Its performance is reported in Table 3. The success rate is omitted since either all instances could be solved or none could (-).

Other settings were tried: no learning at all and learning factors larger than 4. The analysis shows that learning is essential if we have few constraints but it might be skipped if enough constraints are around (Table 3). An intuitive explanation could be that with few blocks the algorithm might split on dependent variables and then discover that this was not necessary. With many constraints, standard heuristics select almost only independent variables and therefore learning contribution to performance is diminished.

Note that the performance of the algorithm improves with the number of blocks composing the instance. Adding more

constraints makes the search for the only (?) existing solution easier. This behavior is consistent with standard cryptographic techniques [Biham & Shamir, 1991; Matsui, 1994a] where having more data improves the chances of success.

Given this promising results, the algorithm has been engineered to accept larger formulae with more variables and tried on the full 16-round DES, also using 1, 2, and 4 blocks. The algorithm didn't return within 12 hours.

A small re-engineering of the algorithm was carried to exploit in a limited manner the knowledge of the domain. After a first selection of potential branching variables, a threshold is used in the original algorithm to reduce their number. The modified algorithm didn't check the threshold if the selected variable was a keybit. In this way the algorithm gives preferences to dependent variable with very good properties or independent variables with medium properties. However, the running time of the algorithm didn't improved substantially.

6 Lessons for SAT Solvers

It is a promising result that SAT solvers can crack a limited version of DES without using any problem-dependent heuristics but this is not enough. We want to solve the full DES.

The first temptation is then to dismiss the SAT solvers themselves: this problem has a non-clausal structure, so it has to be expected that CNF provers perform badly; the right tool should have been BDDs [Bryant, 1986]. Surprisingly, an extensive experimentation reported in [Ascione, 1999] shows that the BDDs cannot solve key search problems any better than SAT-based approaches.

The second conclusion might be that the problem is too constrained: at three rounds there is almost only one solution. This makes the problem harder for local search, but should make it easier for complete algorithms. Indeed, the very characteristics of DES with its avalanche effect (all keybits should affect all ciphertext bits, and a flip in the plaintext should affect all ciphertext bits, etc.) should make this problem easy: if the value of few keybits is wrongly chosen, a cascade of unit propagations should immediately generate an inconsistency. This would implies that formulae encoding more rounds (and more defined variables) should be easier and not harder. Since this is not the case, it seems that with more rounds unit propagation is somehow hindered.

Finding an explanation (and a workaround) for this difficulty is important because the structure of the encoding is common in many hard real problems: the natural formulation of a problem is usually structured in layers, makes use of abbreviations and definitions, and often contains modulo-2 arithmetics (xors). For instance see the parity bit problem mentioned in [Selman et al., 1997] and the IFIP benchmark for hardware verification.

If we look again at the structure of the encoding, we may notice that each round is separated by the next round by a level of xors and that most constraints are in form of xors: a large subpart of the problem is an affine problem, which should be polynomially solvable by Schaefer's theorem. It is precisely this affine subproblem that make the problem hard for current AI techniques. Look again at table 1: the problem becomes difficult as soon as xors start to appear.

In contrast, cryptographic techniques exploits this affine subproblem and even approximate the whole problem into an affine problem [Matsui, 1994a]. Therefore, to crack DES or similar real-word problem *a SAT solver needs the ability to solve affine subproblems*.

7 Conclusions and Future Challenges

In this paper we have seen an application of propositional reasoning and search to a key security problem of industrial relevance. We have also discussed how this approach can optimally provide "real-world" problems where many instances can be randomly generated.

Thus we believe that the whole approach on encoding cryptographic key search as propositional search can be a good answer to the final challenge proposed in [Selman *et al.*, 1997]:

> Develop a generator for problem instances that have computational properties that are more similar to real world instances.

Moreover, the preliminary tests on using SAT-solvers to crack the Data Encryption Standard are promising, although SAT-solvers must be improved to meet the full challenge provided by this benchmark. Thus, a good conclusion of this paper may just be the indication of the future challenges. They are listed in order of feasibility.

The first challenge is to find a key for the commercial 16 rounds Data Encryption Standard in less than 56 hours using off-the-shelf h/w and s/w but specialized search heuristics. This might be the simplest and immediately rewarding challenge, assuming that the 10,000 USD prize of RSA Security for breaking its DES challenges will be there in the year 2000.

Then we may wish to design SAT-solvers that work with every Feistel-type cipher with data independent rounds like DES. If we were able to cope with affine subproblems this would not be a big extension. Since the operations are data independent, a certain amount of preprocessing for the internal rounds could be done off-line.

The third challenge is to find efficient encodings into SAT of data-dependent Feistel-type ciphers like RC5 [Schneier, 1994]. A straightforward encoding is always possible: just translate the cipher into a circuit and this into propositional logic. Unfortunately this is already unworkable for DES.

Last but not least, we may wish to find efficient encodings into propositional (or any) logic of public-key algorithms such as RSA. This challenge, firstly proposed in [Cook and Mitchel, 1997], might prove to be the hardest since number theory is fairly remote from propositional logic.

As for all real problems, there might also be a darker side: the final measure of success might well be the "privilege" (!?) of successful SAT algorithms being denied export licenses as dangerous weapons.

References

[Anderson & Needham, 1996] R. Anderson & R. Needham. Programming satan's computer. In *Computer Science Today - Recent Trends and Developments*, LNCS 1000, pp. 426–440. Springer-Verlag, 1996.

[Andleman & Reeds, 1982] D. Andleman & J. Reeds. On the cryptanalysis of rotor machines and substitution-permutations networks. *IEEE Trans. on Inf. Theory*, 28(4):578–584, 1982.

[Ascione, 1999] M. Ascione. Validazione e benchmarking dei BDD per la criptanalisi del DES. Master's thesis, Facoltà di Ingegneria, Univ. di Roma I "La Sapienza", April 1999. In Italian.

[Bayardo & Schrag, 1997] R. Bayardo & R. Schrag. Using CSP look-back techniques to solve real-world SAT instances. in *Proc. of AAAI-97*. pp. 203–208. AAAI Press/The MIT Press, 1997.

[Biham & Shamir, 1991] E. Biham & A. Shamir. Differential cryptanalisis of DES-like cryptosystems. *J. of Cryptology*, 4(1):3–72, 1991.

[Bryant, 1986] R. Bryant. Graph-based algorithms for boolean function manipulation. *IEEE TOC*, 35(8):677–691, 1986.

[Crawford & Auton, 1996] J. Crawford & L. Auton. Experimental results on the crossover point in random 3SAT. *AIJ*, 81(1-2):31–57, 1996.

[Cook and Mitchel, 1997] S. Cook & D. Mitchel. Finding hard instances of the satisfiability problem: A survey. In *Satisfiability Problem: Theory and Applications*, DIMACS Series in Discr. Math. and TCS, 25:1–17. AMS, 1997.

[DES Search, 1998a] DES key search project information. Technical report, Cryptography Research Inc., 1998. Available on the web at http://www.cryptography.com/des/.

[Feistel *et al.*, 1975] H. Feistel, W. Notz, and L. Smith. Some cryptographic techniques for machine-to-machine data communication. *Proc. of the IEEE*, 63(11):1545–1554, 1975.

[G10, 1996] Committee on Payment, Settlement Systems, and the Group of Computer Experts of the Central Banks of the Group of Ten countries. *Security of Electronic Money*. Bank for International Settlements, Basle, August 1996.

[Kautz *et al.*, 1997] H. Kautz, D. McAllester, and & B. Selman. Exploiting Variable Dependency in Local Search Abstract in *Abstracts of the Poster Sessions of IJCAI-97*, 1997.

[Marraro & Massacci, 1999] L. Marraro & F. Massacci. A new challenge for automated reasoning: Verification and cryptanalysis of cryptographic algorithms. Tech. Rep. 5, Dip. di Informatica e Sistemistica, Univ. di Roma "La Sapienza", 1999.

[Matsui, 1994a] M. Matsui. The first experimental cryptanalysis of the Data Encryption Standard. In *Proc. of CRYPTO-94*, LNCS 839, pp. 1–11. Springer-Verlag, 1994.

[Matsui, 1994b] M. Matsui. Linear cryptanalysis method for des cipher. In *Proc. of Eurocrypt 93*, LNCS 765, pp. 368–397. Springer-Verlag, 1994.

[NIST, 1997] NIST. Data encryption standard. Federal Information Processing Standards Publications FIPS PUB 46-2, National (U.S.) Bureau of Standards, Dec 1997. Supersedes FIPS PUB 46-1 of Jan. 1988 and FIPS PUB 46 of Jan. 1977.

[OECD, 1998] OECD. Emerging market economy forum (EMEF): Report of the ministerial workshop on cryptography policy. OLIS SG/EMEF/ICCP(98)1, Organization for Economic Co-operation and Development, Paris, Feb 1998.

[Ryan & Schneider, 1998] P. Ryan & S. Schneider. An attack on a recurive authentication protocol: a cautionary tale. *IPL*, 65(15):7–16, 1998.

[Schneier, 1994] B. Schneier. *Applied Cryptography: Protocols, Algorithms, and Source Code in C*. John Wiley & Sons, 1994.

[Selman *et al.*, 1994] B. Selman, H. Kautz, and B. Cohen. Noise strategies for local search. In *Proc. of AAAI-94*, pp. 337–343. AAAI Press/The MIT Press, 1994.

[Selman *et al.*, 1997] B. Selman, H. Kautz, and D. McAllester. Ten challenges in propositional resoning and search. In *Proc. IJCAI-97*, pp. n50-54. Morgan Kaufmann, 1997.

SAT-Encodings, Search Space Structure, and Local Search Performance

Holger H. Hoos

University of British Columbia
Department of Computer Science
2366 Main Mall, Vancouver, B.C., Canada V6T 1Z4
hoos@cs.ubc.ca

Abstract

Stochastic local search (SLS) algorithms for propositional satisfiability testing (SAT) have become popular and powerful tools for solving suitably encoded hard combinatorial from different domains like, e.g., planning. Consequently, there is a considerable interest in finding SAT-encodings which facilitate the efficient application of SLS algorithms. In this work, we study how two encodings schemes for combinatorial problems, like the well-known Constraint Satisfaction or Hamilton Circuit Problem, affect SLS performance on the SAT-encoded instances. To explain the observed performance differences, we identify features of the induces search spaces which affect SLS performance. We furthermore present initial results of a comparitive analysis of the performance of the SAT-encoding and -solving approach versus that of native SLS algorithms directly applied to the unencoded problem instances.

1 Introduction

In the past few years, the development of extremely fast stochastic algorithms for the propositional satisfiability problem (SAT) have stirred considerable interest in the AI community. Modern stochastic local search algorithms, like WalkSAT and its more recent variants [McAllester et al., 1997], can solve hard instances with several thousand variables and ten thousands of clauses within minutes of computing time. While only a very few "real-world" problems come as instances of SAT, many of these are combinatorial problems with quite natural CSP-like formulations, which can be easily encoded into SAT. In practice, however, for solving problems by encoding them into SAT and applying state-of-the-art SAT solvers, one has to find encodings which cannot only be efficiently generated, but which are also efficiently solvable by the respective SAT-solvers. While recent successes in solving SAT-encoded planning problems suggest that such efficient encodings can be found, our understanding of how encodings affect the performance of modern SAT algorithms and how good encodings can be found is very limited. "Characterizing the computational properties of different encodings of a real-world problem domain, and/or giving general principles that hold over a range of domains" has

therefore been proposed as a challenge for propositional reasoning at IJCAI'97 [Selman et al., 1997].

We approach this problem by studying the impact of encoding strategies on search space structure and the performance of stochastic local search (SLS) algorithms. In particular, we investigate the following questions:

1. Does it pay off to minimise the number of propositional variables, *i.e.*, are compact encodings which achieve small search spaces preferable to the bigger, but conceptually simpler sparse encodings?

2. Is the generic problem solving approach using SAT-encodings and modern SLS algorithms for SAT competitive with applying SLS algorithms to the un-encoded problem instances?

Our investigation is based on two case-studies, covering sets of hard instances of the NP-hard Constraint Satisfaction Problem (CSP) and Hamilton Circuit Problem (HCP). Building on earlier work on search space structure and SLS performance [Clark et al., 1996; Yokoo, 1997; Frank et al., 1997] and SAT encodings [Ernst et al., 1997], we empirically analyse the impact of different encoding strategies on SLS performance and provide explanations for our observations by identifying search space features correlated with the observed SLS performance. Furthermore, we compare the performance of SLS algorithms on the best SAT-encoding of hard random binary CSP encodings with the performance of the best known native CSP algorithm based on stochastic local search.

As a preview of the results presented in the next sections, we briefly summarise our answers to the questions from above — however, given the general nature of these questions and the limited scope of the underlying empirical evidence these answers are tentative and should be understood as testable hypotheses.

1. According to our results for CSP and HCP, it seems to be much more advisable to use sparse rather than compact encodings, as the search spaces produced by the compact encodings are smaller but have characteristic features which impede local search.

2. When comparing the performance of SLS algorithms for CSP and SLS-based SAT algorithms applied to SAT-encoded CSPs, we observe a surprisingly small advantage for the direct CSP solving approach, which is outweighed by other advantages of the generic SAT-

encoding and solving approach such as the availability of very efficient implementations.

The remainder of this paper is structured in the following way. Section 2 gives some background on SLS algorithms for SAT and introduces the problems classes and test-sets used for our empirical analysis. Section 3 reviews previous work on search space structure and its impact on SLS performance and presents our approach to search space structure analysis. Sections 4–6 present the empirical investigations of the three questions from above, and Section 7 contains some conclusions and points out directions for future research.

2 Background

Stochastic local search approaches for SAT became prominent in 1992, when independently Selman, Levesque, and Mitchell [Selman *et al.*, 1992] as well as Gu [Gu, 1992] introduced algorithms based on stochastic local hill-climbing which could be shown to outperform state-of-the-art systematic SAT algorithms on a variety of hard subclasses of SAT. Since then, numerous other SLS schemes for SAT have been proposed. To date, state-of-the-art SLS algorithms can solve hard SAT problems up to several thousand variables, including SAT-encoded problems from other domains. In the recent past, especially the successful applications of SLS-based SAT algorithms for solving SAT-encoded planning problems, have stirred considerable interest in the AI community [Kautz and Selman, 1996; Ernst *et al.*, 1997; Kautz and Selman, 1998].

The algorithms considered here are model finding algorithms for CNF formulae. The underlying state space is always defined as the set of all assignments for the variables appearing in the given formula. Local search steps modify at most the value assigned to one of the propositional variables appearing in the formula; such a move is called a *variable flip*. The objective function is generally defined as the number of clauses which are unsatisfied under a given variable assignment; thus, the models of the given formula correspond to the global minima of this function. The general idea for finding these is to perform stochastic hill-climbing on the objective function, starting from a randomly generated initial assignment.

The main difference between the individual algorithms lies in the strategy used to select the variable to be flipped next. In this paper, we focus on the well-known WalkSAT family of algorithms [McAllester *et al.*, 1997], which provided a substantial driving force for the development of SLS algorithms for SAT and have been extremely successful when applied to a broad range of problems from different domains. WalkSAT algorithms start from a randomly chosen variable assignment and repeatedly select one of the clauses which are violated by the current assignment. Then, according to some heuristic a variable occurring in this clause is flipped using a greedy bias to increase the total number of satisfied clauses. For the original WalkSAT algorithm, in the following referred to simply as WalkSAT, the following heuristic is applied. If in the selected clause variables can be flipped without violating other clauses, one of these is randomly chosen. Otherwise, with a fixed probability p a variable is randomly chosen from the clause and with probability $1-p$ a variable is picked which minimises the number of clauses which are currently satisfied but would become violated by the variable's flip (number of breaks). The walk probability p (also called the *noise parameter*) has an important influence on the algorithms' overall performance. In this paper, we always use approximately optimal noise parameter settings for evaluating SLS performance; these settings are experimentally determined such that they minimise the expected number of flips for solving the given problem instance.

For the empirical study presented here, we use two well-known classes of combinatorial problems: Random binary Constrained Satisfaction Problems (CSPs) and Random Hamilton Circuit Problems (HCPs). Both binary CSPs and HCPs form NP-complete problem classes. Random binary CSPs have been studied extensively by various researchers, especially in the context of phase transition phenomena and their impact on the performance of CSP algorithms [Smith and Dyer, 1996; Prosser, 1996]. To obtain a test-set of hard problem instances, CSP instances with 20 variables and domain size 10 were sampled from the phase transition region characterised by a constraint graph density of $\alpha = 0.5$ and a constraint tightness of $\beta = 0.38$. Filtering out the insoluble instances with a complete CSP algorithm, test-set `csp20-10`, containing 100 soluble instances from this problem distribution, was generated.

For empirically investigating SLS performance for different SAT-encodings of the HCP, we focussed on the Hamilton Circuit Problem in directed random graphs. For a given graph, the HCP is to find a cyclic tour (Hamilton Circuit) using the edges of the graph which visits every vertex exactly once. In earlier work, when investigating the dependence of the existence of Hamilton Circuits on the average connectivity (edges per vertex), a phase transition phenomenon was observed [Cheeseman *et al.*, 1991]. The associated peak in hardness for backtracking algorithms was located between $\kappa = e/(n \log n) \approx 0.9$ and 1.2, where n is the number of vertices and e the number of edges [Frank and Martel, 1995]. Based on these results, we created a test-set by randomly sampling soluble HCP instances from distributions of directed random graphs with $n = 10$ and $\kappa = 1$. The test-set was generated using a HCP generator and solver developed and provided by Joe Culberson; insoluble instances were filtered out using the integrated systematic HCP solver, such that the final test-set `hcp10` contains 100 soluble instances.

3 Search Space Structure and SLS Performance

Obviously, the behaviour of SLS algorithms is determined by the topology of the search space, *i.e.*, the objective function induced by a specific problem instance. Recently, a growing number of researchers have been investigating the nature of this dependency for SLS-based SAT algorithms [Clark *et al.*, 1996; Yokoo, 1997; Frank *et al.*, 1997]. However, all of the studies we are aware of are restricted to Random-3-SAT, a widely used class of randomly generated SAT problems, while SAT-encoded problems from other domains have not been addressed. In [Clark *et al.*, 1996], it has been shown that for a given problem instance, its number of solutions is strongly negatively correlated with the performance of some SLS algorithms for SAT and CSP based on hill-climbing. This confirms the intuition that instances with a high solution density, *i.e.*, a large number of solutions, tend to be much easier to solve for SLS algorithms than instances with very few solutions. [Yokoo, 1997] explains the peak in local search cost observed at the phase-transition region of Random-3-SAT in terms of the number and size of local minima regions in the search space. His analysis, however, relies on an exhaustive analyses of the search space and is therefore restricted to very small problem instances. [Frank *et al.*, 1997] analyse the topology of search spaces induced by Random-3-SAT formulae, but do not investigate the concrete impact of these features (such as the size of local minima) on SLS performance.

The approach taken here is to compare both the impact of encoding strategies on SLS performance as well as to provide explanations of the observed correlation in terms of search space features induced by the different encodings. To be not restricted to very small problem instances which possibly do not reflect the typical situation as encountered for realistic problems (*i.e.*, instances which can be solved with state-of-the art SLS algorithms), we restrict our analysis to features with can be determined without exhaustive search of large parts of the search space. The features we measure are:

- the solution density (number of solutions/search space size);

- the standard deviation of the objective function (*sdnclu*);

- the local minima branching along SLS trajectories (*blmin*).

As the solution density is known to be an important factor for SLS performance, it should be taken into account although it is generally time-consuming to measure. For counting the number of solutions of a given problem instance, we applied a modified version of the ASAT algorithm [Dubois *et al.*, 1993] to the SAT-encoded instances. To our best knowledge, both *sdnclu* and *blmin* have not been studied before in the context of search space structure.

Intuitively, large *sdnlcu* values should indicate a rugged search space structure for which SLS approaches based on hill-climbing are more effective than for featureless, flat search spaces with many plateaus. To measure *sdnclu* values, we determine the objective function value (number of unsatisfied clauses) for a sample of 100,000 randomly chosen assignments. To improve comparability of the results for different numbers of clauses, we scale objective function values to the interval $[0, 1]$ (by division by the number of clauses). The *sdnclu* value is then computed as the empirical standard deviation over this sample. Although compared to the search space sizes of our test instances the sample size is very small, we get meaningful results — presumably because of the global effects of the encoding strategies on search space topology.

Since it is known that the number and size of local minima plays an important role for SLS performance on Random-3-SAT [Yokoo, 1997], we extended these results by studying the structure of local minima regions. We do this by measuring the average branching of local minima states, *i.e.*, for a given variable assignment, the number of neighbouring assignments[1] with the same objective function value. The

underlying intuition is that highly branched local minima regions are more difficult to escape from, as there are fewer escape routes for random walk and similar plateau escape techniques, but more possibilities for non-deterministic loops to occur in the search trajectory. Local minima states are typically quite rare for the problem instances studied here; thus, *blmin* cannot be measured by randomly sampling the search space. Instead we sampled the local minima states along SLS trajectories, using a sample size of 100,000. Again, to improve comparability of the results between different problem instances, we scale the values thus obtained to the interval $[0, 1]$ (by division by the number of variables).

For a given problem instance, WalkSAT's performance (denoted as *lsc* — local search cost) is measured as the expected number of flips per solution, determined from 100–1,000 runs per instance using an approximately optimal noise setting (see above) and a cutoff parameter high enough to guarantee that in every run a solution was found. [2]

4 Compact versus Sparse Encodings

Many combinatorial problems, such as Number Partitioning, Bin Packing, or Hamilton Circuit, can be quite naturally formulated as discrete constraint satisfaction problems. When encoding such CSP formulations into SAT, perhaps the most intuitive way is to encode each assignment of a value to a CSP variable by a different propositional variable [de Kleer, 1989]. We call this the *sparse encoding*, since it results in relatively sparse constraint graphs[3] for the resulting CNF formulae. This encoding strategy requires $|D| \cdot n$ variables, where $|D|$ is the domain size and n the number of CSP variables.[4]

Given the intuition that high solution densities should facilitate local search (see above), it seems to be worthwhile to consider encodings which minimise the number of propositional variables, and therefore the potential search space size without affecting the number of solutions. One encoding strategy which achieves that is the *compact encoding* obtained by representing each value assignment to a CSP variable binarily using a set of $\lceil log_2|D| \rceil$ propositional variables. Compared to the sparse encoding, this strategy significantly reduces the search space by a factor of $O(n \cdot (|D| - log|D|))$, while the number of clauses is usually similar, as it is usually dominated by clauses encoding the constraint relations (the number of which is identical for both encodings). The compact encoding is well-known from the literature; it has been proposed in the context of SAT variable complexity by [Iwama and Miyazaki, 1994] and is also used in the SAT-based MEDIC planning system, where it is called "factored representation" [Ernst *et al.*, 1997].

To investigate the impact of these two encoding schemes on SLS performance we measured WalkSAT's performance

---

[1]The neighbourhood relation is the same as used by all GSAT-type algorithms, *i.e.*, two assignments are neighbours if and only if they differ in the truth value of exactly one variable.

[2]Our actual experimental methodology is based on measuring run-time distributions (RTDs) as outlined in [Hoos and Stützle, 1998]; the RTD data is not reported here, but can be obtained from the author. A more detailed description of the empirical study and its results can be found in [Hoos, 1998] and will be presented in more detail in an extended version of this paper.

[3]The constraint graph consists of one node for each propositional variable and edges between nodes corresponding to variables which occur together in some clause of the given CNF formula.

[4]For simplicity's sake we assume that the domain sizes for all CSP variables are identical.

on the test-sets of Random Binary CSP and HCP instances described above. The HCP instances are encoded as CSPs by focussing on vertex permutations of the given graph as solution candidates (this idea has been proposed in [Iwama and Miyazaki, 1994]); in particular, for each vertex v we introduce a CSP variable the value of which represents v's position in the permutation. The constraint relations ensure that each vertex appears exactly once (type 1 constraints), *i.e.*, the candidate solution corresponds to a valid permutation of the vertices, and that each pair of neighbouring vertices in this (cyclic) permutation is connected by an edge in the given graph (type 2 constraints).

Figure 1 shows the correlation of the average local search cost (*lsc*) between the different encodings across the test-set `csp20-10`; each data point corresponds to the *lsc* for the sparse *vs* the compact encoding for one problem instance from the original test-set. As can be seen from the scatter plot, there is a strong linear correlation between the logarithm's average local search cost for both encodings (correlation coefficient $r = 0.95$), *i.e.*; instances which are relatively hard for WalkSAT when sparsely encoded also tend to be hard when using the compact encoding. But this analysis also shows that the compact encoding results in instances for which the *lsc* is generally ca. 7 times higher than for the corresponding sparsely encoded instances, although the compact encoding requires less then half the number of variables and significantly fewer clauses than the sparse encoding (*cf.* Table 1). This confirms earlier observations [Ernst *et al.*, 1997] that the compact encoding generates problem instances which are typically extremely hard for stochastic local search.

But what exactly makes this encoding so ineffective? Table 1 shows the solution density, *sdnclu*, and *blmin* values for the easiest, median, and hardest (w.r.t. their *lsc* values for WalkSAT) problem instance from the test-set `csp20-10`. The data confirms that within the test-set, the solution density is the predominant factor affecting local search cost, as earlier observed for Random-3-SAT test-sets [Clark *et al.*, 1996]. However, between the two encodings, this does not hold. Instead, the *sdcnlu* and the *blmin* values indicate that the compact encoding induces a flatter, featureless search space topology characterised by considerably higher branched local minima states. As argued above, intuitively this makes local search more difficult, which is consistent with the considerably higher local search cost observed for WalkSAT on the correspondingly encoded CSP instances. Interestingly, this explanation is also quite consistent with the (relatively big) differences in local search cost within the corresponding test-sets, although the relatively small differences in *sdcnlu* and *blmin* seem to confirm the predominant role of the solution density.

Applying the same analysis to sparsely and compactly encoded versions of the HCP test-set `hcp10` gives exactly analogous results (*cf.* Table 1); the correlation coefficient for the correlation between log(*lsc*) for -s and -c is 0.85) and thus confirms our observations and interpretation given above. Apparently, the compact encoding induces rather flat, featureless search spaces which impede local search and local minima escape to such an extent that WalkSAT's performance is significantly reduced despite the much higher solution density achieved by reducing the number of variables.

There is, however, another factor to be considered. The

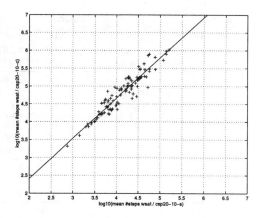

Figure 1: Correlation of average local search cost per instance between sparse (horizontal) and compact SAT-encoding (vertical) for CSP instances from test-set `csp20-10` when using WalkSAT with approx. optimal noise.

CPU-time required for each single flip performed by Walk-SAT is roughly constant for a given problem instance; it depends, however, considerably on the syntactical features of the given formula (especially number and length of clauses). Comparing the CPU-time per variable flip between the formulae generated by the sparse and compact encoding schemes reveals that for the compact encoding also the CPU-time per flip is significantly higher (for both, `csp20-10-c` and `hcp10-c` instances approximately by a factor of 3) than for the sparse encoding. This can be explained by the fact that the compact encoding produces longer and more tightly connected clauses (in terms of number of clauses which share at least one variable with any given clause), such that each variable flip affects potentially more clauses (by breaking or fixing them). So the compact encoding induces both, a syntactic structure (the longer and more tightly connected clauses) and a semantic structure (the search space features discussed above) which reduce WalkSAT's performance by increasing the CPU-time per search step and decreasing the efficiency of these search steps.

5   To Encode or Not to Encode?

The results presented in the preceeding sections suggest that when solving combinatorial problems by encoding them into SAT and applying powerful SLS algorithms, there might be a tradeoff between the size of the representation and SLS performance. Apparently compact encodings can be used to generate formulae with small search spaces; however, these have characteristic features which impede the performance of WalkSAT and similar SAT algorithms. One obvious question therefore is the following. Given a formulation of a combinatorial problem as a CSP, should we encode into SAT at all, or rather apply SLS algorithms for CSP to directly solve the unencoded problem?

Here, we present some initial results on this question. Specifically, we analyse the correlation between the performance of WalkSAT and an WMCH, an analogous algorithm for CSP which is based on the Min Conflicts Heuristic [Minton *et al.*, 1992] and has been introduced in [Steinmann *et al.*, 1997]. Like WalkSAT, WMCH is a SLS algorithm

instance	encoding	variables	clauses	avg. lsc	num sln	sln density	$sdnclu$	$blmin$
csp20-10-s/easy	sparse	200	3,661	775.80	37,297	$2.01 \cdot 10^{-56}$	0.0366	0.015
csp20-10-s/med	sparse	200	4,367	11,162.69	6	$3.73 \cdot 10^{-60}$	0.0361	0.017
csp20-10-s/hard	sparse	200	4,412	134,777.38	2	$1.24 \cdot 10^{-60}$	0.0356	0.017
csp20-10-c/easy	compact	80	2,861	2,249.19	37,297	$3.09 \cdot 10^{-20}$	0.0011	0.131
csp20-10-c/med	compact	80	3,555	77,883.52	6	$4.96 \cdot 10^{-24}$	0.0011	0.157
csp20-10-c/hard	compact	80	3,612	1,000,456.82	2	$1.65 \cdot 10^{-24}$	0.0011	0.161
hc10-s/easy	sparse	100	1,060	215.97	60	$4.73 \cdot 10^{-29}$	0.0504	0.059
hc10-s/med	sparse	100	1,060	781.28	20	$1.58 \cdot 10^{-29}$	0.0502	0.056
hc10-s/hard	sparse	100	1,060	2,562.18	20	$1.58 \cdot 10^{-29}$	0.0502	0.047
hc10-c/easy	compact	40	1,110	548.37	60	$5.46 \cdot 10^{-11}$	0.0017	0.187
hc10-c/med	compact	40	1,110	1,258.55	20	$1.82 \cdot 10^{-11}$	0.0017	0.181
hc10-c/hard	compact	40	1,110	3,294.71	20	$1.82 \cdot 10^{-11}$	0.0016	0.172

Table 1: Easy, median, and hard problem instances from compactly and sparsely encoded CSP and HCP test-sets; the table shows the size of the instances, the expected local search cost for WalkSAT (in steps/solution, using approx. optimal noise), as well as the number of solutions, solution density, normalised $sdnclu$ and average $blmin$ value (for details, see text).

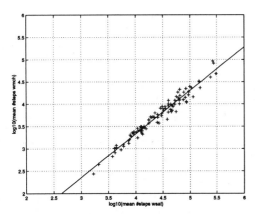

Figure 2: Correlation of average local search cost per instance for WalkSAT *vs* WMCH applied to test-set `csp20-10`; both algorithms use approx. optimal noise, WalkSAT is used with the sparse SAT-encoding.

which iteratively repairs violated constraints following the steepest gradient, but also allows to escape from local minima of the objective function by allowing occasional, randomised uphill moves (for details, see [Steinmann *et al.*, 1997]). Like for WalkSAT, the local search cost (lsc) for WMCH was measured as the expected number of local search steps to find a solution, based on 100 runs of the algorithm for each given problem instance. Generally, we always used approximately optimal noise parameter settings and a cutoff parameter high enough to guarantee that in every run a solution was found.

Analysing the correlation between the average local search cost for WalkSAT (using the sparse encoding) and WMCH across the test-set `csp20-10` reveals an extremely strong linear correlation between the logarithms of the average local search cost for both algorithms (*cf.* Figure 2; correlation coefficient $r = 0.98$), *i.e.*, instances which are relatively hard for WalkSAT also tend to be hard for WMCH and vice versa. A linear regression analysis of this data shows that WalkSAT tends to require ca. 5 times more steps than WMCH for solving the problem instances from our test-set (the coefficients of the regression analysis are $a = 0.98$ and $b = -0.57$).

However, neither WalkSAT nor WMCH are the best known SLS algorithms for SAT and CSP, respectively. We therefore performed the same analysis for the best-performing SLS-based SAT algorithm and the best SLS-based CSP algorithm we are aware of — Novelty [McAllester *et al.*, 1997], one of the most recent variants of WalkSAT, and the tabu search algorithm by Galinier and Hao [Galinier and Hao, 1997].[5] Using optimal noise parameters for both algorithms, we find that when measuring the average number of local search steps per solution, Galinier's and Hao's CSP algorithm has generally only an advantage of a factor between 2 and 4 over Novelty. The correlation between both algorithm's performance is very strong (*cf.* Figure 3; correlation coefficient = 0.96); however, Novelty occasionally gets stuck in local optima which it cannot escape (causing the outliers in the scatter plot 7 instances), while the CSP algorithm shows no such behaviour. But this happens only for 7 of our 100 instances and for these only in a small number of the multiple tries we performed. We conjecture that by exending Novelty with a stronger stochastic escape mechanism, this phenomenon can be eliminated. But except for these outliers, the regression analysis indicates that both algorithms show approximately the same scaling behaviour w.r.t. instance hardness. This is somewhat surprising, since Galinier's and Hao's algorithm and Novelty are conceptually significantly less closely related than WMCH and WalkSAT. When performing an exactly analogous analysis for instances with 30 constraint variables and 10 values, we find a similar situation; only now, the performance advantage of the native CSP algorithm over Novelty is only a factor of ca. 1.7 on average (comparing the number of local search steps). Also, we observe no increased occurence of the outliers mentioned above. This suggests that when increasing the problem size, the SAT-based approach might have a slight scaling advantage over the native CSP algorithm.

Generally, our results from comparing the performance of SLS-based algorithms for CSP and SAT indicate that when measuring the average number of steps per solution, the dif-

---

[5]The considerably more complicated R-Novelty algorithm [McAllester *et al.*, 1997] for SAT, which shows an even better performance than Novelty on Random-3-SAT, is inferior to Novelty for the random binary CSPs used here.

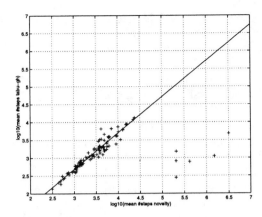

Figure 3: Correlation of average local search cost per instance for Novelty *vs* Galinier's and Hao's tabu search algorithm for CSP applied to test-set `csp20-10`; all algorithms use approx. optimal noise, Novelty is used with the sparse SAT-encoding.

ferences are rather surprisingly small. We deliberately refrained from comparing CPU-times for these algorithms, because the implementations for the SAT algorithms are significantly more optimised. The SAT algorithms generally have the advantage that they are conceptually easier, which facilitates their efficient implementation, evaluation, and further development. Of course, our analysis is too limited to give a conclusive answer, but the results reported here suggest that for solving hard CSP instances, encoding them into SAT and using a state-of-the-art SLS algorithm for SAT to solve the SAT-encoded instances might be very competitive compared to using more specialised SLS-based CSP solvers.

6   Conclusions and Future Work

In this paper we presented an initial investigation of how SAT-encoding strategies affect the topological structure of the induced search spaces and SLS performance. Our empirical results show that for two well-known classes of NP-hard combinatorial problems, random binary CSPs and HCPs in random directed graphs near the solubility phase transition, compact SAT-encodings, which minimise the number of propositional variables for the encoded problem instances, exhibit structural features which impede local search algorithms like WalkSAT. This observation is consistent with earlier observations for planning problems and HCPs, that compact encodings are extremely hard to solve for SLS algorithms. At the same time, it shows that the influence of solution density on SLS performance which has been observed for CSP and SAT, is of minor significance compared to features like the overall ruggedness of the search space (as measured by the standard deviation of the objective function) or the local minima branching. However, consistently with earlier results, it plays an important role in explaining the differences in SLS performance observed across test-sets of randomly generated instances, when using a fixed SAT-encoding. As a consequence of these results, compact encodings should be avoided in the context of using SLS algorithms for solving SAT-encoded combinatorial problems.

Furthermore, when comparing the performance of SLS algorithms directly applied to test-sets of random binary CSP

instances to with the performance of SLS-based algorithms for SAT using the sparse encoding, we found that there is a strong correlation of the expected number of search steps required for finding a solution across the test-set. Although when comparing the best known SLS algorithms for CSP and SAT in this way, the direct CSP algorithm requires fewer local search steps per solution, we feel that this might very well be outweighed by other advantages of the SAT-encoding and solving approach, like the availability of extremely fast implementations or its conceptual simplicity. Also, due to the restrictions of the implementatins of the SAT-based CSP algorithms available for this preliminary study only binary CSP instances could be analysed. For more structured, nonebinary CSP instance, one might encounter a different situation; although it is not clear that (a) existing CSP algorithms can exploit this structure, and (b) even if they could, the same would not also be possible without too much effort for the SAT-encoded problem instances.

It should also be noted that, according to the results reported here and elsewhere [Ernst *et al.*, 1997; Kautz and Selman, 1996], it seems that finding efficient SAT-encodings could very well be significantly easier than developping specialised algorithms for the respective domains. We do not believe that the generic problem solving approach based on SAT-encodings and extremely optimised SAT-algorithms will generally be competitive with specialised algorithms which make use of domain knowledge. However, it is quite possible that it can be established as another generic method for attacking problems for which domain-specific knowledge is not (yet) available or which are too specific and limited in their application to make the development of specialised algorithms worthwhile. In this sense, the SAT-encoding and -solving approach could be compared to other generic problem solving methods, like, e.g., Mixed Integer Programming (MIP), which has become a standard generic solving technique for combinatorial problems in Operations Research.

The novel tools and techniques presented here can be easily applied to other hard combinatorial problems and SAT-encoding schemes. Out investigation can be extended in various directions; in particular, it provides a basis for studying the following research questions:

- Based on the knowledge of the search space structure induced by specific encoding schemes, can we design SAT algorithms which exploit these features?

- Given the knowledge about which features affect SLS performance, can we devise efficient encoding strategies which improve SLS performance?

- For which problem classes is the SAT-encoding and -solving approach, using SLS algorithms for SAT, competitive with analogous, generic SLS algorithms directly applied to the unencoded problem instances?

Thus, while this study does certainly not provide the final answers to the challenge or the more specific questions stated in Section 1, it shows a way for systematically investigating the relation between encodings, search space structure, and SLS performance which will hopefully lead to improved encodings and SAT algorithms, as well as, in the long run, to a realistic assessment of the generic SAT-encoding and -solving approach for solving hard combinatorial problems.

Acknowledgements

The CSP instances used for the experimental part of this paper were generated using software provided by Thomas Stützle whom I also wish to thank for many interesting and stimulating discussions. Furthermore, I thank Bart Selman for his encouraging comments on an earlier version of this paper as well as Wolfgang Bibel and the Intellectics Group at TU Darmstadt for their support during a significant part of this work. Finally, I gratefully acknowledge valuable input by David Poole and the members of the Laboratory of Computational Intelligence at the University of British Columbia. This research was partially supported IRIS Phase-III Project BOU, "Preference Elicitation and Interactive Optimization."

References

[Cheeseman et al., 1991] P. Cheeseman, B. Kanefsky, and W. Taylor. Where the Really Hard Problems Are. In *Proc. IJCAI'91*, pages 331–337, 1991.

[Clark et al., 1996] D. Clark, J. Frank, I. Gent, E. MacIntyre, N. Tomov, and T. Walsh. Local Search and the Number of Solutions. In *Proc. CP'96*, LNCS, vol. 1118 , pages 119–133. Springer Verlag, 1996.

[Dubois et al., 1993] O. Dubois, P. Andre, Y. Boufkhad, and J. Carlier. SAT versus UNSAT. In *2nd DIMACS Implementation Challenge*, 1993.

[de Kleer, 1989] J. de Kleer. A Comparison of ATMS and CSP Techniques. In *Proc. IJCAI'89*. Morgan Kaufmann, 1989.

[Ernst et al., 1997] M. Ernst, T. Millstein, and D. Weld. Automatic SAT-Compilation of Planning Problems. In *Proc. IJCAI-97*, 1997.

[Frank and Martel, 1995] J. Frank C. Martel. Phase Transitions in the Properties of Random Graphs. In *CP'95 Workshop on Studying and Solving Really Hard Problems*, 1995.

[Frank et al., 1997] J. Frank, P. Cheeseman, and J. Stutz. When Gravity Fails: Local Search Topology. *JAIR*, 7:249–281, 1997.

[Galinier and Hao, 1997] P. Galinier and J. Hao. Tabu Search For Maximal Constraint Satisfaction Problems. In *Proc. CP'97*, LNCS, vol. 1330, pages 196–208. Springer Verlag, 1997.

[Gu, 1992] J. Gu. Efficient Local Search for Very Large-scale Satisfiability Problems. *ACM SIGART Bulletin*, 3(1):8–12, 1992.

[Hoos, 1998] Hoos, H. H. 1998. *Stochastic Local Search — Methods, Models, Applications*. Ph.D. Dissertation, Fachbereich Informatik, Technische Universität Darmstadt.

[Hoos and Stützle, 1998] H. H. Hoos and T. Stützle. Evaluating Las Vegas algorithms — pitfalls and remedies. In *Proc. UAI'98*, 1998.

[Iwama and Miyazaki, 1994] K. Iwama and S. Miyazaki. SAT-Variable Complexity of Hard Combinatorial Problems. In *Proc. IFIP World Computer Congress*, pages 253–258. Elsevier Science B.V., North Holland, 1994.

[Kautz and Selman, 1996] H. Kautz and B. Selman. Pushing the Envelope: Planning, Propositional Logic, and Stochastic Search. In *Proc. AAAI'96*, volume 2, pages 1194–1201, 1996.

[Kautz and Selman, 1998] H. Kautz and B. Selman. The role of Domain-specific Knowledge in the Planning as Satisfiability Framework. In . *Proc. AIPS-98*, 1998.

[McAllester et al., 1997] D. McAllester, B. Selman, and H. Kautz. Evidence for Invariants in Local Search. In *Proc. AAAI'97*, pages 321–326, 1997.

[Minton et al., 1992] S. Minton, M.D. Johnston, A.B. Philips, and P. Laird. Minimizing Conflicts: A Heuristic Repair Method for Constraint Satisfaction and Scheduling Problems. *Artificial Intelligence*, 52:161–205, 1992.

[Prosser, 1996] P. Prosser. An Empirical Study of Phase Transitions in Binary Constraint Satisfaction Problems. *Artificial Intelligence*, 81:81–109, 1996.

[Selman et al., 1992] B. Selman, H. Levesque, and D. Mitchell. A New Method for Solving Hard Satisfiability Problems. In *Proc. AAAI'92*, pages 440–446, 1992.

[Selman et al., 1997] B. Selman, H. Kautz, and D. McAllester. Ten Challenges in Propositional Reasoning and Search. In *Proc. IJCAI-97*, 1997.

[Smith and Dyer, 1996] B. Smith and M. Dyer. Locating the Phase Transition in Binary Constraint Satisfaction Problems. *Artificial Intelligence*, 81:155–181, 1996.

[Steinmann et al., 1997] O. Steinmann, A. Strohmaier, and T. Stützle. Tabu Search vs. Random Walk. In *Advances in Artificial Intelligence (KI-97)*, LNAI, vol. 1303, pages 337–348. Springer Verlag, 1997.

[Yokoo, 1997] M. Yokoo. Why Adding More Constraints Makes a Problem Easier for Hill-Climbing Algorithms: Analyzing Landscapes of CSPs. In *Proc. CP'97*, LNCS, vol. 1330, pages 357–370. Springer Verlag, 1997.

CHALLENGE PAPERS

Challenge Papers 3:
Propositional Reasoning and Search/Planning

On the Use of Integer Programming Models in AI Planning

Thomas Vossen   Michael Ball
Robert H. Smith School of Business
and Institute for Systems Research
University of Maryland
College Park, MD 20742   USA
{tvossen, mball}@rhsmith.umd.edu

Amnon Lotem   Dana Nau
Department of Computer Science
and Institute for Systems Research
University of Maryland
College Park, MD 20742   USA
{lotem, nau}@cs.umd.edu

Abstract

Recent research has shown the promise of using propositional reasoning and search to solve AI planning problems. In this paper, we further explore this area by applying Integer Programming to solve AI planning problems. The application of Integer Programming to AI planning has a potentially significant advantage, as it allows quite naturally for the incorporation of numerical constraints and objectives into the planning domain. Moreover, the application of Integer Programming to AI planning addresses one of the challenges in propositional reasoning posed by Kautz and Selman, who conjectured that the principal technique used to solve Integer Programs—the linear programming (LP) relaxation—is not useful when applied to propositional search.

We discuss various IP formulations for the class of planning problems based on STRIPS-style planning operators. Our main objective is to show that a carefully chosen IP formulation significantly improves the "strength" of the LP relaxation, and that the resultant LPs *are* useful in solving the IP and the associated planning problems. Our results clearly show the importance of choosing the "right" representation, and more generally the promise of using Integer Programming techniques in the AI planning domain.

1   Introduction

Although some of the application areas addressed in the fields of Artificial Intelligence (AI) and Operations Research (OR) are very similar (e.g., planning, scheduling), the techniques that are used to solve these problems are oftentimes substantially different. Therefore, it seems only natural that recent research in the interface between AI and OR has focused on comparing the relative merits of the techniques and tools that are used in these areas. In this paper, we further explore the interface between AI and OR by applying Integer Programming (IP), which has a rich history in OR, to a classical AI problem, AI planning.

The possibility of using OR techniques in AI planning has not received much attention so far. Bylander [1997] uses Linear Programming as a heuristic for nonlinear planning; Bockmayr and Dimopoulos [1998] describe domain-dependent IP models for specific problem domains; and Kautz and Walser [1999], who use IP formulations for planning problems with resources, action costs, and complex objective functions. However, theirs is the only work we know of besides ours.

One potential advantage of using Integer Programming for AI planning is that IP formulations quite naturally allow the incorporation of numeric constraints and objectives into planning domains(for example, see Kautz and Walser [1999]). The use of numerical constraints and objectives is not addressed adequately in most existing AI planning systems, but it is critical in real-world planning [Nau *et al.*, 1998].

One difficulty indeveloping Integer Programming formulations for AI planning is that the performance of the resulting IP will depend critically on *how* AI planning problems are formulated as Integer Programs. The purpose of this paper is therefore to develop good domain-independent IP formulations for AI planning. In particular, we discuss various IP formulations for the class of action-based planning problems using STRIPS-style operators. Our main objective is to show that a carefully chosen IP formulation significantly improves the "strength" of the LP relaxation, so that it can provide useful guidance in solving the problem.

Our IP formulations are principally derived from work by Kautz and Selman [1996], which showed that planning problems can be efficiently solved by general propositional satifiablity algorithms. As such, the use of Integer Programming also addresses one of the challenges posed in the paper "Ten Challenges in Propositional Reasoning and Search," by Selman *et al.* [1997]. Specifically, the challenge that we address concerns the development of IP models and methods for propositional reasoning. Selman *et al.* mention that the basic technique used to solve integer programs—that is, the Linear Programming (LP) relaxation of the problem—does not appear to be useful for satisfiability problems, since it usually sets all variables (modulo unit propagation) to the value $\frac{1}{2}$ and therefore does not guide the selection of variables in solving the problem.

Our results are as follows:

- In our experiments, IP formulations derived directly from SAT encodings proposed by Kautz and Selman [1996] performed rather poorly—but an alternative IP formulation that we call the "state-change formulation" was competitive with BlackBox using the systematic Satz solver [Kautz and Selman, 1998], in terms of the number of nodes expanded in the search space. Since the branching rule that is used in systematic satisfiability algorithms is an important factor in reducing the size of the search tree, this indicates that the LP relaxation *does* guide the selection of variables in solving the problem.

- Like Graphplan-based planners such as Blackbox, state-change formulation is guaranteed to find plans that have optimal values for the number of time steps in the plan. However, this formulation also takes into account the number of actions required by the plans (i.e., the plan *length*); and the number of actions obtained using the state-change IP formulation was usually much less than the number of actions in the plans obtained by BlackBox.

The organization of this paper is as follows. In Section 2, we discuss the various IP formulations of the planning problem. Next, Section 3 provides experimental results for these formulations, and a comparison with the systematic satisfiability solver. We conclude in Section 4 with a brief discussion of issues that arise in using IP techniques, and of plans for future work.

2 Integer Programming Formulations

The most effective current approach for solving general integer programs involves the use of branch and bound employing a linear programming (LP) relaxation. Thus, the key to the effectiveness of using integer programming to solve planning problems will lie in the effectiveness of the LP relaxation in improving the underlying tree search. The LP relaxation is typically solved at every node in the search tree. Search can be terminated at a node 1) if LP relaxation value indicates that further search could only uncover solutions with objective function values inferior to the best known, 2) if the LP is infeasible, which in turn implies the integer program is infeasible and 3) if the LP yields an integer solution. Since for planning problems, the objective function is only of secondary consideration, 1) will have little value. On the other hand 2) and 3) can be quite useful in improving search performance for planning problems. In particular, if the initial LP solves integer then no search is necessary. Another role the LP relaxation plays is that it provides information useful in deciding which variables to branch on.

A key issue in the performance of integer programming algorithms is the "strength" of the formulation. In general, there can be many equivalent integer programming formulations for a given problem. One formulation is stronger than another if the feasible region of the LP relaxation more closely approximates the integer program (see [Wolsey, 1998] for more details on this concept). Stronger formulations are more likely to yield integer solutions and produce objective function values closer to the values of the integer program.

In the remainder of this section we discuss two IP formulations for STRIPS-style planning problems. In order to express these formulations, we first introduce the following sets:

- $\mathcal{F}$, the set of *fluents*, that is, the set of all instantiated predicates;
- $\mathcal{A}$, the set of *actions*, that is, the set of all instantiated operators;
- $\mathcal{I} \subseteq \mathcal{F}$. $\mathcal{I}$ represents the set of fluents that hold initially;
- $\mathcal{G} \subseteq \mathcal{F}$. $\mathcal{G}$ represents the set of fluents that have to to hold in the goal state.

We assume that the number of time steps in the plan, t, is given. Furthermore, we introduce the sets

- $\text{pre}_f \subseteq \mathcal{A}$ for all $f \in \mathcal{F}$. pre_f represents the set of actions which have fluent f as a precondition;
- $\text{add}_f \subseteq \mathcal{A}$ for all $f \in \mathcal{F}$. add_f represents the set of actions which have fluent f as an add effect;
- $\text{del}_f \subseteq \mathcal{A}$ for all $f \in \mathcal{F}$. del_f represents the set of actions that delete fluent f.

2.1 SATPLAN-based IP Formulations

Initially, our IP formulations were motivated by the well known SATPLAN encodings, as discussed in [Kautz and Selman, 1996]. In SATPLAN, the problem of determining whether a plan exists, given a fixed number of time steps, is expressed as a satisfiability problem.

It is well known that satisfiability problems can be expressed as integer linear programs. (see for instance [Blair *et al.*, 1986] or [Hooker, 1988]). Usually, this is done by converting the clauses in the CNF representation of the satisfiability problem to 0-1 linear inequalities. For instance, the clause

$$x_1 \vee \neg x_2 \vee x_3$$

is equivalent to the $0 - 1$ inequality

$$x_1 + (1 - x_2) + x_3 \geq 1; x_1, x_2, x_3 \in \{0, 1\}.$$

Our first formulation consisted of this conversion for the SATPLAN encodings that are based on GraphPlan [Blum and Furst, 1996], i.e., we allow for parallel actions and the propagation of fluents using the "no-op" operator. The resulting formulation is summarized as follows:

Variables For all $f \in \mathcal{F}$, $i \in 1, \ldots, t+1$, we have fluent variables, which are defined as

$$x_{f,i} = \begin{cases} 1 & \text{if fluent } f \text{ is true in period } i, \\ 0 & \text{otherwise.} \end{cases}$$

For all $a \in \mathcal{A}$, $i \in 1, \ldots, t$, we have action variables, which are defined as

$$y_{a,i} = \begin{cases} 1 & \text{if action } a \text{ is carried out in period } i, \\ 0 & \text{otherwise.} \end{cases}$$

We remark that the action variables include the "no-op" maintain operators from GraphPlan for each time step and fact, which simply has that fact both as a precondition and as an add effect. "no-op" actions are necessary to propagate the fluent values.

Constraints The constraints are separated into different classes, which can be outlined as follows:

- **Initial/Goal State Constraints** These constraints set the requirements on the initial and final period, i.e.

$$x_{f,1} = \begin{cases} 1 & \text{if } f \in \mathcal{I}, \\ 0 & \text{if } f \notin \mathcal{I}. \end{cases}$$

$$x_{f,t+1} = 1 \quad \text{if} \quad f \in \mathcal{G}.$$

- **Precondition Constraints** Actions should imply their preconditions, which is expressed as follows.

$$y_{a,i} \leq x_{f,i} \qquad \forall a \in \text{pre}_f, i \in 1, \ldots, t.$$

- **Backward Chaining Constraints** Backward chaining is expressed as

$$x_{f,i+1} \leq \sum_{a \in \text{add}_f} y_{a,i} \quad \forall i \in 1, \ldots, t, f \in \mathcal{F}.$$

- **Exclusiveness Constraints** Actions conflict if one deletes a precondition or add effect of the other. The exclusiveness of conflicting actions is expressed as

$$y_{a,i} + y_{a',i} \leq 1,$$

for all $i \in 1, \ldots, t$, and all a, a' for which there exist $f \in \mathcal{F}$ such that $a \in \text{pre}_f$ and $a' \in \text{pre}_f \cup \text{add}_f$.

Objective Function The objective function was set to minimize the number of actions in the plan. It should be noted that in theory we could have chosen any objective function, since the constraints guarantee a feasible solution. In practice however, the choice of an objective function can significantly impact performance.

In addition, we made the following two modifications in the formulation. First of all, we used the notion of clique inequalities to strengthen the formulation. The basic idea behind this is that the inequalities $x_1 + x_2 \leq 1$, $x_2 + x_3 \leq 1$ and $x_1 + x_3 \leq 1$ can be replaced by a single inequality $x_1 + x_2 + x_3 \leq 1$. This leads to a formulation which is not only more compact but also stronger, in the sense that the fractional solution $x_1 = x_2 = x_3 = \frac{1}{2}$ is feasible in the first set of inequalities, but

not in the second. It should be noted that the ability to detect clique inequalities is available in most of today's commercial solvers.

Secondly, we did not restrict all variables to be 0-1 integers. Specifically, the integrality of the fluent variables $x_{f,i}$ was relaxed, that is, the constraints $x_{f,i} \in \{0,1\}$ were replaced by $0 \leq x_{f,i} \leq 1$. This is possible because the integrality of these variables is implied by the integrality of the action variables. We remark that as a consequence, none of the fluent variables will be selected in the branch and bound tree.

2.2 An Alternative Formulation

We now describe an alternative formulation of the planning problem, which we shall refer to as the "state-change formulation". The differences with respect to the formulation described in the previous section are twofold. First of all, the original fluent variables are "compiled away" and suitably defined "state change" variables are introduced instead. As we will see, this results in a stronger representation of the exclusion constraints. Secondly, we more explicitly restrict the possible propagation of fluents through "no-op"-actions, so as to reduce the number of equivalent feasible solutions.

Before giving this formulation, we again first define the variables. The action variables are the same as before, i.e.,

$$y_{a,i} = \begin{cases} 1 & \text{if action } a \text{ is executed in period } i, \\ 0 & \text{otherwise.} \end{cases}$$

for all $a \in \mathcal{A}$, $i \in 1 \ldots t$. Now however, the "no-op" actions are *not* included, but represented separately by variables $x_{f,i}^{\text{maintain}}$, for all $f \in \mathcal{F}$, $i \in 1, \ldots, t$.

In order to express the possible state changes, we introduce auxiliary variables $x_{f,i}^{\text{pre-add}}$, $x_{f,i}^{\text{pre-del}}$ and $x_{f,i}^{\text{add}}$, which are defined logically as

$$x_{f,i}^{\text{pre-add}} \equiv \bigvee_{a \in \text{pre}_f / \text{del}_f} y_{a,i},$$

$$x_{f,i}^{\text{pre-del}} \equiv \bigvee_{a \in \text{pre}_f \cap \text{del}_f} y_{a,i},$$

$$x_{f,i}^{\text{add}} \equiv \bigvee_{a \in \text{add}_f / \text{pre}_f} y_{a,i}.$$

Informally, $x_{f,i}^{\text{pre-add}} = 1$ if and only if an action is executed in period i that has f as a precondition but does not delete it. We note that the execution of such an action at a given time step implicitly asserts that the value fluent f is propagated. Similarly, $x_{f,t}^{\text{pre-del}} = 1$ if and only if an action is executed in period i that has f both as a precondition and a delete effect. $x_{f,i}^{\text{add}} = 1$ if and only if an action is executed in period i that has f as an add effect but not as a precondition.

The logical interpretation of these variables is represented in the IP formulation by the following constraints:

$$\sum_{a\in \text{pre}_f/\text{del}_f} y_{a,i} \geq x_{f,i}^{\text{pre-add}}$$

$$y_{a,t} \leq x_{f,i}^{\text{pre-add}} \quad \forall \quad a \in \text{pre}_f/\text{del}_f$$

$$\sum_{a\in \text{add}_f/\text{pre}_f} y_{a,t} \geq x_{f,i}^{\text{add}}$$

$$y_{a,t} \leq x_{f,i}^{\text{add}} \quad \forall \quad a \in \text{add}_f/\text{pre}_f$$

$$\sum_{a\in \text{pre}_f\cap \text{del}_f} y_{a,t} = x_{f,i}^{\text{pre-del}}$$

for all $f \in \mathcal{F}$, $i \in 1, \ldots, t$. The equality in the definition of $x_{f,i}^{\text{pre-del}}$ follows from the fact that all actions that have f both as a precondition and as an add effect are mutually exclusive. As a consequence these variables can in fact be substituted out, although for reasons of clarity we shall not do so here. The remaining exclusiveness constraints can easily be expressed in terms of the auxiliary variables, by stating that $x_{f,i}^{\text{pre-del}}$ is mutually exclusive with $x_{f,i}^{\text{add}}$, $x_{f,i}^{\text{pre-add}}$, and $x_{f,i}^{\text{maintain}}$. However, in order to strengthen the formulation we furthermore assert that $x_{f,i}^{\text{maintain}}$ is mutually exclusive with $x_{f,i}^{\text{add}}$ and $x_{f,i}^{\text{pre-add}}$. Informally, this means that a fluent can only be propagated at a time step if no action that adds it is executed. The resulting constraints are as follows.

$$x_{f,i}^{\text{add}} + x_{f,i}^{\text{maintain}} + x_{f,i}^{\text{pre-del}} \leq 1$$
$$x_{f,i}^{\text{pre-add}} + x_{f,i}^{\text{maintain}} + x_{f,i}^{\text{pre-del}} \leq 1$$

for all $f \in \mathcal{F}$, $i \in 1, \ldots, t$.

The backward chaining requirements can also be expressed in terms of the auxiliary variables. Since, all auxiliary variable that assert the precondition of a fact f at a certain time step (i.e., $x_{f,i}^{\text{pre-add}}$, $x_{f,i}^{\text{maintain}}$, and $x_{f,i}^{\text{pre-del}}$) are mutually exclusive, we have the following constraint

$$x_{f,i}^{\text{pre-add}} + x_{f,i}^{\text{maintain}} + x_{f,i}^{\text{pre-del}} \leq$$
$$x_{f,i-1}^{\text{add}} + x_{f,i-1}^{\text{pre-add}} + x_{f,i-1}^{\text{maintain}}$$

for all $f \in \mathcal{F}$, $i \in 1, \ldots, t$.

Finally, we can express the initial/goal state constraints as

$$x_{f,t}^{\text{add}} + x_{f,t}^{\text{pre-add}} + x_{f,t}^{\text{maintain}} \geq 1$$

for all $f \in \mathcal{G}$, and

$$x_{f,0}^{\text{add}} = \begin{cases} 1 & \text{if } f \in \mathcal{I}, \\ 0 & \text{otherwise}. \end{cases}$$

The objective function is again set to minimize the number of actions. Also, the integrality requirement of the auxiliary variables variables was again relaxed, as it is implied by the integrality of the action variables.

3 Experimental Results

We tested the IP formulations on a variety of planning problems from the Blackbox software distribution, and compared the results with those obtained by Blackbox using the systematic Satz solver. The integer programs were solved using Cplex 6.0, a widely used LP/IP solver. In solving the integer programs, we used all of Cplex's default settings, except the following: the initial LP optimum was obtained by solving the dual problem, and the variable selection strategy used was "pseudo-reduced cost". In addition, the solver was terminated as soon as a feasible integer solution was found. All problems were run on a Sun Ultra workstation.

The results are shown in Table 1. "Nodes" represents the number of nodes visited in the branch and bound procedure, and "iterations" the number of simplex iterations performed. All times are in seconds. It should be noted that, both for the IP formulations and BlackBox, the results shown are for the problem of finding a feasible solution given the number of time steps (i.e., t is known in advance and given).

As shown in Table 1, the state-change formulation led to a significant improvement in performance. Whereas the SATPLAN-based IP formulation solved only the smallest problems, the state-change formulations solved all, and required both fewer nodes and less computation time. While the systematic BlackBox solver usually required less time than the state-change formulation, both BlackBox and the state-change formulation explored similar numbers of nodes. Moreover, the Black-Box/Satz did not find a feasible solution to the "bw-large.b" blocks-world problem, while the state-change formulation did find a solution, using only 28 nodes.

It should be noted that the introduction of auxiliary variables can possibly introduce a large number of variables and constraints. However, we found that the size of the formulation was significantly reduced by standard IP preprocessing (similar to the use of Graphplan as a preprocessing tool in BlackBox). For example, while the initial formulation of the problem "rocket.a" had 27744 variables and 40018 constraints, preprocessing reduced this to 1573 variables and 3007 constraints. Similar reductions in size were also obtained for the other problems.

A further indication of the strength of respective formulations can be found by examining the value of the LP relaxations. Since the objective function that is used is to minimize the number of actions in the plan, the value of the LP relaxation may also viewed as a lower bound on the number of actions required in the plan. The results for the SATPLAN-based and the state-change formulation are shown in Table 2. In almost all cases, the state-change formulation has a much higher lower bound, which indicates that its formulation is indeed much stronger.

In the SATPLAN and Graphplan framework, the *parallel length* (i.e., the number of time steps) of plans is minimized. The IP formulation follows this framework,

Table 1: Experimental results: IP formulations vs. Systematic BlackBox solver.

Problem	SATPLAN IP			State-change IP			BlackBox/Satz	
	nodes	its.	time	nodes	its.	time	nodes	time
anomaly	59	1471	3.1	3	161	0.1	3	0.55
bw-12step	*	*	*	4	2037	9.7	3	2.42
bw-large.a	*	*	*	4	4261	36	38	20.8
bw-large.b	*	*	*	28	89048	2500	–	–
att-log2	491	2748	4.9	24	177	0.57	7	0.56
att-log3	99	1296	12.1	33	406	4.2	16	0.58
att-log4	1179	20778	101.4	40	961	5.7	23	0.56
rocket.a	*	*	*	213	40877	140	234	3.37
rocket.b	*	*	*	73	18492	67	630	6.38
log-easy	*	*	*	102	2505	5.8	16	0.62
logistics.a	*	*	*	40	9305	80	41	1.66
logistics.b	*	*	*	30	9532	92	46	2.37
logistics.c	*	*	*	285	89760	1400	39297	79.3

– denotes that no plan was found after 10 hours of computation time.
* denotes that the node limit of 2500 was reached without finding a feasible integer solution.

Table 2: LP relaxation values.

Problem	SATPLAN-based	State-change
anomaly	2.62	5
bw-12step	2.33	5
bw-large.a		12
bw-large.b		16
att-log2	2.19	6.75
att-log3	1.57	6.75
att-log4	2.89	10.7
rocket.a	12.73	20.6
rocket.b		20.6
log-easy	5.28	19.25
logistics.a		42.8
logistics.b		30.9
logistics.c		38.9

Table 3: Plan length comparison (total number of actions in plan).

Problem	State-change IP	BlackBox/Satz
rocket.a	30	33
rocket.b	26	29
log-easy	25	25
logistics.a	60	72
logistics.b	47	68
logistics.c	66	90

so it also is guaranteed to minimize the number of time steps. In addition, the IP formulation also explicitly uses minimization of the number of actions in the objective function. Since we set the solver to terminate as soon as the first feasible integer solution was found, the IP solutions were not guaranteed to minimize the possible number of actions. Still, we found that in most cases, the IP formulation found plans with a significantly smaller total number of actions than those obtained by Black-Box. This is shown in Table 3.

4 Conclusions

Although Selman *et al.* [1997] reported difficulty in making effective use of IP techniques for propositional reasoning in general, our results suggest that IP techniques may potentially work well for AI planning problems, for the following reasons.

- First, the IP formulation has the potential to do

efficient planning. In our results, the number of nodes expanded in the search space was typically small, and comparable to a systematic satisfiablity solver. This indicates that the LP relaxation gave significant guidance in the selection of variables in solving planning problems.

- Second, IP models may provide a natural means of incorporating numeric constraints and objectives into the planning formulation. This capability would be important in many application domains, but it is not available in most existing approaches to AI planning. It should be noted, however, that the way in which numeric constraints will be represented may have a significant influence on the performance, much in the same way as we saw with the various IP formulations. Therefore, the development of strong IP representations that capture common numeric constraints that arise in the planning domain is an issue for further research.

We would like to emphasize that so far our main concern has been the development of different IP formulations, rather than improving the efficiency of the LP relaxation itself. While we believe that the state-change formulation is reasonably strong, solving the LP relation at each node is still sometimes computationally expensive. One of the main reasons for this, we believe, is the degeneracy of the LP relaxation (a condition that can cause the LP solver to execute many non-productive iterations). Therefore, we are currently also investigating techniques to resolve this degeneracy, as well as further strengthening of the IP formulation. In particular, we want to investigate the use of constraint and column generation techniques.

References

[Blair *et al.*, 1986] Blair, C.E., Jeroslow, R.G., and J.K. Lowe. 1986. Some results and experiments in programming techniques for propositional reasoning. *Computers and Operations Research* 13:633–645.

[BockMayr and Dimopoulos, 1998] Alexander Bockmayr and Yanis Dimopoulos. 1998. Mixed Integer Programming Models for Planning Problems. *CP'98 Workshop on Constraint Problem Reformulation.*

[Bylander, 1997] T. Bylander. 1997. A Linear Programming Heuristic for Optimal Planning. *Proc. AAAI-97.*

[Blum and Furst, 1997] A. L. Blum and M. L. Furst. 1997. Fast Planning Through Planning Graph Analysis. *Artificial Intelligence*, 90(1–2):281–300.

[Hooker, 1988] J. N. Hooker. 1988. A quantitative approach to logical inference. *Decision Support Systems* 4:45–69.

[Kautz *et al.*, 1996] Henry Kautz, David McAllester, and Bart Selman. 1996. Encoding plans in propositional logic. *Proc. KR-96.*

[Kautz and Selman, 1996] Henry Kautz and Bart Selman. 1996. Pushing the envelope: Planning, propositional logic, and stochastic search. *Proc. AAAI-96.*

[Kautz and Selman, 1998] Henry Kautz and Bart Selman. 1998. BLACKBOX: A New Approach to the Application of Theorem Proving to Problem Solving. *Working notes of the Workshop on Planning as Combinatorial Search, held in conjunction with AIPS-98, Pittsburgh, PA, 1998.*

[Kautz and Walser, 1999] Henry Kautz and Joachim P. Walser. 1999. State-space Planning by Integer Optimization. *Proc. AAAI-99.*

[Nau *et al.*, 1998] D. S. Nau, S. J. Smith and Kutluhan Erol. 1998. Control strategies in HTN planning: theory versus practice. In *AAAI-98/IAAI-98 Proceedings*, 1127–1133, 1998.

[Selman *et al.*, 1997] B. Selman, H. Kautz, and D. McAllester. 1997. Ten challenges in propositional reasoning and search. In *Proc. Fifteenth International Joint Conf. Artificial Intelligence (IJCAI-97)*, Nagoya, Japan.

[Wolsey, 1998] L. Wolsey, *Integer Programming*, 1998, John Wiley, New York.

The LPSAT Engine & its Application to Resource Planning[*]

Steven A. Wolfman   Daniel S. Weld

Department of Computer Science & Engineering
University of Washington, Box 352350
Seattle, WA 98195–2350 USA
{wolf, weld}@cs.washington.edu

Abstract

Compilation to boolean satisfiability has become a powerful paradigm for solving AI problems. However, domains that require metric reasoning cannot be compiled efficiently to SAT even if they would otherwise benefit from compilation. We address this problem by introducing the LCNF representation which combines propositional logic with metric constraints. We present LPSAT, an engine which solves LCNF problems by interleaving calls to an incremental simplex algorithm with systematic satisfaction methods. We describe a compiler which converts metric resource planning problems into LCNF for processing by LPSAT. The experimental section of the paper explores several optimizations to LPSAT, including learning from constraint failure and randomized cutoffs.

1 Introduction

Recent advances in satisfiability (SAT) solving technology have rendered large, previously intractable problems quickly solvable [Crawford and Auton, 1993; Selman *et al.*, 1996; Cook and Mitchell, 1997; Bayardo and Schrag, 1997; Li and Anbulagan, 1997; Gomes *et al.*, 1998]. SAT solving has become so successful that many other difficult tasks are being compiled into propositional form to be solved as SAT problems. For example, SAT-encoded solutions to graph coloring, planning, and circuit verification are among the fastest approaches to these problems [Iˉuutz and Selman, 1996; Selman *et al.*, 1997].

But many real-world tasks have a metric aspect. For instance, resource planning, temporal planning, scheduling, and analog circuit verification problems all require

Figure 1: Data flow in the demonstration resource planning system; space precludes discussion of the grey components.

reasoning about real-valued quantities. Unfortunately, metric constraints are difficult to express in SAT encodings[1]. Hence, a solver which could efficiently handle both metric constraints and propositional formulae would yield a powerful substrate for handling AI problems.

This paper introduces a new problem formulation, LCNF, which combines the expressive power of propositional logic with that of linear equalities and inequalities. We argue that LCNF provides an ideal target language into which a compiler might translate tasks that combine logical and metric reasoning. We also describe the LPSAT LCNF solver, a systematic satisfiability solver integrated with an incremental Simplex algorithm. As LPSAT explores the propositional search space it updates the set of metric requirements managed by the linear program solver; in turn, Simplex notifies the propositional solver if these requirements become unsatisfiable.

We report on three optimizations to LPSAT: learning and backjumping, adapting LPSAT's core heuristic to trigger variables, and using random restarts. The most effective of these is the combination of learning and backjumping; LPSAT learns new clauses by discovering explanations for failure when a branch of its search terminates. The resulting clauses guide backjumping and constrain future truth assignments. In particular, we show that analysis of the state of the linear program solver is crucial in order to learn effectively from constraint conflicts.

To demonstrate the utility of the LCNF approach, we also present a fully implemented compiler for resource planning problems. Figure 1 shows how the components fit together. Their performance is impressive: LPSAT solves large resource planning problems (encoded in a

---

[*]We thank people who provided code, help, and discussion: Greg Badros, Alan Borning, Corin Anderson, Mike Ernst, Zack Ives, Subbarao Kambhampati, Henry Kautz, Jana Koehler, Tessa Lau, Denise Pinnel, Rachel Pottinger, Bart Selman, and the blind reviewers. This research was funded in part by Office of Naval Research Grant N00014-98-1-0147, by the ARCS foundation Barbara and Tom Cable fellowship, by National Science Foundation Grants IRI-9303461 and IIS-9872128, and by a National Science Foundation Graduate Fellowship.

---

[1]Encoding each value as a separate boolean variable is a simple but unwieldy solution; bitwise-encodings produce smaller formulae but ones which appear very hard to solve [Ernst *et al.*, 1997].

$MaxLoad \Rightarrow$ (load $\leq$ 30)	; Statements
$MaxFuel \Rightarrow$ (fuel $\leq$ 15)	; defining
$MinFuel \Rightarrow$ (fuel $\geq$ 7 + load / 2)	; triggered
$AllLoaded \Rightarrow$ (load = 45)	; constraints
$MaxLoad$	; Triggers for load and
$MaxFuel$	; fuel limits are unit
$Deliver$	; The goal is unit
$\neg Move \vee MinFuel$	; Moving requires fuel
$\neg Move \vee Deliver$	; Moving implies delivery
$\neg GoodTrip \vee Deliver$	; A good trip requires
$\neg GoodTrip \vee AllLoaded$	; a full delivery

Figure 2: Portion of a tiny LCNF logistics problem (greatly simplified from compiler output). A truck with load and fuel limits makes a delivery but is too small to carry all load available (the *AllLoaded* constraint). *Italicized* variables are boolean-valued; typeface are real.

variant of the PDDL language [McDermott, 1998] based on the metric constructs used by metric IPP [Koehler, 1998]), including a metric version of the ATT Logistics domain [Kautz and Selman, 1996].

2 The LCNF Formalism

The LCNF representation combines a propositional logic formula with a set of metric constraints. The key to the encoding is the simple but expressive concept of triggers — each propositional variable may "trigger" a constraint; this constraint is then enforced whenever the *trigger variable*'s truth assignment is true.

Formally, an LCNF *problem* is a five-tuple $\langle \mathcal{R}, \mathcal{V}, \Delta, \Sigma, \mathcal{T} \rangle$ in which $\mathcal{R}$ is a set of real-valued variables, $\mathcal{V}$ is a set of propositional variables, Δ is a set of linear equality and inequality constraints over variables in $\mathcal{R}$, Σ is a propositional formula in CNF over variables in $\mathcal{V}$, and $\mathcal{T}$ is a function from $\mathcal{V}$ to Δ which establishes the constraint triggered by each propositional variable. We require that Δ contain a special null constraint which is vacuously true, and this is used as the $\mathcal{T}$-value for a variable in $\mathcal{V}$ to denote that it triggers no constraint. Moreover, for each variable v we define $\mathcal{T}(\neg v) = $ null.

Under this definition, an assignment to an LCNF problem is a mapping, φ, from the variables in $\mathcal{R}$ to real values and from the variables in $\mathcal{V}$ to truth values. Given an LCNF problem and an assignment, the *set of active constraints* is $\{c \in \Delta | \exists v \in \mathcal{V} \ \varphi(v) = \text{true} \wedge \mathcal{T}(v) = c\}$. We say that an assignment *satisfies* the LCNF problem if and only if it makes at least one literal true in each clause of Σ and satisfies the set of active constraints.

Figure 2 shows a fragment of a sample LCNF problem: a truck, which carries a maximum load of 30 and fuel level of 15, can make a *Delivery* by executing the *Move* action. We discuss later why it cannot have a *GoodTrip*.

3 The LPSAT Solver

Our first step in constructing the LPSAT engine was to choose solvers to use as the foundation for its metric and propositional solving portions. The choice was motivated by the following criteria:

1. It must be easy to modify the propositional solver in order to support triggers and handle reports of inconsistency from the constraint reasoner.

2. The metric solver must support incremental modifications to the constraint set.

3. Because a Simplex solve is more expensive than setting a single propositional variable's value, the propositional solver should minimize modifications to the constraint set.

These principles led us to implement the LPSAT engine by modifying the RELSAT satisfiability engine [Bayardo and Schrag, 1997] and combining it with the CASSOWARY constraint solver [Borning *et al.*, 1997; Badros and Borning, 1998] using the method described in [Nelson and Oppen, 1979]. RELSAT makes an excellent start for processing LCNF for three reasons. First, it performs a systematic, depth-first search through the space of partial truth assignments; this minimizes changes to the set of active metric constraints. Second, the code is exceptionally well-structured. Third, RELSAT incorporates powerful learning and backjumping optimizations. CASSOWARY is an appropriate Simplex solver for handling LCNF because it was designed to support and quickly respond to small changes in its constraint set.

In order to build LPSAT, we modified RELSAT to include trigger variables and constraints. This required four changes. First, the solver must trigger constraints as the truth assignment changes. Second, the solver must now check for a solvable constraint set to ensure that a truth assignment is satisfying. Third, the solver must report in its solution not only a truth assignment to the boolean variables, but an assignment of real values to the constraint variables[2]. Finally, since even a purely positive trigger variable may (if set to true) trigger an inconsistent constraint, pure literal elimination cannot act on *positive* trigger variables[3]. Figure 3 displays pseudocode for the resulting algorithm.

4 Incorporating Learning and Backjumping

LPSAT inherits methods for learning and backjumping from RELSAT [Bayardo and Schrag, 1997]. LPSAT's depth-first search of the propositional search space creates a partial assignment to the boolean variables. When the search fails, it is because the partial assignment is inconsistent with the LCNF problem. LPSAT identifies an inconsistent subset of the truth assignments

---

[2]While the assignment to the constraint variables is optimal according to CASSOWARY's objective function, it is not guaranteed to be the globally optimal assignment to the real variables by the same measure; a different assignment to the propositional variables might provide a better solution. So, the specific function used is not vital (we use CASSOWARY's default which minimizes the slack in inequalities).

[3]This restriction falls in line with the pure literal elimination rule if we consider the triggers themselves to be clauses. The trigger $MaxLoad \Rightarrow$ (load $\leq$ 30) from Figure 2 would then become the clause $\neg MaxLoad \vee$ (load $\leq$ 30), and $MaxLoad$ could no longer be purely positive.

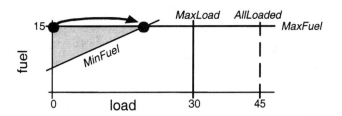

Procedure LPSAT(LCNF problem: $\langle \mathcal{R}, \mathcal{V}, \Delta, \Sigma, \mathcal{T} \rangle$)
1 If $\exists$ an empty clause in Σ or BAD?(Δ), return $\{\bot\}$.
2 Else if Σ is empty, return SOLVE(Δ).
3 Else if $\exists$ a pure literal u in Σ and $\mathcal{T}(u) = $ null,
4   return $\{u\} \cup$ LPSAT($\langle \mathcal{R}, \mathcal{V}, \Delta, \Sigma(u), \mathcal{T} \rangle$).
5 Else if $\exists$ a unit clause $\{u\}$ in Σ,
6   return $\{u\} \cup$ LPSAT($\langle \mathcal{R}, \mathcal{V}, \Delta \cup \mathcal{T}(u), \Sigma(u), \mathcal{T} \rangle$).
7 Else choose a variable, v, mentioned in Σ.
8   Let $\mathcal{A} = $ LPSAT($\langle \mathcal{R}, \mathcal{V}, \Delta \cup \mathcal{T}(v), \Sigma(v), \mathcal{T} \rangle$).
9   If $\bot \notin \mathcal{A}$, return $\{v\} \cup \mathcal{A}$.
10   Else, return $\{\neg v\} \cup$ LPSAT($\langle \mathcal{R}, \mathcal{V}, \Delta, \Sigma(\neg v), \mathcal{T} \rangle$).

Figure 3: Core LPSAT algorithm (without learning or backjumping). BAD? denotes a check for constraint inconsistency; SOLVE returns constraint variable values. $\mathcal{T}(u)$ returns the constraint triggered by u (possibly null). $\Sigma(u)$ denotes the result of setting literal u true in Σ and simplifying.

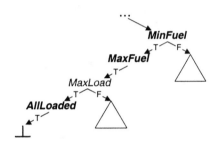

Figure 4: Possible search tree for the constraints from Figure 2. Each node is labeled with the variable set at that node; branchpoints have true (T) and false (F) branches. $\bot$ indicates an inconsistent constraint set. The bold variables are members of the conflict set.

in the partial assignment, a *conflict set*, and uses this subset to learn in two ways. First, since making the truth assignments represented in the conflict set leads inevitably to failure, LPSAT can learn a clause disallowing those particular assignments. For example, in the problem from Figure 2 the constraints triggered by setting *MinFuel*, *MaxFuel*, *MaxLoad*, and *AllLoaded* to true are inconsistent, and *MinFuel*, *MaxFuel*, and *AllLoaded* form a conflict set. So, LPSAT can learn the clause ($\neg MinFuel \vee \neg MaxFuel \vee \neg AllLoaded$). Second, because continuing the search is futile until at least one of the variables in the conflict set has its truth assignment changed, LPSAT can backjump in its search to the deepest branch points at which a conflict set variable received its assignment, ignoring any deeper branch points. Figure 4 shows a search tree in which *MinFuel*, *MaxFuel*, *MaxLoad*, and *AllLoaded* have all been set to true. Using the conflict set containing *MinFuel*, *MaxFuel*, and *AllLoaded*, LPSAT can backjump past the branchpoint for *MaxLoad* to the branchpoint for *MinFuel*, the deepest member of the conflict set which is a branchpoint.

However, while LPSAT inherits methods to *use* conflict sets from RELSAT, LPSAT must *produce* those conflict sets for both propositional and constraint failures while

Figure 5: Graphical depiction of the constraints from Figure 2. The shaded area represents solutions to the set of solid-line constraints. The dashed *AllLoaded* constraint causes an inconsistency.

RELSAT produces them only for propositional failures. Thus, given a propositional failure LPSAT uses RELSAT's conflict set discovery mechanism unchanged, learning a set based on two of the clauses which led to the contradiction [Bayardo and Schrag, 1997]. For a constraint conflict, however, LPSAT identifies an inconsistent subset of the active constraints, and the propositional triggers for these constraint compose the conflict set. We examine two methods for identifying these inconsistent subsets.

In our first method, called *global conflict set discovery*, LPSAT includes the entire set of active constraints in the conflict set. This mechanism is simple but often suboptimal since a smaller conflict set would provide greater pruning action. Indeed, preliminary experiments showed that — while global conflict set discovery *did* increase solver speed over a solver with no learning or backjumping facility — the conflict sets were on average twice as large as those found for logical conflicts.

In our second method, called *minimal conflict set discovery*, LPSAT identifies a (potentially) much smaller set of constraints which are responsible for the conflict. Specifically, our technique identifies an inconsistent conflict set of which every proper subset is consistent.

Figure 5 illustrates the constraints from the example in Figure 2. The constraints *MaxLoad*, *MaxFuel*, and *MinFuel* and the implicit constraints that fuel and load be non-negative are all consistent; however, with the introduction of the dashed constraint marked *AllLoaded* the constraint set becomes inconsistent. Informally, LPSAT finds a minimal conflict set by identifying only those constraints which are, together, in greatest conflict with the new constraint. We now discuss how LPSAT discovers the conflicting constraints in this figure and which set it discovers.

When LPSAT adds the *AllLoaded* constraint to CASSOWARY's constraint set, CASSOWARY initially adds a "slack" version of the constraint which allows error and is thus trivially consistent with the current constraint set. This error is then minimized by the same routine used to minimize the overall objective function [Badros and Borning, 1998]. In Figure 5, we show the minimization as a move from the initial solution at the upper left corner point to the solution at the upper right corner point of the shaded region. The error in the solution is the horizontal distance from the solution point to the new constraint *AllLoaded*. Since no further progress within the shaded region can be made toward *AllLoaded*, the error has been minimized; however, since the error is non-zero, the strict constraint is inconsistent.

At this point, LPSAT uses "marker variables" (which CASSOWARY adds to each original constraint) to establish the conflict set. A marker variable is a variable that was added by exactly one of the original constraints and thus identifies the constraint in any derived equations. LPSAT examines the derived equation that gives the error for the new constraint, and notes that each constraint with a marker variable in this equation contributes to keeping the error non-zero. Thus, all the constraints identified by this equation, plus the new constraint itself, compose a conflict set.

In Figure 5 the *MinFuel* and *MaxFuel* constraints restrain the solution point from coming closer to the *AllLoaded* line. If the entire active constraint set were any two of those three constraints, the intersection of the two constraints' lines would be a valid solution; however, there is no valid solution with all three constraints.

Note that another conflict set (*AllLoaded* plus *MaxLoad*) exists with even smaller cardinality than the one we find. In general, there may be many minimal conflict sets, and our conflict discovery technique will discovery only one of these, with no guarantee of discovering the global minimum. Some of these sets may prove to have better pruning action, but we know of no way to find the best minimal conflict set efficiently. However, the minimal conflict set *is* at least as good as (and usually better than) any of its supersets.

A brief proof that our technique will return a *minimal* conflict set appears in the longer version of this paper [Wolfman and Weld, 1999].

5 The Resource Planning Application

In order to demonstrate LPSAT's utility, we implemented a compiler for metric planning domains (starting from a base of IPP's [Koehler *et al.*, 1997] and BLACKBOX's [Kautz and Selman, 1998] parsers) which translates resource planning problems into LCNF form. After LPSAT solves the LCNF problem, a small decoding unit maps the resulting boolean and real-valued assignments into a solution plan (Figure 1). We believe that this translate/solve/decode architecture is effective for a wide variety of problems.

5.1 Action Language

Our planning problems are specified in an extension of the PDDL language [McDermott, 1998]; we support PDDL typing, equality, quantified goals and effects, disjunctive preconditions, and conditional effects. In addition, we handle metric values with two new built-in types: *float* and *fluent*. A float's value may not change over the course of a plan, whereas a fluent's value may change from time step to time step. Moreover, we support fluent- and float-valued functions, such as ?distance[Nagoya,Stockholm].

Floats and fluents are manipulated with three special built-in predicates: test, set, and influence. Test statements are used as predicates in action preconditions; set and influence are used in effects. As its argu-

```
Action loop_a              Action loop_b
  pre: test fluent1 = 0      pre: test fluent2 = 0
  eff: set fluent2 = 1       eff: set fluent1 = 1
```

Figure 6: Two actions which can execute in parallel, but which cannot be serialized.

ment, test takes a constraint (an equality or inequality between two expressions composed of floats, fluents, and basic arithmetic operations); it evaluates to true if and only if the constraint holds. Set and influence each take two arguments: the object (a float or fluent) and an expression. If an action causes a set to be asserted, the object's value after the action is defined to be the expression's value before the action. An asserted influence changes an object's value by the value of the expression, as in the equation *object := object + expression*; multiple simultaneous influences are cumulative in their effect [Falkenhainer and Forbus, 1988].

5.2 Plan Encoding

The compiler uses a regular action representation with explanatory frame axioms and conflict exclusion [Ernst *et al.*, 1997]. We adopt a standard fluent model in which time takes nonnegative integer values. State-fluents occur at even-numbered times and actions at odd times. The initial state is completely specified at time zero, including all properties presumed false by the closed-world assumption.

Each test, set, and influence statement compiles to a propositional variable that triggers the associated constraint. Just as logical preconditions and effects are implied by their associated actions, the triggers for metric preconditions and effects are implied by their actions.

The compiler must generate frame axioms for constraint variables as well as for propositional variables, but the axiomatizations are very different. Explanatory frames are used for boolean variables, while for real variables, compilation proceeds in two steps. First, we create a constraint which, if activated, will set the value of the variable at the next step equal to its current value plus all the influences that might act on it (untriggered influences are set to zero). Next, we construct a clause which activates this constraint unless some action actually sets the variable's value.

For a parallel encoding, the compiler must consider certain set and influence statements to be mutually exclusive. For simplicity, we adopt the following convention: two actions are mutually exclusive if and only if at least one sets a variable which the other either influences or sets.

This exclusivity policy results in a plan which is correct if actions at each step are executed strictly in parallel; however, the actions may not be serializable, as demonstrated in Figure 6. In order to make parallel actions arbitrarily serializable, we would have to adopt more restrictive exclusivity conditions and a less expressive format for our test statements.

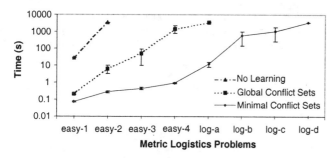

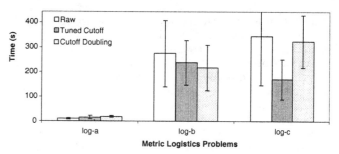

Figure 7: Solution times for three versions of LPSAT in the metric logistics domain. No learning or backjumping is performed in the line marked "No learning." Global conflict sets and minimal conflict sets use progressively better learning algorithms. Note that the final point on each curve reaches the resource cutoff (one hour).

6 Experimental Results

There are currently few available metric planners with which to compare LPSAT. The ZENO system [Penberthy and Weld, 1994] is more expressive than our system, but ZENO is unable even to complete *easy-1*, our simplest metric logistics problem. There are only a few results available for Koehler's metric IPP system [Koehler, 1998], and code is not yet available for direct comparisons.

In light of this, this section concentrates on displaying results for LPSAT in an interesting domain and on describing the heuristics and optimization we used to enhance LPSAT's performance. We report LPSAT solve time, running on a Pentium II 450 MHz processor with 128 MB of RAM, averaged over 20 runs per problem, and showing 95 percent confidence intervals. We do not include compile time for the (unoptimized) compiler since the paper's focus is the design and optimization of LPSAT; however, compile time can be substantial (*e.g.*, twenty minutes on *log-c*).

We report on a sequence of problems in the metric logistics domain, which includes all the features of the ATT logistics domain [Kautz and Selman, 1996]: airplanes and trucks moving packages among cities and sites within cities. However, our metric version adds fuel and distances between cities; airplanes and trucks both have individual maximum fuel capacities, consume fuel to move (the amount is per trip for trucks and based on distance between cities for airplanes), and can refuel at depots. *log-a* through *log-d* are the same as the ATT problems except for the addition of fuel. *easy-1* through *easy-4* are simplifications of *log-a* with more elements retained in the higher numbered problems. We report on highly successful experiments with learning and backjumping as well as two other interesting optimizations.

6.1 Learning and Backjumping

The results in Figure 7 demonstrate the improvement in solving times resulting from activating the learning and backjumping facilities which were described in Section 4. Runs were cut off after one hour of solve time (the minimal conflict set technique ran over an hour only on *log-d*). Without learning or backjumping LPSAT quickly

Figure 8: Solution times for two types of random restarts. Tuned cutoff uses raw experimental data to select a constant cutoff. Cutoff doubling starts with a cutoff of one second and doubles it on each run.

exceeds the maximum time allotted to it. With learning and backjumping activated using global conflict sets, the solver handles larger problems and runs faster. Our best method, minimal conflict sets, quickly solves even some of the harder problems in the metric logistics domain.

6.2 Splitting Heuristic

Line 7 of the LPSAT pseudocode (Figure 3) makes a non-deterministic choice of variable v before the recursive call, and the *splitting heuristic* used to guide this choice can bias performance. We expected the standard RELSAT heuristic to perform poorly (due to a overly strong preference for trigger variables) for two reasons: 1) the trigger itself is an implicit clause which is resolved when a trigger variable is set, and 2) each time the solver modifies a trigger variable, it may call CASSOWARY, and these calls often dominate runtime. We tried several methods of including information about the trigger variables in the splitting heuristic, including adding and multiplying the score of trigger variables by a user-settable preference value. To our surprise, however, we were unable to achieve significant improvement (although *increasing* the preference for trigger variables did slow execution). These results lead us to suspect that either that LCNF problems are generally insensitive to our heuristics or that our compilation of metric planning domains already encodes information about trigger variables in the structure of the problem. Further experiments will decide the issue.

6.3 Random Restarts

Because LPSAT uses a randomized backtracking algorithm and because early experimental results showed a small percentage of runs far exceeded the median runtime, we experimented with random restarts using a process similar to the one described in [Gomes *et al.*, 1998]. We cut off solving at a deadline — which can be either fixed beforehand or geometrically increasing — and restart the solver with a new random seed.

Figure 8 shows the results of these experiments. We first ran the algorithm twenty times on each problem to produce the "Raw" entries[4]. Then, we calculated the

---

[4] All three sets of runs use minimal conflict sets, learning, and backjumping.

| problem | steps | Blackbox | | | | Graphplan |
| | | default | | compress | | |
		clauses	time	clauses	time	
reverse	8	1,347	2 sec	917	3 sec	2 sec
12step	12	25,978	5 sec	6,643	3 sec	3 sec
large.a	12	116,353	13 sec	18,061	5 sec	3 sec
large.b	18	469,993	6.5 min	123,653	28 sec	1.9 min
large.c	28	2,496,832	*	917,402	1.3 hour	—

Table 3: Comparing the default and "compressed" SAT translations produced by blackbox, for blocks world problems where the optimal plan length is input (no parallel actions possible). Solver used by `Blackbox` is "-compact -l -then satz -cutoff 40 -restart 20 -then satz -cutoff 400". Star (*) indicates solver failed due to memory size, and long dash (—) that no solution found after 48 hours.

tion was respectable (no competitor dominated it in on all categories in round 1, and only IPP did so in round 2), we must note that the competition problem instances did not provide a way of distinguishing planning systems that employ plan graphs on the basis of their *search strategies*. Nearly all of the instances were "too easy" in the sense that once a planning graph was generated *any* search strategy could extract a solution, or "too hard" in the sense that the planning graph grew intolerably large *before* conversion to CNF. For example, `Blackbox`'s difficulty in dealing with the "gripper" domain were due to explosion of the initial plan graph, even though the domain is inherently *non*-combinatorial (a linear time domain specific optimal planning algorithm exists). Differences in performance between the various systems was largely due to various graph-pruning strategies each employed, such as the RIFO strategy of IPP (Nebel *et al.* 1997). Many of these strategies can be incorporated into `Blackbox` by simply replacing it's Graphplan front-end with *e.g.* IPP.

The memory required for the SAT encoding can be an issue for running `Blackbox` on small-memory machines (as noted above, ones with less than the 178 MB required for log.d), particularly because the current code does not optimize memory use (*e.g.*, several copies of the wff are kept in core, and memory is not reused when wffs are sequentially generated with larger bounds). Even so, the falling prices for RAM (currently about $1000 for 512MB) support the argument that the approach will only grow more practical with time. A more serious technical challenge comes from recent work on structure sharing techniques for compactly representing large plan graphs (as will appear in the next versions of IPP and STAN (Fox and Long 1998)). How can one translate such representations into SAT without multiplying out all the shared structure? Instead of compiling into pure SAT, one might try to compile the plan graph into a smaller set of *axiom schemas*, that is, a "lifted" form of CNF. The axiom schemas could be passed on to a general lifted SAT solver or further compiled into rules in a constraint logic programming system. The latter alternative appears particularly attractive in the light of good results recently obtained in using constraint logic programming to solve planning problems (van Beek and Chen 1999).

3   The Role of Limited Inference

The plan graph approach to STRIPS planning gains much of its power through its use of mutex computations, as we briefly

| problem | vars | percent set by | | |
		uprop	flit	blit
12step	1191	13%	43%	79%
bw.a	2452	10%	100%	100%
bw.b	6358	5%	43%	99%
bw.c	19158	2%	33%	99%
rocket.a	1337	3%	24%	40%
rocket.b	1413	3%	21%	49%
log.a	2709	2%	36%	45%
log.b	3287	2%	24%	30%
log.c	4197	2%	23%	27%
log.d	6151	1%	25%	33%

Table 4: The number of variables in the encoding of a series of planning problems before simplification, and the percentage determined by simplification by unit propagation (uprop), the failed literal rule (flit), and by the binary failed literal rule (blit). The first set of problems are blocks world and the second set are logistics.

described above. During construction of the plan graph, Graphplan marks a pair of instantiated actions as mutually exclusive if one deletes a precondition or add-effect of the other. It further determines that a pair of facts (predicates fully instantiated at a particular time-instant) are mutually exclusive if all the actions that add one are exclusive of all actions that add the other. Additional mutexes are added between actions if a precondition of one is mutex with a precondition of the other. If one takes the number of preconditions or effects of an operator to be constant then mutex computation can be performed in $O(n^2)$ time, where n is the number of instantiated actions (where an instantiated action specifies all its parameters as well as a particular time step).

Thus mutex computation is simply a specialized form of constraint propagation, *i.e.*, limited deduction. Some nodes can be determined to be inconsistent during instantiation and immediately eliminated from the plan graph. The remaining mutex relations are used to constrain the search over the either the graph or its SAT translation. It is natural to wonder if other forms of limited inference are useful for planning problems. Blum (personal communication) observes that computing higher-order mutexes (between triples of actions, *etc.*) is not very useful. Do the binary mutex computations extract all important "local" information from the problem instances?

We decided to test this hypothesis by experimenting with a series of different limited inference algorithms that work on the the SAT *encodings* of the problems. We used the program "compact" developed by James Crawford, and considered the following options:

unit propagation Apply unit resolution. Requires $O(n)$ time.

failed literal For each literal, try adding the literal to the formula and applying unit resolution. If inconsistency is determined then then literal can be set to false. Requires $O(n^2)$ time.

binary failed literal For each pair of literals, try adding the pair of literals to the formula and applying unit resolution. If inconsistency is determined then the binary clause consisting of the negations of the literals can be added to the formula, and the single failed literal rule applied again. Requires $O(n^3)$ time.

Table 4 shows the result of applying each of these kinds of simplifications to a series of encodings of blocks world and logistics planning problems. For each problem we show the number of variables in the instance and the percentage of those variables whose values are determined by local computation. The results for unit propagation (uprop) seem to confirm the intuition that there is little local information left in these problems. For the blocks world problems only between 2% and 13% of the variables are determined by unit propagation, and for the logistics problems no more than 3% are determined. However, the story changes dramatically for the failed literal rule (flit). In the blocks world from 33% to 100% (*i.e.*, the problem is completely solved!) of the variables are determined. In the logistics domain over 21% of the variables are eliminated. The binary failed literal rule (blit) is even more powerful. All of the blocks world problems were either solved completely or made trivial to solve (less than 131 variables) by this rule. The logistics problems were also further reduced in size, although they remained non-trivial to solve.

These results led us to select the failed literal rule as the default simplification procedure for Blackbox. It runs quickly and greatly decreases the size and hardness of the problem instance. So far the higher overhead ($O(n^3)$ versus $O(n^2)$) for the binary failed literal rule makes it impractical for the domains we have considered: it takes about as long to simplify the problem with the binary rule as to solve it using the unary simplifier and satz-rand. Still, these results suggest that an improved implementation of the binary rule could be of dramatic help in certain domains.

Thus we see that general limited inference computations on the SAT-encoding of planning problems provide a powerful complement to the kind of specialized mutex computations performed by the Graphplan front-end to Blackbox. There is a role both for planning-specific and domain-independent simplification procedures. In future work we plan to see if we can find other polytime simplification algorithms for SAT that take particular advantage of the structure of SAT encodings of planning problems.

4 Conclusions

We have provided an overview of the Blackbox planning system, and described how it unifies the plan graph approach to STRIPS planning with the planning as satisfiability framework. It provides a concrete step toward the *IJCAI Challenge* for unifying planning frameworks (Kambhampati 1997). We discussed empirical results that suggest that new randomized systematic SAT algorithms are particularly suited to solving SAT encodings of planning problems. Finally, we examined the role of limited inference algorithms in the creation and solution of problem encodings.

There is strong evidence that the best current general SAT engines are more powerful than the search (plan extraction) engines used by Graphplan and its descendents. Although it is possible to incorporate the heuristics used by these general solvers back into a specialized planner (see Rintanen (1998) for such an approach), given the rapid development of new SAT engines such a tactic may be premature. As an alternative, Giunchiglia *et al.* (1998) present evidence that it possible to dramatically boost the performance of a general SAT engine by feeding it a tiny amount of information about the structure of the encoding (in particular, identification of the action variables). There is also much work on improving the plan graph generation phase (*e.g.,* Kambhampati *et al.* (1997), Nebel *et al.* (1997)) which could be directly incorporated in Blackbox by replacing its front-end.

Blackbox is an evolving system. Our general goal is to unify many different threads of research in planning and inference by using propositional satisfiability as a common foundation. An important direction that we have not touched on in this paper is the use of *domain specific control knowledge* in planning (Bacchus and Kabanza 1996; Kautz and Selman 1998; Gerevini and Schubert 1998; Fox and Long 1998); see Cheng, Selman and Kautz (1999) for work on adding control knowledge to Blackbox.

References

Bacchus, F. and Kabanza, F. (1996). Using temporal logic to control search in a forward-chaining planner. In *New Directions in Planning*, M. Ghallab and A. Milani (Eds.), IOS Press, 141–153.

Bayardo Jr., R.J. and Schrag, R.C. (1997). Using CSP look-back techniques to solve real world SAT instances. Proc. AAAI-97, Portland, OR.

Baioletti, M. , Marcugini, S., and Milani, A. (1998). C-SATPlan: a SATPlan-based tool for planning with constraints. AIPS-98 Workshop on Planning as Combinatorial Search, Pittsburgh, PA.

van Beek, P. and Chen, X. CPlan: A constraint programming approach to planning. *Proc. AAAI-99*, Orlando, FL.

Blum, A. and Furst, M.L. (1995). Fast planning through planning graph analysis. *Proc. IJCAI-95*, Montreal, Canada.

Chapman, D. (1985). Planning for conjunctive goals. TR AI-TR-802, M.I.T. AI Lab.

Cheng, Y. , Selman, B., and Kautz, H. (1999). Control knowledge in planning: benefits and tradeoffs. *Proc. AAAI-99*, Orlando, FL.

Ernst, M.D., Millstein, T.D., and Weld, D.S. (1997). Automatic SAT-compilation of planning problems. *Proc. IJCAI-97,*

Nagoya, Japan.

Fikes, R. E., and Nilsson, N. 1971. STRIPS: A New Approach to the Application of Theorem Proving to Problem Solving. *Artificial Intelligence* 5(2): 189-208.

Fox, M., and Long, D. 1998. The automatic inference of state invariants in TIM. Forthcoming.

Gerevini, A. and Schubert, L. 1998. Inferring state constraints for domain-independent planning. *Proc AAAI-98*, Madison, WI.

Gomes, C.P., Selman, B., and Kautz, H. (1998). Boosting combinatorial search through randomization. *Proc. AAAI-98,* Madison, WI.

Giunchiglia, E., Massarotto, A., and Sebastiani, R. (1998). Act, and the rest will follow: exploiting determinism in planning as satisfiability. *Proc. AAAI-98*, Madison, WI.

Kambhampati, S. (1997). Challenges in bridging plan synthesis paradigms. *Proc. IJCAI-97*, Nagoya, Japan.

Kambhampati, S., Lambrecht, E., and Parker, E. (1997). Understanding and extending graphplan. *Proc. 4th European Conf. on Planning*, S. Steel, ed., vol. 1248 of *LNAI*, Springer.

Kautz, H., McAllester, D. and Selman, B. (1996). Encoding plans in propositional logic. *Proc. KR-96*, Boston, MA.

Koehler, J., Nebel, B., Hoffmann, J., and Dimopoulos, Y. (1997). Extending planning graphs to an ADL subset. *Proc. 4th European Conf. on Planning*, ibid.

Li, Chu Min and Anbulagan (1997). Heuristics based on unit propagation for satisfiability problems. *Proc. IJCAI-97,* Nagoya, Japan.

Luby, M., Sinclair A., and Zuckerman, D. (1993). Optimal speedup of Las Vegas algorithms. *Information Process. Lett.*, 17, 1993, 173–180.

Kautz, H. and Selman, B. (1992). Planning as satisfiability. *Proc. ECAI-92,* Vienna, Austria, 359–363.

Kautz, H. and Selman, B. (1998). The role of domain-specific axioms in the planning as satisfiability framework. *Proc. AIPS-98,* Pittsburgh, PA.

Kautz, H. and Selman, B. (1996). Pushing the envelope: planning, propositional logic, and stochastic search. *Proc. AAAI-1996,* Portand, OR.

McCarthy, J. and Hayes, P. (1969). Some philosophical problems from the standpoint of artificial intelligence. In *Machine Intelligence 4*, D. Michie, ed., Ellis Horwood, Chichester, England, page 463ff.

McDermott, D., *et al.* (1998). PDDL — the planning domain definition language. Draft.

Nebel, B., Dimopolous, Y., and Koehler, J. (1997). Ignoring irrelevant facts and operators in plan generation. *Proc. 4th European Conf. on Planning*, ibid.

Rintanen, J. (1998). A planning algorithm not based on directional search. *Proc. KR-98*, A.G. Cohn, L.K. Schubert, and S.C. Shapiro, eds., Morgan Kaufmann.

Selman, B., Kautz, H., and Cohen, B. (1994). Noise strategies for local search. *Proc. AAAI-94*, Seattle, WA.

Veloso , M. (1992). *Learning by analogical reasoning in general problem solving*. Ph.D. Dissertation, CMU.

Weld, D. (1999). Recent advances in AI planning. *AI Magazine*, to appear.

Temporal Planning with Mutual Exclusion Reasoning*

David E. Smith
NASA Ames Research Center
Mail Stop 269-2
Moffett Field, CA 94035 USA
de2smith@ptolemy.arc.nasa.gov

Daniel S. Weld
Department of Computer Science & Engineering
University of Washington, Box 352350
Seattle, WA 98195–2350 USA
weld@cs.washington.edu

Abstract

Many planning domains require a richer notion of time in which actions can overlap and have different durations. The key to fast performance in classical planners (*e.g.*, Graphplan, IPP, and Blackbox) has been the use of a disjunctive representation with powerful mutual exclusion reasoning. This paper presents TGP, a new algorithm for temporal planning. TGP operates by incrementally expanding a compact planning graph representation that handles actions of differing duration. The key to TGP performance is tight mutual exclusion reasoning which is based on an expressive language for bounding mutexes and includes mutexes between actions and propositions. Our experiments demonstrate that mutual exclusion reasoning remains valuable in a rich temporal setting.

1 Introduction

For many real world planning domains, the classical STRIPS model of action is inadequate — actions can be simultaneous, can have different durations, and can require metric resources. These characteristics are particularly prevelant in many NASA planning applications. For example, both spacecraft (such as DS1) and planetary rovers (such as Sojourner) use heaters to warm up various components, and these warming actions may span several other actions or experiments. Likewise, data compression and telemetry may overlap with other actions, and these actions may have wildly different durations (from milliseconds to hours).

While previous work on temporal planning has yielded some success [Vere, 1983; Pelavin & Allen, 1987; Penberthy & Weld, 1994; Muscettola, 1994], past systems

---

*We thank Corin Anderon, Keith Golden, Zack Ives, Ari K. Jonsson, Rao Kambhampati, Pandu Nayak and the anonymous reviewers for helpful comments and discussion. This research was funded in part by Office of Naval Research Grant N00014-98-1-0147, and by National Science Foundation Grants IRI-9303461 and IIS-9872128.

either scaled poorly or required humans to set up elaborate temporal constraint networks and specify guidance heuristics. The use of reachability analysis and mutual exclusion reasoning in Graphplan [Blum & Furst, 1995] and descendants such as IPP [Koehler *et al.*, 1997] has yielded spectacular speedup in classical planning, so it is natural to wonder if similar reasoning is extensible to the problem of temporal planning. This paper demonstrates that this extension is indeed possible in the generalized Graphplan context. In particular, we:

- Generalize the planning graph representation to deal with arbitrary time instead of graph levels. To accomplish this, we change to a much more compact cyclic graph, where actions and propositions appear only once in the graph annotated by their earliest possible start times.

- Extend mutual exclusion reasoning to work for actions that can have different durations and can overlap in arbitrary ways. This requires 1) a more general notion of *conditional mutex involving time bounds, and 2) mutex relationships between actions and propositions.*

- *Describe the Temporal Graphplan (TGP) algorithm, which operates incrementally on the generalized planning graph introduced above, and employs extended mutual exclusion reasoning on that graph.*

- *Present empirical evidence that 1) these generalizations do not significantly degrade performance, and 2) mutual exclusion remains valuable (and perhaps vital) in a richer temporal setting.*

2 Graphplan Review

We briefly summarize the Graphplan algorithm [Blum & Furst, 1997], because it forms the basis for TGP. Graphplan solves STRIPS planning problems in a deterministic, fully specified world. Both the preconditions and effects of its action schemata are conjunctions of literals (*i.e.*, denoting the add and delete lists). Graphplan alternates between two phases: *graph expansion* and *solution extraction*. The graph expansion phase extends a *planning graph* until it has achieved a necessary (but in-

Def 5. Let A be an action and P be a proposition. For each precondition Q_i of A, let Φ_i be the condition under which P is mutex with Q_i (true if emutex, ...). For each action B_j possibly supporting P, let Ψ_j be the condition under which A is mutex with B_j.

Let $\Phi = \left(\bigvee_i \Phi_i \right) \vee \left(\bigwedge_j (\Psi_j \vee (B_j] > \lfloor P)) \right) \wedge (\lfloor A < \lceil P)$. If Φ is satisfiable, then *action A and proposition P are cmutex when Φ.*

Loosely speaking, actions A and B are cmutex when A is cmutex with *any* precondition of B *or* vice versa.

Def 6. Let A and B be two actions which are not emutex. For each precondition P_i of B, let Φ_i be the condition under which A is mutex with P_i. For each precondition Q_j of A, let Ψ_j be the condition under which B is mutex with Q_j. Let $\Phi = \bigvee_i \Phi_i \vee \bigvee_j \Psi_j$. If Φ is satisfiable, then *actions A and B are cmutex when Φ.*

To see how these rules work, consider the example of Figure 2. Def 1 shows that X is emutex with $\neg X$. Def 5 further concludes that A is cmutex with Q when $\lfloor A < \lceil Q$, *i.e.* $\lfloor A < 2$; also that B is cmutex with P when $\lfloor B < \lceil P$, *i.e.* $\lfloor B < 1$. Intuitively, this makes sense — if A starts before 2, then it must overlap support for Q (*i.e.*, action B), but A and B are emutex. Finally, Def 4 shows that propositions P and Q are cmutex when $(\lfloor A < 2) \wedge (\lfloor B < 1)$. Adding the action durations to both sides of each inequality yields the following P/Q condition: $(\lceil A] < 3) \wedge (\lceil B] < 3)$. Thus we conclude that P and Q are cmutex when $(\lfloor P < 3) \wedge (\lfloor Q < 3)$, and this simple, symmetric condition is equivalent to a standard Graphplan proposition mutex that expires at time 3.

In bigger examples, the situation gets more complicated and asymmetric. Being able to quickly manipulate and simplify the cmutex conditions is a necessary ability for doing mutex reasoning with actions of varying duration. In Section 7, we describe a canonical form for these asymmetric conditions and explain how to quickly manipulate the conditions. In section 8, we present empirical evidence that mutex reasoning (while complex) yields important speedup.

5 Incremental Graph Expansion

Using the compact representation described above it is possible to update the planning graph in an incremental fashion. More precisely, the planner can keep track of what has changed in the graph, and only examine those propositions, actions and mutex relationships that can be affected by the changes. In particular:

- Adding a proposition node to the graph (*e.g.*, as the novel effect of a newly added action) can result in new actions (*i.e.*, those with the proposition as precondition) being added.
- Adding an action to the graph can cause new propositions (the action's effects) to be added, and/or can provide additional support for existing propositions. This new support can cause an action/proposition cmutex to terminate (by Def 5).

Figure 3: The TGP algorithm uses this *causation diagram* to guide its processing of events. Dark lines denote effects that occur later in time (*i.e.*, after an action execution).

- Terminating a cmutex between propositions P and Q can result in new actions (*e.g.*, actions with both P and Q as preconditions). In addition, it can cause an action/proposition cmutex to end (by Def 5), *e.g.*, between P and a consumer, C, of Q.
- Terminating a cmutex between action A and proposition P can cause a proposition/proposition cmutex to terminate (by Def 4), *e.g.*, between P and an effect, R, of A. In addition, it can cause an action/action cmutex to terminate (by Def 6), *e.g.*, between A and a consumer, C, of P.
- Terminating a cmutex between actions A and B can cause an action/proposition cmutex to end (by Def 5), *e.g.*, between A and an effect, R, of B.

These relationships are illustrated in the causation diagram of Figure 3. This diagram shows the structure of an incremental approach to graph expansion which provides speed gains proportional to the space reductions afforded by the compact representation.

Although the detailed bookkeeping is surprisingly complex, the basic TGP expansion algorithm is straightforward. Starting at time 0, it moves incrementally forward in time, progressively taking care of new propositions, new actions, new support for existing propositions and terminated mutexes. Persistence actions are *not* added explicitly. TGP keeps two main time-ordered priority queues, **NewSupp** and **EndPPMutex**. **NewSupp** contains triples $\langle A, P, t \rangle$ meaning proposition P has new support from action A at time t, and **EndPPMutex** contains pairs $\langle M, t \rangle$ meaning that M is a proposition/proposition cmutex that ended at time t. For efficiency, TGP also keeps a temporary list: **NewProps** is the subset of propositions mentioned in **NewSupp** that are new (*i.e.*, have no prior support).

Given a temporal planning problem (*i.e.*, a set of initial conditions, list of conjunctive goals, and set of ground actions), TGP graph expansion follows a loop with the following steps:

1. Add new actions and their effects to the graph. Note: TGP need only consider actions with a precondition in **NewProps**, or with two preconditions whose cmutex is in **EndPPMutex**. (At time zero, the initial conditions are added by a special instance of this step).

2. Add eternal and conditional mutex relationships for new actions; this includes both action/proposition and action/action mutexes.

3. Increment time to the next interesting entry in the `NewSupp` or `EndPPMutex` queues.

4. Recheck propositions with new support, possibly terminating (*i.e.*, tightening the bound on) action/proposition, action/action, and proposition/proposition cmutexes via a recursive algorithm that traverses the causation diagram.

5. Add action/proposition and proposition/proposition mutexes (both eternal and conditional) that involve new propositions.

6. If all goals are present in the graph, pairwise nonmutex, then call solution extraction. Otherwise (and if solution extraction fails) loop.

6   Solution Extraction

Once the planning graph has been extended to a time, t_G, when all goals are present and are pairwise nonmutex, TGP performs a backward chaining search for a working plan. This search is implemented using two main data structures: `Agenda`, and `Plan`. `Agenda` is a priority queue of $\langle P_i, t_i \rangle$ pairs, where P_i is a (sub)goal proposition and t_i is the time by which the goal must be true. `Agenda` is initialized by enqueuing $\langle G_i, t_G \rangle$ for each top level goal G_i, and the queue is sorted in decreasing temporal order. The second structure, `Plan`, which is initialized empty, stores the plan under construction as a set of $\langle A_i, s_i \rangle$ pairs, where s_i is the start time for action A_i. Persistence actions for a goal, denoted `persist-G`, are considered explicitly since they were not added during incremental graph expansion. The TGP solution extraction loop performs the following steps while `Agenda` is nonempty:

1. Dequeue $\langle G, t \rangle$ from `Agenda`.
2. If $t = 0$ and $G \neq$ initially true, then fail (backtrack). If $t > 0$ then let $\mathcal{S}$ equal the set of actions, $\{A_i\}$, such that each A_i has G as an effect and $A_i] \leq t$.
3. Choose A from $\mathcal{S} \cup \{$`persist-G`$\}$ such that A isn't mutex with any action in `Plan`. Add $\langle A, t - |A| \rangle$ to `Plan`, and for each precondition P of A, add $\langle P, t - |A| \rangle$ to `Agenda`. If no such A exists, backtrack. All such consistent A's must be considered for completeness.[1]

In essence, persistence actions are really just placeholders to ensure that TGP remembers to check all relevant action/proposition mutexes. Unfortunately, the presence of persistence actions adds redundancy to the space of plans, and this can lead to increased search. For a simple example of this, consider the domain of Figure 1 and suppose that the goal is to achieve both P and Q. The shortest plan involves executing actions A and B and requires two units of time. It should also be clear that A could start execution at any time in the interval $[0, 1]$. But TGP should *not* consider all such times, for

there is an uncountable number; indeed, the algorithm above restricts attention to start times which are an integral multiple of the greatest common divisor of the set of action durations, and this does not compromise completeness. For this example, the GCD restriction translates into starting A at time 0 or at time 1.

But TGP applies the following even stronger, completeness-preserving filter: all actions are executed as late as possible, unless this leads to a mutex inconsistency. Intuitively, one may think of this as defining a canonical form for plans by taking a legal plan and "tilting it" so that all actions "slide as far right" as they can go without breaking plan correctness. This completeness-preserving heuristic can be implemented by refusing to choose $A =$ `persist-G` to support subgoal G (in step 3) unless all other choices are inconsistent.

7   Approximating Mutex Conditions

As we mentioned at the end of Section 4, simplifying the logical and inequality formulae that bound the applicability of conditional mutexes is a key component of temporal reasoning and a central aspect of the TGP algorithm. Since these formulae can get arbitrarily complex, we developed the *asymmetric* restricted form in an effort to keep the reasoning tractable. The asymmetric form limits the mutex condition to a simple conjunction of two inequalities, but allows for different bounds in each inequality. For example, X is mutex with Y when $(\lfloor X < t_x) \wedge (\lfloor Y < t_y)$. In contrast with the restrictive symmetric form, when one plugs this representation into Def 4, there is no loss of information. Unfortunately this is not the case for Def 5 and 6. For example,

Def 6a (Asymmetric). Let A and B be two actions which are not emutex. For each precondition P_i of B, let $\Phi_i = (\lfloor A < t_{A_i}) \wedge (\lfloor P_i < t_{P_i})$ be the condition under which A is mutex with P_i. For each precondition Q_j of A, let $\Psi_j = (\lfloor B < t_{B_j}) \wedge (\lfloor Q_j < t_{Q_j})$ be the condition under which B is mutex with Q_j. Let $\Phi = \left(\bigvee_i (\lfloor A < t_{A_i}) \wedge (\lfloor B < t_{P_i}) \right) \vee \left(\bigvee_j (\lfloor B < t_{B_j}) \wedge (\lfloor A < t_{Q_j}) \right)$.

This condition does not simplify to the cannonical asymmetric form because of the $\wedge$ inside the $\vee$. There are several choices here for bounding approximations, and two possibilities are:

$$\Phi = (\lfloor A < \min(t_{A_i}, t_{Q_j})) \wedge (\lfloor B < \max(t_{B_j}, t_{P_i}))$$

and

$$\Phi = (\lfloor A < \max(t_{A_i}, t_{Q_j})) \wedge (\lfloor B < \min(t_{B_j}, t_{P_i}))$$

In practice we do something slightly more sophisticated by using the better of these max/min approximations on each successive pair of disjuncts. More precisely, the binary disjunction

$$((\lfloor A < x_1) \wedge (\lfloor B < y_1)) \vee ((\lfloor A < x_2) \wedge (\lfloor B < y_2))$$

---

[1] If A is the special "persist-G" action, let $|A|$ equal the greatest common divisor of the durations of the set of actions, and test for mutexes with proposition G.

becomes:

$$
\begin{array}{ll}
(\lfloor A < x_1) \wedge (\lfloor B < \max(y_1, y_2)) & \text{if } x_1 = x_2 \\
(\lfloor A < x_1) \wedge (\lfloor B < y_1) & \text{if } x_1 > x_2 \\
(\lfloor A < x_2) \wedge (\lfloor B < y_2) & \text{otherwise}
\end{array}
$$

We note that this form gives an exact result except in two cases, 1) when $x_1 < x_2 \wedge y_1 > y_2$ and 2) $x_1 > x_2 \wedge y_1 < y_2$. In those two cases the result will be a min/max approximation.

Def 5a (Asymmetric). Let A be an action and P be a proposition. For each precondition Q_i of A, let $\Phi_i = (\lfloor P < t_{P_i}) \wedge (\lfloor Q_i < t_{Q_i})$ be the condition under which P is mutex with Q_i. For each action B_j possibly supporting P, let $\Psi_j = (\lfloor A < t_{A_j}) \wedge (\lfloor B_j < t_{B_j})$ be the condition under which A is mutex with B_j. Let $\Phi = (\bigvee_i (\lfloor P < t_{P_i}) \wedge (\lfloor Q_i < t_{Q_i})) \vee \left(\bigwedge_j (\lfloor A < t_{A_j}) \wedge (\lfloor B_j < t_{B_j}) \vee (B_j] > \lfloor P) \right) \wedge (\lfloor A < \lceil P)$. If Φ is satisfiable, then *action A and proposition P are cmutex when Φ.*

As before, this condition does not simplify to our cannonical form; there are several choices here for bounding approximations, and one min/max argument leads to the following:

$$
\begin{aligned}
\Phi = \ & (\lfloor P < \min(t_{P_i}, t_{B_j} + |B_j|)) \wedge \\
& (\lfloor A < \max(t_{Q_i}, \min(\lceil P, t_{A_j})))
\end{aligned}
$$

Again, we improve on this equation by using the better of this and a symmetric max/min approximation on each successive pair of disjuncts.

8 Experimental Results

To date our implementation has been primarily used to verify the correctness and completeness of the cmutex rules; we have put little effort into code optimization. Direct comparison between TGP and other temporal planning systems is difficult for both availability and modularity reasons (HSTS [Muscettola, 1994], for example, is part of a larger embedded system and requires inputs which are radically different from classical representation). Nevertheless, we plan to do direct comparison in the immediate future.

In this section, we report on two experiments. First, we compare the performance of TGP with that of SGP [Weld, Anderson, & Smith, 1998] on plain STRIPS problems in order to see whether TGP's general, temporal framework comes at huge cost. Using a Power Mac G3/400 running Macintosh Common Lisp 4.2 in 68mb memory, we solved each problem ten times with SGP, with full TGP, and also using TGP with cmutex reasoning disabled. All runs were censored after 100 seconds, and we averaged across each set of ten runs to reach a single time for each problem/algorithm combination (Figure 4). TGP generally performs much better than SGP on the harder logistics problems. SGP wins on Med-bw2 and Big-bw2 which are dominated by solution extraction and appear sensitive to goal ordering decisions therein. We conjecture that SGP is faster at solution extraction either

Problem	TGP	No cmutex	SGP
Med-bw1	0.108	0.032	0.090
Big-bw1	0.529	>100.000	0.451
Med-bw2	1.034	46.019	0.418
Big-bw2	20.953	>100.000	4.535
Simple-block-stack	0.012	0.005	0.028
Simple-block1	0.023	0.006	0.042
Simple-block2	0.139	0.221	0.189
Simple-block3	0.723	8.219	0.560
Fix-strips1	0.024	0.011	0.329
Fix-strips2	0.026	1.443	0.546
Fix-strips3	0.026	2.602	0.546
Fix-strips4	0.054	60.079	0.840
Att-log0	0.014	0.010	3.352
Att-log1	0.018	0.015	7.332
Att-log2	0.026	0.115	11.692
Att-log3	1.516	3.453	>100.000
Att-log4	1.516	>100.000	>100.000
Log01	3.415	>100.000	>100.000
Log02	1.568	>100.000	>100.000
Strips-log-y-1	1.203	>100.000	>100.000
Strips-log-y-2	11.760	>100.000	>100.000
Strips-log-y-3	6.009	>100.000	>100.000

Figure 4: TGP with both cmutex and emutex reasoning beats emutex alone, and often beats SGP as well. Times are in seconds.

due to reduced overhead when checking mutexes or because of SGP's use of dynamic variable ordering [Bacchus & van Run, 1995].

In our second experiment we considered TGP's performance on temporal planning problems, and again looked at the contribution of asymmetric cmutex reasoning. In the absence of a test suite of large temporal planning problems, we took 30 STRIPS problems (mostly from ATT logistics domains); for each STRIPS problem we created 10 temporal problems by randomly assigning actions a duration from a normal distribution of integers in the range $[1, x]$. We then ran full TGP as well as TGP without cmutex reasoning on each of the resulting temporal planning problems, censoring after 100 seconds and averaging the results. We repeated this procedure for $x = 2, 4$, and 8. Figure 5 displays the results — clearly, cmutex reasoning provides a substantial gain in performance, especially for difficult problems.

We also note that TGP can handle relatively complex problems: *e.g.*, the solution to Log-4 is a 14-action plan; with emutex and cmutex reasoning combined, generation of the plan takes about 1.5 seconds on average.

9 Exogenous Events & Time Windows

Thus far, our description of temporal planning has focussed on handling actions of extended duration, but several other aspects are equally challenging. A general temporal planner must also handle exogenous events (*e.g.*, a solar eclipse or orbit perigee) and temporally constrained goals (*e.g.*, observations that must be performed during a time window). This section explains how the basic TGP algorithm can be extended with this functionality.

Suppose that as input the planning problem specified

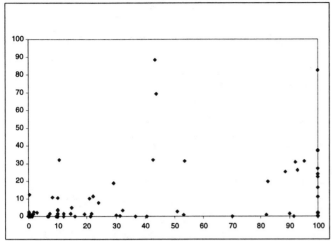

Figure 5: Cmutex reasoning provides substantial speedup on larger problems.

a set of $\langle G, s, e \rangle$ triples instead of a simple set of goals. We wish the planner to ensure that goal G is true at time t such that $s \leq t \leq e$. Handling this representation requires only minor changes to graph expansion and solution extraction. Graph expansion need never proceed past the maximum of the goal's endpoints, and TGP can claim failure without attempting solution extraction if some goal fails to enter the planning graph by its endpoint. Solution extraction is modified as follows:

1. Dequeue $\langle G, s, e \rangle$ from **Agenda**.
2. If $e = 0$ and $G \neq$ initially true, then fail (backtrack). If $e > 0$ then let $\mathcal{S}$ equal the set of actions, $\{A_i\}$, such that each A_i has G as an effect and $A_i] \leq e$.
3. If $s < e$ then add persist-G to $\mathcal{S}$.
4. Choose A from $\mathcal{S}$ such that A isn't mutex with any action in **Plan**. Add $\langle A, e - |A| \rangle$ to **Plan**, and for each precondition P of A, add $\langle P, 0, e - |A| \rangle$ to **Agenda**. If no such A exists, backtrack. All such consistent A's must be considered for completeness.

Note that this algorithm does not preclude G from being made true earlier than s and then persisting into the interval $[s, e]$. If one wishes to ensure that G is *made* true during that interval, one must post $\langle \neg G, 0, e - |A| \rangle$ as a goal in step 4.

There are (at least) two ways to handle exogenous events, and the first is simple. One can model exogenous events with a partial plan. Each event defines a special type of "action" with no preconditions but with the event's effects. Of course the agent has no choice about when these event "actions" are executed — these times are specified in the problem input. We denote the resulting set of $\langle E, t \rangle$ pairs with the variable **Events**. The following simplistic approach to graph expansion now suffices. During the normal process of expanding the planning graph, whenever the time is incremented to the starting time of an event E its effects are added into the graph. Similarly, solution extraction only requires minor modification: instead of initializing **Plan**

to the empty set, it is initialized to equal **Events**. Normal mutex reasoning now ensures that the events will be dealt with correctly.

While correct, this approach is simplistic in its treatment of recurring events (*e.g.*, cyclic periods of blocked communications due to satelite orbits). Instead of storing a single time label on each proposition (and action and mutex) node in the planning graph, one should store a set of time intervals that dictate the times when the proposition is possibly achieveable. As we envision these extensions, the two level plan graph starts to look very much like a temporal CSP network, in which propositions, actions and mutexes "come and go," *i.e.* are active according to sets of allowed time windows. Unfortunately, efficient techniques like arc-consistency are not powerful enough to derive and propagate mutex relationships. For this, k-consistency is required. However, experience shows that general k-consistency reasoning is too unfocused to be practical. Mutex reasoning is a highly-focused form of k-consistency, and we believe it will prove quite valuable in more general temporal planning problems. Extending these techniques to a general temporal CSP is something we have just begun to investigate.

10 Related Work & Discussion

There is a long history of research on temporal planning, but few systems have seen wide use, presumably due to performance limitations. Deviser [Vere, 1983] is an early temporal planner which required a library of HTN schemata and numerous domain-specific heuristics. FORBIN [Dean, Firby, & Miller, 1988] combined HTN reduction and temporal projection to tackle a similar problem, but the system ran on only a few examples. IxTeT [Ghallab & Laruelle, 1994] is a more recent HTN-decomposition temporal planner. Allen *et al.* developed several elegant temporal planners based on temporal logic [Allen & Koomen, 1983; Pelavin & Allen, 1987; Allen, 1991], but none supported metric durations. The Zeno planner [Penberthy & Weld, 1994] used an incremental Simplex algorithm to support actions with metric durations and continuous change, but performance was lacking — TGP is orders of magnitude faster. HSTS [Muscettola, 1994] plans using a dynamic, temporal CSP. When the planner commits to an action, new nodes are added to the CSP corresponding to the action's start and end. Constraints are then added between the various time points in the CSP to specify action duration and to enforce precondition and effect constraints for the action. Since the result is a *simple* temporal network, arc-consistency is sufficient to determine overall consistency [Dechter, Meiri, & Pearl, 1991]. HSTS does not do any form of reachability analysis or mutual exclusion reasoning — it must commit to a particular action or event before it can do any reasoning about consistency. Although it does not handle actions of varying duration, STAN uses an independently developed representation akin to our compact planning graph [Long & Fox, 1999].

We now discuss a method for extending Graphplan to handle temporal actions without new mutex rules or our compact planning-graph representation. Instead, macro-expand each action in the domain into a number of atomic pieces, each the length of the GCD of the set of action durations, and each a regular STRIPS action. This compilation is a bit tricky since it needs to generate new propositions and add them as preconditions and effects of the different pieces in order to ensure that the pieces sequence properly and that two actions don't intercalate inappropriately. Unfortunately, this approach would vastly expand the size of the domain theory, if the ratio of the GCD of action durations is small relative to the longest action — which is inevitable if there is wide variation in action durations.

11 Conclusions

This paper makes several contributions:

- We describe TGP, a fast planner that handles temporally-extended actions.
- TGP incrementally generates a compact planning graph representation.
- The key to TGP's performance is a novel form of reachability analysis for actions with varying duration. We distinguish conditional and eternal mutexes, and introduce action/proposition mutexes.
- We present experiments demonstrating the power of conditional mutex reasoning with an asymmetric condition representation.
- We explain how to extend TGP to handle exogenous events and goals that must be achieved during certain time windows.

We believe that the ideas introduced here can be extended to deal with a richer temporal language that allows: (1) for action preconditions which need not hold throughout execution (*i.e.*, "trigger" preconditions as well as "maintenance" preconditions), (2) for effects that become true during the action (instead of just at the end), and (3) temporary effects of actions (*e.g.*, inexhaustible resource usage). In section 9 we discuss methods for handling (4) exogenous events, and (5) time windows on goals and actions (*e.g.*, for modeling scientific experiments or astronomical observations), and we wish to experiment with the efficiency of these approaches. Yet, even without considering increased action expressiveness there are algorithm improvements to be made. Recall that during the backward chaining solution extraction phase, if a plan is not found then TGP initiates another search starting from a time which is a single GCD increment later. A more sophisticated approach would analyze the memoized nogoods and calculate the next time point when a nogood might vanish and start solution extraction there.

References

[Allen & Koomen, 1983] Allen, J., and Koomen, J. 1983. Planning using a temporal world model. In *Proceedings of the Eighth International Joint Conference on Artificial Intelligence*, 741–747.

[Allen, 1991] Allen, J. 1991. Planning as temporal reasoning. In *Proc. Conf. Knowledge Representation and Reasoning*, 3–14.

[Bacchus & van Run, 1995] Bacchus, F., and van Run, P. 1995. Dynamic variable ordering in csps. In *Proceedings of the 1995 conference on Principles and Practice of Constraint Programming*, 258–275.

[Blum & Furst, 1995] Blum, A., and Furst, M. 1995. Fast planning through planning graph analysis. In *Proceedings of the Fourteenth International Joint Conference on Artificial Intelligence*, 1636–1642. San Francisco, Calif.: Morgan Kaufmann.

[Blum & Furst, 1997] Blum, A., and Furst, M. 1997. Fast planning through planning graph analysis. *Artificial Intelligence* 90(1–2):281–300.

[Dean, Firby, & Miller, 1988] Dean, T., Firby, J., and Miller, D. 1988. Hierarchical planning involving deadlines, travel times, and resources. *Computational Intelligence* 4(4):381–398.

[Dechter, Meiri, & Pearl, 1991] Dechter, R., Meiri, I., and Pearl, J. 1991. Temporal constraint networks. *Artificial Intelligence* 49:61–96.

[Ghallab & Laruelle, 1994] Ghallab, M., and Laruelle, H. 1994. Representation and control in IxTeT, a Temporal Planner. In *Proceedings of the Second International Conference on Artificial Intelligence Planning Systems*, 61–67. Menlo Park, Calif.: AAAI Press.

[Koehler *et al.*, 1997] Koehler, J., Nebel, B., Hoffmann, J., and Dimopoulos, Y. 1997. Extending planning graphs to an ADL subset. In *Proceedings of the Fourth European Conference on Planning*, 273–285. Berlin, Germany: Springer-Verlag.

[Long & Fox, 1999] Long, D., and Fox, M. 1999. The efficient implementation of the plan graph in STAN. *J. Artificial Intelligence Research* 10.

[Muscettola, 1994] Muscettola, N. 1994. HSTS: integrating planning and scheduling. In Zweben, M., and Fox, M., eds., *Intelligent Scheduling*. Morgan Kaufmann.

[Pelavin & Allen, 1987] Pelavin, R., and Allen, J. 1987. A model for concurrent actions having temporal extent. In *Proceedings of the Sixth National Conference on Artificial Intelligence*, 246–250.

[Penberthy & Weld, 1994] Penberthy, J., and Weld, D. 1994. Temporal planning with continuous change. In *Proceedings of the Twelfth National Conference on Artificial Intelligence*. Menlo Park, Calif.: AAAI Press.

[Vere, 1983] Vere, S. 1983. Planning in time: Windows and durations for activities and goals. *IEEE Trans. on Pattern Analysis and Machine Intelligence* 5:246–267.

[Weld, Anderson, & Smith, 1998] Weld, D. S., Anderson, C. R., and Smith, D. E. 1998. Extending graphplan to handle uncertainty and sensing actions. In *Proceedings of the Fifteenth National Conference on Artificial Intelligence*, 897–904. Menlo Park, Calif.: AAAI Press.

COGNITIVE MODELING

COGNITIVE MODELING

Cognitive Modeling 1

An anthropocentric tool for decision making support

Elisabeth Le Saux
Philippe Lenca
Philippe Picouet
Jean-Pierre Barthélemy
LIASC - ENST Bretagne
BP 832
F-29285 BREST CEDEX

Abstract

Nowadays, firms, formerly considering the human operator as the main error source in process control, bend their efforts towards anthropocentric approaches to (re)integrate the human factor, especially the knowledge he/she has been developping, as the essential resource for a high quality decision process.

As the expert operator remains a rare resource and in order to capitalize his/her knowledge and know-how, the development of tools integrating this new dimension has become an important challenge.

This paper deals with a tool for knowledge acquisition under cognitive constraints, assuming that cognitive principles could be sometimes useful to improve machine learning tools results. Additionally, we have to cope with the difficulty linked to the fact that the acquired strategies have to be adapted on-line.

After describing the underlying cognitive principles, we will introduce the decision representation space and its related notations. We will then show the difficulties linked to the search of an optimal representation of the expert strategies set and how the heuristics used by the algorithm studied avoid these NP-complete problems. Finally, the current results and our work perspectives are stated.

1 Introduction

In a context of short time, if not on-line, decision making for the control of industrial processes, we've been led to defining a new method for process control experts decision support. As the classical machine learning and total quality management tools are not fully convenient here because they may not fully account for flexibility and reuse, we have adopted an anthropocentric approach, putting back the expert operator in the center of the decision process so that the algorithm can turn his/her capacities as advantage.

This on-going work has been initialised in the frame of the European Brite-Euram project COMAPS (COgnitive Management of Anthropocentric Production Systems - BE 96-3941).

2 Cognitive model

We distinguish 3 phases in the life cycle of a process (see figure 1 and [Barthélemy *et al.*, 1995]):

- a learning phase: the operator comes from the "novice" state to the "expert" state. During this phase, the operator daily makes trials on the process,

- a maintenance phase: the expert operator applies his/her know-how and adapts the process control rules,

- a reinitialisation phase (breaking/revision phase): the structural changes are so important that a simple adaptation is not enough anymore. A learning phase must be initialised once more.

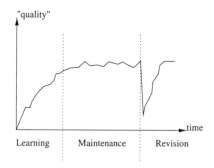

Figure 1: Life cycle of a process

In the frame of Anthropocentric Production Systems, which are forms of advanced manufacturing dependent upon a balanced integration between human skill, collaborative work organisation and adapted technologies, the human being is always *inside the loop* of the industrial process. Consequently, we have to adapt classical machine learning techniques to give back to the expert user the possibility to intervene in the decision process.

The underlying cognitive models we've used in this aim suppose the operator is an expert, applying stabilised process control rules for the usual maintenance of the production process. Once this restriction is cleared, we can apply the two following cognitive models:

- Bounded Rationality as described by Simon in [Simon, 1979],

- Moving Basis Heuristic from Barthélemy and Mullet ([Barthélemy and Mullet, 1992]).

2.1 Bounded Rationality

It assumes that the decision maker shows rationality (for situations in his/her usual domain of expertise) in the way that *something* is optimised. But this rationality is bounded by his/her cognitive abilities (of stocking and computing in short-term memory) and his/her satisfaction.

It also supposes he/she uses a not too large set of stable strategies involving a small number of attributes. These strategies, constructed by his/her experience, are assumed to be stored in his/her long-term memory and they may be rather complex.

In addition, it supposes that some combinations of attributes are used more frequently than others.

As defined, this bounded rationality can be seen as a constraint for the expert to search among aspects (subset of attribute values) for a subcollection that should be short but large enough, with regards to its size and/or to its quality, to achieve decision.

2.2 Moving Basis Heuristic

The Moving Basis Heuristic (MBH) involves three cognitive principles:

- *parsimony*: the decision maker manipulates a short subset of aspects due to his/her short-term memory capacity (storage capacity - there is no intermediate storage in the long-term memory - and computational abilities - strategies are computed in short-term memory -) - see [Aschenbrenner and Kasubek, 1978] and [Johnson and Payne, 1985] -,

- *reliability/warrantability*: the chosen sub-collection of aspects has to be large enough (size and/or quality) for individual or social justification - see [Adelbratt and Montgomery, 1980], [de Hoog and van der Wittenboer, 1986], [Montgomery, 1983] and [Ranyard and Crozier, 1983] -,

- *decidability/flexibility*: the decision maker must effect a choice by appropriate changes in the sub-collection until a decision is taken (he/she has to achieve decision quickly in almost all cases) - see [Huber, 1986], [Montgomery, 1983], [Svenson, 1979]. Consequently, his/her strategies must be stable.

These principles, together with Bounded Rationality, show that the expert operator uses, at the same time, only a small amount of information.

We are not working in the classical expert system frame because:

- the operator modelling and the extraction strategies are following these cognitive principles. The human expert uses complex strategies on a limited knowledge amount whereas expert systems use well-known algorithms on a huge amount of information;

- the operator is always "in the loop", even for the strategies convergence to a pertinent set of process control rules;

- the protocol and the algorithmic techniques are specific to the incremental and iterative aspect underlying the maintenance phase of a process life cycle.

To represent the expert's decision space, we have chosen to use a geometrical paradigm which is now described.

3 Representation space

Experts are taking their decisions among a set X of n parameters X_i together with their related value x_i. We call the tuple $x = (x_1, \ldots, x_i, \ldots, x_n)$ a *parameters setting*. Each parameter X_i has its values domain V_i which can correspond to nominal as well as numerical, discrete or continuous, values set.

On the base of this parameters setting, an expert has to take a decision, that is to say he/she has to answer the question: "What do I have to modify on the process parameters setting to obtain a good quality for my product (which is defined by the product parameters setting) ?". His/her answer consists of assigning a value d to the control parameter D, called *decision outcome* and the couple $cs = (x, d)$ is called a *control situation*.

We work in an n-dimensional space, each point of which corresponds to a parameters setting. The control situations, i.e. parameters settings which have already been examined by the expert, are labelled with the value d of the decision outcome D.

As experts' decisions are taken on a restricted subset of the available parameters that describe the process and/or the product to be manufactured, a process control rule R will have, as premises, a conjunction of a few number p of attributes aspects A_j, i.e. subsets of parameters values domain $(A_j \subset V_j)$. For example a rule R can be:

$$R: \text{ if } (x_\alpha \in A_\alpha) \wedge (x_\beta \in A_\beta) \text{ then } (D = d)$$

This means that the attributes not appearing in these preconditions can take any value without influencing the current decision process. In an n-dimensional space, a rule R can then be seen as a *cylinder* W for which the *dimensions* are all free except those corresponding to the restricted aspects of R's preconditions. This cylinder is labelled with the value of R's decision outcome. Figure 2 shows, in the 3-dimensional space $X = X_1 \times X_2 \times X_3$, the cylinder corresponding to the rule

$$R: \text{ if } (x_1 \in A_1) \text{ and } (x_3 \in A_3) \text{ then} (D = d)$$

The dimension corresponding to X_2 is free, every value of X_2 in V_2 is valid.

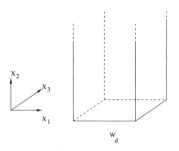

Figure 2: Representation of a cylinder

The *cylinder base* $B(W)$ is the hypercube defined by the rule R preconditions:

$$B(W) = \{(X_j, A_j)/A_j \subset V_j\}$$

It has a *dimension* $d(W)$ corresponding to the number of preconditions $d(W) = |B(W)|$. A set of cylinders is called a *paving* $\mathcal{P}$.

4   COMAPS algorithm

4.1   Three distinct phases

The COMAPS tool has been divided into 3 distinct parts which correspond more or less to the 3 phases of the process life cycle:

- the *learning phase* allows the extraction of an initial cylinders set $\mathcal{P}_0$ from a learning data set - a set of control situations that have already been examined by the expert - , called history and denoted H, using more standard but adapted machine learning - and especially decision tree learning - techniques;

- the *maintenance phase* takes the result $\mathcal{P}_0$ of the learning phase as well as H as inputs and it consists of an on-line update of the paving $\mathcal{P}$ according to new incoming control situations. This phase is the one we will further develop in this paper;

- a *conflict solving phase* is called when no acceptable - for the expert or for the maintenance phase algorithm - modification is found to correctly update the current paving. This kind of conflict mostly appears when important technological changes are observed on the process. For more details concerning this phase, see [Saunier, 1998].

Whereas the learning phase consists of an off-line process, the maintenance phase has to work at least at the pace the expert does: the algorithm is a kind of machine learning algorithm under cognitive constraints. But maintaining a paving consistent with the history to which one adds new control situations leads to face several NP-complete problems.

4.2   NP-complete problems encountered

P_1: **Search for maximal cylinders**

Let $V_1, \ldots, V_n$ n finite sets and $V = V_1 \times \ldots \times V_n$, D a finite set, $H \subseteq V \times D$, m an integer and $j \in D$.

Is there a cylinder W, corresponding to the decision outcome j for H (i.e. W H-compatible with j), of dimension d, so that $|W| \geq m$?

Searching for such a cylinder W, i.e. trying to find a cylinder covering as much control situations as possible, becomes NP-complete since $d \geq 2$.

P_2: **Covering by a minimal number of cylinders having at most d dimensions**

Let $V_1, \ldots, V_n$ n finite sets and $V = V_1 \times \ldots \times V_n$, D a finite set, $H \subseteq V \times D$, s an integer, $j \in D$ and $H^j = \{cs = (x, y) \in H / x \in V \text{ and } y \in D \text{ with } y = j\}$.

Does it exist a set of s cylinders $W_1, \ldots, W_s$ so that $\forall i$, W_i is H-compatible with j, $d(W_i) \leq d$ and $\bigcup_{1 \leq i \leq s} W_i \supseteq H^j$?

The covering problem by a minimal number of cylinders which dimension does not exceed a given integer d is NP-complete since $d \geq 2$.

P_3: **Consistency checking problem**

Let d an integer, $\{W_1, \ldots, W_m\}$ a set of cylinders differently labelled and so that $d(W_i) \geq d$.

Do we have $\bigcap_{1 \leq i \leq m} W_i \neq \emptyset$?

If we have cylinders corresponding to different decision outcome values, we will have to verify the consistency of the paving, checking their intersection is empty and this becomes a NP-complete problem since $d \geq 3$.

Most of the work to tune the maintenance phase consists then in finding heuristics to bypass these NP-complete problems.

4.3   Main notions

Covering notion

Because:

- not every point of the space can be a real parameters setting, some values combinations being impossible or known as giving a far too bad result according to the product quality,

- we are searching for maximal cylinders but their base is bounded according to the extreme parameters values of the control situations in H,

the cylinders space paving is not complete and thus, a control situation - i.e. a labelled point - can have several status:

- **not covered**: the parameters setting doesn't fit with any of the cylinders bases. In any other case, the control situation is **covered**,

- **bad covered**: the control situation is covered but the labelling of the covering cylinder(s) is not the same as its own decision outcome value,

- **well covered**: the control situation is covered and the covering cylinder(s) has (have) the same decision outcome value.

Priority between cylinders

As P_3 is NP-complete, we have decided not to guarantee a paving without any intersection. To cope with potential intersection, we have introduced a notion of priority between cylinders. We say that a cylinder W_1 has the priority over a cylinder W_2, noted $W_1 \mathcal{P}_r W_2$, if

$$|cs = (x,d)/cs \in W_1 \cap W_2| > \sigma$$

and if

$$\frac{|cs = (x,d)/cs \in W_1 \cap W_2 \land d = label(W_1)|}{|cs = (x,d)/cs \in W_1 \cap W_2 \land d = label(W_2)|} > \tau$$

where σ and τ are thresholds either fixed with the tool configuration or adapted dynamically according to the size of H and to the proportion of each label in H.

Two cylinders W_1 and W_2 of different labels can thus intersect without having neither $W_1 \mathcal{P}_r W_2$ nor $W_2 \mathcal{P}_r W_1$ and this can happen if:

- their intersection is empty, i.e. no control situation has already been seen in this area of the space,
- there are not enough control situations in the intersection according to the threshold σ,
- none of the two labels in competition is related to a number of control situations significantly higher according to the threshold τ.

Evaluation of a cylinder accuracy

As we cannot guarantee to generate a paving with cylinders only covering control situations labelled in the same way and without any intersection of differently labelled cylinders, we need to be able to measure the "quality" of the paving and thus the "quality" of a cylinder with regards to H.

The quality of a cylinder, which we call $CF(W)$, is estimated by the ratio between the number of control situations it covers well and the number of control situations it covers:

$$CF(W) = \frac{|cs = (x,d)/cs \in W \land d = label(W)|}{|cs/cs \in W|}$$

Of course, a cylinder W is too weak if $CF(W)$ is not at least equal to the proportion of control situations having $d(cs) = label(W)$. In the same way as for the priority computation, we have defined a threshold β under which a new cylinder to be integrated to the paving can not be accepted.

Furthermore, the global quality of the paving is defined as the average of the n constituting cylinders qualities:

$$CF(\mathcal{P}) = \frac{1}{n} \sum_{i=1}^{n} CF(W_i)$$

As the aim of maintenance phase is to update the current paving, this quality evaluation is also used to determine if a possible modification has to be applied or not. The criterion is then that the quality of the rule after modification is at least as good as the old rule one.

"Wait and see" policy

As the expert's rules are supposed to be stabilised, the algorithm is designed in a way that no action on the current paving is immediately tried. It waits until a sufficient number of control situations have confirmed something has to be modified. The arrival of an inconsistent (i.e. bad or not covered) control situation implies a modification only if there are *enough* control situations with the same decision outcome value in its **neighbourhood**. This neighbourhood can be defined in several ways according to the inconsistent type. For example, for a not covered control situation $cs = ((x_1, \ldots, x_i, \ldots, x_n), d)$, we define it is an hypercube which aspects are $[x_i - \alpha(V_i), x_i + \alpha(V_i)]$, for numerical attributes and $\{x_i\}$ for nominal attributes. If the control situation examined appears at the intersection of at least two rules, this neighbourhood is the intersection itself.

5 The maintenance phase

We remind that its aim is to update continuously the cylinders paving, starting with an initial paving P_0 which is consistent with the history H of the process and taking into account, as they arrive, new control situations the expert user has just added, with regards to the following constraints, highly linked to the cognitive principles which have to be followed:

- remaining consistent with H at each step, i.e. modifying the cylinders so that H is still correctly described by the updated rules set underlying the cylinders paving,
- keeping a small number of dimensions (at most 4 to be compatible with the expert's short-term memory abilities) in the cylinders base - a cylinder can be based on more than 4 dimensions but it should not be more than a temporary state, corresponding for example to a less common situation for the expert, during which he has to adapt a bit further his/her own rules -,
- keeping a small number of cylinders in the paving.

5.1 Cylinders modification functionalities

Different modification functions have been implemented that can be applied to one or several cylinders of the current paving, according to the status of the control situation to be integrated to H:

1. generalisation of an existing cylinder by suppressing one constrained dimension:
   $d(W^t) = d(W^{t-1}) - 1 \quad - \quad W^{t-1} \subset W^t$

2. generalisation of an existing cylinder by extending the possible values over one dimension. For one i so that $A_i \subset V_i$,
   $A_i^{t-1} \subset A_i^t \quad - \quad W^{t-1} \subset W^t$

3. creation a cylinder by dividing a cylinder into two:
   $W^{t-1} \rightarrow W_1^t \oplus W_2^t$ with $label(W_1^t) = label(W^{t-1})$ and $label(W_2^t) \neq label(W^{t-1})$

4. creation a new cylinder, according to the current control situation $cs = (x, d)$, by creating aspects for all the attributes[1] and taking the conjunction of at most four of them to define the new cylinder base, which will have d as a label.

5. restriction of a cylinder that is unnecessarily large by adding some constraints on one dimension:
$$d(W^t) = d(W^{t-1}) + 1 \quad - \quad W^t \subset W^{t-1}$$

6. restriction of a cylinder by restricting the aspect extension on one of its dimension. For one i so that
$A_i \subset V_i$,
$$A_i^t \subset A_i^{t-1} \quad - \quad W^t \subset W^{t-1}$$

7. modification of the priority between the cylinders covering the current control situation by recomputing it.

5.2 Functionalities use

Of course, these modifications are not used in any case.

If the new control situation to be treated is already well covered, the only thing we might try is the first function: as the cylinder is confirmed by the arrival of a well classified example, we can try to see if all its dimensions are needed or if it can be extended without loosing its quality (using function (1.).

For a control situation currently not covered, the algorithm will first try to integrate it to an existing cylinder of the same label using function (2.) and, if it doesn't work, to create a new cylinder to cover it using function (4.).

For a bad covered control situation cs, and according to the inconsistency type with regards to the cylinder(s) involved - i.e. considering the "environment": number of cylinders covering cs, number of different labels, priority value(s), ... - several of these seven modifications can be tried to improve the situation. But, as the expert rules are supposed to be stabilised, the order in which these functions are applied is strongly dependent on how deep the resulting modification is for the paving.

Indeed, according to the cognitive model, cylinders must stay large - i.e. with not too constrained bases, which corresponds to short rule premises conjunction - and not too numerous.

One of the criteria involved while sorting the functions is that they imply local or more global modifications: function (7.) - priority modification - is clearly the one that leads to the most local modification whereas function (4.) - cylinder creation - leads to far deeper changes so it is the last one tested.

Function (1.) is not sorted with the other ones: it is a bit different because it is applied only in case the current control situation is well covered by a too restricted, and thus not satisfying, cylinder - i.e. corresponding to a rule for which there are more than four aspects in the premise -.

---
[1] We don't describe here the way these aspects are computed.

As the modifications implied by function (2.) - extension of an aspect values - remain local, it is the second the algorithm tests. Then, the third alternative is function (3.) - cylinder division -: of course it creates a new cylinder but in an area that is already covered by a more general cylinder.

Finally, functions (5.) and (6.) are tried, in this order, because they both imply smaller cylinders - i.e. more constrained premises for the rules -, which contradicts one of the cognitive principles.

6 Comparison with previous works in this domain

This kind of approach, using Bounded Rationality and MBH principles as underlying cognitive principles to an anthropocentric algorithm, has already been led and validated in [Barthélemy et al., 1995] and [Laurent et al., 1994]. The improvements we've brought for COMAPS are of three kinds:

- we don't assume anymore any hypothesis on the order of the attributes modalities: the previous works were turning this order, which corresponds to the decision maker's attractiveness scales, to advantage because the representation space was derived from Galois' lattices, but these scales are difficult to obtain without using verbalisation techniques and they are different from an expert to another;

- the formerly defined methods were rapidly limited by the number of attributes taken into account for the computation. As for real industrial processes we often have to deal with more than 20 parameters, it was a real need to find a way to push back this limit, especially because we can not afford long computation time for an on-line control;

- the expert is observed in his/her real decision making process: after the initial set of rules has been extracted off-line, every new control situation is given a decision outcome value on-line by the expert and is immediately treated by the algorithm. The former developments were using dynamically computed questionnaires to ask the expert its decision in a given situation but this was not his/her normal task, and if something was changing in his/her decision rules, it could be modified in the computed rules only by starting again to answer a new set of questions.

7 Current results and work perspectives

In the frame of this european project, we have the possibility to test our program on three real industrial processes, in the fields of copper foil production, printed circuit boards manufacturing and brake pads production.

7.1 Current results

Real data being confidential, we've been testing the algorithm through a mockup with coded data. The first tests have been led without the expert, dividing the coded data set into a training set for the learning phase and an incoming situations set for the maintenance phase.

With one of the pilot sites data, we had the possibility to test the behaviour of the maintenance phase facing a known evolution of the process control. Starting from a set of 6 institutional rules and an history of 1086 cs, the rules set has been updating according to 556 new cs.

The results according to the quality of the rules are summarized in Figure 3, the last column corresponding to the type of modification applied according to the list presented in 5.1. All the results have been shown to the expert and they were validated.

Rule	CF Before	CF After	Modification
1	0.41	1	
2	0.84	0.87	
3	0.56	0.87	5.
4	0.57	0.69	6.
5	0.89	0.87	5.
6	0.70	0.88	5. and 6.
7		0.84	4.
8		0.86	4.

Figure 3: Quality of the rules

7.2 Work perspectives

We still have to improve the internal model of priority between cylinders: at this time, it is represented by a boolean matrix where $P(i, j)$ is 1 if $W_i \mathcal{P}_r W_j$ and is 0 otherwise. This doesn't give any information concerning the priority status for an intersection of more than two cylinders and it's not possible to deduce it looking at the priority between every pair of cylinders involved. On the opposite, this kind of deduction could lead to a nonsense: if we have, for example, three cylinders W_1, W_2 and W_3 with $W_1 \mathcal{P}_r W_2$, $W_2 \mathcal{P}_r W_3$ and $W_3 \mathcal{P}_r W_1$, which of them should have the priority ?

In addition, we wait for a prototype, now under development, to be installed (benchmarking in April this year) to be able to make some more tests, but this time in a real decision context and not only with *a posteriori* validation.

Some comparisons between classical machine learning tools, and especially decision tree learning tools like ID3 [Quinlan, 1986] and C4.5 [Quinlan, 1993] are also under way.

References

[Adelbratt and Montgomery, 1980] T. Adelbratt and H. Montgomery. Attractiveness of decision rules. *Acta Psychologica*, (45):177–185, 1980.

[Aschenbrenner and Kasubek, 1978] K.M. Aschenbrenner and W. Kasubek. Challenging the custing syndrome: multi-attribute evaluation of cortison drugs. *Organizational Behaviour and Human Performances*, (22):216–234, 1978.

[Barthélemy and Mullet, 1992] J.-P. Barthélemy and E. Mullet. A model of selection by aspect. *Acta Psychologica*, (79):1–19, 1992.

[Barthélemy et al., 1995] J.-P. Barthélemy, G. Coppin, and F. Guillet. Smelting process control: from experimental design to acquisition of expertise. In *International Conference on Industrial Engineering and Production Management*, volume 2, pages 2–11, March 1995.

[de Hoog and van der Wittenboer, 1986] R. de Hoog and G. van der Wittenboer. Decision justification, information structure and the choice of decision rules. In B. Brehmer, H. Jungermann, P. Lourens, and G. Sevon, editors, *New direction in research on decision making*, North Holland, 1986.

[Huber, 1986] O. Huber. Decision making as a problem solving process. In B. Brehmer, H. Jungermann, P. Lourens, and G. Sevon, editors, *New directions in research on decision making*, 1986.

[Johnson and Payne, 1985] E.J. Johnson and J.W. Payne. Effort and accuracy in choice. *Management Science*, (31):295–314, 1985.

[Laurent et al., 1994] S. Laurent, E. Pichon, and R. Bisdorff. Solving by resolving: cognitive solving approach to finite decision problems in chip. *First European Conference on Cognitive Science in Industry*, pages 53–66, 1994.

[Montgomery, 1983] H. Montgomery. Decision rules and the search for a dominance structure: toward a process model of decision making. In P.C. Humphrey, O. Svenson, and A. Vari, editors, *Analyzing and Aiding Decision Process*, North Holland, 1983.

[Quinlan, 1986] J. R. Quinlan. Induction of decision trees. *Machine Learning*, 1(1):81–106, 1986.

[Quinlan, 1993] J. R. Quinlan. *C4.5: Programs for Machine Learning*. Morgan Kaufmann, San Mateo, CA, 1993.

[Ranyard and Crozier, 1983] R. Ranyard and R. Crozier. Reasons given for risky judgment and choice: a comparison of three tasks. In P.C. Humphrey, O. Svenson, and A. Vari, editors, *Analyzing and Aiding Decision Process*, North Holland, 1983.

[Saunier, 1998] P. Saunier. Comaps: check as you decide paradigm. In *Seventeenth European Conference on Human Decision Making and Manual Control*, December 1998.

[Simon, 1979] H.A. Simon. *Models of thought*. Yale University Press, New Haven, 1979.

[Svenson, 1979] O. Svenson. Process description of decision making. *Organizational behaviour and human performance*, (23):86–112, 1979.

Autonomous Concept Formation

Edwin D. de Jong
Vrije Universiteit Brussel
Artificial Intelligence Lab
Pleinlaan 2, B-1050 Brussels, Belgium
edwin@arti.vub.ac.be
http://arti.vub.ac.be

Abstract

A model for the formation of *situation concepts* is described. A characteristic of this form of concept formation is that it does not require instructive feedback. This renders it suitable for concept formation by autonomous agents. It is experimentally demonstrated that situation concepts constructed independently by several agents can convey useful information between agents through a learned system of communication. A relation was found between the development of the learned system of communication and the duration of the situations.

1 Introduction

The ability to communicate with others is a manifestation of our intelligence. An understanding of communication therefore contributes to the goals of artificial intelligence. A requirement for higher forms of communication, such as human language, is the development of concepts that are to be communicated. In this paper, a model is proposed that describes the formation of a particular type of concepts.

A *situation concept* is a part of the state of an environment that determines how the environment will present itself to a certain agent in response to (possibly absent) actions of that agent. Therefore, a situation concept is an agent specific aspect of the complete state of the environment. In many environments, the state of an environment can not be completely determined from the current sensor inputs. Thus, knowledge about the interaction history with the environment yields extra information about the current state. Situation concepts can be formed by agents by observing patterns in the sequence of inputs from the environment, actions of the agent, and subsequent evaluative feedback. They allow an agent to predict some aspect of the future, e.g. the evaluative feedback that will follow a certain action, or the next input from the environment given the action.

An important characteristic of situation concepts is that they can be developed by autonomous agents, since only evaluative feedback is assumed to be available from the environment. This distinguishes the method from traditional concept learning methods such as decision tree learning (see e.g. [Quinlan, 1990]), which require instructive feedback and thus are a form of supervised learning. [1] Although unsupervised learning methods, such as clustering, can also be viewed as methods for concept formation, these are less suitable as a basis for an agent that has to adapt itself to an environment, since feedback on how well the agent is performing can by definition not be taken into account.

It is assumed here that an autonomous agent should learn to produce successful behavior based on evaluative feedback. This feedback may be provided directly by the environment, as is usually assumed in reinforcement learning, or it may be determined by the agent itself based on its internal state and its interaction with the environment, which seems to correspond better to how humans and animals function. When such an agent adapts its behavior to an environment, its choice of actions will come to depend on its interaction history with that environment. However, the number of possible interaction histories may be large, even if histories of small length are considered, so that the exact same history is unlikely to recur frequently. In the interest of learning, it is therefore necessary to generalize.

Some generalization methods for reinforcement learning can be used as a basis for situation concept formation. A prerequisite is that the representation of the states of the environment is adapted to the learning problem, and provides a division of the interaction space into regions, such that an agent only needs to consider a region within that space, and not the specific interaction history (a point within that region), in order to decide which action to take. A good example of such an algorithm is the U-Tree method [McCallum, 1996], which uses the Kolmogorov-Smirnov test to determine whether the distribution of long-term expected rewards within a region of the state-action space, determined by features on the interaction history, varies or not. However, most generalization methods for reinforcement learning can not be used as a basis, either because the representation of the interaction space is not adapted to the learn-

---

For an exposition of the difference between evaluative and [1]instructive feedback, see e.g. [Sutton and Barto, 1998], pp. 31-33.

ing problem (e.g. plain discretization, CMAC [Albus, 1981]), or because no crisp division of the state-action space is used (e.g. neural networks).

In cognitive science literature, many models for concepts are discussed, see e.g. [Lakoff, 1987; van Orman Quine, 1975; Putnam, 1988]. When viewed as a cognitive model for a specific type of concepts, situation concepts distinguish themselves from other models by the level of detail at which they are specified. Since this level allows direct implementation, their validity can be tested in computational experiments, as testified by this paper. It should be emphasized that situation concepts are an idealized model of a particular class of concepts, and are not claimed to be a general model for the formation of concepts. Nonetheless, the possible forms of situation concepts are diverse, as may be judged from the examples in the paper.

Situation concepts are especially suited to serve as a basis for communication. In the model of language evolution investigated here, concept formation interacts with a process linking concepts to words or signals, see [Steels, 1997; Steels and Vogt, 1997]. In literature on the evolution of language, communication often corresponds directly to actions, which limits communication to the instruction of other agents. Examples include [Werner and Dyer, 1991], where sounds tell agents in a simulation how to move to the emitter of the sound, [Yanco and Stein, 1993], where a leader robot instructs a following robot what way to move, and [Oliphant, 1997], where concepts are abstract and are modeled as having a one to one correspondance with situations. An exception is [MacLennan, 1991], where the term situation is also used to describe what the symbols that are communicated represent. The meaning of those situations is quite different from situation concepts though, since they are equal to the input of the agent, hence no concept formation is involved. In [Billard and Hayes, 1999], an interesting experiment is described where a robot develops concepts as regularities in its own behavior. This is possible because actions are selected by a process independent of concept formation, which explains why the problem mentioned above with relation to unsupervised learning plays no role here. Since the meaning of concepts in that work (objects in the environment of the robots) is fixed in advance for one of the robots (the teacher) though, it does not deal with the initial creation of the concepts, with which we will be concerned here.

Situation concepts are constructed individually by each agent. Since the concepts are based on experience with the same environment, there should be strong similarities between the conceptual systems of different agents, given that they are of the same type or species. This provides a basis for the development of communication. When agents link signals they receive and produce to their current situation, a system of communication may result where the individual situation concepts of agents are associated with shared signals. This principle is demonstrated in a simulated environment. The

question that will be investigated here is whether the communication that results from this process is useful.

The structure of the paper is as follows. Section 2 formally defines situation concepts in general and describes how agents form a specific type of situation concepts in the experiments of this paper. Section 3 describes how agents adapt associations between concepts and signals in order to develop a system of communication. Section 4 explains how agents may utilize situation concepts once a system for communicating them has been learned. The setup of the experiments is described in section 5. In section 6, the benefit of communicating situation concepts is measured. Finally, section 7 presents conclusions drawn from the experiments.

2 Formation of Situation Concepts

In the most general formulation, a situation concept is a subset of the possible histories of an agent's interaction with its environment with the property that knowing to which situation concept the actual history of interaction corresponds, allows the agent to predict some aspect of the future. As an example, let's consider the advent of a thunder storm. Both seeing a flash of lightning and hearing a roaring sound of thunder are indicators that in a few moments, it may start to rain. Thus, these observations may be grouped together to form a situation which has the property that a shower is likely to arrive within short, whereas this possible future event will be less likely in the case of a bright blue sky. In this example, the situation is based on observations in the recent past, and the prediction concerns future observations. Actions of the agent or evaluative feedback played no role. Another example is the *schema* mechanism described in [Drescher, 1991], where the context and an agent's action are used to predict the result of the action. In that framework, a context is specified as a set of conditions and can be viewed as an instantiation of situation concepts, since it defines a subset of the possible histories of interaction (viz. the current input) and has predictive value.

To formally describe interaction histories, time will be discretized here, which is a simplification of situation concepts in general. At time T, the complete interaction history H_{max} is defined as the following set of symbols:

$$\{X_1, X_2, ...X_T, A_1, A_2, ...A_{T-1}, R_1, R_2, ...R_{T-1}\}$$

where for $0 \leq t \leq T$, X_t, A_t and R_t are symbols representing the input, action and reward, an evaluative feedback, at time t. Situation concepts are defined for a subset H of this complete history:

$$H \subseteq H_{max}$$

A situation concept S_p is a membership function that accepts a value for each element of an interaction history H within the corresponding domain ($\mathbf{I}^m$ for X_t, $\mathbf{A}^n$ for A_t and $\mathbf{R}$ for R_t) and yields a boolean value. If and only if this value is *true* at time T, the situation concept S_p applies; equivalently, it may be said in this case that the agent is in situation S_p.

In the rest of the paper, the interaction history of situation concepts will consist of the current input from the environment, so that $H = \{X_T\}$. They are chosen such as to allow to predict the subsequent reward given an action the agent may choose. In the experiments, the formation of situation concepts is based on the Adaptive Subspace algorithm of [de Jong and Vogt, 1998], which recursively splits a space into two halves in a selected dimension, based on some split criterion. The split criterion here is whether the distribution of rewards over the sensor space differs between the two halves, which yields an algorithm similar in function to the previously mentioned U-tree algorithm and the continuous state generalization algorithms in [Uther and Veloso, 1998]. Initially, the complete sensor space is a single region. Regions have a one to one correspondance with situation concepts, and hence there is a single situation concept. When the distribution of rewards varies substantially within a region of the sensor space, this region is split in half, thus replacing it with two half-sized regions. This principle is applied recursively, and terminates when each situation corresponds to a region of the sensor space within which rewards are distributed homogeneously.

The result of concept formation is a tree which divides the sensor space into situations, represented by internal nodes, and for each situation contains a subtree representing possible actions in that situation, where each leaf stores an estimation of the reward following the selection of the corresponding action in that situation. An example of such a tree is shown in figure 1. The actions that are distinguished depend on the situation and are constructed based on the same principle as the situations.

Action selection depends solely on the situation, not on the specific input determining the situation. The tree of situations and actions is traversed from left to right, following the conditions in the nodes that apply to the current input. This yields the current situation, represented as an internal node of the tree. The possible actions are now represented in the leaves of this node's subtree. Greedy action selection would select an action determined by the leaf with the highest estimation of the subsequent reward. For learning though, exploration is necessary. In the experiments here, the choice of explorative actions is based on the estimation error when the action was last selected and the time since it was last selected, and hence combines error based and recency based properties. For an overview of other exploration policies, see [Thrun, 1992].

3   Development of Communication

Situation concepts organize the possible inputs an agent may receive into groups such that experience gained with a certain input influences the reward estimation of similar inputs. Apart from speeding up learning, this form of generalization provides a basis for the development of communication. Although the specific concepts agents create may differ, they result from a search for patterns

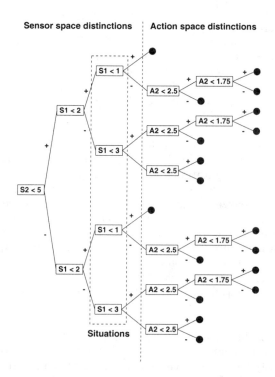

Figure 1: Example of a tree that defines situation concepts. Nodes to the left of the dotted line divide up the sensor space by constraining the range of a sensor (+ and - represent the outcome of the inequality), nodes to the right divide up the action space. The dotted rectangle contains four situation concepts.

in interactions with the same environment. If a relation between the individual concepts of the agents and a shared set of signals can be found, this would allow the agents to 'speak a common language'. To this end, agents maintain a set of signals for each situation. An association between a signal and a situation has a *use* score and a *success* score. When an agent is in situation S, it selects a signal associated with S and emits it. After every agent has produced the signal corrresponding to its situation, every agent receives the collection of signals produced. Upon receiving these signals, each agent increases its use scores for the associations between these signals and the current situation. Since the conceptual systems of agents may differ, the signals associated with a certain state of the environment may differ from agent to agent.

4   Benefitting from Communication

The ability to communicate enables a capacity of gaining knowledge or information that cannot be attained through use of the ordinary perceptual devices. This advantage explains why so many animals, including humans, have retained the faculty to develop communication in the course of evolution once it evolved. An inspiring example is the alarm call system of vervet monkeys. Ingenious experiments involving playing back the calls produced by these monkeys show that these animals have a warning system with specific calls for different kinds of predators [Seyfarth *et al.*, 1980]. This example demonstrates the principle of how situation concepts can be useful when communicated. When a monkey did not detect the threat of an approaching predator, successful interpretation of the alarm calls produced by other community members may induce awareness of its perilous situation. Put in abstract terms, the signals an agent receives from the other agents allow it to deduce that its situation is different from what it had observed using ordinary perception.

It should be understood that the ultimate meaning of a situation concept is determined by its predictive value, and not by the pattern in interaction history that has been observed to be correlated with this aspect of the future. In terms of the alarm calls example, the situation corresponds to the presence of a predator, rather than to the observation of the predator by a monkey, even though situation concepts are by necessity initially constructed as correlations between interaction histories and consequences. Therefore, when a significant aspect of an agent's environment cannot be perceived directly through perception, communication may be the only way to determine the actual situation.

The benefit of communication may surface when sensor information is incomplete. The resulting uncertainty may be partially resolved by means of communication. Once a coherent mapping between situations and signals exists, the likelihood of being in a certain situation given the signals an agent receives can be determined using Bayes' formula:

$$P(\mu \mid \sigma) = \frac{P(\mu \wedge \sigma)}{P(\sigma)} = \frac{P(\mu) \cdot P(\sigma \mid \mu)}{P(\sigma)}$$

where σ is a signal that was perceived, and μ is a situation. If the probability of a certain situation given the signals is high enough, the agent may decide that it is in that situation, and not in the situation indicated by its sensors (or, in general, its interaction history).

The use of Bayes' formula assumes that a coherent mapping between situations and signals is already available. However, since this is initially not the case, agents need to adapt their private associations between situations and signals. Depending on the process of adaptation, a coherent mapping may or may not emerge. Two sources of information are available as input to this adaptation process. Firstly, an agent may use its sensors to determine its situation and update the use scores of the associations between that situation and the signals it receives from the other agents. Secondly, the situation may be determined from the signals emitted by the other agents. To calculate the probability of being in a situation given the signals using Bayes' formula, a linear combination of the use and success scores is filled in for $P(\sigma \mid \mu)$ in the above formula; the remaining two values are obtained from counts of the occurence of situations and signals. This second source of information indicates more directly whether the link between a signal and a situation can increase the performance of the agent. Concretely, the estimated value of the action and

the actual reward following the action are compared to decide whether the determination of the situation was correct or not. If the magnitude of the difference is small, the success scores of the associations between the signals and the situation should be increased. Conversely, if the absolute difference exceeds a threshold, they should be decreased. Sending signals is not followed by evaluation, and hence does not influence scores.

Figure 2 shows an outline of the algorithm specifying when the situation is determined based on signals, and how association use and success are updated.

```
x := receive-input()
sensor-situation := determine-situation-from-sensors(x)
produce-signal(sensor-situation)
signals := receive-signals()
signal-situation := determine-situation-from-signals(signals)
if (P(signal-situation | signals) > random(1.0))
  action := choose-action(signal-situation)
  act(action)
  R := receive-reward()
  if (|R - value(action)| < threshold)
    increase-association-success(signal-situation, signals)
    for ((s in situations) and (not (s = signal-situation)))
      decrease-association-success(s, signals)
  else
    decrease-association-success(signal-situation, signals)
  update-value(action)
else
  all-signals := signals(sensor-situation)
  decrease-association-use(sensor-situation, all-signals)
  increase-association-use(sensor-situation, signals)
  action := choose-action(sensor-situation)
  act(action)
  R := receive-reward()
  update-value(action)
```

Figure 2: An outline of the algorithm. The main choice is whether the agent uses signals or sensors to determine its situation. This choice determines whether to adapt the use or the success of the association between the situation and the signals received from other agents.

5 Experimental Setup

In the experiments, five agents can move horizontally and vertically on a grid, see figure 3. Input consists of the agent's own horizontal and vertical coordinates, and an input indicating the type of a predator that is present or the absence of predators. Actions consist of moving one step left or right or staying, and selecting a vertical position.

A predator of random type is created in 10% of the timesteps at a random horizontal position, provided no predator is present yet. Three different types of predators exist. The vertical position of an agent determines whether it is safe from the predator or not, and since the number of vertical positions is three, each position corresponds to a single type of predator. The horizontal position of an agent determines whether it can see the

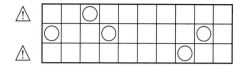

Figure 3: Visualization of the experimental environment. Horizontal positions determine the visibility of the predator, vertical positions function as abstractions of hideaways (only the middle row is safe here).

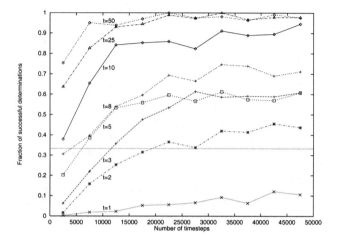

Figure 4: Histograms of the fraction of successful determinations of the situation based on communication when a predator first arrives and is invisible to the agent. Each line is the average of five repetitions of the same experiment. The interval during which a predator is present was varied between t=1 and t=50. The graph shows that when the interval is long enough, agents benefit from communication and determine the right situation in substantially more than the fraction of $\frac{1}{3}$ (dotted line) that would be expected without communication.

predator. The scope of the agents' perception amounts to 90% of the field; hence, for each agent, 10% of the predators are expected to be invisible. When a predator is invisible to an agent at creation time it will remain so until it is removed again, i.e. until the end of the situation.

6 Measuring the Benefit of Communication

The previous section demonstrated how communication may be of benefit to an agent. Our current purpose will be to investigate whether this benefit does indeed arise. If such a benefit can be measured convincingly, this would indicate that an effective system of communication has emerged.

If the predator is invisible to an agent, there is a chance of 1 in 3 that the agent can randomly select the right vertical position. But if the agent has the right vertical position in significantly more than a third of all cases where a predator is present and invisible to the agent,

this is an indication that the agent benefits from the signals it receives from other agents. However, this way of measurement has a possible problem. If a predator arrives and is invisible to an agent, the agent will receive a low success. Since the processes of learning and adaptation are active continuously, the agent's estimation of the position's attractiveness will slowly but surely decrease. When the value of the action corresponding to the position has decreased below another action's value, and the agent will start to choose that other action, and move to another position. The speed of this process may be increased by the exploration mechanism, which will at times select the action of moving to another position upon which the value of that action increases, since its reward is higher than the original estimation. Because the number of positions is limited, the agent will eventually hit the position where it's safe from the predator.

The problem can be circumvented in the following way. At the first timestep after the creation of a predator, the only information available to an agent for which the predator is invisible consists of the signals that are produced by other agents that can see the predator. Thus, if the agent moves to the correct position at this timestep more often than in a third of the cases, it must have extracted information from communication. Since the event that a predator is created and is invisible to an agent that uses the signals to determine its situation at that same moment is rather infrequent, the number of measurements is scarce. Therefore, this information is measured over a period of 50.000 timesteps.

There are numerous factors that influence the course of the experiment, including the increase and decrease of association strengths, removal of infrequent signals, and selection of the signal an agent produces. However, a single factor has been found to be very strongly related to the development of successful communication. This factor is the duration of a situation, and the relationship can, besides the feasibility of learned communication of situation concepts, be seen as a general result of this research.

Experiments have been performed where the duration t of the intervals during which a predator is present varied from a single timestep up to 50 timesteps. To visualise the information, a histogram has been made where the fraction of correct situation determinations is calculated over bins of 5.000 timesteps. In order to get a more reliable estimate, the experiment has been repeated a number of times for each parameter setting. Because of the duration of the experiments, the number of runs per parameter setting was limited to 5. In the graph in figure 4, each line represents the average of five runs with different random seeds for a chosen duration of situations.

The graph shows how the benefit of communication depends on the duration of the interval. When predators stay for only a single timestep, the fraction of successful determinations of the situation based on signals in case of an invisible predator stays well under one third, which means that the agent is doing worse than when it would randomly choose its position. However, as the duration of the intervals increases, so do performance and speed of convergence. For intervals of 3 or more timesteps, the fraction of successful guesses is already higher than a third, and for intervals of 10 or more steps the agents reach perfection in determining which predator is present based on communication.

7 Conclusions

A model for the formation of a particular type of concepts, called *situation concepts*, has been described. Situation concepts capture information about how the environment of an agent will respond to its actions. They can be constructed by analysing patterns in the history of interaction between the agent and its environment. Apart from providing a particularly detailed model of concept formation, situation concepts are especially suited to serve as a basis for communication. Since agents interact with the same environment, successful communication of the situation allows agents to be better informed about their environment than their sensors alone would permit, which improves the ability to select appropriate actions.

Both the formation of situation concepts and the subsequent development of learned communication have been demonstrated in a simulation experiment. Moreover, the possible benefit of communication as an extra information source has been observed in the experiment by monitoring the actions of agents at moments when the sensors provided incomplete information. Finally, a strong relationship was found between the duration of situations and the development of successful communication.

References

[Albus, 1981] J.S. Albus. *Brains, Behavior, and Robotics*. Byte Books, Peterborough, NH, 1981.

[Billard and Hayes, 1999] Aude Billard and Gillian Hayes. Drama, a connectionist architecture for control and learning in autonomous robots. *Adaptive Behavior*, 7(1), 1999.

[de Jong and Vogt, 1998] Edwin D. de Jong and Paul Vogt. How Should a Robot Discriminate Between Objects? A comparison between two methods. In *Proceedings of the Fifth International Conference of The Society for Adaptive Behavior SAB'98*, volume 5, Cambridge, MA, 1998. The MIT Press.

[Drescher, 1991] Gary L. Drescher. *Made-up minds. A constructivist approach to artificial intelligence*. The MIT Press, Cambridge, MA, 1991.

[Lakoff, 1987] G. Lakoff. *Women, Fire, and Dangerous Things. What Categories Reveal about the Mind*. University of Chicago Press, Chicago, 1987.

[MacLennan, 1991] Bruce MacLennan. Synthetic ethology: An approach to the study of communication. In Chris G. Langton, C. Taylor, J.D. Farmer, and S. Rasmussen, editors, *Artificial Life II*, volume X. Addison-Wesley, 1991.

[McCallum, 1996] Andrew K. McCallum. Reinforcement learning with selective perception and hidden state. *Ph.D. Thesis*, 1996.

[Oliphant, 1997] Michael Oliphant. *Formal Approaches to Innate and Learned Communication: Laying the Foundation for Language*. PhD thesis, University of California, San Diego, CA, 1997.

[Putnam, 1988] Hilary Putnam. *Representation and reality*. The MIT Press (A Bradford Book), Cambridge, MA, 1988.

[Quinlan, 1990] J. Ross Quinlan. Induction of decision trees. In Jude W. Shavlik and Thomas G. Dietterich, editors, *Readings in Machine Learning*. Morgan Kaufmann, 1990. Originally published in *Machine Learning* 1:81–106, 1986.

[Seyfarth *et al.*, 1980] R.M. Seyfarth, D.L. Cheney, and P. Marler. Monkey responses to three different alarm calls: Evidence of predator classification and semantic communication. *Science*, 210:801–803, 1980.

[Steels and Vogt, 1997] Luc Steels and Paul Vogt. Grounding adaptive language games in robotic agents. In C. Husbands and I. Harvey, editors, *Proceedings of the Fourth European Conference on Artificial Life*, Cambridge MA and London, 1997. The MIT Press.

[Steels, 1997] Luc Steels. The synthetic modeling of language origins. *Evolution of Communication*, 1(1):1–34, 1997.

[Sutton and Barto, 1998] Richard S. Sutton and Andrew G. Barto. *Reinforcement learning: an introduction*. The MIT Press (A Bradford Book), Cambridge, MA, 1998.

[Thrun, 1992] Sebastian Thrun. *Handbook of Intelligent Control: Neural, Fuzzy and Adaptive Approaches*, chapter The role of exploration in learning control. Van Nostrand Reinhold, Florence, Kentucky, 1992.

[Uther and Veloso, 1998] Willam T.B. Uther and Manuela M. Veloso. Tree based discretization for continuous state space reinforcement learning. In *Proceedings of AAAI-98*, Madison, WI, 1998.

[van Orman Quine, 1975] Willard van Orman Quine. *Word and Object*. MIT Press, Cambridge, Mass., 1975.

[Werner and Dyer, 1991] Gregory M. Werner and Michael G. Dyer. Evolution of communication in artificial organisms. In Chris G. Langton, C. Taylor, J.D. Farmer, and S. Rasmussen, editors, *Artificial Life II*, volume X. Addison-Wesley, 1991.

[Yanco and Stein, 1993] H. Yanco and L. Stein. An adaptive communication protocol for cooperating mobile robots. In H.L. Roitblat Meyer, J-A. and S. Wilson, editors, *From Animals to Animats 2. Proceedings of the Second International Conference on Simulation of Adaptive Behavior*, pages 478–485, Cambridge, MA, 1993. The MIT Press.

Reasoning About Actions in Narrative Understanding

Srinivas Narayanan
CS Division, UC Berkeley and ICSI
snarayan@{cs,icsi}.berkeley.edu

Abstract

Reasoning about actions has been a focus of interest in AI from the beginning and continues to receive attention. But the range of situations considered has been rather narrow and falls well short of what is needed for understanding natural language. Language understanding requires sophisticated reasoning about actions and events and the world's languages employ a variety of grammatical and lexical devices to *construe, direct attention and focus on,* and *control inferences about* actions and events. We implemented a neurally inspired computational model that is able to reason about linguistic action and event descriptions, such as those found in news stories. The system uses an active event representation that also seems to provide natural and cognitively motivated solutions to classical problems in logical theories of reasoning about actions. For logical approaches to reasoning about actions, we suggest that looking at story understanding sets up fairly strong desiderata both in terms of the fine-grained event and action distinctions and the kinds of real-time inferences required.

1 Introduction

Formal approaches to model reasoning about changing environments have a long tradition in AI. This research area was initiated by McCarthy [McCarthy, 1969], who claimed that reasoning about actions plays a fundamental role in common sense. Trying to build language understanding programs not only underscores the importance of reasoning about actions, but also suggests that the the set of situations and the kinds of inferential processes required are richer than has been traditionally studied in formal approaches.

Language understanding requires sophisticated reasoning about actions and events. The world's languages have a variety of grammatical and lexical devices to *construe, direct attention and focus,* and *control infer-*ences about actions and events. Consider the meaning of *stumbling* in the following newspaper headline "Indian Government stumbling in implementing Liberalization Plan". Clearly, the speaker intends to specify that the liberalization plan is experiencing some difficulty. Moreover, the grammatical form *is + VP-ing* suggests that the difficulty facing the plan is **ongoing** and the final outcome of the plan is indeterminate. Compare this to the subtle meaning differences with grammatical and lexical modifiers on the same root verb such as *has stumbled* or *starting to stumble*. Most readers are likely to infer after reading this sentence that the government's liberalization policy is likely to fail, but this is only a default causal inference that is made in the absence of information to the contrary. Finally, how does *stumble*, whose basic meaning is related to spatial motion and obstacles get interpreted in a narrative about international economic policies?

We have implemented a computational model that is able to reason about action and event descriptions from discourse fragments such as the one above. The system uses an active event representation that also seems to provide natural and cognitively motivated solutions to classical problems in logical theories of reasoning about actions. We first present the main features of our representation and show that it provides a computational model for existing formalisms for reasoning about actions. We then suggest how looking at story understanding sets up fairly strong desiderata for logical approaches to reasoning about actions both in terms of the fine-grained event and action distinctions and the kinds of real-time inferences required.

2 The Action Model

Our action theory comprises of two central components; 1) an **executing** representation of *actions* (called **x-schemas**) based on extensions to Petri Nets and 2) a Belief Net model of *state* that captures and reasons about complex dependencies between state variables.

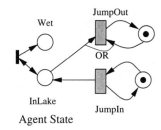

Figure 2: Potatoes in Tailpipes

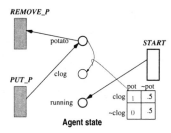

Figure 3: Jumping Into Lakes

3.1 Ramifications, Inertial and Dependent Fluents

Indirect effects are quite naturally handled by our system. Indirect effects that are "inertial fluents" get set by instantaneous transitions. In Figure 3, the direct effect of JumpIn sets the fluent InLake, which instantaneously sets the value of the fluent Wet. Note that the fluent Wet persists unless some other action is taken (like drying) to change the value of this fluent. In contrast, note that in Figure 2, the truth value of the 'dependent fluent" clog is determined by the fluent potato. While the value proposition $\neg potato \land \neg clog$ **after** put_pot ; $remove\_pot$, is not entailed by the description depicted in Figure 2 (from the uniform prior for $P(clog|\neg potato)$); if the domain theory contains the explicit knowledge **initially** $\neg clog \land \neg potato$, the proposition is entailed by the model.[3]

4 Understanding Language About Actions and Events

The frequency with which languages refer to events, the universality of such expressions, and the subtlety in the kinds of distinctions made have made the temporal character of events in language (called linguistic aspect) an object of study since Aristotle. Somewhat more recently, the complex and context-sensitive determination of aspectual status, or the internal temporal shape of an event has been the focus of much work [MS, 1988].

Many languages have a variety of grammatical aspectual modifiers such as the English *progressive* construction

---

[3]More generally, logical entailment can be viewed as the downward closure of the final marking.

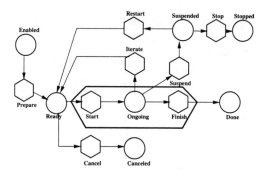

Figure 4: The CONTROLLER x-schema. Actions have rich internal structure that can be referred to by language and used for simulative inferences in language understanding.

($be + V\text{-}ing$) which enable a speaker to focus on the ongoing nature of an underlying process while allowing for inferences that the process has started and that it has not yet completed. Similarly, one use of the *perfect* construction (has $V\text{-}ed$) allows a speaker to specify that some *consequences* of the described situation hold. For instance, the phrase *I have lost my keys* entails that the keys are still missing (unlike the phrase *I lost my keys*). Languages also have a variety of other means to express aspect including aspectual verbs like *start, end, cease, continue,* and *stop* and related grammatical forms.

To model the kinds of subtle semantic distinctions made by languages, actions and events can no more be atomic transitions. In fact, we have found that cross-linguistically language makes reference to a specific structure of actions and events, which captures regularities that are relevant in the evolution of processes (enabling, inception, in-process, completion, suspension, resumption, etc.) We call this structure the CONTROLLER (Figure 4). The controller abstraction seems to capture the basic temporal structure of people's conceptualization of events. The semantics of aspect arises from the dynamic binding between verb-specific x-schemas and a **controller** that captures regularities in the evolution of complex events, shown in Figure 4.

In our language understanding system, the causal domain structure is encoded as connected x-schemas. Our domain model is a dynamic system based on inter-x-schema *activation, inhibition* and *interruption*. In the simulation framework, whenever an executing x-schema makes a CONTROLLER transition, it potentially modifies state, leading to asynchronous and parallel triggering or inhibition of other x-schemas. The notion of state as a graph marking is inherently distributed over the network, so the working memory of an x-schema-based inference system is distributed over the entire set of x-schemas and state fluents. Of course, this is intended to model the massively parallel computation of the brain.

Figure 5 depicts a simplified x-schema model of walking and reacting to obstacles (the domain of *stumbling*).

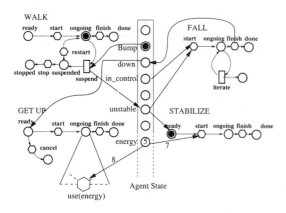

Figure 5: Event Structure is a x-schema simulation environment used for inference.

For instance, during a walk (specified by a token in the *ongoing* phase of the WALK x-schema) encountering an unanticipated **bump**, you become *unstable*. [4] This *may lead* to a FALL unless you are able to simultaneously *expend energy* and STABILIZE, in which case you may *resume* the *interrupted* walk. If you are unable to STABILIZE, and thus FALL, you will be **down** and **hurt**.

Now consider that this complex situation described above can be coded in a single lexical item *stumble*! First, notice that stumble can only occur during a STEP, and that it is a specific kind of interrupt to the step (i.e. the presence of a **bump** or **stumbling block**). But this by itself does not capture the intended meaning of stumble, since the inference (that the agent may fall) is routinely intended by the speaker. Furthermore, note that the fact that stumble is not a planned motion but an interrupt is important to infer that it is unintentional.

It should be clear that to model linguistic distinctions in event structure, we need much finer-grained distinctions than those that been proposed in the literature for reasoning about actions. This is also consistent with the key observation in [MS, 1988] that aspectual phenomena depend on a notion of event structure that captures **contingency** relationships among events. Our framework of an active action semantics embodies a precise model of such inter-event contingency.

While our solutions to the problems of aspect are outside the scope of this paper, the following inter-schema activation, inhibition, and modification relationships are intended to give the reader an idea of the fine-grained nature of contingency relationships involved.

Definition 3 . **Activation**: Activation relationships between schemas correspond to the case where executing one schema causes the *enabling, start* or *continued execution* of another schema. We are able to distinguish *concurrent* from *sequential* activation.

---

[4] In fact, the simulation is of finer granularity in that it is during an ongoing STEP (subschema of WALK), that the interruption occurs. This is not shown to simplify exposition.

X **activates** Y ($Act\,(X,Y) : X, Y \in \mathcal{SS}$) if some subset p of places marked in the result state $P(X_r)$ of X ($p \subseteq P(X_r)$) *enable* the **start** transition of Y ($p \subseteq *T(Y_s)$). X **enables** Y if ($p * T(Y_s)$ i.e. $*T(Y_s) \subseteq P(X_r)$).

seq_enables(X, Y): done(X) $\wedge (p \in P(X_r)) \wedge (p \subseteq *T(Y_e^+))$
conc_enables$(X,Y) : ongoing(X) \wedge (p \in P(X_p)) \wedge (p \subseteq *T(Y_e^+))$
inh_periodic$(X) :$ seq_enables(X,X)
mut_enables$(X,Y) :$ seq_enables$(X,Y) \wedge$ seq_enables(Y,X)

Definition 4 . **Inhibition**: Inhibitory links prevent execution of the inhibited x-schema by **activating** an inhibitory arc. Again, our model is able to distinguish between concurrent and sequential inhibition as well as be able to model mutual inhibition and aperiodicity.

X **inhibits** Y ($Inh\ \ (X,Y) : X, Y \in \mathcal{SS}$) if some subset p of places marked in the *done* state of· X $P(X_r)$ ($p \in P(X_r)$) are *inhibitor* arcs for the start transition of Y ($p \subseteq *T(Y_s)$). X disables Y if ($p * T(Y_s)$ i.e. $*Inh(Y_s) \subseteq P(X_r)$).

seq_disables(X, Y): done(X) $\wedge (p \in P(X_r)) \wedge (p \subseteq *T(Y_e^-))$
conc_disables$(X,Y) : ongoing(X) \wedge (p \in P(X_p)) \wedge (p \subseteq *T(Y_e^-))$
inh_aperiodic$(X) :$ seq_disables(X,X)
mut_disables$(X,Y) :$ seq_disables$(X,Y) \wedge$ **seq_disables(Y,X)**

Definition 5 . **Modification**: Modifying relationships between x-schemas occur when the execution of the modifying x-schema results in setting the Agent State in such a way the the currently active modified x-schema undergoes a **controller** state transition.

interrupts(X, Y): ongoing(Y) $\wedge (p \in P(X))) \wedge (p \supseteq *T(Y_{inh}^+))$
prevents(X,Y) : $enabled(Y) \wedge \neg start(Y) \wedge (p \in P(X_r)) \wedge (p \in *T(Y_s^-))$
terminates(X,Y) : $ongoing(Y) \wedge (p \in P(X_r)) \wedge (p \supseteq *T(Y_f^+))$
resumes(X,Y) : $suspended(Y) \wedge (p \in P(X_r)) \wedge (p \supseteq *T(Y_{int}^+))$
stops(X,Y) : $(suspended(Y) \vee ongoing(Y)) \wedge (p \in P(X_r)) \wedge (p \supseteq *T(Y_{cease}^+))$

Example 3 Examples of contingency relations in the Walking Domain

TRIP seq_enables FALL $\wedge$ STABILIZE.
$\neg in\_control(loc)$ enables FALL
$\neg stable$ enables STABILIZE
GRASPING(x) conc_enables HOLDING(x).
Energy(x) isa_resource for WALK

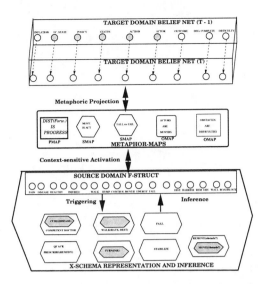

Figure 6: Abstract Domains are mappings from concrete actions

WALK is mut-exclusive to RUN.
STABILIZE seq_disables FALL.
In_control(loc) disables FALL
GETUP resumes WALK.
Standing enables WALK
REACH(X) terminates WALK(X).

■

4.1 Metaphoric Reasoning about Actions and Events

We have seen how the structure of actions and events is grounded in fine-grained, dynamic representations. Another ubiquitous phenomenon in language[Lakoff, 1994], is the routine projection of such fine-grained semantic distinctions across domains. Systematic metaphors project features of these representations (source) onto abstract domains such as economics (target) enabling linguistic devices to use embodied causal terms to describe features of abstract actions and processes.

Figure 6 shows an implemented system that uses projections of the action representation outlined earlier to interpret such sentences. In our model *indirect effects* of x-schema execution now not only propagate to dependent source domain fluents but may also be mapped by metaphor maps to other abstract domains (modeled as a temporally extended Belief Net).

Continuing with the stumble example, notice that in our model effects of spatial inferences such as stumbling *leads to* falling can felicitously be transferred to the abstract domain of economic policy through a conventionalized metaphor that *falling ↦ failure*, enabling the inference of plan failure. This inference context-sensitive and may be overridden by prior knowledge (in the target domain Belief Net) that the liberalization plan is succeeding.

5 Conclusion

This paper described a new framework for reasoning about actions that is motivated from story understanding. One central feature of this framework is an extremely fine-grained action model with a real-time execution semantics that is able to capture a much richer notion of contingency and causality than other models we are aware of. Another key feature is our model of state where complex dependencies between state variables are modeled as a Belief Network. We showed how this framework is able to reason about actions, ramifications with inertial and dependent fluents, as well as inter-domain mappings which are crucial in story understanding. We believe that looking further into issues in narrative (such as into force-dynamics, modals, and mental spaces) can yield valuable insights that can help us build useful theories of reasoning about actions.

6 Acknowledgments

Thanks to J. Feldman, G. Lakoff and the NTL group at UC Berkeley and ICSI.

References

[Gelfond & Lifschitz, 1993] Gelfond, M. & Lifschitz, V. (1993). Representing Action and Change by Logic Programs. *Journal of Logic Programming*, 17:301-322, 1993.

[Giunchiglia & Lifschitz, 1995] Giunchiglia E. & Lifschitz, V. (1995). Dependent Fluents *Proc. Of IJCAI*, 1995: 1964-1969, Morgan Kaufman, Inc. 1995.

[Goldszmidt, 1992] Goldszmidt, M. & Pearl, J. (1992). Rank-based systems. *Proc. Of the Third Conference on Principles of KR and Reasoning*, 1992: 661-672, Morgan Kaufman, Inc. 1992.

[Jensen, 1996] Jensen, F. (1996). *An Introduction to Bayesian Networks*. Springer-Verlag ISBN 0-387-91502-8.

[Lakoff, 1994] Lakoff, G. (1994). What is Metaphor?. *Advances in Connectionist Theory. V3 : Analogical Connections*, V3,1994.

[McCarthy, 1969] McCarthy, J., & Hayes, P. (1969). Some Philosophical Problems From the Standpoint of Artificial Intelligence. *Machine Intelligence* 4 (1969) 463-502.

[Narayanan, 1997] Narayanan, S. (1997). Knowledge-based Action Representations for Metaphor and Aspect (KARMA). *Ph.D. Dissertation* CS Division, EECS Dept. UC Berkeley 1997.

[MS, 1988] Moens, M. & Steedman, M. (1988). Temporal Ontology and Temporal Reference. In *Proc. ACL-88*, V4, Number 2, June 1988, pp. 15-29.

[Reisig, 1985] Reisig, W. (1985). *Petri Nets*. Springer Verlag.

COGNITIVE MODELING

Cognitive Modeling 2

Using a Cognitive Architecture to Plan Dialogs for the Adaptive Explanation of Proofs

Armin Fiedler

FB Informatik, Universität des Saarlandes
Postfach 15 11 50, D-66041 Saarbrücken, Germany
afiedler@cs.uni-sb.de

Abstract

In order to generate high quality explanations in technical or mathematical domains, the presentation must be adapted to the knowledge of the intended audience. Current proof presentation systems only communicate proofs on a fixed degree of abstraction independently of the addressee's knowledge.

In this paper we propose an architecture for an interactive proof explanation system, called *P.rex*. Based on the theory of human cognition ACT-R, its dialog planner exploits a cognitive model, in which both the user's knowledge and his cognitive processes are modeled. By this means, his cognitive states are traced during the explanation. The explicit representation of the user's cognitive states in ACT-R allows the dialog planner to choose a degree of abstraction tailored to the user for each proof step to be explained. Moreover, the system can revise its assumptions about the user's knowledge and react to his interactions.

1 Introduction

A person who explains to another person a technical device or a logical line of reasoning adapts his explanations to the addressee's knowledge. A computer program designed to take over the explaining part should also adopt this principle.

Assorted systems take into account the intended audience's knowledge in the generation of explanations (see e.g. [Cawsey, 1990; Paris, 1991; Wahlster *et al.*, 1993]). Most of them adapt to the addressee by choosing between different discourse strategies. Since proofs are inherently rich in inferences, the explanation of proofs must also consider which inferences the audience can make [Horacek, 1997; Zukerman and McConachy, 1993]. However, because of the constraints of the human memory, inferences are not chainable without costs. Explicit representation of the addressee's cognitive states proves to be useful in choosing the information to convey [Walker and Rambow, 1994].

While a mathematician communicates a proof on a level of abstraction that is tailored to the audience, state-of-the-art proof presentation systems such as *PROVERB*

[Huang and Fiedler, 1997] verbalize proofs in a nearly textbook-like style on a fixed degree of abstraction given by the initial representation of the proof. Nevertheless, *PROVERB* is not restricted to presentation on a certain level of abstraction. Adaptation to the reader's knowledge may still take place by providing the appropriate level of abstraction in the initial representation of the proof.

Drawing on results from cognitive science, we are currently developing an *interactive proof explanation system*, called *P.rex* (for *proof explainer*). In this paper, which extends the work reported in [Fiedler, 1998], we propose an architecture for its dialog planner based on the theory of human cognition ACT-R [Anderson and Lebiere, 1998]. The latter explicitly represents the addressee's knowledge in a declarative memory and his cognitive skills in procedural production rules. This cognitive model enables the dialog planner to trace the addressee's cognitive states during the explanation. Hence, for each proof step, it can choose as an appropriate explanation its most abstract justification that is known by the addressee. Moreover, the system can revise its assumptions about the user's knowledge and react to his interactions.

The architecture of *P.rex*, which is sketched in Section 3, is designed to allow for multimodal generation. The dialog planner is described in detail in Section 4. Since it is necessary to know some of the concepts in ACT-R to understand the macroplanning process, the cognitive architecture is first introduced in the next section.

2 ACT-R: A Cognitive Architecture

In cognitive science several approaches are used to describe the functionality of the cognitive apparatus, e.g. production systems, mental models or distributed neural representations. Production systems that model human cognition are called *cognitive architectures*. In this section we describe the cognitive architecture ACT-R [Anderson and Lebiere, 1998], which is well suited for user adaptive explanation generation because of its conflict resolution mechanism. Further examples for cognitive architectures are SOAR [Newell, 1990] and EPIC [Meyer and Kieras, 1997].

ACT-R has two types of knowledge bases, or *memories*, to store permanent knowledge in: declarative and procedural representations of knowledge are explicitly separated into the declarative memory and the procedural production rule base, but are intimately connected.

Procedural knowledge is represented in production rules (or simply: *productions*) whose conditions and actions are defined in terms of declarative structures. A production can only apply if its conditions are satisfied by the knowledge currently available in the declarative memory. An item in the declarative memory is annotated with an activation that influences its retrieval. The application of a production modifies the declarative memory, or it results in an observable event. The set of applicable productions is called the *conflict set*. A *conflict resolution* heuristic derived from a rational analysis of human cognition determines which production in the conflict set will eventually be applied.

In order to allow for a goal-oriented behavior of the system, ACT-R manages goals in a goal stack. The current goal is that on the top of the stack. Only productions that match the current goal are applicable.

2.1 Declarative Knowledge

Declarative knowledge is represented in terms of *chunks* in the declarative memory. Below is an example for a chunk encoding the fact that $F \subseteq G$, where subset-fact is a concept and F and G are contextual chunks associated to factFsubsetG.

```
factFsubsetG
    isa    subset-fact
    set1   F
    set2   G
```

Chunks are annotated with continuous activations that influence their retrieval. The activation A_i of a chunk C_i consists of its base-level activation B_i and the weighted activations of contextual chunks. In B_i, which is defined such that it decreases logarithmically when C_i is not used, ACT-R models the forgetting of declarative knowledge. Note that the definition of the activation establishes a spreading activation to adjacent chunks, but not further; multi-link-spread is not supported.

The constraint on the capacity of the human working memory is approached by defining a retrieval threshold τ, where only those chunks C_i can be matched whose activation A_i is higher than τ. Chunks with an activation less than τ are considered as forgotten.

New declarative knowledge is acquired when a new chunk is stored in the declarative memory, as is always the case when a goal is popped from the goal stack. The application of a production may also cause a new chunk to be stored if required by the production's action part.

2.2 Procedural Knowledge

The operational knowledge of ACT-R is formalized in terms of *productions*. Productions generally consist of a condition part and an action part, and can be applied if the condition part is fulfilled. In ACT-R both parts are defined in terms of chunk patterns. The condition is fulfilled if its first chunk pattern matches the current goal and the remaining chunk patterns match chunks in the declarative memory. An example for a production is

IF   the current goal is to show that $x \in S_2$ and it is known
       that $x \in S_1$ and $S_1 \subseteq S_2$

THEN conclude that $x \in S_2$ by the definition of $\subseteq$

Similar to the base-level activation of chunks, the strength of a production is defined such that it decreases logarithmically when the production is not used. The time spent to match a production with a chunk depends on the activation of the chunk.[1] It is defined such that it is negative exponential to the sum of the activation of the chunk and the strength of the production. Hence, the higher the activation of the chunk and the strength of the production, the faster the production matches the chunk. Since the activation must be greater than the retrieval threshold τ, τ constrains the time maximally available to match a production with a chunk.

The conflict resolution heuristic starts from assumptions on the probability P that the application of the current production leads to the goal and on the costs C of achieving that goal by this means. Moreover G is the time maximally available to fulfill the goal. The net utility E of the application of a production is defined as

$$E = PG - C. \qquad (1)$$

We do not go into detail on how P, G and C are calculated. For the purposes of this paper, it is sufficient to note that G only depends on the goal, but not on the production.

To sum up, in ACT-R the choice of a production to apply is as follows:

1. The conflict set is determined by testing the match of the productions with the current goal.

2. The production p with the highest utility is chosen.

3. The actual instantiation of p is determined via the activations of the corresponding chunks. If no instantiation is possible (because of τ), p is removed from the conflict set and the algorithm resumes in step 2, otherwise the instantiation of p is applied.

ACT-R provides a learning mechanism, called *production compilation*, which allows for the learning of new productions. We are currently exploring this mechanism for its utility for the explanation of proofs.

3   The Architecture of *P.rex*

P.rex is planned as a generic explanation system that can be connected to different theorem provers. It adopts the following features of the interactive proof development environment ΩMEGA [Benzmüller *et al.*, 1997]:

- Mathematical theories are organized in a hierarchical knowledge base. Each theory in it may contain axioms, definitions, theorems along with proofs, as well as proof methods, and control rules how to apply proof methods.

- A proof of a theorem is represented in a hierarchical data structure. This representation makes explicit the various levels of abstraction by providing several justifications for a single proof node, where each justification belongs to a different level of abstraction. The least abstract level corresponds to a

---

[1]In this context, *time* does not mean the CPU time needed to calculate the match, but the time a human would need for the match according to the cognitive model.

proof in Gentzen's natural deduction (ND) calculus [Gentzen, 1935]. Candidates for higher levels are proof plans, where justifications are mainly given by more abstract proof methods that belong to the theorem's mathematical theory or to an ancestor theory thereof.

An example for a proof is given below. Each line consists of four elements (label, antecedent, succedent, and justification) and describes a node of the proof. The *label* is used as a reference for the node. The *antecedent* is a list of labels denoting the hypotheses under which the formula in the node, the *succedent*, holds.[2] This relation between antecedent and succedent is denoted by $\vdash$.

Label	Antecedent	Succedent	Justification
L_0		$\vdash a \in U \vee a \in V$	J_0
H_1	H_1	$\vdash a \in U$	HYP
L_1	H_1	$\vdash a \in U \cup V$	Def$\cup(H_1)$
H_2	H_2	$\vdash a \in V$	HYP
L_2	H_2	$\vdash a \in U \cup V$	Def$\cup(H_2)$
L_3		$\vdash a \in U \cup V$	$\cup$-Lemma(L_0)
			CASE(L_0, L_1, L_2)

We call $\Delta \vdash \varphi$ the *fact* in the node. The proof of the fact in the node is given by its *justification*. A justification consists of a rule and a list of labels, the *premises* of the node. J_i denotes an unspecified justification. HYP and Def$\cup$ stand for a hypothesis and the definition of $\cup$, respectively. L_3 has two justifications on different levels of abstraction: the least abstract justification with the ND-rule CASE (i.e. the rule for case analyses) and the more abstract justification with the rule $\cup$-Lemma that stands for an already proven lemma about a property of $\cup$. By agreement, if a node has more than one justification, these are sorted from most abstract to least abstract.

The proof is as follows: From $a \in U \vee a \in V$ we can conclude that $a \in U \cup V$ by the $\cup$-Lemma. If we do not know the $\cup$-Lemma, we can come to the conclusion by considering the case analysis with the cases that $a \in U$ or $a \in V$, respectively. In each case, we can derive that $a \in U \cup V$ by the definition of $\cup$.

A formal language for specifying proofs is the interface by which theorem provers can be connected to $P\!rex$. An overview of the architecture of $P\!rex$ is provided in Figure 1.

The crucial component of the system is the ***dialog planner***. It is implemented in ACT-R, i.e. its operators are defined in terms of productions and the discourse history is represented in the declarative memory by storing conveyed information as chunks (details are given in Section 4). Moreover, presumed declarative and procedural knowledge of the user is encoded in the declarative memory and the production rule base, respectively. This establishes that the dialog planner is modeling the user.

In order to explain a particular proof, the dialog planner first assumes the user's supposed cognitive state by updating its declarative and procedural memories. This is done by looking up the user's presumed knowledge

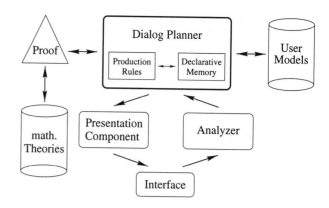

Figure 1: The Architecture of $P\!rex$

in the user model, which was recorded during a previous session. An individual model for each user persists between the sessions.

The individual user models are stored in the database of **user models**. Each user model contains assumptions on the knowledge of the user that are relevant to proof explanation. In particular, it makes assumptions on which mathematical theories the user knows, which definitions, proofs, proof methods and mathematical facts he knows, and which productions he has already learned.

After updating the declarative and procedural memories, the dialog planner sets the global goal to show the conclusion of the proof's theorem. ACT-R tries to fulfill this goal by successively applying productions that decompose or fulfill goals. Thereby, the dialog planner not only produces a multimodal dialog plan (see Section 4.1), but also traces the user's cognitive states in the course of the explanation. This allows the system both to always choose an explanation adapted to the user (see Section 4.2), and to react to the user's interactions in a flexible way: The dialog planner analyzes the interaction in terms of applications of productions. Then it plans an appropriate response.

The dialog plan produced by the dialog planner is passed on to the ***presentation component***. Currently, we use *PROVERB*'s microplanner [Huang and Fiedler, 1997] to plan the scope and internal structure of the sentences, which are then realized by the syntactic generator TAG-GEN [Kilger and Finkler, 1995].

An ***analyzer*** receives the user's interactions and passes them on to the dialog planner. In the current experimental stage, we use a simplistic analyzer that understands a small set of predefined interactions.

4 The Dialog Planner

In the community of NLG, there is a broad consensus that the generation of natural language should be done in three major steps [Reiter, 1994]. First a *macroplanner (text planner)* determines what to say, i.e. content and order of the information to be conveyed. Then a *microplanner (sentence planner)* determines how to say it, i.e. it plans the scope and the internal structure of the sentences. Finally, a *realizer (surface generator)* produces the surface text. In this classification, the dialog

---

[2]As notation we use Δ and Γ for antecedents and φ and ψ for succedents.

planner is a macroplanner for managing dialogs.

As Wahlster *et al.* argued, such a three-staged architecture is also appropriate for multimodal generation [Wahlster *et al.*, 1993]. By defining the operators and the dialog plan such that they are independent of the communication mode, our dialog planner plans text, graphics and speech.

Since the dialog planner in *P.rex* is based on ACT-R, the plan operators are defined as productions. A goal is the task to show the fact in a node n of the proof. A production fulfills the goal directly by communicating the derivation of the fact in n from already known facts or splits the goal into new subgoals such as to show the facts in the premises of n. The derivation of a fact is conveyed by so-called mathematics communicating acts (MCAs) and accompanied by storing the fact as a chunk in the declarative memory. Hence the discourse history is represented in the declarative memory. ACT-R's conflict resolution mechanism and the activation of the chunks ensure an explanation tailored to the user. The produced dialog plan is represented in terms of MCAs.

4.1 Mathematics Communicating Acts

Mathematics communicating acts (MCAs) are the primitive actions planned by the dialog planner. They are derived from *PROVERB*'s *proof communicative acts* [Huang, 1994]. MCAs are viewed as speech acts that are independent of the modality to be chosen. Each MCA at least can be realized as a portion of text. Moreover some MCAs manifest themselves in the graphical arrangement of the text.

In *P.rex* we distinguish between two types of MCAs:

- MCAs of the first type, called *derivational MCAs*, convey a step of the derivation. An example for a derivational MCA with a possible verbalization is:

  ```
  (Derive :Reasons (a ∈ U, U ⊆ V)
          :Conclusion a ∈ V
          :Method Def⊆)
  ```
  "Since a is an element of U and U is a subset of V, a is an element of V by the definition of subset."

- MCAs of the second type, called *structural MCAs*, communicate information about the structure of a proof. For example, case analyses are introduced by:

  ```
  (Case-Analysis :Goal ψ
                 :Cases (φ₁, φ₂))
  ```
  "To prove ψ, let us consider the two cases by assuming φ_1 and φ_2."

4.2 Plan Operators

Operational knowledge concerning the presentation is encoded as productions in ACT-R that are independent from the modality to be chosen. The proof explaining productions are derived from *PROVERB*'s macroplanning operators [Huang, 1994]. Each of those corresponds to one or several productions in *P.rex*.

Each production either fulfills the current goal directly or splits it into subgoals. Let us assume that the following nodes are in the current proof:

Label	Antecedent	Succedent	Justification
P_1	Δ_1	$\vdash \varphi_1$	J_1
		$\vdots$	
P_n	Δ_n	$\vdash \varphi_n$	J_n
C	Γ	$\vdash \psi$	$R(P_1, \dots, P_n)$

An example for a production is:

(P1) IF   The current goal is to show $\Gamma \vdash \psi$
and R is the most abstract known rule justifying the current goal
and $\Delta_1 \vdash \varphi_1, \dots, \Delta_n \vdash \varphi_n$ are known
    THEN   produce   MCA   (Derive :Reasons $(\varphi_1, \dots, \varphi_n)$:Conclusion ψ :Method R)
and pop the current goal (thereby storing $\Gamma \vdash \psi$ in the declarative memory)

By producing the MCA the current goal is fulfilled and can be popped from the goal stack. An example for a production decomposing the current goal into several subgoals is:

(P2) IF   The current goal is to show $\Gamma \vdash \psi$
and R is the most abstract known rule justifying the current goal
and $\Phi = \{\varphi_i | \Delta_i \vdash \varphi_i$ is unknown for $1 \leq i \leq n\} \neq \emptyset$
    THEN   for each $\varphi_i \in \Phi$ push the goal to show $\Delta_i \vdash \varphi_i$

Note that the conditions of (P1) and (P2) only differ in the knowledge of the premises φ_i for rule R. (P2) introduces the subgoals to prove the unknown premises in Φ. As soon as those are derived, (P1) can apply and derive the conclusion.

Now assume that the following nodes are in the current proof:

Label	Antecedent	Succedent	Justification
P_0	Γ	$\vdash \varphi_1 \vee \varphi_2$	J_0
H_1	H_1	$\vdash \varphi_1$	HYP
P_1	Γ, H_1	$\vdash \psi$	J_1
H_2	H_2	$\vdash \varphi_2$	HYP
P_2	Γ, H_2	$\vdash \psi$	J_2
C	Γ	$\vdash \psi$	CASE(P_0, P_1, P_2)

A specific production managing such a case analysis is the following:

(P3) IF   The current goal is to show $\Gamma \vdash \psi$
and CASE is the most abstract known rule justifying the current goal
and $\Gamma \vdash \varphi_1 \vee \varphi_2$ is known
and $\Gamma, H_1 \vdash \psi$ and $\Gamma, H_2 \vdash \psi$ are unknown
    THEN   push the goals to show $\Gamma, H_1 \vdash \psi$ and $\Gamma, H_2 \vdash \psi$ and produce MCA (Case-Analysis :Goal ψ :Cases (φ_1, φ_2))

This production introduces new subgoals and motivates them by producing the MCA.

Since more specific rules treat common communicative standards used in mathematical presentations, they are assigned lower costs, i.e. $C_{(P3)} < C_{(P2)}$ (cf. equation 1).

Moreover, it is supposed that each user knows all natural deduction (ND) rules. This is reasonable, since ND-rules are the least abstract possible logical rules in proofs. Hence, for each production p that is defined such that its goal is justified by an ND-rule in the proof, the probability P_p that the application of p leads to the goal to explain that proof step equals one. Therefore, since CASE is such an ND-rule, $P_{(P3)} = 1$.

Before examining more closely an example explanation of a proof, we look at a production reacting to a user interaction. Consider the case that the user informs the system that he did not understand a step of the derivation. The analyzer receives the user's message and pushes the goal to backtrack to the node n whose explanation was not understood. This goal can be fulfilled by the following production:

(P4)   IF   The current goal is to backtrack to node n and
      THEN   push the subgoals to re-explain the fact in n and to revise the assumption, that the justification J used in its last explanation was known.

A further production (P5), which is omitted here due to space restrictions, performs the revision by decreasing the base-level activation of J.

In order to elucidate how a proof is explained by $P.rex$ let us consider the following situation:

- The following nodes are in the current proof:

Label	Antecedent	Succedent	Justification
L_0		$\vdash a \in U \vee a \in V$	J_0
H_1	H_1	$\vdash a \in U$	HYP
L_1	H_1	$\vdash a \in U \cup V$	Def$\cup(H_1)$
H_2	H_2	$\vdash a \in V$	HYP
L_2	H_2	$\vdash a \in U \cup V$	Def$\cup(H_2)$
L_3		$\vdash a \in U \cup V$	$\cup$-Lemma(L_0)
			CASE(L_0, L_1, L_2)

- the current goal is to show the fact in L_3,
- the rules HYP, CASE, Def$\cup$, and $\cup$-Lemma are known,
- the fact in L_0 is known, the facts in H_1, L_1, H_2, and L_2 are unknown.

The only applicable production is (P1). Since $\cup$-Lemma is more abstract than CASE and both are known, it is chosen to instantiate (P1). Hence, the dialog planner produces the MCA

(Derive :Reasons $(a \in U \vee a \in V)$
         :Conclusion $a \in U \cup V$
         :Method $\cup$-Lemma)

that can be verbalized as "Since $a \in U$ or $a \in V$, $a \in U \cup V$ by the $\cup$-Lemma."

Suppose now that the user interrupts the explanation throwing in that he did not understand this step. The analyzer translates the user's interaction into the new goal to backtrack to L_3, which is pushed on the goal stack. This goal is processed by (P4) pushing the subgoals to re-explain the fact in L_3 and to revise the assumption, that $\cup$-Lemma is known. The latter is fulfilled by (P5) by decreasing the base-level activation of $\cup$-Lemma below the retrieval threshold. This leaves the goal to (re-)explain the fact in L_3 on the top of the goal stack.

Now, since CASE is the most abstract known rule justifying the current goal, both decomposing productions (P2) and (P3) are applicable. Recall that the conflict resolution mechanism chooses the production with the highest utility E (cf. equation 1). Since $P_{(P3)} = 1$ and $P_p \leq 1$ for all productions p, $P_{(P3)} \geq P_{(P2)}$. Since the application of (P2) or (P3) would serve the same goal,

$G_{(P3)} = G_{(P2)}$. Since (P3) is more specific than (P2), $C_{(P3)} < C_{(P2)}$. Thus

$$E_{(P3)} = P_{(P3)}G_{(P3)} - C_{(P3)} > P_{(P2)}G_{(P2)} - C_{(P2)} = E_{(P2)}$$

Therefore, the dialog planner chooses (P3) for the explanation, thus producing the MCA

(Case-Analysis :Goal $a \in U \cup V$
              :Cases $(a \in U, a \in V)$)

that can be realized as "To prove $a \in U \cup V$ let us consider the cases that $a \in U$ and $a \in V$," and then explains both cases. The whole dialog takes place as follows:

> **$P.rex$:** Since $a \in U$ or $a \in V\Gamma a \in U \cup V$ by the $\cup$-Lemma.
> **User:** Why does this follow?
> **$P.rex$:** To prove $a \in U \cup V$ let us consider the cases that $a \in U$ and $a \in V$. Let $a \in U$. Then $a \in U \cup V$ by the definition of $\cup$. Let $a \in V$. Then $a \in U \cup V$ by the definition of $\cup$.

This example shows how a production and an instantiation are chosen by $P.rex$. While the example elucidates the case that a more detailed explanation is desired, the system can similarly choose a more abstract explanation if needed. Hence, modeling the addressee's knowledge in ACT-R allows $P.rex$ to explain the proof adapted to the user's knowledge by switching between the its levels of abstraction as needed.

Having in mind that the MCAs and the explaining productions are derived from $PROVERB$'s macroplanner, it is no surprise that $P.rex$'s dialog planner produces text plan equivalent to $PROVERB$. But while the proof must be provided to $PROVERB$ on an appropriate level of abstraction to satisfy the user, $P.rex$ determines for each proof step which level of abstraction it considers as the most appropriate for the respective audience. Moreover, $P.rex$ can react to interactions by the user and revise both its assumptions about the addressee and its planning decisions.

5   Conclusion and Future Work

In this paper, we proposed to combine the traditional design of a dialog planner with a cognitive architecture in order to strive for an optimal user adaptation. In the interactive proof explaining system $P.rex$, the dialog planner is based on the theory of cognition ACT-R.

Starting from certain assumptions about the addressee's knowledge (e.g. which facts does he know, which definitions, lemmas, etc.) built up in the user model during previous sessions, the dialog planner decides on which level of abstraction to begin the explanation. Since ACT-R traces the user's cognitive states during the explanation, the dialog planner can choose an appropriate degree of abstraction for each proof step to be explained. Furthermore, it can react to user interactions and revise the user model. The rationale behind this architecture should prove to be useful for explanation systems in general.

Moreover, since this architecture can predict what is salient for the user and what he can infer, it could be used as a basis to decide whether or not to include optional information [Walker and Rambow, 1994].

P.rex is still in an experimental stage. It goes already beyond *PROVERB*'s capabilities, since it can not only produce textbook style proofs but also plan explanations tailored to the respective user and react to interactions. We plan to extend the presentation component to multimodality supporting graphics, text, and speech. It should consist of the following subcomponents:

A *multimodal microplanner* plans the scope of the sentences and their internal structure, as well as their graphical arrangement. It also decides, whether a graphical or a textual realization is preferred. Textual parts are passed on to a *linguistic realizer* that generates the surface sentences. Then a *layout component* displays the text and graphics, while a *speech system* outputs the sentences in speech. Hence, the system should provide the user with text and graphics, as well as a spoken output. The metaphor we have in mind is the teacher who explains what he is writing on the board.

Currently, we are examining the knowledge compilation mechanism of ACT-R that could enable the system to model the user's acquisition of proving skills. This could pave the way towards a tutorial system that not only explains proofs, but also teaches concepts and proving methods and strategies.

Moreover, we are planning experiments with users of different levels of expertise in mathematics to evaluate the system.

Acknowledgements

Many thanks go to Jörg Siekmann, Frank Pfenning, Ken Koedinger, and Christian Lebiere for their help in my research. Frank Pfenning, Carsten Schürmann and Chris Scarpinatto read earlier drafts of this paper. I also want to thank the anonymous reviewers for their useful comments.

References

[Anderson and Lebiere, 1998] J. R. Anderson and C. Lebiere. *The Atomic Components of Thought*. Lawrence Erlbaum, 1998.

[Benzmüller *et al.*, 1997] C. Benzmüller, L. Cheikhrouhou, D. Fehrer, A. Fiedler, X. Huang, M. Kerber, M. Kohlhase, K. Konrad, E. Melis, A. Meier, W. Schaarschmidt, J. Siekmann, and V. Sorge. ΩMEGA: Towards a mathematical assistant. In W. McCune, editor, *Proceedings of the 14th Conference on Automated Deduction*, number 1249 in LNAI, pages 252–255, Townsville, Australia, 1997. Springer Verlag.

[Cawsey, 1990] A. Cawsey. Generating explanatory discourse. In R. Dale, C. Mellish, and M. Zock, editors, *Current Research in Natural Language Generation*, number 4 in Cognitive Science Series, pages 75–101. Academic Press, San Diego, CA, 1990.

[Fiedler, 1998] A. Fiedler. Macroplanning with a cognitive architecture for the adaptive explanation of proofs. In *Proceedings of the 9th International Workshop on Natural Language Generation*, pages 88–97, Niagara-on-the-Lake, Ontario, Canada, 1998.

[Gentzen, 1935] G. Gentzen. Untersuchungen über das logische Schließen I & II. *Mathematische Zeitschrift*, 39:176–210, 572–595, 1935.

[Horacek, 1997] H. Horacek. A model for adapting explanations to the user's likely inferences. *User Modeling and User-Adapted Interaction*, 7:1–55, 1997.

[Huang and Fiedler, 1997] X. Huang and A. Fiedler. Proof verbalization as an application of NLG. In M. E. Pollack, editor, *Proceedings of the 15th International Joint Conference on Artificial Intelligence (IJCAI)*, pages 965–970, Nagoya, Japan, 1997. Morgan Kaufmann.

[Huang, 1994] X. Huang. Planning argumentative texts. In *Proceedings of the 15th International Conference on Computational Linguistics*, pages 329–333, Kyoto, Japan, 1994.

[INLG, 1994] *Proceedings of the 7th International Workshop on Natural Language Generation*, Kennebunkport, ME, USA, 1994.

[Kilger and Finkler, 1995] A. Kilger and W. Finkler. Incremental generation for real–time applications. Research Report RR-95-11, DFKI, Saarbrücken, Germany, 1995.

[Meyer and Kieras, 1997] D. E. Meyer and D. E. Kieras. EPIC: A computational theory of executive cognitive processes and multiple-task performance: Part 1. *Psychological Review*, 104:3–65, 1997.

[Newell, 1990] A. Newell. *Unified Theories of Cognition*. Havard University Press, Cambridge, MA, 1990.

[Paris, 1991] C. Paris. The role of the user's domain knowledge in generation. *Computational Intelligence*, 7:71–93, 1991.

[Reiter, 1994] E. Reiter. Has a consensus NL generation architecture appeared, and is it psycholinguistically plausible? In *Proceedings of the 7th International Workshop on Natural Language Generation* [1994], pages 163–170.

[Wahlster *et al.*, 1993] W. Wahlster, E. André, W. Finkler, H.-J. Profitlich, and T. Rist. Plan-based integration of natural language and graphics generation. *Artificial Intelligence*, 63:387–427, 1993.

[Walker and Rambow, 1994] M. A. Walker and O. Rambow. The role of cognitive modeling in achieving communicative intentions. In *Proceedings of the 7th International Workshop on Natural Language Generation* [1994], pages 171–180.

[Zukerman and McConachy, 1993] I. Zukerman and R. McConachy. Generating concise discourse that addresses a user's inferences. In Ruzena Bajcsy, editor, *Proceedings of the 13th International Joint Conference on Artificial Intelligence (IJCAI)*, pages 1202–1207, Chambery, France, 1993. Morgan Kaufmann.

Investigating the Emergence of Speech Sounds

Bart de Boer
Vrije Universiteit Brussel AI-Lab
Pleinlaan 2
1050, Brussels
Belgium
bartb@arti.vub.ac.be

Abstract

This paper presents a system that simulates the emergence of realistic vowel systems in a population of agents that try to imitate each other as well as possible. The agents start with no knowledge of the sound system at all. Although none of the agents has a global view of the language, and none of the agents does explicit optimization, a coherent vowel system emerges that happens to be optimal for acoustic distinctiveness.

The results presented here fit in and confirm the theory of Luc Steels [Steels 1995, 1997, 1998] that views languages as a complex dynamic system and the origins of language as the result of self-organization and cultural evolution.

1 Introduction

Language is considered to be important for the understanding of intelligence. Although animals are often quite capable of behavior that can be described as adaptive or intelligent, they are not capable, with the possible exception of the higher primates, of the more abstract intelligence (abstract reasoning, working with hierarchical structures, learning of arbitrary mappings) that is characteristic of humans. This more abstract kind of intelligence is of a symbolic nature, and therefore associated with language. Understanding the nature and the origin of language is therefore of crucial importance to the understanding of the nature and origin of human intelligence [Steels 1995, 1997, 1998].

1.1 The origins of language

Some scholars have assumed that the human faculty for language is innate and genetically determined in a very specific way [Chomsky 1980; Pinker & Bloom 1990]. It is obviously true that humans have a unique capability for learning and using language. If a bonobo chimpanzee (our evolutionary closest relative) is raised in the same (linguistic) environment as a human child, it will only learn a very rudimentary set of words, and no grammatical structure, whereas the human child will learn the full language. There are also a number of features of human anatomy (lowered larynx, very accurate control of breathing, accurate control of the tongue) that can only be explained as adaptations to language. However, it is questionable whether the human brain is really so specifically adapted to language that it contains a language organ and a set of "principles and parameters" [Chomsky 1980]. Although a couple of areas in the brain (most notably Broca's and Wernicke's area in the left hemisphere) do seem to be used for language processing in most humans, it is quite possible for other areas of the brain to take over their function. For example, children that are born with damage to these areas, or that receive the damage at a very early age, are still able to learn language very well [Johnson 1997]. Also, the neural pathways in the brain do not seem to be determined in sufficient detail genetically to explain something as specific as the proposed language organ.

It seems more likely that humans have a number of general capacities for learning and abstraction that enable them to learn language. How then did language emerge? Steels [1995, 1997, 1998] considers language the product of *cultural evolution*. Language, from his point of view is a distributed, complex and adaptive system. Important properties of language are that it is spoken in a population, where none of the speakers has perfect knowledge or central control. The language is not dependent on the individual speakers; they can enter and leave the population without changing the language. Also, new words and constructions can be adopted and spread in the language. From his point of view, language is not so much determined by an abstract individual grammar, but is rather an emergent phenomenon of a population of speakers. Whenever a group of humans is brought together, they will spontaneously develop a language. This has actually been observed in the emergence of pidgins and creoles and in the emergence of sign languages in communities of deaf people [Senghas 1994].

In Steels' theory, humans developed a need to cooperate and communicate under pressure of environmental circumstances. The first communication systems were developed on the basis of the general intelligence of the speakers. Complexity in the language was increased through innovation under the (conflicting) selection pressures of ease of production and ease of understanding.

The first pressure tends to reduce the utterances, while the second one tends to expand them. Variation will be introduced either through speech errors and reductions or through conscious innovation by the speakers themselves. Reproduction of the language is ensured through learning and imitation. All elements for an evolutionary system are present: reproduction, variation and selection. Therefore the process is called cultural evolution. According to Steels, coherence of the language is maintained through self-organization in the population of language users. In this framework it is not the biological evolution that drives the development of language, but rather the development of language that drives the biological evolution through the Baldwin effect [Baldwin 1896].

1.2 The origin of speech sounds

Steels tries to test all of his theories using computer simulations. A number of aspects of language, such as lexicon formation and formation of meanings have already been modeled, both in computer simulations and on robots [Steels 1995; Steels & Vogt 1997, Steels & Kaplan 1998]. The work presented in this paper applies the theory of language as a complex adaptive system to the emergence of speech sounds and more specifically to the emergence of vowels.

Speech sounds are an ideal test case for the role of self-organization and cultural evolution in the emergence of language. Speech sounds are the most physical aspect of language. It is therefore easy to measure their properties and the properties of human speech production and perception. The constraints on a system that works with speech sounds are therefore much more explicit and less controversial than the constraints on a system that works with e.g. grammar. Earlier work [Liljencrants & Lindblom 1972] has shown that in the case of vowel systems, the constraints are mostly acoustic. At the same time, the kinds of sound systems that can appear in human languages are well researched (see e.g. [Lindblom & Maddieson 1988; Schwartz *et al.* 1997a] and references therein). It is therefore easy to verify whether the sound systems that are predicted by the simulation are realistic or not.

Humans can distinguish a large number of different vowels: phoneticians have found at least 44 different basic vowels in the world's languages and the number of different vowel qualities that humans can distinguish in one single language is at least 15 (in Norwegian). However, vowel systems of the worlds' languages do not use a random subset of these vowels. Almost all languages contain [i], [a] and [u] (they appear in 87%, 87% and 82% of the languages in the UPSID$_{451}$[1] database [Maddieson 1984]) many languages also contain [e] (65%) and [o] (69%). Other sounds are much rarer. Also, if a language contains a back, rounded vowel of a certain height, for example [o], it will usually also contain the front, unrounded vowel of the same height, [e]. In other words, vowel systems tend to be symmetric. Furthermore, the

world's languages have a strong tendency towards systems with five vowels, which is neither the minimum, nor the maximum number of possible vowels. Of course, these are just tendencies, not universal rules. There are always languages that are exceptions.

It has already been known for some time [Liljencrants & Lindblom, 1972] that the symmetry of vowel systems, the abundance of certain vowels and the rarity of others can be explained as the result of optimizing acoustic distinctiveness. This has been shown with computer simulations. However, these simulations do not explain who is doing the optimization. No human language learner actively optimizes the sound system he or she learns. Instead, they try to imitate the sound system as accurately as possible. Until now, simulations of vowel systems were forced to explicitly implement the optimization, even in simulations that were based on populations of agents [Glotin 1995, Berrah 1998]. This paper will show that the optimization is an emergent result of self-organizing interactions in the population.

2 The System

The simulations are based on a population of agents that are each able to produce, perceive and learn realistic vowel sounds. For this purpose, they are equipped with a realistic vowel synthesizer, an associative memory for storing vowel prototypes and a model of vowel perception for calculating the distance between the vowel prototypes and the acoustic signals that the agents receive.

2.1 Production and Perception

The production module is an articulatory synthesizer that takes as input the three major vowel parameters and that produces as outputs the first four formant frequencies of the corresponding vowel. The major vowel parameters [Ladefoged & Maddieson 1996, ch. 9] are tongue height, tongue position and lip rounding. In the model the parameters are real numbers in the range [0,1]. For tongue position, 0 means most to the front, for tongue height 0 means lowest and for lip rounding 0 means least rounded. Thus the parameter setting (0,0,0) (in the order position, height, rounding) generates [a], (0, 1, 0) generates [i] and (1, 1, 1) generates [u]. The formant frequencies are defined as the peaks in the frequency spectrum of the vowel. The precise position of the peaks for different vowels depends on the speaker. The articulatory synthesizer that is used here is based on data from [Vallée 1994 pp. 162–164]. For [a] the formant values are (708, 1517, 2427, 3678), for [i] (252, 2202, 3242, 3938) and for [u] (276, 740, 2177, 3506). The mapping from articulatory to acoustic space is highly non-linear. In order to make the simulations more realistic and more interesting, noise is added to all four formant frequencies as follows:

1) $\quad F_i' = F_i(1 + v_i)$

where F_i is the formant frequency without noise, F_i' is the formant frequency with noise and v_i is a random value taken from the uniform distribution in the range $\left[\dfrac{-noise}{2}, \dfrac{noise}{2}\right]$, where *noise* is the noise level of the simulation.

---

[1] UCLA Phonological Segment Inventory Database with 451 languages.

The perception of vowels is based on a comparison with a list of prototypes. Research into perception of linguistic signals has shown that humans perceive them in terms of prototypes. Therefore each agent maintains a list of vowel prototypes. Whenever it perceives a signal, it compares it with all its vowel prototypes and considers the closest prototype as the one that is recognized. The realism of the simulation depends on the distance function. It is based on work by [Mantakas *et al.* 1986, Schwartz *et al.* 1997b]. It calculates the distance between the acoustic signals of two vowels. This distance is a weighted Euclidean distance between two 2-dimensional vectors that consist of the first formant frequency F_1 of the vowels and their effective second formant frequency F_2'. The effective formant frequency is a non-linear weighted sum of the second to the fourth formant. The idea of the effective second formant stems from the way humans perceive formant patterns. Because of the higher bandwidth of human receptors of higher frequencies, peaks at higher frequencies tend to merge into each other and are perceived as one peak. It is calculated as follows:

$$
2) \quad F_2' = \begin{cases} F_2, \text{if } F_3 - F_2 > c \\ \dfrac{(2-w_1)F_2 + w_1 F_3}{2}, \text{if } F_3 - F_2 \leq c \wedge F_4 - F_2 > c \\ \dfrac{w_2 F_2 + (2 - w_2)F_3}{2} - 1, \text{if } F_4 - F_2 \leq c \wedge F_3 - F_2 < F_4 - F_3 \\ \dfrac{(2+w_2)F_3 - w_2 F_4}{2} - 1, \text{if } F_4 - F_2 \leq c \wedge F_3 - F_2 \geq F_4 - F_3 \end{cases}
$$

where F_2, F_3 and F_4 are the formant frequencies expressed in Bark[2], c is a threshold distance, equal to 3.5 Bark, and w_1 and w_2 are weights, which in the original formulation are based on the strengths of the formants. As the articulatory model does not generate the strengths of the formants, they are considered to be proportional to the distance between the peaks, as follows:

$$
3) \quad w_1 = \frac{c - (F_3 - F_2)}{c}
$$

$$
4) \quad w_2 = \frac{(F_4 - F_3) - (F_3 - F_2)}{F_4 - F_2}.
$$

Finally, the distance D between signal a and signal b is calculated as follows:

$$
5) \quad D = \sqrt{\left(F_1^a - F_1^b\right)^2 + \lambda \left(F_2^{a\prime} - F_2^{b\prime}\right)^2}
$$

where λ is a parameter of the system that determines how the effective second formant frequency should be weighted with respect to the first formant frequency. Investigation of the behavior of this function in prediction of vowel systems [Vallée 1994, Schwartz *et al.* 1997b] as well as observations of human perception suggest a value of 0.3 for this parameter.

---

[2] A (partly) logarithmic frequency scale based on the properties of human perception. An equal interval in Bark corresponds to an equal perceptual distance.

2.2 The imitation game

The interactions between the agents are called imitation games. The intention of the interactions is to develop a coherent and realistic vowel system with which the agents can imitate each other as well as possible from scratch. For each imitation game, two agents are picked from the population at random. One of the agents is the *initiator* of the game, the other the *imitator*. The initiator picks a random vowel from its repertoire. If its repertoire is empty (as is the case at the beginning of the simulation) it adds a random vowel. It then produces the acoustic signal of that vowel. The other agent listens to this signal and finds its closest prototype. If its prototype list is empty, it finds a good imitation by talking and listening to itself, while improving the signal using a hill-climbing heuristic. It then produces the acoustic signal of the vowel it found. The initiator then listens to this signal and finds its closest prototype. If this is the same prototype as the one it used to initiate the game, the game is successful. If it is not the same, it is a failure. It communicates the success or the failure of the game using non-verbal feedback. Explicit non-verbal feedback is usually not given to children that learn language. However, they do get feedback on the quality of their communication through gesture, facial expression or the achievement (or lack thereof) of the communicative goal.

The imitator and the initiator react to the language game in a number of ways. Both update the use count of the vowels they produced. If the game was successful, they also update the success count. On average every ten imitation games, the agents throw away vowels that have been used at least 5 times and have a success/use ratio that is lower than 0.7. They also merge prototypes that are so close together in articulatory space that they will always be confused by the noise that is added.

The imitator also modifies its vowel inventory depending on the outcome of the imitation games. If the imitation game was successful, it shifts the vowel prototype it used closer to the signal it perceived in order to increase coherence. In the case the imitation game was a failure, this can have two reasons: either the initiator has more prototypes than the imitator, causing confusion, or the imitator simply used a bad phoneme. If the success/use ratio of the used vowel is low, then it is considered to be bad, and it is shifted closer to the perceived signal in the hope that it will be improved. If its ratio is high, this means it was used successfully in earlier games, so the reason of the failure was probably confusion. Therefore, a new prototype is added that is a close imitation of the perceived signal, using the same hill-climbing procedure that was used to add first prototypes.

A last possible change of the agents' vowel inventories is random addition of a new vowel (with probability typically 0.01). This is done in order to put a pressure on the agents to increase their number of vowels. In humans this pressure could for example come from a need to express new meanings. Iterating the imitation game in a large enough population of agents results in the emergence of realistic vowel systems.

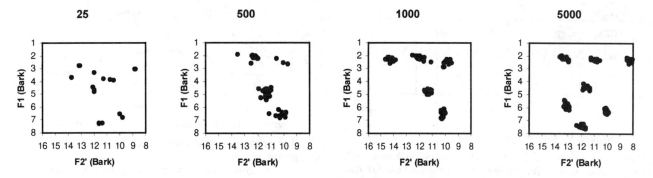

Figure 1: Emergence of a vowel system in a population of 20 agents with 10% noise.

3 The Results

The first result, which is shown in figure 1, is the emergence of a vowel system in a population of twenty agents and a noise level of 10%. In this figure, all vowel prototypes of all agents in the population are plotted in the acoustic space formed by the first and effective second formant. The first formant is plotted on the vertical axis and the effective second formant is plotted on the horizontal axis. The scales of the axes are in Barks. Note that the direction of the axes is reversed with respect to the usual direction of axes in graphs. This has been done in order to put the vowels in positions that correspond to the positions that they are usually given by linguists, with front vowels in the left- and high vowels in the upper part of the graphs. Note also that articulatory limitations cause vowels to be produced only in a roughly triangular region, with the apex at the bottom of the graph.

The leftmost frame of the figure shows the system after 25 imitation games. It can be seen that the distribution of the agents' vowel prototypes is still quite random, although vowel prototypes tend to occur in pairs. This is because the main factors at work are the random addition of vowel prototypes and the direct imitation of these. After 500 imitation games, in the second frame of figure 1, the main factor at work is a clustering of the agents' vowel prototypes. All agents in the population already have a vowel prototype near one of these clusters. Most imitation games will therefore be successful. In response to this the agents will shift their vowel prototypes closer to the corresponding vowel prototypes of the other agents. Because of the noise with which vowels are produced, however, the clusters remain a certain size and do

not reduce to points. Between 1000 and 5000 imitation games, the number of clusters increases until the available acoustic space is filled evenly with vowel clusters. The resulting vowel system consists of [i], [ɛ], [a], [ɔ], [u], [ɨ] and [ə] a system that is natural and that occurs for example in the Sa'ban language of Borneo. The artificial vowel system can be compared with measurements of a real vowel system in figure 2 (note that the scales in this figure are linear!) The system keeps on changing from this stage on, even though the changes are much less rapid. Vowel clusters might change position new and vowel clusters sometimes appear, get merged or split. But the appearance of the system remains the same.

Not all simulations with the same parameter settings result in the same vowel system. Sometimes the number of clusters is smaller, and their position might be different. This is illustrated in figure 3. This figure was generated by running 1000 times a run of 5000 imitation games with the same parameter settings as were used for figure 1. It shows the frequencies of the average sizes of the vowel systems of the agents in each of the populations that resulted from every run of 5000 games. Peaks occur at different integer values. This indicates both that systems of different sizes emerge and that the average size of the population's vowel systems tends towards integer numbers. This is because agents in the same population usually have the same number of vowels, indicating that the emerged vowel systems are coherent.

Vowel systems that emerge for the same parameter settings do not only have different sizes, but within the same system size, different distributions of the vowel prototypes in the acoustic space are found. Figure 4 shows this for systems with five vowel prototypes. The

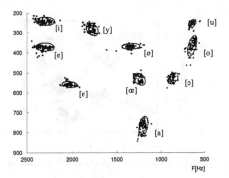

Figure 2: Vowel system of French, [Rober-Ribes 1995]

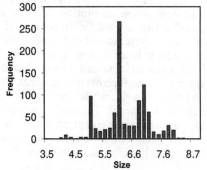

Figure 3: Size distribution of 10% noise systems.

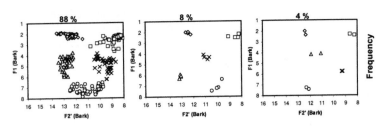

Figure 4: Vowel configurations for five vowel systems.

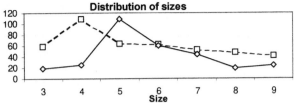

Figure 6: Size distribution in real and artificial systems.

systems were obtained from running the simulation with 15% acoustic noise, for 25 000 imitation games. Of the 100 runs, 49 resulted in populations with on average five vowels per agent. From each of these populations, one agent with the average number of vowels was taken at random. The vowel systems of these agents are shown in the figure, classified by type. It is found that the symmetric type occurs in 88% of the cases, the type with a central vowel and more front vowels occurs in 8% of the cases and the type with a central vowel and more back vowels occurs in 4% of the cases. This agrees very well with what has been found in natural languages. Schwartz *et al.* [1997a] found that in a previous version of UPSID (with 317 languages) 89% of the languages had the symmetric system, while the two types with the central vowel each occur in 5% of the cases. For different system sizes similarly good matches between emerged systems and human vowel systems are found, except for the smallest inventories (of three and four vowels) where discrepancies occur for the less frequent systems.

The outcome of the simulations does not depend very sensitively on the settings of the different parameters. Although the number of vowel clusters and their distribution are different for different parameter settings, their distribution is realistic in the sense that they could occur in human languages. Unfortunately space is too limited to show this in detail (see de Boer, *in preparation*).

A further observation of human languages is that they have a preference for vowel systems consisting of five vowels, and especially the symmetric system shown in figure 4. This is remarkable, because five is neither the minimum, nor the maximum number of vowels found in human languages. Apparently the frequency with which vowel system sizes occur is non-monotonic with respect to the number of vowels. This same phenomenon appears in the simulations. Simulations were run for values of the noise parameter ranging from 8% to 24% with increments proportional to the noise value (so that each parameter change has equal influence). The frequencies of the different vowel system sizes are plotted. This is shown in figure 5. The solid line shows the frequency of sizes of actual human vowel systems and the dashed line shows the frequency (which is of course relative to the total sample size) of sizes of emerged vowel systems. Both lines show a peak, but unfortunately, the peak for human systems occurs at 5 vowels, while the peak for artificial systems occurs at 4 vowels. This can probably be explained by the fact that the perception model is not perfect, so that high front vowels tend to be centered too much. This is probably also the explanation for the fact

that predictions for configurations with 3 and 4 vowels are not accurate.

It has now been shown that self-organization can predict the vowel systems that occur in human languages to a large degree of accuracy. But would it really be as robust as Steels' [1997, 1998] theory claims? It has already been shown that it is robust against changes in the language itself. It is also robust against changes in the population. This is shown in figure 6. The gray squares in this figure show the starting vowel system of a population of 50 agents. The population was then run for 15 000 imitation games. There was a probability of 1% per language game of taking an old agent from the population or inserting a new (empty) one in the population. The black circles show the system afterwards. By that time the whole population has been replaced. The vowel system has simplified a bit, but has remained mostly the same. It can thus be concluded that vowel systems are robust against changes in the population.

4 Conclusion

The simulations of populations that develop vowel systems clearly show that self-organization under constraints of perception and production is able to explain the structure of the vowel systems in human languages. The agents and their interactions form a dynamic system, in the sense described by Steels' [1995, 1997, 1998] theories. The most frequently occurring systems can be considered attractors of this dynamical system. Due to the random influences—noise on the articulations, random choice of agents—the populations never quite settle in exactly one of these attractors. They can settle in several different near-optimal configurations, just as human languages do not always have the optimal systems as predicted by optimization models [Liljencrants & Lindblom 1972; Schwartz *et al.* 1997b]. Although the agents do not have an innate predisposition towards certain vowel configurations, some seem to be preferred over others. This

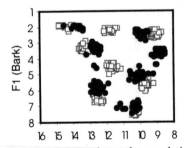

Figure 6: Vowel system conservation under population replacement.

is not, as a naïve observer might think, the result of innate rules and representations, but of self-organization in the population.

Just like human languages, emerged vowel systems also never quite stop changing. The systems that emerge are also robust to changes in the language and to changes in the population, just as required by any realistic model of language. The fact that sound systems can be transferred reliably from one generation to the next opens the possibility of cultural evolution.

Many things still need to be investigated: more complex utterances (so that not only acoustic constraints have to be taken into account, but also articulatory ones) and more realistic signals (so that the predictions match even better with real languages) are the ones that come to mind first. Nevertheless, these simulations already lend strong support to Steels' theory that language is a complex dynamic system and that self-organization and cultural evolution have played important roles in its emergence.

References

[Baldwin 1896] J. Mark Baldwin (1896) A new Factor in Evolution, *The American Naturalist* 30 (June 1896) pp. 441–451, 536–553.

[Berrah 1998] Ahmed Réda Berrah *Évolution Artificielle d'une Société d'Agents de Parole: Un Modèle pour l'Émergence du Code Phonétique*, Thèse de l'Institut National Polytechnique de Grenoble, Spécialité Sciences Cognitives, 1998

[Chomsky 1980] Noam Chomsky, Rules and representations, in *The behavioral and brain sciences* 3, pp. 1–21, 1980

[de Boer, *in preparation*] Bart de Boer *Self Organisation in Vowel Systems*, Vrije Universiteit Brussel AI-Lab Ph. D. thesis, to be defended June 1999.

[Glotin 1995] Hervé Glotin *La Vie Artificielle d'une société de robots parlants: émergence et changement du code phonétique*. DEA sciences cognitives-Institut National Polytechnique de Grenoble 1995

[Johnson 1997] Mark H. Johnson *Developmental Cognitive Neuroscience*, Oxford: Blackwell, 1997

[Ladefoged & Maddieson 1996] Peter Ladefoged and Ian Maddieson *The Sounds of the World's Languages*, Oxford: Blackwell, 1996

[Liljencrants & Lindblom 1972] L. Liljencrants and Björn Lindblom (1972) Numerical simulations of vowel quality systems: The role of perceptual contrast, *Language* 48: 839–862, 1972

[Lindblom & Maddieson 1988] Björn Lindblom and Ian Maddieson, Phonetic Universals in Consonant Systems, in: Larry M. Hyman & Charles N. Li (eds.) *Language, Speech and Mind*, pages 62–78, 1995

[Maddieson 1984] Ian Maddieson *Patterns of sounds*, Cambridge University Press, 1984 [Mantakas *et al.* 1986] Mantakas, M, J.L. Schwartz & P. Escudier *Modèle de prédiction du 'deuxiéme formant effectif' F₂'—application à l'étude de la labialité des voyelles avant du français*. In: Proceesings of the 15th journées d'étude sur la parole. Société Française d'Acoustique, pages 157–161.

[Pinker & Bloom 1990] Steven Pinker and P. Bloom Natural Language and Natural Selection. The *Behavioral and Brain Sciences* 13: 707–784, 1990

[Rober-Ribes 1995] Jordi Rober-Ribes *Modèles d'intégration audiovisuelle de signaux linguistiques*. Thèse de docteur de l'Institut National Polytechnique de Grenoble, 1995

[Schwartz *et al.*. 1997a] Jean-Luc Schwartz, Louis-Jean Boë, Nathalie Vallée and Christian Abry (1997a), Major trends in vowel system inventories, *Journal of Phonetics* **25**: 233–253, 1997

[Schwartz *et al.*. 1997b] Jean-Luc Schwartz, Louis-Jean Boë, Nathalie Vallée and Christian Abry (1997b), The Dispersion-Focalization Theory of vowel systems, *Journal of Phonetics* 25: 255-286, 1997

[Senghas 1994] Ann Senghas Nicaragua's Lessons for Language Acquisition, in: *Signpost* **7**(1), pp. 32–39,1994

[Steels 1995] Luc Steels A Self-Organizing Spatial Vocabulary, *Artificial Life* **2**(3): 319–332, 1995

[Steels 1997] Luc Steels, The Synthetic Modelling of Language Origins, *Evolution of Communication* **1**(1): 1–34, 1997

[Steels 1998] Luc Steels Synthesising the origins of language and meaning using co-evolution, self-organisation and level formation, in: James R. Hurford, Michael Studdert-Kennedy & Chris Knight (eds.) *Approaches to the Evolution of Language*, pages 384–404 Cambridge: Cambridge University Press, 1998

[Steels & Kaplan 1998] Luc Steels and Frédéric Kaplan (1998) Spontaneous Lexicon Change. In: *Proceedings of COLING-ACL 1998, Montreal*, pp. 1243–1249, 1998

[Steels & Vogt 1997] Luc Steels and Paul Vogt (1997) Grounding adaptive language games in robotic agents. In: Husbands, Phil & Harvey, Inman (eds.) *Proceedings of the Fourth European Conference on Artificial Life*, Cambridge (MS): MIT Press, pp. 474–482, 1997

[Vallée 1994] Nathalie Vallée, *Systèmes vocaliques: de la typologie aux prédictions*, Thèse préparée au sein de l'Institut de la Communication Parlée (Grenoble-URA C.N.R.S. no 368) 1994

Computer-Aided Tracing of Children's Physics Learning: a Teacher Oriented View

Filippo Neri
Dipartimento di Scienze e Tecnologie Avanzate
Università del Piemonte Orientale "A. Avogadro"
Corso Borsalino 54
Alessandria, I-15100
ITALY
email: neri@al.unipmn.it

Abstract

For an effective Teacher-Student interaction, the Teacher has to maintain a constant understanding of "what is going on" in the Student's mind. When coming to Physics, the Teacher's ability to propose and to relate explanations at different levels of abstraction - as a chains of causal interactions (deep) or as a set of observable phenomena (shallow) - may determine a successful and lasting learning in the Student.

Here, we describe a knowledge representation to be used by the teacher to depict to herself the student's mental model and to tune her future lessons according to the current student comprehension.

Supported by a cognitive theory of children physics learning, we used the system WHY for modeling the evolution of a student's learning as it appeared at the teacher's eyes. Two of WHY's features turned out to be essential: (a) to deal with explanations having different levels of abstraction, and (b) the possibility to continuously evaluate the coherence of the hypothesized learner's model with respect to her explanation.

In the long term, the work's outcome might contribute to the development of teaching assistant systems that support the teacher in identifying "what has to be explained next".

1 Introduction

For an effective teacher-student interaction, it is essential for the teacher having a continuous understanding of "what is going on" in the student's mind, i.e. to continuously hold a hypothesis about the student's knowledge consistent with her explanations. In addition, when coming to Physics, the teacher's ability to propose and to relate explanations at different levels of abstraction (for instance, as a chains of causal interactions (deep) or just as a set of observable phenomena (shallow)) may determine a successful and lasting learning.

We describe our experience in using the system WHY [Saitta et. al., 1993] for modeling the evolution of a student's learning as it would appear from the point of view of a teacher that is aware of a specific cognitive framework accounting for children learning in physics [Tiberghien, 1994]. The WHY system helps the teacher in inferring and representing the student's model from a sequence of interviews collected along a teaching period. The hypothesized learner's model is structured according to Tiberghien's cognitive framework [1994], derived from psychology results and educational experiences.

Two of WHY's features were determining its choice for this research: (a) its capability to deal with explanations having many levels of abstraction, and (b) its capability to continuously validate the coherence of the learner's model, proposed by the teacher, with respect to her explanations.

The long term work's outcome might possibly contribute to the development of teaching assistant systems supporting the teacher in identifying "what has to be explained next" during a cycle of lessons. At the present time, our research enabled the teacher to better realize and explore the limits involved in the learner's evolving knowledge as observed in a past teaching experience [Tiberghien, 1994]. This *a-posteriori* experience enabled the teacher to consider what-if situation where alternative next lesson topics could be selected in order to canalize the student learning effort towards the acquisition/understanding of scientifically correct physics models.

The paper is organized as follows: in Section 2, we summarize current approaches to the modeling of human learning and we discuss the aspects that differentiate our approach from them. In Section 3 and 4, we describe the considered educational context and the system WHY, respectively. In Section 5, a case study of student modeling is reported, and in Section 6 we compare the student's explanations with respect to the WHY's ones. Finally, in Section 6, some conclusions are drawn.

2 Related works

From the point of view of cognitive science, various aspect of human learning have been identified and studied. Our research mainly related to the study of the phenomena of conceptual change [Tiberghien, 1994; Vosniadou & Brewer, 1994; Caravita & Halldén,1994; Chi et al., 1994; Vosniadou, 1994]. No definition of conceptual change with universal validity has yet been found [White,1994]. But, roughly speaking the term conceptual change describes the evolution of the models of the world used by people to interpret data, to explain phenomena and to make predictions. Conceptual change has been mainly studied in the context of learning Mathematics or Physics [Forbus & Gentner, 1986; diSessa, 1993; Vosniadou, 1994; Chi et al., 1994] because both areas make available a body of knowledge that is enough completed and detailed to allow a formal representation (logic or calculus). All this models use rich and "informal" knowledge representation and have essentially a descriptive nature: they describe mental models or knowledge states, but do not include a description of the "learning strategy", i.e., the actual mechanisms of transition from a knowledge state to another. Trying to represent the evolution of a student's learning by using these rich and informal knowledge models without the help of an automatic system, is almost impossible. Consequently, exploiting these frameworks to hypothesize what a student is learning during a cycle of lessons is a very though and long work.

On the other end, computer scientists also proposed models of human learning [Sleeman et al., 1990; Baffes & Mooney, 1996; Sage & Langley, 1983; Newell, 1990; Schmidt & Ling, 1996; Shultz et al., 1994]. And, they all show a dynamic nature: they are able to coherently match the variations of the learner's performances by exploiting some computer-oriented mechanisms such as backpropagation, theory revision operation, etc.. Unfortunately, the price to be paid for obtaining such automatically evolving systems consists in the use of simple formalisms to represent the learner's knowledge and, in some cases, in the complete carelessness for the kind of changes occurring to the learner's knowledge as only a mimic of her performance is pursued. Then these approaches provide only a limited, if any, support to the teacher in understanding what exactly the student currently knows.

We believe that an important aspect is overlooked in these last models: the strict *interconnection* between the *shallow phenomenological knowledge* in a specific domain and pre-existing *deeper knowledge structures* or theories [Vosniadou, 1994, 1995; Tiberghien, 1994; Chi et al. 1994. This is particularly evident when examining a learner's explanations during learning: shallow and deep pieces of knowledge are mixed again and again by the learner in the effort to develop one coherent view of the world. In addition, human learning is, to a great extent, a search for explanations; then, any model of human learning should provide an explanatory framework, allowing not only to predict questions to answers, but also to put forward reasons in support of those answers.

Our approach intends to address these major aspects in the learner modelization by extending a descriptive model of learning [Tiberghien, 1984] with the explanatory framework provided by the learning system WHY [Saitta, Botta & Neri, 1993]. Note, however, that we do not claim that proposed knowledge representation resembles to the one in the student's mind. On the contrary, we claim that the resulting model is a functional model of the student's understanding of the domain. In our approach, the transitions between successive knowledge states are accomplished through interactive human-computer sessions. During these interactions, the teacher evaluates the coherence of her hypothesized learner's state against the previously collected student's answers and WHY proposes possible knowledge refinement when a student's answer cannot be explained on the basis of the current knowledge.

Finally, we believe that is relevant to clarify the differences between tutoring systems like, for instance, the Andes one [Gertner et al., 1998] and our approach. Tutoring systems are student oriented, our approach is teacher-oriented. In the firsts, the student model is automatically built to select the next most effective hint during problem solving; instead, we help the teacher to described her perceived evolution of the student's model, and we delegate to her experience the choice about the "next lesson" topic. Essentially we chose to operate at a different time scale: days instead of minutes or hours. In addition, we focalize on the effective teaching/learning of (large) theories more than on providing hints to the student while she is solving a specific problem.

3 The Educational Perspective

In education research, results on students' conceptions show difficulties in learning physics [Hestenes, 1987; Duit, 1995; diSessa, 1993]. In [Tiberghien, 1994] a theoretical framework for interpreting such difficulties has been proposed. The framework has its foundation both in pedagogical studies and in the epistemology of science. In experimental sciences, questions are strongly linked to three main factors: the theoretical background, the experimental facts considered, and the explanations produced. In the chosen theoretical framework, interpretation and prediction in physics imply a modelling process articulated on three levels: "theory", "model" and "experimental field" of reference.

Tiberghien [1994] assumes that an explanation of the learner's behaviour can be given by focusing the modelling process on the specific task of understanding the material world, rather than on general logical-mathematical reasoning. In this framework, a basic assumption, concerning the learner's cognitive activities, is made: when the learner is interpreting (or predicting) a material situation, she constructs a "model" of the situation, which depends on her background theory and is also internally coherent.

In [Tiberghien, 1994] no formal definition of these levels was given. A tentative addition of operational specifications is reported in [Neri et al., 1997]. Our basic assumption is that the "theory" level contains a causal model of the domain; thus, an explanation is a *causal attribution*.

The specific learning context considered is the following: students of six classes, at the first and second years of secondary school (11 - 13 year old), participated in a physics course, consisting of 11 sessions (once a week) including experiments, questions, discussion and explicit teaching. The contents of the course were basic concepts and qualitative relations in the domain of *heat transfer* in everyday life situations. Two students of each class were interviewed individually about the subject before and after the set of teaching sessions; and all the students filled two questionnaires, as well. In this paper we focalise our attention on the student David.

4 The Modeling Tool WHY

WHY [Saitta, Botta & Neri, 1993] has been chosen as testbed because of its ability to model both the answers and the causal explanations given by the children.

WHY learns and revises a knowledge base for classification problems using domain knowledge and examples. The domain knowledge consists of a *causal model* C of the domain, stating the relationships among basic phenomena, and a body of *phenomenological theory* P, describing the links between abstract concepts and their possible manifestations in the world.

The causal model provides explanations in terms of causal chains among events, originating from "first" causes. The phenomenological theory contains the semantics of the vocabulary terms, structural information about the objects in the domain, ontologies, taxonomies, domain-independent background knowledge (such as symmetry, spatial and temporal relations). Finally, P contains a set of rules aimed at describing the manifestations of abstractly defined concepts in terms of measurable properties, objects and events in the specific domain of application.

The causal model is represented as a directed, labeled graph. Three kinds of nodes occur in the graphs: *causal* nodes, corresponding to processes or states related by cause-effect relations, *constraint* nodes, attached to edges and representing conditions which must be verified in order to instantiate the corresponding cause-effect relation, and *context* nodes, associated to causal nodes, representing contextual conditions to be added to the cause in order to obtain the effect. The phenomenological theory is represented as a set of Horn clauses.

As said above, WHY's objective is to build up or revise a knowledge base KB of heuristic classification rules. A causal explanation (justification) for any proposed revision to the knowledge base is automatically provided.

It is important to stress the relations between the causal model and the heuristic knowledge base. As reasoning on the causal model is slow, some of the rules in KB act as shortcuts compiled from C. Some other rules, instead, do not have any relations with C. For instance, when KB is not derived from C but is directly acquired by the learner on a pure inductive basis. In the latter case, KB will give classifications (correct or not), for which no explanation exists with respect to C. Exploiting these different types of relations between KB and C, all the learning models emerged in the experimentation could be modeled. In the interplay between KB and C, the knowledge in P supplies the links between the general principles stated in C and the concrete experiments.

WHY relies on a sophisticated algorithm for uncovering errors or incompleteness in its knowledge that can be triggered when one of WHY's explanations does not match the student's ones. This provided useful information to the teacher in discovering where her hypothesized student's model was incoherent with the learner answer.

To model David's knowledge in WHY, we proceeded as follows. Each question answered by David consists of a) the description of an experimental setting for which a prediction about the heating effect has to be made, b) David's prediction and his (shallow or causal) explanation. In WHY, the experimental setting is an example description, the prediction is viewed as the example classification, and the student's explanation is interpreted as a chain of (shallow/deep) relationships determining the experiment outcome.

5 David Learns that Heating Causes Phase Transitions in Objects

As a case study: we compare here two significant knowledge states of David: before and after the teaching course. David's knowledge before teaching has been inferred on the basis of his answers and explanations to questions and interviews done before teaching. Part of David's knowledge before teaching is represented as a causal model in Figure 1. The drawing of the causal model make evident the findings emerging from David's answers. The most important are that David uses a notion of material causality linked to the "substance" of a body to describe what will happen when heating the body: "what happens to the body depends on what it is". For instance, water will eventually boil, if heated, whereas lead or iron or gold will melt, and, for this reason, they will become hot. Similarly, sugar becomes "caramel" and, again, it becomes hot. Questioned on the subject, David shows evidence to believe that "boiling" and "melting" are alternative (and mutually exclusive) behaviors, exhibited by different substance. In fact, he say that iron, gold and lead shall not boil, *because they melt*.

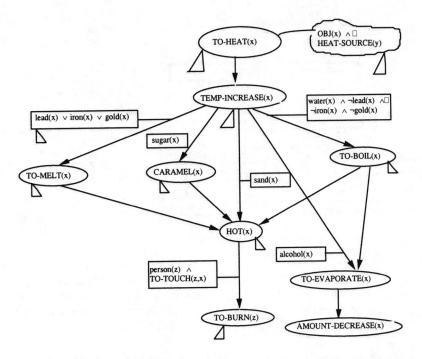

Figure 1 – Causal model hypothesized to represent part of David's knowledge before teaching. Elliptic nodes contain the domain phenomena. Arrows represent causal relationships among them. Rectangle and clouds represent accessory conditions.

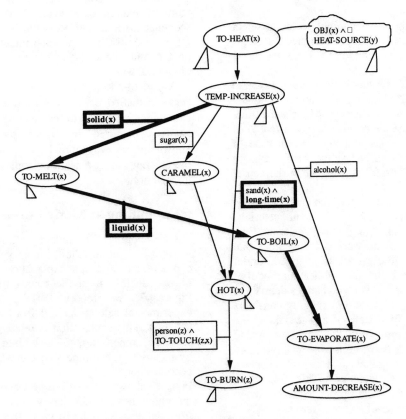

Figure 2 – Part of David's hypothesized knowledge after teaching. The most relevant change is represented by the bold causal path.

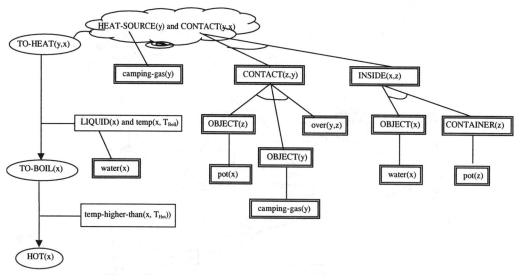

Figure 3 – Explaining with different levels of abstraction the phenomena: "The water becomes hot because of heating". Relations between the causal model and the phenomenological knowledge are outlined. The double thick-rectangles represent predicates occurring in the phenomenological theory. Such predicates are defined using Horn clauses, and, thus, they are depicted using AND/OR graphs.

One of the limits of this model of heating is the student cannot answer questions about materials that he has not experience of: David actually answered "I don't know" about the possibility of diamond, salt and aluminum to become liquid or gaseous.

Aware of this findings, the teacher might decide to select as "next lesson topic" some working experience that stress the independence of the heating effect from the body material.

Up to here the WHY system helped the teacher to develop and to describe her comprehension of David's heating model according to his answers. At the same time, WHY took care to validate the coherence (consistency) of the model with respect to David's answers. In case of incoherence, WHY actives its interactive theory revision module to propose some useful adjustment to the causal model.

After the teaching course, during which David has seen several other experiments involving different materials, he fills the final questionnaire and participates to the final interview. From these latter answers, we may infer that his deep knowledge of the world is changed, under various respect. In Figure 2, the inferred heating model of David after teaching is reported. Two changes deserve to be noted. The first one is that David explicitly considers time in determining the final state of a material. At the beginning, in fact, he simply said that the sand would become hot, when heated. Now, he is able to understand that the effect of heating takes time to happens, suggesting the idea of a "process". This finding is confirmed by the answers like: "in order for the water to start boiling, at least a quarter of an hour is necessary".

However, the most relevant change, with respect to the goal of the teaching course, is that David seems less committed to material causality for determining behaviors. He generalized from "iron", "lead", "gold" and "ice", that any "solid" may become liquid if sufficiently heated. Moreover, "to boil" and "to melt" are not anymore mutually exclusive behaviors, but they are possibly in sequence, as it should be. David's causality shows a shift from the "substance" to some underlying process, which, on the other hand, he is not yet completely capable of pinning down.

Aware of these findings, the teacher may just declare herself satisfied of David's progress. On the other hand, she might even try to evaluate the kind of conceptual changes occurred in David by comparing his two knowledge states (Figure 1 vs Figure 2), or she may plan the teaching of new learning topics exploiting the freshly learned notions.

6 Explaining at Many Levels of Abstraction

For developing the student's model and to trace her learning evolution, the capability to represent and to compare the student's explanations with respect to the ones deducible from the causal model is essential. In Figure 3, we report WHY's explanation for an experimental setting derived from David's model before teaching. This explanation is relative to a simple heating situation: some water, contained into a pot, is being heated by means of a camping gas; the water starts boiling and becomes hot.

Figure 3 shows the relations between the causal model and the phenomenological theory. The causal path explains, from the abstract point of view, that a liquid becomes hot because of the heat transfer produced by an heat source. The phenomenological theory make the explanation concrete: the liquid heated is some water, the water is contained into a pot, the pot is over the heat source, and the heat source is a camping gas.

In fact WHY explanation is a template of explanations where either abstract or concrete concepts may be included to interpret an observed phenomenon. Such explanations can thus be read at many abstraction levels ranging from a pure causal explanation (i.e. deep knowledge based) down to a plain sequence of measurable phenomena (i.e. shallow knowledge based). These explanations template facilitate the task of accounting for David's explanations while the teacher was developing David's model. In fact most of a student's early explanations mix shallow and deep knowledge in the effort to acquire a coherent view of the new subject matter. In the case of the mentioned experiment, David performed the experience by himself (under the teacher's supervision) in the school's laboratory. When he was questioned about the heating phenomenon, he said "The water is a liquid and is over the fire. The fire is hot. Then, the water boils and becomes hot".

7 Conclusion

We proposed a way of interpreting and describing learning progresses during teaching from the point of view of the teacher. In our approach, the tutor constructs and maintains a model of the student while the automatic system support the modeling activity by providing an enhanced knowledge representation framework. The articulated representation allows the modeling of phenomena observed in children learning elementary physics: notably their explanations in terms of simple causality, and the interdependence of "surface" pragmatic knowledge and "deep" causal one. Moreover, the structuring of the knowledge in terms of causal theory, phenomenological knowledge and experimental field provide a valuable framework for evidencing differences between the learner's knowledge and the target physics knowledge.

In the long term, we hope this research may contribute to the development of teaching assistant systems able to support the teacher in identifying "what has to be explained next" in a sequence of lessons.

References

Baffes P. T. and Mooney R. J. (1996). "A Novel Application of Theory Refinement to Student Modelling". *Proc. of Thirteenth National Conference on Artificial Intelligence*, Portland, pp. 403-408.

Caravita S. and Halldén O. (1994). "Re-framing the Problem of Conceptual Change". *Learning and Instruction, 4*, 89-111.

Chi M. T. H., Slotta J. D. and de Leeuw N. (1994). "From Things to Processes: A Theory of Conceptual Change for Learning Science Concepts". *Learning and Instruction, 4*, 27-43.

diSessa A. (1993). "Toward an Epistemology of Physics". *Cognition and Instruction, 10*, 105-225.

Duit R. (1995). "Constraints on Knowledge Acquisition and Conceptual Change the Case of Physics". *Proc. of Symposium on Constraints on Knowledge Construction and Conceptual Change* at 6th European Conference for Research on Learning and Instruction (Nijmegen, The Netherlands).

Forbus K.D. and Gentner D. (1986). "Learning Physical Domains: Toward a Theoretical Framework". In R. Michalski, J. Carbonell & T. Mitchell (Eds.), *Machine Learning: An Artificial Intelligence Approach, Vol. II*, Morgan Kaufmann, Los Altos, CA, pp. 311-348.

Gertner A. S., Conati C, and VanLehn K. (1998). "Procedural help in Andes: generating hints using a Bayesian Network Student Model", Proc. of National Conference on Artificial Intelligence AAAI'98, pp. 106-111.

Hestenes D. (1987). "Toward a Modelling Theory of Physics Instruction". *American Journal of Physics, 55*, 440-454.

Neri F., Saitta L. and Tiberghien A. (1997). "Modelling Physical Knowledge Acquisition in Children with Machine Learning". Proc. of *19th Annual Conference of the Cognitive Science Society*, pp. 566–571.

Newell A. (1990). *Unified Theories of Cognition*, Harvard University Press, Cambridge, MA.

Sage S. and Langley P. (1983). "Modeling Cognitive Development on the Balance Scale Task". *Proc. 8th Int. Joint Conf. on Artificial Intelligence*, pp. 94-96.

Saitta L., Botta M., Neri F. (1993). "Multistrategy Learning and Theory Revision". *Machine Learning, 11*, 153-172.

Schmidt W.C. and Ling C.X. (1996). "A Decision-Tree Model of Balance Scale Development". *Machine Learning, 24*, 203-230.

Shultz T.R., Mareschal D. and Schmidt W. (1994). "Modeling Cognitive Developemnt on Balance Scale Phenomena". *Machine Learning, 16*, 57-86.

Sleeman D., Hirsh H., Ellery I. and Kim I. (1990). "Extending Domain Theories: two case Studies in Student Modeling". *Machine Learning, 5*, 11-37.

Tiberghien A. (1994). "Modelling as a Basis for Analysing Teaching-Learning Situations". *Learning and Instruction, 4*, 71-87.

Vosniadou S. (1994). "Capturing and Modeling the Process of Conceptual Change". *Learning and Instruction, 4*, 45-69.

Vosniadou S. and Brewer W.F. (1994). "Mental Models of the Day/Night Cycle". *Cognitive Science, 18*, 123-183.

White R. T. (1994). "Commentary Conceptual and Conceptional Change". *Learning and Instruction, 4*, 117-121.

COGNITIVE MODELING

Cognitive Modeling 3:
Spatial Reasoning

Diagrammatic Proofs

Norman Y. Foo
Knowledge Systems Group
Department of Artificial Intelligence
School of Computer Science and Engineering
University of New South Wales, NSW 2052
Australia

Maurice Pagnucco and **Abhaya C. Nayak**
Knowledge Systems Group
School of MPCE
Macquarie University
NSW 2109
Australia

Abstract

Diagrammatic reasoning comprises phenomena that range from the so-called "free-rides" (e.g. almost immediate understanding of visually perceived relationships) to conventions about tokens. Such reasoning must involve cognitive processes that are highly perceptual in content. In the domain of mathematical proofs where diagrams have had a long history, we have an opportunity to investigate in detail and in a controlled setting the various perceptual devices and cognitive processes that facilitate diagrammatically based arguments. This paper continues recent work by examining two kinds of diagrammatic proofs, called Categories 1 and 3 by [Jamnik, et. al. 97], the first being one in which generalization of a diagram instance is implied, and the second being one in which an infinite completion is represented by an ellipsis. We provide explanations of why these proofs work, a semantics for ellipses, and conjectures about the underlying cognitive processes that seem to resonate with such proofs.

1 Introduction

The use of diagrams as reasoning aids has a long history, but the serious investigation of what is involved in such reasoning is recent. Valuable insights into mixed-mode or heterogeneous reasoning in which both text and diagrams play essential roles in the instruction of mathematical logic were obtained from the *Hyperproof* system of Barwise and Etchemendy [Barwise and Etchemendy 95]. Shin [Shin 94] undertook a detailed investigation of how far diagrams and diagrammatic constructions can be used in set theory as an alternative to traditional textual expositions. Sowa [Sowa 84] and the conceptual graph community advocate a diagrammatic approach to knowledge representation and computation. There are also the long-established ER diagrams in databases. For more diverse AI applications, the collection of papers [Glasgow, et. al. 95] is representative of the effort to understand what constitutes diagrammatic reasoning and the strengths and weaknesses of this mode. Of particular interest is the idea of "free rides" (see [Shimojima 96] and [Gurr 98] for details), e.g. the processing and understanding of diagrams that yield facts, relationships, etc. with apparently little effort on the part of humans. Not much of this is well-understood because of the complexity of the tasks and the difficulty of designing experiments to test theories. However, in the specialised domain of mathematical proofs there is the intriguing possibility that the tasks are simpler to understand and experiments may be subject to control protocols. This paper should be read from this perspective. We are fortunate that Nelsen [Nelsen 93] has compiled a comprehensive collection of such proofs. Indeed, Jamnik, et. al. [Jamnik, et. al. 97] took a number of Nelsen's examples as challenges that required explanation.

We believe that explanation of the efficacy of a diagrammatic proof of a mathematical theorem has at least two obligations. The first obligation is to give an account – using standard mathematics, meta-mathematics, logic or computation theory – of why that mode of reasoning is sound. The second obligation is to adduce – or, in the absence of an accepted theory, to conjecture – credible cognitive processes for the "free rides" involved.

The *main aim* of this paper is to fulfill these obligations for the chosen examples, and in so doing, pave the way for discovering the principles behind the mechanical generation and/or verification of diagrammatic proofs. Such principles presume an understanding of the aforementioned cognitive processes.

2 Types of Diagrammatic Proofs

Jamnik, et. al., [Jamnik, et. al. 97] have categorized diagrammatic proofs of mathematical theorems according to certain characteristics. They identified three categories. In Category 2 which they examined in recent papers (see also [Jamnik, et. al. 98]), the proofs are schematic. While not requiring induction for the particular proof, one is required to generalize on the size of the diagram. Their central result was to show how a constructive ω-rule could be invoked to do this. The paradigmatic example is the *sum of odd numbers* which Nelsen [op. cit.,p.71] attributes to Nichomachus of Gerasa. As we shall be concerned only with Categories

1 and 3 in this paper, we reproduce their descriptions from Jamnik, et. al. [Jamnik, et. al. 97].

Category 1 Proofs that are not schematic: there is no need for induction to prove the general case. Simple geometric manipulations of a diagram prove the individual case. At the end, generalisation is required to show that this proof will hold for all [parameters]. Example theorem: Pythagoras Theorem.

Category 3 Proofs that are inherently inductive: for each individual concrete case of the diagram they need an inductive step to prove the theorem. Every particular instance of a theorem, when represented as a diagram, requires the use of abstractions to represent infinity. Thus, the constructive ω-rule is not applicable here. Example: Geometric Sum.

In this paper we initiate an examination of both these categories.

3   Category 1 Proofs

Category 1 proofs somehow require generalization from a specific collection of diagrams. The diagrammatic proof of Pythagoras Theorem, attributed by Nelsen [op. cit.,p.3] to the unknown author of the *Chou Pei Suan Ching*, is reproduced as the two diagrams $A(a,b)$ and $B(a,b)$ in Figure 1. The dimensions a and b are the lengths of the two sides of the four right-angled congruent triangles with hypotenuse c, a dependent length. In $A(a,b)$, the smaller square embedded in the larger one has side c, so its area is c^2. It is also the residual region after the four surrounding triangles are excluded. In $B(a,b)$ we have a transformed version, via diagrammatic operations T, of $A(a,b)$ in which the triangles have been moved to the positions shown. The residual region outside the triangles, which must have the same area as the one before, are now the two small squares with areas a^2 and b^2. This proves the theorem for the specific case of these linear dimensions a, b and c.

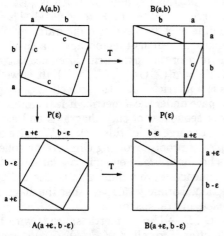

Figure 1: Diagrammatic proofs of Pythagoras: original and its perturbed version

We propose two solutions to the problem of generalization using this example as a paradigm. The first relies on a notion of continuity, while the second is the analog of a powerful meta-theorem in logic. Both of these have precursors in the recent discussion by Hayes and Laforte [Hayes and Laforte 98].

The *continuity* argument has two parts. The first is illustrated in Figure 1 via two additional diagrams $A(a+\epsilon, b-\epsilon)$ and $B(a+\epsilon, b-\epsilon)$. What is argued here is that the second two diagrams are perturbed versions, via a map $P(\epsilon)$, of the first two, but *the same transformation T relation holds*. In fact, this can be made precise by saying that the diagrams *commute* as indicated. This argument shows that the relative ratio $a{:}b$ is not material, but does not meet the criticism that an absolute magnitude for, say a, is used in the diagram. To meet this we need the second part, which is a scaling argument. That is, to the $A(a,b)$ and $B(a,b)$ diagrams and the operations T, we have a *scaled* counterpart $A(ra,rb)$ and $B(ra,rb)$ with the same operations.

The second solution, analogous to logic, is the diagrammatic version of the theorem called "generalization on constants", also known as the *Theorem on Constants* (TOC for short). One statement of it (see, e.g. [Shoenfield 67]) is as follows. Suppose Γ is a set of formulas and $\alpha(x)$ is a formula with free variable x, and the constant d does not appear in any formula in Γ. Further, suppose $\Gamma \vdash \alpha[x/d]$, where the notation $\alpha[x/d]$ signifies the substitution of d for x in $\alpha(x)$. Then we may infer $\Gamma \vdash \alpha(x)$, and hence $\Gamma \vdash \forall x \alpha(x)$.

The discussion below is an *outline* of how the TOC is applied. The details require attention to the admissible operations on, and inferences from, diagrams; these we postpone to a later paper, but see [Hayes and Laforte 98] for some current insights.

The relevance of the TOC as a response to specificity of the diagrammatic proof of the Pythagoras Theorem lies in the implicit *hypotheses* Γ of the proof. We enumerate some members of this Γ: first, there are the Euclidean geometric propositions used, e.g., properties of triangle congruence, the sum of angles of any triangle being 180 degrees, properties of squares, invariance of shapes and areas under rotations and translations. There are also some algebraic identities involving additions and subtraction of areas, and formulas about the area of any square given the length of its side. None of these mention the constants a, b and c. The construction of diagram $A(a,b)$, and the subsequent operations (call them T) to transform it to diagram $B(a,b)$, are the steps in the diagrammatic proof. The conclusion of the proof is $a^2 + b^2 = c^2$, in symbolic notation $\Gamma \triangleright a^2 + b^2 = c^2$, where none of a, b or c occur in Γ. Here $\triangleright$ is the diagrammatic analog of textual proof (i.e., $\vdash$) in diagrams, principally diagrammatic operations supplemented by reasoning about invariants like areas, etc., the details of which we will elucidate in a future paper. The TOC now authorizes generalization of the conclusion $a^2 + b^2 = c^2$ to *arbitrary* values for these constants.

These two responses to Category 1 diagram specificity

extend to many other proofs in which ostensibly particular dimensions are named, e.g., Nelsen's own diagrammatic proof [op. cit.,p.22] of Diophantus' "Sum of Squares Identity".

4   Category 3 Proofs

The main feature of Category 3 proofs is an ellipsis, the classical "$\cdots$" notation used in suggesting the infinite completion of, say, a series such as $a_0 + a_1 + a_2 \cdots$. This ellipsis is used in Category 3 diagrams to similarly suggest that the reasoning applied so far to a finite diagram can be successfully completed to infinity by some implicit induction. The most well-known example of this is the diagrammatic proof of the sum of the geometric series $1/2, 1/2^2, 1/2^3, \cdots$, attributed by Nelsen [op. cit.,p.118] to Page. It is reproduced here as diagram A in Figure 2.

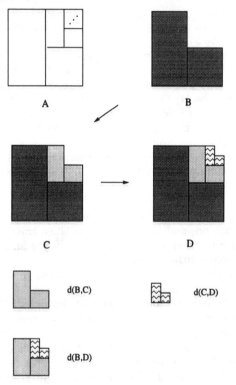

Figure 2: Construction steps in the proof of the sum $\sum 1/2^k$.

We will now provide justifications for the diagrammatic steps in the proof, and a semantics for the ellipsis in the diagram. The key idea is to view the completed square as the limit of a sequence of constructions, each of which is a "monotonic" and "Markovian" addition to its predecessor. It is monotonic because each construction stage adds new information that is distinctly represented without retracting old information. It is Markovian because only the most recent piece of information (construction) is used to construct the next one. The usual diagram with its ellipsis notation is reproduced as diagram A in the figure. The diagram B corresponds to the sum $S_1 = 1/2 + 1/2^2$. The next diagram C corresponds

to the sum $(1/2 + 1/2^2) + (1/2^3 + 1/2^4) = S_1 + S_2$ where S_2 abbreviates the second grouping of summands. Each group is colored differently for ease of viewing. Proceeding likewise, the diagram D corresponds to the sum $S_1 + S_2 + S_3$ where $S_3 = (1/2^5 + 1/2^6)$.

4.1   Meaning of the Ellipsis

This subsection assumes some mathematical background that can be found in standard texts such as [Simmons 84]. Let us denote by A_i the area corresponding to the summand S_i, i.e., each A_i is an L-shaped region typically indicated by the differently colored pieces in Figure 2. The regions can be placed in the first quadrant of co-ordinate axes so that the initial A_1 diagram (B in Figure 2) has the origin at its left bottom corner, and the X- and Y-edges have length 1. The second region A_2 will have its left bottom corner at the point $(1/2, 1/2)$, and edge lengths $1/2$. With this convention, each L-piece in the later pictures can be described as an affine transformation of the preceding L-piece.

Identifying the L-piece A_k with the co-ordinates of its points, this transformation T can be specified as follows, where d_k is the (co-ordinates of the point at the) left bottom corner of A_k:

$$A_{k+1} = \begin{bmatrix} 1/2 & 0 \\ 0 & 1/2 \end{bmatrix} (A_k - d_k) + \begin{bmatrix} 1/2^k \\ 1/2^k \end{bmatrix} + d_k$$

The diagram D in Figure 2 can then be denoted as a union $A_1 \cup A_2 \cup A_3$, which by the definition of the affine transformation can equivalently be written as $(I \cup T \cup T^2)A_1$, where I is the identity operator. Using this notation as a basis we can express the progression from one diagram to the next as a larger transformation F as follows:

$F(A_1 \cup \cdots \cup A_k) = (A_1 \cup \cdots \cup A_k) \cup T(A_k)$.

This is the formal expression of the geometric intuition that the next diagram in the sequence is obtained by gluing a smaller (scaled and translated) L-shape onto it at the appropriate corner, making explicit its Markovian character.

There is an obvious way to describe the difference between, say, diagrams B and C, which is just the additional L-piece A_2 added to B to yield C. This way to view the difference between two diagrams by observing the difference in regions they occupy is a special case of the measure μ of the *symmetric difference* between two sets $d(X, Y) = \mu((X \cup Y) \setminus (X \cap Y))$. It is well-known that this is a metric. Thus, the collection of diagrams is a metric space under the d metric. It is therefore possible to consider sequences of such diagrams and ask if such sequences converge under this metric. We have observed in examples of proofs involving ellipses, the collection of diagrams has been broad enough to guarantee that convergent sequences have a limit that is also a diagram in the collection. Formally this says that the diagram space is a *complete* metric space.

A map $G : U \to U$ on a metric space U with metric d is a *contraction* if for all X, Y $d(GX, GY) \leq k \cdot d(X, Y)$ for some $k < 1$. The Banach Fixed Point (BFP) theorem says that a contraction G in a complete metric space has a unique fixed point, i.e. there is one, and only one, X_0 such that $G(X_0) = X_0$. Moreover, this fixed point can be constructively obtained from an arbitrary initial point Y by repeated application of G starting from Y, i.e., $X_0 = \lim_{n \to \infty} G^n(Y)$. This theorem cannot be directly applied to explicate the efficacy of the diagrammatic proof, but a weaker form of it is relevant. The weaker statement (WFP) still relies on G being a contraction on a subspace $Y_1, Y_2 \cdots$, consisting of the terms in the sequence generated by G starting from a given initial point Y_0. Such a sequence will still converge to a fixed point, a result that follows directly from the standard proof of the BFP theorem.

Observation 1 *The transformation F defined above on the space of T-generated L-shapes is a contraction map. Hence it has a unique fixed point, which is the square A in Figure 2.*

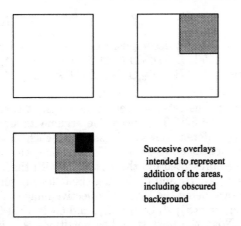

Succesive overlays intended to represent addition of the areas, including obscured background

Figure 3: Summing overlays is perceptually difficult.

The fact that the general form of the BFP is not helpful in explicating the visual persuasiveness of this diagrammatic proof suggests some cognitive hypotheses that cry out for testing. To explain the hypotheses, let us examine the transformation F more closely. Suppose the initial diagram is not a unit edge L-shape but a unit *square* instead. The underlying transformation T as defined before will now work on this square to produce a scaled version of it, then translate this version so that its top right corner coincides with that of the original square. Figure 3 shows the first three members of this sequence. Now, if this is intended to represent the sum of the geometric series $1 + 1/2^2 + 1/2^4 \cdots$, we have to re-define the transformation F to be not the union of the diagram sequence as before, but *the sum of the overlaid areas*, so that multiple overlays are counted area-wise as many times as they occur. With this re-definition the WFP theorem will still hold, so convergence is guaranteed. But unlike Figure 2, the corresponding visual task is no longer easy. Indeed, the area addition at each stage in Figure 3 is not monotonically distinct in terms of representation, as each new piece intersects prior peices. The crucial difference from Figure 2 appears to be

this – the set unions for the L-shaped sequences in Figure 2 are *disjoint unions*, that moreover are contiguous, so that sums of areas are easy to see. We therefore conjecture that disjoint unions, especially contiguous ones, are free ride features.

There is an important point we note about the choice of the initial shape fed into the constructor T. In Figure 2 we chose an L-shape. We could have conceivably chosen, say, the left tall rectangle in diagram B. If we did that, then the second stage will be the addition of the right square in diagram B. This leads to a more complex constructor T which has to be decomposed into two stages – it is no longer Markovian in the strict sense, but is nevertheless still finite memory. In essence, the choice boils down to how long a preceding sequece is needed to define the next piece(s) of the sequence.

So that we can use "$\cdots$" as a meta-notation in our description of ellipses, it is convenient to adopt the alternative notation &c to denote the ending ellipses signifying continuation to the limit in both diagrams and sequential expressions. With these remarks, we propose that the *the semantics of ellipses* be as follows.

Definition 1 *We interpret the meaning of the ellipsis &c in the diagram $A_1 \cup A_2$ &c to be a constructor function application written in "suffix form" with argument the diagram $A_1 \cup A_2$, and whose value is the diagram $A_1 \cup A_2 \cup A_3$ &c. More generally, &c denotes a function &c defined as follows: the diagram $A_1 \cup \cdots \cup A_k$ &c has the intended meaning $\&c(A_1 \cup \cdots \cup A_k)$ which evaluates to the diagram $F(A_1 \cup \cdots \cup A_k)$ &c.*

This has the effect of making &c denote a "lazy expander" of the finite diagram so far constructed. A more formal approach to the semantics of &c appeals to the notion of recursive domains [Stoy 77] in which the diagrams are the solutions (up to isomorphism) of the domain equation

$$Aexp = (A_0 + Aexp \uplus T(end(Aexp))$$

and the "completed" (infinite) diagram, i.e., the square in this case, is the least upper bound of these solutions. Here the function *end* extracts the last component of the instance of $Aexp$, and $\uplus$ is the ordered union operation.

4.2 Construction Invariants

Another example of a Category 3 proof, attributed by Nelsen [op. cit.,p.121] to Ajose, is shown in Figure 4. The diagram A in it is the proof of the sum $1/2^2 + 1/2^4 + 1/2^6$ &c $= 1/3$. Diagrams B, C and D show the analogs of the construction leading to diagram A as was explained for the proof in Figure 2, with the L-shapes as before. As the semantics for the ellipsis &c is similar to that above, we will omit it. However, in this proof a new feature is present that requires justification. As can be seen from the diagrams B,C and D, we have at each stage to "see" that the colored area is 1/3 of the total area (L-shapes) constructed so far, and that eventually the total area is 1. That the eventual area is 1 is reached exactly as in the proof in Figure 2. How do we account for the other piece of inference - that the colored area is always 1/3 of the total? We propose that the underlying idea is a *construction invariant*. This is closely related to the idea of a loop invariant in the semantics of programming languages. There, a first-order formula ϕ is a loop invariant in loop L if its truth at the point of entry into the loop guarantees its truth at the end of it, denoted $\phi \supset [\![L]\!]\phi$. Likewise, in the present construction, let $\phi[area]$ stand for the statement: "colored area = 1/3 total area". Then we have the *visual proof rule*: $\{\phi[A_1 \cup \cdots \cup A_k] \supset \phi[F(A_1 \cup \cdots \cup A_k)]\} \supset \phi[A_1 \cup \cdots \cup A_k \, \&c]$, where F is the one-step constructor above.

The visual proof rule is a formal statement of the conjecture that such *uniform invariants* across uniform constructions are *inductive* "free rides". In other words, such proof rules capture the essence of cognitive induction in diagram completions or fixed points.

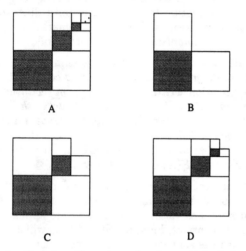

Figure 4: Construction steps in the proof of the sum $\sum 1/2^{2k}$.

5   Schröder-Bernstein Theorem

As yet another instance of a Category 3 type proof which illustrates the ellipsis and construction invariant features, we will now examine the diagrammatic aid to the proof of the Schröder-Bernstein theorem in set theory [Kamke 50]. This theorem states that if there is an injection ψ from set S into set U and also an injection χ from set U into set S, then the sets have the same cardinality, i.e., there is a bijection η between them. The usual proof uses a "back-and-forth" argument, but there is a less well-known proof that establishes a (apparently stronger, but actually equivalent) statement which implies the theorem, and is arguably easier to expound. This statement is as follows: If there is an injection π from set S into a proper subset A_1 of itself, then there is a bijection between S and all subsets S_1 such that $A_1 \subset S_1 \subset S$. It is this latter statement whose proof is usually accompanied by a diagram, the appeal to which is inessential only to the most experienced and sophisti-

cated of set theorists. All others (the authors included) appear to find the diagram indispensable. The use of this diagram further exhibits some of the properties discussed in the preceding sections, and invites similar conjectures.

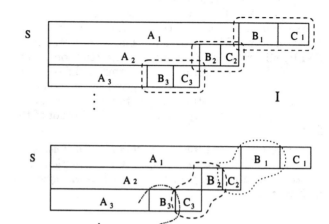

Figure 5: Disjoint decompositions of sets S and S_1
$S = B_1 \cup C_1 \cup B_2 \cup C_2 \cup B_3 \cup C_3 \cup \ \&c \ \cup \bigcap A_i$
$S_1 = B_1 \cup C_2 \cup B_2 \cup C_3 \cup B_3 \cup C_4 \cup \ \&c \ \cup \bigcap A_i$

Figure 5 illustrates the reasoning steps. It is adapted from [Kamke 50]. The successive arguments are represented by different views of the same set, each view being a strip partitioned as shown. For instance, the original set S is (represented by) the first strip, with the labelled partitions A_1, B_1 and C_1 having the following roles: A_1 is as above, being the assumed injective image subset of S, i.e. $A_1 = \pi(S)$; $A_1 \cup B_1 = S_1$; and C_1 is what is "left over". Now, the next strip has partitions A_2, B_2 and C_2 with the following roles: $A_2 = \pi(A_1)$, $B_2 = \pi(B_1)$, and $C_2 = \pi(C_1)$. The subsequent layers are interpreted likewise.

The diagram I shows a way to decompose the set S. It yields the equation $S = B_1 \cup C_1 \cup B_2 \cup C_2 \cup B_3 \cup C_3 \ \&c \cup \bigcap A_i$. The diagram II shows a way to decompose the set S_1 (= $A_1 \cup B_1$). It yields the equation $S_1 = B_1 \cup C_2 \cup B_2 \cup C_3 \cup B_3 \cup C_4 \ \&c \cup \bigcap A_i$. Then by aligning these equations as indicated in Figure 5, we see that the disjoint components are in one-to-one correspondence with each other (bearing in mind that by assumption $C_{k+1} = \pi(C_k)$), thereby establishing the bijection between S and S_1 as required.

What devices have been used in this appeal to the diagrams? First, the layout of the successive strips emphasized the *disjoint* components, much as in the proofs of the sums of series above. Second, the decompositions used the elliptical *&c* as above. Third, the apparently textual alignment of the two decompositions were used to argue for extension of pairwise correspondences between components to the entire set union. We submit that the third device is at least as much diagrammatic as it is textual, depending as it were on appeal to a linear layout and the elliptical *&c* for its "free ride" cogency.

We note in particular the implicit appeal to an invariant and a *visual* proof rule. Let $\phi[S_1, S_2]$ stand for the statement: $S_1 \simeq S_2$, where $\simeq$ means a termwise 1-1 correspondence between the two sequences S_1 and S_2. Then we have the *visual* proof rule: $\{\phi[S_1, S_2] \supset \phi[F([S_1), F(S_2)]]\} \supset \phi[S_1 \, \&c, S_2 \, \&c]$, where F is the one-step constructor for extending the partitions to the next layer.

6 Conjectures for "free rides"

In the preceding analyses we suggested a number of features of diagrams in mathematical proofs that seem to resonate with cognitive ease of processing. It is convenient to summarize them here as challenges for controlled experiments. If validated, they can form the basis for the automation and generation of diagrammatic proof systems, and of related HCI designs for diagrammatic reasoning. Invalidation of any of them will prompt alternatives, and certainly prevent some blind alleys from being pursued. Some diagrammatic features that facilitate proofs are conjectured to be:

- Continuous transformations of proof constructions.
- Disjoint unions or decompositions.
- Contiguous pieces in these unions.
- Monotone sequences of areas with a "Markovian" uniform rule that generates the next element from the last one.
- Limits are upper or lower bounds of such sequences.
- Simply shaped upper or lower bounds.
- Contractive mappings with simple (see below) metrics like symmetric difference.
- Ellipses represent implicit uniform constructions with lazy evaluation semantics.
- Simply perceived relations between areas.
- Relations true in the limit are exactly those invariant with respect to one step uniform (Markovian) constructions.

We end this concluding section by remarking on metrics for sets. It would not have escaped the attention of readers familiar with work in fractals [Peitgen, et. al. 92] that diagrams such as Figures 2 and 4 are reminiscent of such recursively generated images. In fractal topology, the convergence metric normally used is the *Hausdorff metric*. We believe that this is *not* a "free ride" metric, and hence is not simple, for reasons that we will explain elsewhere.

7 Acknowledgements

We thank Donald Michie, Pavlos Peppas, Yusuf Pisan and Yan Zhang for their comments on earlier versions of this paper. This research is supported in part by a grant from the Australian Research Council.

References

[Barwise and Etchemendy 95] Barwise, J. and Etchemendy, J., "Heterogeneous logic", in *Diagrammatic Reasoning: Cognitive and Computational Perspective*, eds. J. I. Glasgow, N. H. Narayanan and B. Chandrasekaran, MIT Press, 1995, 209-232.

[Glasgow, et. al. 95] Glasgow, J. I., Narayanan, N. H. and Chandrasekaran, B. (eds), *Diagrammatic Reasoning: Cognitive and Computational Perspectives*, MIT Press, 1995.

[Gurr 98] Gurr, C. A., "Theories of Visual and Diagrammatic Reasoning: Foundational Issues", Proceedings of the AAAI Fall Symposium on Visual and Diagrammatic Reasoning, Orlando, AAAI Press, October 1998, pp 3-12.

[Hayes and Laforte 98] Hayes, P. J. and Laforte, G. L., "Diagrammatic Reasoning: Analysis of an Example", Proceedings of the AAAI Fall Symposium on Visual and Diagrammatic Reasoning, Orlando, AAAI Press, October 1998, pp 33-37.

[Jamnik, et. al. 97] Jamnik, M., Bundy, A. and Green, I., "Automation of Diagrammatic Reasoning", Proceedings of the Fifteenth International Joint Conference on Artificial Intelligence, IJCAI'97, pp. 528-533, Nagoya, August 1997, Morgan Kaufmann.

[Jamnik, et. al. 98] Jamnik, M., Bundy, A. and Green, I., "Verification of Diagrammatic Proofs", Proceedings of the AAAI Fall Symposium on Visual and Diagrammatic Reasoning, Orlando, AAAI Press, October 1998, pp 23-30.

[Kamke 50] Kamke, E. *Theory of Sets*, Dover Publications, 1950.

[Nelsen 93] Nelsen, R. B., *Proofs without Words*, The Mathematical Association of America, 1993.

[Peitgen, et. al. 92] Peitgen, H-O., Jurgens, H., Saupe, D., *Chaos and Fractals : New Frontiers of Science* Springer-Verlag, 1992.

[Simmons 84] Simmons, G. F. *Introduction to Topology and Modern Analysis* McGraw-Hill, 1984.

[Shin 94] Shin, S. J., *The Logical Status of Diagrams*, Cambridge University Press, 1994.

[Shimojima 96] Shimojima, A., "Operational Constraints in Diagrammatic Reasoning", in *Logical Reasoning with Diagrams*, ed. J. Barwise and G. Allwein, Oxford University Press, New York, 1996.

[Shoenfield 67] Shoenfield, J., *Mathematical Logic*, Addison Wesley, 1967.

[Sowa 84] Sowa, J., *Conceptual Structures*, Addison Wesley, 1984.

[Stoy 77] Stoy, J. E. *Denotational Semantics: the Scott-Strachey Approach to Programming Language Theory*, MIT Press, 1977.

Modeling the Basic Meanings of Path Relations

Christian Kray
German Research Center for
Artificial Intelligence GmbH (DFKI)
Stuhlsatzenhausweg 3
66123 Saarbrücken
Germany
kray@dfki.de

Anselm Blocher
Collaborative Research Center 378
University of Saarbrücken
Postfach 151150
66041 Saarbrücken
Germany
anselm@cs.uni-sb.de

Abstract

In the field of spatial reasoning, point-to-point relations have been thoroughly examined, but only little attention has been payed to the modeling of path relations. We propose a computational model that extends the existing referential semantics for point-to-point relations to path relations. On the linguistic side, we present some research on German path prepositions as well as results on their English counterparts. This analysis of path prepositions is used to extract a semantic model for path relations. On the geometric side, we examine the characteristics of trajectories and propose a computational method to find an appropriate path relation for a given situation. Finally, we show how our findings on the linguistic and the geometric sides can be brought together to form a consistent model.

1 Introduction

Space plays a central role in human cognition, and has therefore been a research focus in different disciplines like (computational) linguistics [Lakoff, 1987], cognitive sciences [Kosslyn, 1994], psychology [Landau and Jackendoff, 1993], and artificial intelligence [Maaß et al., 1993]. Sophisticated conceptual [Egenhofer, 1991] and computational models [Gapp, 1994] have been developed that made it possible to *compute* the appropriateness of spatial relations in specific situations, thereby providing a better understanding of what is meant by certain spatial expressions. These results paved the way for intelligent systems that are able to analyze and generate natural language descriptions of space [Wahlster et al., 1998].

Within the field of spatial relations, so-called *topological* (e.g. near or at) and *projective* relations (like right-of or above) have been most thoroughly examined. Both groups are *point-to-point relations* as they establish a spatial relation between two objects of arbitrary shape. (Between is an exception from this rule as it requires at least three objects to be computed correctly[Habel, 1989].)

A different kind of spatial relations are the so-called *path relations* (e.g. along, around, or past). Much less attention has been payed to their conceptualization [Krüger and Maaß, 1997] and computation than in the case of point-to-point relations. This may be due to the greater complexity: the problem of computing the most appropriate path relation can only be solved if there is a *path* which consists at least of a simple line with a starting point and an ending point. As we will show in section 5, topological, projective, and path relations share nevertheless several (geometric) concepts.

In section 2, we present the basic ideas and concepts we will use throughout the paper. Based on an analysis of the linguistic side of the problem (section 3), we propose a semantic model which is described in section 4. In the following section, we turn to the geometric side, and establish a basic framework for geometric path relations. These two sides are integrated to form a consistent model which then is applied to various examples (section 6). Finally, we summarize our findings and give an outlook on future directions.

2 Key Concepts and Related Work

Following [Herskovits, 1986] we distinguish between the *basic meaning* of a spatial relation and its instantiation in a concrete situation: An *object to be localized (LO)* is set in relation to a *reference object (RO)*. Furthermore, a *frame of reference* has to be established in order to distinguish different spatial relations. Determining the origin and the orientation of the reference frame depends on a multitude of factors such as the point of view of the observer/addressee, or the intrinsic orientation of the RO [Maaß, 1993]. The computation of topological

German preposition	Raw translation	Meaning	Formalization
zu	*towards*	approach	$\mathbf{D} \xrightarrow{D} IM\mathbf{D}$
bis	*up to*	approach	$\mathbf{D} \xrightarrow{*} IM\mathbf{D}$
in	*into*	translation from outside to inside	$M\mathbf{D} \xrightarrow{M} \mathbf{I}$
nach	*to*	approach	$\mathbf{D} \xrightarrow{*} IM\mathbf{D}$
an	*to*	approach until contact	$\mathbf{D} \xrightarrow{D} M\mathbf{D}$
gegen	*against*	approach until contact	$\mathbf{D} \xrightarrow{M} I M$
von	*(away) from*	increase of distance	$IM\mathbf{D} \xrightarrow{*} \mathbf{D}$
aus	*out of*	translation from inside to outside	$\mathbf{I} \xrightarrow{M} M\mathbf{D}$
entlang	*along*	keeping distance (anlong boundary)	$IM\mathbf{D} \xrightarrow{*} IM\mathbf{D}$
vorbei	*past*	approach, increase of distance	$\mathbf{D} \xrightarrow{D} \mathbf{D}$
durch	*through*	approach, entering of interior, leaving of interior	$IM\mathbf{D} \xrightarrow{I} IM\mathbf{D}$
um	*around*	angular movement	$M\mathbf{D} \xrightarrow{MD} M\mathbf{D}$
		approach, passing along boundary, increase of distance	$M\mathbf{D} \xrightarrow{MD} M\mathbf{D}$

Table 1: Several German prepositions used for path description

and projective relations relies on a frame of reference. It is used to extract the two essential parameters that are needed to evaluate the applicability of point-to-point relations: the distance of the LO from the RO (topological relations), and the angle disparity from a prototypical direction (projective relations).

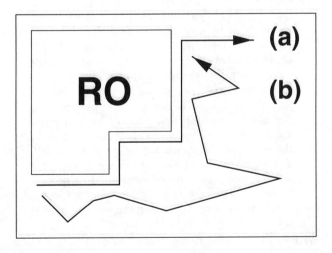

Figure 1: Two trajectories

[Gapp, 1997] proposed a model for spatial relations that is based on a three level *referential semantics*. On the lowest level, only purely visual information is available. This information is abstracted on the semantic level to a geometrical representation which the referential semantic itself relies on. *Idealized meanings* of spatial relations are compared to the actual situation taking into account contextual factors that are modeled on the *conceptual layer*. A *degree of applicability (DA)* is computed that rates how well a relation corresponds to the prototypical meaning, on a scale from 'zero' (not applicable) to 'one' (fully applicable). For a detailed description of the factors and algorithms used to determine the DA of point-to-point relations, refer to [Gapp, 1997].

Path relations differ from their topological and projective counterparts in two ways. On one side, the LO is expected to be path-like: either its shape has to be path-like, or it can be abstracted to a path-like shape. In some cases, this also holds for the RO. (In the computation of the applicability of point-to-point relations, the shape of the LO is of lesser importance.) On the other side, the computation of path relations cannot be reduced to a simple two point problem. Figure 1 illustrates this fact: Trajectory (a) is certainly a better match for a relation along$_1$ (describing a path that follows the form of the RO) than is trajectory (b). But there is no *single* point on either trajectory that can be used to determine the applicability of this relation. (While one may argue about the meaning of "along", along$_1$ might actually capture a meaning facet.)

3 Analysis of German Path Prepositions

From a computational perspective, one of the main problems in understanding natural language is its inherent ambiguity. This is also true for path prepositions: The German path preposition[1] "zu" (roughly "to", "towards"), for example, is used to describe trajectories that lead towards the reference object. The description "der Weg *zu* dem Park" ("the way to the park") can mean different things. It is not obvious where the tra-

---

[1] We use the term '(path) preposition' although, from a strictly linguistic perspective, not all of them are prepositions per se.

jectory starts, nor where it ends: Does it end outside the park, just at the border, or inside? The verbalization process is affected by ambiguity, too: To describe a path that starts within the park and leads outside of it, one could, for example, use "aus" (approx. "out of") or "von" (approx. "from").

Table 1 lists some of the most commonly used German path prepositions. We tried to express the basic meanings of the main uses in natural language and – at a finer level of detail – in a more formal syntax. It should be stated that the table does not contain a complete description of all possible meanings of path prepositions but only *meaning facets*. The formal syntax is based on a subset of Egenhofer's semantics for topological relations [Egenhofer, 1991]. "I" stands for *containment* of the LO within the RO (inside), "M" for *contact* of the boundaries of LO and RO (meet), and "D" for the *disjointness* of them (disjoint). So, a formula like

$$\mathbf{I}\mathbf{M}D \xrightarrow{M} \mathbf{D}$$

is to be read as

"The corresponding relation describes a path that starts either within the border, or on the border, or outside of the RO. On its way, the contact relation becomes true at least once, and it ends outside of the RO."

We use bold style for the main usage, plain style for possible uses, and italics for unlikely (but still possible) uses of a relation. An asterix (*) above the arrow indicates that no special relation has to be fulfilled during transition. Although the table was created with German prepositions in mind, preliminary research on the corresponding English prepositions indicates that a basic set of concepts exists across different languages. Exploratory studies in French and Japanese support this hypothesis, and justify the search for a language independent conceptual model.

4   Basic Semantic Concepts

A first look at the meaning column in Tab. 1 reveals that the majority of the prepositions describes an approach towards an object. Only a few words are available to express an increase of distance (e.g. "von", "aus"). (This is not surprising since one usually follows a path with the target in mind.) Furthermore, there is a concept of angular movement (such as in "um" and "entlang"). So, the two essential parameters (distance and angle) needed for the evaluation of point-to-point relations play an important role in the conceptualization of path relations, too.

A second observation is that the meaning component of some path prepositions (e.g. "in") contains a simple point-to-point relation. This relation is applied to either one of the endpoints of the trajectory (in the case of "in": to the ending point), or to the entire trajectory (e.g. "past"). If we take out that element, we are left with a *simple path relation* that is only related to the *path* but not to a single point.

Based on these observations, we can establish a semantics for path relations which relies on simple path relations. We propose the following five simple path relations as building blocks for more complex ones. They can be combined with each other, and/or with point-to-point relations to form higher order path relations.

- **decrease-distance**: the ending point of the trajectory is closer to the RO than the starting point.
- **increase-distance**: the starting point of the trajectory is closer to the RO than the ending point.
- **maintain-distance**: the distance of every point on the trajectory from the RO is the same.
- **change-angle**: the starting and the ending point form an angle with the RO.
- **maintain-angle**: the starting and the ending point show no angular disparity in relation to the RO.

Since the direction of the angular disparity cannot be expressed easily using path prepositions (at least as far as German, French, and English are concerned), it makes sense to have just one relation expressing undirected change. This is not true in the case of distance, where we consequently differentiate approach and an increase of distance.

5   Geometric path relations

As far as the geometric side of the computation of path relations is concerned, we first want to define clearly the object to be accomplished:

Given an LO in path-like shape (or abstraction) represented by a trajectory, find the path relation which describes best the relation of the LO to an arbitrary reference object (and compute a corresponding degree of applicability).

A trajectory is defined by n points $(p_1...p_i...p_N)$. The endpoints p_1 and p_N denoting beginning and end of the trajectory are defined either by an explicit direction or by the order of the computational analysis itself. This description of the trajectory is provided by the conceptual layer mentioned in section 2. Its construction (e.g. by choosing a specific idealization or by indicating the starting point) is beyond the scope of this paper.

We rely on the following assumptions:

1. **The LO is represented as a trajectory.** This corresponds to the fact that a path preposition can hardly be applied to an object which is not path-like shaped at all (e.g. "the ball along the wall").

2. **We want to describe the trajectory as a whole.** Though it might be preferable to subdivide the trajectory into parts (which analyzed one by one could possibly be associated more evidently with *several* path relations), the entire trajectory has to be analyzed in order to detect possible subdivisions. Therefore, it is appropriate to generate first an overall description using a *single* relation.

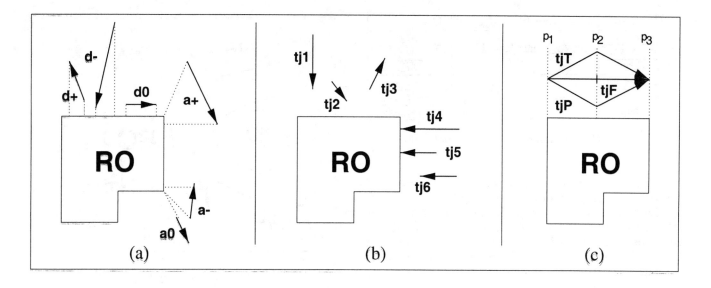

Figure 2: Trajectories: (a) changes (b) qualities (c) curvatures

3. **We want to describe the *course* of a trajectory.** In this case, point-to-point relations are not sufficient and path relations are needed.

4. **We want to extend the computational model of static relations to path relations.** Accordingly, the DAs have to be comparable. This will be ensured by using the same essential parameters – distance and angle –, identically calculated frame of reference, reference points (the nearest points between LO and RO), and intermediate results of the computation of point-to-point relations.

5. **We focus on path relations that correspond to path prepositions.** As the geometric model is linked to linguistic concepts via the reference semantics, path *prepositions* have to be kept in mind while exploring geometric path *relations*.

5.1 Two-point-trajectories

The most basic trajectory consists of exactly two distinct points and is called *two-point-trajectory*. On one hand, more complex trajectories – *n-point-trajectories* – can easily be constructed by concatenating n-1 two-point-trajectories. On the other, even the most complex trajectory can be split into a unique series of two-point-trajectories. This implies that the first step to analyze path relations is to study the relations between two-point-trajectories and the reference object.

Any trajectory can be localized exactly using the concepts of distance and angle. This corresponds to assumption four and to the observations made in section 4. In order to describe the course of a two-point-trajectory as a whole (see asumption three) using distance and angle, the changes of these essential parameters between p_1 and p_2 have to be analyzed: Distance and/or angle can either be increased, maintained or decreased as depicted

in Fig. 2a. This distinction – similar to the one made in the previous section – enables us to define *basic path relations* (see Tab. 2; cw: clockwise, ccw: counter-cw).

Change	Distance		Angle	
Increasing	depart	$d+$	turn-cw	$a+$
Decreasing	approach	$d-$	turn-ccw	$a-$
None	follow	$d0$	no-turn	$a0$

Table 2: Basic path relations (see Fig. 2a)

Figure 2b shows that we can even sort trajectories according to the degree of being an optimal representant of a path relation: $tj1$ is closer to the ideal meaning of **approach** than is $tj2$. Furthermore, we can *compare different* relations: The quality of the relation **depart** represented by $tj3$ lies inbetween the qualities of $tj1$ and $tj2$. To describe the differences between $tj4$ to $tj6$ other factors than course, e.g. the distance to the RO, have to be taken into account. Nevertheless, these trajectories are all optimal representants of the relation **approach** since we assumed that path relations depend on their course only. Consequently, the degree of applicability can be expressed as the difference in the distances (Δd) of p_1 and p_2 with respect to the RO, divided by the length of the trajectory. As the computation of each of these distances corresponds to the one used for point-to-point relations, the resulting DAs are comparable. Table 3 illustrates the computation of the DAs for the basic path relations defined above.

5.2 N-point-trajectories

Actually, in most cases trajectories representing abstractions of real world objects consist of more than two points. In order to extend the use of basic path relations

Relation	Measure ($M_{essParam}$)	DA
depart		M_{dist}
approach	$M_{dist} = \frac{\Delta d_{RO}(p_2,p_1)}{|\overrightarrow{p_1p_2}|}$	$-M_{dist}$
follow		$1 - |M_{dist}|$
turn-cw		M_{angle}
turn-ccw	$M_{angle} = \frac{\Delta \angle_{RO}(p_2,p_1)}{2\pi}$	$-M_{angle}$
no-turn		$1 - |M_{angle}|$

Table 3: Calculation of degrees of applicability

to n-point-trajectories it suffices to build the weighted average over all parts of the trajectory.

However, as shown in Fig. 2c, there are differences in the course of n-point-trajectories we are still not able to describe using the basic path relations defined above: A distinction of the curvature of n-point-trajectories has to be made. Three types can be distinguished:

- tjP first approaches the RO and then departs: this curvature corresponds to the path relation past.

- tjT first departs from the RO and then approaches it again: this curvature corresponds to trip.[2]

- tjF keeps the distance over the whole course, no curvature exists: this equals follow.

There are two possible ways to cope with curvatures: either by finding a suitable segmentation (which contradicts assumption two), or by analyzing the essential parameter distance more thoroughly. A curvature can only exist if a trajectory has at least three points: In this case, the difference of $\Delta d_{RO}(p_2, p_1)$ and $\Delta d_{RO}(p_3, p_2)$ is either positive (trip) or negative (past). The degree of the curvature is measured as follows:

$$sign(\Delta d_{RO}(p_2,p_1) - \Delta d_{RO}(p_3,p_2))\left(1 - \frac{|\overrightarrow{p_1p_3}|}{|\overrightarrow{p_1p_2}| + |\overrightarrow{p_2p_3}|}\right)$$

A n-point-trajectory's curvature can easily be expressed by the weighted curvatures of the inner points.

6 Results

Table 4 integrates the semantic aspects of German path prepositions developed in section 3 and path relations constructed according to section 5. They may be combined with each other, or with point-to-point relations. (Path relations refer to the entire trajectory while point-to-point relations refer to the trajectory point(s) mentioned explicitly in brackets.)

However, there is no 1:1-correspondence between a given preposition and a specific realization. Since a single preposition can be used to describe different situations, and a single situation can be described using different prepositions, there is a n:m-relation between language and geometry. To overcome the vagueness of language, contextual factors can be taken into account. Additionally, vagueness (precision) can be modeled explicitly as proposed in [Kray, 1998].

---

[2]There seems to be no corresponding path preposition neither in German nor in English.

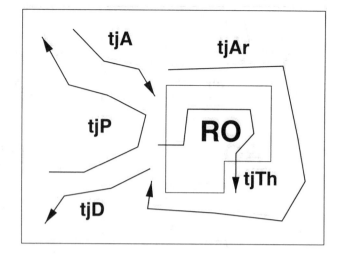

Figure 3: Exemplary trajectories

Table 5 shows exemplary results for the trajectories in Fig. 1 and 3. As expected, the DAs for 1(a) and 1(b) are significantly different. The examples in Fig. 3 also yield reasonable results.

Fig.	Tj.	Relation	DA	Preposition
1	(a)	follow	0.76	"entlang"
1	(b)	follow	0.59	"entlang"
3	tjA	approach	0.68	"nach", "zu"
3	tjD	depart	0.68	"von"
3	tjTh	thru	0.71	"durch"
3	tjAr	turn-cw	0.63	"um"
3	tjAr	past	0.57	"vorbei"

Table 5: Exemplary results

7 Conclusion

The connection between visual and verbal space is an important issue in the development of natural language systems that are concerned with spatial information. In this paper, we presented an analysis of German path prepositions, and used the results to deduce a basic semantics for path relations. Extending the model for spatial relations, we showed how those findings can be integrated with geometric path relations.

Currently, our results are being integrated in a localization agent [Wahlster et al., 1998] and in a mobile tourist [Deep Map, 1999] guide. In addition, their potential for anytime behavior (interruptability with increasing quality over time) [Dean and Boddy, 1988] is being investigated. In the future, we plan to develop segmentation algorithms that are based on the methods proposed in this paper. A subdivision of a complex trajectory may improve the quality of path descriptions due to the finer granularity. Furthermore, we intend to evaluate the meaning facets of path prepositions empirically.

German preposition	Raw translation	Formalization	Path relation (basic or combined)
zu	*towards*	$D \xrightarrow{D} IMD$	approach
bis	*up to*	$D \xrightarrow{*} IMD$	approach
in	*into*	$MD \xrightarrow{M} I$	approach $\wedge$ in(p_N)
nach	*to*	$D \xrightarrow{*} IMD$	approach $\wedge$ in(p_N)
an	*to*	$D \xrightarrow{D} MD$	approach $\wedge$ contact(p_N)
gegen	*against*	$D \xrightarrow{M} IM$	approach $\wedge$ contact(p_N)
von	*away from*	$IMD \xrightarrow{*} D$	depart
aus	*out of*	$I \xrightarrow{M} MD$	in(p_1) $\wedge$ depart
entlang	*along*	$IMD \xrightarrow{*} IMD$	follow
vorbei	*past*	$D \xrightarrow{D} D$	past
durch	*through*	$IMD \xrightarrow{I} IMD$	past $\wedge$ $\exists i : $ in(p_i)
um	*around*	$MD \xrightarrow{MD} MD$	turn-cw $\vee$ turn-ccw
		$MD \xrightarrow{MD} MD$	past $\wedge$ (turn-cw $\vee$ turn-ccw)

Table 4: German path prepositions with their corresponding path relations

Acknowledgments: The research presented in this paper was funded by the Collaborative Research Center 378 at the University of Saarbrücken, the German Research Center for Artificial Intelligence GmbH (DFKI), and the European Media Laboratory GmbH (EML) at Heidelberg, Germany.

References

[Dean and Boddy, 1988] T. Dean and M. Boddy. An Analysis of Time-Dependent Planning. In *Proc. of AAAI-88*, pages 49–54, St. Paul, MN, 1988.

[Deep Map, 1999] Deep Map. Intelligent next-generation Geo-Information Systems. http://www.eml.org/englisch/projekte/deepmap/deepmap.html

[Egenhofer, 1991] M. J. Egenhofer. Reasoning about Binary Topological Relations. In O. Günther and H.-J. Schek, editors, *Advances in Spatial Databases*, pages 144–160. Springer, Berlin, Heidelberg, 1991.

[Gapp, 1994] K.-P. Gapp. Basic Meanings of Spatial Relations: Computation and Evaluation in 3D Space. In *Proc. of AAAI-94*, Seattle, WA, 1994.

[Gapp, 1997] K.-P. Gapp. *Objektlokalisation: Ein System zur sprachlichen Raumbeschreibung.* Studien zur Kognitionswissenschaft. Deutscher Universitätsverlag, Wiesbaden, 1997.

[Habel, 1989] C. Habel. Zwischen-Bericht. In C. Habel, M. Herweg, and K. Rehkämper, editors, *Raumkonzepte in Verstehensprozessen: Interdisziplinäre Beiträge zu Sprache und Raum*, pages 37–69. Niemeyer, Tübingen, 1989.

[Herskovits, 1986] A. Herskovits. *Language and Spatial Cognition. An Interdisciplinary Study of the Prepositions in English.* Cambridge University Press, Cambridge, London, 1986.

[Kosslyn, 1994] S. M. Kosslyn. *Image and Brain.* MIT Press, Cambridge, MA, 1994.

[Kray, 1998] C. Kray. Ressourcenadaptierende Verfahren zur Präzisionsbewertung von Lokalisationsausdrücken und zur Generierung von linguistischen Hecken. Memo 66, Universität des Saarlandes, Sonderforschungsbereich (SFB) 378, 1998.

[Krüger and Maaß, 1997] A. Krüger and W. Maaß. Towards a Computational Semantics of Path Relations. In *Workshop Language and Space, AAAI'97*, pages 101–109, Providence, RI, 1997.

[Lakoff, 1987] G. Lakoff. *Women, Fire, and Dangerous Things. What Categories Reveal about the Mind.* Chicago University Press, Chicago, 1987.

[Landau and Jackendoff, 1993] B. Landau and R. Jackendoff. "What" and "Where" in Spatial Language and Spatial Cognition. *Behavioral and Brain Sciences*, 16:217–265, 1993.

[Maaß et al., 1993] W. Maaß, P. Wazinski, and G. Herzog. VITRA GUIDE: Multimodal Route Descriptions for Computer Assisted Vehicle Navigation. In *Proc. of the Sixth Int. Conf. on Industrial and Engineering Applications of Artificial Intelligence and Expert Systems IEA/AIE-93*, pages 144–147, Edinburgh, Scotland, 1993.

[Maaß, 1993] W. Maaß. A Cognitive Model for the Process of Multimodal, Incremental Route Description. In *Proc. of the European Conference on Spatial Information Theory.* Springer, Berlin, Heidelberg, 1993.

[Wahlster et al., 1998] W. Wahlster, A. Blocher, J. Baus, E. Stopp, and H. Speiser. Ressourcenadaptierende Objektlokalisation: Sprachliche Raumbeschreibung unter Zeitdruck. *Kognitionswissenschaft, Sonderheft zum Sonderforschungsbereich (SFB) 378*, 1998.

CONSTRAINT SATISFACTION

CONSTRAINT SATISFACTION

Constraint Satisfaction 1

A Comparison of Structural CSP Decomposition Methods

Georg Gottlob
Inst. für Informationssysteme
Technische Universität Wien
A-1040 Vienna, Austria
gottlob@dbai.tuwien.ac.at

Nicola Leone
Inst. für Informationssysteme
Technische Universität Wien
A-1040 Vienna, Austria
leone@dbai.tuwien.ac.at

Francesco Scarcello
ISI-CNR
Via P. Bucci 41/C
I-87030 Rende, Italy
scarcello@si.deis.unical.it

Abstract

We compare tractable classes of constraint satisfaction problems (CSPs). We first give a uniform presentation of the major structural CSP decomposition methods. We then introduce a new class of tractable CSPs based on the concept of *hypertree decomposition* recently developed in Database Theory. We introduce a framework for comparing parametric decomposition-based methods according to tractability criteria and compare the most relevant methods. We show that the method of hypertree decomposition dominates the others in the case of general (nonbinary) CSPs.

1 Constraint Satisfaction Problems

An instance of a *constraint satisfaction problem (CSP)* (also *constraint network*) is a triple $I = (Var, U, \mathcal{C})$, where Var is a finite set of variables, U is a finite domain of values, and $\mathcal{C} = \{C_1, C_2, \ldots, C_q\}$ is a finite set of constraints. Each constraint C_i is a pair (S_i, r_i), where S_i is a list of variables of length m_i called the *constraint scope*, and r_i is an m_i-ary relation over U, called the *constraint relation*. (The tuples of r_i indicate the allowed combinations of simultaneous values for the variables S_i). A *solution* to a CSP instance is a substitution $\vartheta : Var \longrightarrow U$, such that for each $1 \le i \le q$, $S_i \vartheta \in r_i$. The problem of deciding whether a CSP instance has any solution is called *constraint satisfiability (CS)*. (This definition is taken almost verbatim from [Jeavons *et al.*, 1997].)

Many problems in Computer Science and Mathematics can be formulated as CSPs. For example, the famous problem of *graph three-colorability (3COL)*, is elegantly formulated as a CSP. Constraint Satisfiability is an NP-complete problem.

It is well-known [Bibel, 1988; Gyssens *et al.*, 1994; Dechter, 1992] that the CS problem is equivalent to various database problems, e.g., to the problem of evaluating *Boolean conjunctive queries* over a relational database [Maier, 1986], or to the equivalent problem of evaluating *join dependencies* on a given database.

This paper is organized as follows. In Section 2 we discuss tractability of CSPs due to restricted structure. In Section 3 we briefly review well-known CSP decomposition methods. In Section 4 we describe the new method of *hypertree decompositions*. In Section 5 we explain our comparison criteria and in Section 6 we present the comparison results for general CSPs. The case of binary CSPs is briefly discussed in Section 7.

2 Tractable classes of CSPs

Much effort has been spent by both the AI and the database communities to indentify *tractable classes* of CSPs. Both communities have obtained deep and useful results in this direction. The various successful approaches to obtain tractable CSP classes can be divided into two main groups [Pearson and Jeavons, 1997]:

1. **Tractability due to restricted structure.** This includes all tractable classes of CSPs that are identified solely on the base of the structure of the constraint scopes $\{S_1, \ldots S_q\}$, independently of the actual constraint relations $r_1, \ldots, r_q$.

2. **Tractability due to restricted constraints.** This includes all classes that are tractable due to particular properties of the constraint relations $r_1, \ldots, r_q$.

The present paper deals with tractability due to restricted structure. The *structure* of a CSP is best represented by its associated *hypergraph* and by the corresponding *primal graph*, defined as follows.

To any CSP instance $I = (Var, U, \mathcal{C})$, we associate a hypergraph $\mathcal{H}_I = (V, H)$, where $V = Var$, and $H = \{var(S) \mid C = (S, r) \in \mathcal{C}\}$, where $var(S)$ denotes the set of variables in the scope S of the constraint C. Since in this paper we always deal with hypergraphs corresponding to CSPs instances, the vertices of any hypergraph $\mathcal{H} = (V, H)$ can be viewed as the variables of some constraint satisfaction problem. Thus, we will often use the term *variable* as a synonym for vertex, when referring to elements of V.

Let $\mathcal{H}_I = (V, H)$ be the constraint hypergraph of a CSP instance I. The *primal graph* of I is a graph $G = (V, E)$, having the same set of variables (vertices) as $\mathcal{H}_I$ and an edge connecting any pair of variables $X, Y \in V$

such that $\{X, Y\} \subseteq h$ for some $h \in H$.

Note that if all constraints of a CSP are binary, then its associated hypergraph is identical to its primal graph.

The most basic and most fundamental structural property considered in the context of CSPs (and conjunctive queries) is *acyclicity*. It was recognized independently in AI and in database theory that *acyclic* CSPs are polynomially solvable. I is an acyclic CSP iff its primal graph G is chordal (i.e., any cycle of length greater than 3 has a chord) and the set of its maximal cliques coincide with $edges(\mathcal{H}_I)$ [Beeri *et al.*, 1983].

A *join tree* $JT(\mathcal{H})$ for a hypergraph $\mathcal{H}$ is a tree whose nodes are the edges of $\mathcal{H}$ such that whenever the same vertex $X \in V$ occurs in two edges A_1 and A_2 of $\mathcal{H}$, then A_1 and A_2 are connected in $JT(\mathcal{H})$, and X occurs in each node on the unique path linking A_1 and A_2 in $JT(\mathcal{H})$.

Acyclic hypergraphs can be characterized in terms of join trees: A hypergraph $\mathcal{H}$ is *acyclic* iff it has a join tree [Bernstein and Goodman, 1981; Beeri *et al.*, 1983; Maier, 1986]. Acyclic CSP satisfiability is not only tractable but also highly parallelizable. In fact, this problem is complete for the low complexity class LOGCFL [Gottlob *et al.*, 1998].

Many CSPs arising in practice are not acyclic but are in some sense or another *close* to acyclic CSPs. In fact, the hypergraphs associated with many naturally arising CSPs contain either few cycles or small cycles, or can be transformed to acyclic CSPs by simple operations (such as, e.g., lumping together small groups of vertices). Consequently, CSP research in AI and in database theory concentrated on identifying, defining, and studying suitable classes of *nearly acyclic* CSPs, or, equivalently, methods for decomposing cyclic CSPs into acyclic CSPs.

3 Decomposition Methods

In order to study and compare various decomposition methods, we find it useful to introduce a general formal framework for this notion.

For a hypergraph $\mathcal{H} = (V, H)$, let $edges(\mathcal{H}) = H$. Moreover, for any set of edges $H' \subseteq H$, let $var(H') = \bigcup_{h \in H'} h$; and for the hypergraph $\mathcal{H}$, let $var(\mathcal{H}) = var(H)$. W.l.o.g., we assume that $var(H) = V$, i.e., every variable in V occurs in at least one edge of $\mathcal{H}$, and hence, any hypergraph can be simply represented by the set of its edges. Moreover, we assume w.l.o.g. that all hypergraphs under consideration are both *connected*, i.e., their primal graph consists of a single connected component, and *reduced*, i.e., no hyperedge is contained in any other hyperedge. All our definitions and results easily extend to general hypergraphs.

Let $\mathcal{HS}$ be the set of all (reduced and connected) hypergraphs. A *decomposition method* (short: DM) D associates to any hypergraph $\mathcal{H} \in \mathcal{HS}$ a parameter *D-width($\mathcal{H}$)*, called the *D-width* of $\mathcal{H}$.

The decomposition method D ensures that, for fixed k, every CSP instance I whose hypergraph $\mathcal{H}_I$ has D-width $\leq k$ is polynomially solvable, i.e., it is solvable in $O(|I|^{O(1)})$ time, where $|I|$ denotes the size of I. For

any $k > 0$, the *k-tractable class* $C(D, k)$ of D is defined by $C(D, k) = \{\mathcal{H} \mid D\text{-width}(\mathcal{H}) \leq k\}$. Thus, $C(D, k)$ collects the set of CSP instances which, for fixed k, are polynomially solvable by using the strategy D. Typically, the polynomial above depends on the parameter k. In particular, for each D there exists a function f such that, for each k, each instance $I \in C(D, k)$ can be transformed in time $O(|I|^{O(f(k))})$ into an equivalent *acyclic* CSP instance (from where it follows that all problems in $C(D, k)$ are polynomially solvable).

Every DM D is complete w.r.t. $\mathcal{HS}$, i.e., $\mathcal{HS} = \bigcup_{k \geq 1} C(D, k)$. Note that, by our definitions, it holds that $D\text{-width}(\mathcal{H}) = \min\{k \mid \mathcal{H} \in C(D, k)\}$.

All major tractable classes based on restricted structure fit into this framework. In particular, we shall compare the following decomposition methods:

- **Biconnected Components** (short: BICOMP) [Freuder, 1985]. Any graph $G = (V, E)$ can be decomposed into a pair $\langle T, \chi \rangle$, where T is a tree, and the labeling function χ associates to each vertex of T a biconnected component of G (a component which remains connected after any one-vertex removal). The *biconnected width* of a hypergraph $\mathcal{H}$, denoted by BICOMP-width($\mathcal{H}$), is the maximum number of vertices over the biconnected components of the primal graph of $\mathcal{H}$.

- **Cycle Cutset** (short: CUTSET) [Dechter, 1992]. A *cycle cutset* of a hypergraph $\mathcal{H}$ is a set $S \subseteq var(\mathcal{H})$ such that the subhypergraph of $\mathcal{H}$ induced by $var(\mathcal{H}) - S$ is acyclic. The CUTSET width of $\mathcal{H}$ is the minimum cardinality over all its possible cycle cutsets.

- **Tree Clustering** (short: TCLUSTER) [Dechter and Pearl, 1989]. The *tree clustering* method is based on a triangulation algorithm which transforms the primal graph $G = (V, E)$ of any CSP instance I into a chordal graph G'. The maximal cliques of G' are then used to build the constraint scopes of an acyclic CSP I' equivalent to I. The *tree-clustering width* (short: TCLUSTER width) of $\mathcal{H}_I$ is 1 if $\mathcal{H}_I$ is an acyclic hypergraph; otherwise it is equal to the maximum cardinality over the cliques of the chordal graph G'.

- **Treewidth** (TREEWIDTH) [Robertson and Seymour, 1986]. We omit a formal definition of graph treewidth here. The TREEWIDTH of a hypergraph $\mathcal{H}$ is the treewidth of its primal graph plus one. As pointed out below, TREEWIDTH and TCLUSTER are two equivalent methods.

- **Hinge Decompositions** (short: HINGE) [Gyssens *et al.*, 1994; Gyssens and Paredaens, 1984], Let $\mathcal{H}$ be a hypergraph, and let $V \subseteq var(\mathcal{H})$ be a set of variables and $X, Y \in var(\mathcal{H})$. X is $[V]$-adjacent to Y if there exists an edge $h \in edges(\mathcal{H})$ such that $\{X, Y\} \subseteq (h - V)$. A $[V]$-path π from X to Y is a sequence $X = X_0, \ldots, X_\ell = Y$ of variables such that: X_i is $[V]$-adjacent to X_{i+1}, for each $i \in [0 \ldots \ell\text{-}1]$. A set $W \subseteq var(\mathcal{H})$ of variables is $[V]$-connected if $\forall X, Y \in W$ there is a $[V]$-path from X to Y. A *[V]-component* is a maximal $[V]$-connected non-empty set of variables $W \subseteq (var(\mathcal{H}) - V)$. For any

$[V]$-component C, let $edges(C) = \{h \in edges(\mathcal{H}) \mid h \cap C \neq \emptyset\}$.

Let $\mathcal{H} \in \mathcal{HS}$ and let H be either $edges(\mathcal{H})$ or a proper subset of $edges(\mathcal{H})$ containing at least two edges. Let $C_1, ..., C_m$ be the connected $[var(H)]$-components of $\mathcal{H}$. Then, H is a *hinge* if, for $i = 1, ..., m$, there exists an edge $h_i \in H$ such that $var(edges(C_i)) \cap var(H)) \subseteq h_i$. A hinge is *minimal* if it does not contain any other hinge. (Our definition of hinge is equivalent to the original one in [Gyssens *et al.*, 1994; Gyssens and Paredaens, 1984].)

A *hinge-decomposition* of $\mathcal{H}$ is a tree T such that all the following conditions hold: (1) the vertices of T are minimal hinges of $\mathcal{H}$; (2) each edge in $edges(\mathcal{H})$ is contained in at least one vertex of T; (3) two adjacent vertices A and B of T share precisely one edge $L \in edges(\mathcal{H})$; moreover, L consists exactly of the variables shared by A and B (i.e., $L = var(A) \cap var(B)$); (4) the variables of $\mathcal{H}$ shared by two vertices of T are entirely contained within each vertex on their connecting path in T.

The size (i.e., the cardinality) of the largest vertex of T is called the *degree of cyclicity* of $\mathcal{H}$. This is precisely what we call here the HINGE *width* of $\mathcal{H}$. It was shown in [Gyssens and Paredaens, 1984] that for any CSP instance I, the HINGE width of $\mathcal{H}_I$ is the cardinality of the largest minimal hinge of $\mathcal{H}_I$.

- **Hinge Decomposition + Tree Clustering** (short: HINGE^{TCLUSTER}) [Gyssens *et al.*, 1994]. It has been shown [Gyssens *et al.*, 1994] that the minimal hinges of a hypergraph can be further decomposed by means of the triangulation technique of the above-described tree-clustering method. This leads to the HINGE^{TCLUSTER} *method*. Let $T = (N, E)$ be a hinge tree of a hypergraph $\mathcal{H}$. For any hinge $H \in N$, let $w(H)$ be the minimum between the cardinality of H and the TCLUSTER width of the hypergraph $(var(H), H)$. The HINGE^{TCLUSTER} width of T is $max_{H \in N}\{w(H)\}$. Define the HINGE^{TCLUSTER} *width* of $\mathcal{H}$ as the minimum HINGE^{TCLUSTER} width over all its hinge decompositions.

For each of the above decomposition methods D it was shown that for any fixed k, given a CSP instance I, deciding whether a hypergraph $\mathcal{H}_I$ has D-width$(\mathcal{H}_I) \leq k$ is feasible in polynomial time and that solving CSPs whose associated hypergraph is of width $\leq k$ can be done in polynomial time. In particular, D consists of two phases. Given a CSP instance I, the (k-bounded) D-width w of $\mathcal{H}_I$ along with a corresponding decomposition is first computed. Exploiting this decomposition, I is then solved in time $O(|I|^{w+1} \log |I|)$ (for most methods this phase consists of the solution of an acyclic CSP instance equivalent to I).

The cost of the first phase is independent on the constraint relations of I; in fact, it is $O(|\mathcal{H}_I|^{c_1 k + c_2})$, where $|\mathcal{H}_I|$ is the size of the hypergraph $\mathcal{H}_I$, and c_1, c_2 are two constants relative to the method D ($0 \leq c_1, c_2 \leq 3$ for the methods above). Observe also that computing the D-width w of a hypergraph in general (i.e., without the bound $w \leq k$) is NP-hard for most methods; while it is polynomial for HINGE, and it is even linear for BICOMP.

Further interesting methods that do not explicitly generalize acyclic hypergraphs are based on a notion of *width* as used in [Freuder, 1982; 1985]. If $\sqsubset$ is a total ordering of the vertices of a graph $G = (V, E)$, then the $\sqsubset$-width of G is defined by $w_{\sqsubset}(G) = max_{v \in V} |\{\{v, w\} \in E \text{ s.t. } w \sqsubset v\}|$. The width of G is the minimum of all $\sqsubset$-widths over all possible total orderings $\sqsubset$ of V. For each fixed constant k, it can be determined in polynomial time whether a graph is of width k. [Freuder, 1982] observed that many naturally arising CSPs are of very low width. Note that bounded width in this sense is a structural property. The following theorem shows that bounded width alone does not entail tractability.

Theorem 3.1 *Constraint solvability remains NP-complete even if restricted to CSPs whose primal graph has width bounded by 4.*

Proof. 3COL remains NP-complete even for graphs of degree 4 (cf. [Garey and Johnson, 1979]). Such graphs, however, have width ≤ 4. The theorem follows by the well-known natural encoding of 3COL as a CSP. ∎

Freuder showed that a CSP of width k whose relations enjoy the property of k'-*consistency*, where $k' > k$, can be solved in a backtrack-free manner, and thus in polynomial time [Freuder, 1982; 1985].

[Dechter and Pearl, 1988] consequently introduce the notion of *induced width* w^* which is – roughly – the smallest width k of any graph G' obtained by triangulation methods from the primal graph G of a CSP such that G' ensures $k + 1$-consistency. Graphs having induced width $\leq k$ can be also characterized as *partial k-trees* [Freuder, 1990] or, equivalently, as graphs having treewidth $\leq k$ [Arnborg *et al.*, 1991]. It follows that, for fixed k, checking whether $w^* \leq k$ is feasible in linear time [Bodlaender, 1997]. If w^* is bounded by a constant, a CSP is solvable in polynomial time. The approach to CSPs based on w^* is referred to as the w^*-Tractability method [Dechter, 1992]. Note that this method is implicitly based on hypergraph acyclicity, given that the used triangulation methods enforce chordality of the resulting graph G' and thus acyclicity of the corresponding hypergraph. It was noted [Dechter and Pearl, 1989; Dechter, 1992] that, for any given CSP instance I, TCLUSTER-width$(\mathcal{H}_I) = w^*(\mathcal{H}_I) + 1$.

4 Hypertree Decompositions of CSPs

A new class of tractable conjunctive queries, which generalizes the class of acyclic queries, has been recently identified [Gottlob *et al.*, 1999]. Deciding whether a given query belongs to this class is polynomial time feasible and even highly parallelizable. In this section, we first generalize this notion to the wider framework of hypergraphs, and then show how to employ this notion in order to define a new decomposition method we will refer to as HYPERTREE.

A *hypertree for a hypergraph* $\mathcal{H}$ is a triple $\langle T, \chi, \lambda \rangle$, where $T = (N, E)$ is a rooted tree, and χ and λ are labeling functions which associate to each vertex $p \in N$

two sets $\chi(p) \subseteq var(\mathcal{H})$ and $\lambda(p) \subseteq edges(\mathcal{H})$. If $T' = (N', E')$ is a subtree of T, we define $\chi(T') = \bigcup_{v \in N'} \chi(v)$. We denote the set of vertices N of T by $vertices(T)$, and the root of T by $root(T)$. Moreover, for any $p \in N$, T_p denotes the subtree of T rooted at p.

Definition 4.1 A *hypertree decomposition* of a hypergraph $\mathcal{H}$ is a hypertree $\langle T, \chi, \lambda \rangle$ for $\mathcal{H}$ which satisfies all the following conditions:

1. for each edge $h \in edges(\mathcal{H})$, there exists $p \in vertices(T)$ such that $var(h) \subseteq \chi(p)$;

2. for each variable $Y \in var(\mathcal{H})$, the set $\{p \in vertices(T) \mid Y \in \chi(p)\}$ induces a (connected) subtree of T;

3. for each $p \in vertices(T)$, $\chi(p) \subseteq var(\lambda(p))$;

4. for each $p \in vertices(T)$, $var(\lambda(p)) \cap \chi(T_p) \subseteq \chi(p)$.

A hypertree decomposition $\langle T, \chi, \lambda \rangle$ of $\mathcal{H}$ is a *complete decomposition* of $\mathcal{H}$ if, for each edge $h \in edges(\mathcal{H})$, there exists $p \in vertices(T)$ such that $var(h) \subseteq \chi(p)$ and $h \in \lambda(p)$.

The *width* of the hypertree decomposition $\langle T, \chi, \lambda \rangle$ is $max_{p \in vertices(T)} |\lambda(p)|$. The HYPERTREE width $hw(\mathcal{H})$ of $\mathcal{H}$ is the minimum width over all its hypertree decompositions.

Intuitively, if $\mathcal{H}$ is a cyclic hypergraph, the χ labeling selects the set of variables to be fixed in order to split the cycles and achieve acyclicity; $\lambda(p)$ "covers" the variables of $\chi(p)$ by a set of edges.

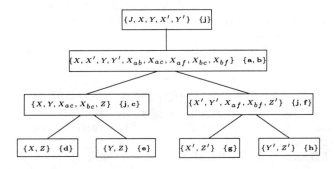

Figure 1: A 2-width hypertree decomposition of $\mathcal{H}_1$

Example 4.2 Consider the following constraint scopes:

$a(X_{ab}, X, X', X_{ac}, X_{af}); b(X_{ab}, Y, Y', X_{bc}, X_{bf});$
$c(X_{ac}, X_{bc}, Z); d(X, Z); e(Y, Z); f(X_{af}, X_{bf}, Z');$
$g(X', Z'); h(Y', Z'); j(J, X, Y, X', Y')$

Let $\mathcal{H}_1$ be their corresponding hypergraph. $\mathcal{H}_1$ is clearly cyclic, and thus $hw(\mathcal{H}_1) > 1$ (as only acyclic hypergraphs have hypertree width 1). Figure 1 shows a (complete) hypertree decomposition of $\mathcal{H}_1$ having width 2, hence $hw(\mathcal{H}_1) = 2$.

It is easy to see that the acyclic CSPs are precisely the CSPs of hypertree width one.

We say that a CSP instance I has k-bounded hypertree-width if $hw(\mathcal{H}_I) \leq k$, where $\mathcal{H}_I$ is the hypergraph associated to I. From the results in [Gottlob *et*

al., 1999], it follows that k-bounded hypertree-width is efficiently decidable, and that a hypertree decomposition of width k can be efficiently computed (if any).

We next show that any CSP instance I is efficiently solvable, given a k-bounded complete hypertree-decomposition HD of $\mathcal{H}_I$. To this end, we define an acyclic CSP instance which is equivalent to I and whose size is polynomially bounded by the size of I.

For each vertex p of the decomposition HD, we define a new constraint scope whose associated constraint relation is the projection on $\chi(p)$ of the join of the relations in $\lambda(p)$. This way, we obtain a join-tree JT of an acyclic hypergraph $\mathcal{H}'$. $\mathcal{H}'$ corresponds to a new CSP instance I' over a set of constraint relations of size $O(n^k)$, where n is the input size (i.e., $n = |I|$) and k is the width of the hypertree decomposition HD. By construction, I' is an acyclic CSP, and we can easily show that it is equivalent to the input CSP instance I. Thus, all the efficient techniques available for acyclic CSP instances can be employed for the evaluation of I', and hence of I.

Theorem 4.3 *Given a CSP I and a k-width hypertree decomposition of $\mathcal{H}_I$, I is solvable in $O(n^k \log n^k) = O(n^k \log n)$ time, where n is the size of I.*

5 Comparison Criteria

For comparing decomposition methods we introduce the relations $\preceq$, $\rhd$, and $\lll$ defined as follows:

$D_1 \preceq D_2$, in words, D_2 *generalizes* D_1, if $\exists \delta \geq 0$ such that, $\forall k > 0$, $C(D_1, k) \subseteq C(D_2, k + \delta)$. Thus $D_1 \preceq D_2$ if every class of CSP instances which is tractable according to D_1 is also tractable according to D_2.

$D_1 \rhd D_2$ (D_1 beats D_2) if there exists an integer k such that $\forall m \; C(D_1, k) \not\subseteq C(D_2, m)$. To prove that $D_1 \rhd D_2$, it is sufficient to exhibit a class of hypergraphs contained in some $C(D_1, k)$ but in no $C(D_2, j)$ for $j \geq 0$. Intuitively, $D_1 \rhd D_2$ means that at least on some class of CSP instances, D_1 outperforms D_2.

$D_1 \lll D_2$ if $D_1 \preceq D_2$ and $D_2 \rhd D_1$. In this case we say that D_2 *strongly generalizes* D_1.

Mathematically, $\preceq$ is a *preorder*, i.e., it is reflexive, transitive but not antisymmetric. We say that D_1 *is $\preceq$-equivalent* to D_2, denoted $D_1 \equiv D_2$, if both $D_1 \preceq D_2$ and $D_2 \preceq D_1$ hold.

The decomposition methods D_1 and D_2 are *strongly incomparable* if both $D_1 \rhd D_2$ and $D_2 \rhd D_1$. Note that if D_1 and D_2 are strongly incomparable, then they are also incomparable w.r.t. the relations $\preceq$ and $\lll$.

6 Comparison Results

Figure 2 shows a representation of the hierarchy of DMs determined by the $\lll$ relation. Each element of the hierarchy represents a DM, apart from that containing *Tree Clustering*, w^*, and *Treewidth* which are grouped together because they are $\preceq$-equivalent as easily follows from the observations in Section 3.

Theorem 6.1 *For each pair D_1 and D_2 of decompositions methods represented in Figure 2, the following holds:*

- *There is a directed path from D_1 to D_2 iff $D_1 \lll D_2$, i.e., iff D_2 strongly generalizes D_1.*

- *D_1 and D_2 are not linked by any directed path iff they are strongly incomparable.*

Hence, Fig. 2 gives a complete picture of the relationships holding among the different methods.

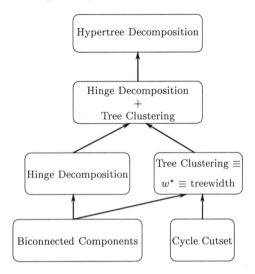

Figure 2: Constraint Tractability Hierarchy

Below we sketch a proof of Theorem 6.1. For space reasons, we report only succinct versions of selected proofs. Detailed proofs of all results are available in the full version of this paper [Gottlob *et al.*, 1999b].

For any $n > 1$ and $m > 0$, let $Circle(n, m)$ be the hypergraph having n edges $\{h_1, \ldots, h_n\}$ defined as follows:

- $h_i = \{X_i^1, \ldots, X_i^m, X_{i+1}^1, \ldots, X_{i+1}^m\}\ \forall 1 \le i \le n-1$;

- $h_n = \{X_n^1, \ldots, X_n^m, X_1^1, \ldots, X_1^m\}$.

For $m = 1$, $Circle(n, 1)$ is a graph consisting of a simple cycle with n edges (like a circle). Note that, for any $n > 1$ and $m > 0$, $Circle(n, m)$ has hypertree width 2; a 2-width hypertree decomposition of $Circle(n, m)$ is shown in Figure 3. Thus, $(\bigcup_{n>1, m>0}\{Circle(n, m)\}) \subseteq C(\text{HYPERTREE}, 2)$

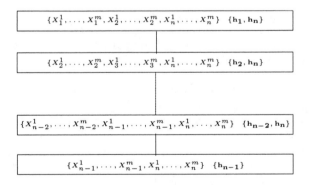

Figure 3: 2-width hypertree decomposition of $Circle(n, m)$

Lemma 6.2 HINGE $\lll$ HYPERTREE.

Proof. (HINGE $\preceq$ HYPERTREE.) Given a hinge decomposition $T = (V, E)$ of $\mathcal{H}$, we build a hypertree decomposition HD of $\mathcal{H}$ having the same width as T. HD has the same tree shape as T; the labels of a vertex p of (the tree of) HD are $\lambda(p) = H$ and $\chi(p) = var(H)$, where H is the hinge corresponding to p in the hinge decomposition.

(HYPERTREE $\rhd$ HINGE.) For any $k > 0$, $C(\text{HYPERTREE}, 2) \supseteq (\bigcup_{n>1}\{Circle(n, 1)\}) \nsubseteq C(\text{HINGE}, k)$. Indeed, for any $n > 1$, the degree of cyclicity of $Circle(n, 1)$ is n [Gyssens *et al.*, 1994]. ∎

Lemma 6.3 TCLUSTER $\lll$ HYPERTREE.

Proof. (TCLUSTER $\preceq$ HYPERTREE.) Let $\mathcal{H} = (V, H)$ be a hypergraph, and $\langle T, \psi \rangle$ be the result of the application of the tree-clustering method on $\mathcal{H}$, where $T = (N, E)$ is a tree, and $\psi : N \to 2^V$ is a labeling function which assigns to each vertex of T a set of variables of $\mathcal{H}$. For any $p \in N$, the set of variables $\psi(p)$ corresponds to a maximal clique identified by the tree-clustering method.

From $\langle T, \psi \rangle$, we define a complete hypertree decomposition $HD = \langle T, \chi, \lambda \rangle$ having the same tree T as the output of the tree clustering method. The labelings χ and λ are defined according to the following procedure.

1. for each $p \in N$, set $\chi(p) = \psi(p)$ and $\lambda(p) = \emptyset$;

2. for each edge $h \in H$, choose a vertex $p \in N$ s.t. $h \subseteq \chi(p)$, and add h to $\lambda(p)$ (i.e., $\lambda(p) := \lambda(p) \cup \{h\}$);

3. While there is a vertex $p \in N$ s.t. $\chi(p)$ contains a variable X not covered by $\lambda(p)$ (i.e., $X \in (\chi(p) - var(\lambda(p)))$), proceed as follows. (A) Find a path π in T linking p to a vertex $q \in N$ s.t. (i) $X \in var(\lambda(q))$ and, (ii) $X \notin var(\lambda(s))$ for every vertex s in $\pi - \{q\}$. (B) Choose an edge $h \in \lambda(q)$ s.t. $X \in h$. (C) Add h to both $\lambda(s)$ and $\chi(s)$, for every vertex $s \in (\pi - \{q\})$ (i.e., $\chi(s) := \chi(s) \cup h$, and $\lambda(s) := \lambda(s) \cup \{h\}$).

We have that HD is a complete hypertree decomposition of $\mathcal{H}$, and its HYPERTREE width is smaller than or equal to the TCLUSTER-width of $\mathcal{H}$.

(HYPERTREE $\rhd$ TCLUSTER.) Let $S = \{Circle(3, m) \mid m > 1\}$. For any $m > 1$, the primal graph G of $Circle(3, m)$ is a clique of $3m$ variables. Thus, G does not need any triangulation, because it is a chordal graph. The TCLUSTER-width of $Circle(3, m)$ is clearly $3m$; while its hypertree width is 2. Hence, for any $k > 0$, $S \nsubseteq C(\text{TCLUSTER}, k)$, whereas $S \subseteq C(\text{HYPERTREE}, 2)$. ∎

Lemma 6.4 HINGE *and* TCLUSTER *are strongly incomparable.*

Proof. (HINGE $\rhd$ TCLUSTER). From the proof above, $S = \{Circle(3, m) \mid m > 1\} \nsubseteq C(\text{TCLUSTER}, k)$, for any $k > 0$. However, $S \subseteq C(\text{HINGE}, 3)$, because every hypergraph in S has only three (hyper)edges.

(TCLUSTER $\rhd$ HINGE). From the proof of Lemma 6.2, $(\bigcup_{n>1}\{Circle(n, 1)\}) \nsubseteq C(\text{HINGE}, k)$, for any $k > 0$. However, $(\bigcup_{n>1}\{Circle(n, 1)\}) \subseteq C(\text{TCLUSTER}, 3)$, because all these graphs can be triangulated in a way that their maximal cliques have cardinality 3 at most. ∎

Interestingly, even the combination of TCLUSTER with HINGE is strongly generalized by the hypertree-decomposition method.

Lemma 6.5 HINGE$^{\text{TCLUSTER}} \precnsim$ HYPERTREE.

Proof. The proof of HINGE$^{\text{TCLUSTER}} \preceq$ HYPERTREE is very similar to that of Lemma 6.3, except that the λ labelings must be initialized in a suitable way (instead of $\emptyset$). To see that HYPERTREE $\triangleright$ HINGE^{TCLUSTER}, note that $(\bigcup_{n>1,m>0} \{Circle(n,m)\}) \not\subseteq C(\text{HINGE}^{\text{TCLUSTER}}, k)$ holds for any $k > 0$; while, $(\bigcup_{n>1,m>0} \{Circle(n,m)\}) \subseteq C(\text{HYPERTREE}, 2)$. ■

7 Binary CSPs

On binary constraint networks, where the constraints relations have arity two, the differences among the decomposition strategies highlighted in Section 6 become less evident. Indeed, bounding the arities of the constraint relations, the k-tractable classes of some decomposition strategies collapse. In particular, as shown in the full version of this paper [Gottlob *et al.*, 1999b], on binary constraints networks, TCLUSTER $\equiv$ HINGE^{TCLUSTER} and HINGE$^{\text{TCLUSTER}} \equiv$ HYPERTREE hold. The relationships among the other decomposition methods remain the same as for the general case (Fig. 2).

To evidentiate the differences of the above decomposition strategies on the domain of binary CSPs, we can compare their respective widths. For each discussed decomposition method D, any CSP instance I is solvable in time $O(|I|^{w+1} \log |I|)$, once the D-width w of $\mathcal{H}_I$ along with a corresponding decomposition have been computed, as noted in Section 3. Thus, the D-width is a measure of the efficiency of a decomposition method: the smaller the D-width of $\mathcal{H}_I$, the more efficient the application of strategy D to I.

Theorem 7.1

1. *For every binary CSP instance I,*
   TCLUSTER-*width*$(\mathcal{H}_I) =$ HINGE^{TCLUSTER}-*width*$(\mathcal{H}_I)$.

2. *For every binary CSP instance I,*
   HYPERTREE-*width*$(\mathcal{H}_I) \leq$ TCLUSTER-*width*$(\mathcal{H}_I)$.

3. *For some CSP instance I,*
   TCLUSTER-*width*$(\mathcal{H}_I) = 2\cdot$HYPERTREE-*width*$(\mathcal{H}_I)$.

Acknowledgments

Research supported by *FWF (Austrian Science Funds)* under the project Z29-INF and by the *CNR (Italian National Research Council)*, under grant n.203.15.07.

References

[Arnborg *et al.*, 1991] S. Arnborg, J. Lagergren, and D. Seese. Problems easy for tree-decomposable graphs. *J. of Algorithms*, 12:308–340, 1991.

[Beeri *et al.*, 1983] C. Beeri, R. Fagin, D. Maier, and M. Yannakakis. On the desirability of acyclic database schemes. *Journal of the ACM*, 30(3):479–513, July, 1983.

[Bernstein and Goodman, 1981] P.A. Bernstein, and N. Goodman. The power of natural semijoins. *SIAM Journal on Computing*, 10(4):751–771, 1981.

[Bibel, 1988] W. Bibel. Constraint Satisfaction from a Deductive Viewpoint. *AIJ*, 35, 401–413, 1988.

[Bodlaender, 1997] H.L. Bodlaender. Treewidth: Algorithmic Techniques and Results. In *Proc. of MFCS'97*, Bratislava. LNCS 1295, Springer, pp. 19-36, 1997.

[Dechter, 1992] R. Dechter. Constraint Networks. In *Encyclopedia of AI*, 2nd ed., Wiley and Sons, pp. 276-285,1992.

[Dechter and Pearl, 1988] R. Dechter and J. Pearl. Network based heuristics for CSPs. *AIJ*, 34(1):1–38, 1988.

[Dechter and Pearl, 1989] R. Dechter and J. Pearl. Tree clustering for constraint networks. *AIJ*, 38:353–366, 1989.

[Freuder, 1982] E.C. Freuder. A sufficient condition for backtrack-free search. *JACM*, 29(1):24–32, 1982.

[Freuder, 1985] E.C. Freuder. A sufficient condition for backtrack-bounded search. *JACM*, 32(4):755–761, 1985.

[Freuder, 1990] E.C. Freuder. Complexity of K-Tree Structured CSPs. *Proc. of AAAI'90*, 1990.

[Garey and Johnson, 1979] M.R. Garey and D.S. Johnson. *Computers and Intractability. A Guide to the Theory of NP-completeness.* Freeman and Comp., NY, USA, 1979.

[Gottlob *et al.*, 1998] G. Gottlob, N. Leone, and F. Scarcello. The Complexity of Acyclic Conjunctive Queries, in *Proc. of FOCS'98*, pp.706–715, Palo Alto, CA, 1998.

[Gottlob *et al.*, 1999] G. Gottlob, N. Leone, and F. Scarcello. "Hypertree Decompositions and Tractable Queries," in *Proc. of PODS'99*, Philadelphia, May, 1999.

[Gottlob *et al.*, 1999b] G. Gottlob, N. Leone, and F. Scarcello. "A Comparison of Structural CSP Decomposition Methods," Tech. Rep. DBAI-TR-99/25, currently available on the web as: `www.dbai.tuwien.ac.at/staff/gottlob/CSP-decomp.ps`

[Gyssens *et al.*, 1994] M. Gyssens, P. Jeavons, and D. Cohen. Decomposing constraint satisfaction problems using database techniques. *AIJ*, 66:57–89, 1994.

[Gyssens and Paredaens, 1984] M. Gyssens and J. Paredaens. A Decomposition Methodology for Cyclic Databases. In *Advances in Database Theory*, volume 2, pp. 85-122. Plenum Press New York, NY, 1984.

[Jeavons *et al.*, 1997] P. Jeavons, D. Cohen, and M. Gyssens. Closure Properties of Constraints. *JACM*, 44(4), 1997.

[Maier, 1986] D. Maier, *The theory of relational databases.* Computer Science Press, Rockville, MD, 1986.

[Pearson and Jeavons, 1997] J. Pearson and P.G. Jeavons. A Survey of Tractable Constraint Satisfaction Problems, CSD-TR-97-15, Royal Holloway Univ. of London, 1997.

[Robertson and Seymour, 1986] N. Robertson and P.D. Seymour. Graph Minors II. Algorithmic aspects of tree width. *Journal of Algorithms*, 7:309–322, 1986.

[Seidel, 1981] R. Seidel. A new method for solving constraint satisfaction problems. In *Proc. of IJCAI'81*, 1981.

Solving Strategies for Highly Symmetric CSPs *

Pedro Meseguer
Inst. Invest. Intel.ligència Artificial
CSIC
Campus UAB, 08193 Bellaterra
Spain

Carme Torras
Inst. Robòtica i Informàtica Industrial
CSIC-UPC
Gran Capità 2-4, 08034 Barcelona
Spain

Abstract

Symmetry often appears in real-world constraint satisfaction problems, but strategies for exploiting it are only beginning to be developed. Here, a rationale for exploiting symmetry within depth-first search is proposed, leading to an heuristic for variable selection and a domain pruning procedure. These strategies are then applied to a highly symmetric combinatorial problem, namely the generation of balanced incomplete block designs. Experimental results show that these strategies achieve a reduction of up to two orders of magnitude in computational effort. Interestingly, two previously developed strategies are shown to be particular instances of this approach.

1 Introduction

Symmetry is present in many natural and artificial settings. A symmetry is a transformation of an entity such that the transformed entity is equivalent to and indistinguishable from the original one. We can see symmetries in nature (a specular reflection of a daisy flower), in human artifacts (a central rotation of 180 degrees of a chessboard), and in mathematical theories (inertial changes in classical mechanics). The existence of symmetries in these systems allows us to generalize the properties detected in one state to all its symmetric states.

Regarding constraint satisfaction problems (CSPs), many real problems exhibit some kind of symmetry, embedded in the structure of variables, domains and constraints. During search, if two or more states of a problem are related by a symmetry, it means that all of them represent *the same state*, so it is enough to visit only one of them. This causes a drastic decrease in the size of the search space, which has a very positive impact on the efficiency of the constraint solver.

In this paper, we propose two strategies for symmetry exploitation, which can speed-up significantly the solving process of CSPs with many symmetries. We have

*This research is supported by the Spanish CICYT proyect TIC96-0721-C02.

used these strategies to solve the problem of generating *balanced incomplete block designs* (BIBD from now on), a combinatorial problem of interest in statistics, coding theory and computer science. With them, we are able to solve the BIBD generation problem with a simple algorithm (FC-CBJ) for a wide set of designs.

This paper is organized as follows. In Section 2, we introduce some basic concepts. In Section 3, we explain two strategies for symmetry exploitation during search. In Section 4, we present the problem of BIBD generation. In Section 5, we formulate the BIBD generation as a CSP and give empirical results. In Section 6, we revise previous approaches to this topic. Section 7 contains conclusions and future work.

2 Basic Definitions

Constraint satisfaction. A finite CSP is defined by a triple $(\mathcal{X}, \mathcal{D}, \mathcal{C})$, where $\mathcal{X} = \{x_1, \ldots, x_n\}$ is a set of n variables, $\mathcal{D} = \{D(x_1), \ldots, D(x_n)\}$ is a collection of current domains where $D(x_i)$ is the finite set of possible values for variable x_i, and $\mathcal{C}$ is a set of constraints among variables. A constraint c_i on the ordered set of variables $var(c_i) = (x_{i_1}, \ldots, x_{i_{r(i)}})$ specifies the relation $rel(c_i)$ of the *allowed* combinations of values for the variables in $var(c_i)$. An element of $rel(c_i)$ is a tuple $(v_{i_1}, \ldots, v_{i_{r(i)}})$, $v_i \in D_0(x_i)$, where $D_0(x_i)$ represents the initial domain of x_i. An element of $D(x_{i_1}) \times \cdots \times D(x_{i_{r(i)}})$ is called a *valid* tuple on $var(c_i)$. A *solution* of the CSP is an assignment of values to variables which satisfies every constraint. A value a is *good* for a variable x_i if a solution includes the assignment (x_i, a). Typically, CSPs are solved by depth-first search algorithms with backtracking. At a point in search, P is the set of assigned or *past* variables, and F is the set of unassigned or *future* variables. The variable to be assigned next is called the *current* variable.

Symmetries. A *symmetry* on a CSP is a collection of bijective mappings $\{\theta, \theta_1, \ldots, \theta_n\}$,

$$\theta : \mathcal{X} \to \mathcal{X}$$

$$\theta_i : D(x_i) \to D(\theta(x_i))$$

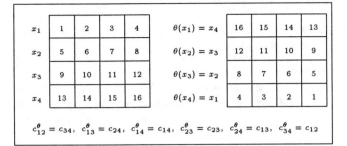

$$c^{\theta}_{12} = c_{34}, \quad c^{\theta}_{13} = c_{24}, \quad c^{\theta}_{14} = c_{14}, \quad c^{\theta}_{23} = c_{23}, \quad c^{\theta}_{24} = c_{13}, \quad c^{\theta}_{34} = c_{12}$$

Figure 1: Central rotation of 180 degrees is a symmetry for the 4-queens problem.

that preserve the set of constraints, i.e., $\forall c_j \in \mathcal{C}$ with $var(c_j) = (x_{j_1}, \ldots, x_{j_{r(j)}})$ and $rel(c_j) = \{(v_{j_1}, \ldots, v_{j_{r(j)}})\}$, the transformed constraint c^{θ}_j with $var(c^{\theta}_j) = (\theta(x_{j_1}), \ldots, \theta(x_{j_{r(j)}}))$ and $rel(c^{\theta}_j) = \{(\theta_{j_1}(v_{j_1}), \ldots, \theta_{j_{r(j)}}(v_{j_{r(j)}}))\}$, is in $\mathcal{C}$.[1]

An example of a symmetry on the 4-queens problem appears in Figure 1. Domains are $D_0(x_1) = \{1, 2, 3, 4\}, D_0(x_2) = \{5, 6, 7, 8\}, D_0(x_3) = \{9, 10, 11, 12\}, D_0(x_4) = \{13, 14, 15, 16\}$. A central rotation of 180 degrees exchanges variables x_1 with x_4 and x_2 with x_3, and value domains are mapped as indicated. This transformation is a symmetry because all the mappings (on variables and domains) are bijective, and the set of constraints is left invariant by the transformation of variables and values. For example, the transformed constraint c^{θ}_{12} is computed as follows,

$$var(c^{\theta}_{12}) = (\theta(x_1), \theta(x_2)) = (x_4, x_3) = var(c_{34}),$$

$$\begin{aligned} rel(c^{\theta}_{12}) &= \{(\theta_1(1), \theta_2(7)), (\theta_1(1), \theta_2(8)), (\theta_1(2), \theta_2(8)), \\ &\quad (\theta_1(3), \theta_2(5)), (\theta_1(4), \theta_2(5)), (\theta_1(4), \theta_2(6))\} \\ &= \{(16, 10), (16, 9), (15, 9), (14, 12), (13, 12), (13, 11)\} \\ &= rel(c_{34}). \end{aligned}$$

Thus, $c^{\theta}_{12} = c_{34}$. Some symmetries leave subsets of variables unchanged. They are of special interest, as we will see in the next paragraph.

Symmetries and depth-first search. A search state s is characterized by an assignment of past variables, plus the current domains of future variables. It defines a subproblem of the original problem, where the domain of each past variable is reduced to its assigned value and the relation $rel(c_i)$ of each constraint c_i is reduced to its valid tuples with respect to current domains. A symmetry *holds* at state s if it is a symmetry of the subproblem occurring at s. A symmetry holding at s is said to be *local* to s if it does not change neither past variables nor their assigned values. A symmetry local to the initial state is a global symmetry of the problem.

The notion of local symmetry is important because of the use of symmetries during search. If a state reports failure, all the states symmetric to it can be removed.

[1]Through an abuse of notation, we denote a symmetry $\{\theta, \theta_1, \ldots, \theta_n\}$ by its variable mapping θ.

Since constraint satisfaction algorithms are based on depth-first search with backtracking, they may only remove states that are in the subtree below the current node, but never above it. Therefore, we are only interested in symmetries connecting states below the current node, that is, leaving the set of past variables unchanged. These symmetries are local to the current node. In the rest of the paper, we will consider local symmetries only.

3 Solving Strategies

In the following subsections, we describe two practical strategies for highly symmetrical CSPs, which can be embedded in any constraint satisfaction algorithm. Both are based on the detection of local symmetries at each search state. Automatic discovery of symmetries is a too complex task to be carried out at run time. Instead, we take a simpler approach. From an initial analysis of the considered problem, we identify a set of symmetries which may appear along the search. When a new state is generated, we check which of these previously identified symmetries are local to this state.

3.1 Breaking Symmetries While Searching

Let s be a search state where the symmetry θ local to s involves a future variable x_i in the following form,

$$x_i \in F, \theta(x_i) \neq x_i \quad \text{or} \quad \forall a \in D(x_i), \theta_i(a) \neq a$$

If x_i is assigned in the next step, symmetry θ no longer holds in the current subproblem after x_i assignment. To see this, it is enough to realize that x_i is now a past variable (which cannot be changed) and θ will change it. In this case, we say that the assignment of x_i *breaks* symmetry θ. If at state s several symmetries $\theta, \phi, \psi, \ldots$ are local to s, all involving variable x_i, assigning x_i will break all these symmetries: no state in the current subproblem will be "repeated" by the action of these symmetries. This positive effect is only due to the assignment of x_i, taken as the current variable. This is the rationale for our variable selection heuristic.

Symmetry-breaking heuristic: Select for assignment the variable involved in the greatest number of symmetries local to the current state.

This greedy heuristic tries to break as many symmetries as possible in the next assignment. When it is applied consistently throughout the search tree, its positive effects accumulate. If x_1 is the variable selected at the first tree level, no matter which value is assigned to it, all symmetries involving x_1 are broken below level 1. If x_2 is the variable selected at the second tree level, no matter which value is assigned to it, all symmetries involving x_1 and x_2 are broken below level 2, and so on.[2] This heuristic tries to maximize the total number of broken symmetries at each level of the search tree. It causes the following benefits.

[2]It could be argued that the assignment of x_2 may restore a symmetry θ broken by the assignment of x_1, if θ exchanges both variables and their values. But now θ is no longer a local symmetry, given that it acts on past variables.

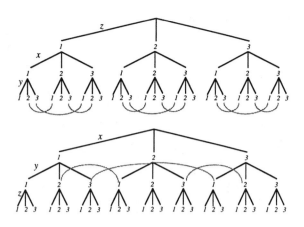

Figure 2: Search tree to solve the equation $xy - z = 4$ with different variable orderings. Symmetric states are connected by shadowed lines.

1. Lookahead of better quality. A lookahead algorithm prunes future domains taking into account past assignments. When symmetries on future variables are present, some of the lookahead effort is unproductive. If there is a symmetry θ such that $\theta(x_j) = x_k$, with $x_j, x_k \in F$, after lookahead on $D(x_j)$, lookahead on $D(x_k)$ is obviously redundant because it will produce results equivalent (through θ) to lookahead on $D(x_j)$. If no symmetries are present, no lookahead effort will be unproductive. Therefore, the more symmetries are broken, the less unproductive effort lookahead performs. When the number of symmetries is high, savings in unproductive lookahead effort could be substantial.

2. Better value selection. Let us suppose a problem with solution. At state s, there is a symmetry $\theta(x_j) = x_k$, with $x_j, x_k \in F$. Let $sol(x_j) = a$ and $sol(x_k) = b$ be the solution values for these two variables. Because of the symmetry, there is another solution with $sol(x_j) = b$ and $sol(x_k) = a$. Therefore, if x_j is selected as current variable, both values a, b are good to bring search to a solution. In a more general setting, this argument supports the fact that a variable involved in many symmetries will have many good values in its domain.

Some of these facts are illustrated in the following example. Let us consider the equation, $xy - z = 4$, where all variables take values in $\{1, 2, 3\}$. There is a symmetry, $\theta(x) = y$, and two solutions $(x = 2, y = 3, z = 2)$ and $(x = 3, y = 2, z = 2)$. Figure 2 displays two search trees for this equation, one following the variable ordering z, x, y and the other x, y, z. In the first tree, symmetry θ is not broken after assigning z, so symmetric states appear inside subtrees at the first level. In the second tree, symmetry θ is broken after assigning x, and symmetric states only appear between subtrees at the first level but not inside them. In addition, $D_0(x)$ has two good values (2 and 3), but $D_0(z)$ has only one (2).

3.2 Value Removal After Failure

Let s be a search state, where x_i is selected as the current variable and value a is tried without success. At this point, a backtracking-based algorithm will try another value for x_i. If θ is a symmetry local to s, we can remove $\theta_i(a)$ (the value symmetric to a) from $D(\theta(x_i))$, because it cannot belong to any solution including the current assignment of past variables. If all values of x_i are tried without success and the algorithm backtracks, all values removed in this way should be restored. If x_i is involved in several symmetries, this argument holds for each of them separately.

This method of value removal after failure provides further support to the symmetry-breaking heuristic of Section 3.1. The more local symmetries a variable is involved in, the more opportunities it offers for symmetric value removal in other domains if a failure occurs. This extra pruning is more effective if it is done at early levels of the search tree, since each pruned value represents removing a subtree on the level corresponding to the variable symmetric to the current one.

An example of this value removal arises in the pigeonhole problem: locating n pigeons in $n - 1$ holes such that each pigeon is in a different hole. This problem is formulated as a CSP by associating a variable x_i to each pigeon, all sharing the domain $\{1, \ldots, n-1\}$, under the constraints $x_i \neq x_j$, $1 \leq i, j \leq n$, $i \neq j$. Among others, this problem has a collection of symmetries in domains,

$$\forall i, \ \forall a, a' \in D(x_i) \ a \neq a', \ \exists \theta, \ \theta = I, \ \theta_i(a) = a'$$

(I is the identity mapping). If search is performed by forward checking and variables and values are assigned lexicographically, the first dead-end occurs when $(x_1, 1), (x_2, 2), \ldots, (x_{n-1}, n-1)$, causing $D(x_n)$ to be empty. $D(x_{n-1})$ has no more values, so backtracking goes back to x_{n-2}. There, it finds that the only remaining value, $n - 1$, is symmetric to $n - 2$ which failed, so $n - 1$ can be pruned and no more values remain in $D(x_{n-2})$. Backtracking goes back to x_{n-3} where, by the same argument, the two remaining values are pruned. This process goes on up to reach x_1, where all its remaining values are pruned and search terminates with failure. Only the leftmost branch of the search tree is generated, and the rest of the tree is pruned.

4 BIBDs

Block designs are combinatorial objects satisfying a set of integer constraints [Hall, 1986; Colbourn and Dinitz, 1996]. Introduced in the thirties by statisticians working on experiment planning, nowadays they are used in many other fields, such as coding theory, network reliability, and cryptography. The most widely used designs are the Balanced Incomplete Block Designs (BIBDs).

Formally, a (v, b, r, k, λ)-BIBD is a family of b sets (called blocks) of size k, whose elements are from a set of cardinality v, $k < v$, such that every element belongs exactly to r blocks and every pair of elements occurs

```
0 1 1 0 0 1 0
1 0 1 0 1 0 0
0 0 1 1 0 0 1
1 1 0 0 0 0 1
0 0 0 0 1 1 1
1 0 0 1 0 1 0
0 1 0 1 1 0 0
```

Figure 3: An instance of (7,7,3,3,1)-BIBD.

exactly in λ blocks. v, b, r, k, and λ are called the parameters of the design. Computationally, designs can be represented by a $v \times b$ binary matrix, with exactly r ones per row, k ones per column, and the scalar product of every pair of rows is equal to λ. An example of BIBD appears in Figure 3.

There are three well-known necessary conditions for the existence of a BIBD:

1. $rv = bk$,

2. $\lambda(v-1) = r(k-1)$, and

3. $b \geq v$ (Fisher's inequality).

However, these are not sufficient conditions. The situation is summarized in [Mathon and Rosa, 1990], that lists all parameter sets obeying these conditions, with $r \leq 41$ and $3 \leq k \leq v/2$ (cases with $k \leq 2$ are trivial, while cases with $k > v/2$ are represented by their corresponding complementaries, which are also block designs). For some parameter sets satisfying the above conditions, it has been established that the corresponding design does not exist; for others, the currently known bound on the number of *non-isomorphic* solutions is provided; and finally, some listed cases remain unsettled. The smallest such case is that with parameters (22,33,12,8,4), to whose solution many efforts have been devoted [Wallis, 1996, Chapter 11].

Some (infinite) families of block designs (designs whose parameters satisfy particular properties) can be constructed analytically, by direct or recursive methods [Hall, 1986, Chapter 15], and the state of the art in computational methods for design generation is described in [Colbourn and Dinitz, 1996; Wallis, 1996]. The aforementioned unsettled case, with $vb = 726$ binary entries, shows that exhaustive search is still intractable for designs of this size. In the general case, the algorithmic generation of block designs is an NP problem [Corneil and Mathon, 1978].

Computational methods for BIBD generation, either based on *systematic* or *randomized* search procedures, suffer from combinatorial explosion which is partially due to the large number of isomorphic configurations present in the search space. The use of group actions goes precisely in the direction of reducing this isomorphism. Although up to our knowledge, BIBD generation has not been tackled from the CSP viewpoint, it appears to be a wonderful instance of highly symmetric CSP, thus offering the possibility to assess the benefits of different search strategies on such problems.

5 Experimental Results

The problem of generating a (v, b, r, k, λ)-BIBD can be formulated as a CSP as follows. Two rows i and j of the BIBD should have exactly λ ones in the same columns. We represent this by λ variables $x_{ijp}, 1 \leq p \leq \lambda$, where x_{ijp} contains the column of the pth one common to rows i and j. There are $v(v-1)/2$ row pairs, so there are $\lambda v(v-1)/2$ variables, all sharing the domain $\{1, \ldots, b\}$. From these variables, the BIBD table T, a $v \times b$ binary matrix, is computed as follows,

$$T[i,c] = \begin{cases} 1 & \text{if } \exists j, p \text{ s.t. } x_{ijp} = c \text{ or } x_{jip} = c \\ 0 & \text{otherwise} \end{cases}$$

Constraints are expressed in the following terms,

$$x_{ijp} \neq x_{ijp'}; \quad \sum_{c=1}^{b} T[i,c] = r; \quad \sum_{i=1}^{v} T[i,c] = k$$

where $1 \leq p, p' \leq \lambda$, $1 \leq i, j \leq v$, $1 \leq c \leq b$. This problem presents many local symmetries. We consider the following ones relating future variables,

1. Variable mapping exchanges x_{ijp} and $x_{ijp'}$, domain mappings are the identity; this symmetry occurs among variables of the same row pair.

2. Variable mapping is the identity, one domain mapping exchanges values c_1 and c_2; this symmetry occurs when $T[l, c_1] = T[l, c_2]$ for $l = 1, \ldots, v$.

3. Variable mapping exchanges x_{ijp} and $x_{i'j'p'}$, domain mappings are the identity; this symmetry occurs when $T[i, c] = T[i', c]$ and $T[j, c] = T[j', c]$ for $c = 1, \ldots, b$.

4. Variable mapping exchanges x_{ij_1p} and $x_{ij_2p'}$, the domain mappings corresponding to these variables exchange values c_1 and c_2; this symmetry occurs when,
$T[j_1, c_1] = T[j_2, c_2] = 1, T[j_1, c_2] = T[j_2, c_1] = 0,$
$T[j_1, c] = T[j_2, c], c = 1, \ldots, b, c \neq c_1, c \neq c_2,$
$T[j, c_1] = T[j, c_2], j = 1, \ldots, v, j \neq j_1, j \neq j_2.$

5. Variable mapping exchanges $x_{i_1j_1p}$ and $x_{i_2j_2p'}$, the domain mappings corresponding to these variables exchange values c_1 and c_2; this symmetry occurs when,
$T[i_1, c_1] = T[i_2, c_2] = 1, T[i_1, c_2] = T[i_2, c_1] = 0$
$T[i_1, c] = T[i_2, c], c = 1, \ldots, b, c \neq c_1, c \neq c_2,$
$T[j_1, c_1] = T[j_2, c_2] = 1, T[j_1, c_2] = T[j_2, c_1] = 0,$
$T[j_1, c] = T[j_2, c], c = 1, \ldots, b, c \neq c_1, c \neq c_2,$
$T[j, c_1] = T[j, c_2], j = 1, \ldots, v, j \neq j_1, j \neq j_2.$

These symmetries have a clear graphical interpretation. Symmetry (1) is inherent to the formulation. Symmetry (2) relates values of the same variable corresponding to equal columns. Symmetry (3) relates variables corresponding to equal rows. Symmetry (4) relates variables sharing row i, and rows j_1 and j_2 that are equal but for two columns c_1 and c_2. These columns are also equal but for rows j_1 and j_2. Exchanging rows j_1 and j_2, and

BIBD	Fc-CBJ		Fc-CBJ-SB		Fc-CBJ-SB-VR	
(v,b,r,k,λ)	Sol	Time	Sol	Time	Sol	Time
7,7,3,3,1	50	1.8e-3	50	3.2e-3	50	3.1e-3
6,10,5,3,2	50	6.8e-3	50	7.1e-3	50	6.9e-3
7,14,6,3,2	49	2.8e-1	50	2.1e-2	50	1.9e-2
9,12,4,3,1	50	5.7e-3	50	1.2e-2	50	1.2e-2
6,20,10,3,4	18	7.0e+0	50	1.5e-1	50	7.5e-2
7,21,9,3,3	19	6.8e+0	50	8.2e-2	50	8.1e-2
6,30,15,3,6	5	1.7e+1	50	5.4e-1	50	2.6e-1
7,28,12,3,4	20	1.0e+1	50	2.1e-1	50	2.0e-1
9,24,8,3,2	42	2.5e+0	50	1.4e-1	50	1.3e-1
6,40,20,3,8	1	3.1e+1	49	2.5e+0	49	1.5e+0
7,35,15,3,5	8	2.5e+1	49	1.3e+0	50	1.2e+0
7,42,18,3,6	5	3.5e+1	49	1.5e+0	50	1.1e+0
10,30,9,3,2	38	5.5e+0	50	3.3e-1	50	2.9e-1
6,50,25,3,10	2	6.1e+1	47	5.1e+0	47	4.6e+0
9,36,12,3,3	26	1.4e+1	50	5.4e-1	50	5.4e-1
13,26,6,3,1	49	5.2e-1	49	1.1e+0	50	3.0e-1
7,49,21,3,7	0	6.8e+1	50	2.2e+0	50	1.3e+0
6,60,30,3,12	0	9.6e+1	48	5.0e+0	50	3.1e+0
7,56,24,3,8	2	8.8e+1	48	5.1e+0	50	2.8e+0
6,70,35,3,14	0	1.2e+2	48	7.3e+0	50	4.4e+0
9,48,16,3,4	16	3.3e+1	50	1.4e+0	50	1.3e+0
7,63,27,3,9	1	1.2e+2	49	5.1e+0	49	4.3e+0
8,56,21,3,6	1	8.1e+1	48	5.3e+0	49	4.4e+0
6,80,40,3,6	0	1.7e+2	48	1.0e+1	48	1.0e+1
7,70,30,3,10	0	1.8e+2	47	9.6e+0	49	7.4e+0
15,35,7,3,1	50	1.0e+0	49	2.7e+0	49	2.6e+0
12,44,11,3,2	45	5.4e+0	50	1.6e+0	50	1.3e+0
7,77,33,3,11	0	2.1e+2	49	9.1e+0	50	6.1e+0
9,60,20,3,5	17	5.8e+1	50	3.2e+0	50	3.2e+0
7,84,36,3,12	0	2.2e+2	48	1.2e+1	49	9.9e+0
10,60,18,3,4	13	5.6e+1	50	3.5e+0	50	3.2e+0
11,55,15,3,3	35	1.9e+1	50	2.8e+0	50	3.2e+0
7,91,39,3,13	0	2.8e+2	48	1.8e+1	50	9.7e+0
9,72,24,3,6	9	8.8e+1	50	5.7e+0	50	4.9e+0
13,52,12,3,2	38	1.5e+1	50	3.5e+0	50	2.6e+0
9,84,28,3,7	6	1.2e+2	49	1.5e+1	50	1.0e+1
9,96,32,3,8	3	1.6e+2	50	1.3e+1	50	1.2e+1
10,90,27,3,6	7	1.3e+2	50	1.4e+1	50	1.4e+1
9,108,36,3,9	2	2.3e+2	49	3.0e+1	50	1.8e+1
13,78,18,3,3	36	3.3e+1	50	1.1e+1	50	8.6e+0
15,70,14,3,2	38	2.5e+1	50	9.1e+0	50	6.4e+0
12,88,22,3,4	35	5.9e+1	50	1.3e+1	50	1.2e+1
9,120,40,3,10	2	3.0e+2	49	3.0e+1	50	2.4e+1
19,57,9,3,1	47	1.0e+1	45	2.2e+1	46	2.1e+1
10,120,36,3,8	3	2.4e+2	50	2.9e+1	50	2.7e+1
11,110,30,3,6	17	1.4e+2	48	3.4e+1	49	3.0e+1
16,80,15,3,2	37	4.4e+1	49	2.2e+1	49	1.8e+1
13,104,24,3,4	27	8.9e+1	50	2.1e+1	50	1.9e+1

Table 1: Performance results of the proposed algorithms.

columns c_1 and c_2, matrix T remains invariant. Symmetry (5) follows the same idea although it is more complex. It occurs when exchanging rows i_1 and i_2, rows j_1 and j_2, and columns c_1 and c_2, matrix T remains invariant. It is worth noting that these symmetries keep invariant matrix T because they are local to the current state, that is, they do not change past variables.

Symmetries are detected dynamically at each visited node. The specific implementation of the symmetry-breaking heuristic performs a weighted sum of the number of symmetries involving each future variable, where symmetries (4) and (5) are considered of less importance than the others.

BIBD generation is a non-binary CSP. We use a forward checking algorithm with conflict-directed backjumping (Fc-CBJ [Prosser, 1993]) adapted to deal with non-binary constraints, with Brelaz heuristic [Brelaz, 1979] for variable selection and random value selection, as reference algorithm. This algorithm is modified to include the symmetry-breaking heuristic for variable selection, with Brelaz as tie-breaker, producing Fc-CBJ-SB. Adding to this algorithm the strategy of value removal after failure, we obtain Fc-CBJ-SB-VR. We compare the performance of these algorithms generating all BIBDs

with $vb < 1400$ and $k = 3$, all having solution. Since the performance of the proposed algorithms depends on random choices, we have repeated the generation of each BIBD 50 times, each with a different random seed. Execution of a single instance was aborted if the algorithm visited more than 50,000 nodes.

Empirical results appear in Table 1, where for each algorithm and BIBD, we give the number of solved problems within the node limit and the average CPU time in seconds for the 50 instances. Comparing Fc-CBJ and Fc-CBJ-SB-VR, we see that Fc-CBJ solves 899 instances while Fc-CBJ-SB-VR solves 2382 out of the 2400 instances executed. Fc-CBJ does not solve any instance for 8 specific BIBDs, while Fc-CBJ-SB-VR provides solution for all BIBDs tested. Regarding CPU time, Fc-CBJ-SB-VR dominates Fc-CBJ in 44 out of the 48 BIBDs considered, and this dominance is of one or two orders of magnitude in 39 cases. These results show clearly that the proposed strategies improve greatly the efficiency of the Fc-CBJ algorithm for BIBD generation.

Fc-CBJ-SB results show that this algorithm almost achieves Fc-CBJ-SB-VR performance. Fc-CBJ-SB solves 2362 instances, 20 less than Fc-CBJ-SB-VR, requiring slightly more time on the average. So, for BIBD generation, the symmetry-breaking heuristic is the main responsible for the savings in search effort, while value removal plays a very secondary role.

We also reimplemented Fc-CBJ adding constraints $x_{ijp} < x_{ijp'}$ if $p < p'$, to break type (1) symmetries. The resulting algorithm, which included the extra pruning capacities caused by these new constraints, runned significantly slower than the original Fc-CBJ in all BIBDs with $\lambda > 1$.

6 Related Work

Previous work on symmetries and CSPs can be classified in two general approaches. An approach, where our work fits in, consists in modifying the constraint solver to take advantadge of symmetries. A modified backtracking algorithm appears in [Brown et al., 1988], testing each node to see whether it is the appropriate representative of those states symmetric to it. Considering specific symmetries, [Freuder, 1991] discusses the pruning of neighborhood interchangeable values of a variable. Another strategy [Roy and Pachet, 1998] considers value pruning between permutable variables. Interestingly, these two strategies are particular cases of the more general strategy presented in Section 3.2. It is easy to show that,

1. Let $x_i \in F, a, b \in D(x_i)$. Values a, b are neighborhood interchangeable iff there exists a symmetry θ such that $\theta(x_i) = x_i, \theta_i(a) = b$.

2. Let $x_i, x_j \in F$. Variables x_i, x_j are permutable iff there exists a symmetry θ such that $\theta(x_i) = x_j, \theta_i(a) = a, a \in D(x_i)$.

So, if a is assigned to x_i and fails, (1) all values neighborhood interchangeable with a in $D(x_i)$, and (2) all values a appearing in future domains of variables permutable with x_i, can be removed. Although developed independently, our strategy of value removal after failure can be seen as a particular case of the symmetry exclusion method introduced by [Backofen and Will, 1998] for concurrent constraint programming, and applied to the CSP context by [Gent and Smith, 1999].

Another approach consists in modifying the symmetric problem to obtain a new problem without symmetries, but keeping the non-symmetric solutions of the original one. To do this, new constraints are added to the original problem in order to break the symmetries. Detecting symmetries and computing the new constraints is performed by hand in [Puget, 1993]. Alternatively, existing symmetries and the corresponding symmetry-breaking predicates (in the context of propositional logic) are computed automatically in [Crawford et al., 1996].

7 Conclusions

In this paper we have analysed how to take symmetry into account to reduce search effort. We have presented two strategies to exploit symmetries inside a depth-first search scheme. These strategies have been tested on a highly symmetric combinatorial problem, namely the generation of BIBDs, an NP problem which has triggered a considerable amount of research on analytic and computational procedures. Its wide variability in size and difficulty makes it a very appropriate benchmark for algorithms aimed at exploiting symmetries in CSPs.

We believe that systematic procedures are more likely to shed light on the solution of difficult instances of the problem, whereas randomized algorithms may be quicker at finding solutions in easier cases. The present work has not been aimed at solving a particular such instance, but instead at proposing and evaluating tools to deal with symmetries. In this respect, the proposed strategies have been shown to be effective in reducing search effort.

It is worth mentioning that there is always a trade-off between the effort spent in looking for and exploiting symmetries, and the savings attained. Thus, instead of considering all possible symmetries, it is advisable to establish a hierarchy of them and try to detect the simplest first, as we have done.

Concerning future work, we plan to compare our strategies with the alternative approach of reformulating the original problem by adding new constraints to break problem symmetries. We also want to assess to what extent our approach depends on the type and number of symmetries occurring in a particular problem. We would like to identify criteria for value selection which complement our symmetry-breaking heuristic for variable selection. Moreover, the experimentation should be extended to other BIBD families, and the benefits obtained validated by applying these strategies to other domains.

Acknowledgements

We thank Javier Larrosa and the anonymous reviewers for their constructive criticisms.

References

[Backofen and Will, 1998] R. Backofen, and S. Will. Excluding symmetries in concurrent constraint programming. In *Workshop on Modeling and Computing with Concurrent Constraint Programming*, 1998.

[Brelaz, 1979] D. Brelaz. New methods to color the vertices of a graph. *Journal of ACM*, **22**(4), 251–256, 1979.

[Brown et al., 1988] C.A. Brown, L. Finkelstein, and P.W. Purdom. Backtrack searching in the presence of symmetry. In *Proc. 6th int. conf. on applied algebra, algebraic algorithms and error correcting codes*, 99–110, 1988.

[Colbourn and Dinitz, 1996] C.H. Colbourn and J.H. Dinitz (Eds.). *The CRC Handbook of Combinatorial Designs*, CRC Press, 1996.

[Corneil and Mathon, 1978] D.G. Corneil and R.A. Mathon. Algorithmic techniques for the generation and analysis of strongly regular graphs and other combinatorial configurations. *Ann. of Discrete Math.*, **2**, 1–32, 1978.

[Crawford et al., 1996] J. Crawford, M. Ginsberg, E. Luks, and A. Roy. Symmetry-Breaking Predicates for Search Problems. In *Proc. of KR-96*, USA, 1996.

[Freuder, 1991] E.G. Freuder. Eliminating interchangeable values in constraint satisfaction problems. In *Proc. of AAAI'91*, pages 227–233, 1991.

[Gent and Smith, 1999] I.P. Gent and B. Smith. Symmetry breaking during search in constraint programming. Research report 99.02, School of Computer Studies, University of Leeds.

[Hall, 1986] M. Hall. *Combinatorial Theory*, Ed. John Wiley & Sons, Second Edition, 1986.

[Mathon and Rosa, 1990] R. Mathon and A. Rosa. Tables of parameters of BIBD with $r \leq 41$ including existence, enumeration and resolvability results: an update. *Ars Combinatoria*, **30**, 1990.

[Prosser, 1993] P. Prosser. Hybrid algorithmics for the constraint satisfaction problem. *Computational Intelligence*, **9**(3), 268–299, 1993.

[Puget, 1993] J.F. Puget. On the satisfiability of symmetrical constrained satisfaction problems. In *Proc. of ISMIS'93*, pages 350–361, Norway, 1993.

[Roy and Pachet, 1998] P. Roy and F. Pachet. Using symmetry of global constraints to speed up the resolution of constraint satisfaction problems. In *Proc. of ECAI'88 workshop on Non-binary constraints*, pages 27–33, Brighton, UK, 1998.

[Wallis, 1996] W.D. Wallis. *Computational and Constructive Design Theory*, Kluwer Academic Publishers, Dordrecht, The Netherlands, 1996.

Extending consistent domains of numeric CSP

Hélène Collavizza, François Delobel, Michel Rueher
Université de Nice–Sophia-Antipolis, I3S — ESSI
930, route des Colles - B.P. 145, 06903 Sophia-Antipolis, France
{helen,delobel,rueher}@essi.fr

Abstract

This paper introduces a new framework for extending consistent domains of numeric CSP. The aim is to offer the greatest possible freedom of choice for one variable to the designer of a CAD application. Thus, we provide here an efficient and incremental algorithm which computes the maximal extension of the domain of one variable. The key point of this framework is the definition, for each inequality, of an *univariate* extrema function which computes the left most and right most solutions of a selected variable (in a space delimited by the domains of the other variables). We show how these univariate extrema functions can be implemented *efficiently*. The capabilities of this approach are illustrated on a ballistic example.

1 Introduction

This paper introduces a new framework for extending the domain of one variable in a consistent CSP [1] which is defined by a set of *non-linear constraints over the reals*. The aim is to offer the greatest freedom of choice of possible values for a variable to the *designer* of a CAD application. For example, one starts from the knowledge of a solution and tries to widen the variations of a variable. This problem occurs in a large class of electro-mechanical engineering and civil engineering applications, where extending the domain of a variable permits the tolerance of any associated component to be enlarged, and therefore to lower the cost of this component. These problems are often under-constrained. So, what the user wants to know is a subset of the solutions. For these applications, classical methods (e.g.,[7; 10]), based on local consistencies and domain splitting, cannot ensure that a solution exists inside the arbitrarily small intervals they compute. Moreover, domain splitting is ineffective if the solution set is not a finite set of isolated solutions but a collection of intervals.

The framework we introduce here allows one to enlarge the domain of a variable while preserving the consistency of the CSP. Sam-Haroud and Faltings [9] have proposed an approach for computing safe solutions of non-linear constraint systems. Roughly speaking, they fill up the solution space with a set of consistent boxes[2]. Their approach could be used to extend the domain of one variable. However, the underlying costs in computation time and space are exponential.

The framework we introduce here is less general but it can be implemented efficiently. Before going into the details, let us outline our framework in very general terms. The main steps of the right extension[3] of the domain of a variable are:

1. Searching for a subset of the solution space; this solution space may be reduced to a single point;

2. Selecting of the variable the domain of which has to be extended;

3. Defining for each inequality of an extrema function that computes the left most solution of the selected variable in a space delimited by the domains of the other variables;

4. Finding the smallest solution of all extrema functions.

The following example illustrates this process.

---

[1] An introduction to CSP and numeric CSP can be found in [4; 7].

[2] Their approach is based upon a classical method used in graphical computing for image synthesis (composition of shapes, of scenes) known as the 2^k trees. The key idea is to classify portions of space in three categories: the black shapes contain no solution at all, the gray shapes contain solutions, but also contain points which are not solutions, and finally, the white shapes contain only points which are solution. The gray shapes are split into smaller one that are again classified into black, white and gray shapes; the decomposition process stops when the size of the shapes becomes smaller than a given value.

[3] Throughout this paper, we will only consider the right extension since the left one can be computed in a symmetrical way.

Example 1 *Let us consider the behavior of an electrical shunt motor, the speed of which may be changed. The maximum speed can be up to 3 times the value of the minimum speed. We only consider two parameters of the motor: the torque C_u, and the rotation speed N. The motor cannot use more than a given power : $N * C_u \leq P_{max}$. Moreover, the motor cannot operate above a given speed and torque: $N \in [1,3]$, $C_u \in [0,4]$.*

We know that the motor is working efficiently for every tuple of values $D_{C_u} \times D_N$ in $[0,1] \times [1,2]$ when $P_{max} = 5$. What we want to compute is the maximum range of values of the torque which is safe with this motor. In other words, we are looking for the maximum domain D_{C_u} such that every tuple in $D_{C_u} \times D_N$ is a solution of the constraint system.

Now, consider equation $N * C_u = 5$ in the space delimited by $N \in [1,3]$, $C_u \in [0,4]$. Its left most solution is the point defined by $C_u = 2.5$ and $N = 2$; this point is obviously an upper bound of the domain D_{C_u}.

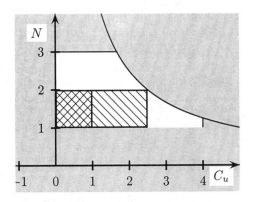

Figure 1: Relation between N and C_u

An initial subset of the solution space can often be found by experimentation. Note that the solution space may be reduced to a single point and the domains of the different variables may successively be extended.

The definition of the univariate extrema functions is a key point of our approach. Optimal univariate extrema functions can trivially be computed for the so-called primitive constraints. For non–primitive constraints, the methods used for computing Box–consistency [1] provide an efficient way to compute a safe approximation of univariate extrema functions.

To define formally the extension of the domain of a variable, we introduce an "internal" consistency, named *i–consistency*, which ensures that every tuple in the Cartesian product of the variable domains is a solution of the constraint system. i–consistency should not be mistaken with arc consistency or approximations of arc consistency [3] (e.g. 2B–consistency[7], Box–consistency[1]). Those consistencies define regions containing all the solutions (and possibly tuples which are not solution) whereas i–consistency defines a region which is a subset of the set of solutions. Figure 2 shows the relations be-

tween these different families of consistencies. Roughly speaking, the smallest external box is the best approximation which can be computed by approximations of arc consistency over continuous domains.

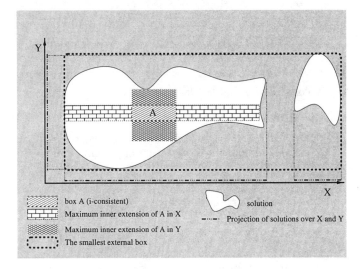

Figure 2: Relations between i–consistency and some partial consistencies

Outline of the paper: Section 2 introduces the notation and recalls the basics on CSP over continuous domains which are needed in the rest of the paper. Section 3 is devoted to the description of the i–consistent extension process. Extrema functions are formally defined and an efficient algorithm is introduced. Section 4 outlines the capabilities of our approach on a ballistic example.

2 Preliminaries

2.1 Notation

We use the following notations, possibly subscripted:

- x, y, z denote variables over the reals;
- u, v denote real constants;
- f, g denote functions over the reals;
- c denotes a constraint over the reals;

The next subsection recalls a few notions of numeric CSP; Details can be found in [2; 10; 3].

2.2 Interval constraint system

A k-ary constraint c is a relation over the reals.

Definition 1 (Interval) *Let $\overline{\mathbb{F}}$ denote a finite subset of $\mathcal{R}$ augmented with the two infinity symbols $\{-\infty, +\infty\}$. An interval $[a,b]$ with $a,b \in \overline{\mathbb{F}}$ is the set of real numbers $\{r \in \mathcal{R} \mid a \leq r \leq b\}$.*

Definition 2 (CSP)
A CSP [8] is a triple $(\mathcal{X}, \mathcal{D}, \mathcal{C})$ where $\mathcal{X} = \{x_1, \ldots, x_n\}$ denotes a set of variables, $\mathcal{D} = \{D_{x_1}, \ldots, D_{x_n}\}$ denotes a set of domains, D_{x_i} being the interval containing all

acceptable values for x_i, and $C = \{c_1, \ldots, c_m\}$ denotes a set of constraints[4].

$\vec{D}$ denotes the Cartesian product $D_{x_1} \times \ldots \times D_{x_n}$. $\vec{v}$ denotes the tuple $(v_{x_1}, \ldots, v_{x_n})$ such that $\vec{v} \in \vec{D}$. $\pi_x(\vec{v})$ denotes the projection over x of $\vec{v}$. $\underline{D_i}$ (resp. $\overline{D_i}$) denotes the lower bound (resp. upper bound) of the interval D_i.

Definition 3 (k-box) *A k-box $I_1 \times \ldots \times I_k$ is the part of a k-dimension space defined by the Cartesian product of intervals $(I_1, \ldots, I_k)$*

By construction, all the k-boxes are convex.

2.3 Local consistencies

Local consistencies over continuous domains are based on arc consistency[8] which was originally defined for finite domains. This section introduces two local consistencies that will be used in the rest of the paper.

Definition 4 (arc consistency) *A CSP P $(\mathcal{X}, \mathcal{D}, \mathcal{C})$ is arc-consistent iff: $\forall D_x \in \mathcal{D}, \forall v_x \in D_x, \forall c \in \mathcal{C}$: $\exists \vec{v} \in \vec{D} \mid \pi_x(\vec{v}) = v_x \wedge c(\vec{v})$*

Davis ([4]) has studied the application of the Waltz algorithm ([12]) over continuous domains and has shown important theoretical limitations. The Waltz algorithm was then extended by Faltings ([5; 6]) in order to deal with ternary constraints defined by continuous and differentiable curves.

Definition 5 (Set Extension) *Let S be a subset of $\mathcal{R}$. The approximation of S —denoted* hull— *is the smallest interval I such that $S \subseteq I$.*

2.4 Box–consistency

Roughly speaking, Box–consistency [1; 10] is a local consistency over continuous domains which computes a safe approximation of the solution of each variable involved in a given constraint.

Definition 6 (Box–consistency) *Let $(\mathcal{X}, \mathcal{D}, \mathcal{C})$ be a CSP and $c \in \mathcal{C}$ a k-ary constraint over the variables $(x_1, \ldots, x_k)$. c is Box-consistent if, for all x_i in $\{x_1, \ldots, x_k\}$ such that $D_{x_i} = [a, b]$, the following relations hold :*
1. $C(D_{x_1}, \ldots, D_{x_{i-1}}, [a, a^+), D_{x_{i+1}}, \ldots, D_{x_k})$,
2. $C(D_{x_1}, \ldots, D_{x_{i-1}}, (b^-, b], D_{x_{i+1}}, \ldots, D_{x_k})$.
where a^+ (resp. a^-) corresponds to the smallest (resp. largest) number of $\overline{\mathbb{F}}$ strictly greater (resp. smaller) than a, and C stands for interval extension of c [3].

The essential point is that the variable x is Box-consistent for constraint $f(x, x_1, \ldots, x_n) = 0$ if the bounds of the domain of x correspond to the leftmost and the rightmost 0 of the optimal interval extension of $f(x, x_1, \ldots, x_n)$.

---

[4]It is worthwhile to notice that the set of constraints $\mathcal{C}$ represents a **conjunction** of constraints that have to be satisfied. Disjunctions may only occur inside a single constraint, e.g. the single constraint $x^2 = y$ is equivalent to the disjunction $(x = \sqrt{y}) \vee (-x = \sqrt{y})$.

3 Extension of the domain of a variable of a CSP

This section introduces the way a domain of a single variable can be extended while preserving consistency of the whole CSP. We start by defining two local consistencies which are needed to characterize the extended domains.

Next, we formally define the univariate extrema functions that actually compute the bounds of the i-consistent extensions of the domain of a variable.

3.1 e–consistency

Various approximations of arc consistency (e.g. 2B-consistency[7], Box–consistency[1]) have been introduced for continuous domains. e–consistency is the best approximation of the solution space which can be computed by these partial consistencies. For instance, e–consistency corresponds to the "smallest external box" on Fig. 2. More formally, e–consistency is defined as follows:

Definition 7 (e–consistency) *Let $P = (\mathcal{X}, \mathcal{D}, \mathcal{C})$ be an arc consistent CSP. A CSP $P' = (\mathcal{X}, \mathcal{D}', \mathcal{C})$ is e-consistent iff $\forall D_i' \in \mathcal{D}' : D_i' = $* hull$(D_i)$

In other words, a CSP $P = (\mathcal{X}, \mathcal{D}, \mathcal{C})$ is e-consistent iff $P' = (\mathcal{X}, \mathcal{D}', \mathcal{C})$ is arc consistent and $\mathcal{D}$ corresponds to the smallest box containing all values of $\mathcal{D}'$. So, for inequality c, e–consistency on the corresponding equation c_{equ} (see section 3.4) yields a box which bounds the maximal extension that can be performed for any variable occurring in c.

3.2 i–consistency

Definition 8 (i–consistency)
Let $P = (\mathcal{X}, \mathcal{D}, \mathcal{C})$ be a CSP. P is i-consistent iff $\forall c \in \mathcal{C}, \forall \vec{v} \in \vec{D} : c(\vec{v})$

In other words, a CSP $P = (\mathcal{X}, \mathcal{D}, \mathcal{C})$ is i–consistent iff $\mathcal{D}$ only contains tuples which are solutions.

Example 2 *Let P be the CSP defined by $\mathcal{X} = \{x, y\}$, $D_x = [-2, 2], D_y = [6, 12], \mathcal{C} = \{x^2 - y \leq 0, -x^2 + 20 \leq y\}$. This system is i-consistent :*
$\forall (v_x, v_y) \in (D_x, D_y) : v_x^2 - v_y \leq 0 \wedge -v_x^2 + 20 \leq v_y$
Now, we want to find the largest $D_x' \supseteq D_x$ such that the CSP defined by replacing D_x by D_x' in P is i-consistent.

Figure 3 shows the original box and the extension of D_x. Both boxes are i-consistent[5]. The domain of y remains unchanged. B is the e-consistent box for equation $x^2 = y$ and gives the upper bound of the extension of D_x.

Ward et al. [13] have proposed four kinds of interval propagation. One of them is related to i–consistency. Each interval D_x is labeled with one of these kinds:

---

[5]Note that we could also perform a fruitful i-consistent extension of D_y to $[6, 14]$ with the new box. But this extension of D_y is much smaller than the one we would have obtained if we had extended the initial box (D_y would have been extended to $[4, 16]$). In general, the result of successive extensions by i-consistency of several variables depends on the processing order of the variables.

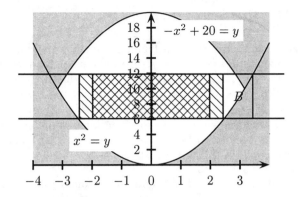

Figure 3: Maximal i–consistent extension of D_x

"only", "every", "some" and "none". If D_x is labeled "only" then solution tuples only take their values for x in D_x. If D_x is "every" then every value of x in D_x gives a tuple solution. If D_x is "some" then there exists at least one solution tuple such that x takes its value in D_x. If D_x is "none" then there is no solution tuple such that the value of x is in D_x.

Labelling every variable with "every" is what we call i–consistency. However, Ward et al.'s inference rules that allow computing labelled interval propagation do not consider the case where two variables are labelled "every". Moreover, these inference rules assume strong monotony and continuity properties of the constraint system.

Now, we formally define what we mean by right i–consistent extension.

3.3 Right i–consistent Extension of D_x
Definition 9 (Right i–consistent extension of D_x)

Let $P = (\mathcal{X}, \mathcal{D}, \mathcal{C})$ be a i–consistent CSP. $P' = (\mathcal{X}, \mathcal{D}', \mathcal{C})$ is a right i–consistent extension of D_x for P iff:

- $\forall D_i \in \mathcal{D} \setminus \{D_x\}$, $D_i = D_i'$
- $D_x \subset D_x'$, $\underline{D_x'} = \underline{D_x}$
- P' is i–consistent

Definition 10 (Maximal right extension)
Let $P = (\mathcal{X}, \mathcal{D}, \mathcal{C})$ be a i–consistent CSP. $P' = (\mathcal{X}, \mathcal{D}', \mathcal{C})$ is a maximal right i–consistent extension of D_x for P iff:

- P' is a right i–consistent extension of D_x for P;
- $\forall P''$, such that P'' is a right i–consistent extension of D_x for P, $P'' \subset P'$ [6]

3.4 Extrema functions
Let c be an inequality, c_{equ} denotes the equation corresponding to c. More precisely, if c is defined by an expression of the form $f(x_1, \ldots, x_n) \leq 0$ or $f(x_1, \ldots, x_n) \geq 0$, then c_{equ} denotes the equation $f(x_1, \ldots, x_n) = 0$.

---

[6]A CSP $P = (\mathcal{X}, \mathcal{D}, \mathcal{C})$ is smaller than a CSP $P' = (\mathcal{X}, \mathcal{D}', \mathcal{C})$ if $\mathcal{D} \subseteq \mathcal{D}'$. $\mathcal{D} \subseteq \mathcal{D}'$ means $D_{x_i} \subseteq D_{x_i'}$ for all $i \in 1..n$.

$F_c^{min(x)}(\mathcal{D})$ is an optimal extremum function of c_{equ} for variable x if $F_c^{min(x)}(\mathcal{D})$ computes the smallest value of x which is a solution of c_{equ} [7] in the space delimited by $\mathcal{D}$.

Definition 11 (Optimal extremum function)
Let $P = (\mathcal{X}, \mathcal{D}, \mathcal{C})$ be a CSP, x a variable of $\mathcal{X}$ and c a constraint of $\mathcal{C}$. The optimal extremum function of constraint c_{equ} for variable x is

$$F_c^{min(x)}(\mathcal{D}) = min(\pi_x(\vec{v}) \mid c_{equ}(\vec{v}) \text{ holds.})$$

By convention, $F_c^{min(x)}(\mathcal{D})$ returns $\overline{D_x}$ when c_{equ} has no solution in the space delimited by $\mathcal{D}$.

Definition 12 (Extremum function approximation)

Let $P = (\mathcal{X}, \mathcal{D}, \mathcal{C})$ be a CSP, c a constraint of $\mathcal{C}$ and $F_c^{min(x)}(\mathcal{D})$ an optimal extremum function of c_{equ} for variable x.
$AF_c^{min(x)}(\mathcal{D})$ is a safe approximation of $F_c^{min(x)}(\mathcal{D})$ iff:
$AF_c^{min(x)}(\mathcal{D}) < F_c^{min(x)}(\mathcal{D})$

3.5 Computing an i–consistent right extension of D_x for P

To define the right i–consistent extension of D_x for a CSP $P = (\mathcal{X}, \mathcal{D}, \mathcal{C})$, we introduce two specific domains, named $\mathcal{D}_{max}$ and $\mathcal{D}_{ext}$:

- $\mathcal{D}_{max}$ is the set of initial domains where D_x has been set to $[\overline{D_x}, \infty)$, i.e., $\mathcal{D}_{max} = \mathcal{D}_{D_x \leftarrow [\overline{D_x}, \infty)}$

- $\mathcal{D}_{ext}$ is the set of initial domains where D_x has been extended to the value of the extremum function of constraint c on x,
  i.e., $\mathcal{D}_{ext} = \mathcal{D}_{D_x \leftarrow [\underline{D_x}, F_c^{min(x)}(\mathcal{D}_{max})]}$

Next proposition defines the right i–consistent extension of D_x for a CSP P with only one single constraint.

Proposition 1 Let $P = (\mathcal{X}, \mathcal{D}, \{c\})$ be an i–consistent CSP with only one inequality constraint c and let x be a variable of $\mathcal{X}$. Then, $P = (\mathcal{X}, \mathcal{D}_{ext}, \{c\})$ is a maximal right i–consistent extension of D_x for P.

Proof:
We assume that c is not a tautology [8] which is true for any value of x. So it results from the definition of the extrema functions (definition 9) that we have either:

$$\forall \vec{v} \in \mathcal{D}_{ext} : c(\vec{v})$$

$$\text{or } \forall \vec{v} \in \mathcal{D}_{ext} : not(c(\vec{v})))$$

Since P is i–consistent, it results that $\forall \vec{v} \in \mathcal{D}_{ext} : c(\vec{v})$.

Proposition 2 Let $P = (\mathcal{X}, \mathcal{D}, \mathcal{C})$ be a i–consistent CSP. Let $P' = (\mathcal{X}, \mathcal{D}', \mathcal{C})$ such that:

- $\forall D_i \in \mathcal{D} \setminus \{D_x\} : D_i = D_i'$

---

[7]Of course, when c_{equ} is not defined in a subpart of $\mathcal{D}$, $F_c^{min(x)}(\mathcal{D})$ returns a value that is strictly smaller than the smallest value of D_x for which c_{equ} is not defined.

[8]Tautologies can be removed in a pre-processing step.

- $D'_x = [\underline{D_x}, min_{c \in C}(F_c^{min(x)}(\mathcal{D}_{max})))$

Then, P' is a right i–consistent extension on x of P. Furthermore, P' is a maximal right i–consistent extension of P on x.

Proof: From proposition 1, it results that $\forall v \in D', \forall c \in C : c(v)$. Since P is a conjunction of constraints, P' is i–consistent.
Let $P'' = (\mathcal{X}, \mathcal{D}'', \mathcal{C})$ be an i–consistent extension of D_x for $P = (\mathcal{X}, \mathcal{D}, \mathcal{C})$. Assume that $P' \subset P''$ and that:

- $\forall D''_i \in \mathcal{D}'' \setminus \{D''_x\} : D'_i = D''_i$

- $D'_x \subset D''_x$

- $\underline{D''_x} = \underline{D'_x} = \underline{D_x}$

Assume that c^k is the constraint such that $\overline{D'_x} = F_{c^k}^{min(x)}(\mathcal{D}_{max})$. So, there exists $\vec{v} \in \vec{\mathcal{D}}_{max}$ such that c^k is false, and that $\underline{D'_x} < \Pi_x(\vec{v}) \leq \overline{D''_x}$. Thus, P'' is not i–consistent.

The algorithm in Figure 4 directly follows from property 2. Note that this algorithm is much simpler than the framework introduced by Sam-Haroud and Faltings [9] to compute a local consistency. Both algorithms select relevant extrema from all extrema including intersections between several curves and intersections between curves and interval extremities. However, in our case, the relevant extrema is simply the left most one since we start from an initial i–consistent box (so we know which portion of the space is a solution) and we extend only one variable domain to the right. This algorithm only searches for the left most extrema, thus, it is linear if the extrema functions can be computed in constant time. The next section shows that the left most extrema can be computed very efficiently.

```
function i-extension(x,Dmax,C): real
I ← Max-Value
for c in C
    I ← Min(I, Fc^min(x)(Dmax))
return I
End function
```

Figure 4: function `i-extension`

3.6 Computing extrema functions

Optimal extrema functions for variable x of constraint c can trivially be computed if c is either a monotonic on x, or if D_x can be decomposed in subdomains where c is monotonic on x. Such constraints are usually called primitive constraints[3]. The set of primitive constraints is infinite and includes the following constraints: $\{x = y, x \leq y, x < y, x \neq y, z = x + y, z = x * y, x = -y, y = sin(x), y = cos(x), y = e^x, y = abs(x), z = x^y, \ldots\}$.

Example 3 *The constraint $x^3 = y$ is primitive: the right extrema function for x is :*

$$F_x^{min}(D_x, D_y) = max(\underline{D_x}, \sqrt[3]{\underline{D_y}})))$$

For a non–primitive constraint c, we will approximate the e–consistent box for c_{equ} in the space delimited by domains $\mathcal{D}_{D_x \leftarrow D_{max}}$. The methods introduced to compute Box–consistency provide an efficient way to compute such a safe approximation of $F_c^{min(x)}(\mathcal{D}_{max})$. The key observation is that extrema functions are *univariate functions* which can be tackled by the *Newton method* implemented in the Box–consistency.
So, consider the i–consistent extension of D_x for CSP $P = (\mathcal{X}, \mathcal{D}, \mathcal{C})$ and an inequality $c \in \mathcal{C}$. To compute a safe approximation of the extrema functions for x of constraint c, we could just compute a Box–consistent interval for x with regard to c_{equ}. Box–consistency would yield an interval D'_x such that $\Pi_x(sol(c_{equ}, \mathcal{D}_{max})) \subset D'_x$. Thus, $\underline{D_x} = AF_c^{min(x)}(\mathcal{D}_{max})$.

As a matter of fact, a complete computation of Box–consistency is not required. The LNAR procedure [11] used in Box–consistency finds the left most zero of the interval extension of the univariate function on x derived from c_{equ} by replacing all variables but x by their domains. Of course, when the function `i-extension` (see. fig. 4) uses approximations of extrema functions, the i–extension of the domain of x may not be maximal.

4 A ballistic example

In this section, we give a small ballistic application which illustrates the capabilities of our system. The problem consists of finding the maximum mechanical tolerances when an object is launched in a uniform gravitational field $\vec{g}$, with an initial speed $\vec{V_i}$ which has an incidence α with the ground (see fig. 5).

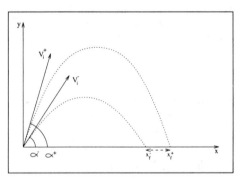

Figure 5: Possible trajectories of the projectile

The strong requirement is that the object must fall inside a predefined interval.

4.1 Modeling of the problem

The initial speed and incidence of the bullet can be stated as follows:

$$x_f = V_x t_f \qquad y_f = -\frac{1}{2}g t_f^2 + V_y t_f$$
$$V_x = V \cos(\alpha) \qquad V_y = V \sin(\alpha)$$

These equations give the impact point (x_f, y_f) of the bullet when $t = t_f$ and $y_f = 0 : t = V_y \frac{2}{g}$

Thus, $x = V_x \frac{2V_y}{g} = \frac{2V^2}{g} \cos(\alpha) \sin(\alpha)$

4.2 Computing i–consistency extension of D_α

The target is defined by the interval $[220, 250]$. Now, assume that the bullet falls on the target when $\alpha \in [32, 35]$ and $V \in [49.2, 50.1]$. So the initial i–consistent box is defined by :

$\forall \alpha \in D_\alpha$:

$$\frac{2}{9.81} * [49.2, 50.1]^2 * cos(\alpha) * sin(\alpha) \geq 220 \qquad (c)$$

$$\frac{2}{9.81} * [49.2, 50.1]^2 * cos(\alpha) * sin(\alpha) \leq 250 \qquad (c')$$

To extend D_α to the right by i–consistency, we have to check whether the box at the right of the i–consistent box is i–consistent. Thus, we have to find the left most bound of D_α for c_{equ} and c'_{equ} with $D_{max} = [35, 90]$. To find these bounds, we have used Numerica [10] to compute Box–consistent intervals for c_{equ} and c'_{equ}. The left most bound of these intervals respectively are 58.4 and 38.4. So, D_α can be extended by i–consistency to interval $[32, 38.4]$ (see Fig. 6).

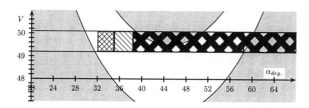

Figure 6: The ballistic constraints and boxes

Now, consider the three dimensional version of this problem where the target is defined by a rectangular area of space $R_x \times R_y \times R_z$ such that $220 \leq R_x \leq 250$, $R_y = 0$ and $-50 \leq R_z \leq 50$. Let β be the angle between $\vec{x}$ and the projection of $\vec{V}$ on the plane defined by $y = 0$. We know that the box defined by $D_\alpha = [34, 35], D_V = [49.2, 50.1]$ and $D_\beta = [0, 0]$ is i–consistent. To extend β by i–consistency, we have computed with Numerica the Box–consistent intervals for the equations derived from the following inequalities :

$$220 \leq \frac{2}{9.81} * V^2 * sin(\alpha) * cos(\alpha) * cos(\beta)$$
$$250 \geq \frac{2}{9.81} * V^2 * sin(\alpha) * cos(\alpha) * cos(\beta)$$
$$-50 \leq \frac{2}{9.81} * V^2 * sin(\alpha) * cos(\alpha) * sin(\beta)$$
$$50 \geq \frac{2}{9.81} * V^2 * sin(\alpha) * cos(\alpha) * sin(\beta)$$

The left most bound of these intervals is 1.4; thus, D_β can be extended by i–consistency to the interval $[0, 1.4]$.

5 Conclusion

This paper has introduced an effective framework for extending the domain of one variable in an already consistent CSP. Extending the domain of one variable is a critical issue in applications where the tolerance of a component determines its cost.

Contrary to Ward et al [13] we do not impose any restrictions on the form of the constraints. The approach suggested by Sam-Haroud and Faltings [9] is more general since they do not know an initial solution but its computation cost is very high. The key point of our framework is the definition of univariate extrema functions which can be computed efficiently.

An interesting way to explore concerns maximizing the size (or volume) of i–consistent boxes.

Acknowledgements

Thanks to Gilles Trombettoni for his careful reading and helpful comments on earlier drafts of this paper. Thanks also to Olivier Lhomme, Jean-Paul Stromboni and Alexander Semenov for interesting suggestions.

References

[1] F. Benhamou, D. McAllester and P. Van Hentenryck. CLP(intervals) revisited. In *Proc. ILPS*. MIT Press, 1994.

[2] F. Benhamou and W. Older. Applying interval arithmetic to real, integer and boolean constraints. *Journal of Logic Programming*, 1997.

[3] H. Collavizza, F. Delobel and M Rueher. A note on partial consistencies over continuous domains. In *Proc. of CP 98*, LNCS 1520, Springer Verlag, 1998.

[4] E. Davis. Constraint propagation with interval labels. *Artificial Intelligence*, 32:281–331, 1987.

[5] B. Faltings. Arc–consistency for continuous variables. *Artificial Intelligence*, 65:363–376, 1994.

[6] B. Faltings and E. Gelle. Local consistency for ternary numeric constraints. *IJCAI'97*, pages 392–397, 1997.

[7] O. Lhomme. Consistency techniques for numeric csp. *Proc. IJCAI93*, pp. 232–238, 1993.

[8] A. Mackworth. Consistency in networks of relations. *Artificial Intelligence*, 8(1):pp. 99–118, 1977.

[9] D.J Sam-Haroud and B. Faltings. Consistency techniques for continuous constraints. *Constraints*, 1(1& 2):85–118, September 1996.

[10] P. Van Hentenryck, Y. Deville and L. Michel. *Numerica. A modeling language for global optimization*. MIT Press, 1997.

[11] D. Kapur, D. McAllester and P. Van Hentenryck. *Solving Polynomial Systems Using a Branch and Prune Approach SIAM Journal on Numerical Analysis*, 34(2), April 1997.

[12] D. Waltz. *The Psychology of Computer Vision*, chap. Understanding line drawing of scenes with shadow. McGraw-Hill, 1975.

[13] A.C. Ward, T. Lozano-Perez and W.P. Seering. Extending the constraint propagation of intervals. In *Proc. of the 11th IJCAI*, pages 1453–1458, 1989.

CONSTRAINT SATISFACTION

Constraint Satisfaction 2

The Difference All-Difference Makes [*]

Kostas Stergiou and **Toby Walsh**
Department of Computer Science
University of Strathclyde
Glasgow, Scotland
{ks,tw}@cs.strath.ac.uk

Abstract

We perform a comprehensive theoretical and experimental analysis of the use of all-different constraints. We prove that generalized arc-consistency on such constraints lies between neighborhood inverse consistency and, under a simple restriction, path inverse consistency on the binary representation of the problem. By generalizing the arguments of Kondrak and van Beek, we prove that a search algorithm that maintains generalized arc-consistency on all-different constraints dominates a search algorithm that maintains arc-consistency on the binary representation. Our experiments show the practical value of achieving these high levels of consistency. For example, we can solve almost all benchmark quasigroup completion problems up to order 25 with just a few branches of search. These results demonstrate the benefits of using non-binary constraints like all-different to identify structure in problems.

1 Introduction

Many real-world problems involve all-different constraints. For example, every fixture for a sports team must be on a different date. Many of the constraint satisfaction toolkits therefore provide specialized algorithms for efficiently representing and, in some case, reasoning about all-different constraints. Alternatively, we can expand all-different constraints into a quadratic number of binary not-equals constraints. However, it is less efficient to do this, and the translation loses some semantic information. The aim of this paper is to show the benefits of keeping with a non-binary representation. We prove that we can achieve much higher levels of consistency in the non-binary representation compared to the binary. We show experimentally that these high levels of consistency can reduce search dramatically.

---
[*]The authors are members of the APES research group, http://www.cs.strath.ac.uk/ apes. We thank our colleagues in the group at the Universities of Strathclyde and Leeds, most especially Paul Shaw. The second author is supported by EPSRC award GR/K/65706.

2 Formal background

A constraint satisfaction problem (CSP) is a triple (X, D, C). X is a set of variables. For each $x_i \in X$, D_i is the domain of the variable. Each k-ary constraint $c \in C$ is defined over a set of variables $(x_1, \ldots x_k)$ by the subset of the cartesian product $D_1 \times \ldots D_k$ which are consistent values. An all-different constraint over $(x_1, \ldots x_k)$ disallows the values $D_1 \times \ldots D_k - \{(a_1, \ldots a_k) \mid a_i \in D_i \,\& \forall u \neq v.a_u \neq a_v\}$. A solution is an assignment of values to variables that is consistent with all constraints.

Many lesser levels of consistency have been defined for binary constraint satisfaction problems (see [Debruyne and Bessiere, 1997] for references). A problem is (i, j)-consistent iff it has non-empty domains and any consistent instantiation of i variables can be extended to a consistent instantiation involving j additional variables. A problem is arc-consistent (AC) iff it is $(1, 1)$-consistent. A problem is path-consistent (PC) iff it is $(2, 1)$-consistent. A problem is strong path-consistent iff it is $(j, 1)$-consistent for $j \leq 2$. A problem is path inverse consistent (PIC) iff it is $(1, \overline{2})$-consistent. A problem is neighborhood inverse consistent (NIC) iff any value for a variable can be extended to a consistent instantiation for its immediate neighborhood. A problem is restricted path-consistent (RPC) iff it is arc-consistent and if a variable assigned to a value is consistent with just a single value for an adjoining variable then for any other variable there exists a value compatible with these instantiations. A problem is singleton arc-consistent (SAC) iff it has non-empty domains and for any instantiation of a variable, the problem can be made arc-consistent.

Many of these definitions can be extended to non-binary constraints. For example, a (non-binary) CSP is generalized arc-consistent (GAC) iff for any variable in a constraint and value that it is assigned, there exist compatible values for all the other variables in the constraint [Mohr and Masini, 1988]. Regin gives an efficient algorithm for enforcing generalized arc-consistency on a set of all-different constraints [Régin, 1994]. We can also maintain a level of consistency at every node in a search tree. For example, the MAC algorithm for binary CSPs maintains arc-consistency at each node in the search tree [Gaschnig, 1979]. As a second example, on a non-binary problem, we can maintain generalized arc-consistency (MGAC) at every node in the search tree.

Following [Debruyne and Bessiere, 1997], we call a consistency property A stronger than B ($A \geq B$) iff in any problem in which A holds then B holds, and strictly stronger ($A > B$) iff it is stronger and there is at least one problem in which B holds but A does not. We call a local consistency property A incomparable with B ($A \sim B$) iff A is not stronger than B nor vice versa. Finally, we call a local consistency property A equivalent to B iff A implies B and vice versa. The following identities summarize results from [Debruyne and Bessiere, 1997] and elsewhere: strong PC > SAC > PIC > RPC > AC, NIC > PIC, NIC $\sim$ SAC, and NIC $\sim$ strong PC.

3 Generalized arc-consistency

All-different constraints are network decomposable [Dechter, 1990] (abbreviated to decomposable in this paper) as they can be represented by binary constraints on the same set of variables. In this section, we give some theoretical results which identify the level of consistency achieved by GAC on decomposable constraints like the all-different constraint.

In general, GAC on decomposable constraints may only achieve the same level of consistency as AC on the binary representation. The problem is that decomposable constraints can often be decomposed into smaller constraints. For example, we can decompose an n-ary all-different constraint into $n(n-1)/2$ binary all-different constraints, and enforcing GAC on these only achieves the same level of consistency as AC on the binary representation. We can achieve higher levels of consistency if we prohibit too much decomposition of the non-binary constraints. For example, we can insist that the constraints are *triangle preserving*. That is, we insist that, if there is a triangle of variables in the constraint graph of the binary representation, then these variables must occur together in a non-binary constraint. Binary constraints can still occur in a triangle preserving set of constraints, but only if they do not form part of a larger triangle. Under such a restriction, GAC is strictly stronger than PIC, which itself is strictly stronger than AC.

Theorem 1 *On a triangle preserving set of decomposable constraints GAC is strictly stronger than PIC on the binary representation.*

Proof: Consider a triple of variables, x_i, x_j, x_k and any value for x_i from its generalized arc-consistent domain. The proof divides into four case. In the first, x_i and x_j appear in one constraint, and x_i and x_k in another. As each of these constraints is arc-consistent, we can find a value for x_j consistent with x_i, and for x_k consistent with x_i. As the (non-binary) constraints are triangle preserving, there is no direct constraint between x_j and x_k so the values for x_j and x_k are consistent with each other. Hence, the binary representation of the problem is PIC. The other three cases follow a similar argument. To show that GAC is strictly stronger, consider an all-different constraint on 4 variables each with domains of size 3. This problem is PIC but not GAC. □

A corollary of this result is that GAC on a triangle preserving set of decomposable constraints is strictly stronger than RPC or AC on the binary representation. We can also put an upper bound on the level of consistency that GAC achieves.

Theorem 2 *NIC on the binary representation is strictly stronger than GAC on a set of decomposable constraints.*

Proof: Consider any variable and value assignment. NIC ensures that we can assign consistent values to the variable's neighbors. However, any (non-binary) constraint including this variable has all its variables in the neighborhood. Hence, the (non-binary) constraint is GAC. To prove strictness, consider a problem with five all-different constraints on $\{x_1, x_2, x_3\}$, on $\{x_1, x_3, x_4\}$, on $\{x_1, x_4, x_5\}$, on $\{x_1, x_5, x_6\}$, and on $\{x_1, x_6, x_2\}$. in which x_1 has the unitary domain $\{1\}$ and every other variable has the domain $\{2, 3\}$. This problem is GAC, but enforcing NIC. shows that it is insoluble. □

Finally, GAC on decomposable constraints, is incomparable to strong PC and SAC, even when restricted to triangle preserving sets of constraints.

Theorem 3 *On a triangle preserving set of decomposable constraints, GAC is incomparable to strong PC and to SAC.*

Proof: Consider an all-different constraint on 4 variables, each with the same domain of size 3. The binary representation of the problem is strong PC and SAC, but enforcing GAC shows that it is insoluble.

Consider the problem in the proof of Theorem 2 with five all-different constraints. This problem is GAC, but enforcing strong PC or SAC shows that it is insoluble.

These results are summarized in Figure 1.

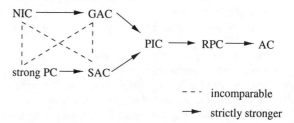

Figure 1: The consistency of GAC on a triangle preserving set of decomposable constraints.

4 Quasigroup problems

Quasigroup problems lend themselves to a non-binary representation using all-different constraints. A quasigroup is a Latin square, a n by n multiplication table in which each entry appears once in every row and column. Quasigroups model a variety of practical problems like tournament scheduling and designing drug tests. Quasigroup completion, the problem of completing a partial filled quasigroup, has been proposed as a constraint satisfaction benchmark [Gomes and Selman, 1997].

An order n quasigroup completion problem can be represented as a non-binary constraint satisfaction problem with n^2 variables, each with a domain of size n. The constraints are $2n$ all-different constraints of size n, one for each row and column, and any number of unitary constraints or preassignments. The special structure of these constraints allows us to prove some tighter results.

Theorem 4 *In quasigroup completion problems, GAC is equivalent to NIC.*

Proof: We need to show that GAC implies NIC. The neighborhood of any variable in an order n quasigroup completion problem are the $2n - 1$ variables that appear in the 2 all-different constraints that contain the variable. As these constraints are GAC, we can find consistent instantiations for each of the variables. In the binary representation, none of these variables have a direct constraint with each other. Hence, this is a consistent instantiation for the neighborhood. □

GAC on quasigroup problems remains strictly stronger than PIC and incomparable to strong PC and to SAC.

Theorem 5 *In quasigroup completion problems, GAC is strictly stronger than PIC.*

Proof: By theorem 1, GAC is stronger than PIC. To show that it is strictly stronger, consider an order 4 quasigroup, in which 3 diagonal elements have domains $\{1\}$, and all the other elements (including the other diagonal element) have domains $\{2, 3, 4\}$. This problem is PIC but is not GAC. □

Theorem 6 *In quasigroup completion problems, GAC is incomparable to strong PC and to SAC.*

Proof: Consider the problem from the last proof. This problem is strong PC and SAC but is not GAC.

Consider an order 3 quasigroup. Let every element have a domain $\{1, 2, 3\}$ except the top right which has the domain $\{1, 2\}$, the bottom left which has the domain $\{1, 3\}$ and the bottom right which has the domain $\{2, 3\}$. This problem is GAC but enforcing strong PC or SAC shows that it is insoluble. □

What can we learn from these results? First, on quasigroup completion problems, we achieve the maximum level of consistency (viz. NIC) possible for a GAC procedure on decomposable constraints. And second, we achieve this at very moderate cost. Regin's algorithm for achieving GAC on a set of all-different constraints has a cost that is polynomial in n. By comparison, enforcing NIC on binary constraints is exponential in the size of the neighborhood (which is $O(n)$ in this case).

5 Maintaining GAC and AC

We now compare an algorithm that maintains GAC on decomposable constraints over one that maintains AC on the binary representation. We say that algorithm A dominates algorithm B if when A visits a node then B also visits the equivalent node in its search tree, and strictly dominates if it dominates and there is one problem on which it visits strictly fewer nodes. Using the previous results, we can reduce our analysis to comparing algorithms that maintain NIC, PIC and AC. In fact, we do better than this and prove some general results about algorithms that maintain any level of consistency stronger than FC in which we just filter domains. This covers algorithms that maintain NIC, PIC and AC, as well those that maintain RPC and SAC. We shall use A-consistent and B-consistent to denote any two such levels of consistency.

We assume throughout a static variable and value ordering. We can then associate each node in the search tree with the

sequence of value assignments made. We say that a node $(a_1, \ldots, a_i)$ is A-compatible with another node $(a_1, \ldots, a_j)$ where $j < i$, if enforcing A-consistency at $(a_1, \ldots, a_j)$ does not remove a_i from the domain of the respective variable. First, we give a necessary and sufficient condition for a node to be visited.

Theorem 7 *A node is visited by an algorithm that maintains A-consistency iff it is consistent, it is A-compatible with all its ancestors, and its parent can be made A-consistent.*

Proof: ($\Rightarrow$) The proofs of the first and third conjuncts are similar to those in [Kondrak and van Beek, 1997]. For the second, suppose that node $(a_1, \ldots, a_i)$ is not A-compatible with one of its ancestors and it is visited. Let $(a_1, \ldots, a_j)$, with $j < i$, be the shallowest of those ancestors. Since $(a_1, \ldots, a_j)$ is an ancestor of $(a_1, \ldots, a_i)$, it is also visited. When we visit node $(a_1, \ldots, a_j)$ and A-consistency is enforced, a_i is pruned out from the domain of x_i. Node $(a_1, \ldots, a_{i-1})$ cannot therefore be extended to $(a_1, \ldots, a_i)$. This is a contradiction.

($\Leftarrow$) WLOG assume that node $(a_1, \ldots, a_{i-1})$ is the shallowest node that can be made A-consistent, its child $(a_1, \ldots, a_i)$ is consistent and A-compatible with all its ancestors, but the child is not visited. Since $(a_1, \ldots, a_i)$ is consistent and A-compatible with all its ancestors, a_i is in the domain of x_i. At node $(a_1, \ldots, a_{i-1})$, we do not annihilate any of the domains of future variables because the node can be made A-consistent. The branch will therefore be extended to the remaining values of the next variable x_i. One of these values is a_i and therefore node $(a_1, \ldots, a_i)$ is visited. □

This results lets us rank algorithms in the hierarchy presented in [Kondrak and van Beek, 1997].

Theorem 8 *If A-consistency is (strictly) stronger than B-consistency then maintaining A-consistency (strictly) dominates maintaining B-consistency.*

Proof: All nodes visited by an algorithm that maintains A-consistency, are A-consistent with all their ancestors and have parents that can be made A-consistent. But as A-consistency is stronger than B-consistency, all these nodes are B-consistent with all their ancestors and have parents that can be made B-consistent. Hence maintaining A-consistency dominates maintaining B-consistency. To show strictness, consider any problem that is B-consistent but is not A-consistent. □

From this result, it follows that MGAC on decomposable constraints strictly dominates MAC on the binary representation, and that MAC itself strictly dominates FC. We can also prove the correctness of MGAC and MAC using the following general result.

Theorem 9 *Maintaining A-consistency is correct.*

Proof: Soundness is trivial as only consistent nodes are visited. For completeness, suppose that some n-level node is consistent. Since this node is consistent, all its ancestors are also consistent. WLOG consider the deepest node $k = (a_1, \ldots, a_i)$, $i \geq 1$ that is not visited, and its parent is visited. When node $(a_1, \ldots, a_{i-1})$ is visited A-consistency is enforced, and since all its descendants are consistent, there is no domain wipe-out. Therefore, k is visited. □

6 Experimental results

To demonstrate the practical relevance of these theoretical results, we ran experiments in three domains.

6.1 Quasigroup completion

Gomes and Selman have proposed random quasigroup completion problems as a benchmark that combines some of the best features of random and structured problems [Gomes and Selman, 1997]. For these problems, there is a phase transition from a region where almost all problems are soluble to a region where almost all problems are insoluble as we vary the percentage of variables preassigned. The solution cost peaks around the transition, with approximately 42% of variables preassigned [Gomes and Selman, 1997].

We encoded the problem in ILOG Solver, a C++ constraint toolkit which includes Regin's algorithm for maintaining GAC on all-different constraints. We used the Brelaz heuristic for variable selection (as in [Gomes and Selman, 1997]) and Geelen's promise heuristic for value ordering (as in [Meseguer and Walsh, 1998]). Gomes et al. observed that search costs to solve random quasigroup completion problems can be modeled by a "heavy-tailed" distribution [Gomes et al., 1997]. We therefore focus on the higher percentiles. Table 1 gives branches explored to complete an order 10 quasigroup with $p\%$ of entries preassigned, maintaining either AC on the binary representation or GAC on the all-different constraints. We see a very significant advantage for MGAC over MAC. With a random value ordering, the worst case for MGAC was also 2 branches. CPU times reflect the difference in explored branches. For example, some instances at the phase transition for quasigroups of order 20 were solved by MGAC in seconds, while MAC took hours.

p	MAC		MGAC	
	100th	90th	100th	90th
10	163	1	1	1
20	*	1	1	1
30	*	15	2	1
35	*	124	2	1
40	*	1726	2	1
42	*	*	2	1
45	*	*	2	1
48	*	2771	2	1
50	5692	1263	2	1
55	324	71	2	1
60	47	7	1	1
70	2	2	1	1
80	2	2	1	1
90	2	2	1	1

Table 1: Percentiles in branches searched to complete a quasigroup of order 10 using either MAC or MGAC. * means that the instance was abandoned after 10000 branches. 100 problems were solved at each data point.

Table 2 shows that, as we increase problem size, almost all the problems remain trivial. The only exception was a single order 25 problem with 42% of its variables preassigned. Search was abandoned at the cutoff limit of 10,000 branches. Apart from this, all instances were solved in less than 5 branches. This is a significant improvement over the results of [Gomes et al., 1997] where, despite the use of random restarts, problems of order 25 were too expensive to solve, especially at the phase transition.

p	order 10		order 15		order 20		order 25	
	100th	90th	100th	90th	100th	90th	100th	90th
10	1	1	1	1	1	1	1	1
20	1	1	1	1	1	1	1	1
30	2	1	1	1	2	1	2	1
40	2	1	2	1	2	1	2	1
42	2	1	2	1	2	1	*	1
45	2	1	3	1	3	1	3	1
48	2	1	2	1	2	1	2	1
50	2	1	2	1	2	1	3	1
60	1	1	1	1	4	1	1	1
70	1	1	1	1	1	1	1	1
80	1	1	1	1	1	1	1	1
90	1	1	1	1	1	1	1	1

Table 2: Percentiles in branches explored to complete quasigroups of order 10, 15, 20 and 25 using MGAC.

6.2 Quasigroup existence

A variety of automated reasoning programs have been used to answer open questions in finite mathematics about the existence of quasigroups with particular properties [Fujita et al., 1993]. Is GAC useful on these problems? We follow [Fujita et al., 1993] and look at the so-called QG3, QG4, QG5, QG6 and QG7 class of problems. For example, the QG5 problems concern the existence of idempotent quasigroups (those in which $a \cdot a = a$ for each element a) in which $(ba \cdot b)b = a$. For the definition of the other problems, see [Fujita et al., 1993]. In these problems, the structure of the constraint graph is disturbed by additional non-binary constraints. These reduce the level of consistency achieved compared to quasigroup completion problems. Nevertheless, GAC significantly prunes the search space and reduces runtimes.

To solve these problems, we again use the Solver toolkit, maintaining either GAC on the all-different constraints, or AC on the binary representation, and the fail-first heuristic for variable ordering. To eliminate some of the symmetric models, as in [Fujita et al., 1993], we added the constraint that $a \cdot n \geq a - 1$ for every element a. Table 3 demonstrates the benefits of MGAC over MAC. In QG3 and QG4, MAC explores twice as many branches as MGAC, in QG5 the difference is orders of magnitude, whilst there is only a slight difference in QG6 and QG7. MGAC dominates MAC in terms of CPU time as well as in terms of explored branches. It would be interesting to identify the features of QG5 that gives MGAC such an advantage over MAC, and those of QG6 and QG7 that lessen this advantage.

We now compare our results with those of FINDER [Slaney, 1992], MACE [McCune, 1994], MGTP [Fujita et

Order	QG3		QG4		QG5		QG6		QG7	
	MAC	MGAC	MAC	MGAC	MAC	MGAC	MAC	MGAC	MAC	MGAC
6	7	4	6	4	0	0	0	0	6	4
7	64	48	59	42	5	3	5	2	67	39
8	1,511	821	1,227	707	15	10	9	3	415	314
9	65,001	31,274	88,460	40,582	30	19	36	26	4,837	4,211
10	-	-	-	-	268	74	199	167	94,433	80,677
11	-	-	-	-	1,107	292	2,221	1,876	-	-
12	-	-	-	-	6,832	910	42,248	34,741	-	-
13	-	-	-	-	>1,000,000	27,265	-	4,730,320	-	-

Table 3: Branches explored using MAC on the binary representation and MGAC on the all-different constraints.

al., 1993], SATO [Zhang and M., 1994], and SEM [Zhang and Zhang, 1995]. Table 4 shows that Solver outperforms MGTP and FINDER by orders of magnitude, and explores less branches than SEM. SEM and SATO have sophisticated branching heuristics and complex rules for the symmetry breaking that are far more powerful than the symmetry breaking constraint we use [Zhang and Zhang, 1995]. It is therefore impressive that our simple Solver program is competitive with well-developed systems like SEM and SATO.

To conclude, despite the addition of non-binary constraints that disturb the structure of the constraint graph, MGAC significantly reduces search and runtimes on quasigroup existence problems. We conjecture that the performance of SEM and SATO could be improved by the addition of a specialized procedure to maintain GAC on the all-different constraints.

6.3 Small-worlds problems

Recently, [Watts and Strogatz, 1998] has shown that graphs that occur in many biological, social and man-made systems are often neither completely regular nor completely random, but have instead a "small world" topology in which nodes are highly clustered, whilst the path length between them is small. Walsh has argued that such a topology can make search problems hard since local decisions quickly propagate globally [Walsh, 1999]. To construct graphs with such a topology, we start from the constraint graph of a structured problem like a quasigroup and introduce randomness by deleting edges at random from the binary representation. Deleting an edge at random breaks up an all-different constraint on n variables into two all-different constraints on $n-1$ variables. For example, if $x_1, x_2, x_3 \ldots, x_k$ are all-different and remove the edge between x_1 and x_2 then we are left with all-different constraints on $x_1, x_3 \ldots, x_k$ and $x_2, x_3 \ldots, x_k$.

Figures 2 and 3 show percentiles in the number of branches explored and in CPU time to find the optimal coloring of order 10 quasigroups in which we delete $p\%$ of edges from the binary representation. The hardest problems had 5% of their edges removed. MGAC dominates MAC by orders of magnitude in the hard region both in terms of branches explored and CPU time. All instances were solved by MGAC within 120 seconds while approximately 10% of the instances could not be solved by MAC within 1 hour. As p increases, problems become very easy and both MGAC and MAC quickly find a solution. MAC starts to outperform MGAC in terms of CPU time as the overhead of GAC on the large number of

all-different constraints is greater.

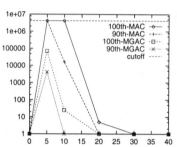

Figure 2: Percentiles in branches explored by MAC and MGAC to color small world problems.

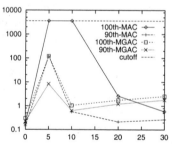

Figure 3: Percentiles of CPU seconds used by MAC and MGAC to color small world problems.

7 Related work

[Gomes and Selman, 1997] solved quasigroup completion problems using the MAC algorithm and a binary representation. They found that a randomization and restart strategy could eliminate the heavy-tailed behavior of the backtracking algorithm. However, they were still not able to consistently solve quasigroup completion problems of order 25 or larger.

[Meseguer and Walsh, 1998] solved quasigroup completion problems using forward checking (FC) on the binary representation. They found that discrepancy and interleaved based methods can reduce the heavy tail. However, their experiments were limited to quasigroups of order 20 and less.

[Bacchus and van Beek, 1998] have compared generalized FC on non-binary constraints with FC on the hidden variable and dual encodings into binary constraints. They show that

Order	Models	Branches					
		MGTP	FINDER	MACE	SATO	SEM	Solver (MGAC)
7	3	9	3	4	5	6	3
8	1	34	13	8	8	11	10
9	0	239	46	14	11	29	19
10	0	7,026	341	37	21	250	74
11	5	51,904	1,728	112	43	1,231	292
12	0	2,749,676	11,047	369	277	8,636	910

Table 4: Branches explored and models found on QG5 problems by a variety of different programs.

a simple extension of FC on the hidden variable encoding dominates generalized FC on the non-binary representation.

8 Conclusions

We have shown experimentally and theoretically the benefits of achieving generalized arc-consistency on decomposable constraints like all-different constraints. Generalized arc-consistency on such constraints lies between neighborhood inverse consistency and, under a simple restriction, path inverse consistency on the binary representation of the problem. On quasigroup completion problems, generalized arc-consistency achieves neighborhood inverse consistency. By generalizing the arguments of [Kondrak and van Beek, 1997], we proved that a search algorithm that maintains generalized arc-consistency on decomposable constraints dominates a search algorithm that maintains arc-consistency on the binary representation. Our generalization also proves the correctness of the algorithms that maintain arc-consistency or generalized arc-consistency. Our experiments demonstrated the practical value of achieving these high levels of consistency. For example, we solved almost all benchmark quasigroup completion problems up to order 25 with just a few branches of search. On quasigroup existence problems, we are competitive with the best programs, despite lacking their specialized branching heuristics and symmetry breaking rules.

What general lessons can be learnt from this study? First, it can be very beneficial to identify structure in a problem by means of a non-binary representation. We can use this structure to enforce higher levels of consistency than can be practical in a binary representation. Second, theory can be motivated by experiment. We were led to attempt our theoretical analysis by the exceptionally good experimental results on quasigroup completion problems. And finally, the all-different constraint really can make a big difference.

References

[Bacchus and van Beek, 1998] F. Bacchus and P. van Beek. On the conversion between non-binary and binary constraint satisfaction problems. In *Proc. of AAAI-98*, pages 311–318. 1998.

[Debruyne and Bessiere, 1997] R. Debruyne and C. Bessiere. Some practicable filtering techniques for the constraint satisfaction problem. In *Proc. of IJCAI-97*, pages 412–417. 1997.

[Dechter, 1990] R. Dechter. On the expressiveness of networks with hidden variables. In *Proc. of AAAI-90*, pages 555–562. 1990.

[Fujita et al., 1993] Masayuki Fujita, John Slaney, and Frank Bennett. Automatic generation of some results in finite algebra. In *Proc. of IJCAI-93*, pages 52–57. 1993.

[Gaschnig, 1979] J. Gaschnig. Performance measurement and analysis of certain search algorithms. Tech. rep. CMU-CS-79-124, Carnegie-Mellon University, 1979. PhD thesis.

[Gomes and Selman, 1997] C. Gomes and B. Selman. Problem structure in the presence of perturbations. In *Proc. of AAAI-97*, pages 221–226. 1997.

[Gomes et al., 1997] C. Gomes, B. Selman, and N. Crato. Heavy-tailed distributions in combinatorial search. In G. Smolka, editor, *Proc. of CP97*, pages 121–135. 1997.

[Kondrak and van Beek, 1997] G. Kondrak and P. van Beek. A Theoretical Evaluation of Selected Backtracking Algorithms. *Artificial Intelligence*, 89:365–387, 1997.

[McCune, 1994] W. McCune. A Davis-Putnam Program and its Application to Finite First-Order Model Search: Quasigroup Existence Problems. Tech. Rep. ANL/MCS-TM-194, Argonne National Laboratory, 1994.

[Meseguer and Walsh, 1998] P. Meseguer and T. Walsh. Interleaved and discrepancy based search. In *Proc. of ECAI-98*. Wiley, 1998.

[Mohr and Masini, 1988] R. Mohr and G. Masini. Good old discrete relaxation. In *Proc. of ECAI-88*, pages 651–656, 1988.

[Régin, 1994] J-C. Régin. A filtering algorithm for constraints of difference in CSPs. In *Proc. of AAAI-94*, pages 362–367. 1994.

[Slaney, 1992] J. Slaney. FINDER, Finite Domain Enumerator: Notes and Guide. Tech. Rep. TR-ARP-1/92, Australian National University, 1992.

[Walsh, 1999] T. Walsh. Search in a small world. In *Proc. IJCAI-99*, 1999.

[Watts and Strogatz, 1998] D.J. Watts and S.H. Strogatz. Collective dynamics of 'small-world' networks. *Nature*, 393:440–442, 1998.

[Zhang and M., 1994] H. Zhang and Stickel M. Implementing the Davis-Putnam Algorithm by Tries. Tech. rep., University of Iowa, 1994.

[Zhang and Zhang, 1995] J. Zhang and H. Zhang. SEM: a System for Enumerating Models. In *Proc. of IJCAI-95*, pages 298–303, 1995.

The Symmetric Alldiff Constraint

Jean-Charles RÉGIN
ILOG
Les Taissounières HB2
06560 Valbonne, FRANCE
e-mail : regin@ilog.fr

Abstract

The *symmetric* alldiff constraint is a particular case of the alldiff constraint, a case in which variables and values are defined from the same set S. That is, every variable represents an element e of S and its values represent the elements of S that are compatible with e. This constraint requires that all the values taken by the variables are different (similar to the classical alldiff constraint) and that if the variable representing the element i is assigned to the value representing the element j, then the variable representing the element j is assigned to the value representing the element i. This constraint is present in many real-world problems, such sports scheduling where it expresses matches between teams. In this paper, we show how to compute the arc consistency of this constraint in $O(nm)$ ($m = \sum_i |D(i)|$), where n is the number of involved variables and $D(i)$ the domain of the variable i. We also propose a filtering algorithm of less complexity ($O(m)$).

1 Introduction

Constraint Satisfaction Problems (CSPs) involve finding values for problem variables subject to constraints on which combinations are acceptable. They are more and more used in real-life applications, such as frequency allocation, crew scheduling, time tabling, car sequencing, etc. [Simonis, 1996].

The general task of finding a solution in a constraint network being NP-hard, many researchers have concentrated on improving the efficiency of solving a CSP.

Currently, it seems that a look-ahead approach is the most promising way. The purpose of this technique is to look at the values of the variables that are not yet instantiated and to remove values that cannot lead to a solution w.r.t. the current partial instantiation. Thus, it anticipates the detection of some failures by using a particular treatment after each modification of domain variables. A filtering algorithm is one such particular treatment. With respect to a partial instantiation, it re-

moves once and for all certain inconsistencies that would have been discovered several times otherwise.

Techniques based on filtering algorithms are thus quite important. Particularly, arc consistency caught the attention of many researchers, who then discovered a large number of algorithms.

Furthermore, it is necessary to deal directly with the arity of the constraints because nonbinary constraints lose much of their semantics when encoded into a set of binary constraints. (See [Régin, 1994].) This encoding leads, for example, to behavior that prunes much less for filtering algorithms handling it.

When the semantics of a nonbinary constraint is not known *a priori*, GAC-Schema [Bessière and Régin, 1997] can be used to achieve arc consistency of the constraint. However, this algorithm does not perform as well with known semantics. In such a situation, it is particularly interesting to develop a specific filtering algorithm, as it was done for the well known alldiff constraint [Régin, 1994]. This approach leads to an important gain in time and in space for solving a CSP, even if the filtering algorithm does not achieve arc consistency. For instance, the diff-n or cumulative constraints are really useful in practice to solve real-world problems, as it has been shown by Simonis, although arc consistency is not achieved for these constraints.

In this paper, we study a new constraint and propose some filtering algorithms for it. Some of those algorithms ensure arc consistency; others are weaker.

The symmetric alldiff constraint

Consider a set of people to be grouped by pairs according to predefined compatibilities such that each person is paired exactly once. This problem can be modeled as a constraint satisfaction problem in which each person is associated with one variable and one value. The domain of a variable associated with a person p is defined by the values which are associated with a person compatible with p. For instance, consider the simple problem defined on a set of three people p_1, p_2, p_3 that are all compatible. The CSP will then involve three variables x_1, x_2, x_3, where x_i is associated with p_i and three values v_1, v_2, v_3, where v_i is associated with

p_i. Moreover, $D(x_1) = \{v_2, v_3\}$, $D(x_2) = \{v_1, v_3\}$ and $D(x_3) = \{v_1, v_2\}$.

Since we want to pair all the variables with different values, we add an alldiff constraint involving all the variables. Constraints stating that "if any variable x is associated with a variable y, then y must be associated with x" can be defined by means of the σ function. This function is defined as follows: $\sigma(x)$ is the value v that is associated with the same person as the variable x, and $\sigma(v)$ is the variable x that is associated with the same person as the value v. Of course, we have $\sigma(x) = v - x = \sigma(v)$. Then, for each variable x and for each value v, we define the constraint: $(x = v - \sigma(v) = \sigma(x))$.

The CSP we have just defined can be viewed as only one constraint that we will call **symmetric alldiff constraint**. This constraint requires that all the values taken by the variables are different (similar to the classical alldiff constraint) and that if the variable representing the element i is assigned to the value representing the element j, then the variable representing the element j is assigned to the value representing the element i.

The example problem we consider has no solution. However, the CSP that has just been built is arc consistent[1]. Thus it is important to be able to efficiently handle symmetric alldiff constraints.

These constraints arise in some problems such crew scheduling (two pilots must be in a cockpit at the same time), nurse rostering (two nurses are required for certain operations) or sports scheduling. In the latter problems, one of the main tasks is to compute a set of matches between teams such that each team plays against another team, and each team plays exactly once for each period of time under consideration. There exist compatibility constraints between teams. For instance, during the winter period, travel has to be limited. Therefore, for a given period, the problem we have to solve for each period is exactly a symmetric alldiff constraint.

A symmetric alldiff constraint can be expressed by a graph, in which nodes represent variables and there is an edge between two nodes x_1 and x_2 if and only if $\sigma(x_1) \in D(x_2)$ and $\sigma(x_2) \in D(x_1)$. (See Figure 1).

Initially this graph corresponds to the compatibility graph. During the search for a solution, it is built from the current domain of the variables.

Since this new constraint corresponds to the definition of a particular CSP involving several constraints, there is an equivalence between the consistency of this new constraint and the existence of a solution for the CSP. This equivalence means that an algorithm checking the consistency of a symmetric alldiff constraint is more efficient for the resolution of the problem than is the conjunction of all the algorithms checking the consistency (or achieving arc consistency) of the other constraints involved in the first model.

It is quite important to emphasize this point in order to understand that there is great interest in defin-

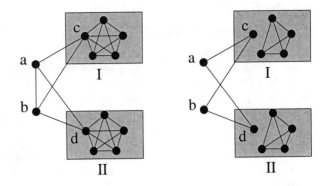

Figure 1: An example of a symmetric alldiff constraint. Nodes represent teams, and edges compatibilities between teams. The left graph is the initial graph, the right graph is the graph obtained after achieving arc consistency.

ing specific global constraints for which efficient algorithms computing the consistency of these constraints are known. For instance, consider the problem given by the left graph in Figure 1 and two models of this problem. First, this problem is represented by a classical alldiff constraint and constraints ensuring the symmetries. Second, the problem is represented by only one symmetric alldiff constraint. The subproblems part I and part II of this graph are odd size cliques. Thus, clearly, if c is not instantiated to neither a nor b then there is no solution[2]. Unfortunately, the CSP defined by the first model is arc consistent, and so no value is removed. The right graph of the figure shows the achievement of arc consistency for the symmetric alldiff constraint.

The consistency of an alldiff constraint can be computed by searching for a maximum matching in a bipartite graph. We will show that the consistency of a symmetric alldiff constraint can also be achieved by searching for a maximum matching in a graph which is not necessarily bipartite. This problem can be easily solved by using, for instance, Edmonds's algorithm [Edmonds, 1965]. We will also present an original algorithm for achieving arc consistency for a symmetric alldiff constraint. Unfortunately, this algorithm is not incremental. Hence, we will propose a filtering algorithm, which does not necessarily achieve arc consistency, but which has a remarkable complexity.

The paper is organized as follows. First we give some preliminaries about constraint network and matching theory. Then, we formally present the symmetric alldiff constraint, and we explain how to compute the consistency of this constraint. In the next section, an algorithm achieving arc consistency for this constraint is fully detailed. After it, we propose a filtering algorithm which has lower complexity. Then we conclude.

---

[1]For instance, $\{(x_1, v_2), (x_2, v_3), (x_3, v_1)\}$ satisfies the alldiff constraint.

[2]When there is no ambiguity we will say that node x is instantiated to y instead of saying node x is instantiated to $\sigma(y)$ and node y is instantiated to $\sigma(x)$.

2 Preliminaries

2.1 Constraint network

A finite **constraint network** $\mathcal{N}$ is defined as a set of n **variables** $X = \{x_1, \ldots, x_n\}$, a set of current finite **domains** $\mathcal{D} = \{D(x_1), \ldots, D(x_n)\}$ where $D(x_i)$ is the finite set of possible **values** for variable x_i, and a set $\mathcal{C}$ of **constraints** between variables. We introduce the particular notation $\mathcal{D}_0 = \{D_0(x_1), \ldots, D_0(x_n)\}$ to represent the set of initial domains of $\mathcal{N}$.[3]

Then, a constraint C on the ordered set of variables $X(C) = (x_{i_1}, \ldots, x_{i_k})$ is a subset $T(C)$ of the Cartesian product $D_0(x_{i_1}) \times \cdots \times D_0(x_{i_k})$ that specifies the **allowed** combinations of values for the variables $x_{i_1} \times \ldots \times x_{i_k}$. An element τ of $D_0(x_{i_1}) \times \cdots \times D_0(x_{i_k})$ is called a **tuple on** $X(C)$ and $\tau[k]$ is the kth value of τ.

$ind(C, x)$ is the position of variable x in $X(C)$; $\#(v, \tau)$ is the number of occurences of the value v in the tuple τ; and $D(X)$ denotes the union of the domain of the variables of X.

A tuple τ on $X(C)$ is **valid** if $\forall (x, a) \in \tau, a \in D(x)$. A value $a \in D(x)$ is **consistent with** C iff $x \notin X(C)$, or $\exists \tau \in T(C)$, such that $a = \tau[ind(C, x)]$ and τ is valid. C is **arc consistent** iff $\forall x \in X(C), D(x) \neq \varnothing$ and $\forall a \in D(x), a$ is consistent with C. We achieve arc consistency of C by removing all values not consistent with C.

The **value graph** of a constraint C is the bipartite graph $GV(C) = (X(C), D(X(C)), E)$ where $\{x_i, a\} \in E$ iff $a \in D(x_i)$.

2.2 Matching theory

Most of these definitions are due to [Tarjan, 1983].

If $\{u, v\}$ is an edge of a graph, then we say that u and v are the **ends** or the **extremities** of the edge. n are the number of nodes and m the number of edges of a graph. $G - \{u, v\}$ denotes the graph G in which the nodes u and v have been removed. $G - \{\{u, v\}\}$ denotes the graph G in which the edge $\{u, v\}$ has been removed. A **matching** M on a graph is a set of edges no two of which have a common vertex. The **size** $|M|$ of M is the number of edges it contains. The **maximum matching problem** is that of finding a matching of maximum size. M **covers** X when every vertex of X is an endpoint of some edge in M.

Let M be a matching. An edge in M is a **matching edge**; every edge not in M is **free**. A vertex is **matched** if it is incident to a matching edge and **free** otherwise. For any matched vertex v, $mate(v)$ denotes the vertex w such that $\{v, w\}$ is a matching edge.

A **path** in a graph **from** v_1 **to** v_k is a sequence of vertices $[v_1, v_2, \ldots, v_k]$ such that $\{v_i, v_{i+1}\}$ is an edge for $i \in [1, \ldots, k-1]$. The path is **simple** if all its vertices are distinct. A path is a **cycle** if $k > 1$ and $v_1 = v_k$. An **alternating path or cycle** is a simple path or cycle whose edges are alternately matching and free. The *length* of an alternating path or cycle is the number of edges it contains.

3 The symmetric alldiff constraint

Definition 1 *Let X be a set of variables and σ be a one-to-one mapping from $X \cup D(X)$ to $X \cup D(X)$ such that*

$\forall x \in X$: $\sigma(x) \in D(X)$; $\forall a \in D(X)$: $\sigma(a) \in X$ *and* $\sigma(x) = a - x = \sigma(a)$.

*A **symmetric alldiff constraint** defined on X is a constraint C associated with σ such that:*

$$T(C) = \{ \tau \text{ such that } \tau \text{ is a tuple on } X$$
$$\text{and } \forall a \in D(X): \#(a, \tau) = 1$$
$$\text{and } a = \tau[ind(C, x)] - \sigma(x) = \tau[ind(C, \sigma(a))]\}$$

It is denoted by symalldiff(X, σ)

The consistency of the classical alldiff constraint is computed by searching for the existence of a matching in the value graph that covers all the variables, and arc consistency is achieved by identifying all the edges that can never belong to a matching that covers all the variables. Our problem is really close to that one with one major difference: the graph under consideration can be nonbipartite.

The problem we have to solve is called symmetric matching. Symmetric matching in a $2n$-node bipartite graph is, indeed, really no different from matching in an n-node nonbipartite graph. Consider the value graph $GV(C)$ of a symmetric alldiff constraint. This graph is bipartite. Now, we can modify this graph by contracting any variable x with value $a = \sigma(x)$ into a single vertex. The edge between x and a is deleted, and the other edges that have x or a as an endpoint are replaced by edges having the contracting vertex as endpoint and their other extremity unchanged. The graph we get in that way, denoted by $CGV(C)$, is no longer bipartite and is called the **contracted value graph** of a symmetric alldiff constraint. More formally: $CGV(C) = (X(C), E)$ where $\{x_1, x_2\} \in E$ iff $\sigma(x_1) \in D(x_2)$ and $\sigma(x_2) \in D(x_1)$.

There is a correspondance between a matching which covers $X(C)$ in $CGV(C)$ and a tuple of $T(C)$.

Proposition 1 *Given $C = $symalldiff$(X, \sigma)$, every tuple of $T(C)$ corresponds to a set A of edges in $CGV(C)$ such that for each vertex $x \in X(C)$, x is an end of exactly one edge. And a matching M in $CGV(C)$ which covers $X(C)$ corresponds to an element of $T(C)$*

proof: An element of $T(C)$ corresponds to a matching that covers $X(C)$ in $CGV(C)$, by construction of $CGV(C)$. And from a matching in $CGV(C)$ covering $X(C)$, we can build a tuple that satisfies the constraint, by definition of the symmetric alldiff constraint.

Therefore, we have:

Corollary 1 *A constraint $C = $symalldiff$(X, \sigma)$ is consistent iff there exists a matching that covers $X(C)$ in $CGV(C)$.*

Since $CGV(C)$ can be nonbipartite, an algorithm searching for maximum matching in a nonbipartite graph has to be used, like the blossom-shrinking algorithm

---

[3]Indeed, we consider that any constraint network $\mathcal{N}$ can be associated with an initial domain $\mathcal{D}_0$ (containing $\mathcal{D}$), on which constraint definitions were stated.

of Edmonds. An implementation of this algorithm in $O(mn)$ is fully detailed in [Tarjan, 1983]. The advantage of this algorithm is its incrementality. Suppose that we start with a matching of size k, and there exists a matching of size $n/2$; then this matching can be computed in $O((n/2 - k)m)$. This point is important if we systematically check the consistency of the constraint during the search for solution.

On the other hand, [Micali and Vazirani, 1980] proposed a complex algorithm in $O(\sqrt{n}m)$.

For computing the consistency of a symmetric alldiff constraint, it is also necessary to update the contracted value graph. Precisely, when a value is removed from the domain of a variable, the corresponding edge must be deleted. All these modifications need at most $O(m)$ operations. Therefore, we can consider that the consistency of a symmetric alldiff constraint can be computed in $O(\sqrt{n}m)$.

3.1 Arc consistency

For the sake of clarity, we will consider that $C = $ symalldiff(X, σ) is a symmetric alldiff constraint. We will also consider that the consistency of C has been checked; thus M a matching which covers $X(C)$ in $CGV(C)$ is known.

First, for every variables x and y of $X(C)$, we have to ensure that if $\sigma(y)$ is removed from $D(x)$ then $\sigma(x)$ is also removed from $D(y)$. This can be easily done in $O(1)$ for each deletion.

From proposition 1 and by definition of arc consistency, we have:

Corollary 2 *A value a of a variable x is consistent with C if and only if the edge $\{x, \sigma(a)\}$ belongs to a matching that covers $X(C)$ in $CGV(C)$.*

Thus, the arc consistency of C is achieved by removing all the values (x, a) such that the edge $\{x, \sigma(a)\}$ does not belong to any matching that covers $X(C)$ in $CGV(C)$. Therefore, there is a simple algorithm achieving arc consistency: For each free edge $\{u, v\}$, we search for a matching in $CGV(C) - \{u, v\}$ that covers $X(C) - \{u, v\}$. If such a matching exists, then the edge $\{u, v\}$ belongs to a matching that covers $X(C)$; otherwise, it does not. To compute the matchings that cover $X(C) - \{u, v\}$ in $CGV(C) - \{u, v\}$, we start from $M - \{\{u, mate(u)\}, \{v, mate(v)\}\}$. So we need only $O([n/2 - (n/2 - 2)]m) = O(m)$ operations. Since there are m edges in $CGV(C)$, the complexity to achieve arc consistency is $O(m^2)$.

We can improve this complexity by using the following proposition which has been used for efficiently computing arc consistency in the classical alldiff constraint. This proposition, indeed, does not depend on whether the graph is bipartite or not.

Proposition 2 ([Berge, 1970]) *An edge belongs to some but not all maximum matchings, iff, for an arbitrary maximum matching, it belongs to either an even alternating path which begins at a free vertex, or an even alternating cycle.*

```
ArcConsistency(CGV(C), M)
  for each vertex x in CGV(C) do
    searchForEvenAlternatingCycle(x, CGV(C), M)
    for each edge {u, x} not marked valid do
      remove {u, x} from CGV(C)
      remove σ(u) from D(x) and σ(x) from D(u)
```

Algorithm 1: An arc consistency algorithm for a symmetric alldiff constraint.

M is a matching which covers $X(C)$; thus no vertex of $X(C)$ is free. Therefore, a value a of a variable x is consistent with C iff the edge $\{x, \sigma(a)\}$ belongs to an even alternating cycle. If the edge $\{x, \sigma(a)\}$ belongs to M, then the value a of x is consistent with C. Thus, the value a of x is not consistent with C if and only if the edge $\{x, \sigma(a)\}$ is free and if it does not belong to an alternating cycle. Such an alternating cycle is formed by an alternating path $[x, \sigma(a), ..., mate(x)]$ and the matched edge $\{mate(x), x\}$. Therefore the problem of the search for an alternating cycle is equivalent to the problem of the search for an alternating path from x to $mate(x)$ in $CVG - \{\{mate(x), x\}\}$.

We can give the algorithm achieving arc consistency. For each matching edge $\{u, v\}$ in $CGV(C)$, we search for an alternating path from u to v in $CGV(C) - \{\{v, u\}\}$, but we do not stop if we reach an edge with v as its extremity. If such an edge is reached, it is marked as "valid" and the algorithm continues as if the edge does not exist. When there are no more edges to study, the algorithm stops. All edges $\{v, y\}$ different from $\{v, u\}$ that are not marked valid cannot belong to an even alternating cycle. Afterwards, we apply the same reasoning by starting from v in order to identify the valid edges $\{x, u\}$. (See Algorithm 1.)

The problem which remains is the computation of alternating paths.

An alternating path from x to $mate(x)$ in $CGV(C) - \{\{mate(x), x\}\}$ can be found by applying the following procedure due to Edmonds. x is marked even; then we mark *even* a vertex reached from a matching edge, and *odd* a vertex reached from a free edge. Thus, from any even vertex u, we traverse the free edge having an extremity in u. And from any odd vertex v, we traverse the matching edge linked to v. Note that a vertex is even if it is at an even distance from the starting vertex and odd otherwise. This method works fine for a bipartite graph because there is no odd-length cycle, so a vertex marked even can never be reached from a vertex also marked even.

On nonbipartite graphs, there is a subtle difficulty: a vertex can appear on an alternating path in either parity. (See Figure 2.) Such an anomaly can occur only if G contains an alternating path p from a vertex s to an even vertex u and an edge from u to another even vertex w on p. The odd-length cycle formed by $\{u, w\}$ and the part of p from w to u is called a **blossom**. In Figure 2, $\{c, d, e, f, g\}$ form a blossom.

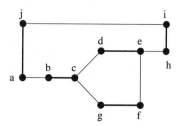

Figure 2: The problem with nonbipartite graphs. Suppose that we search whether $\{a, b\}$ belongs to an alternating cycle. $[a, b, c, d, e]$ marks e even, whereas $[a, b, c, g, f, e]$ marks e odd and h cannot be reached.

Edmonds proposed an algorithm that is able to deal with this difficulty. Since any vertex in a blossom can be reached from an alternating path from the base in either parity, it should be possible to traverse any free edge that has a vertex in the blossom if we do not want to miss an alternating path. As noted by Edmonds, this can be easily obtained by marking all the vertices of a blossom as even.

Algorithm 2 proposes an adaptation to our purpose of Edmonds's algorithm. Since Edmonds's algorithm cannot miss any alternating paths the arc consistency algorithm that we have proposed is exact.

Algorithm 2 traverses each edge at most twice, because the arc (u, w) is introduced in the list of arcs to study when u is marked even and a node is marked even only once. Moreover, when an arc is traversed it is removed from $ArcsToStudy$. Thus, the complexity of this algorithm depends on the functions belongToDifferentBlossom(u, v) and computeNewBlossom(u, v).

The function belongToDifferentBlossom(u, v) determine whether u and v belongs to different blossoms. If this function is true, then a new blossom is detected. The function computeNewBlossom(u, v) determines the nodes involved in the new blossom and updates internal data structures needed by the first function. Tarjan has proposed an efficient and beautiful implementation of them based on a union-find structure. We will not present it here because it is fully detailed in [Tarjan, 1983] p 121–122. This particular implementation leads to an algorithm in $O(m)$. Thus, we will consider that the complexity of Algorithm 2 is $O(m)$.

Therefore, the complexity of the arc consistency algorithm is $O(nm)$ because there are $2n$ calls to Algorithm 2. However, this algorithm is not incremental. In fact, each time arc consistency is achieved, it will be necessary to call a procedure $2n$ times in $O(m)$. For certain problems, this complexity can prevent this algorithm from being systematically used during the search for solutions. Thus, in the next section, we propose a filtering algorithm that does not necessarily ensure arc consistency, but it has a complexity that allows its systematic use during the search for solutions.

SEARCHFOREVENALTERNATINGCYCLE$(x, CGV(C), M)$
  // each edge $\{v, w\}$ is also represented by
  // two arcs (v, w) and (w, v)
  mark all vertices unreached
  mark all edges not traversed and not valid
  remove the matching edge $\{x, mate(x)\}$ from $CGV(C)$
  $ArcsToStudy \leftarrow \varnothing$
  mark $mate(x)$ even and add all arcs $(mate(x), w)$ in $ArcsToStudy$
  while $ArcsToStudy \neq \varnothing$ do
    pick (u, v) in $ArcsToStudy$ and remove it (u is even)
    mark $\{u, v\}$ traversed
    if $v = x$ then mark $\{u, v\}$ valid
    else
      if v *is unreached* then
        mark v odd, $mate(v)$ even and add all arcs $(mate(v), w)$ in $ArcsToStudy$
      if v *is even* and belongToDifferentBlossom(u, v) then
        // a new blossom is discovered
        $blossomNodes \leftarrow$ computeNewBlossom(u, v)
        for *each odd node* $o \in blossomNodes$ do
          mark o even
          add all arcs (o, w) in $ArcsToStudy$

Algorithm 2: A modification of the blossom-shrinking algorithm of Edmonds applied to search for even alternating cycles containing a vertex x.

3.2 Another filtering algorithm

Property 1 *Let $\{u, mate(u)\}$ be a matching edge. If $\{u, mate(u)\}$ is traversed by Algorithm 2, then all edges that belong to an even alternating cycle containing $\{u, mate(u)\}$ are also traversed by the algorithm.*

This property holds because Edmonds's algorithm cannot miss any alternating paths.

Proposition 3 *Let M be matching that covers $X(C)$ in $CGV(C)$. Then any free edge $\{u, v\}$ such that at least one of its ends is reached by Algorithm 2 and $\{u, v\}$ is not traversed by Algorithm 2 cannot belong to a maximum matching.*

proof: The ends of $\{u, v\}$ cannot be even; otherwise, this edge would have been traversed by Algorithm 2. Consider that v has been reached, then v is marked odd. The matching covers all the vertices and v is odd, thus the matching edge $\{mate(v), v\}$ has been traversed. v belongs to only one matching edge, so every alternating cycle containing $\{u, v\}$ contains also $\{mate(v), v\}$. Furthermore, by Property 1, all the edges that belong to an even alternating cycle containing $\{v, mate(v)\}$ are traversed by the algorithm. Hence, if $\{u, v\}$ is not traversed by the algorithm then $\{u, v\}$ does not belong to any maximum matching.

From this proposition, we propose a filtering algorithm. We choose any vertex x; then we apply Algorithm 2 to it. Each free edge $\{x, u\}$ which is not marked valid is removed. Then, each edge which satisfies Proposition 3 is also removed. If at least one edge is removed

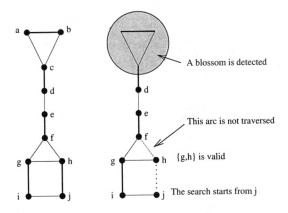

Figure 3: An example of the filtering algorithm for a symmetric alldiff constraint. The bold edges represent the matching edges. The edge $\{f,h\}$ is not traversed, so $\sigma(f)$ is removed from $D(h)$, and $\sigma(h)$ is removed from $D(f)$.

by the previous procedures, then we choose any other vertex that has not already been chosen, and we repeat the previous operation. If no edge is removed, we stop the algorithm. (See Figure 3.) If no deletion occurs, the complexity of the algorithm is $O(m)$, and for each deletion, the complexity of this algorithm is also $O(m)$. The advantage of this approach is that the complexity can be amortized for each deletion.

FILTERINGALGORITHM$(CGV(C), M)$
    $S \leftarrow X(C)$; $credit \leftarrow 1$
    do
        pick a vertex x in S and remove it
        $credit \leftarrow credit - 1$
        $searchForEvenAlternatingCycle(x, CGV(C), M)$
        for *each edge $\{u,x\}$ not marked valid* **do**
            remove $\{u,x\}$ from G
            remove $\sigma(u)$ from $D(x)$ and $\sigma(x)$ from $D(u)$
            $credit \leftarrow credit + 1$
        for *each not traversed free edge $\{u,v\}$ s.t. u or v has been reached* **do**
            remove $\{u,v\}$ from G
            remove $\sigma(u)$ from $D(v)$ and $\sigma(v)$ from $D(u)$
            $credit \leftarrow credit + 1$
    while $credit > 0$ **and** $S \neq \varnothing$

Algorithm 3: A filtering algorithm.

However, we can obtain a better amortization. Suppose that during one pass of the previous algorithm 10 edges are removed. Then, if the next 10 passes delete no edges, the amortized complexity will remain $O(m)$ per deletion. Algorithm 3 is a possible implementation of this idea.

This algorithm does not ensure arc consistency because Algorithm 2 traverses some edges that do not belong to an even alternating path.

In practice, this algorithm can also be improved by using some heuristics. It is important to take care about the possible creation of new connected components when some edges are removed. The previous algorithm can be independently applied to each connected component of the graph. On other hand, note that if $CGV(C)$ contains a connected component with an odd number of nodes, then there is no solution. This observation means that if there is a 2-connected component with an odd number of nodes and containing exactly one cutpoint of the graph[4], then this cutpoint cannot be matched with another node of the component. Similarly, if there is a 2-connected component with an even number of nodes and containing exactly one cutpoint of the graph, then this cutpoint cannot be matched with a node that does not belong to the 2-connected component. Such components can be identified easily in $O(m)$. Moreover, if a node in $CGV(C)$ has only two neighbors, then these two neighbors cannot be matched together. Furthermore, it is also interesting to use the classical alldiff constraint and arc consistency for this constraint.

4 Conclusion

In this paper we have presented the symmetric alldiff constraint. This constraint is present in many real-life applications. We have shown how arc consistency for this constraint can be achieved in $O(nm)$. We have also proposed a filtering algorithm that does not ensure arc consistency but has a complexity that can be used in practice because it can be amortized for each deletion ($O(m)$ per deletion).

References

[Berge, 1970] C. Berge. *Graphe et Hypergraphes*. Dunod, Paris, 1970.

[Bessière and Régin, 1997] C. Bessière and J-C. Régin. Arc consistency for general constraint networks: preliminary results. In *Proceedings of IJCAI'97*, pages 398–404, Nagoya, 1997.

[Edmonds, 1965] J. Edmonds. Path, trees, and flowers. *Can. J. Math.*, 17:449–467, 1965.

[Micali and Vazirani, 1980] S. Micali and V.V. Vazirani. An $O(\sqrt{|V|}|E|)$ algorithm for finding maximum matching in general graphs. In *Proceedings 21st FOCS*, pages 17–27, 1980.

[Régin, 1994] J-C. Régin. A filtering algorithm for constraints of difference in CSPs. In *Proceedings AAAI-94*, pages 362–367, Seattle, Washington, 1994.

[Simonis, 1996] H. Simonis. Problem classification scheme for finite domain constraint solving. In *CP96, Workshop on Constraint Programming Applications: An Inventory and Taxonomy*, pages 1–26, Cambridge, MA, USA, 1996.

[Tarjan, 1983] R.E. Tarjan. *Data Structures and Network Algorithms*. CBMS-NSF Regional Conference Series in Applied Mathematics, 1983.

---

[4] A cutpoint is a node whose deletion increases the number of connected components of the graph.

Branch and Bound with Mini-Bucket Heuristics

Kalev Kask and Rina Dechter

Department of Information and Computer Science
University of California, Irvine, CA 92697-3425
{kkask,dechter}@ics.uci.edu

Abstract

The paper describes a branch and bound scheme that uses heuristics generated mechanically by the mini-bucket approximation. This scheme is presented and evaluated for optimization tasks such as finding the Most Probable Explanation (*MPE*) in Bayesian networks. The mini-bucket scheme yields monotonic heuristics of varying strengths which cause different amounts of pruning, allowing a controlled tradeoff between preprocessing and search. The resulting Branch and Bound with Mini-Bucket heuristic (BBMB), is evaluated using random networks, probabilistic decoding and medical diagnosis networks. Results show that the BBMB scheme overcomes the memory explosion of bucket-elimination allowing a gradual tradeoff of space for time, and of time for accuracy.

1 Introduction

This paper proposes a new scheme for augmenting branch-and-bound search with heuristics generated automatically by the *Mini-Bucket* algorithms. Mini-bucket is a class of parameterized approximation algorithms based on the recently proposed bucket-elimination framework. The approximation uses a controlling parameter which allows adjustable levels of accuracy and efficiency [Dechter and Rish, 1997]. The algorithms were presented and analyzed for deterministic optimization tasks and probabilistic tasks, such as finding the most probable explanation (*MPE*), belief updating, and finding the maximum a posteriori hypothesis. Encouraging empirical results were reported for *MPE* on randomly generated noisy-or networks, on medical-diagnosis CPCS networks, and on coding problems [Rish *et al.*, 1998]. In some cases, however, the approximation was largely suboptimal, even when using the highest feasible accuracy level.

One way of improving the mini-bucket scheme is by embedding it in a general search algorithm. The intermediate functions created by the mini-bucket scheme can be interpreted as a heuristic evaluation function and used by any heuristic search algorithm. For instance, an upper bound on the probability of the best possible extension of any partial assignment in an MPE task can be derived. The tightness of these bounds can be controlled by the accuracy parameter of the mini-bucket scheme.

In this paper we evaluate this idea using Branch-and-Bound search which searches the space of partial assignments in a depth-first manner. It expands a partial assignment only if its upper-bounding heuristic estimate is larger than the currently known best lower bound. The virtue of branch-and-bound compared to best-first search, is that it requires a limited amount of memory and can be used as an anytime scheme - when interrupted, Branch-and-Bound outputs the best solution found so far. In [Kask and Dechter, 1999a] we apply this approach to Best-First search and compare the two schemes.

The resulting search algorithm, BBMB (Branch and Bound with Mini-Bucket heuristics) is evaluated and compared against other algorithms (such as bucket elimination, the mini-bucket scheme and iterative belief propagation), on a number of test problems, including coding networks, random networks, and CPCS networks. We show that the BBMB scheme is effective for a larger range of problems because of its gradual trade-off between preprocessing and search, and time and accuracy. Unlike bucket elimination, BBMB does not suffer from memory explosion and is often quicker to find an optimal solution. We investigated this approach for the optimization task of finding the *Most Probable Explanation* (MPE).

Section 3 presents an overview of the relevant algorithms. In Section 4 we describe our branch-and-bound scheme and its guiding heuristic function. Section 5 presents empirical evaluations, while Section 6 provides discussion and conclusions. For space reasons we omit all proofs. For more details see [Kask and Dechter, 1999a].

1.1 Related work

MPE appears in applications such as medical diagnosis, circuit diagnosis, natural language understanding and probabilistic decoding. For example, given data on clinical findings, MPE can postulate on a patient's probable affliction. In decoding, the task is to identify the most likely input message transmitted over a noisy channel

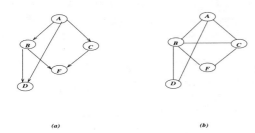

(a)   (b)

Figure 1: belief network $P(f,d,c,b,a) = P(f|c,b)P(d|b,a)\,P(b|a)P(c|a)$

given the observed output. Researchers in natural language consider the understanding of text to consist of finding the most likely facts (in internal representation) that explains the existence of the given text. In computer vision and image understanding, researchers formulate the problem in terms of finding the most likely set of objects that explains the image. Scientific theories are models that attempt to fit the given observations, and so on.

It is known that solving the MPE task is NP-hard. Complete algorithms for MPE use either the *cycle cutset* technique or the *join-tree-clustering* [Pearl, 1988] and the bucket-elimination scheme [Dechter, 1996]. However, these methods work well only if the network is sparse enough to allow small cutsets or small clusters. Following Pearl's stochastic simulation algorithms for the MPE task [Pearl, 1988], the suitability of Stochastic Local Search (SLS) algorithms for MPE was studied in the context of Medical diagnosis applications [Peng and Reggia, 1986], [Peng and Reggia, 1989] and more recently in [Kask and Dechter, 1999b]. Best first search algorithms were also proposed [Shimony and Charniak, 1991] as well as algorithms based on linear programming [Santos, 1991].

2 Background

2.1 Notation and definitions

Belief Networks provide a formalism for reasoning about partial beliefs under conditions of uncertainty. They are defined by a directed acyclic graph over nodes representing random variables of interest.

DEFINITION **2.1 (Belief Networks)** *Given a set,* $X = \{X_1, \ldots, X_n\}$ *of random variables over multivalued domains* $D_1, \ldots, D_n$, *a belief network is a pair* (G, P) *where* G *is a directed acyclic graph and* $P = \{P_i\}$. $P_i = \{P(X_i \mid pa(X_i))\}$ *are conditional probability matrices associated with* X_i. *The set* $pa(X_i)$ *is called the parent set of* X_i. *An assignment* $(X_1 = x_1, \ldots, X_n = x_n)$ *can be abbreviated to* $x = (x_1, \ldots, x_n)$. *The BN represents a probability distribution* $P(x_1, \ldots, x_n) = \Pi_{i=1}^n P(x_i \mid x_{pa(X_i)})$, *where,* x_S *is the projection of* x *over a subset* S. *An evidence set* e *is an instantiated subset of variables. The argument set of a function* h *is denoted* $S(h)$.

DEFINITION **2.2 (Most Probable Explanation)** *Given a belief network and evidence e, the Most Probable Explanation (MPE) task is to find an assignment* $(x_1^o, \ldots, x_n^o)$ *such that*

$$P(x_1^o, \ldots, x_n^o) = max_{X_1, \ldots, X_n} \prod_{k=1}^{n} P(X_k \mid pa(X_k), e)$$

DEFINITION **2.3 (graph concepts)** *An ordered graph is a pair* (G, d) *where* G *is an undirected graph and* $d = X_1, \ldots, X_n$ *is an ordering of the nodes. The* width *of a node in an ordered graph is the number of its earlier neighbors. The* width w(d) *of an ordering* d, *is the maximum width over all nodes. The induced width of an ordered graph,* $w^*(d)$, *is the width of the induced ordered graph obtained by processing the nodes recursively, from last to first; when node* X *is processed, all its earlier neighbors are connected. The* moral graph *of a directed graph* G *is the undirected graph obtained by connecting the parents of all the nodes in* G *and then removing the arrows. An example of a belief network is given in Figure 1a, and its moral graph in Figure 1b.*

2.2 Bucket and mini-bucket algorithms

Bucket elimination is a unifying algorithmic framework for dynamic-programming algorithms applicable to probabilistic and deterministic reasoning [Dechter, 1996]. The input to a bucket-elimination algorithm consists of a collection of functions or relations (e.g., clauses for propositional satisfiability, constraints, or conditional probability matrices for belief networks). Given a variable ordering, the algorithm partitions the functions into buckets, each placed in the bucket of its latest argument in the ordering. The algorithm has two phases. During the first, top-down phase, it processes each bucket, from the last variable to the first by a variable elimination procedure that computes a new function, placed in a lower bucket. For MPE, this procedure computes a product of all probability matrices in the bucket and maximizes over the bucket's variable. During the second, bottom-up phase, the algorithm constructs a solution by assigning a value to each variable along the ordering, consulting the functions created during the top-down phase.

THEOREM **2.1** *[Dechter, 1996] The time and space complexity of Elim-MPE, the bucket elimination algorithm for MPE, are exponential in the induced width* $w^*(d)$ *of the network's ordered moral graph along ordering* d. $\square$

The *Mini-bucket elimination* is an approximation scheme designed to avoid the space and time problems of full bucket elimination. In each bucket, all the functions are first partitioned into smaller subsets called mini-buckets which are then processed independently. Here is the rationale. Let $h_1, \ldots, h_j$ be the functions in $bucket_p$. When *Elim-MPE* processes $bucket_p$, it computes the function h^p: $h^p = max_{X_p} \Pi_{i=1}^j h_i$. The mini-bucket algorithm, on the other hand, creates a partitioning $Ql = \{Q_1, \ldots, Q_r\}$ where the mini-bucket Q_l contains the functions $h_{l_1}, \ldots, h_{l_k}$. The approximation will compute $g^p = \Pi_{l=1}^r max_{X_p} \Pi_{l_i} h_{l_i}$. Clearly, $h^p \leq g^p$. Thus,

Algorithm Approx-MPE(i) (MB(i))
Input: A belief network $BN = \{P_1, ..., P_n\}$; ordering d;
Output: An upper bound on the MPE, an assignment and the set of ordered augmented buckets.
1. **Initialize:** Partition matrices into buckets. Let $S_1, ..., S_j$ be the subset of variables in $bucket_p$ on which matrices (old or new) are defined.
2. **(Backward)** For $p \leftarrow n$ downto 1, do
• If $bucket_p$ contains $X_p = x_p$, assign $X_p = x_p$ to each h_i and put each in appropriate bucket.
• else, for $h_1, h_2, ..., h_j$ in $bucket_p$, generate an (i)-partitioning, $Q' = \{Q_1, ..., Q_r\}$. For each $Q_l \in Q'$ containing $h_{l_1}, ... h_{l_t}$ generate function h^l, $h^l = max_{X_p} \Pi_{i=1}^{t} h_{l_i}$. Add h^l to the bucket of the largest-index variable in $U_l \leftarrow \bigcup_{i=1}^{j} S(h_{l_i}) - \{X_p\}$.
3. **(Forward)** For $i = 1$ to n do, given $x_1, ..., x_{p-1}$ choose a value x_p of X_p that maximizes the product of all the functions in X_p's bucket.
4. Output the ordered set of augmented buckets, an upper bound and a lower bound assignment.

Figure 2: algorithm *Approx-MPE(i)*

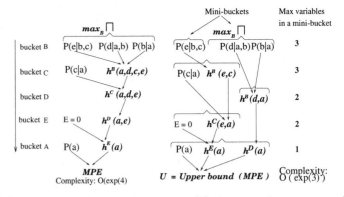

(a) A trace of *Elim-MPE*   (b) A trace of *approx-mpe(3)*.

Figure 3: (a) Algorithm *approx-mpe(i,m)* and (b) a trace of the algorithm's execution.

the algorithm computes an upper bound on the probability of the MPE assignment. Subsequently, in its second phase, the algorithm computes an assignment that provides a lower bound. The quality of the upper bound depends on the degree of the partitioning into mini-buckets. Given a bound parameter i, the algorithm creates an i-partitioning, where each mini-bucket includes no more than i variables. Algorithm *Approx-MPE(i)* (sometimes called MB(i)) is described in Figure 2. The algorithm outputs not only an upper bound on the MPE and an assignment (whose probability yields a lower bound), but also the collection of augmented buckets. By comparing the upper bound to the lower bound we can always have a bound on the error for the given instance.

THEOREM 2.2 *[Dechter and Rish, 1997] Algorithm Approx-MPE(i) generates an upper bound on the exact MPE and its time and space complexity is $O(exp(i))$.*

When the bound i is large enough (i.e. when $i \geq w^*$), the algorithm coincides with full bucket elimination.

Example 2.3 *Figure 3(b) illustrates how algorithms Elim-MPE and Approx-MPE(i) for $i = 3$ process the network in Figure 1(a) along the ordering (A, E, D, C, B). Elim-MPE records new functions $h^B(a, d, c, e)$, $h^C(a, d, e)$, $h^D(a, e)$, and $h^E(a)$ during its backwards phase. Then, in the bucket of A, it computes MPE $= max_a P(a) h^E(a)$. Subsequently, an MPE assignment $(A = a', B = b', C = c', D = d', E = 0)$ ($E = 0$ is an evidence) is computed by maximizing the product functions in each bucket. Namely, $a' = \arg \max_a P(a) h^E(a)$, $e' = 0$, $d' = \arg \max_d h^C(a', d, e = 0)$, and so on. The approximation Approx-MPE(3) splits bucket B into two mini-buckets each containing no more than 3 variables, and generates $h^B(e, c)$ and $h^B(d, a)$. An upper bound U on the MPE value is computed in A's bucket, $U = max_a P(a) \cdot h^E(a) \cdot h^D(a)$. A suboptimal MPE tuple*

is computed by assigning a value to each variable that maximizes the product of functions in the corresponding bucket, given the values of preceding variables.

3 Heuristic Search with Mini-Bucket

3.1 Notation

Given an ordered set of augmented buckets generated by the mini-bucket algorithm along $d = X_1, ..., X_n$, we use the following convention

• P_{p_j} denotes an input conditional probability matrices placed in bucket p, (namely, its highest-ordered variable is X_p).

• h_{p_j} denotes an arbitrary function in bucket p generated by the mini-bucket algorithm.

• h_j^p denotes a function created by the j-th mini-bucket in bucket p.

• λ_{p_j} denotes an arbitrary function in bucket p.

We denote by $buckets(1..p)$ the union of all functions in the bucket of X_1 through the bucket of X_p. Remember that $S(f)$ denotes the set of arguments of function f.

3.2 The idea

We will now show that the new functions recorded by the mini-bucket algorithm can be used to express upper bounds on the most probable extension of any partial assignment. Therefore, they can serve as heuristics in an evaluation function which guides either a *best-first search* or a *branch-and-bound search*.

DEFINITION 3.1 (**Exact Evaluation Function**)
Let $\bar{x} = \bar{x}^p = (x_1, ..., x_p)$. The probability of the most probable extension of $\bar{x}^p$, denoted $f^*(\bar{x}^p)$ is:

$$max_{\{X_{p+1}, ..., X_n | X_i = x_i, \ \forall i, \ 1 \leq i \leq p\}} \prod_{k=1}^{n} P(X_k \mid pa(X_k), e)$$

The above product defining f^* can be divided into two smaller products expressed by the functions in the ordered augmented buckets. In the first product all the arguments are instantiated, and therefore the maximization operation is applied to the second product only. Denoting

$$g(\bar{x}) = \prod_{P_i \in \ buckets(1..p)} P_i(\bar{x}_{S(P_i)})$$

and

$$H^*(\bar{x}) = max_{\{X_{p+1},...,X_n | X_i = x_i, \ \forall \ 1 \le i \le p\}} \prod_{P_i \in buckets(p+1..n)} P_i,$$

we get

$$f^*(\bar{x}) = g(\bar{x}) \cdot H^*(\bar{x})$$

During search, the g function can be evaluated over the partial assignment $\bar{x}^p$, while H^* can be estimated by a heuristic function. Our first proposal is to estimate $H^*(\bar{x}^p)$ by a function $H_1 = \prod_j h_{p_j}$ which is the product of all h functions generated by the mini-bucket algorithm which reside in bucket p. It can be shown, using properties of mini-bucket scheme, that this product indeed provides an upper bound on H^*, yielding an *admissible* heuristic.

However, the heuristic function H_1 is non-monotonic. In fact, even if provided with augmented buckets that are generated by exact full bucket elimination, this heuristic may still be nonmonotonic. A heuristic function is *monotonic* if the evaluation function along any path in the search tree is not increasing.

We next modify H_1 to make it monotone and more accurate. The *modified* heuristic function H_2 adds to the product of H_1 all those h functions in buckets(1..p-1) that were generated in buckets processed before bucket p. The rationale is that some conditional probability matrices in H^* are approximated by h functions that are placed below bucket p (because they are not defined over X_p).

DEFINITION **3.2** *Given an ordered set of augmented buckets, the heuristic function $H_2(\bar{x}^p)$, is the product of all the h functions that satisfy the following two properties: 1) They are generated in buckets $(p+1,...,n)$, and 2) They reside in buckets 1 through p. Namely, $H_2(\bar{x}^p) = \prod_{i=1}^{p} \prod_{h_j^k \in bucket_i} h_j^k$, where $k > p$, (i.e. h_j^k is generated by a bucket processed before bucket p.)*

THEOREM **3.1** (Mini-Bucket Heuristic) *For every partial assignment $\bar{x} = \bar{x}^p = (x_1,...,x_p)$, of the first p variables, the evaluation function $f(\bar{x}^p) = g(\bar{x}^p) \cdot H_2(\bar{x}^p)$ is: 1) Admissible - it never underestimates the probability of the best extension of $\bar{x}^p$. 2) Monotonic, namely $f(\bar{x}^{p+1})/f(\bar{x}^p) \le 1$.* □

The following proposition shows how $g(\bar{x}^{p+1})$ and $H(\bar{x}^{p+1})$ can be updated recursively based on $g(\bar{x}^p)$ and $H(\bar{x}^p)$ and functions residing in bucket $p+1$. (From now on we will use H to mean H_2.)

Proposition 1 *Given a partial assignment $\bar{x}^p = (x_1,...x_p)$, both $g(\bar{x}^p)$ and $H(\bar{x}^p)$ can be computed recursively by*

$$g(\bar{x}^p) = g(\bar{x}^{p-1}) \cdot \Pi_j P_{p_j}(\bar{x}^p_{S(P_{p_j})}) \qquad (1)$$

Algorithm BBMB(i)
Input: A belief network $BN = \{P_1,...,P_n\}$; ordering d.
Output: An MPE assignment, or a lower bound and an upper-bound on the MPE.
1. **Initialize:** Run MB(i) algorithm which generates a set of ordered augmented buckets and an upper-bound on MPE. Set lower bound L to 0. Set current variable index p to 0.
2. **Search:** Execute the following procedure until variable X_1 has no legal values left.
• **Expand:** Given a partial instantiation $\bar{x}^p$, compute all partial assignments $\bar{x}^{p+1} = (\bar{x}^p, v)$ for each value v of X_{p+1}. For each node $\bar{x}^{p+1}$ compute its heuristic value $f(\bar{x}^{p+1}) = g(\bar{x}^{p+1}) \cdot H(\bar{x}^{p+1})$ using $g(\bar{x}^{p+1}) = g(\bar{x}^p) \cdot \Pi_j P_{p+1_j}$ and $H(\bar{x}^{p+1}) = H(\bar{x}^p) \cdot \Pi_k h_{p+1_k}/\Pi_j h_j^{p+1}$. Prune those assignments $\bar{x}^{p+1}$ for which $f(\bar{x}^{p+1})$ is smaller than the lower bound L.
• **Forward:** If X_{p+1} has no legal values left, goto Backtrack. Otherwise let $\bar{x}^{p+1} = (\bar{x}^p, v)$ be the best extension to $\bar{x}^p$ according to f. If $p+1 = n$, then set $L = f(\bar{x}^{p+1})$ and goto Backtrack. Otherwise remove v from the list of legal values. Set $p = p+1$ and goto Expand.
• **Backtrack:** If p = 1, Exit. Otherwise set $p = p-1$ and repeat the Forward step.

Figure 4: Algorithm *BBMB(i)*

$$H(\bar{x}^p) = H(\bar{x}^{p-1}) \cdot \Pi_k h_{p_k}/\Pi_j h_j^p \qquad (2)$$

3.3 Search with Mini-Bucket Heuristics

The tightness of the upper bound generated by the mini-bucket approximation depends on its i-bound. Larger values of i yield better upper-bounds, but require more computation. Therefore, Branch-and-Bound search, if parameterized by i, allows a controllable tradeoff between preprocessing and search, or between heuristic strength and its overhead.

In Figure 4 we present algorithm BBMB(i). This algorithm is initialized by running the mini-bucket algorithm, producing the set of ordered augmented buckets. It then traverses the search space in a depth-first manner, instantiating variables from first to last. Throughout the search, the algorithm maintains a lower bound on the probability of the MPE assignment, which corresponds to the probability of the best full variable instantiation found thus far. It uses the heuristic evaluation function $f(\bar{x}^p)$ to prune the search space. Search terminates when it reaches a time-bound or when the first variable has no values left. In the latter case, the algorithm has found an optimal solution.

The heuristic function generated by the mini-bucket approximation can also be used to guide any A* type algorithm. For a description of *Best-First* search with mini-bucket heuristics see [Kask and Dechter, 1999a].

4 Experimental Methodology

We tested the performance of our scheme on sev-

N C,P,K	Elim MPE #[time] w^*	opt	MB / BBMB i=2 #[time]	MB / BBMB i=4 #[time]	MB / BBMB i=6 #[time]	MB / BBMB i=8 #[time]	MB / BBMB i=10 #[time]	MB / BBMB i=12 #[time]	MB / BBMB i=14 #[time]
256 100,2,2	91[4.91] 14.6	>0.95	14[0.03] 89[6.30]	30[0.03] 100[1.04]	44[0.04] 100[0.21]	**50[0.07]** 100[0.13]	63[0.15] 100[0.18]	68[0.40] 100[0.45]	81[1.20] 100[1.28]
256 105,2,2	69[7.11] 15.8	>0.95	6[0.03] 83[8.86]	20[0.03] 99[1.38]	29[0.04] 100[0.69]	**42[0.08]** 100[0.19]	47[0.17] 100[0.26]	67[0.49] 100[0.52]	75[1.54] 100[1.63]
256 110,2,2	41[9.06] 17.5	>0.95	8[0.04] 77[14.1]	15[0.03] 100[3.68]	23[0.04] 99[1.07]	33[0.08] 100[0.41]	**47[0.18]** 100[0.35]	55[0.57] 100[0.70]	67[1.85] 100[1.98]
256 115,2,2	17[12.3] 19.1	>0.95	6[0.03] 71[17.5]	10[0.03] 98[5.74]	16[0.05] 100[1.78]	22[0.09] 100[0.85]	**43[0.21]** 100[0.71]	37[0.66] 100[0.84]	51[2.17] 100[2.34]
256 120,2,2	11[9.99] 20.3	>0.95	4[0.04] 57[20.4]	10[0.04] 95[6.50]	10[0.05] 97[2.60]	29[0.08] 100[1.96]	**30[0.22]** 100[0.97]	39[0.66] 100[1.00]	53[2.10] 100[2.35]
256 125,2,2	2[21.1] 22.4	>0.95	2[0.03] 49[21.5]	8[0.04] 86[9.44]	9[0.05] 95[4.79]	21[0.09] 96[2.17]	28[0.25] 100[1.62]	**35[0.78]** 100[1.52]	35[2.50] 100[3.34]

Table 1: Random MPE. Time bound 30 sec. 100 samples.

eral types of networks. On each problem instance we ran bucket elimination (Elim-MPE), mini-bucket approximation with various i-bounds (MB(i)) and branch and bound with some levels of mini-bucket heuristics (BBMB(i)).

The main measure of performance of the approximation algorithm given a fixed time bound, is the accuracy ratio $opt = P_{alg}/P_{MPE}$ between the probability of the solution found by the test algorithm (P_{alg}) and the probability of the optimal solution (P_{MPE}), whenever P_{MPE} is available. We also record the running time of each algorithm.

We report the distribution of problems with respect to 5 predefined ranges of accuracy : $opt \geq 0.95$, $opt \geq 0.5$, $opt \geq 0.2$, $opt \geq 0.01$ and $opt < 0.01$. We recorded the number of problems that Elim-MPE solved as well as the average induced width w^* of the test problems. Because of space restrictions in most cases we report only the number of problems that fall in the highest accuracy range $opt \geq 0.95$. However, since most problems were solved by BBMB optimally, we lose only minimal information.

In addition, during the execution of BBMB we also stored the current lower bound L at regular time intervals. Comparing the lower bound against the optimal solution, allows reporting the accuracy of BBMB as a function of time.

4.1 Random Bayesian Networks and Noisy-OR Networks

Random Bayesian networks and Noisy-OR networks were randomly generated using parameters (N, K, C, P), where N is the number of variables, K is their domain size, C is the number of conditional probability matrices and P is the number of parents in each conditional probability matrix.

The structure of each test problem is created by randomly picking C variables out of N and for each, randomly selecting P parents from preceding variables, relative to some ordering. For random Bayesian networks, each probability table is generated randomly. For Noisy-OR networks, each probability table represents an OR-function with a given noise and leak probabilities :
$P(X = 0|Y_1, ..., Y_P) = P_{leak} \times \Pi_{Y_i=1} P_{noise}$.

Tables 1 and 2 present results of experiments with random Bayesian networks and Noisy-OR networks respectively. In each table, parameters N, K and P are fixed, while C, controlling network's sparseness, is changing. For each C, we generate 100 problem instances. Each entry in the table reports the number of instances that fall in a specific range of accuracy, as well as the average running time of each algorithm (note that BBMB time includes the preprocessing time by MB).

For example, Table 1 reports the results with random problems having N=256, K=2, P=2. There are 5 horizontal blocks, each corresponding to a different value of C. Each block has two rows, one for MB and one for BBMB, reporting the number of problems in accuracy range of 0.95 and the average running time.

The second column reports the results of Elim-MPE, namely the number of instances it solved, their average w^* and running time. The rest of the columns report results of MB and BBMB for various levels of i. Looking at the first line in Table 1 we see that in the best accuracy range, $opt \geq 0.95$, MB with $i = 2$ solved only 14 problems using 0.03 seconds on the average. BBMB with $i = 2$ solved 89 instances in this range while using 6.30 seconds on the average. Note that Elim-MPE on the other hand solved 91 instances using much more time than BBMB with any i-bound.

Each row demonstrates a tradeoff between preprocessing by MB and subsequent search by BBMB. As expected, MB can solve more instances as i increases while its average time increases. At the same time, the search time of BBMB decreases as i increases. We observe that the total BBMB time improves when i increases until a threshold point and then worsens. We have highlighted the best performance point in each row. Below this threshold, the heuristic function is weak, resulting in long search. Above the threshold, the extra preprocessing is not cost effective. As problems become harder BBMB achieves its best performance at higher thresholds. For example, when C is 100 and 105, the threshold is $i = 8$, when C is 110, 115 and 120, it is $i = 10$, and when C is 125, it is $i = 12$.

Table 2 reporting on Noisy-OR shows similar results (based on $opt \geq 0.95$ range). On this class BBMB is very effective and solved all problems exactly, while Elim-

N C,P	Elim MPE #[time] w^*	opt	MB / BBMB i=2 #[time]	MB / BBMB i=6 #[time]	MB / BBMB i=10 #[time]	MB / BBMB i=14 #[time]
128 90,2	6[10.9] 20.4	>0.95	31[0.04] 100[0.54]	**42[0.05]** 100[0.11]	49[0.22] 100[0.25]	71[2.22] 100[2.22]
128 95,2	1[7.67] 21.5	>0.95	26[0.02] 99[0.78]	**36[0.04]** 100[0.11]	44[0.22] 100[0.27]	59[2.45] 100[2.46]
128 100,2	0[-] 23.6	>0.95	10[0.05] 98[1.01]	**26[0.06]** 100[0.25]	44[0.27] 100[0.33]	57[2.77] 100[2.79]
128 105,2	0[-] 24.7	>0.95	16[0.03] 99[2.18]	29[0.04] 100[0.45]	**38[0.26]** 100[0.37]	48[3.17] 100[3.20]

Table 2: Noisy-OR MPE. Noise 0.2, Leak 0.01. Time bound 30 sec. 100 samples. 10 evidence.

MPE solved almost none. For $i \geq 6$ BBMB can solve all 100 instances, with threshold $i = 6$.

In Figures 5 and 6 we provide an alternative view of the performance of BBMB(i). Let $F_{BBMB(i)}(t)$ be the fraction of the problems solved completely by BBMB(i) by time t. Each graph in Figures 5 and 6 plots $F_{BBMB(i)}(t)$ for some specific value i. Figure 5 shows the distribution of $F_{BBMB(i)}(t)$ for random Bayesian networks when N=256, C=125, K=2 and P=2 (corresponding to the last row in Table 1), whereas Figure 6 shows the distribution of $F_{BBMB(i)}(t)$ for Noisy-OR networks when N=128, C=95 and P=2 (corresponding to the second row in Table 2).

Figures 5 and 6 display a trade-off between preprocessing and search. Clearly, if $F_{BBMB(i)}(t) > F_{BBMB(j)}(t)$, then $F_{BBMB(i)}(t)$ completely dominates $F_{BBMB(j)}(t)$. For example, in Figure 5 BBMB(10) completely dominates BBMB(6). When $F_{BBMB(i)}(t)$ and $F_{BBMB(j)}(t)$ intersect, they display a trade-off as a function of time. For example, if we have only few seconds, BBMB(6) is better than BBMB(14). However, when sufficient time is allowed, BBMB(14) is superior to BBMB(6).

The same pattern appears in Figure 6. BBMB(6) completely dominates BBMB(2), while there is a trade-off between BBMB(2) and BBMB(14) depending on the amount of time allowed.

4.2 Random Coding Networks

Our random coding networks fall within the class of *linear block codes*. They can be represented as four-layer belief networks (Figure 7). The second and third layers correspond to input information bits and parity check bits respectively. Each parity check bit represents an XOR function of input bits u_i. Input and parity check nodes are binary while the output nodes are real-valued. In our experiments each layer has the same number of nodes because we use code rate of R=K/N=1/2, where K is the number of input bits and N is the number of transmitted bits.

Given a number of input bits K, number of parents P for each XOR bit and channel noise variance σ^2, a coding network structure is generated by randomly picking parents for each XOR node. Then we simulate an input signal by assuming a uniform random distribution of information bits, compute the corresponding values of the parity check bits, and generate an assignment to

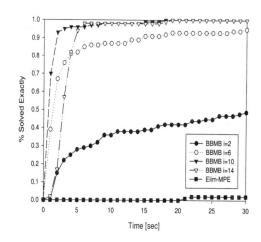

Figure 5: Random Bayesian. N=256, C=125, K=2, P=2. 100 samples.

N=100 K=50 σ	opt	MB / BBMB i=6	MB / BBMB i=10	MB / BBMB i=14	IBP
0.22	>0.95	1727[0.06] 1998[0.13]	1830[0.40] 2000[0.42]	**1936[4.54]** 2000[4.55]	2000 [0.08]
0.28	>0.95	1081[0.08] 1977[0.75]	1306[0.38] 1996[0.69]	1627[4.55] 1999[4.63]	1996 [0.08]
0.32	>0.95	660[0.08] 1908[1.77]	899[0.39] 1972[1.28]	1247[4.54] 1990[4.82]	1993 [0.08]
0.40	>0.95	172[0.06] 1522[6.19]	272[0.37] 1779[4.24]	450[4.46] 1900[6.51]	1741 [0.08]
0.51	>0.95	21[0.06] 811[17.0]	35[0.37] 1175[13.4]	84[4.41] 1435[11.9]	616 [0.08]

Table 3: Random coding. Time 30 sec. 2000 samples.

the output nodes by adding Gaussian noise to each information and parity check bit. The decoding algorithm takes as input the coding network and the observed real-valued output assignment and recovers the original input bitvector by computing or approximating an MPE assignment.

We tested two sets of random coding networks - K=50 and K=100 input bits. Table 3 reports results on random coding networks having K=50. In addition to Elim-MPE and BBMB, we also ran Iterative Belief Propagation (IBP) which was recently observed as the best performing decoding algorithm. It is identical to iterative application of Pearl's belief updating on tree-like networks [Pearl, 1988]. For each σ we generated and tested 2000 samples divided into 200 different networks each simulated with 10 different input bit vectors.

In Table 3 we observe a familiar pattern of preprocessing-search tradeoff. For each level of noise σ there is an empirical optimal i balancing preprocessing cost and search. For $\sigma = 0.22$ the threshold is 6. As noise increases, the threshold increases. Also, as noise increases, the role of search becomes more significant. Although IBP is superior (because it is faster) for small

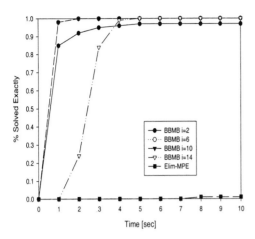

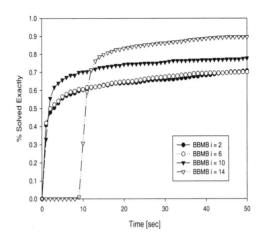

Figure 6: Noisy-OR. N=128, C=95, P=2. 100 samples.

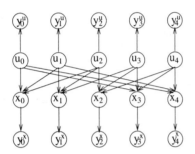

Figure 7: Belief network for structured (10,5) block code with parent set size P=3

noise, it has a shortcoming for high noise levels since its performance cannot be improved with extra time while BBMB can.

Table 4 reports the Bit Error Rate (BER) for MB/BBMB(14) and IBP. BER is a standard measure used in the coding literature denoting the fraction of input bits that were decoded incorrectly. When compared using BER, IBP is about the same as BBMB(14) when the noise is small, but slightly better when the noise is large.

Figure 8 shows the distribution of $F_{BBMB(i)}(t)$ for Random Coding networks when K=100 and $\sigma = 0.28$. We observe that no algorithm completely dominates any other algorithm. However, we can see a trade-off depend-

σ	MB / BBMB i = 14	IBP
0.22	0.0012/0.00024	0.00024
0.28	0.010/0.0015	0.0015
0.32	0.025/0.0041	0.0034
0.40	0.090/0.021	0.016
0.51	0.184/0.102	0.084

Table 4: Random coding BER.

Figure 8: BBMB Random Coding. K=100, $\sigma = 0.28$. 500 samples.

ing on the time available. When the time allowed is small (less then 10 seconds), BBMB(i) with i less than 14 is better. However, when more time is allowed, BBMB(14) is clearly superior.

4.3 CPCS Networks

As another realistic domain, we used the CPCS networks derived from the Computer-Based Patient Care Simulation system, and based on INTERNIST-1 and Quick Medical Reference expert systems [Pradhan et al., 1994]. The nodes in CPCS networks correspond to diseases and findings. Representing it as a belief network requires some simplifying assumptions, 1) conditional independence of findings given diseases, 2) noisy-OR dependencies between diseases and findings, and 3) marginal independencies of diseases. For details see [Pradhan et al., 1994].

In Table 5 we have results of experiments with two binary CPCS networks, cpcs360b (N = 360, C = 335) and cpcs422b (N = 422, C = 348), with 1000 and 150 instances respectively. Each instance had 10 evidence nodes picked randomly.

Since cpcs360b network is solved quite effectively by MB we see that BBMB added search time is small, serving primarily to prove the optimality of the MB solution. On the other hand, on cpcs422b MB can solve a third of the instances accurately when i is small, and more as i increases. BBMB can solve all instances accurately for $i \geq 12$ when search takes little additional time.

5 Discussion and Conclusion

Our experiments demonstrate that combining branch-and-bound with mini-bucket heuristics (BBMB) provides a powerful method of attacking optimization problems such as the MPE.

CPCS360b 1000 samples	MB / BBMB i=4	MB / BBMB i=8	MB / BBMB i=12	MB / BBMB i=16
>0.95	939[0.94] 1000[0.96]	950[0.96] 1000[0.97]	983[2.04] 1000[2.04]	991[16.4] 1000[16.4]
>0.50	13[0.94] 0[-]	8[0.96] 0[-]	6[2.01] 0[-]	6[16.1] 0[-]
>0.20	44[0.95] 0[-]	38[0.97] 0[-]	11[2.03] 0[-]	3[16.6] 0[-]
>0.01	4[0.94] 0[-]	4[0.96] 0[-]	0[-] 0[-]	0[-] 0[-]
<0.01	0[-] 0[-]	0[-] 0[-]	0[-] 0[-]	0[-] 0[-]

CPCS422b 150 samples	MB / BBMB i=4	MB / BBMB i=8	MB / BBMB i=12	MB / BBMB i=16
>0.95	56[23.1] 144[25.5]	67[23.1] 148[24.5]	78[23.2] 150[23.4]	98[39.9] 150[40.0]
>0.50	14[22.9] 1[45.0]	8[22.9] 0[-]	19[23.4] 0[-]	22[40.1] 0[-]
>0.20	12[23.0] 0[-]	16[22.9] 0[-]	23[23.4] 0[-]	17[40.1] 0[-]
>0.01	34[23.1] 2[45.0]	27[23.1] 2[45.0]	15[23.2] 0[-]	8[40.0] 0[-]
<0.01	34[23.1] 3[45.0]	32[22.9] 0[-]	15[23.0] 0[-]	5[40.0] 0[-]

Table 5: CPCS networks. Time 30 and 45 resp.

On the one hand it avoids the storage bottleneck of full bucket elimination while frequently solving problems optimally. On the other hand, it improves output quality substantially over the mini-bucket approximation, especially when the former is highly suboptimal. However, the most important feature of BBMB is the ability to control the balance between preprocessing (for heuristic generation) and search, using its bounding parameter i. Pure search (low i) and pure bucket-elimination (high i) are two extremes ends of that spectrum.

In all our experiments, including random Bayesian networks, Noisy-OR networks, coding networks and medical diagnosis CPCS networks, we observed that optimal performance (measured by time within a certain accuracy range) occurred at an intermediate threshold point of i. Weaker heuristics, lying below the threshold, and stronger heuristics, lying above the threshold, were less cost-effective. We also observed that as problems grew harder, stronger heuristics became more cost-effective. The control of the gradual change of space-time-accuracy tradeoff of BBMB now makes a larger set of problem solvable.

Although the best threshold point may not be predictable for every problem instance, a preliminary empirical analysis can be informative when given a class of problems that is not too heterogeneous.

We have also tested the mini-bucket heuristic function with Best-First search. We found that if we are interested in the optimal solution only, BFMB(i) is often significantly faster than BBMB(i) when given sufficient time and space. However, unlike BBMB, BFMB is not an anytime algorithm [Kask and Dechter, 1999a].

References

[Dechter and Rish, 1997] R. Dechter and I. Rish. A scheme for approximating probabilistic inference. In *Proceedings of Uncertainty in Artificial Intelligence (UAI97)*, pages 132–141, 1997.

[Dechter, 1996] R. Dechter. Bucket elimination: A unifying framework for probabilistic inference algorithms. In *Uncertainty in Artificial Intelligence (UAI-96)*, pages 211–219, 1996.

[Kask and Dechter, 1999a] K. Kask and R. Dechter. On the power of mini-bucket heuristics for improved search. *UCI Technical report*, 1999.

[Kask and Dechter, 1999b] K. Kask and R. Dechter. Stochastic local search for bayesian networks. In *Workshop on AI and Statistics (AISTAT99)*, 1999.

[Pearl, 1988] J. Pearl. *Probabilistic Reasoning in Intelligent Systems*. Morgan Kaufmann, 1988.

[Peng and Reggia, 1986] Y. Peng and J.A. Reggia. Plausability of diagnostic hypothesis. In *National Conference on Artificial Intelligence (AAAI86)*, pages 140–145, 1986.

[Peng and Reggia, 1989] Y. Peng and J.A. Reggia. A connectionist model for diagnostic problem solving. *IEEE Transactions on Systems, Man and Cybernetics*, 1989.

[Pradhan et al., 1994] M. Pradhan, G. Provan, B. Middleton, and M. Henrion. Knowledge engineering for large belief networks. In *Proc. Tenth Conf. on Uncertainty in Artificial Intelligence*, 1994.

[Rish et al., 1998] I. Rish, K. Kask, and R. Dechter. Approximation algorithms for probabilistic decoding. In *Uncertainty in Artificial Intelligence (UAI-98)*, 1998.

[Santos, 1991] E. Santos. On the generation of alternative explanations with implications for belief revision. In *Uncertainty in Artificial Intelligence (UAI-91)*, pages 339–347, 1991.

[Shimony and Charniak, 1991] S.E. Shimony and E. Charniak. A new algorithm for finding map assignments to belief networks. In *P. Bonissone, M. Henrion, L. Kanal, and J. Lemmer Eds. Uncertainty in Artificial Intelligence*, volume 6, pages 185–193, 1991.

CONSTRAINT SATISFACTION

Constraint Satisfaction 3

Improving search using indexing: a study with temporal CSPs

Nikos Mamoulis and **Dimitris Papadias**
Department of Computer Science
Hong Kong University of Science and Technology
Clear Water Bay, Hong Kong
http://www.cs.ust.hk/{~mamoulis, ~dimitris}

Abstract

Most studies concerning constraint satisfaction problems (CSPs) involve variables that take values from small domains. This paper deals with an alternative form of temporal CSPs; the number of variables is relatively small and the domains are large collections of intervals. Such situations may arise in temporal databases where several types of queries can be modeled and processed as CSPs. For these problems, systematic CSP algorithms can take advantage of temporal indexing to accelerate search. Directed search versions of chronological backtracking and forward checking are presented and tested. Our results show that indexing can drastically improve search performance.

1 Introduction

Many problems in a variety of application domains can be modeled and solved as constraint satisfaction problems (CSPs). A binary CSP is defined by:

- a set of n variables $v_1, \ldots, v_n$
- for each variable v_i a domain D_i of m_i values: $\{u_{i1}, \ldots, u_{im_i}\}$
- for each pair of variables $\{v_i, v_j\}$, $i \neq j$, a binary constraint C_{ij}, which is a subset of $D_i \times D_j$.

An assignment $\{v_i \leftarrow u_{ia_i}, v_j \leftarrow u_{ja_j}\}$ is consistent if $(u_{ia_i}, u_{ja_j}) \in C_{ij}$. The goal is to find one or all solutions, i.e., n-tuples $(u_{1a_1}, \ldots, u_{ia_i}, \ldots, u_{ja_j}, \ldots, u_{na_n})$ such that for each $\{i,j\}$, $i \neq j$, $\{v_i \leftarrow u_{ia_i}, v_j \leftarrow u_{ja_j}\}$ is consistent.

Several systematic search heuristics that aim to minimize the number of consistency checks have been proposed. Based on the general idea of *backtracking,* these methods try to improve the *backward step,* e.g. *backjumping,* or the *forward step,* e.g. *forward checking* [Haralick and Elliot, 1980]. Hybrid algorithms combine different types of backward and forward steps [Prosser, 1993]. The aforementioned search methods apply exhaustive search in the variable domains while assigning or pruning values. When the number of potential values for a variable is small (i.e. less than 100) linear scan suf-fices; for large domains, however, the overhead can be significant due to repetition of scan.

In this paper we study how indexing may be utilized by CSP algorithms to direct search and avoid linear scan of domains. As an application, we deal with CSPs, where the values are temporal intervals and the constraints are disjunctions of temporal relations as defined in [Allen, 1983]. Such problems may occur in planning or temporal databases. A previous work that uses indexing in temporal databases is [Dean, 1989]. In contrast to our method, where intervals are indexed according to their position in space, that method directs search using a conceptual hierarchical structure, the *discrimination tree.* Algorithms that combine CSP search and indexing to facilitate retrieval of structural queries in large spatial databases were presented in [Papadias *et al.*, 1998]. Here, we extend this work by investigating the application of directed search in temporal databases and study the performance gain of directed search under various problem conditions using different CSP algorithms.

The rest of the paper is organized as follows. Section 2 introduces data structures and search methods for temporal intervals. Section 3 shows how conventional methods for solving CSPs can be modified to accelerate search using indexing. Section 4 experimentally compares directed search algorithms with methods that do not use indexing. Finally, Section 5 concludes the paper with directions for future work.

2 Temporal CSPs

The class of problems that we deal with in this paper includes CSPs where domain values are well defined intervals in *discrete* time, and each binary constraint C_{ij} is a disjunction of the permissible set of Allen's [1983] temporal relations between v_i and v_j. Notice that the current issue is different from traditional temporal reasoning problems (e.g. [van Beek, 1992]) where the aim is to identify a consistent scenario for a set of continuous variables, given information about their relationships. Here, we *search* into domains of intervals for variable assignments that satisfy the given constraints.

This temporal CSP can be solved by employing traditional search techniques. Each time a variable is visited,

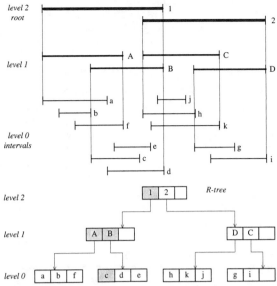

Figure 1: Organizing a set of intervals into a 1-d R-tree

Relation	Illustration	I.left	I.right
b: q before x		unbounded	> q.right
m: q meets x		≤ q.right	> q.right
o: q overlaps x		< q.right	> q.right
s: q starts x		≤ q.left	> q.right
d: q during x		< q.left	> q.right
f: q finishes x		< q.left	≥ q.right
e: q equal x		≤ q.left	≥ q.right
fi: q finished by x		< q.right	≥ q.right
di: q contains x		< q.right	> q.left
si: q started by x		≤ q.left	> q.left
oi: q overlapped by x		< q.left	> q.left
mi: q met by x		< q.left	≥ q.left
bi: q after x		< q.left	unbounded

Table 1: Bounding conditions for intermediate node entries

its whole domain has to be scanned in order to identify consistent assignments. When the variable domains are small, classic CSP algorithms behave well, but as the domain size increases, linear scan for consistent values is expensive.

CSP algorithms can avoid linear scans by employing interval-based data structures that index the variable domains. The search for solutions can be *directed* upon *satisfaction* of the temporal constraints, using the data structure to minimize the number of consistency checks. Since search through the domains is repeated a large number of times, directed search has a significant effect on performance.

For the indexing of variable domains we use R-trees [Guttman, 1984], a data structure aimed at indexing multidimensional rectangles in spatio-temporal databases. The data rectangles are stored into leaf nodes; each intermediate node contains a pointer to a lower level node and the *minimum bounding rectangle* of the rectangles in this node. We chose R-trees because they are becoming a standard in both research and industry (e.g., Illustra, Informix) due to their efficiency, dynamic nature and relatively simple implementation. Alternatively, any interval-based data structure, such as interval trees and segment trees [Preparata and Shamos, 1985], can be employed.

Figure 1 illustrates how a 1-dimensional R-tree can be used for interval storage and retrieval, assuming maximum tree node capacity equal to 3. The data intervals (*a* to *k*) are stored in the leaf nodes. Artificial intervals in the higher tree nodes are formulated by grouping intervals from the level below (e.g., *a,b* and *f* are grouped in *A*). The end points of an intermediate node interval are the leftmost and rightmost end points of the intervals it indexes. The R-tree for a static set of intervals can be built in a bottom-up fashion after sorting them with respect to one end-point, e.g. in this example the left one

(*R-tree packing*). Thus, the R-tree construction for n intervals costs $O(n \log n)$.

R-trees are very efficient in answering *range intersection* queries, i.e., find all intervals that intersect (share a common point with) a *query interval*. In addition, the hierarchical nature of R-tree facilitates general selection queries, i.e., retrieval of intervals that satisfy any temporal condition with respect to a query interval. As an example, consider the query: "find all intervals that start *immediately* after interval *b*" applied to the R-tree of Figure 1. Retrieval starts from the root of the tree; due to the relative positions of *b* and *2*, there can be no interval indexed by the root entry *2* that starts immediately after *b*. Thus the sub-tree under *2* is pruned. On the other hand, entry *1* can contain qualifying intervals and is recursively searched. Both entries *A* and *B* may point to a query answer and they are followed; the only solution is interval *c*. Typically, the retrieval cost is proportional to the number of solutions; when this is small, worst case performance is logarithmic to the number of stored intervals.

Let $q=[q.left, q.right]$ be a query interval; Table 1 shows, for each temporal relation, the *bounding conditions* that an *intermediate-level* interval I should satisfy in order to potentially point to a query answer x. This is the criterion of following an R-tree node during retrieval. In the previous example (*b meets x*) the intermediate nodes to be searched should satisfy $I.left \le b.right$ and $I.right > b.right$. Intermediate interval *2* is pruned because it violates $2.left \le b.right$. When the query is a disjunction of temporal relations, the disjunction of the bounding conditions is applied during search. For instance, if the search predicate is *starts ∨ during ∨ finishes*, the bounding conditions for an intermediate level entry I are $I.left \leq q.left$ and $I.right \geq q.right$. Although for the examples throughout the paper we use the tree of Figure 1, for our implementation we assume that each variable domain is different and indexed by a separate R-tree. The next section describes algorithms that use these indexes to prune the search space (the methods can be easily applied when some domains/trees are common).

3. Directed Search for Temporal CSPs

Classic local consistency methods, like *arc* and *path consistency*, perform well for small domains, because in this case there is a high probability that a value will be pruned. However, for large variable domains and dense constraint graphs usually they do not pay-off. Therefore, we do not consider conventional local consistency methods for pre-processing, but apply the temporal network maintenance algorithm from [Allen, 1983] prior to search in order to infer undefined constraints and refine the existing ones. This is equivalent to a path consistency algorithm that does not check value consistency, but *constraint graph consistency*, and its complexity is, therefore, independent from the domain sizes. For instance, consider a constraint graph of three variables, where C_{12} = *meets*, C_{23} = *during*, and C_{13} is undefined. The *implied* constraint C_{13} is then *overlap* $\vee$ *starts* $\vee$ *during*. If C_{13} was defined, then the *updated* constraint is $C_{13} \wedge \{overlap \vee starts \vee during\}$. Notice that this reasoning method detects inconsistency prior to search, e.g. when $C_{13} \wedge \{overlap \vee starts \vee during\} = \varnothing$.

Efficiency of CSP search depends on the order by which variables are instantiated [Dechter and Meiri, 1994]. The usual rule for *static variable ordering* (SVO) schemes is to "place the most constrained variable first". A simple way to apply this rule is to sort the variables in decreasing order of their degree in the constraint graph. Since in our problem the constraint edges do not have the same tightness, we follow another method: instead of "adding 1" for each edge that goes out from a variable, we add a *weight* that represents the tightness of the constraint edge. For a temporal relation r, weight(r) is the inverse of the probability[1] $P(r)$ that r will be satisfied between two arbitrary intervals. In typical cases, the relation with the largest weight is *equal*, and the relations with the smallest, *before* and *after*. If a constraint is a disjunction of primitive relations, the weight is the inverse sum of the relation weights that participate in the disjunction, e.g.,

$$weight(meets \vee starts) = \frac{1}{P(meets) + P(starts)}$$

The weight of a variable is then the sum of the weights of all constraint edges adjacent to it. SVO will instantiate the "heaviest" variable first and the one with the smallest weight last. Whenever dynamic variable ordering (DVO)

is employed, the above method is used to find the variable with the largest weight and place it first. The order of subsequent variables is dynamically changed according to their domain sizes during search.

3.1 Directed Search Backtracking

Integration of directed search into backtracking (BT) is rather simple. Whenever a variable v_j is visited, its consistent values are retrieved from the corresponding R-tree R_j by applying the instantiations of the previous variables v_i, $i<j$, as query intervals, and the constraints C_{ij} as retrieval conditions. During retrieval, the conjunction of bounding conditions, defined by each v_i, direct the search at intermediate R-tree levels. At the leaf level, the entries that satisfy the constraint C_{ij} with each variable v_i, are retrieved as consistent values for v_j.

To clarify the retrieval procedure, consider the following example. Let the query *overlap*$(v_1,v_3) \wedge$ *overlapped by* (v_2,v_3) and the instantiations $v_1 \leftarrow f$, $v_2 \leftarrow h$ in Figure 1 (i.e., v_3 should overlap f to the right and h to the left). In order to retrieve all consistent values for v_3, first the bounding conditions (*BC*) according to v_1 and v_2 are calculated using Table 1; BC_{13} = {$I.left < f.right$ and $I.right > f.right$} and BC_{23} = {$I.left < h.left$ and $I.right > h.left$}. The conjunction of the above constraints results in the bounding conditions {$I.left < f.right$ and $I.right > h.left$}, used to guide R-tree search. Retrieval starts from the root, where entry 2 is pruned as it does not satisfy $2.left < f.right$. Similarly, entry A violates $A.right > h.left$ and the sub-tree below is pruned. Only intervals under entry B can satisfy both C_{13} and C_{23}. Finally, d and e constitute the consistent assignments for v_3. Notice that the whole process costs 4 consistency checks at the intermediate levels and 6 at the leaf level (each interval under B is tested against both v_1 and v_2), whereas a linear scan would cost 14 consistency checks.

The above method can be applied with alternative forms of backtracking (e.g., backjumping, dynamic backtracking) using information about *nogoods*. In the next subsection we illustrate how forward checking can employ the index to prune the domains of future variables.

3.2 Directed Search Forward Checking

After a variable instantiation, forward checking (FC) *marks* in the domains of all future variables the values that are consistent with the current variable (*check-forward*). When a subsequent variable is to be instantiated only the marked values will be considered. This marking mechanism can be thought of as a *linear index* in the variable domain that points to the consistent values. Assume that an intermediate variable v_i is being instantiated. The domain of each future variable v_j (i<j) has already been pruned by the instantiation of variables before v_i. As the linear indexes of some variables may still be large, check-forward during instantiation of v_i can be rather costly. For these variables we apply directed

---

[1] The probabilities of temporal relations can be estimated either by sampling the input data, or by using probabilistic estimation formulae given the distribution of interval positions and sizes.

search using the R-tree and filter the results using the linear index. Filtering with respect to the linear index is needed, because directed search is performed on the whole domain (i.e., an interval which satisfies the current constraint with v_i may have been pruned out by a previous instantiation). The issue to be investigated is when to apply directed search instead of linear scan.

A good heuristic is to employ directed search at a future variable only when the number of remaining consistent values is large, and the search constraint is tight, so the search would benefit from the R-tree. For example, let $C_{13} = before$ and $C_{23} = equal$. After v_1 is instantiated, directed search is applied to prune the domains of v_2 and v_3. When v_2 is given a value it is worth applying directed search again while checking forward for consistent values of v_3, because the domain of v_3 is still large and C_{23} is a tight constraint. The results of directed search that do not satisfy $before$ with respect to the value of v_1 are filtered out. Now let $C_{13} = equal$ and $C_{23} = before$. After v_1 is given a value, the domain of v_3 is expected to become very small; thus, during instantiation of v_2, linear scan of D_3 is cheaper than using the tree.

This mechanism is called a *double index*, in the sense that we keep both the whole domain R-tree and the linear index of consistent values and use either both, or only the linear index. Directed search is applied when the *expected* number of values that satisfy the search conditions is smaller than the number of values in the linear index. The number of retrieved values is estimated using the temporal relation probabilities. For instance, if $C_{ij} = overlap$, $P(overlap) = 0.02$ and $|D_j| = 1000$, then 20 intervals in the domain of v_j are expected to be consistent with the value of a previous variable v_i. If while instantiating v_i, the remaining consistent values of v_j from former checks is smaller than 20, linear scan at $check\_forward(v_i, v_j)$ will be preferred to directed search.

Alternatively, versions of the variable R-trees could be maintained at each instantiation level, where only consistent values would remain in the data structure, and search could be performed at each check-forward. We do not use this method because dynamic operations on data structures (i.e. insertion, deletion, construction) are usually expensive.

4   Experiments

In this section we compare the performance of *directed BT* (dirBT) and *directed FC* (dirFC) with plain versions of the algorithms based on linear scan. FC and dirFC use the *fail first* (FF) DVO heuristic [Haralick and Elliot, 1980]. BT and dirBT apply the SVO heuristic described in Section 3, because, as suggested in [Bacchus and van Run, 1995], BT with DVO does at least as much work as FC with DVO, thus it is just a FC-DVO algorithm with redundant checks.

The problems were randomly generated by modifying the parameters $<n, m, p_1, p_2>$ (see [Dechter and Meiri, 1994]), where n is the number of variables, m the cardinality of the domains, p_1 the probability that a random pair of variables is constrained (*constraint network density*), and p_2 the probability that a random assignment for a constrained pair is inconsistent (*constraint tightness*). The centers of the intervals in the variable domains are uniformly distributed and their sizes take values with an average 1.5% of the workspace. The intervals in each domain are indexed by R-trees with node capacity equal to 20.

In order to identify the hard region of the problems we use the *constrainedness* measure [Gent et al., 1996]:

$$\kappa = 1 - \frac{\log_2(Sol)}{\log_2 \prod_{i=1}^{n} m_i} = 1 - \frac{\log_2(Sol)}{n \log_2 m} \qquad (1)$$

The hard region for an ensemble of problems is when $\kappa \approx 1$, whereas problems with $\kappa << 1$ and $\kappa >> 1$ are *easy and soluble* and *easy and insoluble*, respectively. The denominator of eq. (1) denotes the *size* of the problem and *Sol* denotes the number of solutions in a random problem of the class. If the binary constraints are independent, *Sol* can be estimated by:

$$Sol = \prod_{v=1}^{n} m_v \cdot \prod_{1 \le i, j \le n, i \ne j} P(C_{ij}) \qquad (2)$$

where $P(C_{ij})$, as described in the previous section, is the probability that two intervals from D_i and D_j satisfy C_{ij}. The first product in (2) corresponds to the total number of n-tuples of intervals, while the second one to the probability that a tuple constitutes a solution. For acyclic networks the constraints are independent and (2) will give a good estimation of the problem solutions. When cycles exist the constraints are no longer independent, but applying (2) for the minimum spanning tree of the graph (w.r.t. the constraint tightness) will give an overestimation of the expected solutions.

We first tested the performance improvement achieved by the path consistency (PC) method of Section 3 for *acyclic* networks ($p_1 = (n-1)/(n(n-1)/2) = 2/n$), by running experiments for $n=10$ and $m=1000$, and several values of p_2 around the hard region. For each value of p_2 we solved an ensemble of 100 problems and measured the average cost for finding one solution. Usually, random CSPs are generated with every constraint having exactly the same tightness. Because this cannot be done for the current problem, we chose disjunctions of temporal relations which may be different for each constraint, but have average tightness within $\pm 10^{-4}$ of the target value p_2. The hard region ($\kappa = 1$) is when $p_2 \approx 0.99953$. This large value of p_2 is due to the large domain size and the sparseness of the graph. In general, problems with sparse graphs are easy [Dechter and Pearl, 1987] and the few

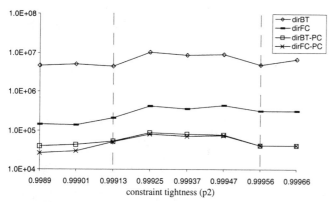

Figure 2: cost of directed search with and without PC

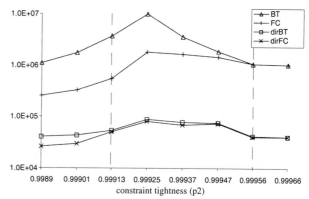

Figure 3: comparison of directed and plain search for trees

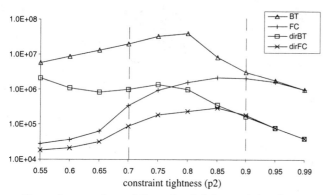

Figure 4: comparison of directed and plain search for cliques

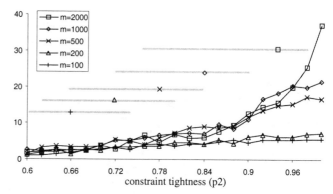

Figure 5: Performance gain of dirFC for various domain sizes

existing constraints must be very tight in order to generate a small number of solutions.

Figure 2 shows the cost (in terms of consistency checks[2]) of directed search BT and FC, with and without PC. The dotted vertical lines include the phase transition, i.e. the first ensemble that included an insoluble problem (left line) and the last ensemble that included a soluble one (right line). As expected, the performance gain of PC is significant since the inferred constraints drastically prune the search space. In the sequel we use PC for both directed search and plain versions of the algorithms. The nearest point to 50% solubility (crossover point) was at $p_2 = 0.99925$ ($\kappa = 0.93748$), where 54% of the problems were soluble.

The second set of experiments compares the cost of directed versus undirected search for tree ($p_1 = 2/n$) and clique ($p_1 = 1$) graphs. The experimental settings are the same as in the previous experiments ($n=10$ and $m=1000$; each ensemble contains 100 problems for each value of p_2 around the hard region). Figure 3 illustrates the cost for tree graphs. The directed search versions outperform the original algorithms by more than one order of magnitude. Tree constraint graphs can alternatively be solved by the application of *arc consistency* prior to search,

which would lead to backtrack-free search [Dechter and Pearl, 1987]. This method is also expected to profit from indexing.

For cliques, the hard region cannot be estimated using (1), due to the dependency of the constraints. In order to identify it, we experimented with various values of p_2. The diagram of Figure 4 illustrates the behavior of algorithms for a wide scope of tightness values. Notice that the hard region corresponds to a larger range of p_2 than in the case of tree graphs. While the cost difference between directed and regular versions of the algorithms is again about an order of magnitude for large p_2, their performance converges as the constraints become loose. When $p_2 < 0.7$ most of the constraints contain relations *before* or *after*. On the average, each such constraint prunes out around 50% of the values in a domain, and directed search is only about twice as fast as linear scan.

As a general conclusion, the performance gain of directed search in comparison to linear scan grows with the constraint tightness p_2. dirFC is, as expected, more efficient than dirBT due to its relevance with FC which in most cases outperforms BT. In the sequel we focus on the performance gain of dirFC with respect to FC for various problem settings.

The next experiment compares FC and dirFC for $n=10$, clique topology, and various values of m and p_2. Figure 5 shows how many times dirFC is faster than FC (average

---

[2] We consider as consistency checks the comparisons that take place at all levels of the R-trees.

of 50 instances per experimental setting). The gray horizontal lines present the phase transition for each m, and the symbol on the line indicates the position of the crossover point. With the exception of m=100-200 and very small tightness values (p_2<0.65), dirFC outperforms FC several times. For small domains the constraints should be very tight in order for the intermediate R-tree node comparisons to pay-off. However, directed search is intended for large domains (e.g., in spatio-temporal databases the cardinality often exceeds 10^5), and in such cases the performance gain is significant. For this experiment, we limited m to 2000, so that FC could terminate in reasonable time.

#vars	p_2	%soluble	FC	dirFC	gain
5	0.9996	58%	562466	21974	25.6
10	0.75	42%	2118699	299047	7.1
15	0.68	43%	2715124	848629	3.2
20	0.61	46%	4660763	2922984	1.6
25	0.58	42%	8570553	6619067	1.3

Table 2: Performance gain of dirFC compared to FC for various number of variables

In order to test the implication of the number of variables, we fixed m=1000, p_2 to be around the crossover point, the graph topology to clique, and generated 100 random problems for several values of n. Table 2 presents, for each ensemble, the value of p_2, the percentage of soluble problems, and the mean consistency checks of FC and dirFC. The last row of the table shows how many times dirFC was faster than FC. As the number of variables increases, the value of p_2 at the crossover point decreases. As a result, the costs of dirFC and FC converge due to the relaxation of constraints which deteriorates R-tree search, making it comparable to linear scan.

5 Discussion

This paper studies a specific CSP problem, where variable domains are large collections of well defined intervals and constraints are temporal relations. We show how systematic CSP algorithms can take advantage of indexing to accelerate search. Although we experimented with two representative algorithms, chronological backtracking and forward checking, directed search can be applied with a variety of algorithms and heuristics (e.g. arc consistency). In typical database applications, where m is in the order of 10^5 or above and n<10, the performance gain of directed search is large.

Application of data structures is not limited to the temporal CSP discussed here. Any problem, where variables have large domains and the nature of constraints facilitates directed search, can benefit from it. This particularly applies for spatial and multimedia databases where several types of content-based queries can be modeled as CSPs (e.g., find all triplets (v_1, v_2, v_3) of objects such that v_2 is *inside* v_1, and v_1 is *northeast* of v_3). An alternative approach that solves the above problem by hierarchically applying CSP algorithms at each R-tree level is described in [Papadias *et al.*, 1999].

Acknowledgement

This work was supported by grant HKUST 6151/98E from Hong Kong RGC and grant DAG97/98.EG02.

References

[Allen, 1983] James F. Allen. *Maintaining Knowledge about Temporal Intervals*. Communications of the ACM 26(12): 832-843, 1983.

[Bacchus and van Run, 1995] Fahiem Bacchus, Paul van Run. *Dynamic variable reordering in CSPs*. In Proceedings of CP-95, 1995.

[Dean, 1989] Thomas Dean. *Using Temporal Hierarchies to Efficiently Maintain Large Temporal Databases*. Journal of ACM 36(4): 687-718, 1989.

[Dechter and Meiri, 1994] Rina Dechter, Itay Meiri. *Experimental Evaluation of Preprocessing Algorithms for Constraint Satisfaction Problems*. Artificial Intelligence 68(2): 211-241, 1994.

[Dechter and Pearl, 1987] Rina Dechter, Judea Pearl. *Network-Based Heuristics for Constraint-Satisfaction Problems*. Artificial Intelligence 34(1): 1-38, 1987.

[Gent *et al.*, 1996] Ian P. Gent, Ewan MacIntyre, Patrick Prosser, Toby Walsh. *The Constrainedness of Search*. In Proceedings of AAAI-96, 1996.

[Guttman, 1984] Antonin Guttman. *R-trees: A Dynamic Index Structure for Spatial Searching*. In Proceedings of ACM SIGMOD, 1984.

[Haralick and Elliot, 1980] Robert M. Haralick, Gordon L. Elliott. *Increasing tree search efficiency for constraint satisfaction problems*. Artificial Intelligence 14(3): 263-313, 1980.

[Papadias *et al.*, 1998] D. Papadias, N. Mamoulis and V. Delis. *Querying by Spatial Structure*. In Proceedings of VLDB, 1998.

[Papadias *et al.*, 1999] D. Papadias, P. Kalnis, N. Mamoulis. *Hierarchical Constraint Satisfaction in Spatial Databases*. In Proceedings of AAAI-99, 1999.

[Preparata and Shamos, 1985] F. Preparata, M. Shamos. *Computational Geometry*. Springer, 1985.

[Prosser, 1993] Patrick Prosser. *Hybrid Algorithms for the Constraint Satisfaction Problem*. Computational Intelligence, 9(3): 268-299, 1993.

[van Beek, 1992] Peter van Beek. *Reasoning about qualitative temporal information*. Artificial Intelligence 58: 297-324, 1992.

A new tractable subclass of the rectangle algebra

P. Balbiani
Laboratoire d'informatique de Paris-Nord
Avenue J.-B. Clément
F-93430 Villetaneuse, France
balbiani@lipn.univ-paris13.fr

J.-F. Condotta, L. Fariñas del Cerro
Institut de recherche en informatique de Toulouse
118 route de Narbonne
F-31062 Toulouse Cedex 4, France
{condotta,farinas}@irit.fr

Abstract

This paper presents the 169 permitted relations between two rectangles whose sides are parallel to the axes of some orthogonal basis in a 2-dimensional Euclidean space. Elaborating rectangle algebra just like interval algebra, it defines the concept of convexity as well as the ones of weak preconvexity and strong preconvexity. It introduces afterwards the fundamental operations of intersection, composition and inversion and demonstrates that the concept of weak preconvexity is preserved by the operation of composition whereas the concept of strong preconvexity is preserved by the operation of intersection. Finally, fitting the propagation techniques conceived to solve interval networks, it shows that the polynomial path-consistency algorithm is a decision method for the problem of proving the consistency of strongly preconvex rectangle networks.

1 Introduction

Spatial representation and reasoning concern many areas of artificial intelligence: computer vision, geographic information, natural language understanding, computer-aided design, mental imagery, etc. These last ten years, numerous formalisms for reasoning about space were proposed [Egenhofer *et al.*, 1991; Mukerjee *et al.*, 1990; Freska, 1992; Randell *et al.*, 1992]. We can mention as an example the well-known model of the regions proposed by Cohn, Cui and Randell [Randell *et al.*, 1992] whose objects are the regions of a topological space and relations are eight topological relations, and for which Renz and Nebel [Renz *et al.*, 1997] characterize a maximal tractable subclass of relations. Although this formalism is very attractive, it suffers from the impossibility of expressing orientation relations.

An example which enables this is the rectangle algebra (RA) [Güsgen, 1989; Mukerjee *et al.*, 1990; Balbiani *et al.*, 1998]. It is an extension for the space of the better known model for reasoning about time: the interval algebra (IA) proposed by Allen [Allen, 1983]. The basic objects of this spatial formalism are the rational rectangles whose sides are parallel to the axes of some orthogonal basis in a 2-dimensional Euclidean space. Though restrictive, it is sufficient for applications in domains like architecture or geographic information. The relations between these objects are the 13×13 pairs of atomic relations which can hold between two rational intervals. These relations are very expressive, with them we can express both directional relations such as *left-of*, *right-of*, *above*, etc., and topological relations such as *disjoint*, *overlap*, etc., between two rectangles.

In RA, spatial information are represented by spatial constraint networks which are special constraint satisfaction problems (CSPs). In these CSPs, each variable represents a rational rectangle and each constraint is represented by a relation of RA.

Given a spatial constraint network, the main problem is to know whether or not it is consistent, i.e, whether or not the spatial information represented by the network is coherent. Generally, this problem is NP-complete, but we can find subsets of the whole relations of RA for which this problem is polynomial, as in IA [Nebel *et al.*, 1994; Beek, 1992]. Notably, in [Balbiani *et al.*, 1998], Balbiani et al. presented a tractable set of relations called saturated-preconvex relations. In this paper, we present a new tractable set: the set of strongly-preconvex relations. This set contains the saturated-preconvex relations. We also prove that the well-known method, the path-consistency method, is complete for this set. To prove these results, we introduce a new method, called the weak path-consistency method, which is almost the path-consistency method.

The remainder of the paper is organised as follows. In Section 2, we make some recalls about RA, moreover we introduce the weakly-preconvex relations. Section 3 is concerned with some properties of fundamental operations: composition, intersection and inverse. In Section 4, we discuss spatial constraint network and we present the weak path-consistency method. Section 5 is concerned with the tractability results. In section 6, we define the strongly-preconvex relation and Section 7 concludes with suggestions for further extensions.

2 The rectangle algebra

The considered objects are the rectangles whose sides are parallel to the axes of some orthogonal basis in a 2-dimensional Euclidean space. The basic relations between these objects are defined from the basic relations of the interval algebra (denoted by $\mathcal{B}_{int}$ and represented in the figure 2) in the following way :

$$\mathcal{B}_{rec} = \{(A,B) : A,B \in \mathcal{B}_{int}\}.$$

$\mathcal{B}_{rec}$ constitutes the exhaustive list of the relations which can hold between two rational rectangles. For example, in figure 1, two rational rectangles satisfy the basic relation (m,p) of $\mathcal{B}_{rec}$. The set of the relations of the rect-

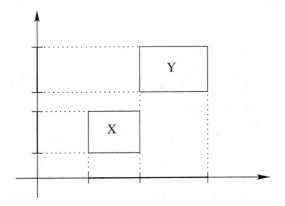

Figure 1: Two rational rectangles satisfying the basic relation (m,p).

angle algebra is defined as the power set of $\mathcal{B}_{rec}$. Each relation of $2^{\mathcal{B}_{rec}}$ can be seen as the union of its basic relations. We obtain 2^{169} relations. Let R be a rectangle relation of $2^{\mathcal{B}_{rec}}$, we call the projections of R the two relations of $2^{\mathcal{B}_{int}}$, denoted by R_1 and R_2 and defined by:

$$R_1 = \{A : (A,B) \in R\} \text{ and } R_2 = \{B : (A,B) \in R\}.$$

Relation	Symbol	Reverse	Meaning	Dim
precedes	p	pi	x ―― y ――	2
meets	m	mi	x ―― y ――	1
overlaps	o	oi	x ―― y ――	2
starts	s	si	x ―― y ――	1
during	d	di	x ―― y ――	2
finishes	f	fi	x ―― y ――	1
equals	eq	eq	x ―― y ――	0

Figure 2: The set $\mathcal{B}_{int}$ of the basic relations of IA.

Ligozat [Ligozat, 1994] arranges the basic relations of the interval algebra in a partial order $\leq$ which defines a

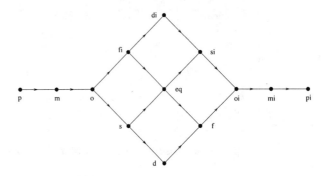

Figure 3: The interval lattice $(\mathcal{B}_{int}, \leq)$.

lattice called the interval lattice (see fig. 3). From this partial order we define the partial order $\preceq$ on $\mathcal{B}_{rec}$: $(A,B) \preceq (C,D)$ iff $A \leq C$ and $B \leq D$, with (A,B), $(C,D) \in \mathcal{B}_{rec}$.

$(\mathcal{B}_{rec}, \preceq)$ defines a lattice that we call the rectangle lattice. The convex relations of IA and RA correspond to the intervals in the interval lattice and in the rectangle lattice respectively. We can prove that a convex relation R of RA is the cartesian product of its projections and that its projections are both convex relations of IA.

For each relation R of IA and RA, there exists a smallest convex relation of IA and RA respectively, which contains R. According to Ligozat's notation, we denote this relation by $I(R)$ (the convex closure of R). We can easily prove the following proposition:

Proposition 1 Let $R \in 2^{\mathcal{B}_{rec}}$ be, $I(R) = I(R_1) \times I(R_2)$.

In [Ligozat, 1994], a basic relation of IA is represented by a region of the Euclidean plane and a relation of IA by the union of the regions representing its basic relations. With this representation two concepts are defined – the dimension and the topological closure of a relation of IA – in the following way:

- the dimension of a basic relation A (see figure 2), denoted by $dim(A)$, corresponds to the dimension of its representation in the plane, i.e. 0, 1 or 2. The dimension of a relation R is the maximal dimension of its primitives.

- The topological closure of a basic relation A, denoted by $C(A)$ is the relation which corresponds to the topological closure of the region of A (see Table 1). For a relation R, $C(R)$ is the union of the topological closure of its basic relations.

These definitions use a geometrical representation of the basic relations, but we shall express them differently. In IA, each basic relation forces zero, one or two endpoint equalities. For example, between two intervals the basic relation eq imposes the first and the second endpoints to be equal whereas the basic relation p imposes no equality. We can use the following definition:

Definition 1 *the dimension of a basic relation A of $\mathcal{B}_{int}$ is the maximal number of equalities which can be imposed by a basic relation (i.e. 2) minus the number of equalities imposed by the basic relation A.*

Relation	Topological closure	Relation	Topological closure
p	$\{p, m\}$	pi	$\{pi, mi\}$
m	$\{m\}$	mi	$\{mi\}$
o	$\{m, o, fi, s, eq\}$	oi	$\{mi, oi, f, si, eq\}$
s	$\{s, eq\}$	si	$\{si, eq\}$
d	$\{d, s, f, eq\}$	di	$\{di, si, fi, eq\}$
f	$\{f, eq\}$	fi	$\{fi, eq\}$
eq	$\{eq\}$		

Table 1: The topological closure of the atomic relations of IA.

Then we can easily extend this definition to RA:

Definition 2 *the dimension of a basic relation of $\mathcal{B}_{rec}$ is the maximal number of endpoint equalities that a basic relation can impose between the orthogonal axe projections of two rectangles (i.e. 4) minus the number of endpoint equalities imposed by the basic relation.*

For example, the dimension of the basic relation (m, p) (see figure 1) is 3. The dimension of a relation R of $2^{\mathcal{B}_{rec}}$ is the maximal dimension of its basic relations, and we suppose that the dimension of the empty relation is -1. It is easy to prove the following facts:

Proposition 2

- *let (A, B) be a basic relation of $\mathcal{B}_{rec}$, $dim((A, B)) = dim(A) + dim(B)$;*
- *let $R \in 2^{\mathcal{B}_{rec}}$ be a convex relation, $dim(R) = dim(R_1) + dim(R_2)$.*

To extend the definition of the topological closure to RA we use directly the topological closure of the atomic relations of IA (see Table 1) by the following ways:

Definition 3

- *let $(A, B) \in \mathcal{B}_{rec}$ be, $C((A, B)) = C(A) \times C(B)$;*
- *let $R \in 2^{\mathcal{B}_{rec}}$ be, $C(R) = \bigcup \{C((A, B)) : (A, B) \in R\}$.*

Although speaking of topological closure doesn't make any sense because we don't use regions to represent the relations of RA, we shall continue to use the term as in IA. We can prove the following proposition :

Proposition 3

- *let $R, S \in 2^{\mathcal{B}_{rec}}$ be, $C(R) \circ C(S) \subseteq C(R \circ S)$;*
- *let R be a convex relation of $2^{\mathcal{B}_{rec}}$, $C(R) = C(R_1) \times C(R_2)$;*
- *let R be a convex relation of $2^{\mathcal{B}_{rec}}$, for all $(A, B) \in R$ there exists $(C, D) \in R$ such that $dim((C, D)) = dim(R)$ and $(A, B) \in C((C, D))$.*

Proof.(Sketch) Ligozat proves the first part of this proposition for two relations of IA. Using this result we can also prove this for RA. The proof of the second part is obvious. To prove the third one, first we prove it for IA by examining the exhaustive list of the convex relations of IA. And from this result and the first two parts we prove the result for RA. □

In [Ligozat, 1994], the preconvex relations of IA are defined in the following way: a relation R of IA is a preconvex relation iff $dim(I(R) \setminus R) < dim(R)$ – an equivalent definition is: R is a preconvex relation iff $I(R) \subseteq C(R)$. The set of preconvex relations coincides with the set of the well known ORD-Horn relations, which is the maximal tractable set of IA which contains all basic relations [Nebel *et al.*, 1994]. Using the convex closure and the dimension of a relation of RA, now, we are ready to define the preconvex relations in RA. We shall call these relations the weakly-preconvex relations.

Definition 4 *Let $R \in 2^{\mathcal{B}_{rec}}$ be, R is a weakly-preconvex relation iff $dim(I(R) \setminus R) < dim(R)$.*

Using proposition 3, we can prove:

Proposition 4 *A relation R of RA is a weakly-preconvex relation iff $I(R) \subseteq C(R)$.*

From this proposition it follows that:

Proposition 5 *A relation R of RA is a weakly-preconvex relation iff $C(R)$ is a convex relation.*

Proof. Let R be a weakly-preconvex relation of RA. From proposition 4, $R \subseteq I(R) \subseteq C(R)$. So, $C(R) \subseteq C(I(R)) \subseteq C(C(R))$. Since $C(C(R)) = C(R)$, we deduce that $C(R) = C(I(R))$. Given that every convex relation of IA has a convex topological closure [Ligozat, 1996], from propositions 1 and 3 we deduce that $C(I(R))$ is convex. Let $R \in 2^{\mathcal{B}_{rec}}$ be such that $C(R)$ is convex. Since $R \subseteq C(R)$, by definition of I we deduce that $I(R) \subseteq C(R)$. □

3 Fundamental operations

The set $2^{\mathcal{B}_{rec}}$ is enriched with the fundamental relational operations, the binary operations, intersection ($\cap$), composition ($\circ$) and the unary operation inverse ($^{-1}$). The composition of two basic relations and the inverse of a basic relation in RA can be computed from the same operations in IA in the following way : $(A, B) \circ (C, D) = (A \circ C) \times (B \circ D)$ and $(A, B)^{-1} = (A^{-1}, B^{-1})$. Composition between two relations in $2^{\mathcal{B}_{rec}}$ is defined by : $R \circ S = \bigcup \{(A, B) \circ (C, D) : (A, B) \in R, (C, D) \in S\}$. The inverse of a relation in $2^{\mathcal{B}_{rec}}$ is the union of the inverse of its basic relations. $2^{\mathcal{B}_{rec}}$ is stable for these three operations. Considering a subset of $2^{\mathcal{B}_{rec}}$, firstly we must look whether this subset is stable for these operations. We can easily prove the following proposition:

Proposition 6 *for every relation $R, S, T, U \in 2^{\mathcal{B}_{int}}$,*

- *$(R \times S) \cap (T \times U) = (R \cap T) \times (S \cap U)$;*
- *$(R \times S) \circ (T \times U) = (R \circ T) \times (S \circ U)$;*
- *$(R \times S)^{-1} = R^{-1} \times S^{-1}$.*

Consequently, the set of the convex relations of $2^{\mathcal{B}_{rec}}$ is stable for the operations: intersection, composition and inverse. Hence the set of the convex relations of $2^{\mathcal{B}_{rec}}$ is a subclass of RA. From all this it follows that:

Proposition 7 *For all relations R and $S \in 2^{\mathcal{B}_{rec}}$, $I(R \circ S) \subseteq I(R) \circ I(S)$.*

Indeed, $I(R) \circ I(S)$ is a convex relation and contains the relation $R \circ S$.

Now, let us consider the subset of the weakly-preconvex relations, we denote this set by $\mathcal{W}$. We have the following result:

Proposition 8 $\mathcal{W}$ *is stable for the operations* $\circ$, $^{-1}$ *but it is not stable for the operation* $\bigcap$.

Proof. The proof of the stability of the composition is the same as the one given in [Ligozat, 1994] for the stability of the preconvex relations of IA: for all relations $R, S \in \mathcal{W}$, $I(R \circ S) \subseteq I(R) \circ I(S) \subseteq C(R) \circ C(S) \subseteq C(R \circ S)$. Hence, $R \circ S$ is a weakly-preconvex relation. We notice that for all basic relation $(A, B) \in \mathcal{B}_{rec}$, we have $C((A, B)^{-1}) = C((A, B))^{-1}$, so for all relation $R \in 2^{\mathcal{B}_{rec}}$, $C(R^{-1}) = C(R)^{-1}$. Moreover, owing to the symetry of the rectangle lattice, we have $I(R^{-1}) = I(R)^{-1}$. From these results, the stability of $\mathcal{W}$ for the operation inverse is obvious. $\square$

Unlike the case of IA, the weakly-preconvex relations in RA are not stable for the intersection. We can see it with the following counter-example. Let consider the two weakly-preconvex relations R, S of $2^{\mathcal{B}_{rec}}$ defined by $R = \{(o, o), (eq, s), (s, eq)\}$ and $S = \{(d, d), (eq, s), (s, eq)\}$. $R \cap S$ is the relation $\{(eq, s), (s, eq)\}$, this relation is not weakly-preconvex. This lack of stability – as we may see in the sequel – will raise some problem.

4 Constraints networks

We start this section with some reminders about constraints networks of RA [Balbiani *et al.*, 1998]. A rectangle network $\mathcal{N}$ is a structure (V, C), where $V = \{V_1, \ldots, V_n\}$ is a set of variables which represent rational rectangles, and C is a mapping from $V \times V$ to the set $2^{\mathcal{B}_{rec}}$ which represent the binary constraints between the rational rectangles. C is such that :

- for every $i \in \{1, \ldots, |V|\}$, $C_{ii} = \{(eq, eq)\}$;
- for every $i, j \in \{1, \ldots, |V|\}$, $C_{ij} = C_{ji}^{-1}$.

An interval network is defined in the same way except that V represents a set of rational intervals and C is to $2^{\mathcal{B}_{int}}$.

Let $\mathcal{N} = (V, C)$ be a rectangle network, the consistency and the path-consistency of $\mathcal{N}$ is defined in the following way:

- $\mathcal{N}$ is consistent iff there exists a mapping m from V to the set of rational rectangles such that, for every $i, j \in \{1, \ldots, |V|\}$, there exists a basic relation P such that $P \in C_{ij}$ and m_i and m_j satisfy P. We call such a mapping m, a satisfying instanciation of the network $\mathcal{N}$.

- $\mathcal{N}$ is path-consistent when, for every $i, j \in \{1, \ldots, |V|\}$, $C_{ij} \neq \{\}$ and for every $i, j, k \in \{1, \ldots, |V|\}$, $C_{ij} \subseteq C_{ik} \circ C_{kj}$.

We have the same definitions for the interval networks. A convex (respectively weakly-preconvex) network is a network which contains only convex relations (respectively weakly-preconvex relations).

We define another property, the weak path-consistency. A weakly path-consistent network is an almost path-consistent network:

Definition 5 *A rectangle (or interval) network is weakly path-consistent when, for every* $i, j \in \{1, \ldots, |V|\}$, $C_{ij} \neq \{\}$ *and for every* $i, j, k \in \{1, \ldots, |V|\}$, $C_{ij} \subseteq I(C_{ik} \circ C_{kj})$.

A path-consistent network is obviously weakly path-consistent, the contrary is not true.

A well-known polynomial method to see whether a network $\mathcal{N} = (V, C)$ is consistent, is the path-consistency method [Allen, 1983]. It consits to iterate on the network the triangulation operation: $C_{ij} := C_{ij} \cap (C_{ik} \circ C_{kj})$ for all $i, j, k \in \{1, \ldots, |V|\}$, until we obtain a stable network. It is sound but not complete as a decision procedure for the issue of the consistency of a network. Indeed, if after applying the method we obtain the empty relation then the network is not consistent, in the contrary case we do not know whether the network is consistent.

Similarly, we define a weaker method that we call the weak path-consistency method. It consists to iterate the weak triangulation operation $C_{ij} := C_{ij} \cap I(C_{ik} \circ C_{kj})$. The time complexity is the same as the one of the path-consistency method. Moreover, since $(C_{ik} \circ C_{kj}) \subseteq I(C_{ik} \circ C_{kj})$, this method is sound but not complete like the path-consistency method.

5 Results of tractability

Let $\mathcal{N} = (V, C)$ be a network and m be a satisfying instanciation of $\mathcal{N}$, we shall say that m is maximal iff for all $i, j \in \{1, \ldots, |V|\}$, $dim(P) = dim(C_{ij})$, with P the basic relation satisfied between m_i and m_j.

Ligozat [Ligozat, 1994] proves this important theorem:

Theorem 1 *Let* $\mathcal{N}$ *be an interval network which contains only preconvex relations, if* $\mathcal{N}$ *is path-consistent then there exists a maximal instanciation of* $\mathcal{N}$.

From this theorem we can prove the following lemma :

Lemma 1 *Let* $\mathcal{N} = (V, C)$ *be a convex rectangle network, if* $\mathcal{N}$ *is path-consistent then there exists a maximal instanciation of* $\mathcal{N}$.

Proof. Let $\mathcal{N}' = (V', C')$ and $\mathcal{N}'' = (V'', C'')$ be two interval networks defined by $V = V' = V''$ and for all $i, j \in \{1, \ldots, |V|\}$, $C'_{ij} = (C_{ij})_1$ and $C''_{ij} = (C_{ij})_2$. We can prove that $\mathcal{N}'$ and $\mathcal{N}''$ are path-consistent ,see [Balbiani *et al.*, 1998]. Moreover they are convex (a fortiori preconvex [1]). So there exists a maximal instanciation of $\mathcal{N}'$ and $\mathcal{N}''$, let us call them m' and m'' respectively. Let us consider the instanciation m of $\mathcal{N}$ such that for every $i, j \in \{1, \ldots, |V|\}$, m'_{ij} is the projection of the rational rectangle m_{ij} onto the horizontal axis and m''_{ij} is the projection of m_{ij} onto the vertical axis.

---

[1] We remind that the set of the preconvex relations contains the set of the convex relations in IA.

It is easy to see that m is a satisfying instantiation of $\mathcal{N}$. Moreover, m_i' (respectively m_i'') and m_j' (respectively m_j'') satisfy a basic relation A (respectively B) such that $dim(A) = dim(C_{ij}')$ (respectively $dim(B) = dim(C_{ij}'')$). So m_i and m_j are such that $dim((A, B)) = dim(C_{ij})$ because C_{ij} is a convex relation. So, m is a maximal instantiation of $\mathcal{N}$. $\square$

Consequently, for the weakly-preconvex relations of $2^{\mathcal{B}_{rec}}$, we have the following result:

Lemma 2 *Let $\mathcal{N} = (V, C)$ be a weakly-preconvex rectangle network, if $\mathcal{N}$ is weakly path-consistent then $\mathcal{N}$ is consistent, moreover there exists a maximal instantiation of $\mathcal{N}$.*

Proof. Let $\mathcal{N}' = (V', C')$ be the rectangle network such that $V' = V$ and for all $i, j \in \{1, \ldots, |V|\}$, $C_{ij}' = I(C_{ij})$. First, let us prove that $\mathcal{N}'$ is a path-consistent network: for all $i, j, k \in \{1, \ldots, |V|\}$ we have: $C_{ij} \subseteq I(C_{ik} \circ C_{kj})$, then $I(C_{ij}) \subseteq I(I(C_{ik} \circ C_{kj}))$, consequently $I(C_{ij}) \subseteq I(C_{ik} \circ C_{kj})$ and because $I(R \circ S) \subseteq I(R) \circ I(S)$ for all relations $R, S \in 2^{\mathcal{B}_{rec}}$, we obtain the result $I(C_{ij}) \subseteq I(C_{ik}) \circ I(C_{kj})$. So, $C_{ij}' \subseteq C_{ik}' \circ C_{kj}'$, hence $\mathcal{N}'$ is path-consistent.
$\mathcal{N}'$ is convex and path-consistent then there exists a maximal instantiation m of $\mathcal{N}'$. For each $i, j \in \{1, \ldots, |V|\}$, m_i and m_j satisfy a basic relation P of C_{ij}' such that $dim(P) = C_{ij}'$. C_{ij} is weakly-preconvex then $dim(I(C_{ij}) \setminus C_{ij}) < C_{ij}$. Moreover, remind that $C_{ij}' = I(C_{ij})$, consequently $P \in C_{ij}$ and $dim(P) = dim(C_{ij})$. Hence, m is also a maximal instantiation of the rectangle network $\mathcal{N}$. $\square$

Because a path-consistent network is also weakly path-consistent too, this lemma is true as well for a weakly-preconvex network $\mathcal{N}$ which is path-consistent instead of weakly path-consistent.
When we apply the path-consistency method from a weakly-preconvex network, we are not sure to obtain a weakly-preconvex network, because the set of the weakly-preconvex relations is not stable for the operation intersection, likewise with weak path-consistency method because the intersection between a weakly-preconvex relation and a convex relation is not always a weakly-preconvex relation. For example, the intersection between the weakly-preconvex relation $\{(d, d), (eq, s), (s, eq)\}$ and the convex relation $\{(s, s), (eq, s), (s, eq), (eq, eq)\}$ is $\{(s, eq), (eq, s)\}$ which is not weakly-preconvex. Hence, despite the previous lemma, we cannot assert that the path-consistency method or the weak path-consistency method are decision procedures for the issue of the consistency of a rectangle network which contains only weakly-preconvex relations. But we can characterise some subsets of $2^{\mathcal{B}_{rec}}$ for which it works:

Theorem 2 *(Main result) Let $E \subset \mathcal{W}$, stable for the intersection with the convex relations.*
The weak path-consistency method is a decision procedure for the issue of the consistency of a rectangle network which contains just constraints in E.

Proof. From the previous lemma the proof is direct. Let $\mathcal{N}$ be a rectangle network whose constraints are in E. After applying the weak path-consistency method from $\mathcal{N}$, we obtain a network $\mathcal{N}'$ whose constraints are always in E and consequently which is weakly-preconvex. Moreover, $\mathcal{N}'$ is equivalent to $\mathcal{N}$, so if $\mathcal{N}'$ contains the empty relation then $\mathcal{N}'$ and $\mathcal{N}$ are not consistent. Else, from the previous lemma we deduce that there exists a maximal instantiation of $\mathcal{N}'$ and consequently $\mathcal{N}'$ and $\mathcal{N}$ are consistent. $\square$

Moreover, we can assert that path-consistency method is also complete for rectangle networks whose relations are in such a set E.

Let us denote by $\overline{F}$ the closure of a set F of relations by the operations intersection, composition and inverse. Nebel and Bürckert [Nebel *et al.*, 1994] show that from an interval network whose constraints are in $\overline{F}$ we can construct, in polynomial time, another interval network whose constraints are in F and such that the former network is consistent if and only if the latter is consistent. We can prove the same thing in RA. Hence, if E is a set of rectangle relations having the properties of the previous theorem, then the problem of the consistency of the networks whose relations belong to $\overline{E}$ is a polynomial problem.

6 The strongly-preconvex relations

In this section, first, we are going to define a new set with the properties of theorem 2: the set of the strongly-preconvex relations of RA. Then, we shall prove that this set is the maximal set for these properties.

The strongly-preconvex relations of RA are defined by:

Definition 6 *Let R be a relation of $2^{\mathcal{B}_{rec}}$, R is a strongly-preconvex relation if, and only if, for all convex relations S, $R \cap S$ is a weakly-preconvex relation.*

The universal relation of $2^{\mathcal{B}_{rec}}$ is a convex relation, from this we deduce that a strongly-preconvex relation is a weakly-preconvex relation. We denote the set of the strongly-preconvex relations by $\mathcal{S}$. The convex relations are stable for the intersection and are weakly-preconvex relations. So, they belong to $\mathcal{S}$. What is more:

Proposition 9 *If $R, S \in \mathcal{S}$ then $R \cap S \in \mathcal{W}$.*

Proof. First, we are going to prove that $I(C(R \cap S)) = C(R \cap S)$. Let us denote $I(C(R \cap S))$ by T.
We have $R \cap S \subseteq T$, so $R \cap S \subseteq T \cap R$ and $R \cap S \subseteq T \cap S$. Consequently $T \subseteq I(C(T \cap R))$ and $T \subseteq I(C(T \cap S))$. Because R and S are strongly-preconvex relations and T is a convex relation, $T \cap R$ and $T \cap S$ are two weakly-preconvex relations. Consequently $C(T \cap R)$ and $C(T \cap S)$ are two convex relations hence, $T \subseteq C(T \cap R)$ and $T \subseteq C(T \cap S)$. When we compute the topological closure of a relation, we add only basic relations of lower dimension. So, $dim(T) = dim(C(T \cap R))$ and $dim(T) = dim(C(T \cap S))$. Le P be a basic relation such $P \in T$ and $dim(P) = dim(T)$. From the previous results we deduce that $P \in C(T \cap R)$, $P \in C(T \cap S)$, and $dim(P) = dim(C(T \cap R)) = dim(C(T \cap S))$. So, as $T \cap R$ and

$T \cap S$ are weakly-preconvex relations, $P \in T \cap R$ and $P \in T \cap S$, hence $P \in C(R \cap S)$. Let Q be any basic relation belonging to T, from proposition 3, we can deduce too that $Q \in C(R \cap S)$. Hence $T \subseteq C(R \cap S)$.
$C(R \cap S) \subseteq I(C(R \cap S)) \subseteq C(R \cap S)$, so $R \cap S$ is a weakly-preconvex relation of $2^{\mathcal{B}_{rec}}$. □

Moreover, we can prove the following result:

Proposition 10 S *is stable for the intersection with the convex relations of* $2^{\mathcal{B}_{rec}}$.

Proof. Let R and S be two relations of $2^{\mathcal{B}_{rec}}$ such that R is a strongly-preconvex relation and S a convex relation. Let us prove that $R \cap S$ is a strongly-preconvex relation. Let T be any convex relation, we have : $(R \cap S) \cap T = R \cap (S \cap T)$. $S \cap T$ is a convex relation too. R is a strongly-preconvex relation, we can deduce that $R \cap (S \cap T)$ is a weakly-preconvex relation, hence $R \cap S$ is a strongly-preconvex relation. □

Consequently, we can apply theorem 2 on the set S. From the last two propositions we can easily prove that S is stable for the intersection. S is stable for the inverse operation too. But we have not yet succeeded in proving the composition stability, so perhaps $\overline{S} = S$. Moreover, let E be a set with the properties of theorem 2, we can easily prove that $E \subseteq S$. From all this it follows:

Theorem 3 S *is tractable and* S *is the maximal set included in* W *and stable for the intersection with the convex relations.*

Hence, S is the maximal set with the properties of theorem 2.

A saturated-preconvex relation of $2^{\mathcal{B}_{rec}}$ corresponds to the cartesian product of two preconvex relations of $2^{\mathcal{B}_{int}}$ [Balbiani *et al.*, 1998]. By using this and the fact that the set of the saturated-preconvex relations is stable for the intersection [Balbiani *et al.*, 1998], from proposition 3 we can prove that the set of the saturated-preconvex relations is a subset of S. Moreover, it is a proper subset of S. For example, let us consider the relation $\{(o, o), (s, eq), (eq, s), (s, s)\}$ which is strongly-preconvex but not saturated-preconvex. So, now $\overline{S}$ is the largest known set to be a tractable set which contains the basic relations. This result provides also another proof of the tractability of saturated-preconvex relations.

7 Conclusion

The subclass generated by the set of the strongly-preconvex relations is now the biggest known tractable set of RA which contains the 169 atomic relations. An open question is: is this subclass a maximal tractable subclass which contains the atomic relations ?

Another future development is to extend RA to a greater dimension than two. For dimension n ($n \geq 3$), the considered objects will be the blocks whose sides are parallel to the axes of some orthogonal basis in a n-dimensional Euclidean space. The atomic relations between these objects are the 13^n relations obtained by the cartesian product of atomic relations of IA. A first attempt shows that the previous tractability results of RA can be easily extended to this structure.

References

[Allen, 1983] J. Allen. *Maintaining knowledge about temporal intervals.* Communications of the ACM, Volume 26, 832–843, 1983.

[Balbiani *et al.*, 1998] P. Balbiani, J-F. Condotta and L. Fariñas del Cerro. *A model for reasoning about bidimensional temporal relations.* A.G. Cohn, L. Schubert, and S.C. Shapiro (editors), KR'98. Proc. of the 6th Int. Conf., 124–130, Morgan Kaufmann, 1998.

[Egenhofer *et al.*, 1991] M. Egenhofer and R. Franzosa. *Point-set topological spatial relations.* International Journal of Geographical Information Systems 5(2), 161–174, 1991.

[Freska, 1992] C. Freska. *Using orientation information for qualitative spatial reasoning.* A.U. Frank, I. Campari, and U. Formentini (editors), Theories and Methods of Spatio-Temporal Reasoning in Geographic Space, Proc. of the Int. Conf. GIS - From Space to Territory, 162–178, Springer Verlag, 1992.

[Güsgen, 1989] H. Güsgen. *Spatial reasoning based on Allen's temporal logic.* Report ICSI TR89-049, International Computer Science Institute, 1989.

[Ligozat, 1994] G. Ligozat. *Tractable relations in temporal reasoning: pre-convex relations.* ECAI-94. Workshop on Spatial and Temporal Reasoning, 99-108, 1994.

[Ligozat, 1996] G. Ligozat. *A new proof of tractability for ORD-Horn relations.* AAAI-96. Proc. of the 13th Nat. Conf. on Artificial Intelligence, Volume one, 395–401, AAAI Press and MIT Press, 1996.

[Nebel *et al.*, 1994] B. Nebel, H.-J. Bürckert. *Reasoning about temporal relations : a maximal tractable subclass of Allen's interval algebra.* AAAI-94. Proc. of the 12th Nat. Conf. on Artificial Intelligence, Volume one, 356–361, AAAI Press and MIT Press, 1994.

[Mukerjee *et al.*, 1990] A. Mukerjee, G. Joe. *A Qualitative Model For Space.* AAAI-90. Proc. of the 8th Nat. Conf. on Artificial Intelligence, Volume two, 721–727, AAAI Press and MIT Press, 1990.

[Randell *et al.*, 1992] D. Randell, Z. Cui, T. Cohn. *An interval logic for space based on "connection".* B. Neumann (editor), ECAI-92. Proc. of the 10th European Conf. on Artificial Intelligence, 394–398, Wiley, 1992.

[Renz *et al.*, 1997] J. Renz, B. Nebel. *On the complexity of qualitative spatial reasoning: a maximal tractable fragment of the region connection calculus.* M. Polack (editor), IJCAI-97. Proc. of the 15th Int. Joint Conf. on Artificial Intelligence, Volume one, 522–527, Morgan Kaufmann, 1997.

[Beek, 1992] P. van Beek. *Reasoning about qualitative temporal information.* Artificial Intelligence, 58(1-3), 297–321, 1992.

Maximal Tractable Fragments of the Region Connection Calculus: A Complete Analysis

Jochen Renz

Institut für Informatik, Albert-Ludwigs-Universität
Am Flughafen 17, 79110 Freiburg, Germany

Abstract

We present a general method for proving tractability of reasoning over disjunctions of jointly exhaustive and pairwise disjoint relations. Examples of these kinds of relations are Allen's temporal interval relations and their spatial counterpart, the RCC8 relations by Randell, Cui, and Cohn. Applying this method does not require detailed knowledge about the considered relations; instead, it is rather sufficient to have a subset of the considered set of relations for which path-consistency is known to decide consistency. Using this method, we give a complete classification of tractability of reasoning over RCC8 by identifying two large new maximal tractable subsets and show that these two subsets together with $\widehat{\mathcal{H}}_8$, the already known maximal tractable subset, are the only such sets for RCC8 that contain all base relations. We also apply our method to Allen's interval algebra and derive the known maximal tractable subset.

1 Introduction

In qualitative spatial and temporal reasoning, knowledge is often represented by specifying the relationships between spatial or temporal entities. Of particular interest are disjunctions over a set of jointly exhaustive and pairwise disjoint (JEPD) relations. JEPD relations are also called *base relations*. Since any two entities are related by exactly one of the base relations, they can be used to represent definite information with respect to the given level of granularity. Indefinite information can be specified by disjunctions of possible base relations.

An important reasoning problem is deciding consistency of a set of constraints using these relations, which is in many cases NP-hard. Sometimes deciding consistency is tractable if only a subset of all possible disjunctions is used. If this subset contains all base relations, then instances of the NP-hard consistency problem can be solved by backtracking over tractable subinstances [Ladkin and Reinefeld, 1992; Nebel, 1997].

Larger tractable subsets often lead to more efficient solutions (cf. [Renz and Nebel, 1998]). The goal is to identify the boundary between tractable and NP-hard subsets, i.e., all maximal tractable subsets containing all base relations.

Two examples of these types of relations are Allen's interval algebra [Allen, 1983] mainly used for temporal reasoning and their spatial counterpart, Randell, Cui, and Cohn's [1992] Region Connection Calculus RCC-8. In the former case, the only maximal tractable subset containing all base relations has been identified [Nebel and Bürckert, 1995], in the latter case, only one maximal tractable subset has been identified so far [Renz and Nebel, 1999]. It was previously unknown whether there are others containing all base relations. For both subsets path-consistency is sufficient for deciding consistency. Tractability and sufficiency of path-consistency have been proven by reducing the consistency problem to a tractable propositional satisfiability problem which requires very detailed knowledge about the considered set of relations and complicated proofs.

We present a new method for proving tractability and showing sufficiency of path-consistency for this kind of problem which does not require detailed knowledge about the considered set of relations. Applying this method, we identify two large new maximal tractable subsets of RCC-8 and show that these subsets together with the already known maximal tractable subset are the only such sets for RCC-8 that contain all base relations. We consider only sets containing all base relations, since only these sets enable efficient backtracking algorithms.

The paper is structured as follows. In Section 2 we introduce RCC-8. In Section 3 we present the new method for proving tractability. In Section 4 we identify two large subsets of RCC-8 which are candidates for maximal tractable subsets, and apply our new method in Section 5 to show that both sets are tractable. In Section 6 the new method is used for finding a consistent scenario. In Section 7 we apply the method to Allen's interval algebra after which we discuss and summarize our results. Some of our proofs are computer assisted. The programs are available at http://www.informatik.uni-freiburg.de/~sppraum.

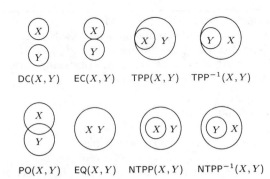

Figure 1: Examples for the eight base relations of RCC-8

2 The Region Connection Calculus RCC8

The Region Connection Calculus RCC-8 [Randell *et al.*, 1992] is a language for qualitative spatial representation and reasoning where *spatial regions* are regular subsets of a topological space. Regions themselves do not have to be internally connected, i.e., a region may consist of different disconnected pieces.

RCC-8 contains eight JEPD base relations and all 2^8 possible disjunctions thereof. The base relations are denoted by DC, EC, PO, EQ, TPP, NTPP, TPP^{-1}, and $NTPP^{-1}$, with the meaning of *DisConnected, Externally Connected, Partial Overlap, EQual, Tangential Proper Part, Non-Tangential Proper Part*, and their converses. Two-dimensional examples of the base relations are shown in Figure 1. In the following we write sets of base relations to denote disjunctions of base relations. The disjunction of all base relations is called the *universal relation*. The subset of RCC-8 consisting of the eight base relations is denoted by $\mathcal{B}$.

An important reasoning problem in this framework, denoted by RSAT, is deciding *consistency* of a set Θ of constraints of the form xRy, where R is an RCC-8 relation and x, y are spatial variables. The domain of spatial variables is the set of all spatial regions of the considered topological space. Θ is consistent if it has a *solution*, which is an assignment of spatial regions to the spatial variables of Θ in a way that all constraints are satisfied. When only relations of a specific subset $\mathcal{S} \subseteq$ RCC-8 are used in Θ, the corresponding reasoning problem is denoted by RSAT($\mathcal{S}$). RSAT is NP-complete in general. Consistency of Θ can be approximated by using an $O(n^3)$ time *path-consistency* algorithm, which makes Θ *path-consistent* by eliminating all the impossible labels (base relations) in every subset of constraints involving three variables [Mackworth, 1977]. If the empty relation occurs during this process, then Θ is inconsistent, otherwise the resulting set is path-consistent.

Renz and Nebel [1999] identified a tractable subset of RCC-8 (denoted by $\widehat{\mathcal{H}}_8$) containing all base relations which is maximal with respect to tractability, i.e., if any other RCC-8 relation is added to $\widehat{\mathcal{H}}_8$, the consistency problem becomes NP-complete. They further showed that enforcing path-consistency is sufficient for deciding RSAT($\widehat{\mathcal{H}}_8$). $\widehat{\mathcal{H}}_8$ contains 148 relations, i.e., about 60% of all RCC-8 relations.

3 A New Method for Proving Tractability of Sets of Relations

In this section we develop a new method for proving tractability of reasoning over disjunctions of a JEPD set of binary relations over a domain $\mathcal{D}$. Let $\mathcal{A}$ be a finite set of JEPD binary relations. We assume in the following that there is a relation $Id \in \mathcal{A}$ such that $Id(d, d)$ is satisfied for all $d \in D$. Id is called *identity relation*. The consistency problem CSPSAT($\mathcal{S}$) for sets $\mathcal{S} \subseteq 2^{\mathcal{A}}$ over a domain $\mathcal{D}$ is defined as follows [Renz and Nebel, 1999]:

Instance: A set V of variables over a domain D and a finite set Θ of binary constraints xRy, where $R \in \mathcal{S}$ and $x, y \in V$.

Question: Is there an instantiation of all variables in Θ such that all constraints are satisfied?

$\widehat{\mathcal{S}}$ denotes the closure of $\mathcal{S}$ under composition ($\circ$), intersection ($\cap$) and converse ($\smile$). CSPSAT($\widehat{\mathcal{S}}$) can be polynomially reduced to CSPSAT($\mathcal{S}$) if the universal relation is contained in $\mathcal{S}$ [Renz and Nebel, 1999]. Therefore, we consider in the following only sets $\mathcal{S} \subseteq 2^{\mathcal{A}}$ with $\mathcal{S} = \widehat{\mathcal{S}}$.

Before we present our new method for showing that CSPSAT($\mathcal{S}$) is tractable for a set $\mathcal{S}$, we define some terminology. A *refinement* of a constraint xRy is a constraint $xR'y$ such that $R' \subseteq R$. For instance, the constraint $x\{DC, TPP\}y$ is a refinement of the constraint $x\{DC, EC, PO, TPP\}y$. A refinement of a set of constraints Θ is a set of constraints Θ' that contains a refinement of every constraint of Θ. Every solution of Θ' is also a solution of Θ. A *consistent scenario* Θ_s of Θ is a refinement of Θ such that Θ_s is consistent and contains only constraints over relations of $\mathcal{A}$. We assume that a set of constraints Θ contains n ordered variables $x_1, \ldots, x_n$. The following definition will be central for our new method.

Definition 1 (reduction by refinement)
Let $\mathcal{S}, \mathcal{T} \subseteq 2^{\mathcal{A}}$. $\mathcal{S}$ can be reduced by refinement to $\mathcal{T}$, if the following two conditions are satisfied:

1. *for every relation $S \in \mathcal{S}$ there is a relation $T_S \in \mathcal{T}$ with $T_S \subseteq S$,*

2. *every path-consistent set Θ of constraints over $\mathcal{S}$ can be refined to a set Θ' by replacing $x_iSx_j \in \Theta$ with $x_iT_Sx_j \in \Theta'$ for $i < j$,[1] such that enforcing path-consistency to Θ' does not result in an inconsistency.*

Lemma 2 *If path-consistency decides CSPSAT($\mathcal{T}$) for a set $\mathcal{T} \subseteq 2^{\mathcal{A}}$, and $\mathcal{S}$ can be reduced by refinement to $\mathcal{T}$, then path-consistency decides CSPSAT($\mathcal{S}$).*

Proof. Let Θ be a path-consistent set of constraints over $\mathcal{S}$. Since $\mathcal{S}$ can be reduced by refinement to $\mathcal{T}$, there is

---

[1]Note that we only refine constraints x_iSx_j for $i < j$. This is no restriction, as by enforcing path-consistency the converse constraint $x_jS^{\smile}x_i$ will also be refined. Rather it offers the possibility of refining, e.g., converse relations to other than converse sub-relations, i.e., if, for instance, R is refined to r, we can refine $R^{\smile}$ to a relation other than $r^{\smile}$.

by definition a set Θ' of constraints over $\mathcal{T}$ which is a refinement of Θ such that enforcing path-consistency to Θ' does not result in an inconsistency. Path-consistency decides $\mathsf{CSPSAT}(\mathcal{T})$, so Θ' is consistent, and, hence, Θ is also consistent. ∎

Since path-consistency can be enforced in cubic time, it is sufficient for proving tractability of $\mathsf{CSPSAT}(\mathcal{S})$ to show that $\mathcal{S}$ can be reduced by refinement to a set $\mathcal{T}$ for which path-consistency decides $\mathsf{CSPSAT}(\mathcal{T})$. Note that for refining a constraint xSy ($S \in \mathcal{S}$) to a constraint xT_Sy ($T_S \in \mathcal{T}$), it is not required that T_S is also contained in $\mathcal{S}$. Thus, with respect to common relations, the two sets $\mathcal{S}$ and $\mathcal{T}$ are independent of each other.

We will now develop a method for showing that a set of relations $\mathcal{S} \subseteq 2^{\mathcal{A}}$ can be reduced by refinement to another set $\mathcal{T} \subseteq 2^{\mathcal{A}}$. In order to manage the different refinements, we introduce a *refinement matrix* that contains for every relation $S \in \mathcal{S}$ all specified refinements.

Definition 3 (refinement matrix) *A refinement matrix M of $\mathcal{S}$ has $|\mathcal{S}| \times 2^{|\mathcal{A}|}$ Boolean entries such that for $S \in \mathcal{S}$, $R \in 2^{\mathcal{A}}$, $M[S][R] = true$ only if $R \subseteq S$.*

For example, if the relation $\{\mathsf{DC}, \mathsf{EC}, \mathsf{PO}, \mathsf{TPP}\}$ is allowed to be refined only to the relations $\{\mathsf{DC}, \mathsf{TPP}\}$ and $\{\mathsf{DC}\}$, then $M[\{\mathsf{DC}, \mathsf{EC}, \mathsf{PO}, \mathsf{TPP}\}][R]$ is *true* only for $R = \{\mathsf{DC}, \mathsf{TPP}\}$ and for $R = \{\mathsf{DC}\}$ and *false* for all other relations $R \in 2^{\mathcal{A}}$. M is called the *basic refinement matrix* if $M[S][R] = true$ if and only if $S = R$.

We propose the algorithm CHECK-REFINEMENTS (see Figure 2) which takes as input a set of relations $\mathcal{S}$ and a refinement matrix M of $\mathcal{S}$. This algorithm computes all possible path-consistent triples of relations R_{12}, R_{23}, R_{13} of $\mathcal{S}$ (step 4) and enforces path-consistency (using a standard procedure PATH-CONSISTENCY) to every refinement $R'_{12}, R'_{23}, R'_{13}$ for which $M[R_{ij}][R'_{ij}] = true$ for all $i, j \in \{1, 2, 3\}, i < j$ (steps 5,6). If one of these refinements results in the empty relation, the algorithm returns $\mathtt{fail}$ (step 7). Otherwise, the resulting relations $R''_{12}, R''_{23}, R''_{13}$ are added to M by setting $M[R_{ij}][R''_{ij}] = true$ for all $i, j \in \{1, 2, 3\}, i < j$ (step 8). This is repeated until M has reached a fixed point (step 9), i.e., enforcing path-consistency on any possible refinement does not result in new relations anymore. If no inconsistency is detected in this process, the algorithm returns $\mathtt{succeed}$.

A similar algorithm, GET-REFINEMENTS, returns the revised refinement matrix if CHECK-REFINEMENTS returns $\mathtt{succeed}$ and the basic refinement matrix if CHECK-REFINEMENTS returns $\mathtt{fail}$. Since $\mathcal{A}$ is a finite set of relations, M can be changed only a finite number of times, so both algorithms always terminate.

Lemma 4 *Let Θ be a path-consistent set of constraints over $\mathcal{S}$ and M a refinement matrix of $\mathcal{S}$. For every refinement Θ' of Θ with $x_i R' x_j \in \Theta'$ only if $x_i R x_j \in \Theta$, $i < j$, and $M[R][R'] = true$: if CHECK-REFINEMENTS$(\mathcal{S}, M)$ returns $\mathtt{succeed}$, enforcing path-consistency to Θ' does not result in an inconsistency.*

Algorithm: CHECK-REFINEMENTS
Input: A set $\mathcal{S}$ and a refinement matrix M of $\mathcal{S}$.
Output: $\mathtt{fail}$ if the refinements specified in M can make a path-consistent triple of constraints over $\mathcal{S}$ inconsistent; $\mathtt{succeed}$ otherwise.

1. $changes \leftarrow true$
2. *while* changes *do*
3. $oldM \leftarrow M$
4.   *for every* path-consistent triple
        $T = (R_{12}, R_{23}, R_{13})$ of relations over $\mathcal{S}$ *do*
5.   *for every* refinement $T' = (R'_{12}, R'_{23}, R'_{13})$ of T
         with $oldM[R_{12}][R'_{12}] = oldM[R_{23}][R'_{23}] = $
         $oldM[R_{13}][R'_{13}] = true$ *do*
6. $T'' \leftarrow$ PATH-CONSISTENCY(T')
7.   *if* $T'' = (R''_{12}, R''_{23}, R''_{13})$ contains the empty
          relation *then return* $\mathtt{fail}$
8.   *else do* $M[R_{12}][R''_{12}] \leftarrow true$,
             $M[R_{23}][R''_{23}] \leftarrow true$,
             $M[R_{13}][R''_{13}] \leftarrow true$
9.   *if* $M = oldM$ *then* changes $\leftarrow false$
10. *return* $\mathtt{succeed}$

Figure 2: Algorithm CHECK-REFINEMENTS

Proof. Suppose that CHECK-REFINEMENTS$(\mathcal{S}, M)$ returns $\mathtt{succeed}$ and GET-REFINEMENTS$(\mathcal{S}, M)$ returns the refinement matrix M'. Suppose further that enforcing path-consistency to Θ' results in an inconsistency which is detected first for the three variables x_a, x_b, x_c. Suppose that for every pair of variables x_i, x_j, $x_i R_{ij} x_j \in \Theta$ and $x_i R'_{ij} x_j \in \Theta'$. Enforcing path-consistency to Θ' can be done by successively enforcing path-consistency to every triple of variables of Θ'. Suppose that we start with the triple x_1, x_2, x_3. We have that $M'[R_{ij}][R'_{ij}] = true$ for every $i, j \in \{1, 2, 3\}, i < j$. After enforcing path-consistency to this triple we obtain the relations R''_{ij} for which again $M'[R_{ij}][R''_{ij}] = true$, otherwise CHECK-REFINEMENTS$(\mathcal{S}, M)$ would have returned $\mathtt{fail}$. The same holds when we proceed with enforcing path-consistency to every triple of variables, we always end up with relations R^*_{ij} for which $M'[R_{ij}][R^*_{ij}] = true$. Therefore, for all possible relations $R^*_{ab}, R^*_{bc}, R^*_{ac}$ we can obtain by enforcing path-consistency to Θ' we have that $M'[R_{ij}][R^*_{ij}] = true$ for all $i, j \in \{a, b, c\}, i < j$. If this triple of relations were inconsistent, CHECK-REFINEMENTS$(\mathcal{S}, M)$ would have returned $\mathtt{fail}$. ∎

If CHECK-REFINEMENTS returns $\mathtt{succeed}$ and GET-REFINEMENTS returns M', we have pre-computed all possible refinements of every path-consistent triple of variables as given in the refinement matrix M'. Thus, applying these refinements to a path-consistent set of constraints can never result in an inconsistency when enforcing path-consistency.

Theorem 5 *Let $\mathcal{S}, \mathcal{T} \subseteq 2^{\mathcal{A}}$, and let M be a refinement matrix of $\mathcal{S}$. GET-REFINEMENTS$(\mathcal{S}, M)$ returns the refinement matrix M'. If for every $S \in \mathcal{S}$ there is a $T_S \in \mathcal{T}$ with $M'[S][T_S] = true$, then $\mathcal{S}$ can be reduced by refinement to $\mathcal{T}$.*

Proof. By the given conditions, we can refine every path-consistent set Θ of constraints over $\mathcal{S}$ to a set Θ' of constraints over $\mathcal{T}$ such that $M'[R_{ij}][R'_{ij}] = true$ for every $x_i R_{ij} x_j \in \Theta$ and $x_i R'_{ij} x_j \in \Theta'$, $i < j$, $R'_{ij} \in \mathcal{T}$. M' is a fixed point with respect to GET-REFINEMENTS, i.e., GET-REFINEMENTS$(\mathcal{S}, M')$ returns M', thus it follows from Lemma 4 that enforcing path-consistency to Θ' does not result in an inconsistency. ∎

By Lemma 2 and Theorem 5 we have that the procedures CHECK-REFINEMENTS and GET-REFINEMENTS can be used to prove tractability for sets of relations.

Corollary 6 *Let* $\mathcal{S}, \mathcal{T} \subseteq 2^{\mathcal{A}}$ *be two sets such that path-consistency decides* CSPSAT$(\mathcal{T})$, *and let* M *be a refinement matrix of* $\mathcal{S}$. GET-REFINEMENTS$(\mathcal{S}, M)$ *returns* M'. *If for every* $S \in \mathcal{S}$ *there is a* $T_S \in \mathcal{T}$ *with* $M'[S][T_S] = true$, *then path-consistency decides* CSPSAT$(\mathcal{S})$.

In the following sections we apply this method to the Region Connection Calculus RCC-8 and to Allen's interval algebra for proving certain subsets to be tractable. For RCC-8 it will help us make a complete analysis of tractability by identifying two large new maximal tractable subsets. Later, it will turn out that the new method can be used for identifying the fastest possible algorithms for finding a consistent scenario.

4 Candidates for Maximal Tractable Subsets of RCC8

In order to identify maximal tractable subsets of a set of relations with an NP-hard consistency problem, two different tasks have to be done. On the one hand, tractable subsets have to be identified. On the other hand, NP-hard subsets have to be identified. Then, a tractable subset is maximal tractable if any superset is NP-hard. If tractability has not yet been shown for certain subsets, the NP-hardness results restrict the number of different subsets that still have to be analyzed for tractability.

In this section we present new NP-hardness results for RCC-8 and identify those subsets that are candidates for maximal tractable subsets, i.e., if any other relation is added to one of those candidates they become NP-hard. Before this, we summarize Renz and Nebel's [1999] NP-hardness proofs that were necessary for showing that $\widehat{\mathcal{H}}_8$ is a maximal tractable subset of RCC-8.

Lemma 7 (Renz and Nebel, 1999) RSAT$(\mathcal{B} \cup \{R\})$ *is NP-hard if* $R \in \mathcal{N} \subseteq$ RCC-8, *where:*

$$\mathcal{N} = \{R \mid \{\text{PO}\} \not\subseteq R \text{ and } \{(\text{N})\text{TPP}, (\text{N})\text{TPP}^{-1}\} \subseteq R\}.$$

(N)TPP *indicates either* TPP *or* NTPP.

Renz and Nebel [1999] proved maximality of $\widehat{\mathcal{H}}_8$ by showing that RSAT$(\widehat{\mathcal{H}}_8 \cup \{\text{EQ, NTPP}\})$ is NP-hard and that the closure of $\widehat{\mathcal{H}}_8$ plus any relation of RCC-8 $\setminus (\widehat{\mathcal{H}}_8 \cup \mathcal{N})$ contains the relation $\{\text{EQ, NTPP}\}$. This NP-hardness proof, however, does not make use of all relations of $\widehat{\mathcal{H}}_8$, but only of the relations $\{\text{EC, TPP}\}$ and $\{\text{EC, NTPP}\}$.

Thus, any set of RCC-8 relations that contains all base relations plus the relations $\{\text{EC, TPP}\}$, $\{\text{EC, NTPP}\}$, and $\{\text{EQ, NTPP}\}$ is NP-hard.

This result rules out a lot of subsets of RCC-8 to be tractable, but still leaves the problem of tractability open for a large number of subsets. We found, however, that it is not necessary that both relations, $\{\text{EC, TPP}\}$ and $\{\text{EC, NTPP}\}$, must be added to $\{\text{EQ, NTPP}\}$ in order to enforce NP-hardness. It is rather sufficient for NP-hardness that only one of them is added to $\{\text{EQ, NTPP}\}$.

This is shown in the following two lemmata. They are proven by reducing 3SAT, the NP-hard satisfiability problem of propositional formulas that contain exactly three literals per clause [Garey and Johnson, 1979], to the respective consistency problem. Both reductions are similar to the reductions given in [Renz and Nebel, 1999]: every literal as well as every literal occurrence L is reduced to a constraint $X_L R Y_L$ where $R = R_t \cup R_f$ and $R_t \cap R_f = \emptyset$. L is true iff $X_L R_t Y_L$ holds and false iff $X_L R_f Y_L$ holds. "Polarity constraints" enforce that $X_{\neg L} R_t Y_{\neg L}$ holds iff $X_L R_f Y_L$ holds, and *vice versa*. "Clause constraints" enforce that at least one literal of every clause is true.

Lemma 8 *If* $(\mathcal{B} \cup \{\{\text{EQ, NTPP}\}, \{\text{EC, NTPP}\}\}) \subseteq \mathcal{S}$, *then* RSAT$(\mathcal{S})$ *is NP-complete.*

Proof Sketch. Transformation of 3SAT to RSAT$(\mathcal{S})$. $R_t = \{\text{NTPP}\}$ and $R_f = \{\text{EQ}\}$. Polarity constraints:

$$X_L\{\text{EC}\}X_{\neg L}, Y_L\overline{\{\text{DC, EC}\}}Y_{\neg L},$$
$$X_L\{\text{EC, NTPP}\}Y_{\neg L}, X_{\neg L}\{\text{EC, NTPP}\}Y_L.$$

Clause constraints for each clause $c = \{i, j, k\}$: $Y_i\{\text{NTPP}^{-1}\}X_j, Y_j\{\text{NTPP}^{-1}\}X_k, Y_k\{\text{NTPP}^{-1}\}X_i$. $\overline{\{\text{DC, EC}\}}$ is contained in $\widehat{\mathcal{S}}$. ∎

Lemma 9 *If* $(\mathcal{B} \cup \{\{\text{EQ, NTPP}\}, \{\text{EC, TPP}\}\}) \subseteq \mathcal{S}$, *then* RSAT$(\mathcal{S})$ *is NP-complete.*

Proof Sketch. Transformation of 3SAT to RSAT$(\mathcal{S})$. $R_t = \{\text{NTPP}\}$ and $R_f = \{\text{EQ}\}$. Polarity constraints:

$$X_L\{\text{DC, EC, TPP}\}Y_{\neg L}, X_L\{\text{DC, NTPP}^{-1}\}X_{\neg L},$$
$$Y_L\{\text{EC, TPP}\}Y_{\neg L}, X_{\neg L}\{\text{DC, EC, PO, TPP, NTPP}\}Y_L.$$

Clause constraints for each clause $c = \{i, j, k\}$: $Y_i\{\text{NTPP}^{-1}\}X_j, Y_j\{\text{NTPP}^{-1}\}X_k, Y_k\{\text{NTPP}^{-1}\}X_i$. All the above relations are contained in $\widehat{\mathcal{S}}$. ∎

Using these results, four other relations can be ruled out to be contained in any tractable subset of RCC-8, since the closure of the base relations plus one of the four relations contains $\{\text{EQ, NTPP}\}$ as well as $\{\text{EC, TPP}\}$.

Definition 10 *The two sets* $\mathcal{NP}_8$ *and* $\mathcal{P}_8$ *are defined as follows:*

- $\mathcal{NP}_8 = \mathcal{N} \cup \{\{\text{EC, NTPP, EQ}\}, \{\text{EC, NTPP}^{-1}, \text{EQ}\}, \{\text{DC, EC, NTPP, EQ}\}, \{\text{DC, EC, NTPP}^{-1}, \text{EQ}\}\}$.

- $\mathcal{P}_8 = $ RCC-8 $\setminus \mathcal{NP}_8$.

$\mathcal{NP}_8$ contains 76 relations, $\mathcal{P}_8$ contains 180 relations.

Corollary 11 RSAT$(\mathcal{B} \cup \{R\})$ *is NP-hard, if* $R \in \mathcal{NP}_8$.

Lemmata 8 and 9 give us a sufficient but not necessary condition of whether a subset of $\mathcal{P}_8$ is NP-hard, namely, if $\mathcal{B} \subseteq \widehat{\mathcal{S}} \subseteq \mathcal{P}_8$ contains $\{EQ, NTPP\}$ and one of $\{EC, TPP\}$ or $\{EC, NTPP\}$, $RSAT(\mathcal{S})$ is NP-hard, otherwise the complexity of $RSAT(\mathcal{S})$ remains open.

We computed all subsets of $\mathcal{P}_8$ that are candidates for maximal tractable subsets with respect to the above two NP-hardness proofs, i.e., we enumerated all subsets $\mathcal{S} \subseteq \mathcal{P}_8$ with $\mathcal{S} = \widehat{\mathcal{S}}$ that contain all base relations and the universal relation, and checked whether they fulfilled the following two properties:

1. $\mathcal{S}$ does not contain ($\{EQ, NTPP\}$ and $\{EC, TPP\}$) or ($\{EQ, NTPP\}$ and $\{EC, NTPP\}$), and

2. the closure of $\mathcal{S}$ plus any relation of $\mathcal{P}_8 \setminus \mathcal{S}$ contains ($\{EQ, NTPP\}$ and $\{EC, TPP\}$) or ($\{EQ, NTPP\}$ and $\{EC, NTPP\}$).

To our surprise, this resulted in only three different subsets of $\mathcal{P}_8$, of which $\widehat{\mathcal{H}}_8$ is of course one of them. The other two subsets are denoted by $\mathcal{C}_8$ and $\mathcal{Q}_8$.[2]

$$\widehat{\mathcal{H}}_8 = \mathcal{P}_8 \setminus \{R \mid (\{EQ, NTPP\} \subseteq R \text{ and } \{TPP\} \not\subseteq R) \\ \text{or } (\{EQ, NTPP^{-1}\} \subseteq R \text{ and } \{TPP^{-1}\} \not\subseteq R)\}$$

$$\mathcal{C}_8 = \mathcal{P}_8 \setminus \{R \mid \{EC\} \subset R \text{ and } \{PO\} \not\subseteq R \text{ and } \\ R \cap \{TPP, NTPP, TPP^{-1}, NTPP^{-1}, EQ\} \neq \emptyset\}$$

$$\mathcal{Q}_8 = \mathcal{P}_8 \setminus \{R \mid \{EQ\} \subset R \text{ and } \{PO\} \not\subseteq R \text{ and } \\ R \cap \{TPP, NTPP, TPP^{-1}, NTPP^{-1}\} \neq \emptyset\}$$

$\mathcal{C}_8$ contains 158 different RCC-8 relations, $\mathcal{Q}_8$ contains 160 different relations. We have that $\widehat{\mathcal{H}}_8 \cup \mathcal{C}_8 = \mathcal{P}_8$.

Lemma 12 *For every subset $\mathcal{S}$ of RCC-8: If $RSAT(\mathcal{S})$ is tractable, then $\mathcal{S} \subseteq \widehat{\mathcal{H}}_8$, $\mathcal{S} \subseteq \mathcal{C}_8$, or $\mathcal{S} \subseteq \mathcal{Q}_8$.*

Proof. By computing the closure of every set containing the base relations, the universal relation, and two arbitrary RCC-8 relations, the resulting set is either contained in one of the sets $\widehat{\mathcal{H}}_8$, $\mathcal{C}_8$, or $\mathcal{Q}_8$, or is NP-hard according to Lemma 8, Lemma 9, or Corollary 11. ∎

So far we did not say anything about tractability of $\mathcal{C}_8$ or $\mathcal{Q}_8$ or subsets thereof. It might be that both sets are NP-hard or that there is a large number of different maximal tractable subsets that are contained in the two sets. What we obtained so far is, thus, only a restriction of the number of different subsets we have to check for tractability. However, we will see in the next section that both $\mathcal{C}_8$ and $\mathcal{Q}_8$ are in fact tractable.

5   A Complete Analysis of Tractability

In [Renz and Nebel, 1999] tractability of $\widehat{\mathcal{H}}_8$ was shown by reducing $RSAT(\widehat{\mathcal{H}}_8)$ to HORNSAT. This was possible because $\widehat{\mathcal{H}}_8$ contains exactly those relations that are transformed to propositional Horn formulas when using

---

[2] The names were chosen, since all $\mathcal{P}_8$-relations not contained in $\mathcal{C}_8$ contain E$\underline{C}$, and all $\mathcal{P}_8$-relations not contained in $\mathcal{Q}_8$ contain E$\underline{Q}$.

the propositional encoding of RCC-8. This propositional Horn encoding of $\widehat{\mathcal{H}}_8$ was also used for proving that path-consistency decides $RSAT(\widehat{\mathcal{H}}_8)$ [Renz and Nebel, 1999], by relating positive unit resolution, which is a complete decision method for propositional Horn formulas, to path-consistency. The propositional encoding of $\mathcal{C}_8$ and $\mathcal{Q}_8$ is neither a Horn formula nor a Krom formula (two literals per clause), so it is not immediately possible to reduce the consistency problem of these subsets to a tractable propositional satisfiability problem. Therefore we have to find other ways of proving tractability.

Let us have a closer look at the relations of the two sets $\mathcal{C}_8$ and $\mathcal{Q}_8$ and how they differ from $\widehat{\mathcal{H}}_8$.

Proposition 13 *For all relations $R \in \mathcal{P}_8 \setminus \widehat{\mathcal{H}}_8$ we have that $\{EQ\} \subset R$. For all refinements R' of R with $R' \cup \{EQ\} = R$ and $\{EQ\} \not\subseteq R'$ we have that $R' \in \widehat{\mathcal{H}}_8$.*

$\mathcal{C}_8$ and $\mathcal{Q}_8$ are both subsets of $\mathcal{P}_8$, so if we can prove the following conjecture, then both sets are tractable:

Conjecture 14 *Let Θ be a path-consistent set of constraints over $\mathcal{C}_8$ or over $\mathcal{Q}_8$. If Θ' is obtained from Θ by eliminating the identity relation $\{EQ\}$ from every constraint $xRy \in \Theta$ with $R \in \mathcal{P}_8 \setminus \widehat{\mathcal{H}}_8$, then enforcing path-consistency to Θ' does not result in an inconsistency.*

If we can prove this conjecture, then, by Proposition 13, Θ' contains only constraints over $\widehat{\mathcal{H}}_8$. Since path-consistency decides $RSAT(\widehat{\mathcal{H}}_8)$, we then have that if Θ is path-consistent, Θ' is consistent and, therefore, Θ is also consistent, i.e., path-consistency decides consistency for sets of constraints over $\mathcal{C}_8$ and over $\mathcal{Q}_8$. In [Gerevini and Renz, 1998] it was shown that the relation $\{EQ\}$ can always be eliminated from every constraint of a path-consistent set of constraints over $\widehat{\mathcal{H}}_8$ without changing consistency of the set. This was, again, shown by applying positive unit resolution to the propositional Horn encoding of $\widehat{\mathcal{H}}_8$, a method which is not applicable in our case. Instead, we can now apply the new method developed in Section 3, namely, we can check whether $\mathcal{C}_8$ and $\mathcal{Q}_8$ can be reduced by refinement to $\widehat{\mathcal{H}}_8$. Conjecture 14 gives the refinement matrix we have to check. We define this particular refinement matrix for arbitrary sets $\mathcal{S}$ of disjunctions over a set $\mathcal{A}$ of JEPD relations:

Definition 15 (identity-refinement matrix) $M^{\neq}$ is the identity-refinement matrix of a set $\mathcal{S} \subseteq 2^{\mathcal{A}}$ if for every $S \in \mathcal{S}$, $M^{\neq}[S][S'] = true$ iff $S' = S \setminus Id$, where $Id \in \mathcal{A}$ is the identity relation.

Proposition 16

- CHECK-REFINEMENTS$(\mathcal{C}_8, M^{\neq})$ returns succeed.
- CHECK-REFINEMENTS$(\mathcal{Q}_8, M^{\neq})$ returns succeed.

Theorem 17 *Path-consistency decides $RSAT(\mathcal{C}_8)$ as well as $RSAT(\mathcal{Q}_8)$.*

Proof. It follows from Proposition 13 and Proposition 16 that Theorem 5 can be applied with $\mathcal{T} = \widehat{\mathcal{H}}_8$. Since path-consistency decides $RSAT(\widehat{\mathcal{H}}_8)$, it follows from Corollary 6 that path-consistency decides $\text{RSAT}(\mathcal{C}_8)$ as well as $\text{RSAT}(\mathcal{Q}_8)$ ∎

Together with Lemma 12 it follows that $\widehat{\mathcal{H}}_8$, $\mathcal{C}_8$, and $\mathcal{Q}_8$ are the only maximal tractable subsets of RCC-8 that contain all base relations.

Theorem 18 *For every subset $\mathcal{S}$ of RCC-8 that contains all base relations and the universal relation: $\text{RSAT}(\mathcal{S})$ is tractable iff $\mathcal{S} \subseteq \widehat{\mathcal{H}}_8$, $\mathcal{S} \subseteq \mathcal{C}_8$, or $\mathcal{S} \subseteq \mathcal{Q}_8$.*

6 Finding a Consistent Scenario

Gerevini and Renz [1998] gave an $O(n^3)$ time algorithm for computing a consistent scenario for a set of constraints over $\widehat{\mathcal{H}}_8$. Their algorithm is based on first eliminating $\{\text{EQ}\}$ from every constraint and then successively refining constraints to constraints over base relations in a particular order and enforcing path-consistency in between. As shown in the previous section it is also possible to eliminate $\{\text{EQ}\}$ from all constraints over $\mathcal{C}_8$ and over $\mathcal{Q}_8$, so it is possible to apply Gerevini and Renz's algorithm also for $\mathcal{C}_8$ and $\mathcal{Q}_8$. By applying the method developed in Section 3 we can, however, improve this algorithm for all three maximal tractable subsets of RCC-8.

Lemma 19 $\widehat{\mathcal{H}}_8$, $\mathcal{C}_8$, *and* $\mathcal{Q}_8$ *can be reduced by refinement to $\mathcal{B}$, the set of all RCC-8 base relations.*

This gives us the possibility of computing a consistent scenario of a path-consistent set of constraints over a tractable subset by a simple table lookup scheme, which is the fastest possible way.

Lemma 20 *Let $\mathcal{S}$ be one of $\widehat{\mathcal{H}}_8$, $\mathcal{C}_8$, $\mathcal{Q}_8$. For every relation $R \in \mathcal{S}$, $base(R)$ is the following base relation:*

(1) If $R \in \mathcal{B}$, then $base(R) = R$;

(2) else if $\{\text{DC}\} \subseteq R$, then $base(R) = \{\text{DC}\}$;

(3) else if $\{\text{EC}\} \subseteq R$ and $\mathcal{S} = \mathcal{Q}_8$ or $\mathcal{S} = \widehat{\mathcal{H}}_8$, then $base(R) = \{\text{EC}\}$;

(4) else if $\{\text{PO}\} \subseteq R$, then $base(R) = \{\text{PO}\}$;

(5) else if $\{\text{NTPP}\} \subseteq R$ and $\mathcal{S} = \mathcal{C}_8$, then $base(R) = \{\text{NTPP}\}$;

(6) else if $\{\text{TPP}\} \subseteq R$, then $base(R) = \{\text{TPP}\}$;

(7) else $base(R) = base(R^\smile)$.

Theorem 21 *A consistent scenario Θ_s of a path-consistent set Θ of constraints over $\widehat{\mathcal{H}}_8$, $\mathcal{C}_8$, or over $\mathcal{Q}_8$ can be computed in $O(n^2)$ time, by replacing every constraint $xRy \in \Theta$ with $xR'y \in \Theta_s$, where $R' = base(R)$.*

7 Applying the New Method to Allen's Interval Algebra

The method developed in Section 3 can also be applied to Allen's interval algebra [Allen, 1983] which consists of the 13 JEPD relations *before* (<), *meets* (m), *overlaps* (o), *starts* (s), *during* (d), *finishes* (f), their converse relations >, mi, oi, si, di, fi, and the identity relation *equal* (=) that describe the possible relationships between two

convex intervals. The full algebra consists of the 2^{13} possible disjunctions of the base relations and has an NP-complete consistency problem. Tractable subclasses of the interval algebra for which path-consistency decides consistency were identified by Vilain et al. [1989], the "Pointisable" subclass $\mathcal{P}$ (about 2% of the full algebra), and by Nebel and Bürckert [1995], the "ORD-Horn" subclass $\mathcal{H}$ (about 10% of the full algebra) which is the only maximal tractable subclass of the interval algebra that contains all base relations.

Since the only maximal tractable subclass of the interval algebra containing all base relations has already been identified, we cannot provide any new results on that topic. We can, however, validate the usefulness of our new method by showing that tractability of the ORD-Horn subclass and sufficiency of path-consistency for deciding consistency for this subclass can also be proven using our method. For this we apply the same strategy as for $\mathcal{C}_8$ and $\mathcal{Q}_8$, namely, we use the identity-refinement matrix $M^{\neq}$ (cf. [Ligozat, 1996]).

Proposition 22 GET-REFINEMENTS$(\mathcal{H}, M^{\neq})$ *returns $M^{\mathcal{P}}$ which has the following property: For every $R \in \mathcal{H}$ there is an $R' \in \mathcal{P}$ such that $M^{\mathcal{P}}[R][R'] = true$.*

This was computed in less than 25 minutes on a Sun Sparc Ultra1. We can now apply Theorem 5:

Theorem 23 $\mathcal{H}$ *can be reduced by refinement to $\mathcal{P}$.*

Not all of the 188 pointisable relations are necessary for this refinement, but only 30 of them which are obtained according to the following refinement scheme.

Lemma 24 *For every relation $R \in \mathcal{H}$, $point(R)$ is the following pointisable relation where $R^{\neq} = R \setminus \{=\}$ and $R' = R \cap \{<, >, o, oi, d, di\}$:*

(1) If $R = \{=\}$, then $point(R) = R$;

(2) else if $R' \neq \{\}$, then $point(R) = R'$;

(3) else $point(R) = R^{\neq}$.

Using this refinement scheme, every path-consistent set Θ of constraints over ORD-Horn can be refined to a path-consistent set Θ' by replacing every constraint $xRy \in \Theta$ with $xR'y \in \Theta'$, where $R' = point(R)$. This can be useful for some tasks such as finding a consistent scenario (cf. [Gerevini and Cristani, 1997]).

8 Discussion & Further Work

The method we developed for proving tractability of reasoning over sets of relations is very simple, does not require detailed knowledge about the considered relations, and seems to be very powerful. The only difficulty of this method is finding an adequate refinement matrix. However, the simple heuristic of eliminating all identity relations was successful for all maximal tractable fragments of RCC-8 and Allen's interval algebra which contain all base relations. This leads to an interesting question, namely, whether it is a general property of sets of relations containing all base relations for which path-consistency decides consistency that the identity relation can be eliminated from all constraints of a path-consistent set without making the set inconsistent.

The complete analysis of tractability for RCC-8 gives the possibility to develop more efficient algorithms for deciding consistency. As Renz and Nebel [1998] have shown in an empirical study, running different strategies in parallel is very effective; almost all apparently hard instances of the phase-transition region up to a certain size were solved in a few seconds. The two maximal tractable subsets of RCC-8 identified in this paper suggest several new strategies that should be empirically studied. Both subsets are larger than $\widehat{\mathcal{H}}_8$, but their average branching factor is higher ($\mathcal{C}_8$: 1.523, $\mathcal{Q}_8$: 1.516, $\widehat{\mathcal{H}}_8$: 1.438).

9 Summary

We developed a general method for proving sufficiency of path-consistency for deciding consistency of disjunctions over a set of JEPD relations. We applied this method to the Region Connection Calculus RCC-8 and identified two large new maximal tractable subsets. Together with $\widehat{\mathcal{H}}_8$, the already known maximal tractable subset, these are the only such sets for RCC-8 that contain all base relations and can, hence, be used to increase efficiency of backtracking algorithms for reasoning over NP-hard subsets. We also applied our method to Allen's interval algebra which resulted in a simple proof of tractability of reasoning in the ORD-Horn subclass.

Acknowledgments

This research was supported by DFG as part of the project FAST-QUAL-SPACE, which is part of the DFG special research effort on "Spatial Cognition". I want to thank Christoph Dornheim and Bernhard Nebel for their helpful comments.

References

[Allen, 1983] James F. Allen. Maintaining knowledge about temporal intervals. *Communications of the ACM*, 26(11):832–843, 1983.

[Garey and Johnson, 1979] Michael R. Garey and David S. Johnson. *Computers and Intractability—A Guide to the Theory of NP-Completeness*. Freeman, San Francisco, CA, 1979.

[Gerevini and Cristani, 1997] Alfonso Gerevini and Matteo Cristani. On finding a solution in temporal constraint satisfaction problems. In *Proceedings of the 15th International Joint Conference on Artificial Intelligence*, pages 1460–1465, Nagoya, Japan, 1997.

[Gerevini and Renz, 1998] Alfonso Gerevini and Jochen Renz. Combining topological and qualitative size constraints for spatial reasoning. In *Proceedings of the 4th International Conference on Principles and Practice of Constraint Programming*, Pisa, Italy, 1998. Springer.

[Ladkin and Reinefeld, 1992] Peter B. Ladkin and Alexander Reinefeld. Effective solution of qualitative interval constraint problems. *Artificial Intelligence*, 57(1):105–124, 1992.

[Ligozat, 1996] Gerard Ligozat. A new proof of tractability for ORD-Horn relations. In *Proceedings of the 13th National Conference of the American Association for Artificial Intelligence*, pages 715–720, Portland, OR, August 1996. MIT Press.

[Mackworth, 1977] Alan K. Mackworth. Consistency in networks of relations. *Artificial Intelligence*, 8:99–118, 1977.

[Nebel and Bürckert, 1995] Bernhard Nebel and Hans-Jürgen Bürckert. Reasoning about temporal relations: A maximal tractable subclass of Allen's interval algebra. *Journal of the Association for Computing Machinery*, 42(1):43–66, 1995.

[Nebel, 1997] Bernhard Nebel. Solving hard qualitative temporal reasoning problems: Evaluating the efficiency of using the ORD-Horn class. *CONSTRAINTS*, 3(1):175–190, 1997.

[Randell *et al.*, 1992] David A. Randell, Zhan Cui, and Anthony G. Cohn. A spatial logic based on regions and connection. In *Principles of Knowledge Representation and Reasoning: Proceedings of the 3rd International Conference*, pages 165–176, Cambridge, MA, 1992. Morgan Kaufmann.

[Renz and Nebel, 1998] Jochen Renz and Bernhard Nebel. Efficient methods for qualitative spatial reasoning. In *Proceedings of the 13th European Conference on Artificial Intelligence*, pages 562–566, Brighton, UK, August 1998. Wiley.

[Renz and Nebel, 1999] Jochen Renz and Bernhard Nebel. On the complexity of qualitative spatial reasoning: A maximal tractable fragment of the Region Connection Calculus. *Artificial Intelligence*, 108(1-2):69–123, 1999.

[Vilain *et al.*, 1989] Marc B. Vilain, Henry A. Kautz, and Peter G. van Beek. Constraint propagation algorithms for temporal reasoning: A revised report. In D. S. Weld and J. de Kleer, editors, *Readings in Qualitative Reasoning about Physical Systems*, pages 373–381. Morgan Kaufmann, San Mateo, CA, 1989.

CONSTRAINT SATISFACTION

Constraint Satisfaction 4

Path Consistency on Triangulated Constraint Graphs*

Christian Bliek
ILOG
1681 Route des Dolines
06560 Valbonne, France
bliek@ilog.fr

Djamila Sam-Haroud
Artificial Intelligence Laboratory
Swiss Federal Institute of Technology
1015 Lausanne, Switzerland
haroud@lia.di.epfl.ch

Abstract

Among the local consistency techniques used in the resolution of constraint satisfaction problems (CSPs), *path consistency* (PC) has received a great deal of attention. A constraint graph G is PC if for any valuation of a pair of variables that satisfy the constraint in G between them, one can find values for the intermediate variables on any other path in G between those variables so that all the constraints along that path are satisfied. On complete graphs, Montanari showed that PC holds if and only if each path of length two is PC. By convention, it is therefore said that a CSP is PC if the completion of its constraint graph is PC. In this paper, we show that Montanari's theorem extends to triangulated graphs. One can therefore enforce PC on sparse graphs by triangulating instead of completing them. The advantage is that with triangulation much less universal constraints need to be added. We then compare the pruning capacity of the two approaches. We show that when the constraints are convex, the pruning capacity of PC on triangulated graphs and their completion are identical on the common edges. Furthermore, our experiments show that there is little difference for general non-convex problems.

1 Introduction

The constraint satisfaction paradigm allows for a natural formulation of a wide variety of practical problems. It consists of representing a problem as a set of variables taking their values in particular domains, subject to constraints which specify consistent value combinations. Solving a CSP amounts to assigning to the variables, values from their domains, so that all the constraints are satisfied. Backtrack search is the principal mechanism for solving a CSP. It is commonly combined with local consistency techniques to limit the combinatorial explosion. These techniques reduce the size of the search space by removing local inconsistencies.

---

*Authors are listed in alphabetical order.

This paper considers a particular form of local consistency called *path consistency* (PC). The work presented

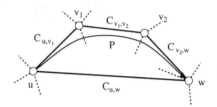

Figure 1: Path Consistency

considers binary CSPs and builds on their classical *constraint graph* representation, where the vertices represent the variables and the edges represent the constraints between the variables.

A path $P = \langle u, \ldots, v_i, \ldots, w \rangle$ in a constraint graph G is PC if for all pairs of values for (u, w) that satisfy the constraint $C_{u,w}$ in G one can find values for the intermediate variables v_i so that all the constraints $C_{u,v_1}, \ldots, C_{v_i,v_{i+1}}, \ldots, C_{v_k,w}$ in G along the path are satisfied (see figure 1). A constraint graph is PC iff all paths in the graph are PC [Mackworth, 1977]. In this paper we make the distinction between enforcing PC on CSPs and on constraint graphs. A CSP is PC if the completion of its constraint graph is PC. A CSP will be said to be *partially* PC (PPC) if its constraint graph is PC.

In practice, we know how to enforce PC on complete graphs thanks to the following theorem:

Theorem 1 *(Montanari, 1974) A network with a complete graph is PC iff every path of length two is PC.*

As a result, existing algorithms first complete sparse graphs by adding universal binary constraints, then enforce PC on each path of length two. The algorithms with the best time complexity [Mohr and Henderson, 1986; Han and Lee, 1988] run in time $O(n^3 d^3)$. n is the number of variables and d the maximum domain size.

Despite its relatively high computational complexity, PC on complete graphs has been shown to be a central notion for certain classes of problems. In effect, it has been shown to be equivalent to global consistency for convex binary problems. This means that if a binary convex CSP is PC, its solutions can be derived backtrack-free. The PC property has also received particular attention in the area of temporal reasoning [Schwalb and Dechter, 1997] where lower forms of consistency prove to be of less interest.

In this paper we show that Montanari's theorem extends to triangulated constraint graphs. Triangulated constraint graphs can be made PC by ensuring that every path of length two is PC. In this case there is no need for additional constraints to be synthesized. This allows us to devise an algorithm for making a CSP with a triangulated constraint graph PPC in time $O(\delta e d^3)$. δ is the maximum degree of the graph and e is the number of edges in the graph. When the original constraint graph is not triangulated, we can triangulate it by adding universal edges. It is important to note that for sparse problems, the number of edges added by triangulation is much less than by completion.

Given an incomplete constraint graph, we then compare the pruning capacity of PC depending on whether it is enforced on a triangulation or a completion of the graph. We prove that for convex problems, the pruning capacity of the two is identical on the common edges. This means that, in this case, the extra edges synthesized for completion do not affect the labeling of the common edges. We also propose an algorithm for filling in these extra edges.

Finally, we present some experiments illustrating that significant gains in computational effort can be obtained using our algorithms. Furthermore it appears that there is little difference in the pruning capacity of PPC and PC for general non-convex CSPs with triangulated constraint graphs.

2 Background

In this paper, we consider binary CSPs (V, C, D) where V is the set $\{1, \ldots, i, \ldots, n\}$ of variables, D is the set $\{D_1, \ldots, D_i, \ldots, D_n\}$ of domains and variable i takes its value in domain D_i. The variables of V are subject to a set of constraints $C = \{C_{i,j} \mid C_{i,j}$ represent the legal value combinations from $D_i \times D_j\}$. We use the $(0,1)$ matrix representation of constraints proposed in [Montanari, 1974] and assume that $C_{i,j}$ is always the transposition of $C_{j,i}$. $C_{i,j} = D_i \times D_j$ is called a *universal* constraint. A constraint is *connected row-convex* (CRC) if after removing the empty rows from its matrix representation it is row-convex and connected, i.e. all the 1 entries in a row are consecutive and two successive rows either intersect or are consecutive [Deville *et al.*, 1997].

A CSP is *strongly* PC if in addition to PC it also is *arc consistent* (AC). A CSP is *globally* consistent if any partial instantiation of a subset of variables can be extended to a solution without backtracking.

Let us now recall the necessary background from graph theory. An undirected graph G is *triangulated* if every cycle of length strictly greater than 3 possesses a chord, that is, an edge joining two non-consecutive vertices of the cycle. For a graph $G = (V, E)$, with $|V| = n$, an ordering $[v_1, \ldots, v_i, \ldots, v_n]$ of V is a bijection of $\{1, \ldots, n\}$ onto V. For each v in V, the adjacency set Adj(v), is defined as $\{w \in V \mid (v, w) \in E\}$. A vertex v is *simplicial* if Adj(v) is complete. Every triangulated graph has a simplicial vertex. A triangulated graph remains triangulated after removing a simplicial vertex and its incident edges from the graph. The order in which simplicial vertices are successively removed is called a *perfect elimination order*. For a given perfect elimination order, we will use the notation $S_i = \{v_{n-i+1}, \ldots, v_n\}$, and G_i will denote the subgraph of G induced by S_i. $F_i = \{v_k \in$ Adj$(v_{n-i}) \mid v_{n-i} < v_k\}$ where $<$ is the precedence relation of the given order. Observe that since the elimination order is perfect, the subgraph of G induced by F_i is complete.

The material cited below is taken from [Kjærulff, 1990]. A perfect elimination order can be found in $O(n+e)$ time using the *maximum cardinality search* algorithm. A non-triangulated graph can always be transformed into a triangulated one by adding edges. Finding a *minimal* triangulation, where every edge is necessary for the graph to be triangulated can be done in $O(n(e+f))$ time, where f is the number of added edges. This bound is improved on average by a procedure called *recursive thinning* which we use in this work.

3 PC on Triangulated Constraint Graphs

In this section we extend theorem 1 to triangulated graphs. We show the following result:

Theorem 2 *A triangulated constraint graph G is PC iff every path of length 2 is PC.*

Proof: Since G is triangulated, we can find a perfect elimination order which defines S_i, G_i and F_i as discussed above. We demonstrate that G is PC by induction on i. Since every path of length 2 is PC, we know by construction that G_3 is PC. Assuming that G_i is PC, we set out to prove that G_{i+1} is PC. We do this by showing that any path P from u to w in G_{i+1} is PC.

If P is in G_i then P is PC by assumption. So we need to consider two cases. Either 1) as illustrated on the left in figure 2, v_{n-i} is an endpoint of P, e.g. $v_{n-i} = w$ or 2) P goes through v_{n-i} as shown on the right in figure 2.

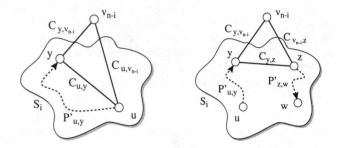

Figure 2: Two cases of inductive proof

Let us consider these two cases below:

1. This path is considered for PC only if there is a constraint $C_{u,v_{n-i}}$. Let us show that one can find values for the intermediate variables so that all the constraints along a path P are satisfied. Let y be the variable that precedes v_{n-i} in P. So in addition to the constraint $C_{u,v_{n-i}}$ we also have a constraint $C_{y,v_{n-i}}$. Since G is triangulated, the graph induced by F_i is complete. So there is a constraint $C_{u,y}$. Now in G every path of length 2 is PC, so for every pair of values that satisfy $C_{u,v_{n-i}}$ we can find a value for v that satisfies $C_{u,y}$ and $C_{y,v_{n-i}}$. The part $P'_{u,y}$ of the path P between u and y is in G_i and is therefore PC by assumption. So for the pair of values found for (u,y) we know that we can find values for the intermediate variables on this path $P'_{u,y}$. Hence we are able to find a set of values for all the intermediate variables between u and v_{n-i} that satisfy the constraints along P.

2. If P goes through v_{n-i} then let y and z be the variables that respectively precede and follow v_{n-i} in the path P. Note that both y and z are in S_i. Since there is a constraint $C_{y,v_{n-i}}$, a constraint $C_{v_{n-i},z}$ and that the graph induced by F_i is complete, we know that there is a constraint $C_{y,z}$. Now consider the path $P'_{u,y}; P'_{z,w}$ that goes directly from y to z without passing through v_{n-i}. $P'_{u,y}; P'_{z,w}$ is in G_i and therefore by assumption PC. This means that for any pair of values for (u,w) we can find values for the intermediate variables so that all the constraints along $P'_{u,y}; P'_{z,w}$ are satisfied. Since in G every path of length 2 is PC, we also know that for the pair of values found for (y,z) we can find a value for v_{n-i} that satisfies both $C_{y,v_{n-i}}$ and $C_{v_{n-i},z}$. By doing so we just have found a set values that satisfy all the constraints along the original path P. □

4   From Triangulated to Completed Graphs

Given the result in the previous section, the question arises whether more pruning can be obtained by completing a triangulated graph. As demonstrated in section 6 this may indeed occasionally occur. However, in this section we show that for the class of convex problems, no additional pruning is obtained by completing the graph. The notion of convexity we refer to is a broad one. It includes the conventional definition of convexity in continuous domains, as well as its CRC extension to the discrete case. This extended convexity property is closed under composition and intersection of constraints.

To show our result on convex problems we need the following lemma.

Lemma 1 *If $G = (V, E)$ is an incomplete triangulated graph, then one can add a missing edge (u, w), with $u, w \in V$ so that*

1. *the graph $G' = (V, E \cup \{(u,w)\})$ is triangulated and*

2. *the graph induced by $X = \{x \mid (u,x),(x,w) \in E\}$ is complete.*

Proof: Since G is triangulated, it has a perfect elimination order defining S_i, G_i and F_i. Let i be the smallest index such that G_i is complete. Consider a variable $v_j \in S_i$ for which there is no edge (v_{n-i}, v_j) in G. By taking $(u, w) = (v_{n-i}, v_j)$ we now prove the two claims of the lemma.

1. Since G_i is complete, there is an edge between v_j and every variable in F_i. The graph induced by F_i in $G' = (V, E \cup \{(v_{n-i}, v_j)\})$ therefore remains complete. As a result, the considered elimination order is also perfect for G'. Since a graph with a perfect elimination order is triangulated, G' is triangulated.

2. Let us first show that $X = F_i$. Suppose it is not. In that case we necessarily have that a $y \in X$ that precedes v_{n-i} for which $(v_{n-i}, y), (y, v_j) \in E$. But then, since G is triangulated, there would also be an edge (v_{n-i}, v_j) which contradicts our assumption. Finally, since $X = F_i$ and G is triangulated, we know that the graph induced by X is complete. □

This lemma is illustrated in figure 3. In this case

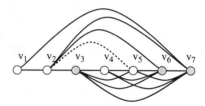

Figure 3: Completing Triangulated Graphs

$S_i = \{v_3, v_4, v_5, v_6, v_7\}$, $v_{n-i} = v_2$ and $F_i = \{v_3, v_6, v_7\}$. The variables of F_i are colored gray. The construction would for example add the dashed edge (v_2, v_5) which is currently missing.

Let us now turn to the main result of this section.

Theorem 3 *For a convex CSP with a triangulated constraint graph G, strong PC on G is equivalent to strong PC on the completion of G.*

By *equivalent* we mean that the relations computed for the constraints in G are identical.

Proof: Suppose we have a triangulated graph $G = (V, E)$ that is strongly PC. We will add to G the missing edges one by one until the graph is complete. To prove the theorem, we show that the relations of the constraints can be computed from the existing ones so that each intermediate graph, including the completed graph, is strongly PC.

To add the edges, we use the construction proposed for the proof of lemma 1. At all times during the constraint addition process, the graph therefore remains triangulated. After the addition of a single edge (v_{n-i}, v_j) to G, we obtain $G' = (V, E \cup \{(v_{n-i}, v_j)\})$. For this edge the new relation C_{v_{n-i}, v_j} is computed as follows:

$$C_{v_{n-i}, v_j} = \bigcap_{v_k \in F_i} C_{v_{n-i}, v_k} \otimes C_{v_k, v_j} \qquad (1)$$

where $\otimes$ is the composition operator. For example, in figure 3, C_{v_2,v_5} is obtained by intersecting the compositions obtained via the variables in $F_i = \{v_3, v_6, v_7\}$. C_{v_{n-i},v_j} is the universal relation when $F_i = \emptyset$.

If after making G strongly PC the relations in G are empty, the construction above would, as desired, compute the empty relations for the missing edges. In what follows we therefore assume that the relations in G after strong PC are not empty.

We now show that G' is PC. Since G' is triangulated, by theorem 2 it is sufficient to prove that every path of length 2 is PC. By assumption, paths of length 2 that do not go through v_{n-i} and v_j are PC. So let us consider paths of length 2 that go through v_{n-i} and v_j. By lemma 1 and the construction used in its proof, we know that the set of intermediate variables on the relevant paths is F_i and that F_i induces a complete subgraph of G. This situation is illustrated in figure 4, where the variables in F_i are colored gray. Note that by construction the graph A induced by $\{v_{n-i}\} \cup F_i$ and the graph B induced by $F_i \cup \{v_j\}$ are complete. We have to consider

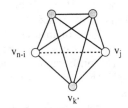

Figure 4: Added edges are PC

two cases[1]. With $v_{k'} \in F_i$, either 1) $P = \langle v_{n-i}, v_j, v_{k'} \rangle$ or 2) $P = \langle v_{n-i}, v_{k'}, v_j \rangle$. Let us consider each of these cases in turn.

1. If $P = \langle v_{n-i}, v_j, v_{k'} \rangle$ we need to prove that for every pair of values for $(v_{n-i}, v_{k'})$ that satisfies $C_{v_{n-i},v_{k'}}$ we can find a value for v_j so that C_{v_{n-i},v_j}, as defined by (1), and $C_{v_j,v_{k'}}$ are satisfied.

   A is complete, strongly path-consistent and convex, it is therefore also globally consistent [Sam-Haroud and Faltings, 1996]. So that for every pair of values that satisfy $C_{v_{n-i},v_{k'}}$ we can find values for all the variables in $F_i - \{v_{k'}\}$ so that all other edges in A are also satisfied (see figure 4). Similarly, since B is complete, strongly path-consistent and convex it is globally consistent. This means that for the above values of the variables in F_i, we can find a value for v_j so that all constraints in B are satisfied. For the considered values the constraint $C_{v_j,v_{k'}}$ is therefore satisfied. For any pair of values for $C_{v_{n-i},v_{k'}}$ we are hence able to find values for the variables in $(F_i - \{v_{k'}\}) \cup \{v_j\}$ so that all constraints in $A \cup B$ are satisfied. For the values for (v_{n-i}, v_j), the relations C_{v_{n-i},v_k} and C_{v_k,v_j} participating in (1) are therefore satisfied by the values for the variables in F_i. The values for (v_{n-i}, v_j) therefore satisfy C_{v_{n-i},v_j}.

2. If $P = \langle v_{n-i}, v_{k'}, v_j \rangle$ the relation C_{v_{n-i},v_j} of the new edge ensures by definition that for every pair of values in C_{v_{n-i},v_j} we can find a value for $v_{k'}$ so that the $C_{v_{n-i},v_{k'}}$ and $C_{v_{k'},v_j}$ are verified.

We now show that G' is AC. When $|F_i| \geq 1$, since G' is PC we know that for every value pair in $C_{v_{n-i},v_{k'}}$ or in $C_{v_{k'},v_j}$ we can find a value pair that satisfies C_{v_{n-i},v_j}. Since G is AC this means that for any support respectively on $C_{v_{n-i},v_{k'}}$ or on $C_{v_{k'},v_j}$ we are able to find a support on C_{v_{n-i},v_j}. As a consequence G' is not only PC but also AC. When $|F_i| = 0$, $C_{v_{n-i},v_j} = D_{v_{n-i}} \times D_{v_j}$. Since G is AC, G' will therefore be AC as well. $\square$

Corollary 1 is a direct consequence of theorem 3.

Corollary 1 *For convex problems, insolubility is detected using PC by graph completion iff it is detected using PC by graph triangulation.*

5 Algorithms

By theorem 2 we know that triangulated graphs can be made PC by enforcing that every path of length two is PC. For problems with a triangulated constraint graph we can therefore make the CSP PPC by a simple modification of existing PC algorithms[2]. The resulting algorithm is Algorithm 1. The procedure *Related-*

---

algorithm PPC

> $Q \leftarrow E$
> **Until** Q *is empty* **do**
> > $q \leftarrow \text{Dequeue}(Q)$
> > **for** $(v_i, v_k, v_j) \in$ *Related-Triplets*(q) **do**
> > > $C_{v_i,v_j} \leftarrow C_{v_i,v_j} \cap (C_{v_i,v_k} \otimes C_{v_k,v_j})$
> > > **if** C_{v_i,v_j} *has changed* **then**
> > > > $\text{Enqueue}((v_i, v_j), Q)$
> > >
> > > **end**
> >
> > **end**
>
> **end**

end.

Algorithm 1: PPC

Triplets(q) returns all those triplets in which q participates and that correspond to actual triangles in G. The difference with a classical PC algorithm, referred to as PC in the rest of the paper, is that PC revises all possible triplets, not only those corresponding to triangles in G. To determine the complexity of this algorithm for discrete problems, consider the number of revisions that can be made based on each edge (v_i, v_j). Revisions based on C_{v_i,v_j} will be made only when a pair of values is removed. If d is the maximum domain size, then one can remove at most d^2 pairs from any relation. Each removal

---

[1] The reasoning is the same for the symmetrical cases.

[2] PPC is close to Schwalb and Dechter's PLPC algorithm from which it borrows the name. PLPC (Partial Loose PC) enforces a partial form of path consistency on disjunctive temporal CSPs. It only considers the paths of length two with at least two non-universal constraints.

prompts revisions only of the 2 neighboring edges in each triangle. If δ_{v_k} is the degree of variable v_k, a modification of C_{v_i,v_j} will prompt at most $2 \min\{\delta_{v_i} - 1, \delta_{v_j} - 1\}$ revisions. Summing over all edges we find that at most

$$\sum_{(v_i,v_j) \in E} 2 \min\{\delta_{v_i} - 1, \delta_{v_j} - 1\} d^2 = O(\delta e d^2)$$

revisions will be performed, where δ is the maximum degree. This should be compared to the $O(n^3 d^2)$ revisions performed by the classical PC algorithm. Using the results presented in [Chiba and Nishizeki, 1985], one may use the arboricity α of G instead of δ, resulting in a number of revisions $O(\alpha e d^2)$. The same reference also presents upper bounds on α both for general graphs and for specific types of graphs.

For the experiments below we report the number of revisions since this measure is independent of the specific techniques one might use for updating the relations. In practice one can for example use the techniques based on the principle of minimal support used in PC-6 [Chmeiss, 1996]. In this case at most $O(e d^2)$ value pairs may be deleted in the relations. Per value pair at most $O(\delta d)$ supports may be visited leading to a time complexity of $O(\delta e d^3)$. However, per value pair only $O(\delta)$ support information concerning the smallest supporting element is stored, resulting in a $O(\delta e d^2)$ space complexity. In case of CRC constraints one can use the techniques described in [Deville *et al.*, 1997] to obtain a time complexity of $O(\delta e d^2)$ and a space complexity of $O(\delta e d)$.

The PPC algorithm makes CSPs with triangulated constraint graphs PPC. CSPs whose constraint graph is not triangulated can be made PPC by triangulating the graph with universal constraints before running PPC. For convex problems PPC is equivalent to PC. If desired, the relations of the missing edges can be computed as proposed in the proof of theorem 3. This fill algorithm is shown in Algorithm 2 below.

---

algorithm Fill
  for $i \leftarrow 1$ **to** n **do**
    Until G_i *is complete* **do**
      let (v_{n-i}, v_j) be a missing edge in G_i
      $C_{v_{n-i},v_j} \leftarrow \bigcap_{v_k \in F_i} C_{v_{n-i},v_k} \otimes C_{v_k,v_j}$
    end
  end
end.

Algorithm 2: Fill

The variables are assumed to be ordered according to a perfect elimination order. Observe that it is not required to update the sets F_i when G changes, since the order in which the edges are added to G_i does not matter.

Algorithm 2 computes at most $n(n-1)/2$ relations. Since each relation is computed by intersecting at most 2δ compositions, the number of revisions Algorithm 2 needs to perform is therefore $O(\delta n^2)$. For CRC constraints one can, as before, use the techniques described in [Deville *et al.*, 1997] to perform the actual computations. In this case the missing relations can be filled in in time $O(\delta n^2 d^2)$.

6 Experiments

In this section, we report some preliminary experiments that compare the number of revision steps carried out by PC and PPC for three types of randomly generated problems. The convex case is illustrated by tests on linear continuous and CRC problems, the non-convex one by tests on randomly generated discrete problems. For the linear problems, the constraints generated are inequalities. They are discretized similarly to what is described in the work of [Sam-Haroud and Faltings, 1996] and represented by $(0, 1)$ matrices. The constraint graph of each generated instance is triangulated before running PPC. The domain size is 8 for all the types of problems. Each test is averaged over 25 instances.

Table 1 shows the comparison for different sizes of constraint graphs and a fixed density p. The density chosen ($p = 0.1$) corresponds to sparse graphs and illustrates the most favorable case for PPC. Table 2 compares PC and PPC for problems of fixed size ($n = 20$) and different densities. Since PPC is of interest on sparse CSPs, we report the experiments on sparse graphs ($p \leq 0.5$). For higher densities, the number of revisions of PPC approaches that of PC. Note that PPC and PC are identical for complete graphs.

By theorem 3 for convex problems the relations computed by PPC and PC on the common edges are identical. For non-convex problems, we also compare the pruning capacity of PPC to the one of PC. ρ is the ratio between the number of tuples removed by PPC over the number of tuples removed by PC on the common edges. For the tests conducted on random problems, insolubility detected by PC was also detected by PPC.

The tests reported for non-convex problems are generated in the phase transition [Grant and Smith, 1996] as this seems to best illustrate the difference of behavior between PPC and PC. Indeed, several hundreds of tests run out of the phase transition showed no difference of pruning between PC and PPC on the common edges. Note that the randomly generated linear and CRC problem instances do not necessarily fall in the phase transition.

It is worth mentioning that despite the worst case complexity of $O(n(e + f))$ for triangulation algorithms, the effective time devoted to triangulation is negligible compared to the running time of PPC.

More experiments clearly need to be conducted for better stating the effectiveness of PPC. The preliminary results we report are however encouraging enough to warrant PPC being investigated as alternative to PC for sparse problems.

7 Conclusion

Path consistency is an important notion in constraint satisfaction. A new algorithm, called PPC, is proposed that makes triangulated constraint graphs PC. PC can

Linear

n	p	PC	PPC
10	0.1	1,944	211
15	0.1	10,293	334
20	0.1	33,220	550
25	0.1	85,463	644
30	0.1	183,253	1,641
35	0.1	356,825	4,532
40	0.1	619,999	9,666

CRC

n	p	PC	PPC
10	0.1	1,827	222
15	0.1	9,117	374
20	0.1	32,213	559
25	0.1	84,796	950
30	0.1	185,807	1,825
35	0.1	361,000	5,160
40	0.1	624,314	14,621

Random

n	p	PC	PPC	ρ (%)
10	0.1	1,971	339	99.75
15	0.1	13,870	407	99.51
20	0.1	32,366	749	99.65
25	0.1	97,180	1,388	99.84
30	0.1	143,116	5,441	99.80
35	0.1	348,399	5,477	100.0
40	0.1	665,871	33,623	99.92

Table 1: Revisions performed by PC and PPC on sparse graphs for different problem sizes

Linear

n	p	PC	PPC
20	0.1	33,220	550
20	0.2	37,440	1,660
20	0.3	38,187	5,329
20	0.4	38,719	8,907
20	0.5	39,054	13,736

CRC

n	p	PC	PPC
20	0.1	32,213	559
20	0.2	37,593	2,257
20	0.3	38,393	5,692
20	0.4	38,811	8,919
20	0.5	39,043	13,339

Random

n	p	PC	PPC	ρ (%)
20	0.1	32,366	749	99.65
20	0.2	35,017	3,263	99.98
20	0.3	55,330	13,982	100.0
20	0.4	112,986	45,979	100.0
20	0.5	223,459	148,330	100.0

Table 2: Revisions performed by PC and PPC on given problem size for different densities

thus be enforced on incomplete constraint graphs by triangulating instead of completing them. When the problem is sparse, this spares a significant amount of work compared to the classical PC algorithm. We have also shown that for convex CSPs with triangulated constraint graphs, the PPC and PC algorithms will compute the same labeling on the common edges.

Excessive memory requirements of existing PC algorithms limit their applicability [Chmeiss and Jégou, 1996]. Since on sparse graphs PPC has a lower space complexity than PC, PPC might prove to be a viable alternative when memory is a limiting factor.

For non-convex problems, PPC exhibits a good pruning capacity compared to PC and can be computed much more efficiently than PC on sparse graphs. We therefore expect that it might be beneficial to interleave it with backtrack algorithms to search for solutions. This will be a topic of future research.

8 Acknowledgments

We would like to thank Jean-Charles Régin for pointing out the results on arboricity. Most of this work was performed at the Artificial Intelligence Laboratory of the Swiss Federal Institute of Technology in Lausanne where Christian Bliek was sponsored by the Swiss National Science Foundation under project number 2000-52363.97 through the ERCIM Fellowship Program.

References

[Chiba and Nishizeki, 1985] N. Chiba and T. Nishizeki. Arboricity and subgraph listing algorithms. *SIAM Journal on Computing*, 14, 1985.

[Chmeiss and Jégou, 1996] A. Chmeiss and P. Jégou. Path-consistency: When space misses time. In *AAAI-96*, pages 196–201, Portland, Oregon, 1996.

[Chmeiss, 1996] A. Chmeiss. Sur la consistance de chemin et ses formes partielles. In *Actes du Congrès RFIA-96*, pages 212–219, Rennes, France, 1996.

[Deville et al., 1997] Y. Deville, O. Barette, and P. Van Hentenryck. Constraint satisfaction over connected row convex constraints. In *IJCAI-97*, pages 405–410, Nagoya, Japan, 1997.

[Grant and Smith, 1996] S. A. Grant and B. Smith. The arc and path consistency phase transitions. In *CP-96*, pages 541–542, 1996.

[Han and Lee, 1988] C. Han and C. Lee. Comments on Mohr and Henderson's path consistency algorithm. *Artificial Intelligence*, 36, 1988.

[Kjærulff, 1990] U. Kjærulff. Triangulation of graphs – algorithms giving small total state space. Research Report R-90-09, Aalborg University, Denmark, 1990.

[Mackworth, 1977] A.K. Mackworth. Consistency in networks of relations. *Artificial Intelligence*, 8:99–118, 1977.

[Mohr and Henderson, 1986] R. Mohr and T.C. Henderson. Arc and path consistency revisited. *Artificial Intelligence*, 28:225–233, 1986.

[Montanari, 1974] Ugo Montanari. Networks of constraints: Fundamental properties and applications to picture processing. *Information Science*, 7:95–132, 1974.

[Sam-Haroud and Faltings, 1996] D. Sam-Haroud and B.V. Faltings. Consistency techniques for continuous constraints. *Constraints*, 1:85–118, 1996.

[Schwalb and Dechter, 1997] E. Schwalb and R. Dechter. Processing disjunctions in temporal constraint networks. *Artificial Intelligence*, 93:29–61, 1997.

A New Method to Index and Query Sets

Jörg Hoffmann and **Jana Koehler**
Institute for Computer Science
Albert Ludwigs University
Am Flughafen 17
79110 Freiburg, Germany
hoffmann|koehler@informatik.uni-freiburg.de

Abstract

Let us consider the following problem: Given a (probably huge) set of sets S and a query set q, is there some set $s \in S$ such that $s \subseteq q$? This problem occurs in at least four application areas: the matching of a large number (usually several 100,000s) of production rules, the processing of queries in data bases supporting set-valued attributes, the identification of inconsistent subgoals during artificial intelligence planning and the detection of potential periodic chains in labeled tableau systems for modal logics. In this paper, we introduce a data structure and algorithm that allow a compact representation of such a huge set of sets and an efficient answering of *subset* and *superset* queries. The algorithm has been used successfully in the IPP system and enabled this planner to win the ADL track of the first planning competition.

1 Introduction

The problem of how to effectively index and query sets occurs in various computer applications:

Researchers in **object oriented databases** have among others stressed the need for richer data types, in particular set-valued attributes such as for example the set of keywords in a document, the set of classes a student is enrolled in, etc. Typical queries to such an enriched database require to determine all *supersets* or *subsets* of a given query. For example, given a set of classes C, to find all students taking at least these classes the *supersets* of C need to be determined. Or as another example, given that a student has passed some basic courses C, which advanced courses become possible? The answer is found by retrieving all advanced courses whose prerequisite course set is a *subset* of C.

Machine learning is highly concerned with the *utility problem*, i.e., the problem of learning new knowledge in such a way that the learning costs do not exceed the savings in the system's performance that are achieved through learning. A key factor in a good learning algorithm is to effectively match sets of attributes against each other, for example in the form of *preconditions* of large sets of *production rules*. In order to decide which rules apply to a particular situation, all precondition sets have to be determined that are *subsets* of the query set describing the situation.

Artificial intelligence planning is concerned with the problem of constructing a sequence of actions that achieves a set of goals given a particular initial state in which the plan is scheduled for execution. Even in its simplest form, the problem is known to be PSPACE-complete [Bylander, 1991], i.e., planning algorithms are worst-case exponential and techniques to effectively prune the search space are mandatory. Since millions of goal sets are constructed when searching larger state spaces for a plan, it is important to know in advance when a goal set can never be satisfied. This is the case when at least one *subset* of the current goal set has previously been shown to be unsatisfiable.

Modal logics are often formalized using labeled tableau methods, where one is sometimes confronted with infinite branches in the tableau. To guarantee termination, one needs to identify potential periodic chains of labels [Gore, 1997].

In its abstract form, these and other applications have to deal with the following problem: Given a set of sets S stored in some data structure and a query set q, does there exist a set $s \in S$ such that $q \supseteq s$ (or sometimes $q \subseteq s$ depending on the application). Though this seems to be a trivial problem to handle, its difficulty comes from the dimensions in which it occurs: S will quite often contain millions of sets and some applications require to handle a huge sequence of queries q_i over a dynamically changing S.

2 The UBTree Algorithm

The key to a fast set query answering algorithm lies in an appropriate data structure to index a large number of sets of varying cardinality.

2.1 The UBTree Data structure

A node (see Figure 1) N in UBTree consists of three components:

- $N.e$: the element it represents
- $N.T$: the sons, a set of other tree nodes
- $N.EoP$: the End-of-Path marker.

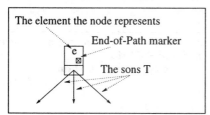

Figure 1: Representation of a single node.

The UBTree is now simply represented by a set T of such nodes and can be seen as a forest. Note that we are speaking about *sets* of tree nodes, i.e., neither the number of trees nor the number of sons any node can have is limited. That is where the UBTree got its name from: Unlimited Branching Tree.

Based on this data structure, the following functions will be defined below:

- insert(set s, tree T) inserts a set s into the tree T.
- lookup_first(set q, tree T) tells us whether *any subset $s \subseteq q$* is stored in T.
- lookup_subs(set q, tree T) determines *all subsets* for a given query set q from T.
- lookup_sups(set q, tree T) determines *all supersets* for a given query set q from T.

The only assumption on which our algorithm relies is the existence of a total ordering over all elements that can possibly occur in the sets.

2.2 The insert Function

To insert a set s into a forest T, the insert function (Figure 2) creates a *path* starting in T corresponding to that set. In principle, this path is just a series of connected tree nodes corresponding to the ordered elements of s.

Definition 1 *Let $s = \{e_0, \ldots, e_{n-1}\}$ be an ordered set, T be a forest.*
A path $\Phi(s)$ in T corresponding to s is a non-empty tuple of tree nodes $N_0, \ldots, N_{n-1}$ such that

1. $N_0 \in T \wedge N_0.e = e_0$
2. $\forall i \in 1 \ldots n-1 : (N_i \in N_{i-1}.T \wedge N_i.e = e_i)$
3. $N_{n-1}.EoP = \mathsf{TRUE}$

When the insert function is called, T is initialized with the root nodes of the forest. The function then tries to look up the elements of s one after the other (remember that the sets get ordered before they are inserted) and, doing this, follows paths that have been created by other, previously inserted sets. If there is no corresponding node for some element e_i in the set T of nodes (implying that no set starting with $\{e_0, \ldots, e_i\}$ has been inserted before), it creates a new path at that point, i.e., a new son is added to the current node N. Finally, the last node (the one that represents e_{n-1}) is marked as the end of a path. Note that we assume s to be non-empty, i.e., $n > 0$, otherwise there would be no element e_{n-1} and, consequently, no node N to represent it.[1]

```
sort(s) /* now s = {e_0,...,e_{n-1}} */
for all elements e_i ∈ s do
    N := the node in T corresponding to e_i
    if there is no such N then
        insert a new node N corresponding to e_i into T
    endif
    T := N.T
endfor
mark N as the end of a path
```

Figure 2: insert(s,T)

Figure 3 shows how a forest T with two trees evolves when the 4 (already ordered) sets $s_0 = \{e_0, e_1, e_2, e_3\}$, $s_1 = \{e_0, e_1, e_3\}$, $s_2 = \{e_0, e_1, e_2\}$, and $s_3 = \{e_2, e_3\}$ are inserted one after the other.

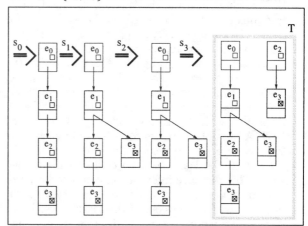

Figure 3: Iterative insertion of 4 sets

2.3 The lookup Functions

We now show how the set of sets S stored in a forest T can be used to answer questions about the query set q.

Let us begin with the lookup_first function, which decides if there is *any* set $s \in S$ in T with $s \subseteq q$. The function simply tries to reach a node N in the

---

[1]We make this assumption just for simplification, the UBTree algorithm can easily be extended to deal with possibly empty sets.

tree that is marked as the end of a path, using the elements in q as "money" to pay its travel costs. This is to say, given a set of tree nodes T and a set $q = \{e_0, \ldots, e_{n-1}\}$, it finds all nodes $N \in T$ corresponding to an element $e_i \in q$. If any such N is marked as the end of a path, lookup_first succeeds in finding a subset to the query set. Otherwise, the ongoing search is a recursive instance with the set of sons, $N.T$, and the remaining elements $\{e_{i+1}, \ldots, e_{n-1}\}$ as parameters.[2] See Figure 4 for a formal description of the lookup_first function.

```
M := all nodes N ∈ T that match an element eᵢ ∈ q
while M is non-empty do
        choose a node N ∈ M
        if N is the end of a path then succeed endif
        /* else:  call search on next tree
        and remaining elements */
        lookup_first(N.T, {e_{i+1}, ..., e_{n-1}})
endwhile
/* all elements have failed */
fail
```

Figure 4: lookup_first(q,T)

The function is initially called on the (previously ordered) query set q and the forest T. It is important to notice and crucial to the performance of UBTree that, in using the "money" method, large fractions of the search space can be excluded: for a query set $q = \{q_0, \ldots, q_{n-1}\}$ of length n, 2^n possible subsets need to be considered. Half of them (those that contain q_0) lie in the tree rooted in the node corresponding to q_0. If there is no such node, the search space is immediately reduced to 2^{n-1}.

Note that the function is non-deterministic with respect to which matching node $N \in M$ is chosen first. A possible heuristic could store in each node the distance to the next end-of-path node. The node with the least distance could then be tried first. This distance information can also be used, and in fact is used in our implementation to cut unnecessary branches out of the search tree. If the distance stored in a search node N is greater than the number of elements we have left at that stage of search, we can back up (i.e., **fail**) right away. In this case the query set does not contain enough elements to reach an end-of-path marker.

The lookup_subs function, as given in Figure 5, works in a very similar way. Instead of terminating after identifying one end-of-path marker, i.e., the first matching subset, it has to work its way through *all* nodes it can reach. Again, the function uses the "money" method, i.e., passes only those

---
[2]No nodes representing any of the elements in $\{e_0, \ldots, e_i\}$ can exist in a subtree starting in e_i due to the total ordering of the elements.

nodes for which it has matching elements in the query. Every time it finds a node that is the end of a path, it adds the path ending in this node to a global answer set Q. The function is initially called with the ordered query set q and the forest T as parameters, the answer set is initialized with the empty set $Q := \emptyset$. Upon termination of lookup_subs, Q contains all sets $s \in S$ with $s \subseteq q$.

```
M := all nodes N ∈ T that match an element eᵢ ∈ q
for all nodes N ∈ M do
        if N is the end of a path then
            Q := Q ∪ { the set on the path to N }
        endif
        lookup_subs(N.T, {e_{i+1}, ..., e_{n-1}})
endfor
```

Figure 5: lookup_subs(q,T)

Finally, we show how to retrieve all supersets $s \in S$, $s \supseteq q$ from T. This can be done by finding all paths in T that comprise the path corresponding to q as a (possibly disconnected) subpath. The lookup_sups algorithm is shown in Figure 6. Again, the answer set is initialized with $Q := \emptyset$ and the function is called with the ordered query set q and the forest T as input parameters.

```
M := all nodes N ∈ T matching e with e < e₀
call lookup_sups(q, N.T) on all nodes N ∈ M
if a node N ∈ T corresponds to e₀ then
        if {e₁, ..., e_{n-1}} ≠ ∅ then
            lookup_sups({e₁, ..., e_{n-1}}, N.T)
        else
            P := all end-of-path nodes N' in the tree under N
            Q := Q ∪ {s | s is represented by a node N' ∈ P}
        endif
endif
```

Figure 6: lookup_sups(q,T)

At each stage of the search, lookup_sups does the following: First, it searches all trees that start with an element *preceding* the first element in the query set; these are trees that can possibly contain nodes for the whole set. If there is a node $N \in T$ that directly corresponds to the first element in the (possibly already reduced) query set, the query set gets further reduced by this element. Now the function only needs to find matching nodes for the remaining elements. If there are no such elements left, the search has succeeded, i.e., every end-of-path node that can be reached from N will yield a superset to the query. Otherwise, search needs to be continued with the reduced query set and the appropriate set of nodes.

3 Theoretical Properties of UBTree

We state the soundness and completeness of the lookup_first function in the following theorem.

Theorem 1 *Let T be a forest UBTree that has been constructed by iteratively inserting all sets $s \in S$. The lookup_first function, as defined in Section 2, succeeds on a query set q and T if and only if there exists a set $s \in S$ with $s \subseteq q$.*

A similar theorem stating the soundness and completeness of the lookup_subs and lookup_sups functions can be proven.

To analyze the runtime behavior of the lookup_subs and lookup_first functions, let us re-examine the algorithm in Figure 5 from a different perspective. At each stage, the function tries to find a node N in T that matches the *first* element e_0 of q. If this node is found, there is a new recursive instance, with $N.T$ and $q \setminus \{e_0\}$ as parameters; afterwards, the function works on T and $q \setminus \{e_0\}$. If on the other hand, no node in T matches e_0, the function simply skips e_0 and continues with $q \setminus \{e_0\}$. From these observations, we get the following recursive formula for the number of search nodes that are visited by lookup_subs (which is an upper limit to the number of nodes visited by lookup_first):

$$E(i) = P^N * (1 + 2 * E(i-1)) + (1 - P^N) * E(i-1)$$
$$= P^N + (1 + P^N) * E(i-1)$$

Here, P^N denotes the *probability* that the node N matching e_0 is in T, and $E(i)$, consequently, denotes the *expected* number of visited search nodes with i elements to go. Obviously, $E(1) = P^N$. It is easily proven that the recursion results in:

$$E(n) = P^N * \sum_{i=0}^{n-1} (1 + P^N)^i$$
$$= P^N * \frac{(1 + P^N)^n - 1}{(1 + P^N) - 1}$$
$$= (1 + P^N)^n - 1 \qquad (1)$$

The probability P^N at each stage of the search is equal to the probability that there is a set $s \in S$ which *starts* with the elements that would be represented on a path to N. It is an open question, how an upper limit for P^N can be determined. In the worst-case, when all nodes N are present in the tree, we get $P^N = 1$ and $E(n) = 2^n - 1$ search nodes for a query set of size n.[3]

---

[3]It should be noticed, that, when matching rules or determining unsatisfiable goals in planning, the query sets are small while $|S|$ is very large. Thus, searching 2^n nodes is still much better than checking $|S|$ sets for inclusion.

The number of nodes visited by the lookup_sups function is only dominated by the total number of nodes that are in the forest. Let e_{max} denote the maximal element with respect to the total ordering, i.e., $e < e_{max}$ for all $e \neq e_{max}$. Trying to find all supersets of the query set $\{e_{max}\}$, lookup_sups has to search the whole structure. Consequently, we determine an upper bound for the total number of nodes in the tree.

Theorem 2 *Let T be a forest in which exactly the sets $s \in S$ have been iteratively inserted. If the total number of distinct elements in all of the sets $s \in S$ is P, then the total number of nodes in T is at most $2^P - 1$.*

The worst case occurs if and only if *all* sets containing e_{max} are contained in S.

4 Empirical Evaluation

To demonstrate the effectiveness of the approach, we discuss examples taken from the use of UBTree in the IPP planning system [Koehler *et al.*, 1997]. Following [Hellerstein *et al.*, 1997], the *workload* for UBTree is determined by the following factors:

- the *domain*, which is the set of all possible sets, i.e., given P logical atoms to characterize states, the domain comprises 2^P sets,
- an *instance* of the domain is the finite subset $S \subseteq 2^P$ that is currently stored in T,
- the *set of queries*, which is the set of goals that are constructed during planning.

Note that the workload is *dynamic*. Starting with an empty UBTree structure T, a generated goal set is added if no plan was found by the planning system, i.e., T is monotonically growing containing $|S|$ sets at the end.

Since it is extremely difficult to make distribution assumptions for instances and query sets in a planning system, we use the following parameters to characterize the size of a UBTree:

- P : the total number of distinct logical atoms in S.
- $|S| = |\{s_0, \ldots, s_{k-1}\}|$: the number of all stored sets.
- $|T|$: the total number of nodes in the forest T.
- $C = \frac{|T|}{\sum_{i=0}^{k-1} |s_i|}$: the storage cost, which would be equal to 1 in a trivial data structure simply representing all sets separately.
- $|Q|$: the total number of queries that have been answered during the process.

Figure 7 shows the parameters for forests of increasing size in two different planning domains (the *blocksworld* shown in the upper part and the *briefcase world* shown in the lower part of the table).

The larger **UBTree** grows (reflected by increasing $|S|$ and $|T|$) and the smaller P is, the better values are obtained for the storage cost.

P	$|S|$	$|T|$	C	$|Q|$
71	4846	55035	0.69	8778
96	56398	584015	0.61	112337
115	324628	3042203	0.55	669127
33	1618	4370	0.36	5291
46	22044	59743	0.29	61909
46	92971	210666	0.23	243175
61	1058930	2007326	0.16	24369798

Figure 7: Typical sizes of **UBTree**.

Figures 8, 9, 10, and 11 illustrate the runtime behavior of the query functions reflected in the number of searched nodes for a given query-set size $|q|$ and $|S|$. Note that $|S|$ is shown on a logarithmic scale in all figures.

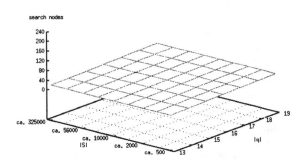

Figure 8: The average number of visited search nodes as a function of query-set size $|q|$ and instance size $|S|$ (shown on a logarithmic scale) for the **lookup_first** function in the positive case where the query succeeds.

Figure 8 indicates that the **lookup_first** function needs significantly less search time on queries where it can retrieve a subset than on those where it must fail. In fact, the average runtime behavior in the positive case was **linear** in the size of the query set and completely **independent** of the instance size throughout all our experiments. The function never visited more than an average of $|q| * 2.5$ search nodes on positive queries. In the general case, the behavior tends to be logarithmic in the instance size. The behavior with respect to the query-set size varied in different domains: sometimes clearly polynomial, even sub-

linear; sometimes, as in the case of Figure 9, possibly exponential, but to a small degree(as indicated by equation 1).

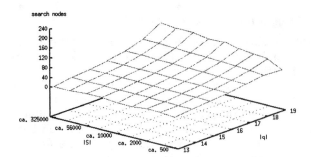

Figure 9: The average number of visited search nodes as a function of query-set size $|q|$ and instance size $|S|$ (shown on a logarithmic scale) for the **lookup_first** function averaged over all, i.e., succeeding and failing, queries.

A behavior as shown in Figure 10 is typical for the **lookup_subs** function: clearly logarithmic in $|S|$ and probably exponential, to a small degree, in the query set size.

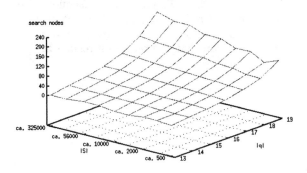

Figure 10: Number of search nodes for **lookup_subs**, averaged over all queries.

Figure 11 shows a typical picture for **lookup_sups** that we found in all investigated domains. It turns out that the performance of this function decreases for small query sets. This happens because small sets are likely to have more supersets than big ones. The behavior with respect to the instance size tends to be linear. Note that again, S is shown on a *logarithmic* scale and that the z scale is different here.

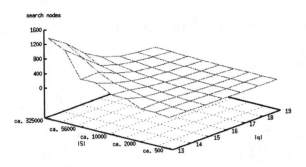

Figure 11: Number of search nodes for lookup_sups, averaged over all queries.

5 Related Work

In order to deal with set queries in *planning*, a partial subset test that only considers sets of size $|q| - 1$ to a given query set of size $|q|$ has been developed in [Blum and Furst, 1997]. Obviously, this can be done in linear time, but such a test must be inherently incomplete. With UBTree, a complete test is available that runs in almost linear time in practice despite its exponential worst-case behavior.

For *databases*, RD trees [Hellerstein and Pfeffer, 1994] have been proposed as an effective means in answering superset queries, but they are very limited in handling subset queries. In contrast to UBTree where a set is spread over several nodes, an RD tree is organized such that the leaf nodes contain the sets and non-leaf nodes contain supersets (of different size) of their children nodes to effectively guide search. To handle subset queries, inverted RD trees are used which are equivalent to RD trees on the complements of the base sets. Two serious problems occur in this approach. First, a non-leaf node needs to be recomputed if a new set is inserted into one of its leaf-children. Second, even if only small sets are stored in the leaves, their complements and their supersets in the corresponding parent nodes grow impractically large. UBTree avoids both problems.

An optimized implementation of the RETE *pattern matching* algorithm [Forgy, 1982] to handle large numbers of production rules is described in [Doorenbos, 1994]. The indexing structure for preconditions of rules is similar to UBTree, but the way how the elements of the query set match the stored sets in the indexing structure is quite different because the preconditions can contain variables, while UBTree deals with sets of ground atoms only. Thus, the problem of *null activations*, where rule nodes are activated though not all of their preconditions are satisfied by the current input, can occur in RETE, but not in UBTree, which would index all ground instances of pattern matching rules instead.

6 Conclusion

Depending on the particular requirements of an application, UBTree can be further optimized. For example, if one is only interested in keeping *minimal* sets, all non-minimal sets can be pruned from the tree. Furthermore, if all sets $s \in S$ are constructed from a finite and fixed domain of elements, an implicit bitmap representation of the sets can further reduce memory consumption and query times.

As we saw in Section 4, the worst-case behavior of the algorithms, especially of the lookup_sups function, depends on the ordering of the elements. In application areas where one has information about the likelihood of appearance of the elements in any set s, it should be possible to generate a total ordering that minimizes the number of tree nodes. One simply orders elements with high likelihood of appearance *before* those with low values. Thereby, both storage and search costs can be reduced.

References

[Blum and Furst, 1997] A. Blum and M. Furst. Fast planning through planning graph analysis. *Artificial Intelligence*, 90(1–2):279–298, 1997.

[Bylander, 1991] T. Bylander. Complexity results for planning. In *IJCAI-91*, pages 274–279. Morgan Kaufmann, San Francisco, CA, 1991.

[Doorenbos, 1994] R. Doorenbos. Combining left and right unlinking for matching a large number of learned rules. In *AAAI-94*, pages 451–458. Morgan Kaufmann, San Francisco, CA, 1994.

[Forgy, 1982] C. Forgy. Rete: A fast algorithm for the many pattern/many object pattern match problem. *Artificial Intelligence*, 19:17–37, 1982.

[Gore, 1997] R. Gore. Tableau methods for modal and temporal logics. Technical report, Australian National University, 1997.

[Hellerstein and Pfeffer, 1994] J. Hellerstein and A. Pfeffer. The RD-Tree: An index structure for sets. Technical Report 1252, University of Wisconsin Computer Sciences Department, 1994.

[Hellerstein et al., 1997] J. Hellerstein, C. Papadimitriou, and E. Koutsoupias. On the analysis of indexing schemes. In *PODS-97*, pages 249–256. ACM, 1997.

[Koehler et al., 1997] J. Koehler, B. Nebel, J. Hoffmann, and Y. Dimopoulos. Extending planning graphs to an ADL subset. In *ECP-97*, volume 1348 of *LNAI*, pages 273–285. Springer, 1997.

Constraint Propagation and Value Acquisition: why we should do it Interactively

E.Lamma, P.Mello, M.Milano
DEIS
University of Bologna
V.le Risorgimento, 2
40136 Bologna ITALY

R. Cucchiara
DSI
University of Modena
Via Campi 213/b
41100 Modena ITALY

M.Gavanelli, M. Piccardi
Dip. Ingegneria
University of Ferrara
Via Saragat, 1
44100 Ferrara ITALY

Abstract

In Constraint Satisfaction Problems (CSPs) values belonging to variable domains should be completely known before the constraint propagation process starts. In many applications, however, the acquisition of domain values is a computational expensive process or some domain values could not be available at the beginning of the computation. For this purpose, we introduce an Interactive Constraint Satisfaction Problem (ICSP) model as extension of the widely used CSP model. The variable domain values can be acquired when needed during the resolution process by means of Interactive Constraints, which retrieve (possibly consistent) information. Experimental results on randomly generated CSPs and for 3D object recognition show the effectiveness of the proposed approach.

1 Introduction

The Constraint Satisfaction Problem (CSP) formalization has been widely used within Artificial Intelligence and related areas. A CSP is defined on a finite set of variables each ranging on a finite domain of objects of arbitrary type and a set of constraints. A solution to a CSP is an assignment of values to variables which satisfies all the constraints. Propagation algorithms [4] (e.g., forward checking, look ahead) have been proposed in order to reduce the search space.

A basic hypothesis for a CSP model is that variable domain values are completely specified at the beginning of the constraint propagation process. We can consider the problem solving activity as the result of the cooperation of two software components (depicted in figure 1): a generator of domain values GEN and a constraint solver CS. The classical CSP formalization leads to a sequential use of this architecture, where GEN produces all domain values and the CS module processes constrained data. The generation or the acquisition of variable domain values should be completed before the constraints on variables are imposed and propagated.

However, in many applications the acquisition of domain values is a computational expensive process. Thus, it is *not convenient* to acquire all domain values, but a pipelined behaviour is preferable. Take, for example, a visual system as GEN module. The acquisition of visual features (such as segments and surfaces) as domain values for the CS is a computational expensive task. In other applications, not all values are available at the beginning of the computation. Thus, it is *not possible* to acquire all the domain values at the beginning of the computation. Suppose we are processing an image representing a box of possibly overlapped pieces that a robot should handle one by one. We have no information on occluded pieces (and thus on the corresponding visual features) until the robot has picked up the emerging pieces occluding the underlying ones.

We argue that interleaving the generation/acquisition of domain values and their processing could greatly increase the performances of the problem solving strategy in some cases, and can be the only way of processing in presence of unknown information. Domain values acquisition can be performed *on demand* only when values are effectively needed or available, as previously suggested by Sergot in [11] in the Logic Programming setting.

Furthermore, in many applications the GEN module is able to focus its attention on significant domain values (i.e., domain values satisfying some properties) or even provide consistent values when guided by means of constraints which we call *interactive constraints*.

For this purpose, the classical CSP model should be extended in order to (i) cope with partially or fully unknown variable domains; (ii) dynamically acquire domain values *on demand* while the constraint propagation process is in progress; (iii) drive the domain value acquisition by means of *interactive constraints*; (iv) incrementally process new information without restarting a constraint propagation process from scratch each time new information is available. The resulting framework has been called *Interactive Constraint Satisfaction Problem* (ICSP) model.

In this paper, we present the ICSP model and corresponding propagation algorithms based on the *Forward Checking* (FC) [4] and *Minimal Forward Checking* (MFC) [2] which we call respectively *Interactive For-*

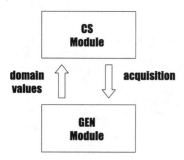

Figure 1: Two modules architecture

ward Checking (IFC) and *Interactive Minimal Forward Checking* (IMFC). If the GEN module is able to focus on significant domain values or even to provide consistent values when guided by constraints, on average the number of acquisition greatly decreases with respect to the standard case. Otherwise, we have the same number of data acquisition of the standard case.

2   The ICSP model

In this section, we first recall some CSP-related concepts. Then, we present the interactive constraint satisfaction framework. We focus on binary CSPs. A binary CSP is a tuple (V, D, C) where V is a finite set of variables $X_1, \dots, X_n$ ranging on domains of objects of arbitrary type $D_1, \dots, D_n$. We call $D_i = [v_{i_1}, \dots, v_{i_n}]$ the domain of X_i. C is a finite set of constraints on pairs of variables in V. A constraint c on variables X_i and X_j, i.e., $c(X_i, X_j)$, defines a subset of the cartesian product of variable domains $D_i \times D_j$ representing sets of possible assignments of values to variables. A *solution* to a CSP is an assignment of values to variables which satisfies all the constraints. A constraint c on variables X_i, X_j is *satisfied* by a pair of values v_i, v_j if $(v_i, v_j) \in c$.

We now extend the CSP definition in order to allow constrained variables to range on partially or completely unknown domains.

Definition 2.1 *An interactive domain of a variable X_i $D_i = [v_{i_1}, v_{i_2}, \dots, v_{i_k} | X_i']$ is a set of possible values which can be assigned to that variable. We refer to $Known_i$ as the list of values representing the known domain part $[v_{i_1}, v_{i_2}, \dots, v_{i_k}]$, and to $UnKnown_i$ as a variable X_i' representing a list of not yet available values for variable X_i. Declaratively, the association of a domain to a variable $X_i :: [v_{i_1}, v_{i_2}, \dots, v_{i_k} | X_i']$ holds iff*

$X_i = v_{i_1} \lor X_i = v_{i_2} \lor \dots \lor X_i = v_{i_k} \lor X_i :: X_i'$
Both $Known_i$ and $UnKnown_i$ can be possibly empty lists[1]. Also, for each i, the intersection of $Known_i$ and $UnKnown_i$ is empty: this follows from the fact that the interactive domain is a set.

The *interactive domain* of variable X_i can be either completely known, e.g, $D_i = [3, 4, 5]$, or only partially known, e.g., $D_i = [3, 4, 5 | X_i']$, where X_i' is a variable

representing a list of values which will be eventually retrieved in the future if needed, or completely unknown, e.g., $D_i = X_i'$.

The notion of interactive domains has some similarities with the concept of streams [12] widely used for communication purposes in Concurrent Prolog. A stream is a communication channel which can be assigned to a term that contains a message and an additional variable. From this perspective, *interactive domains* represent communication channels between the GEN module and the CS module. The unknown part of the domain contains a message (one retrieved value) and an additional variable for future acquisitions.

The strength of the interactive approach concerns the fact that the CS module can guide knowledge acquisition (i.e., the GEN module) by means of constraints, called *interactive constraints*, and incrementally process new information without restarting a constraint propagation process from scratch each time new values are available. With no loss of generality, we define binary interactive constraints.

Definition 2.2 *An interactive binary constraint c on variables X_i and X_j, i.e., $c(X_i, X_j)$, defines a possibly partially known subset of the cartesian product of variable interactive domains $D_i \times D_j$ representing sets of possible assignments of values to variables. Declaratively, given the domains of $X_i :: [v_{i_1}, \dots, v_{i_n} | X_i']$ and $X_j :: [v_{j_1}, \dots, v_{j_m} | X_j']$, the constraint $c(X_i, X_j)$ is satisfied iff*

$\bigvee_{k=1..n, l=1..m} c(v_{i_k}, v_{j_l}) \quad \lor \quad \bigvee_{k=1..n} c(v_{i_k}, X_j') \quad \lor$
$\bigvee_{l=1..m} c(X_i', v_{j_l}) \lor c(X_i', X_j')^2$
where $c(v_{i_k}, X_j')$ (resp. $c(X_i', v_{j_l})$) is satisfied iff for each future acquired value v_j' for X_j' $(v_{i_k}, v_j') \in c$.

Definition 2.3 *A binary Interactive CSP (ICSP) is a tuple (V, D, C) where V is a finite set of variables $X_1, \dots, X_n$, D is set of interactive domains $D_1, \dots, D_n$ and C is a set of interactive (binary) constraints. A solution to the ICSP is an assignment of values to variables which is consistent with constraints.*

3   Search strategies

In this section, we define the *Interactive Forward Checking* and the *Interactive Minimal Forward Checking* procedures. With no loss of generality, both the algorithms start by considering an ICSP where all variables range on a completely unknown domain, i.e., no value is available for any variable. Thus, all variables initially range on a completely unknown domain, and are chosen in the following instantiation order: $X_1, \dots, X_i, \dots, X_n$. The *current variable* X_i is the variable to be instantiated and D_i is its current interactive domain. We refer to *future connected* variables to X_i as the ordered subset of

---

[1]When both are empty an inconsistency arises.

[2]With an abuse of notation, we impose the constraint c on variables representing a list. For the sake of readability, we have omitted the definition of a new variable $X_{new} :: X_i'$ on which constraints should be imposed.

```
procedure IFC(Var, Domain);
begin
for all X_i ∈ Var do
    begin
        I-label(i);
        I-propagation-acquisition(i,future_connected_vars);
    end;
end;
```

Figure 2: The IFC algorithm

```
procedure I-label(i);
begin
known[i] := known(Domain[i]); % known part of Var[i]
unknown[i] := unknown(Domain[i]); % unknown part of Var[i]
if unknown[i] ≠ [] % Var[i] domain is fully unknown
    then begin
        collect all unary constraints C on Var[i];
        impose C on unknown[i];
        acquire_one_val(i,C);
    end;
    if known[i] = []
        then fail;
        else begin % Now known[i] is surely defined
            select a value v_i from known[i];
            assign Var[i] = v_i;
            end;
end;
```

Figure 3: The labeling procedure

$X_{i+1}, \ldots, X_n$ containing those variables linked to X_i by means of a constraint.

3.1 Interactive Forward Checking

In standard CSPs, the forward checking strategy [4] interleaves a labeling step which instantiates variable X_i to a value v in its domain with a constraint propagation process. This second step removes from the domains of future connected variables values which are not consistent with v.

The interactive version of the FC (figure 2) is divided in two steps as well. A *labeling move* is used to find an instantiation for the current variable, and a *propagation/acquisition* step is used to remove (already acquired) values inconsistent with the current labeling, or to acquire new consistent values.

The labeling step, called `I-label` (figure 3), takes as input the index of the variable X_i to be instantiated and either selects a value v in its known domain part if it exists, or retrieves one value v for X_i consistent with the unary constraints on X_i. `I-label` then assigns $X_i = v$.

The propagation/acquisition step (figure 4) takes as input the index i of the current variable and the set of future connected variables. For each future connected variable X_j, a classical FC propagation step is performed in order to remove inconsistent values if the domain of X_j is known. Otherwise, an acquisition is performed in order to retrieve **all** the values consistent with v. After the acquisition, the domain of X_j is completely known.

The main difference with the classical FC algorithm is achieved if the *GEN* module is able to be guided by means of constraints in order to retrieve consistent values. For instance, in a visual recognition system [1], constraints exploiting some form of *locality*, such as *touches(X1,X2)* where $X1$ and $X2$ are segments, could

```
procedure I-propagation-acquisition(i,future_connected_vars);
begin
for each Var_j in future_connected_vars
do begin
    known[j] := known(Domain[j]);
    unknown[j] := unknown(Domain[j]);
    if known[j] = [v_{j_1}, \ldots, v_{j_m}]
        then begin
            for each v_{j_k} in known[j] do
            if not consistent(v_i, v_{j_k})
                then begin
                    remove v_{j_k} from known[j];
                    if known[j] = [] then fail;
                end
        else begin
            impose_constraints on unknown[j]
            acquire_all_values(unknown[j])
        end;
    end ;
end;
```

Figure 4: The propagation algorithm

guide the knowledge acquisition in order to let the *GEN* module to focus only on semantically significant image parts. If this capability could be exploited, the number of data acquisition performed by IFC is significantly smaller than those performed by FC.

3.2 Interactive Minimal Forward Checking

In the previous section, we have described the IFC algorithm which performs, when needed, the acquisition of all domain values consistent with a given assignment.

As argued in [2], a more efficient algorithm finds and maintains only **one** consistent value in the domain of each future variable, suspending forward checks until other values are required by the search. In the interactive version of the MFC we retrieve only one value for each future connected variable, consistent with a given assignment. In addition, we impose new constraints on the unknown part of the domain for eventual future acquisitions. The algorithm is the same as the one described in figure 2. The `I-propagation-acquisition` step reported in figure 5 is different from the IFC since we acquire only one value by the *GEN* module and produce constraints on the unknown domain parts which will be used in backtracking for acquiring further values. Posing new constraints on the variables representing the unknown domain parts is a crucial point in our framework that allows newly acquired data to be processed without starting the constraint propagation process from scratch each time new values are available.

As an example, consider the constraint $X_1 < X_2$, where variable X_1 is instantiated to 3 and the domain of variable X_2 completely unknown, i.e., $X_2 :: X_2'$. When the constraint is checked, a knowledge acquisition is performed for X_2. Suppose that value 5 is retrieved. The domain of X_2 becomes $X_2 :: [5|X"_2]$ and on $X"_2$ a set of constraints is imposed, stating that $X"_2 \neq 5$ and $X"_2 > 3$. These constraints are taken into account if value 5 is removed from the domain of X_2 during constraint propagation. In this case, another consistent value for X_2 is retrieved satisfying the imposed constraints on $X"_2$.

```
procedure I-propagation-acquisition(i,future_connected_vars);
begin
for each Var_j in future_connected_vars
do begin
    known[j] := known(Domain[j]); % contains at most one value
    unknown[j] := unknown(Domain[j]);
    if known[j] = [v_j]
        then begin
            if not consistent(v_i, v_j)
            then begin
                remove v_j from known[j];
                impose_constraints on unknown[j];
                acquire_one_value(unknown[j]);
            end;
        else impose_constraints on unknown[j]
    else begin % the domain of Var_j is fully unknown
        impose_constraints on unknown[j]
        acquire_one_value(unknown[j])
        end;
    end ;
end;
```

Figure 5: The IMFC propagation

4 Heuristics

One important issue is the ordering in which variables
are labelled and the ordering in which values are assigned
to each variable. Decisions in these orderings significantly affect the efficiency of the search strategy.

As concerns variable selection, a widely used CSP
heuristics, called *first fail principle*, selects first the variable with the smallest domain. When coping with partially or fully unknown domains, we cannot know in advance how many values will be contained in the domain.
Thus, we partially disable variable selection heuristics
which depend on domain size. A general criterion which
can be followed in the interactive framework tends to
minimize knowledge acquisitions. Thus, we first select
variables with a completely known domain and among
those, then partially known variables, and finally, completely unknown variables.

As concerns the domain value choice, the only heuristic used concerns the selection of a value belonging to
the known part of a domain before the selection of the
unknown part that results in an unguided knowledge acquisition.

5 Experimental Results

In order to test ICSP algorithms, we performed a series of experiments based on randomly generated CSPs.
Each CSP is defined by a 4-tuple $< n, m, p, q >$, where n
is the number of variables, m is the size of every domain,
p is the probability that a binary constraint is imposed
on a pair of variables (constraint density), and q is the
conditional probability that two values in a constraint
are consistent.

We consider both the number of constraint checks performed by the high-level system and the number of constraint checks performed by the low-level system during
interaction. Each time a single value is requested for one
variable domain (function `acquire_one_value`), first we
check if an already acquired value is consistent w.r.t.
the interactive constraints (and we count the number of

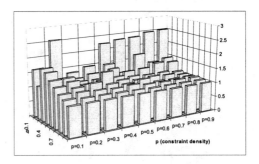

Figure 6: Constraint check ratio FC/IFC

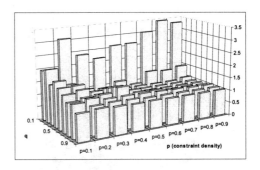

Figure 7: Constraint check ratio MFC/IMFC

constraint checks needed); if the element is not found we
perform acquisition.

Figure 6 shows the ratio of the number of constraint
checks performed by FC and by IFC (the higher the bars,
the better is the interactive approach). The test was
performed generating a number of problems with $n = 10$,
$d = 10$, and varying p and q. Each bar is calculated on
the average of 20 problems.

We can see that the number of constraint checks performed by IFC is always less than plain FC and is considerably lower when the constraint tightness is high (i.e.,
low values of q). This depends on the fact that, when
binding a variable, the IFC algorithm acquires only the
values consistent with constraints, so, if the constraint is
tight, only few acquisitions will be performed.

Analogous considerations can be done for Minimal
Forward Checking algorithm: as the constraint tightness
grows, the interactive approach outperforms the non interactive one.

Since in most applications the value extraction is usually the most expensive task, the comparison based on
the number of extracted values is more significant than
a comparison based on constraint checks. In Figure 9 we
show the percentage of extracted elements for the IMFC
algorithm in problems generated with $n = 10$, $d = 10$,
varying p and q from 10% to 90%. We can see that
in more than half of the cases the number of extracted
elements is less than 50% of the number of elements extracted by CSP methods. The number of acquired values
is very low if the constraints are tight, as every interactive constraint will acquire only few values and this will

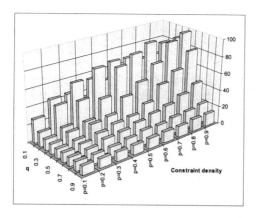

Figure 8: IFC percentage of extracted elements.

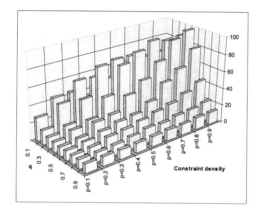

Figure 9: IMFC percentage of extracted elements.

be enough to demonstrate that the whole problem is inconsistent.

The number of acquisitions is higher in IFC, because it extracts all values consistent with an interactive constraint (Figure 8). The displayed graph is quite similar to that in Figure 9, but shows a higher number of acquisitions when q grows. If almost every value in a domain is consistent w.r.t. the interactive constraints, then it is likely that every acquisition will lead to a full extraction, i.e. every acquisition will extract nearly all the d values which can be assigned to a given variable.

5.1 3D Visual Object Recognition

In this section, we show some results obtained in 3D object recognition by using the ICSP framework, [1]. We model 3D objects by means of constraint graphs: nodes represent object parts (say surfaces) and constraints geometric and topological relations among them. A graph representation of object models has been used in many different contexts of 2D shapes [9], and extended to the 3D scene recognition [7],[6]. Solving the 3D object recognition problem as a standard CSP involves the extraction from the image of all surfaces $S_0 \ldots, S_m$ which are put in variable domains $D_0 \ldots D_n$. Then, we have to find an assignment of surfaces to variables satisfying all

constraints.

The CSP-based approach for object recognition suffers of a severe limitation in term of efficiency when applied to real vision applications: surface extraction is a time consuming step working on range images. Thus, useless acquisitions should be avoided and the adoption of ICSP leads to a significant performance improvement. The ICSP-based recognition executes the following steps: (i) the constraint solver queries the low-level image processing system for retrieving an unconstrained surface (S1); (ii) the interacting constraint propagation starts, and whenever a variable domain is not known, new variable values satisfying constraints are requested. In this case, the *GEN* module is able to acquire visual features being guided by spatial constraints such as `get_surface_touching(Xi)` so that only adjacent surfaces to `Xi` are directly computed. This improves the ICSP performances since variable domains turn to be smaller and, more important, the visual system focusses only on significant image parts. Thus, the guided interaction prevents the low-level system from acquiring many useless surfaces.

Several tests are performed on a specific data-base of range images: we have created a modified version of the Washington State University database [5] by assembling several images in order to obtain new ones containing many different possibly overlapped objects.

Image	ICSP	CSP	Speedup
B_1 (320x320) *	136.60	279.66	2.04
B_2 (320x320) *	129.80	276.07	2.12
B_3 (320x320)	125.01	256.51	2.05
B_4 (320x320)	39.93	263.50	6.59
B_5 (320x320) *	156.50	309.90	1.98
B_6 (320x320)	34.89	301.43	8.63
B_7 (400x400)	178.77	442.51	2.47
B_8 (400x400)*	549.10	518.59	0.94
B_9 (400x400)	215.85	555.76	2.57

Table 1: Computational results

Results in Table 1 refer to a database of 9 images and describe the time (in seconds) spent for extracting the first 3D object with an L-shape: the CSP and the ICSP approaches are compared. Some images (marked with *) do not contain the object. In those cases the whole image has been explored and all surfaces computed for both approaches. When all the surfaces are extracted in the image, the performance gain using an interactive approach is not particularly high (in one case the ICSP is even slower since it uses more check points): nevertheless, in images containing the modelled 3D object, a speedup ranging between 2 to 8 has been obtained.

6 Related Work

The general idea that in many applications it is both unreasonable and unrealistic to force the user to provide in advance all information required to solve the problem was argued by Sergot [11] who proposed an extension of Prolog allowing interaction with the user. From an algorithmic perspective, our starting points are the FC [4] and the MFC [2] algorithms. They have been extended with the notion of interaction between a constraint solver and a low level module producing constrained data to be processed.

Dynamic Constraint Satisfaction (DCS) [8] is a field of AI taking into account dynamic changes of the constraint store such as the addition, deletion of values and constraints. The difference between DCS and our approach concerns the way of handling these changes. DCS approaches propagate constraints as if they work in a *closed world*. DCS solvers record the dependencies between constraints and the corresponding propagation in proper data structures so as to tackle modifications of the constraint store. In this perspective, we also cope with changes in the sense that the acquisition of new variable values can be seen as a modification of the constraint store. However, we work in an *open world* where domains are left *opened* thanks to their unknown part. Unknown domain parts intensionally represent future acquisition, i.e., future changes. Thus, the propagation we perform is less powerful than that performed by dynamic approaches, but we do not need to store additional information for restoring the constraint store consistency as done by DCS approaches.

Other related approaches concern constraint-based reactive systems [3]. Reactive programs are programs that react with their environment, are usually stateful, and have to make decisions before their consequences are known. They interleave information accumulation and decision making activities. Also in our approach data acquisition and its processing are interleaved. However, in reactive programs the constraint solver computes a solution for a given set of (incrementally added) variables starting from an already committed system state. Thus, the computation of a single query is performed with no interaction with the (GEN) system. In our approach, instead, interactions between the system (the GEN module) and the constraint solver take place during the execution of a single query.

As a final remark, in the field of programming languages, concurrent constraint programming [10] represents a framework which is based on the notions of consistency and entailment for computing with partial information. Computation emerges from the interaction of concurrently executing agents communicating by means of constraints on shared variables. In a sense, the work on concurrent constraint programming concentrates on the algorithms without paying attention to the semantics of the external world. With our approach we add this semantics. Concurrent constraint programming can be used as an effective language for implementing the interactive constraint solver.

7 Conclusion and Future work

We have presented a model for interactive CSP which can be used when data on the domain is not completely known at the beginning of the computation, but can be dynamically acquired on demand by a low level system.

More important, it is used in order to guide the search by generating new constraints at each step. We have implemented the framework by extending the ECL^{i}PS^e CLP(FD) library. We have shown results on randomly generated CSPs and in the field of 3D object recognition.

Future work concerns the extension of other constraint propagation algorithms, like arc-consistency, to the interactive case. In addition, we are investigating other fields such as planning and user interfaces which could benefit from the proposed approach.

Acknowledgements
This work has been partially supported by MURST Project on "Intelligent Agents: Interaction and Knowledge Acquisition".

References
[1] R. Cucchiara, E. Lamma, P. Mello, and M. Milano. An interactive constraint-based system for selective attention in visual search. In *Proceedings ISMIS'97*, LNAI, 1997.

[2] M.J. Dent and R.E. Mercer. Minimal forward checking. In *Proceedings of ICTAI94*, 1994.

[3] M. Fromherz and J. Conley. Issues in reactive constraint solving. In *Proceedings of COTIC'97 - Workshop in CP'97*, 1997.

[4] P. Van Hentenryck. *Constraint Satisfaction in Logic Programming*. MIT Press, 1989.

[5] A. Hoover, G. Jean-Baptiste, X. Jiang, P.J. Flynn, H.Bunke, D.B.Goldgof, K. Bowyer, D.W. Eggerf, A.Fitzgibbon, and R.B. Fisher. An experimental comparison of range image segmentation algorithms. *IEEE Transactions on PAMI*, 18(7):673–689, 1996.

[6] M.Herman and T.Kanade. Incremental reconstruction of 3D scene from multiple complex image. *Artificial Intelligence*, 30:289–341, 1986.

[7] M.H.Yang and M.Marefat. Constrained based feature recognition: handling non uniquitess in feature interaction. In *IEEE International Conference on Robotics and Automations*, 1996.

[8] S. Mittal and B. Falkenhainer. Dynamic constraint satisfaction problems. In *Proc. of AAAI-90*, 1990.

[9] J.A. Murder, A.K.Mackworth, and W.S.Havens. Knowledge structuring and constraint satisfaction: the MAPSEE approach. *IEEE Trans. on PAMI*, 10(6):866–879, 1988.

[10] V.A. Saraswat. *Concurrent Constraint Logic Programming*. MIT Press, 1993.

[11] M. Sergot. A query-the-user facility for logic programming. In P. Degano and E. Sandewall, editors, *Integrated Interactive Computing Systems*, pages 27–41. North-Holland, 1983.

[12] E. Shapiro, editor. *Concurrent Prolog - Vol. I*. MIT Press, 1987.

DISTRIBUTED
ARTIFICIAL INTELLIGENCE

DISTRIBUTED ARTIFICIAL INTELLIGENCE

Multi-Agent Systems 1

Sequential Optimality and Coordination in Multiagent Systems

Craig Boutilier

Department of Computer Science
University of British Columbia
Vancouver, B.C., Canada V6T 1Z4
cebly@cs.ubc.ca

Abstract

Coordination of agent activities is a key problem in multiagent systems. Set in a larger decision theoretic context, the existence of coordination problems leads to difficulty in evaluating the utility of a situation. This in turn makes defining optimal policies for sequential decision processes problematic. We propose a method for solving sequential multiagent decision problems by allowing agents to reason explicitly about specific *coordination mechanisms*. We define an extension of value iteration in which the system's state space is augmented with the state of the coordination mechanism adopted, allowing agents to reason about the short and long term prospects for coordination, the long term consequences of (mis)coordination, and make decisions to engage or avoid coordination problems based on expected value. We also illustrate the benefits of mechanism generalization.

1 Introduction

The problem of coordination in multiagent systems (MASs) is of crucial importance in AI and game theory. Given a collection of agents charged with the achievement of various objectives, often the optimal course of action for one agent depends on that selected by another. If the agents fail to *coordinate* the outcome could be disastrous. Consider, for instance, two agents that each want to cross a bridge that can support the weight of only one of them. If they both start to cross, the bridge will collapse; coordination requires that they *each* "agree" which one of them should go first.

Coordination problems often arise in *fully cooperative MASs*, in which each agent shares the same utility function or *common interests*. This type of system is appropriate for modeling a team of agents acting on behalf of a single individual (each tries to maximize that individual's utility). In the bridge example above, it may be that neither agent cares whether it crosses first, so long as they both cross and pursue their objectives. In such a setting, coordination problems generally arise in situations where there is some flexibility regarding the "roles" into which agents fall. If the abilities of the agents are such that it makes little difference if agent $a1$ pursues objective $o1$ and $a2$ pursues $o2$, or vice versa, the agents run the risk of both pursuing the same objective—with consequences ranging from simple delay in goal achievement to more drastic outcomes—unless they coordinate. This issue arises in many team activities ranging from logistics planning to robotic soccer.

An obvious way to ensure coordination is to have the agents' decision policies constructed by a central controller (thus defining each agent's role) and imparted to the agents. This is often infeasible. Approaches to dealing with "independent" decision makers include: (a) the design of conventions or social laws that restrict agents to selecting coordinated actions [9, 15]; (b) allowing communication among agents before action selection [16]; and (c) the use of learning methods, whereby agents learn to coordinate through repeated interaction [5, 6, 8, 11].

Unfortunately, none of these approaches explicitly considers the impact of coordination problems in the context of larger sequential decision problems. If the agents run the risk of miscoordination at a certain state in a decision problem, how should this impact their policy decisions at *other states*? Specifically, what is the long-term (or sequential) *value* of being in a state at which coordination is a potential problem? Such a valuation is needed in order for agents to make rational decisions about whether to even put themselves in the position to face a coordination problem.

Unfortunately, there are no clear-cut definitions of sequential optimality for multiagent sequential decision processes in the general case. Most theoretical work on coordination problems assumes that a simple repeated game is being played and studies methods for attaining equilibrium in the stage game. In this paper, we argue that optimal sequential decision making requires that agents be able to reason about the specific coordination mechanisms they adopt to resolve coordination problems. With this ability, they can make optimal decisions by considering the tradeoffs involving probability of (eventual) coordination, the consequences of miscoordination, the benefits of coordination, the alternative courses of action available, and so on. We develop a dynamic programming algorithm for computing optimal policies that accounts not only for the underlying system state, but also the *state of the coordination mechanism being adopted*. Specifically, we show how the underlying state space can be expanded minimally and dynamically to account for specific coordination protocol being used.

With this definition of state value *given* a coordination mechanism, one can tackle the problem of defining good coordination mechanisms for specific decision problems that offer good expected value (we but will make a few remarks near the end of the paper on this point). Our framework therefore provides a useful tool for the design of conventional, communication and learning protocols [15].

We focus on fully cooperative MASs, assuming that a common coordination mechanism can be put in place, and that agents have no reason to deliberate strategically. However, we expect most of our conclusions to apply *mutatis mutandis* to more general settings. We introduce Markov decision processes (MDPs) and *multiagent MDPs* (MMDPs) in Section 2. We define coordination problems and discuss several coordination mechanisms in Section 3. In Section 4 we describe the impact of coordination problems on sequential optimality criteria, show how to expand the state space of the MMDP to reason about the state of the specific mechanisms or protocols used by the agents to coordinate, and develop a version of value iteration that incorporates such considerations. We illustrate the ability of generalization techniques to enhance the power of coordination protocols in Section 5, and conclude with some remarks on future research directions in Section 6.

2 Multiagent MDPs

2.1 Markov Decision Processes

We begin by presenting standard (single-agent) *Markov decision processes* (MDPs) and describe their multiagent extensions below (see [3, 13] for further details on MDPs). A fully observable MDP $M = \langle \mathcal{S}, \mathcal{A}, \mathrm{Pr}, R \rangle$ comprises the following components. $\mathcal{S}$ is a finite set of *states* of the system being controlled. The agent has a finite set of *actions* $\mathcal{A}$ with which to influence the system state. Dynamics are given by $\mathrm{Pr} : \mathcal{S} \times \mathcal{A} \times \mathcal{S} \rightarrow [0,1]$; here $\mathrm{Pr}(s_i, a, s_j)$ denotes the probability that action a, when executed at state s_i, induces a transition to s_j. $R : \mathcal{S} \rightarrow \Re$ is a real-valued, bounded *reward function*. The process is fully observable: though agents cannot predict with certainty the state that will be reached when an action is taken, they can observe the state precisely once it is reached.

An agent finding itself in state s^t at time t must choose an action a^t. The *expected value* of a course of action π depends on the specific objectives. A *finite horizon* decision problem with horizon T measures the value of π as $E(\sum_{t=0}^{T} R(s^t)|\pi)$ (where expectation is taken w.r.t. Pr). A *discounted, infinite horizon* problem measures value as $E(\sum_{t=0}^{\infty} \beta^t R(s^t)|\pi)$. Here $0 \leq \beta < 1$ is a discount factor that ensures the infinite sum is bounded.

For a finite horizon problem with horizon T, a *nonstationary* policy $\pi : S \times \{1, \cdots, T\} \rightarrow A$ associates with each state s and stage-to-go $t \leq T$ an action $\pi(s, t)$ to be executed at s with t stages remaining. An *optimal* nonstationary policy is one with maximum expected value at each state-stage pair. A *stationary* policy $\pi : S \rightarrow A$ for an infinite horizon problem associates actions $\pi(s)$ with states alone.

A simple algorithm for constructing optimal policies (in both the finite and infinite horizon cases) is *value iteration* [13]. Define the t-stage-to-go value function V^t by setting

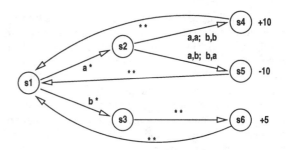

Figure 1: A Simple MMDP with a Coordination Problem.

$V^0(s_i) = R(s_i)$ and:

$$V^t(s_i) = R(s_i) + \max_{a \in \mathcal{A}} \{\beta \sum_{s_j \in \mathcal{S}} \mathrm{Pr}(s_i, a, s_j) V^{t-1}(s_j)\} \quad (1)$$

For a finite horizon problem with horizon T, we set $\beta = 1$ (no discounting) and during these calculations set $\pi(s_i, t)$ to the action a maximizing the right-hand term, terminating the iteration at $t = T$. For infinite horizon problems, the sequence of value functions V^t produced by value iteration converges to the optimal value function V^*. For some finite t, the actions a that maximize the right-hand side of Equation 1 form an optimal policy, and V^t approximates its value.

2.2 The Multiagent Extension

We now assume that a collection of agents is controlling the process. The individual actions of agents interact in that the effect of one agent's actions may depend on the actions taken by others. We take the agents to be acting on behalf of some individual; therefore, each has the same utility or reward function R. The system is fully observable to each agent.

We model this formally as a *multiagent Markov decision process* (MMDP). MMDPs are much like MDPs with the exception that actions (and possibly decisions) are "distributed" among multiple agents. An MMDP $M = \langle \alpha, \{A_i\}_{i \in \alpha}, \mathcal{S}, \mathrm{Pr}, R \rangle$ consists of five components. The set α is a finite collection of n agents, with each agent $i \in \alpha$ having at its disposal a finite set A_i of *individual actions*. An element $\langle a_1, \cdots, a_n \rangle$ of the *joint action space*, $\mathcal{A} = \times A_i$, represents the concurrent execution of the actions a_i by each agent i. The components $\mathcal{S}$, Pr and R are as in an MDP, except that Pr now refers to joint actions $\langle a_1, \cdots, a_n \rangle$.

Taking the joint action space to be the set of basic actions, an MMDP can be viewed as a standard (single-agent) MDP. Specifically, since there is a single reward function, the agents do not have competing interests; so any course of action is equally good (or bad) for all. We define optimal *joint policies* to be optimal policies over the joint action space: these can be computed by solving the (standard) MDP $\langle \mathcal{A}, \mathcal{S}, \mathrm{Pr}, R \rangle$ using an algorithm like value iteration.

Example An example MMDP is illustrated in Figure 1. The MMDP consists of two agents $a1$ and $a2$, each with two actions a and b that can be performed at any of the six states. All transitions are deterministic and are labeled by the joint actions that induce that transition. The joint action $\langle a, b \rangle$ refers to $a1$ performing a and $a2$ performing b, and others similarly (with * referring to any action taken by the corresponding agent). At the "source" state s_1, $a1$ alone decides whether the system moves to s_2 (using a) or s_3 (using b). At s_3, the agents are guaranteed a move to s_6 and a reward of 5 no matter what joint action is executed. At s_2 both agents must choose action a or both must choose b in order to move to s_4 and gain a reward of 10; choosing opposite actions results in a transition to s_5 and a reward of -10. The set of optimal joint policies are those where $a1$ chooses a at s_1 ($a2$ can choose a or b), and $a1$ and $a2$ choose either $\langle a, a \rangle$ or $\langle b, b \rangle$ at s_2.

The value function determined by solving the MMDP for the optimal joint policy is the *optimal joint value function* and is denoted $\widetilde{V}$. In the example above, an infinite horizon problem with a discount rate of 0.9 has $\widetilde{V}(s_1) = 29.9$, while for a finite horizon problem, $\widetilde{V}^t(s_1)$ is given by $10 \lfloor \frac{t+1}{3} \rfloor$.

MMDPs, while a natural extension of MDPs to cooperative multiagent settings, can also be viewed as a type of stochastic game as formulated by Shapley [14]. Stochastic games were originally formulated for zero-sum games only (and as we will see, the zero-sum assumption alleviates certain difficulties), whereas we focus on the (equally special) case of cooperative games.

3 Coordination Problems and Coordination Mechanisms

The example MMDP above has an obvious optimal joint policy. Unfortunately, if agents $a1$ and $a2$ make their decisions independently, this policy may not be implementable. There are two optimal joint action choices at s_2: $\langle a, a \rangle$ and $\langle b, b \rangle$. If, say, $a1$ decides to implement the former and $a2$ the latter, the resulting joint action $\langle a, b \rangle$ is far from optimal. This is a classic coordination problem: there is more than one optimal joint action from which to choose, but the optimal choices of at least two agents are mutually dependent (we define this formally below). Notice that the uncertainty about how the agents will "play s_2" makes $a1$'s decision at s_1 rather difficult: without having a good prediction of the expected value at s_2, agent $a1$ is unable to determine the relative values of performing a or b at s_1 (more in this in Section 4).

In the absence of a central controller that selects a single joint policy to be provided to each agent, ensuring coordinated action choice among independent decision makers requires some *coordination mechanism*. Such a mechanism restricts an agent's choices among the potentially individually optimal actions, perhaps based on the agent's history. We describe some of these below, including learning, conventional and communication techniques.

In the remainder of this section, we focus on *repeated games*, returning to general MMDPs in the next section. An identical-interest repeated game can be viewed as an MMDP with only one state—joint actions are played at that state repeatedly. An immediate reward $R(a)$ is associated with each joint action. Our aim is to have the individual actions selected by each agent constitute an optimal joint action. Formally, a

stage game G comprises action sets A_i for each agent i, joint action space $\mathcal{A}$, and reward function R. The stage game is played repeatedly.

Definition Joint action $a \in \mathcal{A}$ is *optimal* in stage game G if $R(a) \geq R(a')$ for all $a' \in \mathcal{A}$. Action $a_i \in A_i$ is *potentially individually optimal* (PIO) for agent i if some optimal joint action contains a_i. We denote by PIO_i the set of such actions for agent i.

Definition Stage game $G = \langle \alpha, \{A_i\}_{i \in \alpha}, R \rangle$ induces a *coordination problem* (CP) iff there exist actions $a_i \in PIO_i$, $1 \leq i \leq n$, such that $\langle a_1, \cdots, a_n \rangle$ is not optimal.

Intuitively, a CP arises if there is a chance that each agent selects a PIO-action, yet the resulting joint action is suboptimal.

CPs in repeated games can often be "reduced" by eliminating certain PIO-actions due to considerations such as dominance, risk (e.g., see the notions of risk-dominance and tracing used by Harsanyi and Selten to select equilibria [7]), or focusing on certain PIO-actions due to certain asymmetries. These reductions, if embodied in protocols commonly known by all agents, can limit choices making the CP "smaller" (thus potentially more easily solved), and sometimes result in a single "obvious" action for each agent. We do not consider such reductions here, but these can easily be incorporated into the model presented below.

A *coordination mechanism* is a protocol by which agents restrict their attention to a subset of their PIO-actions in a CP. A mechanism has a *state*, which summarizes relevant aspects of the agent's history and a *decision rule* for selecting actions as a function of the mechanism state. While such rules often select actions (perhaps randomly) from among PIO-actions, there are circumstances where non-PIO-actions may be selected (e.g., if the consequences of uncoordinated action are severe). Mechanisms may guarantee immediate coordination, eventual coordination, or provide no such assurances. To illustrate, we list some simple (and commonly used) coordination methods below. In Section 4, we will focus primarily on randomization techniques with learning. However, communication and conventional methods can be understood within the framework developed below as well.

Randomization with Learning This is a learning mechanism requiring that agents select a PIO-action randomly until coordination is achieved (i.e., an optimal joint action is selected by the group). At that point, the agents play that optimal joint action forever. We assume that actions are selected according to a uniform distribution.[1] The mechanism has $k + 1$ states, where k is the number of optimal joint actions: k states each denote coordination on one of the optimal actions, and one denotes lack of coordination. The state changes from the uncoordinated state to a coordinated state as soon as an optimal action is played. This requires that agents be able to observe actions or action outcomes.

We can model this protocol as a finite-state machine (FSM). The FSM for the CP at s_2 in Figure 1 is illustrated in

---

[1] In this and other mechanisms, reduction methods can be used to reduce the number of actions considered by each agent.

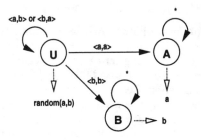

Figure 2: A simple FSM for the randomization mechanism: solid arrows denote state transitions, labeled by inputs (observed joint actions); dashed arrows indicate outputs (action choices).

Figure 2. When the agents are uncoordinated (state U), they each choose action a and b randomly. If the observed joint action is not coordinated, the remain in state U; but if they coordinate, they move to the appropriate state (A or B) and stay there (executing the corresponding action).

For many problems, we can view the mechanism as having only two states: coordinated (C) and uncoordinated (U). If C, we simply require that the agent memorize the action on which the group coordinated. For the purposes of computing expected value below, we often need only distinguish between C and U states (without regard to the actual action chosen). We note that randomization works quite well if there is a small group of agents with few actions to choose from; but as these sets grow larger, the probability of transitioning from U to C gets exponentially smaller. Randomization ensures eventual coordination, at a rate dictated by the number of agents and number of choices available to them.

Fictitious play (FP) is a related learning technique commonly studied in game theory [4, 6] where each agent i observes the actions played in the past by other agents and plays a best response given the empirical distribution observed. We refer to [6] for details, but note that the state of the mechanism consists of "counts" of the PIO-actions played by other agents; thus FP has an infinite number of states. For fully cooperative games, FP converges to an optimal joint action if attention is restricted to PIO-actions and agents randomize over tied best responses [2, 12].[2] It also has the property that once a coordinated action is played, it is played forever. Unlike randomization, FP tends to lead to *faster* coordination as the number of agents and actions increase [2].

Lexicographic Conventions Conventions or social laws (e.g., driving on the right-hand side of the road) are often used to ensure coordination [9, 15]. *Lexicographic conventions* can be applied to virtually any CP. Given some commonly-known total ordering of both agents and individual actions, the set of optimal actions can be totally ordered in several different ways. Lexicographic conventions ensure immediate coordination, but can have substantial overhead due to the requirement that each agent have knowledge of these orderings

---

[2] Hence, it might best be described as a learning technique with randomization, rather than a randomization technique with learning.

of both agents and actions. This may be reasonable in a fixed setting, but may be harder to ensure over a variety of decision problems (e.g., involving different collections of agents). In contrast, the learning models described above can be viewed as "meta-protocols" that can be embodied in an agent once and applied across multiple decision problems.

Communication Finally, a natural means of ensuring coordination is through some form of communication. For example, one agent may convey its intention to perform a specific PIO-action to another, allowing the other agent to select a matching PIO-action. There are a number of well-known difficulties with devising communication and negotiation protocols, involving issues as varied as synchronization and noisy channels. We do not delve into such issues here. We assume that some agreed upon negotiation protocol is in place. Realistically, we must assume that communication has some cost, some risk of failure or misinterpretation, and delays the achievement of goals. As such, we model communication as actions in an MMDP which have effects not on the underlying system state, but on the "mental state" of the agents involved. Rather abstractly, we can say that the state of a communicative coordination mechanism for an agent i is its estimate of the "mental state" of other agents. For example, after negotiation, agent $a1$ may believe that $a2$ is committed to performing action b. The "mental state" of other agents will generally only be partially observable, and the state of the mechanism will be estimated by each agent.

4 Dynamic Programming with Coordination

4.1 Sequential Optimality and State Value

CPs arise at specific states of the MMDP, but must be considered in the context of the sequential decision problem as a whole. It is not hard to see that CPs like the one at s_2 in Figure 1 make the joint value function misleading. For example, $\widetilde{V}^1(s_2) = 10$ and $\widetilde{V}^1(s_3) = 5$, suggesting that $a1$ should take action a at s_1 with 2 stages-to-go. But $\widetilde{V}^1(s_2)$ assumes that the agents will select an optimal, coordinated joint action at s_2. As discussed above, this policy may not be implementable. Generally, the optimal joint value function $\widetilde{V}$ will overestimate the value of states at which coordination is required, and thus overestimate the value of actions and states that lead to them.

A more realistic estimate $V^1(s_2)$ of this value would account for the means available for coordination. For instance, if a lexicographic convention were in place, the agents are assured of optimal action choice, whereas if they randomly choose PIO-actions, they have a 50% chance of acting optimally (with value 10) and a 50% chance of miscoordinating (with value -10). Under the randomization protocol, we have $V^1(s_2) = 0$ and $V^1(s_3) = 5$, making the optimal decision at s_1, with two stages to go, "opting out of the CP:" $a1$ should choose action b and move to s_3.

Unfortunately, pursuing this line of reasoning (assuming a randomization mechanism for coordination) will lead the $a1$ to always choose b at s_1, no matter how many stages remain. If we categorically assert that $V^1(s_2) = 0$, we must have that $V^t(s_3) > V^t(s_2)$ for any stage $t \geq 1$. This ignores the fact that the coordination mechanism in question does not require the agents to randomize at *each* interaction: once they have coordinated at s_2, they can choose the same (optimal) joint action at all future encounters at s_2. Clearly, the $V^1(s_2)$ *depends on the state of the coordination mechanism*. If the agents have coordinated in the past, then $V^1(s_2) = 10$, since they are assured coordination at this final stage; otherwise $V^1(s_2) = 0$. By the same token, $V^t(s_2)$ depends on the state of the mechanism for arbitrary $t \geq 1$, as does the value of other states.

The optimal value function V is not a function of the system state alone, but also depends on the state of the mechanism. By expanding the state space of the original MMDP to account for this, we recover the usual value function definition. In this example, we define the *expanded MMDP* to have states of the form $\langle s, c \rangle$, where s is some system state and c is the state of the randomization mechanism. We use C and U to refer to coordinated and uncoordinated states of the mechanism, respectively (with C standing for either A or B in the FSM of Figure 2). Transitions induced by actions are clear: each action causes a system state transition as in the MMDP, while the coordination state changes from U to C only if the agents choose action $\langle a, a \rangle$ or $\langle b, b \rangle$ at s_2 (and never reverts to U). The coordination protocol also restricts the policies the agents are allowed to use at s_2. If they find themselves at (expanded) state $\langle s_2, U \rangle$, they must randomize over actions a and b. As such, the transition probabilities can be computed easily: $\langle s_2, U \rangle$ moves to both $\langle s_4, C \rangle$ and $\langle s_5, U \rangle$ with probability 0.5.[3]

The expanded MMDP can be viewed a combination of the original MMDP and the partially specified controller shown in Figure 2. The state space of the expanded MMDP is given by the cross-product of the MMDP and FSM state spaces, while the FSM restricts the choices that can be made when the agents are at state s_2 (for each state A, B or U of the FSM). Generally speaking, the protocol restricts action choices at the state where the CP arose, while optimal choices should be made at all other states. Notice that these choices are optimal *subject to the constraints imposed by the protocol (or finite-state controller)*.

With this expanded state space, we can trace value iteration on our running example to illustrate how the agents reason about sequential optimality in a way that accounts for the CP and the coordination mechanism. We assume a finite horizon problem without discounting.

Example For all stages $t > 0$, obviously $V^t\langle s_2, C \rangle > V^t\langle s_3, C \rangle$; so if the agents are in a state of coordination, $a1$ should choose action a at s_1 and "opt in" to the CP by moving to s_2. Matters are more complex if the agents are uncoordinated. For all stages $t < 8$, $V^t\langle s_2, U \rangle < V^t\langle s_3, U \rangle$. So with 8 or fewer stages remaining, $a1$ should choose to "opt out" (choose b) at $\langle s_1, U \rangle$. For all stages $t > 10$, however, $V^t\langle s_2, U \rangle > V^t\langle s_3, U \rangle$ (e.g., $V^{11}\langle s_2, U \rangle = 22.5$ while $V^{11}\langle s_3, U \rangle = 20$.)[4] Thus, $a1$ should "opt in" to the

CP at $\langle s_1, U \rangle$ if there are 12 or more stages remaining.

This example shows how knowledge of the state of the coordination mechanism allows the agents to make informed judgments about the (long term) benefits of coordination, the costs of miscoordination, and the odds of (immediate or eventual) coordination. Because of the cost of miscoordination (and its 50% chance of occurrence), the agents avoid s_2 with fewer than eight stages to go. The safe course of action is deemed correct. However, with eight or more stages remaining, they move from $\langle s_1, U \rangle$ to $\langle s_2, U \rangle$: the 50% chance of coordination not only provides the agents with a 50% chance at the reward of 10, but also with a 50% chance at least two more passes through s_4. The *long term* benefits of coordination (with a sufficient horizon) make the risk worthwhile when compared to the safe alternative.

It is important to note that the state of the coordination mechanism must be taken into account at each (system) state of the MMDP. For instance, though the state of the mechanism can have no influence on what the agents do at state s_3 (there is only one "choice"), it is relevant to determining the value of being at state s_3.

In general, reasoning with coordination mechanisms allows one to account for the factors mentioned above. Naturally, the tradeoffs involving long term consequences depend on the decision problem horizon or discount factor. The key factor allowing computation of value in this case is an understanding of the coordination mechanism used to (stochastically) select joint actions in the presence of multiple equilibria, and the ability to associate a value with any state of the MMDP (given the state of the mechanism). Shapley's stochastic games [14] provide a related sequential multiagent decision model with a a well-defined value for game states. This value, however, is a consequence of the zero-sum assumption, which removes the reliance of state value on the selection of a (stage game) equilibrium. In particular, it does not apply to fully cooperative settings where CPs arise.

4.2 Value Iteration with State Expansion

Value iteration can be revised to construct an optimal value function and policy based on any given coordination mechanism. A straightforward version is specified in Figure 3. We discuss several optimizations below.

A list *CP* of state-game CPs and associated mechanisms is kept as they are discovered. A CP exists if the set of optimal joint actions at a state/stage pair (the Q-values in step 3(a)i) induces a CP in the sense defined earlier. Notice that CPs are defined using the value function V^t, not immediate reward. We assume that each CP is associated with a state and the collection of actions involved in the optimal joint actions. Any state s_i with a CP will have the availability of actions involved in the CP restricted by the state of the mechanism. The set $PA(s_i)$ is the set of actions permitted at s_i given the mechanism state—this may include randomization actions as well (if s_i has no CP, this set is just $\mathcal{A}$); and agents can only use permitted actions (step 3(a)i). If a CP is discovered among the maximizing (permitted) actions at s_i, a new mechanism C is introduced and the state is split and replaced by all pairs of states $\langle s_i, c \rangle$ (where c is some state of C).

---

[3] More precisely, $\langle s_2, U \rangle$ transitions to states $\langle s_4, A \rangle$ and $\langle s_4, B \rangle$ with probability 0.25 each.

[4] The values $V^t\langle s_2, U \rangle$ and $V^t\langle s_3, U \rangle$ are equal for $8 \leq t \leq 10$.

1. Let $V^0(s) = R(s)$ for all $s \in \mathcal{S}$.

2. Set $t = 0; \mathcal{S}^1 = \mathcal{S}^0 = \mathcal{S}; CP = \emptyset$.

3. While $t < T$ do:

 (a) For each $s_i \in \mathcal{S}^{t+1}$

 i. For each $a \in PA(s_i)$, compute
 $$Q^{t+1}(s_i, a) = R(s_i) + \{\textstyle\sum_{s_j \in \mathcal{S}^t} \Pr(s_i, a, s_j) V^t(s_j)\}$$

 ii. Let $Opt^{t+1}(s_i)$ be the set of actions with max Q-value

 iii. If $Opt^{t+1}(s_i)$ induces a *new* CP at s_i, introduce mechanism C: (a) add C to CP; (b) replace s_i in $\mathcal{S}^{t+1}$ with states $\langle s_i, c \rangle$, where c ranges over states of C; (c) Recompute $Q^{t+1}(\langle s_i, c \rangle, a)$ for each new state (according to rules of C); (d) return to step ii. to check for new CPs.

 iv. Let $V^{t+1}(s_i) = \max_a Q^{t+1}(s_i, a)$ and $\pi^{t+1}(s_i)$ be any maximizing action (if s_i was split, do this for all $\langle s_i, c \rangle$).

 (b) $t = t + 1; \mathcal{S}^{t+1} = \mathcal{S} \times CP$.

Figure 3: Value Iteration with State Expansion

To illustrate, suppose the value function V^t induces the following choices at s_i:

	a	b	c
a	10	0	0
b	0	10	0
c	0	0	7

If randomization is used to coordinate on a/b, expected value is 5 (and the mechanism requires agents to randomize over their PIO-actions). In contrast, the Q-value of $\langle c, c \rangle$ is better than that of attempting to coordinate, thus the value of s_i is defined as 7 if the agents are uncoordinated (and 10 if they are coordinated). Notice that new CPs may be introduced at the same state and the process can be iterated.[5] In this problem, each state s is split into three states: $\langle s, A \rangle$ (agents have coordinated on joint action $\langle a, a \rangle$ at s_i), $\langle s, B \rangle$ (coordinated on $\langle b, b \rangle$), and $\langle s, U \rangle$ (have not coordinated w.r.t. a and b).

If a mechanism has been introduced for the same state and actions at an earlier stage, a new mechanism is not generated. Value (and policy choice) is defined by comparing the value of actions *not* involved in the CP and the value of behaving according to the rules of the mechanism (step 3(a)iv). At the next iteration all states are split according all mechanisms introduced, since this may be required to predict the value of reaching state s_i. If multiple CPs exist, each underlying system state is expanded many times in this (naive) algorithm.

Implicit in this discussion is that assumption that the transitions induced by a coordination protocol over the expanded state space are well defined: this will generally involve extending the underlying system dynamics by rules involving mechanism state evolution. The mechanism designer must provide such rules (as discussed in Section 3.2).

An important optimization is to have the algorithm only expand states with mechanisms whose state is required to predict value. This can be effected rather easily. If *system* state s_i transitions to state s_j, and s_j has been split in $\mathcal{S}^t$ to involve some mechanism in CP, s_i must be split in state $\mathcal{S}^{t+1}$. But if s_i moves only to states that are unaffected by some (or all) CPs, s_i need not be split using the state of those CPs. This

---

[5] However, the splitting must eventually terminate.

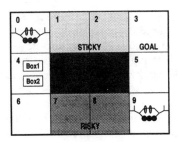

Figure 4: A More Complex Coordination Problem.

allows one to only refer to the state of a mechanism when it is necessary for predicting value: the state space need not be split uniformly.

Other optimizations of the algorithm are possible. For example, one can "cluster" together states of the coordination mechanism together that provide for the same optimal action and value at a given state. For instance, though FP has an infinite number of distinct states, for any finite number of stages-to-go, only a finite number of distinction are relevant (much like state abstraction methods used in MDPs and reinforcement learning [1, 3]). Finally, we note that modeling communcation protocols requires introducing communication actions, in addition to the state-splitting mechanism above.

4.3 Examples

We describe the results of applying the algorithm to several small test problems in this section. We focus here on the use of the simple randomization mechanism described above.

Testing a finite horizon version of the problem in Figure 1 shows that a single CP exists (at state s_2). The state space is eventually expanded so that each state is split into two (referring to coordination or lack of it at s_2). The optimal decision at $\langle s_1, U \rangle$ is to "opt out" with fewer than eight stages to go and "opt in" with eight or more stages remaining. The infinite horizon version of this problem gives rise to stationary policies. When the discount rate $\beta = 0.9$ (or higher), $a1$ "opts in" at $\langle s_1, U \rangle$; but for $\beta = 0.85$ (or lower), $a1$ "opts out" and avoids the CP—because of discounting, the delay in expected payoff of coordination ensures that "opting in" is not worth the cost. With $\beta = 0.9$, the value of opting in is 17.14 and opting out is 16.54 (assuming the agents act optimally thereafter), while with $\beta = 0.85$, the value of opting in is 8.62 and opting out is 9.36 (within tolerance 0.001).

A more complex example is illustrated in Figure 4. Two agents have independent tasks. Agent $a1$ moves box $b1$ and $a2$ moves $b2$ to the goal state repeatedly. Once a box is dropped at the goal, a reward is received and a new box appears in the original location (so the problem is a continuous, infinite horizon MMDP). While the objectives are independent, both agents are rewarded with the same constant reward whenever either of their boxes is delivered. The optimal policies are not independent however. The dark shaded region at the bottom is "risky:" if both agents are in the region, a large (variable) penalty is given. They must coordinate their moves to ensure that no more than one agent is in the risky region at any time. The agents' actions are stochastic: they can move in any (feasible) compass direction but with probability 0.1 they fail to move (they can also stay in place intentionally). Complicating the problem is the fact that the light shaded region is "sticky:" the agents' moves are more prone to failure (with varying probability). If stickiness is low, the optimal policy is for both agents to traverse the top of the grid repeatedly. But if stickiness is relatively high (or the problem is heavily discounted, making speedy delivery more important), one or both agents will want to traverse the risky area, in which case coordination is needed. The problem has 900 nominal states (though a number of these are not reachable) and 25 joint actions.

We give a brief summary of the results in this domain with the following specific parameter settings: a reward of 5 is given for each box delivered; a penalty of -20 is given whenever both agents are in the risky area; stickiness (the probability of not moving) is 0.7 in the sticky region; and $\beta = 0.95$. With these settings, the optimal joint policy (roughly) requires that one agent move across the top of the grid and one move across the bottom.[6] Generally, if an agent is closer to the top it will move across the top; but if both agents are close (and equally close) to the bottom, they must coordinate (since either could move to the top).

CPs arise at eight states of the MMDP. Thus there are eight coordination mechanisms needed to solve this problem, expanding the state space by a factor of 256 (no distinctions need be made among coordinated choices, so each mechanism has only two states). We focus on two MMDP states where CPs arise and their interaction: $s_{4,4} = \langle h1, h2, 4, 4 \rangle$, where both agents are located at grid cell 4 each holding boxes, and $s_{6,6} = \langle h1, h2, 6, 6 \rangle$, which is similar, but with both agents at location 6. The optimal joint policy at $s_{4,4}$ requires one agent to move up (to traverse the sticky region) and the other to move down (to traverse the risky region) on the way to the goal. The optimal policy at $s_{6,6}$ is similar: one agent should move up, the other right. The optimal joint value function has $\widetilde{V}(s_{4,4}) = 11.54$ and $\widetilde{V}(s_{6,6}) = 11.83$.

If the agents have coordinated at all other states where CPs arise, we have the following optimal values for the four states of the expanded MMDP corresponding to each of $s_{4,4}$ and $s_{6,6}$ (here we use u_4 to denote that the agents have not coordinated at $s_{4,4}$, and c_4 to denote that they have coordinated at $s_{4,4}$; similarly for $s_{6,6}$):

	u_4u_6	u_4c_6	c_4u_6	c_4c_6
$s_{4,4}$	10.4419	11.3405	11.5356	11.5356
$s_{6,6}$	7.1866	11.8339	7.3983	11.8340

In both states ($s_{4,4}$ or $s_{6,6}$), if the agents are uncoordinated, the optimal policy requires them to randomize, regardless of the state of the other coordination mechanism. Notice that the values for most of the expanded states where the agents are uncoordinated are less than the corresponding values for the optimal joint policy (which is identical to the expected values at the states where c_4c_6 holds), as expected. The one

exception is at $s_{4,4}$: when c_4 holds, expected value is identical whether or not c_6 holds, since the optimal policy will never take the agents from $s_{4,4}$ to $s_{6,6}$. In contrast, when u_4 holds, the status of c_6 has a dramatic impact on expected value: if the agents are uncoordinated at $s_{4,4}$ they will randomize and with probability 0.25 both choose to move down (hence to $s_{6,6}$). Their state of coordination at $s_{6,6}$ is thus important to predicting expected value. Being uncoordinated at $s_{6,6}$ has very low value, since randomization has a good chance of moving both agents to the risky area—the risk is worthwhile, however, so randomization is the optimal choice at $s_{6,6}$.[7] Also when the agents are coordinated at $s_{6,6}$, the status of c_4 has a rather small effect on value. Because coordination at $s_{6,6}$ ensures that one agent takes the "sticky" route to the goal region, the agents get "out of synch" and the odds of them both reaching the pickup location (cell 4) at the same time (within a reasonable time frame) is quite small. Hence, whether or not the agents are coordinated at $s_{4,4}$ has little impact on expected value at $s_{6,6}$.

Randomization is an important aspect of this problem. If the agents were to choose from among their PIO actions independently, but deterministically, without reasoning about the consequences of miscoordination, they can end up in cycles that never reach the goal state.

5 Generalization of Coordination Decisions

One difficulty with the algorithm above is the potential for uninhibited state expansion, and the corresponding computational cost. In the simple experimental domain with two agents collecting boxes in a grid world, eight CPs occurred across the 900 problem states, requiring the state space to be increased by a factor of 256 (to 230,400 states). Fortunately, in many circumstances we can introduce a single coordination mechanism to deal with multiple, related CPs. In the grid problem, for example, once the agents coordinate at a state by one agent moving up and the other down, they can maintain these "roles" at other states exhibiting similar CPs.

We do not propose a method for constructing such generalizations automatically—this could use, say, generalization techniques from reinforcement learning [1]—but we illustrate potential benefits with the simple example shown in Figure 5. It is similar to the MMDP in Figure 1 except that miscoordination at s_2 has a larger penalty, and an analogous "low cost" CP has been added. If a single mechanism is used for both CPs (at s_2 and s_7), once coordination is attained at s_7, it is automatic at s_2. As in the original MMDP, with fewer than 12 stages-to-go, the optimal action at $\langle s_1, U \rangle$ is to "opt out" and take the sure reward 5. With 12 or more stages remaining, the optimal action at $\langle s_1, U \rangle$ is $\langle a, a \rangle$: the agents move to the low risk CP and try to coordinate there. Never do the agents move to s_2 in an uncoordinated state. Even though there is no immediate benefit to moving to s_7, it gives the agents an opportunity to "train," or learn to coordinate with minimal risk. Once they coordinate, they immediately exploit this learned protocol and choose $\langle a, b \rangle$ at $\langle s_1, C \rangle$ (thereby moving to $\langle s_2, C \rangle$). Reasoning about the long term

---

[6] If the penalty is negligible or if the stickiness is even higher, the agents will both tend to move across the bottom, perhaps with one waiting for the other. If the stickiness is negligible, then both agents will traverse the top of the grid.

[7] Though with higher penalties, it is not.

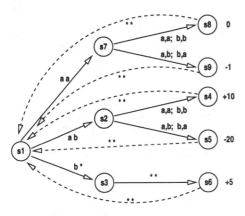

Figure 5: An MMDP with Similar Coordination Problems

prospects of coordination and its costs, the agents realize that risk-free training is worthwhile.

If we retain the original penalty of -10 at s_5, this reasoning fails: there is essentially less risk involved in training at the high stakes CP, so the agents will never move to s_7 to train.

The infinite horizon problem is similar. With a discount rate of 0.95, the optimal policy requires the agents to move to s_7 until they coordinate, at which point they repeatedly move to s_2. Interestingly, adding the "training states" increases the expected reward accrued by the agents. Without the training states, $V(\langle s_1, U \rangle) = 46.68$ since the agents accept the risk of getting several -20 rewards to ensure coordination. With the training states, they can learn to coordinate without the severe penalties, and $V(\langle s_1, U \rangle) = 49.57$.

6   Concluding Remarks

We have introduced a novel method of defining value functions (and consequently, optimal policies) for multiagent decision problems that accounts for specific means of coordination. We also defined a value iteration algorithm for computing optimal policies that recognizes and reasons about CPs.

Further experimentation is needed with other coordination mechanisms and their impact on policy value. We have described experiments in this paper using randomization, and have begun to investigate communication methods, and hope to explore other models like FP. We intend to introduce economic models (such as auctions) so that agents may integrate reasoning about their activity in markets into their decision processes. We must explore automated generalization methods further; it has the potential to substantially reduce the required number of mechanisms, alleviate computational difficulties, and increase objective policy value.

We would also like address the problem of designing robust, computationally effective and value-increasing coordination protocols in the framework. In a certain sense, such an undertaking can be viewed as one of designing *social laws* [15]. It is also related to the issues faced in the design of protocols for distributed systems and the distributed control of discrete-event systems [10]. But rather than designing protocols for specific situations, metaprotocols that increase value

over a wide variety of CPs would be the target. The framework developed here can also help decide whether sophisticated protocols are worthwhile. For instance, a lexicographic protocol induces immediate coordination with a measurable (in our model) increase in expected value over (say) a randomization method. This increase can then be used to decide whether the overhead of incorporating a lexicographic convention (e.g., ensuring agents have common orderings) is worthwhile. Similar remarks can be applied to the design of agents (e.g., is communicative ability worthwhile given the class of decision problems they will face).

Acknowledgements

This research was supported by the DARPA Co-ABS program (through Stanford University contract F30602-98-C-0214), NSERC Research Grant OGP0121843, and IRIS Phase-III Project BAC. Thanks to Ronen Brafman for discussion of these issues.

References

[1] D. P. Bertsekas and J.. N. Tsitsiklis. *Neuro-dynamic Programming.* Athena, Belmont, MA, 1996.

[2] C. Boutilier. Learning conventions in multiagent stochastic domains using likelihood estimates. *Proc. 12th Conf. on Uncertainty in Artif. Intel.*, pages 106–114, Portland, OR, 1996.

[3] C. Boutilier, T. Dean, and S. Hanks. Decision theoretic planning: Structural assumptions and computational leverage. *Journal of Artif. Intel. Research*, 1998. To appear.

[4] G. W. Brown. Iterative solution of games by fictitious play. In T. C. Koopmans, editor, *Activity Analysis of Production and Allocation*. Wiley, New York, 1951.

[5] D. Fudenberg and D. K. Levine. Steady state learning and Nash equilibrium. *Econometrica*, 61(3):547–573, 1993.

[6] D. Fudenberg and D. K. Levine. *The Theory of Learning in Games.* MIT Press, Cambridge, MA, 1998.

[7] J. C. Harsanyi and R. Selten. *A General Theory of Equilibrium Selection in Games.* MIT Press, Cambridge, 1988.

[8] E. Kalai and E. Lehrer. Rational learning leads to Nash equilibrium. *Econometrica*, 61(5):1019–1045, 1993.

[9] D. K. Lewis. *Conventions, A Philosophical Study.* Harvard University Press, Cambridge, 1969.

[10] F. Lin and W. Wonham. Decentralized supervisory control of discrete-event systems. *Info. Sciences*, 44:199–224, 1988.

[11] M. L. Littman. Markov games as a framework for multi-agent reinforcement learning. *Proc. 11th International Conf. on Machine Learning*, pages 157–163, New Brunswick, NJ, 1994.

[12] D. Monderer and L. S. Shapley. Fictitious play property for games with identical interests. *Journal of Economic Theory*, 68:258–265, 1996.

[13] M. L. Puterman. *Markov Decision Processes: Discrete Stochastic Dynamic Programming.* Wiley, New York, 1994.

[14] L. S. Shapley. Stochastic games. *Proc. National Academy of Sciences*, 39:327–332, 1953.

[15] Y. Shoham and M. Tennenholtz. On the synthesis of useful social laws for artificial agent societies. *Proc. 10th National Conf. on Artif. Intel.*, pages 276–281, San Jose, 1992.

[16] G. Weiß. Learning to coordinate actions in multi-agent systems. *Proc. 13th International Joint Conf. on Artif. Intel.*, pages 311–316, Chambery, FR, 1993.

A Protocol-Based Semantics for an Agent Communication Language

Jeremy Pitt and **Abe Mamdani**

Intelligent & Interactive Systems Group, Dept. of Electrical & Electronic Engineering
Imperial College of Science Technology and Medicine, London SW7 2BT, England
Email: {j.pitt,a.mamdani}@ic.ac.uk   URL: http://www-ics.ee.ic.ac.uk

Abstract

There are fundamental limitations on using mental attitudes to formalise the semantics of an Agent Communication Language (ACL). Instead, we define a general semantic framework for an ACL in terms of protocols. We then argue that the proper role of mental attitudes is to link what an agent 'thinks' about the content of a message to what it 'does' in response to receiving that message. We formalise this connection through normative and informative specifications and demonstrate its use in communication between two BDI-style agents.

1 Introduction

The growing ease of network connectivity of computers provided the enabling technology for the agent paradigm. From the computing perspective, agents are autonomous, asynchronous, communicative, distributed and possibly mobile processes. From the AI perspective, they are communicative, intelligent, rational, and possibly intentional entities.

The common feature of communication has determined that some kind of message passing between agents is required. To provide inter-operability between heterogeneous agents, a commonly understood agent communication language (ACL) is used: examples include KQML [Finin *et al.*, 1995], Arcol [Breiter and Sadek, 1996], and FIPA's ACL [FIPA, 1997]. To ensure that it is commonly understood, a formal semantics for the ACL is required. From the AI perspective, the semantics has typically been characterised in terms of speech act theory and framed in terms of the intentional stance, i.e. mentalistic notions such as beliefs, desires and intentions [Cohen and Levesque, 1995; Breiter and Sadek, 1996; FIPA, 1997].

An intentional formalisation of an ACL semantics often involves the axiomatisation of the felicity conditions of Searle and the conversational maxims of Grice. Grice's analysis of conversational implicatures was underpinned by the sincerity condition to support the co-operativity principle. For agents to converse co-operatively (e.g. for negotiation, co-ordination, etc.), the sincerity condition is a reasonable requirement, but is often hard-wired into the semantics as a feasibility precondition on performing a simple speech act, e.g. KQML tell and FIPA inform. Thus an agent believes what it says and only says what it believes.

However, by defining the meaning of a performative in isolation through an axiomatisation that implicitly expects the performative to be used in conversation, there is a risk of being exclusive. In isolation, we could motivate the behaviour of a sincere agent by the axiom:

$$\models \mathcal{B}_s\phi \land \mathcal{D}_s\mathcal{B}_r\phi \to \mathcal{I}_s(\text{DONE}(<s, inform(r, \phi)>))$$

Here $\mathcal{B}$, $\mathcal{D}$ and $\mathcal{I}$ are respectively the beliefs, desires (goals) and intends modalities, and DONE is an operator on actions. This axiom therefore states that if the agent s believed ϕ and wanted another agent r to believe ϕ, then s would generate the intention to inform r of ϕ, after which action r may also come to believe ϕ. Alternatively we could define the behaviour of a 'rapacious' agent by the axiom:

$$\models \mathcal{D}_s\psi \land \mathcal{B}_s(\text{DONE}(A) \to \psi) \to \mathcal{I}_s\text{DONE}(A)$$

This axiom states that if s desires (wants) ψ and believes that doing A will achieve ψ then s will intend to do A. If $\psi = \mathcal{B}_r\phi$, the same communication occurs (A is $<s, inform(r, \phi)>$), without s having an explicitly held belief in ϕ.

Any formalisation of communication based on the mental states of the participants must deal with what is fundamentally a process of revision and updating of those states. It is unlikely that a single set of axioms will cover all eventualities because communication is inherently context-dependent. What works in one application may be inappropriate in another. Furthermore, intentionality is concerned with agent internals and a communicative act is an external phenomenon: mental attitudes can only give a possible reason for and not the definitive meaning of the performative. Therefore there are considerable limitations of intentionality as a basis for defining the semantics of an ACL (cf. [Singh, 1998]).

This paper develops an alternative semantic framework for an ACL from the computing perspective, with an emphasis on protocols. Mental attitudes are used now to link what an agent 'thinks' about the message content to what it 'does' in response to receiving that message.

2 A Layered Semantics

Consider the situation illustrated in Figure 1. It shows two agents, each embedded in an environment, which partially overlap. However, rather than communicating by changing the environments, they can communicate by using speech acts and the ACL protocols.

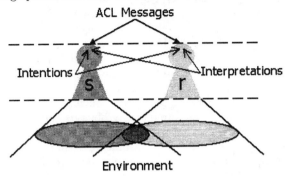

Figure 1: Communicating Agents

We identify three layers of semantics here:

i The content level semantics, which is concerned with interpreting and understanding the content of a message, and is internal to an agent;

ii The action level semantics, which is concerned with replying in appropriate ways to received messages, and is external to the agents;

iii The intentional semantics, which is concerned with making a communication in the first place, and with replying, and again is internal to the agent.

We would argue that the current FIPA ACL semantics for example, is level 3, and because it is internal to an agent, its usefulness in standardisation has been questioned [Wooldridge, 1998; Singh, 1998]. The only part of the communication that is amenable to standardisation is the observable tip of the iceberg: namely the communication itself. Note that this properly includes ontologies, so that there may be a standard interpretation, but the actual interpretation of the content of the message is once again internal to the agent.

3 Generic Semantics for Performatives

We define a standard semantics for performatives by an input-output relationship at the action level (level (ii) above). We define the meaning of a speech act (as input) as the intention to perform another speech act (as output). In computing this functional relationship we can take into account the agent's mental state, without proscribing that state or how it should be implemented.

We base the relationship on how the object-level content of a message induces a change in the information state of the receiver, and how the meta-level action descriptor of a message (the performative itself) induces a response from the receiver. Our proposal is that the semantics of performatives can be characterised in these terms, and that this is the semantics that should be specified for a standard agent communication language. This means specifying, for the content, what it 'means' for an agent (receiving a message) to add its interpretation of that content to its current information state; and for the speech act, the space of possible responses an agent may make, one of which it is committed to make.

For the specification that follows in this section, let c and σ be sets of integers, and let Δ, *content_meanings*, and *speech_acts* be, respectively, possibly infinite sets of agent information states, the agent's interpretation of the content of a message, and speech acts.

An ACL is defined by a 3-tuple $<$Perf, Prot, *reply*$>$ where Perf is a set of performative names, Prot is a set of protocol names, and *reply* is a partial function given by:

$$reply : \text{Perf} \times \text{Prot} \times \sigma \mapsto \wp(\text{Perf})$$

For the FIPA ACL, for example, Perf would be the set of all FIPA ACL performatives, and Prot would be the set of all FIPA ACL protocols, used for negotiations, calls-for-proposals, etc., for example:

$$\text{Perf} = \{inform, confirm, disconfirm, \ldots, \textbf{null}, \ldots\}$$
$$\text{Prot} = \{negotiate, cfp, \ldots, \textbf{no\_protocol}, \ldots\}$$

Note we include a null performative which is a 'do nothing' (no reply) performative (cf. *silence* as used in Smith *et al.* [1998]), and require an empty protocol **no_protocol**: agents can communicate using one-shot speech acts irrespective of a particular protocol.

Each element of Prot names a finite state diagram. Then *reply* is a (partial) function from performatives, protocols and protocol states to the power set of performatives. This states for each performative, 'uttered' in the context of a conversation following a specific protocol, what performatives are acceptable replies. The *reply* function can be constructed from inspection of the protocol state diagrams, and vice versa, although more formal characterizations are possible (e.g. [Kuwabara *et al.*, 1995]).

This 3-tuple is standard for all agents using the ACL. To fully characterise the semantics, we need three further functions which are relative to an agent a, and specify what an agent does with a message, not how it does it:

$$add_a : \quad \text{Perf} \times \text{Prot} \times content\_meanings \times \Delta \rightarrow \Delta$$
$$select_a : \quad \wp(\text{Perf}) \times \Delta \rightarrow speech\_acts$$
$$conv_a : \quad c \mapsto \sigma$$

Here, add_a is agent a's own procedure for computing the change in its information state from the content of an incoming message using a particular performative 'uttered' in the context of a particular protocol. add_a then converts a's (a-type) information state into a new (a-type) information state. $select_a$ is agent a's own procedure for selecting a performative from a set of performatives (valid replies), and from its current information state generating a complete speech act for this performative which will be its (intended) reply. Finally, we require that agents keep track of the state of each conversation in which it is involved, and uniquely identify each conversation with some identifier, i.e. an agent may be involved in more than one conversation and uses the identifier to distinguish between them. $conv_a$ then maps a conversation identifier onto the current state of the protocol being used to conduct the conversation. (Note that FIPA ACL has message attributes (reply-with, in-reply-to and conversation-id) to serve such purposes, but they are not accommodated in the formal semantics.)

An agent s communicates with (and communicates information to) an agent r via a speech act. This is represented by:

$$< s, \mathsf{perf}(r, (C, L, O, p, i, t_{snd})) >$$

This is saying that s does (communicates with) performative perf with content C in language L using ontology O, in the context of a conversation identified by i which is following protocol p, at the time of sending t_{snd}.

Define a function f which for any speech act sa returns the performative used in that speech act. The meaning of a speech act is then given by:

$$[\![< s, \mathsf{perf}(r, (C, L, O, p, i, t_{snd})) >]\!] = \mathcal{I}_r < r, sa >$$

$$\text{such that} f(sa) \in reply(\mathsf{perf}, p, conv_r(i))$$

This defines the meaning of the speech act by sender s to be an intention of receiving agent r to perform some other speech act. The performative used in the speech act as the response is selected from $reply(\mathsf{perf}, p, conv_r(i))$, i.e. it is constrained to be one of the performatives allowed by the protocol. The speech act is generated from r's information state at the time of selection $\Delta_{r,t_{now}}$ and the state of the conversation i according to the protocol p, using r's $select_r$ function:

$$sa = select_r(reply(\mathsf{perf}, p, conv_r(i)), \Delta_{r,t_{now}})$$

where $\Delta_{r,t_{now}}$ is given by:

$$\Delta_{r,t_{now}} = add_r(\mathsf{perf}, p, L_r[\![C]\!]_{L,O}, \Delta_{r,t_{rcv}})$$

This states that r's information state after receiving the message is the result of adding, using r's own procedure add_r, r's own interpretation (content meaning) of the content C in language L using ontology O to its database at the time of receipt, $\Delta_{r,t_{rcv}}$.

Note that for a speech act performed as part of a conversation identified by i, both sending and receiving agents are expected to update their respective $conv$ mapping from conversation identifiers to current state (as defined by the protocol). The sending agent will do this on performing the speech act, the receiving agent after creating the intention to reply. This means that after a message has been sent and before it has been processed, the two parties of the conversation will (for a while) be in different states, and this can be useful in error recovery as a result of lost messages, for example.

It is possible, with a little care, to describe FIPA ACL as a 3-tuple as defined above. FIPA ACL has a small set of basic performatives and just a few protocols, most with fewer than 10 states. However, more work is required for protocols where there are more than two participants, the sequence of speech acts is not simple turn-taking, there are timing constraints which affect allowable replies, and so on. It may also be that a protocol, if not infinite, may nevertheless have a 'very large' number of states. Therefore a further generalisation of the specification may be required, by defining rules for generating speech acts between two players (i.e. a game).

To summarise, all agents should react to a speech act, and we try to constrain and predict the possible reactions with protocols. These, we argue, are the normative standard items: what an agent can do, not how it does it. add_a and $select_a$ are specifying what agent a should do, not how it should do it. However, even if an ACL with a standard external semantics can be agreed, it is unlikely to be testable as the agents are complex entities. It does impose a requirement that agents involved in a conversation behave according to a protocol, but 'anti-social' behaviour may not be immediately obvious and the history of communications needs logging, and a means of auditing, policing and accountability is required. Standardising the protocols alone will not achieve this.

4 The Proper Role of Belief States

We have seen how an agent's information state (belief state) can be used to guide the selection of a response to a message, and this formed the core of our proposed semantics for the ACL. This would be a normative specification. How then do agents choose which speech acts to perform in the first place? It is in answer to this question that speech act theory, as originally conceived, and agent belief states, can contribute to an informative specification. We specify add_a and $select_a$ with respect to beliefs, desires and intentions, i.e. by giving an intentional semantics at level (iii) of Section 2.

For example, reconsider our 'sincerity' axiom:

$$\models \mathcal{B}_s\phi \wedge \mathcal{D}_s\mathcal{B}_r\phi \rightarrow \mathcal{I}_s(\text{DONE}(< s, inform(r, \phi) >))$$

The 'logical operation' of this axiom is closely related to the BDI agent architecture of Kinny *et al.* [1995], where the combination of beliefs and desires trigger intentions. As an informative specification, it guides agent developers as to the circumstances under which inform speech acts could (or should) be performed, but does not constrain them to use BDI architectures.

We then provide, as an informative specification, that:

$$add_a(\mathsf{inform}, \textbf{no\_protocol}, \phi, \Delta_a) = \Delta_a \cup \{\phi\}$$

which is to say that the basic intuition behind receiving, from a sincere agent, an inform message not in the context of any protocol, is just to add the content to the agent's information state. However, the implementation of add_a for a particular agent a need not be so trusting, also it could do 'its own thing' in dealing with additional inferential effects, inconsistency, multiple sources of information, belief revision (non-monotonic logic), copies of ϕ (resource logics), and so on.

We illustrate this idea in the next section. We conclude this section with the observation that the extent to which agents wish to expose their behaviour by publicising their *add* and *select* functions, also defines the extent to which this behaviour can be verified. Otherwise, all that is required, to be compliant to a standard, for example, is that an agent should make an appropriate response to a particular input, as given by the *reply* function, and this can be verified with relative ease.

5 A BDI Implementation

In this section, we discuss an operational model of the BDI agent architecture as suggested in [Kinny *et al.*, 1995], enhanced to accommodate BDI-reasoning about agent–agent communication protocols based on the semantics described in the previous section.

5.1 The BDI Architecture

Kinny *et al.'s* [1995] BDI-agent architecture consists of the modules illustrated in Figure 2. Here, the belief database contains facts about 'the world'; the desires module contains goals to be realized; the plan library consists of plans, which are sequences of actions which achieve goals; and the intention structures contains instances of those plans chosen for execution (and currently being executed). The interpreter executes intentions, updates beliefs, modifies goals, and chooses plans.

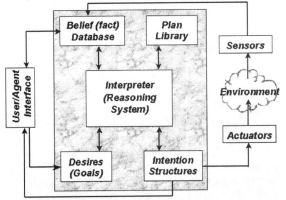

Figure 2: BDI Agent Architecture

The interpreter execution cycle is as follows: At time t: certain goals are established, and certain beliefs are held. Event(s) occur that alter the beliefs or modify goals, and the new combination of goals and beliefs trigger action plans. One or more action plans are selected and placed on the intention structures. An executable plan is selected and one step is executed, whereby the agent performs the action. Performing the action changes the environment and may establish new goals and beliefs, and so the interpreter execution cycle starts again.

We now describe how we envisaged the BDI architecture working in conjunction with the ACL semantics, for a pair of communicating agents.

5.2 A Semantic Specification

Consider again the communicating agents in Figure 1. Suppose they are telling each other when they have changed something in the environment in which they are embedded. To ensure that their perceptions of the environment are aligned, they will use a mutually agreed protocol, called *datasync*. This protocol is illustrated as a finite state diagram in Figure 3.

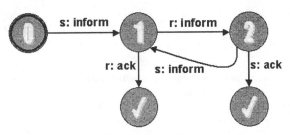

Figure 3: *datasync* Protocol

The idea is for one agent to inform the other agent of changes in the environment, and for this other agent to agree the change (via the acknowledge speech act ack), or correct it via another inform speech act.

We can formalise this as part of our ACL semantics as follows, by specifying, inter alia:

$$
\begin{aligned}
\text{Perf} \ &= \ \{\text{inform}, \text{ack}, \mathbf{null}, \ldots\} \\
\text{Prot} \ &= \ \{datasync, \mathbf{no\_protocol}, \ldots\} \\
reply \ : \ & \text{inform} \times datasync \times 0 \to \{\text{inform}, \text{ack}\} \\
& \text{inform} \times datasync \times 1 \to \{\text{inform}, \text{ack}\} \\
& \text{inform} \times datasync \times 2 \to \{\text{inform}, \text{ack}\} \\
& \text{ack} \times datasync \times 1 \to \{\mathbf{null}\} \\
& \text{ack} \times datasync \times 2 \to \{\mathbf{null}\}
\end{aligned}
$$

The *reply* function therefore specifies the acceptable replies to messages sent in the context of the *datasync* protocol. The protocol is initiated by an inform message, and terminated (with success) by an ack message.

Ignoring for now issues like language, time, ontology and protocol, an agent designer could specify an agent a's behaviour for reacting to an inform message with content ϕ from an agent s using the *datasync* protocol to be:

$$
add_a(\text{inform}, datasync, \phi, \Delta_a) = \Delta'_a, \text{where}
$$

$$
\begin{aligned}
\phi \in \Delta_a \ &\to \ \Delta'_a = \Delta_a \\
\phi \notin \Delta_a \ &\to \ \Delta'_a = \Delta_a \cup \{\phi, \mathcal{D}_a \mathcal{B}_s \mathcal{B}_a \phi\} \\
& \quad \text{if } \Delta_a \cup \{\phi\} \text{ is consistent} \\
&\to \ \Delta'_a = \Delta_a \cup \{\phi^c, \mathcal{D}_a \mathcal{B}_s \phi^c\} \\
& \quad \text{if } \Delta_a \cup \{\phi\} \text{ is inconsistent} \\
\phi^c \in \Delta_a \ &\to \ \Delta'_a = \Delta_a - \{\phi^c\} \cup \{\phi, \mathcal{D}_a \mathcal{B}_s \mathcal{B}_a \phi\} \\
& \quad \text{if } belief\_revise_a(\Delta_a, \phi, \phi^c) = \phi \\
&\to \ \Delta'_a = \Delta_a \cup \{\mathcal{D}_a \mathcal{B}_s \phi^c\} \\
& \quad \text{otherwise}
\end{aligned}
$$

This is only an exemplary specification in a semi-formal notation. Note the formula ϕ^c denotes the complement of formula ϕ. It treats each of the three cases: when the content of the inform is already known, new, or contradictory. The function $belief\_revise_a$ is a gloss on a's belief revision for contradictory statements (cf. [Galliers, 1992]), and we are not saying how the agent ensures its database is consistent (but there are algorithms for doing this, e.g. forward chaining).

This intentional reading of informing agent a of some information can be paraphrased informally as follows (where all replies are intuitively *intentions*, to be consistent with the ACL semantics):

If you tell me something I already know,
  then I'll stay as I am;
If you tell me something I don't know, then
  if it is consistent with my database Δ,
    I'll add it to Δ and acknowledge it
  else if it is inconsistent with Δ
    I'll inform you that I disagree;
If you tell me something that I disagree with, then
  if I prefer your version,
    I'll revise Δ and acknowledge it
  else if I prefer my version
    I'll keep Δ as it is and inform you otherwise

This is of course just one formulation: the treatment of new and contradictory information may not be treated in the same way, for example. It is also easy to refine such a specification to incorporate elements of trust. Furthermore, since the sincerity condition is predicated on the notion of co-operation; and all speech acts involve the receiver recognizing an intention on the part of the sender, agents are free (but not forced) to make further inferences about the other agent's beliefs and intentions. Different inferences may be more appropriate for particular types of agents in different kinds of application.

However, we can now appreciate the potential utility of intentionality for individual agents: indeed, we can even imagine 'publishing' this behavioural interface in an open system. It then becomes effectively a social commitment on the receiving agent's part (cf. [Singh, 1998]). The intriguing possibility then is that the 'standard' behaviour (sought by the FIPA97 specification) could actually be an emergent property of the system. For now, we show how this specification operates in the communicating agents example of section 2, where each agent is (at least specified as) a BDI agent.

5.3   The Semantics in Operation

In the plan library, we posit plan axiom schema of two types, which we call proactive and reactive. The two types of plan both generate intentions. The first type is the type of plan schema that triggers a dialogue, with the agent as the initiator of that dialogue. The second type is the plan schema that an agent uses to reply to messages that have been received, determining, for example, if there were a protocol, which possible responses would conform to the protocol.

We suppose that both agents have plan axiom schema in the plan library, which for agent a (where a could be sender s or receiver r, although it need not be the same for both) are:

$$\mathcal{B}_a\phi \wedge \mathcal{D}_a\mathcal{B}_R\phi \rightarrow \mathcal{I}_a < a, \mathsf{inform}(R, \phi, datasync) >$$
$$[R, \mathsf{inform}(a, \phi, datasync)]\mathcal{B}_a\phi \wedge \mathcal{D}_a\mathcal{B}_R\mathcal{B}_a\phi \rightarrow$$
$$\mathcal{I}_a < a, \mathsf{ack}(R, \mathcal{B}_a\phi, datasync) >$$
$$[R, \mathsf{inform}(a, \phi, datasync)]\mathcal{B}_a\phi^c \wedge \mathcal{D}_a\mathcal{B}_R\phi^c \rightarrow$$
$$\mathcal{I}_a < a, \mathsf{inform}(R, \phi^c, datasync) >$$

The first plan axiom schema is proactive and states that if agent a believes ϕ and has the goal that another agent R share that belief (the preconditions for action), then agent a will form the intention to inform R of ϕ, using the *datasync* protocol. The other two plan axiom schema are reactive and determine replies. The former states that after some agent R has informed agent a of some information ϕ, if agent a believes the proposition and wants the original sender to believe this, then it will form an intention to reply with an acknowledgement. Similarly, if the informed agent disagrees with the content it will inform the originator of this. It should be clear that the latter two axioms specify the decision making for response making in the *datasync* protocol if add_a has been implemented as described above.

We now logically animate this specification for a sending and a receiving agent. For the sending agent s, in its belief database there are facts, such as p (implicitly $\mathcal{B}_s p$), and modal action schema. These state the beliefs that an agent will have after performing an action. For example, for agent s, we could have:

$$\mathcal{B}_s: \quad p \qquad\qquad\qquad \text{(fact } p)$$
$$[a, \mathsf{inform}(R, \phi, \_)]\mathcal{B}_R\phi \quad \text{(after } s \text{ informs } R \text{ of } \phi,$$
$$s \text{ believes } R \text{ believes } \phi)$$

Here R and ϕ are any agent and formula respectively. The post-condition of the modal action schema specifies the intended rational effect of the action which the agent will believe after doing the action (if the agent later discovers it is not true, it will need to do belief revision). This formula concerns the inform performative, irrespective of the protocol it is used in.

In the desire database, there are goals. For example, if the goal of s is for r to believe p, we have $\mathcal{D}_s : \mathcal{B}_r p$.

Beliefs and desires are used to trigger a plan action schema and create instances which will be executable plans. In the case of s, the following simple plan will be placed on the intention structures:

$$\mathcal{I}_s :< s, \mathsf{inform}(r, p, datasync) >$$

When the intention is chosen for execution by the interpreter, the intention is fulfilled, the belief state changes according to the appropriate instance of the action axiom schema, i.e. $[s, \mathsf{inform}(r, p)]\mathcal{B}_r p$, the goal is discharged and withdrawn from the desire database, so we end up, in this case, with:

$$\mathcal{B}_s: \quad p \qquad\qquad\qquad \mathcal{D}_s : \emptyset \quad \mathcal{I}_s : \emptyset$$
$$\mathcal{B}_r p$$
$$[a, \mathsf{inform}(R, \phi,)]\mathcal{B}_R\phi$$

This is the situation with agent s. For agent r, who receives the message, the database prior to receipt might have been entirely empty:

$$\mathcal{B}_r : \emptyset \quad \mathcal{D}_r : \emptyset \quad \mathcal{I}_r : \emptyset$$

Now it receives the message $< s, \mathsf{inform}(r, p, datasync) >$. The interpreter of r runs its procedure add_r on this input and this database; being a new conversation, the protocol state is 0. If add_r is implemented as specified above, then r will add p to its belief database (p is not present and adding it is consistent), and generate the goal for the sender to believe that it believes it:

$$\mathcal{B}_r : p \quad \mathcal{D}_r : \mathcal{B}_s\mathcal{B}_rp \quad \mathcal{I}_r : \emptyset$$

From the reactive plan axiom schema in the plan library, after an inform r will have the intention to send an acknowledge or an inform. The BDI interpreter is effectively applying the $select_r$ function, and as with the sending agent beliefs and desires are used to trigger a plan action schema and create instances which will be executable plans. The appropriate intention is placed on the intention structures:

$$\mathcal{B}_r : p \quad \mathcal{D}_r : \mathcal{B}_s\mathcal{B}_rp \quad \mathcal{I}_r :< r, \mathsf{ack}(s, p, datasync) >$$

Now we see that the meaning of the speech act is indeed the intention to reply with a valid performative in the context of a protocol, as specified in sections 3 and 4.

6   Conclusions and Further Work

With growing investment in open, agent-based system design and deployment, there is a need for software standards defining the interface between agents. The FIPA standardisation body is probably the most important recent development in the agents field and offers significant potential advantages for developers of open, heterogeneous, and interoperable agent systems.

However, there are considerable limitations of using mental attitudes for standardising the semantics of the ACL [Singh, 1998]. Intentionality is concerned with agent internals and a communicative act is an external phenomenon: mental attitudes only give a reason for and not the meaning of the performatives. They can give guidance to developers but may be too strong a constraint for heterogenous agents in varying applications.

The protocols specified by FIPA can give purpose and meaning to individual performatives but only in the context of a conversation that has an identifiable objective. However, there appears to be a growing consensus that conversations, protocols, and social context are the important factors to consider in defining an ACL's formal semantics [Singh, 1998; Labrou and Finin, 1998; Smith et al., 1998].

Our own experience of applying the FIPA specifications suggests that interactions in a multi-agent system could be designed on the basis of the standard performatives and protocols. This work has gone one step further and formalised the normative use of performatives in specific protocols. Furthermore, the relationship between what an agent 'thinks' about the content of a message to what it 'does' in response to receiving that message is formalised through informative specifications expressed in terms of beliefs, desires and intentions.

The semantic framework described here actually defines a *class* of ACLs. The challenges ahead then include: extending an ACL specification with new protocols and performatives, and customising with intentional specifications for particular applications; describing conversation states by structures which are affected by speech acts; allowing for multi-party conversations; identifying a way for agents to publicise thier understanding and use of new performatives and protocols (so-called brown pages); and providing a mechanism for agents to discover and learn a new dialect. The issues of social behaviour and time also need to be addressed as these are both significant factors in why and when agents communicate.

In the meantime, we have submitted this work to FIPA as a proposal for the ACL semantics in FIPA99.

Acknowledgements

This research has been undertaken in the context of the UK EPSRC/Nortel Networks joint funded project CASBAh (GR/L34440) and the EU funded ACTS project MARINER (AC333). We are grateful for the constructive comments of the anonymous reviewers.

References

[Breiter and Sadek, 1996] P. Breiter and M. Sadek. A rational agent as a kernel of a co-operative dialogue system. In *Proceedings ECAI'96 ATAL Workshop*, pp261–276. Springer-Verlag, 1996.

[Cohen and Levesque, 1995] P. Cohen and H. Levesque. Communicative actions for artificial agents. In V. Lesser, ed., *Proceedings ICMAS95*. AAAI Press, 1995.

[Finin et al., 1995] T. Finin, Y. Labrou, and J.Mayfield. KQML as an agent communication language. In J. Bradshaw, ed., *Software Agents*. MIT Press, 1995.

[FIPA, 1997] FIPA. FIPA'97 Specification Part 2: ACL. FIPA, http://drogo.cselt.stet.it/fipa/, 1997.

[Galliers, 1992] J. Galliers. Autonomous belief revision and communication. In P. Gardenfors, ed., *Belief Revision*. Cambridge University Press, 1992.

[Kinny et al., 1995] D. Kinny, M. Georgeff, J. Bailey, D. Kemp, and K. Ramamohanarao. Active databases and agent systems: A comparison. In *Proc. 2nd International Rules in Database Systems Workshop*. 1995.

[Kuwabara et al., 1995] K. Kuwabara, T. Ishida, and N. Osato. AgenTalk: Describing multiagent coordination protocols with inheritance. In *Proc. 7th IEEE ICTAI95*, pp460–465. 1995.

[Labrou and Finin, 1998] Y. Labrou and T. Finin. Semantics and conversations for an agent communication language. In M. Huhns and M. Singh, eds., *Readings in Agents*, pp235–242. Morgan Kaufmann, 1998.

[Singh, 1998] M. Singh. Agent communication languages: Rethinking the principles. *IEEE Computer*, pp40–47, December, 1998.

[Smith et al., 1998] I. Smith, P. Cohen, J. Bradshaw, M. Greaves, and H. Holmback. Designing conversation policies using joint intention theory. In Y. Demazeau, ed., *Proceedings ICSMAS98*. 1998.

[Wooldridge, 1998] M. Wooldridge. Verifiable semantics for agent communication languages. In Y. Demazeau, ed., *Proceedings ICMAS98*. 1998.

Towards Flexible Multi-Agent Decision-Making Under Time Pressure

Sanguk Noh and **Piotr J. Gmytrasiewicz**
Department of Computer Science and Engineering
University of Texas at Arlington
Arlington, TX 76019, Box 19015
{noh, piotr}@cse.uta.edu

Abstract

To perform rational decision-making, autonomous agents need considerable computational resources. In multi-agent settings, when other agents are present in the environment, these demands are even more severe. We investigate ways in which the agent's knowledge and the results of deliberative decision-making can be compiled to reduce the complexity of decision-making procedures and to save time in urgent situations. We use machine learning algorithms to compile decision-theoretic deliberations into condition-action rules on how to coordinate in a multi-agent environment. Using different learning algorithms, we endow a resource-bounded agent with a tapestry of decision making tools, ranging from purely reactive to fully deliberative ones. The agent can then select a method depending on the time constraints of the particular situation. We also propose combining the decision-making tools, so that, for example, more reactive methods serve as a pre-processing stage to the more accurate but slower deliberative decision-making ones. We validate our framework with experimental results in simulated coordinated defense. The experiments show that compiling the results of decision-making saves deliberation time while offering good performance in our multi-agent domain.

1 Introduction

It is desirable that an autonomous agent, operating under uncertainty in complex environments, be able to make optimal decisions about which actions to execute. Rational decision-making under such circumstances using, for instance, the paradigm of expected utility maximization, is costly [Horvitz, 1988; Russell and Wefald, 1991; Russell and Subramanian, 1995; Zilberstein and Russell, 1996]. In our work, we consider additional complexities presented by multi-agent environments. In these settings, an agent has to make decisions as to the rational course of action considering not only the possibly complex and not fully known state of its environment, but also considering the beliefs, goals, intentions and actions of the other agents. Clearly, these demands may lead to its failure to decide an action within the time constraint.

To cope with time constraints imposed by various decision-making situations in complex and uncertain multi-agent settings, we endow an agent with a tapestry of decision-making procedures, from strictly reactive to purely deliberative. The reactive procedures are constructed by compiling the deliberative decision-theoretic reasoning into condition-action rules. The compilation process exploits the regularities of the decision-theoretic reasoning and avoids costly deliberations in urgent situations. The rules are obtained from machine learning algorithms, which, as inputs, use the results of full-blown decision-theoretic computations performed offline. Each of the compiled methods is assigned a performance measure that compares it to the full-blown decision-theoretic benchmark. The various compilations available, and their combinations with more deliberative methods, constitute a spectrum of approaches to making decisions under the constraints of available computational (and cognitive) resources, and under time pressure.

Given the various decision-making methods at its disposal, an agent should consider a number of factors to choose the appropriate decision-making mechanism for the situation at hand. The key factors include *the quality of the decision* provided by a method, *the method's running time*, and *the urgency of the situation at hand*. Intuitively, when a situation is not urgent, the agent can afford the luxury of full-blown decision-theoretic reasoning since it results in highest quality of the choice made. If the situation is very urgent, the agent should save as much time as possible by using a crude but fast reactive tool. If the situation is somewhat urgent, the agent should use methods that are somewhat sophisticated although not necessarily optimal.

Interestingly, the spectrum between the purely reactive and fully deliberative decision-making tools can be spanned by combining these two varieties of methods. For example, the agent can use fast reactive rules as a pre-processing stage to narrow down the set of viable alternatives. These alternatives can then be passed on to a deliberative decision-making method that uses all of the agent's detailed knowledge to compute the expected utility of these few courses of action.

In this paper, we develop a suite of decision-making procedures for agents operating in multi-agent environments, and we measure their performance and running time. We use a particular multi-agent domain in which automated agents have to decide how to coordinate their attempts to intercept multiple incoming threats (as in anti-air defense), but we believe that lessons learned in this domain generalize to other multi-agent domains.

2   Background and Related Work

Our prior work on deliberative decision-theoretic method includes the Recursive Modeling Method (RMM) [Gmytrasiewicz, 1996; Gmytrasiewicz *et al.*, 1998; Noh and Gmytrasiewicz, 1997; 1998]. We have implemented a full-blown version of RMM which allows an agent to compute its best action given what is known about the other agents and about their states of knowledge and capabilities. In the task of coordinating agents in a simulated

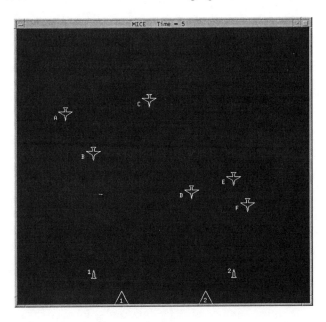

Figure 1: An example anti-air defense scenario.

anti-air defense domain (such as in Figure 1) the performance of RMM agents was comparable to or better than the human performance. Figure 2 presents these results in terms of the average total damage suffered by each of the coordinating defense teams. We show the performance of three different teams: RMM-RMM, RMM-Human, and Human-Human team. We experimented with all the teams in cases when communication was, and was not, available. When the communication was available, the performance achieved by three teams was improved, with the all-RMM team performing slightly

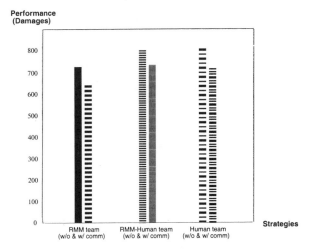

Figure 2: The performance of RMM, RMM-Human, and Human teams in anti-air defense, without and with communication, respectively.

better than the others. However, since the RMM decision procedure considers all of the combinations of the agents' alternative actions, it is not surprising that its complexity is, in the worst case, exponential in the number of agents present. As the complexity of the multi-agent situation increases, as in Figure 3, the running time of RMM grows to over one hour (our current implementation is in Lisp running on a P90 machine). It is clear that the full-blown RMM needs to be supplemented by other, more reactive, methods for more complex and time-critical scenarios.

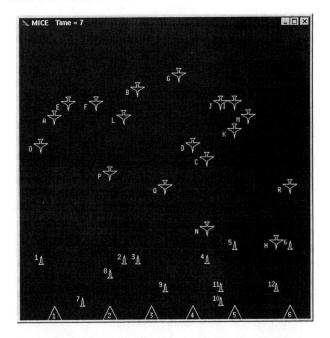

Figure 3: A complex anti-air defense scenario.

Our present work builds on a body of related research. Fox et al. [Fox and Krause, 1991] provides a theoretical framework for symbolic reasoning as reactive decision procedure. Other rigorous efforts to make decision-theoretic systems computationally tractable include work on the use of metareasoning procedures to control inference [Horvitz, 1988; Horvitz *et al.*, 1989], and anytime algorithms [Dean and Boddy, 1988; Russell and Subramanian, 1995; Zilberstein and Russell, 1996]. In yet another approach Bratman [Bratman *et al.*, 1988] describes an agent's architecture that includes both means-end reasoning and decision-theoretic reasoning. For a resource-bounded agent, the agent's beliefs, desires, and intentions (BDI) involve the formation, revision, and execution of plans to constrain the deliberation process. Rao et al. [Rao and Georgeff, 1995] explore the applicability of reactive and deliberative behavior provided by the BDI architecture, and use it for air-traffic management system (OASIS). Ephrati and collaborators [Ephrati *et al.*, 1995] apply a filtering strategy to the multi-agent tileworld system. The filtering is accomplished using rules provided by the system designer, and it only guides the agent's role allocation. Our condition-action rules, on the other hand, represent learning over the results of agent's rational decisions in sample scenarios obtained from a deliberative method. Our filtering strategy is to accumulate agents' knowledge and effectively use it to limit deliberation in urgent situations.

In the following sections of this paper we propose a compilation process that explores the regularities of a deliberative decision making, and show how an autonomous agent can use the compiled information, given performance metrics and time constraints. Then, we validate our framework empirically, and discuss the experimental results. In conclusion, we summarize our results and further research issues.

3 Formalism of Compilation and Filtering

To reduce the complexity and time needed for decision making in time constrained situation, we compile the results of deliberative decision-making into a set of reactive condition-action rules with numerous machine learning algorithms. An autonomous agent can use the compiled knowledge [Russell, 1989; Zilberstein, 1995] and either eliminate the deliberative decision-making all together, or constrain the number of alternative actions considered by excluding the ones that are likely to be suboptimal.

We propose an *adaptive and deliberative agent* (ADA) architecture, as consisting of compiled and deliberative decision procedures that allow the agent's bounded rationality to emerge from their combined usage. Let N be the set of agents, A_i, $i \in N$, be the set of actions of agent i, and S_i, $i \in N$, be the set of world states that the $i-th$ agent can discriminate among. For each action $a_i^k \in A_i$ we define $condition(a_i^k, S_i)$ to be the abstraction of the world state that includes only the parameters relevant for this action. For example, if the action is to pick up a block (shoot at a given threat), then the corresponding abstraction specifies the location and other parameters of the block (threat). Finally, let L_i, $i \in N$, be the set of compilation methods (learning algorithms) that the agent i employs.

Given a learning method $l \in L_i$, a compiled decision-making procedure of an adaptive and deliberative agent implements a function $\rho_{i[l]}$: $condition(a_i^k, S_i) \mapsto \{Yes, No\}$, representing that the action a_i^k is (or is not) recommended in the state S_i. Thus, various machine learning algorithms compile decision-theoretic models into different functions $\rho_{i[l]}$. As we mentioned, we generated the training examples for these learning algorithms from deliberative reasoning performed by RMM.

To allow for further flexibility in the ADA agents, we allow the procedures to be combined depending on circumstances at hand. Clearly, when the agents have enough time, they should try to make a deliberatively rational decision that maximizes their expected utility. In a time-critical situation, however, agent's decision-making is bounded by the available computation time. For an adaptive and deliberative agent, therefore, we use the set of compiled rules to remove from consideration the likely unprofitable actions, and to reduce the deliberation cost. This strategy is represented by the agent i's filtering criterion $\delta_{i[l]}$: $S_i \times A_i \mapsto A_i'$, where $A_i' \subseteq A_i$. Intuitively, the value of δ is the set of plausible actions the agent should consider in situation S_i. The filtering criterion $\delta_{i[l]}$ results from applying the rules in the function $\rho_{i[l]}$ to the current state to obtain the plausible alternatives. For example, if $\delta_{i[l]}(s_i^1, \{a_i^j, a_i^k, a_i^m\}) = \{a_i^k, a_i^m\}$, then a_i^k and a_i^m are plausible, and a_i^j is not, in situation s_i^1.

Given the set of plausible actions, our agent maximizes the expected utility among them:

$$\arg \max_{a_i^j \in A_i'} EU(a_i^j) \qquad (1)$$

We now apply the above formalism to agents making coordinated decisions in the anti-air defense domain.

4 Deliberation About Action in Anti-Air Defense Domain

Our specific domain, the anti-air domain, consists of a number of attacking targets, labelled A and B in Figure 4, and a number of defending units, labelled 1 and 2.[1] The mission of the defense units is to attempt to intercept attacking targets so as to *minimize damages* to the defended ground area. Let us note that this situation makes coordination necessary. The defense batteries do not want to miscoordinate and attempt to intercept the same threat, both due to the wasted ammunition and due to the increase in likelihood that the remaining threat will reach its destination and cause damage proportional to its warhead size.

Given these factors, the expected benefit of shooting at a threat can be quantified as a product of the size of

---

[1] In the figure, the left top corner of the screen is (0,0), x is pointing right, and y is pointing down.

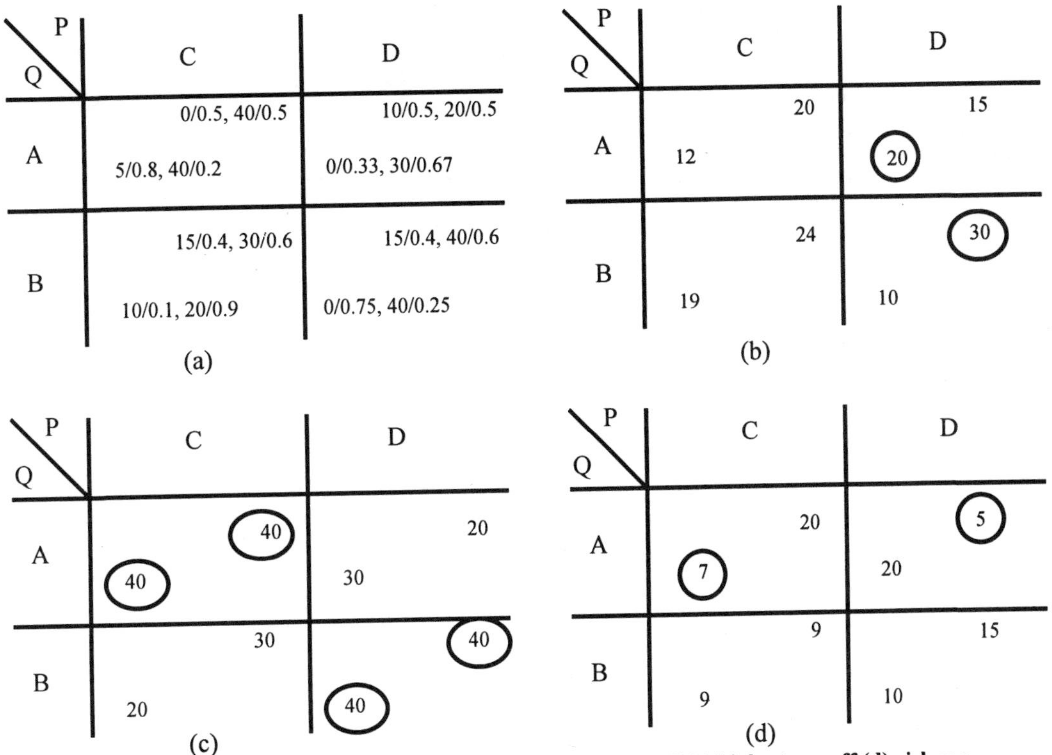

Figure 2. An uncertain game matrix (a) and its (b) expected payoff (c) highest payoff (d) risk matrix forms respectively

strategy has the highest dominance of other agents. However, there is still a problem, how agents reach some particular outcome that is the Pareto-efficient and Nash equilibrium? It needs a negotiation protocol to coordinate agents to reach a stable outcome.

3 Risk Control in a Multi-agent Negotiation Protocol

By taking the risk preference into consideration, the negotiation decision making will be based on the new notion of dominance instead of payoff as in the previous work. Here, we describe how the two communication actions can be used in a negotiation protocol to achieve the Pareto-efficient Nash equilibrium in the sense of dominance.

3.1 An Example of Negotiation Protocol

For simplicity, in the following communication protocol descriptions, the trusted third party is literally ignored.

Consider an uncertain game matrix in Figure 2(a). Figure 2(b)(c)(d) are the corresponding expected payoff, the highest payoff and the risk matrix forms respectively. The circles in Figure 2(b)(c)(d) indicate the most desirable states in its corresponding game matrix. There is no Nash equilibrium in Figure 2(b) and Figure 2(d) while two in Figure 2(c). Therefore, it is necessary for rational agents to negotiate a

stable result. If both P and Q are risk-neutral, then this game can be solved according to the guarantee/compensation negotiation protocol based on the expected payoff matrix in Figure 2(b). Q will pay guarantee 8 not to play strategy A and will also pay a compensation 7 to ask P to play strategy C. This resulted in a new expected payoff game matrix in Figure 3(a). It can be shown that the strategy combination (B, C) is Pareto-efficient and the Nash equilibrium.

If Q is risk-averse and P is risk-seeking. Q may pay a guarantee 8 not to play strategy B and this results in a new game matrix in Figure 3(b). In Figure 3(b), the strategy combination (A, C) is a Pareto-efficient and Nash equilibrium subjected to the risk preference conditions that Q takes the minimum risk in Figure 2(d) and P gets the highest possible payoff in Figure 2(c). If Q is risk-natural and P is risk-averse. Q may pay a guarantee 8 not to play strategy B and P may pay a guarantee 6 not to play D and it forms the strategy combination (A, D) a Pareto-efficient and Nash equilibrium. If Q is risk-seeking and P is risk-neutral, Q may pay a guarantee 11 not to play strategy A and P may pay a guarantee 6 not to play D and it forms the strategy combination (B, D) also Pareto-efficient and the Nash equilibrium.

It turns out that in the above example, with the negotiation protocol, all strategy combinations (A, C), (A, D), (B, C), (B, D) can be made as a unique Pareto-efficient and Nash equilibrium point, depending on different combination of the risk preference of both agents. Therefore, the rational agent can control the final negotiated state they will reach. The final state may satisfy the different risk preference of each agent. But, of course, the expected payoff may be affected in each encounter of agents who have different risk preference from risk-neutral one.

3.2 General Negotiation Protocol for Risk Control

The general protocol of the negotiation is:
Procedure: Negotiation Protocol for Risk Control
Input: the game matrix with payoff/probability entries
Output: a game matrix with a unique Pareto-efficient and Nash equilibrium

1. Construct the three game matrices (Expected Payoff, Risk, Highest Payoff)
2. Make a proposal that using guarantee or compensation communication actions based on the preference and rational assumption of other agents.
3. If the game still doesn't have a unique Pareto-efficient and Nash equilibrium, then go to step 2.
4. Play the game.

End of the Protocol

Note that **Step 2** is different from the previous work. In the previous work, agents just need to analyze one matrix, but in this paper, an agent must analyze on an appropriate game matrix under the risk preference and find out the highest dominance that is consistent with risk preference. If no dominant strategy can be found under the new dominance concept, then the agent needs to adopt asking guarantee or offering compensation negotiation actions to create one.

4. Discussion

In this paper, we define the risk in terms of a quantity that is calculated as the difference between the expected payoff and the least possible payoff. The definition of the risk can be a problem since the risk of losing or gaining certain amount of payoff may mean differently and non-linear to people. In fact, the risk measurement of certain amount of payoff was pointed out be a logarithm function [Bernoulli 1954]. The model of the risk preference discussed only three extreme types of the risk preference. It is too simple to reflect the true human risk preference in reality. Different functions of mapping payoff to utility will lead to different risk preference agents. A risk-averse agent maps less utility for a marginal payoff while a risk-seeking agent maps more utility for a marginal payoff [Hertz, 1983]. However, it is hard to obtain such an individual non-linear mapping function.

A risk preference can be a mixed weighting combination of three criteria: 1. Maximizing the expected value, 2.

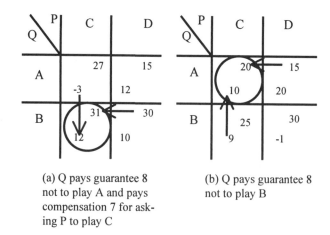

(a) Q pays guarantee 8 not to play A and pays compensation 7 for asking P to play C

(b) Q pays guarantee 8 not to play B

Figure 3. The resulting game matrix after negotiation to get a Pareto-efficient and Nash equilibrium based on the expected payoff, if (a) both P and Q are risk-neutral. (b) Q is risk-averse and P is risk-seeking.

Minimizing the expectation variance, and 3 Minimize the probability of an unacceptable low value [Fabrycky 1980]. A moderate risk-averse agent, for example, may also have a tolerance bound on risk. If the risk is under the tolerance bound then he will take the risk to seek for a higher expected payoff. On the other hand, if the risk is over her tolerance bound, he will not play the strategy. Including such a tolerance bound into agent's decision making will indeed cause a more complex reasoning for the negotiation protocol to come up with a stable outcome. We leave it as future work.

The assumption of rationality of agents is redefined in the new notion of dominance instead of the expected payoff. Therefore an agent is still rational if he always maximizes the expected payoff that is subjected to his risk preference. But he sometimes would be treated as irrational in the old sense of rationality that is trying to maximize the expected payoff only.

We can prove that the proposed negotiation procedure with risk control will end within finite time. A similar convergence theorem as well as the one of the feasibility of creating a unique Pareto-efficient and Nash equilibrium using the guarantee/compensation negotiation protocol via trusted third party can be proved [Wu and Soo, 1999].

5 Conclusions

We separated the risk preference from utility function as another dimension other than the expected payoff. To model the preference of taking risk, we defined three types of agents with different risk preferences. In this way, in game decision making, we redefined the concept of dominance so that the optimal strategy that agents select can take risk into account. As illustrated in the above examples, we showed that different risk preference agents in the same uncertain game could lead to different outcomes that satisfy the agent's risk preference. Therefore the agent can in some sense control the risk of the outcomes of his decision making.

The purpose of agent negotiation is for the agents to reach a stable and efficient result. Under the risk preference model, agents negotiate to control not only the expected payoff but also the risk. The mechanisms of communication actions of guarantee and compensation help agents to reduce the risk due to unpredictable behaviors of other agents in games, especially in situations of there is no unique Nash equilibrium or there is a unique Nash equilibrium but not Pareto-efficient, e.g. prisoner's dilemma. The separation of the risk from the payoff and the redefinition of dominance in terms of different risk preferences allow agents to take risk control into decision making can reduce the risk due to the uncertainty of a nature move.

Acknowledgements

This work was financially supported by the National Science Council of Taiwan, Republic of China, under grant No. NSC88-2213-E-007-057.

Reference

[Axelrod, 1984] R. Axelrod, *The Evolution of Cooperation*, Basic Books Inc., New York, 1984.

[Brafman and Tennenholtz, 1997] R.I. Brafman and M. Tennenholtz, Modeling Agents as Qualitative Decision Makers, *Artificial Intelligence*, Vol.94, pp217-268, 1994

[Bernoulli, 1954] D. Bernoulli, Exposition of a New Theory of the Measurement of Risk, *Econometrica*, Vol. 22, pp. 23-36.

[Durfee et al., 1993] E.H. Durfee, J. Lee, and P.J. Gmytrasiewicz, Overeager Reciprocal Rationality and Mixed Strategy Equilibria, *In Proceedings of the Eleventh National Conference on Artificial Intelligence (AAAI-93)*, pp.225-230, 1993.

[Fabrycky, 1980] W.J. Fabrycky and G.J. Thuesen, *Economic Decision Analysis* 2nd ed. 1980.

[Gmytrasiewicz et al., 1991] P.J. Gmytrasiewicz, E.H. Durfee and D.K. Wehe, The Utility of Communication in Co-ordinating Intelligent Agents, in *Proceedings of the Ninth National Conference on Artificial Intelligence* (AAAI-91), pp.166-172, 1991.

[Haynes and Sen, 1996] T. Haynes and S. Sen, Satisfying User Preferences while Negotiating Meetings, *in Proceeding of the Second International Conference on Multi-Agent Systems (ICMAS-96)*, 1996.

[Hertz, 1983] D. B. Hertz, *Risk Analysis and its Applications, Chichester*, John Wiley & Sons, 1983.

[Koller and Pfeffer, 1997] D. Koller and A. Pfeffer, Representations and Solutions for Game-theoretic Problems, *Artificial Intelligence*, Vol.94, pp 167-215, 1997.

[March and Shapira, 1992] James G. March and Zur Shapira, Variable Risk Preferences and the Focus of Attention, *Psychological Review*, 99(1), pp. 172-183, January, 1992.

[Mor and Rosenschein, 1995] Y. Mor and J. S. Rosenschein, Time and the Prisoner's Dilemma, *In Proceeding of the First International Conference of Multi-Agent System (ICMAS-95)*, pp.276-282, 1995.

[Nash 1951] J. F. Nash, Non-cooperative Games, *Ann. of Math.* 54, pp.286-295, 1951.

[Rasmusen 1989] E. Rasmusen, *Games and Information: An Introduction to Game Theory*, Basil Blackwell, Oxford, 1989.

[Rosenschein and Genesereth, 1985] J.S. Rosenschein, M.R. Genesereth, Deals among Rational Agents, *in Proceedings of the ninth international conference on Artificial Intel*ligence(*IJCAI-85*), pp.91-99. 1985.

[Rosenschein and Zlotkin, 1994] J.S. Rosenschein and G. Zlotkin, *Rules of Encounter*, MIT Press, Cambridge, 1994.

[Sandholm and Lesser, 1995] T.W. Sandholm and V.R. Lesser, Issues in Automated Negotiation and Electronic Commerce: Extending the Contract Net Framework, in *Proceedings of the First International Conference on Multi-Agent Systems (ICMAS-95)*, pp.328-335, MIT Press, 1995.

[Shehory and Kraus, 1998] O. Shehory and S. Kraus, Methods for Task Allocation via Agent Coalition Formation, *Artificial Intelligence*, Vol.101, pp.165-200, 1998.

[Tennenholtz 1998] M. Tennenholtz, On Stable Social Laws and Qualitative Equilibria, *Artificial Intelligence*, Vol.102, pp.1-20, 1998.

[Vidal and Durfee, 1995] J.M. Vidal and E.H. Durfee, Recursive Agent Modeling using Limited Rationality, in *Proceedings of the First International Conference on Multi-Agent Systems (ICMAS-95)*, pp. 376-383, MIT Press, 1995.

[Wu and Soo, 1998a] S. Wu, V. Soo, Escape from a Prisoners' Dilemma by Communication with a Trusted Third Party, in *Proceeding of the Tenth International Conference on Tools with Artificial intelligent (ICTAI'98)*, pp.58-65, 1998.

[Wu and Soo, 1998b] S. Wu, V. Soo, A Fuzzy Game Theoretic Approach to Multi-Agent Coordination, *Pacific Rim international workshop of on Multi-Agent (PRIMA'98)*, 1998.

[Wu and Soo, 1999] S. Wu, V. Soo, Game Theoretic Reasoning in Multi-agent Coordination by Negotiation with a Trusted Third Party, in *Proceeding of the Third International Conference on Autonomous Agents (Agents'99)*, Seattle, Washington, 1999.

Shopbots and Pricebots

Amy R. Greenwald and Jeffrey O. Kephart
IBM Institute for Advanced Commerce
IBM Thomas J. Watson Research Center
Yorktown Heights, NY 10598
amygreen@cs.nyu.edu,kephart@watson.ibm.com

Abstract

Shopbots are agents that automatically search the Internet to obtain information about prices and other attributes of goods and services. They herald a future in which autonomous agents profoundly influence electronic markets. In this study, a simple economic model is proposed and analyzed, which is intended to quantify some of the likely impacts of a proliferation of shopbots and other economically-motivated software agents. In addition, this paper reports on simulations of *pricebots* — adaptive, price-setting agents which firms may well implement to combat, or even take advantage of, the growing community of shopbots. This study forms part of a larger research program that aims to provide insights into the impact of agent technology on the nascent information economy.

1 Introduction

Shopbots, agents that automatically search the Internet for goods and/or services on behalf of consumers, herald a future in which autonomous agents become an essential component of nearly every facet of electronic commerce [Chavez and Maes, 1996; Kephart *et al.*, 1998; Tsvetovatyy *et al.*, 1997]. In response to a consumer's expressed interest in a specified good or service, a typical shopbot can query several dozen web sites, and then collate and sort the available information for the user — all within seconds. For example, www.shopper.com claims to compare 1,000,000 prices on 100,000 computer-oriented products! In addition, www.acses.com compares the prices and expected delivery times of books offered for sale on-line, while www.jango.com and webmarket.junglee.com offer everything from apparel to gourmet groceries. Shopbots can out-perform and out-inform even the most patient, determined consumers, for whom it would take hours to obtain far less coverage of available goods and services.

Shopbots deliver on one of the great promises of electronic commerce and the Internet: a radical reduction in the cost of obtaining and distributing information. It is generally recognized that freer flow of information will profoundly affect market efficiency, as economic friction will be reduced significantly [Lewis, 1997; DeLong and Froomkin, 1998]. Transportation costs, menu costs — the costs to firms of evaluating, updating, and advertising prices — and shopping costs — the costs to consumers of seeking out optimal price and quality — will all decrease, as a consequence of the digital nature of information as well as the presence of autonomous agents that find, process, collate, and disseminate that information at little cost. What are the implications of the widespread use of shopbots and related types of autonomous agents in electronic marketplaces, and how might species of computational agents evolve?

DeLong and Froomkin [1998] qualitatively investigate the ongoing emergence of shopbots; in particular, they note that short of violating anti-trust laws, firms will be hard pressed to prevent their competitors from sponsoring shopbots, in which case those who do not do so will experience decreased sales. In this paper, we utilize quantitative techniques to address the aforementioned questions. We propose, analyze, and simulate a simple economic model designed to capture the present role of shopbots as agents of economic change, particularly with regard to consumer preferences, as they decrease the cost of obtaining information in markets known to exhibit price dispersion. Looking ahead several years into the future, we project that shopbots will evolve into economic entities (*i.e.*, utility maximizers) in their own right, interacting with billions of other self-interested software agents. Moreover, we predict the emergence of *pricebots* — economically-motivated agents that set prices so as to maximize the profits of firms, just as shopbots seek prices that minimize costs for consumers. Accordingly, we study adaptive price-setting algorithms which pricebots might utilize to combat the growing community of shopbots, in a full-fledged agent-based economy.

This paper is organized as follows. The next section, Section 2, presents our model, which is analyzed in Section 3 from a game-theoretic point of view. Section 4 describes various adaptive price-setting algorithms and the results of their simulation under the prescribed model. A possible evolution of shopbots and pricebots is discussed Section 5. Concluding remarks and ideas for future work appear in Section 6.

2 Model

We consider an economy in which there is a commodity that is offered for sale by S sellers and of interest to B buyers, with $B \gg S$. Each buyer b generates purchase orders at random times, with rate ρ_b, while each seller s resets its price p_s at random times, with rate ρ_s. The value of the good to buyer b is v_b; the cost of production for seller s is c_s.

A buyer b's utility for a good is a function of price:

$$u_b(p) = \begin{cases} v_b - p & \text{if } p \leq v_b \\ 0 & \text{otherwise} \end{cases} \quad (1)$$

This states that a buyer purchases a good from a given seller if and only if the seller's price is less than the buyer's valuation of the good; if price equals valuation, we make the behavioral assumption that a transaction occurs. We do not assume that buyers are utility maximizers; instead we assume that they consider the prices offered by sellers using one of the following strategies:

1. *Any Seller:* buyer selects seller at random, and purchases the good if the price charged by that seller is less than the buyer's valuation.

2. *Bargain Hunter:* buyer checks the offer price of all sellers, determines the seller with the lowest price, and purchases the good if that lowest price is less than the buyer's valuation. (This type of buyer corresponds to those who take advantage of shopbots.)

The buyer population consists of a mixture of buyers employing one of these strategies, with a fraction w_A using the *Any Seller* strategy and a fraction w_B using the *Bargain Hunter* strategy; $w_A + w_B = 1$. Buyers employing these respective strategies are referred to as type A and type B buyers.

A seller s's expected profit per unit time π_s is a function of the price vector $\vec{p}$:

$$\pi_s(\vec{p}) = (p_s - c_s)D_s(\vec{p}) \quad (2)$$

where $D_s(\vec{p})$ is the rate of demand for the good produced by seller s. This rate of demand is the product of the overall buyer rate of demand $\rho = \sum_b \rho_b$, the likelihood of a given buyer selecting seller s as their potential seller, $h_s(\vec{p})$, and the fraction of buyers whose valuations satisfy $v_b \geq p_s$, denoted $g(p_s)$:

$$D_s(\vec{p}) = \rho B h_s(\vec{p})g(p_s). \quad (3)$$

Note that $g(p_s) = \int_{p_s}^{\infty} \gamma(x)dx$, where $\gamma(x)$ is the probability density function describing the likelihood that a given buyer has valuation x. If $v_b = v$ for all buyers b, then $\gamma(x)$ is the Dirac delta function $\delta(v - x)$, and the integral yields a step function $g(p_s) = \Theta(v - p_s)$:

$$\Theta(v - p_s) = \begin{cases} 1 & \text{if } p_s \leq v \\ 0 & \text{otherwise} \end{cases} \quad (4)$$

Without loss of generality, we define the time scale such that $\rho B = 1$. It follows that $D_s(\vec{p}) = h_s(\vec{p})g(p_s)$, and π_s is seller s's expected profit per unit sold systemwide.

The probability $h_s(\vec{p})$ that buyers select seller s as their potential seller depends on the distribution of the buyer population, namely (w_A, w_B). In particular,

$$h_s(\vec{p}) = w_A f_{s,A}(\vec{p}) + w_B f_{s,B}(\vec{p}) \quad (5)$$

where $f_{s,A}(\vec{p})$ and $f_{s,B}(\vec{p})$ are the probabilities that seller s is selected by buyers of type A and B, respectively. The probability that a buyer of type A select a seller s is independent of the ordering of sellers' prices; in particular, $f_{s,A}(\vec{p}) = 1/S$. Buyers of type B, however, select a seller s if and only if s is one of the lowest price sellers. Given that the buyers' strategies depend on the relative ordering of the sellers' prices, it is convenient to define the following functions:

- $\lambda_s(\vec{p})$ is the number of sellers charging a lower price than s, and

- $\tau_s(\vec{p})$ is the number of sellers charging the same price as s, excluding s itself.

Now buyers of type b select seller s iff s is s.t. $\lambda_s(\vec{p}) = 0$, in which case a buyer selects a particular such seller s with probability $1/(\tau_s(\vec{p}) + 1)$. Therefore,

$$f_{s,B}(\vec{p}) = \frac{1}{\tau_s(\vec{p}) + 1} \delta_{\lambda_s(\vec{p}),0} \quad (6)$$

where $\delta_{i,j}$ is the Kronecker delta function, equal to 1, whenever $i = j$, and 0, otherwise.

The preceding results can be assembled to express the profit function π_s for seller s in terms of the distribution of strategies and valuations within the buyer population. In particular, assuming (as we do from here forward) that all buyers share the same valuation v, and all sellers share the same cost c, then

$$\pi_s(\vec{p}) = \begin{cases} (p_s - c)h_s(\vec{p}) & \text{if } p_s \leq v \\ 0 & \text{otherwise} \end{cases} \quad (7)$$

where

$$h_s(\vec{p}) = w_A \frac{1}{S} + w_B \frac{1}{\tau_s(\vec{p}) + 1} \delta_{\lambda_s(\vec{p}),0} \quad (8)$$

3 Analysis

In this section, we perform a game-theoretic analysis assuming sellers are profit maximizers. In particular, we first show that there is no pure strategy Nash equilibrium, and we then compute and describe the symmetric mixed strategy Nash equilibrium. Recall that $B \gg S$; in particular, the number of buyers is assumed to be very large, while the number of sellers is a great deal smaller. In accordance with this assumption, it is reasonable to consider the strategic decision-making of the sellers alone, since their relatively small number suggests that the behavior of individual sellers indeed influences market dynamics, while the large number of buyers renders the effects of individual buyers' actions negligible. A Nash equilibrium is a vector of prices $\vec{p}^*$ at which sellers maximize their individual profits and from which

yields $\pi_s^{MY} = 0.053125$ in this instance. The simulation results match this closely: the average profit per time step is 0.0515, which is just over twice the average profit obtained via the game-theoretic pricing strategy.

Since prices fluctuate over time, it is of interest to compute the probability distribution of prices. Fig. 4(a) depicts the cumulative distribution function for myopti-mal pricing. This measured cumulative density function has exactly the same endpoints $p^* = 0.53125$ and $v = 1$ as those of the mixed strategy equilibrium, but the linear shape between those endpoints (which reflects the linear price war) is quite different from what is displayed in Fig. 1(a).

DF Pricing Strategy

Fig. 2(b) shows the price dynamics that result when 5 derivative followers are pitted against one another. Recall that derivative followers do not base their pricing decisions on any information that pertains to other agents in the system — neither sellers' price-setting tendencies nor buyers' preferences. Nonetheless, their behavior tends towards what is in effect a collusive state in which *all* sellers charge nearly the monopolistic price. This is tacit collusion as defined, for example, in Tirole [1988], so-called because the agents do not communicate at all and there is consequently nothing illegal about their collusive behavior. Note that DF sellers accumulate greater profits than myoptimal or game-theoretic sellers. According to Fig. 3(b), sellers that are currently lowest-priced can expect an average profit of 0.30 to 0.35, while the others can expect roughly the game-theoretic profit of 0.025. Averaging over the last 90 million time steps (to eliminate transient effects), we find that the average profit per seller is 0.0841. This is near the absolute collusive limit of $(1/S)(v - c) = 0.10$, which would be obtained if all sellers were to fix their prices at 1.

How do derivative followers manage to collude? Like myoptimal sellers, DF sellers are capable of engaging in price wars; such dynamics are visible in Fig. 2(b). However, these price wars tend to involve only two sellers, and the positive feedback that drives them depends critically on both the sequence of price increments and the timing of the asynchronous moves by the sellers. Downward trends are therefore very easily disrupted. For example, if A's price is currently above B's, but A reduces its price by an amount insufficient to undercut B, then A's profits decrease, so that A raises its price in subsequent time steps. Soon after A breaks the downward cycle, B discovers that it can improve profits by increasing its price, and does so. Simulations clearly show that upward trends in price are much faster and more certain than downward trends. The tendency of a society of DF sellers to reach and maintain high prices is reflected in the cumulative distribution function, shown in Fig. 4(b).

It is also of interest to study the interplay among GT, MY, and DF sellers. Typically, we find that, when a myoptimal seller is introduced into a population of DF or GT sellers, it substantially outplays them, and their profits decline significantly.

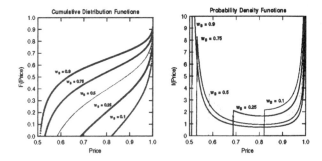

Figure 1: Nash Equilibria for $S = 5, v = 1, c = .5$, and $w_B \in \{.1, .25, .5, .75, .9\}$

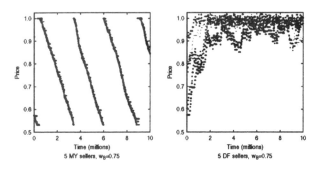

Figure 2: Price dynamics for a) 5 MY sellers and b) 5 DF sellers during the first 10 million time steps.

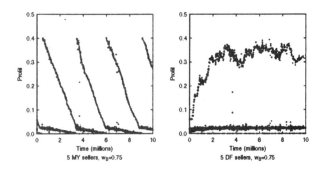

Figure 3: Profit dynamics for a) 5 MY sellers and b) 5 DF sellers during the first 10 million time steps.

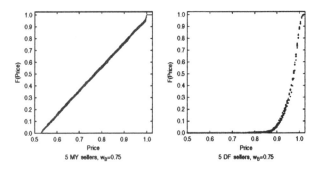

Figure 4: Cumulative distribution functions for a) 5 MY sellers and b) 5 DF sellers, derived from prices observed between times 10 million and 100 million.

5 Evolution of Shopbots and Pricebots

In additional simulations, we investigated a situation in which all five sellers use identical pricing strategies, but one of the sellers resets its price more quickly than the others. We observed that the faster price-setter earns substantially more profit than the others because, for example, in the case of myoptimal agents, it undercuts far more often than it itself is undercut. In the absence of any throttling mechanism, it is advantageous for sellers to re-price their goods as quickly as possible, but this could potentially lead to an arms race in which sellers do so with ever-increasing frequency. In such a world, a human price setter would undoubtedly be too slow and costly, and would be replaced with a pricebot (likely one based on a more sophisticated algorithm than any explored in Section 4!). Almost certainly, this strategy would make use of information about the buyer population, which could be purchased from other agents. Even more likely, however, the strategy would require knowledge of competitors' prices. How would the pricebot obtain this information? From a shopbot, of course!

With each seller seeking to re-price its products faster than its competitors, shopbots would quickly become overloaded with requests. A pricebot representing amazon.com might submit a million or more queries (one per book title) to a shopbot every hour — or maybe even every minute! Since shopbots must query individual sellers for prices, they would in turn pass this load back to amazon.com's competitors: *e.g.*, barnesandnoble.com, kingbooks.com. The rate of pricing requests made by sellers could easily dwarf the rate at which similar requests would be made by human buyers, eliminating the potential of shopbots to ameliorate market frictions.

A typical solution to an excess demand for shopbot services would be for shopbots to charge pricebots for price information. Today, shopbots tend to make a living by selling advertising space on their Web pages. This appears to be an adequate business model so long as requests are made by humans. Agents, however, are unwelcome customers because they are are not influenced by advertisements; as a result, agents are either barely tolerated or excluded intentionally. By charging for the information services they provide, shopbots would be economically-motivated agents, creating the proper incentives to deter excess demand, and welcoming business from other agents. Once shopbots begin to charge for pricing information, it would seem natural for sellers — the actual owners of the desired information — to themselves charge the shopbots for their information. The sellers could use another form of pricebot to dynamically price this information. This scenario illustrates how the need for agents to dynamically price their services could quickly percolate through an entire economy of software agents. The alternative is "meltdown" due to overload which could occur as agents become more prevalent on the Internet. Rules of etiquette followed voluntarily today by web crawlers and related programs could be trampled in the rush for competitive advantage.

6 Conclusion

Game-theoretic analysis of a model of a simple commodity market established a quantitative relationship between the degree of shopbot usage among buyers and the degree of price competition among sellers. This motivated a comparative study of various *pricebot* algorithms that sellers might employ in an effort to gain an edge in a market in which shopbots have increased the level of competition. Pricebots were shown to be capable of inducing price wars, yet even so they may earn profits that are well above game-theoretic equilibrium levels. Future work will explore the dynamics of markets in which more sophisticated shopbots base their search on product attributes as well as price, and in which pricebots use more sophisticated learning algorithms such as Q-learning.

References

[Chavez and Maes, 1996] Anthony Chavez and Pattie Maes. Kasbah: an agent marketplace for buying and selling goods. In *Proceedings of the First International Conference on the Practical Application of Intelligent Agents and Multi-Agent Technology*, London, U.K., April 1996.

[Cournot, 1838] A. Cournot. *Recherches sur les Principes Mathematics de la Theorie de la Richesse*. Hachette, 1838.

[DeLong and Froomkin, 1998] J. Bradford DeLong and A. Michael Froomkin. The next economy? In Deborah Hurley, Brian Kahin, and Hal Varian, editors, *Internet Publishing and Beyond: The Economics of Digital Information and Intellecutal Property*. MIT Press, Cambridge, Massachusetts, 1998.

[Greenwald et al., 1998] A. Greenwald, E. Friedman, and S. Shenker. Learning in network contexts: Results from experimental simulations. *Submitted for Publication*, May 1998.

[Kephart et al., 1998] J. O. Kephart, J. E. Hanson, D. W. Levine, B. N. Grosof, J. Sairamesh, R. B. Segal, and S. R. White. Dynamics of an information filtering economy. In *Proceedings of the Second International Workshop on Cooperative Information Agents*, 1998.

[Lewis, 1997] T. G. Lewis. *The Friction-Free Economy: Marketing Strategies for a Wired World*. Hardcover HarperBusiness, 1997.

[Nash, 1951] J. Nash. Non-cooperative games. *Annals of Mathematics*, 54:286–295, 1951.

[Tirole, 1988] Jean Tirole. *The Theory of Industrial Organization*. The MIT Press, Cambridge, MA, 1988.

[Tsvetovatyy et al., 1997] M. Tsvetovatyy, M. Gini, B. Mobasher, and Z. Wieckowski. MAGMA: an agent-based virtual market for electronic commerce. *Applied Artificial Intelligence*, 1997.

[Varian, 1980] H. Varian. A model of sales. *American Economic Review, Papers and Proceedings*, 70(4):651–659, September 1980.

Be Patient and Tolerate Imprecision: How Autonomous Agents can Coordinate Effectively*

Sudhir K. Rustogi and Munindar P. Singh
Department of Computer Science
North Carolina State University
Raleigh, NC 27695-7534, USA
skrustog@eos.ncsu.edu, singh@ncsu.edu

Abstract

A decentralized multiagent system comprises agents who act autonomously based on local knowledge. Achieving coordination in such a system is nontrivial, but is essential in most applications, where disjointed or incoherent behavior would be undesirable. Coordination in decentralized systems is a richer phenomenon than previously believed. In particular, five major attributes are crucial: the extent of the local knowledge and choices of the member agents, the extent of their shared knowledge, the level of their inertia, and the level of precision of the required coordination. Interestingly, precision and inertia turn out to control the coordination process. They define different regions within each of which the other attributes relate nicely with coordination, but among which their relationships are altered or even reversed. Based on our study, we propose simple design rules to obtain coordinated behavior in decentralized multiagent systems.

1 Introduction

Coordination is key to the design of multiagent systems. Often, the multiagent systems must be *decentralized*—whose member agents act autonomously based on local information. Such systems are essential in a number of applications where the agents may not wish to or be able to communicate or have a common plan.

Coordination has been studied before. In the context of distributed problem-solving and generalized partial planning, many good results have been obtained [Decker and Lesser, 1995; Durfee, 1999]. However, the key features of decentralized systems and their relationship to coordination have not yet been fully explored. Their study is the theme of this paper.

Let's begin with a brief historical overview. The early work on coordination considered knowledge as a key factor. Although decentralized systems of the kind we study were not always considered, the community's folklore is that more knowledge leads to better coordination. It is also recognized that the locally best actions would not always lead to the best payoff for an individual agent much less for the system as a whole.

Schaerf *et al.* consider multiagent reinforcement learning in the context of load balancing in distributed systems [1995]. In their framework, the agents share a number of resources, which they autonomously select to use. When all agents are noncooperative, e.g., by always selecting their most preferred resources, they all stand to lose. However, when individuals sometimes select the less desirable resources, the entire population benefits. In this system, communication may not be useful in improving the performance of the population and may in fact be detrimental.

In a simpler framework, Sen *et al.* also study coordination among agents sharing resources [1996]. Coordination corresponds to achieving equilibrium. Sen *et al.* argue that, contrary to conventional wisdom, giving the interacting agents additional knowledge causes the coordination to slow down. Baray uses the same framework, but applies genetic algorithms to show how coordination can be speeded up [1998].

Rustogi & Singh study coordination in a similar framework [1999]. They show that in addition to knowledge, the choices available and the extent of the knowledge shared by the agents are also important. Rustogi & Singh show that coordination slows down when the available choices increase. When shared knowledge increases, then too coordination slows down. There is no direct contradiction with Sen *et al.*, because their results correspond to the case where the agents' knowledge also increases.

The present paper advances the above program of research by bringing in additional features of decentralized systems in order to better characterize the outcome of coordination. Our experiments indicate that perfect coordination is often inordinately more time-consuming than slightly imperfect coordination. Usually, if the agents exhibit higher patience or inertia in terms of not jumping to another resource, they can coordinate faster.

*Supported by the NCSU College of Engineering, the National Science Foundation under grant IIS-9624425 (Career Award), and IBM corporation.

Organization Section 2 describes our experimental setup. Section 3 describes the main experimental results we obtained. Section 5 discusses some relevant conceptual issues, mentions some related literature, and concludes with a description of some open problems.

2 Experimental Setup

Our setup (Figure 1) consists of an array of equivalent resources. Each agent uses exactly one resource, but a resource can support several agents. The agents prefer resources that support fewer other agents. The agents know the occupancy of a certain number (Kn) of other resources besides their own. They can elect to move to any of a certain number (Ch) of resources. The agents move only to resources that appear better. They gradually disperse from the more crowded resources toward the less crowded ones.

Equilibrium is achieved when the agents are uniformly distributed over all resources, and none move. Equilibrium corresponds to perfect coordination, because it means the agents have achieved a locally and globally optimal sharing of resources. Note that the present setting requires the same or complementary decisions. In general, complementary decisions are more interesting, because they cannot be hardwired in some trivial mechanism.

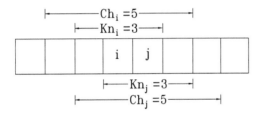

Figure 1: Knowledge (Kn), choice (Ch), and knowledge sharing of agents at resources i and j

2.1 Decision Protocol

Each agent stochastically decides whether to move and where. All agents use the same decision function and only move to better resources. The expressions used by an agent to compute the probability of moving from current resource i to another resource j in its choice window are given as follows. The f_{ij} are treated as weights.

$$f_{ij} = \begin{cases} 1 & \text{if } i = j \\ 0 & \text{if } i \neq j \text{ and } r_i \leq r_j \\ 1 - \frac{1}{1+\tau \exp\left(\frac{r_i - r_j - \alpha}{\beta}\right)} & \text{otherwise} \end{cases}$$

where α, β, and τ are control parameters, and r_i and r_j the number of agents at resources i and j, respectively. In our experiments, we set $\alpha = 5$, $\beta = 2$, and $\tau = 1$ unless otherwise specified.

The weights are normalized to yield probabilities. Thus, the probability of an agent moving from resource i to resource j is given by

$$p_{ij} = \frac{f_{ij}}{\sum_j f_{ij}}$$

Intuitively, when the choices are limited (as when small problems are considered), the agent typically has only a few good alternatives. Each good alternative gets a small positive weight; each undesirable alternative gets a weight of 0. Thus, the value of p_{ii} comes out fairly high. As the distribution of the agents levels out, their p_{ii} values increase until each of them becomes 1 meaning that none of the agents can move.

2.2 Key Concepts

This simple framework provides enough structure to capture a variety of interesting concepts.

Choice. The number of actions an agent may choose from. A rational agent may find it has fewer realistic choices when it comes to know more facts, but that aspect is not directly measured here. If resource j is not in the choice window, then r_j is not used, and $p_{ij} = 0$.

Knowledge. The number of resources whose occupancy is known to the agent. Thus, the knowledge of an agent increases as the agent is given information about an increasing number of resources.

The variables r_i and r_j give the occupancy of resources i and j. They are accurate for resources within the agent's knowledge window. For other resources, they are estimated based on the total number of agents and the occupancy of the known part of the world.

$$r_j = \begin{cases} \text{occupancy of } j & \text{if } j \text{ is in knowledge window} \\ (N - K)/u & \text{otherwise} \end{cases}$$

where N is the total number of agents, K is the number of agents in the knowledge window, and u is the number of resources that are not known about. Thus, N and u are a form of global knowledge in the system. Since eliminating them would complicate the present experiment considerably, that aspect is deferred to future work.

Inertia. This is the tendency of an agent to stay in its resource even if better alternatives are known. Greater inertia means that the probability p_{ii} is higher. In our setup, inertia is controlled by α. As remarked above, if all p_{ii} values increase to 1, coordination is achieved. Thus inertia can facilitate coordination. A system whose agents have low inertia may exhibit chaotic behavior, and never achieve coordination. On the other extreme, very high inertia would lead to an inactive system, with a similar result.

Sharing. Shared knowledge corresponds to overlapping knowledge windows. Rustogi & Singh estimate the total amount of sharing in the system as roughly proportional to the cube of the size of the knowledge window.

Under a homogeneous strategy (as here), shared knowledge would tend to lead to similar decisions, which could influence coordination.

Precision. Imprecision is the distance from a perfectly coordinated state, i.e., the minimum number of agent relocations required to coordinate. Given an acceptable level of imprecision, we control the simulations to halt when that level is reached. Introducing precision into the experimental framework had important consequences. First, because coordination is achieved much faster when imprecision is allowed, we could simulate much larger configurations than otherwise possible. Second, allowing some imprecision made the trends more robust by reducing the likelihood of pathological situations in which the system may get stuck. Third, imprecision helps us study the above pathological situations, which are interesting in their own right. This is the basis for some technical results presented later.

3 Results

The following figures indicate our results. The tuple in each caption indicates, respectively, the number of resources, the number of agents, the initial deviation (distance of the agent distribution from a coordinated state), and the imprecision tolerated.

Know-ledge	Choice							
	2	4	6	8	10	12	14	16
2	64	21	22	31	44	110	127	74
4		17	20	20	59	115	139	174
6			17	31	103	180	254	366
8				51	142	194	518	931
10					339	710	1007	1464
12						1096	2464	7270
14							5257	10550
16								21069

Table 1: Number of steps to coordination $\langle 16, 48, \pm 24, \pm 4 \rangle$

We compute the tables only for the upper triangular submatrix, because the lower triangular submatrix is readily determined from it. The lower triangular submatrix corresponds to the knowledge window being a superset of the choice window. In our decision protocol, this extra knowledge is useless and harmless, because it does not affect the agent's decisions. Thus, the values are essentially constant along each column below the principal diagonal. (In simulations, the randomization can cause minor variations.)

3.1 Sharing of Knowledge

Figure 2 is based on the last column of Table 1. Figure 2 shows that the time to achieve coordination has the same order as the sharing metric. To reduce clutter, we only show the graphs for a cubic polynomial that was fit to the data, and data corresponding to the last

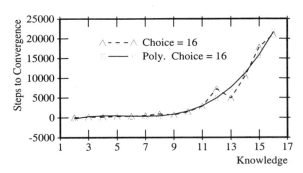

Figure 2: Effect of sharing of knowledge $\langle 16, 48, \pm 24, \pm 4 \rangle$

column (constant, maximal choice) of Table 1. This figure indicates that sharing may have a significant role to play in the final understanding of coordination in decentralized systems where the agents are homogeneous and coordination calls for complementary decisions, as here.

3.2 Precision

Reducing the required precision enhances the scalability of coordination. In other words, as the quality of the coordination increases, the cost in terms of time becomes extremely high. We studied this observation further by delineating the effect of the deviation from coordination at the start of each simulation run. In our setup, the deviation ranges from 1 (almost coordinated) to 15 (maximally uncoordinated).

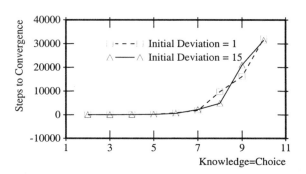

Figure 3: Effect of initial deviation $\langle 10, 30, \pm 0 \rangle$

Figure 3 demonstrates that it takes far fewer steps to progress from maximal uncoordination to almost perfect coordination than to go from almost perfect coordination to perfect coordination. The last little bit of precision consumes almost all of the effort.

The previous result suggests that the time to coordinate increases exponentially as the allowed imprecision is reduced to zero. Figure 4 supports this claim. The exponential variation occurs as inertia drops significantly, resulting in increasing instability. The exponential variation described above, however, does not manifest itself when the agents have little choice, because in such scenarios, the agents cannot move around much anyway. Instead, as Figures 5 and 6 demonstrate, for small choice

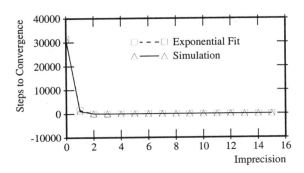

Figure 4: Effect of imprecision $\langle 10, 30, \pm 15 \rangle$

3.3 Inertia

Recall that inertia refers to the tendency of an agent to stay in its present resource even if it knows of better resources. From the probability calculations of section 2, it should be clear that, in general, as the number of choices increase, $\sum_j f_{ij}$ increases, and consequently the inertia (i.e., p_{ii}) decreases. This reason, especially when coupled with an imprecision of 0, can prevent coordination for moderately large dimensions.

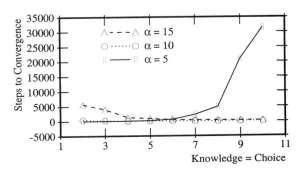

Figure 7: Effect of inertia (α) $\langle 10, 30, \pm 15, \pm 0 \rangle$

windows, the time for coordination increases only polynomially with reducing allowed imprecision. In these figures, to help visualize the trends better, each curve is normalized to 1 with respect to its maximum value. It should be obvious, however, that for low values of imprecision (including 0), the actual time to coordinate increases with choice. For higher values, the time to coordinate is practically independent of the choices available to the agents or the knowledge possessed by them.

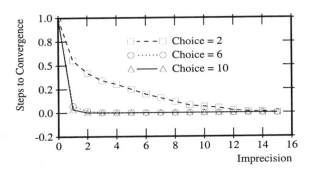

Figure 5: Effect of choice relative to imprecision $\langle 10, 30, \pm 15 \rangle$ (each curve is normalized to 1)

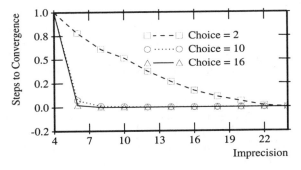

Figure 6: Effect of choice relative to imprecision $\langle 16, 48, \pm 24 \rangle$ (each curve is normalized to 1)

In our setup, inertia is characterized by the parameter α. The preceding results were based on $\alpha = 5$; now we vary α above and below this value. Figure 7 shows that increasing the inertia facilitates coordination. This is because when the agents are less likely to move, a low occupancy resource will not suddenly by occupied by several agents. Conversely, decreasing the inertia to a low value can make coordination extremely slow. The agents appear to jump about too much and system takes longer and longer to converge. For such cases, the detrimental effect of shared knowledge still applies; thus adding knowledge slows coordination.

Interestingly, for high inertia, an increase in knowledge or choice further improves the coordination. This relationship is a reversal from when the inertia is low. It appears that the trend changes, because higher inertia limits agent movement to such an extent that the benefits of additional local knowledge in decision-making overshadow the usual ill effects of increased sharing of knowledge.

The improvement of coordination due to increasing inertia is observed only if the inertia is not too high. Increasing the inertia to a very high value results in slow coordination. This is because very high inertia causes the agents to freeze in whatever resources they occupy.

3.4 Other Variants Considered

Our interest is in understanding the phenomenon of coordination in general, not analyzing the specific setup used in our experiments. Thus we emphasize the trends observed in the simulations, and the qualitative relationships among the trends, such as whether the number of steps is increasing or decreasing and if so at what polynomial order. Our experiments included complex scenarios, but which also yield the same trends as the simple scenarios on which the above results are directly based.

- Our results hold for several decision functions, but we present only the simple decision function used by Sen *et al.*

- Like Rustogi & Singh, we observed that keeping the knowledge and choice windows of an agent symmetrically distributed around its current resource yield the same trends as when the windows are skewed with respect to each other; therefore, we focus on the simpler situation.

- To enable convergence, we set an integral ratio of agents to resources. This is not strictly necessary when imprecise coordination is allowed, but changing the ratio has no effect on the trends, so we report only the integral situations here.

- Except when precision itself is a variable, we can make do with lower precision, because it yields faster convergence without affecting the qualitative nature of the trends.

- We studied the role of inertia and its interplay with knowledge and choice, by altering the control parameters (α, β, and τ) in our protocol. The results highlighted an interesting interplay among the various bases of coordination. Varying α alone, however, provides representative results.

4   Mapping the Terrain

Our experimental study of decentralized multiagent systems brought out a number of important factors that affect coordination. Some of these factors—inertia and precision—have not been empirically studied in such systems. Others—knowledge and choice—have been studied but, as our analysis showed, the trends relating to these are richer than believed. Trends due to inertia and precision can dominate and sometimes reverse the simpler trends.

The following simple rules summarize our qualitative results.

R1. Low inertia & low imprecision $\implies$ knowledge sharing governs $\implies$ local knowledge & limited choice performs better

R2a. Moderately high inertia $\implies$ extent of knowledge or choice is less important

R2b. High imprecision $\implies$ extent of knowledge or choice is less important

R3. Very high inertia $\implies$ system inactivity

The above rules demarcate the most important regions of our terrain. Figure 8 illustrates the corresponding regions. Rule *R1* supported by Figure 2, is mapped to Region *I* in Figure 8. To achieve effective coordination in this region, agents must limit their knowledge as well as choice. The results of Sen *et al.* and Rustogi & Singh lie within this region. Figures 5-6 and 7 support the

rules *R2b* and *R2a*, respectively. The results of Baray lie within this region—this is the reason he obtains much faster coordination than Sen *et al.* These rules, mapped to region *II* of Figure 8, imply that knowledge and choice are less relevant for coordination. Rule *R3* is intuitively obvious and is represented by region *III* in Figure 8.

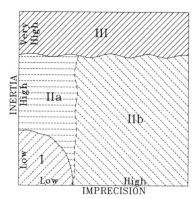

Figure 8: Mapping the terrain of decentralized systems

The study of coordination is interesting from a practical engineering standpoint. The above rules yield heuristics to aid in the engineering of a multiagent system. Our first conclusion is that for maximal scalability, we should allow some imperfection in coordination. Even a slight imperfection improves performance considerably. A moderately high value of inertia is desirable. Selecting the right value is nontrivial, especially because it will change in a dynamic system. An open problem is to devise online learning techniques to adapt to the right inertia during execution.

Interestingly, for most of the situations in our setup, local information performs better than global information. Even when local information gives suboptimal results, for many applications, it can provide a reasonable tradeoff with the cost incurred in acquiring the global information.

5   Discussion

In addition to the works mentioned above, some interesting relevant approaches are known in the literature. For instance, Kuwabara *et al.* present a market-based approach in which agents controlling different resources set their prices based on previous usage, and buyer agents choose which resources to use [1996]. The buyer agent can use more than one resource concurrently, and seeks to minimize the total price. As in our approach, the buyer's decision-making is probabilistic. Although Kuwabara *et al.*'s model is similar to ours, they do not study the reasons for achieving effective coordination.

Rachlin *et al.* show how agents, using the A-Team architecture, can achieve coordination without explicit communication [1999]. An A-Team is an asynchronous team of agents that shares a population of solutions that evolve over time into an optimal set of solutions.

Through sharing of the solution population, cooperative behavior between agents may emerge leading to better solutions than any one agent could produce. Often, however, a human agent may be necessary to help achieve coordination by imparting domain-specific knowledge.

Results by Hogg & Huberman indicate the potential benefits of introducing heterogeneity of different forms [1991]. These agree with the intuition that in homogeneous settings, the sharing of knowledge may have an undesirable effect on coordination. This is especially so when the agents must make complementary decisions so as to coordinate, i.e., move to different resources. This problem is closely related to the emergence of conventions for resource sharing [Lewis, 1969].

There are some limitations of the present experimental setup. It focuses on cases where the resource conflicts are direct and immediately perceived, the resources are homogeneous, the agents all use the same decision-making protocol, and the agents do not communicate directly. Further, there are well-known limitations of reinforcement learning in terms of time taken to learn even simple concepts. The present experiments leave open the possibility that more sophisticated agents in more flexible environments, where their learning is supervised in certain ways might discover better ways of coordination, which may turn out to have different characteristics in terms of the influence of knowledge and choice.

Although we introduced some interesting considerations, a lot remains to be done. Choice and inertia bear an interesting relationship to the notion of commitments. It appears that the two are complementary in that the greater the agent's choice the lower its commitment to a particular decision. Previous experimental work appears especially relevant. Kinny & Georgeff empirically investigate how the agents' commitment to their current plan contributes to their effective behavior [1991]. The agents in their work are characterized as bold, normal, or cautious based on the extent of their commitment (akin to inertia here), ranging from high to low, in that order. The cautious agents continually reconsider their plan at every step, in the face of a dynamic environment, and therefore exhibit the least commitment. For the most part, bold agents, despite their higher degree of blind commitment, perform better than normal and cautious agents except when the rate of change is very high. Kinny & Georgeff, however, do not study the effectiveness of behavior when the degree of commitment is very high.

We identified several of the key attributes affecting coordination in a way that agrees with but subsumes previous results. We also give some heuristics to develop decentralized multiagent systems. To cover additional applications, we need to consider communication among agents and to determine the circumstances under which it helps or disrupts coordination. We need to consider systems whose membership involves agents being removed and added back.

References

[Baray, 1998] Cristobal Baray. Effects of individual decision schemes on group behavior. In *Proceedings of the 3rd International Conference on Multiagent Systems (ICMAS)*, pages 389–390. July 1998.

[Decker and Lesser, 1995] Keith Decker and Victor Lesser. Designing a family of coordination algorithms. In *Proceedings of the International Conference on Multiagent Systems*, pages 73–80, 1995.

[Durfee, 1999] Edmund Durfee. Distributed problem solving and planning. In Gerhard Weiß, editor, *Multiagent Systems: A Modern Approach to Distributed Artificial Intelligence*. MIT Press, Cambridge, MA, chapter 3, pages 121–164. 1999.

[Hogg and Huberman, 1991] Tad Hogg and Bernardo Huberman. Controlling chaos in distributed systems. *IEEE Transactions on Systems, Man, and Cybernetics*, 21(6):1325–1332, 1991.

[Kinny and Georgeff, 1991] David Kinny and Michael Georgeff. Commitment and effectiveness of situated agents. In *Proceedings of the International Joint Conference on Artificial Intelligence (IJCAI)*, pages 82–88, 1991.

[Kuwabara et al., 1996] Kazuhiro Kuwabara, Toru Ishida, Yoshiyasu Nishibe, and Tatsuya Suda. An equilibratory market-based approach for distributed resource allocation and its applications to communication network control. In Scott Clearwater, editor, *Market Based Control: A Paradigm for Distributed Resource Allocation*. World Scientific, 1996.

[Lewis, 1969] David Lewis. *Convention*. Harvard University Press, Cambridge, MA, 1969.

[Rachlin et al., 1999] John Rachlin, Richard Goodwin, Sesh Murthy, Rama Akkiraju, Fred Wu, Santhosh Kumaran, and Raja Das. A-Teams: An agent architecture for optimization and decision-support. In *Intelligent Agents V: Proceedings of the 5th International Workshop on Agent Theories, Architectures, and Languages (ATAL-98)*, pages 261–276. Springer-Verlag, 1999.

[Rustogi and Singh, 1999] Sudhir Rustogi and Munindar Singh. The bases of effective coordination in decentralized multiagent systems. In *Intelligent Agents V: Proceedings of the 5th International Workshop on Agent Theories, Architectures, and Languages (ATAL-98)*, pages 149–162. Springer-Verlag, 1999.

[Schaerf et al., 1995] Andrea Schaerf, Yoav Shoham, and Moshe Tennenholtz. Adaptive load balancing: A study in multi-agent learning. *Journal of Artificial Intelligence Research*, 2:475–500, 1995.

[Sen et al., 1996] Sandip Sen, Shounak Roychoudhury, and Neeraj Arora. Effect of local information on group behavior. In *Proceedings of the International Conference on Multiagent Systems*, pages 315–321, 1996.

DISTRIBUTED ARTIFICIAL INTELLIGENCE

Economic Models 1

Efficiency and Equilibrium in Task Allocation Economies with Hierarchical Dependencies

William E. Walsh   Michael P. Wellman

Artificial Intelligence Laboratory
University of Michigan
1101 Beal Avenue, Ann Arbor, MI 48109-2110 USA
{wew, wellman}@umich.edu

Abstract

We analyze economic efficiency and equilibrium properties in decentralized task allocation problems involving hierarchical dependencies and resource contention. We bound the inefficiency of a type of approximate equilibrium in proportion to the number of agents and the bidding parameters in a particular market protocol. This protocol converges to an approximate equilibrium with respect to all agents, except those which may acquire unneeded inputs. We introduce a decommitment phase to allow such agents to decommit from their input contracts. Experiments indicate that the augmented market protocol produces highly efficient allocations on average.

1 Introduction

We consider task allocation problems in which competing agents desire to accomplish tasks, which may require complex chains of production activity. In order to perform a particular task, an agent may need to achieve some subtasks, which may in turn be delegated to other agents, forming a supply chain through a hierarchy of task achievement. Constraints on the task assignment arise from *resource contention*, where agents would need a common resource (e.g., a subtask achievement, or something tangible like a piece of equipment) to accomplish their own tasks. We assume that agents are self-interested and have private information, and so we must allocate in a decentralized manner.

We take a market-based approach to decentralized resource allocation, utilizing the large body of solution methods and analytical techniques from economics. Auctions mediate negotiation and determine prices and allocations. Prices indicate relative values of resources to guide local agent decisions. Experience with the *market-oriented programming* approach has verified that it works predictably and effectively in convex domains [Wellman, 1993]. Discrete problems, such as the task allocation domain considered here, provide additional challenges.

In previous work [1998], we proposed a market protocol that reliably constructs supply chains in a decentralized manner. In this paper we generalize the model and protocol to account for multiple competing demands for multiple end tasks. We bound the inefficiency of a type of approximate equilibrium in proportion to the number of agents and the bidding parameters in a particular market protocol. This protocol converges to an approximate equilibrium with respect to all agents, except those which may acquire unneeded inputs. We introduce a decommitment phase to allow such agents to decommit from their input contracts. Experiments indicate that the augmented market protocol produces highly efficient allocations on average.

We describe the task allocation problem in Section 2. We discuss price systems and competitive equilibrium in Section 3, and survey some market protocols for decentralized resource allocation in Section 4. In Section 5 we analyze the equilibrium properties of the extended protocol, and in Section 6 we examine its efficiency. We describe related task allocation work in Section 7.

2 Problem Description

Tasks are performed on behalf of particular agents; if two agents need a subtask then it would have to be performed twice to satisfy them both. In this way, tasks are the same as any other discrete resource. Hence we make no distinction in our model, and use the term "good" to refer to both.

We describe the problem in terms of bipartite graphs. A *task dependency network* is a directed, acyclic graph, (V, E). The vertices are $V = G \cup A$, where G is the set of goods, $A = C \cup \Pi \cup S$ is the set of agents, C is the set of consumers, Π is the set of producers, and S is the set of suppliers. The edges, E, connects agents with goods they can use or provide. There exists an edge $\langle g, a \rangle$ from $g \in G$ to $a \in A$ when agent a can make use of one unit of g, and an edge $\langle a, g \rangle$ when a can provide one unit of g. When an agent can acquire or provide multiple units of a good, we represent each unit as a separate edge. The goods can be traded only in integer quantities.

A *consumer* wishes to acquire one unit of one good from a set of some high-level goods. A *producer* can produce a single unit of an **output** good conditional on acquiring a certain number each of some fixed set of **input** goods. A producer's input requirements are **complementary** in that it must acquire each of its inputs; it cannot accomplish anything with only a partial set. A **supplier** can supply a set of goods, up to some maximum quantity for each, without requiring any input goods.

An **allocation** is a subgraph $(V', E') \subseteq (V, E)$. For $g \in G$, an edge $\langle a, g \rangle \in E'$ means that agent a provides g, and $\langle g, a \rangle \in E'$ means a acquires g. An agent is in an allocation graph iff it acquires or provides a good. A good is in an allocation graph iff it is bought or sold.

A producer is **active** iff it provides its output. A **producer is feasible** iff it is inactive or acquires all its inputs. Consumers and suppliers are always feasible. An **allocation is feasible** iff all producers are feasible and all goods are in **material balance**, that is the number of edges into a good equals the number of edges out.

A **solution** is a feasible allocation such that one or more consumers acquire a desired good. If $c \in C \cap V'$ for solution (V', E'), then (V', E') is a **solution for** c.

Each supplier s has some **opportunity cost** $oc_s(g)$ for supplying one unit $\langle s, g \rangle$ of good g. The total opportunity cost to s for allocation E' is $oc_s(E') \equiv \sum_{\langle s,g \rangle \in E'} oc_s(g)$.[1] The cost might represent the value s could obtain from putting the goods to some other use, or some actual, direct cost incurred in supplying the goods.

We assume that a consumer has preferences over different possible goods, but wishes to obtain only a single unit of one good.[2] Thus, a consumer c obtains **value** $v_c(g)$ for obtaining a single unit of good g, and, for allocation E', obtains value $v_c(E') \equiv \max_{\langle g,c \rangle \in E'} v_c(g)$.

Definition 1 (value of an allocation) *The* value *of allocation* (V', E') *is:*

$$value((V', E')) \equiv \sum_{c \in C} v_c(E') - \sum_{s \in S} oc_s(E').$$

Definition 2 (efficient allocations) *The set of* efficient allocations *contains all feasible allocations* (V^*, E^*) *such that* $value((V^*, E^*)) = \max_{(V', E')}(value((V', E')) \mid (V', E')$ *is feasible*$)$.

---

[1] We overload the notation for opportunity cost and agent value, using as an argument either a single good or a set of edges.

[2] More complicated consumer value functions can be expressed through combinations of multiple consumers and producers. For instance, a group of consumers, each desiring a single separate good, effectively represents an additive value function over the set of goods. If a consumer has preferences over *bundles* of goods, the bundles can be represented as output goods of producers, with the inputs of a producer corresponding to the components of the respective output bundle. Note that transformations such as this may not be strategically equivalent, in that the group of consumers may not behave as would the single agent they represent.

One could find efficient allocations using centralized search techniques, but we assume that we are constrained to solve the problem in a decentralized fashion. In the following, we examine an abstract framework for how a price system can guide decentralized task allocation. We also examine market protocols for decentralized task allocation.

3 Price Systems and Competitive Equilibrium

In the general-equilibrium approach to economic resource allocation, we posit a **price system** p, which assigns to each good g a nonnegative number $p(g)$ as its **price**. Intuitively, prices indicate the relative global value of the goods. Therefore, agents may use the prices as a guide to their local decision making.

We assume each agent has a **quasilinear** utility function. Its utility is the sum of the "money" it holds and the value (or negative cost) obtained from its allocation of goods. Agents wish to maximize their **surplus**.

Definition 3 (surplus) *The* surplus, $\sigma(a, E', p)$, *of agent a with allocation E' at prices p, is the utility gain from E', defined as follows:*

- $v_a(E') - \sum_{\langle g,a \rangle \in E'} p(g)$, *if $a \in C$,*
- $\sum_{\langle a,g \rangle \in E'} p(g) - \sum_{\langle g,a \rangle \in E'} p(g)$, *if $a \in \Pi$,*
- $\sum_{\langle a,g \rangle \in E'} p(g) - oc_a(E')$, *if $a \in S$.*

Informally, an allocation (V', E') is a **competitive equilibrium** at prices p if (V', E') is feasible and assigns to each agent an allocation that optimizes the agent's surplus at p. A competitive equilibrium allocation is stable in the sense that no agent would want a different allocation at the equilibrium prices.

We should generally expect that iterative auction protocols with discrete bid adjustments would overshoot exact equilibria by at least a small amount. However, approximate equilibrium is a useful concept for analyzing such protocols [Demange *et al.*, 1986; Walsh *et al.*, 1998]. We define and discuss properties and existence of a λ-δ-**competitive equilibrium**—a particular type of approximation equilibrium relevant to task dependency networks. The λ and δ parameterize an agent's maximum error in surplus optimization.

Denote as $H_a(p)$, the maximum surplus that agent a can obtain in (V, E), at some prices p, subject to feasibility. That is,

$$H_a(p) \equiv \max_{E' \subseteq E} \sigma(a, E', p)$$

such that a is feasible at E'.

Definition 4 (λ-δ-competitive equilibrium) *Given the parameters:*

- $\delta \in \Re^+ \cup \{0\}$,
- $\lambda_\pi \in \Re^+ \cup \{0\}$ *for all $\pi \in \Pi$,*
- N_π, *the number of input units required by $\pi \in \Pi$*

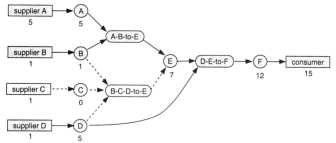

Figure 1: A λ-δ-equilibrium for $\lambda_{\text{B-C-D-to-E}} = \delta = 1$.

an allocation (V', E') is in λ-δ-competitive equilibrium at prices p iff:

1. *For all $a \in A$, $\sigma(a, E', p) \geq 0$.*
2. *For all $c \in C$, $\sigma(c, E', p) \geq H_c(p) - \delta$.*
3. *For all $\pi \in \Pi$, $\sigma(\pi, E', p) \geq H_\pi(p) - (N_\pi \lambda_\pi + \delta)$, and π is feasible at E'.*
4. *For all $s \in S$, $\sigma(s, E', p) = H_s(p)$.*
5. *All goods are in material balance at p.*

Figure 1 shows a λ-δ-equilibrium for $\lambda_{\text{B-C-D-to-E}} = \delta = 1$. Goods are indicated by circles, consumers and suppliers are represented as boxes, and producers are indicated by curved boxes. A solid arrow from a good to an agent indicates that the agent buys the good, and a solid arrow from an agent to a good indicates that the agent sells the good. Dashed arrows indicate input/output capabilities not part of the allocation. Shaded agents receive non-null allocations. Agent values and good prices are shown under their respective nodes. Note that for $\pi = \text{B-C-D-to-E}$, $\sigma(\pi, E', p) = 0 \geq H_\pi(p) - (N_\pi \lambda_\pi + \delta) = 1 - 4$. Thus π obeys the producer conditions for λ-δ-competitive equilibrium.

A λ-δ-competitive equilibrium corresponds to the standard notion of a competitive equilibrium when $\lambda_\pi = \delta = 0$ for all producers π. Bikhchandani and Mamer [1997] and Gul and Stacchetti [1997] show that, in an exchange economy, any competitive equilibrium set of prices supports an optimal allocation. We extend this result below to the class of production economies represented by task allocation economies. We show this by proving the more general result that a λ-δ-competitive equilibrium is suboptimally efficient by a fixed bound, $\sum_{\pi \in \Pi}[N_\pi \lambda_\pi + \delta] + |C|\delta$.

Lemma 1 *The value of a feasible allocation (V', E'), at any prices p, can be expressed as:*

$$value((V', E')) = \sum_{a \in A} \sigma(a, E', p). \quad (1)$$

Proof sketch.[3] Since supply equals demand in a feasible allocation, all the price terms cancel out and we are

---

[3]Complete proofs of all results appear at `http://www-personal.engin.umich.edu/~wew/Papers/ijcai99-extended.ps.Z`.

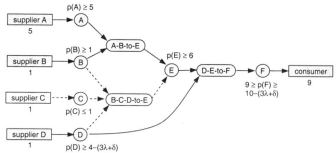

Figure 2: An economy with a λ-δ-competitive equilibrium solution when $3\lambda_{\text{B-C-D-to-E}} + \delta > 1$.

left with the original formula for the value of a solution (Definition 1). $\square$

Theorem 2 *If (V', E') is a λ-δ-competitive equilibrium for (V, E) at some prices p, then (V', E') is a feasible allocation with a nonnegative value that differs from the value of an efficient allocation by at most $\sum_{\pi \in \Pi}[N_\pi \lambda_\pi + \delta] + |C|\delta$.*

Proof sketch. We can compare the value of (V', E') to another feasible allocation (V^*, E^*), agent-wise, using Equation (1). The λ-δ-competitive equilibrium conditions imposed on the agents imply a global value difference that obeys the stated bound. $\square$

Not all task allocation economies have competitive equilibria (technically, this is due to complementarity of inputs for producers). However, we can always specify δ and λ_π values such that a λ-δ-competitive equilibrium exists, even when a competitive equilibrium does not exist. For example, we can do this by setting prices of the goods desired by the consumers higher than their values, and the prices of all other goods to zero (if there are any suppliers that could sell directly to consumers with positive surplus on both sides, we can set the prices so that only these suppliers trade with those consumers). We then set δ and the λ_π values sufficiently high such that $H_\pi(p) - (N_\pi \lambda_\pi + \delta) \leq 0$ for all $\pi \in \Pi$. Hence producers could obey the λ-δ-competitive equilibrium conditions by being inactive. Unfortunately, we cannot generally specify a λ-δ-competitive equilibrium for some fixed, problem-independent values of δ and λ_π. Indeed, the necessary values to obtain a *non-solution* λ-δ-equilibrium are proportional to the highest consumer value and the depth of the network.

Figure 2 shows the constraints on $\lambda_{\text{B-C-D-to-E}}$ and δ in order to have a *solution* in λ-δ-competitive equilibrium for a particular economy. The only solution involves all agents except B-C-D-to-E. The constraints on the prices of goods A and B ensure that suppliers A and B sell their goods. The constraint on the price of good C ensures that supplier C does not sell its good. The constraint on the price of good E ensures that A-B-to-E is active. The constraint on the price of good D ensures that B-C-D-to-E does not trade any goods. Fi-

Sequential Auctions for the Allocation of Resources with Complementarities

Craig Boutilier
Dept. of Computer Science
University of British Columbia
Vancouver, BC V6T 1Z4
cebly@cs.ubc.ca

Moisés Goldszmidt and Bikash Sabata
SRI International
333 Ravenswood Ave.
Menlo Park, CA 94025
{moises,sabata}@erg.sri.com

Abstract

Market-based mechanisms such as auctions are being studied as an appropriate means for resource allocation in distributed and multiagent decision problems. When agents value resources in combination rather than in isolation, one generally relies on *combinatorial auctions* where agents bid for resource bundles, or *simultaneous auctions* for all resources. We develop a different model, where agents bid for required resources *sequentially*. This model has the advantage that it can be applied in settings where combinatorial and simultaneous models are infeasible (e.g., when resources are made available at different points in time by different parties), as well as certain benefits in settings where combinatorial models are applicable. We develop a dynamic programming model for agents to compute *bidding policies* based on estimated distributions over prices. We also describe how these distributions are updated to provide a learning model for bidding behavior.

1 Introduction

A great deal of attention has been paid to the development of appropriate models and protocols for the interaction of agents in distributed and multiagent systems (MASs). Often agents need access to specific resources to pursue their objectives, but the needs of one agent may conflict with those of another. A number of market-based approaches have been proposed as a means to deal with the resource allocation and related problems in MASs [5, 21].

Of particular interest are *auction mechanisms*, where each agent bids for a resource according to some protocol, and the allocation and price for the resource are determined by specific rules [13]. Auctions have a number of desirable properties as a means for coordinating activities, including minimizing the communication between agents and, in some cases, guaranteeing Pareto efficient outcomes [13, 21].

An agent often requires several resources before pursuing a particular course of action. Obtaining one resource without another—for example, being allocated trucks without fuel or drivers, or processing time on a machine without skilled labor to operate it—makes that resource worthless. When resources exhibit such *complementarities*, it is unknown whether simple selling mechanisms can lead to efficient outcomes [21, 1]. Moreover, groups of resources are often *substitutable*: obtaining the bundle needed to pursue one course of action can lower the value of obtaining another, or render it worthless. For instance, once trucks and drivers are

obtained for transporting material in an optimal fashion, helicopters and pilots lose any value they may have had.

Two methods for dealing with complementarities have been studied: simultaneous auctions for multiple goods [1, 17]; and *combinatorial auctions* in which agents submit bids for *resource bundles* [16, 18, 19, 9, 21]. Specific models sometimes deal (possibly implicitly) with substitution effects, and sometimes not. In this paper, we explore a model that combines features of both simultaneous and combinatorial auctions. Our *sequential auctions model* supposes that the set of resources of interest are auctioned in sequence. Agents bid for resources in a specific, known order, and can choose how much (and whether) to bid for a resource depending on past successes, failures, prices, and so on.

Our model has several advantages over standard combinatorial and simultaneous models. The chief benefit of such a model is that is can be applied in situations where combinatorial and simultaneous models cannot. Specifically, when multiple sellers offer various resources of interest, or when the resources are sold at different points in time, one does not have the luxury of setting up either combinatorial or simultaneous auctions. As such, our model is suitable for agents who are required to interact with multiple suppliers over time. Even in settings where combinatorial models can be applied, there may be some advantages to using a sequential model. Unlike combinatorial models, our model relieves the (computational) burden of determining a final allocation from the seller, effectively distributing computation among the buyers (as in the simultaneous case); note that determining an optimal allocation that maximizes the seller's revenue is NP-hard [18]. Our sequential model also has the advantage that buyers are not required to reveal information about their valuations for specific resource bundles that they do not obtain. Furthermore, it has greater flexibility in that agents can enter and leave the market without forcing recomputation of entire allocations. In contrast to simultaneous models, agents in the sequential model may lessen their exposure. If an agent does not obtain a certain resource early in the sequence, it need not expose itself by bidding on complementary resources occurring later in the sequence. Agents are typically bidding in a state of greater knowledge in the sequential model, at least in later stages; however, in earlier stages agents may have lesser information than they would in a simultaneous model.

One difficulty that arises in the sequential model is how an agent computes bids for individual resources (the same difficulty arises in simultaneous models). An agent has a valuation for a particular resource bundle $b = \{r_1, \cdots, r_k\}$, but has no independent assignment of value to the individual resources.[1] While auction theory can tell us how an agent should bid as a function of its valuation of resource r_i for specific auction mechanisms, in our setting no such valuation exists. If b is worth $v(b)$, how is an agent to "distribute the value" among the resources r_i in order to compute bids?

In this paper, we develop a dynamic programming algorithm for doing just this. We assume that each agent has a probabilistic estimate of the size of the maximum bids for each resource (excluding its own). It can then compute a *bidding policy* that maximizes its expected utility, and apply this policy as dictated by its initial endowment. Bids for resources early in the sequence are computed as a function of the odds of being able to obtain their complements and substitutes, while bids for later resources are conditioned on the resources obtained early in the sequence.

We also interested in adaptive bidding behavior, and to this end investigate a *repeated sequential auction model* in which agents repeatedly bid for the same resources over time. We consider the problem of estimating the probability distributions over maximal bids in this repeated scenario. If agents persistently find themselves requiring resources to pursue their aims, we want them to learn which resources they will be able to obtain and which they will not. This is related to recently proposed learning models for auctions [11, 12], though our focus is on learning prices and its effect on the valuation of individual resources in bundles.

The problem we study is part of a more general research program designed to study the impact of specific resource allocation schemes on the solution of sequential multiagent decision problems. We motivate the problem studied here as follows. We suppose that a number of agents have certain tasks and objectives to pursue, and for any objective there may exist a number of potential courses of action that are more or less suitable. For instance, an agent may construct a policy for a Markov decision process [15, 2], from which it can determine the value of various courses of action, their likelihood of success, and so on. Any specific course of action will require certain resources, say, bundle b^k, whose value can be determined as a function of the expected value of that course of action (and the expected value of alternative courses of action). As such, we suppose each bundle b^k has an associated value $v(b^k)$ and that the agent will use only one bundle (the one associated with the highest-valued course of action among those bundles it possesses). It is from these valuations that the agent must determine its bidding policy for individual resources. This is the problem considered here.

Ultimately, the decision problem we hope to study is far more complex. Determining appropriate courses of action will depend on perceived probability of obtaining requisite resources, uncertainty in that course of action, alternatives available and so on. We envision very sophisticated reasoning emerging regarding the interaction bidding behavior and

---

[1] In fact, we will assume that several bundles can be valued, with possible overlap. This accounts for possible substitution effects.

"base-level" action choice (in the MDP), such as taking a few critical steps along a specific course of action before deciding to enter the market for the corresponding resources (e.g., perhaps because this policy is fraught with uncertainty). We also foresee interesting interactions with other coordination and communication protocols.

In Section 2 we describe the basic sequential bidding model. We note a number of dimensions along which our basic model can vary, though we will focus only on specific instantiations of the model for expository reasons. We describe our dynamic programming model for constructing bidding policies in Section 3. We also describe the motivation for using the specific model proposed here instead of using explicit equilibrium computation. We discuss *repeated* sequential auctions in Section 4, focusing on the problem of highest-bid estimation. In Section 5 we describe some preliminary experimental results, and conclude in Section 6 with discussion of future research directions.

While bidding strategies for sequential auctions would seem to be an issue worthy of study, there appears to have been little research focussed on this issue. What work exists (see, e.g., [8, 10]) tends to focus the seller's point of view— for example, will simultaneous or sequential sales maximize revenue—and does not address the types of complementarities we consider here. Generally, existing work assumes that single items are of interest to the buyer.

2 Basic Model

We assume we have a finite collection of agents, all of whom require resources from a pool of n resources $R = \{r_1, \cdots, r_n\}$. We denote by R^t the subset $\{r_1, \cdots, r_t\}$, $t \leq n$, with $R^0 = \emptyset$ by convention. We describe the quantities relevant to a specific agent a below, assuming that these quantities are defined for each agent. Agent a can use exactly one bundle $b^i = \{r_1^i, \cdots, r_{|b^i|}^i\}$ of resources from a set of k *possible bundles*: $B = \{b^1, \cdots, b^k\}$. We denote by $U(a) = \cup B$ the set of *useful resources* for our agent.

Agent a has a positive valuation $v(b^i)$ for each resource bundle $b^i \in B$. Suppose the *holdings* of a, $H(a) \subseteq U(a)$, are those resources it is able to obtain. The value of these holdings is given by $v(H(a)) = \max\{v(b^i) : b^i \subseteq H(a)\}$; that is, the agent will be able to use the resource bundle with maximal value from among those it holds in entirety, with the others going unused. This is consistent with our interpretation given in Section 1 where resource bundles correspond to alternative plans for achieving some objective (though other value combinators can be accommodated).

The resources will be auctioned sequentially in a commonly known order: without loss of generality, we assume that this ordering is $r_1, r_2, \cdots, r_n$ We use A_i to denote the auction for r_i. We refer to the sequence of auctions $A_1, A_2, \cdots, A_n$ as a *round* of auctions. There may be a single round, some (definite or indefinite) finite numbers of rounds, or an infinite number of rounds.

Supposing for the moment only one round, we assume that agent a is given an initial endowment e which it can use to obtain resources. At the end of the round, a has holdings $H(a)$

and d dollars remaining from its endowment.[2] We assume that the utility of being in such a state at the end of the round is given by $v(H(a)) + f(d)$, where f is some function attaching utility to the unused portion of the endowment. Other utility functions could be considered within this framework.

There are a wide range of options one could consider when instantiating this framework. We define a specific model here, but list the options that could be explored. We develop the algorithms in this paper for the specific model, but where appropriate, indicate how they should be modified for other design choices. The main design choices are:

- What auction mechanism is used for the auctions A_i?
- What rules are instituted for reselling or speculation?
- What information is revealed to the agents? When?
- What information do agents have when a round begins?

We assume that the individual auctions will be first-price, sealed-bid—each agent will provide a single bid and the highest bidder will be awarded the resource for the price bid. We adopt this model because of the ease with which it fits with our approach to bid computation; however, we believe our model could be adapted for other auction protocols. We also assume that bids are discrete (integer-valued); but we do describe the appropriate amendments to deal with continuous bids. Agents, once obtaining a resource, cannot resell that resource to another agent. This, of course, means that an agent may obtain one resource r_i, but later be unable to obtain a complementary resource r_{i+k}, essentially being "stuck" with a useless resource r_i. We do this primarily for simplicity, though in certain settings this assumption may be realistic. We are currently exploring more sophisticated models where agents can "put back" resources for re-auctioning, or possibly resell resources directly to other agents.

Each agent is told the winning price at the end of the each auction (and whether it was the winner). We could suppose that no information (other than winning or losing) is provided, that the distribution over bids is announced, or that the bids of specific individuals are made public; our assumption seems compatible with the first-price, sealed-bid model.

Finally, agent a believes that the highest bid that will be made for resource r_i, excluding any bid a might make, is drawn from some unknown distribution $\overline{Pr}^i$. Because bids are integer-valued, this unknown distribution is a multinomial over a non-negative, bounded range of integers.[3] To represent a's uncertainty over the parameters of this distribution, we assume a has a prior probability distribution Pr^i over the space of bid distributions. Agent a models Pr^i as a Dirichlet distribution with parameters $\beta_0^i, \cdots, \beta_{m_i}^i$ [6], where m_i is the (estimated) maximum possible bid for r_i. We elaborate on this probability model in Sections 3 and 4.

We make two remarks on this model. First, if the space of possible bids is continuous, a suitable continuous PDF (e.g.,

Gaussian) could be used to model bid distributions and the uncertainty about the parameters of this PDF. More questionable is the implicit assumption that bids for different resources are uncorrelated. By having distributions Pr^i rather than a joint distribution over *all* bids, agent a is reasoning as if the bids for different resources are independent. When resources exhibit complementarities, this is unlikely to be the case. For instance, if someone bids up the price of some resource r_i (e.g., trucks), they may subsequently bid up the price of complementary resource r_j (e.g., fuel or drivers). If agent a does not admit a model that can capture such correlations, it may make poor bids for certain resources. Again, we make this assumption primarily for ease of exposition. Admitting correlations does not fundamentally change the nature of the algorithms to follow, though it does raise interesting modeling and computational issues (see Section 4).

3 Computing Bids by Dynamic Programming

In this section we focus on the decisions facing an agent in a single round of auctions. A key decision facing an agent at the start of a round is how much to bid for each resource that makes up part of a useful bundle b_i. In standard single item auctions (e.g., first/second-price, sealed bid) rational agents with an assessment of the valuations of other agents can compute bids with maximum expected utility [13]. For example, in first-price, sealed bid auctions, an agent should bid a some amount below its true valuation, where this amount is given by its beliefs about the valuations of others.

Unfortunately, the same reasoning cannot be applied to our sequential setting, since individual resources cannot be assessed a well-defined valuation. For instance, if bundle $b^i = \{r_1^i, r_2^i\}$ has valuation $v(b^i)$, how should agent a apportion this value over the two resources? Intuitively, if there is a greater demand for r_1^i, a larger "portion" of the value should be allotted for bidding in the first auction rather than the second. If the agent fails to obtain r_1^i, the value of r_2^i goes to zero (ignoring other bundles). In contrast, should a obtain r_1^i, it is likely that the agent should offer a substantial bid for r_2^i, approaching the valuation $v(b^i)$, since the price paid for r_1^i is essentially a "sunk cost." Of course, if the agent expects this high price to be required, it should probably not have bid for r_1^i in the first place. Finally, the interaction with other bundles requires the agent to reason about the relative likelihood of obtaining any specific bundle for an acceptable price, and to focus attention on the most promising bundles.

3.1 The Dynamic Programming Model

These considerations suggest that the process by which an agent computes bids should not be one of assigning value to individual resources, but rather one of constructing a *bidding policy* by which its bid for any resource is conditioned on the outcome of events earlier in the round. The sequential nature of the bidding process means that it can be viewed as a standard sequential decision problem under uncertainty. Specifically, the problem faced by agent a can be modeled as a fully observable Markov decision process (MDP) [15, 2]. The computation of an optimal *bidding policy* can be implemented using a standard stochastic dynamic programming al-

---

[2] If speculation or reselling is allowed, there is the possibility that $d > e$, depending on the interaction protocols we allow. We will mention this possibility below, but we will examine only protocols that disallow it.

[3] We assume that a bound can be placed on the highest bid.

gorithm such as value iteration.

We emphasize that agents are computing optimal *bids*, not true valuations for individual resources. Thus issues involving revelation of truthful values for resources are not directly relevant (but see Section 4 on multiple rounds).

We assume the decision problem is broken into $n + 1$ stages, n stages at which bidding decisions must be made, and a terminal stage at the end of the round. We use a time index $0 \leq t \leq n$ to refer to stages—time t refers to the point at which auction A_{t+1} for r_{t+1} is about to begin. The *state* of the decision problem for a specific agent a at time t is given by two variables: $H^t(a) \subseteq R^t$, the subset of resources R^t held by agent a; and d^t, the dollar amount (unspent endowment) available for future bidding. We write $\langle h, d \rangle^t$ to denote the state of a's decision problem at time t. Note that although we could distinguish the state further according to which agents obtained which resources, these distinctions are not relevant to the decision facing a.[4]

The dynamics of the decision process can be characterized by a's estimated transition distributions. Specifically, assuming that prices are drawn independently from the stationary distributions $\overline{Pr}^i$, agent a can predict the effect of any action (bid) z available to it. If agent a is in state $\langle h, d \rangle^t$ at stage t, it can bid for r_{t+1} with any amount $0 \leq z \leq d^t$ (for convenience we use a bid of 0 to denote nonparticipation). Letting w denote the highest bid of other agents, if a bids z at time t, it will transition to state $\langle h \cup \{r_{t+1}\}, d - z \rangle^{t+1}$ with probability $\overline{Pr}^{t+1}(w < z)$ and to $\langle h, d \rangle^{t+1}$ with $\overline{Pr}^{t+1}(w \geq z)$.[5]

This does not form an MDP *per se*, since a may be uncertain about the true distribution $\overline{Pr}^{t+1}$, having only a Dirichlet distribution $\langle \beta_1^{t+1}, \cdots, \beta_{m_{t+1}}^{t+1} \rangle$ over the possible parameters of $\overline{Pr}^{t+1}$. However, the expectation that the highest bid is w is given by the relative weight of parameter β_w^{t+1}; thus,

$$\mathrm{Pr}^{t+1}(w < z) = \frac{\sum_{i=0}^{z-1} \beta_i^{t+1}}{\sum_{i=0}^{m_{t+1}} \beta_{i+1}^t}$$

While the observation of the true winning bid can cause this estimated probability to change (properly making this a partially observable MDP), the change cannot impact *future* transition probability estimates or decisions: we have assumed that the high bid probabilities are independent. Thus, treating this as a fully observable MDP with transition probabilities given by *expected* transition probabilities is sound.

The final piece of the MDP is a reward function q. We simply associate a reward of zero with all states at stages 0 through $n - 1$, and assign reward $v(h) + f(d)$ to every terminal state $\langle h, d \rangle^n$. A *bidding policy* π is a mapping from states into actions: for each legal state $\langle h, d \rangle^t$, $\pi(\langle h, d \rangle^t) = z$ means that a will bid z for resource r_{t+1}. The *value* $V^\pi(\langle h, d \rangle^t)$ of policy π at any state $\langle h, d \rangle^t$ is the expected reward $E_\pi(q(\langle H(a), d \rangle^n)|\langle h, d \rangle^t)$ obtained by executing π. The expected value of π given the agent's initial

state $\langle \emptyset, e \rangle^t$ is simply $V^\pi(\langle \emptyset, e \rangle^t)$. An *optimal bidding policy* is any π that has maximal expected reward at every state.

We compute the optimal policy using value iteration [15], defining the value of states at stage t using the value of states at stage $t + 1$. Specifically, we set

$$V(\langle h, d \rangle^n) = v(h) + f(d)$$

and define, for each $t < n$:

$$
\begin{aligned}
Q(\langle h, d \rangle^t, z) &= \mathrm{Pr}^{t+1}(w < z) \cdot V(\langle h \cup \{r_t\}, d - z \rangle^{t+1}) \\
&\quad + \mathrm{Pr}^{t+1}(w \geq z) \cdot V(\langle h, d \rangle^{t+1}) \\
V(\langle h, d \rangle^t) &= \max_{z \leq d} Q(\langle h, d \rangle^t, z) \\
\pi(\langle h, d \rangle^t) &= \arg\max_{z \leq d} Q(\langle h, d \rangle^t, z)
\end{aligned}
$$

Given that V is defined for all stage $t + 1$ states, $Q(\langle h, d \rangle^t, z)$ denotes the value of bidding z at state $\langle h, d \rangle^t$ and acting optimally thereafter. $V(\langle h, d \rangle^t)$ denotes the optimal value at state $\langle h, d \rangle^t$, while $\pi(\langle h, d \rangle^t)$ is the optimal bid.

Implementing value iteration requires that we enumerate, for each t, all possible stage t states and compute the consequences of every feasible action at that state. This can require substantial computational effort. While linear in the state and action spaces (and in the number of stages n), the state and action spaces themselves are potentially quite large. The number of possible states at stage t could potentially consist of any subset of resources R^t together with any monetary component. The action set at a state with monetary component d has size $d+1$. Fortunately, we can manage some of this complexity using the following observations: first, a never needs to bid for any resource outside the useful set $U(a)$, so its state space (at stage t) is restricted to subsets of $U^t(a)$; and second, if a resource r_t requires a complementary resource $r_{t'}$, $t' < t$, (that is, all bundles containing r_t also contain $r_{t'}$), then we need never consider a state where a has r_t but not $r_{t'}$.[6] Reducing the impact of the number of possible bids is more difficult. We can certainly restrict the state and action space to dollar values no greater than a's initial endowment e. If the PDF is well-behaved (e.g., concave), pruning is possible: e.g., once the expected value of a larger bids starts to decrease, search for a maximizing bid can be halted.[7]

This dynamic programming model deals with the complementarities and substitutability inherent in our resource model; no special devices are required. Furthermore, it automatically deals with issues such as uncertainty, dynamic valuation, "sunk costs," and so on. Given stationary, uncorrelated bid distributions, the computed policy is optimal.

3.2 Extensions of the Model

While the assumptions underlying our (single-round) model are often reasonable, there are two assumptions that must be relaxed in certain settings: the requirement for discrete bids

---

[4] This is true under the current assumptions, but may not be under different models; see below.

[5] For expository purposes, the model assumes ties are won. Several rules can be used for ties; none complicate the analysis.

[6] This reasoning extends to arbitrary subset complementarities.

[7] If we move to a continuous action space, the value function representation and maximization problems may become easier to manage for certain well-behaved classes of probability distributions and utility functions (see Section 3.2 and [3]).

and the prohibition of reselling or returning resources for resale. We are currently exploring these relaxations.

Continuous bidding models are important for computational reasons. Though money is not truly continuous, the increments that need to be considered generally render explicit value calculations for all discrete bids infeasible. Continuous function maximization and manipulation techniques are often considerably more efficient that discrete enumeration, and approximately optimal "integer" bids can usually be extracted. We are currently exploring specific continuous models, specifically using parameterized bid distributions (such as Gaussian and uniform distributions) and linear utility functions (as described above). The key difficulty in extending value iteration is determining an appropriate value function representation. While the maximization problem (over bids) for a specific state is not difficult, we must represent V^t as a function of the continuous state space. This function is linear (in d) at all states where the remaining endowment d is greater than the maximal worthwhile bid. But a different function representation is needed for states with endowment less than the best bid. We are currently exploring a value function representation with piecewise, continuous representations of V for each (discrete) set of holdings $H(a)$ [3].

Reselling may be appropriate in many settings and can allow agents to bid more aggressively with less risk. We are currently developing a simple model in which agents are allowed, at the end of a round, to "put back" resources for re-auction that are not needed (e.g., are not part of the agent's max-valued complete bundle).[8] Several difficulties arise in this setting, including the fact that agents may need to estimate the probability that an unobtained resource may be returned for re-auction.

3.3 Equilibrium Computation

The model described above does not allow for strategic reasoning on the part of the bidding agent. The agent takes the expected prices as given and does not attempt to compute the impact of its bids on the behavior of other agents, how they might estimate its behavior and respond, and so on; that is, no form of equilibrium is computed. Standard models in auction theory generally prescribe bidding strategies that are in Bayes-Nash equilibrium: when each agent has beliefs about the *types* of other agents (i.e., how each agent values the good for sale), and these beliefs are common knowledge, then the agents' bidding policies can be prescribed so that no agent has incentive to change its policy.[9] This, for instance, is the basis for prescribing the well-known strategies for bidding in first- and second-price auctions [20].

Our approach is much more "myopic." There are several reasons for adopting such a model rather that a full Bayes-Nash equilibrium model. First, equilibrium computation is often infeasible, especially in a nontrivial sequential, multi-resource setting like ours. Second, the information required on the part of each agent, namely a distribution over the possible types of other agents, is incredibly complex—an agent type in this setting is its set of valuations for *all* resource bundles, making the space of types unmanagable. Finally, the common knowledge assumptions usually required for equilibrium analysis are unlikely to hold in this setting.

We expect that the MDP model described here could be extended to allow for equilibrium computation. Rather than do this, we consider an alternative, adaptive model for bidding in which agents will adjust their estimates of prices—hence their bidding policies—over time. Implicitly, agents learn how others value different resources, and hopefully some type of "equilibrium" will emerge. We turn our attention to this process of adaptation.

4 Repeated Auctions and Value Estimation

In certain domains, agents will repeatedly need resources drawn from some pool to pursue ongoing objectives. We model this by assuming that the same resource collection is auctioned repeatedly in rounds. While agents could compute a single bidding policy and use it at every round, we would like agents to use the behavior they've observed at earlier rounds to update their policies. Specifically, observed winning prices for resource auctions A_i in the past can be used by an agent to update its estimate of the true distribution $\Pr^i$ of high bids for r_i. Its bidding strategy at the next round can be based on the updated distributions.

If each agent updates its bidding policy based on past price observations, the prices observed at earlier rounds may not be reflective of the prices that will obtain at the next round. This means that the agents are learning based on observations drawn from a nonstationary distribution. This setting is common in game theory, where agents react to each others past behavior. Myopic learning models such as *fictitious play* [4] (designed to learn strategy profiles) can be shown to converge to a stationary distribution despite the initial nonstationarity. This type of learning model has been applied to repeated (single-item) auctions and shown to converge [11]. Our model is based on similar intuitions—namely, that learning about prices will eventually converge to a steady state. Hu and Wellman [12] also develop a related model for price learning in a somewhat different context.

The advantage of a learning model is that agents can come to learn which resources they can realistically obtain and focus their bidding on those. If agents A and B have similar endowments and both equally value having either r_1 or r_2, they may learn over time not to compete for r_1 and r_2; instead they may learn to anticipate (implicitly, through pricing) each other's strategy and (implicitly) coordinate their activities, with one pursuing r_1 and the other r_2. If one agent has a greater endowment than another (e.g., it may have higher priority objectives in a distributed planning environment), the poorer agent should learn that it can't compete and focus on less contentious (and perhaps less valued) resources. Another important feature of learning models is that they can be used to overcome biased or weak prior assessments.

Given the form of the probabilistic model described in Section 3, an agent can update its estimate of a bid distribution rather easily. Suppose agent a has parameters $\langle \beta_1^t, \cdots, \beta_{m_t}^t \rangle$

---

[8]More complicated models that allow agents to put back resources during the round or resell directly are also possible.

[9]We use *type* here in the sense used in game theory for games with incomplete information [14].

that characterize its distribution $\Pr^t$ over the true distribution $\overline{\Pr}^t$ of high bids for resource r_t. After auction A_t the winning bid w is announced to each agent.[10] If a fails to win the resource, it should update these Dirichlet parameters by setting β_w^t to $\beta_w^t + 1$; at the next round, its estimate that the highest bid will be w is thus increased. If a wins resource r_t for price z, the only information it gets about the highest bid (excluding its own) is that it is less than z. The Dirichlet parameters can then be updated with an algorithm such as EM [7]. Roughly, the expectation step computes an update of the parameters of the Dirichlet using current estimates to distribute the observation over the parameters $\beta_1^t, \cdots, \beta_{z-1}^t$: each β_j^t ($j < z$) is increased by $\beta_j^t / \sum_{i=0}^{z-1} \beta_i^t$. The maximization step corresponds to the actual update followed by the substitution of these parameters in $\Pr$. Whereas the EM algorithm requires an iteration of these two steps until convergence, we performed this iteration about 10 times.[11]

In the specific probability model developed here, agents cannot profitably use this updated estimate during the current round. Because prices are assumed independent, learning about one price cannot influence an agent's bidding strategy for other resources.[12] Thus the agent continues to implement the bidding policy computed at the start of the round. The updated bid distributions are used prior to the start of the next round of auctions to compute an new bidding policy.

As mentioned above, the price-independence assumption may be unrealistic. If prices are correlated, the observed price of a resource can impact the estimated price of another resource that will be available later in the round. Agents in this case should revise their bidding policies to reflect this information. Two approaches can be used to deal with correlations. First, agents can simply recompute their bidding policies during a round based on earlier outcomes. An alternative is to model this directly within the MDP itself: this entails making the MDP partially observable, which can cause computational difficulties.

One thing we do not consider is agents acting strategically within a round to influence prices at subsequent rounds. Agents are reasoning "myopically" within a specific round. By formulating multi-round behavior as a sequential problem, we could have agents attempting to manipulate prices for future gain. Our current model does not allow this.

5 Results

We now describe the results of applying this model to some simple resource allocation problems. These illustrate interesting qualitative behavior such as adaptation and coordination. We also explain why such behavior arises. In all runs, multiple rounds are considered and remaining endowment d

---

[10] Our model can accommodate both more (e.g., the bids of all agents) and less (e.g., only whether an agent won or lost) revealed information about the auction outcome rather easily.

[11] Preliminary experiments showed this sufficient.

[12] With correlated prices, an agent could attempt to provide misleading information about its valuation of one resource in order to secure a later resource at a cheaper price. This type of deception, studied for identical item auctions in [10], cannot arise within a single round in our current model, even if strategic reasoning is used.

is valued at $0.5d$ ($\alpha = 0.5$). Agent priors have slightly increasing weights on higher bids.[13]

The first series of examples illustrates bidding behavior in allocation problems with specific parameter settings.

Example There are two agents whose optimal bundles are disjoint: a_1 requires $b_1^1 = \{r_1, r_3\}$ (value 20) or $b_2^1 = \{r_4, r_5, r_6\}$ (value 30), while a_2 requires $b_1^2 = \{r_2, r_3\}$ (value 20) or $b_2^2 = \{r_7, r_8, r_9\}$ (value 30). Initially, both agents focus on the smaller (and lower-valued) bundles. At the first round, a_1 obtains b_1^1, while a_2 gets "stuck" with r_2 (a_1 outbid it for r_3). The next round sees a_2 bid less for r_2, and more for r_3 (outbidding a_1). Since it obtains b_1^2, it does not attempt to bid for b_2^2. But without b_1^1, and its estimated prices for resources in b_2^1 lowered, a_1 now bids for and gets b_2^1 (its optimal bundle). Up to the 14th round, one of the agents gets its best bundle and the other its worst. At the 14th round, each gets its best bundle, and after the 16th round, the *socially optimal* allocation (the one with maximal total bundle value) is reached each time: the agents (more or less) "realize" that they need not compete. The agents do "hedge their bets" and still keep bidding for resources r_1, r_2 and r_3. They also offer fairly high bids for the nonconflicting resources, though these bids are reduced over time.

This first example shows that optimal allocations will emerge when agents are not in direct competition. It also illustrates general behavioral phenomenon that occur in almost all examples. (1) Agents tend to bid more aggressively (initially) for resources in bundles with smaller size, since the odds of getting all resources in a larger bundle are lower. (2) Agents tend to bid more aggressively for resources that occur later in the sequence. Once an agent obtains all resources in a bundle but one, the last resource is very valuable (for example, in round 16 above, a_1 obtains b_2^1 by paying 1 for r_4 and r_5, and 27 for r_6). (3) Agents tend to initially offer high bids for certain resources, and gradually lower their bids over time (realizing slowly that there is no competition). For example, a_1 reduces its bid for r_6 to 26 only at round 36. This is a consequence of the simple priors and belief update rules we use, and the lack of information it obtains when it wins the resource consistently: it is not told what the next highest bid is (it is zero), and can only conclude that it was less than 27, making belief update slow. The equivalent sample size of our priors also makes adjustment somewhat slow. Domain-specific (more accurate) priors, and the use of exponential decay (or finite histories) in price-estimation would alleviate much of this slowness of response.

Example There are 25 resources and five agents with four bundles each (with an average of four resources per bundle). There exists an allocation of five disjoint bundles, one to each agent. For each agent three of the resources occur only in its bundles, so the agents are competing for only 10 of the 25 resources. The socially optimal allocation has value 100. Over fifty rounds, the agents generally find very good (but not optimal) allocations. Figure 1 shows the value of the allocations obtained at each round,

---

[13] More realistic priors could reflect perceived demand.

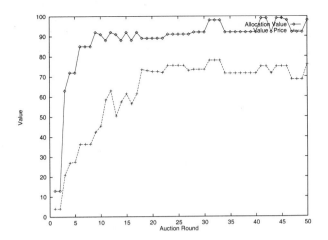

Figure 1: Behavior over 50 Auction Rounds: 5 agents with disjoint bundles (optimal allocation has value 100).

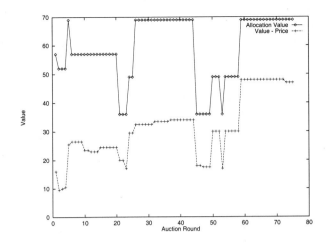

Figure 2: Sample Behavior over 75 Auction Rounds: 5 agents (optimal allocation has value 69)

as well as the collective "surplus" (total value minus α-adjusted prices paid). The agents quickly find good allocations (by the ninth round, no allocation has value less than 88), and also learn to pay less for the resources.

Example An interesting phenomenon emerges in a two-agent example of [21] that has no price equilibrium: assume resources r_1, r_2, with a_1 valuing bundle $\{r_1, r_2\}$ at 6, and a_2 valuing either of r_1, r_2 at 4. The agents have equal endowments. Though there is no price equilibrium, in our adaptive protocol a_2 wins one of its bundles much more frequently than a_1. It bids for r_1, and if it wins it need not bid for r_2; if it loses it can outbid a_1 for r_2 (since a_1 has paid for r_1). a_2 experiments with r_1 and wins it occasionally. a_2 gradually lowers its bid for r_2 and, since it does not model correlations in prices, occasionally loses r_2, allowing a_1 to get both r_1 and r_2. When this occurs, a_2 will quickly raise its bids and win one of the resources again. By modeling price correlations, or estimating the requirements of a_1, agent a_2 *could* guarantee that it obtains one of its resources (see Section 6).

Example We have 3 resources and 2 agents, each valuing $\{r_1, r_2\}$ at 10 and r_3 at 5, but differing in initial endowment: a_1 begins with 6, a_2 with 8. Initially, a_1 gets the first (higher-valued) bundle (at prices 2 and 5) and a_2 the second (at price 3). By the fourth round, a_2 realizes that it can win r_1 with bids of 3 and 5. It spends 8 on $\{r_1, r_2\}$, leaving a_1 to bid 4 for r_3. These prices persist, with a_2 not bidding on r_3 and a_2 eventually not bidding on r_1 or r_2. This illustrates that agents with larger endowments (or less relative value for money compared to bundles) have greater odds of obtaining their most important bundles, leaving "poorer" agents to get what is left.[14]

---

[14] This last property is useful for teams if agents with higher priority objectives are given larger endowments.

We also studied the bidding behavior on randomly generated allocation problems. Here we describe two sets of experiments. In problem set Ps1, five allocation problems were randomly generated with the following characteristics: four agents are competing for 12 resources with an initial endowment of 30 each; each agent has a random number of needed bundles (normally distributed with mean 4 and s.d. 1); each bundle contains a random number of resources (normally distributed with mean 3 and s.d. 1, where the resources are themselves drawn uniformly from the set of 12); and the value of each bundle is random (normally distributed with mean 16 and s.d. 3). Problem set Ps2 is identical except there are five agents and the mean number of resources per bundles is 4: hence problems in Ps2 are more constrained, with more competition among the agents.

Typical behavior for one trial from Ps2 (the more constrained problem set) is shown in Figure 2, which plots the the value of the allocations obtained at each round, as well as the collective surplus. The agents find good allocations in this problem, reaching the (socially) optimal allocation (with value 69) at many of the rounds. On average, over the 75 rounds, the allocation obtained has value 59 (85% of optimal). Note that once the agents "find" a good allocation, they may not stick with it—generally such allocations are not in equilibrium in the sequential game induced by a round of auctions. At the very least, agents have a tendency to attempt to lower the prices they bid after consistently winning a good, due to the lack of information about what other agents bid and how they update their beliefs (as mentioned above). This itself can cause some instability. The greater cause of instability however is the fact that a socially optimal allocation does not generally make self-interested agents happy.

Other trials illustrate similar qualitative behavior. When comparing Ps1 (the less constrained problem set) to Ps2 (the more constrained), we find that the allocations in Ps1 have value that is, on average, within 87% of the optimal, while with Ps2, allocations are within 80% of optimal. This suggests that for less constrained problems, sequential auctions among self-interested agents can lead to allocations with higher social welfare value. Given that agents "discover" many different allocations, one might view sequential auctions as a heuristic search mechanism for combinatorial auctions.[15] However, we emphasize that the main goal of our model is to compute bidding policies when combinatorial and simultaneous auctions are not possible.

6 Concluding Remarks

We have described a model for sequential auctioning of resources that exhibit complementarities for different agents and described a dynamic programming algorithm for the computation of optimal bidding policies. We have also illustrated how price learning can be used to allow agents to adapt there bidding policies to those of other agents. The sequential model can be applied in settings where combinatorial and simultaneous models are infeasible (e.g., when agents enter or leave markets over time, or when agents require resources from multiple sellers). Preliminary results are encouraging and suggest that desirable behavior often emerges.

We have suggested several possible extensions of the model, some of which we are currently exploring. These include developing continuous bidding models, models with reselling/return, incorporating correlated bid distributions and exploring the interactions between decision theoretic planning and bidding for the resources needed to implement plans and policies.

There are several more immediate directions we hope to pursue. One is the investigation of models where prices are estimated with greater weight placed on more recent prices. Along with correlated price distributions, the use of limited "opponent" models may be helpful: by identifying which agents tend to need which resources, a bidder can make more informed decisions. Additional revealed information about specific auctions (such as who bid what amount) could also lead to more informed decisions. This information may be appropriate in team situations, where distributed decision makers are not directly in competition.

Apart from such myopic mechanisms, we would also like to develop a Bayes-Nash equilibrium formulation of the sequential model, and study the extent to which myopic models like our simple learning scheme approximate it. The conditions under which our model converges to interesting allocations (socially optimal allocations, equilibria, etc.) is also worthy of exploration. Other avenues to be considered are the development of different auction ordering heuristics to maximize social welfare, seller's revenue or other objective criteria; and the development of generalization methods to speed up dynamic programming. We are also integrating the sequential auction model for resource allocation into the general planning context described in Section 1.

Acknowledgments Craig Boutilier and Moisés Goldszmidt acknowledge partial support from the DARPA Co-ABS program (through Stanford University contract F30602-98-C-0214). Bikash Sabata was funded by DARPA through the SPAWARSYSCEN under Contract Number N66001-97-C-8525. Craig Boutilier was partially supported by NSERC Research Grant OGP0121843. Thanks to Bill Walsh, Piero La Mura, Tuomas Sandholm, Yoav Shoham and Mike Wellman for their helpful comments, suggestions and pointers to relevant literature.

References

[1] S. Bikhchandani and J. W. Mamer. Competitive equilibria in and exchange economy with indivisibilities. *J. Econ. Theory*, 74:385–413, 1997.

[2] C. Boutilier, T. Dean, and S. Hanks. Decision theoretic planning: Structural assumptions and computational leverage. *J. Artif. Intel. Res.*, 1999. To appear.

[3] C. Boutilier, M. Goldszmidt, and B. Sabata. Continuous value function approximation for sequential bidding policies. manuscript, 1999.

[4] G. W. Brown. Iterative solution of games by fictitious play. T. C. Koopmans, ed., *Activity Analysis of Production and Allocation*. Wiley, New York, 1951.

[5] S. Clearwater, ed. *Market-based Control: A Paradigm for Distributed Resource Allocation*. World Scientific, San Mateo, 1995.

[6] M. H. Degroot. *Probability and Statistics*. Addison-Wesley, New York, 1986.

[7] A. P. Dempster, N. M. Laird and D. B. Rubin Maximum likelihood from incomplete data via the EM algorithm. *J. Roy. Stat. Soc.*, B-39:1–39, 1977.

[8] R. Engelbrecht-Wiggans and R. J. Weber. A sequential auction involving assymetrically informed bidders. *Intl. J. Game Theory*, 12:123–127, 1983.

[9] Y. Fujisima, K. Leyton-Brown, and Y. Shoham. Taming the computational complexity of combinatorial auctions. *IJCAI-99*, Stockholm, 1999. To appear.

[10] D. B. Hausch. Multi-object auctions: Sequential vs. simultaneous sales. *Mgmt. Sci.*, 32(12):1599–1610, 1986.

[11] S. Hon-Snir, D. Monderer, and A. Sela. A learning approach to auctions. *J. Econ. Theory*, 82(1):65–88, 1998.

[12] J. Hu and M. P. Wellman. Online learning about other agents in a dynamic multiagent system. *2nd Intl. Conf. Auton. Agents*, Minneapolis, 1998.

[13] R. P. McAfee and J. McMillan. Auctions and bidding. *J. Econ. Lit.*, 25:699–738, 1987.

[14] R. B. Myerson. *Game Theory: Analysis of Conflict*. Harvard, 1991.

[15] M. L. Puterman. *Markov Decision Processes*. Wiley, 1994.

[16] S. J. Rassenti, V. L. Smith, and R. L. Bulfin. A combinatorial auction mechanism for airport time slot allocation. *Bell J. Econ.*, 13:402–417, 1982.

[17] M. H. Rothkopf. Bidding in simultaneous auctions with a constraint on exposure. *Operations Research*, 25:620–629, 1977.

[18] M. H. Rothkopf, A. Pekeč, and R. M. Harstad. Computationally manageable combinatorial auctions. *Mgmt. Sci.*, 1998. To appear.

[19] T. Sandholm. An algorithm for optimal winner determination in combinatorial auctions. *Proc. of IJCAI-99*, Stockholm, 1999. To appear.

[20] W. Vickrey. Counterspeculation, auctions, and competitive sealed tenders. *J. Finance*, 16(1):8–37, 1961.

[21] M. P. Wellman, W. E. Walsh, P. R. Wurman, and J. K. MacKie-Mason. Auction protocols for decentralized scheduling. (manuscript), 1998.

---

[15] This is reminiscent of the mechanism suggested in [9].

Algorithms for Optimizing Leveled Commitment Contracts*

Tuomas Sandholm, Sandeep Sikka, and Samphel Norden
{sandholm,sikka,samphel}@cs.wustl.edu
Department of Computer Science
Washington University
St. Louis, MO 63130-4899

Abstract

In automated negotiation systems consisting of self-interested agents, contracts have traditionally been binding. Leveled commitment contracts—i.e. contracts where each party can decommit by paying a predetermined penalty—were recently shown to improve Pareto efficiency even if agents rationally decommit in Nash equilibrium using inflated thresholds on how good their outside offers must be before they decommit. This paper operationalizes the four leveled commitment contracting protocols by presenting algorithms for using them. Algorithms are presented for computing the Nash equilibrium decommitting thresholds and decommitting probabilities given the contract price and the penalties. Existence and uniqueness of the equilibrium are analyzed. Algorithms are also presented for optimizing the contract itself (price and penalties). Existence and uniqueness of the optimum are analyzed. Using the algorithms we offer a contract optimization service on the web as part of *eMediator*, our next generation electronic commerce server. Finally, the algorithms are generalized to contracts involving more than two agents.

1 Introduction

In multiagent systems consisting of self-interested agents, contracts have traditionally been binding [Rosenschein and Zlotkin, 1994; Sandholm, 1993; Kraus, 1993]. Once an agent agrees to a contract, she has to follow through no matter how future events unravel. Although a contract may be profitable to an agent when viewed *ex ante*, it need not be profitable when viewed after some future events have occurred, i.e. *ex post*. Similarly, a contract may have too low expected payoff *ex ante*, but in some realizations of the future events, it may be desirable when viewed *ex post*. Normal full commitment contracts are unable to take advantage of the possibilities that such future events provide.

On the other hand, many multiagent systems consisting of cooperative agents incorporate some form of decommitment in order to allow agents to accommodate new events. For example, in the original Contract Net Protocol [Smith, 1980], the agent that contracts out a task could send a termination message to cancel the contract even when the contractee had partially fulfilled it. This was possible because the agents were not self-interested: the contractee did not mind losing part of its effort without a monetary compensation. Similarly, the role of decommitment among cooperative agents has been studied in meeting scheduling [Sen, 1993].

Contingency contracts have been suggested for utilizing the potential provided by future events among self-interested agents [Raiffa, 1982]. The contract obligations are made contingent on future events. In some games this increases the expected payoff to both parties compared to any full commitment contract. However, contingency contracts are often impractical because the space of combinations of future events may be large and unknown. Also, when events are not mutually observable, the observing agent can lie about what transpired.

Leveled commitment contracts are another method for capitalizing on future events [Sandholm and Lesser, 1996]. Instead of conditioning the contract on future events, a mechanism is built into the contract that allows unilateral decommitting. This is achieved by specifying in the contract the level of commitment by decommitment penalties, one for each agent.[1] If an agent wants to decommit—i.e. to be freed from the obligations of the contract—it can do so simply by paying the decommitment penalty to the other party. The method requires no explicit conditioning on future events: each agent can do her own conditioning dynamically. No event verification mechanism against lying is required either.

Principles for assessing decommitment penalties have been studied in law [Calamari and Perillo, 1977; Posner, 1977], but the purpose has been to assess a penalty on the agent that has breached the contract *after the breach has occurred*. Similarly, penalty clauses for partial failure—such as not meeting a deadline—are commonly used in contracts, but the purpose is usually to motivate the agents to follow the contract. Instead, in leveled commitment contracts, explicitly allowing decommitment from the contract for a predetermined price is used as an active method for utilizing the potential provided by an uncertain future.[2] The decommitment possibility increases each agent's expected payoff under very

---

*This material is based upon work supported by the National Science Foundation under CAREER Award IRI-9703122, Grant IRI-9610122, and Grant IIS-9800994.

[1][Sandholm and Lesser, 1995] present an example protocol that uses this feature.

[2]Decommitting has been studied in other settings, e.g. where

general assumptions [Sandholm and Lesser, 1996].

We analyze contracting situations from the perspective of two risk neutral agents each of which attempts to maximize his own expected payoff: the *contractor* who pays to get a task done, and the *contractee* who gets paid for handling the task. Handling a task can mean taking on any types of constraints. The method is not specific to classical task allocation. The contractor tries to minimize the contract price ρ that he has to pay. The contractee tries to maximize the payoff ρ that she receives.

We study a setting where the future of the agents involves uncertainty. Specifically, the agents might receive outside offers.[3] The contractor's best outside offer $\breve{a}$ is only probabilistically known *ex ante* by both agents, and is characterized by a probability density function $f(\breve{a})$. If the contractor does not receive an outside offer, $\breve{a}$ corresponds to its best outstanding outside offer or its fallback payoff, i.e. payoff that it receives if no contract is made. The contractee's best outside offer $\breve{b}$ is also only probabilistically known *ex ante*, and is characterized by a probability density function $g(\breve{b})$. If the contractee does not receive an outside offer, $\breve{b}$ corresponds to its best outstanding outside offer or its fall-back payoff.[4] The variables $\breve{a}$ and $\breve{b}$ are assumed statistically independent.

The contractor's options are either to make a contract with the contractee or to wait for $\breve{a}$. Similarly, the contractee's options are either to make a contract with the contractor or to wait for $\breve{b}$. The two agents could make a full commitment contract at some price. Alternatively, they can make a leveled commitment contract which is specified by the contract price, ρ, the contractor's decommitment penalty, a, and the contractee's decommitment penalty, b. We restrict our attention to contracts where $a \geq 0$ and $b \geq 0$, i.e. agents do not get paid for decommitting. The contractor has to decide on decommitting when he knows his outside offer $\breve{a}$ but does not know the contractee's outside offer $\breve{b}$. Similarly, the contractee has to decide on decommitting when she knows her outside offer $\breve{b}$ but does not know the contractor's. This seems realistic from a practical automated contracting perspective.

The theory of these leveled commitment protocols was presented by [Sandholm and Lesser, 1996], but to date no algorithms have been presented for agents to compute when they should decommit given a contract, or for agents to choose beneficial contracts. This paper operationalizes leveled commitment contracts by presenting an algorithm for computing how the agents should de-

commit (Section 2), and an algorithm for constructing the optimal leveled commitment contract for any given setting defined by $f(\breve{a})$ and $g(\breve{b})$ (Section 3).

2 Nash equilibria for a given contract

One concern is that a rational agent is reluctant in decommitting because there is a chance that the other party will decommit, in which case the former agent gets freed from the contract, does not have to pay a penalty, and collects a penalty from the breacher. [Sandholm and Lesser, 1996] showed that despite such insincere decommitting the leveled commitment feature increases each contract party's expected payoff, and enables contracts in settings where no full commitment contract is beneficial to all parties. To set the context, we first review their analysis of how rational agents would decommit, i.e. we derive the Nash equilibrium (NE) [Nash, 1950] of the decommitting game where each agent's decommitting strategy is a best response to the other agent's decommitting strategy. The new contributions begin in Section 2.3.

The contractor decommits if he gets a low enough outside offer, e.g., he can get his task handled at a low cost. We denote his decommitting threshold by $\breve{a}^*$, so his decommitting probability is

$$p_a = \int_{-\infty}^{\breve{a}^*} f(\breve{a}) da \qquad (1)$$

The contractee decommits if she gets a high enough outside offer, e.g., gets paid for handling a task. We denote her decommitting threshold by $\breve{b}^*$, so her decommitting probability is

$$p_b = \int_{\breve{b}^*}^{\infty} g(\breve{b}) db \qquad (2)$$

2.1 Sequential decommitting (SEQD) game

In our sequential decommitting (SEQD) game, one agent has to reveal her decommitting decision before knowing whether the other party decommits. While our implementation analyzes both orders of decommitting, due to space limitations we only discuss the setting where the contractee has to decide first. The case where the contractor decides first is analogous. There are two alternative leveled commitment contracts that differ on whether or not the agents have to pay the penalties if both decommit.

If the contractee has decommitted, the contractor's best move is not to decommit because $-\breve{a} - a + b \leq -\breve{a} + b$ (because $a \geq 0$). This also holds for a contract where neither agent has to pay a decommitment penalty if both decommit since $-\breve{a} \leq -\breve{a} + b$. In the subgame where the contractee has not decommitted, the contractor's best move is to decommit if $-\breve{a} - a > -\rho$, i.e.

$$\breve{a}^* = \rho - a \qquad (3a)$$

The contractee gets $\breve{b} - b$ if she decommits, $\breve{b} + a$ if she does not but the contractor does, and ρ if neither decommits. Thus the contractee decommits if $\breve{b} - b > p_a(\breve{b} + a) + (1 - p_a)\rho$. If $p_a = 1$, this is equivalent to $-b > a$ which is false because $a \geq 0$ and $b \geq 0$. In other words, if the contractee surely decommits, the contractor does not. On the other hand, the above is equivalent to

there is a constant inflow of agents, and they have a time cost for searching partners of two types: good or bad [Diamond and Maskin, 1979].

[3] The framework can also be interpreted to model situations where the agents' cost structures for handling tasks and for getting tasks handled change e.g. due to resources going off-line or becoming back on-line.

[4] Games where at least one agent's future is certain, are a subset of these games. In such games all of the probability mass of $f(\breve{a})$ and/or $g(\breve{b})$ is on one point.

$$\check{b} > \rho + \frac{b + ap_a}{1 - p_a} \stackrel{\text{def}}{=} \check{b}^* \quad \text{when } p_a < 1 \tag{4a}$$

2.2 Simultaneous decommitting games

In our simultaneous decommitting games, agents have to reveal their decommitment decisions simultaneously. We first discuss the variant (SIMUDBP) where both have to pay the penalties if both decommit. The contractor decommits if $p_b \cdot (-\check{a} + b - a) + (1 - p_b)(-\check{a} - a) > p_b \cdot (-\check{a} + b) + (1 - p_b)(-\rho)$. If $p_b = 1$, this equates to $a < 0$, but we already ruled out contracts where an agent gets paid for decommitting. On the other hand, this equates to

$$\check{a} < \rho - \frac{a}{1 - p_b} \stackrel{\text{def}}{=} \check{a}^* \quad \text{when } p_b < 1 \tag{3b}$$

The contractee decommits if $(1 - p_a)(\check{b} - b) + p_a(\check{b} - b + a) > (1 - p_a)\rho + p_a(\check{b} + a)$. If $p_a = 1$, this equates to $b < 0$, but we ruled out contracts where an agent gets paid for decommitting. However, this equates to

$$\check{b} > \rho + \frac{b}{1 - p_a} \stackrel{\text{def}}{=} \check{b}^* \quad \text{when } p_a < 1 \tag{4b}$$

In a SIMUDNP game, neither agent has to pay if both decommit. The contractor decommits if $p_b \cdot (-\check{a}) + (1 - p_b)(-\check{a} - a) > p_b \cdot (-\check{a} + b) + (1 - p_b)(-\rho)$. If $p_b = 1$, this equates to $b < 0$, but we already ruled out contracts where an agent gets paid for decommitting. On the other hand, this equates to

$$\check{a} < \rho - a - \frac{bp_b}{1 - p_b} \stackrel{\text{def}}{=} \check{a}^* \quad \text{when } p_b < 1 \tag{3c}$$

The contractee decommits if $(1 - p_a)(\check{b} - b) + p_a\check{b} > (1 - p_a)\rho + p_a(\check{b} + a)$. If $p_a = 1$, this equates to $a < 0$, but we ruled out contracts where an agent gets paid for decommitting. However, this equates to

$$\check{b} > \rho + b - \frac{ap_a}{1 - p_a} \stackrel{\text{def}}{=} \check{b}^* \quad \text{when } p_a < 1 \tag{4c}$$

For each game, calculating the Nash equilibria amounts to solving the simultaneous equations (3) and (4) which use (1) and (2).

2.3 Existence of a Nash equilibrium

We now discuss existence of the NE. Denote the support of $f(\check{a})$ by $[\check{a}_1, \check{a}_n]$, and the support of $g(\check{b})$ by $[\check{b}_1, \check{b}_m]$.

Proposition 2.1
SEQD: *A NE exists if $\check{a}_1 \le \rho - a \le \check{a}_n$. No NE exists if $\rho - a > \check{a}_n$. Only a trivial NE with $p_a = 0$ exists if $\rho - a < \check{a}_1$.*
SIMUDBP: *A NE exists if $\rho - a \ge \check{a}_n$ and $\rho + b \le \check{b}_1$. Only a trivial NE with $p_a = 0$ exists if $\rho - a < \check{a}_1$ and $\rho + b > \check{b}_1$. Only a trivial NE with $p_b = 0$ exists if $\rho + b > \check{b}_m$ and $\rho - a < \check{a}_n$. Otherwise a NE may or may not exist.*
SIMUDNP: *A NE exists if $\rho - a \ge \check{a}_n$ and $\rho + b \ge \check{b}_m$. Only a trivial NE with $p_a = 0$ exists if $\rho - a < \check{a}_1$ and $\rho + b > \check{b}_1$. Only a trivial NE with $p_a = 0$ and $p_b = 0$ exists if $\rho - a < \check{a}_1$ and $\rho + b > \check{b}_m$. No NE exists if $\rho + b < \check{b}_1$. Otherwise a NE may or may not exist.*
Proof. For each of the three games, the curves defined by (3) and (4) are continuous.
SEQD: From (3a): $\check{a}^* = \rho - a$. For (4a), when $\check{a}^* = \check{a}_1, \check{b}^* = \rho + b$ and in the limit $\check{a}^* \to \check{a}_n, \check{b}^* \to \infty$. Thus

the curves intersect if $\check{a}_1 \le \rho - a \le \check{a}_n$. For (4a) if $\rho - a < \check{a}_1$ then $\check{b}^* = \rho + b$, and so (3a) intersects with (4a) such that $p_a = 0$. For $\rho - a > \check{a}_n$ (3a) and (4a) do not intersect.
SIMUDBP: For (3b), in the limit $\check{b}^* \to \check{b}_1, \check{a}^* \to -\infty$ and when $\check{b}^* = \check{b}_m, \check{a}^* = \rho - a$. For (4b), when $\check{a}^* = \check{a}_1, \check{b}^* = \rho + b$ and in the limit $\check{a}^* \to \check{a}_n, \check{b}^* \to \infty$. Thus the curves intersect if $\rho - a \ge \check{a}_n$ and $\rho + b \le \check{b}_1$. For (4b) if $\check{a}^* < \check{a}_1$ then $\check{b}^* = \rho + b$, and so the two curves will intersect with $p_a = 0$ if $\rho + b > \check{b}_1$. Similarly for (3b) if $\check{b}^* > \check{b}_m$ then $\check{a}^* = \rho - a$, and so the two curves will intersect with $p_b = 0$ if $\rho - a < \check{a}_n$. Otherwise they may or may not intersect.
SIMUDNP: For (3c), in the limit $\check{b}^* \to \check{b}_1, \check{a}^* \to -\infty$ and when $\check{b}^* = \check{b}_m, \check{a}^* = \rho - a$. For (4c), when $\check{a}^* = \check{a}_1, \check{b}^* = \rho + b$ and in the limit $\check{a}^* \to \check{a}_n, \check{b}^* \to -\infty$. Thus the curves intersect if $\rho - a \ge \check{a}_n$ and $\rho + b \ge \check{b}_m$. For (4c) if $\check{a}^* < \check{a}_1$ then $\check{b}^* = \rho + b$, and so the two curves intersect with $p_a = 0$ if $\rho + b > \check{b}_1$. Further if $\rho + b > \check{b}_m$ then p_b also equals 0. The curves do not intersect if $\rho + b \le \check{b}_1$. Otherwise they may or may not intersect. □

2.4 Uniqueness of the Nash equilibrium

We now consider uniqueness of the Nash equilibrium.
Proposition 2.2 *For the sequential games, the NE is unique. For the simultaneous games the NE need not be unique.*
Proof. For the sequential games, uniqueness follows from the forms of (3) and (4): One threshold is expressed as a function of ρ and a penalty, and the other is defined as a function of this threshold. Fig. 1 shows an example where multiple equilibria exist for a SIMUDBP game. We constructed a similar example for SIMUDNP. □

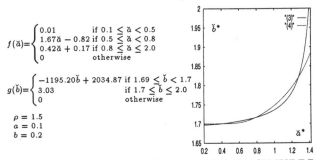

$$f(\check{a}) = \begin{cases} 0.01 & \text{if } 0.1 \le \check{a} < 0.5 \\ 1.67\check{a} - 0.82 & \text{if } 0.5 \le \check{a} < 0.8 \\ 0.42\check{a} + 0.17 & \text{if } 0.8 \le \check{a} \le 2.0 \\ 0 & \text{otherwise} \end{cases}$$

$$g(\check{b}) = \begin{cases} -1195.20\check{b} + 2034.87 & \text{if } 1.69 \le \check{b} < 1.7 \\ 3.03 & \text{if } 1.7 \le \check{b} \le 2.0 \\ 0 & \text{otherwise} \end{cases}$$

$\rho = 1.5$
$a = 0.1$
$b = 0.2$

Figure 1: Example with 3 Nash equilibria for SIMUDBP.

2.5 Algorithm for finding the Nash equilibria

We now discuss the algorithm for computing the Nash equilibria. We assume that the probability density functions $f(\check{a})$ and $g(\check{b})$ are piecewise linear with n and m pieces respectively. This is reasonable since any continuous function can be approximated arbitrarily closely by a piecewise linear curve, and piecewise linear curves are easy for the user to input.

The algorithm for computing the equilibrium of a sequential game is straightforward. It simply substitutes the contract parameters (ρ, a, b) into (3) and (4).

In the simultaneous games this substitution gives a system of two nonlinear simultaneous equations. These equations may have multiple solutions and all of them need to be found. This rules out iterative procedures that only find one solution. That motivated us to design a fast analytic algorithm that finds all solutions. We decompose the search space into rectangles. Since $f(\breve{a})$ and $g(\breve{b})$ are piecewise linear, the simultaneous equations can be solved analytically within each rectangle. The rectangles are $[\breve{a}_i, \breve{a}_{i+1}] \times [\breve{b}_j, \breve{b}_{j+1}]$ where $1 \leq i < n$ and $1 \leq j < m$, i.e. the boundaries are the end points of each linear segment of f and g. Within each rectangle, the algorithm

1. Solves (1) and (2) to get $p_a(\breve{a}*)$ and $p_b(\breve{b}*)$. These functions are quadratic because $f(\breve{a})$ and $g(\breve{b})$ are linear within the rectangle.
2. Substitutes $p_a(\breve{a}*)$ into (4), and $p_b(\breve{b}*)$ into (3).
3. Substitutes $\breve{a}^*$ from (3) into (4).
4. Reduces the resulting equation to a cubic polynomial in $\breve{b}^*$.
5. Solves for the roots of this polynomial.
6. Calculates the corresponding values for $\breve{a}^*$ using (3).
7. Accepts the solutions that lie within the rectangle.

The algorithm runs in $O(nm)$ time because it is $O(1)$ within each rectangle, and there are $O(nm)$ rectangles.

Of all the equilibria found, it presents social welfare maximizing one(s) to the user, i.e. the one(s) that maximize the sum of the agents' expected payoffs. It can also present all equilibria.

3 Optimizing the contract

So far we discussed how rational agents would decommit under a given contract. Now we take this further by optimizing the contract itself—taking into account that agents will decommit insincerely in Nash equilibrium. Specifically, we present an algorithm and analysis for finding the optimal contract price and decommitment penalties in any given setting for all three protocols.

3.1 Analysis

We first describe the optimization problem. Let π_a be the contractor's expected utility, and π_b the contractee's. For shorthand, we define T_1, T_2, T_3, and T_4:
$T_1 = \int_{\breve{b}^*}^{\infty} g(\breve{b})db$, $T_2 = \int_{\breve{b}^*}^{\infty} bg(\breve{b})db$
$T_3 = \int_{\breve{a}^*}^{\infty} f(\breve{a})da$, $T_4 = \int_{\breve{a}^*}^{\infty} af(\breve{a})da$
We now derive π_a and π_b for each of the games.

SEQD:

$$\pi_a = \int_{\breve{b}^*(\rho,a,b)}^{\infty} g(\breve{b}) \int_{-\infty}^{\infty} f(\breve{a})[-\breve{a}+b]d\breve{a}d\breve{b}$$
$$+ \int_{-\infty}^{\breve{b}^*(\rho,a,b)} g(\breve{b})[\int_{-\infty}^{\rho-a} f(\breve{a})[-\breve{a}-a]d\breve{a} + \int_{\rho-a}^{\infty} f(\breve{a})[-\rho]d\breve{a}]d\breve{b}$$
$$= \breve{b}^*T_3T_1 - E[\breve{a}] + T_4 - T_1T_4 - \breve{a}^*T_3 + \breve{a}^* - \rho$$

$$\pi_b = \int_{\breve{b}^*(\rho,a,b)}^{\infty} g(\breve{b})[\breve{b}-b]d\breve{b} + \int_{-\infty}^{\breve{b}^*(\rho,a,b)} g(\breve{b})[\int_{-\infty}^{\rho-a} f(\breve{a})[\breve{b}+a]d\breve{a} + \int_{\rho-a}^{\infty} f(\breve{a})\rho d\breve{a}]d\breve{b}$$
$$= -\breve{b}^*T_3T_1 - E[\breve{b}](1-T_3) + T_2T_3 + \breve{a}^*T_3 - \breve{a}^* + \rho$$

SIMUDBP:

$$\pi_a = \int_{\breve{b}^*(\rho,a,b,\breve{b}^*)}^{\infty} g(\breve{b})[\int_{-\infty}^{\breve{a}^*(\rho,a,b,\breve{b}^*)} f(\breve{a})[-\breve{a}+b-a]d\breve{a} + \int_{\breve{a}^*(\rho,a,b,\breve{b}^*)}^{\infty} f(\breve{a})[-\breve{a}+b]d\breve{a}]d\breve{b}$$
$$+ \int_{-\infty}^{\breve{b}^*(\rho,a,b,\breve{a}^*)} g(\breve{b})[\int_{-\infty}^{\breve{a}^*(\rho,a,b,\breve{b}^*)} f(\breve{a})[-\breve{a}-a]d\breve{a} + \int_{\breve{a}^*(\rho,a,b,\breve{b}^*)}^{\infty} f(\breve{a})[-\rho]d\breve{a}]d\breve{b}$$
$$= -E[\breve{a}] + \breve{b}^*T_1T_3 + \breve{a}^*(1-T_1)(1-T_3) + T_4(1-T_1)$$
$$-\rho(1-T_3+T_1T_3)$$

$$\pi_b = \int_{\breve{b}^*(\rho,a,b,\breve{a}^*)}^{\infty} g(\breve{b})[\int_{-\infty}^{\breve{a}^*(\rho,a,b,\breve{b}^*)} f(\breve{a})[\breve{b}-b+a]d\breve{a} + \int_{\breve{a}^*(\rho,a,b,\breve{b}^*)}^{\infty} f(\breve{a})[\breve{b}-b]d\breve{a}]d\breve{b}$$
$$+ \int_{-\infty}^{\breve{b}^*(\rho,a,b,\breve{a}^*)} g(\breve{b})[\int_{-\infty}^{\breve{a}^*(\rho,a,b,\breve{b}^*)} f(\breve{a})[\breve{b}+a]d\breve{a} + \int_{\breve{a}^*(\rho,a,b,\breve{b}^*)}^{\infty} f(\breve{a})[\rho]d\breve{a}]d\breve{b}$$
$$= E[\breve{b}](1-T_3) - \breve{b}^*T_1T_3 - \breve{a}^*(1-T_1)(1-T_3) + T_3T_2$$
$$+\rho(1-T_3+T_1T_3)$$

SIMUDNP:

$$\pi_a = \int_{\breve{b}^*(\rho,a,b,\breve{a}^*)}^{\infty} g(\breve{b})[\int_{-\infty}^{\breve{a}^*(\rho,a,b,\breve{b}^*)} f(\breve{a})[-\breve{a}]d\breve{a} + \int_{\breve{a}^*(\rho,a,b,\breve{b}^*)}^{\infty} f(\breve{a})[-\breve{a}+b]d\breve{a}]d\breve{b}$$
$$+ \int_{-\infty}^{\breve{b}^*(\rho,a,b,\breve{a}^*)} g(\breve{b})[\int_{-\infty}^{\breve{a}^*(\rho,a,b,\breve{b}^*)} f(\breve{a})[-\breve{a}-a]d\breve{a} + \int_{\breve{a}^*(\rho,a,b,\breve{b}^*)}^{\infty} f(\breve{a})[-\rho]d\breve{a}]d\breve{b}$$
$$= -E[\breve{a}] + T_4(1-T_1) + a(-1+T_1+T_3-T_1T_3) + bT_1T_3$$
$$-\rho(1-T_1)T_3$$

$$\pi_b = \int_{\breve{b}^*(\rho,a,b,\breve{a}^*)}^{\infty} g(\breve{b})[\int_{-\infty}^{\breve{a}^*(\rho,a,b,\breve{b}^*)} f(\breve{a})[\breve{b}]d\breve{a} + \int_{\breve{a}^*(\rho,a,b,\breve{b}^*)}^{\infty} f(\breve{a})[\breve{b}-b]d\breve{a}]d\breve{b}$$
$$+ \int_{-\infty}^{\breve{b}^*(\rho,a,b,\breve{a}^*)} g(\breve{b})[\int_{-\infty}^{\breve{a}^*(\rho,a,b,\breve{b}^*)} f(\breve{a})[\breve{b}+a]d\breve{a} + \int_{\breve{a}^*(\rho,a,b,\breve{b}^*)}^{\infty} f(\breve{a})[\rho]d\breve{a}]d\breve{b}$$
$$= E[\breve{b}](1-T_3) + T_2T_3 - a(-1+T_1+T_3-T_1T_3) - bT_1T_3$$
$$+\rho(1-T_1)T_3$$

For each of the three protocols the social welfare, π, is

$$\pi = \pi_a + \pi_b = -E[\breve{a}] + E[\breve{b}](1-T_3) + T_2T_3 + T_4 - T_1T_4$$

We define the optimal contract to be the contract that maximizes social welfare, i.e. $max_{(\rho,a,b)}\pi$. The expression above shows that π is the same for all three games. Also, π is a function of $(\breve{a}^*, \breve{b}^*)$. So, the original problem of optimizing over a 3-dimensional space (ρ, a, b) reduces to optimizing over a 2-dimensional space $(\breve{a}^*, \breve{b}^*)$.

A rational agent only accepts a contract if it does not decrease his expected payoff. These individual rationality (IR) constraints, $\pi_a \geq E[-\breve{a}]$ and $\pi_b \geq E[\breve{b}]$, define a feasible set in the 3-dimensional space $(\breve{a}^*, \breve{b}^*, \rho)$.

We first derive the unconstrained optima, and then verify that they belong to the feasible set. The necessary conditions for unconstrained optima are: [5]
$\frac{\partial \pi}{\partial \breve{a}^*} = 0 \Leftrightarrow f(\breve{a}^*)(E[\breve{b}] - T_4 - \breve{a}^* + \breve{a}^*T_3) = 0$
$\frac{\partial \pi}{\partial \breve{b}^*} = 0 \Leftrightarrow g(\breve{b}^*)(\breve{b}^*T_1 - T_2) = 0$
These equalities are trivially satisfied if $f(\breve{a}^*) = 0$ or $g(\breve{b}^*) = 0$, i.e. if the optimal decommitting thresholds

---

[5]In deriving the formulas on the right, the derivative of an integral with respect to its limits is calculated using the Leibnitz formula [Arfken and Weber, 1995].

DISTRIBUTED ARTIFICIAL INTELLIGENCE

Economic Models 2:
Auctions

An Algorithm for Optimal Winner Determination in Combinatorial Auctions

Tuomas Sandholm*
sandholm@cs.wustl.edu
Department of Computer Science
Washington University
St. Louis, MO 63130-4899

Abstract

Combinatorial auctions, i.e. auctions where bidders can bid on combinations of items, tend to lead to more efficient allocations than traditional auctions in multi-item auctions where the agents' valuations of the items are not additive. However, determining the winners so as to maximize revenue is $\mathcal{NP}$-complete. We present a search algorithm for optimal winner determination. Experiments are shown on several bid distributions. The algorithm allows combinatorial auctions to scale up to significantly larger numbers of items and bids than prior approaches to optimal winner determination by capitalizing on the fact that the space of bids is necessarily sparsely populated in practice. We do this via provably sufficient selective generation of children in the search and by using a method for fast child generation, heuristics that are accurate and optimized for speed, and four methods for preprocessing the search space.

1 Introduction

Auctions are popular, efficient, and autonomy preserving ways of allocating items among agents. This paper focuses on auctions with multiple items to be allocated.

In a *sequential auction*, the items are auctioned one at a time. If a bidder has preferences over bundles, i.e. combinations of items (as is often the case e.g. in electricity markets, equities trading, bandwidth auctions [McAfee and McMillan, 1996], and transportation exchanges [Sandholm, 1993]), bidding in such auctions is difficult. To determine her valuation for an item, the bidder needs to guess what items she will receive in later auctions. This requires speculation on what the others will bid in the future because that affects what items she will receive. Furthermore, what the others bid in the future depends on what they believe others will bid, etc. This counterspeculation introduces computational cost and other wasteful overhead. Moreover, in auctions with a reasonable number of items, such lookahead in the game tree is intractable, and then there is no known way to bid rationally. Bidding rationally would involve optimally trading off the cost of lookahead against the gains it provides, but that would again depend on how others strike that tradeoff. Furthermore, even if lookahead were computationally manageable, usually uncertainty remains about the others' bids because agents do not have exact information about each other. This often

---

*Patent pending since 10/27/1998.

leads to inefficient allocations where bidders fail to get the combinations they want and get ones they do not.

In a *parallel auction* the items are open for auction simultaneously and bidders may place their bids during a certain time period. This has the advantage that the others' bids partially signal to the bidder what the others' bids will end up being so the uncertainty and the need for lookahead is not as drastic as in a sequential auction. However, the same problems prevail as in sequential auctions, albeit in a mitigated form.

Combinatorial auctions can be used to overcome the need for lookahead and the inefficiencies that stem from the uncertainties [Rassenti *et al.*, 1982, Sandholm, 1993]. In a combinatorial auction bidders may place bids on combinations of items. This allows the bidders to express complementarities between items instead of having to speculate into an item's valuation the impact of possibly getting other, complementary items. For example, the Federal Communications Commission saw the desirability of combinatorial bidding in their bandwidth auctions, but it was not allowed due to perceived intractability of winner determination. This paper focuses on winner determination in combinatorial auctions where each bidder can bid on bundles of indivisible items, and any number of her bids can be accepted.

2 Winner determination

Let M be the set of items to be auctioned, and let $m = |M|$. Then any agent, i, could place any bid $b_i(S)$ for any combination $S \subseteq M$. The relevant bids are:

$$\bar{b}(S) = \max_{i \in \text{ bidders}} b_i(S)$$

Let n be the number of these bids. Winner determination is the following problem, where the goal is to maximize the auctioneer's revenue:

$$\max_{\mathcal{X}} \sum_{S \in \mathcal{X}} \bar{b}(S)$$

where $\mathcal{X}$ is a valid outcome, i.e. an outcome where each item is allocated to only one bidder: $\mathcal{X} = \{S \subseteq M | S \cap S' = \emptyset$ for every $S, S' \in \mathcal{X}\}$.

If each combination S has received at least one bid of positive price, the search space will look like Fig. 1.

Proposition 2.1 *The number of allocations is $O(m^m)$ and $\omega(m^{m/2})$.*

The proof is long, and is presented in [Sandholm, 1999].

The graph can be searched more efficiently than exhaustive enumeration by dynamic programming, which takes $\Omega(2^m)$ and $O(3^m)$ steps [Rothkopf *et al.*, 1998]. This is still too complex to scale up above about 25 items. Also, dynamic programming executes the same

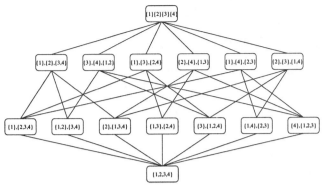

Figure 1: Space of allocations in a 4-item example. Each node represents one possible allocation $\mathcal{X}$.

algorithmic steps regardless of which bids have actually been submitted.

Some combinations of items may not have received any bids, so some of the allocations in the graph need not be considered. Unfortunately no algorithm can find the optimal allocation in polynomial time in n, the number of bids submitted, unless $\mathcal{P} = \mathcal{NP}$:

Proposition 2.2 *Winner determination is $\mathcal{NP}$-complete.*

Proof. Winner determination is weighted set packing, and set packing is $\mathcal{NP}$-complete [Karp, 1972]. □

Even approximate winner determination is hard:

Proposition 2.3 *No polytime algorithm can guarantee an allocation within a bound $\frac{1}{n^{1-\epsilon}}$ from optimum for any $\epsilon > 0$ (unless $\mathcal{NP}$ equals probabilistic polytime).*

The proof is based on [Håstad, 1999], and is presented in the full length version of this paper [Sandholm, 1999].

If the bids exhibit special structure, better approximations can be achieved in polynomial time [Chandra and Halldórsson, 1999, Halldórsson, 1998, Hochbaum, 1983, Halldórsson and Lau, 1997], but even these guarantees are so far from optimum that they are irrelevant for auctions in practice [Sandholm, 1999].

Polynomial time winner determination can be achieved by restricting the combinations on which the agents are allowed to bid [Rothkopf *et al.*, 1998]. However, because the agents may then not be able to bid on the combinations they want, similar economic inefficiencies prevail as in the non-combinatorial auctions.

3 Our optimal search algorithm

The goals of our approach to winner determination are:

- allow bidding on all combinations.
- strive for the optimal allocation.
- completely avoid loops and redundant generation of vertices when searching the allocation graph, Fig. 1.
- capitalize heavily on the sparseness of bids. In practice the space of bids is necessarily extremely sparsely populated. For example, if there are 100 items, there are $2^{100} - 1$ combinations, and it would take longer than the life of the universe to bid on all of them even if every person in the world submitted a bid per second. Sparseness of bids implies sparseness of the allocations $\mathcal{X}$ that need to be checked.

Our algorithm constructively checks each allocation $\mathcal{X}$ that has positive value exactly once, and does not construct the other allocations. Therefore, unlike dynamic programming, the algorithm only generates those parts of the search space which are actually populated by bids. The disadvantage then is that the run time depends on the bids received.

To achieve these goals, we use a search algorithm that generates a tree, Fig. 2. Each path in the tree consists of a sequence of disjoint bids, i.e. bids that do not share items. As a bid is added to the path, the bid price is added to the g-function. A path terminates when all items have been used on that path. At that point the path corresponds to a feasible allocation, and the revenue from that allocation, i.e. the g-value, can be compared to the best one found so far to determine whether the allocation is the best one so far. The best so far is stored, and once the search completes, that allocation is optimal.

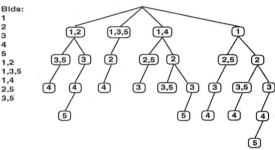

Figure 2: A search tree generated by our algorithm.

The naive method of constructing the search tree would include all bids (that do not include items that are already on the path) as the children of each node. Instead, the following proposition enables a significant reduction of the branching factor by capitalizing on the fact that the order of the bids on a path does not matter.

Proposition 3.1 *Every allocation will be explored exactly once in the tree if the children of a node are those bids that*

- *include the item with the smallest index among the items that are not on the path yet, and*
- *do not include items that are already on the path.*

Proof. We first prove that each allocation is generated at most once. The first bullet leads to the fact that an allocation can only be generated in one order of bids on the path. So, for there to exist more than one path for a given allocation, some bid would have to occur multiple times as a child of some node. However, the algorithm uses each bid as a child for a given node only once.

What remains to be proven is that each allocation is generated. Assume for contradiction that some allocation is not. Then, at some point, there has to be a bid in that allocation such that it is the bid with the item with the smallest index among those not on the path, but that bid is not inserted to the path. Contradiction □

Our search algorithm restricts the children according to the proposition, Fig. 2. This can be seen for example at the first level because all the bids considered at the first level include item 1. The minimal index does not coincide with the depth of the search tree in general.

The auctioneer's revenue can increase if he can keep items. That can be profitable if some item has received no bids on its own. For example, if there is no bid for item 1, a \$5 bid for item 2, and a \$3 bid for the combination of 1 and 2, it is more profitable for the auctioneer to keep 1, and to allocate 2 alone. Such optimization can be implemented by placing dummy bids of price zero on those individual items that received no bids alone, Fig. 2. For example, if item 1 had no bids on it alone and dummies were not used, the tree under 1 would not be explored and optimality could be lost. When dummy bids are used, the resulting search generates each allocation that has positive revenue exactly once (and searches through no other allocations). This guarantees that the algorithm finds the optimal solution. Throughout the rest of the paper, we use this dummy bid technique.

3.1 Optimized generation of children

The main search algorithm uses a secondary depth-first-search (DFS) to quickly determine the children of a node. The secondary search occurs in a data structure which we call the *Bidtree*. It is a binary tree in which the bids are inserted up front as the leaves. Only those parts of the tree are generated for which bids are received, Fig. 3. What makes the data structure special is the use of a

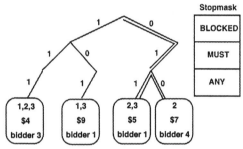

Figure 3: The Bidtree data structure.

Stopmask. The Stopmask is a vector with one variable for each auctioned item. If the variable corresponding to an item has the value BLOCKED, those parts of the Bidtree are pruned instantaneously (and in place) that contain bids containing that item. In other words, search in the Bidtree will never progress left at that level. If the item's variable has the value MUST, all other parts of the Bidtree are pruned instantaneously and in place, i.e. search cannot progress right at that level. The value ANY corresponds to no pruning based on that item: the search may go left or right.

To start, the first item has value MUST in the Stopmask, and the others have ANY. The first child of any given node in the main search is determined by a DFS from the top of the Bidtree. The siblings of that child are determined by backtracking in the Bidtree after the main search has explored the tree under the first child. As a bid is appended to the path of the main search, BLOCKED is inserted in the Stopmask for each item of that bid. That implements the branching reduction of the main search based on the second bullet of Prop. 3.1.

MUST is inserted at the unallocated item with the smallest index. That implements the branching reduction of the main search based on the first bullet of Prop. 3.1. These MUST and BLOCKED values are changed back to ANY when backtracking a bid from the path of the main search, and MUST is reallocated to the place where it was before that bid was appended to the path.

The secondary search can be implemented to execute in place, i.e. without memory allocation during search. That is accomplished via the observation that recursion or an open list is not required because in DFS, to decide where to go next, it suffices to know where the search focus is now, and from where it most recently came.

3.2 Anytime winner determination via depth-first-search (DFS)

We first implemented the main search as DFS which executes in linear space. The depth-first strategy causes feasible allocations to be found quickly (the first one is generated in linear time when the first search path ends), and the solution improves monotonically since the algorithm keeps track of the best solution found so far. This implements the anytime feature: if the algorithm does not complete in the desired amount of time, it can be terminated prematurely, and it guarantees a feasible solution that improves monotonically over time. When testing the anytime feature, it turned out that in practice most of the revenue was generated early on as desired, and there were diminishing returns to computation.

3.3 Preprocessing

Our algorithm preprocesses the bids in four ways to make the main search faster without compromising optimality. The next subsections present the preprocessors in the order in which they are executed.

PRE1: Keep only the highest bid for a combination
As a bid arrives, it is inserted into the Bidtree. If a bid for the same S already exists in the Bidtree, only the bid with the higher price is kept, and the other bid is discarded. We break ties in favor of the earlier bid.

PRE2: Remove provably noncompetitive bids
This preprocessor removes bids that are provably non-competitive. A bid (*prunee*) is noncompetitive if there is some disjoint collection of subsets of that bid such that the sum of the bid prices of the subsets exceeds or equals the price of the prunee bid. For example, a \$10 bid for items 1, 2, 3, and 4 would be pruned by a \$4 bid for items 1 and 3, and a \$7 bid for items 2 and 4.

To determine this we search, for each bid (potential prunee), through all combinations of its disjoint subset bids. This is the same DFS as the main search except that it restricts the search to those bids that only include items that the prunee includes (Fig. 4): BLOCKED is kept in the Stopmask for other items.

Especially with bids that contain a large number of items, PRE2 can take more time than it saves in the main search. In the extreme, if some bid contains all items, the preprocessing search with that bid as the prunee is the same as the main search (except for one main search

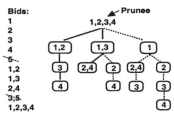

Bids:
1
2
3
4
5
1,2
1,3
2,4
3;5
1,2,3,4

Figure 4: A search tree generated for one prunee in PRE2. The dotted paths are not generated because pruning occurs before they are reached.

path that contains that bid only). To save preprocessing time, PRE2 is carried out partially. Some of the noncompetitive bids are left unpruned, but that will not affect optimality of the main search—although it can make it slower. We implemented two ways of restricting PRE2:

1. A cap, Γ, on the number of pruner bids that can be combined to try to prune a particular prunee bid. This limits the depth of the search in PRE2 to Γ.

2. A cap, Φ, on the number of items in a prunee bid. Longer bids would then not be targets of pruning. This entails a cap, Φ, on tree depth. It also tends to exclude wide trees because long prunees usually lead to trees with large branching factors.

With either method PRE2 takes $O(nn^{cap}m)$ time, which is polynomial for a constant cap (there are n prunees, the tree for each is $O(n^{cap})$, and finding a child in the Bidtree is $O(m)$). The latter method is usually preferable. It does not waste computation on long prunees which take a lot of preprocessing time and do not significantly increase the main search time. This is because the main search is shallow along the branches that include long bids: each item can only occur once on a path and a long bid uses up many items. Second, if the bid prices are close to additive, the former method does not lead to pruning when a path is cut prematurely based on the cap.

PRE3: Decompose bids into connected sets

The bids are partitioned into sets such that no item is shared by bids from different sets. PRE4 and the main search are then done in each set of bids independently, and using only items included in the bids of the set. The sets are determined as follows. We define a graph where bids are vertices, and two vertices share an edge if the bids share items. We generate an adjacency list representation of the graph in $O(mn^2)$ time. We use DFS to generate a depth-first forest of the graph in $O(n + m)$ time. Each tree is then a set with the desired property.

PRE4: Mark noncompetitive tuples of bids

Noncompetitive tuples of disjoint bids are marked so that they need not be considered on the same path in the main search. For example, the pair of bids \$5 for items 1 and 3, and \$4 for items 2 and 5 is noncompetitive if there is a bid of \$3 for items 1 and 2, and a bid of \$7 for items 3 and 5. Noncompetitive tuples are determined as in PRE2 except that now each prunee is a virtual bid that contains the items of the bids in the tuple, and the prunee price is the sum of the prices of those bids.

For computational speed, we only mark 2-tuples, i.e. pairs of bids. A pair of bids is excluded also if the bids

share items. PRE4 is used as a partial preprocessor like PRE2, with caps Γ' or Φ' instead of Γ or Φ. PRE4 runs in $O(n^2 n^{cap} m)$ time. Handling 3-tuples would increase this to $O(n^3 n^{cap} m)$, etc. Handling large tuples also slows the main search because it needs to ensure that noncompetitive tuples do not exist on the path.

As a bid is appended to the path, it excludes from the rest of the path those other bids that constitute a noncompetitive pair with it. Our algorithm determines this quickly as follows. For each bid, a list of bids to exclude is determined in PRE4. In the main search, an exclusion count is kept for each bid, starting at 0. As a bid is appended to the path, the exclusion counts of those bids that it excludes are incremented. As a bid is backtracked from the path, those exclusion counts are decremented. Then, when searching for bids to append to the main search path from the Bidtree, only bids with exclusion count 0 are accepted.[1]

3.4 IDA* and heuristics

We sped up the main search by using an iterative deepening A* (IDA*) search strategy [Korf, 1985] instead of DFS. The search tree, use of the Bidtree, and the preprocessors stay the same. At each iteration of IDA*—except the last—the IDA* threshold gives an upper bound on solution quality. It can be used, for example, to communicate search progress to the auctioneer.

Since winner determination is a maximization problem, the heuristic function h should never underestimate the revenue from the items that are not yet allocated in bids on the path because that could lose optimality. We designed two heuristics that never underestimate:

1. $$h = \sum_{i \in \text{unallocated items}} c(i) \text{ where } c(i) = \max_{S|i \in S} \frac{\bar{b}(S)}{|S|}$$

2. As above, but accuracy is increased by recomputing $c(i)$ every time a bid is appended to the path since some combinations S are excluded: some of their items are on the path, or they constitute a noncompetitive pair with some bid on the path.

We use (2) with several methods for speeding it up. A tally of h is kept, and only some of the $c(i)$ values in h need to be updated when a bid is appended to the path. In PRE4 we precompute for each bid the list of items that must be updated: items included in the bid and in bids that are on the bid's exclude list. To make the update even faster, we keep a list for each item of the bids in which it belongs. The $c(i)$ value is computed by traversing that list and choosing the highest $\frac{\bar{b}(S)}{|S|}$ among the bids that have exclusion count 0. So, recomputing h

---

[1]PRE2 and PRE4 could be converted into anytime preprocessors without compromising optimality by starting with a small cap, conducting the searches, increasing the cap, reconducting the searches, etc. Preprocessing would stop when it is complete (cap $= n$), the user decides to stop it, or some other stopping criterion is met. PRE2 and PRE4 could also be converted into approximate preprocessors by allowing pruning when the sum of the pruners' prices exceeds a fixed fraction of the prunee's price. This would allow more bids to be pruned which can make the main search faster, but it can compromise optimality.

takes $O(mn)$ time, where m is the number of items that need to be updated, and n is the (average or greatest) number of bids in which those items belong.[2]

On the last IDA* iteration, the IDA* threshold is always incremented to equal the revenue of the best solution found so far in order to avoid futile search. In other words, once the first solution is found, the algorithm converts to branch-and-bound with the same heuristic.

4 Experimental setup

Not surprisingly, the worst case complexity of the main search is exponential in the number of bids. However, unlike dynamic programming, this is complexity in the number of bids actually received, not in the number of allowable bids. To determine how the algorithm does in practice, we ran experiments on a regular uniprocessor workstation (360MHz Sun Ultra 60 with 256 MRAM) in C++ with four different bid distributions:

- **Random:** For each bid, pick the number of items randomly from $1, 2, ..., m$. Randomly choose that many items without replacement. Pick the price randomly from $[0, 1]$.
- **Weighted random:** As above, but pick the price between 0 and the number of items in the bid.
- **Uniform:** Draw the same number of randomly chosen items for each bid. Pick the prices from $[0, 1]$.
- **Decay:** Give the bid one random item. Then repeatedly add a new random item with probability α until an item is not added or the bid includes all m items. Pick the price between 0 and the number of items in the bid.

If the same bid was generated twice, the new version was deleted and regenerated. So if the generator was asked to produce e.g. 500 bids, it produced 500 different bids.

We let all the bids have the same bidder. This conservative method causes PRE1 to prune no bids. In practice, the chance that two agents bid on the same combination of items is often small anyway because the number of combinations is large ($2^m - 1$). However, in some cases PRE1 is very effective. For example, it prunes all of the bids except one if all bids are placed on the same combination by different bidders.

5 Experimental results

We focus on IDA* because it was two orders of magnitude faster than DFS. We lower the IDA* threshold between iterations to 95% of the previous threshold or to the highest $f = g + h$ that subceeded the previous threshold, whichever is smaller. Experimentally, this tended to be a good rate of decreasing the threshold.

---

[2] PRE2 and PRE4 use DFS because due to the caps their execution time is negligible compared to the main search. Alternatively they could use IDA*. Unlike in the main search, the $c(i)$ values should be computed using only combinations S that are subsets of the prunee. The threshold for IDA* can be set to the prunee bid's price (or a fraction thereof in the case of approximation), so IDA* will complete in one iteration. Finally, care needs to be taken that the heuristic and the tuple exclusion are handled correctly since they are based on the results of the preprocessing itself.

If it is decreased too fast, the overall number of search nodes increases because the last iteration becomes large. If it is decreased too slowly, the number of search nodes increases because new iterations repeat a large portion of the search from previous iterations.

For PRE2, the cap $\Phi = 30$ gave a good compromise between preprocessing time and main search time. For PRE4, $\Phi' = 20$ led to a good compromise. These values are used in the rest of the experiments. With these caps, the hard problem instances with short bids get preprocessed completely, and PRE2 and PRE4 take negligible time compared to the main search because the trees under such short prunees are small. The caps only take effect in the easy cases with long bids. In the uniform distribution all bids are the same length, so PRE2 does not prune any bids because no bid is a subset of another.

PRE3 saved significant time on the uniform and decay distributions by partitioning the bids into sets when the number of bids was small compared to the number of items, and the bids were short. In almost all experiments with random and weighted random, all bids fell in the same set because the bids were long. In real world combinatorial auctions it is likely that the number of bids will significantly exceed the number of items which would suggest that PRE3 does not help. However, most bids will usually be short, and the bidders' interests often have special structure which leads to some items being independent of each other, and PRE3 capitalizes on that.

The main search generated 35,000 nodes per second when the number of items was small, e.g. 25, and the bids were short. This rate decreased slightly with the number of bids, but significantly with the number of items and bid size. With the random distribution with 400 items and 2000 bids, the search generated only 9 nodes per second. However, the algorithm solved these cases easily because the search paths were short and the heuristic focused the search well. Long bids make the heuristic and exclusion checking slower but the search tree shallower which makes them easier for our algorithm than short bids overall. This observation is further supported by the results below. Each point in each graph represents an average over 20 problem instances. The search times presented include all preprocessing times.

The random distribution was easy, Fig. 5, since the search was shallow because the bids were long. The weighted random distribution was even easier. The curves become closer together on the logarithmic value axis as the number of items increases, which means that search time is polynomial in items. In the weighted random case, the curves are sublinear meaning that search time is polynomial in bids as well, while in the unweighted case they are roughly linear meaning that search time is exponential in bids.

The uniform distribution was harder, Fig. 6 left. The bids were shorter so the search was deeper. The curves are roughly linear so complexity is exponential in bids. The spacing of the curves does not decrease significantly indicating that complexity is exponential in items also. Fig. 6 right shows complexity decrease as bids get longer.

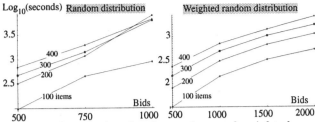

Figure 5: Search time for the random and weighted random distributions. In the random distribution, the point with 1,000 bids and 200 items is unusually high due to one hard outlier among the 20 problem instances.

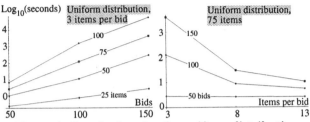

Figure 6: Search time for the uniform distribution.

The decay distribution was also hard, Fig. 7 left. However, the curves get closer together as the number of items increases: complexity is polynomial in items. Complexity first increases in α, and then decreases, Fig. 7 right. Left of the maximum, PRE3 decomposes the problem leading to small, fast searches. The hardness peak moves left as the number of bids grows because the decomposition becomes less successful. Right of the maximum, all bids are in the same set. The complexity then decreases with α because longer bids lead to shallower search.

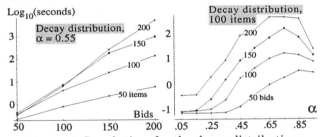

Figure 7: Search time for the decay distribution.

6 Conclusions and generalizations

We presented a search algorithm for optimal winner determination in combinatorial auctions. It allows combinatorial auctions to scale up to significantly larger numbers of items and bids than previous approaches to optimal winner determination. The IDA* search can also be distributed across multiple computers for additional speed. We believe that our algorithm will make the difference between being able to use a combinatorial auction design in many practical markets and not.

The algorithm can also be used to solve weighted set packing, independent set, and maximum clique problems because they are in fact the same problem. So is coalition structure generation in characteristic function games.

The methods discussed so far are based on the common assumption that bids are superadditive: $\bar{b}(S \cup S') \geq$ $\bar{b}(S) + \bar{b}(S')$. But what happens if agent 1 bids $b_1(\{1\}) = \$5$, $b_1(\{2\}) = \$4$, and $b_1(\{1,2\}) = \$7$, and there are no other bidders? The auctioneer could allocate items 1 and 2 to agent 1 separately, and that agent's bid for the combination would value at $\$5 + \$4 = \$9$ instead of $\$7$. So, the current techniques focus on capturing synergies (positive complementarities) among items. In practice, local subadditivities can occur as well. For example, when bidding for a landing slot for a plane, the bidder is willing to take any one of a host of slots, but does not want more than one. To address this we developed a protocol where the bidders can submit *XOR-bids* in our auction server, i.e. bids on combinations such that only one of the combinations can get accepted. This allows the bidders to express general preferences with both positive and negative complementarities, see also [Rassenti *et al.*, 1982]. The winner determination algorithm of this paper can be easily generalized to XOR-bids by marking (as in PRE4) noncompetitive those pairs of bids that are mutually exclusive. These extra constraints cause the algorithm to run faster for XOR-bids than for the same number of nonexclusive bids.

Our server also allows there to be multiple units of each item. The winner determination algorithm then needs to keep track of the sum of the units consumed for each item separately on the main search path. For the multi-unit setting, the h-function can be improved to differentiate between the potential future contributions of units of different items.

Currently we are developing winner determination algorithms for combinatorial double auctions which include multiple buyers and multiple sellers.

References

[Chandra and Halldórsson, 1999] B Chandra and M Halldórsson. Greedy local search and weighted set packing approximation. In *SIAM-ACM Symposium on Discrete Algorithms*.

[Halldórsson and Lau, 1997] M Halldórsson and H Lau. Low-degree graph partitioning via local search with applications to constraint satisfaction, max cut, and 3-coloring. *J. of Graph Alg. Appl.* 1(3):1–13.

[Halldórsson, 1998] M Halldórsson. Approximations of independent sets in graphs. In *Intl. Workshop on Approximation Algorithms for Combinatorial Optimization Problems*, p. 1–14, Aalborg, Denmark. Springer LNCS 1444.

[Håstad, 1999] Johan Håstad. Clique is hard to approximate within $n^{1-\epsilon}$. *Acta Mathematica*, 1999. To appear. Draft: Royal Institute of Tech., Sweden, 8/11/98. Early version: FOCS-96, 627—636.

[Hochbaum, 1983] Dorit S. Hochbaum. Efficient bounds for the stable set, vertex cover, and set packing problems. *Discrete Applied Mathematics*, 6:243–254.

[Karp, 1972] R Karp. Reducibility among combinatorial problems. In Raymond Miller and James Thatcher, editors, *Complexity of Computer Computations*, pages 85–103. Plenum Press, NY.

[Korf, 1985] R Korf. Depth-first iterative-deepening: An optimal admissible tree search. *Artificial Intelligence*, 27(1):97–109.

[McAfee and McMillan, 1996] R P McAfee and J McMillan. Analyzing the airwaves auction. *J. of Econ. Perspectives*, 10(1):159–175.

[Rassenti *et al.*, 1982] S Rassenti, V Smith and R Bulfin. A combinatorial auction mechanism for airport time slot allocation. *Bell J. of Economics* 13:402–417.

[Rothkopf *et al.*, 1998] M Rothkopf, A Pekeč, and R Harstad. Computationally manageable combinatorial auctions. *Management Science*, 44(8):1131–1147. Draft: Rutgers Center for OR report 13-95.

[Sandholm, 1993] T Sandholm. An implementation of the contract net protocol based on marginal cost calculations. In *AAAI*, p. 256–262.

[Sandholm, 1999] T Sandholm. An algorithm for optimal winner determination in combinatorial auctions. WUCS-99-01, Washington University, Dept. of Computer Science, January.

Taming the Computational Complexity of Combinatorial Auctions: Optimal and Approximate Approaches

Yuzo Fujishima, Kevin Leyton-Brown and Yoav Shoham
Robotics Laboratory, Computer Science Department,
Stanford University, Stanford CA, 94305

fujisima@ccs.mt.nec.co.jp (visiting from NEC Corporation)
kevinlb@cs.stanford.edu
shoham@cs.stanford.edu

Abstract

In combinatorial auctions, multiple goods are sold simultaneously and bidders may bid for arbitrary combinations of goods. Determining the outcome of such an auction is an optimization problem that is NP-complete in the general case. We propose two methods of overcoming this apparent intractability. The first method, which is guaranteed to be optimal, reduces running time by structuring the search space so that a modified depth-first search usually avoids even considering allocations that contain conflicting bids. Caching and pruning are also used to speed searching. Our second method is a heuristic, market-based approach. It sets up a virtual multi-round auction in which a virtual agent represents each original bid bundle and places bids, according to a fixed strategy, for each good in that bundle. We show through experiments on synthetic data that (a) our first method finds optimal allocations quickly and offers good anytime performance, and (b) in many cases our second method, despite lacking guarantees regarding optimality or running time, quickly reaches solutions that are nearly optimal.

1 Combinatorial Auctions

Auction theory has received increasing attention from computer scientists in recent years.[1] One reason is the explosion of internet-based auctions. The use of auctions in business-to-business trades is also increasing rapidly [Cortese and Stepanek, 1998]. Within AI there is growing interest in using auction mechanisms to solve distributed resource allocation problems. For example, auctions and other market mechanisms are used in network bandwidth allocation, distributed configuration design, factory scheduling, and operating system memory allocation [Clearwater, 1996]. Market-oriented programming has been particularly influential [Wellman, 1993; Mullen and Wellman, 1996].

The value of a good to a potential buyer can depend on what other goods s/he wins. We say that there exists complementarity between goods g and h to bidder b if $u_b(\{g,h\}) > u_b(\{g\}) + u_b(\{h\})$, where $u_b(G)$ is the utility to b of acquiring the set of goods G. If goods g and h were auctioned separately, it is likely that neither of the typically desired properties for auctions—efficiency and revenue maximization—would hold. One way to accommodate complementarity in auctions is to allow bids for combinations of goods as well as individual goods. Generally, auctions in which multiple goods are auctioned simultaneously and bidders place as many bids as they want for different bundles of goods are called combinatorial auctions[2].

It is also common for bidders to desire a second good less if they have already won a first. We say that there exists substitutability between goods g and h to bidder b when $u_b(\{g,h\}) < u_b(\{g\}) + u_b(\{h\})$. A common example of substitutability is for a bidder to be indifferent between several goods but not to want more than one. In order to be useful, a combinatorial auction mechanism should provide some way for bidders to indicate that goods are substitutable.

Combinatorial auctions are applicable to many real-world situations. In an auction for the right to use railroad segments a bidder desires a bundle of segments that connect two particular points; at the same time, there may be alternate paths between these points and the bidder needs only one [Brewer and Plott, 1996]. Similarly, in the FCC spectrum auction bidders may desire licenses for multiple geographical regions at the same frequency band while being indifferent to which particular band they receive [Milgrom, 1998]. The same situation also occurs in military operations when multiple units each have several alternate plans and each plan may require a different bundle of resources.

---

[1] Funded in part by DARPA under the CoABS program, contract #F30602-98-C-0214.

[2] Auctions in which combinatorial bidding is allowed are alternately called *combinatorial* and *combinational*.

While economics and game theory provide many insights into the potential use of such auctions, they have little to say about computational considerations. In this paper we address the computational complexity of combinatorial auctions.

2 The complexity problem

There has been much work in economics and game theory on designing combinatorial auctions. The Clarke-Groves-Vickrey mechanism (also known as the Generalized Vickrey Auction, or GVA) has been particularly influential [Mas-Colell et al., 1995; Varian, 1995]. It is beyond the scope of this paper to review such mechanisms, but they share a central problem: given a collection of bids on bundles, finding a set of non-conflicting bids that maximizes revenue. (A more precise definition is given in Section 3.) This problem is easily shown to be NP-complete[3] [Rothkopf et al., 1995].

Several methods have been conceived to cope with the computational complexity of combinatorial auctions, most aiming to ease the difficulty of finding optimal allocations. They can be classified into three categories based on the strategies they use.

One strategy is to restrict the degree of freedom of bidding to simplify the task of finding optimal allocations. Rothkopf et al. show that an optimal allocation can be found in polynomial time if (1) each bid contains no more than two goods; (2) for any two bids, either they are disjoint or one is a subset of the other; or (3) each bid contains only consecutive goods given a one-dimensional ordering of goods [Rothkopf et al., 1995].

Another strategy is to shift the burden of finding an optimal allocation to bidders. [Banks et al., 1989] and [Bykowsky et al., 1995] have reported a mechanism called AUSM in which non-winning bids are pooled in a stand-by queue. Bidders can combine their bids with other bids currently in the queue to form new allocations. A new allocation is adopted if it generates more revenue than the previously best allocation.

A third strategy is to attempt to find an optimal allocation but to be satisfied with a sub-optimal allocation when the expenditure of further resources becomes unacceptable. In other words, the optimality of the allocation is traded-off with the resources required, especially time.

In this paper we present two algorithms. The first is an anytime algorithm that attempts to exploit a problem's particular bid structure to reduce the size of the search. It also reduces search time by caching partial results and by pruning the search tree. The second algorithm uses a market-based approach to determine an acceptable allocation, although it is not guaranteed to find an optimal one. We then show results of experiments with synthetic data suggesting that these methods, though not provided with formal guarantees, appear to have surprisingly good performance. Additionally, the market-based approach appears to produce allocations that are always optimal or nearly optimal.[4]

3 Precise Problem Statement

In this paper we propose two methods for finding desirable allocations based on bids submitted. We start by formally defining the optimization problem. Denote the set of goods by G and the set of non-negative real numbers by R^+. A bid $b=(p_b,G_b)$ is an element of $S=R^+\times(2^G-\{\varnothing\})$. Let B be a subset of S. A set $F\subseteq B$ is said to be feasible if $\forall b,c\neq b\in F\ G_b\cap G_c=\varnothing$. Denote the set of all feasible allocations for B by $\Phi(B)$. Further, let $G(B)=\cup_{b\in B}G_b$ be the set of goods contained in the bids of B.

[Problem] Find an allocation $W\in\Phi(B)$ such that $\forall F\in\Phi(B)\ \sum_{b\in F}p_b\leq\sum_{b\in W}p_b$. Such an allocation is said to be optimal or revenue maximizing.

What kind of value interrelation between goods can be represented by the bids defined above? Clearly, complementary values are easily accommodated. Suppose a bidder bids \$20 for each of $\{g\}$ and $\{h\}$, and \$50 for $\{g,h\}$. In this case any revenue-maximizing algorithm will correctly select the $\{g,h\}$ bid instead of $\{g\}$ and $\{h\}$.

This bid format is also sufficient for representing substitutability through an encoding trick. Suppose a bidder is willing to pay \$20 for $\{g\}$ and \$30 for $\{h\}$ but only \$40 for $\{g,h\}$. In this case, bids cannot be submitted as before since the revenue-maximizing algorithm would select the pair $\{g\}$ and $\{h\}$ over $\{g,h\}$, charging the bidder \$50 instead of \$40 for g and h. However, this problem can be solved by the introduction of 'dummy goods'—virtual goods that enforce an exclusive-or relationship. (Each dummy good must appear only in a single bidder's bids.) In our example, the bidder could submit the following bids: (\$20, $\{g,d\}$), (\$30, $\{h,d\}$), and (\$40, $\{g,h\}$) where d is a new, unique dummy good. The first two bids are now mutually exclusive and so will never be allocated together. This technique can lead to a combinatorial explosion in the number of bids if many goods are substitutable, but in many interesting cases this does not arise.

4 CASS Algorithm

When the number of goods and bids is small enough, an exhaustive search can be used to determine the optimal allocation. We propose an algorithm, Combinatorial Auction Structured Search (CASS), presented as a naïve brute-force approach followed by four improvements. CASS considers fewer partial allocations than the brute-force method because it structures the search space to avoid considering allocations containing conflicting bids.

---

[3] The GVA has the additional shortcoming of requiring bidders to submit an unreasonably large number of bids, but we do not address this issue here.

[4] We do not analyze the impact of the approximation on the equilibrium strategies in auction mechanisms such as GVA; we will address this issue in a future paper.

It also caches the results of partial searches and prunes the search tree. Finally, it may be used as an anytime algorithm, as it tends to find good allocations quickly.

4.1 Brute-Force Algorithm

Suppose there are $|G|$ goods 1, 2, ..., $|G|$, and $|B|$ bids 1, 2, ..., $|B|$. First, bids that will never be part of an optimal allocation are removed. That is, if for bid $b_k=(p_k,G_k)$ there exists a bid $b_l=(p_l,G_l)$ such that $p_l > p_k$ and $G_l \subseteq G_k$, then b_k is removed because it can always be replaced by b_l, increasing revenue. Then for each good g, if there is no bid $b=(x,\{g\})$ a dummy bid $b=(0,\{g\})$ is added.

Our brute-force algorithm examines all feasible allocations through a depth-first search. Let x be the first bid and y be the last bid. Our implementation follows:

1. If x does not conflict with the current allocation, add x to the current allocation
2. Increment x
3. If more bids can be added to the allocation, go to 2.
4. Update best revenue and allocation observed so far.
5. If y is contained in the current allocation, remove it, set x=y+1 and repeat from 2.
6. Decrement y.
7. If y is not the first bid, go to 5.

4.2 Improvement #1: Bins

A great deal of unnecessary computation is avoided in the brute-force algorithm by checking whether bids conflict with the current allocation before they are added. However, work is still required to determine that a combination is infeasible and to move on to the next bid. It would be desirable to structure the search space to reduce the number of infeasible allocations that are considered in the first place.

We can reduce the number of infeasible allocations considered by sorting bids into bins, D_i, containing all bids b where good $i \in G_b$ and for all j such that $j \in [1, i-1]$, $j \notin G_b$. Rather than always trying to add each bid to our allocation, we add at most one bid from every bin since all bids in a given bin are mutually exclusive.

In fact, we can often skip bins entirely. While considering bin D_i, if we observe that good $j>i$ is already part of the allocation then we do not need to consider any of the bids in D_j. In general, instead of considering each bin in turn, skip to D_k where $k \notin G(F)$ and $\forall i<k, i \in G(F)$.

4.3 Improvement #2: Caching

Let F_i be the partial allocation under consideration when D_i is reached during a search. Define $C_i \subseteq G(F_i)$ where $\forall j \in G(F_i), j>i \leftrightarrow j \in C_i$. Note that there are many different partial allocations F_{i1}, F_{i2}, etc., that share the same C_i, and that if $C_{i1}=C_{i2}$ then the search trees for F_{i1} and F_{i2} are identical beyond D_i. It is therefore possible to cache partial searches based on C_i. However, caching all possible values of C_i would require a cache of size $2^{|G|-(i-1)}$, which would quickly become infeasible. Therefore, we only cache when C_i in-

cludes no more than k goods, where k is a threshold defined at runtime for each bin. D_i requires a cache of size $\sum_{j=0}^{k} \binom{i}{j}$.

4.4 Improvement #3: Pruning #1

Performance can be improved by backtracking whenever a given search path is provably unable to lead to a new best allocation. We can prune whenever $C(F_{i1}) \subset C(F_{i2})$ and $p(F_{i2}) + p(cache(F_{i1})) \leq bestAllocation$. In this case, the sum of the revenue from the cached path beyond F_{i1} and the revenue leading up to F_{i2} is less than the revenue from the best allocation seen so far. Since F_{i1} allocates a superset of the goods allocated in F_{i2} (thus overestimating revenue), a better allocation would not be found by expanding F_{i2}.

4.5 Improvement #4: Pruning #2

We can also backtrack when it is provably impossible to add any bids to the current allocation to generate more revenue than the current best allocation. Before starting the search we calculate an overestimate of the revenue that can be achieved with each good, $o(g) = \max_{g \in b} p(b)/|G_b|$. $o(g)$ is the largest average price per bid of bids containing good g. We backtrack at any point during the search with allocation F if $p(F) + \sum_{g \notin F} o(g) \leq$ $p(best\_allocation)$. This technique is most effective when good allocations are found quickly. Finding good allocations quickly is also useful if a solution is required before the algorithm has completed (i.e., if CASS is used as an anytime algorithm). We have found that good allocations are found early in the search when the bids in each bin are ordered in descending order of average price per good. Similarly, the pruning technique is most effective when the unallocated goods are those with the lowest $o(g)$ values. To achieve this, we reorder bins so that for any two bins i and j, $o(g_i) > o(g_j) \leftrightarrow i < j$.

5 VSA Algorithm

Our second algorithm is called Virtual Simultaneous Auction (VSA). This market-based method was inspired by market-oriented programming [Wellman, 1993; Mullen and Wellman, 1996] and the simultaneous ascending auction [Milgrom, 1998]. VSA generates a virtual simultaneous auction from the bids submitted in a real combinatorial auction, then runs a simulation for the virtual auction to find a good allocation of goods in the real auction.

5.1 Algorithm

First, a virtual simultaneous auction is generated based on the bids submitted in a real combinatorial auction. For each bid $b=(p_b,G_b)$ a virtual bidder v_b is created. The virtual bidders compete in a virtual simultaneous auction that has multiple rounds. Each virtual bidder v_b tries to win all the goods in G_b for the price p_b on an all-or-nothing basis. The virtual auction starts with no goods allocated and the prices of all goods set to zero. The simultaneous auction is repeated round by round until either an optimal allocation is found or a pre-set time deadline is reached. In the latter case the current best allocation is adopted as the final result.

Each round of VSA has three phases: the virtual auction phase, the refinement phase and the update phase. In the virtual auction phase each virtual bidder bids for the goods they want. Each individual good is allocated to the highest bidder. If a bidder succeeds in winning all desired goods, that bidder becomes a temporary winner. Otherwise the bidder becomes a temporary loser and returns all allocated goods to the auctioneer. In the refinement phase each of the losers is examined in a random order to see whether making that agent a temporary winner (and consequently making a different winner into a loser) would increase global revenue. If so, the list of winners is updated. Finally in the update phase the current highest price of each good is changed to reflect the price that its current winner bid. The current highest price for unallocated goods is reset to zero.

Virtual bidders in VSA follow a simple strategy. If a bidder was the temporary winner in the previous round, the bidder does not bid in the current round. Otherwise, agents calculate the sum of the current highest prices of the goods required. If the sum exceeds an agent's budget, the agent does not bid because the agent will not be able to acquire all the goods simultaneously. If the sum is less than the budget, the agent bids such that the surplus (budget - sum) is equally divided among the goods.

5.2 Properties

In certain circumstances, VSA will find an optimal allocation. Additionally, it is sometimes possible to detect if an optimal allocation has been found, allowing the virtual auction to end before the deadline.

[Theorem] If no virtual bidder bids in a round in the virtual auction, the current set of winners is optimal.

[Proof] Assume that no agents bid in a given round. Define the function that calculates the revenue of an allocation F by $r(F)=\sum_{b\in F}p_b$ and let O denote the optimal set of winners. Split the current set of winners W into two parts O_1 and W_2 such that $O_1=O\cap W$ and $W_2=W\cap\neg O_1$. Also split O into O_1 and O_2 such that O_1 is defined as before and $O_2 = O \cap \neg O_1$. Further, split G into G_1 and G_2 such that $G_1=\cup_{b\in O_1}G_b$ and $G_2=G\cap\neg G_1$. By the assumption, for each currently losing bidder, the sum of the current highest prices of the goods needed exceeds the bidder's budget. This is especially true for bidders in O_2, i.e., $\forall b\in O_2 \; p_b<\sum_{g\in Gb}h_g$ where h_g is the current highest price of good g. It follows that $r(O_2) = \sum_{b\in O2}p_b \leq \sum_{b\in O2}\sum_{g\in Gb}h_g \leq \sum_{g\in G2}h_g = \sum_{b\in W2}\sum_{g\in Gb}h_g = \sum_{b\in W2}p_b = r(W_2)$. (Remember that the minimum price of a good that is not allocated to any agent is zero and agents always bid their entire

budgets.) The inequality means that W is optimal because $r(O) = r(O_1)+r(O_2) \leq r(O_1)+r(W_2) = r(W)$.

However, there is no guarantee that auctions will always finish, even if an optimal allocation is found.

[Theorem] There exists a set of bids B such that at least one virtual bidder always bids in every round of the virtual auction no matter what bidding strategy is used.

[Proof] Suppose $B=\{a,b,c\}$ where $a=\{p_a, \{1,2\}\}$, $b=\{p_b, \{2,3\}\}$, and $c=\{p_c, \{3, 1\}\}$. Suppose further that $p_a < p_b + p_c$, $p_b < p_c + p_a$, and $p_c < p_a + p_b$. Because the real bids are mutually exclusive, at most one virtual bidder becomes the temporary winner. If none is winning, $h_1=h_2=h_3=0$ and all the bidders bid in the current round. Assume here that bidder a is currently winning. Then $h_1+h_2=p_a$ and $h_3=0$. Assume that neither b nor c bids in the current round. Then for each of b and c, the sum of the prices of goods needed must be larger than or equal to the budget, i.e., $h_2+h_3=h_2\geq p_b$ and $h_3+h_1=h_1\geq p_c$. This means that $p_a = h_1+h_2\geq p_b+p_c$ and contradicts $p_a<p_b+p_c$. This argument doesn't depend on the bidding strategy as long as an agent bids if and only if their budget exceeds the sum of the minimum prices of the goods needed.

It is this property that makes the refinement phase of VSA important. Consider the case $B=B_1\cup B_2\cup...$ where $\forall i,j \; G(B_i)\cap G(B_j)=\varnothing$, $|B_i|=3$ and each B_i satisfies the condition from the proof above. If we omit the refinement phase then the winner in each subset changes every round except the case where there is no winner. Therefore, an optimal global allocation is examined only when in every subset the optimal winner is temporarily winning. Such synchronization is unlikely to occur unless the number of subsets is very small. The refinement phase causes the optimal winners to become the temporary winners in every round, leading to an optimal allocation even though it is not detected as optimal. (In some cases where $\exists i,j$ $G(B_i)\cap G(B_j)\neq\varnothing$ or $|B_i| > 3$ an optimal allocation may be impossible to achieve regardless of the time limit.)

6 Experimental Evaluation

As we have not yet determined each algorithm's formal complexity characteristics we conducted empirical tests. We evaluated (1) how running time varies with the number of bids, and (2) how percentage optimality of the best allocation varies with time, given a particular bid distribution and a fixed number of goods.

6.1 Assumptions and Parameters

The space of this problem is large. Roughly speaking it has three degrees of freedom: the number of goods, the number of bids and the distribution of bids. Most problematic among these is the distribution. Precisely because of the computational complexity of combinatorial auctions there is little or no real data available. In the absence of such data we tested our algorithms against bids drawn randomly from specific distributions.

Throughout the experiment we use the following two distribution functions to determine how often a bid for n goods appears. The first is binomial, $f_b(n)=p^n(1-p)^{N-n}N!/(n!(N-n)!)$, $p=0.2$, in which the probability of each good being included in a given bid is independent of which other goods are included. The second distribution is of exponential form, $f_e(n)=Ce^{-x/p}$, $p=5$, representing the case where a bid for $n+1$ goods appears $e^{-1/p}$ times less often than a bid for n goods. The prices of bids for n goods is uniformly distributed between $[n(1-d), n(1+d)]$, $d=0.5$.

We do not present any experiments varying the number of goods in this paper because of space constraints. The results presented here are qualitatively similar to results we observed varying the number of goods.

We ran our experiments on a 450MHz Pentium II with 256MB of RAM, running Windows NT 4.0. 30 MB of RAM was used for the CASS cache. All algorithms were implemented in C++.

6.2 Results

To answer question (1) we measured the running time of CASS, VSA and the brute-force algorithm. Since VSA is not guaranteed to reach the optimal revenue, it was passed this value—calculated by CASS—and stopped when it found an allocation with revenue of at least 95% of optimal. All the results reported here are averages over 10 different runs. Figure 1 shows running time as a function of the number of bids with a binomial distribution, with the number of goods fixed at 30. Figure 2 shows the same thing for an exponential distribution, without the brute-force algorithm.

To answer question (2), we measured the optimality of the output of both VSA and CASS as a function of time. Figure 3 shows both algorithms' performance with 1500 bids for 150 goods, again averaged over 10 runs, with a binomial distribution.

6.3 Discussion

CASS demonstrates excellent performance both in finding optimal allocations and as an anytime algorithm. The effectiveness of CASS's "improvements" are strongly influenced by the distribution of bids, particularly as the number of goods increases. If bids contain k goods on average, improvement #1 will have a great effect because on average k bins will be skipped between every pair of bins that are considered, eliminating the need to individually consider all the bids in those bins. However, the caching scheme described in improvement #2 favors distributions with small bids because they increase the likelihood that partial allocations will be cacheable. The main advantage of the pruning technique described in 4.4 is that it reduces the number of nodes that are cached, reducing memory consumption and making CASS feasible for larger problems. The pruning technique in 4.5 often improves performance by two orders of magnitude, though it is most effective when the variance of average

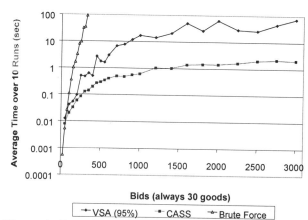

Figure 1: Running Time Comparison (Binom. Dist.)

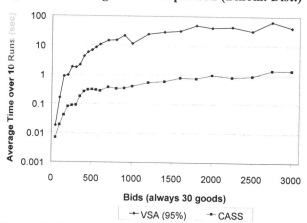

Figure 2: Running Time Comparison (Exp. Dist.)

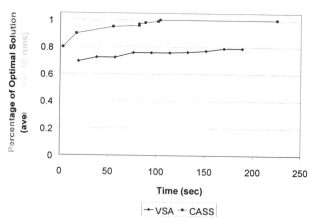

Figure 3: Anytime Behavior (Binom. Dist.)

price per bid is relatively small. This technique also reduces the optimal cache size, further reducing memory consumption. When using pruning techniques we have not found the amount of memory available for caching to be a limiting factor in CASS's performance.

VSA is interesting for two reasons. Firstly, it was the first heuristic method we applied to this problem. Secondly, it provides a case study in the power of market-based optimization. Further work is needed to reach firm conclusions, but it appears that as a centralized optimization method VSA is overshadowed by other techniques. However, other attractions of market-based optimization—in particular its inherent distributed nature and robustness to change in problem specification—may make VSA attractive for some domains. There is also some evidence that VSA provides better anytime performance than CASS when the number of goods is very large. Both of these properties are topics for future study.

7 Related and Ongoing Work

As far as we are aware, the work most directly relevant to the ideas presented here is a paper by Sandholm [1999] that appears in these proceedings. Sandholm's Bidtree algorithm appears to be closely related to CASS, but important differences hold. In particular, Bidtree performs a secondary depth-first search to identify non-conflicting bids, whereas CASS's structured approach allows it to avoid considering most conflicting bids. Bidtree also performs no pruning analogous to our Improvement #3 and no caching. On the other hand, Bidtree uses an IDA* search strategy rather than CASS's branch-and-bound approach, and does more preprocessing. We intend to continue studying the differences between these algorithms, including differences in experimental settings.

Our problem can of course be abstracted away from the auction motivation and viewed as a straightforward combinatorial optimization. This suggests a wealth of literature that could be applied. We are currently implementing some of these techniques and comparing them to our present results. We are especially interested in comparisons with mixed-integer programming and greedy methods. In particular, we have been investigating a new algorithm that orders bids in descending order according to average price per good.[5] It performs a depth-first search, backtracking when the current revenue plus the average price of the next bid times the number of unallocated goods is less than the best allocation. This algorithm appears to offer performance similar to CASS.

8 Conclusion

We have proposed two novel algorithms to mitigate the computational complexity of combinatorial auctions.

Our CASS algorithm determines optimal allocations very quickly, and also provides good anytime performance. In the future we intend to pursue a formal analysis of CASS's computational complexity, and to test both CASS and VSA with data collected from real bidders.

Our VSA algorithm can determine near-optimal allocations even in cases with hundreds of goods and tens of thousands of bids. Since it has been infeasible to run CASS on much larger problems we do not yet know how

close VSA comes to optimality in these cases. An investigation of VSA's limits remains an area for future work.

References

[Banks, et al., 1989] Jeffrey S. Banks, John O. Ledyard, and David P. Porter. Allocating uncertain and unresponsive resources: an experimental approach. *RAND Journal of Economics*, 20(1): 1-25, 1989.

[Brewer and Plott, 1996] P.J. Brewer and C.R. Plott. A binary conflict ascending price (BICAP) mechanism for the decentralized allocation of the right to use railroad tracks. *International Journal of Industrial Organization*, 14:857-886, 1996]

[Bykowsky et al., 1995] Mark M. Bykowsky, Robert J. Cull, and John O. Ledyard. Mutually destructive bidding: the FCC auction design problem. Social science working paper 916, California Institute of Technology, 1995.

[Clearwater, 1996] Scott H. Clearwater, editor. *Market-Based Control: A Paradigm for Distributed Resource Allocation*. World Scientific, 1996.

[Cortese and Stepanek, 1998] Amy E. Cortese and Marcia Stepanek. Good-bye to fixed pricing? *Business Week*, pages 71-84, May 4, 1998.

[Mas-Colell et al., 1995] Andreu Mas-Colell, Michael D. Whinston, and Jerry R. Green. *Microeconomic Theory*. Oxford University Press, New York, 1995.

[Milgrom, 1998] Paul Milgrom. Putting auction theory to work: the simultaneous ascending auction. Working paper 98-002, Dept. Economics, Stanford University, 1998.

[Mullen and Wellman, 1996] Tracey Mullen and Michael P. Wellman. Some issues in the design of the market-oriented agents. In M.J. Wooldridge, J.P. Muller, and M. Tambe, editors, *Intelligent Agents II: Agent Theories, Architectures, and Languages*. Springer-Verlag, 1996.

[Rothkopf et al., 1995] Michael H. Rothkopf, Aleksandar Pekeč, and Ronald M. Harstad. Computationally manageable combinatorial auctions. DIMACS Technical Report 95-09, April 1995.

[Sandholm, 1999] Tuomas Sandholm. An algorithm for optimal winner determination in combinatorial auctions. Proceedings of the International Joint Conference on Artificial Intelligence (IJCAI-99), Stockholm, 1999.

[Varian, 1995] Hal R. Varian. Economic mechanism design for computerized agents. In *Proceedings of the First Usenix Conference on Electronic Commerce*, New York, July 1995.

[Wellman, 1993] Michael P. Wellman. A market-oriented programming environment and its application to distributed multicommodity flow problems. *Journal of Artificial Intelligence Research*, 1:1-23, 1993.

---

[5] This ongoing work is joined by Liadan O'Callaghan and Daniel Lehmann

Speeding Up Ascending-Bid Auctions*

Yuzo Fujishima†, David McAdams‡, and Yoav Shoham†
Computer Science Department (†) and Graduate School of Business (‡)
Stanford University
Stanford, CA 94305

Abstract

In recent years auctions have grown in interest within the AI community as innovative mechanisms for resource allocation. The primary contribution of this paper is to identify a family of hybrid auctions, called *survival auctions*, which combine the benefits of both sealed-bid auctions (namely, quick and predictable termination time) and ascending-bid auctions (namely, more information revelation often leading, among other things, to better allocations and greater expected revenue). Survival auctions are multi-round sealed-bid auctions with an information-revelation component, in which some bidders are eliminated from the auction from one round to the next. These auctions are intuitive, easy to implement, and – most importantly – provably optimal. More precisely, we show that (a) the survival auction in which all but the lowest bidder make it into the next round (the auction lasts for $(n-1)$ rounds when there are n bidders) is strategically equivalent to the Japanese ascending-bid auction, which itself has been proven to be optimal in many settings, and that (b) under certain symmetry conditions, even a survival auction in which only the two highest bidders make it into the next round (the auction lasts only two rounds) is Nash outcome equivalent to the Japanese auction.

1 Introduction

Auction theory has recently captured the attention of computer scientists and especially of AI researchers. One reason, of course, is the explosion of auctions on the internet and to facilitate business-to-business trade [Hansell, 1998; Cortese and Stepanek, 1998]. A more specific reason for interest within AI, however, is the use of auctions as a distributed protocol to solve resource allocation problems. For example, auctions as well as other market mechanisms are used in parts configuration design, factory scheduling, operating system memory allocation, ATM network bandwidth allocation, and distributed QoS allocation. [Clearwater, 1996; Yamaki *et al.*, 1996]. Within AI, market-oriented programming (MOP) [Wellman, 1993; Mullen and Wellman, 1996] has excited many researchers with the prospect of market-based control.

MOP and related approaches leverage ideas from economics and game theory, but these ideas provide little help with computational issues. This paper is concerned with the speed with which an auction terminates. (In the following we assume familiarity with some auction theory. Unfamiliar readers should consult the brief primer provided in Section 2.)

Sealed-bid auctions are attractive since they last exactly one round, but in some situations they have substantial disadvantages. Bidders in an auction often possess information that would be useful to other bidders to assess the value of the good for sale. Sealed bidding denies bidders the opportunity to learn about others' information during the course of the auction, which (as we discuss later) can lead to bad outcomes. In particular, the wrong bidder will sometimes win, the auction will tend to yield lower revenues, and winners will be subjected to more uncertain payoffs. In such situations, an ascending-bid auction is generally preferable on information-revelation grounds. In an ascending-bid auction, bidders with high estimates of a good's value can see the drop-out points of other bidders who have lower estimates. This information – a sense of just how bad is the worst information of others – helps bidders to assess the good's worth to them. For example, in an auction of a purported Rembrandt painting, very aggressive bidding by several experts should convince a non-expert that the painting is unlikely to be a fake. In a sealed-bid auction, bidders can not similarly condition their bidding behavior on the behavior (and hence information) of others.

Yet ascending-bid auctions have a distinct disadvantage. They can take a long and unpredictable amount of time to terminate. This shortcoming can be devastating, for example, when using auctions to allocate time-shared resources in real-time environments.

*This work was supported in part by the DARPA CoABS program, contract number F30602-98-C-0214

The primary contribution of this paper is to present and analyze a new sort of auction, the "survival auction", which shares the information-revelation property of ascending-bid auctions but which looks essentially like a multi-round sealed-bid auction. Here is how a survival auction works. In the first round, all bidders submit a sealed bid. As a function of these bids, the auctioneer announces which bidders "survive" to the second round, a minimum bid for the second round, and, most importantly, all losing bids.

In the final round of a survival auction, the remaining bidders have seen bids submitted by all of the others. Before making their final bids, therefore, they have some sense of the information possessed by the others. In the final stage of an ascending-bid auction, similarly, the last two bidders have seen drop-out points of all of the others, from which they can and should infer similar information.

The usual challenge of auction design is not so much to propose a reasonable-looking scheme as to analyze its equilibrium properties – in particular, its success in allocating the good optimally and in raising maximal revenue. One advantage of survival auctions over other sorts of "accelerated auctions" is that we are able to analyze them with the tools of game theory.

We show that one survival auction is strategically equivalent to the Japanese ascending-bid auction. In this survival auction, all bidders except the lowest survive each round and the minimum bid for each round is the losing bid of the previous round. We call this "the $(n-1)$-round survival auction" since it requires $(n-1)$ rounds to complete when there are n bidders. Strategic equivalence of two auctions implies that, as long as bidders behave rationally and do not care about the superficial details of the auction in which they are participating (which would not be true, for example, if bidders derive "entertainment value" only out of ascending-bid mechanisms), the same bidder will always win and pay the same amount in both auctions. Other survival auctions have the advantage of ending even more quickly than the $(n-1)$-survival auction, but are not strategically equivalent to the Japanese auction. If we impose certain symmetry assumptions, however, these survival auctions are still "Nash outcome equivalent" to the Japanese auction. This includes an auction which lasts only two rounds.

The rest of the paper is organized as follows. Section 2 is an auction primer, which includes a description of the most common types of single-good auctions, a brief literature review pertaining to the comparison of ascending-bid and sealed-bid auctions, and an introduction to the two principles of rational bidding most essential to our equilibrium analysis in Section 3.2. Section 3 introduces survival auctions and presents our results. The first result, in subsection 3.1, is that the $(n-1)$-round survival auction is strategically equivalent to the Japanese ascending-bid auction. The second result, in subsection 3.2, is that all of our survival auctions are Nash outcome-equivalent to the Japanese auction in the context of a model with several symmetry assumptions.

Section 3.3 outlines how our results can be extended to the setting of multiple-good auctions. We conclude with a few comments about the relevance of our results.

2 Auction Primer

The most common auctions fall into three categories: ascending-bid auctions, descending-bid auctions, and sealed-bid auctions. Ascending-bid and descending-bid auctions are known together as open outcry auctions.

Ascending-bid auctions are the most prevalent in practice, accounting for an estimated 75% of all auctions worldwide [Cassady, 1967]. In the English auction, participants make successively higher bids. The winner is the last bidder and pays the last bid. Another common, ascending-bid auction is the Japanese auction. Here, the auctioneer continuously raises the price. Each bidder decides when to drop out, and once a bidder drops out he can not reenter. The last bidder to remain is the winner and pays the final price.

In a sealed-bid auction, all bidders submit a single bid to the auctioneer in ignorance of others' bids. The winner is the one who submitted the highest bid. Payment is made as a function of the bids. The most common sealed-bid auctions are the first- and the second-price. In the first-price auction, the winner pays his own bid. In the second-price auction, the winner pays the second-highest bid.

Descending-bid auctions are the least common in practice. The most familiar descending-bid auction is the Dutch auction. The auctioneer continuously lowers the price until a bidder expresses willingness to buy. That bidder wins and pays the final price.

Auction theorists have shown that under certain symmetry assumptions, when bidders are risk-neutral, do not care about the information possessed by others, and receive statistically independent information, all of the common auctions described above are optimal in the sense that they all allocate the good optimally (the bidder with the highest value for the good always gets the good) and all raise the highest possible expected revenue (see for example [McAfee and McMillan, 1987]). Relaxing various of these assumptions induces rank orderings of the common auctions, both in allocation and revenue terms. In particular, when bidders care about the information possessed by others, ascending-bid auctions outrank sealed-bid auctions in three important settings.

(1) Let $v_i(s_1, ..., s_n)$ represent bidder i's valuation for the good, which is allowed to be a function of all bidders' information. When $\frac{\delta v_i}{\delta s_i}(\vec{s}) \geq \frac{\delta v_j}{\delta s_i}(\vec{s})$ for all $j \neq i$ and for all $\vec{s} = (s_1, ..., s_n)$, ascending-bid auctions are always efficient whereas sealed-bid auctions are not [Dasgupta and Maskin, 1998].

(2) In the model of Section 3.2, when bidders are risk averse the ascending-bid auction has higher expected revenue than the second-price auction. In an ascending-bid auction, the drop-out points of losing bidders reveals information that helps remaining bidders make a tighter estimate of the good's value to them. Since winning

bidders are thus exposed to less risk, all bidders will be willing to bid more aggressively on average for the chance to win. (For more on this, see the discussion of extensions of the Revenue Equivalence Theorem to risk averse bidders in any auction or game theory text, such as [Fudenberg and Tirole, 1991].)

(3) In the model of Section 3.2, when bidders are risk neutral with affiliated private information the ascending-bid auction has higher expected revenue than any sealed-bid auction [Milgrom and Weber, 1982]. Roughly speaking, affiliation means that the more optimistic a given bidder's information, the more likely other bidders are to have more optimistic information. See Milgrom and Weber for a rigorous exposition.

Finally, our analysis presumes that bidders are aware of and act in accordance with the principles of rational bidding. For example, each bidder should reflect: "I make a payment only if I win the auction. Thus, when I choose how much to bid, I ought to presume that I will be the winner". We will call this *the winning bidder principle*. When bidders fail to abide by this principle, they will suffer from "the winner's curse". Typically, the bidder to win an auction is the one with the most optimistic information. If a bidder works off of the presumption that his information is average, he will systematically overvalue the good those times when he does win.

More subtlely, each bidder should reflect upon the marginal relevance of his bid. In the Japanese auction, a bidder considering dropping out at price p when there are k other bidders left in the auction should reflect: "Why should I drop out exactly now? If I stay in the auction and drop out instead at $p + \triangle$, I will still not win unless all other bidders drop out in between p and $p + \triangle$." When deciding to drop out at p, therefore, a savvy bidder will presume that all other remaining bidders will drop out immediately. We will call this *the marginal bid relevance principle*.

3 Survival Auctions

First, we describe the class of multi-round single-good auctions that we have named "survival auctions". Each survival auction is characterized by a survival rule, a minimum bid rule, and a final price rule. The survival rule specifies which bidders are allowed to continue in later rounds of the auction. Once excluded from participating in a given round, a bidder is not allowed to return in later rounds. An initial bid minimum is in effect in the first round; in all later rounds, the minimum bid is set as a function of the bids in earlier rounds. The final price rule specifies the winner's payment.

1. All bidders are active. The auctioneer announces an initial minimum bid.

2. Each active bidder submits a sealed bid. The bid must be no less than the minimum bid.

3. The auctioneer announces which of the active bidders remain active.

4. If only one bidder remains active, this is the winner. The auctioneer announces how much he must pay.

5. If more than one bidder remains active, then the auctioneer announces a minimum bid for the next round and all bids of those who have become inactive. Repeat from 2.

Although some of our results extend to a broader family of survival auctions, we will focus in this paper on a special subclass of survival auctions, called "our survival auctions", in which: (1) the number of survivers in the second round, the third round, and so on is commonly known in advance; (2) the bidders who survive are those who submit the highest bids; (3) the minimum bid is always equal to the *lowest* losing bid in the previous round (and the initial minimum bid is $-\infty$); and (4) the final round has two bidders.

3.1 $(n-1)$-round Survival Auction

Consider the specific survival auction in which only one bidder is eliminated at a time and the minimum bid in each round is the losing bid of the previous round. We call this the "$(n-1)$-round survival auction" since it takes $(n-1)$ rounds to complete when there are n bidders. In this section we prove that the $(n-1)$-round survival auction is "strategically equivalent" to the Japanese auction. Strategic equivalence is the strongest possible formal relationship to establish between two auction mechanisms.

Two auctions are strategically equivalent if there exists an isomorphism between their strategy spaces which preserves payoffs. A strategy z_i of bidder i maps each of bidder i's decision points (also known as action nodes or information sets) into a feasible action. Each of these decision points corresponds to the information that bidder i will possess if he reaches a certain potential moment of decision. For example, suppose that in the first round of the $(n-1)$-round survival auction bidder 1 bids b_1 and is eliminated. In this scenario, bidders $2, ..., n$ each have a second-round decision point at which they have the information "bidder 1 bid exactly b_1 in the first round while all other bidders bid at least b_1 in the first round". The set of feasible actions of each of these bidders at these decision points is simply the set of bids no lower than b_1. The strategy space Z_i of bidder i is the set of all of his strategies. For formal convenience we will include in a bidder's set of decision points the set of his "terminal points". Each of these corresponds to information the bidder can have when the auction terminates. (No decision is made at a terminal point.) A bidder's payoff from an auction is a function both of the auction outcome and of the information available to that bidder at the end of the auction. An outcome consists of an allocation of the good and payments by the bidders.

To show that there exists an isomorphism between the strategy spaces of two auctions preserving payoffs, one must show that: (1) An isomorphism exists between each bidder's sets of decision points in the two auctions. The structure which must be preserved by the isomorphism is that of decision point precedence. One decision point precedes another iff the follower decision point can only be reached if the precedent decision point is reached first. We will say that decision points in the two auctions are "the same" if they are related by this isomorphism. Note that (1) implies that there must be a bijection between the sets of information that each bidder can acquire immediately after every pair of same decision points; (2) There exists an isomorphism between feasible action sets at same decision points which is consistent with the precedence structure. That is to say, there is a set of (vectors of) actions which are consistent with each follower decision point being reached after its immediate precedent. The isomorphism must induce a bijection between all such sets for all same follower-precedent pairs. We will say that actions in the two auctions are "the same" if they are related by this isomorphism; and (3) Bidder payoffs are always the same at same terminal points. That is to say, if $g(\cdot), h(\cdot)$ are the isomorphisms of feasible actions and decision points, then each bidder's payoff at a terminal point t following actions $\vec{a}$ in the first auction must be the same as his payoff at the same terminal point $h(t)$ following the same actions $g(\vec{a})$ in the second auction.

Theorem 1 *The $(n-1)$-round survival auction is strategically equivalent to the Japanese ascending-bid auction.*

[Proof] We follow the proof outline established above.

(1) In the survival auction, the new information that bidder i receives in between rounds k and $k+1$, if he survives round k, is the identity of the loser in round k and the losing bid in that round. Each of his decision points in the $(k+1)$st round can thus be described by the $2k$-dimensional vector of all losing bidders and losing bids in the first k rounds. In the Japanese auction, the new information that bidder i receives in between the $(k-1)$st and kth drop-out, if he is not himself the one to be the kth drop-out, is the identity of the kth bidder to drop out and his drop-out point. His decision after the kth drop-out can thus be described by the $2k$-dimensional vector of the first k bidders to drop out and their drop-out points in the first k rounds.[1]

The isomorphism of decision point sets is the identity mapping. Thus, for example, we will say that a bidder's decision of what to bid in the second round of the survival auction after observing that bidder 1 lost with a bid of b_1 in the first round is the same as his decision of how long to wait before being the next to drop out in

---

[1] The possibility that bidders can drop out simultaneously in the Japanese auction presents a wrinkle. If we presume that bidders can react instantaneously to others' drop-outs, however, then this does not change the analysis. Sometimes, based on one bidder's drop-out, another bidder wants to drop out immediately. We allow such immediate reaction, with the proviso that the bidder who dropped out first can not reverse his decision to drop out after observing the other bidder's drop-out. This way, every bidder is faced with a new decision (and new information) after every drop-out.

the Japanese auction after observing that bidder 1 is the very first to drop out at the price b_1. (A decision in the Japanese auction is not how long to wait until dropping out but how long to wait before being the next one to drop out. If someone else drops out first, a bidder should revise his willingness to remain in the bidding.)

(2) In the survival auction, each bidder in the $(k+1)$st round can make any bid higher than the minimum allowable bid in that round, which equals the losing bid in the kth round. In the Japanese auction, each bidder after the kth drop-out can decide to wait until any price higher than the last drop-out before being the next to drop out. Thus, the feasible action sets are identical and consistency with the decision point isomorphism is obvious.

(3) If play in the two auctions reaches the same terminal point, then all actions will have been same actions at same decision points. Thus, (a) the same bidder will win, (b) this bidder will pay the same amount, and (c) the information available to all bidders at the end of the auction will be the same. ♣

Since strategic equivalence implies outcome equivalence, all of the allocation and revenue advantages of the Japanese auction over sealed-bid auctions carry over to the $(n-1)$-round survival auction. Since the $(n-1)$-round survival auction predictably takes $(n-1)$ rounds whereas an ascending-bid auction can conceivably require hundreds or even thousands of rounds of communication, this marks a significant improvement in speed and reliability.

3.2   2-round Survival Auction

Can we do better than the $(n-1)$-round survival auction? For example, can we construct a survival auction which requires $O(1)$ rounds to terminate and which is strategically equivalent to the Japanese auction? Unfortunately, No. In any survival auction which takes less than $n-1$ rounds, the winner makes fewer than $n-1$ decisions. Thus, requirement (1) of strategic equivalence can not be met. Nonetheless, under certain symmetry assumptions, we can prove that all of our survival auctions are "Nash outcome equivalent" to the Japanese.

Two auctions are Nash outcome equivalent if each auction possesses a Nash equilibrium such that, when those Nash equilibria are played out, the same bidder wins and pays the same price after every realization of uncertainty. Nash outcome equivalence is weaker than strategic equivalence since it is model-specific. Furthermore, bidders may not coordinate on Nash equilibrium play, especially if there are multiple equilibria.

Consider the following model. Each bidder i possesses one-dimensional private information s_i. All signals $\{s_i\}$ are drawn from a common distribution and possess a symmetric correlation structure. (The conditional distribution of all signals $\{s_j\}_{j \neq i}$ given $s_i = x$ is symmetric in all of the other signals and the same as the conditional distribution of all signals $\{s_j\}_{j \neq k}$ given $s_k = x$ for all $k \neq i$. Similarly, all conditional distributions given two signals, three signals, and so on are symmetric and equal.)

Each bidder i's willingness to pay for the good is a function of all private information, $v(s_i; \{s_j\}_{j \neq i})$. For each bidder, this function is symmetric in all other bidders' information, increasing in all signals, and satisfying

$$\frac{\partial v_i}{\partial s_i}(\vec{s}) \geq \frac{\partial v_j}{\partial s_i}(\vec{s}) \; \forall j \neq i \; \forall \vec{s}$$

This inequality states (loosely) that "Each bidder always cares about his own information more than others do." Thus, given any set of information available to both bidders i and j, bidder i has a higher valuation of the good iff his signal is higher. Finally, bidders have identical expected utility functions defined over the difference between valuation and payment. That is to say, there exists a function $u : R \to R$ such that bidder i's utility from getting the good at price p when his valuation is v_i equals $u(v_i - p)$. This allows bidders to be risk averse or risk loving, as $u''(\cdot) < 0$ or $u''(\cdot) > 0$.

Theorem 2 *In the model of this section, all of our survival auctions are Nash outcome equivalent to the Japanese auction.*

[Proof] Recall that in "our survival auctions" the minimum bid equals the lowest losing bid of the previous round and the final round always has two bidders. To conserve space, some details have been left to the reader.

First, we construct a symmetric equilibrium of the Japanese auction. By the principles of rational bidding (see the primer) and model symmetry, at every decision point each bidder chooses the price at which he wants to be the next to drop out by working off of the presumption that all remaining bidders have the exact same signal as he does. Thus, in any symmetric equilibrium, bidder n must choose $v(s_n; s_n..., s_n)$ as the price at which he will be the first to drop out. (The $n-1$ signals to the right of the semi-colon are those of bidders 1 through $n-1$, since this is bidder n's valuation function.) Now, if bidder 1 drops out first at b_1, all remaining bidders should infer that his signal s_1^* satisfies $v(s_1^*; s_1^*, ..., s_1^*) = b_1$. Bidder n must then wait until the price $v(s_n; s_1^*, s_n, ..., s_n)$ before being the next to drop out. And so on after every subsequent drop-out.

Consider now the one of our survival auctions with R rounds and k_r survivors of the rth round ($n > k_1 > ... > k_{R-1} = 2$). Again, by the principles of rational bidding and model symmetry, each bidder in round r must work off of the presumption that his signal is highest and equal to k_r others in any symmetric equilibrium. To minimize notational complexity, we will continue the proof under an additional assumption of risk neutral bidders.[2]

In the first round, then, bidder n wants to bid

$$E[v(s_n; s_1, ..., s_{n-1} | s_n \text{ high, } k_1 \text{ equal})]$$

___
[2] If a bidder is not risk neutral, in round r he ought to bid so as to maximize his expected utility from paying his bid and winning the good given that his signal is the highest and equal to k_r other signals.

if all others follow a similar strategy, where "s_1 high, k_1 equal" means "$s_n \geq s_j \; \forall j$ and $s_n = s_{j_1} = ... = s_{j_{k_1}}$ for some set of k_1 other bidders, $\{j_1, ..., j_{k_1}\}$". Suppose that bidders $1, ..., n - k_1$ lose in the first round with bids $b_1, ..., b_{n-k_1}$. Given the specified first round bid strategy, all remaining bidders should infer each of their signals, $\{s_i, i = 1, ..., n - k_1\}$, by the relation

$$E[v(s_i; \{s_j\}_{j \neq i} | s_i \text{ high, } k_1 \text{ equal})] = b_i.$$

Similarly, in the second round, bidder n wants to bid

$$E[v(s_n; s_1^*, ..., s_{n-k_1}^*, s_{n-k_1+1}, ..., s_{n-1} | s_n \text{ high, } k_2 \text{ equal})]$$

if all others do the same, and so on in all subsequent rounds. These second-round bids will always be feasible since they will never be less than the lowest bid in the first round. ($s_n \geq s_1^*, ..., s_{n-k_1}^*$ and bidder n knows in the second round that $s_{n-k_1+1}, .., s_n \geq s_1^*, ..., s_{n-k_1}^*$ whereas the lowest losing bidder based his first round bid on less optimistic presumptions.) Thus, bidders have no incentive to bid less aggressively in the first round to avoid a possibly disadvantageous position in the second round, nor similarly in later rounds, and these strategies do indeed form a Nash equilibrium.

The winner in this equilibrium is always the same as in the equilibrium of the Japanese auction, since it is the bidder with the highest signal. Finally, in both equilibria the price when n wins and $n-1$ is second equals the final drop-out point / bid of $n - 1$,

$$p = v(s_{n-1}; s_1^*, ..., s_{n-2}^*, s_n | s_n = s_{n-1}),$$

since the final round of the survival auction has two bidders. ♣

Define the "2-round survival auction" to be the one in which only two bidders survive to the second round and in which the minimum bid is the lowest losing bid. This auction always takes two rounds to complete.

Corollary 1 *The 2-round survival auction is Nash outcome equivalent to the Japanese auction.*

3.3 Extension to Multiple Goods

All of our arguments in the context of single-good auctions easily extend to prove analogous claims about multiple-good auctions. In particular, consider the "k-good Japanese auction" in which each bidder may receive any number of units of the good at auction. Each bidder begins by choosing a number of "active bids". As the price rises, each bidder can lower his number of active bids. The auction ends when exactly k active bids remain. Similarly, define "k-good survival auctions" to be those in which each bidder can have multiple active bids and in which the last k active bids win. In particular, define the one-at-a-time k-good survival auction to be the one which eliminates one active bid at a time. (The number of rounds that this auction takes depends on the initial number of active bids.) Also, let "our k-good survival auctions" be those in which: (1) the number of surviving active bids in each round is known in advance as a function of the number of initial active bids; (2) the highest bidders survive; (3) the minimum bid equals the lowest losing bid in the last round; and (4) the final round has $k + 1$ bidders.

Theorem 3 *The one-at-a-time k-good survival auction is strategically equivalent to the k-good Japanese ascending-bid auction.*

[Proof] The proof is analogous to that of Theorem 1, but accounting for the richer strategy spaces of bidders since each must first choose his number of active bids. ♣

Theorem 4 *In the model of subsection 3.2, all of our k-good survival auctions are Nash outcome equivalent to the k-good Japanese auction.*

[Proof] The proof is analogous to that of Theorem 2, also accounting for the richer strategy space. ♣

It is important to note, however, that the k-good Japanese auction in the k-good setting does not share all of the desirable theoretical properties of the Japanese auction in the 1-good setting. In particular, the k-good Japanese auction will not always get the k goods to the bidders who value them most. Which multiple-unit auctions always allocate k-goods optimally is, as far as we are aware, still an open question.

4 Conclusion

There is a reason why the vast majority of auctions are ascending-bid auctions; they reveal information. Given rational bidding, this information revelation leads to better allocations and higher revenue, or, given irrational bidding, can at least mitigate the severity of the winner's curse. Their main practical disadvantage is a long and uncertain termination time. We have proposed a new class of auctions, *survival auctions,* which combine the speed and predictability of sealed-bid auctions with the desirable properties of ascending-bid auctions.

Other sorts of auctions appear to offer a similar blend. For example, in what we call "the binary price-search auction", the auctioneer queries all bidders whether they are willing to pay a given price. If only one bidder answers Yes, he gets the good at that price. If zero or more than one answer Yes, another query follows at a lower or higher price, in such a way to converge at logarithmic speed to a price that exactly one bidder will be willing to pay. Unfortunately, this and other "accelerated auctions" are difficult to analyze with the tools of game theory.

In any event, one should be cautious about applying our pure analysis in real-world situations, especially in consumer-based auctions. For example, it is not realistic to expect all bidders to be present at the very beginning of an auction, and it seems likely that psychological factors may lead human bidders to behave differently in auctions which are game-theoretically equivalent. We do believe, however, that survival auctions should provide a more desirable protocol than ascending-bid auctions in resource allocation problems with computerized agents.

5 Acknowledgments

We are grateful to participants of the Stanford CoABS and Stanford GSB Game Theory seminars for their helpful feedback, in particular Craig Boutilier, Moises Goldszmidt, Leonardo Rezende, Michael Schwarz, Robert Wilson, and Muhamet Yildiz. We especially thank Jeremy Bulow for his insightful comments.

References

[Cassady, 1967] R. Cassady. *Auctions and Auctioneering.* U. California Press, Berkeley, 1967.

[Clearwater, 1996] Scott H. Clearwater, editor. *Market-Based Control: A Paradigm for Distributed Resource Allocation.* World Scientific, 1996.

[Cortese and Stepanek, 1998] Amy E. Cortese and Marcia Stepanek. Good-bye to fixed pricing?: How electronic commerce could create the most efficient market of them all. *Business Week*, pages 71–84, May 4 1998.

[Dasgupta and Maskin, 1998] Partha Dasgupta and Eric Maskin. Efficient auctions. Technical report, Harvard University, 1998.

[Fudenberg and Tirole, 1991] Drew Fudenberg and Jean Tirole. *Game Theory.* MIT Press, Cambridge, Mass., 1991.

[Hansell, 1998] Saul Hansell. Auctions of goods and services thrive on internet. *New York Times*, April 2 1998.

[McAfee and McMillan, 1987] R. Preston McAfee and John McMillan. Auctions and bidding. *Journal of Economic Literature*, 25:699–738, June 1987.

[Milgrom and Weber, 1982] Paul R. Milgrom and Robert J. Weber. A theory of auctions and competitive bidding. *Econometrica*, 50(5):1089–1122, September 1982.

[Mullen and Wellman, 1996] Tracey Mullen and Michael P. Wellman. Some issues in the design of market-oriented agents. In M.J. Wooldridge, J.P. Muller, and M. Tambe, editors, *Intelligent Agents II: Agent Theories, Architectures, and Languages.* Springer-Verlag, 1996. Also available at http://ai.eecs.umich.edu/people/mullen/atal-revised.ps.Z.

[Wellman, 1993] Michael P. Wellman. A market-oriented programming environment and its application to distributed multicommodity flow problems. *Journal of Artificial Intelligence Research*, 1:1–23, 1993. Avaliable at http://www.jair.org/.

[Yamaki et al., 1996] Hirofumi Yamaki, Michael P. Wellman, and Toru Ishida. A market-based approach to allocating qos for multimedia applications. In *The Second International Conference on Multi-Agent Systems (ICMAS-96)*, pages 385–392, 1996.

COMPUTER GAME PLAYING

COMPUTER GAME PLAYING

Game Playing 1

Temporal Coherence and Prediction Decay in TD Learning

Don F. Beal and Martin C. Smith
Department of Computer Science
Queen Mary and Westfield College
University of London
Mile End Road
London E1 4NS
UK

Abstract

This paper describes improvements to the temporal difference TD(λ) learning method. The standard form of the TD(λ) method has the problem that two control parameters, learning rate and temporal discount, need to be chosen appropriately. These parameters can have a major effect on performance, particularly the learning rate parameter, which affects the stability of the process as well as the number of observations required. Our extension to the TD(λ) algorithm automatically sets and subsequently adjusts these parameters. The learning rate adjustment is based on a new concept we call temporal coherence (TC). The experiments reported here compare the extended TD(λ) algorithm performance with human-chosen parameters and with an earlier method for learning rate adjustment, in a complex game domain. The learning task was that of learning the relative values of pieces, without any initial domain-specific knowledge, and from self-play only. The results show that the improved method leads to better learning (i.e. faster and less subject to the effects of noise), than the selection of human-chosen values for the control parameters, and a comparison method.

1 Introduction

Two major parameters that control the behaviour of Sutton's [1988] temporal difference algorithm TD(λ) are the learning rate (or step-size), α, and the temporal discount parameter, λ.

The choice of these parameters can have a major effect on the efficacy of the learning algorithm, and in practical problems they are often determined somewhat arbitrarily, or else by trying a number of values and 'seeing what works' (e.g. Tesauro [1992]). Another widely used method is to use a learning rate that decreases over time, but such systems still require the selection of a suitable schedule.

Sutton and Singh [1994] describe systems for setting both α and λ, within the framework of Markov-chain models. However these methods assume relatively small numbers of distinct states, and acyclic graphs, and so are not directly applicable to more complex real-world problems. Jacobs [1988] presented the 'delta-bar-delta' algorithm for adjusting α during the learning process. We compared the performance of delta-bar-delta with our algorithm on our sample domain. More recently, Almeida [1998] and Schraudolph [1998] have presented other methods for α adaptation for stochastic domains and neural networks respectively.

We describe a new system which automatically adjusts α and λ. This system does not require any *a priori* knowledge about suitable values for learning rate or temporal discount parameters for a given domain. It adjusts these parameters according to the learning experiences themselves. We present results that show that this method is effective, and in our sample domain yielded better learning performance than our best attempt to find optimum choices of fixed α and λ, and better learning performance than delta-bar-delta.

2. Temporal difference learning

Temporal difference learning methods are a class of incremental learning procedures for learning predictions in multi-step prediction problems. Whereas earlier prediction learning procedures were driven by the difference between the predicted and actual outcome, TD methods are driven by the difference between temporally successive predictions.

Sutton's TD(λ) algorithm can be summarised by the following formula. Given a vector of adjustable weights, w, and a series of successive predictions, P, weight adjustments are determined at each timestep according to:

$$\Delta w_t = \alpha \left(P_{t+1} - P_t \right) \sum_{k=1}^{t} \lambda^{t-k} \nabla_w P_k$$

where α is the parameter controlling the learning rate, $\nabla_w P_k$ is the partial derivative of P_k with respect to w, and P_t is the prediction at timestep t. The temporal discount parameter, λ, provides an exponentially decaying weight for more distant predictions.

The formula shows that TD(λ) is parameterised by α, the learning rate, and λ, the temporal discount factor.

Both parameters, and especially α, can have a major effect on the speed with which the weights approach an optimum. In Sutton's paper, learning behaviour for different α and λ values in sample domains is presented, but no method for determining suitable values *a priori* is known. Learning rates too high can cause failure to reach stable values and learning rates too low can lead to orders of magnitude more observations being necessary. Methods of choosing suitable α and λ values before or during the learning are therefore advantageous. There have been several algorithms proposed for adjusting α in supervised and TD learning: ours is based on a new principle that we call temporal coherence.

3. Temporal Coherence: adjusting α

Our system of self-adjusting learning rates is based on the concept that the learning rate should be higher when there is significant learning taking place, and lower when changes to the weights are primarily due to noise. Random noise will tend to produce adjustments that cancel out as they accumulate. Adjustments making useful adaptations to the observed predictions will tend to reinforce as they accumulate. As weight values approach their optimum, prediction errors will become mainly random noise.

Motivated by these considerations, our Temporal Coherence (TC) method estimates the significance of the weight movements by the relative strength of reinforcing adjustments to total adjustments. The learning rate is set according to the proportion of reinforcing adjustments as a fraction of all adjustments. This method has the desirable property that the learning rate reduces as optimum values are approached, tending towards zero. It has the equally desirable property of allowing the learning rate to increase if random adjustments are subsequently followed by a consistent trend.

Separate learning rates are maintained for each weight, so that weights that have become close to optimum do not fluctuate unnecessarily, and thereby add to the noise affecting predictions. The use of a separate learning rate for each weight allows for the possibility that different weights might become stable at different times during the learning process. For example, if weight A has become fairly stable after 100 updates, but weight B is still consistently rising, then it is desirable for the learning rate for weight B to be higher than that for weight A. An additional potential advantage of separate learning rates is that individual weights can be independent when new weights are added to the learning process. If new terms or nodes are added to an existing predictor, independent rates make it possible for the new weights to adjust quickly, whilst existing weights only increase their learning rates in response to perceived need.

The TC learning rates are determined by the history of *recommended* adjustments to each weight. We use the term 'recommended change' to mean the temporal difference adjustment prior to multiplication by the learning rate. This detachment of the learning rate enables the TC algorithm to respond to the underlying adjustment impulses, unaffected by its own recent choice of learning rate. It has the additional advantage that if the learning rate should reach zero, future learning rates are still free to be non-zero, and the learning does not halt.

The *recommended change* for weight w_i at timestep t is defined as:

$$r_{i,t} = (P_{t+1} - P_t)\sum_{k=1}^{t} \lambda^{t-k} \nabla_{w_i} P_k$$

The actual change made to weight w_i after game is:

$$\Delta w_i = c\,\alpha_i \sum_{t=1}^{end-1} r_{i,t}$$

where α_i is the individual learning rate for weight w_i and c is a learning rate for the whole process.

For each weight we are interested in two numbers: the accumulated *net change* (the sum of the individual recommended changes), and the accumulated *absolute change* (the sum of the absolute individual recommended changes). The ratio of net change, N, to absolute change, A, allows us to measure whether the adjustments to a given weight are mainly in the same 'direction'. We take reinforcing adjustments as indicating an underlying trend, and cancelling adjustments as indicating noise from the stochastic nature of the domain (or limitations of the domain model that contains the weights). The individual learning rate, α_i for each weight w_i is set to be the ratio of net recommended change to absolute recommended change:

$$\alpha_i = \frac{|N_i|}{A_i}$$

with the following definitions and update rules:

$$N_i \leftarrow N_i + \sum_{t=1}^{end-1} r_{i,t}$$

$$A_i \leftarrow A_i + \sum_{t=1}^{end-1} |r_{i,t}|$$

$r_{i,t}$ = recommended change for weight w_i at prediction t
$P_1..P_{end-1}$ are predictions, P_{end} is the final outcome

The operational order is that changes to w_i are made first, using the previous values of N_i, A_i and α_i, then N_i, A_i and α_i are updated. The parameter c has to be chosen, but this does not demand a choice between fast learning and eventual stability, since it can be set high initially, and the α_i then provide automatic adjustment during the learning process. All the α_i are initialised to 1 at the start of the learning process.

The foregoing formulae describe updating the weights and learning rates at the end of each sequence. The method may be easily amended to update more frequently (e.g. after each prediction), or less frequently (e.g. after a batch of sequences). For the experiments reported in this paper, update at the end of each game sequence is natural and convenient to implement.

4. Prediction Decay: determining λ

We determine a value for the temporal discount parameter, λ, by computing a quantity ψ we call *prediction decay*. Prediction decay is a function of observed prediction values, indexed by temporal distance between them, described in more detail in appendix A. An exponential curve is fitted to the observed data, and the exponential constant, ψ, from the fitted curve is the *prediction decay*. We set $\lambda = 1$ initially, and $\lambda = \psi$ thereafter.

The use of $\lambda = \psi$ has the desirable characteristics that (i) a perfect predictor will result in $\psi = 1$, and TD(1) is an appropriate value for the limiting case as predictions approach perfection, (ii) as the prediction reliability increases, ψ increases, and it is reasonable to choose higher values of λ for TD learning as the prediction reliability improves. We make no claim that setting $\lambda = \psi$ is optimum. Our experience is that it typically performs better than human-guessed choice of a fixed λ a priori.[1]

The advantage of using prediction decay is that it enables TD(λ) to be applied effectively to domains without prior domain knowledge, and without prior experiments to determine an effective λ. When combined with our method for adjusting learning rates, the resulting algorithm performs better than the comparison method, and better than using fixed rates, in both test domains.

Prediction decay is the average deterioration in prediction quality per timestep. A *prediction quality* function measures the correspondence between a prediction and a later prediction (or end-of-sequence outcome). The observed prediction qualities for each temporal distance are averaged. An exponential curve is then fitted to the average prediction qualities against distance (Figure 1 shows an example), and the exponential constant of that fitted curve is the prediction decay, ψ. We set the TD discount parameter λ, to 1 initially, and $\lambda = \psi$ thereafter. In the experiments reported, ψ (and hence λ) were updated at the end of each sequence.

The *prediction quality* measure, $Q_d(p, p')$ we used is defined below. It is constructed as a piece-wise linear function with the following properties:

i. When the two predictions p and p', are identical, $Q_d = 1$. (The maximum Q_d is 1)
ii. As the discrepancy between p and p' increases, Q_d decreases.
iii. When one prediction is 1 and the other is 0, then $Q_d = -1$. (The minimum Q_d is -1)
iv. For any given p, the average value of Q_d for all possible values of p', such that $0 \le p' \le 1$, equals 0. (Thus random guessing yields a score of zero.) This property is achieved by the quadratic equations in the definition below.

We achieve all these properties by defining:

$$Q_d(p,p') = \begin{cases} p \ge .5 & : & F(p,p') \\ p < .5 & : & F(1-p, 1-p') \end{cases}$$

---

[1] By expending sufficient computation time to repeatedly rerun the experiments we found somewhat better values for λ.

$$F(p,p') = \begin{cases} p \le s & : & \begin{cases} r \le x & : & 1 - r/x \\ r > x & : & -p(r-x)/(p-x) \end{cases} \\ p > s & : & \begin{cases} r \le y & : & 1 - r/y \\ r > y & : & -p(r-y)/(p-y) \end{cases} \end{cases}$$

where:

$r = |p - p'|$

s = solution of $2s^2 - 5s + 1 = 0$

x = solution of $2(1+p)x^2 - 4px + p = 0$

y = solution of $(1+p)y^2 + (2-2p-p^2)y - (1-p)^2 = 0$

p is the current prediction, p' is an earlier prediction, and d refers to the temporal distance between p and p'. Predictions lie in the range [0, 1].

It is assumed that the learning occurs over the course of many multi-step sequences, in which a prediction is made at each step; and that the sequences are independent. To form a prediction pair, both predictions must lie within the same sequence.

$\overline{Q}_d$ is the average prediction quality over all prediction pairs separated by distance d observed so far. For this purpose, the terminal outcome at the end of the sequence is treated as a prediction. At every prediction, the $\overline{Q}_d$ are incrementally updated.

An example graph from our experimental results is given in Figure 1. This example is typical of the fit to the observed data in the test domain. The exponential curve is fitted to the average prediction quality by minimising the mean squared error between the exponential curve and the observed $\overline{Q}_d$ values. ψ was fairly stable in the range 0.990 - 0.993 during the test runs.

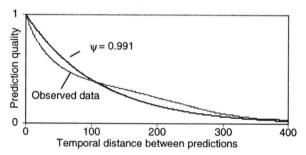

Figure 1: Fit of the prediction quality temporal decay to observed data from the game domain, after 2000 games.

To prevent rarely occurring distances from carrying undue weight in the overall error, the error term for each distance is weighted by the number of observed prediction pairs. Thus we seek a value of ψ which minimises:

$$\sum_{d=0}^{l} \left(\overline{Q}_d - \psi^d \right)^2 N_d$$

where $\overline{Q}_d$ is the average prediction quality for distance d, and N_d is the number of prediction pairs separated by that distance, and l is the length of the longest sequence in the observations so far.

we used meta-parameters of $\kappa = 0.035$, $\phi = 0.333$, $\theta = 0.7$ and $\varepsilon_0 = 0.05$, guided by data presented by Jacobs [1988] and preliminary experiments in this domain. For λ, which DBD does not set, we used $\lambda = 0.95$ derived from our experience with the fixed rate runs. We tried a number of other meta-parameter settings, none of which performed better than the chosen set. It is possible that a comprehensive search for a better set of meta-parameters might have improved the performance of the delta-bar-delta algorithm, but given the computational cost of a single run of 2000 sequences, we were unable to attempt a systematic search of all the meta-parameter values.

Figure 4 shows the average weights obtained using temporal coherence. It can be seen from the figure that all traces have approached their final values after about 900 sequences (some weights much sooner). Comparing with figures 2 and 3 it can be seen that the TC algorithm is faster to approach final values, and more stable once they are reached. In addition, the traces in figure 4 are smoother than in figures 2 and 3, representing less variation due to noise in the individual runs.

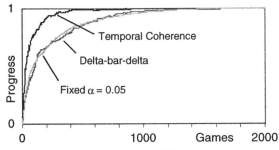

Figure 5: Progress over an average of 10 runs

Figure 5 shows the average piece values over 10 runs for the various methods, combined into a single term measuring progress toward the values achieved at the ends of the runs. From this figure we can see that delta-bar-delta does not improve much on a carefully-chosen fixed learning rate, and that temporal coherence clearly produces faster learning. The TC and fixed-α final weights were not significantly different.

To confirm that the learning process had produced satisfactory values, a match was played pitting the learnt values against the values widely quoted in elementary chess books Q=9, R=5, N/B=3, P=1. One program used those values, the other used the weights learnt using temporal coherence, as a check that the learnt values were at least as good as the standard ones. In a match of 2,000 games the TC values achieved a score of 58% against the standard values (won=1,119 lost=781 drawn=100).

7. Conclusions

We have described two new extensions, temporal coherence, and prediction decay, to the temporal difference learning method that set and adjust the major control parameters, learning rate and temporal discount, automatically as learning proceeds. The resulting TD algorithm has been tested in depth on a complex domain.

The results demonstrated both faster learning and more stable final values than a previous algorithm and the best of the fixed learning rates. The test domain was one in which values were learnt without supplying any domain-specific knowledge. We also tested the TC algorithm in a bounded walk domain [Sutton, 1998], and found similar advantages.

In our comparisons with the delta-bar-delta algorithm, we tried to find good parameter sets for DBD, which requires four meta parameters instead of the one control parameter, α. We tried several different (meta-) parameter sets in each domain, but were unable to find a set of parameters that improved performance over the results presented in sections 5.1 and 6.2. It is possible that a systematic search for better set of meta-parameters in each of the domains might improve performance. However, it is a major drawback for the method that it requires its meta-parameters to be tuned to the domain it is operating in. The methods presented here do not require a search for good parameter values.

The experimental results demonstrated that the temporal coherence plus prediction decay algorithm achieved three benefits: (1) automatic setting and adjustment of parameters (2) faster learning and (3) more stable final values.

References

Almeida, Langlois, & Amaral, 1998, On-Line Step Size Adaptation, *Technical Report RT07/97 INESC*, 9 Rua Alves Redol, 1000 Lisbon, Portugal.

Beal, D. F., and Smith, M.C., 1997, Learning piece values using temporal differences. *International Computer Chess Association Journal*, *20* (3): 147-151.

Beal, D.F., and Smith, M.C., 1998, Temporal Difference Learning for Heuristic Domains. *JCIS'98 Proceedings Vol(1), Oct 23-28, 1998*: 431-434.

Jacobs, R.A., 1988. Increased rates of convergence through learning rate adaptation. *Neural Networks*, *1*: 295-307.

Schraudolph, N.N., 1998, Online Local Gain Adaptation for Multi-layer Perceptrons, *Technical Report IDSIA-09-98*, IDSIA, Corso Elvezia 36, 6900 Lugano, Switzerland.

Sutton, R.S., 1988. Learning to predict by the methods of temporal differences. *Machine Learning*, *3*: 9-44.

Sutton, R.S., 1992. Adapting bias by gradient descent: an incremental version of delta-bar-delta. *Proceedings of the Tenth National Conference on Artificial Intelligence*, 171-176.

Sutton, R.S., and Singh, S.P., 1994. On step-size and bias in temporal-difference learning. *Proceedings of the Eighth Yale Workshop on Adaptive and Learning Systems*, 91-96.

Tesauro, G., 1992. Practical issues in temporal difference learning. *Machine Learning*, *8*: 257-277.

Domain-Dependent Single-Agent Search Enhancements

Andreas Junghanns and Jonathan Schaeffer
Department of Computing Science
University of Alberta
Edmonton, Alberta
CANADA T6G 2H1
Email: {andreas, jonathan}@cs.ualberta.ca

Abstract

AI research has developed an extensive collection of methods to solve state-space problems. Using the challenging domain of Sokoban, this paper studies the effect of search enhancements on program performance. We show that the current state of the art in AI generally requires a large programming and research effort into domain-dependent methods to solve even moderately complex problems in such difficult domains. The application of domain-specific knowledge to exploit properties of the search space can result in large reductions in the size of the search tree, often several orders of magnitude per search enhancement. Understanding the effect of these enhancements on the search leads to a new taxonomy of search enhancements, and a new framework for developing single-agent search applications. This is used to illustrate the large gap between what is portrayed in the literature versus what is needed in practice.

Keywords: single-agent search, IDA*, Sokoban

1 Introduction

The AI research community has developed an impressive suite of techniques for solving state-space problems. These techniques range from general-purpose domain-independent methods such as A*, to domain-specific enhancements. There is a strong movement toward developing domain-independent methods to solve problems. While these approaches require minimal effort to specify a problem to be solved, the performance of these solvers is often limited, exceeding available resources on even simple problem instances. This requires the development of domain-dependent methods that exploit additional knowledge about the search space. These methods can greatly improve the efficiency of a search-based program, as measured in the size of the search tree needed to solve a problem instance.

This paper presents a study on solving challenging single-agent search problems for the domain of Sokoban.

Sokoban is a one-player game and is of general interest as an instance of a robot motion planning problem [Dor and Zwick, 1995]. Sokoban is analogous to the problem of having a robot in a warehouse move specified goods from their current location to their final destination, subject to the topology of the warehouse and any obstacles in the way. Sokoban has been shown to be NP-hard [Culberson, 1997; Dor and Zwick, 1995].

Previously we reported on our attempts to solve Sokoban problems using the standard single-agent search techniques available in the literature [Junghanns and Schaeffer, 1998c]. When these proved inadequate, solving only 10 of a 90-problem test suite, new algorithms had to be developed to improve search efficiency [Junghanns and Schaeffer, 1998b; 1998a]. This allowed 47 problems to be optimally solved, or nearly so. Additional efforts have since increased this number to 52. The results here show the large gains achieved by adding application-dependent knowledge to our program *Rolling Stone*. With each enhancement, reductions of the search tree size by several orders of magnitude are possible.

Analyzing all the additions made to the Sokoban solver reveals that the most valuable search enhancements are based on search (both on-line and off-line) by improving the lower bound. We classify the search enhancements along several dimensions including their generality, computational model, completeness and admissibility. Not surprisingly, the more specific an enhancement is, the greater its impact on search performance.

When presented in the literature, single-agent search (usually IDA*) consists of a few lines of code. Most textbooks do not discuss search enhancements, other than cycle detection. In reality, non-trivial single-agent search problems require more extensive programming (and possibly research) effort. For example, achieving high performance at solving sliding tile puzzles requires enhancements such as cycle detection, pattern databases, move ordering and enhanced lower bound calculations [Culberson and Schaeffer, 1996]. In this paper, we outline a new framework for developing high-performance single-agent search programs.

This paper contains the following contributions:

1. A case study showing the evolution of a Sokoban

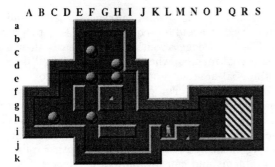

Figure 1: Problem #1 of the Test Set

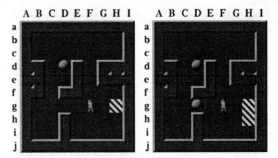

Figure 2: Two Simple Sokoban Problems

solver's performance, beginning with a domain-independent solver and ending with a highly-tuned, application-dependent program.

2. A taxonomy of single-agent search enhancements.

3. A new framework for single-agent search, including search enhancements and their control functions.

2 Sokoban

Figure 1 shows a sample problem of Sokoban. The goal is simple: use the man to push all the stones in the maze to the shaded goal squares. Only one stone can be pushed at a time. These rather simple rules belie the difficulty of Sokoban problems, especially with respect to computer solutions. We identified several reasons why Sokoban is so difficult [Junghanns and Schaeffer, 1998c]:

- The graph underlying Sokoban problems is directed; some moves are not reversible. Consequently, there are *deadlock* states from which no solution is reachable. Deadlocks represent a challenge for anytime algorithms: when committing to a move, how can we make sure that no deadlock is introduced?

- The combination of long solution lengths (up to 674 stone pushes in the test set) and potentially large branching factors make Sokoban difficult for conventional search algorithms to solve. 20×20 Sokoban offers the challenge of a large search space ($\approx 10^{98}$).

- Sokoban solutions are inherently sequential; only limited parts of a solution are interchangeable. Subgoals are often interrelated and thus cannot be solved independently.

- A "simple", effective lower bound on the solution length of a Sokoban problem remains elusive. The best lower bound estimator is expensive to calculate, and is often ineffective.

None of the above obstacles are found in the "standard" single-agent test domains, such as $N \times N$-puzzles and Rubik's Cube.

3 Application-Independent Techniques

Ideally, applications should be specified with minimal effort and a "generic" solver would be used to compute the solutions. In small domains this is attainable (e.g., if it is easily enumerable). For more challenging domains, there have recently been a number of interesting attempts at domain-independent solvers (e.g., *blackbox* [Kautz and Selman, 1996]). Before investing a lot of effort in developing a Sokoban-specific program, it is important to understand the capabilities of current AI tools. Hence, we include this information to illustrate the disparity between what application-independent problem solvers can achieve, compared to application-dependent techniques.

The Sokoban problems in Figure 2 [McDermott, 1998] were given to the program *blackbox* to solve. *Blackbox* was the winner of the AIPS'98 fastest planner competition. The first problem was solved within a few seconds and the second problem was solved in over an hour.

Clearly, domain-independent planners, like *blackbox*, have a long way to go if they are to solve the even simplest problem in the test suite (Figure 1). Hence, for this application domain we have no choice but to pursue an application-dependent implementation.

4 Application-Dependent Techniques

As reported in [Junghanns and Schaeffer, 1998c], we implemented IDA* for Sokoban. We gave the algorithm a fixed node limit of 1 billion nodes for all experiments (varying from 1 to 3 hours of CPU time on a single 195 MHz processor of an SGI Origin 2000). After adding an enhancement, *Rolling Stone* was run on 90 test problems (http://xsokoban.lcs.mit.edu/xsokoban.html) to find out how many could be solved and how much search effort was required to do so.

Figure 3 presents the experimental results for different versions of *Rolling Stone*. Version *R0* is the program using only IDA* with the lower bound; RA contains all the search enhancements. The logarithmic vertical axis shows the number of search nodes needed to solve a problem. The horizontal axis shows how many problems can be solved (out of 90), ordering the problems by search tree size. The performance lines in the figure are sorted from left to right with an increasing number of search enhancements.

Lower Bound (0 solved): To obtain an admissible estimate of the distance of a position to a goal, a minimum-cost, perfect bipartite matching algorithm is used. The matching assigns each stone to a goal and returns the total (minimum) distance of all stones to their goals. The algorithm is $O(N^3)$ in the number of stones N. IDA* with this lower bound cannot solve any of the test problems within one billion search nodes.

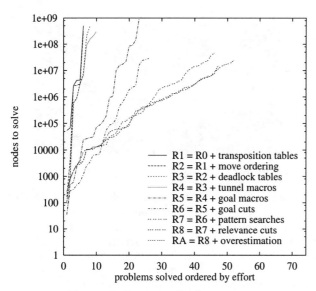

Figure 3: Program Performance

Transposition Table (6 solved): The search space of Sokoban is a graph, rather than a tree, so repeated positions and cycles are possible. A *transposition table* was implemented to avoid duplicate search effort. Positions that have the same stone locations and equivalent man locations (taking man reachability into account) are treated as the same position. Transposition tables reduces the search tree size by several orders of magnitude, allowing *Rolling Stone* to solve 6 problems.

Move Ordering (6 solved): Children of a node are ordered based on their likelihood of leading to a solution. *Move ordering* only helps in the last iteration. Even though move ordering results in no additional problems being solved, less search effort is used to solve each problem.

Deadlock Table (8 solved): The pattern database is a recent idea that has been successfully used in the $N \times N$-puzzles [Culberson and Schaeffer, 1996] and Rubik's Cube [Korf, 1997]. An off-line search enumerated all possible stone/wall placements in a 4×5 region and searched them to determine if deadlock was present. These results are stored in *deadlock tables*. During an IDA* search, the table is queried to see if the current move leads to a local deadlock. Thus, deadlock tables contain search results of partial problem configurations and are general with respect to all Sokoban problems.

Tunnel Macros (10 solved): A Sokoban maze often contains "tunnels" (such as the squares *Kh*, *Lh*, *Mh* and *Nh* in Figure 1). Once a stone is pushed into a tunnel, it must eventually be pushed all the way through. Rather than do this through search, this sequence of moves can be collapsed into a single macro move. By collapsing several moves into one, the height of the search tree is reduced. *Tunnel macros* are identified by pre-processing.

Goal Macros (23 solved): Prior to starting the search, a preliminary search is used to find an appropriate order in which to fill in the goal squares. In many cases this is a non-trivial computation, especially when the goal area(s) has several entrances. A specialized search is used to avoid fill sequences that lead to a deadlock. The knowledge about the goal area is then used to create goal macros, where stones are pushed directly from the goal area entrance(s) to the final goal square avoiding deadlocks. For example, in Figure 1, square *Gh* is defined as the entrance to the goal area; once a stone reaches it, a single macro move is used to push it to the next pre-determined goal square. These macro moves significantly reduce the search depth required to solve problems and can dramatically reduce the search tree size. Whenever a goal macro move is possible, it is the only move considered; all alternatives are *forward pruned*.

Goal Cuts (26 solved): *Goal cuts* effectively push the goal macros further up the search tree. Whenever a stone can be pushed to a goal entrance square, none of the alternative moves are considered. The idea behind these cuts is that if one is confident about using macro moves, one might as well prune alternatives to pushing that stone further up in the search tree.

Pattern Search (46 solved): *Pattern searches* [Junghanns and Schaeffer, 1998b] are an effective way to detect lower bound inefficiencies. Small, localized conflict-driven searches uncover patterns of stones that interact in such a way that the lower bound estimator is off by an arbitrary amount (even infinite, in the case of a deadlock). These patterns are used throughout the search to improve the lower bound. Patterns are specific to a particular problem instance and are discovered on the fly using specialized searches. Patterns represent the knowledge about dynamic stone interactions that lead to poor static lower bounds, and the associated penalties are the corrective measures.

Pattern searches lead to dramatic improvements of the search: many orders of magnitude vanish from the search tree size and 20 more problems can be solved. Note that tree sizes reported include the pattern search nodes.

Relevance Cuts (47 solved): *Relevance cuts* [Junghanns and Schaeffer, 1998a] are an attempt to cut down the branching factor using forward pruning. If moves are "inconsistent" to the previous move history, they are pruned. This heuristic is unsafe, since it has the potential to prune solution paths. However, it does decrease search tree sizes, and can be a beneficial trade-off.

Overestimation (52 solved): Given the difficulty of solving Sokoban problems, *any* solution, even a non-optimal one, is welcome. The patterns that *Rolling Stone* discovers indicate when potentially "difficult" situations arise. To ensure admissibility, some patterns that match are not always used to increase the lower bound. Overestimation allows every pattern to add to the lower bound. In principle, this can be interpreted as the program "avoiding" difficult situations. We prefer to describe it as a knowledge-driven postponement of search: the additional penalty only postpones when the search will explore a certain part of the tree, it will not cut branches indefinitely. In this respect, this method preserves completeness, but not solution optimality.

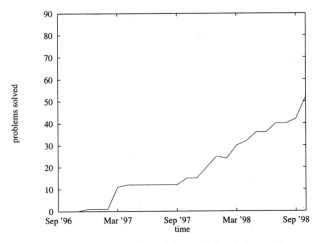

Figure 4: Number of Problems Solved Over Time

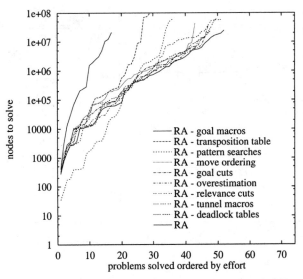

Figure 5: Effort Graphs For Methods Turned Off

The performance gap between the first and last versions of *Rolling Stone* in Figure 3 is astounding. For example, consider extrapolating the performance of *Rolling Stone* with transposition tables so that it can solve the same number of problems as the complete program (52). 10^{50} (not a typo!) seems to be a reasonable lower bound on the difference in search tree sizes.

The preceding discussion closely corresponds to the order in which enhancements were initially added to *Rolling Stone* (although most enhancements have been continually refined). Figure 4 shows how these results were achieved over the 2-year development time. The development effort equates to a full-time PhD, a part time professor, a full-time summer student, and feedback from many people. Additionally, a large number of machine cycles were used for tuning and debugging. It is interesting to note the occasional *decrease* in the number of problems solved, the result of (favorable) bugs being fixed. The long, slow, steady increase is indicative of the reality of building a large system. Progress is incremental and often painfully slow.

The results in Figure 3 may misrepresent the importance of each feature. Figure 5 shows the results of taking the full version of *Rolling Stone* and disabling single search enhancements. In the absence of a particular method, other search enhancements can compensate to allow a solution to be found. Most notably, while the lower bound function alone cannot solve a single problem, neither can the complete system solve a single problem without the lower bound function.

Figure 5 shows that turning off goal macros reduces the number of problems solved by 35, more than 66%! Turning off transposition tables loses 23 problems. Turning off pattern searches reduces the number of solved problems by 16. Other than the lower bound function, these three methods are the most important for *Rolling Stone*; losing any one of them dramatically reduces the performance. While other enhancements don't have as dramatic an effect, turning any one of them off loses at least one problem.

5 Knowledge Taxonomy

In looking at the domain-specific knowledge used to solve Sokoban problems, we can identify several different ways of classifying the knowledge:

Generality. Classify based on how general the knowledge is: *domain* (e.g., Sokoban), *instance* (a particular Sokoban problem), and *subtree* (within a Sokoban search).

Computation. Differentiate how the knowledge was obtained: *static* (such as advice from a human expert) and *dynamic* (gleaned from a search).

Admissibility/Completeness. Knowledge can be: *admissible* (preserve optimality in a solution) or *non-admissible*. Non-admissible knowledge can either preserve *completeness* of the algorithm or render it *incomplete*. Admissible knowledge is necessarily complete.

Figure 6 summarizes the search enhancements used in *Rolling Stone*. Other enhancements from the literature could easily be added into spaces that are still blank, e.g. perimeter databases [Manzini, 1995] (dynamic, admissible, instance). Note that some of the enhancement classifications are fixed by the type of the enhancement. For example, any type of forward pruning is incomplete by definition, and move ordering always preserves admissibility. For some enhancements, the properties depend on the implementation. For example, overestimation techniques can be static or dynamic; goal macros can be admissible or non-admissible; pattern databases can be domain-based or instance-based.

It is interesting to note that, apart from the lower bound function itself, the three most important program enhancements in terms of program performance (Figure 5) are all dynamic (search-based) and instance/subtree specific. The static enhancements, while of value, turn out to be of less importance. Static knowledge is usually rigid and does not include the myriad of exceptions that search-based methods can uncover and react to.

Classification		Domain	Instance	Subtree
Static	admissible	lower bound	tunnel macros	move ordering
	complete			
	incomplete		relevance cuts	goal cuts
Dynamic	admissible	deadlock tables		pattern searches
				transposition table
	complete			overestimation
	incomplete		goal macros	

Figure 6: Taxonomy of Search Enhancements in Sokoban

6 Control Functions

There is another type of application-dependent knowledge that is critical to performance, but receives scant attention in the literature. *Control functions* are intrinsic parts of efficient search programs, controlling when to use or not use a search enhancement. In *Rolling Stone* numerous control functions are used to improve the search efficiency. Some examples include:

Transposition Table: Control knowledge is needed to decide when new information is worth replacing older information in the table. Also, when reading from the table, control information can decide whether the benefits of the lookup justify the cost.

Goal Macros: If a goal area has too few goal squares, then goal macros are disabled. With a small number of goals or too many entrances, the search will likely not need macro moves, and the potential savings are not worth the risk of eliminating possible solutions.

Pattern Searches: Pattern searches are executed only when a non-trivial heuristic function indicates the likelihood of a penalty being present. Executing a pattern search is expensive, so this overhead should be introduced only when it is likely to be cost effective. Control functions are also used to stop a pattern search when success appears unlikely.

Implementing a search enhancement is often only one part of the programming effort. Implementing and tuning its control function(s) can be significantly more time consuming and more critical to performance. We estimate that whereas the search enhancements take about 90% of the coding effort and the control functions only 10%, the reverse distribution applies to the amount of tuning effort needed and machine cycles consumed.

A clear separation between the search enhancements and their respective control functions can help the tuning effort. For example, while the goal macro creation only considers which order the stones should be placed into the goal area, the control function can determine if goal macros should be created at all. Both tuning efforts have very different objectives: one is search efficiency,

```
IDA*() {
   /** Compute the best possible lower bound **/
   lb = ComputeLowerBound();
   lb += UsePatterns();        /** Match Patterns **/
   lb += UseDeadlockTable();
   lb += UseOverestimate( CntrlOverestimate() );
   if( cutoff ) return;
   /** Preprocess **/
   lb += ReadTransTable();
   if( cutoff ) return;
   PatternSearch( CntrlPatternSearch() );
   lb += UsePatterns();
   if( cutoff ) return;
   /** Generate searchable moves **/
   movelist = GenerateMoves();
   RemoveDeadMoves( movelist );
   IdentifyMacros( movelist );
   OrderMoves( movelist );
   for( each move ) {
      if( Irrelevant( move, CntrlIrrelevent() )) next;
      solution = IDA*();
      if( solution ) return;
      if( GoalCut() ) break;
      UpdateLowerBound();      /** Use New Patterns **/
      if( cutoff ) return;
   }
   /** Post-process **/
   SaveTransTable( CntrlTransTable() );
   return;
}
```

Figure 7: Enhanced IDA*

the other risk minimization. Separating the two seems natural and convenient.

7 Single-Agent Search Framework

As presented in the literature, single-agent search consists of a few lines of code (usually IDA*). Most textbooks do not discuss search enhancements, other than cycle detection. In reality, non-trivial single-agent search problems require a more extensive programming (and possibly research) effort.

Figure 7 illustrates the basic IDA* routine, with our enhancements included (in *italics*). This routine is specific to *Rolling Stone*, but could be written in more general terms. It does not include a number of well-known single-agent search enhancements available in the literature. Control functions are indicated by parameters to search enhancement routines. In practice, some of these functions are implemented as simple *if* statements controlling access to the enhancement code.

Examining the code in Figure 7, one realizes that there are really only three types of search enhancements:

1. Modifying the lower bound (as indicated by the updates to *lb*). This can take two forms: optimally increasing the bound (e.g. using patterns) which reduces the distance to search, or non-optimally (using overestimation) which redistributes where the search effort is concentrated.

2. Removing branches unlikely to add additional infor-

```
for( each domain ) {
  /** Preprocess **/
  BuildDeadlockTable( CntrlDeadlockTable() );
  for( each instance ) {
    /** Preprocess **/
    FindTunnelMacros();
    FindGoalMacros( CntrlGoalMacros() );
    while( not solved ) {
      SetSearchParamaters();
      IDA*();
    }
    /** Postprocess **/
    SavePatterns( CntrlSavingPatterns() );
  }
}
```

Figure 8: Preprocessing Hierarchy

mation to the search (the *next* and *break* statements in the *for* loop). This forward pruning can result in large reductions in the search tree, at the expense of possibly affecting the completeness.

3. Collapsing the tree height by replacing a sequence of moves with one move (for example, macros).

Some of the search enhancements involve computations outside of the search. Figure 8 shows where the pre-search processing occurs at the domain and instance levels. Off-line computation of pattern databases or pre-processing of problem instances are powerful techniques that receive scant attention in the literature (chess endgame databases are a notable exception). Yet these techniques are an important step towards the automation of knowledge discovery and machine learning. Preprocessing is involved in many of the most valuable enhancements that are used in *Rolling Stone*.

Similar issues occur with other search algorithms. For example, although it takes only a few lines to specify the alpha-beta algorithm, the *Deep Blue* chess program's search procedure includes numerous enhancements (many similar in spirit to those used in *Rolling Stone*) that cumulatively reduce the search tree size by several orders of magnitude. If nothing else, the *Deep Blue* result demonstrated the degree of engineering required to build high-performance search-based systems.

8   Conclusions

This paper described our experiences working with a challenging single-agent search domain. In contrast to the simplicity of the basic IDA* formulation, building a high-performance single-agent searcher can be a complex task that combines both research and engineering. Application-dependent knowledge, specifically that obtained using search, can result in an orders-of-magnitude improvement in search efficiency. This can be achieved through a judicious combination of several search enhancements. Control functions are overlooked in the literature, yet are critical to performance. They represent a significant portion of the program development time and most of the program experimentation resources.

Domain-independent tools offer a quick programming solution when compared to the effort required to develop domain-dependent applications. However, with current AI tools, performance is commensurate with effort. Domain-dependent solutions can be vastly superior in performance. The trade-off between programming effort and performance is the critical design decision that needs to be made.

9   Acknowledgements

This research was supported by a grant from the Natural Sciences and Engineering Research Council of Canada. Computational resources were provided by MACI. This paper benefited from interactions with Yngvi Björnsson, Afzal Upal and Rob Holte.

References

[Culberson and Schaeffer, 1996] J. Culberson and J. Schaeffer. Searching with pattern databases. In G. McCalla, editor, *Advances in Artificial Intelligence*, pages 402–416. Springer-Verlag, 1996.

[Culberson, 1997] J. Culberson. Sokoban is PSPACE-complete. Technical Report TR97–02, Dept. of Computing Science, University of Alberta, 1997. ftp.cs.ualberta.ca/pub/TechReports/1997/TR97–02.

[Dor and Zwick, 1995] D. Dor and U. Zwick. SOKOBAN and other motion planning problems, 1995. At: http://www.math.tau.ac.il/~ddorit.

[Junghanns and Schaeffer, 1998a] A. Junghanns and J. Schaeffer. Relevance cuts: Localizing the search. In *The First International Conference on Computers and Games*, pages 1–13, 1998. To appear in: *Lecture Notes in Computing Science*, Springer Verlag.

[Junghanns and Schaeffer, 1998b] A. Junghanns and J. Schaeffer. Single-agent search in the presence of deadlock. In *AAAI*, pages 419–424, 1998.

[Junghanns and Schaeffer, 1998c] A. Junghanns and J. Schaeffer. Sokoban: Evaluating standard single-agent search techniques in the presence of deadlock. In R. Mercer and E. Neufeld, editors, *Advances in Artificial Intelligence*, pages 1–15. Springer Verlag, 1998.

[Kautz and Selman, 1996] H. Kautz and B. Selman. Pushing the envelope: planning, propositional logic and stochastic search. In *AAAI*, pages 1194–1201, 1996.

[Korf, 1997] R.E. Korf. Finding optimal solutions to Rubik's Cube using pattern databases. In *AAAI*, pages 700–705, 1997.

[Manzini, 1995] G. Manzini. BIDA*: An improved perimeter search algorithm. *Artificial Intelligence*, 75:347–360, 1995.

[McDermott, 1998] Drew McDermott. Using regression-match graphs to control search in planning, 1998. Unpublished manuscript.

COMPUTER GAME PLAYING

Game Playing 2

Decomposition Search: A Combinatorial Games Approach to Game Tree Search, with Applications to Solving Go Endgames

Martin Müller

Electrotechnical Laboratory
Tsukuba, Japan
mueller@etl.go.jp

Abstract

We develop a new method called *decomposition search* for computing minimax solutions to games that can be partitioned into independent subgames. The method does not use traditional minimax search algorithms such as alpha-beta, but relies on concepts from combinatorial game theory to do locally restricted searches. This divide-and-conquer approach allows the exact solution of much larger problems than is possible with alpha-beta.

We show an application of decomposition search to the game of Go, which has been traditionally regarded as beyond the range of exact search-based solution methods. Our experiments with solving endgames show that alpha-beta searches already become impractical in positions with about 15 remaining moves. However, an endgame solver based on decomposition search can solve a much larger class of endgame problems with solution lengths exceeding 60 moves.

1 Introduction

In two-player games with perfect information, minimax-based search methods have been very successful. Games such as 4-in-a-row, gomoku or nine men's morris have been solved, and heuristic game-playing programs have reached world championship level in a number of popular games. In chess and checkers, endgame databases constructed using retrograde analysis have uncovered a wealth of new information and forced the rewriting of the textbooks.

Today, the conditions under which these standard approaches are successful are well understood. One class of games in which they have not succeeded is combinatorial games. Such a game can be represented as a combinatorial *sum* of local games, called *subgames*.

Decomposition search is a new computational method for solving combinatorial games. Decomposition search decomposes a game into a sum of subgames, performs a particular kind of local search for each subgame, applies

combinatorial game theory to evaluate the resulting local game graphs, and determines overall optimal play from the combinatorial game values of subgames.

By reducing the scope of searches from global to local, the new method can compute minimax solutions and determine optimal play in such games much faster than classical techniques such as alpha-beta, which can not exploit the extra structure given by the decomposition.

The structure of this paper is as follows: Section 2 reviews several existing divide-and-conquer approaches to solving games, including the combinatorial game-theoretical approach to the analysis of games with decomposable state. Section 3 introduces *decomposition search*, a four step algorithm for finding the minimax solution and optimal play in combinatorial games. Section 4 applies decomposition search to Go endgames, and Section 5 compares the performance of decomposition search with standard alpha-beta game tree search, using Go endgames as examples.

2 Divide-and-Conquer Approaches to Solving Games

Research in game tree search follows two general goals: reducing the size of the search space, and traversing the space in clever ways in order to find solutions early. For solving games with large state spaces, divide-and-conquer approaches are attractive: the idea is to identify simpler subproblems that can be solved more easily, and can contribute to an overall solution.

2.1 Heuristic Problem Decomposition: Identifying Subgoals

In complex games, the ultimate goal of the game is difficult to reach directly. Therefore, players identify subgoals and search specifically to achieve these goals. For example, bridge players analyze single-suit play, and chess players seek ways to capture a particular piece or break through a pawn chain. A narrowly focused search to achieve a subgoal is typically much easier than full width game search, yet achieving a subgoal can have a significant impact on the outcome of the game.

2.2 Splitting a Game Vertically: Endgame Databases

A very successful divide-and-conquer method in the computational analysis of games has been the construction of endgame databases. In this approach, a game is split vertically into progressively simpler games along the time axis. *Converging* games such as checkers, nine men's morris or chess can be split in this way, because they simplify towards the end of the game when fewer and fewer pieces remain on the board.

Endgame databases are built bottom-up, starting from the simplest subgames, by retrograde analysis [Thompson, 1986]. The optimal play outcome, and optionally the distance to a win or conversion to another subgame, is computed for all positions in the subgame. Databases are used during heuristic search: whenever search hits a database position, the exact value can be used in place of the heuristic evaluation.

2.3 The Mathematics of Decomposition: The Combinatorial Game Approach to the Analysis of Games

Combinatorial game theory [Conway, 1976; Berlekamp *et al.*, 1982] provides the mathematical basis for a more radical divide-and-conquer method: it breaks up game positions into pieces and analyzes the overall game in terms of these smaller local subgames.

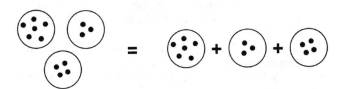

Figure 1: A three heap *Nim* position and its subgames

Each move in the game corresponds to a move in one subgame and leaves all other subgames unchanged. A game ends when all subgames have ended, and the final outcome of the game can be determined from the subgame outcomes. A well-known example of a combinatorial game is *Nim*, shown in Figure 1, which is played with heaps of tokens. At each move, a player removes an arbitrary number of tokens from a single heap, and whoever runs out of moves first loses. Each Nim heap constitutes one subgame. While winning a single subgame is trivial, winning the *sum* of several heaps requires either exhaustive analysis, or, much more efficiently, a computation using the calculus of combinatorial games.

3 Decomposition Search

This section develops decomposition search as a framework for solving games through decomposition, a particular kind of local search named *local combinatorial game search (LCGS)* and the analysis of the resulting local game graphs by applying combinatorial game theory.

3.1 Definition of Decomposition Search

Let G be a game that decomposes into a sum of subgames $G_1 + \ldots + G_n$. Let the combinatorial game evaluation of G be $C(G)$. *Decomposition search* is defined as the following four step algorithm for determining optimal play of G:

1. Game decomposition and subgame identification: given G, find an equivalent sum of subgames $G_1 + \ldots + G_n$.

2. Local combinatorial game search (LCGS): for each G_i, perform a search to find its game graph $GG(G_i)$.

3. Evaluation: for each game graph $GG(G_i)$, evaluate all terminal positions, then find the combinatorial game evaluation of all interior nodes, leading to the computation of $C(G_i)$.

4. Sum game play: through combinatorial game analysis of the set of combinatorial games $C(G_i)$, select an optimal move in $G_1 + \ldots + G_n$.

The following subsections describe the four steps of decomposition search in more detail, discuss how to use the results of decomposition search during game play, and describe limitations of the method.

3.2 Game Decomposition and Subgame Identification

The precondition for applying decomposition search to a game position is that it can be split into subgames which fit the combinatorial games model outlined in Section 2.3. The specific decomposition procedure depends on the game rules.

In some games, such as Nim, Amazons and many of those analyzed in the book Winning Ways [Berlekamp *et al.*, 1982], a suitable decomposition follows directly from the rules of the game. Figure 1 shows the decomposition of a Nim position. In other games, such as Go, more game-specific knowledge is necessary to find a good decomposition of a given position.

3.3 Local Combinatorial Game Search

Local combinatorial game search (LCGS) is the main information gathering step of decomposition search. It is performed independently for each subgame. LCGS generates a game graph representing all relevant move sequences that might be played locally in the course of a game. LCGS works differently from minimax tree search in a number of ways, including move generation and recognition of terminal positions.

Differences Between LCGS and Minimax Search
The game graph built by LCGS differs from the tree generated by minimax search. In the case of minimax, players move alternately, so each position is analyzed with respect to the player on move. In contrast, there is no player-to-move-next in a subgame. All possible local move sequences must be included in the analysis, including sequences with several successive moves by the same

player, because players can switch between subgames at every move.

Another difference between local and full state search is the treatment of cycles. To prevent infinite games, the repetition of a game position is forbidden in most games, or limited to a small number as in chess. However, the same local position can re-occur repeatedly as long as the whole game keeps changing. Combinatorial game evaluation is defined only for games without cycles. Therefore, decomposition search deals only with locally acyclic games, and with those cyclic games where cycles do not enter into optimal play.

Move Generation

LCGS must generate all legal local moves for both players, except in a terminal position or if moves can provably be pruned. Such exact pruning rules are game-specific. Examples are restricting the number of equivalent moves generated to a single one, or pruning locally bad moves which are dominated by other moves.

Terminal Positions and Local Scoring

Termination rules decide when a position can be evaluated without further expanding the game graph. LCGS defines the following termination rules:

- No legal moves
- No good move, game recognized as constant
- Value of position already known

The first two cases represent local terminal positions, which evaluate to an integer. This number, the *local score*, is game-specific and computed according to the rules of the game.

In the third case, if the value of a position is already known from another source, such as a transposition table, game-specific knowledge, or a precomputed local position database, LCGS can be terminated as well. The value retrieved for such a position is a combinatorial game, which has previously been computed by local evaluation as discussed in the next section.

3.4 Local Evaluation: Mapping Game Graphs to Combinatorial Games

Local evaluation computes the combinatorial game value of a given acyclic local game graph with evaluated leaf nodes. Let the players be Black and White, with positive scores good for Black. If from a local position p Black can move to $b_1 \ldots b_n$ and White can move to $w_1 \ldots w_m$, and if the evaluations of these follow-up positions are already known, then the evaluation $C(p)$ is given by the combinatorial game expression

$$C(p) = \{\, C(b_1), \ldots, C(b_n) \mid C(w_1), \ldots, C(w_m) \,\}.$$

This expression can be brought into a canonical form using standard rules of combinatorial game theory. Repeated bottom-up application of the formula eventually yields an evaluation of each node in the game graph.

Cycles that do not Affect the Game Value

Cycles can occur during LCGS, even if they have no effect on optimal play. If evaluation fails due to cycles, bounds are computed by forbidding one player all moves that would repeat a position. This transforms the game graph into an acyclic graph, a different one for each player. If both bounds coincide, optimal play does not depend on cycles. Otherwise, decomposition search stops and indicates a local evaluation failure.

3.5 Sum Game Play

To find an optimal move in a sum game, the final step of decomposition search selects a move which most improves the position. This improvement is measured by a combinatorial game called the *incentive* of a move. The incentives of all moves in all subgames are computed locally. If one incentive dominates all others, an optimal move has been determined. This is the usual case for games with a rich set of values such as Go.

Since incentives are combinatorial games and therefore only partially ordered, it can happen that more than one nondominated candidate move remains. In this case, an optimal move is found by a more complex procedure involving the combinatorial summation of games [Conway, 1976].

Since such a summation can be an expensive operation, there is no worst case guarantee that decomposition search is always more efficient than minimax search. In practice, it seems to work much better. The algorithm presents many opportunities for complexity reduction of intermediate expressions during local evaluation as well as during summation.

Even though all search and most analysis is local, decomposition search yields globally optimal play, which can switch back and forth between subgames in very subtle ways, as in the example of Figure 8.

3.6 Reusing Decomposition Search Results During Play

The result of decomposition search is a complete description and evaluation of all reasonable local play sequences, which makes perfect overall play possible. Results of local analysis can be saved in a database. During play, each full board position corresponds to a set of matching local positions, one from each subgame. Positions and their combinatorial game values are retrieved from the database.

As long as the opponent follows analyzed lines, followup moves can be played from the information stored in the database, without further search. If the opponent plays a less-than-optimal move that was pruned during LCGS and reaches an unevaluated position, the corresponding subgame is re-searched from the new position.

3.7 Limitations of Decomposition Search

There are two types of limitations for decomposition search: cyclic subgames and bounded computational resources. As discussed in Section 3.4, cyclic subgames can be handled only in the case where cycles don't affect optimal play.

Resource exhaustion is detected during algorithm execution if any of the following hold: game decomposition fails or results in very large subgames, LCGS exceeds a preset time or space limit, or intermediate combinatorial game expressions become too complex. Practical limits are highly game-specific, and depend on the shape of local game graphs built during LCGS and on the complexity of the combinatorial games involved. For example, *impartial* games such as Nim are generally easier to evaluate than *partizan* games such as Go.

4 Applying Decomposition Search to Go Endgames

This section discusses how to apply decomposition search to the game of Go. Game decomposition is achieved through the recognition of safe stones and territories and the resulting board partition. Other Go-specific aspects are pruning moves during LCGS and scoring of terminal positions.

4.1 Subgame Identification in Go by Board Partition

A Go position can be decomposed when parts of the board are isolated from the rest by walls of safe stones. Moves in one part have no effect on other parts across such a wall. Figures 2 and 3 show the two decomposition steps: first, finding safe stones and territories, and then identifying subgames as the connected components of the remaining points on the Go board.

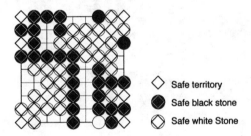

Figure 2: Recognition of safe stones and territories

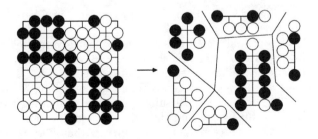

Figure 3: Decomposition of Go endgame position

Finding Safe Stones and Territories

Safe territories are 'finished' subgames: they can be evaluated by a number, the size of the territory. Areas which are completely surrounded by one player are candidate territories. Territories are found by goal-directed search, applying the techniques of [Müller, 1995; 1997] to prove the safety of candidate territories.

Play in territories that have been proven safe is simple. The player never plays first in any territory. If the opponent attacks the player's territory, a goal-directed search is performed to find a refutation which restores the safety of the area.

4.2 LCGS in Go

An endgame area consists of unsettled stones, and of empty points which are not territory. Safe stones, usually of both colors, surround each endgame area, as shown in Figure 3. During endgame play, unsettled stones either become safe or are captured. Empty points will either be occupied or become part of a safe territory. A rare special case are shared empty points in *seki*.

Scoring Local Terminal Positions in Go

Scoring assigns an integer to each terminal position. In Chinese rules, scoring measures the difference between how many stones and empty points belong to either color. In Japanese rules, territory and prisoners are counted. Both kinds of scoring are straightforward in a terminal position since the status of all stones and empty points is known exactly.

Pruning Moves

In contrast to the speculative pruning in selective search methods, only moves that are provably worse-or-equal than others can be eliminated. For example, if a move achieves control of all points in the local area, it is optimal, and all other moves can be pruned. In almost surrounded areas such as the one shown in Figure 4, the move at the entrance at *a* is the only good move for either player.

Figure 4: Area with unique best move at *a*

4.3 Full Board Move Selection in Go

Full board move selection in Go distinguishes three cases:

1. If the opponent just made a threat in player's territory, reply as in Section 4.1 to keep territory and stones safe.

2. Otherwise, if the combinatorial game is not finished yet, play the sum game as in Section 3.5.

3. Otherwise, perform a cleanup phase: fill in the final neutral points to finish the game.

5 Experiments

The performance of decomposition search is compared with standard full board alpha-beta search on two representative examples from a set of Go endgame puzzles in [Berlekamp and Wolfe, 1994]. In the examples, territories have been slightly strengthened to make it easier to prove their safety. The endgames are equivalent to the original version. In each experiment, the full board problem was solved from scratch. No precomputed database of subgames was used.

5.1 Full-board Minimax Search

The minimax implementation used a standard alpha-beta search. The size of the transposition table was 32k entries for the small problems, 4M entries for the big ones. Since naive full-board search would be too expensive, alpha-beta search was allowed to use the same knowledge about safe territories and the same local pruning rules as LCGS.

In contrast to LCGS, pass moves must be generated, because in positions where there is no good move, players must be allowed to pass, instead of being forced to damage their own position.

5.2 First Example: 20 Point Problem

The first Go endgame example, on a 9×9 board, is based on problem C.9 of [Berlekamp and Wolfe, 1994]. After computing safe stones and territories, the total remaining endgame area is 20 points. There are six regions labeled A to F, with sizes ranging from 2 to 6.

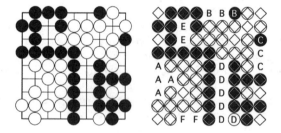

Figure 5: Problem C.9 and its decomposition

This problem is trivial for decomposition search, yet already challenging for minimax. For more detailed testing, a series of simplified problems was created, in which several local endgame situations were replaced by constant territories. Figure 6 shows such a simplified problem of size 10 consisting of areas A, B and C. Areas D, E and F have been 'played out' and replaced by constant territories, as shown by the markings in the figure.

White is to play first in all problems. Table 1 shows the total node count for the LCGS phase of decomposition search, followed by the node count and solution time in seconds for alpha-beta, as measured on a Macintosh G3/250. The solution times for decomposition search are not shown, since they were all very similar at 0.2 - 0.3 seconds. The size of the transposition table (4M entries) was insufficient for the full 20 point problem, resulting in an enormous increase in solution time to over 28 hours.

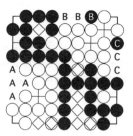

Figure 6: Problem C.9 reduced to areas A+B+C

Areas (Size)	Nodes DS	Nodes $\alpha\beta$	Time $\alpha\beta$
A (4)	21	39	<0.1
A+B (7)	26	526	0.1
A+B+C (10)	31	5905	1.9
A+B+C+D (16)	42	1097589	295.9
A+B+C+D+E (18)	45	10243613	2461.0
A+B+C+D+E+F (20)	48	463941123	103406.2

Table 1: Comparison of decomposition search and alpha-beta in problem C.9

5.3 Second Example: 89 Point Problem

The second example, C.11 of [Berlekamp and Wolfe, 1994], is a Go endgame problem on a 19×19 board. Figure 7 shows the initial position and its partition into subgames. After determining safe stones and territories, 89 unsettled points remain, partitioned into 29 distinct endgame areas of sizes 1 to 6.

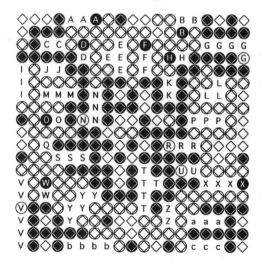

Figure 7: C.11: an 89 point endgame problem

An optimal 62 move solution sequence computed by decomposition search is shown in Figure 8. On the system described above, the complete solution takes 1.1 seconds, including 0.4 seconds for LCGS searching a total of 420 nodes in the 29 subgames. The remaining time is taken up by proving the safety of territories and by operations on combinatorial games. Alpha-beta search behaved as in the first example. Node counts and solution times for the first few subproblems are shown in Table 2.

Areas (Size)	Nodes DS	Nodes $\alpha\beta$	Time $\alpha\beta$
A (3)	5	15	<0.1
A+B (6)	10	178	<0.1
A+B+C (8)	13	899	0.3
A+B+C+D (10)	16	2663	0.7
A+B+C+D+E (14)	21	45446	16.7
A+B+C+D+E+F (17)	26	209815	66.1
A+B+C+D+E+F+G (22)	35	10350151	3192.9
A+B+C+D+E+F+G+H (24)	38	78629573	25044.2

Table 2: Performance of alpha-beta on problem C.11

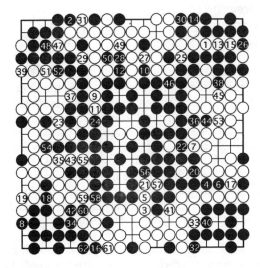

Figure 8: An optimal solution to problem C.11

As a final test two games starting from the initial position of C.11 were played against the current world champion Go program *The Many Faces of Go*. Playing Black, the decomposition search program gained one point over the game-theoretically optimal result. Playing White, it gained five points. Considering the small differences in value of the endgame plays involved, the total gain of six points in two experiments is significant.

5.4 Discussion

The discussion compares decomposition search and alpha-beta in terms of time requirements, results generated and information on alternative moves.

Time Requirement
The fundamental disadvantage of alpha-beta relative to decomposition search is clearly demonstrated by the results: alpha-beta requires time that is exponential in the size of the *whole problem*, while LCGS' worst case time is exponential in the size of the *biggest subproblem*. If local combinatorial game evaluations can be computed and compared without too much overhead, a dramatic speedup results.

Reusing Partial Results
Another advantage of decomposition search over alpha-beta is that it generates useful partial results in the form of evaluated subgames. Frequently occurring games and their combinatorial game evaluation can be stored in a persistent database. If some local searches can be

avoided or terminated early by a database hit, further speedups result. This method works for any combinatorial game, whereas in the case of minimax search databases can be built only for the endgame phase of converging games.

Information on Alternative Moves
Alpha-beta returns the best move and the minimax score of a position. Evaluating alternative moves requires more search. On the other hand, data generated during decomposition search easily yields further information such as other optimal moves and the amount by which a bad move is inferior to an optimal one.

6 Summary

Decomposition search is a new computational method to find minimax solutions of combinatorial games. The method provides a framework to restrict search to subgames, and uses powerful mathematical techniques of combinatorial game theory to combine the local results and achieve globally optimal play. As a divide-and-conquer method, decomposition search results in vast improvements compared to alpha-beta search.

An application of decomposition search to Go has demonstrated perfect play in long endgame problems, which far exceed the capabilities of conventional game tree search methods.

References

[Berlekamp and Wolfe, 1994] E. Berlekamp and D. Wolfe. *Mathematical Go: Chilling Gets the Last Point*. A K Peters, Wellesley, 1994.

[Berlekamp et al., 1982] E. Berlekamp, J. Conway, and R. Guy. *Winning Ways*. Academic Press, London, 1982.

[Conway, 1976] J. Conway. *On Numbers and Games*. Academic Press, London/New York, 1976.

[Müller, 1995] M. Müller. *Computer Go as a Sum of Local Games: An Application of Combinatorial Game Theory*. PhD thesis, ETH Zürich, 1995. Diss.Nr.11.006.

[Müller, 1997] M. Müller. Playing it safe: Recognizing secure territories in Computer Go by using static rules and search. In H. Matsubara, editor, *Proceedings of the Game Programming Workshop in Japan '97*, pages 80–86, Computer Shogi Association, Tokyo, Japan, 1997.

[Thompson, 1986] K. Thompson. Retrograde analysis of certain endgames. *ICCA Journal*, 9(3):131–139, 1986.

GIB: Steps Toward an Expert-Level Bridge-Playing Program

Matthew L. Ginsberg

CIRL

1269 University of Oregon

Eugene, OR 97403-1269

ginsberg@cirl.uoregon.edu

Abstract

This paper describes GIB, the first bridge-playing program to approach the level of a human expert. (GIB finished twelfth in a hand-picked field of thirty-four experts at an invitational event at the 1998 World Bridge Championships.) We give a basic overview of the algorithms used, describe their strengths and weaknesses, and present the results of experiments comparing GIB to both human opponents and other programs.

1 Introduction

Of all the classic games of mental skill, only card games and Go have yet to see the appearance of serious computer challengers. In Go, this appears to be because the game is fundamentally one of pattern recognition as opposed to search; the brute-force techniques that have been so successful in the development of chess-playing programs have failed almost utterly to deal with Go's huge branching factor. Indeed, the arguably strongest Go program in the world (Handtalk) was beaten by 1-dan Janice Kim (winner of the 1984 Fuji Women's Championship) in the 1997 Hall of Champions after Kim had given the program a monumental 25 stone handicap.

Card games appear to be different. Perhaps because they are games of imperfect information, or perhaps for other reasons, existing poker and bridge programs are extremely weak. World poker champion Howard Lederer (Texas Hold'em, 1996) has said that he would expect to beat any existing poker program after five minutes' play.[1] Perennial world bridge champion Bob Hamman, six-time winner of the Bermuda Bowl, once summarized all of the commercial bridge programs by saying that, "They would have to improve to be hopeless."[†]

In poker, there is reason for optimism: the GALA system [Koller and Pfeffer, 1995], if applicable, promises to produce a computer player of unprecedented strength by reducing the poker "problem" to a large linear optimization problem which is then solved to generate a strategy that is nearly optimal in a game theoretic sense. Schaeffer, author of the world champion checkers program CHINOOK [Schaeffer, 1997], is also reporting significant success in this domain [Billings et al., 1998].

The situation in bridge has been bleaker. In addition, because the American Contract Bridge League (ACBL) does not rank the bulk of its players in meaningful ways, it is difficult to compare the strengths of competing programs or players.

In general, performance at bridge is measured by playing the same deal twice or more, with the cards held by one pair of players being given to another pair during the replay and the results then being compared.[2] A "team" in a bridge match thus typically consists of two pairs, with one pair playing the North/South (N/S) cards at one table and the other pair playing the E/W cards at the other table. The results obtained by the two pairs are added; if the sum is positive, the team wins this particular deal and if negative, they lose it.

In general, the numeric sum of the results obtained by the two pairs is converted to International Match Points, or IMPs. The purpose of the conversion is to diminish the impact of single deals on the total, lest an abnormal result on one particular deal have an unduly large impact on the result of an entire match.

Jeff Goldsmith[†] reports that the standard deviation on a single deal in bridge is about 5.5 IMPs, so that if two roughly equal pairs were to play the deal, it would not be surprising if one team beat the other by about this amount. It also appears that the difference between an average club player and a world class expert is about 2 IMPs (per deal played). The strongest bridge playing programs thus far appear to be slightly weaker than average club players.

Progress in computer bridge has been slow. A recent incorporation of planning techniques into Bridge Baron,

---

[1]Many of the citations here are the results of personal communications. Such communications are indicated simply by the presence of a [†] in the accompanying text.

[2]Space restrictions prevent my describing the rules of bridge. Descriptions can be found in other AI papers dealing with bridge, and there are many excellent texts available [Sheinwold, 1996]. Articles on chess-playing programs never describe the rules; hopefully bridge will be treated similarly as it becomes a more regular topic for AI research.

for example, appears to have led to a performance increment of approximately 1/3 IMP per deal [Smith *et al.*, 1996]. This modest improvement still leaves Bridge Baron far shy of expert-level (or even good amateur-level) performance.

Existing programs have attempted to duplicate human bridge-playing methodology in that their goal has been to recognize the class into which any particular deal falls: finesse, end play, squeeze, etc. Smith et.al.'s work uses planning to extend this approach, but the plans continue to be constructed from human bridge techniques. In retrospect, perhaps we should have expected this approach to have limited success; certainly chess-playing programs that have attempted to mimic human methodology, such as PARADISE [Wilkins, 1980], have fared poorly.

GIB works differently. Instead of modeling its play on techniques used by humans, GIB uses brute-force search to analyze the situation in which it finds itself. Monte Carlo techniques are then used to suggest plays by combining the results of analyzing instances of bridge's perfect-information variant. This approach appears to have been first suggested by Levy [Levy, 1989].

Card play is only half of bridge; there is bidding as well. It is possible to use search-based techniques here also, although there is no escaping the fact that a large database of bids and their meanings is needed by the program. (Bidding is, after all, a communicative process; the meanings of the bids need to be agreed upon.) GIB's success here has been more modest; the overall approach is promising but is, for technical reasons that we will describe, unusually vulnerable to gaps or other inaccuracies in the bidding database itself.

GIB currently seems to be about halfway between Bridge Baron and world class, beating Bridge Baron by something over 2 IMPs per deal played and losing to strong human players by approximately half that. Unlike previous programs, however, it it still improving rapidly; there are many straightforward additions that are likely to enhance its performance substantially.

The outline of this paper is as follows: We begin in the next section by describing a Monte Carlo approach to card play, outlining its strengths and weaknesses, and providing details on its performance. Section 3 describes the use of a similar approach to bidding, explaining why it is so vulnerable to database errors and describing several possible ways around this vulnerability. We end with a summary of the GIB project, including details on its overall performance and suggestions for future work.

2 Card play

In order to understand the card play phase of a bridge deal, consider first bridge's perfect information variant, the game where all of the players are playing "double dummy" in that they can see which cards the other players hold. In this case, the game tree is a fairly straightforward minimax tree, although there are some minimizing nodes with minimizing children, since the player playing last to one trick may well play first to the next. The raw

branching factor of the tree appears to be about four; alpha-beta pruning and the introduction of a transposition table bring it down to about 1.7. Augmenting the move ordering heuristic to exploit narrowness[3] reduces the branching factor further to approximately 1.3, corresponding to a search space of some 10^6 nodes per deal. The introduction of partition search [Ginsberg, 1996] and the killer heuristic reduce the space further to some 18,000 nodes per deal.

One way in which we might now proceed in a realistic situation would be to deal the unseen cards at random, biasing the deal so that it was consistent both with the bidding and with the cards played thus far. We could then analyze the resulting deal double dummy and decide which of our possible plays was the strongest. Averaging over a large number of such Monte Carlo samples is one possible way of dealing with the imperfect nature of bridge information.

Algorithm 1 (Monte Carlo card selection) *To select a move from a candidate set M of such moves:*

1. *Construct a set D of deals consistent with both the bidding and play of the deal thus far.*
2. *For each move $m \in M$ and each deal $d \in D$, evaluate the double dummy result of making the move m in the deal d. Denote the score obtained by making this move $s(m, d)$.*
3. *Return that m for which $\sum_d s(m, d)$ is maximal.*

The Monte Carlo approach has drawbacks that have been pointed out by a variety of authors, including Koller[†] and others [Frank and Basin, 1998]. Most obvious among these is that the approach never suggests making an "information gathering play." After all, the perfect-information variant on which the decision is based invariably assumes that the information will be available by the time the next decision must be made! Instead, the tendency is for the approach to simply defer important decisions; in many situations this may lead to information gathering inadvertently, but the amount of information acquired will generally be far less than other approaches might provide. In spite of this, GIB's card play is at the level of a human expert.

Performance was measured initially using *Bridge Master* (BM), a commercial program developed by Gitelman. BM contains 180 deals at 5 levels of difficulty. Each of the 36 deals on each level is a problem in declarer play. If you misplay the hand, BM moves the defenders' cards around if necessary to ensure your defeat.

BM was used for the test instead of randomly dealt deals because the signal to noise ratio is far higher; good plays are generally rewarded and bad ones punished. Every deal also contains a lesson of some kind; there are

---

[3]The narrowness heuristic suggests placing early in the move ordering those moves to which the opponents have few legal responses, thereby keeping the size of the game tree small. This heuristic is apparently well known in the chess community but is poorly cited in the academic literature. A recent paper [Plaat *et al.*, 1996] suggests that the idea is rooted in that of conspiracy search [McAllester, 1988].

no completely uninteresting deals where the line of play is irrelevant or obvious. There are drawbacks to testing GIB's performance on nonrandomly dealt deals, of course, since the BM deals may in some way not be representative of the problems a bridge player would actually encounter at the table.

The test was run under Microsoft Windows on a 200 MHz Pentium Pro. As a benchmark, Bridge Baron (BB) version 6 was also tested on the same deals using the same hardware.[4] BB was given 10 seconds to select each play, and GIB was given 90 seconds to play the entire deal with a Monte Carlo sample size of 50.[5] New deals were generated each time a play decision needed to be made.

These numbers approximately equalized the computational resources used by the two programs; BB could in theory take 260 seconds per deal (ten seconds on each of 26 plays), but in practice took substantially less. GIB was given the auctions as well; there was no facility for doing this in BB. This information was critical on a small number of deals. (The *auction* is the sequence of bids made by the players.)

Here is how the two systems performed:

Level	BB	GIB
1	16	31
2	8	23
3	2	12
4	1	21
5	4	13
Total	33	100
	18.3%	55.6%

Each entry is the number of deals that were played successfully by the program in question.

GIB's mistakes are illuminating. While some of them are of the sort that have already been mentioned (failing to gather information), most are quite different.

GIB is very good (nearly optimal, in fact) at identifying specific possibilities that will allow a contract to be made or defeated, since such possibilities are overlooked only if they don't appear in the Monte Carlo sample being used. What it is weak at is *combining* such possibilities. As an example, suppose that you are playing a hand and you can take one of four possible lines. Each of the first two banks on a specific (but different) distribution of the opposing cards. The third line simply defers the guess by doing something random, and the fourth line is a clever one that succeeds in either of the first two cases, independent of which actually transpires.

GIB chooses randomly between the third and fourth possibilities in this situation, assuming that if it can defer the guess, it will make it correctly in the future! (And

on a double dummy basis, it would.) This pattern accounts for virtually all of GIB's mistakes; as BM's deals get more difficult, they more often involve combining a variety of possibly winning options and that is why GIB's performance falls off at levels 2 and 3.

At still higher levels, however, BM typically involves the successful development of complex end positions, and GIB's performance rebounds. This appeared to happen to BB as well, although to a much lesser extent. It was gratifying to see GIB discover for itself the complex end positions around which the BM deals are designed, and more gratifying still to witness GIB's recent discovery of a maneuver that had hitherto not been identified in the bridge literature.

Experiments such as this one are tedious, because there is no text interface to a commercial program such as Bridge Master or Bridge Baron. As a result, information regarding the sensitivity of GIB's performance to various parameters tends to be only anecdotal.

GIB solves an additional 16 problems (bringing its total to 64.4%) given additional resources in the form of extra time (up to 100 seconds per play, although that time was very rarely taken), a larger Monte Carlo sample (100 deals instead of 50) and hand-generated explanations of the opponents' bids and opening leads. Each of the three factors appeared to contribute equally to the improved performance.

Other authors are reporting comparable levels of performance. Forrester, working with a different but similar benchmark [Blackwood, 1979], reports[6] that GIB solves 68% of the problems given 20 seconds/play, and 74% of them given 30 seconds/play. Deals where GIB has outplayed human experts are the topic of a series of articles in the Dutch bridge magazine *IMP* [Eskes, 1997, and sequels].[7] Based on these results, GIB was invited to participate in an invitational event at the 1998 world bridge championships in France; the event involved deals similar to Bridge Master's but substantially more difficult. GIB joined a field of 34 of the best card players in the world, each player facing twelve such problems over the course of two days. GIB was leading at the halfway mark, but played poorly on the second day (perhaps the pressure was too much for it), and finished twelfth.

The human participants were given 90 minutes to play each deal, although they were penalized slightly for playing slowly. GIB played each deal in about ten minutes, using a Monte Carlo sample size of 500. Michael Rosenberg, the eventual winner of the contest and the pretournament favorite, in fact made one more mistake than did Bramley, the second place finisher. Rosenberg played just quickly enough that the time penalties gave him the victory. The scoring method thus favors GIB slightly.

There are two important technical remarks that must be made about the Monte Carlo algorithm before proceeding. First, note that we were cavalier in simply saying, "Construct a set D of deals consistent with both the

---

[4]The current version is Bridge Baron 9 and could be expected to perform guardedly better in a test such as this. Bridge Baron 6 does not include the Smith enhancements.

[5]GIB's Monte Carlo sample size is fixed at 50 in most cases, which provides a good compromise between speed of play and accuracy of result.

---

[6]Posting to rec.games.bridge on 14 July 1997.

[7]http://www.imp-bridge.nl

bidding and play of the deal thus far."

To construct deals consistent with the bidding, we first simplify the auction as observed, building constraints describing each of the hands around the table. We then deal hands consistent with the constraints using a deal generator that deals unbiased hands given restrictions on the number of cards held by each player in each suit. This set of deals is then tested to remove elements that do not satisfy the remaining constraints, and each of the remaining deals is passed to the bidding module to identify those for which the observed bids would have been made by the players in question. This process typically takes one or two seconds to generate the full set of deals needed by the algorithm.

To conform to the card play thus far, it is impractical to test each hypothetical decision against the cardplay module itself. Instead, GIB uses its existing analyses to identify mistakes that the opponents might make. As an example, suppose GIB plays the ♠5. The analysis indicates that 80% of the time that the next player (say West) holds the ♠K, it is a mistake for West not to play it. If West in fact does not play the ♠K, Bayes' rule is used to adjust the probability that West holds the ♠K at all. The probabilities are then modified further to include information revealed by defensive signalling (if any), and the adjusted probabilities are finally used to bias the Monte Carlo sample, replacing the evaluation $\sum_d s(m,d)$ with $\sum_d w_d s(m,d)$ where w_d is the weight assigned to deal d. More heavily weighted deals thus have a larger impact on GIB's eventual decision.

The second technical point regarding the algorithm itself involves the fact that it needs to run quickly and that it may need to be terminated before the analysis is complete. For the former, there are a variety of greedy techniques that can be used to ensure that a move m is not considered if we can show $\sum_d s(d,m) \leq \sum_d s(d,m')$ for some m'. The algorithm also uses iterative broadening [Ginsberg and Harvey, 1992] to ensure that a low-width answer is available if a high-width search fails to terminate in time. Results from the low- and high-width searches are combined when time expires.

Also regarding speed, the algorithm requires that for each deal in the Monte Carlo sample and each possible move, we evaluate the resulting position exactly. Knowing simply that move m_1 is not as good as move m_2 for deal d is not enough; m_1 may be better than m_2 elsewhere and we need to compare them quantitatively. This approach is aided substantially by the partition search idea, where entries in the transposition table correspond not to single positions and their evaluated values, but to *sets* of positions and values. In many cases, m_1 and m_2 may fall into the same entry of the partition table long before they actually transpose into one another exactly.

3 Bidding

The purpose of bidding in bridge is twofold. The primary purpose is to share information about your cards with your partner so that you can cooperatively select an optimal final contract. A secondary purpose is to disrupt the opponents' attempt to do the same.

In order to achieve this purpose, a wide variety of bidding "languages" have been developed. In some, when you suggest clubs as trumps, it means you have a lot of them. In others, the suggestion is only temporary and the information conveyed is quite different. In all of these languages, *some* meaning is assigned to a wide variety of bids in particular situations; there are also default rules that assign meanings to bids that have no specifically assigned meanings. Any computer bridge player will need similar understandings.

Bidding is interesting because the meanings frequently overlap; there may be one or more bids that are suitable (or nearly so) on any particular set of cards. Existing computer programs have simply tried to find the bid that is the best match for the cards that the machines hold, but world champion Chip Martel reports[†] that human experts take a different approach.[8,9]

Although expert bidding is based on a database such as that used by existing programs, close decisions are made by simulating the results of each candidate action. This involves projecting how the bidding is likely to proceed and evaluating the play in one of a variety of possible final contracts. An expert gets his "judgment" from a Monte Carlo-like simulation of the results of possible bids, often referred to in the bridge-playing community as a *Borel* simulation. GIB takes a similar approach.

Algorithm 2 (Borel simulation) *To select a bid from a candidate set B, given a database Z that suggests bids in various situations:*

1. *Construct a set D of deals consistent with the bidding thus far.*
2. *For each bid $b \in B$ and each deal $d \in D$, use the database Z to project how the auction will continue if the bid b is made. (If no bid is suggested by the database, the player in question is assumed to pass.) Compute the double dummy result of the eventual contract, denoting it $s(b,d)$.*
3. *Return that b for which $\sum_d s(b,d)$ is maximal.*

As with the Monte Carlo approach to card play, this approach does not take into account the fact that bridge is not played double dummy. Human experts often choose not to make bids that will convey too much information to the opponents in order to make the defenders' task as difficult as possible. This consideration is missing from the above algorithm.

Unfortunately, there are more serious problems also. Suppose that the database Z is somewhat conservative

---

[8]The 1994 Rosenblum Cup World Team Championship was won by a team that included Martel and Rosenberg.

[9]Frank suggests [Frank, 1997] that the existing machine approach is capable of reaching expert levels of performance. While this appears to have been true in the early 1980's [Lindelöf, 1983], modern expert bidding practice has begun to highlight the disruptive aspect of bidding, and machine performance is no longer likely to be competitive.

in its actions. The projection in step 2 leads each player to assume his partner bids conservatively, and therefore to bid somewhat aggressively to compensate. The partnership as a whole ends up *over*compensating.

Worse still, suppose that there is an omission of some kind in Z; perhaps every time someone bids $7\diamondsuit$, the database suggests a foolish action. Since $7\diamondsuit$ is a rare bid, a bidding system that matches its bids directly to the database will encounter this problem infrequently.

GIB, however, will be much more aggressive, bidding $7\diamondsuit$ often on the grounds that doing so will cause the opponents to make a mistake. In practice, of course, the bug in the database is unlikely to be replicated in the opponents' minds, and GIB's attempts to exploit the gap will be unrewarded or worse.

This is a serious problem, and appears to apply to any attempt to heuristically model an adversary's behavior: It is difficult to distinguish a good choice that is successful because the opponent has no winning options from a bad choice that *appears* successful because the heuristic fails to identify such options.

There are a variety of ways in which this problem might be addressed, none of them perfect. The most obvious is simply to use GIB's aggressive tendencies to identify the bugs or gaps in the bidding database, and to fix them. Because the database is large (some 7400 rules),[10] this is a slow process.

Another approach is to try to identify the bugs in the database automatically, and to be wary in such situations. If the bidding simulation indicates that the opponents are about to achieve a result much worse than what they might achieve if they saw each other's cards, that is evidence that there may be a gap in the database. Unfortunately, it is also evidence that GIB is simply effectively disrupting its opponents' efforts to bid accurately.

Finally, restrictions could be placed on GIB that require it to make bids that are "close" to the bids suggested by the database, on the grounds that such bids are more likely to reflect improvements in judgment than to highlight gaps in the database.

All of these techniques are used, and all of them are useful. GIB's bidding is substantially better than that of earlier programs, but not yet of expert caliber.

The bidding was tested as part of the 1998 Baron Barclay/OKBridge World Computer Bridge Championships. Each program bid deals that had previously been bid and played by experts; a result of 0 on any particular deal meant that the program bid to a contract as good as the average expert result. There were 20 deals in the contest; although card play was not an issue, the deals were selected to pose challenges in bidding and a standard deviation of 5.5 IMPs/deal is still a reasonable estimate. One standard deviation over the 20 deal set could thus be expected to be about 25 IMPs.

GIB's final score in the bidding contest was +2 IMPs, as it narrowly edged out the expert field against which it

was compared.[11] The next best program finished with a score of -35 IMPs, not dissimilar from the -37 IMPs that had been sufficient to win the bidding contest in 1997.

4 Overall remarks

4.1 GIB compared

GIB participated in the 1998 World Computer Bridge Championships, along with six other computer programs, including Bridge Baron. The event consisted of a complete round robin, with each program playing each other and the results being converted to "victory points." After the round robin, the four leading programs advanced to a knockout phase, which was designed to favor slightly the program that won the round robin.

GIB won every match it played in the round robin, accumulating 95 out of a possible 120 victory points. In the knockout phase, it beat Bridge Baron by 84 IMPs over 48 deals (a 2.2 standard deviation event had the programs been evenly matched) and then beat Q-Plus Bridge in the finals by 63 IMPs over 64 deals (a 1.4 standard deviation event). GIB also played a 14 deal demonstration match against human world champions Zia Mahmood and Michael Rosenberg[12], losing by a total of 6.4 IMPs (a 0.3 standard deviation event). GIB also plays on OKBridge, an internet bridge club with some 15,000 members.[13] After playing thousands of deals against human opponents of various levels, it is losing at the rate of 0.2 IMPs/deal.

4.2 Other games

This has been very much a paper about bridge; I have left essentially untouched the question of to what extent the basic Monte Carlo technique could be applied to other games of imperfect information. Although I can make educated guesses in this area, the experimental work on which this paper is based deals with bridge exclusively.

The primary drawback of the Monte Carlo approach appears to be that it does not encourage information gathering actions, instead tending to defer decisions on the grounds that perfect information will be available later. This leads to small but noticeable errors in GIB's cardplay. Hearts appears to be similar to bridge in this area, and I would expect it to be possible to translate GIB's success from one game to the other.

The Monte Carlo approach is known to be successful in both backgammon and Scrabble, where the strongest machine players simulate possible dice rolls or tile draws

---

[10]GIB uses the database that is distributed with Meadowlark Bridge.

[11]This is in spite of the earlier remark that GIB's bidding is not of expert caliber. GIB was lucky in the bidding contest in that all of the problems involved situations that it understood. When faced with a situation that it does not understand, GIB's bidding deteriorates drastically.

[12]Mahmood and Rosenberg have won, among other titles, the 1995 Cap Volmac World Top Invitational Tournament. As remarked earlier, Rosenberg would also go on after the GIB match to win the Par Competition in which GIB finished 12th.

[13]http://www.okbridge.com

several moves ahead in order to select a move. These games clearly meet the criteria of the previous paragraph, since it is impossible to gather information in advance about the stochastic processes underlying the game.

For other games, however, the problems may be more severe. Poker, for example, depends heavily on the ability to make information gathering maneuvers. How effective Monte Carlo techniques are in cases such as this remains to be seen.

4.3 Future work

GIB has matured to the point that new ideas can be tested by having it play itself overnight over 100 deals. The chess community has already observed that it is easy to use this approach to overfit, so GIB's self-testing is used only to evaluate coarse features of the approach such as the question of whether a Monte Carlo simulation be used during the bidding at all.[14]

There are a variety of straightforward extensions to GIB that should also improve its performance substantially. Principal among these is the further development of GIB's (i.e., Meadowlark's) bidding database, and the inclusion of a facility that allows GIB to think on its opponents' time. None of these modifications requires substantial technical innovation; it's simply a matter of doing it. Martel has predicted that GIB will achieve expert levels of performance around 2000, and be stronger than any human player within two or three years after that. The prospects for doing this seem fairly bright.

Acknowledgement

The GIB work has been supported by Just Write, Inc; during its development, I have received invaluable help from members of both the bridge and computer science communities. I am especially indebted to Chip Martel, Rod Ludwig, Alan Jaffray, Hans Kuijf and Fred Gitelman, but also to Bob Hamman and Eric Rodwell, to David Etherington, Bart Massey and the other members of CIRL, to Jonathan Schaeffer and Rich Korf, and to Jeff Goldsmith, Thomas Andrews and many other members of the rec.games.bridge community.

The work has also been supported by DARPA and AFRL under agreements F30602-97-1-0294 and F30602-98-2-0181. The U.S. Government is authorized to reproduce and distribute reprints for Governmental purposes notwithstanding any copyright annotation hereon. The views and conclusions contained herein are those of the author and should not be interpreted as necessarily representing the official policies or endorsements, either expressed or implied, of DARPA, AFRL, or the U.S. Government.

References

[Billings et al., 1998] Darse Billings, Dennis Papp, Jonathan Schaeffer, and Duane Szafron. Opponent modeling in poker. In *Proceedings of the Fifteenth National Conference on Artificial Intelligence*, pages 493–499, 1998.

[Blackwood, 1979] Easley Blackwood. *Play of the Hand with Blackwood*. Bobbs-Merrill, 1979.

[Eskes, 1997] Onno Eskes. GIB: Sensational breakthrough in bridge software. *IMP*, 8(2), 1997.

[Frank and Basin, 1998] Ian Frank and David Basin. Search in games with incomplete information: A case study using bridge card play. *Artificial Intelligence*, 100:87–123, 1998.

[Frank, 1997] Ian Frank. Bridge. Technical report, ETL, 1997.
http://www.etl.go.jp/etl/suiron/ ianf/Publications/bridge.

[Ginsberg and Harvey, 1992] Matthew L. Ginsberg and William D. Harvey. Iterative broadening. *Artificial Intelligence*, 55:367–383, 1992.

[Ginsberg, 1996] Matthew L. Ginsberg. Partition search. In *Proceedings of the Thirteenth National Conference on Artificial Intelligence*, 1996.

[Koller and Pfeffer, 1995] Daphne Koller and Avi Pfeffer. Generating and solving imperfect information games. In *Proceedings of the Fourteenth International Joint Conference on Artificial Intelligence*, pages 1185–1192, 1995.

[Levy, 1989] David N.L. Levy. The million pound bridge program. In D.N.L. Levy and D.F. Beal, editors, *Heuristic Programming in Artificial Intelligence*, Asilomar, CA, 1989. Ellis Horwood.

[Lindelöf, 1983] Torbjörn Lindelöf. *COBRA: The Computer-Designed Bidding System*. Gollancz, London, 1983.

[McAllester, 1988] David A. McAllester. Conspiracy numbers for min-max searching. *Artificial Intelligence*, 35:287–310, 1988.

[Plaat et al., 1996] Aske Plaat, Jonathan Schaeffer, Wim Pijls, and Arie de Bruin. Exploiting graph properties of game trees. In *Proceedings of the Thirteenth National Conference on Artificial Intelligence*, pages 234–239, 1996.

[Schaeffer, 1997] Jonathan Schaeffer. *One Jump Ahead: Challenging Human Supremacy in Checkers*. Springer-Verlag, New York, 1997.

[Sheinwold, 1996] Alfred Sheinwold. *Five Weeks to Winning Bridge*. Pocket Books, 1996.

[Smith et al., 1996] Stephen J.J. Smith, Dana S. Nau, and Tom Throop. Total-order multi-agent task-network planning for contract bridge. In *Proceedings of the Thirteenth National Conference on Artificial Intelligence*, Stanford, California, 1996.

[Wilkins, 1980] David E. Wilkins. Using patterns and plans in chess. *Artificial Intelligence*, 14:165–203, 1980.

---

[14] The simulation does appear to be useful; GIB bidding with it beats GIB without it by 1 IMP/deal.

KNOWLEDGE-BASED
APPLICATIONS

KNOWLEDGE-BASED APPLICATIONS

Applications 1

An Effective Ship Berthing Algorithm

Andrew Lim
Department of Computer Science
National University of Singapore
Lower Kent Ridge Road
Singapore 119260

Abstract

Singapore has one of the busiest ports in the world. Ship berthing is one of the problems faced by the planners at the port. In this paper, we study the ship berthing problem. We first provide the problem formulation and study the complexity of the problem with different restrictions. In general, the ship berthing problem is NP-complete, although, some of its variants may be solved quickly. While a geometrical model is intuitive, the model cannot be easily extended to handle clearance constraints and berth restriction. Rather than solving the problem geometrically, we transform the problem into the problem of fixing directions of edges in graph to form directed acyclic graph with minimal longest path. Since the problem is NP-complete, solving the problem exactly in polynomial time is highly unlikely. As a result, we devise a fast and effective greedy algorithm to can generate good solutions. The greedy method together with a tabu search like post optimization algorithm is able to return optimal or near optimal solutions.

1 Introduction

Situated at the crossroads of the world, the Port of Singapore is one of the world's busiest port. Every few minutes a ship arrives or departs the port. Every month the port handles more than one million transhipment containers.

When a ship arrives at the port, the planners must first decide where to berth the ship for the unloading and loading of containers. For the containers that are to be unloaded, the planners must decide where to place these containers in the yard. The wharf line of the port is divided into sections, and no ship can be berthed across any two sections. Which section to assign a ship to and exactly where to berth a ship within a section depend on factors like the locations of containers to be loaded and unloaded, the physical (i.e. depth of the berth) and resource limitations (i.e. suitably of quay crane) of each berth. A sketch of a port is given in Figure 1. The allocation of ships to sections and placement of containers in the yard is studied by Lim [Lim, 1998]. The approach used is a variant of graph partitioning problem. Allocation of vessels to sections were also studied by Brown[Brown et al., 1994; 1997].

One of the subproblems in [Lim, 1998] is the ship berthing problem. The ship berthing problem was studied by Heng[Heng, Khoong, and Lim, 1996] using a mixed integer linear programming model. Their model assumed constant inter-ship clearance distance and constant end-berth clearance distance. While their model worked reasonably well on historical test data, it did quite badly on fully packed test cases. Their approach is also computationally intensive. As the ship berthing problem is only a subproblem which is called many times in the berth yard planning system, it needs to be computationally efficient. Heng's version of the problem is also very closely related to the offline version of the dynamic storage allocation problem [Wilson et al., 1995]. Because the dynamic storage allocation problem is a special case of the ship berthing problem, the ship berthing problem is NP-Complete [Garey and Johnson, 1979]

2 Problem Formulation

Ships come in different lengths and they arrive at the port at different times to be berthed. Every ship has an expected duration of stay which may be different from another ship. To berth a ship is to place the ship along the wharf line of a section. Once a ship is berthed, it will not be moved until its departure time. When two ships are berthed side by side, a certain minimum inter-ship clearance distance must be observed. Each ship has an inter-ship clearance distance which is dependent on the ship's length. The minimum inter-ship clearance distance of two ships berthed side by side is the larger of the two ships' inter-ship clearance distances. If a ship is berthed at the end of a section, a certain end-berth clearance distance must be observed. This end-berth clearance distance is not fixed and is dependent on the ship. A ship can also be given a fixed berthing location within a section. A ship may also be prohibited from

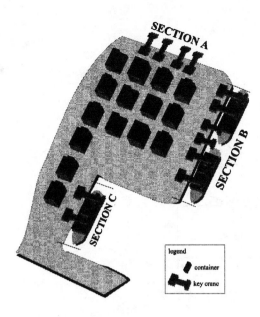

Figure 1: Sketch of a port

berthing at certain parts of a section. A berth plan for a set of ships in a section is the exact locations of ships within the section.

We can represent a *ship* geometrically by a rectangle such that the height of the rectangle is the length of the ship and the length of the rectangle is the duration of its stay. The left edge of the rectangle represents the arrival time of the ship. The right edge represents the departure time of the ship. A *section* can be represented geometrically by an infinitely long rectangle where its height represents the length of the section and the length represents the time axis. We can associate a coordinate with the left bottom corner of the geometric representation of each ship. The x-coordinate is fixed as it represents time of arrival, but the y-coordinate is not known unless the ship has a preassigned berth location. The Ship Berthing Problem is to decide the y-coordinates of the set of boxes in the long rectangle of the section such that all rectangles representing ships are non-overlapping and are within the rectangle of the section with all clearance distances are satisfied. Figure 2 clarifies the transformation.

Let us define the problem formally. Let $\mathcal{S}$ be the set of ships $\{S_1, S_2, \ldots, S_n\}$. Let $b_i, l_i, t_i, d_i, c_i^s, c_i^b$, and F_i be the start wharf mark of the berthing location, length, arrival time, duration of stay, inter-ship clearance distance, end-berth clearance distance, and the set of forbidden berth positions respectively of Ship S_i. When S_i is berthed at b_i, S_i will occupy wharf mark from b_i to $b_i + l_i$ from time t_i to time $t_i + d_i$. F_i is a set of intervals in the section in which ship i cannot be berthed. If S_i is berthed at b_i, the interval $[b_i, b_i + l_i]$ should not intersect with any interval in F_i. For a clearer picture of the above definitions, please refer to Figure 2.

The optimization version of the Ship Berthing Problem

(SBP) is defined Figure 2, where L is the wharf length:

The decision version of the Ship Berthing Problem is similar to the **SBP** problem. All we need to do is to remove the objective function to Minimize L and assume that L is given.

2.1 Complexity

Lemma 1 *If* $\forall S_i \in \mathcal{S}, l_i = C_1, c_i^s = C_2, c_i^b = C_3$, *where* C_1, C_2 *and* C_3 *are constants, the ship berthing problem can be solved in* $O(n \log n)$ *time.*

Proof: The above problem can be transformed to the problem of coloring of interval graphs by first partitioning the section into $\lfloor \frac{L - 2C_3 + C_2}{C_1 + C_2} \rfloor$ fixed berths and sorting the ships, in non-decreasing order based on the arrival times, followed by assigning the ships in the sorted order to the fixed berths using the criteria of most recently used available berth. This algorithm takes $O(n \log n)$ time. □

Biro[Biro *et al.*, 1992] showed that 1-precoloring of interval graph is polynomial time solvable and 2-precoloring is NP-Complete. Using his results, if $\forall S_i \in \mathcal{S}, l_i = C_1, c_i^s = C_2, c_i^b = C_3$, where C_1, C_2 and C_3 are constants, and if some of the ships are preassigned to a single berth, then the problem remains polynomial time solvable. If some of the ships are preassigned to 2 berths, then the problem becomes NP-complete even if the ships have the same length and clearance distances.

In the next section, we will show the that berth planning problem is NP-complete. Our reduction uses the PARTITION problem which is known to be NP-Complete. The definition of the partition problem is given below:

PARTITION Given a finite set $A = \{a_1, a_2, \ldots, a_x\}$ and a size $s(a) \in Z^+$ for each $a \in A$, is there a subset $A' \subseteq A$ such that $\sum_{a \in A'} s(a) = \sum_{a \in A - A'} s(a)$?

Lemma 2 *The berth planning problem is NP-Complete.*

Proof: If we set all inter-ship clearances and end-berth clearances to be zero the berth planning problem is exactly the same as the dynamic storage allocation problem [Garey and Johnson, 1979]. The dynamic storage allocation problem has been shown to be NP-complete by Stockmeyer using the 3-PARTITION problem. However, this result is not published[Garey and Johnson, 1979]. In this section, we shall sketch a simple reduction using the PARTITION problem. Let $T = \sum_{a \in A} s(a)$. We use the triple (l_i, t_i, d_i) to represent the ship S_i, where l_i, t_i, d_i are the length, arrival time and the duration of stay of the ship repectively. Let $\mathcal{S} = \mathcal{S}_A \cup \mathcal{S}_B$. $\mathcal{S}_A = \{S_1, S_2, S_3, \ldots, S_9\}$, where

$$S_1 = (T + 2, 0, 1) \qquad S_2 = (1, 0, 3)$$
$$S_3 = (\frac{T}{2} + 1, 1, 1) \qquad S_4 = (1, 1, 3)$$
$$S_5 = (\frac{T}{2}, 1, 1) \qquad S_6 = (1, 2, 3)$$
$$S_7 = (\frac{T}{2}, 3, 1) \quad S_8 = (\frac{T}{2} + 1, 3, 1)$$

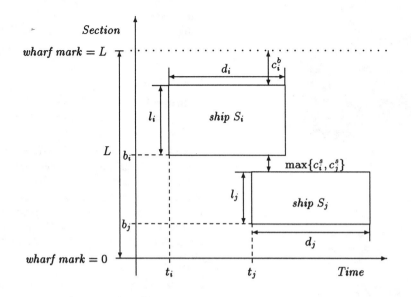

Figure 2: Geometric Representation to Graph Transformation

Minimize L
Subject to :

$$c_{ij} \geq c_i^s \quad \forall S_i, S_j \in \mathcal{S} \quad \text{s.t.} \quad t_i \leq t_j \leq t_i + d_i \quad \text{or} \quad t_j \leq t_i \leq t_j + d_j$$
$$c_{ij} \geq c_j^s \quad \forall S_i, S_j \in \mathcal{S} \quad \text{s.t.} \quad t_i \leq t_j \leq t_i + d_i \quad \text{or} \quad t_j \leq t_i \leq t_j + d_j$$
$$b_i + l_i + c_{ij} \leq b_j + (1 - x_{ij})M \quad \forall S_i, S_j \in \mathcal{S} \quad \text{s.t.} \quad t_i \leq t_j \leq t_i + d_i \quad \text{or} \quad t_j \leq t_i \leq t_j + d_j$$
$$b_j + l_j + c_{ij} \leq b_i + x_{ij}M \quad \forall S_i, S_j \in \mathcal{S} \quad \text{s.t.} \quad t_i \leq t_j \leq t_i + d_i \quad \text{or} \quad t_j \leq t_i \leq t_j + d_j$$
$$x_{ij} \in \{0, 1\} \quad \forall S_i, S_j \in \mathcal{S} \quad \text{s.t.} \quad t_i \leq t_j \leq t_i + d_i \quad \text{or} \quad t_j \leq t_i \leq t_j + d_j$$
$$c_i^b \leq b_i \leq L - l_i - c_i^b \quad \forall S_i \in \mathcal{S}$$
$$b_i + l_i \leq p + (1 - x_{if_j})M \quad \forall S_i \in \mathcal{S} \quad \forall f_j = [p, q] \in F_i$$
$$q \leq b_i + x_{if_j}M \quad \forall S_i \in \mathcal{S} \quad \forall f_j = [p, q] \in F_i$$
$$x_{if_j} \subseteq \{0, 1\} \quad \forall S_i \in \mathcal{S} \quad \forall f_j \in F_i$$
$$M \quad \text{is a constant} \quad > \sum_{\forall i} l_i + \max\{c_i^b, c_i^s\}$$

Figure 3: Mathematical Model of the Problem

$$S_9 = (T + 2, 4, 1)$$

For the set $\mathcal{S}_A$, if $L \leq T + 3$, there are only 2 berth plans (in fact one is a reflection of the other). In both of these plans, there are two unoccupied regions of equal size. One is from wharf mark 1 to $\frac{T}{2} + 1$, from time unit 2 to time unit 3. The other is from wharf mark $\frac{T}{2} + 2$ to $T + 2$ from time unit 2 to unit 3. Let $\mathcal{S}_B = \{S_{10}, S_{11}, \ldots, S_{9+|A|}\}$ where $S_i = (s(a_{i-9}), 2, 1)$. Clearly, if there is a berth plan where $L \leq T + 3$ then the set $\mathcal{S}_B$ must be partitioned into two disjoint subsets such that the sum of lengths of ships in the two subsets are the same. It is clear that the transformation will only take polynomial time. It is also clear that the problem is in NP. Hence, the berth planning problem is NP-complete. □

Since the berth planning problem is NP-Complete, it is highly unlikely that a fast algorithm can be devised to solve the problem optimally.

3   Graph Model

While the geometrical model is visually attractive, it cannot be extended to handle clearance constraints and berth restriction constraints easily. In this section, we shall transform our geometrical representation of the Ship Berthing Problem to a graph, $\mathcal{G}$. For each ship $S_i \in \mathcal{S}$, we have a vertex v_i in $\mathcal{G}$. The weight of vertex v_i is set to l_i which is the length of the ship S_i. If two ships $S_i, S_j \in \mathcal{S}$ have time overlap, then there is an edge (v_i, v_j) linking the 2 vertices v_i and v_j. The weight of the edge (v_i, v_j) is the larger of the two ships inter-ship clearance distances, i.e. $\max\{c_i^s, c_j^s\}$. For each ship S_i, there are 2 additional vertices v_i^{et} and v_i^{eb}. These vertices have weights 0. There is a directed edge $< v_i^{eb}, v_i >$ and another directed edge $< v_i, v_i^{et} >$. The weight of these directed edges is the end-berth clearance c_i^e.

If a ship S_j is required to be fixed at a particular berth location k (i.e. $b_j = k$ and S_j will occupy wharf mark from k to $k + l_j$) within the section, we will add two vertices u_1 and u_2 and two edges $< u_1, v_j >$ and $< v_j, u_2 >$. u_1 and u_2 will have vertex weight of 0. $< u_1, v_j >$ and $< v_j, u_2 >$ will have edge weight of k and $L - (k + l_j)$. Similarly, a ship S_j may not be permitted to berth from wharf mark p to wharf mark q. We can handle this situation by creating a fictitious ship which is fixed at location p with length $q - p - c_j^s$ which has a hypothetical time overlap with only ship j. Using such a transformation, berth restrictions for ships can be handled consistently.

At the end of the transformation, we have a graph consisting of directed and undirected edges. Let us pick an undirected edge $e_{ij} = (v_i, v_j)$. e_{ij} exists because ship S_i and ship S_j have a time overlap. This implies that both ship S_i and ship S_j cannot share any part of the section. If ship S_i is berthed at a lower wharf mark, (a wharf mark is a particular position in a section) than ship S_j, we will set the edge (v_i, v_j) to become $< v_i, v_j >$. Similarly, if ship S_j is berthed at a lower wharf mark than

ship S_i, we will set the edge e_{ij} to go from vertex v_j to vertex v_i, i.e. $< v_j, v_i >$. The ship berthing problem has been transformed to a problem of setting the directions of undirected edges in the graph such that the graph becomes directed acyclic and the longest path in the graph is minimized. The length of a path in our graph is the sum of all vertex weights and edge weights of all vertices and edges in the path.

The directed acyclic condition of the graph is important as the directions of the edges represent relative berth locations, therefore it is impossible to have a situation such that ship S_i is berthed at a lower location than ship S_j, and ship S_j is berthed at a lower location than ship S_k, and ship S_k is berthed at a lower location than ship S_i. Therefore, when we set the direction of the undirected edges we must not create any cycle. The length of the longest path in the directed acyclic graph created is the minimum length required in the section to berth the set of ships $\mathcal{S}$.

Lemma 3 *The Ship Berthing Problem can be transformed to a problem of fixing the directions of some edges in a graph such that the graph becomes directed acyclic and the longest path in the graph is no more than the section length.*

Proof: Obvious from the above discussion.□

It is clear that the optimization version of the Ship Berthing Problem can be transformed to a problem of fixing the directions of edges in a graph such that the graph becomes directed acyclic and the longest path in the graph is minimized. In the worst case, only $O(n)$ of the decision versions of the problem need to be solved through the use of binary search on L.

4   An Effective Greedy Algorithm

In this section, we shall discuss our heuristic for fixing the edge directions in our graph representation to create a DAG with the minimum longest path. Before describing the algorithm, let us define the following. Let e_{ij} be the edge between vertices v_i and v_j. If e_{ij} is undirected, it can be set in two directions, namely from v_i to v_j or from v_j to v_i.

Let β_{ij} and β_{ji} be defined as follows :

$$\beta_{ij} = L_{In}(v_i) + w(v_i) + w(e_{ij}) + w(v_j) + L_{Out}(v_j)$$

$$\beta_{ji} = L_{In}(v_j) + w(v_j) + w(e_{ij}) + w(v_i) + L_{Out}(v_i)$$

$L_{In}(v_i)$ is the longest incoming path of vertex v_i. $L_{Out}(v_i)$ is the longest outgoing path from vertex v_i. $w(v_i)$ and $w(e_{ij})$ are the weights of vertex v_i and edge (i, j) respectively.

For every undirected edge, e_{ij}, the potential of edge, $\Phi(e_{ij})$ is given by $\max\{\beta_{ij}, \beta_{ji}\}$. The algorithm of our heuristic is given in Figure 4. The algorithm first computes the potential of every undirected edge. Next the algorithm selects the undirected edge with the highest potential. In the event of a tie, a second criterion is used. This criterion is $|\beta_{ij} - \beta_{ji}|$, the larger the better. Once the edge is selected, the direction of the edge is set such that the longest path through that edge is as small as possible. In the event of a tie, the edge is set from the vertex with lower degree to the vertex with higher degree. Next, the algorithm updates the longest incoming paths and outgoing paths, and potentials of all affected edges. This may be computed by doing 2 topological sweeps (2 passes, computing the longest incoming path for each vertex in one pass and computing the longest outgoing path for each vertex in the second pass). A topological sweep takes $O(|V(\mathcal{G})| + |\mathcal{E}(\mathcal{G})|)$ time. Updating will take significantly less time in practice even though the worst case time complexity stays the same. Repeat the process of finding the edge with the highest potential, fixing its direction and updating the potential of the rest of the undirected edges until the directions of all edges are set. The longest path in the graph defines the minimum section length needed. The longest incoming path of a vertex v_i defines the wharf mark whereby the ship i is to be berthed.

We shall use a simple example to illustrate our heuristic. In our example, we assume that all clearance distances are zero, i.e. no clearance needed. Note that at the end of the iterations, the longest incoming path for each vertex, v_i will determine the wharf mark of the ship S_i.

It can be easily seen that our algorithm takes at most $O(|E(\mathcal{G})|(|\mathcal{E}(\mathcal{G})| + |\mathcal{V}(\mathcal{G})|))$. In practice, our algorithm runs in $O(|V(\mathcal{G})|^2)$ time.

Lemma 4 *Algorithm Greedy Berth-Planner does not create a cycle from a path.*

Proof: Let us consider a cycle $C = v_1 v_2 \ldots v_{k-1} v_k v_1$. Without loss of generality, let us assume that the edge e_{k1} is the last edge to fix its direction in C, which is from v_k to v_1, to create the cycle C. From our graph construction, it is clear that the length of the path $|p_{1k}| > 0$ as $p_{1k} = v_1 v_2 \ldots v_k$. To set the edge e_{k1} to go from v_k to v_1, β_{k1} must be less than or equal to β_{1k} (see algorithm). This implies

$$L_{In}(v_k) + L_{Out}(v_1) \leq L_{In}(v_1) + L_{Out}(v_k)$$

But,

$$L_{In}(v_k) \geq L_{In}(v_1) + |p_{1k}|$$
$$L_{Out}(v_1) \geq |p_{1k}| + L_{Out}(v_k)$$

This implies that

$$L_{In}(v_k) + L_{Out}(v_1) \geq L_{In}(v_1) + L_{Out}(v_k) + 2|p_{1k}|$$

Since $|p_{1k}| > 0$,

$$L_{In}(v_k) + L_{Out}(v_1) > L_{In}(v_1) + L_{Out}(v_k)$$

From the above, it is clear that our algorithm will never turn a path to a cycle. □

Since the algorithm does not create any cycle, there will not be a situation where the algorithm is stuck, i.e. no matter which direction you fix an edge, you get a cycle. To be in such a situation, you must first have a cycle. From the above lemma, cycle detection is not needed in our heuristic.

Algorithm Greedy Berth-Planner
Step 1: $\forall v_i \in V(\mathcal{G})$ set $LongestIn(v_i) = 0$
and $LongestOut(v_i) = 0$
Step 2: $\forall e_{ij} \in E(\mathcal{G})$ compute $\Phi(e_{ij})$
Step 3: Find the undirected edge, e_{ij}, with the highest potential $\Phi(e_{ij})$.
If there is a tie in the highest potential, pick the edge with the largest $|\beta_{ij} - \beta_{ji}|$.
Step 4: If $(\beta_{ij} < \beta_{ji})$
then set edge to go from v_i to v_j
else if $(\beta_{ij} > \beta_{ji})$
then set edge to go from v_j to v_i
else if $deg(v_i) < deg(v_j)$
then set edge to go from v_i to v_j
else set edge to go from v_j to v_i
Step 5: Update the affected longest incoming and outgoing paths of vertices
Step 6: Update the potential of affected undirected edges
Step 7: If there is an undirected edge, goto 3
Step 8: End

Figure 4: Ship Berthing Heuristic

5 Local Search Post Optimization

Using our graph model, every arrangement is represented by at least an acyclic labeling. Given an acyclic labeling, the longest path and the berth position of every ship can be found in $O(|V(\mathcal{G})| + |\mathcal{E}(\mathcal{G})|)$ time. Our local search improvement approach is based on the Tabu Search method introduced by Glover [Glover, 1989; 1990]. It is applied to the solution generated by the greedy algorithm.

Given an acyclic labeling, AL, of a graph, we define the neighborhood solution of AL to be the set of acyclic labelings reachable from AL by swapping the acyclic labels of two vertices. Among all the possible swaps, we pick the swap that improves best result seen so far. If that is not possible, we will pick the swap, that is not forbidden by the tabu list, that returns the best result. Our tabu list's length is 10. It stores the 10 most recent swaps. The iterative improvement will be performed until the stopping criterion is reached. The stopping criterion is satisfied if there is no improvement of the best solution after 10 iterations or the current solution equals the lower bound.

6 Experimental Results

We have implemented our greedy heuristic and the local search algorithm in C++ using Microsoft Visual C++ development environment. We ran all our experiments on a pentium II 300MHz machine with 128 MBytes of memory. We tested our algorithms on 2 data sets and compare our algorithm with the lower bound. The lower bound is given by the maximum density. Density is given by the largest of all the sums of lengths of vessels at all points on the x (time) axis in the geometric representation. The first data set is the historical data from the Port. The second is manually generated. Each test case

Historical Test Set				
Size	LB	Greedy Algorithm	Local Search PostOpt	
			Result	Time
150	772	903	772	9
29	161	161	–	–
165	726	887	803	8
57	144	144	–	–
72	308	308	–	–
231	774	858	810	23
185	720	829	743	12
173	813	898	856	11
118	632	682	682	7
59	511	511	–	–
149	767	898	787	9

Table 1: Historical Test Data

Compact Test Set				
Size	LB	Greedy Algorithm	Local Search PostOpt	
			Result	Time
15	20	20	–	–
20	26	26	–	–
30	25	32	25	2
26	24	29	24	1
40	25	29	27	6
50	20	25	22	10
100	20	26	23	19

Table 2: Fully Packed Manually Generated Test Data

in the second data set is generated by first defining a rectangle and cutting smaller rectangles from the original rectangle for each test set. In the experiments, all clearance distances are set to 0. This is to facilitate easy checking of the quality of the solutions generated. The results are summarized in Table 1 and 2.

The first column of the tables is the number of ships. The second is the density. The third is the result obtained by the greedy method. The greedy took less than 1 seconds for all the test cases in our experiment. The fourth and fifth columns are the result and time taken in seconds respectively by the local search algorithm.

A sample solution of a test case is given in Figure 5.

7 Conclusion

In this paper, we formulated the ship berthing problem, analyzed its complexity and transformed the geometric version of the problem into a graph problem. We also proposed a fast and effective greedy algorithm which when used with a tabu search like post optimization routine can return optimal or near optimal solutions.

8 Acknowledgment

This research was motivated by a project the first author had with the Port of Singapore Authority. This

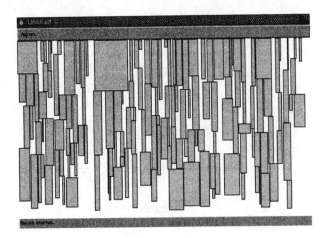

Figure 5: A Solution to a Real World Test Data with 149 ships

research was supported in part by the NUS Research Grant RP3972679.

References

[Biro et al., 1992] M. Biro, M. Hujter, and Zs. Tuza. Precoloring extension. I. Interval Graphs. *Discrete Mathematics*, 100, 1992.

[Garey and Johnson, 1979] M. Garey and D. Johnson. *Computers and Intractability*. W. H. Freeman and Company, 1979.

[Brown et al., 1997] G.G. Brown, K.J. Cormican, S. Lawphongpanich, and D.B. Widdis. Optimizing Submarine Berthing with a Persistence Incentive. *Naval Research Logistics*, 44:301–318, 1997.

[Brown et al., 1994] G.G. Brown, S. Lawphongpanich, and K.P. Thurman. Optimizing Ship Berthing. *Naval Research Logistics*, 41:1–15, 1994.

[Glover, 1989] F. Glover. Tabu Search - part I. *ORSA Journal on Computing*, 1(3):190–206, 1989.

[Glover, 1990] F. Glover. Tabu Search - part II. *ORSA Journal on Computing*, 2(1):4–32, 1990.

[Heng, Khoong, and Lim, 1996] K. Heng, C. Khoong, and A. Lim. A Forward Algorithm Strategy for Large Scale Resource Allocation. In *First Asia-Pacific DSI Conference*, pages 109–117, 1996.

[Lim, 1998] A. Lim. Algorithms for Yard-Berth Scheduling. manuscript, 1998.

[Wilson et al., 1995] P.R. Wilson, M.S. Johnstone, M. Neely, and D. Boles. Dynamic Storage Allocation: A Survey and Critical Review. In *Lecture Notes in Computer Science 986*, pages 1–116, 1995.

A Distributed Case-Based Reasoning Application for Engineering Sales Support

Ian Watson
AI-CBR
University of Salford
Salford, M7 9NU
UK
ian@ai-cbr.org
www.ai-cbr.org

Dan Gardingen
Western Air Ltd.
McCabe Street, North Fremantle
Fremantle
Western Australia

Abstract

This paper describes the implementation of a distributed case-based reasoning application that supports engineering sales staff. The application operates on the world wide web and uses the XML standard as a communications protocol between client and server side Java applets. The paper describes the distributed architecture of the application, the two case retrieval techniques used, its implementation, trial, roll-out and subsequent improvements to its architecture and retrieval techniques using introspective reasoning to improve retrieval efficiency. The benefits it has provided to the company are detailed.

1 Introduction

Western Air is a distributor of HVAC (heating, ventilation and air conditioning systems in Australia with a turnover in 1997 of $25 million (US dollars). Based in Fremantle the company operates mainly in Western Australia, a geographic area of nearly two million square miles. The systems supported range from simple residential HVAC systems to complex installations in new build and existing factories and office buildings.

Western Air has a distributed sales force numbering about 100. The majority of staff do not operate from head office but are independent, working from home or a mobile base (typically their car). Until recently, sales staff in the field would gather the prospective customer's requirements using standard forms and proprietary software, take measurements of the property and fax the information to Western Air in Fremantle. A qualified engineer would then specify the HVAC system. Typically the engineer would have to phone the sales staff and ask for additional information and the sales staff would have to make several visits to the customer's building and pass additional information back to the head office engineer.

Western Air felt that basing a quote on the price of a previous similar installation gave a more accurate estimation than using prices based on proprietary software, catalogue equipment prices and standard labour To try to help engineers make use of all the past installations a database was created to let engineers search for past installations. The database contained approximately 10,000 records, each with 60 fields describing the key features of each installation and then a list of file names for the full specification. Initially the engineers liked the database and it increased the number of past installations they used as references. However, after the honeymoon ended, they started to complain that it was too hard to query across more than two or three fields at once. And that querying across ten or more fields was virtually impossible. In fact most of them admitted to using the database to laboriously browse through past installations until they found one that looked similar to their requirements.

2 Implementation

Western Air decided that merely improving the efficiency of the engineers in Fremantle would not solve the whole problem. Ideally they would like the sales staff to be able to give fast accurate estimates to prospective customers on the spot. However, they were aware that there was a danger that the less knowledgeable sales staff might give technically incorrect quotes.

2.1 The Team

The development team comprised:
- a senior engineer from Western Air (one of the firms owners) as project champion,
- an engineer from Western Air to act as project manager and domain expert,
- a consultant Java/HTML programmer,
- a consultant from AI-CBR to advise on CBR issues (resident in the UK), and
- a part-time data entry clerk.

2.2 Implementation Plan

The project had the direct involvement of one of the firms owners so management commitment was not a problem. It was also decided that creating a partially functional prototype was not sensible since the system would either work or not. However. a carefully controlled and monitored trial was considered essential for two reasons:

1. It was still not certain that sales staff could create technically sound first estimates and therefore a small carefully monitored trial was essential to avoid losing the firm money.
2. There were resource implications since although all sales staff had portable PCs, some were old 486 Windows 3.1 machines and few had modems or Internet accounts.

A fixed (non-negotiable) budget was given to the project of $32,000 and it was decided that six months would be given for development and trial of the system. The project started in October of 1997 and the trial was planned for March of 1998.

It was decided initially to deal with moderately complex residential HVAC systems because it was felt that this would provide a reasonable test of the system without undue risk. Western Air felt that it was commercially unwise to risk experimentation on high value commercial contracts. Western Air realised they wanted a system that could find similar installations without making the query too complex for the engineers. Web based CBR applications have been demonstrated for a few years now such as the FAQFinder and FindME systems [Hammond et al., 1996] and those at Broderbund and Lucas Arts [Watson, 1997].

The solution they envisaged was to set up a web site that sales staff could access from anywhere in the country. Through a forms interface the prospect's requirements could be input and would be passed to a CBR system that would search the library of past installations and retrieve similar installations. Details of the similar installations along with the FTP addresses of associated files would then be available to the sales staff by FTP. The sales staff could then download the files and use these to prepare an initial quote. All this information would then be automatically passed back to an engineer to authorise or change if necessary. Once an installation was completed its details would be added to the library and its associated files placed on the ftp server.

Since a simple nearest neighbour retrieval algorithm would suffice implementing our own system was a viable option. Java (Visual Café) was chosen as the implementation language for both the client and server side elements of the CBR system. XML (eXtensible Markup Language) [WWW Consortium, 1997] was used as the communication language between client and server-side applets. The World-Wide Web Consortium (W3C) finalised XML 1.0 in December 1997 as a potential successor to HTML [WWW Consortium].

2.3 System Architecture

On the sales staff (client) side a Java applet is used to gather the customer's requirements and send them as XML to the server. On the server side another Java applet (a *servlet*) uses this information to query the database to retrieve a set of relevant records. The Java servlet then converts these into XML and sends them to the client side applet that uses a nearest neighbour algorithm to rank the set of cases. A schematic of the architecture is shown in Figure 1.

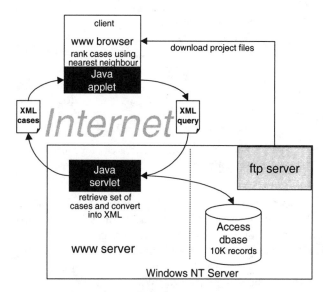

Figure 1. System Architecture

2.4 Case Representation

Cases are stored within a database. Each record (case) comprises 60 fields used for retrieval and many more used to describe the HVAC installations. In addition, links to other files on the FTP server are included to provide more detailed descriptions. Once retrieved from the database the records are ranked by a nearest neighbour algorithm and dynamically converted into XML for presentation to the client browser. An XML case representation is used by our system [Shimazu, 1998]. XML pages can contain any number of user defined tags defined in a document type definition (DTD) file. Tags are nested hierarchically from a single root tag that can contain any number of child tags. Any child tag in turn can contain any number of child tags. Each tag contains a begin statement (e.g. <Case>) and an end statement (e.g. </Case>). This is illustrated in Figure 4.

2.5 Case Retrieval

Case retrieval is a two stage process. In stage one the customer's requirements are relaxed through a process of *query relaxation*. This process takes the original query and relaxes terms in it to ensure that a useful number of records are retrieved from the database. This is similar to the technique used by Kitano & Shimazu [1996] in the SQUAD system at NEC, although as is discussed in section 3, we have improved it efficiency using an introspective learning heuristic.

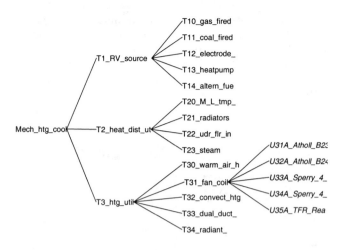

Figure 2. A Portion of a Symbol Hierarchy for Mechanical Heating & Cooling Systems

For example, assume we are trying to retrieve details of installations using Athol B23 equipment. An SQL query that just used "Athol_B23" as a search term might be too restrictive. Using an ordered symbol hierarchy (as in Figure 2) our system knows that "Athol B23" is a type of "Fan Coil" system so the query is relaxed to "Where (((EquipmentReference) = "T31_fan_coil"")..)). This query will include equipment from Athol, Sperry and TFR. An ordering of each set of symbols in the hierarchy is obtained through the reference number suffixes to each symbol (e.g. T10, T11, T12, T13, T14 as shown in Figure 2). The symbol hierarchies are stored in a table in the database.

Other specific criteria, elevations or temperatures that are numbers (integers or reals) can be relaxed by using simple ranges (e.g. a temperature of 65° F. could be relaxed to "Between 60 And 70"). Knowledge engineering was required to determine by what amounts numeric features should be relaxed. The relaxation is expressed as a term ± a percentage (e.g., "Relax_Temp = ± 10%"). These relaxation terms are stored in a table in the database. An example of a relaxed SQL query is shown in Figure 5.

In the second stage of retrieval the small set of retrieved records are compared by the client-side applet with the original query and similarity is calculated using the simple nearest neighbour algorithm shown in Figure 3. The resulting similarity measure is normalised to give a percentage range of 0% (i.e. completely dissimilar) to 100% (i.e. completely similar). The weighting on the features by default is set to 1 (i.e., all features are by default considered of equal importance) However, the sales engineers can change the feature weightings to reflect client priorities or their own preferences.

$$Similarity(T, S) = \sum_{i=1}^{n} f(T_i, S_i) \times w_i$$

where:
T is the target case
S is the source case
n is the number of features in each case
i is an individual feature from 1 to n
f is a similarity function for feature i in cases T and S and
w is the importance weighting of feature I

Figure 3 The Nearest Neighbour Algorithm

Once an HVAC installation is completed its details are added to the database and its associated files placed on the FTP server. Having a database management system for the case repository has proved essential since it makes it easier to generate management reports and ensure data integrity. It would be almost impossible to maintain a collection of 10,000 cases without a DBMS.

2.4 Interface Design

The interface to the system is a standard Java enabled web browser (Netscape or Internet Explorer). The forms within the Java applet were designed to look as similar to the original forms, HVAC specification tools and reports that the sales staff were already familiar with. Microsoft FrontPage 98 and Macromedia's DreamWeaver were the primary tools used to create the web site. A sample screen from the client side Java applet can be seen in Figure 6.

2.4 Testing, Roll Out & Benefits

Two weeks before trial five test scenarios were created that were representative of the range of more complex residential installations the system would be expected to handle in use. These were given to the five sales staff who would initially use the system and they were asked to test the system. Out of the 25 tests (5x5) 22 were correct. Although the remaining three were not specified as expected they were felt to be technically acceptable solutions.

The system was rolled out for trial to the five sales staff in March of 1998. Acceptance of the system from the five sales staff was very good once they understood what it was doing. During the month's trial the system dealt with 63 installations all of which were felt to be technically sound. The sales staff had not had to use the expertise of the HVAC engineers at all for this work although the engineers checked the final specifications.

```
<?xml version="1.0" encoding="shift_jis"?>
<!DOCTYPE SYSTEM "http://case/query.dtd"
<Query Structure>
     <Ref Number> 1024 </Ref Number>
<Location>
     <Reference City> Perth </Reference City>
     <Conditions>
          <Daily Temp Range> L </Daily temp Range>
          <Latitude> 33 </Latitude>
          <Elevation> 0 </Elevation>
          <Elevation Factor>
               <Sensible> 1 </Sensible>
               <Total> 1 </Total>
          </Elevation Factor>
          ...
     </Conditions>
...
</Location>
...
</Query Structure>
```

query.xml

```
<!ELEMENT Case Structure
     (Ref Number, Location, ...)>
<!ELEMENT Location
     (Reference City, Conditions,...)>
<!ELEMENT Conditions
     (Daily Temp Range, Latitude, Elevation,
          Elevation Factor,...)>
<!ELEMENT Elevation Factor
     (Sensible, Total)>
...
```

query.dtd

Figure 4. A Sample of the XML Case Description

```
SELECT Location.ReferenceRegion, Location.DailyTempRange, Location.Lattitude, Location.Elevation, Lo-
cation.ElevationFactorS, Location.ElevationFactorT, Location.DryBulbTempWin, Location.DryBulbTempSum,
Location.WetBulbTemp,
...
FROM Location
WHERE (((Location.ReferenceRegion)="SW") AND ((Location.Elevation) Between 0 And 100) AND ((Loca-
tion.DryBulbTempWin) Between 50 And 60) AND ((Location.DryBulbTempSum) Between 60 And 70))
...
```

Figure 5. Example of an SQL Query That Has Been Relaxed

During the trial month the five sales staff were able to handle 63 installation projects without having an HVAC engineer create the specification. This resulted in a considerable saving in engineers time allowing them more time to deal with complex high value commercial HVAC contracts.

It was estimated that margins had been increased by nearly 2% while still remaining competitive. Based on this Western Air has invested $127,000 in purchasing Pentium notebook PCs for its sales staff. The system was rolled out to the entire sales staff in May of 1998. In the first ten months since the system has been fully operational sales compared with the same period last year are up 10% and margins have increased by 1.75%. Western Air expect the system to make $476,000 in its first year. A return of $253,855 on an investment of $222,145 (all amounts are in US dollars).

One of the firm's senior engineers commented that: *"Since this system went live I've had much more time to spend on my own contracts. I used to hate going into the office because I always had a string of problems to handle from the mob out in the field. Now I feel I have the time to really help when I do get a problem to deal with."*

A member of the sales engineering staff said that: *"This is just great. It used to be really frustrating waiting for them back in Fremantle to deal with our problems. I always had to give 'em aggro and when we did finally get an answer the bloody customer changed his mind. Then they whinge because we can't give them an answer on the spot. Now I can even use their phone and get good answers real quick. It really impresses them!"*

3 System Enhancements

Since its roll-out the original implementation of the system has experienced increasing load performance problems. The Java servlet approach suffered from poor performance because the web server loads, executes and terminates a new servlet program for each user access. Large data sets and complex queries especially burden the system because data querying takes place via the Java servlet program rather than directly via the database. This coupled with the fact that MS Access is not a particularly fast database caused time out problems as the server load increased. To rectify this problem the database was ported to mySQL (http://www.tcx.se) a freeware database with much better performance.

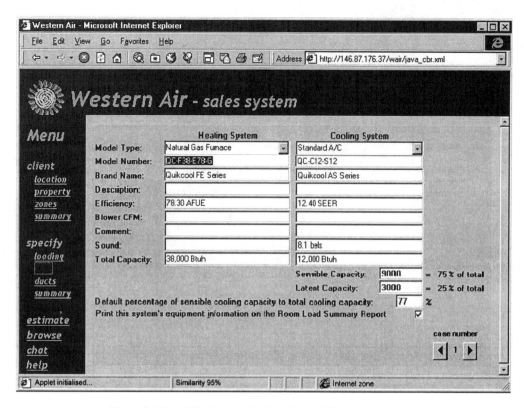

Figure 6. Client Side Java Applet Showing Retrieved HVAC Case

In addition Netscape's LiveWire database integration tool was used. This product has excellent database query functions, and importantly, because the LiveWire engine runs within the Netscape Web Server process it can share database connections across all Web accesses.

3.1 Introspective Learning

The initial query relaxation method of first performing a precise query and then relaxing the query through successive iterations until a sufficiently large set of cases was retrieved also compounded the performance problems. A suggestion was made to turn this process around – namely, why not relax the initial query far enough to ensure that a large set of cases would be retrieved (e.g., several hundred cases) and then refine the query to reduce the sub-set to around twenty cases). The obvious speed advantage in this approach is that an increasingly small sub-set of cases is searched in any subsequent iterations as opposed to the entire database in the original query relaxation approach.

However, deciding how much to relax the query was not straightforward so an introspective learning approach was taken. This is an approach in CBR where the reasoning system itself learns over time to modify its internal representation to improve its performance [Markovitch & Scott, 1993]. For example, CBR systems may learn to modify feature weights, adaptation rules [Leake, et al., 1995; Hanney &

Keane, 1996], or even learn to forget redundant cases [Smyth & Cunningham, 1996]. In our implementation the system logs each time it needs to relax a query. When the same query term is encountered again the query is automatically relaxed by the previous amount. Whilst not a guaranteed improvement this heuristic, combined with the improvements in server side architecture, has reduced the server side retrieval time on average by almost 50%. Moreover, since the amount of query relaxation is controlled dynamically by the introspective learning heuristic it can reflect changes in the case-base due to the addition (or removal) of cases.

4 Conclusions

This implementation has shown how a distributed CBR system can be created on the web in a relatively short space of time (six months). Implementing the system for web delivery made the system much more viable. Just a few years ago we would have had to install the entire system (including the database of 10,000 records) on each of the sales staffs PCs. We would then have had to regularly send them updates to the database. This would have significantly increased the operational costs of the system. Thus the web is an ideal medium for delivering intelligent support of all types.

The project was most certainly helped by having a ready made case library. Although knowledge engineering work was still required in determining valid ways of relaxing the SQL queries and creating similarity metrics. This was not surprising as the similarity measure is one of the most important *knowledge containers* of any CBR system [Richter, 1998].

XML is a useful communications protocol enabling large packets of formatted information to be exchanged thereby reducing network traffic. As a possible replacement to HTML it should help the web support intelligent applications [Hayes, et al., 1998; Doyle, et al., 1998]. However, we have demonstrated that implementing a simple CBR system is not difficult and is a viable alternative to purchasing a commercial tool. We will see CBR systems playing an increasingly important role in product selection and specification on-line, since similarity-based retrieval is very useful for Internet e-commerce systems [Wilke, et al., 1998].

On another level this implementation confirms the growing realisation that CBR is a methodology for problem solving that can use a wide variety of approaches [Kamp et al., 1998; Watson, 1998]. Our system first uses SQL retrieval to obtain a set of broadly similar cases and then uses nearest neighbour retrieval to rank those cases. Further work is planned to investigate the possibility of providing support or possibly automating some aspects of case adaptation.

References

[Doyle, et al., 1998] Doyle, M., Ferrario, M.A, Hayes, C., Cunningham, P., Smyth, B. (1998). CBR Net: Smart Technology Over a Network, Internal Report Trinity College Dublin, TCD-CS-1998-07.
http://www.cs.tcd.ie/Padraig.Cunningham/publications.html

[Hammond et al., 1996] Hammond, K.J., Burke, R., & Schmitt, K. (1996). A Case-Based Approach to Knowledge Navigation. In, Case-Based Reasoning: Experiences, Lessons, & Future Directions. Leake, D.B. (Ed.) pp.125-136. AAAI Press/The MIT Press Menlo Park, Calif., US.

[Hanney & Keane, 1996] Hanney, K. & Keane, M. (1996). Learning Adaptation Rules From a Case-Base. Advances in Case-Based Reasoning, Smith, I. & Faltings, B. (Eds.) Lecture Notes in AI # 1168 pp.179-192. Springer-Verlag, Berlin.

[Hayes, et al., 1998] Hayes, C., Doyle, M., Cunningham, P., (1998). Distributed CBR Using XML, Internal Report Trinity College Dublin, TCD--CS-1998-06.
http://www.cs.tcd.ie/Padraig.Cunningham/publications.html

[Kamp et al., 1998] Kamp, G. Lange, S. & Globig, C. (1998). Case-Based Reasoning Technology: Related Areas. In, Case-Based Reasoning Technology: From Foundations to Application. Lenz, M. et al (Eds.) LNAI # 1400 pp.325-351. Springer-Verlag, Berlin.

[Kitano & Shimazu, 1996] Kitano, H., & Shimazu, H. (1996). The Experience Sharing Architecture: A Case Study in Corporate-Wide Case-Based Software Quality Control. In, Case-Based Reasoning: Experiences, Lessons, & Future Directions. Leake, D.B. (Ed.) pp.235-268. AAAI Press/The MIT Press Menlo Park, Calif., US.

[Leake, et al., 1995] Leake, D.B., Kinley, A. & Wilson, D. (1995). Learning to Improve Case Adaptation by Introspective Reasoning and CBR. In, Case-Based Reasoning Research & Development, Veloso, M. & Aamodt, A. (Eds.), Lecture Notes in AI # 1010, pp.229-240. Springer-Verlag, Berlin.

[Markovitch & Scott, 1993] Markovitch, S. & Scott, P.D. (1993). Information Filtering. Selection mechanisms in Learning Systems. Machine Learning, 10, pp.113-151.

[Richter, 1998] Richter, M. (1998). Introduction - the basic concepts of CBR. In, Case-Based Reasoning Technology: from foundations to applications. Lenz, M., Bartsch-Sporl, B., Burkhard. H-D. & Wess, S. (Eds.). Lecture Notes In AI # 1400 Springer-Verlag, Berlin.

[Shimazu, 1998] Shimazu, H. (1998). Textual Case-Based Reasoning System using XML on the World-Wide Web. To appear in the Proc. Of the 4th European Workshop on CBR (EWCBR98), Springer Verlag LNAI.

[Smyth & Cunningham, 1996]. Smyth, B., & Cunningham,). (1996). The Utility Problem Analysed: A Case-Based Reasoning Perspective. Advances in Case-Based Reasoning, Smith, I. & Faltings, B. (Eds.) Lecture Notes in AI # 1168 pp.392-399. Springer-Verlag, Berlin.

[Watson, 1997] Watson, I. (1997). Applying Case-Based Reasoning: techniques for enterprise systems. Morgan Kaufmann Publishers Inc. San Francisco, CA.

[Watson, 1998] Watson, I. (1998). Case-Based Reasoning is a Methodology not a Technology. Research & Development in Expert Systems XV, Mile, R., Moulton, M. & Bramer, M. (Eds.), pp.213-223. Springer-Verlag, London.

[Wilke, et al., 1998] Wilke, W. Lenz, M. Wess, S. (1998). Intelligent Sales Support with CBR. In, Case-Based Reasoning Technology: from foundations to applications. Lenz, M., Bartsch-Sporl, B., Burkhard. H-D. & Wess, S. (Eds.). Lecture Notes In AI # 1400 91-113. Springer-Verlag, Berlin.

[WWW Consortium 1997] World Wide Web Consortium, (1997). Extensible Markup Language 1.0, recommendation by W3C: www.w3.org/TR/PR-xml-971208

[WWW Consortium] World Wide Web Consortium home page: www.w3.org

Knowledge Modeling and Reusability in $E_x Claim$

Liviu Badea
AI Research Lab
Research Institute for Informatics
8-10 Averescu Blvd., Bucharest, Romania
e-mail: badea@ici.ro

Abstract

This paper presents $E_x Claim$, a hybrid language
for knowledge representation and reasoning. Originally developed as an operationalization language
for the KADS knowledge based systems (KBS) development methodology, $E_x Claim$ has a meta-level
architecture: it structures the knowledge on three
levels, namely the domain, inference and task level.
An extension of a description logic is used for implementing the domain level. The inference and task
levels are general logic programs integrated with
the domain level by means of upward and downward reflection rules which describe the automatic
domain operations performed whenever arguments
of inferences or tasks are accessed. Inferences and
tasks support non-deterministic reasoning, which
in turn requires a non-monotonic domain level.

Description logics offer a set of inference services
(some not available in other knowledge representation languages) which are extremely useful in
knowledge modeling. Such inference services include domain-level deduction, semantic consistency
verification and automatic classification of concepts. We argue that such validation and verification facilities are important in assisting a knowledge engineer in developing models. These models
are *reusable* due to the layered architecture as well
as to the possibility of writing generic inferences
using a reified membership relation.

1 Introduction

Knowledge based systems (KBS) are typically large and complex software systems aiming at solving difficult problems
in knowledge-intensive domains. *Knowledge engineering* in
general and KBS development in particular are notoriously
difficult not only because of the sheer size of the problem
description, but also because they typically involve complex
ontologies, which are usually not easily representable in a
single knowledge representation formalism.

In order to assist the knowledge engineer in developing
KBSs, a large number of KBS development tools have been
built since the eighties. Two main tendencies were followed
in the early years.

On one hand, a great number of expert system "shells"
were put forward. Systems like KEE, ART, Knowledge Craft,
Nexpert Object etc. were successfully used in building a large
number of expert systems. These "shells", however, had an
important drawback: they used a given symbol-level representation (for instance a frame-based system augmented with
rules, daemons, message passing, etc.), which is usually not
appropriate for describing reusable knowledge-level models.

An alternative approach to building KBS development
tools was inspired by the traditional software engineering
(SE) tools. SE tools are nevertheless inappropriate as KBS
tools since the domain knowledge (the ontology) is much
more complex in the case of a KBS than in the case of a
typical software system.

The remarks above suggest the need for a knowledge-level
KBS development tool that would provide at least some of
the nice simulation facilities offered by traditional SE tools.
Such facilities are much harder to develop in the case of
KBSs, since, as already mentioned above, we are dealing
with much more complex domain knowledge. An extreme
approach would be to use full predicate logic as a domain
description language and to support the reasoning involved
with a full first order logic theorem prover. This approach can
be very inefficient in complex cases. Also, the readability of
model specifications may sometimes be quite low, especially
when dealing with complex logic formulae.

In order to support knowledge-level knowledge modeling,
a series of methodologies and specification languages have
been put forward, the most important ones being the KADS
methodology [10], KIF and Ontolingua, etc. A number of
KADS operationalization languages and environments have
been developed for supporting the KADS methodology with
executable tools: $Si(ML)^2$, OMOS, MoMo, KARL, MODEL-
K, FORKADS [5], etc. Most of these languages are either
very expressive, formally sound but computationally inefficient (sometimes even intractable), or they have a more procedural semantics, being less expressive, but more tractable.

This paper presents a hybrid architecture aiming at integrating description logics (viewed as domain description languages) and logic programming (used for representing inference and control knowledge) in a declarative knowledge modeling environment. The main byproduct of this declarative
approach is the possibility of developing reusable libraries of
problem solving methods.

1.1 Brief description of $E_x Claim$

$E_x Claim$ (Executable CommonKADS Language for Integrated Modeling) is a knowledge modeling environment integrating description logics (used for representing domain
knowledge) and logic programming (for dealing with inference and control knowledge). Originally developed as an op-

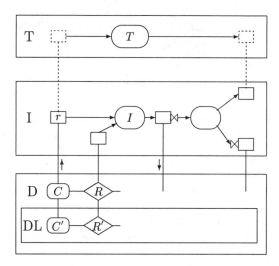

Figure 1: The $E_x Claim$ architecture

Concept	Symbolic	Semantic interpretation
top	$\top$	$\Delta^{\mathcal{I}}$
bottom	$\bot$	$\emptyset$
$and(C_1, C_2)$	$C_1 \wedge C_2$	$C_1^{\mathcal{I}} \cap C_2^{\mathcal{I}}$
$or(C_1, C_2)$	$C_1 \vee C_2$	$C_1^{\mathcal{I}} \cup C_2^{\mathcal{I}}$
$not(C)$	$\neg C$	$\Delta^{\mathcal{I}} \setminus C^{\mathcal{I}}$
$all(R, C)$	$\forall R{:}\,C$	$\{x \in \Delta^{\mathcal{I}} | \forall y.(x,y) \in R^{\mathcal{I}} \to y \in C^{\mathcal{I}}\}$
$exists(R, C)$	$\exists R{:}\,C$	$\{x \in \Delta^{\mathcal{I}} | \exists y.(x,y) \in R^{\mathcal{I}} \wedge y \in C^{\mathcal{I}}\}$
$atleast(n, R)$	$\geq_n R$	$\{x \in \Delta^{\mathcal{I}} | |R^{\mathcal{I}}(x)| \geq n\}$
$atmost(n, R)$	$\leq_n R$	$\{x \in \Delta^{\mathcal{I}} | |R^{\mathcal{I}}(x)| \leq n\}$
$exactly(n, R)$	$=_n R$	$\{x \in \Delta^{\mathcal{I}} | |R^{\mathcal{I}}(x)| = n\}$
Relation	**Symbolic**	**Semantic interpretation**
$and(R_1, R_2)$	$R_1 \wedge R_2$	$R_1^{\mathcal{I}} \cap R_2^{\mathcal{I}}$
$inv(R)$	R^{-1}	$\{(y,x) | (x,y) \in R^{\mathcal{I}}\}$
$domrestr(R, C)$	$C \lfloor R$	$\{(x,y) | (x,y) \in R^{\mathcal{I}} \wedge x \in C^{\mathcal{I}}\}$
$restrict(R, C)$	$R \rfloor C$	$\{(x,y) | (x,y) \in R^{\mathcal{I}} \wedge y \in C^{\mathcal{I}}\}$

Table 1: Concept/relation constructors

Terminological axiom		Semantics
`defconcept(CN,C)`	$CN = C$	$CN^{\mathcal{I}} = C^{\mathcal{I}}$
`defrelation(RN,R)`	$RN = R$	$RN^{\mathcal{I}} = R^{\mathcal{I}}$
`defattribute(AN,A)`	$AN = A$	$AN^{\mathcal{I}} = A^{\mathcal{I}}$
`defprimeconcept(CN,C)`	$CN \subset C$	$CN^{\mathcal{I}} \subset C^{\mathcal{I}}$
`defprimerelation(RN,R)`	$RN \subset R$	$RN^{\mathcal{I}} \subset R^{\mathcal{I}}$
`defprimeattribute(AN,A)`	$AN \subset A$	$AN^{\mathcal{I}} \subset A^{\mathcal{I}}$
`inclusion(C₁,C₂)`	$C_1 \subset C_2$	$C_1^{\mathcal{I}} \subset C_2^{\mathcal{I}}$
`equal(C₁,C₂)`	$C_1 = C_2$	$C_1^{\mathcal{I}} = C_2^{\mathcal{I}}$
`disjoint([CN₁,...,CNₙ])`	$\bigwedge\limits_{j=1}^{n} CN_j = \bot$	$\bigcap\limits_{j=1}^{n} CN_j^{\mathcal{I}} = \emptyset$
Assertional axiom		**Semantics**
`assert_ind(IN,C)`	$IN \in C$	$IN^{\mathcal{I}} \in C^{\mathcal{I}}$
`assert_ind(IN₁,IN₂,R)`	$(IN_1, IN_2) \in R$	$(IN_1^{\mathcal{I}}, IN_2^{\mathcal{I}}) \in R^{\mathcal{I}}$

Table 2: Terminological and assertional axioms

erationalization language for the CommonKADS knowledge based systems methodology [2], $E_x Claim$ has a meta-level architecture which structures the knowledge corresponding to a model on three levels, namely the *domain*, *inference* and *task* level. Figure 1 presents a graphical representation of the $E_x Claim$ architecture (which is typical for the KADS expertise model). Although the decomposition of a given model in the three knowledge levels may not be unique, it is usually relatively easy to map an informal description of the model onto this three-level architecture.

The *domain level* encodes the domain ontology. The domain knowledge is mainly expressed in a description logic (DL) which provides fairly sophisticated inference services (such as domain-level deduction, semantic consistency checking, automatic classification of concepts, knowledge structuring and indexing).

The *inference level* consists of a set of primitive problem solving actions, whose internal functioning is irrelevant from the point of view of the conceptual problem solving model. Inferences (represented graphically as ovals) have a set of input and output *roles* (depicted in diagrams as rectangles), which denote, roughly speaking, the arguments of the inference. (Inference roles represent a kind of meta-level abstraction of domain level objects (concepts, relations, etc).)

Although the execution of inferences induces domain level operations, inferences do not manipulate domain level objects directly. Since they refer to domain object only *indirectly via inference roles*, (partial) models in which the domain-level has been stripped off can be easily reused in a different domain. Reusability is thus a key feature of KADS expertise models as it enables the construction of domain-independent libraries of models.

The inference structures represent the data-flow of a given model. The control of the various inferences is accomplished at the *task level*.

2 The domain level

The $E_x Claim$ domain level is an extension of a description logic (DL), with the *concept, relation and attribute constructors* from Table 1 and the *terminological and assertional axioms* shown in Table 2. (The DL implementation used in $E_x Claim$ is the Motel system [6].) Unlike most implemented

logical and database systems[1], DLs use the *open world assumption* (it is not automatically assumed that all the individuals known at one moment are all possible individuals).

The *inference services* provided by the DL include satisfiability (consistency) and subsumption testing, automatic classification of concepts in a hierarchy and instance retrieval.

In a language including concept negation, all of the above services make use of the knowledge base consistency algorithm [3]. For example, subsumption testing `subsumes(C,D)` reduces to unsatisfiability testing of the concept `and(not(C),D)`.

2.1 The domain level extension

In order to be usable in real-life applications, our KR&R language will have to be able to describe *collections* of objects (such as sets or lists of instances/tuples). However, existing (implemented) DL systems usually lack constructors for sets or lists of objects[2] and we therefore have to *extend* the description logic with such collections of concept instances or relation tuples. This does not affect the completeness of the DL inferences since the terminological and assertional levels of the DL are completely separated (it is impossible to

---

[1] which usually use a form of closed world semantics

[2] Some description logics provide the $one\_of(IN_1, \ldots, IN_n)$ construct which denotes the concept whose extension is given by the set of instances $\{IN_1, \ldots, IN_n\}$. However, what we need is a concept construct whose *instances* denote sets or lists of other instances (or tuples).

have a DL instance that represents a collection of other DL instances).

This domain extension leads to a *hybrid* domain level in which *simple* instances are represented in the DL, while *collections* (sets or lists) are stored in the extension.

The internal representation of a so-called *domain store* element is the following:

$$domain\_store\left(simple, \frac{concept}{relation}, \frac{C}{R}, (IN', IN'')\right)$$

$$domain\_store\left(set/list, \frac{concept}{relation}, \frac{C}{R}, \frac{[IN_1, IN_2, \ldots]}{[(IN_1', IN_1''), \ldots]}\right).$$

A domain-level concept or (binary) relation can have an associated DL description, represented as

$$DL\_description\left(\frac{concept}{relation}, \frac{C}{R}, \frac{DL\_C}{DL\_R}\right).$$

Here C and R stand for domain level concept/relation names, while DL_C and DL_R represent their associated DL descriptions.

3 The inference level

Inferences are primitive problem solving actions which perform elementary problem solving operations (i.e. operations whose internal functioning is irrelevant from the point of view of the conceptual model).

Inferences operate on *inference roles*[3], which can be either inputs or outputs. Inference roles represent a kind of meta-level abstraction of domain level objects (concepts, relations, etc). In order to enhance the flexibility of the mapping between inference roles and domain level objects, the following types of inference role *domain links* have been introduced:

- *simple* (the role refers a single DL instance)

- *set* (the role refers a single domain level instance representing a set of DL instances)

- *list* (the role refers a single domain level instance representing a list of DL instances).

Domain links are represented in $E_x Claim$ as:

$$domain\_link\left(InferenceRole, \frac{simple}{set}, \frac{concept}{relation}, \frac{C}{R}\right).$$

Input roles implement the *upward reflection* rules of the meta-level architecture, i.e. they are responsible, broadly speaking, for retrieving domain level instances. More precisely, input roles can perform the following types of *domain operations*:

- *retrieve* (retrieve an instance of the domain level object linked to the input role, but do not remove the instance afterwards)

- *noretrieve* (no instances are retrieved from the domain, as if no domain operation was performed; the value of the role is set in the call of the inference rather than retrieved from the domain)

- *delete* (retrieves a domain level instance and subsequently removes it; the domain level description logic must provide facilities for knowledge revision in order to support this operation).

---

[3]In KADS, the arguments of inferences are called *roles*.

Figure 2: Role mapping types

Output roles implement the *downward reflection* rules of the meta-level architecture since they are responsible mainly for storing object instances in the domain level. More precisely, output roles can perform the following types of domain operations:

- *store* ("instances" of the given output role are asserted in the domain)

- *nostore* (the "instances" of the output role are not reflected in the domain; instead, their value is passed to the caller of the inference).

Inferences perform *automatic domain operations* on their input/output roles. Since no direct domain reference is made in inferences (or tasks), these levels of the model are domain-independent and thus reusable (the code of the inference can remain exactly the same even after changing the domain level).

The automatic domain operations in inferences can be regarded as a more evolved form of parameter passing in an inference call. For instance, the operation types "noretrieve" and "nostore" perform no actual domain operations and rely on the explicit parameter passing mechanism in the call of the inference. On the other hand, the operation types "delete" and "store" perform domain operations and should be backtrackable if we intend to provide a non-deterministic computation model. This in turn requires the *non-monotonicity* of the domain level and the existence of *knowledge revision* facilities in the corresponding description logic.

The *backtrackability* of domain operations requires that whenever the inference (that performed the corresponding domain operation) fails, the state of the domain store and the description logic is restored to the state before the call of the failing inference. The same happens when new solutions are sought for by backtracking.

In order to further enhance the flexibility of the inference level primitives, two types of *role mappings* have been provided (see also Figure 2):

- *simple* (refers to a single domain store element associated with the inference role)

- *set* (refers to the set of all simple domain store elements associated with the inference role)

The $E_x Claim$ representation of role mappings and the associated role operations is:

$$role\_mapping\left(Inference, \frac{InputRole}{OutputRole}, simple/set, \frac{noretrieve/retrieve/delete}{nostore/store}\right).$$

Note that a "simple" role operation involves a *single*[4] domain store element of the form:

$$domain\_store\left(\frac{simple}{set}{list}, \frac{concept}{relation}, \frac{C}{R}, Instance\right).$$

---

[4]irrespective of the domain link type, which can be: simple, set or list.

From the conceptual point of view, inferences are primitive problem solving actions and their internal structure as well as their functioning need not be further detailed. However, if we are aiming at an operational system, the knowledge engineer would have to provide the "code" of the inference in order to be able to execute the model.

In $E_x Claim$, inferences are *normal logic programs*, i.e. sets of clauses of the form (we are using a Prolog syntax):

```
inference_name([input_role_i = Value_i, ...],
               [output_role_j = Value_j, ...]) :-
    inference_body.
```

The heads of such clauses have two arguments representing the lists of input and output role bindings. A *role binding* is a term of the form role_name = RoleValue (RoleValue can be a variable or a (partially) instantiated Prolog term). The order of the role bindings in the binding lists is irrelevant.

An inference body can contain calls to other inferences or tasks, but this is not recommended as a good modeling approach (since inferences should be thought of as primitive executable objects).

In $E_x Claim$, inferences are executed using the following primitive:

```
exec_inference(inference_name,
               [input_role_i = InputValue_i, ...],
               [output_role_j = OutputValue_j, ...]).
```

which performs the following operations:

- unify the input arguments of the inference with those of the call
- perform domain operations for the input roles (noretrieve, retrieve, delete)
- execute the inference body
- unify the output arguments of the inference with those of the call
- perform domain operations for the output roles (nostore, store).

All the above steps of exec_inference are backtrackable. As already mentioned, backtracking to a domain operation may involve domain level knowledge revision too.

4   The task level

The task level embodies the *control knowledge* of a model. Tasks do not perform domain operations since they are viewed as composite executable objects (only the primitive executable objects, i.e. the inferences, are allowed to perform domain operations).

Since no domain operations are associated to task roles, tasks are, from an operational point of view, like inferences with "*noretrieve*" input roles and "*nostore*" output roles.

One and the same role can be an inference role and a task role at the same time. (For example, the input role of a composite task can also be the input role of a component inference or subtask. The actual domain operations are performed when the inference is executed.)

Parameter passing in tasks is done explicitly in the call of the task. From the programmer's point of view, tasks have the same syntax as inferences:

```
task_name([input_role_i = InputValue_i, ...],
          [output_role_i = OutputValue_j, ...]) :-
    task_body.
```

Task bodies can, of course, contain calls to other inferences and subtasks. Executing a task with

```
exec_task(task_name,
          [input_role_i = InputValue_i, ...],
          [output_role_j = OutputValue_j, ...])
```

amounts to

- unifying the input arguments of the task with those of the call
- executing the body
- unifying the output arguments of the task with those of the call.

All the above execution steps of exec_task are backtrackable.

5   A simple example

A very simple example of a resource allocation problem will be used to illustrate the facilities of $E_x Claim$. In a university department there is a set of classes to be taught by a set of lecturers. Classes can be either courses or seminars (but not both), while lecturers are either professors or assistants (but not both). Let us further assume that assistants are allowed to teach only seminars and that the list of classes familiar to (known by) the various lecturers is also given. Of course, a lecturer can teach a given class only if he knows it. Also, we require that each class should be taught by a lecturer and that a lecturer cannot teach more than one class (of course, there may be lecturers that don't teach any class at all). The goal of the problem is to find an assignment of lecturers (resources) to classes (requests) such that all the above constraints are verified.

The most straightforward conceptualization of this problem involves defining the following concepts and relations:

```
defconcept(lecturer, or(prof, assistant)).
defprimeconcept(prof, lecturer).
defprimeconcept(assistant, all(teaches, seminar)).
disjoint([prof, assistant]).
defconcept(class, or(course, seminar)).
defprimeconcept(course, class).
defprimeconcept(seminar, class).
disjoint([course, seminar]).
defprimerelation(knows).
defprimerelation(teaches).
```

The relations *teaches* and *knows* link a lecturer with the course he teaches or knows respectively.

Given the relation *knows*, one must find the relation *teaches* subject to all the problem constraints. Some of these constraints are easily expressible in the description logic (like the ones presented above). Other constraints may not be expressible in the DL and we may have to take them into account at the inference level. For instance, the constraint mentioning that "a lecturer can teach a given class only if he knows it" cannot be represented in the DL unless the particular DL we are using allows the famous role-value map constructor:

```
equal(subset(teaches, knows), top).
```

However, since role-value maps (together with relation composition and concept conjunction) induce the *undecidability* of the DL inference services [9], they are usually not provided in implemented DL systems with complete algorithms. Therefore, we will have to encode this constraint at the higher levels of the model (inference and/or task level).

On the other hand, the constraints that each class should be taught by a lecturer and that a lecturer cannot teach more than one class could easily be represented in existing DLs as:

```
defprimeconcept(class, exists(inv(teaches), lecturer)).
defprimeconcept(lecturer, atmost(1, teaches)).
```

In fact, if all the problem constraints could be represented in the description logic, we could use the DL inference services to solve our problem without additional support from the inference or task level (DL inference services are usually reducible to the knowledge base consistency test, which typically works by constructing models of the KB. The model constructed while proving the KB consistency can then be used to extract the solution of the problem).

However, not all constraints are expressible in a given DL, so that the additional levels are really necessary. Also, we may wish to exert a tighter control on the problem solving process and thus inference and task levels are again needed (relying entirely on the description logic inference services may turn out to be too expensive from a computational point of view).

Last, if we are trying to develop reusable models, having separate domain, inference and task levels turns out to be again very useful. For instance, stripping off the domain level from our simple allocation example leads to a reusable problem-solving model for general resource allocation problems (lecturers are abstracted as *resources*, while classes are viewed as *requests*). We could also reuse the domain model in a different problem involving lecturers and classes.

After having completely described the domain level of our simple model, we proceed to the construction of the inference level. An extremely simple non-deterministic approach will be followed.

Assume that a partial assignment (of the *teaches* relation) has been constructed up to this point and that we are currently attempting to extend this partial assignment with a new tuple for *teaches* chosen from the tuples of *knows* and linking a class that has not already been assigned and a lecturer who is still free (teaches no other class). The corresponding inference structure is depicted in Figure 3. Note that we have used generic (abstract) names for the inference roles denoting lecturers, classes and the relations *teaches* and *knows*. Classes are regarded as requests, whereas lecturers are the resources to be allocated to these requests. The tuples of *teaches* are thought of as assignments, whereas the tuples of *knows* are just candidate_assignments.

The inference get_request chooses a request that has not been assigned yet. This chosen_request is passed on to assign_resource, which tries to retrieve a candidate_assignment for this request. If it succeeds, the assignment is stored in the domain level. The whole process is repeated (at the task level) until there are no more unassigned requests (case in which it terminates with success) or until a failure occurs (case in which the system automatically backtracks to a previous state). Backtracking involves not only the inference and task levels, but also the domain level since the DL has to be restored to its previous state (before the call).

Inference and task bodies are extremely simple since we are heavily relying on the automatic domain operations performed by inferences. We are also relying on the powerful description logic inference mechanisms (mainly when doing domain store retrieval but also when checking for global consistency after a solution has been found).

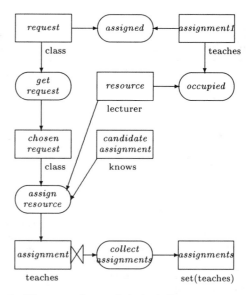

Figure 3: The non-deterministic inference structure for the lecturer allocation problem

Note that the problem-solving process involves computations (deduction) at two different levels: (1) at the domain level (DL deduction) and (2) at the inference and task levels (execution of inferences and tasks).

This observation shows that not only the description of the problem, but also the problem-solving process itself is distributed at different levels. We feel that this separation of computations (performed while solving the problem) is extremely useful and natural, leading to a higher reusability of the models. For instance, a change in the domain model does not require modifications at the inference or task levels. Let us illustrate this with an example.

Consider a problem instance in which there are only two lecturers (l_1 and l_2), two classes (a *course* c_1 and another class c_2) and in which l_1 and l_2 know both c_1 and c_2.

If we are not told whether l_1 or l_2 are professors or assistants, the system will return two alternative allocations, namely $[(l_1, c_1), (l_2, c_2)]$ and $[(l_1, c_2), (l_2, c_1)]$.

However, if we now specify that l_1 is an *assistant*, only the second assignment will be retained as a consistent one, since an assistant (l_1) cannot teach a course (c_1).

6 Generic inferences and reification

For achieving reusability of the models we need to open the possibility of writing *generic* inferences, i.e. inferences parametrized by the types of their arguments, which will be known only at runtime.

Consider, for example, the following situation. If we want to describe the staff of some research institute, we may want to introduce concepts like *director*, *secretary*, *researcher* and instances like *Tom, Joan, Mary, Peter, Fred* etc: *Tom* ∈ *director*, *Joan* ∈ *secretary*, *Mary* ∈ *secretary*, *Peter* ∈ *researcher*, *Fred* ∈ *researcher*. Note that the concepts *director*, *secretary* and *researcher* represent positions in the research institute. They are therefore not only concepts, but also *instances* of the (meta-level) concept *position*: *director* ∈ *position*, *secretary* ∈ *position*, *researcher* ∈ *position*.

The meta-level concept *position* should not be confused

with the concept *employee*, which is a super-concept of *director*, *secretary* and *researcher director* ⊂ *employee*, *secretary* ⊂ *employee*, *researcher* ⊂ *employee*.

Now suppose we would like to write separate inferences for retrieving directors, secretaries and researchers. This would amount to writing three separate pieces of code that are extremely similar. For instance, the inference for retrieving secretaries would be described by

```
domain_link(candidate, simple, concept, secretary).
role_mapping(choose_secretary, candidate, simple, retrieve).
domain_link(chosen_candidate, simple, concept, secretary).
role_mapping(choose_secretary, chosen_candidate, simple, nostore).

choose_secretary([candidate = Cand], [chosen_candidate = Cand]).
```

If we would like to avoid writing three separate pieces of code, we would have to write a *generic* inference that would be parametrized by the *position* of the person we'd like to choose. This can be accomplished by using an input role, called *type*, linked to the concept *position* and which is supposed to specify the position of the person to be chosen.

```
domain_link(candidate, simple, concept, employee).
role_mapping(generic_choose, candidate, simple, retrieve).
domain_link(type, simple, concept, position).
role_mapping(generic_choose, type, simple, retrieve).
domain_link(in, simple, relation, in).
role_mapping(generic_choose, in, simple, retrieve).
domain_link(chosen_candidate, simple, concept, employee).
role_mapping(generic_choose, chosen_candidate, simple, nostore).

generic_choose([candidate = Cand, in = [Cand,Type],
                type = Type, [chosen_candidate = Cand]).
```

Note that we are making use of the built-in relation *in* (*in* links an instance X with a concept C whenever X is an instance of C). It is usually enough to have a single role called *in* (and linked to the predefined relation *in*) since all inferences that need to refer to it can do so. Of course, *in* can be used as input and output role at the same time.[5] Whenever the role *in* is used as an input (output) role, it retrieves (stores) tuples of the form $[X, C]$ whith $X \in C$.

The predefined relation *in* allows therefore a kind of meta-level (generic) inferences which are sometimes very important for writing domain-independent and reusable models.[6] This is achieved by abstracting not only the arguments of inferences, but also their "types". (More theoretical details on reification can be found in [1].)

7 Related approaches and conclusions

The following advantages of the approach presented in this paper can be mentioned:
• the meta-level architecture of the system enables the development of reusable domain-independent problem solving models (PSMs) and of application-independent ontologies.
• the possibility of developing domain-independent executable libraries of PSMs, as in [2].
• supporting the process of KBS validation by using the inference services offered by the domain-level language: semantic

---

[5] It can be an input for some inferences and an output role for others.
[6] By using a generic inference in our example, we don't have to write any more separate inferences for each type of position (*director*, *secretary* or *researcher*). Not only is it cumbersome to have three identical pieces of code, but these pieces of code would depend on the domain level (the types of positions – *director*, *secretary* and *researcher* are domain-dependent; we cannot change the domain level, for example by introducing a new position, without having to modify the inference level too, since we would have to add a new inference for the new position type. On the other hand, if we are using the generic inference above, we would only have to change the domain link of the role *type*).

consistency checking, domain level deduction automatic concept classification, knowledge structuring and indexing. Most KBS development tools do not provide all of these inference services. Also, most of the existing tools provide symbol-level inference services, as opposed to $E_x Claim$, in which knowledge is represented at the knowledge-level (due to its clean integration of the domain-level description logic with the inference and task-level logic programs).
• the description logic used at the domain level can be regarded as a reasonable compromise between expressiveness, readability of formulas and runtime efficiency.
• $E_x Claim$ provides non-deterministic inference and task levels, which rely on a non-monotonic domain level. The lack of non-determinism in a KBS is, in our opinion, an important drawback, since algorithms in KBSs (as opposed to traditional software engineering environments) are complex and usually non-deterministic.
• $E_x Claim$ provides the reified membership relation *in* which can be used to write *generic* inferences. These inferences increase the domain-independence and reusability of models.

Several previous works have dealt with hybrid representation languages combining description logics with logic programming, for example AL-log [4], CARIN [8], F-logic [7]. However, none of these systems allows the KBS developer to specify reusable models, as in $E_x Claim$.

The main goal of this research is the creation of domain-independent executable libraries of problem solving models.

Acknowledgments

The research presented in this paper has been partly supported by the European Community project PEKADS (CP93-7599). I am indebted to Doina Ţilivea for developing the graphical user interface of $E_x Claim$, to Jan Wielemaker for support on using the XPCE environment [11] as well as to Ullrich Hustadt and Renate Schmidt for permitting the use of the Motel terminological system [6] in this research.

References

[1] Badea Liviu. *Reifying Concepts in Description Logics*. Proc. IJCAI-97, 142-147.

[2] Breuker J., Van de Velde J. *CommonKADS Library for Expertise Modelling. Reusable Problem Solving Components*. IOS 1994.

[3] Buchheit M., Donini F.M., Schaerf A. *Decidable Reasoning in Terminological Knowledge Representation Systems*. J. of AI Research 1 (1993), 109-138.

[4] Donini F., Lenzerini M., Nardi D., Schaerf A. *A hybrid system integrating datalog and concept languages*. LNAI 549, 1991.

[5] Fensel D., van Harmelen F., *A comparison of languages which operationalize and formalize KADS models of expertise*. Report 280, Universität Karlsruhe, September 1993.

[6] Hustadt U., Nonnengart A., Schmidt R., Timm J. *Motel User Manual*. Max Planck Institute Report MPI-I-92-236, Sept. 1994.

[7] Kifer M., Lausen G., Wu J. *Logical foundations of object-oriented and frame-based languages*. J. of the ACM, May 1995.

[8] Levy A., Rousset M.C. *CARIN: a representation language integrating rules and description logics*. Proc. ECAI'96.

[9] Schmidt-Schauß M. *Subsumption in KL-ONE is undecidable*. Proceedings KR-89, pp. 421-431.

[10] Schreiber G., Wielinga B., Breuker J. *KADS: A Principled Approach to Knowledge-Based System Development*. Academic Press, 1993.

[11] Wielemaker J., Anjewierden A. *Programming in PCE/Prolog*. University of Amsterdam, 1992.

KNOWLEDGE-BASED APPLICATIONS

Applications 2

Verifying Integrity Constraints on Web Sites

Mary Fernández
AT&T Research
180 Park Ave.
Florham Park, NJ 07932 USA
mff@research.att.com

Daniela Florescu
INRIA
BP.105 Rocquencourt
Le Chesnay cedex, France
dana@rodin.inria.fr

Alon Levy
Dept. of Computer Science
University of Washington
Seattle, WA. 98195 USA
alon@cs.washington.edu

Dan Suciu
AT&T Research
180 Park Ave.
Florham Park, NJ 07932 USA
suciu@research.att.com

Abstract

Data-intensive Web sites have created a new form of knowledge base, as richly structured bodies of data. Several novel systems for creating data-intensive Web sites support declarative specification of a site's structure and content (i.e., the pages, the data available in each page, and the links between pages). Declarative systems provide a platform on which AI techniques can be developed that further simplify the tasks of constructing and maintaining Web sites. This paper addresses the problem of specifying and verifying integrity constraints on a Web site's structure. We describe a language that can capture many practical constraints and an accompanying sound and complete verification algorithm. The algorithm has the important property that if the constraints are violated, it proposes fixes to either the constraints or to the site definition. Finally, we establish tight bounds on the complexity of the verification problem we consider.

1 Introduction

Data-intensive Web sites have created a new form of knowledge base. They typically contain and integrate several bodies of data about the enterprise they are describing, and these bodies of data are linked into a rich structure. For example, a company's internal Web site may contain data about its employees, linked to data about the products they produce and/or to the customers they serve. The *data* in a Web site and the *structure* of the links in the site can be viewed as a richly structured knowledge base.

The management of data-intensive Web sites has received significant attention in the database community [Fernandez *et al.*, 1998; Atzeni *et al.*, 1998; Arocena and Mendelzon, 1998; Cluet *et al.*, 1998; Paolini and Fraternali, 1998]. The key insight of recent systems is to specify the structure and content of sites declaratively. These systems separate and provide direct support for the three primary steps of site creation: (1) identifying and accessing the data served at the site, (2) defining the site's structure (i.e., the pages, the data in each page, and the links between pages), and (3) specifying

the HTML rendering of the site's pages. Step 2 is usually supported by a declarative, specification language.

Web-site management systems based on declarative representations offer several benefits. First, since a site's structure and content are defined declaratively, not procedurally by a program, it is easy to create multiple *versions* of a site. For example, it is possible to build internal and external views of an organization's site or to build sites tailored to novice or expert users. Currently, creating multiple versions requires writing multiple sets of programs or manually creating different sets of HTML files. Second, these systems support the evolution of a site's structure. For example, to reorganize pages based on frequent usage patterns or to extend the site's content, we simply rewrite the site's specification. Another advantage is efficient update of a site when its data sources change.

Declarative Web-site management systems also allow us to view a site's definition and its content as a knowledge base. A natural next step is to consider how reasoning techniques can further improve the process of building and maintaining Web sites. We consider the reasoning problem of verifying integrity constraints over Web sites. Specifically, when the structure of a site becomes complex, it is hard for a designer to ensure that the site will satisfy a set of desired properties. For example, we may want to enforce that all pages are reachable from the root, every organization homepage points to the homepages of its sub-organizations, or proprietary data is not displayed on the external version of the site. A study on the usability of on-line stores [Lohse and Spiller, 1998] provides other constraints that if followed, would improve the site design.

For a verification tool to be useful, it must verify constraints against a site definition, *not* a particular instance of the site, because (1) we do not want to verify the constraints every time the site instance changes, and (2) if a Web site is dynamically generated, an instance is never completely materialized making it is impossible to check the constraints. Verifying the constraints on the site definition ensures that as long as the site is generated according to the definition, the constraints will be satisfied. For this reason, the verification problem requires reasoning, and not just applying a procedure to the site. Furthermore, when the integrity constraints are not verified, the system should automatically propose a set of candidate modifications to the site definition. This raises a search problem in the space of possible modifications.

This paper makes the following contributions. First, we identify an important class of integrity constraints relevant to Web sites. Second, we describe a sound and complete algorithm for verifying the integrity constraints and an analysis of their complexity. The key feature of our algorithms is that they consider only the *specification* of the site's structure and content, not a particular instance of a site. Hence, the verification is independent of changes to the underlying site, as long as they are generated by the same specification. Finally, in cases where the verification algorithm shows that the constraints may be violated, it proposes a set of corrections to the Web site's definition.

The problem we consider is closely related to the problem of knowledge-base verification (see [VVT'98, 1998] for a recent workshop). We follow the paradigm proposed in [Levy and Rousset, 1998], where algorithms for verification are based on query containment. However, whereas in [Levy and Rousset, 1998] there was a 1-1 translation between the verification problem and query containment, a challenge in our case is to perform the appropriate transformation.

We believe that Web-site management tools based on declarative specifications will pose several important AI research problems in the near future. Hence, one of the contributions of this paper is to bring the problem to the attention of our community. In the last section, we mention other research problems in this context.

2 Declarative Management of Web Sites

Declarative systems for Web-site management are based on the principle of separating three tasks: (1) the management of the data underlying the site, (2) the definition of the site's structure and the content, and (3) the graphical presentation of the site. The first step requires identifying the sources that contain the site's data. We refer to this data as the *raw data*. These sources may include databases, structured files, or pre-existing sites. We assume that we interact with each of these sources via a *wrapper* program that produces the necessary data in tabular form. Here, we assume that the raw data is stored in a single relational database system. In the rest of the paper, we use an example that is a small fragment of a publication's Web site. Fig. 1 contains the schema of the raw data and sample data.

The second step in building a Web site requires specifying the site's structure. We describe a formalism for specifying this structure that captures features common to many declarative systems for Web-site management [Fernandez *et al.*, 1998; Atzeni *et al.*, 1998; Arocena and Mendelzon, 1998; Cluet *et al.*, 1998; Paolini and Fraternali, 1998]. We emphasize that the declarative specification is concerned with the *logical* model of the site as a set of nodes and links, not its *graphical* pre-

Person

persid	name
p1	"john"
p2	"mary"

Author

persid	artid
p1	a1
p1	a2
p2	a2
p2	a3

Article

artid	title	year
a1	"title1"	1995
a2	"title2"	1998
a3	"title3"	1998

PsFile

artid	psfile
a2	"file2.ps"
a3	"file3.ps"

Figure 1: The schema and data underlying the publication Web site.

sentation (i.e., how each node is translated to HTML). When using the systems above, the site designer also specifies the graphical presentation of each page, usually by a set of HTML templates, each of which applies to a group of related pages.

2.1 Specifying Web-site Structure

In order to specify a site's structure, we need to state (1) what pages exist (2) what data is available in each page, and (3) what links exist between pages. We specify the structure of site in a *site definition*. Given a site definition and a database instance, applying the definition to the database produces an instance of the site, called a *site graph*. Fig. 2 contains our example site definition and Fig. 3 contains the resulting site graph.

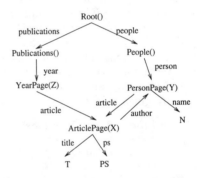

Figure 2: The site definition for our example site.

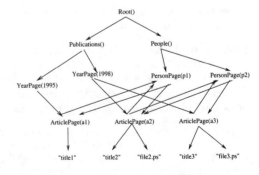

Figure 3: The example site graph.

A site definition is a graph whose nodes are labeled by variables or by functional terms of the form $f(\bar{X})$, where

$\bar{X}$ is a (possibly empty) tuple of variables. Functional nodes in the site definition represent *sets* of pages in the site graph. In our example, the node PersonPage(Y) represents the set of pages PersonPage(p) where p is a constant in the database. Non-functional nodes are leaves and have one incoming edge. They represent the data contained in the page that points to them. For example, the node N represents the name of the person Y. Functional nodes that have no arguments represent unique pages, such as the root.

Each functional node is labeled with a Horn rule that defines the conditions for the existence of instances of the node. A rule's head is an atom of the form Node(f(X)), where Node is a special predicate. For example, the rule for YearPage specifies that there will be a node for a year Z if some article was published in year Z. The rules for our example site are:

$Node(Root()) : -true.$
$Node(Publications()) : -true.$
$Node(People()) : -true.$
$Node(YearPage(Z)) : -Article(\_, \_, Z).$
$Node(PersonPage(Y)) : -Person(Y, \_).$
$Node(ArticlePage(X)) : -Article(X, \_).$

Edges in the site definition represent sets of links in the site graph. Each edge has an associated a Horn rule, which specifies the conditions for existence of a link between instances of source and destination nodes. The Horn rules use the special predicate Link. For example, the rule fourth below specifies that there is a link in the site graph between the page PersonPage(Y) and the page ArticlePage(X) if Y is an author of paper X. The third argument of the predicate Link is the link's label in the site graph.[1] We assume that in all of the rules this argument is always a constant. The rules for the links in our example are given below.

$Link(Root(), Publications(), \text{``}publications\text{''}) : -true.$
$Link(Root(), People(), \text{``}people\text{''}) : -true.$
$Link(Publications(), YearPage(Z), \text{``}year\text{''}) : -Article(\_, \_, Z).$
$Link(People(), PersonPage(Y), \text{``}person\text{''}) : -Person(Y, \_).$
$Link(PersonPage(Y), ArticlePage(X), \text{``}article\text{''}) : -$
$\quad Author(Y, X), Article(X, \_, \_).$
$Link(YearPage(Z), ArticlePage(X), \text{``}article\text{''}) : -$
$\quad Article(X, \_, Z).$
$Link(ArticlePage(X), PersonPage(Y), \text{``}author\text{''}) : -$
$\quad Author(Y, X), Person(Y, \_).$

Finally, the data contained in each page is also specified by Horn rules. For every leaf associated with a functional node, we associate a Horn rule defining the contents of the leaf. The first rule below specifies that the name of a person will be contained in the appropriate person page:

$Link(PersonPage(Y), N, \text{``}name\text{''}) : -Person(Y, N).$
$Link(ArticlePage(X), T, \text{``}title\text{''}) : -Article(X, T, \_).$
$Link(ArticlePage(X), PS, \text{``}ps\text{''}) : -Article(X, \_, \_),$
$\quad PsFile(X, PS).$

---

[1] This string denotes the name of the relationship between the nodes in the site graph, and not the anchor that will appear on the link in the actual site. Anchors are omitted for clarity.

Declarative specification of a Web site offers many advantages: rapid modification of the site's structure; creation of multiple versions of the site for different classes of users; and, as we explore next, the ability to reason globally about the site's structure. In principle, restructuring a site or building another version requires modifying the set of rules that define the site, instead of modifying each page and its hard-wired links.

3 Specifying Integrity Constraints

Although declarative specification can simplify the task of creating complex sites, the specification of a richly structured site can be long. For example, the specification of a customer-billing site using the Strudel specification language [Fernandez *et al.*, 1998] is 474 lines. The specification is more concise than the equivalent implementation in a scripting language, but still too large to determine without automated reasoning whether global constraints on the site are satisfied. [Lohse and Spiller, 1998] describes Web sites for on-line stores. They argue that enforcing integrity constraints on such sites is critical to customer satisfaction and describe a set of such constraints. Our goal is to take advantage of a site's declarative definition and develop algorithms for verifying that a given definition only produces sites that satisfy the given set of constraints. For our example, some possible constraints include:

IC1: All article pages are reachable from the root page.

IC2: For every article, there is a link from its article page to its PostScript source.

IC3: If two articles have a common author, there is a path between the corresponding article pages.

IC4: If two articles have been published in the same year, there is a path between the corresponding article pages.

We may also want to specify constraints that limit the length of a path between two nodes, or that force every path to a node to go through some distinguished set of nodes. We define our language for specifying these kinds of integrity constraints and formally define the verification problem.

Integrity constraints express properties we would like the Web site to have. Since the Web site is modeled as a graph, integrity constraints should be able to express the existence of certain paths between pages in the site. We express such paths using *regular-path expressions*. A regular-path expression over the set of constants $\mathcal{C}$ is formed by the following grammar (R, R_1 and R_2 denote regular-path expressions):

$$R := a \mid \text{not } (a) \mid \_ \mid (R_1.R_2) \mid (R_1 \mid R_2) \mid R^+.$$

In the grammar, a denotes a constant in $\mathcal{C}$; not (a) matches any constant in $\mathcal{C}$ different from a. An $\_$ denotes any constant in $\mathcal{C}$; a period denotes concatenation, and $\mid$ denotes alternation. R^+, denotes 1 or more repetitions of R. For example, $a.b.\_.c^+$ denotes the set of paths beginning with ab, then an arbitrary element of $\mathcal{C}$ and then any number of occurrences of c. We use $*$ as a shorthand for $(\_)^+$, meaning an arbitrary path of length 1 or more.

Regular-path expressions are used in *path atoms* of the form $X \to R \to Y$, where R is a regular-path expression, and X and Y are terms. The atom $X \to R \to Y$ is satisfied in a labeled directed graph G by each pair of nodes X, Y for which there is path from X to Y that satisfies the regular path expression R.

In principle, we can express integrity constraints using arbitrary formulas in first-order logic. However, our main goal here is to identify a more restricted language for which it is possible to develop sound and complete verification algorithms and which is expressive enough to model integrity constraints that are of practical interest. We consider integrity constraints that have the form $\phi \Rightarrow \psi$, where ϕ and ψ are conjunctions of path atoms, atoms of the relations of the raw data, and atoms of the relation Node. Variables that appear in both ϕ and ψ are assumed to be universally quantified, while the others are existentially quantified. The following sentences express the integrity constraints in our example.

IC1: $Article(X, \_, \_) \Rightarrow Root() \to * \to ArticlePage(X)$

IC2: $Article(X, \_, \_) \Rightarrow ArticlePage(X) \to \text{``}ps\text{''} \to Y$

IC3: $Article(X, \_, \_), Article(Y, \_, \_),$
     $Author(Z, X), Author(Z, Y) \Rightarrow$
     $ArticlePage(X) \to * \to ArticlePage(Y)$

IC4: $Article(X, \_, Z), Article(Y, \_, Z) \Rightarrow$
     $ArticlePage(X) \to * \to ArticlePage(Y)$

Given a particular site graph, it is straightforward to test whether an integrity constraint holds. However, our goal is to verify at the *intentional level* whether an integrity constraint is guaranteed to hold, i.e., given a site definition $\mathcal{R}$, test whether the integrity constraint will hold for *all* Web sites that can be generated by $\mathcal{R}$, for any possible database state. Formally, our problem is the following.

Definition 1: *Let $E_1, \ldots, E_n$ be the relations in the schema of the raw data, $\mathcal{R}$ be a site definition. Let IC be an integrity constraint. We say that $\mathcal{R}$ satisfies IC if, for any given extension $\mathcal{I}$ of the relations $E_1, \ldots, E_n$, IC is satisfied in the site graph resulting from $\mathcal{R}$ and $\mathcal{I}$.*

In our example, IC1 is satisfied, because every article has a year of publication, and therefore is reachable through the YearPage. Similarly, IC3 is also. satisfied. IC2 is not satisfied, because some articles may not have PostScript sources. Although IC4 is satisfied by the site graph in Fig. 3, it is not necessarily satisfied for *every* site graph.

Next, we describe a sound and complete verification algorithm, and show how the complexity of the verification problem changes with the form of the integrity constraints considered.

4 Verification Algorithm

The crucial step of our verification algorithm is to translate the integrity constraint $\phi \Rightarrow \psi$ into a pair of Datalog programs Q_ϕ and Q_ψ. Datalog [Ullman, 1997] is a database query language where queries are specified by sets of Horn rules, and the meaning of the query is given by the least fixpoint model of the database and the rules. Our translation has the property that the integrity constraint is satisfied if and only if the datalog program Q_ϕ is *contained* in the program Q_ψ. Informally, given two queries Q_1 and Q_2 the query Q_1 *contains* the query Q_2 if Q_1's result is a superset of Q_2's result for *any* database instance. Algorithms for query containment have been studied extensively in the database literature [Ullman, 1997]. These algorithms can be viewed as logical-entailment algorithms for specific classes of logical sentences, which is why they are useful in our context.

Our algorithm has two steps.

1. Given the integrity constraint, $\phi \Rightarrow \psi$, and the site definition, $\mathcal{R}$, create a pair of Datalog queries Q_ϕ and Q_ψ.

2. We use an extended query containment algorithm to test whether Q_ϕ is contained in Q_ψ. If the containment holds, then the integrity constraint is guaranteed to hold. If not, the containment algorithm returns a set of *candidate fixes*.

We describe each step in more detail.

The algorithm in Fig. 4 translates either ϕ or ψ into a Datalog program. This step relies heavily on the possible paths specified in the structure of the site definition in order to generate Q_ϕ and Q_ψ. The subtle part of the translation concerns the path atoms. Given a path atom $X \to R \to Y$, the translation builds in a bottom-up fashion a Datalog program that defines a relation corresponding to each of the subexpressions of R. The translation varies slightly depending on whether X and Y are variables, functional terms, and whether there is another conjunct of the form $Node(X)$ $(Node(Y))$. In the figure, we show only the case when X and Y are unary functional terms.

If our extended query-containment algorithm reports that Q_ϕ is contained in Q_ψ, then then the integrity constraint is guaranteed to hold. Otherwise the containment algorithm returns a set of candidate fixes. The algorithm considers four kinds of fixes:

- Add conditions to ϕ in the integrity constraint,

- Remove conditions from the rules in the site definition $\mathcal{R}$,

- Modify $\mathcal{R}$ by adding back arcs in the site definition, and

- Suggest a set of integrity constraints to enforce on the raw data, which guarantee that the constraints on the site will hold.

The fixes are reported to the site designer, who can then decide how to proceed. Due to space limitations, we only illustrate this phase of the algorithm through the example below. Intuitively, the fixes are generated by searching through the possible modifications to Q_ϕ and Q_ψ such that for the modified queries, the containment holds.

Algorithm IC-translate($\tau, \mathcal{R}, \bar{X}$)
Input: τ is either the LHS or RHS of an IC.
$\mathcal{R}$ is the site definition.
$\bar{X}$ are the universally quantified variables in the IC.
Output: a Datalog program defining the relation $Q_\tau(\bar{X})$.

Let τ be of the form $A_1, \ldots, A_m$.
For $1 \leq i \leq m$, let P_{A_i} be the set of Horn rules returned by
atomToProg($A_i, \mathcal{R}$), with query predicate q_{A_i},
return atomToProg($A_1, \mathcal{R}$) $\cup \ldots \cup$ atomToProg($A_m, \mathcal{R}$)
and the rule $Q_\tau(\bar{X}) : -q_{A_1}(\bar{X}_1), \ldots, q_{A_m}(\bar{X}_m)$
where
if A_i is of the form $p(\bar{Y})$ **then** $\bar{X}_i = \bar{Y}$
if A_i is of the form $f(X) \to R \to g(Y)$, **then** $\bar{X}_i = (X, Y)$.
end IC-translate.

// $A(\bar{X})$ is an atom; $\mathcal{R}$ is a site definition.
Algorithm atomToProg($A, \mathcal{R}$)
if A is of the form $p(\bar{X})$
then return the Datalog program: $q_A(\bar{X}) : -p(\bar{X})$.
if A is of the form $f(X) \to R \to g(Y)$ **then**
return the Datalog program constructed as follows:
for every rule $r \in \mathcal{R}$ of the form
$Link(f_1(X_1), f_2(X_2), "a") : -body$
where the rules for f_1 and f_2 have bodies
$body_1, body_2$ respectively, add the following rule:
$a(f_1, X_1, f_2, X_2) : -body, body_1, body_2$
Define an IDB predicate for R by structural induction on R:
if R is of the form $"a"$, **then**
$Q_a(f_1, X_1, f_2, X_2) : -a(f_1, X_1, f_2, X_2)$.
if R is of the form $R_1.R_2$ **then**
$Q_{R_1.R_2}(f_1, X_1, f_2, X_2) : -$
$Q_{R_1}(f_1, X_1, f_3, X_3), Q_{R_1}(f_3, X_3, f_2, X_2)$
if R is of the form $R_1 \mid R_2$ **then**
$Q_{R_1 \mid R_2}(f_1, X_1, f_2, X_2) : -Q_{R_1}(f_1, X_1, f_2, X_2)$.
$Q_{R_1 \mid R_2}(f_1, X_1, f_2, X_2) : -Q_{R_2}(f_1, X_1, f_2, X_2)$.
if R is of the form R^* **then**
$Q_{R^*}(f_1, X_1, f_2, X_2) : -Q_R(f_1, X_1, f_2, X_2)$.
$Q_{R^*}(f_1, X_1, f_2, X_2) : -$
$Q_R(f_1, X_1, f_3, X_3), Q_{R^*}(f_3, X_3, f_2, X_2)$.
the query predicate of the Datalog program is defined by:
$q_A(X, Y) : -Q_R(f, X, g, Y)$.
end atomToProg

Figure 4: Algorithm for translating the LHS or RHS of an integrity constraint into a Datalog program.

Consider the constraint IC1 in our example, that requires a path from the root page to any article page. The translation step produces the following two Datalog programs, whose query predicates are Q_{lhs} and Q_{rhs}. Since the RHS of the constraint involves a path atom with the regular expression $*$, the Datalog program of Q_{rhs} defines a predicate $Q_*(X_1, f_1, X_2, f_2)$ (the transitive closure of Q_-), which describes the possible paths in the site graph between nodes of the form $f_1(X_1)$ and $f_2(X_2)$. We also use the rules defining Q_* in the other parts of the example.

$Q_{lhs}(X) : -Article(X, \_, \_)$.

$Q_{rhs}(X) : -Q_*("Root", [], "ArticlePage", X)$.
$Q_*(X, Y, Z, W) : -Q_*(X, Y, T, R), Q_-(T, R, Z, W)$.
$Q_*(X, Y, Z, W) : -Q_-(X, Y, Z, W)$.
$Q_-("Root", [], "Publications", []) : -true$.
$Q_-("Root", [], "People", []) : -true$
$Q_-("Publications", [], "YearPage", X) : -Article(\_, \_, X)$.
$Q_-("People", [], "PersonPage", X) : -Person(X, \_)$.
$Q_-("YearPage", X, "ArticlePage", Y) : -Article(Y, \_, X)$.
$Q_-("PersonPage", X, "ArticlePage", Y) : -Person(X, \_),$
$Author(X, Y), Article(Y, \_, \_)$.
$Q_-("ArticlePage", X, "PersonPage", Y) : -Person(Y, \_),$
$Author(Y, X), Article(X, \_, \_)$.

Since the containment check will show that Q_{lhs} is contained in Q_{rhs}, the verification test succeeds. For IC2, the algorithm produces the following two programs, for which the containment fails.

$Q_{lhs}(X) : -Article(X, \_, \_)$.
$Q_{rhs}(X) : -Q_{ps}("ArticlePage", X, \_, Y)$.
$Q_{ps}("ArticlePage", X, \_, Y) : -Article(X, \_, \_), PsFile(X, Y)$.

However, in this case, the algorithm will propose a correction to the integrity constraint, namely adding the conjunct $PsFile(X, Y)$ to the left hand side (meaning that the constraint needs to hold only on articles that have a PostScript source).

Finally, IC4 would result in the two programs:

$Q_{lhs}(X, Y) : -Article(X, \_, Z), Article(Y, \_, Z)$.
$Q_{rhs}(X, Y) : -Q_*("ArticlePage", X, "ArticlePage", Y)$.

In this case, the containment does not hold because paths between article pages in the site only go through the author pages, not through the year pages. Hence, the algorithm will suggest to add a link from ArticlePage to either Root(), the Publications(), or to the corresponding YearPage, and would propose the appropriate query to put on the new link.

5 Complexity of Verification

The algorithm described in the previous section provides a sound and complete verification algorithm in many important cases. This section characterizes these cases and establishes the complexity of the algorithm and of the verification problem. Note that in all of the results, the complexity is measured in the size of the site definition and *not* the size of the underlying raw data.

The following theorem considers the case in which there are no cycles in the nodes in the site definition.

Theorem 1: *Let $\mathcal{R}$ be a site definition and IC be an integrity constraint of the form $\phi \Rightarrow \psi$. Assume that there are no cycles between nodes in the site definition. Then, our verification algorithm is sound and complete and runs in non-deterministic polynomial time. The verification problem under these conditions is NP-complete.*

The following theorem permits cyclic site definitions, but requires that the left-hand side of the integrity constraint does not contain path atoms with Kleene star.

This is a common case, because the left-hand side usually refers to conditions on the raw data, not on the site graph.

Theorem 2: *Let $\mathcal{R}$ be a site definition and IC be an integrity constraint of the form $\phi \Rightarrow \psi$, where ϕ does not contain path atoms with Kleene star. Then, our verification algorithm is sound and complete and it runs in non-deterministic polynomial time. The verification problem under these conditions is NP-complete.*

The proof of the theorems is based on the fact that the size of Q_ϕ and Q_ψ is polynomial in the size of $\mathcal{R}$, and the complexity of the corresponding containment algorithms. Note that in general, containment of arbitrary recursive Datalog is undecidable [Shmueli, 1993], but in the cases considered above Q_ϕ is always non-recursive. Note that if $\mathcal{R}$ contains the interpreted predicates $\leq, <, \neq$, then the complexity of the problems in the theorems is Π_2^p-complete.

6 Conclusions and Related Work

Web-site management systems based on declarative representations offer many opportunities for applying AI research to improve the Web-site construction and maintenance process. This paper considered the first such problem, namely the specification and verification of integrity constraints. We described a language for specifying a wide class of constraints and a sound and complete algorithm for verification. In addition, our algorithm suggests fixes to the site definition when the integrity constraint does not hold.

Our work can be viewed as an extension of verification methods for rule-based knowledge-base systems. Of that work, the most related·to ours is [Levy and Rousset, 1998] which first showed how to use query containment techniques for knowledge-base verification. In contrast to that work, where there was a direct mapping from the knowledge base to a query containment problem, an added challenge in our context is to develop the translation to containment. [Schmolze and Snyder, 1997] considers the verification problem where rules may have side-effects, but those to not appear in our context. [Rousset, 1997] proposes an *extensional* approach to verifying constraints on snapshots of Web sites (i.e., directly on the site graphs).

Finally, we mention two additional opportunities for new AI problems in this context. The first, a generalization of the work we described here, is to specify the structure of Web sites at an even higher level. Whereas in our work we only checked whether certain integrity constraints hold for a given site definition, there may be cases that we would want to specify *only* integrity constraints for the site. The system would then consider the constraints and would propose a definition of the structure for the Web site. The challenge is to choose among multiple structures that satisfy the given constraints.

The second problem concerns automatically restructuring Web sites. The short experience in building Web sites has already shown that it is a highly iterative process. Even after the Web site is up, designers will frequently want to restructure it after understanding the patterns with which users browse the site. Perkowitz and Etzioni [Perkowitz and Etzioni, 1997] have proposed the notion of *adaptive* Web sites that restructure themselves automatically. We argue that declarative representations of Web sites provide a basis on which to build adaptive Web site techniques. In particular, once we have a model of a Web site, we can analyze the user browsing patterns and propose meaningful ways to restructure the model, and hence the site itself.

References

[Arocena and Mendelzon, 1998] Gustavo Arocena and Alberto Mendelzon. WebOQL: Restructuring documents, databases and webs. In *Intl. Conf. on Data Engineering (ICDE)*, Orlando, Florida, 1998.

[Atzeni *et al.*, 1998] P. Atzeni, G. Mecca, and P. Merialdo. Design and maintenance of data-intensive web sites. In *Conf. on Extending Database Technology (EDBT)*, Valencia, Spain, 1998.

[Cluet *et al.*, 1998] S. Cluet, C. Delobel, J. Simeon, and K. Smaga. Your mediators need data conversion. In *SIGMOD Conf. on Management of Data*, Seattle, WA, 1998.

[Fernandez *et al.*, 1998] M. Fernandez, D. Florescu, J. Kang, A. Levy, and D. Suciu. Catching the boat with Strudel: Experiences with a web-site management system. In *SIGMOD Conf. on Management of Data*, Seattle, WA, 1998.

[Levy and Rousset, 1998] A. Levy and M. Rousset. Verification of knowledge bases based on containment checking. *Artificial Intelligence*, 101(1-2):227–250, 1998.

[Lohse and Spiller, 1998] Gerald Lohse and Peter Spiller. Electronic shopping. *Comm. of the ACM*, 41(7), July 1998.

[Paolini and Fraternali, 1998] P. Paolini and P. Fraternali. A conceptual model and a tool environment for developing more scalable, dynamic, and customizable web applications. In *Conf. on Extending Database Technology (EDBT)*, 1998.

[Perkowitz and Etzioni, 1997] Mike Perkowitz and Oren Etzioni. Adaptive web sites: an AI challenge. In *Proc. of the 15th International Joint Conference on Artificial Intelligence*, 1997.

[Rousset, 1997] Marie-Christine Rousset. Verifying the web: a position statement. In *Proceedings of the 4th European Symposium on the Validation and Verification of Knowledge Based Systems (EUROVAV-97)*, 1997.

[Schmolze and Snyder, 1997] J. Schmolze and W. Snyder. Detecting redundant production rules. In *Proc. of the National Conference on Artificial Intelligence*, 1997.

[Shmueli, 1993] Oded Shmueli. Equivalence of datalog queries is undecidable. *Journal of Logic Programming*, 15:231–241, 1993.

[Ullman, 1997] Jeffrey D. Ullman. Information integration using logical views. In *Intl. Conf. on Database Theory (ICDT)*, Delphi, Greece, 1997.

[VVT'98, 1998] *Proceedings of the AAAI Workshop on Verification and Validation of Knowledge-Based Systems*, Madison, Wisconsin, July 1998.

Discovering chronicles with numerical time constraints from alarm logs for monitoring dynamic systems

Christophe Dousson and **Thắng Vũ Dương**
France Telecom CNET, 2 avenue Pierre Marzin
F-22307 Lannion Cedex - France
{christophe.dousson, thang.vuduong}@cnet.francetelecom.fr

Abstract

We address the problem of knowledge acquisition for alarm correlation in a complex dynamic system like a telecommunications network. To reduce the amount of information coming from telecommunications equipment, one needs to preprocess the alarm stream and we propose here a way to acquire some knowledge to do that. The key idea is that only the frequent alarm sets are relevant for reducing the information stream: we aggregate frequent relevant information and suppress frequent noisy information. We propose algorithms for analysing alarm logs: first stage is to discover frequently occurring temporally-constrained alarm sets (called *chronicles*) and second stage is to filter them according to their interdependency level. We also show experimental results with an actual telecommunications ATM network.

Areas: knowledge acquisition, discovery, temporal reasoning, applications, monitoring.

1 Introduction

Telecommunications networks are growing in size and complexity, which means that a bigger and bigger volume of notifications needs to be handled by the management system. Most of this information is produced spontaneously by equipment (e.g., status change and dysfunction detection) and this message flow must be preprocessed to make effective management possible.

Filters based on a per-notification basis fail to perform an adequate information preprocessing required by human operators or by management application software, which are not able to process such amount of events. A preprocessing stage must decrease this information stream by suppressing superfluous notifications and/or by aggregating relevant ones.

Some papers deal with different approaches and propose more or less complex intelligent filtering: one can use some efficient rule-based languages (like in [Möller et al., 1995]), and/or object-based techniques like ECXpert (Event Correlation eXpert) which builds alarm correlation trees according to some handwritten rules [Nygate, 1995]. More specific techniques are also studied to capture time constraints between alarms [Dousson et al., 1993; Jakobson and Weissman, 1995].

In any case, the problem of expertise acquisition remains the same: how to feed the filtering system? Which aggregation rules are relevant? Since time information is apropos for the telecommunications alarm propagation, we also have to be able to deal with numerical time constraints. One way for such a knowledge acquisition is model-based approaches like [Bibas et al., 1995] or [Laborie and Krivine, 1997], which use models to build a simulator for generating relevant faulty scenarios.

Our approach is more akin to data mining techniques: it is based on a frequency analysis of actual alarm logs of the supervised system (the telecommunications network) to discover some frequent chronicles. The frequent chronicle approach is relevant to reach the aim of reducing the alarm stream: if a chronicle corresponds to a dysfunction, we aggregate the set of alarms for the human operator and if not, we only hide the corresponding alarms. At the moment, we do not use any extra knowledge, so the rule qualification (aggregation or suppression) must be performed by an expert.

The original idea stands in [Mannila et al., 1995] but their work focuses only on two types of chronicles (which are called episodes): the parallel ones (alarms are not ordered) and the serial ones (alarms are completely ordered). Some extensions for a more complex chronicle structure are proposed (but not tested) by combining serial and parallel chronicles. Moreover, only a user given upper bound of chronicle duration was allowed to be a time constraint. We extend our frequency analysis with a time representation, which is able to deal with numerical time constraints.

We present in this paper a system (called FACE - Frequency Analyser for Chronicle Extraction) that enables an expert to process some powerful analyses of alarm logs and to identify some recurrent phenomena. In Section 2, we expose some definitions for later use. Section 3 details the first stage of our log analyser, where frequently occurring chronicles in alarm logs are discovered; Section 4 corresponds to the second stage where a graph of dependencies between chronicles is established. Then in Section 5, before concluding, we show some results about an experiment with an actual ATM network.

2 Representation and Definitions

2.1 Time

We based our alarm correlation system on CRS, a Chronicle Recognition System similar to IxTeT[1], described in [Dousson, 1996], because of its real-time capabilities to deal with numerical time constraints.

For complexity reasons, this system relies on time-points as elementary primitives and considers the time as a linearly ordered set of discrete events. A time constraint between two time-points t_1 and t_2 is represented by an interval, $[I^-, I^+]$, which corresponds to the lower and upper bounds on the temporal distance from t_1 to t_2. We also define a time constraint graph $\mathcal{T}$ as a set of time-points with time constraints between them (constraint between i and j is an interval denoted by $K_{\mathcal{T}}(i \rightarrow j)$). We define a partial order (*tighter than*, denoted by $\subseteq$) among constraint graphs as follows:
$$\mathcal{T} \subseteq \mathcal{T}' \equiv_{def} \forall (i,j) \in \mathcal{T}, K_{\mathcal{T}}(i \rightarrow j) \subseteq K_{\mathcal{T}'}(i \rightarrow j)$$
A constraint graph may have many equivalent representations. In particular, there is a unique equivalent constraint graph, which is *minimal* (with respect to $\subseteq$) and its computation (and its consistency check) is ensured by the well-known path consistency *Floyd-Warshall*'s algorithm with the complexity of $O(n^3)$ [Dechter *et al.*, 1991]. We do not allow disjunctive constraints since this problem becomes NP-hard.

In the following sections, we systematically apply this algorithm, and so, we always deal with the minimal time constraint graph.

2.2 Alarm

Alarm: an alarm is a pair (A, t) where A is the *alarm type* and t is the time instant (i.e., occurrence date) of the alarm.

Alarm occurrence: an alarm occurrence is a time-stamped alarm (e.g., $(A, 4)$).

Alarm log: an alarm log $\mathcal{L}$ is a time-ordered list of alarm occurrences. For example, $(A, 1)(B, 3)(A, 4)$ $(C, 4)(A, 7)(B, 8)(C, 9)(B, 10)(B, 12)$.

Due to time-point primitives, an alarm has no duration. If we need some, we can introduce two alarm types corresponding to the beginning and the end of an alarm. For instance, in the telecommunications management, one usually uses a LOS_{active} when the alarm *Loss Of Signal* appears, and a LOS_{clear} when it disappears.

We also suppose that alarms are correctly time-stamped in logs (which is often the case). The message propagation delay in a network must only be taken into account during the on-line recognition stage and this feature is actually performed by CRS.

---

[1]The main differences between them are the heuristics used during the recognition because CRS is specially developed for telecommunications networks, but it does not matter here because we use it as a black box.

2.3 Chronicle Model and Instance

Chronicle model: a chronicle model $\mathcal{C}$ is a pair $(\mathcal{S}, \mathcal{T})$ where $\mathcal{S}$ is a set of alarms and $\mathcal{T}$ is a constraint graph of their instants. We also denote $\mathcal{C}^N$ a chronicle with N alarms (N is called the *size* of $\mathcal{C}^N$).

For example, Figure 1 shows a breakdown link chronicle, where LOS stands for *Loss Of Signal* and LOF stands for *Loss Of Frame*.

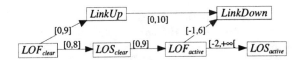

Figure 1: A breakdown link chronicle.

Unconstrained chronicle model: an unconstrained chronicle model (denoted by $(\mathcal{S}, \cdot)$) is a chronicle model with no time constraint and *no order* between alarms. We also use alarm types for the simplified notation of an unconstrained chronicle model as in the following example: ABB stands for $((A, t_1), (B, t_2), (B, t_3), \cdot)$[2].

Chronicle instance: a chronicle instance c of a chronicle model $\mathcal{C}$ is a set of alarm occurrences which is consistent with the time constraints of $\mathcal{C}$. For example, $\{(A, 1)(B, 3)(A, 7)\}$ is an instance of the left chronicle of Figure 2.

Subchronicle instance: an instance c is a subchronicle instance of an instance c' *iff* c is a subset of c' (e.g., $\{(A, 1)(C, 6)\}$ is a subchronicle instance of $\{(A, 1)(B, 3)(C, 6)\}$ but not of $\{(A, 3)(C, 6)\}$).

Subchronicle model: a model $\mathcal{C}$ is a subchronicle model of $\mathcal{C}'$ (denoted by $\mathcal{C} \sqsubseteq \mathcal{C}'$) *iff* from any instance of $\mathcal{C}'$, we can extract a chronicle instance of $\mathcal{C}$ (e.g., in Figure 2 the two right chronicle models are subchronicle models of the left one). This relation defines a partial order on chronicle models.

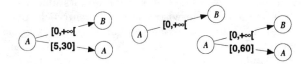

Figure 2: Chronicle and subchronicles models.

Superchronicle: c (resp. $\mathcal{C}$) is a superchronicle instance (resp. model) of c' (resp. $\mathcal{C}'$), which is denoted by $c \sqsupseteq c'$ (resp. $\mathcal{C} \sqsupseteq \mathcal{C}'$), *iff* c' (resp. $\mathcal{C}'$) is a subchronicle instance (resp. model) of c (resp. $\mathcal{C}$).

Theorem 1 *A chronicle model* $\mathcal{C} = (\mathcal{S}, \mathcal{T})$ *is a subchronicle model of* $\mathcal{C}' = (\mathcal{S}', \mathcal{T}')$ *iff* $\mathcal{S} \subseteq \mathcal{S}'$ *and* $\mathcal{T} \sqsupseteq \mathcal{T}'$.

For brevity, hereafter *chronicle* stands for *chronicle model* and *instance* stands for *chronicle instance*.

---

[2]Of course, ABB is equivalent to BAB or BBA.

2.4 Instance Set and Frequency

Given an alarm log $\mathcal{L}$ and a recognition process, we denote $\mathcal{I}_{\mathcal{C}}(\mathcal{L})$ the set of instances of $\mathcal{C}$ recognized in $\mathcal{L}$. Of course, this set depends strongly on the strategy implemented in the used recognition tool.

For our algorithms, we only need that the strategy guarantees the following property:

Property 2 $\forall c \in \mathcal{I}_{\mathcal{C}}(\mathcal{L}),\ c' \in \mathcal{I}_{\mathcal{C}}(\mathcal{L}),\ c \cap c' = \emptyset$.

This property means that an alarm occurrence can't belong to two instances of the *same* chronicle model.

For instance, with $\mathcal{L}$ given in Section 2.2, the instance set of the unconstrained chronicle AB could be:

- $\{\{(A,1)(B,3)\}, \{(A,4)(B,8)\}, \{(A,7)(B,10)\}\}$
- $\{\{(A,1)(B,12)\}, \{(B,3)(A,7)\}, \{(A,4)(B,10)\}\}$
- etc.

Frequency of chronicle: given an alarm log $\mathcal{L}$, the frequency $fq(\mathcal{C}, \mathcal{L})$ of a chronicle $\mathcal{C}$ in $\mathcal{L}$ is the cardinal of $\mathcal{I}_{\mathcal{C}}(\mathcal{L})$. For example, with $\mathcal{L}$ given in Section 2.2, the frequency of the unconstrained chronicle AB is 3.

Frequent chronicle: given a threshold fq_{min}, $\mathcal{C}$ is frequent in $\mathcal{L}$ if $fq(\mathcal{C}, \mathcal{L}) \geq fq_{min}$. We suppose that the threshold fq_{min} is defined by the user.

As our algorithms work with only one alarm log at a time, we now use the simplified notations $\mathcal{I}_{\mathcal{C}}$ and $fq(\mathcal{C})$ instead of respectively $\mathcal{I}_{\mathcal{C}}(\mathcal{L})$ and $fq(\mathcal{C}, \mathcal{L})$.

3 Discovering Frequent Chronicles

This section presents algorithms to discover all the sets of frequent chronicles of size i (denoted by Φ^i).

Lemma 3 *If a chronicle $\mathcal{C}$ is frequent in $\mathcal{L}$, all its subchronicles are also frequent in $\mathcal{L}$.*

A chronicle $\mathcal{C}^i$ won't be frequent if one of its subchronicles is infrequent. Otherwise, if all the subchronicles of $\mathcal{C}^i$ are frequent, $\mathcal{C}^i$ will be a *candidate* for Φ^i (i.e., $\mathcal{C}^i$ *may be* frequent). For example, with the unconstrained chronicle ABC, if one of its subchronicles A, B, C, AB, AC, BC is infrequent, ABC is also infrequent; otherwise, ABC may be frequent and is a candidate. In fact, if we know that AB is frequent, we also know that A and B are frequent. Thus we only need to check the frequency of AB, AC, BC (chronicles of size $i-1$). We denote Φ^i_c the set of candidate chronicles for Φ^i ($\Phi^i_c \supseteq \Phi^i$).

So the intuitive solution to compute Φ^i_c is to generate all the possible chronicles $\mathcal{C}^i$ of size i from one of its frequent subchronicle of size $i-1$ (if AB is infrequent, we do not need to generate AAB, ABB or ABC!) and then to check its frequency.

Based on these analyses, our main algorithm builds iteratively the exhaustive set of all frequent chronicles (see Figure 3). It starts by computing Φ^1, which corresponds

to the set of all the frequent alarms in $\mathcal{L}$. At an iteration i, it first computes the set Φ^i_c from Φ^{i-1} (function *generateCandidate*). It then calculates the frequency of each candidate and keeps only the frequent ones in Φ^i. Its main loop ends at the iteration i where there is no frequent chronicle of size i ($i \leq |\mathcal{L}|$).

$\Phi^1 \leftarrow \{((A, t_A), \cdot)\ |\ A \in \mathcal{L}, fq(A) \geq fq_{min}\}$
while $\Phi^{i-1} \neq \emptyset$ **do**
    $\Phi^i_c \leftarrow generateCandidate(\Phi^{i-1})$
    Calculate $fq(\mathcal{C})$ for all the chronicles $\mathcal{C}$ of Φ^i_c
    $\Phi^i \leftarrow \{\mathcal{C} \in \Phi^i_c\ |\ fq(\mathcal{C}) \geq fq_{min}\}$
    $i \leftarrow i + 1$
endwhile

Figure 3: Main algorithm

The following sections only give algorithms for the chronicle generation stage because we use CRS to calculate the frequency: chronicles are modeled into CRS, which receives $\mathcal{L}$ as alarm input stream and then the number of times of recognition performed by CRS for each chronicle gives us the frequency of the chronicle.

3.1 Candidate Generation

This section presents the algorithms to compute Φ^i_c from Φ^{i-1}.

There are two subtasks to build a candidate $\mathcal{C}^i$: computing a set of i alarms occurring frequently together (i.e., a frequent unconstrained chronicle) and establishing the time constraints between these alarms. Therefore, in order to compute Φ^i_c, we first compute the set Ψ^i_c of the candidate unconstrained chronicles of size i that *may* be frequent. The set Ψ^i of frequent unconstrained chronicles of size i is then computed from Ψ^i_c. Eventually, we establish time constraints between alarms of Ψ^i to generate the final candidates of Φ^i_c (see Figure 4).

---

proc *generateCandidate*(Φ^{i-1})
    $\Psi^i_c \leftarrow generateUnconstrainedCandidates(\Phi^{i-1})$
    Calculate $fq(\mathcal{C})$ for all the chronicles $\mathcal{C}$ of Ψ^i_c
    $\Psi^i \leftarrow \{\mathcal{C}\ |\ \mathcal{C} \in \Psi^i_c$ and $fq(\mathcal{C}) \geq fq_{min}\}$
    $\Phi^i_c \leftarrow generateConstrainedCandidates(\Psi^i, \Phi^{i-1})$
return(Φ^i_c)

Figure 4: Candidate generation

The frequency of unconstrained chronicles is easily computed by using the following lemma:

Lemma 4 *With an unconstrained chronicle $\mathcal{C}$ we have:*
$$fq(\mathcal{C}) = \left[\min_{A_i \in \mathcal{C}} \left(\frac{fq(A_i)}{N(A_i)} \right) \right], \text{ where } N(A_i) \text{ is the number}$$
of alarms (of $\mathcal{C}$) whose type is A_i.[3]

---

[3]Here, $[r]$ stands for the greatest integer less than or equal to a real number r.

For example, with the alarm log given in Section 2.2, the frequency of the unconstrained AAB is:
$$\left[min \left\{ \frac{fq(A)}{N(A)} = \frac{3}{2}, \frac{fq(B)}{N(B)} = \frac{4}{1} \right\} \right] = 1.$$

Unconstrained Candidate Generation

First, Φ^{i-1} is used to construct the set Γ of the unconstrained chronicles corresponding to the chronicles of Φ^{i-1} (obviously, $\Gamma \subseteq \Psi^{i-1}$). We then compute the set Ψ_c^i from Γ. Lemma 3 enables us to suppress any chronicle including an infrequent subchronicle (see Figure 5).

---

proc *generateUnconstrainedCandidates*(Φ^{i-1})
$\quad \Gamma = \{ (\mathcal{S}, \cdot) \mid \exists \mathcal{T}, (\mathcal{S}, \mathcal{T}) \in \Phi^{i-1} \}$
$\quad \Omega = list \ of \ alarm \ types \ used \ in \ chronicles \ of \ \Gamma$
$\quad \Psi_c^i \leftarrow \emptyset$
$\quad$ **for** *each* $(\mathcal{S}, \cdot)$ *of* Γ **do**
$\quad\quad$ **for** *each alarm type A of* Ω **do**
$\quad\quad\quad \mathcal{S}' = \mathcal{S} \cup \{ (A, t_i) \}$
$\quad\quad\quad$ **if** *all subchronicles of* $(\mathcal{S}', \cdot)$ *are in* Γ **then**
$\quad\quad\quad\quad \Psi_c^i \leftarrow \Psi_c^i \cup \{ (\mathcal{S}', \cdot) \}$
$\quad$ **return**(Ψ_c^i)

Figure 5: Unconstrained candidate generation

For example, with the alarm log given in Section 2.2, $fq_{min} = 2$ and $i = 3$, we have $\Gamma = \{ AB, AC, BC, BB \}$ and thus, $\Omega = \{ A, B, C \}$. By adding to AB each element of Ω, one by one, we generate the three candidates AAB, ABB, ABC for Ψ_c^3, but AAB is suppressed because one of its subchronicles, AA, is infrequent. We process similarly for AC, BC, BB and finally obtain $\Psi_c^3 = \{ ABB, ABC, BBC \}$.

With this exhaustive generation, one chronicle may be generated many times from those of Γ before checking its candidature for Ψ_c^i (e.g., BBC is generated twice, from BB and from BC). To avoid this redundancy and also to reduce the number of generated chronicles, our optimized algorithm orders completely the alarm types of Ω (e.g. in lexical order) and only adds to a chronicle $(\mathcal{S}, \cdot)$ of Γ an alarm whose type is greater than or equals to the greatest alarm type of S (see example in Figure 6). It can be proved that this optimization reduces in half the number of chronicles for which one needs checking the candidature for Ψ_c^i.

Establishing Time Constraints

Once Ψ^i is computed, the time constraints between the alarms of its chronicles are established by using Theo-

Γ	exhaustive generation	optimized generation
AB	$AAB, \mathbf{ABB}, \mathbf{ABC}$	$\mathbf{ABB}, \mathbf{ABC}$
AC	$AAC, \mathbf{ABC}, ACC$	ACC
BB	$\mathbf{ABB}, BBB, \mathbf{BBC}$	$BBB, \mathbf{BBC}$
BC	$\mathbf{ABC}, \mathbf{BBC}, BCC$	BCC

Figure 6: Exhaustive vs. optimized generation for Ψ_c^3 (The bold chronicles are the candidates in Ψ_c^3).

rem 1. The idea is that the time constraints between two alarms in the chronicles of Φ_c^i are deduced from the time constraints between these alarms in the chronicles of Φ^{i-1} (see Figure 7).

---

proc *generateConstrainedCandidates*(Ψ^i, Φ^{i-1})
$\quad \Phi_c^i \leftarrow \emptyset$
$\quad$ **for** *each* $(\mathcal{S}, .)$ *of* Ψ^i **do**
$\quad\quad \mathcal{T}$ *is a constraint graph so that* : $\forall (A, B) \in \mathcal{S},$
$\quad\quad K_\mathcal{T}(t_A \rightarrow t_B) = \bigcup_{(\mathcal{S}', \mathcal{T}') \in \Phi^{i-1}} K_{\mathcal{T}'}(t_A \rightarrow t_B)$
$\quad\quad$ **if** $\mathcal{T}$ *is consistent* **then**
$\quad\quad\quad \Phi_c^i \leftarrow \Phi_c^i \cup (\mathcal{S}, \mathcal{T})$
$\quad$ **return**(Φ_c^i)

Figure 7: Computing Φ_c^i from Ψ^i and Φ^{i-1}

For example, suppose that in Φ^2 we have $K(t_A \rightarrow t_B) = [2, 5]$, $K(t_B \rightarrow t_C) = [1, 1]$, $K(t_A \rightarrow t_C) = [1, 5]$, and the unconstrained chronicle $ABC \in \Psi^3$. The constraint graph $\mathcal{T}$ constructed from $\{ A, B, C \}$ with these constraints is consistent (see Figure 8), so $(\{ (A, t_A), (B, t_B), (C, t_C) \}, \mathcal{T})$ is a candidate in Φ_c^3.

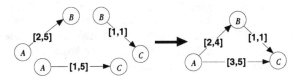

Figure 8: Establishing time constraints.

3.2 Discovering Chronicles of Size 2

The time constraints for the alarms are originally established at this stage and then are used to correlate alarms in the chronicles of size greater than 2. Using the same strategy as described above, our algorithm computes firstly Ψ^2, then establishes the time constraints between alarms of the chronicles of Ψ^2.

Based on the distinct instances of a frequent chronicle AB in the alarm log, we establish the time constraint between A and B. A constraint $[I^-, I^+]$ can be accepted as the time constraint between A and B if *all* the instances of $\mathcal{I}_{AB}$ respect $[I^-, I^+]$. But if *all* the instances of $\mathcal{I}_{AB}$ are used, some noises may be taken into account. In order to avoid noises, one should use an *instance threshold* it_{min} $(0 < it_{min} \leq 1)$, i.e., only $\lceil it_{min} \times fq(AB) \rceil$ instances of $\mathcal{I}_{AB}$ should be considered.

Among these *acceptable* time constraints, one should use some criteria to select the *good* ones for A and B. In order to find only tight constraints between alarms, we select only the constraints so that their *duration* and the *distance* between A and B are as small as possible since alarm effects are rapidly propagated in telecommunications network. More concretely:

- From the acceptable constraints, select $[I^-, I^+]$ so that $(I^+ - I^-)$ is the smallest (criterion of the tightest constraint).

- From the selected constraints, select $[I^-, I^+]$ so that $max\{|I^-|, |I^+|\}$ is the smallest (criterion of the shortest distance).

Searching good constraints (at most two) can be done using the algorithm A^*. These constraints can be considered as the *disjunctive* constraint between A and B. For example, with the instance threshold $it_{min} = 1$ and the alarm log $\mathcal{L} = (A,1)(B,3)(A,4)(B,5)(A,7)(B,8)(A,10)$, it is easy to find that $[-2,-1]$ and $[1,2]$ are two good time constraints between A and B.

In fact, CRS does not accept disjunctive constraints, therefore such ones will be unified to obtain the constraint for CRS. In the above example, the constraint $K(t_A \rightarrow t_B)$ will be $[-2,2]$ instead of $[-2,-1] \cup [1,2]$ for CRS. Another possibility could be to define two chronicles AB in CRS, one with $[-2,-1]$ and another with $[1,2]$.

3.3 Discovering Frequent Chronicles with Chronicles Known by Experts

If we have some expertise, we can use it to improve the discovery process: all known chronicles of size i are added to Φ^i. Moreover, in order to determine whether the chronicle $\mathcal{C}$ is frequent, we use Theorem 1 to check if $\mathcal{C}$ is a subchronicle of one of the known chronicles. If it is, we already know that $\mathcal{C}$ is frequent. Otherwise, we have to calculate the frequency of $\mathcal{C}$. Taking this remark into account, the number of chronicles to calculate the frequency may be much reduced.

3.4 Complexity

At an iteration i, the global complexity of our algorithms is the sum of the following complexities:

Unconstrained chronicle generation (Figure 5): for each unconstrained chronicle $(S', \cdot)$ of size i, checking if one of its subchronicles of size $i-1$ belongs to Γ can be done in time $O(i.\log|\Gamma|)$ with binary search; because $(S', \cdot)$ has i unconstrained subchronicles of size $i-1$, checking the candidature of $(S', \cdot)$ for Ψ_c^i can be done in time $O(i^2.\log|\Gamma|)$. The number of unconstrained chronicles to check the candidature for Ψ_c^i is $|\Gamma|.|\Omega|$. In fact, $|\Gamma|$ can be overvalued to $|\Psi^{i-1}|$, so this complexity can be overvalued to $O(|\Psi^{i-1}|.|\Omega|.i^2.\log|\Psi^{i-1}|)$, which is a little better than one of [Mannila *et al.*, 1995].

Unconstrained chronicles frequency calculation: it requires $O(i)$ time for a unconstrained candidate of size i (Lemma 4); so this complexity is $O(|\Psi_c^i|.i)$.

Establishing time constraints (Figure 7): for each unconstrained chronicle $(S, \cdot)$ of Ψ^i, establishing the time constraint for one of its $\frac{i(i-1)}{2}$ pairs of alarms can be done in time $|\Phi^{i-1}|$; so, constructing a constraint graph corresponding to $(S, \cdot)$ requires $O(i^2.|\Phi^{i-1}|)$ time. In addition to this complexity, checking the consistency of a constraint graph of i nodes takes $O(i^3)$ time. Therefore this complexity is $O(|\Psi^i|.(i^2.|\Phi^{i-1}| + i^3))$.

Constrained chronicle frequency calculation : [Dousson, 1996] had shown that: for a chronicle of size i, the propagation when one of its alarms arrives requires $O(i^2)$ time; so we have a complexity of $O(i^3)$ for the chronicle; as the internal mechanism of CRS generates on average i instances for one recognized (and i^2 in the worst case), the average complexity of the frequency calculation is $O(i^4)$ (and $O(i^5)$ in the worst case). So this complexity is $O(|\Phi_c^i|.i^4)$ (and $O(|\Phi_c^i|.i^5)$ in the worst case).

4 Dependency Filtering

The number of frequent chronicles is always great. Thus, once these chronicles are discovered, one should filter them to find the relevant ones. What should be the criteria of relevance? Recall that our goal is to discover expertise for monitoring, so the discovered chronicles have to be able to identify phenomena produced during the functioning of the system. The question here is: does a chronicle signify itself a phenomenon or is it always included in a more complex one? For instance, is AB a phenomenon or does AB *always* come with other alarms (and so, the relevant chronicles may be ABC or ABB)?

We base the dependency relationship between a chronicle and one of its subchronicles on the alarms of the subchronicle that are not included in any instance of the superchronicle.

We define the *independent* instance set between two chronicles $\mathcal{C}$ and $\mathcal{C}'$ as follows:

$$\mathcal{I}_{\mathcal{C} \sqsubseteq \mathcal{C}'}^{\star} = \begin{cases} \{c \in \mathcal{I}_{\mathcal{C}} \mid (c \cap \bigcup_{c_i \in \mathcal{I}_{C_i}, \mathcal{C} \sqsubseteq C_i \sqsubseteq \mathcal{C}'} c_i) = \emptyset\} & \text{if } \mathcal{C} \neq \mathcal{C}' \\ \mathcal{I}_{\mathcal{C}} & \text{if } \mathcal{C} = \mathcal{C}' \end{cases}$$

And so, the *independent* frequency $fq^{\star}(\mathcal{C} \sqsubseteq \mathcal{C}')$ is defined as the number of elements of $\mathcal{I}_{\mathcal{C} \sqsubseteq \mathcal{C}'}^{\star}$.

In term of dependency level, one can say that the chronicle $\mathcal{C}'$ *depends completely* on all its subchronicles, i.e., the phenomenon corresponding to $\mathcal{C}'$ included the phenomena corresponding to all its subchronicles. If there is $\mathcal{C}$ so that $fq^{\star}(\mathcal{C} \sqsubseteq \mathcal{C}')$ is high, one can say that the influence of $\mathcal{C}$ is not only showed in $\mathcal{C}'$, but also outside $\mathcal{C}'$. Therefore, if $\mathcal{C}'$ is a relevant chronicle, $\mathcal{C}$ is also relevant. On the other hand, if $fq^{\star}(\mathcal{C} \sqsubseteq \mathcal{C}')$ is low, one can say that outside $\mathcal{C}'$, the influence of $\mathcal{C}$ is not remarkable. In other words, $\mathcal{C}$ should only be considered as an excerpt of $\mathcal{C}'$.

Theorem 5 $fq^{\star}(\mathcal{C} \sqsubseteq \mathcal{C}') \leq fq(\mathcal{C}) - \sum_{\mathcal{C} \sqsubset \mathcal{C}_i \sqsubseteq \mathcal{C}'} fq^{\star}(\mathcal{C}_i \sqsubseteq \mathcal{C}')$

Proof: This is due to the fact that for any instance c_i of $\mathcal{C}_i$ ($\mathcal{C}_i$ is superchronicle of $\mathcal{C}$), there is at least one *dependent* instance c of $\mathcal{C}$ (i.e., $c \subset c_i$). $\square$

Corollary 6 *The following recursive formula gives an upper bound of* $fq^{\star}(\mathcal{C} \sqsubseteq \mathcal{C}')$:

$$\widetilde{fq}(\mathcal{C} \sqsubseteq \mathcal{C}') = \begin{cases} fq(\mathcal{C}) & \text{if } \mathcal{C} = \mathcal{C}' \\ fq(\mathcal{C}) - \sum_{\mathcal{C} \sqsubset \mathcal{C}_i \sqsubseteq \mathcal{C}'} \widetilde{fq}(\mathcal{C}_i \sqsubseteq \mathcal{C}') & \text{if } \mathcal{C} \sqsubset \mathcal{C}' \end{cases}$$

Proof: Recursively: suppose that the formula is true for any superchronicle $\mathcal{C}'$, Theorem 5 gives it for $\mathcal{C}$. ☐

Let us suppose that the recognition process is contructed so that the instances of chronicles are recognized as soon as possible (*first-coming* instances). Namely, the process guarantees the following property (CRS does):

Property 7 *For any chronicle $\mathcal{C}$, its instance set $\mathcal{I}_\mathcal{C}$ is totally ordered by the relation $\prec$ (*before*) between two instances of $\mathcal{C}$, where $\prec$ is defined as follows:*

$$c = \{(A_i, t_i)\}, c' = \{(A_i, t'_i)\}, c \prec c' \text{ iff } \forall i, t_i < t'_i.$$

For example, with the alarm log given in Section 2.2, the instance set $\mathcal{I}_{AB}$ is the following: $\{\{(A,1)(B,3)\}, \{(A,4)(B,8)\}, \{(A,7)(B,10)\}\}$.

With our algorithms, we can prove the following theorem:

Theorem 8 *For any frequent chronicle $\mathcal{C}'$ with distinct alarm types and $\mathcal{C}$ one of its subchronicles, if $\mathcal{I}_\mathcal{C}$ has Property 7, we have: $\widetilde{fq}(\mathcal{C} \sqsubseteq \mathcal{C}') = fq^\star(\mathcal{C} \sqsubseteq \mathcal{C}')$.*

Thanks to Theorem 8, we can easily calculate the independent frequencies for chronicles with distinct alarm types. For the other kind of chronicles[4], we can calculate their independent frequencies by *exhaustive* algorithm (i.e., using the definition) and/or calculate the upper bounds for estimating purposes.

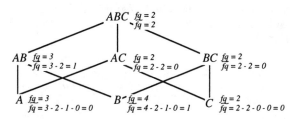

Figure 9: Calculation of $\widetilde{fq}(\mathcal{C} \sqsubseteq ABC)$ (with $fq_{min} = 2$).

Output of the Filtering Process

Based on the above analyses, the output of the filtering process is a graph G representing the dependency relationship between the frequent chronicles. There will be a link from $\mathcal{C}'$ to $\mathcal{C}$ if $\mathcal{C} \sqsubseteq \mathcal{C}'$ and $fq^\star(\mathcal{C} \sqsubseteq \mathcal{C}') = 0$. [5]

A chronicle $\mathcal{C}$ is considered as *independent* if its independent frequencies against *all* its independent superchronicles greater than zero, i.e., $\mathcal{C}$ has no links with its independent superchronicles in G. All the chronicles that have no superchronicle are independent.

Figure 10 shows the dependency graph, which is computed from the alarm log $\mathcal{L}$ given in Section 2.2 with $fq_{min} = 2$. We exhibit here four independent chronicles ABB, AB, ABC and BBC (to simplify the figure, the corresponding constraint graphs are not shown).

---

[4]Fortunately, first experimental results show that this kind of chronicles is relatively rare.

[5]One can define a dependency threshold for filtering.

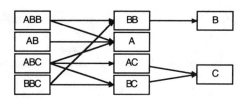

Figure 10: Dependency graph of the frequent chronicles.

5 Experiment and Results

The first experiment of our approach was with the data from the French packet switching telecommunications network. The input data was a log of 2900 alarms of 36 different types and corresponded to a duration of 20 hours. One run of our algorithms (i.e., for one given value of fq_{min}) took about 2 minutes, and many runs exhibited a dozen of independent relevant chronicles (due to the size of the input, frequent phenomena are relatively rare). Since the network is well known, this was more a validation experiment than an actual knowledge acquisition. In spite of that, one of the discovered chronicles was unknown but relevant to experts. Moreover, it was a non-trivial chronicle in the sense that it was out of usual monitoring knowledge: this chronicle showed the influence of a non-telecom unit – a secondary power supply failure – with an alarm indicating the too high temperature on an equipment (the reason is that the air conditionning system was out of order since it was plugged on the secondary power supply).

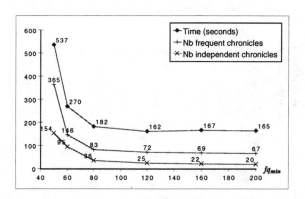

Figure 11: Experiment with ATM network data.

The second application is related to the first experimental national ATM (Asynchronous Transfer Mode) network. As this network is more recent, the challenge for our algorithms is to help efficiently experts with monitoring knowledge acquisition. The amount of data is more significant since we have a one month log with about forty thousand alarms dispatched through about 3800 different types. For this application, an alarm type consists of the actual alarm type and its localisation: for instance, if telecommunications equipment are able to emit a *LOS* (Loss of Signal), we define a *LOS_Lyon* for the Lyon switch, a *LOS_Paris* for the Paris switch and so on [6]. Figure 11 shows some experimental results. Moreover, we can notice that we have very few chronicles containing twice the same alarm type or more; hence, Theorem 8 (Section 4) gives us the exact independent frequency.

At this stage, we already know that some of them are relevant and some others must be filtered during on-line monitoring. Figure 1 (at the beginning of the paper) shows such a discovered chronicle: the first group (LOF_{clear}, LOS_{clear}, $LinkUp$) corresponds to the connection re-establishment and the second group (LOF_{active}, LOS_{active}, $LinkDown$) indicates a connection breakdown; this chronicle signifies an unstable connection link, which fails in the 10 seconds following the re-establishment; this is a particular chronicle of the network and it is unpredictable according to the rules of recommendations of telecommunications management since it is a recurrent malfunctionning phenomenon. However, to improve the results, we need more investigations with telecommunications monitoring experts.

6 Conclusion

We present a chronicle discovery process that is very helpful for experts to discover monitoring knowledge from alarm logs. It is based on the key idea that a chronicle is frequent only if its subchronicles are frequent (like the work of [Mannila *et al.*, 1995] but the chronicle formalism is more expressive than their episode-rule structure). Our process is also able to take into account and to establish numerical time constraints between alarms since this information could be discrepant for the fault detection.

The use of the same chronicle recognition system and the same chronicle model guarantees that semantics of recognition remains the same during the off-line (knowledge acquisition) and on-line processing (monitoring).

We also propose a method for sorting the discovered chronicles and exhibiting the most relevant ones. The main advantage is to focus the attention of an expert on few (about one third) discovered chronicles to understand and to be categorized for the monitoring process.

The first experiments show that our algorithms are able to deal with an amount of data compatible with the requirement of a discovery process and the preliminary results are quite promising since many discovered chronicles could be explained by the corresponding ITU[7] recommendations. We will interact with equipment experts to validate more chronicles but we already know that this is a good way to acquire knowledge for monitoring a telecommunications network (like ATM). We noticed that the approach also exhibits some non-trivial scenarios, which are very rarely modelled by experts.

Future work will focus on addition of variables in discovered chronicles and on introduction of some knowledge in the telecommunications domain to ease the chronicle generation stage. Experiments with the ATM network will also be pursued and another test on a SDH (Synchronous Digital Hierarchy) network is planned.

7 Acknowledgements

Thang Vu Duong is currently a Ph.D. student at the CNET (R&D centre of France Telecom), and is grateful to his advisor, Malik Ghallab (LAAS/CNRS, Toulouse), for helpful suggestions.

The authors would like to thank Thierry Vidal (ENIT, Tarbes), the GASPAR project team for useful discussions and especially, Philippe Dague (LIPN/CNRS, Paris) for valuable comments on this paper.

References

[Bibas *et al.*, 1995] S. Bibas, M.O. Cordier, P. Dague, F. Lévy, and L. Rozé. Scenario generation for telecommunication network supervision. *Workshop on AI in Distributed Information Networks*, August 1995. Montréal, Québec, Canada.

[Dechter *et al.*, 1991] R. Dechter, I. Meiri, and J. Pearl. Temporal constraint networks. *Artificial Intelligence, Special Volume on Knowledge Representation*, 49(1-3):61–95, 1991. Elsevier Science B.V.

[Dousson *et al.*, 1993] C. Dousson, P. Gaborit, and M. Ghallab. Situation recognition: Representation and algorithms. *Proc. of the 13th IJCAI*, pages 166–172, August 1993. Chambéry, France.

[Dousson, 1996] C. Dousson. Alarm driven supervision for telecommunication networks : II- On-line chronicle recognition. In *Annals of Telecommunications*, 9/10:51, pages 501–508. CNET, France Telecom, October 1996.

[Jakobson and Weissman, 1995] G. Jakobson and M. Weissman. Real-time telecommunication network management: extending event correlation with temporal constraints. *Proc. 4th ISNIM*, pages 290–301, May 1995.

[Laborie and Krivine, 1997] P. Laborie and J.P. Krivine. Automatic generation of chronicles and its application to alarm processing in power distribution systems. *8th international workshop of diagnosis (DX'97)*, September 1997. Mont Saint-Michel, France.

[Mannila *et al.*, 1995] H. Mannila, H. Toivonen, and A. I. Verkamo. Discovering frequent episodes in sequences. *Proc. 1st KDD*, pages 210–215, August 1995. Montréal, Québec, Canada.

[Möller *et al.*, 1995] M. Möller, S. Tretter, and B. Fink. Intelligent filtering in network-management systems. *Proc. 4th ISNIM*, pages 304–315, May 1995.

[Nygate, 1995] Y.A. Nygate. Event correlation using rule and object based techniques. *Proc. 4th ISNIM*, pages 279–289, May 1995.

---

[6]This is a limitation of our algorithms: we only discover chronicles that correspond to the phenomena repeating on the same equipment. In future work, we will introduce variables in chronicles to capture similar phenomena occuring on different places in the network.

[7]International Telecommunication Union

Integrating Problem-Solving Methods into Cyc

James Stuart Aitken
Artificial Intelligence Applications Institute
Division of Informatics
University of Edinburgh
Edinburgh EH1 1HN, Scotland
Email: stuart@aiai.ed.ac.uk

Dimitrios Sklavakis
School of Artificial Intelligence
Division of Informatics
University of Edinburgh
Edinburgh EH1 1HN, Scotland
Email: dimitris@dai.ed.ac.uk

Abstract

This paper argues that the reuse of domain knowledge must be complemented by the reuse of problem-solving methods. Problem-solving methods (PSMs) provide a means to structure search, and can provide tractable solutions to reasoning with a very large knowledge base. We show that PSMs can be used in a way which complements large-scale representation techniques, and optimisations such as those for taxonomic reasoning found in Cyc. Our approach illustrates the advantages of task-oriented knowledge modelling and we demonstrate that the resulting ontologies have both task-dependent and task-independent elements. Further, we show how the task ontology can be organised into conceptual levels to reflect knowledge typing principles.

1 Introduction

Developing reusable ontologies which specify the structure and content of domain knowledge has become a central problem in the construction of large and scalable knowledge based systems. For example, a key step in KBS construction using the Cyc system [Lenat and Guha, 1990] is to extend the existing upper-level ontology by creating new classes and representations. Methodologies for ontology development have been proposed [Lenat and Guha, 1990; Uschold and Gruninger, 1996; Blázquez *et al.*, 1998]. However, many unsolved problems remain. Other important issues concern the relationship between the domain representation and its intended use [Wielinga *et al.*, 1994; van Heijst *et al.*, 1997]. We shall concentrate on the representational and performance issues focusing initially on the reasoning processes, and reflect on the implications for domain representation in the light of these findings.

Versions of Cyc are currently being used as an integration platform by the DARPA-funded High Performance Knowledge Bases (HPKB) program. Key issues on the HPKB program are the **scalability**, **robustness**, and **reusability** of knowledge-based system solutions. Cyc is unique in that it has potential solutions to each of these problems.

Cyc uses a resolution-based inference procedure that has a number of optimisations that improve the scalability of the architecture. For example, a specialised taxonomic reasoning module replaces the application of the logical rule for transitivity of class membership. Where specialised modules are not implemented, Cyc makes use of weak search methods to perform inference. Cyc lacks any principles for structuring inference at a conceptual level. Problem-solving methods provide precisely this structure, hence the importance of integrating structuring principles into a scalable KBS architecture.

Robustness and reusability are related properties of the knowledge representation scheme and the inference rules: Predicates such as *bordersOn* and *between*, defined in the upper-level ontology, can be reused in many different contexts. The combination of predicate properties (such as symmetry) and existing inference rules means that the use of these predicates is robust. Reconciling units of measure is a similar problem. In this case, Cyc has sufficient knowledge to prove *(greaterThan (Meter 1) (Centimeter 2))* using its existing definitions and rules about units of measure. Reusability is also an important motivation for defining a upper-level ontology as the basis of knowledge representation. The upper-level ontology can be shared among more specialised reasoning contexts or applications. Extensions to the upper-level can themselves be shared, and can be regarded as ontologies in their own right.

We describe the implementation of a PSM for fault diagnosis in Cyc. The diagnostic method was applied to two different domains to investigate whether the potential for method reuse was actually achievable. As implementation was preceded by a significant amount of domain and task analysis, this work allows us to review the value of the methodological approach and to investigate issues such as the task-dependence of the ontologies constructed. This paper begins with an introduction to the component technologies used—CommonKADS and Cyc—and then describes the implementation of the PSM and the associated knowledge modelling.

2 Component Technologies

2.1 PSMs: The CommonKADS View

In CommonKADS, problem-solving methods are the product of expertise analysis - one of several analysis steps which are specified by the methodology. PSMs are also used in Protege [Puerta *et al.*, 1992], and in Expect [Gil and Melz, 1996] (although in different forms). PSMs define distinct methods for performing a task, for example, diagnosis can be modelled as involving a heuristic association between observations and solutions, or as a process of decomposing a system and testing its subcomponents for correct operation. In addition to specifying an inference procedure, PSMs require that domain knowledge be modelled in particular ways, i.e. a method ontology is associated with a PSM.

CommonKADS is a methodology for KBS development which addresses not only the desired problem-solving performance of the end system, but the context in which it will operate. A number of models are constructed in the analysis phase: an *organisational model* represents the processes, structure, and resources of the organisation which is to use the KBS, a *task model* describes the activities of the process of interest, an *agent model* represents the agents involved in the process and their capabilities, a *communication model* describes agent (human and machine) communication, an *expertise model* defines domain and problem-solving knowledge, and, finally, a *design model* describes the structure and function of the system that will implement the knowledge-based task. More details of the various models, and appropriate modelling techniques can be found in [Kingston *et al.*, 1997].

CommonKADS is relatively neutral on questions of implementation. However, expertise modelling does make a number of assumptions about knowledge representation constructs and their interaction. The expertise model has three layers: the domain layer represents knowledge about the domain, the inference layer defines the procedures applied during problem solving, and the task layer specifies the ordering of inference steps. As the expertise model is the only CommonKADS model that captures expert problem-solving behaviour, we shall limit our attention to representing this model in Cyc.

2.2 Cyc

Cyc is a very large, multi-contextual knowledge-based system which is currently being used commercially by **Cycorp**. Cyc is also used for research purposes, and, in the HPKB program, Cyc is being used as a platform for technology integration.

The arguments for Cyc proposed in Lenat and Guha [1990] remain the cornerstones of the Cyc project; namely, the need to overcome the brittleness of traditional expert systems, and the means of achieving this through the development of a shared ontology representing 'consensus reality'. The upper-level ontology, which constitutes the basis of knowledge representation in Cyc, has been made publicly available. However, this represents only a fraction of the knowledge which has been entered into Cyc.

The upper-level ontology is represented in a variant of first-order logic known as *CycL*. The ontology includes: classes used for constructing representations, for example *SetOrCollection* and *Predicate*; classes for high-level concepts such as *Event* and *Agent*; and more specific classes representing commonly occurring objects and events such as *Book* and *BirthEvent*.

Assertions in CycL are always associated with a *microtheory* context. The *BaseKB* contains the upper-level ontology and new contexts can be defined which specialise this theory. Multiple inheritance of microtheory contexts is allowed. Alternative specialisations of a microtheory need not be consistent with each other: a microtheory can contain ontology extensions and assertions which are inconsistent with those defined in a different theory - providing neither context is defined as subsuming the other. The microtheory mechanism plays an important role in structuring inference.

Cyc performs inferencing in response to a query by the user (by backward chaining) or in response to an assertion (by forward chaining with rules which are explicitly specified to be forward rules). Queries are made in a specific microtheory which forms the local search context. Typically, a microtheory will be a specialisation of one or more theories and in this case search will progress out to wider contexts should a solution not be found locally. Queries are treated in a purely logical manner: the order of conjuncts is not considered to be significant and may be changed by optimisations operating at the clause-form level. The preconditions of rules are also treated in this way - prohibiting the user from influencing the search process in a predictable way. The dependencies between derived facts, rules and assertions are recorded and maintained by a truth maintenance mechanism.

Cyc's purely declarative treatment of rules differs from other approaches to logic-based knowledge representation, such as Prolog, where the ordering of clauses, and of literals within clauses, is used to determine the order of search.

The Cyc system includes a number of tools for viewing and browsing the ontology. In common with other browsers, including that for Loom [MacGregor, 1994], terms in the ontology are hyperlinked in a web-based interface. This allows the user to explore the concepts which define, or are subsidiary to, the concepts currently being displayed.

The Cyc system also gives the KBS developer access to a LISP-like environment where new procedures can be defined in the *SubL* language. The Cyc knowledge base and inference engine can be accessed via the SubL functions *ask* and *assert*. Due to the treatment of rules described above, imposing structure on the search process necessarily requires SubL coding.

3 Systematic Diagnosis in Cyc

This section describes the expertise modelling process and presents its products. The implementation of these models in Cyc is then outlined. We begin with a brief introduction to the domain and the diagnostic task.

The task of diagnosis was selected because a set of well understood methods for solving such tasks already exists [Wielinga *et al.*, 1992]. An important part of expertise modelling is the selection between alternative methods - with their accompanying behaviours and assumptions. The choice of a specific diagnostic method was not made prior to domain analysis. It is readily apparent that we have chosen a problem type that falls within the scope of the methodology we intend to apply. However, it is not at all obvious that diagnosis—which is inherently an incremental procedure requiring information gathering—can be adequately implemented by backward chaining driven by a query-based interaction (i.e. by the default environment provided by Cyc). We shall return to this point below.

Fault finding in personal computers (PCs) was chosen as the primary task domain. This task can be modelled accurately, i.e. the actual behaviour of human experts is known and has been documented [Kozierok, 1998], yet the amount of electronics knowledge required is low as fault finding never progresses to a level where sophisticated test equipment is required. The second domain chosen was fault finding in an automobile ignition system. This task ought to be soluble by the method developed for PC diagnosis, despite differences in the characteristics of the domain and in the method ontology.

3.1 Modelling Expertise

The selection of a problem-solving method is one of the central modelling decisions in CommonKADS. This will typically have an impact on domain representation. Following this approach, the PC-diagnosis problem was addressed by investigating candidate PSMs. As PSMs may be refined in several different ways, alternative instantiations were also investigated. This is a notable contrast with a domain-oriented approach which would focus on developing an ontology of the domain being reasoned about, PC systems and their components in this case.

The systematic diagnosis PSM was found to match the expert reasoning process most closely. The generic model had to be adapted to reflect expert reasoning more faithfully. The central steps in systematic diagnosis are the decomposition of the system being diagnosed into subsystems, and the testing of the subsystems for correct operation by making tests and comparing the observed with the predicted outcomes. The subsystem currently being tested is said to play the role of the current *hypothesis*. Testing may rule out this hypothesis, in which case another subsystem becomes the hypothesis. Testing may yield an inconclusive result, in which case more tests are required, or testing may indicate a fault, in which case the diagnosis is concluded—if the current hypothesis cannot be further decomposed (i.e. it is a component), or diagnosis continues at a lower level of

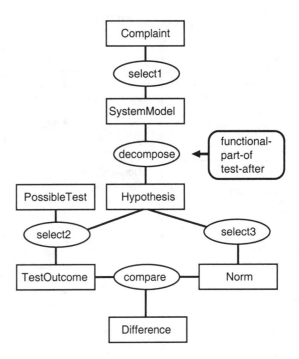

Figure 1: PSM for systematic diagnosis

system decomposition—if the current hypothesis can be decomposed (i.e. it is a system). The system model may describe how the system is decomposed into (physical) parts, or may describe the functional relationships between systems.

It was discovered that the the *part-of* model, which lies at the heart of systematic diagnosis, had to be instantiated to *functional-part-of* in the PC diagnosis domain. That is, problem solving requires a functional view of the system, rather than a component/subcomponent view. The *functional-part-of* predicate is clearly a representational construct at the domain level, and is one of several part-of views that might be taken of a system. In fact, there was no need to represent the *physical-part-of* relation in order to solve this problem.

Another important refinement of the generic model was the addition of theories of test ordering. Where there are several decompositions of a system, the model permits any subsystem to play the role of hypothesis. However, in PC diagnosis it is important to establish first, for example, that the power system is operational, then that the video system is operational. Once the video system is known to work we can be sure that the results of BIOS system tests are being displayed correctly. Similar ordering constraints were found for all subsystems, and at all levels of decomposition. Consequently, there is a need to impose an order on hypothesis selection (or, equivalently, system decomposition) and we chose to represent this knowledge in a heuristic fashion via a *testAfter* predicate. Figure 1 shows the specialised PSM in a diagrammatic form.

Determining the overall view of the desired problem-solving behaviour aided knowledge acquisition, much of

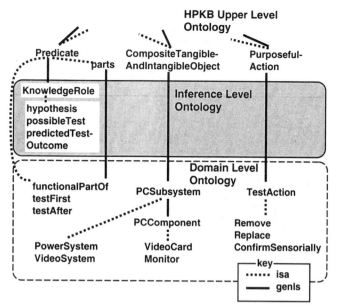

Figure 2: Upper-Level ontology extensions - distinguished by level

which concerned the extraction and structuring of information from an on-line source [Kozierok, 1998]. Our experience confirmed the claimed advantages of the modelling approach. In addition to specifying an inference-level procedure, knowledge acquisition also requires the content and scope of domain knowledge to be determined. The task of representing domain knowledge in Cyc followed the standard procedure of extending the ontology by defining new collections and predicates, and linking these to existing constants. We now describe the Cyc implementation in more detail.

3.2 Cyc Implementation

Diagnosis requires interactive data gathering, and the subsequent evaluation of test results and updating of the current hypothesis. Such a procedure cannot be implemented by logical inference alone, and so it is clearly necessary to use Cyc's LISP-like language, SubL, to implement a control regime. In CommonKADS, control knowledge is divided between the inference layer, where knowledge roles and inference steps are defined, and the task layer, where the order of application of inference steps is specified. Our aim was to represent the levels of the expertise model in Cyc in as faithful a manner as possible. We begin by considering domain knowledge.

Domain knowledge was represented by extending existing collections where possible. Figure 2 shows a small illustrative set of the extensions made. The collection PCSubsystem was added as a subcollection of CompositeTangibleAndIntangibleThing, and PCComponent was defined as a specialisation of it. Both types of object have a tangible component, and may carry information hence have an intangible component also. TestAction was defined as a new collection of PurposefulAction, and the instances of Remove, Replace, and ConfirmSensorially (i.e. confirm by observation) were added [Sklavakis, 1998]. functionalPartOf was introduced to represent the functional decomposition of a system, and stated to generalise to parts, being the most general existing *part-of* predicate in the upper ontology[1]. Other specialisations of parts include physicalDecompositions and timeSlices.

The predicates testFirst and testAfter were introduced as predicates to represent the test ordering theory. A test is defined by three components: a TestAction, a PCSubsystem and a PossibleObservable. The collections PossibleObservable, PossibleObservableValue, and ResultType were defined as subcollections of AttributeValue. The representation of testing knowledge can be made more robust by grounding it extensively in the upper ontology. In contrast, part-of facts are not likely to be derivable by appeal to background knowledge.

At the inference level, knowledge roles are represented by predicates, and inference steps are rules which have knowledge roles as preconditions and conclusions. Figure 2 shows the introduction of the KnowledgeRole collection, a specialisation of the Predicate class of the upper ontology. Instances of KnowledgeRole predicates take domain-level formulae or collections as arguments. Examples include; the unary predicate hypothesis - applicable to PCSubsystem - denotes the current hypothesis, possibleTest holds of applicable tests, and the relation predictedTestOutcome holds of a test, PossibleObservableValue and a ResultType. More complex mappings to the inference level, and the definition of additional collections and terms, are also possible within this approach. The CycL language is sufficiently expressive to allow complex mappings of the type described in [Wielinga *et al.*, 1994] where the inference-level ontology (in our terminology) might define relations holding of domain-level ontology, e.g. we could express the fact that PhysicalPartOf is a relation: *relation(PhysicalPartOf)*.

In a similar way, the currently invoked inference step (e.g. *decompose, select*) is also explicitly asserted in the KB by predicates which belong to the inference level.

Inference steps are invoked by querying or asserting knowledge roles. For example, the role *hypothesis* holds of the subsystem currently playing the role of the hypothesised fault. The rules for selecting the test ordering theory depend on the current hypothesis, for example:

```
F: (implies (and (hypothesis PCSystem)
                 (plausibleInference Decompose))
        (and (testFirst PowerSystem)
             (testAfter PowerSystem VideoSystem))).
```

This is a forward rule which fires when *hypothesis* and *plausibleInference* are asserted. The current hypothesis assertion must be deleted and replaced as diagnosis proceeds. These operations are implemented in SubL by

---

[1]Note that terms defined in the ontology, or its extension, are written in sans-serif, following the Cyc convention, names of collections begin with a capital letter and predicates begin with a lower case letter.

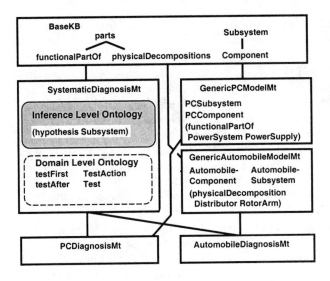

Figure 3: Microtheory structure

functional-interface functions, within the larger structure of the systematic diagnosis task function. The user could make this series of deductions themselves, and in the implemented system, the user is able to inspect the state of the reasoning process as it progresses. As an example, the following SubL code is called at the start of diagnosis and simply asserts that the entire system is the hypothesis, and then calls another SubL function, sd-select2-3, which performs system decomposition.

```
(define sd-select1 (system)
(fi-assert (#$hypothesis system) *defaultMt*)
(sd-select2-3))
```

We have achieved an explicit representation of knowledge roles and of inference steps in Cyc that reflects the knowledge typing principles advocated in [van Heijst *et al.*, 1997]. Control over the search process is achieved by making a series of simple queries, structured to implement the pattern of inference of the PSM. We found no need to extend the functionality of Cyc, or the expressivity of its representation language(s) in order to implement the PSM. The central problem was to combine the available features into structured architecture, in order to to take advantage of the model-based approach to problem solving.

We tested the reusability of the domain and inference level definitions, and of the SubL code, by considering diagnosis in the domain of automobile ignition systems. This experience is discussed in the wider context of the reusability, scalability, and robustness of our approach.

4 Representation and Reasoning

4.1 Domain Ontologies

The view of domain ontology construction which results from the prior selection and adaption of an explicit problem solving method is more focussed on concepts relevant to problem solving than a task-neutral view would be. The resulting domain ontology is not task-specific in its

formalisation, e.g. the definition of the *functional-part-of* relation has no intrinsic task-related properties. But, the coverage of the resulting ontology may only be partial – we did not need to elicit *physical-part-of* knowledge.

Had we taken a view that focussed on the domain alone, we would have had no explicit guidance as to which concepts were or were not relevant to the ontology definition effort. We have gained experience of constructing ontologies where the primary aim was to represent the domain, with ontology definition only informally guided by considering the task. Under these conditions it is difficult to determine the relevance of a potential domain concept, and the distinction between concepts that are intrinsic to the representation of the domain, and those that are related to the task to be performed was difficult to make.

Reusability of domain knowledge is an important issue, and our approach has been to use the microtheory mechanism of Cyc to encapsulate the generic components of the extended ontology. The resulting mircotheory structure, shown in Figure 3, places the generic system models for PCs and automobile systems in distinct microtheories, that are extensions of the BaseKB, and are included in the specific diagnosis microtheories. Strictly speaking, these microtheories are not extensions of the ontology as they make no new specifications. Instead, the BaseKB is extended by adding the definitions of the functionalPartOf predicate and the collections Subsystem and Component as these concepts are sufficiently general to be reusable across domains. The method-specific ontology, comprising domain and inference level components, is also a specialisation of the BaseKB, and this theory is shared by both PC and Automobile diagnosis theories. The microtheory structure shows that the generic system models can be used in any context which includes the (now extended) BaseKB, and that these theories can be thought of as parameters of the diagnosis microtheories.

4.2 Inference Knowledge

The application of systematic diagnosis to the automobile domain required a change in system theory from *functionalPartOf* to *physicalDecomposition*. While this is a significant change in the modelling of the diagnostic process (physical parts play the role of hypotheses) there were few implications for formalisation of the inference level as no new knowledge roles were found. Similarly, the SubL code was only modified to take the specific diagnosis microtheory as a parameter. In future, we aim implement other PSMs and this may permit us to generalise inference-level theories across PSMs.

4.3 Scalability

The domain and inference level knowledge representations that we have used are extensions of the basic representation, and can make use of the existing optimisations for indexing large KBs, performing taxonomic reasoning and theory structuring. Our approach to PSM implementation is based on structuring a series of queries and assertions to implement a problem-solving method. As the individual queries are simple, the space searched is small (we can specify the depth of search to be 1–3 levels). This contrasts with the basic query mechanism where the only means of getting an answer to query which requires many rules to be combined is to increase the depth of search - with the resulting exponential increase in search space.

4.4 Robustness

At present we are unable to reason about inference structures or about the mappings from the domain to the inference level within Cyc. There are no rules which allow PSMs to be modified or to be configured. Consequently, the system lacks robustness as it cannot fall back to first principles when an existing method is not immediately applicable. The problems of PSM modification and configuration are significant, even for human experts, but we believe that automatically specialising PSMs is a feasible proposition. We also plan to explore the idea of falling back to more general methods, when more specific methods are inapplicable, to regain robustness.

Inference steps (implemented by rules) require proving domain-level predicates, and robustness at the level of reasoning about domain knowledge occurs exactly as in Cyc.

5 Discussion

We have described an approach to implementing problem-solving methods in Cyc which makes use of the existing optimisations developed for large-scale knowledge bases, and adds additional structure to the inference process. Extensions to the existing ontology distinguished generic extensions to the upper-level ontology, extensions to the knowledge base, and task-related extensions. Knowledge typing principles were used within the task-related ontology to further structure problem-solving knowledge.

Our investigation of diagnostic problem solving has not only raised issues of knowledge reuse and scalability, but also of system-environment interaction. Intelligent systems cannot rely on large amounts of background knowledge alone as many classes of problems require information gathering or user interaction. If such interaction is to happen in an intelligent fashion then there is a requirement to represent and reason about the inferences which require interaction.

Acknowledgments

This work is sponsored by the Defense Advanced Research Projects Agency (DARPA) under grant number F30602-97-1-0203. The U.S. Government is authorised to reproduce and distribute reprints for Governmental purposes notwithstanding any copyright annotation hereon. The views and conclusions contained herein are those of the authors and should not be interpreted as necessarily representing official policies or endorsements, either express or implied, of DARPA, Rome Laboratory or the U.S. Government.

References

[Blázquez et al., 1998] M. Blázquez, M. Fernández, J.M. Garcia-Pinar, and A. Gómez-Pérez. Building ontologies at the knowledge level using the ontology design environment. In *Proceedings of KAW'98*, 1998.

[Gil and Melz, 1996] Y. Gil and E. Melz. Explicit representations of problem-solving strategies to support knowledge acquisition. In *Proceedings of the Thirteenth National Conference on Artificial Intelligence*, 1996.

[Kingston et al., 1997] J. Kingston, A. Griffith, and T. Lydiard. Multi-perspective modelling of the air campaign planning process. In *Proceedings of the 15th International Joint Conference on Artificial Intelligence*, pages 668–673, 1997.

[Kozierok, 1998] C.M. Kozierok. Troubleshooting expert, 1998. URL: http://www.pcguide.com.

[Lenat and Guha, 1990] D.B. Lenat and R.V. Guha. *Building large knowledge-based systems. Representation and inference in the Cyc project*. Addison-Wesley, 1990.

[MacGregor, 1994] R.M. MacGregor. A description classifier for the predicate calculus. In *Proceedings of the Twelfth National Conference on Artificial Intelligence*, pages 213–220, 1994.

[Puerta et al., 1992] A.R. Puerta, J.W. Egar, S.W. Tu, and M.A. Musen. A multiple-method knowledge-acquisition shell for the automatic generation of knowledge-acquisition tools. *Knowledge Acquisition*, 4:171–196, 1992.

[Sklavakis, 1998] D. Sklavakis. Implementing problem solving methods in Cyc. Master's thesis, Division of Informatics, University of Edinburgh, 1998.

[Uschold and Gruninger, 1996] M. Uschold and M. Gruninger. Ontologies: principles, methods and applications. *Knowledge Engineering Review*, 11(2):93–136, 1996.

[van Heijst et al., 1997] G. van Heijst, A.T. Schreiber, and B.J. Wielinga. Explicit representations of problem-solving strategies to support knowledge acquisition. *International Journal of Human-Computer Studies*, 46(2/3):183–292, 1997.

[Wielinga et al., 1992] B.J. Wielinga, T. Schreiber, and J.A. Breuker. KADS: A modelling approach to knowledge engineering. *Knowledge Acquisition*, 11(2):93–136, 1992.

[Wielinga et al., 1994] B.J. Wielinga, G. Schreiber, W. Jansweijer, A. Anjewierden, and F. van Harmelen. Framework and formalism for expressing ontologies, 1994. KACTUS Project Report (Esprit Project 8145) DO1b.1-Framework-1.1-UvA-BW+GS+WJ+AA, University Of Amsterdam.

KNOWLEDGE-BASED APPLICATIONS

Applications 3

Visual Planning: A Practical Approach to Automated Presentation Design

Michelle X. Zhou

IBM T. J. Watson Research Center
30 Saw Mill River Rd. Rt. 9A
Hawthorne, NY 10532
mzhou@watson.ibm.com

Abstract[†]

Based on a set of design principles, automated visual presentation systems promise to simplify an application programmer's design tasks by automatically constructing appropriate visual explanations for different information. However, these automated presentation systems must be equipped with a powerful inference approach to suit practical applications. Here, we present a planning-based, practical inference approach that can design a series of connected visual presentations in interactive environments. Our emphasis here is on a set of important visual planning features and how they facilitate visual design. This set of features includes a knowledge-rich representation of visual planning variables and constraints, a novel object-decomposition model that can be used with action decomposition to simplify the visual synthesis process, and practical temporal and spatial reasoning capabilities to facilitate coherent visual design and presentation. In addition, we have implemented our visual planning approach in a visual planner called PREVISE, as part of our automated presentation testbed system. A set of examples is also given to illustrate the necessity and utility of our visual planning approach.

1 Introduction

Automated visual presentation systems rely on a powerful inference engine to generate desired presentations efficiently. In this paper, we present a practical inference method that uses a planning approach to infer visual designs in interactive environments.

A visual design ultimately appears in the form of a *visual discourse* that consists of sequences of temporally ordered visual actions [Zhou, 1998]. Visual actions are encoded visual techniques, which may render a collection of graphics objects on the screen (e.g., action Display), or animate a graphical transformation (e.g., Enlarge). Since such a pattern is reminiscent of the result produced by AI planning, we model visual design as a planning problem. In particular,

the communicative goals are accomplished as planning goals, visual design guidelines are maintained as planning constraints, and visual actions are employed as planning operators to construct a visual plan (a visual discourse).

The core of our visual planning is a least-commitment, top-down hierarchical decomposition partial-order planning approach [Young et al., 1994]. Combined with a set of visual design heuristics [Zhou and Feiner, 1997], this approach helps minimize costly redesign, eases knowledge encoding by reusing visual actions, and ensures global and local design coherency. Furthermore, we have equipped the core approach with an additional set of features. Specifically, we provide a versatile visual planning representation formalism to express and manage progressively refined visual plans. To simplify visual object synthesis and knowledge management, we explicitly address object decomposition. We also augment visual planning with temporal and spatial reasoning capabilities to maintain temporal and spatial constraints [Allen, 1983; Freeman-Benson, 1993]. In addition, we have implemented our approach in a visual planner called PREVISE (Planning in REactive VISual Environments), which is part of an automated presentation testbed system.

In the rest of the paper, we focus on illustrating these important features of our visual planning approach. But first we briefly describe several related works, followed by an example that is planned by PREVISE to illustrate the visual planning problem. We then describe four important visual planning features and explain how they facilitate automated visual design. Finally, we present our conclusions and indicate some future research directions in visual planning.

2 Related Work

While most automated presentation systems employ simple search-based approaches (e.g., [Seligmann and Feiner, 1991]), a few have used planning approaches (e.g., [Andre and Rist, 1993; Karp and Feiner, 1993; Bares and Lester, 1997]). However, systems using planning approaches either deal with static presentations [Andre and Rist, 1993] or focus on planning camera movements [Karp and Feiner, 1993; Bares and Lester, 1997]. Furthermore, these systems usually handle premade graphics objects at a high level without worrying about low-level visual object composition (e.g., composing a visual object using basic visual ele-

[†] This work was conducted at Columbia University, as part of the author's Ph.D. thesis in the Dept. of Computer Science.

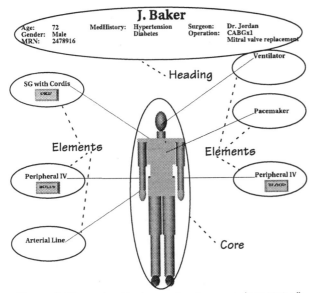

Figure 1. Present patient overview to nurse (annotated)

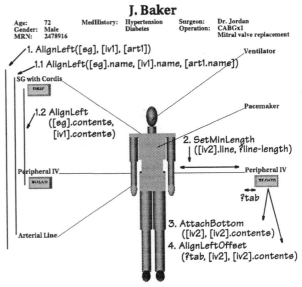

Figure 3. Present patient overview to nurse (annotated)

ments such as color and shape).

Aiming to create a coherent visual discourse from scratch, our work involves both visual composition and transformation. Thus, we have designed a more sophisticated visual planning approach. This approach, implemented in PREVISE, is based in part on two planning systems: DPOCL [Young et al., 1994] and SIPE [Wilkins, 1988; Wilkins et al., 1994]. DPOCL is the first system to explicitly address top-down action decomposition with partial-order planning, while SIPE can plan in a reactive environment. From DPOCL, PREVISE inherits the top-down action-decomposition strategy and amplifies it to accommodate object-decomposition; and from SIPE, PREVISE partly adopts its plan and action representation formalisms, but further expands them to allow more knowledge rich representations.

3 Example

We use one complex example, shown in Figure 1 and Figure 2, to illustrate the characteristics of visual planning. In this example, our task is to present a patient's information to a nurse after the patient's coronary artery bypass graft (CABG) operation. As the final presentation contains coordinated text, speech, and graphics, here we only concentrate on how the graphics presentations are planned.

In this task, PREVISE must accomplish two goals. The first goal is to create an overview of patient information, and the second is to elaborate the patient information details based on the created overview. To achieve the first goal, PREVISE plans to construct a structure diagram (Figure 1) that organizes various information (e.g., IV lines) around a *core* component (e.g., represented by the patient's body). This decision is made based on the fact that nurses prefer to see all information arranged relative to the patient's body. In a top-down design manner, PREVISE first creates an "empty" structure diagram. This empty diagram is then defined through its individual components by recursively partitioning and encoding the patient information into different groups. As shown in Figure 1, the patient's demographics information, including name, age, and gender as a group, is encoded as the *heading* of the diagram; the patient's physical body serves as the *core*, and the rest of the information is arranged around the core as diagram *elements*. To express the partial designs and their refinement, PREVISE uses variables and constraints to represent the progressively refined diagram at different levels of detail. In addition, PREVISE must formulate and satisfy a set of spatial constraints to determine the sizes and locations of various diagram components (Figure 3).

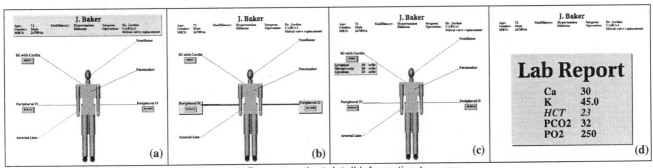

Figure 2. Present patient detail information to nurse

To accomplish the second goal, PREVISE plans a series of visual actions to allow certain information to be reinforced or revealed based on the overview. Figure 2(a–b) are created to reinforce the patient's demographics information and IVs using the visual action Highlight, while Figure 2(c–d) are planned to reveal the drip (intravenously administered drug) and lab report details. To introduce new information (e.g., drip details) into an existing display, PREVISE reasons about the spatial arrangement of existing objects and the placement of new objects. Finally, PREVISE ensures that all visual actions are temporally coordinated to produce a coherent presentation; for example, the highlighting on the demographics in Figure 2(a) should be turned off before the IVs are highlighted in Figure 2(b).

4 Visual Planning

In this section, we concentrate on illustrating four distinct visual planning features and explain how they aid visual design. To facilitate a flexible and efficient planning environment, we first present a knowledge-rich and object-oriented representation formalism for visual planning. Using this representation, we describe how to explicitly employ object decomposition with action decomposition to simplify visual synthesis. To create both temporally and spatially coherent presentations, we address temporal and spatial reasoning issues in visual planning.

4.1 Visual Planning Representation Formalism

Using a top-down design strategy, a visual planning process must deal with partially specified visual plans at multiple levels of abstraction. To capture and manage these complex partial plans, we have developed a knowledge-rich object-oriented representation formalism based on previous work (e.g., [KRSL, 1993; Wilkins and Myers, 1995; Tate, 1996]). Specifically, our representation formalism permits the efficient usage of complex planning variables and constraints, and allows a rich expression of planning operators (visual actions). For illustration purpose, all examples given below are presented in a simplified frame-like representation formalism, where brackets [ ] are added around symbols to indicate object instances.

Planning Variables and Constraints

Unlike any of other planning variables used in complex planning systems (e.g., [Currie and Tate, 1991; Wilkins and Myers, 1995]), visual planning variables are first *declared* in s-expressions, and are then *created* and managed as object

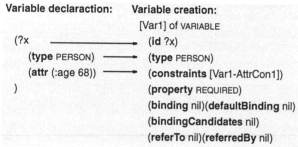

Figure 4. Variable declaraction and creation

instances. Figure 4 shows how a PREVISE variable may be declared with a symbolic id, a specific binding type, and a set of constraints. The symbolic id can either be in a form of ?x or $?y to distinguish a single valued variable (x) from a multi-valued one (y). When created, a variable instance is assigned a binding property to indicate how it should be managed [KRSL, 1993]. For example, a REQUIRED variable must be bound during planning, while an OPTIONAL variable may not be bound at all through the entire planning process. A variable may be created with or without a binding, a set of binding-Candidates, or even a defaultBinding. Moreover, this variable instance may *refer* to another variable instance or be *referred* by others during planning.

Having a separate variable declaration and creation eases both knowledge encoding and planning. In particular, variables are declared in s-expressions during knowledge encoding without dealing with the details of object creation and management. On the other hand, variables are easily handled as objects in planning without repeatedly processing complex symbolic representations. In addition, our visual planner can rely on various variable attributes described above, including variable property and references, to efficiently decide when and how to update variables. For example, using the variable reference information, if a variable binding is updated, so are all the variables that refer to this one.

It is worth noting that we also allow a special type of *dynamic variables* in visual planning. During planning, these variables may be continuously updated by a numerical constraint solver called STM [Gleicher, 1994]. Hence we refer to them as to STM-VAR. Unlike dynamic variables in other systems (e.g., [Wilkins and Myers, 1995]), a STM-VAR is more flexible in use (e.g., we do not need to explicitly specify its rebinding), and more efficient in representation. For example, a STM-VAR, used to represent a 3D bounding box, can be used to capture the changing geometry of a 3D object through five other variables (center, objCenter, width, height, and depth).

In visual planning, a PREVISE variable is usually accompanied by a set of constraints, which are also handled in the similar fashion as variables. In other words, visual planning constraints are specified initially in s-expressions, and are instantiated and managed as object instances during planning. To facilitate constraint management, we classify constraints based on their *origination* (e.g., META or SUFFICIENCY constraints in [Tate, 1996]) and *duration* (e.g., ONE-TIME or ALWAYS constraints in [KRSL, 1993]). Moreover, we assign constraints with *strength* (e.g., REQUIRED or PREFERRED) and *type* (ATOMIC or ABSTRACT) to organize them into a hierarchy [Borning et al., 1992]. This constraint hierarchy not only allows object relationships to be expressed at multiple levels of abstraction, but also allows for a more efficient constraint management (see Sections 4.3 and 4.4).

Visual Action

In visual planning, a visual action captures both the properties of a planning operator and a visual technique. As a visual technique, a visual action can be a *formational* action that creates a visual object from scratch (Figure 5a),

```
DesignTableChart (is-a FORMATION-ACTION)                    (a)
  (operands (?x (type DOMAIN-OBJECT) (?t (type TABLE-CHART)))
  (localParameters (?heading (type VISUAL-UNITY)
                              (property OPTIONAL)) ...)
  (purposes ENCODE | TABULATE)
  (effects (effect1 (Encode ?x ?t)) (effect2 (Table ?t))) ...

Move (is-a TRANSFORMATION-ACTION)                           (b)
  (operands (?v (type VISUAL-OBJECT)))
  (localParameters (?src (type VECTOR)) (?dest (type VECTOR)))
  (purposes TRANSFORM | REPOSITION)
  (preconditions (cond1 (Existing ?v)) (cond2 (At ?v ?src))...)
  (effects (effect1 (At ?v ?destination))) ...
```

Figure 5. A visual action definition

or a *transformational* action that modifies an existing visual object (Figure 5b). Since formational actions do not actually perform graphics rendering, they are not included in the final plan but their results might be. For example, the formational action, DesignTableChart, itself does not appear in the final plan, but its result—the created table chart may appear in the final plan with a Display action.

We also assign purposes to each visual action to summarize its functions at different levels of abstraction. For example, the purposes specified in the action Move indicate that it can be used to transform a visual object in general, specifically to reposition a visual object (Figure 5b). In addition, we use the purposes to index visual actions and create partitioned search space to reduce search time. This helps us cope with a large number of visual actions efficiently during planning. For example, when searching for a proper visual action to accomplish a transformation task, PREVISE only searches among the visual actions that have Transform as one of their purposes. Otherwise, PREVISE must examine the postconditions of *all* visual actions to find a match.

Much like a SIPE operator [Wilkins and Myers, 1995], visual action arguments are represented as variables with constraints on their binding types or properties. For example, the variable ?heading is optionally bound to a particular visual object (Figure 5a). But unlike SIPE, visual action arguments are separated into two groups: operands and local parameters. Whereas *operands* provide the uniform interface to access an action, *local parameters* describe a set of attributes specific to that action. In particular, formational actions use operands to specify their input and output (e.g., ?x is the input and ?t is the output of DesignTableChart in Figure 5a), and transformational actions use operands to indicate their recipients (e.g., ?v of Move in Figure 5b). On the other hand, both formational and transformational actions use localParameters to record all needed parameters to complete the action (e.g., ?heading of DesignTableChart, or ?dest of Move). Separating the operands from local parameters simplifies the action instantiation process since PREVISE needs to consider only the operands during this stage. This allows the instantiations of local parameters to be delayed; for example, PREVISE is not concerned with local parameters, such as ?dest (the destination of the movement) in Move, at a high

level of the design.

To simplify the planning process, plan goals in PREVISE are also specified similar to actions. For example, the communicative goal to create a summary of patient information, achieved in Figure 1, is notated as a rhetorical act, Summarize<?patient-info>. Based on the domain-specific nurse preference rule, this general act is then refined to a visual goal Structure<?patient-info> that requires all information to be structured in a specific way. This visual goal is in fact an abstract visual act, which can be accomplished by other visual actions (e.g., action DesignStructureDiagram) [Zhou and Feiner, 1998].

4.2 Object Decomposition

As a planning operator, a visual action may be a *primitive* action that can be directly executed by a plan agent, or a *composite* action that contains a set of partially specified subplans and must be replaced by the subplans during planning. PREVISE usually uses composite actions to sketch a design at a high level, and refines the vague parts of the design into more detailed ones using primitive visual actions. During such a design refinement, action and object decomposition may both be required. For example, a DesignTableChart action may be decomposed into a set of subactions that define individual table components. In the meantime, the input (the data ?x) used to produce the table chart must also be decomposed into smaller units that can be used by the subactions. Although in certain cases object decomposition could be implicitly handled by action decomposition, entangled action and object decomposition makes visual planning extremely difficult (e.g., a data object may be decomposed into different subparts under different situations). Thus, we explicitly introduce object decomposition in visual planning

```
DesignTableChart (is-a FORMATION-ACTION)
  (actionDecomSchemata [actD1] ...)
  (objDecomSchemata [objD1] [objD2] [objD3] ...)
  (objDecompPreferences
    (preference1 (:condition (is-itemize ?x)) (:prefer [objD1]))
    (preference2 (:condition (is-overview ?x)) (:prefer [objD2]))
    (always [objD3]))
[actD1] of ACT-DECOMPOSITION-SCHEMA
  (subactions (:loop ?i (:range 1 ?n)(:update (bind ?i (+ 1 ?i)))
    (Subaction<?i> (:expr (DesignVisRep ?x<?i> ?t<?i>)))))
[objD1] of OBJECT-DECOMPOSITION-SCHEMA
  (objId ?x) (numParts ?n = :(get-numOfIndividual))
  (subParts (:loop ?i (:range 1 ?n) ?x<?i> = :(get-individual ?i)))
[objD2] of OBJECT-DECOMPOSITION-SCHEMA
  (objId ?x) (numParts ?n = :(get-numOfGroup))
  (subParts (:loop ?i (:range 1 ?n) ?x<?i> = :(get-group ?i)))
[objD3] of OBJECT-DECOMPOSITION-SCHEMA
  (objId ?t)
  (subParts (:loop ?i (:range 1 ?n)
    IF (is-identifier ?x<?i>)) THEN (put-heading ?t ?t<?i>)
    ELSE (put-cells ?t ?t<?i>)))
```

Figure 6. A visual action and its decomposition schemata

using a set of object decomposition schemata.

An object decomposition schema uses objectId to identify the object to be decomposed, subParts to specify a set of components that the object is decomposed to, and numParts to indicate the total number of subparts (Figure 6). Unlike action decomposition where only *one* decomposition schema can be used at one time, *more than one* object decomposition schemata may be applied simultaneously. For example, PRE-VISE may use [objD1] in Figure 6 to decompose the data ?x, but *always* uses [objD3] to determine the structural relationships between the table chart itself (?t) and its components (?t<?i>). To determine which and when an object decomposition schema should be used, PREVISE uses preference constraints stored in objDecompPreferences. Moreover, variables are used extensively in decomposition schemata to express partial plans and objects, or to represent unknown situations (e.g., ?n).

In general, two types of object decomposition occur in visual planning. In the first case, a completely specified object (e.g., a piece of data to be conveyed) needs to be decomposed into smaller units to be manipulated (e.g., decomposition schemata [objD1] and [objD2] in Figure 6). In the second case, a partially specified object (e.g., a visual object to be defined) must be decomposed into subparts so it can be refined through the subparts (e.g., [objD3]). Both types of object decomposition promote a simpler and more general knowledge encoding and management.

Using the first type of object decomposition, we can easily handle the uncertainty involved in action decomposition. For example, during knowledge encoding, the number of subactions in [actD1] may be unknown, depending on how the data (?x) will be processed in the actual planning process. In this case, before instantiating subactions in [actD1], PREVISE can establish the needed variables (e.g., ?n) by selecting an object decomposition schema (e.g., [objD1]) based on objDecompPreferences (e.g., preference1). This approach allows a simple and general representation of action decomposition, which only needs to specify the unknowns using variables (e.g., ?n in [actD1]).

The second type of object decomposition also helps generalize and simplify action decomposition. Without the object decomposition schema [objD3], for example, we must replace the general action DesignVisRep with more specific subactions, such as DesignTableHeading and DesignTableCell, to define various table constituents. In addition, we must consider all the possible combinations of these specific subactions to construct different subplans (e.g., a subplan may require a subaction DesignTableHeading, but another may not). This not only requires a number of different actions to be defined, but also increases the complexity of knowledge management. Considering the case of defining a new action DesignBarChart, we need to introduce a set of new actions (e.g., DesignAxes and DesignBar) for various bar chart constituents. We must also ensure that each subaction is supplied with the proper data components to guarantee the design correctness. For example, only quantitative data components may be involved in the subaction DesignBar.

Therefore, separating the object decomposition from the action decomposition allows simpler and more general representations for action decomposition. More importantly, these simpler and more general representations improve PRE-VISE's applicability by easing its tasks of knowledge encoding and management.

4.3 Temporal Reasoning

During a visual presentation, visual actions can occur concurrently or over extended time intervals. To create a temporally coherent visual presentation, we have integrated temporal reasoning into PREVISE to ensure that visual actions are temporally coordinated. Compared to other systems (e.g., [Tate et al., 1994; Wilkins and Myers, 1995; Andre and Rist, 1996]), PREVISE uses multilevel topological and metric time constraints to describe actions at a finer granularity during planning generation. It also employs a novel scheduler to ensure that all temporal constraints are met during planning execution.

Temporal Constraint Specification

PREVISE deals with two types of temporal constraints: *Inter-action* constraints specify temporal relations *between* two visual actions, and *intra-action* constraints describe temporal relations *within* a visual action.

Inter-Action Temporal Constraints. PREVISE uses topological constraints to represent temporal relationships between two visual actions qualitatively. These constraints can be represented as either time-point or time-interval constraints. In general, PREVISE allows three types of time-point constraints: BeforeAt, AfterAt, and EquatAt; and permits time interval constraints, containing any subset of the thirteen basic temporal relations defined in [Allen, 1983]. When described in time-point constraints, visual actions may be considered *instantaneous*. In contrast, visual actions have distinct starting and finishing times when specified using time-interval constraints.

Allowing both time-point and time-interval constraints not only enables PREVISE to represent different temporal relationships accurately, but also helps to handle temporal constraints efficiently by exploiting a multilevel constraint representation. Usually, we can use concise time-point constraints to specify incomplete temporal relations at a high level, and employ time-interval constraints to express more refined temporal relationships at a low level. For example, PREVISE can use a simple time-point constraint to assert that action A must start before B at a high level, without knowing their finishing times:

(BeforeAt A B)

Later, this constraint can be refined using one of the three more specific time-interval constraints based on their finishing times:

1. A finishes before B: (Overlap A B)
2. A finishes after B: (Contain A B)
3. A and B finishes at the same time: (FinishedBy A B)

This multilevel temporal constraint representation helps avoid computationally complex temporal reasoning at a high level, hence improves planning efficiency.

Intra-Action Temporal Constraints. In addition to temporal constraints between visual actions, we also describe temporal relationships within an action. Unlike inter-action temporal relationships, these relations are described quantitatively using metric time constraints (usually in seconds).

In general, a PREVISE action has a startTime and an endTime to regulate when and how long the desired visual effects should appear on the screen. But we add subtime intervals in a transformational action to describe its animation subacts. In particular, animOnDuration controls the time taken to turn on the desired visual effects (e.g., gradually changing the color of an object to highlight it), holdingDuration specifies how long the current effect should remain on the screen (e.g., holding the highlighting effect), and animOffDuration limits the time taken to reverse the visual transformation (e.g., turning off the highlighting). Using these subintervals, we can describe and control a finer-grained visual action and its execution. Moreover, we can specify an animation with its reverse without explicitly introducing a set of undo actions (e.g., unhighlight).

To facilitate temporal media coordination (e.g., coordinating a graphics animation with speech) in a multimedia presentation, we also allow more flexible time-window constraints. For example, we may specify that a Highlight action needs a minimum of 1s or maximum of 2s to turn on the highlight, and another 3s to 4s to hold the highlighting. To coordinate the highlighting with speech, a media coordinator can use the time window to compute a time interval acceptable for both graphics and speech.

Temporal Constraint Satisfaction

We deal with temporal constraints in both plan generation and execution. In plan generation, we use a simple constraint solver to process qualitative time constraints based on transitive closures. Conversely, we use a constraint solver based on *Metric/Allen Time System (*MATS*)* [Kautz, 1991] to process quantitative temporal constraints.

Execution Scheduler. In plan execution, we have implemented a time queue to schedule visual actions. All visual actions are first entered in the time queue by their starting times. The scheduler then uses a global alarm clock to invoke actions when their starting times are reached. A local timer is also maintained within each visual action to signal its termination when its finishing time approaches.

This approach works fine until this problem arises: Two closely scheduled actions (e.g., actions A and B in Figure 7a) may overlap as the scheduler cannot guarantee a *full* stop in previous action (e.g., A) when its local timer expires. This is because the local timer does not account for the time spent for executing various implicit finishing acts. For example,

action A may call an *instantaneous* undo act (animOffDuration is 0.0s) when its local timer expires. Thus, there is no guarantee that A's undo act will be finished *before* B starts.

To fix this problem, each action is required to signal the scheduler when it is truly finished. In addition, we insert a dummy finishing act for each action in the time queue by its finishing time to ensure that the global clock be stopped if the previous action is not finished. As shown in Figure 7(a), when the global clock reaches the dummy act A_end, it would not be advanced to action B_start until it receives A's finishing signal.

The above approach only fixes half of our problem: it works for actions scheduled one *after* another (e.g., A and B in Figure 7a), but not for actions scheduled *right next* to each other (e.g., B and C). In this case, the plan agent is expected to execute two tasks *simultaneously*: finishing the previous action (B) and starting a new action (C). Since it is physically impossible for uniprocessor machines to process two tasks at the same time, the tasks will be executed in a nondeterministic order. This may result in undesirable visual effects. Suppose B and C are both highlighting actions, and B must finish by removing its highlight *before* C starts to put on a new highlight. Because of the nondeterministic execution order, C might be started *before* B finishes to cause an undesired visual effect: two objects highlighted at the same time instead of in sequence.

To ensure desired visual effects, we add *sub-order* temporal constraints to serialize simultaneous actions using heuristics. For example, one heuristic rule in PREVISE asserts that all dummy finishing acts precede any other action scheduled at the same time. In the above example, the plan agent will process B_end before C_start, as if the time point t is *expanded* into a time interval [t, t+Δ] (Figure 7b). This ensures that all objects in action B are unhighlighted before any new object is highlighted in action C.

4.4 Spatial Reasoning

PREVISE performs spatial reasoning in two situations. In *spatial composition*, PREVISE regulates the size and placement of visual objects to ensure a valid visual composition. In *spatial transformation*, PREVISE controls the spatial modification of existing visual objects and the integration of new visual objects to maintain a coherent visual transformation.

Spatial Composition

A visual composition is considered *valid* if all syntactic constraints are satisfied during visual object synthesis [Zhou, 1998]. Among these syntactic constraints, some regulate spatial relationships between visual objects. Figure 3 is annotated to show a set of spatial constraints that must be satisfied in a structure diagram. Moreover, these constraints are specified at different levels of abstraction to capture multi-level spatial relationships. For example, constraint 1 is an abstract spatial constraint, defined at a high level to describe vague spatial relationships between complex visual objects. In contrast, constraints 1.1 and 1.2 express more concrete visual relationships. To be evaluated, an abstract constraint (e.g., constraint 1), must be replaced by a set of more concrete constraints (e.g., constraints 1.1 and 1.2). One

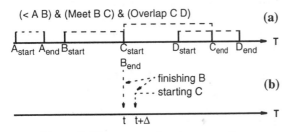

Figure 7. Time queue for plan execution

distinct advantage of using abstract constraints is to achieve planning efficiency by postponing overwhelming details involved in lower level constraints to a later time.

By evaluating a set of constraints, PREVISE can determine the size and placement of visual objects involved. For example, the locations or sizes of various texts in Figure 3 can be determined. In PREVISE, we model spatial constraints using mathematical equations and inequalities, which are eventually solved by STM using a numerical optimization method. Since the optimization method requires a set of proper initial values, we must supply these values for STM to start with. For example, we need to supply the proper initial values for ?line-length and ?tab in constraints 2 and 4 (Figure 3). Currently, these values are obtained based on empirical analyses of many existing graphical representations (e.g., hand-made or machine-made structure diagrams). For example, to best illustrate the spatial ratio between the patient body and the lines, we have learned that the length of various lines in the picture is usually at least 1/3 of the diagonal length of the body's bounding box.

Spatial Transformation

In addition to ensuring a valid visual composition, PREVISE also uses spatial constraints to control the integration of new information into an existing presentation. In one approach, PREVISE directly adds the new information to the existing scene as *visual extensions* of existing objects. For example, to reveal drip details (Figure 2c), PREVISE directly adds a pull-down menu as an extension of the drip button in the overview (Figure 1). To determine the size and the placement of new objects (e.g., the pull-down menu) in relation to the existing objects (e.g., the button), PREVISE reasons about the spatial geometry of the existing scene, including the objects' size, orientation, and topology, by issuing queries. It then formulates constraints based on design heuristics. In our case, based on the current geometry of the drips button, PREVISE formulates spatial constraints to regulate the size and position of the added pull-down menu.

To avoid unnecessary spatial rearrangement, we also assert a set of spatial constraints *in advance* to prepare for potential visual changes. For example, a button is usually expected to bring up a pull-down menu when pressed. Therefore, when a button is created, a spatial constraint is asserted to ensure that there is enough room reserved below the button for placing a pull-down menu (e.g., the space below the drips button in Figure 3).

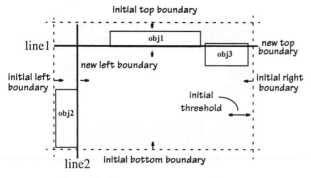

Figure 8. Space management diagram

In general, directly adding new objects to the existing scene is relatively simple since PREVISE deals with a confined space with rigid spatial constraints (e.g., placing a pull-down menu near a button). However, in many cases, PREVISE may need to modify the existing scene dramatically for integrating new information. In this case, PREVISE must determine how to make spatial changes for the new objects. For example, to produce Figure 2(d), PREVISE decides to keep the table chart at the top (e.g., name, age, and gender) of Figure 2(c) to provide the necessary context information, while replaces the rest of representation with the lab report.

PREVISE currently deals with relatively simple space-management cases. Our approach assumes that all existing visual objects will be replaced except the objects that must be kept to provide necessary background or context information. Once PREVISE determines what to keep or to remove, it will plan the size and the placement of the new objects (e.g., the table chart for lab report) using an iterative-adjustment algorithm. To utilize space efficiently and produce a balanced layout, the algorithm assumes that the kept objects usually reside in the shaded area to leave the middle area for the new objects (Figure 8).

The shaded areas are initially defined by a set of threshold values to guarantee that at least 2/3 of the display area in the middle be reserved for the new visual objects. The algorithm then iteratively computes the bounding box for each object kept in the scene and determines the region containing this object. If the object falls in only one of the eight shaded regions (e.g., obj1 and obj2 in Figure 8), the algorithm adjusts the current boundaries by pushing them toward the center to define unoccupied space. For example, the initial top boundary is pushed down into line 1, and the initial left boundary becomes line 2 in Figure 8. If the object does not completely fall in any of the eight regions (e.g., obj3) and the threshold values are adjustable, the algorithm recursively increases the current threshold values to recompute new boundaries. If the threshold values are not adjustable, the current existing objects may be modified to create enough room for new objects. Eventually, the algorithm returns four boundaries to define the dimension and position of the area for placing the new objects.

5 Implementation

PREVISE is implemented using both CLIPS [JSC-25012, 1993] and C++, currently running on SGIs and PCs under Windows NT. The rendering component is written in C++ and Open Inventor, an object-oriented 3D interactive graphics toolkit [Wernecke, 1994]. On a SGI Indigo 2 with a 250 MHz R4400 processor, it takes about 25 seconds to plan the overview of patient record shown in Figure 1, and about 45 seconds to plan the entire detail view of patient record, partly shown in Figure 2.

6 Conclusions & Future Work

In this paper, we have presented a practical visual planning approach to automated visual presentation design. In particular, we model visual actions as planning operators, and visual design principles as planning constraints. On top of our core top-down hierarchical decomposition partial-order planning approach, we add a set of visual planning features. These features include a powerful visual planning representation, an explicit object decomposition method, and temporal and spatial reasoning capabilities. Moreover, this approach is implemented in a planner, PREVISE, as part of our automated visual presentation testbed system.

Currently, we are working in two areas to improve the visual planning approach. To allow user interaction during planning generation and execution, we are planning to incorporate reactive planning strategies [Wilkins et al., 1994]. For example, users may suggest changes to the design decisions made by PREVISE, or interactively alter the course of the execution to selectively view the presentation (e.g., executing visual actions out of sequence). Thus, our current approach must be extended to recognize the inadequacy of a current plan, and correct it to meet the new conditions.

To perform spatial analysis and management for more complicated situations, we would also like to enhance the spatial reasoning capability. For example, developing a general and efficient algorithm to query the spatial density of a scene so we can place new objects on the location where the spatial density is low to avoid possible object occlusions.

Acknowledgments

I would like to thank my thesis advisor, Professor Steven Feiner, for his constant support on this work. I would also like to thank Rahamad Dawood for implementing the scheduler, Blaine Bell for porting the entire system to PCs, and Bill Yoshimi, Keith Houck, and Po Yu for proofreading this paper. This research was supported in part by DARPA Contract DAAL01-94-K-0119, the Columbia University Center for Advanced Technology in High Performance Computing and Communications in Healthcare (funded by the New York State Science and Technology Foundation), the Columbia Center for Telecommunications Research under NSF Grant ECD-88-11111, and ONR Contract N00014-97-1-0838.

References

Allen, J. (1983). Maintaining knowledge about temporal intervals. *Communications of the ACM*, 26(11):832–843.

Andre, E. and Rist, T. (1993). The design of illustrated documents as a planning task. In Maybury, M., editor, *Intelligent Multimedia Interfaces*, chapter 4, pages 94–116. AAAI Press/The MIT Press, Menlo Park, CA.

Andre, E. and Rist, T. (1996). Coping with temporal constraints in multimedia presentation planning. In *Proc. AAAI '96*. AAAI.

Bares, W. and Lester, J. (1997). Realtime generation of customized 3d animated explanations for knowledge-based learning environments. In *Proc. AAAI '97*, pages 347–354.

Borning, A., Freeman-Benson, B., and Wilson, M. (1992). Constraint hierarchies. *List and Symbolic Computation*, 5(3):223–270.

Currie, K. and Tate, A. (1991). O-plan: The open planning architecture. *Artificial Intelligence*, 51(1):49–86.

Freeman-Benson, B. (1993). Converting an exising user interface to use constraints. In *Proc. UIST '93*, pages 207–215. ACM.

Gleicher, M. (1994). *A Differential Approach to Graphical Interaction*. PhD thesis, School of Computer Science, Carnegie Mellon University, Pittsburgh, PA 15213-3891.

JSC-25012 (1993). *CLIPS Reference Manual*. Software Technology Branch, Lyndon B. Johnson Space Center. CLIPS Version 6.0, JSC-25012.

Karp, P. and Feiner, S. (1993). Automated presentation planning of animation using task decomposition with heuristic reasoning. In *Proceedings of Graphics Interface '93*, pages 118–127.

Kautz, H. (1991). *MATS (Metric/Allen Time System) Documentation*. AT&T Bell Laboratories.

KRSL (1993). *Knowledge Representation Specification Language Reference Manual*. DARPA/Rome Laboratory Planning and Scheduling Initiative Knowledge Representation and Architecture Issue Working Group. Version 2.0.2.

Seligmann, D. and Feiner, S. (1991). Automated generation of intent-based 3D illustrations. *Computer Graphics*, 25(4):123–132.

Tate, A. (1996). Representing plans as a set of constraints: the I-N-OVA model. In *Proc. AIPS '96*, Edinburgh, UK. AAAI Press.

Tate, A., Drabble, B., and Kirby, R. (1994). O-plan2: An open architecture for command, planning and control. In Fox, M. and Zweben, M., editors, *Intelligent Scheduling*. Morgan Kaufmann.

Wernecke, J. (1994). *The Inventor Mentor: Programming Object-Oriented 3D graphics with Open Inventor*. Addison Wesley, Reading, MA.

Wilkins, D. (1988). *Practical Planning: Extending Classical AI Paradigm*. Morgan Kaufmann, San Mateo, CA.

Wilkins, D. and Myers, K. (1995). A common knowledge representation for plan generation and reactive execution. *J. of Logic and Computation*, 5:731–761.

Wilkins, D., Myers, K., Lowrance, J., and Wesley, L. (1994). Planning and reacting in uncertain and dynamic environments. *Journal of Experimental and Theoretical AI*, 6:197–227.

Young, R., Pollack, M., and Moore, J. (1994). Decomposition and causality in partial-order planning. In *2nd Int. Conf. on AI Planning Systems: AIPS-94*, pages 188–193. Chicago, IL.

Zhou, M. (1998). *Automated Generation of Visual Discourse*. PhD thesis, Columbia University, New York, NY.

Zhou, M. and Feiner, S. (1997). Top-down hierarchical planning of coherent visual discourse. In *Proc. IUI '97*, pages 129–136, Orlando, FL.

Zhou, M. and Feiner, S. (1998). Visual task characterization for automated visual discourse synthesis. In *Proc. CHI '98*, pages 292–299, Los Angeles, CA. ACM.

A Case Based Approach to the Generation of Musical Expression

Taizan Suzuki   **Takenobu Tokunaga**   **Hozumi Tanaka**

Department of Computer Science
Tokyo Institute of Technology
2–12–1, Oookayama, Meguro, Tokyo 152-8552, Japan.
E-mail: {taizan, take, tanaka}@cs.titech.ac.jp

Abstract

The majority of naturally sounding musical performance has musical expression (fluctuation in tempo, volume, etc.). Musical expression is affected by various factors, such as the performer, performative style, mood, and so forth. However, in past research on the computerized generation of musical expression, these factors are treated as being less significant, or almost ignored. Hence, the majority of past approaches find it relatively hard to generate multiple performance for a given piece of music with varying musical expression.

In this paper, we propose a case-based approach to the generation of expressively modulated performance. This method enables the generation of varying musical expression for a single piece of music. We have implemented the proposed case-based method in a musical performance system, and, we also describe the system architecture and experiments performed on the system.

1 Introduction

Almost all musicians play music with musical expression (varying of tempo, volume, etc.). They consider how the target pieces should be played, and they elaborate upon it with tempo curves and change in volume. Thus, musical expression is a highly significant element in making performance pleasant and attractive.

Many past research efforts have focused on the computerized generation of musical expression. The majority of them employ musical expression rules, which define relations between phrase characteristics and musical expression (Figure 1). Past approaches have used rules of musical expression manually acquired by human researchers ([Frydén and Sundberg, 1984], [Friberg and Sundberg, 1986], [Friberg, 1991], and [Noike et al., 1992]). Here, expressively modulated performance is generated by applying these rules to the target piece. Some recent research efforts have introduced learning mechanisms into the acquisition of rules ([Bresin et al., 1992], [Chafe, 1997], [Widmer, 1993b], [Widmer, 1993a], and [Widmer, 1995]). These approaches extract rules of musical expression from sample performance data played by human musicians. Since the above methods generate and apply rules of musical expression, they are called *rule-based approaches*.

One advantage of rule-based approaches is, once the rule set is established, it is applicable to any piece of music. Another advantage is transparency in that users can

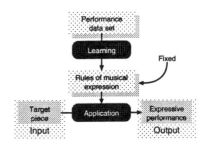

Figure 1: The basic mechanism employed by rule-based approaches

access rules for musical expression used in the generation process. These rules are useful for cognitive research.

On the other hand, rule-based approaches have some drawbacks. The most serious one is that these approaches are hard to adapt to the generation of performances with different styles.

Generally, musical expression has vast freedom and a broad range of tolerance. Musical expression varies according to various factors, for instance, the performer, style (e.g. "Baroque", "Romantic", etc.), mood (e.g. "lively", "calm", etc.), and so forth. We call these factors *performance conditions*.

To generate suitable musical expression by computer, these performance conditions must be taken into consideration. However, as was seen for rule-based approaches, it is hard to introduce these factors into the process of generation. Besides, performance conditions are difficult to describe in term of rules of musical expression, since they consist of various elements and each element continuously changes. Thus, there is little research which has considered such factors ([Canazza et al., 1997]).

On the other hand, there is very little research which has employed non-rule-based approaches. Arcos, et al. applied case based reasoning (CBR) to the generation of musical expression ([Arcos et al., 1997]). Their approach uses a performance data set as a musical expression knowledge base. For each note in the target piece, it retrieves similar notes from the knowledge base, analyzes musical expression in these similar notes, and applies to the target piece. However, Arcos, et al. do not take any kind of performance conditions into account, such that, their approach cannot generate performance variety, similarly to rule-based approaches.

We aim to develop a method of computerized generation of natural musical expression which incorporates a range of performance conditions. To overcome the problems faced by conventional methods, we propose a new case-based method for the generation of musical expression. The advantage of this method is that it can easily consider performance conditions, to be able to generate various kinds of musical expression for a single piece of music in accordance with performance condition settings. We have implemented the case-based method proposed in this paper in a music performance system. In the remainder of this paper, we present our case-based method for the generation of musical expression, and discuss the architecture of the performance system incorporating this method, and experiments on it.

2 Case-based method for musical expression generation

2.1 Concept

Figure 2 shows a rough outline of our method. Our method uses a *performance data set* consisting of pre-analyzed musical pieces, from which an *example data set* is extracted for use as the musical expression knowledge base. An example data set is acquired for each inputted target piece. Moreover, we evaluate the significance of each example piece to the input piece by considering the structural resemblance of the two pieces and similarity between performance conditions for the input and example piece. The resultant performance is generated based on the example data set and the various significance values. Hence, even if the example pieces are fixed, the generated performance will change according to the input performance conditions. This mechanism realizes our aim of generating varying musical expression.

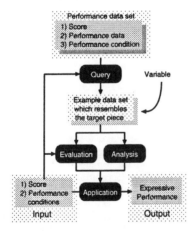

Figure 2: Rough outline of our case-based method for musical expression generation

2.2 Algorithm

This section describes the basic architecture used in our case-based method. Figure 3 shows the algorithm of our method.

Our method requires a performance data set, which is a set of musical performance data performed by human musicians. Each data component has not only a record of the event sequence (note on, note off, pedal control, etc.) but also the musical score of the performed piece and the performance conditions under which the data was

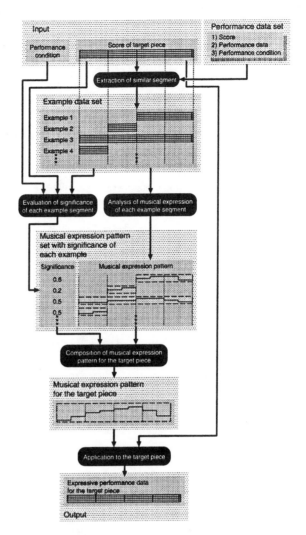

Figure 3: Overview of the case-based method for musical expression generation

recorded. This performance data set must be collected beforehand.

Our method comprises the following stages: 1) input the musical score of the target piece and performance condition settings, 2) extract similar parts (called the example segment set) from the performance data set, 3) analyze musical expression in each example segment, 4) evaluate the significance of each example segment, 5) compose the musical expression pattern for the target piece, and, 6) apply the musical expression pattern to the target piece.

Input data consists of information about the target piece taken from the musical score and performance condition settings. The musical score information is not only the information about note sequence but also accompanying information (e.g. beats, bars, repetitions, pauses, etc.). The performance condition settings are parameters which decide the characteristics and mood of the generated performance. A description of the performance condition settings is presented in Section 3.2.

In the extraction stage, our method divides both the target piece and each example piece in the performance data set into segments (e.g. parts, phrases, bars, etc.) (see Section 3.1 for details). Then, the similarity between each segment of the target piece and all sample segments is evaluated, and similar sample segments are obtained as the *example data set* for the target piece.

In the analysis stage, our method compares the record of the performance sequence and the musical score for each example segment, and analyzes variances in tempo, volume, and so on. Variance in musical expression is represented as a curve of the relative diversity, called the *musical expression pattern (MEP)* (see Section 3.3 for details). Patterns for all example data segments are stored in the *MEP set*.

In the evaluation stage, our method calculates a significance score for each example segment. This score indicates how useful the example data is expected to be in the generation of musical expression for the target piece. It is determined principally from similarity in musical score and performance conditions.

As a result of the analysis and evaluation stages, an MEP set with significance scores is obtained. In the composition stage, these MEPs are integrated into a musical expression value for the whole target piece (see Section 3.3 for details). The first step of this stage is the calculation of the MEPs for each segment of the target piece. This is achieved through the average of example MEPs for that segment. The average is weighted by the significance of each MEP. The second step is the integration of segments MEPs. In this step, averaged MEPs for each target piece segment are unified as the integrated MEP.

Finally, in the application stage, our method applies the integrated MEP to the musical score of the target piece, and outputs the resultant performance data.

3 Component technologies

3.1 Segmentation of musical pieces

Generally speaking, one possible serious problem faced by the case-based method is shortfalls in the example data set. Our methods extracts available example segments from the example data set, analyzes them, and applies them to the target piece. Thus, if the size of available example data is insufficient, the proceeding processes will not function satisfactorily.

Arcos et al. used single notes as their segment granularity, and introduced cognitive musical structure to relate neighboring notes. This is based on Narmour's implication/realization model ([Narmour, 1990]), and Lerdahl and Jackendoff's generative theory of tonal music ([Lerdahl and Jackendoff, 1983]). This is a good way to avoid shortfalls in the example data set. However, such an approach is insufficient to generate musical expression variance over longer stretches of music. Therefore, as mentioned above, our method extracts sequence of notes instead of single notes as the example data, and does not rely on the cognitive musical structure. It is obvious that the cognitive structure has a good effect on the generation of musical expression. However, since there may be individual differences between some of these structures, it is undesirable to rely solely on this knowledge type. Moreover, we think that the cognitive structure can equally be acquired with a case-based method similar to that proposed here. So, in this research, we chose the more challenging path, that is the generation without cognitive musical structure.

In our method, the most desirable example type is performance data on the target piece. However, it is unreal-istic to expect that such examples can be obtained, and close-fitting examples for all portions of the target piece are also rarely found. In other words, it is likely that enough examples could not be found simply by querying a piece which is similar throughout.

To avoid this problem, as briefly mentioned above (cf. Section 2.1), we divide the target piece into segments, and extract an example data set for each segment.

So as to extract examples extensively for all parts of the target piece, queries should be made at various granularities of division. Ideally, all possible methods of division should be tried. However, the number of plausible segment lengths reaches exponential order on the number of notes which appear in the target piece, making such exhaustive computation unrealistic from the viewpoint of computational cost. Hence, our method uses a number of consistent approaches to division, which are based on the musical structure described in the musical score.

Most music pieces have a hierarchical musical structure consisting of musically meaningful segments (e.g. motives, repetitions, phrases, bars, etc.). The musical structure mentioned in this paper is not cognitive, but a combination of parts which constitute musical pieces. This structure consists of multiple layers of variably sized segmentation units. The segmentation unit at the bottom layer is the smallest sized segments, i.e. the single note. The segmentation unit at the next layer up is one size larger, which is usually a beat. Still higher layers consist of much larger segments, such as a half bar, bar, phrase, sequence of phrases, repetition, motive, and so on. The top layer is composed of the whole piece. The segmentation of a musical piece is described in the musical score to some extent, and likely to be unaffected by factors other than musical score information. In dividing the target piece into segments, the possibility of finding appropriate examples increases.

3.2 Performance conditions

This section explains performance conditions and the associated method of comparison.

Performance conditions are described as a set of *features*. Each feature is made up of *key* and *value*. The key indicates the particular feature in the form of a keyword. The value is the degree of the feature, and given as a real number in the range -1 to 1. For instance, "an elegant and bright performance" has two features. One feature has the key "elegant", and the other has the key "bright". The value of each feature is between 0 and 1. In the case of "elegant and very bright performance", the value of the feature "bright" is close to 1. In contrast, in the case of "somewhat bright performance", the value of the feature "bright" is close to 0. In the case of "non-bright performance", the feature "bright" has a negative value. If the feature "bright" is not given, it is considered that this performance implicitly has the feature "bright" with value 0.

Not only the information on the feel to the performance but also information on the performer and performance style are also described in this form. For example, performance data from musician "A" has feature "performer A". The value of this feature is 1. In the case of musician A imitating musician B, the performance conditions consist of feature "performer A" and "performer B", with values slightly closer to 0 than in the previous case.

Now, considering the key and value of each feature as unit vector and the norm of that vector, respectively, performance conditions are the sum of vectors on a vector space which covers each unit vector key. This summation of the vectors is named the *performance condition vector*. Equation 1 shows performance condition vector v

$$v = \sum_{i \in V} a_i \cdot i \qquad (1)$$

where V is the set of keys of features which constitute the performance conditions, and a_i is the value of key i.

By introducing the concept of the performance condition vector, similarity in performance conditions can be evaluated through the distance between the performance conditions vectors. Equation 2 shows the resemblance value of performance condition vectors v and u. The numerator is the dot product of the performance vectors. The denominator is the square of the length of the larger vector, hence normalizing the degree of resemblance.

$$\text{Resemblance}(v, u) = \frac{v \cdot u}{\max\{|v|^2, |u|^2\}} \qquad (2)$$

3.3 Musical expression pattern

This method uses *musical expression patterns (MEPs)* in the generation process. This section describes analysis and composition of MEPs.

Analysis of MEPs

This method uses the ratio of "the musical expression value (tempo, volume, and so on) of the target example segment" to "the average value of the next segment up (parent segment)" as a representation of variance in musical expression. The MEP of an example segment is the set of the ratios for each type of musical expression (tempo, volume, etc.). Equation 3 shows this calculation. $P_{exp}(s)$ is the MEP of musical expression type exp (seconds/crotchet (see below), volume, etc.) for a segment s, $s_{i,j}$ is a segment of the target piece, i is the depth of the segmentation layer (c.f Section 3.1), j and k are segment indices within the given segmentation layer, $s_{i,j}$ is a sub-phrase of $s_{i-1,k}$, and $exp(s)$ is the musical expression value of segment s. The average MEP over all segments composing one segment size up is always 1.

$$P_{exp}(s_{i,j}) = \frac{exp(s_{i,j})}{exp(s_{i-1,k})} \qquad (3)$$
$$s_{i,j} \subset s_{i-1,k}$$

The following example shows the calculation of MEP for a performance data segment of a 4 bar phrase (Figure 4). This performance data is played at an average tempo of 120 (0.5 seconds/crotchet). In the case of human performance, the tempo varies with musical expression, so that the tempo of most notes in the phrase will be other than 120. In this example, the average tempo of each bar is, respectively, 115 (0.52 seconds/crotchet), 133 (0.45 seconds/crotchet), 150 (0.4 seconds/crotchet), and 95 (0.63 seconds/crotchet). (Note that the average of these tempos will not be 120, since the average tempo is the reciprocal of total performance time.) As mentioned above, MEP is the ratio of the expression value of the target segment to the value of the next segment up. In this case, target segments are made up of each bar, and the parent will generally be the whole phrase

(4 bars) or a half phrase (2 bars). The parent is decided in accordance with the segmentation strategy. In the case of tempo, the MEP is calculated from the seconds/crotchet value, instead of the tempo value, since the tempo value is inconsistent in some calculations (e.g. the mean of tempo values and the average tempo value usually differ).

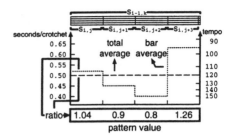

Figure 4: An example of MEP calculation for tempo

Assuming that the next segment up is the whole phrase, the tempo MEP for each segment (each bar) is the ratio of the seconds/crotchet tempo of each bar (0.52, 0.45, ...) to the seconds/crotchet tempo of the whole phrase (0.5). In this way, the MEP for the bars are 1.04, 0.9, 0.8, and 1.26, respectively.

MEP composition

In the composition stage, these MEPs are integrated into a single MEP for the whole target piece. As mentioned in Section 2.1, the composition stage consists of two steps. The first step is the calculation of the MEP for each segment of the target piece. The MEP of each segment of the target piece is the weighted mean of MEPs of all examples for that. Equation 4 is a formalization of this process. In this equation, $s_{i,j}$ refers to a segment of target piece, $E_{i,j}$ is the overall example data set for segment $s_{i,j}$, and $W(s)$ is the weight of example segment s, which is calculated from the significance of each segment.

$$P_{exp}(s_{i,j}) = \frac{\sum_{s \in E_{i,j}} W(s) \cdot P_{exp}(s)}{\sum_{s \in E_{i,j}} W(s)} \qquad (4)$$

The second step is the integration of the individual MEPs. In this step, for each note of the target piece, the MEPs of all ancestral segments are multiplied. An ancestral segment of a note is any segment which contains that note. Equation 5 shows the integrated MEP for the mth note n_m. S_i is the set of segments in ith layer, and n is number of layers, where the segmentation unit of the nth layer is a single note (i.e. $s_{n,m} = n_m$).

$$P_{exp}(n_m) = \prod_{1 < i \le n} P_{exp}(s_{i,j}) \ \{j | n_m \in s_{i,j}\} \qquad (5)$$

Figure 5 shows a simple example of this calculation. The MEP for a half bar segment is the ratio of the value of the half bar to the value of full length containing bar, and the MEP for a bar segment is the ratio of the bar value to the whole 4 bar phrase value. Thus, the integrated MEP indicates the ratio of the value of each note to the value of the whole phrase.

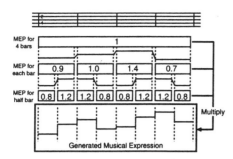

Figure 5: An example of MEP generation for a 4 bar phrase

4   Musical expression generation system

4.1   Outline

We have been developing a musical expression generation system called *Kagurame*, which uses the case-based method described above. Kagurame Phase–I, the first stage of Kagurame, is intended to estimate the system capability and possibilities of our method. For the sake of simplicity, the types of musical pieces and performance conditions the system can handle have been limited. For example, the target piece and sample data are limited to single note sequences.

4.2   Architecture

Figure 6 shows the architecture of Kagurame Phase–I. The following section describes the basic mechanism and algorithm for each component.

Input

As input, this system uses: 1) musical score information of the target piece, 2) the musical structure of the target piece, and 3) performance condition settings. The musical score information is a sequence of detailed parameters for each note (e.g. position, beat length, key value, etc.). The musical structure is information on segment boundaries, used to divide the target piece into segments (cf. Section 3.1). The performance condition settings are given in the form of a performance condition vector (cf. Section 3.2). This combined information is given in an originally formatted text file.

Performance data set

Each performance data set consists of: 1) musical score information, 2) musical structure, 3) performance conditions, and 4) performance data. The musical score information, musical structure, and performance conditions are given in the same format as described for the system input. The performance data is a sequential record of a human performance. It is given as a standard MIDI format file (SMF). The SMF is a sequence record of note event information, which consists of the time, key value, and strength ("velocity"). This format file is easily obtained from a computer and electronic keyboard. Each data type is divided into segments beforehand for convenience of calculation at the extraction stage.

Extraction of examples

In the extraction process, first of all, the target piece is divided into segments according to the musical structure information. The similarity score between a given target segment and each performance data segment is then

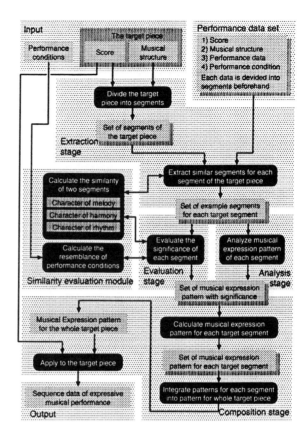

Figure 6: The system architecture of our performance system

calculated, and high scoring segments are used as the example data set for the target segment. This extraction process is carried out for all segments of the target piece.

Evaluation of similarity

The similarity score used at the extraction stage is calculated by the similarity evaluation module. This estimation is based on the resemblance of the characteristics of the concerned segments. The system currently uses three factors as segment characteristics: melody, harmony, and rhythm. Melody is the tendency for fluctuation in the melody. It is calculated as the difference between the average pitch of the first half of the segment and that of the latter half. Equation 6 shows the melody characteristic function $C_m(s)$ for segment s, where N_f is the set of notes in the first half of the segment, N_l is the set of notes in the latter half, and $p(n)$ is the pitch of note n. The characteristic of harmony is the chord component of the segment. This is a set of 12 values. Each value is a count of given pitch set. Equation 7 shows the ith value of the harmony characteristic function $C_{h,i}(s)$. The characteristics of rhythm is the beat length of the segment.

$$C_m(s) = \frac{\sum_{n \in N_l} p(n)}{|N_l|} - \frac{\sum n \in N_f p(n)}{|N_f|} \quad (6)$$

$$C_{h,i}(s) = \frac{|\{n | n \in N, p(n) \text{ is } i\text{th pitch on the scale}\}|}{|N|} \quad (7)$$

$$D_h(s_1, s_2) = \sum_{1 \leq i \leq 12} |C_{h,i}(s_1) - C_{h,i}(s_2)| \quad (8)$$

For each factor, the system evaluates the characteristic parameters of target segments, calculates the resemblance of these parameters, and normalizes them. Resemblance of melody is the difference between $C_m(s)$ for two segments. Resemblance of harmony is the summation of the difference of $C_{h,i}(s)$ for each i (Equation 8). Resemblance of rhythm is the ratio of beat length. If this value calculates to less than 1, the inverse is used. The summation of these resemblances is used as the similarity between segments.

Analysis of MEPs

Then, this system analyzes the MEP of each example segment. Details of this process are given in Section 3.3.

Evaluation of significance

The significance of each example segment is the product of similarity with the target segment, similarity with neighbor segments, similarity with ancestral segments, and resemblance of performance conditions. The similarity of target segments is calculated in the same way as for the extraction process, and likewise for the similarity of neighbor or ancestral segments. Resemblance of performance conditions is the dot product of the performance condition vectors in question (cf. Section 3.2).

Composition of musical expression

The application process consists of: 1) calculation of MEP for the each segment of the target piece, 2) integration of segment MEPs for the whole target piece, and 3) generation of expressive performance data for the target piece. Details of the calculation and integration process are given in Section 3.3. The weight for the calculation of MEP of each segment ($W(s)$ in Equation 4) is an exponential function on the significance of that segment. As a result of this process, the integrated MEPs for the overall target piece are generated.

In the generation process, the system multiplies the integrated MEPs by the average for each musical expression over the whole piece. For example, in the case of tempo, the average seconds/crotchet value for the piece is multiplied in its entirety with each integrated MEP. The overall average value is based on example data for segments of the overall piece and notation on the musical score of target piece. All types of musical expression are generated in same way. Finally, the system applies the overall musical expression to each note of the target piece, and outputs the resultant performance data as an SMF file.

Handling of musical expression

Kagurame Phase–I handles three types of musical expression: local tempo, duration, and volume. Local tempo is the tempo of each note. Duration is the ratio of the time from note on until note off to the given length of the note. Duration of 1 means the note is played for its full length. (there is no pause or overlap). In the case of staccato, the duration will be close to 0, and in the case of legato, it will exceed 1. Volume is a measure of the strength of sound. These parameters are easily accessible from the SMF file.

5   Evaluation

We generated some expressive performance data with Kagurame Phase–I, and evaluated the resultant performance. This section describes the experiments and evaluation of the performance generated by Kagurame Phase–I.

5.1   Experiments

A relatively homogeneous set of 21 short etudes from Czerny's "160 Kurze Übungen" and "125 Passagenübungen" were used for the experiment. Performance data was prepared for each piece. All performance data was derived from a performance by an educated human musician, and each piece was played in two different styles: 1) Romantic style and 2) Classical style. The performance conditions for each piece has the single feature of "Romantic" or "Classical" with a value of 1.

Out of the 21 pieces, one piece was selected as test data, and performance data for all the remaining pieces (20 pieces) was used as the performance data set. As such, the human performance data for the test piece was not included in the sample data set (i.e. evaluation is open). Two styles (those described above) of performance data were generated for the test piece by Kagurame Phase–I based on the performance data set. The test piece was varied iteratively (similar to cross-validation), and performance data was generated for all the pieces. All generated SMF data was played with a YAMAHA Clavinova CLP–760 and recorded on an audio tape for the listening experiments.

5.2   Evaluation of performance results

We evaluated the resultant performance through a listening test and numerical comparison. In the listening test, the resultant performances were presented to several human musicians for their comments. Some of them were players of sample data. In the numerical comparison, the difference between human performance and the generated performance was calculated, and rating was also made of the difference between performance data for the two styles.

The following are comments from the listeners. From the viewpoint of satisfaction of performance, the resultant performances sounded almost human-like, and musical expression was acceptable. There were some overly weak strokes caused by misplay in the sample data, but these misplays were not obvious in the resultant performance. It is hard to determine which performance (human or system) is better, since it relies heavily on the listener's taste. But, if forced to say one way or the other, human performance was better than the system one.

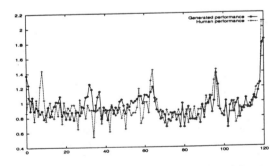

Figure 7: The tempo curve of the system and human performance of "No. 1, 160 Kurze Übungen"

Human listeners pointed out that the curve of the generated performance tended to be similar to that of the human performance particularly at characteristic points. (e.g. the end of each piece). Numerical comparison between the human performance and generated performance also showed that fluctuations in musical expression for the system performance resembled human performance in many respects. Figure 7 shows the comparative tempo curves for the generated performance and human performance of "No. 1, 160 Kurze Übungen" in the "Romantic" style (Of course, this is not the best resultant data but an average case). In this graph, it observable that the peaks of the graph coincide (e.g. around 65, 100, the ending, and so on). In some portions, however, differences in the curve behavior are noticeable. Human listeners judged some of these differences to be permissible and not critical errors. They seem to represent variance of musical expression within the same style.

The difference between the generated performance for the two styles was clear in each case. In the listening test, very high percentages of correct answers were obtained when listeners were asked to identify the performance style of the piece. Figure 8 shows the tempo curve of the "Romantic" and "Classical" styles for the generated performance. The target piece is "No. 1, 160 Kurze Übungen". This graph also evidences differences in the generated tempo curve. The range of fluctuation for the "Romantic" style is much broader than the "Classical" style. Since a broad range of rubato is known as a typical characteristic of the "Romantic" style, the broader fluctuation seen for the "Romantic" performance seems to be appropriate. Based on this result, at least these two styles were discriminated in performance.

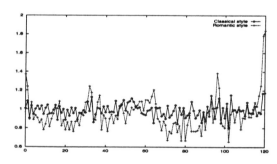

Figure 8: The tempo curve of the "Romantic" and "Classical" style performances of "No. 1, 160 Kurze Übungen"

6 Conclusion

This paper described a case-based method for the generation of musical expression, and detailed a music performance system based on the case-based method proposed in this paper. The advantage of the proposed method is that it can model performance conditions during the generation process. This makes it easy to generate various kinds of musical expression for a single piece of music in accordance with the performance condition settings.

According to a listening test, the resultant performance of the described system was judged to be almost human-like and acceptable as a naturally expressed performance. Particularly, at characteristic points of the target piece, musical expression tended to be remarkably similar to human performance. By testing different styles of system performance, it was proved that our system can generate different musical expression for a given piece of music. Moreover, most of the generated musical expression was judged to be appropriate for the given style.

As a result of these experiments on the system, the case-based method presented in this paper can be seen to be useful for the generation of expressive performance. It was also confirmed that this method can generate varying musical expression for a single piece of music through changing the performance condition settings.

References

[Arcos et al., 1997] J. L. Arcos, R. L. de Mántaras, and X. Serra. SaxEx : a case-based reasoning system for generating expressive musical performances. In *Proceedings of the 1997 International Computer Music Conference*, pages 329–336. International Computer Music Association, 1997.

[Bresin et al., 1992] R. Bresin, G. De Poli, and A. Vidolin. Symbolic and sub-symbolic rules system for real time score performance. In *Proceedings of the 1992 International Computer Music Conference*, pages 211–214. International Computer Music Association, 1992.

[Canazza et al., 1997] S. Canazza, G. De Poli, A. Rodà, and A. Vidolin. Analysis by synthesis of the expressive intentions in musical performance. In *Proceedings of the 1997 International Computer Music Conference*, pages 113–120. International Computer Music Association, 1997.

[Chafe, 1997] C. Chafe. Statistical pattern recognition for prediction of solo piano performance. In *Proceedings of the 1997 International Computer Music Conference*, pages 145–148. International Computer Music Association, 1997.

[Friberg and Sundberg, 1986] A. Friberg and J. Sundberg. A lisp environment for creating and applying rules for musical performance. In *Proceedings of the 1986 International Computer Music Conference*, pages 1–3. International Computer Music Association, 1986.

[Friberg, 1991] A. Friberg. Generative rules for music performance: a formal description of a rule system. In *Computer Music Journal*, volume 15, number 2, pages 56–71. MIT Press, 1991.

[Frydén and Sundberg, 1984] L. Frydén and J. Sundberg. Performance rules for melodies. origin, functions, purposes. In *Proceedings of the 1984 International Computer Music Conference*, pages 221–224. International Computer Music Association, 1984.

[Lerdahl and Jackendoff, 1983] F. Lerdahl and R. Jackendoff. *A Generative Theory of Tonal Music*. MIT Press, 1983.

[Narmour, 1990] E. Narmour. *Analysis and Cognition of Basic Melodic Structures*. The University of Chicago Press, 1990.

[Noike et al., 1992] K. Noike, N. Takiguchi, T. Nose, Y. Kotani, and H. Nisimura. Automatic generation of expressive performance by using music structures. In *Proceedings of the 1992 International Computer Music Conference*, pages 211–214. International Computer Music Association, 1992.

[Widmer, 1993a] G. Widmer. The synergy of music theory and AI: Learning multi-level expressive interpretation. In *Proceedings of the Twelfth National Conference on Artificial Intelligence*, pages 114–119. American Association for Artificial Intelligence, 1993.

[Widmer, 1993b] G. Widmer. Understanding and learning musical expression. In *Proceedings of the 1993 International Computer Music Conference*, pages 268–275. International Computer Music Association, 1993.

[Widmer, 1995] G. Widmer. Modeling the rational basis of musical expression. In *Computer Music Journal*, volume 19, number 2, pages 76–96. MIT Press, 1995.

Using Focus Rules in Requirements Elicitation Dialogues

Renaud Lecœuche [*†]   and   **Dave Robertson**[†]   and   **Catherine Barry**[*]

renaudl@dai.ed.ac.uk   dr@dai.ed.ac.uk   greboval@insa-rouen.fr

Abstract

Requirements engineering is a complex task which benefits from computer support. Despite the progress made in automatic reasoning on requirements, the tools supporting requirements elicitation remain difficult to use. In this paper we propose a novel approach where a tool's reasoning is intimately linked to the dialogue it has with its users. Because the dialogue is guided by rules ensuring coherence, the interaction with the tool is more natural. We discuss in detail the rules we use to organise the dialogue and how we apply them to the requirements elicitation tool. We present an evaluation of this approach demonstrating improvements in usability during the elicitation process.

1   Introduction

Requirements elicitation is a difficult part of software engineering in which the specifications for a new system are discussed with potential users. Because verifying that requirements are correct is a complex task, computer support is beneficial. This support requires formal specifications. However people are usually not trained to use formal specification languages. Task or domain specific languages smooth the learning curve to write formal specifications but the elicitation process often remains error prone. Users need more support while writing specifications. In particular, a tool which interacts with them and helps them express their requirements in a domain specific way could lower the number of requirements elicitation errors. However, the interaction between the requirements engineer or future users and requirements elicitation tools has often been neglected. This is a problem since the easiest way to acquire the information for the requirements elicitation tools is often not the most acceptable in terms of human dialogue. Adapting the dialogue so that users can make sense of the information provided by the tools is therefore important. On the other hand we do not want to force requirements elicitation tools to be aware of dialogue

---
[*]PSI-LIRINSA, I.N.S.A., Place Emile Blondel, 76130 Mont-Saint-Aignan, France

[†]Department of Artificial Intelligence, 80 South Bridge, Edinburgh EH1 1HN, Scotland

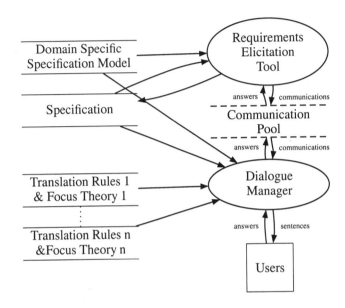

Figure 1: System data flow diagram

management strategies. A solution to this problem is to separate requirements elicitation tools and dialogue managers but make them interact and constrain each other.

We have developed a system which deals with this issue. This system communicates with its users to acquire requirements interactively. Its main feature is to organise the dialogue it has with users in order to ensure a coherent interaction. It is composed of two parts: a requirements elicitation tool and a dialogue manager as shown in figure 1 [Ward, 1986, details the graphical notation used].

The *Requirements Elicitation Tool* checks that the requirements entered by users are correct. It also provides guidance by making deductions on the requirements. It uses a *Domain Specific Specification Model* which contains the domain knowledge of the system about what can be elicited. It also accesses a *Specification* which represents the requirements that have been elicited so far. The specification is the instantiation of the domain specific specification model for the specific situation the users have described.

In our system, the requirements elicitation tool and the dialogue manager interact by means of "communications". The

Communication Pool contains the communications to be output by the the dialogue manager and the answers provided by the users. The requirements elicitation tool puts communications in the communication pool depending on the deductions it makes and the dialogue manager puts users' answers to the communications as they become available.

The *Dialogue Manager* outputs the communications created by the requirements elicitation tool in natural language. It also enables users to write English sentences that are then transformed into a notation appropriate for the tool. It organises how the communications are output by means of *Focus Theories*. Focus can be defined informally as "the set of all the things to which participants in a dialogue are attending at a certain point in the dialogue and the point of view they have on these things" [Lecœuche *et al.*, 1998]. Focus theories ensure that the guidance provided by the tool is appropriate to the users' current task. The dialogue manager has access to different focus theories that can be "plugged-in" the system. Therefore we can adapt the level of text structure by using different focus theories. Focus theories seem well-suited for organising the kind of dialogues we consider here. Other techniques, such as those based on the intentions underlying the dialogue, would require the dialogue manager to know what the elicitation system is trying to achieve and what its plan is. For some elicitation systems, this knowledge may not be available. Focus theories require less information and allow a stronger separation between the elicitation system and the dialogue manager.

We have tested our system with two theories: a global focus theory organising the dialogue at a high level and a local focus theory (not presented here but based on centering [Grosz and Sidner, 1986]) organising the sentence-by-sentence flow of the dialogue. The dialogue organisation depends also on the communications available in the communication pool and therefore on the requirements elicitation tool. Conversely, the reasoning of this module is dependent on which communications the dialogue manager outputs since this directly influences users' answers. The focus theories have access, through the dialogue manager, to the specification and the specification model in order to re-use the knowledge represented in these data stores. The access to these datastores is mediated by *Translation Rules*.

In this paper, we present in section 2 one of the focus theories we use in our system. We advocate the use of a formal focus theory independent of any domain. Because the theory is formal, we can prove properties about the dialogues it allows. In section 3, we describe some translation rules we use to transform the domain knowledge used by our requirements elicitation tool into a form suitable to our formal focus theory. We show in section 4 an example of a requirements elicitation dialogue when using our dialogue manager. In that example, our system enables users to specify how to present a research group WWW site. We then summarise an evaluation of the effectiveness of this approach for requirements elicitation dialogues in section 5. The fact that focus rules improve the quality of texts is usually taken for granted and very few approaches provide a precise evaluation of their role. Finally we conclude the paper in section 6.

2 Focus Rules

In this section we present the formal focus theory that our system uses. The theory ensures that dialogues between the tool and its users are globally coherent. It is based on a simplification of Reichman's global focus theory [Reichman, 1985]. The basic idea is that the dialogue is supported by a sequence of changes to a focus spaces set. The focus space set contains focus spaces which represent the information in focus during part of the dialogue. If $S = \{\mathcal{F}_1\}$ is the initial focus space set, only containing the initial focus space $\mathcal{F}_1$ at the beginning of the dialogue, then the set when some communications have been output is $S = \{\mathcal{F}_1, \ldots, \mathcal{F}_n\}$ where each $\mathcal{F}_i$ contains some of the things spoken about in the dialogue. We may need to create several focus spaces since the dialogue may deal with more than one topic. Focus spaces have different activation levels. We use three activation levels in our formalisation:

Active This is the space to which current communications are added. This space is unique at any given point in the dialogue.

Controlling These are the spaces expected to become active again when the space they control is closed. The controlling spaces form a tree: each space is at most controlled by one other space and a space cannot control a space already controlling it or controlling any of its controlling spaces.

Closed These are the spaces which have been dealt with and are not expected to be returned to.

Communications cause things to be included in the active focus space. They can also cause focus space activations to be modified and focus spaces to be created. In our theory, communications have one main subject which is a thing to be discussed, and possibly some other subjects which provide some context for the communication.

Our theory is composed of seven rules. The focus rules define the possible ways the dialogue may develop. Associated with an ordering, they represent what we expect to say next in the dialogue. The rules are based on four relations between the things that can be mentioned in the dialogue:

Direct relation There is a direct relation from one thing to another if the other is closely related to it and can be mentioned in the same focus space.

Specialisation relation There is a specialisation relation from one thing to another if the other is more specific than it. In that case the more specific thing can be discussed in the perspective of the more generic one.

Generalisation relation There is a generalisation relation from one thing to another if there is a specialisation relation in the other direction between the two things and no direct or specialisation relation already links the first thing to the other.

Simple relation There is a simple relation from one thing to another if it is related to the other and no direct, specialisation or generalisation relation already links it to the other.

The exact nature of these relations depends on the application domain. The translation from the domain relations to these relations is discussed in section 3.

Expression	Interpretation
$\mathcal{F}_i$	A focus space.
$active(\mathcal{F}_i)$	Focus space $\mathcal{F}_i$ is active.
$cont(\mathcal{F}_i, \mathcal{F}_j)$	Focus space $\mathcal{F}_i$ is controlling focus space $\mathcal{F}_j$.
$closed(\mathcal{F}_i)$	Focus space $\mathcal{F}_i$ is closed.
C	C is a communication to be output.
$subject(C,X)$	X is a subject of communication C.
$main(C,X)$	X is the main subject of communication C. The communication main subject is a communication subject.
$dir(D,X_1,X_2)$	X_1 is in direct relation D with X_2.
$spe(S,X_1,X_2)$	X_1 is in specialisation relation S with X_2.
$gen(G,X_1,X_2)$	X_1 is in generalisation relation G with X_2.
$sim(R,X_1,X_2)$	X_1 is in simple relation R with X_2.

Table 1: Notation used to formalise the global focus rules

Because focus rules only indicate what changes in the focus spaces (most things stay the same), we are faced with a simple version of the frame problem, i.e., how to indicate what changes and what does not. We tackle this problem by indicating the time during which a relation holds rather than asserting and deleting the relation itself [Kowalski and Sergot, 1986]. In particular, we represent the time in the dialogue as the sequence of communications and their associated focus moves performed since the beginning of the dialogue. For example, at the start of the dialogue, the time is the empty sequence $\langle\rangle$, and after communications C_1, C_2 and C_3 have been output with their associated moves m_1, m_2 and m_3 respectively, the time is the sequence $\langle m_1(C_1), m_2(C_2), m_3(C_3)\rangle$.

We define the $\succeq$ relation on time in the following way: $t_1 \succeq t_2 \Leftrightarrow \exists t_3.(t_1 = t_2 \cdot t_3)$ where $\cdot$ is the sequence concatenation operator. The $\succ$ relation is then defined as $t_1 \succ t_2 \Leftrightarrow t_1 \succeq t_2 \wedge \neg(t_1 = t_2)$. Relations that begin to hold at a certain time are noted $start(P,t)$ where P is the relation and t the time. Relations that stop holding at a certain time are noted $end(P,t)$. In order to know if a relation holds at a certain time, we define the predicate $hold(P,t)$. The definition of this predicate is

$$hold(P,t) \Leftrightarrow \exists t_s. \left(\begin{array}{c} t \succeq t_s \wedge start(P,t_s) \wedge \\ \neg \exists t_e.(t \succeq t_e \wedge t_e \succ t_s \wedge end(P,t_e)) \end{array} \right).$$

Because the notation used above is quite cumbersome, we will write $hold(P(A_1,\ldots,A_n),t)$ as $P_t(A_1,\ldots,A_n)$. The same applies for infix operators. For example, inclusion in a set at time t is noted $\in_t$. We will ignore the time if it does not influence the truth value of the predicate.

The notation used to represent the rules is expressed in our simplified notation in table 1.

In the following rules, the time variable, t, and the communication variable, C, are universally quantified. All other variables are assumed to be existentially quantified unless explicitly universally quantified. When a new space is created, it is assigned an unused number. This number is computed by the function $new(t)$ where t is the dialogue time from which the number of existing focus spaces can be deduced.

Rule 2.1 (No change) *The focus space does not change and new information is added to it. This rule is used to speak*

about things closely related to the things in the current active focus space.

$$\left(\begin{array}{c} active_t(\mathcal{F}_i) \wedge \\ X_1 \in_t \mathcal{F}_i \wedge \\ main(C,X_2) \wedge \\ dir_t(D,X_1,X_2) \end{array} \right) \rightarrow \left(\begin{array}{c} \forall X.(subject(C,X) \\ \rightarrow start(X \in \mathcal{F}_i,t')) \end{array} \right)$$

where t' stands for $t \cdot \langle no\,change(C)\rangle$.

Rule 2.2 (Resetting) *A new focus space is created. This rule is used to speak about more abstract things than the ones in the current active focus space. It may therefore serve to give background information on the things in the current active focus space.*

$$\left(\begin{array}{c} active_t(\mathcal{F}_i) \wedge \\ X_1 \in_t \mathcal{F}_i \wedge \\ main(C,X_2) \wedge \\ gen_t(G,X_1,X_2) \end{array} \right) \rightarrow \left(\begin{array}{l} end(active(\mathcal{F}_i,t') \\ \wedge\, start(closed(\mathcal{F}_i),t') \\ \wedge\, start(active(\mathcal{F}_{new(t')}),t') \\ \wedge\, \forall X.(subject(C,X) \\ \quad \rightarrow start(X \in \mathcal{F}_{new(t')},t')) \end{array} \right)$$

where t' stands for $t \cdot \langle resetting(C)\rangle$.

Rule 2.3 (Additive) *A new focus space is created. It is controlled by the current active space. Entities in the current active space are copied to the new space. This rule is used to speak about things that are more precise than the ones in the current active focus space. The new things are discussed from the perspective of the current active focus space.*

$$\left(\begin{array}{c} active_t(\mathcal{F}_i) \wedge \\ X_1 \in_t \mathcal{F}_i \wedge \\ main(C,X_2) \wedge \\ spe_t(S,X_1,X_2) \end{array} \right) \rightarrow \left(\begin{array}{l} end(active(\mathcal{F}_i),t') \\ \wedge\, start(active(\mathcal{F}_{new(t')}),t') \\ \wedge\, start(cont(\mathcal{F}_i, \mathcal{F}_{new(t')}),t') \\ \wedge\, \forall X.(X \in_t \mathcal{F}_i \\ \quad \rightarrow start(X \in \mathcal{F}_{new(t')},t')) \\ \wedge\, \forall X.(subject(C,X) \\ \quad \rightarrow start(X \in \mathcal{F}_{new(t')},t')) \end{array} \right)$$

where t' stands for $t \cdot \langle additive(C)\rangle$.

Rule 2.4 (Generating) *A new focus space is created. Entities in the current active space are copied to the new space. Any controlling relation is passed from the current active space to the newly created space since we may not expect to come back to the current active space but we still expect to come back to its potential controlling space. This rule is used to speak about things related to the things in the current active focus space but not closely associated with them.*

$$\left(\begin{array}{c} active_t(\mathcal{F}_i) \wedge \\ X_1 \in_t \mathcal{F}_i \wedge \\ main(C,X_2) \wedge \\ sim_t(R,X_1,X_2) \end{array} \right) \rightarrow \left(\begin{array}{l} end(active(\mathcal{F}_i),t') \\ \wedge\, start(closed(\mathcal{F}_i),t') \\ \wedge\, start(active(\mathcal{F}_{new(t')}),t') \\ \wedge\, \forall X.(X \in_t \mathcal{F}_i \\ \quad \rightarrow start(X \in \mathcal{F}_{new(t')},t')) \\ \wedge\, \forall X.(subject(C,X) \\ \quad \rightarrow start(X \in \mathcal{F}_{new(t')},t')) \\ \wedge\, cont_t(\mathcal{F}_j, \mathcal{F}_i) \\ \quad \rightarrow start(cont(\mathcal{F}_j, \mathcal{F}_{new(t')}),t') \end{array} \right)$$

where t' stands for $t \cdot \langle generating(C)\rangle$.

Rule 2.5 (Pop) *A controlling space becomes active again. This rule is used to come back to a space that was expected* to be reactivated. This rule does not output any communications. It is always used in conjunction with one of the other rules which outputs a communication.

$$\left(\begin{array}{c} active_t(\mathcal{F}_i) \wedge \\ cont_t(\mathcal{F}_j, \mathcal{F}_i) \end{array} \right) \rightarrow \left(\begin{array}{c} end(active(\mathcal{F}_i), t') \\ \wedge\, start(closed(\mathcal{F}_i), t') \\ \wedge\, start(active(\mathcal{F}_j), t') \end{array} \right)$$

where t' stands for $t \cdot \langle pop(C) \rangle$.

Rule 2.6 (Digressing) *A new focus space is created. It is controlled by the current active space. This rule is used to change the focus of the dialogue for a period of time after which the dialogue will resume where it was interrupted.*

$$\left(\begin{array}{c} active_t(\mathcal{F}_i) \wedge \\ main(C, X_1) \wedge \\ \forall j.(X_1 \notin_t \mathcal{F}_j) \wedge \\ \forall R.(\neg \exists X.(X \in_t \mathcal{F}_i \wedge \\ (dir_t(R, X, X_1) \\ \vee spe_t(R, X, X_1) \\ \vee gen_t(R, X, X_1) \\ \vee sim_t(R, X, X_1)))) \end{array} \right) \rightarrow \left(\begin{array}{c} end(active(\mathcal{F}_i), t') \\ \wedge\, start(\\ \quad active(\mathcal{F}_{new(t')}), t') \\ \wedge\, start(\\ \quad cont(\mathcal{F}_i, \mathcal{F}_{new(t')}), t') \\ \wedge\, \forall X.(subject(C, X) \\ \quad \rightarrow start(X \in \mathcal{F}_{new(t')}, t')) \end{array} \right)$$

where t' stands for $t \cdot \langle digressing(C) \rangle$.

Rule 2.7 (Reopening) *An old space becomes active again. This rule is used to come back to a topic that was considered dealt with. There are two ways a topic may be re-introduced in a dialogue: (1) we realise we forgot to say something about it and come back to it (2) the topic is discussed from another perspective. The reopening move only addresses the first type of re-introduction. For the second type a new focus space would be created since the dialogue context (i.e., the controlling space) has changed.*

$$\left(\begin{array}{c} active_t(\mathcal{F}_i) \wedge \\ closed_t(\mathcal{F}_j) \wedge \\ main(C, X_1) \wedge \\ X_1 \in_t \mathcal{F}_j \wedge \\ \forall R.(\neg \exists X.(X \in_t \mathcal{F}_i \wedge \\ (dir_t(R, X, X_1) \\ \vee spe_t(R, X, X_1) \\ \vee gen_t(R, X, X_1) \\ \vee sim_t(R, X, X_1)))) \end{array} \right) \rightarrow \left(\begin{array}{c} end(active(\mathcal{F}_i, t') \\ \wedge\, start(closed(\mathcal{F}_i), t') \\ \wedge\, end(closed(\mathcal{F}_j), t') \\ \wedge\, start(active(\mathcal{F}_j), t') \\ \wedge\, \forall X.(subject(C, X) \\ \quad \rightarrow start(X \in \mathcal{F}_j, t')) \end{array} \right)$$

where t' stands for $t \cdot \langle reopening(C) \rangle$.

The dialogue starting state for this theory is $active_{\langle\rangle}(\mathcal{F}_1)$ with $\mathcal{F}_1 =_{\langle\rangle} \{\}$.

Now that the rules have been formalised, it is possible to prove properties of them. For example, we can verify that in any dialogue, there is exactly one active space. This can be shown by induction on the dialogue time. At time $t = \langle\rangle$, the property is verified since there is only one focus space and this space is active. If we then suppose that for any time $t \prec T$, the property holds, it also holds at time $t = T$ because (1) every move starting a new active relation ends the current active relation, (2) no move ends the current active relation without starting a new one. Checking these properties is difficult in most other focus theories because they are not formalised.

2.1 Rule ordering

Several rules may have their preconditions satisfied at the same time. We prefer then to apply the rule that maintains the focus if possible, or minimises its movement. We minimise the focus movements by presenting general concepts before specialised ones and by avoiding references to unrelated concepts. Rules are therefore applied in the following preference order:

> no change > resetting > additive > generating > pop > digressing > reopening.

This means that we first try to find a communication to be output which would allow a no change move. If such a communication does not exist, we try to find a resetting communication and so on until a communication is found.

There is an exception to this ordering. If the main subject of a communication to output is already a member of a space controlling the current active space then a pop is the preferred move. This avoids reintroducing concepts that we are expecting to return to later in the dialogue.

3 From Domain Knowledge to Focus Rule Representation

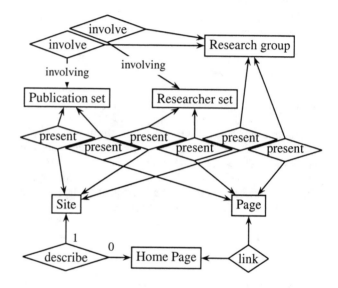

Figure 2: Specification model example

Because the focus rules we presented in section 2 are based on generic concepts such as direct, specialisation, generalisation or simple relations which are not necessarily used in the application domain of the system, we need to bridge the gap between the representation used in this domain and the representation used by the focus rules. This is done by "translation rules". These rules allow the use of this focus theory in different domains and for different applications.

We have created a set of translation rules to map the specification model used by our requirements elicitation tool to the generic concepts used by our formalised focus theory. In our system, the specification model is represented by an

Entity-Relationship (ER) model [Chen, 1976]. A part of the model used to check the specification of a WWW site describing a research group is presented in figure 2 [Wieringa, 1996, details the graphical notation used]. A research group involves a set of researchers and a set of publications. These three entities can be presented by a single WWW page or by a WWW site, i.e., a group of pages. Sites can be described by a home page. Pages and home pages can be linked together.

The main idea behind the translation rules is to allow things that are related to the current focus and cannot be accessed easily otherwise to be mentioned immediately. We only present here two examples of such rules (These rules can be formalised [Lecœuche, 1999]. We do not show the formalisation here as it would require us to also explain the formal framework used to represent the specification model):

- An entity is in direct relation with another if it may not exist at all and if it cannot exist without the other one. In our example, a home page is an optional entity whose existence requires the existence of a site. There is therefore a direct relation from the site to the home page.

- If an entity can be linked to several others playing the same role, then there is a relation of specialisation from this entity to the others. In our example, the research group involves the researcher set and the publication set which fill the same role `involving`. These two elements are therefore in a specialisation relation with the research group.

Using the translation rules, the ER relations presented in figure 2 are associated with the following focus relations:

Direct relations: `present` from publication set, researcher set and research group to site and page, `describe` from site to home page.

Specialisation relations: `involve` from research group to publication set and researcher set, `link` from home page to page and conversely.

Generalisation relations: `involve` from publication set and researcher set to research group, `present` from site and page to publication set, researcher set and research group.

Simple relations: All other relations.

Basing the global focus relations on the specification model is a great advantage since it enables us to re-use the domain knowledge of the tool checking the specification. Moreover the translation rules we presented here are dependent on the ER model structure but not on the application domain itself. This makes them more generic. As a consequence we have been able to use them in other domains than the WWW site design one. In particular we have applied our system for a simple library loan process description tool and for a more generic ER model acquisition tool. The translation rules could however be made more domain dependent if need be.

4 Example

In this section we present an example of a requirements elicitation dialogue. Our system enables users to specify how

S:	Research group #rg1 is the research group. Do you want a site presenting it?
U:	Yes
S:	A site presents the research group. Which site presents the research group?
U:	A new site.
S:	Site #s1 presents the research group. Do you want a home page describing site #s1?
U:	Site #s1 is described by a new home page.
S:	Home page #hp1 describes site #s1. What is the title of home page #hp1?
U:	"Research group".
S:	Do you want a page linked from it?
U:	I want to speak about the researcher set
S:	OK. Researcher set #rs1 is the researcher set. It is involved by the research group. Do you want a page presenting it?

Table 2: Dialogue example

to present a research group by a WWW site. Once this has been done, the specification can be transformed into HTML and the site can be displayed by a WWW browser. Our system allows users' intervention in the elicitation process but we show here an example where it has the initiative and is in charge of acquiring the requirements.

The system uses templates to generate sentences and interpret users' answers. Depending on the focus information available, the templates can be adapted to produce pronouns, or definite noun phrases. Entities introduced in the dialogue can be referred to using a unique identifier provided in the dialogue by the system.

Using the results of the translation rules, the system tries to keep elements in direct relation together as explained in section 2.1. This is shown in the example presented in table 2. The system first deals with everything directly related to the research group, i.e., site and home page, in the same focus space, $\mathcal{F}_1$. Then it selects a specialisation relation from the home page to a page. This move opens a new focus space, $\mathcal{F}_2$, under the control of the previous one. However, the user redirects the dialogue by choosing another specialisation relation from research group to researcher set. This move closes the controlled focus space and opens another one, $\mathcal{F}_3$, under the control of the first focus space. The final state of the dialogue is presented graphically in figure 3. This dialogue is more coherent than a dialogue where the system is free to choose the topic and could possibly shift randomly between

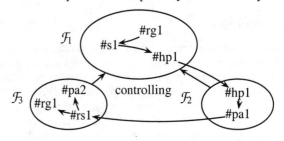

Figure 3: Dialogue evolution

Local and global theories order	39
Global theory order	34
Elicitation module order	17
Local theory order	10
	100

Table 3: Evaluation

research group, home page, site and researcher set.

5 Evaluation

A detailed evaluation of our focus theories has been carried out [Lecœuche, 1999]. In this section we summarise the results of initial tests with users.

We tested our system by asking people to read transcripts of requirements elicitation dialogues generated with and without focus theories and asking them to compare the dialogues pair-wise for coherence [Saaty, 1990]. Transformations can then be made on these comparisons to compute the overall ranking of the theories. For example, a theory with a value of 60 is considered three times more coherent than a theory with a value of 20. The values of all the theories add up to 100.

The experiment involved six persons for 90 minutes. Six dialogues were evaluated. Each participant compared four dialogues, resulting in 36 pair-wise comparisons. The results are presented in table 3. (The consistency ratio is equal to 0.0993 which indicates reliable results. The participants may however not be representative of the whole user community.) They show that our global focus theory was judged to improve the global coherence of the dialogue compared to following the requirements elicitation tool order, i.e., without using focus rules. The results also show that the local theory we use in our system performs badly on its own. This may be explained by the tendency of local theories to produce "spaghetti" dialogues without global structure. The local and global theories together perform somewhat better than the global theory alone. This can be explained by the local theory improving the transitions between communications in each global focus spaces and the transition between global focus spaces themselves.

This evaluation shows that our approach provides improvements in perceived dialogue quality. However using any individual focus theory may not be sufficient to achieve this result as demonstrated by the poor evaluation of the local focus theory on its own.

6 Conclusion

We have presented an interactive system for requirements elicitation dialogue. Our system uses focus rules to improve the quality of its interaction with users. Focus rules have rarely been used in interactive systems, especially to direct the system's reasoning. Other systems used for requirements elicitation [Rolland and Ben Achour, 1998; Reubenstein, 1990] do not take them into account and leave users in charge of picking up the relevant information from the system output. We have discussed a formal focus theory. Because of its

formality, properties of the theory can be proven mathematically. We then presented "translation" rules, bridging the gap between the representation used by the focus theory and the representation used for the domain knowledge. We then presented an example of dialogue showing the influence of the focus theory. Finally, we showed that our approach was judged to improve the perceived quality of requirements elicitation dialogues. Although we presented our results in the domain of requirements engineering, we believe that our theory could be used in other domains where the quality of interaction with users is important. We now plan to investigate how the theory presented in this paper could be integrated with other techniques (such as intentional ones in case the elicitation system is able to indicate its plan) and to use it in multi-agent systems where one of the agent would be in charge of the natural language interation with users.

References

[Chen, 1976] Peter Pin-Shan Chen. The entity-relationship model – Toward a unified view of data. *ACM Transactions on Database Systems*, 1(1):9–36, March 1976.

[Grosz and Sidner, 1986] Barbara J. Grosz and Candace L. Sidner. Attention, intentions, and the structure of discourse. *Computational Linguistics*, 12(3):175–204, 1986.

[Kowalski and Sergot, 1986] Robert Kowalski and Marek Sergot. A logic-based calculus of events. *New Generation Computing*, 4:67–95, 1986.

[Lecœuche *et al.*, 1998] Renaud Lecœuche, Chris Mellish, Catherine Barry, and Dave Robertson. User-system dialogues and the notion of focus. *The Knowledge Engineering Review*, 4(13):381–408, 1998.

[Lecœuche, 1999] Renaud Lecœuche. *Formalisation and Evaluation of Focus Theories for Requirements Eliciation Dialogues in Natural Language*. PhD thesis, University of Edinburgh, 1999. (forthcoming).

[Reichman, 1985] Rachel Reichman. *Getting Computers to Talk Like You and Me*. The MIT Press, Cambridge, MA, USA, 1985.

[Reubenstein, 1990] Howard B. Reubenstein. Automated acquisition of evolving informal descriptions. Technical Report TR-1205, MIT Artificial Intelligence Laboratory, June 1990.

[Rolland and Ben Achour, 1998] Colette Rolland and Camille Ben Achour. Guiding the construction of textual use case specifications. *Data and knowledge engineering journal*, 25(1–2):125–160, March 1998.

[Saaty, 1990] Thomas L. Saaty. How to make a decision: The Analytic Hierarchy Process. *European Journal of Operational Research*, 48:9–26, 1990.

[Ward, 1986] Paul T. Ward. The transformation schema: An extension of the data flow diagram to represent control and timing. *IEEE Transactions on Software Engineering*, 12(2):198–210, 1986.

[Wieringa, 1996] Roel J. Wieringa. *Requirements Engineering – Frameworks for understanding*. John Wiley & Sons, 1996.